D0712855

COMPARATIVE POLITICS

Delegation and Accountability in Parliamentary Democracies

COMPARATIVE POLITICS

Comparative politics is a series for students and teachers of political science that deals with contemporary issues in comparative government and politics. As Comparative European Politics it has produced a series of high quality books since its foundation in 1990, but now takes on a new form and new title for the the millennium—Comparative Politics. As the process of globalization proceeds, and as Europe becomes ever more enmeshed in world trends and events, so it is necessary to broaden the scope of the series. The General Editors are Max Kaase, Vice President and Dean of Humanities and Social Sciences, International University, Bremen, and
Kenneth Newton, Professor of Government,
University of Southampton. The series is published in association with the European Consortium for Political Research.

OTHER TITLES IN THIS SERIES

Coalition Governments in Western Europe
Edited by Wolfgang C. Müller and Kaare Strøm

Political Institutions: Democracy and Social Choice
Josep M. Colomer

Extreme Right Parties in Western Europe
Piero Ignazi

Environmental Protest in Western Europe
Christopher Rootes

Democracy Transformed?: Expanding Political Opportunities in Advanced Industrial Democracies
Edited by Bruce E. Cain, Russell J. Dalton and Susan E. Scarrow

Social Movements and Networks: Relational Approach to Collective Action
Edited by Mario Diani and Doug McAdam

Delegation and Accountability in Parliamentary Democracies

Edited by
KAARE STRØM
WOLFGANG C. MÜLLER
TORBJÖRN BERGMAN

OXFORD
UNIVERSITY PRESS

OXFORD
UNIVERSITY PRESS

Great Clarendon Street, Oxford OX2 6DP

Oxford University Press is a department of the University of Oxford.
It furthers the University's objective of excellence in research, scholarship,
and education by publishing worldwide in

Oxford New York

Auckland Bangkok Buenos Aires Cape Town Chennai
Dar es Salaam Delhi Hong Kong Istanbul Karachi Kolkata
Kuala Lumpur Madrid Melbourne Mexico City Mumbai Nairobi
São Paulo Shanghai Taipei Tokyo Toronto

Oxford is a registered trade mark of Oxford University Press
in the UK and in certain other countries

Published in the United States
by Oxford University Press Inc., New York

First published 2003

Publication of this book has been supported by a grant from the
Austrian Bundesministerium für Bildung, Wissenschaft und Kultur.

Publication of this book has been supported by a grant from the
project on Constitutional Change and Parliamentary Democracy
(Bank of Sweden Tercentenary Foundation 1996-0801)

British Library Cataloguing in Publication Data

Data available

Library of Congress Cataloging in Publication Data

Data available

ISBN 0-19-829784-X (hbk.)

1 3 5 7 9 10 8 6 4 2

Typeset by Newgen Imaging Systems (P) Ltd., Chennai, India
Printed in Great Britain
on acid-free paper by
Biddles Ltd., Guildford and King's Lynn

Acknowledgements

Some academic projects are sustained by their intellectual rewards as well as by the good companionship that goes into their creation. Such has been the case with this volume. It has been long in the making. Each one of us has, in his own way and throughout his career, been centrally concerned with governance in parliamentary democracies. Indeed, we have worked jointly as well as individually in this field of research. Yet, the labour that has resulted in this book began in earnest with a conference in Umeå in June 1997, at which the very first drafts of the chapters were presented. For each of us, this conference represented the largest scholarly enterprise we had ever launched, both in terms of the sheer number of collaborators involved and in terms of our scholarly ambitions. We were therefore suitably awed, and we have surely wandered down our share of blind alleys, for which we apologize to our patient contributors.

Recent years have witnessed a great and most gratifying revival in theoretically ambitious and empirically comprehensive cross-national studies of democratic institutions. We have nothing but the greatest respect for those scholars who are capable of producing such works single-handedly. In our own study of European parliamentary democracies, however, we were from the beginning convinced that teamwork was essential and indispensable. At the same time, we have been acutely aware of the administrative complications and potential inconsistencies that such forms of scholarship imply. Therefore, our approach has been one that has combined a great deal of collaboration with an elaborate and very detailed agenda.

Hence, the bulk of the data presented in this volume has been collected and compiled by a set of country specialists. In some cases, our specialists have been teams of scholars; in other cases, they have been individuals. In either case, they have collected and presented their data according to very specific guidelines. Thus, the country chapters in this volume are based on a much more detailed set of questions than is usually the case. We have surely occasionally driven our country experts to exasperation with our long and numerous lists of open-ended as well as fixed-format questions about institutional details in their respective national governance processes.

Generating this framework for our research was not a one-way process. The country authors helped define the questions that we asked in the first place and thus contributed to our theoretical agenda as well as to the data that we present. The same set of information was collected for each of our seventeen countries and for each year in the 1945–2000 period (or for as much of that period as these countries have been continuously democratic). These questions were dutifully answered by our country specialists, who altogether prepared more than 250 draft tables. For the purposes of economy and presentation, and again with the help of the contributors, most of this information has now been compiled in the cross-national tables that constitute the backbone of Chapter 4. Through these tremendous efforts, our collaborators have helped us provide information about practically all postwar institutional changes that impinge on the democratic delegation process in the parliamentary democracies of Western Europe. We gratefully acknowledge their efforts.

The main sponsor of this scholarship has been the Bank of Sweden Tercentenary Foundation, which through a grant to Torbjörn Bergman and the project on 'Constitutional Change and Parliamentary Democracy' (Project No. 1996-0801) made the whole effort possible. In addition, we have had more help and assistance than we can probably remember to acknowledge. We want to thank especially all those who made our first meeting in Umeå such a success. Also, let us mention Joseph B. Board, Gunnel Gustafsson, Michael Metcalf, and Nelson W. Polsby—four individuals who in various ways made lasting contributions at the formative stage of this project.

Since the original Umeå conference, we have enjoyed numerous opportunities to meet with our contributors as our work progressed. The Political Academy (Vienna) and its Director Günther Burkert Dottolo have supported this book by twice enabling us to meet and develop our project. In 1998, we were also able to meet at the annual meetings of the European Consortium for Political Research at the University of Warwick. The same year, the University of Siena graciously hosted a group meeting at its beautiful conference centre. We are indebted to Maurizio Cotta and to Luca Verzichelli for this wonderful opportunity. The University of Kent similarly supported a group meeting in 2000. We are grateful to the university and especially to Thomas Saalfeld, who was hugely helpful in organizing this meeting. All of these meetings were used at least in part to push forward our work on this volume. The Center of German and European Studies at the University of California has supported the book through several research assistantship grants, as has the Center for the Study of Democracy at the University of California, Irvine. Last but certainly not least, we are grateful to the Rockefeller Foundation, which, by granting a fellowship for collaborative residence to Müller and Strøm, and graciously welcoming Bergman to join in, allowed us to meet in the sunmer of 2001 at its beautiful and serene Villa Serbelloni in Bellagio, where we completed many of the intellectual tasks of this volume.

Several individuals deserve special thanks for their contributions to the project. Cindy Kite skillfully language edited the country chapters into more complete accounts and more felicitous prose. Although such thanks must be kept to a minimum, we simply have to acknowledge the help of the two most prominent scholars on the Swedish constitution, Erik Holmberg and the late Nils Stjernquist. And we gratefully acknowledge the constructive suggestions of numerous colleagues who have commented on earlier drafts of these papers, including James E. Alt, John D. Huber, and Mona Lyne. Last, but certainly not least, we are indebted to Magnus Blomgren, Scott Kastner, and Benjamin Nyblade for their painstaking and most conscientious research assistance as well as for their creative and genuine contributions to our project.

All academics know about the perils of publishing. In this project, we have had nothing but favourable experiences with the good offices of Oxford University Press. We especially wish to thank our editor Dominic Byatt for his enthusiasm for our project and his continuous support, and Alison Heard, Claire M. Croft, and Stuart Fowkes for their warm and supportive efficiency in guiding our bulky volume through the various stages of publication.

And to our fellow authors as well as our research assistants we would like to say that while we—in what has been sometimes been referred to as the 'troika'—are very happy to see this book completed, we will always take pleasure in having worked with you. It was great fun!

June 2003   Kaare Strøm
                                         Wolfgang C. Müller
                                         Torbjörn Bergman

Contents

III. ANALYSIS AND CONCLUSION

List of Figures

List of Tables

List of Contributors

Rudy B. Andeweg is Professor of Political Science at the University of Leiden, the Netherlands.

Torbjörn Bergman is Senior Lecturer in Political Science at Umeå University, Sweden.

Magnus Blomgren is Ph.D. Candidate in Political Science at Umeå University, Sweden.

Erik Damgaard is Professor of Political Science at the University of Aarhus, Denmark.

Lieven De Winter is Professor of Political Science at the Université Catholique de Louvain, Louvain-la-Neuve, Belgium.

Patrick Dumont is Ph.D. Candidate in Political Science at the Université Catholique de Louvain, Louvain-la-Neuve, Belgium.

Carlos Flores Juberías is Professor of Constitutional Law at the University of Valencia, Spain.

Svanur Kristjánsson is Professor of Political Science at the University of Iceland.

Arthur Lupia is Professor of Political Science at the University of Michigan, USA.

Paul Mitchell is Lecturer in European Politics in the Government Department at the London School of Economics and Political Science, UK.

Wolfgang C. Müller is Professor of Political Science at the University of Mannheim, Germany.

Hanne Marthe Narud is Professor of Political Science at the University of Oslo, Norway.

Octavio Amorim Neto is Assistant Professor of Political Science at the Graduate School of Economics at the Getulio Vargas Foundation, Rio de Janeiro, Brazil.

Benjamin Nyblade is Ph.D. Candidate in Political Science at the University of California, San Diego, USA.

Tapio Raunio is Professor of Political Science at the University of Tampere, Finland.

Thomas Saalfeld is Senior Lecturer in Political Science at the University of Kent, UK.

Kaare Strøm is Professor of Political Science at the University of California, San Diego, USA.

Jean-Louis Thiébault is Professor of Political Science and Director of the Institute of Political Studies, Lille, France.

Arco Timmermans is Lecturer in Political Science at the University of Twente, the Netherlands.

Georgios Trantas is Legal Councilor on Constitutional and Administrative Law and Independent Researcher in Athens, Greece.

Luca Verzichelli is Professor of Political Science at the University of Siena, Italy.

Matti Wiberg is Professor of Political Science at the University of Turku, Finland.

Paraskevi Zagoriti is Ph.D. Student in Political Science at the University of Athens, Greece.

PART I

INTRODUCTION AND THEORY

1

Parliamentary Democracy: Promise and Problems

WOLFGANG C. MÜLLER, TORBJÖRN BERGMAN, AND
KAARE STRØM

INTRODUCTION

Democracy is neither simple nor straightforward, but it is feasible. While the twentieth century witnessed some of the greatest political atrocities in human history, it was also the century in which democracy was gradually established and consolidated in large parts of the world. At the end of the millennium, there were more stable democracies than ever before, and there was no continent in which democracy was entirely foreign (Lijphart 1999; Przeworski *et al.* 2000).

To fulfill its promise, democratic government must be benign as well as effective. Many distinguished political thinkers have been fortunate enough to be able to presume government effectiveness—hence their major concern has been to be tame and constrain government power. Yet, democratic government cannot exist without a government capable of enforcing law and order, as Weber (1972) reminded us, and securing revenue, as Schumpeter (1954 [1918]) has pointed out. At the same time, democracy must mean limited government—the exist-ence of a protected private sphere in which the government is prohibited from regulating, and a set of human and civil rights that it is obligated to respect. While the precise boundaries between the public and the private sphere are constantly revised, there must be some form of private sphere and some commitment to a set of citizen rights (Dahl 1971).

Popular government may take many forms, but contemporary exemplars are predominantly *representative* democracies. Thus, popular sovereignty is exercised through *delegation* from citizens to individual politicians and collective actors, in particular political parties. Just as citizens in democratic societies may delegate important tasks in their private lives to specialists (e.g. their medical treatment to physicians and the education of their children to teachers), they delegate the greater part of their public life to politicians.[1] Moreover, those who are directly elected in turn delegate to specialists

---

[1] Or, to be more precise, such acts of delegation have happened in the past, or are assumed to have taken place. Indeed, most citizens face a set of rules of delegation that was set up without their formal participation.

many of their more specific tasks. It is politicians who deliberate, make laws, and take other political decisions. And, eventually, these decisions are implemented by bureaucrats that politicians recruit and supervise.

You cannot always trust politicians, or, for that matter, anyone else to whom you delegate. Hence, delegation is inherently risky. The danger of any delegation is that it may turn into abdication, that the person who delegates may lose control rather than get help. To avoid such disasters, delegation to politicians needs to be coupled with some mechanism of accountability, some way in which these politicians can be checked and controlled, and if necessary removed, if their behaviour or performance in office is unsatisfactory. Democracy therefore means effective but limited government containing mechanisms of *delegation* as well as *accountability* (Manin, Przeworski, and Stokes 1999: 29; Powell 2000; Strøm 2000).

Parliamentary government, which we shall formally define later in this chapter, is the most common way to organize delegation and accountability in contemporary democracies. Of the thirty-six states with a minimum of 19 years of democratic experience covered in Lijphart's magisterial *Patterns of Democracy* (1999), as of 2003 only five—the United States, Switzerland, Colombia, Costa Rica, and Venezuela—are not parliamentary by our standards (see below).[2] Woldendorp, Keman, and Budge (2000), who apply less restrictive criteria and claim to have excluded only tiny states, count forty-five parliamentary states by our criteria (though not necessarily by theirs). In fact, about a third of the world's population live under this regime form, a larger proportion than for any other system of government. The states that feature parliamentary constitutions span all continents and include some of the largest countries in the world (India), as well as some of the most economically advanced and powerful (Japan), and some of those commonly considered to have the highest qualities of life (Canada, New Zealand). Yet, Europe remains the heartland of parliamentarism. In Western Europe (leaving aside microstates such as the Vatican), only Switzerland is not parliamentary. And by and large, the great majority of European citizens accept their parliamentary constitutions as legitimate vehicles for popular representation.

This volume examines political delegation and accountability in the parliamentary democracies of Western Europe. Our aim is to add to our understanding of parliamentary democracy both empirically and theoretically. Empirically, we survey the institutions that govern political delegation and accountability in seventeen Western European parliamentary democracies. Electoral and governmental institutions in Western Europe display great variation, with consequences for democratic delegation and accountability. While such observations are commonplace, our knowledge of the range that parliamentary institutions take is still remarkably unsystematic and incomplete. *Delegation and Accountability in Parliamentary Democracies* is certainly the most ambitious, as well as the most comprehensive, account of the institutions of democratic delegation in

---

[2] Lijphart (1999) also classifies Israel as non-parliamentary after the introduction of a directly elected Prime Minister in 1996. A recent institutional reform has once again removed this anomaly, however, and returned Israel to the set of parliamentary systems.

Western European parliamentary democracies. Indeed, to our knowledge it is the only contemporary survey in the English language.[3]

Yet, much as we believe that such a comprehensive institutional survey is a significant contribution to the study of parliamentary regimes, we are even more convinced that our understanding of such governments needs to recognize the ways in which government institutions serve to express and constrain the voice of the citizens. What are the governance problems to which different institutional configurations are a response? How effectively do the institutions in the parliamentary repertoire address such problems? Do the various parliamentary institutions in themselves give rise to any governance problem? And can we observe any changes over time in the ways in which parliamentary systems confront the delegation issues facing them?

These are, broadly speaking, the questions which this volume will address. In order thus to illuminate important facets of the policy processes of parliamentary democracy, we employ agency theory, or the principal–agent approach (see e.g. Moe 1984, 1997; Pratt and Zeckhauser 1985; Furubotn and Richter 1997). There are three reasons, we believe, why this is a fruitful approach to the study of parliamentary democracy and popular representation more generally. One is that it gives us a general framework by which a variety of apparently unrelated representation issues can be understood. One of the main messages we wish to convey is that the same framework can be used to answer questions that have hitherto often been studied in mutual isolation, by different scholarly communities, and in needlessly complex and diverse sets of terms. A second virtue of this framework is its simplicity and parsimony, which will permit us to spend less time on cloudy and confusing definitional debates. Finally, and very importantly, this is a framework that lends itself to rigorous and precise theoretical reasoning. Indeed, a substantial body of theoretical results concerning delegation and accountability has been developed in the social sciences. Yet, agency theory has not been applied to parliamentary systems of government in any comprehensive manner. Adapting agency theory to the study of parliamentary democracy and applying it to the political institutions of Western Europe is a huge task that in this volume we can only begin. We do hope, however, that we can lay foundations on which other, more specialized studies can build.

The rest of this chapter is organized as follows. In the next section we look at the historical origins of parliamentary government and show how the term sometimes denotes a historic system of government in which the parliament had wrested control

---

[3] This, of course, is not to say that the agency problems of representative democracy have previously gone unnoticed. Dennis C. Mueller's impressive *Constitutional Democracy* largely shares our normative concerns and analytical perspective, seeing democracy as a giant agency problem (1996: 17). The empirical research that comes closest to our concerns, although it does not share our analytical foundations, is the British Democratic Audit project (Weir and Beetham 1999), which measures British democracy against a set of democratic standards and covers all steps in the chain of delegation. Finally, numerous individual authors, mainly examining a single step in the chain of delegation in a single country, have identified problems of delegation and accountability stemming from preference divergence and information asymmetries (see Chapters 2 and 3). They have provided valuable information on delegation and accountability in their respective countries, as can be seen from the references in the seventeen country chapters. We build on all this work.

over much of national politics out of the hand of a hereditary monarchy. This historical meaning of the term parliamentary government (or parliamentarism) often creates
confusion when it is used in reference to modern representative democracies. This problem is addressed in the section titled Parliamentary Government. In the following
section, we compare the regime type of parliamentary democracy with its main rival,
presidentialism. Even though there has been a heated debate about the relative merits
of parliamentary versus presidential government, surprisingly little is known about
the strengths and weaknesses of parliamentary democracy as a mechanism of delegation from voters via politicians to civil servants. We then begin to develop our own
principal–agent approach to the challenges of delegation and accountability in parliamentary democracies. The final section outlines the rest of the book.

THE HISTORY OF PARLIAMENTARY GOVERNMENT

Unlike American federalism or presidentialism, parliamentary government was not the
product of deliberate institutional design. Rather, it gradually evolved in Britain over
several centuries.[4] Norton (1981: 12) identifies 1688 as the beginning of parliamentary
dominance, when Parliament prevailed in its conflict with King James II, who was
forced to flee the country. Parliament was then in 1689 effectively able to select the new
King, William of Orange, and to impose significant constraints on his powers.
According to Lowell (1896: 3), the roots of parliamentary government can be traced
back to 1693, when the King first appeased the House of Commons by appointing a
government out of the party (the Whigs) that enjoyed a majority there. Important further developments occurred in the late eighteenth century, when William Pitt the
Younger, based on solid support in the House of Commons, established the leading
role of the cabinet vis-à-vis parliament and, in conducting its daily business, vis-à-vis the
monarch. At that time the cabinet was still that of the Crown, though as a rule cabinets
were appointed that could count on the support of the House of Commons. Yet, the
Commons was still dominated by the King and the aristocracy, who controlled access
to the vast majority of seats.

In 1830, however, the House of Commons forced Wellington to resign over his
unwillingness, due to a deep split among the Tories, to engage in parliamentary reform.
Earl Grey's subsequent Whig Cabinet persuaded the King to dissolve Parliament and
then won the general election on the issue of parliamentary reform. The reform passed
the House of Commons but was held up by the House of Lords. Grey then asked the
King to create enough new peers to force the reform through the Lords. When the
King refused, Grey, backed by the Whigs, tendered the cabinet's resignation. The King
unsuccessfully tried to install a new Wellington cabinet but eventually had to invite the
Whigs back into office and accept their terms. In the end, the House of Lords

---

[4] See, for example, Mackintosh (1968); Kluxen (1983); Norton (1981); Judge (1993) ch. 1; Cox (1987); see
also Goldsworthy (1999).

pre-empted the appointment of many Whig peers and passed the reform bill—The Representation of the People Act—which eliminated or reduced the weight of small boroughs, where elections were often corrupt, and created new seats in towns and cities. The electorate increased from 220,000 to more than 500,000. By 1866, increasing wealth had swollen the ranks of voters to more than one million.

After the 1832 Reform Act, the Crown appears to have had scant influence over cabinet appointments or deliberations—and thus became the 'dignified part' of the British Constitution (Bagehot 1963 [1867]). The House of Commons, on the other hand, criticized and could dismiss the cabinet and in most cases also determine cabinet appointments. Over the subsequent decades, party government was established, and the cabinet came to dominate the House of Commons. According to Gary Cox (1987), this was an indirect response to heightened electoral competitiveness. Members of Parliament (MPs) became more active because their re-election increasingly depended on their visibility and constituency service. Yet, while parliamentary activism was individually rational, it was collectively self-defeating. Too many active and ambitious MPs seeking position-taking and credit-claiming opportunities threatened to overburden the parliamentary agenda and induce institutional paralysis. Hence, those procedural rights that had been abused by visibility-seeking MPs were abolished and the cabinet's agenda control strengthened.

Parliamentary behaviour also became more party-based as the larger constituencies required both a different kind of campaigning and greater activity in Parliament. This process accelerated with the electoral reform acts of 1867 and 1884, which enfranchised a much larger electorate. Now the fate of cabinets was no longer decided on the floor of the House of Commons, as it had been in the 'golden age' of parliamentary government (1832–67), but by the general electorate. 'Members of Parliament were gradually relegated to being representatives of that opinion, and their freedom of parliamentary action was correspondingly diminished' (Norton 1981: 16). Consequently, cabinet members and MPs began to address the general electorate rather than the House of Commons. Procedural reform continued and led to the evolution of a government-managed parliament (Norton 1981: 19–20).

The Swedish Experience

Britain was the birthplace of parliamentary government, and it is first and foremost through the British influence that this form of government has spread throughout the world. Yet, as early as the eighteenth century there were other and largely independent precursors of modern parliamentary and party government. In a less robust and eventually less influential form, parliamentary government existed in Sweden between 1719 and 1772 (Roberts 1986). This period, the 'Age of Liberty', began when after the wars of the early eighteenth century, the Swedish King lost his country's great-power status and a considerable amount of his own powers vis-à-vis the Riksdag (the Swedish Parliament, which then consisted of four Estates Chambers). The new constitution placed the King's Council (rather than the King himself) at the core of executive power.

The King was free to appoint the members of the Council, but only from among the three candidates suggested by the Riksdag. In the Riksdag, one of the four Estates, the Nobility, dominated the proceedings, and the committee system played a major role.

Parliamentary groups at least resembling parties developed by the late 1730s, when some nobles began to form an opposition group known as the Hats (an allusion to the military background common to many in this group). They later extended their organization to the other Estates. The Hats referred to the established Riksdag leadership as the Caps (after Night-Cap) because they considered them to be old and tired. The Hats also more actively sought to regain the military great-power status that had been lost earlier in the century. In 1738 the Hats were strong enough to take control of the Riksdag. They also took control of the King's Council (the cabinet of the time) by refusing to approve the conduct of ministers who allegedly had failed to follow Riksdag decisions. In modern terms, this was essentially a vote of no confidence (or censure) against these ministers (Linnarsson 1943). When the King asked for new candidates for the Council, only candidates from the Hat 'party' were nominated. By 1739, power in the Council was firmly in the hands of the Hats. Metcalf (1977: 7) thus aptly describes the first decades of the Age of Liberty, '[s]tep by step since 1720, the Estates and the Council had introduced limitations on the King's constitutional rights and privileges— not through any formal amendment of the constitution, but through de facto expansion of their own powers and the subsequent evolution of constitutional usage'.

The Hats kept this power for 26 years, at times using a name stamp when the King refused to sign documents, until by 1765 the Caps mustered enough support to wrest control of the Riksdag out of their hands. But even though they were stronger supporters of the King, the Caps did not refrain from taking control of the Council for themselves. The Hats regained power in 1769, and the Caps again in 1771, but by now economic troubles and infighting among the parties and the Estates had eroded support for the system. That year the old King died, and only a year later the new King (Gustav III), supported by the army, ended the 'party system' and restored the powers of the monarchy (Hadenius 1994).

Parliamentary Government Conquers Europe

Parliamentary government later spread through the British Empire 'organically' and to other parts of Europe by diffusion. Yet, there was certainly no 'tidal wave' of parliamentarism until the second half of the nineteenth century. Since the development towards parliamentary government was often irregular, with both incremental and revolutionary steps as well as reversals, the national 'birth dates' are often difficult to pinpoint precisely. France introduced ministerial accountability to parliament in 1792. Most other European countries followed in the late nineteenth or early twentieth century. Parliamentary government (in this sense of ministerial accountability) was thus first introduced in Belgium and Luxembourg in 1830, The Netherlands in 1848, Italy in 1867, Spain in 1869, Norway in 1884, Denmark in 1901, with Austria, Finland, Germany, Iceland, and Ireland following after the First World War (Gerlich 1973: 100–1). At the same time, wealth requirements for representatives gradually disappeared (Manin 1997: ch. 4).

In some countries parliamentary *democracy*, based on universal (or, at least, universal male) suffrage, followed only after considerable delay (e.g. Norway 1897, The Netherlands 1917, Sweden 1917, Britain 1918, Italy 1919, Belgium 1919, and Luxembourg 1919), while in other countries the breakthrough of parliamentary government and full adult suffrage coincided. The latter pattern was particularly prevalent in those countries that had a regime change after First World War, most notably Germany and Austria. In some countries, the enfranchisement of women was delayed even more (Italy 1945, France 1946, and Belgium 1948) (Colomer 2001).

Since the Second World War especially, parliamentary government has proven itself to be a highly resilient regime type, as there have been few cases of authoritarian back-sliding once parliamentarism has been introduced (Stepan and Skach 1993; Przeworski *et al.* 2000). Yet, in several countries the first wave of democratization failed (e.g. Germany, Austria, Spain, and Italy), and a few countries have a record of more than one failed attempt to establish parliamentary government and/or democracy (Greece, Spain) (von Beyme 1973, 1999; Colomer 2001: 217). Such cases indeed account for the parliamentary democracies represented in this volume—Greece, Portugal, and Spain— which in their present form date from the 1970s.

PARLIAMENTARY GOVERNMENT

The terms *parliamentarism, parliamentary government*, and *parliamentary democracy* are often used interchangeably, and so far we have not established any explicit distinction between them. Before we engage in a more substantive discussion of parliamentary government and democracy, however, we need to clarify our use of these key terms. Let us first consider *parliamentary government* as a positive term denoting a particular institutional arrangement.

The term parliamentary government was not used until 1832 in Britain and the late 1830s on the continent (von Beyme 1999: 29–33). Competing terms include representative government (J. S. Mill 1984 [1861]), responsible government, and cabinet government (Bagehot 1963 [1867]). Note that the term parliamentary government conventionally focuses on the relationship between parliament and government. There is no necessary connection to citizens and full universal suffrage. Parliamentary government is thus possible without democracy. Indeed, such early theorists of parliamentary government (though they did not use this term) as John Stuart Mill and Walter Bagehot favoured a limited franchise.

Parliamentary regimes are characterized by a number of specific and interrelated institutional features, upon which its dynamics hinge. To illuminate these institutional effects, a number of authors, most notably Bryce (1921), Loewenstein (1957, 1975), Verney (1959), and von Beyme (1973, 1999), have sought to provide comprehensive definitions of parliamentary government. Their mutual differences notwithstanding, these definitions collectively include the following criteria:

1. There is a dual executive (split between the head of government and the head of state).
2. Parliament has formal or informal investiture powers.

3. The cabinet is a collective decision-making body.
4. Cabinet Ministers are usually also members of parliament.
5. The cabinet is politically responsible to the parliamentary majority.
6. Parliament has means of control (interpellations, committees of inquiry, etc.) over the cabinet.
7. The parliamentary majority can force the cabinet to resign.
8. This power is in most cases balanced by the Prime Minister's power to dissolve parliament.

The properties listed above certainly jointly describe a number of salient features of parliamentary government. Yet, while such a comprehensive conception enhances our configurative understanding, it does not cleanly differentiate between parliamentary government and other regime forms. It is commonly acknowledged that not all parliamentary systems exhibit this list of features in its entirety, and conversely that some of these properties adhere to non-parliamentary systems as well. But a characterization that specifies neither necessary nor sufficient conditions is not very helpful analytically. Moreover, it is not clear whether some of these properties are simply the behavioural consequences of others. Most comprehensive definitions do not make it clear what are definitional properties of parliamentary government and what are contingent features or mere behavioural regularities. Even if in principle these conceptual problems could be solved, the problem remains that some of these criteria are difficult to operationalize. And the more (necessary) definitional criteria we add, the more likely we exclude from the parliamentary category constitutions that otherwise have very much in common.

Minimal Definitions

We believe in the virtues of simple and unambiguous classifications, and hence will not attempt to provide a comprehensive definition. Rather, we prefer a minimal definition, which should provide the simplest and sharpest analytical tool by which we can distinguish parliamentary systems from others. Several such minimal definitions have been proposed. Lijphart (1984: 68, drawing on Epstein 1968) defines parliamentary government as 'a form of constitutional democracy in which executive authority emerges from, and is responsible to, legislative authority'. The 'emergence' criterion denotes that Prime Ministers are selected by parliament, though Lijphart includes in this category cases in which the head of state appoints the Prime Ministers, who 'emerge from interparty bargaining' (1984: 69).[5] Similarly, Sartori (1997: 101) states that 'parliament is sovereign' under parliamentarism and that this regime type requires 'government to be appointed, supported and, as the case may be, dismissed, by parliamentary vote'.

Stepan and Skach (1993: 3) define a parliamentary regime as a system of mutual dependence: '(1) The chief executive power must be supported by a majority in the

---

[5] In a later publication Lijphart (1999: 116–8) adds 'collective or collegial executives' as a third criterion, and thus moves a step away from a minimal definition.

legislature and can fall if it receives a vote of no confidence. (2) The executive power (normally in conjunction with the head of state) has the capacity to dissolve the legislature and call for elections'. And Shugart and Mainwaring (1997: 14–5) thus define parliamentary in contrast to presidential democracy: 'While in presidential systems the head of government is popularly elected, this is not the case with the Prime Minister in parliamentary systems. Furthermore, the electoral terms of the government and the assembly are fixed in presidential systems but not in parliamentary systems'.

Useful as these contrasting definitions are, they are not quite satisfactory. There are three problems. One is analytical: some of the terms of these definitions are ambiguous, or do not effectively partition the world's democratic regimes. The second problem is empirical: Some definitions, if taken seriously, would lead us to categorize particular political systems in ways that few analysts seem to find compelling. The third and most important problem is theoretical: None of these definitions tell us what is *democratic* about parliamentary democracies. We shall address the first two of these problems below, and the third and most important one later in this chapter.

The first (analytical) problem is thus that many existing definitions of parliamentary government are operationally ambiguous. Different scholars using the same criteria may classify the same political systems differently, as Robert Elgie (1998) has amply demonstrated. Also, there are political systems that by common agreement are neither parliamentary nor presidential. Indeed, much of the literature on regime types has concerned itself with such hybrids as the French Fifth Republic or Switzerland. In the case of the French Fifth Republic, the executive does not emerge from the legislature, whereas in Switzerland it does not depend on the legislature's confidence. How, then, do we categorize France? Is it parliamentary or presidential? And what about Switzerland? Or Poland? Or Russia? In fact, a growing number of constitutions do not fit the standard definitions. These constitutions, and the French Fifth Republic in particular, have spawned a growing literature on 'semi-presidential' or 'premier-presidential' government (Duverger 1980; Shugart and Carey 1992; Sartori 1997; Elgie 1998, 1999).

The second (empirical) problem is that if parliament's role in the 'emergence' (Lijphart) or 'appointment' (Sartori) of the cabinet means some form of active selection, then this criterion simply does not very faithfully describe the process of government formation in systems conventionally labelled as parliamentary. It is true that in some such systems, for example Ireland, parliament actually elects a Prime Minister by majority vote. In other systems, such as Italy, parliament must, after a new Prime Minister has been appointed, approve the incoming cabinet in an investiture vote. In most cases, however, there is simply no mechanism by which parliament directly selects the Prime Minister or cabinet. Britain, the birthplace of modern parliamentary democracy, has no such institutional vehicle. Nor does Austria, Denmark, Finland, The Netherlands, or Norway, just to name a few (for empirical surveys, see Laver and Schofield 1990; Bergman 1993; De Winter 1995: ch. 4; and Chapter 4 of this volume). In the real world, then, parliamentary government rarely means that the legislature actually elects or appoints the executive (von Beyme 1973: 41–3). A similar problem is that those definitions that include the executive's dissolution power (e.g. Stepan and Skach 1993; Shugart and Mainwaring 1997) by implication exclude cases that are normally understood as parliamentary. In declining order of severity, this problem applies to Norway, whose constitution simply does not permit early parliamentary dissolution, Germany, in which it is limited to rare circumstances explicitly described in the constitution, and Sweden, where dissolution is contained by the strong disincentive that a new parliament would be elected only for the remainder of the dissolved parliament's term.

The Accountability Criterion

To avoid such definitional problems, a number of authors have resorted to a truly minimalist concern with cabinet accountability. Is his monumental *The History of Government*, S. E. Finer (1997: 1590), drawing on the nineteenth century Swiss constitutional lawyer Johann Kaspar Bluntschli, distinguishes parliamentary government from constitutional monarchy by the responsibility of ministers. While under constitutional monarchy the cabinet ministers 'are appointed by and dismissed by the monarch and are responsible to him alone', under parliamentary government 'they are responsible to the legislature which can force them to retire, or, if the legislature is very strong, can actually impose them on the monarch'. The same definition of parliamentary government has been used to distinguish it, not from its historical predecessor, but from other democratic regime types, in particular presidentialism. Hence, to Strong (1963: 73–5), if the assembly has the power to remove the executive, the regime is parliamentary. Likewise, Steffani's (1979: 39) defining criterion is that the government can be removed from office by parliament. Finally, according to Riggs (1988: 252) the crucial difference between parliamentary and presidential constitutions is 'whether or not the head of government can be replaced by an assembly vote'.[6]

What thus characterizes parliamentary government is that the cabinet must be tolerated by the parliamentary majority, not that the latter actually plays any direct role in the selection of the cabinet. This preserves a core element of all the definitions discussed above, namely the idea of executive accountability to parliament, whereas it disregards the question of selection. Political systems that we conventionally label as parliamentary have much more in common with respect to the former criterion (cabinet accountability) than with respect to the latter (cabinet selection). It is also not clear that the way a cabinet emerges matters as much as its accountability. Diermeier and Feddersen (1998), for example, argue that it is the confidence relationship, the threat of being voted out of office, that accounts for greater party cohesiveness in parliamentary systems than under presidentialism (see also Huber 1996; Baron 1998). These are issues to which we shall return at length later in this volume.

In this volume we adopt this minimal definition. Hence, *parliamentary government* refers to the institutional arrangement by which the executive is accountable, through a confidence relationship, to any parliamentary majority. Thus, in our minimal definition,

---

[6] Riggs (1988: 252) also mentions presidential veto rights and the possibility of executive policies not endorsed by the assembly as 'natural consequences' of presidentialist systems. However, they are 'not the essence of presidentialism'.

parliamentary government is a system of government in which the Prime Minister and his or her cabinet are accountable to any majority of the members of parliament and can be voted out of office by the latter, through an ordinary or constructive vote of no confidence.[7] For simplicity, we shall also use *parliamentarism* as a shorthand for a parliamentary system of government.[8]

PARLIAMENTARY VERSUS PRESIDENTIAL GOVERNMENT

Rules matter to the extent that they affect the game that is played. So also with political regime types such as parliamentarism. Much of the current literature on parliamentary government is concerned with its political effects compared to other regime types. The most frequent alternative is presidentialism, and there is a sizeable literature comparing their respective effects and merits.[9] Bryce (1921: ii. 464–76) was probably the first scholar systematically to assess the comparative merits of modern parliamentarism and presidentialism (plus the Swiss executive council). Bryce compared these regime types along three dimensions, captured in three questions:

1. Which of them best succeeds in giving prompt and full effect to the Will of the People?
2. Which is best calculated to guard against errors into which the people may fall by ignorance, haste, or passion?
3. Which secures the highest efficiency in administration?

Bryce did not provide a clear answer to his third question. Yet, in his words,

the Presidential system leaves more to chance than does the Parliamentarian. A Prime Minister is only one out of a Cabinet, and his colleagues may keep him straight and supply qualities wanting in him, but everything depends on the character of the individual chosen to be President. He may be strong or weak, wise or short-sighted. He may aim at standing above party and use his authority and employ his patronage with a single eye to the nation's welfare, or may think first of his own power and his party's gain,... (Bryce 1921: ii. 469)

In modern parlance, variance in governance will tend to be greater under presidentialism, and this may lead risk-averse citizens to prefer parliamentarism. Yet, it is unclear how significant this variance will be.

Bryce did, however, provide influential answers to his first two questions. He considered parliamentary government superior with regard to 'giving prompt and full effect to the Will of the People': 'Efficiency is most likely to be secured by the

---

[7] For systems with bicameral legislatures, it suffices for the Prime Minister and cabinet to be accountable to the majority in one chamber. Empirically, this is typically the lower chamber. Constitutions under which the Prime Minister and cabinet are accountable to both chambers, such as Italy, are the exception.

[8] We are aware that this common usage can be criticized because an 'ism' typically refers to a normative perspective or movement. Indeed, in the nineteenth century parliamentarism was a democratic movement against autocratic rule (Schütt-Wetschky 1984: 38–9).

[9] Other democratic alternatives are assembly (or convention) government (Loewenstein 1957, 1975; von Beyme 1973, 1999) and Swiss directoral government.

Parliamentary system, because whatever the Executive needs it is sure to obtain from its majority in the Assembly, subject of course, to any check which the existence of a Second Chamber may provide'[10] (Bryce 1921: ii. 475). With regard to Bryce's second question—which system guards better against errors caused by ignorance, haste, or passion—he favoured presidentialism: 'by dividing power between several distinct authorities, it provides more carefully than does the Parliamentary [system] against errors on the part either of Legislature or Executive, and retards the decision by the people of conflicts arising between them' (1921: ii. 474).

Before arriving at his verdict, Bryce discussed at some length the merits and demerits of parliamentarism and presidentialism. In the present context it may suffice to summarize his judgement on parliamentarism. Parliamentary government, according to Bryce,

concentrates the plenitude of popular power in one body, the Legislature, giving to its majority that absolute control of the Executive which enables the latter, when supported by the Legislature, to carry out the wishes of the majority with the maximum of vigour and promptness... The essence of the scheme is that the Executive and the majority in the Legislature work together, each influencing the other; the Cabinet being in fact an Executive Committee of the Legislature... The working of the scheme presupposes not only the existence of parties, but a sentiment of party unity strong enough to induce the majority in the Legislature to entrust a large discretion to the Cabinet, and to support it, except now and then in very grave matters, with a trustful loyalty which assumes its action to have been right till proved to have been wrong. (Bryce 1921: ii. 465)

This description led Bryce to identify the following merits of parliamentary government: It is

calculated to secure swiftness in decision and vigour in action, and enables the Cabinet to press through such legislation as it thinks needed, and to conduct both domestic administration and foreign policy with the confidence that its majority will support it against the attacks of the Opposition. To these merits there is to be added the concentration of Responsibility. For any faults committed the Legislature can blame the Cabinet, and the people can blame both the Cabinet and the majority. (Bryce 1921: ii. 465–6)

However, these merits of parliamentarism 'are balanced by serious defects' (Bryce 1921: ii. 466), among which Bryce counts excessive partisanship and erratic policy making. In his view, parliamentary government nurtures an 'unhealthy' competition between politicians and parties: 'The system intensifies the spirit of party and keeps it always on the boil.[11] Even if there are no important issues of policy before the nation there are always the Offices to be fought for. One party holds them, the other desires them, and the conflict is unending, for immediately after a defeat the beaten party begins its campaign to dislodge the victors' (Bryce 1921: ii. 466).

---

[10] Obviously, Bryce did not consider minority governments, which account for 37% of Western European governments in the 1945–99 period (Müller and Strøm 2000: 561). Under this type of government, parliaments are less likely to be the willing executor of government policies.

[11] Bryce (1921: ii. 335) attributed the 'decline of parliaments', his famous thesis, to the rise of party machines and the multiplication of parties, which, in turn, was said to cause cabinet instability and faulty compromises in policy-making.

Bryce also seriously questioned the capacity of parliamentary governments to generate policy outputs that are in the long-term public interest. First, the accountability to parliament would force cabinets to think first and foremost about the short-term popularity of their policy proposals. A cabinet, he argued, is disposed 'to think too much of what support it can win by proposals framed to catch the fancy of the moment, and to think too little of what the real needs of the nation are' (1921: ii. 467). Moreover, Bryce suggested that parliamentary government would encourage hasty and half-baked decisions: 'Lastly, the very concentration of power and swiftness with which decisions can be reached and carried into effect is a source of danger. There is no security for due reflection, no opportunity for second thoughts. Errors may be irretrievable'. Presidential government, on the other hand, 'was built for safety, not for speed' (Bryce 1921: ii. 468).

Although Bryce's analysis has largely been eclipsed by more recent scholarship, we find it incisive and rich in intuition. As later chapters will show, the choice of regime type does in fact involve a trade-off between such concerns as efficiency and the risk of faulty (counter-productive or, at least, suboptimal) decisions. Moreover, this trade-off is associated with regime type much in the way that Bryce suggests. Also, Bryce's concern with the connection between parliamentary government and partisan-ship continues to be valid. Yet, whereas Bryce could only speculate about these relationships in somewhat imprecise terms, we can examine delegation and its con-comitant problems in much more precise and rigorous ways, and examine an empirical record that is much larger and better documented. But before we embark on our main project, let us briefly examine the more recent debate that these improvements in our understanding have occasioned.

The Contemporary Debate

The contemporary literature on the merits of parliamentary government is character-ized by three substantive concerns and three approaches. The three substantive con cerns are the effects of regime types on (1) regime stability, (2) policy outputs and their fit with citizen preferences, and (3) the process of governance. The first approach to these questions maintains the classical distinction between presidential and parliamen-tary systems and attempts to identify the relative merits of one versus the other. The second approach similarly maintains this classification of regime types but then adds further criteria so as to differentiate subtypes within each of these main categories. For scholars in the third tradition, however, the presidential–parliamentary distinction is epiphenomenal or simply less consequential than other differences between demo-cratic constitutions.

The influential work of Linz (1994) exemplifies the first approach above. Linz argues that the 'temporal rigidity' of presidentialism potentially undermines democratic stability. Under presidential government, citizens are stuck with their agents (the President and the legislature) until their respective terms expire. Under the worst-case scenario, the 'Linzian nightmare' (Ackerman 2000: 645), the constitutional design of presidentialism results in divided government, deadlock, crises of governability, and eventually the breakdown of democracy. Parliamentary government compares favourably, because it allows the removal at any time of executive office holders who have lost the trust of the legislature.

As Kaiser (1997: 422–3) has observed, the subsequent debate over the advantages and disadvantages of parliamentary and presidential democracy is characterized by its asymmetrical focus on the inherent problems of presidential constitutions. Several contributions have lent theoretical (Colomer 1995; Riggs 1997) or empirical (Stepan and Skach 1993; Przeworski *et al.* 2000) support to Linz's negative assessment of the effects of presidentialism on regime stability. Colomer (2001: 213), who differentiates between parliamentary systems with majoritarian versus proportional electoral systems, shows that the regime survival rate of proportional-parliamentary democracies is considerably greater than that of presidential democracies, which, in turn, do better than majoritarian parliamentary ones. Other studies, however, place presidential democracy in a more favourable light (Shugart and Carey 1992; Mainwaring and Shugart 1997; von Mettenheim 1997). Lane and Ersson (2000: 117–42), for instance, show that parliamentary systems clearly outperform presidential ones in democratic stability and socio-economic development. However, if socio-economic development is understood not as a consequence of regime type, but rather its environment, much of the difference between presidential and parliamentary government disappears.

Regime stability may be a necessary condition for good government, but citizens in many advanced industrial democracies perceive little systemic threat. In such circumstances, debate over regime performance often shifts to more specific policy outcomes. Scholars interested in this second major concern often emphasize dimensions that cross-cut the presidential–parliamentary distinction. Thus, Powell (1982, 2000), Lijphart (1984, 1999), and Tsebelis (1995, 2002) create their own regime typologies.

Powell (1982) examines electoral participation, government stability, and political order (the absence of turmoil and violence) in twenty-nine democracies between 1958 and 1976. Distinguishing three regime types—presidential systems, majoritarian parliamentary systems, and representational parliamentary systems—Powell concludes that '[e]ach of the constitutional arrangements has some advantages and disadvantages', which in large part reflect their political party systems (1982: 218). In his more recent study, Powell (2000) distinguishes more simply between majoritarian and proportional systems. His only presidential system, the United States, is classified as mixed because of the combined impact of the (majoritarian) single-member plurality electoral system, low party discipline, and separation-of-powers institutions. Powell finds proportionalism more conducive to the formation of governments close to the median citizen (2000: 41).

Focusing on a broad range of performance indicators for stable democracies around the world, Arend Lijphart (1984, 1999) argues that the combination of parliamentary government and proportional representation (PR) electoral systems is optimal. More specifically, Lijphart (1995, 1999) finds that 'consensus democracies' (which feature parliamentary government and PR elections) perform slightly better than majoritarian systems (presidential systems and parliamentary systems with majoritarian elections) macro-economically, but 'a great deal better with regard to many qualitative aspects of democracy: the representation of women and minorities, income equality, voter participation, citizens' satisfaction with democracy, and the proximity between the government and the median voter' (Lijphart 1999: 258–93, 2000: 168–9).

We shall return to several of these concerns later in this volume (see especially chapter 23). Note, however, that some of the advantages that Lijphart reports for consensus democracies may reflect the fact that several of his performance indicators directly or indirectly privilege polities with expansive governments and a large public sector. Such an explanation would be consistent with the work of Persson and Tabellini (1999), who contend that in presidential systems, the chief executive will seek support from those legislators that are 'cheapest to buy'. In parliamentary systems, on the other hand, the members of the executive are forced to sustain the majority that keeps them in power. They are not free to seek support where it is least expensive but must instead embark on more ambitious government programs. Hence, parliamentary systems foster a more expansive and expensive public sector. Empirically, Persson and Tabellini show that, even when they control for per capita income, openness of the economy, age of the population, and ethno-linguistic fractionalization, presidential systems indeed have smaller government shares of gross domestic product (GDP) (see also Boix 2001).

The third major focus of the contemporary literature is on governance and policy-making itself. This is in many ways the approach that is closest to our own concerns in this volume. Moe and Caldwell (1994) thus argue that systems of parliamentary government distinguish themselves with regard to policy efficiency. Legislators, they argue, have incentives to respond to the particularistic demands of interest groups. Under presidential government this leads to the creation of comparatively ineffective bureaucratic structures. Once successful, interest groups prefer to insulate government agencies from future democratic control. In order to protect their policy gains, they lobby for excessive regulation of the agencies, which, in turn, renders these administrative units ineffective (see also McCubbins, Noll, and Weingast 1987). In contrast, parliamentary systems of the Westminster type do not allow for such entrenchment of institutions, since any new parliamentary majority can dismantle the regulations. Hence, there is no incentive to 'overregulate' government agencies and thus cripple them. However, Moe and Caldwell (1994) concede that they compare US presidentialism with the most contrasting type of parliamentarism—the 'Westminster model'—and suggest that coalitional parliamentary systems may be much more similar to presidential ones.

In their study of government capabilities, Weaver and Rockman (1993) distinguish three tiers of explanation. The first tier distinguishes presidential from parliamentary systems. Since the United States is their only case, Weaver and Rockman do not further distinguish between presidential regimes, but they do provide a sub-classification of parliamentary systems. The second tier thus comprises what they call 'regime' and 'government type'(multiparty coalitions versus alternating single-party government versus dominant-party). The third tier includes other institutional features such as federalism, bicameralism, judicial review, and non-institutional factors such as political culture.

Weaver and Rockman's comparison focuses on the impact of institutional arrangements on the government's steering functions (policy innovation, resource targeting, loss imposition, priority setting, coordinating of conflicting objectives, and policy implementation), maintenance functions (policy stability, maintaining international commitments), and political tasks (representing and reconciling diversity, managing conflict, and representing new interests). They conclude that 'the distinction between parliamentary systems and the US system of checks and balances...captures only a small part of potential institutional influences on governmental capacity' (Weaver and Rockman 1993: 445–6). The 'effects of specific institutional arrangements...are neither uniform nor unidirectional' (Weaver and Rockman 1993: 454). In some cases concentrated power is better, in some cases the institutional arrangements make no difference, and in some cases concentrated power is worse.

Similarly, in his review of policy output differences between parliamentary and presidential systems, Eaton (2000) examines the effects of veto players, the visibility of policy negotiations, the systems' biases toward collective or particularistic goods, the accountability of individual office holders, interest group strategies, and delegation to bureaucrats. He concludes that although there are systematic differences between presidential and parliamentary systems, these 'in most cases...tend to wash out' when variation within each regime type is considered (2000: 371).

George Tsebelis' (1995, 2002) contributions are in some ways much in the spirit of Weaver and Rockman, but within a much simpler and more parsimonious theoretical framework. Tsebelis maintains that the critical regime characteristics are the number and preferences of veto players. Presidential governments tend to have more veto players than parliamentary ones. But the distinction between parliamentary and presidential systems is epiphenomenal to the dynamics of democratic policy-making. Whether parliamentary or presidential, Tsebelis argues, systems with few and ideologically homogeneous veto players are more conducive to policy change than those with many and heterogeneous ones.

To put the contemporary regime literature in a nutshell: scholars disagree as to whether parliamentary government is superior to presidentialism with respect to such substantive concerns as regime stability and policy performance, or whether there are no meaningful differences. While some merits of presidentialism have also been identified, this regime type has found fewer enthusiastic defenders. There is broad agreement that substantial differences exist among parliamentary democracies (see e.g. Loewenstein 1957, 1975; Verney 1959: 18; Steffani 1979: 43–4; Sartori 1997: 101), and yet surprisingly few efforts have been made to map out the variety of parliamentary institutions and to carefully assess their implications. Moreover, while the contemporary literature thus has shed considerable light on the systemic as well as policy consequences of different regime types, it has paid scant attention to what makes parliamentary democracy, or for that sake any other form of democracy, *democratic*. In other words, we still need to address the *theoretical* problem identified earlier in this chapter. It is to this concern that we now turn.

THE PARLIAMENTARY CHAIN OF DELEGATION

The policy process in contemporary democracies, from voters all the way to the civil servants that ultimately implement public policy, can be viewed as a process of *delegation*, in which those authorized to make political decisions conditionally designate others to make such decisions in their name and place. The basic normative assumption is that policy-makers in a democracy should do what the citizens want them to do.[12]

In democratic societies, citizens delegate to politicians first and foremost through elections. *Democratic* elections need to satisfy a number of criteria. They must be held under conditions of political competition (freedom to form and join organizations freedom of expression, alternative sources of information, and freedom of candidacy), and there must be an independent and competent administration, as well as appropriate judicial bodies, to implement the election law (for the 'classic' argument, see Dahl 1956: 84, 1971: 3, 1989: 221–2; for a recent application, see Choe 1997).

As the primary democratic institution, elections have a double nature, allowing for delegation as well as accountability (Powell 2000). As mechanisms of delegation, elections vest politicians and parties with a mandate, and as instruments of accountability they provide the opportunity to hold politicians and parties responsible for their actions in office. In the former (mandate) perspective, parties and politicians present their programmes and credentials to the voters and are elected on the basis of the voters' policy choices and their own perceived competence.

Elections can induce accountability to that extent that elective offices are attractive and that incumbents therefore generally would like to remain incumbents or even to rise in the political hierarchy, the motivation identified by Schlesinger (1966) as progressive ambition. The fear of electoral punishment is a strong incentive for incumbents to remain in tune with their voters' demands (see e.g. Sartori 1987: 156). Even if representatives have no ambition to run again, or when term limits prohibit them from doing so, the salutary effects of electoral accountability may operate indirectly. In such cases, the electoral connection constrains politicians through their collective affiliation with political parties, which seek to remain in business well beyond the terms of individual politicians, and hence do their best to make incumbents with discrete ambition (i.e. ambition that does not extend beyond their current term of office) behave *as if* they would face the electorate again (Schlesinger 1991; Wittman 1995; Carey 1996; Müller 2000).

Yet, democratic elections are only the first step in the delegation process. John Stuart Mill's prescription for the 'proper office of a representative assembly' thus stresses the need for parliamentary delegation to the cabinet. Since 'no body of men...is fit for

---

[12] There are at least three arguments which can be made against this assumption. First, because of the problems of preference aggregation, it may simply be impossible to know what citizens want (Riker 1982). Second, if doing what the citizens want means doing what the majority (or plurality) of citizens want, there are normative limits to majority rule (human rights). Third, elitists may claim that leaders know their followers' interests better than the latter do themselves (see Manin, Przeworski, and Stokes 1999). We return to these issues in Chapter 3.

action', parliaments 'ought not to administer' (Mill 1984 [1861]: 249), 'or to dictate in detail to those who have the charge of administration' (1984 [1861]: 250). A parliament 'is as little fitted for the direct business of legislation as for that of administration', Mill (1984 [1861]: 254) maintained. Accordingly, it 'has never been thought desirable that Parliament should itself nominate even the members of a Cabinet' (Mill 1984 [1861]: 253). Hence, parliament should not make administrative decisions, select ministers (or even civil servants), or even legislate in a substantive sense.

Instead of the function of governing, for which it is radically unfit, the proper office of a representative assembly is to watch and control the government: to throw the light of publicity on its acts: to compel a full exposition and justification of all of them which any one considers questionable; to censure them if found condemnable, and, if the men who compose the government abuse their trust, or fulfil it in a sense which conflicts with the deliberate sense of the nation, to expel them from office, and either expressly or virtually appoint their successors. (Mill 1984 [1861]: 258).

Mill favoured a system in which parliament delegates extensively and limits itself to the tasks of controlling the executive and to be an arena for public debate. There are, however, many ways in which citizens can delegate to politicians, and many ways in which politicians can delegate among each other. Let us therefore consider more systematically the nature of democratic delegation from voters to those who govern. This is a chain in which we can identify at least four discrete steps:

1. Delegation from voters to their elected representatives.
2. Delegation from legislators to the executive branch, specifically to the head of government (the Prime Minister).
3. Delegation from the head of government (Prime Minister) to the heads of different executive departments.
4. Delegation from the heads of different executive departments to civil servants.

This chain of delegation is mirrored by a corresponding chain of accountability that runs in the reverse direction. Thus, democratic constitutions contain mechanisms that allow principals to delegate and that make agents accountable. Indeed, what makes democratic regimes democratic is precisely that they contain mechanisms by which the citizens can select and control their representatives.

This view of representative democracy as delegation and accountability is, of course, a simplification (see Chapter 3). Yet, building on this framework, we can now spell out an ideal-typical definition of *parliamentary democracy*. We will use this term for two specific purposes: (1) to anchor our understanding of parliamentary institutions in a conception of popular sovereignty, and (2) to flesh out a configurative model from which we can most easily understand how this form of government differs from alternative constitutions, and particularly presidentialism. Yet, we should stress that this model is an ideal type, designed to capture in an extreme form a bundle of attributes that are positively associated with parliamentary regimes, though not necessary ingredients.

In its ideal-typical form, then, parliamentary democracy is a chain of delegation and accountability, from the voters to the ultimate policy-makers, in which at each link (stage), a *principal* (in whom authority is originally) delegates to an *agent*, whom the principal has conditionally authorized to act in his or her name and place. The parliamentary chain has the following characteristics:

1. It is *indirect*, in that voters (the ultimate principal) directly elect only their parliamentary representatives. All other agents are only indirectly elected and accountable to the citizens.

2. Thus, parliamentary democracy means a particularly *simple* form of delegation.[13] In each link of the parliamentary chain, a single principal delegates to a single agent (such as a member of parliament).[14] Voters in a presidential system, in contrast, typically elect multiple competing agents (such as, for example, a President and members of two separate legislative chambers).

3. In a similar fashion, under parliamentary democracy agents are accountable to a single (though not necessarily individual or unique) principal. Cabinet Ministers, for example, report to a single master (the Prime Minister), and ultimately to a parliament in which a single committee controls their jurisdiction. Likewise, civil servants have a single principal, their respective Cabinet Minister. In a presidential system, on the other hand, agents may have multiple principals. Civil servants, for example, may report to the President as well as to both legislative chambers. Parliamentary democracy, then, means simple accountability as well as simple delegation.

The ideal-typical *parliamentary democracy* thus features an indirect chain of command, in which at each stage a single principal delegates to only one agent (or several non-competing ones), and where each agent is accountable to one and only one principal. Thus, *indirectness* and *singularity* set parliamentarism apart from other constitutional designs, such as presidentialism.

PROBLEMS OF DEMOCRATIC DELEGATION

Delegation is often problematic, and delegation in national governments is no exception. Such problems have not gone unnoticed. Robert Michels, for example, was both aware of the need to delegate to party leaders and highly critical of its effects: 'democracy is inconceivable without organization', he wrote, yet organization 'gives birth to the domination of the elected over the electors, of the mandataries over the mandators, of the delegates over the delegators. Who says organization says oligarchy' (Michels 1962: 61, 365). In the same spirit Robert De Jouvenil ([1914] quoted in Loewenberg and Patterson 1979: 21) coined the well-known dictum that two

---

[13] Note that if we take the idea of singular agents to its logical extreme, the ideal-typical parliamentary democracy is also a unitary state (such as Britain, New Zealand, or Sweden, but not Austria or Canada), with a unicameral parliament (such as the Nordic countries or, again, New Zealand).

[14] In our elaboration of this framework in Chapter 3, we recognize that even under an ideal-typical parliamentary democracy, principals sometimes delegate to multiple agents. Yet, these agents do not generally compete with one another.

revolutionaries, only one of whom is a member of parliament, have less in common than two members of parliament, only one of whom is a revolutionary. There are also numerous references to 'downstream' delegation problems between ministers and civil servants, from Max Weber (1972: 572–4), who in naming ministers 'dilettantes' and civil servants 'experts' clearly indicated agency problems, all the way to the popular television comedy series *Yes, Minister* (Lynn and Jay 1981).

The contemporary literature continues to express concern about delegation, though perhaps in a more disaggregated fashion than in the classical literature. Yet, larger claims about the possibility of democratic delegation have by no means been abandoned. They range from those who hail the virtues of democratic delegation to those who think that delegation equals abdication. Among those who celebrate the successes of parliamentary delegation are Klingemann, Hofferbert, and Budge (1994), who find that government expenditure in several policy areas responds to party manifestos. Among the less sanguine analysts, there are those who claim that delegation works, but only at election time. One important strand of modern democratic theory, the competitive model, puts great store in accountability at election time. All voters can do is to choose a set of politicians who appear more likely to do the 'right things' and to punish politicians who have not done so (see Schumpeter 1942; Riker 1982). In a more cynical formulation, then, the people rule directly only on election day; otherwise they are ruled by the politicians to whom they have delegated the task of making authoritative decisions (Schattschneider 1960: ch. VIII; Sartori 1987: 28–31, 86–9).

But even this view is too positive for some. Even if delegation works on election day, it may have unintended and negative consequences. According to Mayhew (1974) the 'electoral connection' triggers legislative behaviour that is individually rational (by enhancing re-election prospects) but that does not contribute to, and may even undermine, the collective goals of the United States Congress. Hence, individual congressmen engage in 'advertising', 'credit claiming', and 'position taking'. The 'electoral connection' thus induces members to shirk their legislative responsibilities, in which credit claiming is more difficult. Similarly, Fiorina (1977: 39–47) argues that congressmen devote their time and energy to casework and pork-barrel politics rather than legislation. While legislation is likely to be controversial to at least some voters, pork-barrel politics and casework are largely popular. In the most cynical interpretation, the lack of emphasis that representatives put on legislation creates problems that are then resolved piecemeal by the same politicians whose re-election is guaranteed by exactly these services.

Finally, the message of the most severe critics, is that delegation simply does not work. Politicians and other public officials are autonomous, and citizens have no real influence on what their representatives are doing. Consequently, politicians may misbehave in one of two ways: policy drift or rent-seeking. In the former case, 'Politicians may want to pursue their own ideas even if these differ from those of citizens' (Manin, Przeworski, and Stokes 1999: 40). In the latter case, they may use political power to chase material advantage. The 'grabbing hand' perspective in economics argues that politicians do not maximize social welfare but instead pursue their own selfish objectives (Shleifer and Vishny 1998: 4). The literature on rent-seeking politicians indeed claims that 'governments transfer wealth not just among subgroups of citizens but also directly to themselves' (McChesney 1997: 35). Rent extraction by politicians becomes more likely when institutions allow them to cloud responsibility for inefficient government action. And according to influential theories of bureaucracy, non-elected public officials are also likely to behave in ways that defy the voters' preferences (Downs 1967; Niskanen 1971).[15]

Problems of delegation thus give rise to some of the most scathing criticisms of modern democracies. Although much of this scholarship does not focus squarely on parliamentary government, and although we may differ with many of its premises, it holds major implications for our investigation of parliamentarism. Parliamentary systems certainly face their own delegation problems, with critical implications for our assessment of contemporary democracies. But although it is hugely consequential whether parliamentary delegation does or does not work, we need sharper tools and a more detailed plan of campaign before we can properly return to this debate. It is to these needs that we next attend.

Agency Problems

Let us now return to the problems of delegation under parliamentary democracy. We shall discuss these problems in the language of agency theory. The difference between what the principal wants and what the agent delivers is known as agency loss (the technical definition will be made clear in the Chapter 2). Principals (in our case, citizens) may be poorly served by their agents (politicians) for either of two reasons (or both). One problem is that the agents may have preferences that differ from those of the principals. The other problem is that the principals may not know enough about their potential agents to get the best possible deal from them. The latter, informational, problem may in turn come in two forms. First, principals may not be able to choose the right agents in the first place (*adverse selection*). Second, principals may not be able to keep their agents honest and diligent (*moral hazard*). In the Chapters 2 and 3, we shall expand on these problems and their application to the chain of delegation in parliamentary democracies. In this section we briefly review the extent to which the literature on parliamentary democracy has identified adverse selection and moral hazard problems. While the initial and final stages of the parliamentary chain of delegation have traditionally been seen as beset with delegation problems, much less concern has been given to delegation from the parliamentary majority to a Prime Minister or cabinet, or to delegation within the cabinet. Yet, agency loss can occur in any link in the parliamentary chain of delegation, and only if the whole chain works can the democratic promise be fulfilled.

Adverse Selection

After the first wave of European democratization crested immediately following the First World War, problems of parliamentary democracy soon figured prominently in

---

[15] For a theoretical critique of Niskanen (1971), see, for example, McLean (1987: 89–100) or Dunleavy (1991). For an assessment of the empirical fit of Niskanen's theory, see Blais and Dion (1991).

the political debate. Among the principal protagonists in this debate were Gaetano Mosca and Carl Schmitt, whose contributions had a more lasting impact than most others. A core element of their critique was that parliament had been robbed of its power. Although, of course, he never used this label, Gaetano Mosca was centrally concerned with the problem of adverse selection, specifically with the dominance of parliament by societal elites. In his view, elections were controlled by organized minorities, leaving the great majority of people little effective choice of candidates (Mosca 1950: 135–6). Consequently, parliaments would represent the interests of wealthy and powerful elites rather than the popular majority. Mosca also saw this selection problem as a cause of patronage politics. 'Influential voters', that is societal elites, would make MPs intervene in administrative and judicial processes. Because the MPs would depend on the 'influential voters', and the government, in turn, on the MPs, 'all moral and legal considerations' would be pushed to the background. The government and the representatives' 'permanent and obvious conflict between duties and interests' would lead to a situation in which 'the bureaucracy and the elected bodies, which are meant to check each other, corrupt each other' (Mosca 1950: 217).

As Mosca presented his concerns, they do not pertain specifically to parliamentary regimes. The charge that powerful societal elites control elected politicians can be levelled against any system of representation (see, for instance, Mills' (1956) critique of the United States). Mosca most likely associated these problems with parliamentary government because it was the regime under which he lived. At the end of his career, however, Mosca (1947, 1950: 215) conceded that parliamentarism had to be compared with other real-world regimes, in particular those that preceded or succeeded it (i.e. constitutional monarchy and Fascism, respectively). In this comparison, the delegation problems of parliamentarism seem less damning. Mosca also suggested remedies for the problems of parliamentary government (Mosca 1950: 219–22), namely

- greater independence and security of judges,
- greater independence of audit offices,
- government decentralization, and
- more civic engagement among the well-educated and wealthy.

In the terms with which this volume will examine parliamentary democracy, most of these suggested remedies constitute constraints on the agents in the democratic chain of delegation. As we shall see in later chapters, it is intriguing to note the striking ways in which much of Mosca's reform agenda is being heeded, more than half a century later. But that is a story to which we shall return in Chapters 4 and 22.

Moral Hazard

Mosca does not seem to have seriously considered the ways in which mass political parties might help solve the delegation problems with which he was concerned by elevating the representatives of more humble classes. Yet, although political parties might have helped counter adverse selection, they brought their own problems.

Writing in a time when parties had already become the dominant political players, Ostrogorski (1907: ii. 712–17) lamented that they had practically destroyed political accountability. Under party-based parliamentary government, he claimed, 'the responsibility which is supposed to govern parliamentary relations comes to nothing but general irresponsibility', because the MP's responsibility 'disappears in that of the party'... 'however incompetent or culpable' ministers may be, 'it is impossible to punish one of them without punishing all'. Given party cohesion, under party government the fall of a cabinet could only happen by 'accident'. In between elections the government 'can do very much what it likes'. Parliamentary control 'is almost non-existent'. Thus, Ostrogorski's main point is the lack of accountability under party-based parliamentary government. In a word, his complaint is that parties foster moral hazard.

Likewise, in his famous *English Government and Politics*, Frederic Austin Ogg argued that executive agenda control in practice had eroded the cabinet's accountability to parliament: 'Armed with paramount rights of initiative, supported by procedural rules drawn in their favour, and holding the power of life and death over Parliament itself, the cabinet indicates what is to be done; and Parliament, on its part...dreading the consequences of refusal, complies' (Ogg 1936: 461).

Echoing the concerns of Ostrogorski, Carl Schmitt regretted the abandonment of a separation of powers between parliament and government. In his view, 'narrow and narrowest committees of parties and party coalitions make decisions behind closed doors' (Schmitt 1969 [1923]: 52). Note his concern here with what the principal–agent approach labels 'hidden action', which can be a source of moral hazard. Like ourselves, Schmitt conceived of parliamentary democracy as a chain of delegation, with parliament as a committee of the people and the cabinet a committee of parliament. To him, the value of parliamentary government stemmed from rational and public discussion among the MPs. Once all the relevant information had been tabled and discussed, this should lead to 'true and right policies'. Clearly, under 'proper parliamentarism' some learning and enlightenment would take place. This, however, would no longer be the case if parliamentary debate were a mere 'façade'. Thus, the fusion of executive and legislative powers creates severe accountability problems. In Chapter 3 we shall return to similar concerns about transparency.

Yet important early twentieth-century authors, in particular Max Weber and Hans Kelsen (see also Herman Finer 1931), defended parliamentary government against real-world alternatives that were all non-democratic. Weber's writings on parliamentary democracy were essentially an attempt to convince his more reluctant German fellow citizens of its virtues.[16] In contrast, Kelsen (1926, 1929) gave a more balanced assessment. He considered parliamentary government the only possible way to realize the idea of democracy in the world of his day (Kelsen 1926: 5). Yet, he also identified delegation problems and suggested remedies. Specifically, Kelsen called parliamentary government a 'compromise between the democratic demand for freedom and the principle of the division of labour', hence delegation (Kelsen 1926: 7, 1929: 29). According

---

[16] See 'Wahlrecht und Demokratie in Deutschland' (1917) and 'Parlament und Regierung im neugeordneten Deutschland' (1918), both reprinted in Weber (1988).

to Kelsen, parliamentary government is characterized by a 'fiction of representation' that consists of two components: (1) the idea that parliament is only the representative ('Stellvertreter') of the people and (2) that the people can issue their will only in parliament and through parliament, despite the fact that they do not give the MPs binding instructions. This leaves the parliament legally sovereign and hence the decisions of parliament may deviate from the preferences of the voters (Kelsen 1926: 10, 1929: 30). Thus the problem is the 'irresponsibility of the MP vis-à-vis his voters' (Kelsen 1926: 14).

Kelsen's concerns resonate with many subsequent authors, for whom the fusion of the parliamentary majority and the chief executive creates special accountability problems, especially on 'minor' issues. While the electoral connection may secure accountability on major issues, it is likely to be inadequate when issues fall short of catching the voters' attention or causing their alienation. In other words, accountability breaks down when the ultimate principals, the voters, have a severe information problem. Their direct representatives, the Members of Parliament, whose information is considerably better, are bound by party loyalty (or discipline) and hence may not wish to 'rock the government's boat' (King 1976). In this respect, parliamentary government perverts the representatives' incentives: Were government MPs to take seriously their duty to hold the executive accountable, they might raise the voters' attention to the wrongdoings of their co-partisans in the executive branch, with likely adverse electoral consequences. The fusion of legislative and executive powers may also cause bad policies, if the parliamentary majority invariably is willing to turn all government proposals into law. Thus, policy failures are likely to result from the abandonment of parliamentary scrutiny.

Phrased in the terms employed in this volume, Kelsen thought the main problem of parliamentary government to be moral hazard and considered the electoral accountability mechanisms to be insufficient. Consequently, he suggested three remedies:

- the referendum,
- political parties that allow for participation between elections, and
- special corporatist parliaments, which assemble expertise not available in parliament.

These suggested remedies empower the ultimate principal, the voters, and aim at overcoming the information problems vis-à-vis MPs. Note that, in language that Lupia develops in the Chapter 2, Kelsen's remedies focus in large part on *ex ante* mechanism of agency control, whereas Mosca largely favoured *ex post* instruments (see Kiewiet and McCubbins 1991). The debate between these competing vehicles of popular sovereignty continues to this day.

THE ROAD AHEAD

Representative democracy means delegation, and delegation is problematic for several reasons. In this chapter, we have briefly identified some delegation problems that will be discussed at greater length in the following chapters. Preference divergence and asymmetric information may make a mockery out of political representation and lead to such problems as adverse selection and moral hazard. Because such agency problems exist, democracy requires not only delegation, but also accountability. The aim of this volume is to explore the ways in which delegation and accountability works in the parliamentary systems of Western Europe and thus to understand the conditions that favour and constrain popular sovereignty. We focus on those political institutions that impinge on delegation and accountability throughout the democratic chain of delegation. As subsequent chapters will show, institutions can solve or at least ameliorate agency problems in several ways.

The co-editors and contributors to *Delegation and Accountability in Parliamentary Democracy* have had two main objectives. The first aim is to identify the problems of delegation that parliamentary democracy implies and to identify and assess the institutional solutions that might be brought to bear on them. Our second goal is to provide a comprehensive and theoretically guided survey of the institutions of parliamentary democracies, and to describe in greater detail how the democratic process of delegation and accountability operates in the Western European heartland of parliamentary democracy. With regard to both aims we try to identify trends over time. These are interrelated objectives, but they are not modest ones.

Our empirical investigation includes all Western European countries that meet our minimal definition of parliamentary government, that is, all those in which the chief executive (generically referred to in this study as the Prime Minister) is accountable to, and can be removed for purely political reasons by, any parliamentary majority. By this criterion, the only West European country (apart from some mini-states) that during 2003 fails to enter our sample is Switzerland. Of course, by casting our net so widely, we are including a set of political systems that are dissimilar in many ways. Thus, we are including majoritarian as well as consensus democracies (Lijphart 1999), systems with few or many veto players (Tsebelis 1995, 2002), systems with unrestricted versus highly restrictive dissolution powers (Strøm and Swindle 2002), and systems with single-member district as well as proportional electoral systems (Cox 1997).

Some may find that the most consequential and controversial of our decisions is that we include countries oftentimes referred to as semi-presidential (Duverger 1980; Elgie 1998, 1999). It is customary to regard France, Finland (at least until the constitutional reform of 2000), and Portugal (until the constitutional reform of 1982) as semi-presidential, based on the Presidents' direct election and the authority they have exercised in legislation or policy-making and/or over the formation and termination of cabinets as well as over the calling of elections. For the 1975–85 period Greece may be added to the list of semi-presidential regimes, since the President—although not directly elected—was vested with important powers. There is a broader category of semi-presidentialism to which also Austria, Iceland, Ireland, and Portugal (since 1982)—even though their respective *effective* presidential powers seem much more limited—belong by virtue of the fact that their heads of state are popularly elected. Yet, we include all of these countries in the present study because we believe that their common mechanisms of delegation and accountability, and particularly the accountability of the chief executive to parliament (our minimal definition of parliamentarism), are more important than the features that set them apart. That is not to say that these distinctions are unimportant, however, and in fact a central concern of ours will be to demonstrate how and to what extent they actually do shape popular governance.

This volume consists of three major sections. The first section contains two additional theoretical chapters. Chapter 2, by Arthur Lupia, discusses the general problem of delegation versus abdication and introduces the principal–agent framework within which we seek to understand parliamentary democracies. Chapter 3, by Kaare Strøm, brings together this analytical approach and our empirical project. It elaborates a conception of the democratic chain of delegation, contrast the governance mechanisms that character-ize parliamentary versus presidential systems, and discusses the implications of these institutional differences for the problems of democratic delegation and accountability.

The second section, and the bulk of this book, consists of eighteen chapters. In the first of these chapters (Chapter 4), we detail the most important mechanisms of delega-tion and accountability that exist at each stage of the parliamentary chain. This chapter is cross-national and presents a wealth of information in tabular form. It also discusses the broad range of variation in institutional structures that we find across Western Europe. Chapters 5–21 apply our perspective and questions to seventeen West European countries, beginning with Austria and proceeding alphabetically through to the United Kingdom. The country chapters all have a common structure and address the same sets of questions. They cover the entire post-Second World War period (or the period since the latest introduction of democratic government) and report relevant changes in the rules and conventions governing the governance process. These eighteen chapters present the most systematic and detailed cross-national survey that is available on institutional arrangements (accountability mechanisms) in parliamentary democracies, in 2003.

Each chapter focuses on four discrete stages in the delegation process: (1) delegation from voters to parliamentary representatives, (2) delegation from parliament to the Prime Minister and cabinet, (3) delegation within the cabinet, and (4) delegation from individual cabinet members to civil servants. These detailed discussions are followed by a section on external constraints, that is, constitutional and other mechanisms that impinge on democratic delegation and limit the discretion of the relevant constitu-tional actors. The country chapters give a full account of the mechanisms of delega-tion and accountability. They also discuss how effective they are in solving the problems of delegation.

In Chapters 22 and 23, as we return to the broader picture of parliamentary democracy today, we assess our lessons. We are here particularly concerned with the prominence of certain agency problems and with the growing importance of constraints. As we will argue, the relationship between parliamentary democracy and institutional constraints is becoming increasingly complex. While this may accentuate certain agency problems, cur-rent trends also point toward certain promising developments. And while the historical les-sons presented in this chapter remind us that parliamentarism has been and still is a very robust system of government, the parliamentary democracies of Western Europe are fac-ing a number of very important challenges.

REFERENCES

Ackerman, Bruce (2000). 'The New Separation of Powers'. *Harvard Law Review*, 113: 633–729.

Bagehot, Walter (1963 [1867]). *The English Constitution*. London: Fontana/Collins.

Baron, David P. (1998). 'Comparative Dynamics of Parliamentary Governments'. *American Political Science Review*, 92: 593–609.

Bergman, Torbjörn (1993). 'Formation Rules and Minority Governments'. *European Journal of Political Research*, 23: 55–66.

Blais, André and Dion, Stéphane (eds.) (1991). *The Budget-Maximizing Bureaucrat. Appraisals and Evidence*. Pittsburgh: Pittsburgh University Press.

Boix, Carles (2001). 'Democracy, Development, and the Public Sector'. *American Journal of Political Science*, 45: 1–17.

Bryce, James (1921). *Modern Democracies*. New York: Macmillan.

Carey, John M. (1996). *Term Limits and Legislative Representation*. Cambridge: Cambridge University Press.

Choe, Yonhyok (1997). *How to Manage Free and Fair Elections*. Göteborg: Göteborg University.

Colomer, Josep M. (1995). 'The Blame Game of Presidentialism', in H. E. Chehabi and A. Stepan (eds.), *Politics, Society, and Democracy*. Boulder: Westview.

——(2001). *Political Institutions*. Oxford: Oxford University Press.

Cox, Gary W. (1987). *The Efficient Secret*. Cambridge: Cambridge University Press.

—— (1997). *Making Votes Count*. Cambridge: Cambridge University Press.

Dahl, Robert A. (1956). *A Preface to Democratic Theory*. Chicago: University of Chicago Press.

——(1971). *Polyarchy*. New Haven: Yale University Press.

——(1989). *Democracy and Its Critics*. New Haven: Yale University Press.

De Winter, Lieven (1995). 'The Role of Parliament in Government Formation and Resignation', in Herbert Döring (ed.), *Parliaments and Majority Rule in Western Europe*. Frankfurt am Main: Campus and New York: St. Martin's Press.

Diermeier, Daniel and Feddersen, Timothy J. (1998). 'Cohesion in Legislatures and the Vote of Confidence Procedure'. *American Political Science Review*, 92: 611–21.

Downs, Anthony (1967). *Inside Bureaucracy*. Boston: Little, Brown.

Dunleavy, Patrick (1991). *Democracy, Bureaucracy and Public Choice*. New York: Harvester Wheatsheaf.

Duverger, Maurice (1980). 'A New Political System Model: Semi-Presidential Government'. *European Journal of Political Research*, 8: 165–87.

Eaton, Kent (2000). 'Parliamentarism versus Presidentialism in the Policy Arena'. *Comparative Politics*, 32: 355–76.

Elgie, Robert (1998). 'The Classification of Democratic Regime Types: Conceptual Ambiguity and Contestable Assumptions'. *European Journal of Political Research*, 33: 219–38.

——(ed.) (1999). *Semi-Presidentialism in Europe*. Oxford: Oxford University Press.

Epstein, Leon D. (1968). 'Parliamentary Government', in David L. Sills (ed.), *International Encyclopedia of the Social Sciences*. New York: Macmillan and Free Press.

Finer, Herman (1931). *The Theory and Practice of Modern Government*. London: Methuen.

Finer, Samuel E. (1997). *The History of Government From the Earliest Times*. Oxford: Oxford University Press.

Fiorina, Morris P. (1977). *Congress. Keystone of the Washington Establishment*. New Haven: Yale University Press.

Furubotn, Eirik G. and Richter, Rudolf (1997). *Institutions and Economic Theory: An Introduction to and Assessment of the New Institutional Economics*. Ann Arbor: University of Michigan Press.

Gerlich, Peter (1973). 'The Institutionalization of European Parliaments', in Allan Kornberg (ed.), *Legislatures in Comparative Perspective*. New York: David McKay.

Goldsworthy, Jeffrey (1999). *The Sovereignty of Parliament*. Oxford: Oxford University Press.

Hadenius, Stig (1994). *Riksdagen. En svensk historia*. Stockholm: Riksdagen.

Huber, John D. (1996). *Rationalizing Parliament*. Cambridge: Cambridge University Press.

Judge, David (1993). *The Parliamentary State*. London: Sage.

Kaiser, André (1997) 'Types of Democracy? *Journal of Theoretical Politics*, 9: 419–44.

Kelsen, Hans (1926). *Das Problem des Parlamentarismus*. Vienna: Braumüller.

——(1929). *Vom Wesen und Wert der Demokratie*, 2nd edn., Tübingen: Mohr.

Kiewiet, D. Roderick and McCubbins, Mathew D. (1991). *The Logic of Delegation*. Chicago: University of Chicago Press.

King, Anthony (1976). 'Modes of Executive–Legislative Relations: Great Britain, France, and West Germany'. *Legislative Studies Quarterly*, 1: 11–36.

Klingemann, Hans-Dieter, Hofferbert, Richard I., and Budge, Ian (1994). *Parties, Policies, and Democracy*. Boulder, CO: Westview Press.

Kluxen, Kurt (1983). *Geschichte und Problematik des Parlamentarismus*. Frankfurt am Main: Suhrkamp.

Lane, Jan-Erik and Ersson, Svante (2000). *The New Institutional Politics. Performance and Outcomes*. London: Routledge.

Laver, Michael and Schofield, Norman (1990). *Multiparty Government: The Politics of Coalition in Europe*. Oxford: Oxford University Press.

Lijphart, Arend (1984). *Democracies: Patterns of Majoritarian and Consensus Government in Twenty-One Countries*. New Haven: Yale University Press.

——(1995). 'The Virtues of Parliamentarism: But Which Kind of Parliamentarism?', in H. E. Chehabi and Alfred Stepan (eds.), *Politics, Society, and Democracy: Comparative Studies*. Boulder: Westview Press.

——(1999). *Patterns of Democracy*. New Haven: Yale University Press.

——(2000). 'The Future of Democracy: Reasons for Pessimism, but Also Some Optimism'. *Scandinavian Political Studies*, 23: 265–73.

Linnarsson, Lennart (1943). *Riksrådens licentiering. En studie i frihetstidens parlamentarism*. Uppsala: Almqvist & Wiksells Boktryckeri AB.

Linz, Juan J. (1994). 'Presidential or Parliamentary Democracy: Does It Make a Difference?', in Juan J. Linz and Arturo Valenzuela (eds.), *The Failure of Presidential Democracy*, Vol. 1. Baltimore: John Hopkins University Press.

Loewenberg, Gerhard and Patterson, Samuel C. (1979). *Comparing Legislatures*. Boston: Little, Brown.

Loewenstein, Karl (1957). *Political Power and the Governmental Process*. Chicago: University of Chicago Press.

——(1975). *Verfassungslehre*, 3rd edn. Tübingen: Mohr.

Lowell, A. Lawrence (1896). *Governments and Parties in Continental Europe*. London: Longmans, Green, and Co.

Lynn, Jonathan and Jay, Anthony (1981). *The Complete YES MINISTER. The Diaries of a Cabinet Minister*. London: BBC Books.

Mackintosh, John P. (1968). *The British Cabinet*, 2nd edn. London: Methuen.

Mainwaring, Scott and Shugert, Matthew Soberg (eds.) (1997). *Presidentialism and Democracy in Latin America*. Cambridge: Cambridge University Press.

Manin, Bernard (1997). *The Principles of Representative Government*. Cambridge: Cambridge University Press.

——, Przeworski, Adam, and Stokes, Susan C. (1999). 'Elections and Representation', in Adam Przeworski, Susan C. Stokes, and Bernard Manin (eds.), *Democracy, Accountability, and Representation*. Cambridge: Cambridge University Press.

Mayhew, David R. (1974). *Congress. The Electoral Connection*. New Haven: Yale University Press.

McChesney, Fred S. (1997). *Money for Nothing. Politicians, Rent Extraction, and Political Extortion*. Cambridge, MA: Harvard University Press.

McCubbins, Mathew D., Noll, Roger D., and Weingast, Barry R. (1987). 'Administrative Procedures as Instruments of Political Control'. *Journal of Law, Economics, and Organization*, 3: 243–77.

McLean, Iain (1987). *Public Choice. An Introduction*. Oxford: Basil Blackwell.

Metcalf, Michael M. (1977). *Russia, England and Swedish Party Politics 1762–1766. The interplay between Great Power Diplomacy and Domestic Politics during Sweden's Age of Liberty*. Stockhom: Almqvist & Wiksell International.

Michels, Robert (1962). *Political Parties*. New York: Free Press.

Mill, John Stuart (1984 [1861]). 'Considerations on Representative Government', in John Stuart Mill. *Utilitarianism. Liberty. Representative Government*. London: Dent.

Mills, C. Wright (1956). *The Power Elite*. New York: Oxford University Press.

Moe, Terry M. (1984). 'The New Economics of Organization'. *American Journal of Political Science*, 28: 739–77.

——(1997). 'The Positive Theory of Public Bureaucracy', in Dennis C. Mueller (ed.), *Perspectives on Public Choice. A Handbook*. Cambridge: Cambridge University Press.

——and Caldwell, Michael (1994). 'The Institutional Foundations of Democratic Government: A Comparison of Presidential and Parliamentary Systems'. *Journal of Institutional and Theoretical Economics*, 150: 171–95.

Mosca, Gaetano (1947). *Elementi di scienza politica*, 4th edn. Bari: Gius Laterza & Figli.

——(1950). *Die herrschende Klasse*. Munich: Leo Lehnen Verlag.

Mueller, Dennis C. (1996). *Constitutional Democracy*. Oxford: Oxford University Press.

Müller, Wolfgang C. (2000). 'Political Parties in Parliamentary Democracies: Making Delegation and Accountability Work'. *European Journal of Political Research*, 37: 309–33.

——and Strøm, Kaare (2000). 'Conclusions: Coalition Governance in Western Europe', in Wolfgang C. Müller and Kaare Strøm (eds.), *Coalition Governments in Western Europe*. Oxford: Oxford University Press.

Niskanen, William A. (1971). *Bureaucracy and Representative Government*. Chicago: Aldine-Atherton.

Norton, Philip (1981). *The Commons in Perspective*. Oxford: Basil Blackwell.

Ogg, Frederic Austin (1936). *English Government and Politics*, 2nd edn. New York: Macmillan.

Ostrogorski, M. (1907). *Democracy and the Organization of Political Parties*. London: Macmillan.

Persson, Torsten and Tabellini, Guido (1999). 'The Size and Scope of Government: Comparative Politics with Rational Politicians'. *European Economic Review*, 43: 699–735.

Powell, G. Bingham, Jr. (1982). *Contemporary Democracies. Participation, Stability, and Violence*. Cambridge, MA: Harvard University Press.

——(2000). *Elections as Instruments of Democracy. Majoritarian and Proportional Visions*. New Haven: Yale University Press.

Pratt, John W. and Zeckhauser, Richard J. (eds.) (1985). *Principals and Agents: The Structure of Business*. Boston: Harvard Business School Press.

Przeworski, Adam, Alvarez, Michael E., Cheibub, José Antonio, and Limongi, Fernando (2000). *Democracy and Development*. Cambridge: Cambridge University Press.

Riggs, Fred W. (1988). 'The Survival of Presidentialism in America: Para-constitutional Practices'. *International Political Science Review*, 9: 247–78.

——(1997). 'Presidentialism versus Parliamentarism: Implications for Representativeness and Legitimacy'. *International Political Science Review*, 18: 253–78.

Riker, William H. (1982). *Liberalalism Against Populism*. San Francisco: W. H. Freeman.

Roberts, Michael (1986). *The Age of Liberty. Sweden 1719–1772*. Cambridge: Cambridge University Press.

Sartori, Giovanni (1987). *The Theory of Democracy Revisited: The Comtemporary Debate*. Chatham: Chatham House.

Sartori, Giovanni (1997). *Comparative Constitutional Engineering*, 2nd edn. Houndmills: Macmillan.

Schattschneider, E. E. (1960). *The Semisovereign People*. New York: Holt, Rinehart, and Winston.

Schlesinger, Joseph A. (1966). *Ambition and Politics*. Chicago: Rand McNally.

——(1991). *Political Parties and the Winning of Office*. Ann Arbor: University of Michigan Press.

Schmitt, Carl (1969 [1923]). *Die geistesgeschichtliche Lage des heutigen Parlamentarismus*. Berlin: Duncker & Humblot.

Schumpeter, Joseph A. (1942). *Capitalism, Socialism and Democracy*. New York: Harper & Brothers.

——(1954 [1918]). 'The Crisis of the Tax State', in Alan T. Peacock, Ralph Turvey, Wolfgang F. Stopler, and Elizabeth Henderson (eds.), *International Economic Papers*. New York: Macmillan.

Schütt-Wetschky, Eberhard (1984). *Grundtypen parlamentarischer Demokratie*. Freiburg: Verlag Karl Alber.

Shleifer, Andrei and Vishny, Robert W. (1998). *The Grabbing Hand. Government Pathologies and Their Cures*. Cambridge, MA: Harvard University Press.

Shugart, Matthew S. and Carey, John (1992). *Presidents and Assemblies*. Cambridge: Cambridge University Press.

—— and Mainwaring, Scott (1997) 'Presidentialism and Democracy in Latin America: Rethinking the Terms of Debate; in Scott Mainwaring and Matthew Soberg Shugart (eds.) *Presidentialism and Democracy in Latin America*. Cambridge: Cambridge University Press.

Steffani, Winfried (1979). *Parlamentarische und präsidielle Demokratie*. Opladen: Westdeutscher Verlag.

Stepan, Alfred and Skach, Cindy (1993). 'Constitutional Frameworks and Democratic Consolidation: Parliamentarism versus Presidentialism'. *World Politics*, 46: 1–22.

Strøm, Kaare (2000). 'Delegation and Accountability in Parliamentary Democracies.' *European Journal of Political Research*, 37: 261–89.

—— and Swindle, Stephen M. (2002). 'Strategic Parliamentary Dissolution'. *American Political Science Review*, 575–91.

Strong, C. F. (1963). *A History of Modern Political Constitutions*. New York: G. P. Putnam's Sons.

Tsebelis, George (1995). 'Decisionmaking in Political Systems: Veto Players in Presidentialism, Parliamentarism, Multicameralism, and Multipartyism'. *British Journal of Political Science*, 25: 289–325.

——(2002). *Veto Players: An Introduction to Institutional Analysis*. Princeton: Princeton University Press and the Russell Sage Foundation.

Verney, Douglas V. (1959). *The Analysis of Political Systems*. London: Routledge & Kegan Paul.

von Beyme, Klaus (1973). *Die parlamentarischen Regierungssysteme in Europa*. Munich: Piper.

——(1999). *Die parlamentarischen Regierungssysteme in Europa*, 3rd edn. Opladen: Westdeutscher Verlag.

von Mettenheim, Kurt (1997). *Presidential Institutions and Democratic Politics*. Baltimore: Johns Hopkins University Press.

Weaver, R. Kent and Rockman, Bert A. (eds.) (1993). *Do Institutions Matter? Government Capabilities in the United States and Abroad*. Washington, DC: The Brookings Institution.

Weber, Max (1972). *Wirtschaft und Gesellschaft*. Tübingen: Mohr.

——(1988). *Gesammelte politische Schriften*. Tübingen: Mohr.

Weir, Stuart and Beetham, David (1999). *Political Power and Democratic Control in Britain*. London: Routledge.

Wittman, Donald A. (1995). *The Myth of Democratic Failure*. Chicago: University of Chicago Press.

Woldendorp, Jaap, Keman, Hans, and Budge, Ian (2000). *Party Government in 48 Democracies (1945–1998)*. Dordrecht: Kluwer.

2

Delegation and its Perils

ARTHUR LUPIA

INTRODUCTION

Delegation is a central concept in the conduct and the study of politics. Governments great and small use delegation to increase the range of services that they can provide. National governments, for example, delegate to defence ministries the task of maintaining national security and delegate to finance ministries the task of managing the economy. Indeed, the modern nation-state could not exist without delegation—for without delegation, lawmakers would be forced personally to implement and enforce every single law that they make. With delegation, national governments can address a wide range of social issues simultaneously.

In most polities, the most prominent form of delegation is from lawmakers (e.g. parliaments) to government agencies (e.g. economic, security, and public welfare agencies). Such agencies house the persons responsible for enforcing laws and tend to employ the nation's leading experts in the agency's policy area (e.g. economic agencies employ leading economists). In many places, these agencies are known collectively as *the bureaucracy*. In some places, people who work within these agencies are called *bureaucrats* or *civil servants*.

We define delegation as an act where one person or group, called a *principal*, relies on another person or group, called an *agent*, to act on the principal's behalf. This volume's purpose is to examine delegation problems that exist in parliamentary democracies. Table 2.1 displays prominent forms of delegation in these democracies.

Delegation allows political principals to accomplish desired ends with reduced personal cost and effort. Implementing a single ministerial directive, for example, can require more time and effort than any minister can muster. Only by delegating—getting subordinates to do most of the work—can any high-level government official achieve multiple objectives. Similarly, most citizens are not sufficiently qualified to provide the social services that improve their lives (e.g. education, health care). Only by delegating— getting specialists to do most of the work—can any citizen enjoy such services.

I thank Torbjörn Bergman, Sean E. Cain, Christopher DenHartog, James N. Druckman, Elisabeth R. Gerber, Simon Hug, Mathew D. McCubbins, Wolfgang C. Müller, and Kaare Strøm for helpful comments. I worked on this chapter while I was a fellow at the Center for Advanced Study in the Behavioral Sciences and I thank them for their support.

Table 2.1. *Common Forms of Delegation*

Principal	Agent
Voter	A Member of Parliament and/or a party (depending on the ballot list system)
Members of Parliament, Parties	The government
Government	Cabinet Ministers
Cabinet Ministers	Civil Service
Civil service directors	Civil service employees

While delegation allows principals to benefit from the expertise and abilities of others, it can also be perilous. The perils arise from the fact that delegation entails a transfer of power—every time lawmakers delegate to bureaucrats, they give away a portion of their authority to govern. A great danger is that the people to whom power is delegated will abuse the power they receive. Consider, for example, Weber's famous treatise about what happens when legislatures delegate to bureaucrats:

Under normal conditions, the power position of a fully developed bureaucracy is always over-towering. The 'political master' finds himself in the position of the 'dilettante' who stands opposite the 'expert', facing the trained official who stands within the management of administration. This holds whether the 'master' whom the bureaucracy serves is a 'people', equipped with the weapons of 'legislative initiative', the 'referendum', and the right to remove officials, or a parliament, elected on a more aristocratic or more 'democratic' basis and equipped with the right to vote a lack of confidence... (Weber, quoted in Gerth and Mills 1946: 232)

If this danger is realized, then those entrusted with the responsibility of governing lose control of what is done in the government's name and anarchy can ensue.

While delegation is not a perfect means for political principals to achieve their objectives, it is the only feasible means. Anyone who wants to govern or provide services to mass populations must find agents to carry out their plans. Therefore, understanding the relations between principals and agents is critical to answering many questions about parliamentary governance.

In this chapter, I present a theoretical framework that clarifies when principals can, and cannot, use delegation to accomplish desired ends. I use the framework to clarify how a number of factors, including political institutions, affect the success of delegation. In subsequent chapters, other authors use the framework to examine the empirical relationship between delegation and accountability in 17 West European parliamentary democracies.

I continue as follows. In the section titled Measures of What Delegation Accomplishes, I offer important definitions and terms. In the section that follows, I introduce the theoretical framework. In the section on the Consequences of Delegation, I use the framework to clarify when agents will act in their principals' interests. In section titled How Institutions Affect Agency Loss, I explain how political institutions can alleviate the perils of delegation. In the conclusion, I link this chapter's insights to broader questions.

MEASURES OF WHAT DELEGATION ACCOMPLISHES

In this section, I introduce needed definitions. I begin by defining delegation and accountability. Delegation, as noted in this chapter's opening sentences, is an act where one person or group, called a *principal*, relies on another person or group, called an *agent*, to act on the principal's behalf. Defining *accountability* is not as simple.

People use the term *accountability* to characterize the effectiveness or efficiency of governance, in general, and delegation acts, in particular. A problem with the term is that it is used in different ways. For some, accountability is *a process of control*. In this view, civil servants are accountable to ministers only if the ministers can influence a civil servant's actions. For others, accountability is *a type of outcome*. In this view, civil servants are accountable to ministers only if the agent acts in the minister's interests.

The 'control' and 'outcome' definitions of accountability mean different things. A civil servant can provide outcomes that a minister likes without the minister exercising any control. This happens when a civil servant and minister share the same policy goals, the civil servant completely ignores ministerial directives, and pursuing her own interests leads her to take actions that favour the minister nevertheless. Conversely, a minister can exercise great control over a civil servant without achieving a desired outcome. This happens when a minister can remove a civil servant if a certain level of service is not achieved and the servant lacks the skills needed to achieve the goal.

This book adopts the 'control' definition of accountability. An agent is accountable to a principal if the principal can exercise control over the agent and delegation is not accountable if the principal is unable to exercise control. If a principal in situation A exerts more control than a principal in situation B, then accountability is greater in situation A than it is in situation B.

Having defined accountability in this way, I should now restate this chapter's goal. In what follows, I will clarify what delegation accomplishes by using a theoretical framework to examine how common processes of control (i.e. the rules or institutions under which delegation commonly occurs) affect the outcome of an act of delegation.

To describe outcomes, I employ two metrics—agency loss and success/failure. *Agency loss* is the difference between the actual consequence of delegation and what the consequence would have been had the agent been 'perfect'. By perfect, I mean a hypothetical agent who does what the principal would have done if the principal had unlimited information and resources to do the job herself.

Agency loss describes the consequence of delegation from the principal's perspective. To say that agency loss is high is to say that the outcome of delegation is different from the principal's ideal outcome. To say that agency loss decreases is to say that the outcome of delegation moves closer to the principal's ideal.

The agency loss metric, though simple, is easy to misinterpret. Agency loss is zero when the agent takes actions that the principal would have taken *given unlimited information and resources*. If people forget this fact when using the agency loss metric, then delegation often seems to be a bad idea (e.g. 'This act of delegation caused agency loss. Therefore, it is bad.'). However, most political principals do not have unlimited information and resources. Therefore, it is impossible for them to be perfect agents for themselves (e.g. doctors are agents that are employed to maintain good health; consider what would happen if you tried to serve as your own doctor). Indeed, many principals who try to do all that agents can do will experience delegation outcomes far inferior to the ones that a hypothetical perfect agent would provide. Therefore, finding that delegation causes agency loss does not imply that the outcome is bad or even suboptimal.

A coarser metric for describing delegation outcomes is success and failure. Delegation is *successful* if the outcome of delegation improves the principal's welfare relative to what would have happened if the principal had chosen not to delegate. Following common parlance, I call the consequence of an agent's inaction the status quo. Delegation *fails* if it decreases the principal's welfare relative to this status quo.

Throughout the chapter, I use both metrics to describe delegation outcomes. I use agency loss when I want to make comparative statements about how differences between the principal and agent or variations in political institutions affect the degree to which the outcome of delegation reflects the principal's desires. I use the success/failure metric when I want to make simple statements about whether or not an act of delegation makes the principal better or worse off than the status quo.

I should also note that my use of the term status quo is equivalent to the common usage of the term *reversion point*. That is, if the agent fails to act, then the outcome of delegation *reverts* back to the status quo. While I will stick with the term status quo, authors of some later chapters prefer the term reversion point to mean the same thing.

THEORETICAL FRAMEWORK

I now introduce a framework that clarifies the relationship between delegation, mechanisms of accountability, agency loss, delegation success, and delegation failure. The framework builds on three simple premises.

1. *Parliamentary democracy entails a chain of delegation*

In such a chain, each link attaches a principal to an agent. The ideal–typical delegation chain resembles a straight line and includes a link: that attaches voters to members of Parliament; a link that attaches members of Parliament to the government; a link that attaches the government to individual ministers; and a link that attaches ministers to civil servants. In other words, citizens occupy one end of the ideal–typical chain while civil servants who implement government edicts occupy the chain's other end. In this view, the effectiveness of institutional accountability mechanisms can be measured by the extent to which agents at one end of the chain 'feel a tug' when principals at the other end 'pull the chain'.

Of course, most parliamentary democracies are not simple, singular delegation chains. Sometimes multiple principals delegate to a single agent or prin-cipals grant agents overlapping jurisdictions. Such practices change a chain of delegation's shape. Since most countries engage in such practices at least some of the time, we observe delegation chains varying widely in size and shape when we compare democracies empirically. Such variations are a product and a cause of each country's unique experience with democracy. It is, however, important to note that alongside such differences are common properties that all delegation chains share, which leads to our framework's second premise.

2. *Common properties make general conclusions possible*
Three such properties are as follows:

- Every delegation involves a principal and an agent.
- Many delegations entail *the possibility of conflicting interests*.
- Many delegations contain *the possibility of limited information*.

While the first of these properties is obvious, the latter two require explanation. The possibility of conflicting interests implies that the agent need not have the same policy objectives or prefer the same outcomes as principals. An agent may want to help the elderly while his principal detests them (i.e. the principal and agent desire different policies). A principal may prefer that an agent work hard on a complex problem, while the agent may prefer to spend afternoons fishing or at a bar (i.e. the principal and agent may desire the same policy but differ in who should exert effort to achieve that policy objective). Either difference is important because each can provide an agent with reasons to act contrary to his principal's desires.

The possibility of limited information implies that the principal, agent, or both are not omniscient. When an agent lacks information, one possible result is incompetence (e.g. the agent does not know how to do what a principal asks). Students of politics, however, pay much more attention to what happens when principals lack information. Indeed, it is commonly assumed that political principals, particularly voters and backbench MPs, are ignorant of their agents' activities. Our treatment of how limited information affects delegation will share this focus—we shall concentrate primarily on what happens when the principal lacks information about what her agent is doing.

While these three common properties are far from a complete description of any delegation act, they are sufficient for us to derive some important results what delegation accomplishes later in the chapter.

3. *Formal models provide important insights*
The relationships between principals and agents can be complex. When attempting to derive the properties of complex systems, logical devices such as formal models can be helpful ways to derive simple insights from complex observations. In several areas of political science and economics, formal models have helped scholars better understand the relationship between institutions, information, and political decision-making (e.g. Williamson 1975; Shepsle 1979; North 1981).

In the following two sections, I will use a framework built on these three premises to clarify what delegation accomplishes. I will highlight factors that cause agency loss and I will describe the conditions under which well-known accountability mechanisms can reduce agency loss. In the following chapters, the volume's contributors will use this same framework as the foundation of a wide array of empirical analyses.

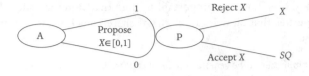

Figure 2.1. A Delegation Model.

THE CONSEQUENCES OF DELEGATION

I now use insights from several formal models to clarify what delegation accomplishes. I begin with a simple model that focuses on a single act of delegation. While this model has origins in economics (e.g. Niskanen 1971), the version I present is due to Romer and Rosenthal (1978). The sequence of events in their model is as follows and as depicted in Fig. 2.1.[1]

Romer and Rosenthal model an act of delegation as a game between a principal and an agent. To simplify my explanation of this and subsequent models, I henceforth refer to the principal as a female and the agent as a male. In the Romer–Rosenthal model, the agent moves first by choosing whether or not to change what was done in the past (i.e. the agent chooses whether or not to act). A civil servant, for example, acts when he interprets a government directive differently than it had been interpreted before. Put another way, Romer and Rosenthal study an act of delegation after the principal has already chosen to delegate.

Romer and Rosenthal conceive of the agent's possible actions as points on a line. They represent the agent's choice of action as the choice of a point, X, on the line $[0, 1]$. This choice may or may not be the same as the pre-existing status quo—denoted as $SQ \in [0, 1]$. SQ represents the outcome of delegation when the agent chooses not to act.

After the agent chooses whether or not to act and, if so, which action to take, the principal reacts by accepting the action or rejecting it in favour of the status quo (i.e. the principal chooses X or SQ). You can think of the principal's decision to reject the agent's action as an outright veto of an agent's decision or as a sanction against the agent that is sufficient to induce him to undo what he has done.

Romer and Rosenthal assume that the principal and agent have preferences over the possible outcomes of delegation. These preferences are represented by assuming that each player maximizes a single-peaked utility function. The peak of each player's utility function is his or her ideal policy. So it is equivalent to say that each player's objective is to achieve a delegation outcome that is as close as possible to his or her ideal policy.

I denote the principal's ideal policy as $P \in [0, 1]$ and the agent's ideal policy as $A \in [0, 1]$. Given our definition of agency loss and this notation, we can also say that P, the principal's ideal policy, is the point at which agency loss is zero. Agency loss grows as does the distance between P and the final outcome of the principal's and agent's interaction.

---

[1] Throughout the chapter, I present theoretical insights with a minimum amount of mathematical notation. For those interested in the mechanics of these theories, I provide citations throughout the text. Some of the material in this section follows directly from an argument first published in Lupia (2000).

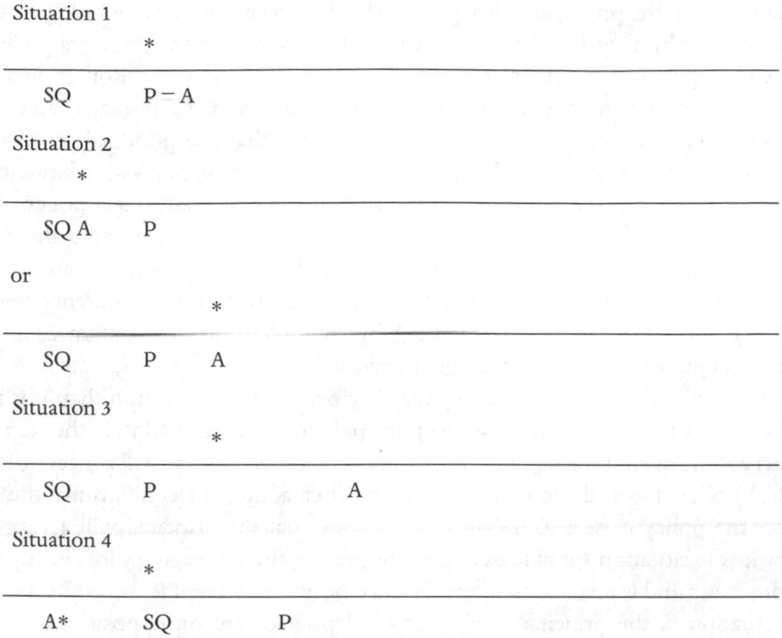

Situation 1
      *

_____

SQ   P − A

Situation 2
    *

_____

SQ A   P

or

        *

_____

SQ   P   A

Situation 3
      *

_____

SQ   P   A

Situation 4
    *

_____

A*   SQ   P

Figure 2.2. Graphical Depictions of the Possible Situations. The star indicates the predicted outcome of delegation in the (complete information) Romer and Rosenthal model.

A key assumption in the Romer–Rosenthal model is that the principal and agent have complete information. This assumption simplifies the model considerably and allows important insights to be derived efficiently. After stating these results, I will describe other models where limited information plays a key role.

The Romer–Rosenthal model reveals fundamental causes of agency loss. It does so by separating four mutually exclusive and collectively exhaustive situations. Each situation provides a distinct insight about the optimal actions of principal and agent given their beliefs about the other's response. I depict each situation in Fig. 2.2.

In situation 1, the principal and agent have identical ideal policies. As a result, they are in perfect agreement about what the agent should do. Thus, the model predicts that agent proposes the principal's (and his own) ideal policy and the principal accepts it. In this situation, there is no agency loss.

In all other situations, the outcome of delegation is different. That is, in any case where the principal and agent do not have identical ideal points, the outcome of delegation in the Romer–Rosenthal model entails some agency loss. In situations 2 and 3, for example, the principal and agent have different ideal policies, but both players' ideal policies are on the same side of the status quo. In these situations, the principal and agent agree on the desired direction of policy change but not on the magnitude of change (e.g. both prefer higher taxes but disagree on the rate of increase).

In situation 2, the principal's ideal policy is farther from the status quo than it is from the agent's ideal policy. In other words, this is the case where the principal prefers the agent's ideal policy, A, to the status quo, SQ. In this situation, the Romer–Rosenthal model predicts that the agent chooses his ideal policy and the principal accepts the agent's action. This occurs because the agent knows that the principal prefers some degree of change (i.e. A) to no change at all (i.e. SQ). The agency loss in situation 2 is the distance between the agent's ideal policy and the principal's ideal policy. To see why, note that if the agent proposes $X = A$ and the principal accepts the agent's proposal, then agency loss is the negative of the difference between A and P. If the agent rejects this action, then agency loss is the negative of the difference between P and SQ. Since A is closer to P than SQ, by the definition of situation 2, then the principal is better off accepting the agent's action.

In situation 3, the principal's ideal policy is closer to the status quo than it is to the agent's ideal policy. This means that the principal would rather maintain the status quo than accept the agent's ideal policy. Since the agent knows this, he *will not* act to achieve his ideal policy. He will, however, choose another action. In equilibrium, the agent chooses the policy closest to his own ideal policy that the principal will accept.[2] The agency loss in situation 3 is at least as great or greater than the agency loss in any of the previous cases and is just less than the distance between SQ and P.

In situation 4, the principal and agent ideal policies are on opposite sides of the status quo (e.g. the principal wants higher taxes, the agent wants lower taxes). Here, no agent action is mutually agreeable to the principal and the agent. Therefore, the outcome is the status quo and the agency loss is the distance between SQ and P.

Comparing these situations to each other offers two insights. First, as we move from a lower numbered situation to a higher numbered situation, agency loss increases if it changes. Second, moving from lower numbered situations to higher numbered situations implies either an increase in the distance between A and P or an increase in the distance between P and SQ relative to the distance between A and P. Put another way, if the agent's ideal policy or the status quo moves away from the principal's ideal policy then agency loss can grow. That agency loss grows with the distance between P and A is straightforward—as the agent finds himself sharing fewer interests with the principal, he gains fewer rewards from serving the principal's interests. That agency loss can grow with the distance between P and SQ follows from the fact that a bad status quo makes a wider range of proposals attractive to the principal (i.e. beggars can't be choosers).

It is worth emphasizing that the Romer–Rosenthal model's predictions depend heavily on two simplifying assumptions. The first assumption is that the principal can only accept or reject the agent's action. If the principal is given greater powers relative to the agent (i.e. she can force the agent to take actions closer to P), then agency loss will decrease. Similarly, if the principal is given lesser power relative to the agent (i.e. she cannot reject agent actions), agency loss will increase.

---

[2] If SQ is greater than A and P, then the agent will propose $P - |SQ - P| + \varepsilon$, where $\varepsilon > 0$ and small. If SQ is less than A and P, then the agent will propose $P + |SQ - P| - \varepsilon$.

The second simplifying assumption is that the principal and agent have complete information. For many acts of delegation, this assumption is wholly unrealistic. I now focus on what delegation accomplishes when information is incomplete. I define information as incomplete when a person is unable to predict the consequence of their actions with certainty. Within a delegation relationship, a principal, agent, or both can have incomplete information.

Principals and agents make use of two kinds of information.

- *Information about actions*: They want to know what the other has done.
- *Information about people and their context*. If people lack information about others' actions, they can often use information about a person (i.e. their skills or preferences) or their circumstances to deduce that person's actions.

If a principal or agent lacks either kind of information, the consequences of delegation can change dramatically. The extent to which the agent will attempt to act in accordance with the principal's preferences is particularly sensitive to whether or not principal and agent have asymmetric information. Information is asymmetric when one person knows more about the consequences of their actions than does the other.

As is customary in the literature on delegation, I will focus on the case where the principal knows less than the agent. While agents can lack information about their principals, students of democracy are far more concerned about the extent to which limited information hinders political principals' abilities to delegate successfully. Indeed, when principals do not know enough to track their agents' actions, the transfer of power inherent in an act of delegation can cause it to be equivalent to abdication—a concern that motivates much of the cited work on delegation. I adopt the same emphasis here.

When principals know less than agents, two kinds of problems arise: *moral hazard* and *adverse selection*. Rasmusen (1989: 133) describes these terms as follows:

- *Moral hazard with hidden actions*: Smith and Brown begin with symmetric information and agree to a contract, but then Smith takes an action unobserved by Brown . . .
- *Adverse selection*: [Smith knows things about himself that Brown does not.] Smith and Brown then agree to a contract. Information is incomplete.

The classic example of moral hazard comes from the realm of insurance. When a person buys a life insurance policy, he knows that his insurance company will pay for possible outcomes of risky behaviours. Since the insurer cannot prevent its clients from all risks, it faces a moral hazard problem—its clients may take riskier actions after a policy is issued. Moral hazard causes delegation problems when it gives the agent an opportunity to take actions of which the principal would not otherwise approve.

Adverse selection problems arise when an agent has *attributes* that a principal cannot observe. A classic example of adverse selection arises in the context of health insurance. As Kreps (1990: 626–7) notes: 'If premiums are set at actuarially fair rates for the population as a whole, insurance may be a bad deal for healthy people, who will then refuse to buy. Only the sick and dying will sign up. And premium rates must then be set to reflect this.' Also see Akerlof (1970) about similar properties in used car markets.

Adverse selection is a problem in many aspects of delegation—most notably elections. To see this problem, suppose that only two types of people choose to run for elective office—those who are truly public-spirited and those who line their own pockets with public resources. If candidates know their type and voters do not, the problem of adverse selection exists. If voters want only to elect public-spirited individuals, then all candidates have an incentive to portray themselves as public-spirited. The extent of agency loss for voters in this delegation will depend on the extent to which they can separate the dutiful from the knaves.

In what follows, I will first use a model to show how moral hazard affects delegation. Then, I will use similar logic to clarify the impact of adverse selection.

How Moral Hazard Affects Delegation

Lupia (1992) shows how moral hazard affects agency in the Romer–Rosenthal model. He finds that if the principal lacks information about the agent's action, then the agent never benefits from choosing any action other than his own ideal point. Such behaviour differs from that found in the Romer–Rosenthal model, particularly in situation 3.

In Romer and Rosenthal's situation 3, the agent proposes an alternative to the status quo that represents a compromise between himself and the principal. He offers the compromise because he knows that if he proposes his own ideal policy, the principal will reject it. In situation 3 with moral hazard added, the agent deals with a relatively ignorant principal and lacks any incentive to compromise.

The principal, in turn, reacts as if the agent can commit only to choosing his own ideal policy. Indeed, she bases her decision about whether to accept or reject the agent's action on her knowledge of the agent's ideal policy. If the expected utility from choosing the agent's ideal policy is greater than the utility from choosing the status quo, then the principal accepts the agent's action; otherwise she does not.

Table 2.2 displays the complete effect of moral hazard in tabular form (also see Lupia and McCubbins 2000). The left side of the table repeats Romer–Rosenthal's conclusions, while the rightmost two columns follow from Lupia (1992). The middle columns of the table show how moral hazard affects agency loss in the best possible case. In the best case, the principal guesses the agent's behaviour correctly despite her inability to observe his actions. The columns on the right display the effect of agency loss in the worst possible case. In the worst case, the principal's lack of information leads her to make mistakes—to reject agent actions that would benefit her and accept agent actions that hurt her. Within each set of columns, I show the policy outcome of delegation as well as its corresponding agency loss.

Table 2.2 shows that, in the worst case, the moral hazard increases agency loss significantly. In fact, situation 4's worst case scenario generates the greatest agency loss possible in the model (i.e. the agent takes actions that are bad for the principal that the principal then accepts). The rest of the table, however, reveals that moral hazard is not sufficient to cause agency loss. Indeed, if the principal can find a substitute for the information about agent actions that he lacks—enough information to make the best case scenario likely, then the impact of moral hazard can be reduced, if not eliminated entirely.

Table 2.2. *How Moral Hazard Potential Affects Agency Loss*

	Complete information: Romer–Rosenthal 1978		Incomplete information: Best case—Lupia 1992		Incomplete information: worst case—Lupia 1992	
	Outcome	Agency loss	Outcome	Δ Loss versus comp. info.	Outcome	Δ Loss versus comp. info.
Situation 1	P	None	P	0	SQ	$|P-SQ|$
Situation 2	A	$-|A-P|$	A	0	SQ	$|A-SQ|$
Situation 3	ε closer to P than SQ	$-|SQ-P|-\varepsilon$	SQ	ϵ	A	$|A-(|SQ-P|+\varepsilon)|$
Situation 4	SQ	$-|SQ-P|$	SQ	0	A*	$|A^\star-SQ|$

Notes: A* denotes the agent's ideal point in the situation where he and the principal's ideal point are on opposite sides of SQ. In this situation, A* is worse for the principal than SQ. ϵ denotes a number that is greater than zero, but very small. Note that $-|X-P|$ refers to the utility level of the principal given ideal policy, P, and delegation outcome, X. So, for example, when the outcome of delegation is the principal's ideal policy, as it is in the complete information version of situation 1, then the principal's utility is $-|P-P|$ or 0. When the outcome of delegation is the agent's ideal policy, as it is in several instances in the table, then the principal's utility is $-|A-P|$.

The main lesson, therefore, is that a principal lacking information about actions is not sufficient to cause agency loss. What matters more is whether or not the principal *can learn* enough to wield whatever power she may have over the agent effectively. In the following section, I explain when accountability mechanisms can, and cannot, provide such information.

How Adverse Selection Affects Delegation

Adverse selection entails a principal who lacks information about her agent's skills and preferences. Such information asymmetries matter because they correspond directly to the two reasons why an agent will fail to take actions that are consistent with his principals' interests.

- *The agent is unwilling*: An agent may be unwilling to pursue a principal's interests because she desires a different outcome. She may desire a different outcome because she and her principal have policy disagreement or because she and her agent disagree about how much of her own resources (i.e. time and effort) she should expend pursuing the principal's interests (see Brehm and Gates 1997).
- *The agent is unable*: An agent is unable to pursue a principal's interests because her resources are insufficient. Her ability will be a product of the complexity of the situation relative to her resources.

If an agent is willing but unable, she may want to satisfy the principal but cannot. If an agent is able but not willing, then she will choose not to work on the principal's behalf. To reduce agency loss, it is helpful for a principal to know if an agent is both willing and able. The theoretical study of adverse selection reveals how lacking either kind of information about an agent affects a principal's ability to delegate successfully.

To see the effects of adverse selection, it is helpful to refer back to Table 2.2 as a baseline. Now suppose that the otherwise fully informed principal in the Romer–Rosenthal model lacks information about the agent's willingness to accomplish the outcome she desires (i.e. she is uncertain about the location of A on the line [0, 1] in Fig. 2.2). Because the principal does not suffer from incomplete information about agent's actions (there is no moral hazard as in the Lupia model), the principal knows enough to accept actions that are better for her than the status quo and to reject those that are worse for her. Knowing this, the agent has no incentive to deviate from the actions he chose in the Romer–Rosenthal model. Therefore, *the outcome of delegation in this case is identical to the outcome in the Romer–Rosenthal model.*

If the principal lacks information about an agent's ability, by contrast, the outcome can differ. While the principal retains the ability to veto agent actions that are worse for her than the status quo, the agent's lack of information may lead him to choose different actions than was the case in the Romer–Rosenthal model and, therefore, Fig. 2.2. Indeed such an agent may choose an action that does not maximize his own utility—which would change the alternative to the status quo that the principal must consider. Depending on the nature of the agent's inability, the change in agent actions can either increase or decrease agency loss (i.e. the agent's mistakes about how to pursue his own self-interests may induce him to choose actions closer to or farther from P).

The outcome of delegation is less favourable for the principal when adverse selection and moral hazard appear together. To see why, refer back to the Lupia model (Table 2.2). Now suppose that in addition to lacking information about the agent's action, the principal also lacks information about his willingness to accomplish the outcome she desires (i.e. she is uncertain about the location of A on the line [0, 1]). In this case, the principal's best response is to base her decision regarding the agent's action on her beliefs about the location of A. If she believes that A is close to P (i.e. if she thinks it very likely that she and the agent want the same things), then she approves the agent's action. If her beliefs about the agent are correct, then the outcome of delegation resembles the best-case scenario in the Lupia model. If her beliefs are incorrect, however, then the outcome of delegation can be worse than Table 2.2's worst-case scenario. Specifically, a principal who faces adverse selection and moral hazard may approve actions with high agency loss and reject actions with low agency loss. To reduce agency loss in these cases, a principal must find some way to reduce her uncertainty about the agent's actions or the agent himself. In what follows, I describe conditions under which common political institutions can provide such information.

HOW INSTITUTIONS AFFECT AGENCY LOSS

Moral hazard and adverse selection give the principal an incentive to gather information about her agent. One means by which such information can be generated is institutions. Institutions affect incentives and can be constructed in ways that affect agent's incentives to reveal information about their motivations or actions. In the 1980s and 1990s, formal theorists spent considerable effort attempting to clarify what kinds of institutional designs can help delegation succeed. In this section, I highlight a few of these insights.

Formal theorists classify institutional designs that affect the provision of information to political principals as *ex ante* or *ex post* mechanisms.

- Principals use *ex ante* mechanisms to learn about their agents *before they act*, typically as they select particular individuals to serve as their agents. Such mechanisms are appropriate if a principal anticipates adverse selection problems.
- Principals use *ex post* mechanisms to learn about an agent's actions after the fact. Such mechanisms are a way to deal with moral hazard problems.

The most common forms of *ex ante* control are screening and selection rules. Screening and selection rules are devices that principals can use to sort good agents from bad before delegating to them. Such rules are an important part of the political institutions that govern many delegation relationships. Consider, for example, the extensive review process endured by candidates for cabinet ministries and, supreme courts and or Prime Ministerial candidates.

Contracts—task or time specific agreements between principals and agents—are also a common means for *ex ante* control. The point of such agreements is to establish shared interests between principals and agent, for example, by giving the agent a cut of any gain that the principal experiences as a result of the agent's efforts. It is common for contracts to specify an *ex post* mechanism of control (e.g. a clause such as 'If at date x, you have performed task y, I will reward you. Otherwise, I will sanction or sue you.').

In what follows, I survey models that reveal the conditions under which common *ex ante* control mechanisms such as those just described can help political principals reduce agency loss. I then discuss the effects of some *ex post* mechanisms.[3]

Ex Ante *Mechanisms: Screening*

A common screening mechanism in the context of delegation involves institutions that instigate competition between potential candidates for agent positions. A common supposition is that such competition always helps the principal choose her agents more effectively. The relationship between such screening practices and agency loss, however, is not so simple—as a comparison of three simple cases suggests.

Case 1: Romer–Rosenthal revisited　Refer back to Fig. 2.2 and to the Romer–Rosenthal model. Now suppose that we add additional agents to the model, remembering that it assumes complete information. Then, we can see that competition decreases agency loss. To see why, place the ideal policy of a second agent, say $A_2 \in [0, 1]$, anywhere on the line in any of situations 1–4. If A_2 is between P and A, then the effect of multiple agents is to move the outcome of delegation closer to P. That is, A_2 maximizes his utility by proposing an alternative to the status quo that is at least as close to P as is X,

---

[3] Readers who are interested in a more comprehensive theoretical treatment of how information and institutions affect choices such as those inherent in delegation can consult introductory texts such as McMillan (1992: parts II and III), intermediate texts such as Kreps (1990: chs 16 and 17) and Salanié (1998), advanced texts such as Laffont and Tirole (1993), or seminal articles such as Crawford and Sobel (1982), Milgrom and Roberts (1986), Farrell and Gibbons (1989), Banks (1991), Farrell and Rabin (1996).

the alternative that the first agent proposed when lacking competition. If A_2 is not between P and A, then adding A_2 has no effect. Therefore, in the complete information setting of the Romer–Rosenthal model, setting up a competition between agents can reduce agency loss.

Case 2: Competition Sometimes Fails   Competition need not have the same effect when the principal faces information problems. To see why, consider the analogy of the government putting up for auction the right to be an agent. Such a selection procedure occurs when a government hires a private firm to perform a public service (e.g. municipal construction projects). One could also use an auction analogy to characterize the battles for cabinet positions that occur during coalition formation negotiations.

When a principal forces potential agents to compete for the right to be her agent, she can induce the potential agents to reveal information about themselves—in particular their ability and willingness to perform the tasks she asks of them. The conditions under which such a competition best reduces agency loss are as follows:

- it is easy to determine whether or not the agent can perform the task in question,
- potential agents know whether or not they are willing and able to perform the task in question,
- potential agents know whether or not other potential agents are willing and able to perform the task in question,
- it is relatively easy and costless for the principal to punish the agent for failing to accomplish the task *ex post*.

If all of these conditions are met, then potential agents have an incentive to truthfully report their willingness and ability to serve the principal. In equilibrium, the most efficient potential agent becomes the actual agent. This outcome occurs because it solves the adverse selection problem. In this case, no agent has an incentive to make a false claim about his attributes (in the form of his bid) just to win the auction. In this situation, auctioning the right to be an agent minimizes agency loss.

If, however, any of these conditions are not met, then competition need not have such a pleasant effect. For example, if the principal cannot easily determine whether the agent has done what he promised to do, then the moral hazard problem reappears. Alternatively, if potential agents are uncertain about their own ability or their competitors' abilities, then they may gain an incentive to understate or overstate their own desire for the job. Such an outcome can lead to increased agency loss.

Case 3: The Hold-Up Problem   Moreover, if the principal lacks information about the agent's abilities and cannot punish the agent, then the principal is exposed to an extreme form of moral hazard known as the 'hold up' problem (e.g. see Williamson (1989) and Salanié (1998: ch. 7)). In a 'hold up' problem, a question arises about who will obtain the benefits from resources already committed to a particular activity.

To see how a hold up problem works, suppose that when a principal selects a particular person to be her agent, that agent then acquires valuable expertise that those who were not selected to be the agent cannot acquire. This agent can then use his expertise as leverage to renegotiate the terms of his relationship with the principal and extract additional benefits for himself. Consider, for example, a person who becomes identified with excellent service in a particular cabinet post. Upon achieving such a status, the 'excellent' minister may seek increased power in a wider range of government decisions. As the government's effectiveness or public standing becomes increasingly dependent on the 'excellent' minister's performance, they may have a greater incentive to let this agent have his way—even if it increases agency loss.

At this point, any reduction in agency loss that may have resulted from earlier competition may be lost. In sum, while competition among agents may seem like a natural solution to adverse selection and moral hazard problems, the benefits of competition are realized only if certain informational and institutional conditions are met.

Additional Caveats

Several additional factors work against competition among agents as a means of increasing accountability and decreasing agency loss. First, competition can preclude the most qualified potential agents from seeking the job. For if the skills required to be an effective agent differ from the skills required to win the competition (as is sometimes alleged in mass elections) or if the most skilled candidates for a position lack the resources needed to prevail in competition for a job (as may be the case with qualified experts in a field who lack political connections or the field of candidates who choose to run for the US presidency), then competition may produce a suboptimal outcome (also see Aghion and Tirole 1997 for a more general discussion of participation constraints). Second, competition among agents can entail negative externalities. In the rush to provide a particular service, for example, competition may cause efforts to be duplicated and lead to inefficiency. Such caveats are not meant to imply that competition is the wrong way to seek accountability or reduce agency loss. However, focusing on these caveats reminds us that means such as competition do not automatically produce desired ends (see Salanié 1998 for a recent and more technical review).

Ex Ante *Mechanisms: Selection*

By selection, I mean to describe cases where one person (e.g. an agent) chooses an action that reveals to other players (e.g. a principal) a previously hidden personal characteristic. By taking a firm public stand on a controversial issue, for example, a member of parliament may reveal to others the depth of his or her concern about the issue. By doing so, the MP 'selects' a public identity that may reveal previously unknown characteristics. Such selection mechanisms can help principals to learn about their agents and delegate successfully.

Economic *signaling models* are efficient means for understanding the general properties of selection mechanisms. The seminal signaling model (Spence 1974) focuses on the plight of an employer who needs to hire a new worker. While the employer prefers to hire a skilled applicant, she cannot initially observe an applicant's skill level. However, she knows that skilled applicants can obtain a tangible good—formal education—with less effort than can unskilled applicants (i.e. unskilled applicants are more likely to drop out of school before obtaining a degree). The question Spence poses is: If the employer can observe whether a particular applicant obtained an education and bases her hiring decision on the applicant's education, will she hire high-skilled applicants?

The model's conclusion is that the diploma convinces the employer of the applicant's skill level only if unobservable skill levels and observable education levels are highly correlated. Such logic clarifies important aspects of political interactions—it reveals that factors such as the agent's reputation for taking particular actions persuade the principal of the agent's skill level only if unobservable skill levels and observable reputations are sufficiently correlated. For example, if a background in economics correlates with ability to be an effective finance minister, then governments that want an effective finance minister have an incentive to give more serious consideration to ministerial candidates with an economics backgrounds.

Ex Ante *Mechanisms: Contract Design*

Laffont and Tirole (1993) are among a group of economists whose work on contracts clarifies an analogous means of *ex ante* agent selection. They show how offering potential agents a 'menu of contracts' can induce agents to reveal things about themselves that then help the principal limit the extent of agency loss. While their work is multifaceted, I paraphrase the basic insight of their efforts as follows. When structuring an agent's incentives, *ex ante*, a principal faces a trade-off between risk-sharing—which prevents the agent's rewards from depending too strongly on observable outcomes—and incentives—which induce the principal to condition the agent's rewards on observable outcomes.

The concept of risk-sharing is important when the principal asks the agent to perform tasks about which the agent is not completely informed. For example, certain military exercises may be required to satisfy a critical domestic agenda. In this case, the military is the agent of principals in the government. Suppose, however, that the outcome of a military operation is often uncertain *ex ante* and that there is a national interest in having the military take certain risks. A military officer's incentive to take such risks will then be conditioned on how the government treats him in the event that things go wrong. If the government cannot credibly commit to take some responsibility for bad outcomes (e.g. casualties of battle), then military officers have less of an incentive to take risky actions, even if the rewards of such an action—if successful—would be great for everyone.

In such a case, the polity may benefit by the government committing to share some of the military's risk. But they can go too far. If, for example, the government commits to assume all of the risk—by holding itself and not the military fully responsible for military actions—then the military has an incentive to take potentially beneficial actions. However, accountability then wanes.

While many of the problems of delegation may seem easily solved by forcing agents to assume the consequences of every outcome with which they are involved, this appearance is illusory. For if observable outcomes depend on some factors that are outside of an agent's control, then tying the agent's fate to outcomes can dissuade the agent from performing valuable services—and can actually increase agency loss.

Ex Post *Mechanisms*

In many democratic delegations, a principal may lack the information she needs to distinguish agent actions that help her from agent actions that hurt her (i.e. she may lack knowledge sufficient to reduce agency loss).[4] Such principals have three ways to gain information about her agent's actions: direct monitoring, attending to the *what the agent says* about his activities, or attending to *third party testimony* about agent actions.

Relying on others for information can be advantageous because it requires less of the principal's time and effort than does conducting her own investigation. Such dependence, however, can also entail substantial peril. Not all people from whom principals can seek advice are trustworthy or knowledgeable. Therefore, a principal who wants to exert some degree of control over her agent's actions must be very selective about which advice she follows. She has an incentive to seek information providers who provide credible reports of agent activities and to avoid information providers who provide vague or misleading reports.

Some procedural requirements, for example, attempt to induce interested third parties to share information with the principal that the principal might not otherwise receive, as is the case when government officials hold public hearings on agency actions and invite affected interests to provide reports or give testimony. McCubbins and Schwartz (1984) call this process 'fire alarm oversight' because of its similarity to concerned citizens pulling fire alarms to alert firefighters about dangerous activities. Such processes allow interested individuals to 'signal' political principals about what an agent is doing. It is useful to note McCubbins and Schwartz contrast fire alarm oversight with 'police patrol oversight' in which principals do much of the oversight themselves.

If a principal can achieve the same quality of oversight using fire alarms and police patrols, fire alarm oversight would be preferred because others pay the cost of learning about the agent's activities. The institutional context in which fire alarm oversight is attempted can have a great effect on a principal's ability to learn about her agent's activities. Fire alarm oversight is most effective when it occurs amongst institutions that feature a means for assessing the information provider's credibility. Institutions can affect what people *choose* to say and what people *choose* to believe. When they have this effect on people who signal principals, they affect the principals' ability to judge the credibility of others.

To clarify how institutions affect delegation, I describe the results of a model (Lupia and McCubbins 1998) that includes the potential for moral hazard described in Lupia (1992), and adds a third party who can send signals to the principal about what the agent is doing.

In the model, principals may be uncertain about the quality of the third party's advice. Specifically, Lupia and McCubbins assume that principals may be uncertain about how much these advice givers know about the agent's actions and about whether or not the third party is attempting to mislead the principal. They further assume that

---

[4] The following argument draws extensively from a parallel one in Lupia and McCubbins (2000).

signals are sent in the context of institutional forces including the threat of verification (i.e. a device that helps the principal distinguish true claims from false claims). Such threats can affect what people *choose* to say and what people *choose* to believe. When institutions have this effect on people who signal principals, they affect the principals' ability to judge the credibility of others.

Institutions increase the likelihood of verification when they provide new actors with incentives to provide information about an agent's actions. An institution such as the European Union (EU), for example, can now provide information about domestic level activities (see Lupia 2000). A domestic agent who, absent the threat of verification, will pursue a personal agenda, rather than the agenda of his principal (in his own country), must now consider the potentially verifying activities of actors in other EU nations. When EU membership increases the population of potential verifiers, domestic agents are faced with a higher likelihood that their principals will detect and reject his actions. In such a case, the emergence of the European Union can reduce agency loss domestically.

Using the model described earlier, Lupia and McCubbins (1998, paraphrased) generate the following result about when the principal can use signals to overcome moral hazard problems with her agent:

Proposition 1.   *The principal can distinguish agent actions that are better for her than the SQ from those that are worse only if:*

- *the principal's prior knowledge is sufficient for this task or*
- *she can* correctly perceive *a third party to have common interests and the knowledge she desires or*
- *institutional factors, such as verification, provide effective substitutes for her lack of knowledge about the third party's knowledge and interests.*

This proposition implies that the principal need not know very much about what her agent is doing in order to delegate successfully. Indeed, if institutional forces are sufficient to induce the principal to follow the third party's advice, then delegation can succeed even if the principal initially lacks knowledge about her agent, and even if she believes that any third party from which she could learn has conflicting interests.

Put another way, if a principal has access to reliable advisers then she need not be very knowledgeable about her agent to act as if she was so knowledgeable. Moreover, in cases where a principal may lack information about those who attempt to advise her, institutions can substitute for the type of information she lacks. Consider, for example, the position of someone—a juror or a judge—who must render a verdict in a trial. There will be cases when the juror is presented with a witness whose motives or knowledge she cannot verify on her own. However, if the principal is in a setting where factors such as a high likelihood of verification are present (e.g. when a valuable reputation is at stake and cross-examination is likely), then she need know little about the witness's interests to make a reliable credibility assessment. The incentives imposed on the witness by the institutional context in which she testifies may be sufficient for the principal to render an accurate judgement about the witness's credibility.

Another common form of *ex post* accountability mechanism is what Kiewiet and McCubbins (1991: 34) call 'institutional checks'. Such checks are means by which principals can reduce agency loss by increasing the likelihood of verification for those who provide information about agent actions as Kiewiet and McCubbins attest: 'Rather than striving for an unbiased source of information, a principal may do better obtaining biased reports from different agents who have conflicting incentives. The view that legal proceedings should be adversarial rather than administrative is based on the same logic. Conversely, checks are disabled when agents' incentives cease to be in conflict.'

When it is possible to construct such checks, many problems caused by the principal's lack of direct information about an agent's activities can be alleviated. However, like contracts, institutional checks are not always feasible or effective. As was the case with contract design, if such checks prevent agents or information providers from undertaking risky but potentially beneficial activities, then agents and third parties will avoid such actions, which may lead to increased agency loss *ex post*.

CONCLUSION AND IMPLICATIONS

It is impossible to provide a simple statement that describes how common accountability mechanisms affect delegation and its perils. However, reviewing the insights of this chapter can clarify when delegation is capable of accomplishing particular things.

- When a principal and agent desire precisely the same policy outcome and the agent is willing and able to put forth the work needed to achieve the objective, then delegation succeeds and there is no agency loss.
- As the agent's willingness or ability to serve the principal decreases, then the possibility for agency loss arises.
- When an agent is not fully willing or able to serve the principal, the principal can minimize agency loss if she has complete information about the agent's actions.
- If the principal lacks such information, then her ability to reduce agency loss depends on her ability to acquire other kinds of information.
- Through *ex ante* mechanisms, principals can attempt to learn about important agent attributes such as their policy motivations, the extent to which they are willing to exert effort on the principal's behalf, and their ability. With such information in hand principals can reduce agency loss. In many cases, however, such mechanisms are impossible to construct (i.e. sometimes it is impossible to learn what you need to know about an agent in advance) and *ex ante* strategies will be less effective.
- Through *ex post* mechanisms, principals can attempt to learn about agent actions from others. With such information to hand, principals can effectively distinguish agent actions that benefit them from actions that do not—a skill that allows them to reduce agency loss. Institutions can help by clarifying for principals whose reports of agent actions are credible.

Political principals delegate with the hope that their agents will work towards ends they desire. While delegation can have this effect, it need not always. In cases where agents are willing and able to serve their principals, delegation increases those principals' abilities to accomplish their goals. Otherwise, the perils of delegation arise. Given the many demands on voters, members of parliament, and members of government, it is unrealistic to expect them to have detailed information about their agents' preferences or actions. The perils commonly associated with such information asymmetries, however, are not inevitable. *Ex ante* and *ex post* accountability mechanisms can be made part of a country's political institutions—and those entrusted with the responsibility of governing can retain control of what is done in the government's name.

I conclude this chapter by describing what such insights imply about delegation chains. As we look across the parliamentary democracies of Western Europe, we see within it delegation chains of many shapes. While these chains differ in important ways, it is important to recognize that the links in these chains are all constructed from the same basic material—principal–agent relationships that are affected by information and institutions in systematic ways.

To see the effect of this insight on delegation chains, I begin with a simple example. Suppose, for a moment, that a country's chain of delegation is a straight line—one link connects voters to MPs, one link connects MPs to governments, and so on. In such a chain, a broken link implies a broken chain. So, for citizens at one end of the chain to hold accountable civil servants at the other end, every link of the chain must be strong. Reducing agency loss in such cases requires that the necessary conditions for successful delegation are satisfied at every link in the chain.

If this condition is not satisfied, the chain is broken. As a result, principals on one side of the break have no direct control over agent actions on the other side of the break. The agents on the other side may, if such principals are lucky, take actions that are good for the principal with the result being a minimum of agency loss. This happy outcome is not accountability as defined above because the principal has no direct control.

What would it take to satisfy this condition? Not as much as a follower of Weber might think. Citizens at one end of a straight chain holding accountable civil servants at the other end does not, for example, require that every principal have complete information about the actions of their agents. Instead, if at each link in such a chain of delegation, *any* of the conditions in Proposition 1 hold, principals have control over their agents—and agency loss can be no worse than if the principals had never delegated. If, moreover, a policy exists that both the principal and agent prefer to the status quo (as is the case in situations 1–3 in Fig. 2.2 and Table 2.2) at every stage in the chain, then delegation will make all principals better off than if they had not delegated.

But what happens if a country's delegations are not linked in a serial fashion? The answer depends on whether failed delegation at one link in the chain can be remedied by actions at a later link. If so, then it is easier to reduce agency loss—the conditions for successful delegation must be satisfied at only one of the two substitutable links. Consider, for example, cases where a policy-maker has the option of working with any of several bureaucratic agencies to perform a particular task. If the policy-maker cannot delegate successfully to agency A, delegation may nevertheless succeed if he can delegate the task to an agency B. If the strength of the delegation chain depends on this policy-maker's ability to delegate successfully, he need only find one reliable agent to keep the chain strong.

As important as the width of the chain is its length. In many cases, the longer the chain, the greater the likelihood of agency loss. Consider, for example, a government's attempt to affect what teachers say to children. In this case, the chain of delegation extends from the government to cabinet ministers to high-level civil servants in the nation's capital to possibly many additional stages all the way until a directive arrives in a classroom itself. If a teacher simply ignores the mandate, then delegation fails. Indeed, for certain policies, it may be necessary that *all* agents in the chain approve of the change. When such a requirement holds, the length of the chain becomes increasingly relevant as more links entails more people who have a veto, and greater difficulty for voters or MPs who want agents to 'feel a tug' when they pull the chain.

The chapters that follow give empirical flesh to this theoretical backbone. When these kinds of knowledge are combined, thy should increase the extent to which students and real-world observers understand the most effective and efficient ways to delegate. If they do, then volumes such as this will continue to give governments large and small ability to delegate successfully—a product of great value in an increasingly complex world.

REFERENCES

Aghion, Philippe and Tirole, Jean (1997). 'Formal and Real Authority in Organizations'. *Journal of Political Economy*, 105: 1–29.

Akerlof, George (1970). 'The Market for Lemons: Quality Uncertainty and the Market Mechanism'. *Quarterly Journal of Economics*, 89: 488–500.

Banks, Jeffrey S. (1991). *Signaling Games in Political Science*. Chur, Switzerland: Harwood Academic Publishers.

Brehm, John and Gates, Scott (1997). *Working, Shirking, and Sabotage: Bureaucratic Response to a Democratic Public*. Ann Arbor: University of Michigan Press.

Crawford, Vincent P. and Sobel, Joel (1982). 'Strategic Information Transmission'. *Econometrica*, 50: 1431–51.

Dahl, Robert A. (1967). *Pluralist Democracy in the United States: Conflict and Consent*. Chicago: Rand McNally.

Farrell, Joseph and Gibbons, Robert (1989). 'Cheap Talk with Two Audiences'. *American Economic Review*, 79: 1214–23.

Farrell, Joseph and Rabin, Matthew (1996). 'Cheap Talk'. *Journal of Economic Perspectives*, 10: 103–18.

Gerth, H. H. and Mills, C. Wright (eds.) (1946). *From Max Weber: Essays in Sociology*. New York: Oxford University Press.

Harsanyi, John (1967). 'Games with Incomplete Information Played by "Bayesian" Players, I: The Basic Model'. *Management Science*, 14: 159–82.

Kiewiet, D. Roderick and McCubbins, Mathew D. (1991). *The Logic of Delegation*. Chicago: The University of Chicago Press.

Kreps, David M. (1990). *A Course in Microeconomic Theory*. Princeton: Princeton University Press.

Laffont, Jean-Jacques and Tirole, Jean (1993). *A Theory of Incentives in Procurement and Regulation*. Cambridge, MA: MIT Press.

Lupia, Arthur (1992). 'Busy Voters, Agenda Control, and the Power of Information'. *American Political Science Review*, 86: 390–404.

——(2000). 'The EU, the EEA, and Domestic Accountability: How Outside Forces Affect Delegation within Member States'. *Journal of Legislative Studies*, 6: 15–32.

Lupia, Arthur and McCubbins, Mathew D. (1998). *The Democratic Dilemma: Can Citizens Learn What they Need to Know?* Cambridge: Cambridge University Press.

——and McCubbins, Mathew D. (2000). 'When is Delegation Abdication: How Citizens Use Institutions to Help Delegation Succeed'. *European Journal of Political Research*, 37: 291–307.

McCubbins, Mathew D. and Schwartz, Thomas (1984). 'Congressional Oversight Overlooked: Police Patrols versus Fire Alarms'. *American Journal of Political Science*, 28: 165–79.

McMillan, John (1992). *Games, Strategies, and Managers: How Managers can use Game Theory to Make Better Business Decisions*. New York: Oxford University Press.

Milgrom, Paul and Roberts, John (1986). 'Relying on the Information of Interested Parties'. *Rand Journal of Economics*, 17: 18–31.

Niskanen, William A. (1971). *Bureaucracy and Representative Government*. Chicago: Aldine-Atherton.

North, Douglass C. (1981). *Structure and Change in Economic History*. New York: Norton.

Rasmusen, Eric (1989). *Games and Information: An Introduction to Game Theory*. Oxford: Blackwell.

Romer, Thomas and Rosenthal, Howard (1978). 'Political Resource Allocation, Controlled Agendas, and the Status Quo'. *Public Choice*, 33: 27–44.

Salanié, Bernard (1998). *The Economics of Contracts: A Primer*. Cambridge, MA: MIT Press.

Shepsle, Kenneth A. (1979). 'Institutional Arrangements and Equilibrium in Multidimensional Voting Models'. *American Journal of Political Science*, 23: 27–60.

Spence, A. Michael (1974). *Market Signaling: Informational Transfer in Hiring and Related Screening Processes*. Cambridge, MA: Harvard University Press.

Williamson, Oliver E. (1975). *Markets and Hierarchies: Analysis and Antitrust Implications*. New York: The Free Press.

——(1989). 'Transaction Cost Economics', in Richard Schmalensee and Robert D. Willig (eds.), *Handbook of Industrial Organization, Volume I*. Amsterdam: North-Holland.

3

Parliamentary Democracy and Delegation

KAARE STRØM

In framing a government which is to be administered by men over men, the great difficulty lies in this: you must first enable the government to control the governed; and in the next place oblige it to control itself.

(James Madison, Federalist No. 51)

INTRODUCTION

Madison's dilemma has been the greatest challenge of modern politics, and it is the central concern of this volume. Democracy, as we argue in Chapter 1, seeks to solve it in various ways making the governors responsible to the citizens. Among such designs for popular sovereignty parliamentary government is most common. But even though parliamentary systems have progressively empowered their citizens, they rarely feature much direct popular governance. Not only do citizens typically not make most policy decisions themselves, they often do not even select or instruct the actual decision-makers, but delegate in ways that can be disconcertingly indirect.

Parliamentary democracy, then, implies *delegation* and a corresponding need for *accountability*. As Chapter 2 has demonstrated, all delegation, before and after we grant authority to others to act in our name and place, entails potential agency problems. Indeed, since antiquity political observers have commented on the dangers of representation and delegation. The choice and design of a parliamentary system has particular implications for the forms and severity of political agency problems. And what makes parliamentary and other regimes democratic is precisely the mechanisms by which citizens, the ultimate principals, can select and control their representatives. This book examines the generic features of parliamentary delegation and accountability, as well as its myriad gradations and variations.

I am grateful to Torbjörn Bergman, Gary W. Cox, Robert L. Brown, James N. Druckman, Simon Hix, Carl LeVan, Arthur W. Lupia, Mona Lyne, Wolfgang C. Müller, Benjamin Nyblade, Bjørn E. Rasch, and Asbjørn Skjæveland for helpful comments and suggestions.

In this chapter, I first identify three motivations for political delegation and then discuss the agency problems that may arise and the need for mechanisms of accountability, such as constraint and competition. In its ideal–typical form, parliamentary democracy is a particular regime of delegation and accountability, with two salient properties: singularity and indirect delegation. These institutional features, and the prevalence of cohesive political parties, help explain the commonly observed phenomenon that under parliamentary government, the executive branch dominates policy-making through its control of the political agenda. Yet, by no means are all parliamentary systems the same and the chapter identifies various subtypes of parliamentary democracy. Subsequent chapters will indeed demonstrate a great deal of institutional variation among European parliamentary systems, as well as a contemporary trend towards weaker political parties and stronger alternative accountability mechanisms.

Building on the ideal–typical features of parliamentary democracy identified above, I develop a delegation model in which I show that agency loss, in the form of policy slippage, is greater than under either of two versions of presidentialism. The focus then shifts to two other causes of democratic agency problems, namely non-policy motivations, such as leisure-shirking and rent seeking, and incomplete information. When information is scarce, the perils of delegation include *adverse selection* and *moral hazard*. I discuss various institutional remedies and show that parliamentary democracy prioritizes one of these agency problems, adverse selection, and facilitates accountability primarily through *ex ante* screening by cohesive political parties. On the other hand, parliamentary democracy is not equally well protected against moral hazard. All told, its distinctive properties render parliamentary democracy *efficient* but often lacking in *transparency*.

WHY DELEGATE?

Delegation is a feature of all modern governments. Since delegation means voluntarily giving over authority to others, we must ask why anybody would do so, and indeed why everybody (or at least every large-scale political system) does. I assume that citizens in democratic societies delegate for reasons that satisfy their criteria of good governance. As Robert A. Dahl puts it, 'I have three main criteria for judging whether I shall accept as valid and rightful, and therefore binding on me a process for making decisions on matters that affect me. First, a process may insure that decisions correspond with my own personal choice. Second, a process may insure decisions informed by a special competence that would be less likely under alternative procedures. Third, a process may be less perfect than other alternatives according to the first two criteria but, on balance, more satisfactory simply because it economizes on the amount of time, attention, and energy I must give to it' (Dahl 1970: 8).

While the first consideration, which Dahl calls the Criterion of Personal Choice, militates against delegation, the two others (the Criterion of Competence and the Criterion of Economy, respectively) constitute key parts of its rationale. In addition, the social choice literature has demonstrated some general pitfalls of decision-making in large groups, such as the problems of preference aggregation, collective preference intransitiv-ities, and collective action. Citizens may thus decide to delegate power because they face problems of (1) *capacity* (including Dahl's Criterion of Economy), (2) *competence*, or (3) *social choice* or *collective action* (for a similar argument, see Rasch 2000).

Capacity

Although popular sovereignty means that in a general sense the citizenry rules, these citizens are not always capable of making all (or most) necessary decisions. Their capacity to do so is limited by a variety of resource constraints, one of which is simply time: 'The amount of time devoted to making decisions is limited both by the unwillingness of the people involved to spend an inordinate amount of time on decisions and by deadlines set by events that will not wait. Because time has value, scheduled meetings often have a more or less fixed amount of time within which to do their business; the cost of not completing the agenda during that meeting is another meeting or not getting it done at all' (Dahl 1970: 44–5).

Hence, citizens may often be persuaded to delegate their authority simply to save time, and to ensure that necessary decisions are made. One specific version of such concerns is what economists call transaction costs. Applied to politics, transaction costs refer to any costs that collective decision-making bodies, such as voters or parliamentarians, confront in reaching, implementing, and enforcing policy decisions. These costs may be considerable, particularly when it is difficult to anticipate all the contingencies that might arise, and they may suffice to persuade these political actors to delegate their decisions (Epstein and O'Halloran 1999).

Competence

A second motivation for delegation is competence, or rather the principal's lack of such. This is the classic motivation for delegation between private citizens and various professionals. Competence is, for example, the main reason that most people take their medical concerns to a physician and their legal matters to a lawyer (and not, for example, vice versa). The knowledge and skills advantages that such professionals possess motivate ordinary citizens to demand their services at substantial cost. Increasingly, competence motivates political delegation as well. Most ordinary citizens recognize that they do not have the requisite insight to determine production and safety standards for the energy industry or to select the optimal interest rate for government lending. As Dahl puts it, 'I should not like to be a surgical patient in an operating room governed by the principle that one man's opinion is as much entitled to a hearing as another's. I do not want to be tried in a court where every question of procedure might be appealed to a vote of judge, jury, attorneys, news-papermen, spectators—and defendant. I do not want a referendum to decide what drugs and food additives are safe enough to be made available to the public' (Dahl 1970: 30–1). Contrary to other motivations for delegation, however, the concern for competence does not drive delegation from voters to elected representatives as much as it does delegation further 'downstream', especially between cabinet ministers and civil servants.

Social Choice and Collective Action Problems

Finally, delegation may be motivated by social choice and collective action problems in collective decision-making. The first of these problems has to do with the ability of collectivities, such as citizenries, to form consistent collective preferences. *Preference aggregation problems* exist because a group preference (e.g. the will of San Diego voters) cannot always be inferred from the preferences of individual members (each voter in this city). Even when each individual in a group is fully rational, it may be impossible to generate a transitive preference ordering for the group as a whole. Indeed, the Condorcet paradox shows that collective preference cycles, or the lack of a 'Condorcet winner' (one that can defeat any other option in pairwise majority voting), can occur with as few as three players and three alternatives (Arrow 1951; for introductions to social choice theory, see Riker 1982; Shepsle and Bonchek 1997). The likelihood of collective preference cycles increases with the number of players and with the number of ordered outcomes (Niemi and Weisberg 1968; Riker and Ordeshook 1973).

Extensive social choice research in the 1970s and 1980s established several generic 'chaos' or 'impossibility' results, one of which is that in *n*-dimensional policy space where there is no Condorcet winner, every alternative can by majority vote be defeated by some other point (McKelvey 1976). Social choice theorists soon recognized the devastating implications of McKelvey's result and subsequent extensions. Absent any procedural restrictions, collective and majoritarian decision-making bodies could produce endless voting cycles. The upshot would seem to be radical instability, with no credible equilibrium. The flip side of this result is that the outcome of any such collective choice process depends critically on the way and order in which the alternatives are considered. Hence, control of the political *agenda* is crucial.

Even if groups can avoid, or find ways to solve, their social choice problems, their members may still encounter *collective action* or *coordination* problems. Collective action problems exist when individual members of a group have incentives to behave in ways that lead to collectively suboptimal (inefficient) outcomes (Olson 1965). In the tragedy of the commons, for example, each villager has an incentive to graze his or her cattle on the commons, regardless of how many other members of the community do the same thing. Over time, more and more cattle are added, until the commons is overgrazed and ultimately destroyed (Hardin 1968). Coordination problems are somewhat less nasty, as the participants face a choice between multiple efficient equilibria (several different options, each of which would yield an outcome from which no player would unilaterally defect). The trick, however, is that to realize any of these happy outcomes, the group members must behave in mutually consistent ways. Thus, for highway safety it does not much matter whether motorists drive on the right-hand side or the left-hand side of the road. The crucial point is that everyone does the same thing. One purpose of delegation is precisely to avoid collectively self-defeating behaviours in such situations.

THE PRINCIPAL–AGENT FRAMEWORK

Delegation is an extremely general, and consequential, way in which citizens in all sorts of societies try to respond to such challenges. Representative democracy implies a *chain of delegation* from voters to those who govern. In this chain, those authorized to make political decisions (*principals*) conditionally designate others (*agents*) to act in their name and place. The agency-theoretic research tradition, also known as the principal–agent approach, has generated a growing set of models to illuminate delegation and its effects. As Lupia has shown in Chapter 2, principal–agent models are a powerful tool for political analysis.

Yet, no model does full justice to reality, and our view of representative democracy implies a number of assumptions which to some readers may be controversial, and which I therefore spell out:

1. The *political community* is *given and bounded*. Of course, in the real world this is never strictly true. As the 'garbage can' model of decision-making suggests, many political organizations have fluid boundaries and decision-makers that come and go, grow in importance, or fade into the background (Cohen, March, and Olsen 1972; for a critique see Bendor, Moe, and Shotts 2001). In this book, the political communities are the respective nation-states of Western Europe. But although national political institutions in Western Europe remain the most important arenas of decision-making, many decisions are reached through a tug-of-war between national, subnational, and supranational agents. We discuss these issues below and in subsequent chapters.

2. The *preferences* of principals as well as agents are *exogenously given* (i.e. not explained within our models). Delegation models thus pay no attention to the formation of preferences.

3. All principals and agents *act rationally* on the information available to them. Rational behaviour implies that actors have complete and transitive preferences over the potential outcomes and that they consistently act so as to obtain more-preferred outcomes over less-preferred ones. The rationality assumption is less a hard empirical fact than the most fruitful benchmark for thinking about institutional design and performance. Generally, the verisimilitude of the rationality assumption increases with the professionalism of the political actors. Thus, political rationality may, for example, more reasonably be attributed to leading cabinet members than to ordinary voters. This simply reflects the relative costs of behaving irrationally. A voter may suffer no serious repercussions if she acts erratically or irrationally in the voting booth. A Prime Minister behaving similarly in front of the parliamentary opposition may have much more reason to regret such acts.

4. *Principals face information scarcities*, and *information is critical*. Informational assumptions are key to delegation models, which yield particularly acute insights when information is scarce and consequential.

5. Politics is *hierarchical*, and the principal's preferences are privileged. The role of the agent is to propose means among which the principal can choose, not to help the principal determine her political goals.[1] Moreover, it is the principal's preferences alone that are the benchmark of such concepts as agency loss or slack. Thus, the principal's most preferred policy position (ideal point) is not only analytically critical but also normatively privileged. When the ultimate principals are the voters, then there is indeed strong normative reason to be concerned with whether or not their preferences find expression. But, as we shall discuss below, even in a democracy it is not obvious that the voters' desires should always be decisive.

In this book, we apply the delegation framework to parliamentary democracies. Note, however, that delegation may be neither sufficient nor necessary to solve the collective decision-making problems that I have discussed. Collective agents may face the same problems of preference aggregation, collective action, and coordination as their principals.

Delegation can also be jeopardized by constraints on the agent, when for reasons beyond his own abilities or preferences, the agent cannot satisfy the principal's demands. Here we shall ignore constraints that arise from, for example, the mortality of human beings, the scarcities of life on earth, or the laws of physics. The more relevant *political* constraints may be rules that prohibit certain forms of agency (for example, no democratic agent can be forced to commit crimes against humanity), or that force agents into behaviour that neither they nor their principals would have freely chosen.

For example, even if parliamentarians or cabinet members may indeed consider themselves to be agents of their voters, they also have other constitutionally prescribed roles to play. Many constitutions, for example the German (Article 38) and Italian (Article 67) ones, explicitly designate parliamentarians as representatives of all citizens, and not simply those that elected them. Such broad constitutional accountability is typically unenforceable, but it can at least give elected officials a normative justification for ignoring their voters' preferences. And politicians do indeed tend to embrace this conception of their agency (Wessels 1999).[2]

Moreover, *liberal* democracies may have constitutional norms that disallow the representation of certain popular preferences (e.g. racial discrimination, cruel punishment, or confiscatory government takings). Often, such norms are entrenched in a constitutional document or a bill of rights. The constitution may also insist on certain principles, such as the sovereignty or indivisibility of the nation, that were particularly

---

[1] For simplicity, when I henceforth refer generically to principals or agents, I shall, unless otherwise noted, assume that both principal and agent are individuals and that the principal is female and the agent male.

[2] In their study of role perceptions among Swedish members of parliament, for example, Esaiasson and Holmberg note that 'one alternative from the history of representational doctrine is missing, however— Burke's famous credo of "the nation as a whole". The reason for this is quite simply that Burke has been too successful; the norm that national interests come first is so well-established in most European parliaments that scholars consider it meaningless to probe parliamentary representatives on this matter' (Esaiasson and Holmberg 1996: 62).

dear to its framers. In such cases, government officials represent not only their voters and other superiors, but also the constitutional founders or some set of rights and liberties to which the constitution is committed.

Thus, office-holders in parliamentary democracies are *constrained* and frequently *common* agents, with manifold responsibilities and accountabilities. When we nevertheless consider the agency framework a powerful tool with which to analyse parliamentary government, it is because political institutions and the normative ideas of popular sovereignty can help keep politicians from ignoring their obligations to their principals.

Institutions are often constructed expressly for the purpose of aggregating preferences in a manageable and reasonably time-efficient manner. Electoral systems do so for citizen preferences, and voting rules and procedures for legislators. Although all institutions can be manipulated and none is universally fair, many do give defensible and predictable expression to the more inchoate desires and beliefs of large numbers of individual principals. Institutions are also often deliberately designed to allow political principals to overcome their coordination and collective action problems. This is, for example, the role that the literature on legislatures assigns to committees (Shepsle and Weingast 1987; Mattson and Strøm 1995). Arguably, the more consistently an institution (such as an electoral system) both gives defensible expression to popular preferences and promotes decisional efficiency, the more likely it is to survive. Thus, the demand for popular control and governmental effectiveness helps select suitable institutions.

Delegation models all simplify and distort reality. Yet that may be a price worth paying if such simplifications help us shed light on modern democratic constitutions. As in the case of the rationality assumption, I shall in the following suspend disbelief, as the proof of the framework is in the 'eating'.

AGENCY PROBLEMS AND ACCOUNTABILITY

> A good politician is quite as unthinkable as an honest burglar.
>
> H. L. Mencken (1880–1956)

Any delegation of authority entails the risk that the agent may not faithfully pursue the principal's interests. If the agent has preferences and incentives that are not perfectly compatible with those of the principal, delegation may generate *agency problems*, as discussed by Lupia in Chapter 2. Agency loss occurs when agents take action that is different from what the principal would have done, had she been in the agents' place. As Lupia tells us, for agency loss to occur there must be some minimum of preference divergence between principals and agents as well as asymmetric information. If principals are fully informed about their agents' behaviour, or if they have identical preferences, there is no reason to worry about agency loss. Alas, in politics principals often face both preference heterogeneity and asymmetric information at the same time.

Agency problems under incomplete information may take the form of *hidden information* (principals do not fully know the competencies or preferences of their agents or the exact demands of the task at hand) and/or *hidden action* (principals cannot fully observe the actions of their agents). The former condition can give rise to *adverse selection*, the latter to *moral hazard*. The former problem may lead principals to select the 'wrong' agents, who do not have the most appropriate skills or preferences. The problem of moral hazard, on the other hand, arises when agents, once selected, have incentives and opportunity to take unobservable action contrary to the principal's interests.

Agents may 'misbehave' in several different ways. Brehm and Gates (1997) differentiate between dissent-shirking (failing to serve the principal due to differences in policy preferences), leisure-shirking (failing to serve the principal due to a preference for leisure over policy goals), and sabotage (actively undermining the principal's policy goals). Here, I shall distinguish between (1) policy divergence (or policy slippage), (2) leisure-shirking, and (3) rent seeking. I shall discuss these forms of agency loss in greater detail below. Next, however, let us consider the mechanisms by which principals may seek to counteract such problems.

Accountability

As Lupia points out in Chapter 2, we can think of accountability as a property of political procedures or as an outcome. In this chapter, our focus will largely be on the former meaning. Political accountability, then, refers to mechanisms by which agency loss may be contained. As Fearon puts it, 'relations involving accountability are agency relations, in which one party is understood to be an "agent"' who makes some choices on behalf of a 'principal' who has powers to sanction or reward the agent (Fearon 1999: 55. An agent is *accountable* to his principal if (1) he is obliged to act on her behalf, and (2) she is empowered to reward or punish him for his performance in this capacity (Fearon 1999: 55; Lupia in Chapter 2). And in the words of Manin, Przeworski, and Stokes, 'Governments are accountable if citizens can discern representative from unrepresentative governments and can sanction them appropriately...An "accountability mechanism" is thus a map from the outcomes of actions (including messages that explain these actions) of public officials to sanctions by citizens' (Manin, Przeworski, and Stokes 1999: 10).

Accountability implies that principals have two kinds of rights vis-à-vis agents: a right to demand information, and a capacity to impose sanctions. Three salient forms of sanction are the ability to (1) block or amend decisions made by the agent (veto power), (2) deauthorize the agent (remove him from office or curtail his authority), and (3) impose specific (monetary or other) penalties. Principals may have one of these rights (e.g. some form of veto power, or the right to obtain information) without the others. Accountability varies in the comprehensiveness of the principal's right to information and sanctions, as well as in its exclusiveness. Governance structures in which the principal's rights are comprehensive and exclusive, that is to say, where for each agent there is only one principal, and where that principal has extensive information rights and sanctions, conform to the classic model of a *hierarchy*. Where, on the other hand, there are multiple principals with less comprehensive rights toward the agent, we can speak instead of a *plurarchy*.

Strictly speaking, accountability focuses on the rights and sanctions (oversight) that the principal retains after she has contracted with the agent. Yet, in a broader sense principals can accomplish some of their control objectives even before delegating. In Chapter 2, Lupia identifies several means by which principals can contain agency costs, such as (1) contract design, (2) screening and selection mechanisms, (3) monitoring and reporting requirements, and (4) institutional checks (Lupia in Chapter 2; also Kiewiet and McCubbins 1991; Aghion and Tirole 1997).

The former two are mechanisms by which principals seek to contain agency losses *ex ante*, that is, before entering any agreement. Principals may then subject potential agents to careful scrutiny and/or insist on retaining as much residual power as possible. *Contract design* typically seeks to establish shared interests, or incentive compatibility, between principals and agents, so that their preferences are aligned. *Screening and selection* represent efforts to sort out good agents from bad ones before a contract is made. In the case of screening, the principal does the sorting, whereas selection refers to costly action (for example, the acquisition of recognized credentials) by which the agent demonstrates his suitability. In politics, parties help voters screen candidates for public office and parliament screens potential cabinet members. Selection occurs when aspiring politicians seek minor offices, or run for hopeless seats, to prove their worthiness for more attractive offices. Also, particular educational institutions, such as the ENA (in France) or Christ Church college, Oxford (in Britain), may offer valuable political credentials.

The remaining control mechanisms operate *ex post facto*. That is to say, they are ways to contain agency losses after the contract has been made, by providing the principal with information that she might not otherwise receive. Such *ex post* accountability may rely on information produced by the principal (known as *monitoring* or *police patrols*), by the agent (*reporting*), or by some third party (*institutional checks* or *fire alarms*). In politics, legislators may seek to control executive agencies through committee hearings in which ministers or civil servants have to appear and testify (see Mattson and Strøm 1995). Alternatively (or additionally), executive agencies may regularly have to report to parliament. Finally, parliaments employ institutional checks when they subject executive agencies to legal scrutiny or external audits, or in some other way submit them to the veto powers of a third party. As the concept implies, such practices are particularly common in checks-and-balances (collegial or veto player) systems, but by no means confined to such.

Many important control mechanisms serve as vehicles of *ex ante* as well as *ex post* control. They can be used both to select agents in the first place and to subject them to sanctions and possible 'deselection' after the fact. The most basic mechanism of representative democracy, elections, is clearly of this kind. Voters use elections both prospectively (to select office-holders) and retrospectively (to sanction incumbents).

Principals face two serious constraints on oversight. First, even though the principal may find some forms of oversight (such as selection, reporting, fire alarms) less burdensome than others, for example because they rely on third-party efforts, all oversight is costly. And reliance on third-party oversight provides no free lunch, since it introduces additional agency problems (when can you trust the reports you get?) (Lupia and McCubbins 1994). Since oversight is costly, the principal obviously wants to maximize its effectiveness relative to its cost. Second, principals may face collective action and coordination problems with respect to their oversight activities. For example, in most large-scale societies, voters cannot actively deliberate over the selection and supervision of all their agents. And while it is typically in the interest of all principals that someone bears the cost of monitoring their agents, no individual principal may have an incentive to do so.

These problems notwithstanding, principals possess a substantial menu of oversight mechanisms that facilitate accountability. In the larger picture, political regime types are designed to facilitate accountability (as an outcome) through either or both of two major mechanisms: *competition* and *constraint*. Roughly speaking, in a competition regime the dominant sanction is deauthorization, whereas a constraints regime is more beholden to veto powers and penalties (see above). Parliamentary democracy differentiates itself from presidentialism in its affinity for competition relative to constraint. But as we shall see, we can also distinguish subtypes of parliamentary as well as presidential constitutions on the basis of their reliance on these respective mechanisms.

PARLIAMENTARY DEMOCRACY AND DELEGATION

Let us now consider more explicitly the institutions of parliamentary democracy as a framework for delegation and accountability. There are many ways in which the distinction between parliamentarism and other regime forms, such as presidentialism, could be drawn (see Chapter 1). Our approach in this volume is two-pronged. First, we seek a minimal definition that differentiates as cleanly and parsimoniously as possible between parliamentarism and other constitutional designs. Chapter 1 thus defines *parliamentary government* as a constitution in which any majority of the members of parliament can vote the Prime Minister and his or her cabinet out of office at virtually any time and for whatever reason they deem sufficient.

While this minimal definition allows us to distinguish as cleanly as possible between parliamentary and other constitutions, it does not tell us much about their policy processes. For this purpose, we need a second, ideal–typical conception. We thus identify the policy process of *parliamentary democracy* as a chain of delegation that includes four discrete steps or links:

1. From voters to elected representatives (legislators and others),
2. From legislators to the chief executive (the Prime Minister) and his or her cabinet,
3. From the cabinet and the chief executive to the 'line ministers' (typically individual cabinet members) that head the different executive departments, and
4. From cabinet members, in their capacity as heads of different executive departments (ministries), to civil servants within their agencies.

This chain of delegation consists of a series of agency relationships. For example, the Prime Minister is both the agent of the parliamentary majority and the principal of the line ministers in his cabinet. Democracy as popular sovereignty means that ordinary citizens are the ultimate principal. There is a reverse chain of accountability that

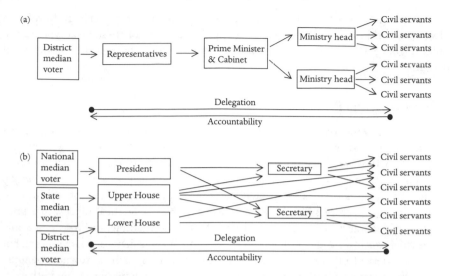

Figure 3.1. Delegation and Accountability Under Parliamentary and Presidential Government: (a) single-chain delegation model of a parliamentary system; (b) multiple-chain delegation model of a US style presidential system.

mirrors the chain of delegation, from civil servants and other office-holders back to the voters. In Chapter 1 we defined parliamentary democracy in its ideal–typical form as *a chain of delegation and accountability, from the voters to the ultimate policy-makers, in which at each link a single principal delegates to one and only one agent, or to several non-competing ones, and in which each agent is accountable to one and only one principal.* Figure 3.1 gives a stylized representation of the chain of delegation under parliamentary democracy, compared with presidentialism of the US variety.

Under either constitution, the chain of delegation approximates the shape of an hourglass (turned horizontal). Representation begins with a multitude of principals (the citizens) and ends with a large number of agents (civil servants). In between, however, the parliamentary chain narrows down more than does the presidential one. Simply put, parliamentary delegation relationships take the form of a long and singular chain, whereas presidential ones look more like a grid. Specifically, the parliamentary chain narrows down to a single link in which the cabinet connects the elected representatives of the people and the administrators of the state. It is thus in the relationship between the legislative majority and the executive that the two regime forms most clearly diverge. This relationship, of course, is also the focal point of our minimal definition of parliamentary government. Note also the singularity of principals and agents in the parliamentary system, as compared with the more complex presidential model (for a similar conception, see Palmer 1995). In short, classical parliamentarism tends to be hierarchical, whereas presidentialism typically means plurarchy.

There are two critical institutional features implicit in our very definition of parliamentary democracy, namely *indirect delegation* and *singularity*. On both dimensions, presidentialism is an interesting counterpoint. It is, then, also possible and useful to place real-world cases on a continuum that spans from one of these ideal types to the other. Figure 3.1 captures these prominent and important contrasts in constitutional design.

Indirect Delegation

Parliamentary democracy implies *indirect* delegation and accountability, as few agents are directly elected by, or accountable to, the citizens. In the classical Westminster model, the voters directly elect members of the House of Commons only. All other agents of the people are indirectly appointed and accountable, often in several stages. Presidential systems such as the United States fall towards the other end of this continuum in that the voters directly elect a large number of political offices. In a presidential and federal system such as the United States, for example, this is true not only of the chief executive at different levels of government (Presidents and Governors), but also of a variety of other executive officers at the state level, such as attorneys general, secretaries of state, education commissioners, insurance commissioners, and others.

There are thus in parliamentary democracies several stages of delegation from voters to ultimate policy-makers. Hence, the challenge is to ensure effective representation across several links in an indirect chain of delegation and accountability. In reality, of course, parliamentary systems vary in the range of elective offices and thus in the directness of delegation. Some parliamentary systems may resemble presidential systems in having more directly elective political offices, although nowhere in our sample does this include the Prime Minister or any other cabinet member.

Singularity

A second notable and distinctive feature of parliamentary democracy is the *singularity* principle. It implies that each principal employs a single agent (who may, however, consist of several individuals), or a set of non-competing agents, and that each agent reports to a single principal. Parliamentary democracy in its pure form thus implies an absence of mutual constraint among agents. Westminster democracies approximate this conception, and may indeed have served as the model for Laver and Shepsle's (1996) conception of parliamentary government: an executive branch organized into a set of mutually exclusive jurisdictions, each headed by a single and supreme minister exercising autonomous jurisdictional control. Again, reality exhibits variation among parliamentary as well as presidential systems, as the singularity principle is nowhere perfectly legislated or observed. Two or more agents, such as executive agencies, may compete for the attention of the same principal, for example a particular cabinet member. Or an agent may see himself as accountable to two or more principals at different stages of the delegation process. For example, the Prime Minister may at the same time seek to satisfy the parliamentary and the popular majority. I shall discuss variations on the parliamentary theme below. First, however, let us consider some of the specific challenges that follow from a typically parliamentary constitution.

ACCOUNTABILITY UNDER PARLIAMENTARY DEMOCRACY

Let us now identify some characteristic features of accountability (oversight) under-parliamentary democracy. A long and singular chain of delegation offers ample opportunities for agency loss. As Lupia points out in Chapter 2, with some caveats, the longer the chain of delegation, the greater the potential for agency loss. Also, the singularity of agents means that principals cannot rely on agents to check one another, or to make competing bids from which she can choose. To counteract these dangers, the *Westminster model* of parliamentary democracy (although no longer found in its pure form in Britain) relies heavily on a mechanism that *ex ante* sorts agents by preferences and subjects them to centralized authority. This mechanism is party government.

Political Parties and Ex Ante Control

One way to contain agency problems in democratic delegation is through a mechanism that aligns the preferences of the candidates for key political offices. The secret of Westminster parliamentarism is thus *centralized, cohesive, policy-oriented political parties.* As Cox (1987) has demonstrated, party government and parliamentary government evolved simultaneously and symbiotically into the 'efficient secret' of British government (Bagehot 1963[1867]): political organizations that align the preferences of the occupants of the most important political offices (parliament, the cabinet, and the heads of the different executive agencies) and subordinate them to centralized control. This is precisely what political parties do. Party leaders can then present to the democratic principals (the voters) a package of candidate agents whose policy preferences are fairly well understood, and whose behaviour will be strictly policed by this semi-public organization. Moreover, even though the voter can only directly influence the selection of parliamentarians, the 'downstream' consequences of a victory for one team or another are straightforward and predictable. As Palmer puts it, 'The Westminster model of government similarly involves the holding of a competition (an election) between competing organizations (parties) for the virtually unconstrained right to exercise a monopoly power (by government, over legitimate coercion). The electorate seeks competing bids from parties in terms of promises to govern according to particular policy preferences and leadership characteristics. By appointing one disciplined party as its agent, the electorate accepts, by majority vote, what it judges to be the best bid' (Palmer 1995: 168).

Under parliamentary democracy, parties influence all stages of the chain of delegation. In particular, they generally control delegation from voters to representatives, as well as from representatives to the chief executive (Müller 2000). Party control means extensive screening of prospective parliamentarians as well as potential cabinet members. Before candidates gain access to higher office, they must acquire the proper party credentials and prove themselves in lesser offices. But the effects of party attenuate as we move 'downstream' the policy chain (see Fig. 3.2). Their reach into administrative agencies is either tenuous or controversial, since partisanship in the civil service often conflicts with cherished values such as competence, neutrality, or simply 'clean

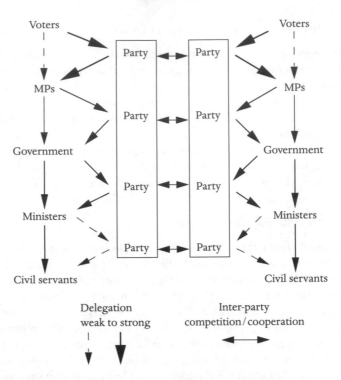

Figure 3.2. Political Parties in the Parliamentary Chain of Delegation: An Empirical Assessment.

Source: Müller (2000).

government'. As Müller puts it, 'Parties are least able to control the final stage in the delegation chain—the behaviour of civil servants. The fact that the role of political parties deteriorates the more the delegation chain develops, reflects increasing informational asymmetries and the relevance of normative constraints' (Müller 2000: 330).

Political parties are complex collaborative devices for mutual gain, formed because candidates for public office and voters find them useful for their respective purposes. But to serve these purposes, political parties have to satisfy two incentive conditions. First, they have to provide sufficient inducements for political office-holders to submit to the cohesion (discipline) that they impose. Second, the policy cohesion that parties induce among office-holders must be sufficient that voters find the party label inform- ative and useful. In addition, it is helpful (though not strictly necessary) for parties to attract activists that can help them in the recruitment, training, and selection of potential candidates for office, as well as provide inexpensive campaign labour.

The first of these conditions means that party leaders must control the recruitment (election and appointment) of government personnel, as well as government policy- making. For party government to be efficient, parties must be the only, or at least the preferred, way in which legislators realize their main political goals: re-election, political power, and policy objectives. John Aldrich (1995) identifies three sets of incentives among politicians for party formation: collective action problems, social choice problems, and political ambition (see also Cox and McCubbins 1993). I have already discussed collective action and social choice problems as motivations for delegation, and such incentives exist among legislators as well as among citizens at large. To provide effective answers to these challenges, parties must be able to structure the legislative and executive arenas so as to facilitate effective decision-making, and they must control access to the offices to which politicians aspire.

At the same time, the second condition implies that parties must be sufficiently effective 'informational economizing devices' that voters and activists will sustain them. Voters can only rely on party labels, or in other words delegate policy aggregation to party leaders, if these are capable of enforcing policy agreement in government. If legislative politics is anarchic, then party labels can be of no use to the voters. Furthermore, as Michael F. Thies points out, the policies underpinning the party label must resonate with voter preferences: 'Mixing apples and oranges is fine if you can sell yourselves as the fruit party, but if voters still like apples or oranges, but not both, they will no longer be able to learn much from the "Fruit Party" label that will help them with their vot ing decisions' (Thies 2000: 249). The evolution of meaningful party labels in Europe was facilitated by the profound social cleavages generated by the industrial and national revolutions (Lipset and Rokkan 1967). In Britain, due to the prior resolution of religious conflict and the temporary suppression of ethno-national ones, the predominance of the class cleavage helped foster two successive two-party systems with strong partisan attachments.

Finally, for voters to attach themselves to political parties, there must also be electoral institutions that translate popular votes into partisan representation in a reasonably meaningful and transparent way. In the classical Westminster model, this is indeed the case. Under a competitive two-party system and plurality single-member districts, the electoral menu is simple and the process transparent. Moreover, the process is non-perverse in that voters can never hurt themselves (would never experience rational *ex post* regret) if they vote for their most-preferred party.

Two institutional features of parliamentary democracy reinforce centralized party authority: the confidence vote and the dissolution power. We have already noted that it is the parliamentary majority's dismissal power, through a vote of no confidence, that fundamentally sets parliamentary government apart from other regime types. But paradoxically, the flip side of this procedure enables the cabinet and the party leadership to dominate the legislative branch. The *confidence vote* enables the Prime Minister to attach the cabinet's fate to some bill before parliament. This is indeed a 'doomsday device' (Lupia and Strøm 1995), by which the entire cabinet can be removed in one fell swoop. Yet, this ability to raise the stakes and redefine the parliamentary agenda often enables Prime Ministers to quell policy dissent within their respective parties or coalitions. It also allows them to manipulate the legislative policy process (Huber 1996).

The *dissolution power* is another doomsday device that similarly allows the Prime Minister or cabinet to threaten the parliament with an immediate electoral verdict. Most parliamentary democracies feature some provision for early dissolution. In the

Westminster model, within the limits of the maximum constitutional term, the election date is fully controlled by the Prime Minister and his party. Consequently, this dissolution power can be used strategically for partisan purposes (Strøm and Swindle 2002).

Consequences of Partisanship

The prominence of partisanship in parliamentary democracies has important ramifications. One has to do with the pool from which political agents are selected. In parliamentary democracies, *ex ante* screening is reinforced through *internal selection of agents* such as parliamentary candidates and cabinet members, particularly in socially cohesive (often externally created) parties. The stronger the 'partyness' of society (Sjöblom 1987), and the more parties represent distinct social groups, the more they tend to rely on prior screening devices, such as strong extra-parliamentary membership organizations, to make sure that candidates represent 'their kind' and the best of their kind. Thus, candidates for office are recruited by and from the party organization.

The second arena in which internal selection is used is parliament. In many parliamentary democracies, such as the United Kingdom, law or convention requires that cabinet members simultaneously hold parliamentary office. Thus, the cabinet is a true subset of parliament. This is a common form of contract design in Westminster systems, and some observers see it as the defining feature of parliamentary government (e.g. Hernes and Nergaard 1989; Lane and Narud 1992).[3] Even in countries without such requirements, cabinet members often have substantial parliamentary experience (for cross-national surveys, see Andeweg and Nijzink 1995; Saalfeld 2000).

Governance through cohesive political parties helps align preferences, and to some extent information, along the chain of delegation. The purpose of the concomitant practice of selecting agents internally is mainly informational. Internal, rather than external, selection of agents has obvious informational advantages, which, as Juan Linz laments, may not be available in presidential systems: 'The presidential candidates do not need and often do not have any prior record as political leaders. They may not be identified with a party with an ideology or program and record, and there may be little information about the persons likely to serve in the cabinet' (Linz 1994: 11).

Another consequence of Westminster parliamentarism is that the cabinet enjoys virtually *monopolistic agenda control*. Agenda control, or the ability to control the set of policy options under deliberation, can be a source of great power. McKelvey's (1976) famous 'chaos' theorem shows that an agenda setter can be a virtual policy dictator. Yet, the value of agenda control depends on the context. Thus, Tsebelis (2002) shows that the power of agenda setters generally declines (or at least does not increase) with the number of veto players.

In agency models, as Lupia points out in Chapter 2, generally the agent proposes and the principal disposes. That is to say, when we select an agent, we simultaneously vest

---

[3] Applied to the relationship between voters and parliamentarians, internal delegation implies a residence requirement for elected representatives. Although such rules, or at least norms, exist in some countries, they are not uniquely associated with parliamentarism. Since the introduction of civil service reforms, internal delegation is not generally a feature of the relationship between cabinet members and civil servants.

that person (or group or organization) with agenda powers. Thus, for example, when a cabinet member (she) delegates a policy issue to a civil servant (he), she specifically asks him to prepare a policy proposal that she may later approve or veto. This recognition helps us reconcile two apparently contradictory facets of the democratic policy process. On the one hand, constitutions prescribe a process of delegation that moves from voters and 'downstream'. On the other hand, students of decision-making often point out that reality looks more like our 'upstream' process of accountability: proposals are initiated by agents and work their way back to the ultimate principals for final approval. Delegation in fact means that authorization moves in a forward direction (from principals to agents) and policy proposals backwards. To put it baldly, *agents have agenda control and principals veto power*.

The simple delegation scheme of parliamentary democracy implies a concentration of agenda control in the cabinet. That is to say, since voters delegate along a singular chain of delegation, agenda control over the policy process is placed squarely, and indeed almost monopolistically, in the cabinet. The cabinet's agenda control can be derived directly from the parliamentary chain of delegation. Policy initiative rests with the executive because the cabinet is the sole agent of the parliamentary majority. Co-partisanship supports such delegation by aligning political preferences and incentives. The fact that civil servants generally are not partisan means that cabinet members will be more reluctant to delegate broadly to agents further 'downstream'.

Under presidentialism, the legislature and the executive are instead coequal agents of the citizens. Since the President is not accountable to the legislators, they are under-standably reluctant to grant him exclusive policy initiative. Yet, since there is simply no hierarchy between legislature and executive, it is not obvious that agenda control instead rests with the former. Rather, legislators may still look to the President and the executive branch for expertise and policy initiatives, but will delegate to the executive only when such delegation can be sustained by common partisan bonds, that is, when a single, cohesive party controls both the legislature and the executive branch (as, for example, in the United States during the New Deal and after the 2002 elections). In such situations, the preferences of President and legislature are likely to be well aligned. Otherwise, we might instead see a tug-of-war between legislature and executive over agenda control.[4]

Ineffective Oversight

Whereas Westminster parliamentary democracy thus relies heavily on partisanship and internal selection to contain agency problems, it makes far less use of another class of accountability mechanisms, namely oversight after the fact of delegation. We can think about a continuum of vehicles of *ex post* oversight, from those that are integral to the chain of parliamentary delegation (consisting of the voters' representatives or their

---

[4] In his veto player analysis, George Tsebelis (2000, 2002) similarly argues that in parliamentary systems agenda control rests with the executive branch, whereas under presidentialism it is lodged with the legis-lature. As suggested above, I agree with the first part of this argument, but not necessarily with the latter.

direct agents), to those that are most clearly external (not directly or indirectly account-able to the voters). Internal mechanisms include such procedures as parliamentary committee hearings. The usefulness of such mechanisms will depend heavily on the degree to which agent preferences are aligned through effective partisanship. The more effectively partisanship works, the less incentive for politicians to use these mechanisms. *Ex post* constraint comes in two forms: (1) multiple (or partitioned) democratic principals, and (2) external checks (such as constitutional courts) that are outside the direct popular chain of delegation. Presidential systems, such as the United States, typically feature a policy process with both multiple principals and external checks or constraints.

Parliamentary systems are less likely to have such a plethora of external constraints. Recall that in its pure form, parliamentary democracy implies a singularity of principals (as well as agents) and more generally a lack of external constraints or checks on policy mak-ers. The Westminster model in fact comes close to this ideal type. In Dicey's (1959: 39–40) formulation, for example, parliamentary sovereignty means that Parliament 'has the right to make and unmake any law whatever; and, further, that no person or body is recognized by the law of England as having a right to override or set aside the legislation of Parliament'.[5] Any democratic constraint in such a system would thus have to be internal.

Yet, in a Westminster parliamentary system, even internal, *ex post* oversight tends to be weak and ineffectual. This claim may at first encounter sound odd, since it is the very *ex post* accountability of the cabinet to the parliamentary majority that defines parliamentary government. But this *ex post* accountability depends almost entirely on electoral competition. And the indeterminacy of election dates under most parliamentary constitutions also complicates *ex post* electoral accountability. In the pure Westminster model, within the limits of the maximum constitutional term, the Prime Minister and his or her party fully control the election date. Consequently, this dissolution power can be used strategically for partisan purposes (Strøm and Swindle 2002). The manipulability of election dates reduces the effectiveness of *ex post* electoral accountability and adds to the informational asymmetry between ins and outs.

Between elections, accountability is tenuous for three reasons. First, parliamentary democracy lacks institutional mechanisms for credible *ex post* oversight. Second, par-liamentary systems (at least in their pure form) lack the capacity to determine when sanctions are appropriate. Third, and most critically, party government implies that the parliamentary majority lacks motivation to sanction its agents. Let us consider these issues in turn.

First, while the hallmark of parliamentarism, the no confidence vote is blunt and unwieldy and there are few alternative sanctions. The impeachment procedure (which elsewhere has been employed not just in the United States, but also in Brazil and Venezuela) has in most parliamentary systems fallen into disuse. Nor are other and less severe forms of censure or reprimand common. And recall provisions, which feature in some presidential constitutions, are essentially unknown (see Chapter 4).

A second problem is that parliamentary systems do not have the monitoring capacity necessary to determine when sanctions might be appropriate. Presidential systems tend

---

[5] As quoted in Norton (1994: 63).

to feature institutions that facilitate active oversight, of either the police-patrol (committee hearings) or the fire alarm (audits, judicial institutions) variety (McCubbins and Schwartz 1984). Such institutions are much less prominent, and have much less teeth, in the parliamentary system. Parliamentary committees, for example, have much lower oversight capacity, and in the Westminster model this capacity is almost entirely absent (see Mattson and Strøm 1995). One interesting vehicle for *ex post* parliamentary oversight is the ombudsman (or parliamentary commissioner), a Swedish 'whistle-blower' innovation that has found acceptance in a number of parliamentary systems. Yet, the ombudsman typically has only advisory powers.

Yet, the most important cause of the weakness of *ex post* accountability under parliamentarism lies in political parties. The institutions of parliamentary democracy empower parties to an extent that is generally not found under presidentialism. But as parties gain importance as mechanisms of bonding (Palmer 1995), they reduce incentives for *ex post* parliamentary oversight of the executive, as Ostrogorski observed almost a century ago (see Chapter 1). The alignment of policy preferences along the chain of delegation means that members of the parliamentary majority have no meaningful incentive to scrutinize the behaviour of their fellow party members in the executive branch (unless the latter were to engage in electorally embarrassing behaviour). Thus, parliamentarism fails to satisfy Madison's concern that 'Ambition must be made to counteract ambition. The interest of the man must be connected with the constitutional rights of the place' (Federalist No. 51). Consequently, as Palmer observes:

The characteristic that distinguishes franchise bidding from other regulatory solutions to natural monopoly also distinguishes the classic Westminster constitution from other systems: the absence of significant *ex post* behavioural regulation—binding checks-and-balances. Once an election has been held, the successful party in a pure model of the Westminster system is effectively entitled to exercise power as it sees fit, subject only to the incentives provided by the prospect of another electoral competition (Palmer 1995: 168).

VARIETIES OF PARLIAMENTARY GOVERNMENT

Parliamentary democracy, we have noted, typically features strong *ex ante* partisan control of democratic agents, and few and weak *ex post* checks and constraints. Yet, not all parliamentary democracies are typical. Indeed, real-world parliamentary systems exhibit substantial variation in accountability regimes along two critical dimensions. One ranges from the cohesive and competitive party government depicted above to a weaker and more fragmented pattern. The other dimension runs from the lack of external accountability mechanisms to greater structural constraint. And while these two dimensions are analytically distinct, there is reason to believe that they may be empirically and historically correlated, in the sense that a weakening of partisan bonds has contributed to an evolution towards more effective constraint (see Chapter 22).

Political scientists have, of course, duly noted this variation. Weaver and Rockman's (1993) insightful work divides parliamentary systems into three different subtypes. The key to this differentiation is the partisan composition of governments, which in turn is driven by differences in electoral systems and accounts for substantial differences in policy performance. Similarly, Arend Lijphart's (1984, 1999) influential work differentiates between Westminster and consensus democracy along two dimensions. The first dimension, which Lijphart seems to privilege, has much to do with the electoral system and the number of political parties. Finally, in a seminal series of publications, George Tsebelis (1995, 2000, 2002) argues that with respect to the capacity for policy change, 'the logic of decision-making in presidential systems is quite similar to the logic of decision-making in multiparty parliamentary systems' (Tsebelis 1995: 292). The critical variable is not regime type but the number of veto players. All else equal, the larger the number of veto players, the lower the capacity for policy change. Like Lijphart and Weaver and Rockman, Tsebelis distinguishes between two-party and coalitional parliamentary systems. Contrary to the latter, however, he goes on to claim that the multiple veto players of coalitional multiparty parliamentary democracies generate policy-making dynamics akin to presidential systems. A further implication of Tsebelis' argument is that deviation from our ideal–typical model along either dimension (party cohesion and external constraint, respectively) should have similar consequences.[6]

These issues are certainly worthy of our attention. To the extent that parliamentary systems deviate from the Westminster model, by having lesser party cohesion or greater *ex post* constraint, how is democratic delegation affected? Below, I therefore discuss party cohesion first and institutional constraint subsequently.

Party Cohesion

Real-world parliamentary systems have been drifting away from the simplicities of the Westminster model, towards less cohesive parties, for about a hundred years. The most important causes of this evolution have been the introduction of proportional representation (PR) and the consequent fragmentation of parliamentary party systems (Rokkan 1970; Boix 1999). Since about First World War, most parliamentary systems, and particularly those in continental Europe, have not been competitive two-party systems. Concomitantly, multiparty government has become the norm (see Müller and Strøm 2000).

As noted, political parties are especially critical to the operation of parliamentary systems, as they function as devices of *ex ante* screening and preference alignment. Hence, the question is whether regimes that involve many (perhaps four or five)

---

[6] Tsebelis acknowledges that the vetoes of institutional veto players are enforceable in ways that those of partisan veto players are not. If one party in a coalition government, for example, refuses to go along with a particular policy proposal, it cannot prevent the rest of the governing parties from passing the bill anyway, provided they can gather enough support on the floor of parliament. Tsebelis argues that the dissenting party can effectively prevent such outcomes by threatening to withdraw from the coalition and thus forcing a resignation or renegotiation. While there are surely cases in which a coalition party can have its way by threatening to withdraw, it is far from obvious that all governing parties have such bargaining power. In fact, a dissenting coalition party should be able to veto policy a proposal only if its threat to bring down the government is credible, that is to say, if its walk-away value is sufficiently high (see Lupia and Strøm 2004). Some parties have high walk-away values because they are pivotal and have other potential coalitions that they could join. But others are not so privileged, for example, if they are surplus parties in an 'oversized' coalition, of if their policy preferences are relative extreme.

parties simultaneously in executive policy-making differ from those in which one party controls the cabinet. The answer is not entirely straightforward. The value of parties is determined not by their official status, but by their ability to condition the behaviour of voters and their agents. The fact that for a long time Christian Democrats in Italy were organized as a single party (the DC), whereas in Germany there were two such parties (the CDU and the CSU), does not mean that the former served as a more effective vehicle of agency control than the latter. The contrary is probably closer to the truth. Thus, the 'partyness' of a given polity is determined less by the number and size of political parties than by the policy cohesion and electoral competition they generate.

The value of partisanship hinges on the incentives that it offers politicians on the one hand and voters on the other. These factors are in turn a function of rules concerning ballot access, electoral seat allocation, legislative agenda control, confidence relationships, parliamentary dissolution, and other choices that matter to politicians. They also depend on the organization and strategies of the political parties themselves. Parties have developed a range of devices by which they induce cohesion by controlling access to a range of perquisites that politicians desire, such as ballot access, coveted committee assignments, campaign funds, and the like.

The PR system directly affects the relationship between voters and parliamentarians less than the relationship between parliament and the cabinet. At least closed-list PR systems do nothing to weaken the internal cohesion of political parties. Such electoral systems may, however, jeopardize the cabinet cohesion that is traditionally found in the Westminster system. Interparty coalitions must strive hard to generate and control similar inducements and then to distribute them in such a way as to foster coalitional cohesion. Such coalition governance institutions are feasible, but not simple or universally effective. Coalition parties often sign extensive policy agreements and set up institutional arrangements, such as coalition committees, inner cabinets, or party summits, to enforce them. Yet, such agreements are notoriously difficult to enforce, and there are numerous cases in which they have failed (Strøm and Müller 1999).

The generally lower level of cohesion in multiparty systems is due not just to enforcement problems, but also to a lack of suitable incentives for politicians. As Palmer (1995) notes, interparty coalitions are unlikely to align electoral incentives as effectively as a single political party. Whereas the cohesion of copartisans is brought about in large part by the expectation of a common electoral fate, this tie is much less likely to bind in multiparty coalitions. Some electoral systems, such as the German mixed-member system or those with apparentement provisions, permit politicians to make coalitions more 'party-like' by forging pre-electoral agreements that effectively allow voters to treat the coalition as if it were a party. But even though such institutions may help, electoral coalitions are typically too fragile to be genuine substitutes for parties. Under the most common electoral systems, members of interparty coalitions are much more likely than copartisans to be in mutual competition for votes. Although the electoral fortunes of coalition parties are likely to be positively correlated, there are many examples of parties that benefit at the expense of their coalition partners (Rose and Mackie 1983).

Party system fragmentation also affects voter incentives. To the extent that interparty coalitions are unstable, of course, such commitments become less valuable to the voters.

The more parties break their own commitments, the less reason voters have to count on them. Party cohesion helps voters control access to the executive branch through the ballot box. Multiparty politics clouds and complicates the relationship between electoral contests and executive power. Voters can no longer assume that voting for their most preferred party will necessarily be their best strategy. Moreover, the entire linkage between electoral results and control of the executive branch may become tenuous. In extreme cases (as in Italy 1945–87), the *responsiveness* of government formation to electoral results may become negative, meaning that parties that lose votes in elections subsequently are more likely to enter government than those that gain (Strøm 1990).

These problems of transparency and responsiveness are more severe in some multiparty systems than in others. In terms of their competitive characteristics, multiparty systems may usefully be subdivided into alternational versus pivotal types. In *alternational* systems, two blocs of parties (internally cemented, perhaps, by effective agreements) compete for the voters' favour and alternate in power much in the way that individual parties do in classical two-party systems. In *pivotal* systems, on the other hand, there is a single party, or occasionally a bloc of smaller parties, that forms of the core of the governing coalition, often because it controls the median legislator on the dominant policy dimension. This pivotal party may occasionally change coalition partners, but there is no wholesale alternation in power as a result of electoral contests. It is in pivotal systems that the bond of partisanship is most severely tested. Institutions such as the German mixed-member system or the French double ballot may drive multiparty systems towards the alternational subtype. Yet, particularly in pivotal party systems, coalition partners cannot assume that they are doomed to sink or swim together and often have electoral incentives to defect. Hence, the glue that keeps politicians in line and subjects them to popular control is particularly suspect in pivotal party systems.

Institutional Constraints

The Westminster model of parliamentary democracy concentrates power in the hands of a virtually unconstrained democratic executive. Yet, in the real world many parliamentary systems have a larger number of constitutional constraints on the power of the Prime Minister and his or her cabinet. Germany is an obvious example, where the power of the chief executive is constrained by an indirectly elected Bundesrat, by a federal constitution, by a constitutional court, by the institutions of the European Union, including an enterprising judiciary and an autonomous central bank, and by a practice of social partnership. As noted above, constraints come in two basic forms: partitions and checks. *Partitions*, such as federalism, consociationalism, or corporatism, subdivide democratic principals into different subgroups. *Checks*, such as judicial review, presidential vetoes, or abrogative referendums, subject the decisions of democratic agents to various veto gates. In principal-agent terms, the former category corresponds to a situation of multiple principals, whereas the latter (at least in some cases) is akin to one of multiple, checking agents.

Such constraints may play a role similar to that of political parties in containing agency costs in the democratic chain of delegation. Yet, they do so in different ways and at different stages. For reasons I have already discussed, party cohesion subverts the effects of internal constraints. Yet, many constraints, such as referendums or constitutional courts, are largely outside the democratic chain of delegation and much less likely to be rendered ineffective by common bonds of copartisanship. It is therefore more likely that external *ex post* agency controls might coexist with cohesive political parties than that internal ones would do so.

If partisan cohesion deteriorates, we might instead expect to see multiparty parliamentary democracies resort to external constraints. But even though partisan control and external constraints are to some extent mutual substitutes, they are not mutually exclusive. It is perfectly possible for a polity to score high on both, as the United States increasingly seems to do. And a system that scores low on both dimensions may simply be low on agency control. Even among parliamentary democracies, there are coalitional multiparty systems with few institutional checks (Denmark) and there are systems with significant institutional checks but little history of multiparty government (Canada). The correlation between the two is, of course, ultimately an empirical question to which we shall return in subsequent chapters.

As Tsebelis has shown, identifying veto players and their interaction can give us powerful insights into the importance of constraints in parliamentary and other regimes. Yet, for our purposes, finer distinctions may be necessary, as not all veto players are created equal. Indeed, it is often useful to distinguish between four different forms of privileged political actors. Thus, in a given policy process, a particular player's agreement may be necessary for a particular decision to be made, sufficient, both, or neither. We call a player whose consent is both necessary and sufficient a *dictator*, one whose support is only necessary a *veto player*, and one whose consent is only sufficient a *decisive player*. Even players whose agreement is neither necessary nor sufficient are not necessarily irrelevant, however. If A can credibly threaten to take action that will affect the payoffs of a dictator, veto player, or decisive player, then A is a *powerful player*. Democratic constitutions typically feature many or all of these powers simultaneously.[7]

Tsebelis distinguishes between *institutional* (legislative chambers, presidents, courts, federal institutions, etc.) and *partisan* veto players (the various parties represented in the cabinet) but argues that a proliferation of either has similar consequences for policy stability. While this is in general terms likely to be the case, it is for our purposes useful to differentiate between institutional and partisan veto players. A proliferation of the former conforms to what I shall call *constrained parliamentarism*. Where the latter is in generous supply, I shall speak instead of *multiparty parliamentarism*, of which the most distinctive subtype is the *pivotal* one (see above).

---

[7] A President in a parliamentary state, for example, can have each of these powers in different domains. He can be a dictator as commander of the armed forces, for example, or in some of his appointment powers. He can be a veto player with respect to ordinary legislation. Of course, we could further distinguish between presidents whose vetoes are only suspensory, those whose vetoes could relatively easily be overriden, and those whose vetoes are nearly impossible to override (see Shugart and Carey 1992). Furthermore, the President can be a decisive player with respect to parliamentary dissolution if he can freely dissolve parliament but there are other circumstances in which parliament may also be dissolved without his involvement (see Strøm and Swindle 2002). Finally, in areas in which he has no constitutional powers, a President can be a powerful player, if by expressing his endorsement or displeasure, giving exhortatory speeches, or dragging his feet, he can affect that benefits that other players derive from particular initiatives.

INSTITUTIONS AND POLICY DIVERGENCE

Having laid out the institutional features of parliamentary versus presidential constitutions, it is now time to consider their implications for specific democratic agency problems. In discussing specific agency problems in contemporary democracies, I proceed in three steps. First, I develop a delegation model in which I assume complete information and thus isolate agency problems that stem strictly from policy preference divergence between principals and agents. The model will highlight specific agency problems that arise from the institutional features of parliamentary and other constitutions. Next I consider, in a less formal way, agency problems associated with various non-policy motivations. Finally, I discuss two critical agency problems, adverse selection and moral hazard, that may arise under asymmetric information, when principals lack certain critical information about their agents.

Let us, then, first examine parliamentary agency problems that may arise even when the democratic principal is fully informed about the preferences of her agent. Consider Fig. 3.3, which illustrates a delegation game, loosely in the tradition of Romer and Rosenthal (1978) and Lupia in Chapter 2, but with one principal and two agents. This

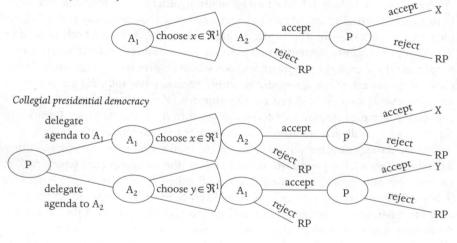

Parliamentary democracy

Collegial presidential democracy

Competitive presidential democracy

Figure 3.3. Agency Loss (Policy Divergence) Under Parliamentary and Presidential Government.

game may take three different forms, depending on the relationship between the two agents: a *hierarchical* model, in which one agent is subordinated to the other, a *competitive* model, in which the agents contest for the favour of the principal, and a *collegial* model, in which both agents have to approve any proposal that is made to the principal, but in which no agent is systematically subordinated to the other.

These models roughly correspond to major contemporary regime types. We can identify the principal as the median voter, and the agents as the median member of the national legislature and cabinet, respectively. (For simplicity, I here ignore the civil service.) The hierarchical model then corresponds to a parliamentary regime, and the two latter models to what I shall call *competitive* and *collegial presidentialism*, respectively.

The common features of these models are as follows: One or both agents are allowed to make policy proposals. The principal can either accept one proposal, or reject any or all proposals. If the principal accepts some proposal, that proposal is implemented and the game ends. If no proposal is accepted, a reversion point (which could represent the status quo) prevails. I assume that any proposal can be represented by a point on a policy continuum and that all players have Euclidean preferences and a most-preferred position (an ideal point) on this policy dimension. The solution concept is subgame perfect Nash equilibrium.

For simplicity, I set the value of the reversion point (status quo) to zero. For the same reason, I assume that no player is indifferent between any proposals, and that no player has an ideal point identical to that of any other player, or to the reversion point. Relaxing any or all of these restrictions should add complexity but not change any of the general results. All players are assumed to have full information concerning all aspects of the game. I further assume that it is costless to make or accept proposals, but that if indifferent between a proposal and the reversion point, any player will opt for the latter. Under these assumptions, no agent will make or endorse a proposal that will not be accepted, or that will not represent an improvement for him, relative to the reversion point. Similarly, if the principal is indifferent between a proposal and the reversion point, she will reject the proposal.

The three games differ in their structure. The *parliamentary* game proceeds as follows: Agent 1 decides whether to propose. If he does, agent 2 either rejects or endorses the proposal. If agent 1 fails to make a proposal, or if agent 2 rejects it, the game ends and the reversion point prevails. If, however, agent 1 proposes and agent 2 endorses, then the principal either accepts or rejects that proposal as it is. Under *competitive presidentialism*, on the other hand, agents 1 and 2 decide separately and independently whether to propose. The principal can then choose between any proposals and the reversion point. Finally, under *collegial presidentialism*, the principal initially vests agenda control in one of her two agents. Along either branch of the game tree, the subgame that follows is identical to the parliamentary game. In other words, the agent vested with agenda control may propose, the other agent endorses or vetoes this proposal, and if the second agent endorses, the principal finally accepts or rejects that proposal.

The two versions of presidentialism differ in their reliance on competition and constraint, respectively. The collegial model may be the more familiar representation of real-world checks-and-balances systems. Yet, even the competitive model captures important elements of procedural choice inherent in presidential regimes. Under US presidentialism, for example, legislators may establish a range of different executive agencies with similar or overlapping jurisdictions. They sometimes design these institutions so as to allow some choice over which agents to utilize. And particularly in federal systems, policy advocates may have some choice whether to press their concerns in state or federal institutions. In the United States, for example, anti-tobacco activists, gun control advocates, and right-to-life groups are among those that have used different channels of access in such a competitive fashion.

The model allows us to examine the magnitude of policy divergence under different institutions and preference configurations. I measure this loss as the distance between the outcome (whether an accepted proposal or the reversion point) and the principal's ideal point.[8] Table 3.1 presents the outcomes of all three games under the ten different preference configurations under which they vary.[9] For each preference configuration and regime type (institutional rule), Table 3.1 reports the magnitude of agency loss. Note that in some cases the rank ordering of the ideal points and the reversion point does not suffice to precisely determine the equilibrium. Rather, the latter depends on the relative distance between these points. Because of these complications, I report two sets of values for each preference configuration: one representing a best-case scenario (minimal policy divergence) and one a worst-case scenario (maximum policy divergence).

The general lessons of these games can be fairly easily summarized: the parliamentary regime is susceptible to greater agency loss than either presidential model. Out of the latter, competitive presidentialism generally minimizes policy divergence, with the collegial model between parliamentarism and competitive presidentialism. There is no arrangement of preferences under which agency loss is greater under either presidential model than under parliamentary institutions. Under most preference configurations, agency loss under parliamentarism varies within the same bounds as under collegial presidentialism. Yet, there are two configurations (numbers VII and X) under which the latter presents a more favourable best-case scenario. These are both cases in which all players favour a change in the same direction relative to the reversion point, but in which the parliamentary agenda setter (agent 1) has the most status quo-oriented preferences. The contrast between parliamentarism and competitive presidentialism is more clear-cut: this presidential variety is superior (has smaller policy divergence in either the best- or the worst-case scenario, or both) in seven out of ten configurations

---

[8] As Lupia points out in Chapter 2, agency loss could be measured either against the reversion point or against the principal's ideal point. Since in this model I am assuming complete information as well as rationality, the principal will not accept a proposal that is inferior to the reversion point. Hence, only the second measure of agency loss is meaningful in a model of this kind.

[9] In all, there are twenty-four different ordinal preference configurations—different ways in which the reversion point and the ideal points of the various players can be arrayed. Note that we shall be concerned only with the magnitude, but not the direction, of policy divergence. Therefore, we can disregard half of these preference configurations, since each of them is simply a 'mirror image' of one other configuration, in which the order of the ideal points is reversed. For simplicity, I also ignore any preference ordering in which both agents are at the opposite side of the reversion point from the principal. In no such situation would rational and fully informed players adopt any alternative to the reversion point, regardless of institutions. That leaves us with the ten preference configurations represented in Table 3.1.

Table 3.1. *Policy Divergence Under Different Regime Types*

Preference configuration	Parliamentary—best case	Parliamentary—worst case	Competitive presidential—best case	Competitive presidential—worst case	Collegial presidential—best case	Collegial presidential—worst case
(I): $A_1 > A_2 > P > 0$	None	$|P-\epsilon|$	None	$|P-\epsilon|$	None	$|P-\epsilon|$
(II): $A_1 > P > A_2 > 0$	None	$|P-\epsilon|$	None	None	None	$|P-\epsilon|$
(III): $A_1 > P > 0 > A_2$	$|P|$	$|P|$	None	None	$|P|$	$|P|$
(IV): $A_1 > 0 > A_2 > P$	$|P|$	$|P|$	$|\epsilon|$	$|P-\epsilon|$	$|P|$	$|P|$
(V): $A_1 > 0 > P > A_2$	$|P|$	$|P|$	None	None	$|P|$	$|P|$
(VI): $A_2 > A_1 > P > 0$	None	$|P-\epsilon|$	None	$|P-\epsilon|$	None	$|P-\epsilon|$
(VII): $A_2 > P > A_1 > 0$	$|\epsilon|$	$|P-\epsilon|$	None	None	None	$|P-\epsilon|$
(VIII): $A_2 > 0 > A_1 > P$	$|P|$	$|P|$	$|\epsilon|$	$|P-\epsilon$	$|P|$	$|P|$
(IX): $P > A_1 > A_2 > 0$	$|\epsilon|$	$|P-\epsilon|$	$|\epsilon|$	$|P-\epsilon$	$|\epsilon|$	$|P-\epsilon|$
(X): $P > A_2 > A_1 > 0$	$2\epsilon|$	$|P-\epsilon|$	$|\epsilon|$	$|P-2\epsilon|$	$|\epsilon|$	$|P-\epsilon|$

Note: The entries in each cell represent the magnitude of policy divergence, measured as the absolute distance between the equilibrium and the principal's ideal point. Vertical bars denote absolute values. See the text and Fig. 3.2 for descriptions of the models.

Table 3.2. *Policy Divergence Under Different Regime Types: Numerical Example*

Preference configuration	Parliamentary	Competitive presidential	Collegial presidential
(I): $A_1 > A_2 > P > R$	0.32	0.32	0.32
(II): $A_1 > P > A_2 > R$	0.02	0	0.02
(III): $A_1 > P > R > A_2$	0.34	0	0.34
(IV): $A_1 > R > A_2 > P$	0.67	0.33	0.67
(V): $A_1 > R > P > A_2$	0.34	0	0.34
(VI): $A_2 > A_1 > P > R$	0.32	0.32	0.32
(VII): $A_2 > P > A_1 > R$	0.34	0	0.02
(VIII): $A_2 > R > A_1 > P$	0.67	0.33	0.67
(IX): $P > A_1 > A_2 > R$	0.35	0.33	0.33
(X): $P > A_2 > A_1 > R$	0.67	0.33	0.35
Mean values	0.404	0.196	0.338

Note: R represents the reversion point. The entries in each cell represent the magnitude of policy divergence, measured as the absolute distance between the equilibrium and the principal's ideal point. In each case, the numerical values of the various positions are 1, 0.67, 0.33, and 0, respectively. See the text and Fig. 3.2 for descriptions of the models.

and is otherwise equal. In a majority of best-case scenarios (six out of ten), competitive presidentialism generates no agency loss at all. The corresponding numbers are four for collegial presidentialism and three for parliamentarism. Moreover, there are four configurations in which competitive presidentialism never exhibits any agency loss, whereas this is never true for parliamentarism or for collegial presidentialism.

To make the results more accessible, Table 3.2 presents a set of numerical examples. Here I have placed the reversion point and all three player ideal points, in every preference configuration represented in Table 3.1, on a policy scale from zero to one, and roughly equidistant from one another. Specifically, the numerical values of the different positions are 0, 0.33, 0.67, and 1, respectively. Note that the reversion point in this example is allowed to vary, rather than being set to zero. Agents are allowed to make policy proposals with precision down to the second decimal point (e.g. 0.51). Otherwise, all features of this example are identical to those represented in Table 3.1. The numerical results are no great surprise, though the advantages of collegial presidentialism over parliamentarism are a bit more obvious here.

The greater policy divergence under parliamentary institutions is largely due to the agenda power of the agenda-setting (first) agent (the cabinet). Parliamentarism is particularly susceptible to agency loss when this agent has relatively extreme preferences, while at the same time the reversion point is unattractive to the principal. While these results may at first blush seem abstract and arcane, it is not difficult to find empirical examples that conform. Unattractive reversion points are particularly likely to obtain immediately after such events as regime transitions and major international crises (such as war). Then, parliamentary cabinets may indeed use their agenda control to push policies that are controversial to fairly large numbers of voters, as seems to have been the case with the Vaclav Klaus post-transition cabinet in the Czech Republic, or with some social democratic post-Second World War cabinets, such as Clement Attlee's in Britain or Einar Gerhardsen's in Norway, or even Margaret Thatcher's administration in the wake of the British 1978–9 'winter of discontent'. This is not to say that such radical policy departures may not occasionally be desirable for economic or political reasons, as many transition theorists have indeed maintained. Yet, the monopolistic agenda control, which characterizes parliamentary democracy, leads to a substantial potential for policy choice that deviates from the preferences of the median voter.

In the discussion above, I have considered only the magnitude, but not the direction, of policy divergence from the principal's ideal point. If in a less abstract setting we consider democratic delegation as an ongoing process, however, we may want to examine also the direction in which adopted policies tend to deviate. If in repeated delegation we think of the mean absolute value of policy divergence as the *efficiency* of representation, then we can think of a measure that also captures the direction of this divergence as capturing *bias*. In a competitive two-party system in which the parties do not converge to the position of the median voter, there may over time be considerable inefficiency, but potentially no significant bias. Pivotal parliamentary systems may have quite different characteristics. Since the pivotal party (bloc) is typically fairly centrist, such systems may be less susceptible than Westminster polities to the large inefficiencies that may result from vesting agenda control in a cabinet with relatively extreme preferences. Yet, the pivotal system may exhibit more bias, particularly if the pivotal party is non-centrist on secondary dimensions of political competition.[10] Constrained systems, whether parliamentary or presidential, may also tend to exhibit more bias than those based on accountability through competition, since constraining institutions (e.g. courts) may have systematically different preferences from those of the median voter.

NON-POLICY MOTIVATIONS

So far I have implicitly assumed that politicians care only about policy outcomes. Although there is good reason to begin our exploration here, this assumption cannot give us a fully satisfactory account of democratic agency problems. We need to consider other motivations that political agents may have. In doing so, I shall proceed more informally than above, so as to discuss a variety of concerns in delegation, rather than rigorously modelling the effects of each in isolation. Readers who are differently inclined may take the discussion that follows as theoretical conjecture.

Non-policy motivations in politics may encompass a great swath of the human condition, including such powerful forces as love, jealousy, compassion, vanity, spite, and greed, as much of the classical literature has indeed recognized. Here, however, I shall focus on a few motivations that are particularly common, generalizable, and liable to cause agency problems, namely (1) lack of effort and (2) the pursuit of, and use of public office for, private advantage.

[10] In the Italian First Republic (1948–92), for example, the DC was consistently able to dominate the cabinet through its median position on the economic left–right axis. Because of DC dominance, however, Italians also had to accept very traditional social policies (e.g. on divorce) and a much cosier relationship with the Vatican than the median voter might have preferred.

Leisure-shirking is certainly not unknown in politics. There are plenty of folk tales about lazy bureaucrats, or about elected politicians that use their offices to enjoy the 'good life' (junkets, lavish receptions, and possibly worse) rather than to serve their constituents. Many delegation models seek to capture such distractions by recognizing that political service is costly and that agents thus pay a cost (in leisure opportunities, for example) for developing policy proposals that can be presented to their principals. For delegation to work, it is thus necessary not only that the agent is able to make proposals that serve the principal's interests, but also that doing so is worth the agent's effort. In more technical terms, the agent's incentive conditions have to be satisfied. This is clearly a non-trivial consideration in real-world representational politics. In many societies, there is widespread concern that the rewards from public service simply do not suffice to motivate the 'best and brightest' to pay the large personal and sometimes financial costs of political involvement. In this respect, however, the distinctive features of parliamentary democracy would seem to count in its favour. While its singularity of representation and the concentration of agenda power may exacerbate agency losses, they simultaneously enhance the agents' incentives to get involved. Moreover, vigorous electoral competition may effectively sanction lazy politicians, whereas judicial and other constraints are less likely to work (inactivity is rarely illegal). Thus, Westminster parliamentarism should be particularly favoured.

Yet, the trade-off between leisure and service to the principal still does not fully capture the range of concerns facing individuals in public office. Clearly, they frequently have options other than either serving the public interest or slacking off. One complication in democratic delegation is the presence of political *rents*. A rent, according to James M. Buchanan, 'is that part of the payment to an owner of resources over and above that which those resources could command in any alternative use' (Buchanan 1980: 4). Political rents, then, are whatever a public official can gain by virtue of holding that office, over and above what he or she would otherwise receive from voluntary transactions. Political office-holders may, for example, be able to gain speaker's fees or honoraria, memberships in exclusive associations, campaign contributions, business contracts, or even cold, hard cash, that they would not otherwise have received. Such rents may be offered quasi-voluntarily by favour-seekers, or politicians may extract them through various forms of extortion, such as threats of regulation or taxation (McChesney 1997). Any office that allows its occupant to make discretionary political decisions with significant distributional consequences is likely to carry some value in rents. The closer to the apex of executive decision-making, the greater the rents that tend to attach to political offices. And the greater the rents, the greater the temptations towards self-serving behaviour. Hence, the risk of agency problems.

If political agents are self-interested and respond to political and economic incentives, then rent-seeking behaviour should covary positively with the magnitude of available rents and negatively with the expected payoffs from alternative uses of their resources. Hence, societies may be particularly susceptible to rent-seeking if they feature (1) a generous public sector (Goel and Nelson 1998), (2) few alternative opportunities for social advancement, and (3) ineffective constraints on the ability of politicians to use their offices for private gain. Sadly, this description fits certain resource-rich developing societies, such as Nigeria, to a tee, and rent-seeking is by all accounts correspondingly rampant.

This may also explain why, as Susan Rose-Ackerman (1999: 1) notes, political corruption is such a depressingly persistent feature of the world's poorest societies, regardless of the promises that may surround new office-holders (see also Montinola and Jackman 2002). For those who wish to 'better themselves' economically, many poor countries simply offer few alternatives to rent-seeking political activities. Corruption is a special form of rent extraction, in which public offices are not only exploited for private advantage, but in which public favours are also traded or conferred in ways that are contrary to the law.

Asymmetric information may foster corruption, and vice versa. Corrupt officials have strong incentives to withhold information about their actions. Once an agent has violated the law, or in other ways the trust of the principal, transparency can be fatal. This tendency prevails not only because incumbents develop large asymmetries of information, but also because becoming corrupt is a bit like losing one's virginity: there is no going back. Once a politician has succumbed to such a temptation, he is unlikely to find the straight-and-narrow path enticing, as his career will continue to be at risk. Since penalties for corruption are often insensitive to the number of violations the agent has committed, each additional act of betrayal often carries a minimal marginal cost. Hence, sadly, honest politicians may become corrupt over time, but corrupt ones rarely become honest. This is probably the best argument in favour of term limits, which otherwise detract from electoral accountability (see Carey 1996).

Do parliamentary systems foster rent-seeking political behaviour that may undermine representational ideals? Clearly, although some parliamentary systems (e.g. Italy and Belgium) have decidedly mixed reputations, most are not among the rent-seeking basket cases of this world. One reason may be comparatively effective judicial checks. A second reason may lie in the strength of civil society and independent mass media. An even more critical factor may be the fact that most parliamentary countries have wealthy and diverse economies that offer many opportunities for social betterment outside of politics. On the other hand, many parliamentary systems, particularly in Europe, have large and well-financed public sectors that may attract rent seekers (see Boix 2001). The overall picture for our countries is thus mixed, with one generally unfavourable and two favourable conditions. Hence, the challenge that rent-seeking poses may vary significantly from one parliamentary system to another, but should not be extreme in Western Europe.

Yet, it is ex ante typically more difficult to gauge a candidate's rent-seeking propensities than his or her policy preferences. This is both because candidates are more likely to lie about the former, and because agency loss in the form of rent-seeking or corruption, rather than policy divergence, is more likely to result from temptation rather than design. Hence, it is difficult to contain rent-seeking behaviour strictly through ex ante controls, and parliamentary systems that are weak both in external constraints and electoral competitiveness, such as pivotal ones, should be particularly vulnerable.

INFORMATIONAL PROBLEMS

So far, I have considered only such challenges to parliamentary governance as stem from the preferences and incentives of politicians. There is, however, a whole other source of agency problems, namely information. Democratic representation can be jeopardized not only when agents have interests and desires that go against those of their principals, but also when principals cannot easily figure out what their agents are up to. Preference divergence between principal and agent is frequently accompanied and exacerbated by asymmetric information favouring the agent, and it is typically the interaction of divergent preferences and poor information that causes the really significant agency problems.

Agency problems under incomplete information may take the form of *hidden information* (principals do not fully know the competencies or preferences of their agents or the exact demands of the task at hand) and/or *hidden action* (principals cannot fully observe the actions of their agents). The former condition can give rise to *adverse selection*, the latter to *moral hazard*. The former problem may lead principals to select the 'wrong' agents, who do not have the most appropriate skills or preferences. The problem of moral hazard, on the other hand, arises when agents, once selected, have incentives and opportunity to take unobservable action contrary to the principal's interests.

Adverse Selection

> The city where those who rule are least eager to do so will be the best governed.
>
> (Plato)

Adverse selection is one generic problem facing democratic principals. In selecting agents, principals look for candidates that have the necessary information and skills. Separating qualified candidates from unqualified ones is no great problem if political qualifications and predispositions are easily discernible. But the problem of many delegation relationships is precisely that the principal does not know very much about the task at hand or the aptitude that it requires. At the same time, and perhaps for the same reasons, the qualifications of potential agents may be very difficult to judge. Furthermore, potential agents must also have the requisite motivation. Simply put, agents must be willing as well as able, and in order to attract such agents, principals must offer adequate incentives. The trouble is that the incentives that principals offer may sometimes systematically attract the least desirable agents.

As Lupia notes, the classical illustration of adverse selection derives from the insurance business. An insurance company, in this case the principal, offers insurance to motorists (the agents). To succeed, the insurance company has to set its rates sufficiently high to recover the claims that will be made, but not so high that it fails to attract any customers. Yet, some motorists are inherently less desirable customers than others. Even though there is considerable randomness in traffic accidents, certain drivers are much more likely to be involved than others, because they have poor skills, little experience, bad driving habits, or risk-acceptant personalities. The problem is that the insurance company is much less likely to be able to identify them than the bad drivers themselves. Even though motorists may flatter themselves about their driving skills, many problem drivers recognize their liabilities, but conceal them from the insurance company as best as they can. At the same time, these customers will use their private information to shop for insurance. If the insurance company is unable to discriminate between good and bad drivers, the latter customers will crowd out the former. Whatever level the insurance company sets its rates, it will attract motorists for whom that is favourable. And the higher these premiums are set, the more systematically it will adversely select only the very worst motorists.

Adverse selection has been recognized as a political problem at least since Plato, whose observation is quoted above. Delegating power to politicians is risky because the individuals most attracted to politics may not be the most desirable rulers. Indeed, it may be precisely the most power-hungry or greedy, and perhaps those most likely to abuse authority, that are drawn to politics. Although most people would prefer to be ruled by the likes of Cincinnatus rather than Macbeth, sadly the latter may be in greater supply.

Hence, many students of political representation see the selection of 'good' agents as the primary democratic challenge. Brehm and Gates (1997: 202) find that in federal, state, and local bureaucracies in the United States, 'the problem of adverse selection trumps the problem of moral hazard'. James Fearon (1999) similarly maintains that the most important task for voters is to select 'good types' for office: 'a candidate with similar policy preferences, who is relatively honest and principled (hard to buy off), and who is skilled' (Fearon 1999: 68). It is not difficult to agree with Fearon's desiderata, and deviation from any of these ideals is indeed a serious real-world concern. Democracy is jeopardized if aspiring politicians have atypical preferences, are disproportionately willing to sacrifice honesty and policy principles, or are lacking in skills. The latter problem, one sometimes hears, is that those people become politicians who lack the ability to succeed elsewhere.

Glenn R. Parker (1996) paints a disturbing picture of how adverse selection has contributed to the moral and political decline of the US Congress. Over time, he argues, the intrinsic rewards of congressional service, such as the value of producing public goods, have declined relative to the opportunities for rent extraction.

As a result, those legislators who gain the most from intrinsic rewards (i.e. those with long tenure in Congress, since intrinsic returns are a function of longevity in office) exit. As Congress becomes populated by rent-seeking legislators, through both recruitment and attrition, institutional rules and arrangements are manipulated to facilitate wealth-earning opportunities... If adverse selection is afflicting our political institutions, the market for politicians may come to resemble George Akerlof's characterization of the market for used cars in the United States—a market for 'lemons'. (Parker 1996: 48)[11]

The highly respected Nigerian writer Chinua Achebe likewise holds adverse selection responsible for many of his country's woes: 'Nigeria...is a country where it would be difficult to point to *one* important job being held by the most competent person we have...We have displayed a consistent inclination since we assumed management of our own affairs to opt for mediocrity and compromise, to pick a third and fourth eleven to play for us. And the result: we have always failed and will always fail to make it to the world league'. (Achebe 1983: 19–20. Emphasis in the original.)

Moral Hazard

> Power tends to corrupt, and absolute power corrupts absolutely.
>
> (Lord Acton (1834–1902))

---

[11] In this context, a 'lemon' is a low-quality used car.

Moral hazard is an equally basic problem in delegation. Whereas adverse selection stems from the agent's private information, moral hazard has to do with hidden action on his part. That is to say, moral hazard arises when the principal cannot, after entering a contract, fully observe the agent's actions that may affect the outcome. Such information asymmetry may jeopardize successful delegation as much as adverse selection does. To return to the automobile insurance example, moral hazard refers to the behaviour of drivers after they have obtained insurance. The problem is that although the insurance company wants its policy holders to take all reasonable precautions while driving, it cannot actually observe whether they do so. This problem is compounded by the drivers' incentives. Once insured, they no longer face the same financial risk. In the event of an accident, the insurance company will pay (except, perhaps, for a minor deductible). Even previously good drivers may be tempted to relax their precautions and take greater risks, with obvious adverse consequences for the insurer.

Again, it is not difficult to see the political analogue. Once politicians have been elected, and especially after they have been elevated to executive office, they face a myriad of temptations. The most innocuous ones may be to use their authority to advance their own political agenda, rather than the platform on which they were elected or their constituents' preferences. A more sinister possibility is that politicians use their offices and influence covertly for personal gain or to benefit their families, friends, business associates, fellow tribesmen, or other acquaintances.

The magnitude of moral hazard is likely to be systematically related to certain significant parameters of delegation. First, the larger the potential political rents, the more serious the problem of moral hazard. That is to say, the more attractive the spoils of office are relative to alternative social rewards, the more we should worry about moral hazard. Second, the greater discretion politicians are granted, and the more generous the spoils under their control, the more severely their character will be tested. Recall Lord Acton's pithy formulation above. Third, the weaker the oversight mechanisms, the larger the threat of moral hazard. Finally, the longer incumbents stay in office, the more serious the moral hazard problem may become, especially with respect to corruption and other abuses of office.

Representative democracy clearly entails problems of moral hazard, which is indeed the motivation for John Ferejohn's (1986) model of electoral competition (see also Barro 1973). Dominant models of electoral competition, Ferejohn notes, have a 'disturbing feature', namely the possibility that 'once in office, the politician's preferences may diverge from those of his constituents and that he may therefore choose policies at variance from his platform' (Ferejohn 1986: 5). Ferejohn's concern is with the extent to which electoral accountability can constrain such behaviour. He assumes the politician to be 'an agent of the electorate whose behaviour is imperfectly monitored...In other words, the voter's problem is to police moral hazard rather than to find and select the more capable of benevolent officeholders' (Ferejohn 1986: 11–2).

Agency problems stemming from incomplete information can thus prevent citizens in contemporary democracies from getting fully satisfactory service from their political agents. Let us now more specifically consider informational challenges in the parliamentary chain of delegation. Recall that this policy process can be divided into at least four distinct stages of delegation, namely those from voters to parliamentarians, from parliamentarians to the cabinet and its chief executive (Prime Minister), from the cabinet to individual ministers, and finally from individual cabinet members to civil servants. Each stage has its informational perils.

Electing Parliamentarians

The simple act of voting enables a relatively small number of representatives to be chosen from among the many that may feel the call. Yet, picking good agents is far from easy. Candidates may well have preferences that differ from those of the voters, especially as regards their leisure and political rents. As Manin, Przeworski, and Stokes (1999: 40) put it:

Politicians may want to pursue their own ideas even if these differ from those of citizens. Some may care most about advancing their careers against fellow politicians, within the government or the same party. Some may seek perks. Some may want to get rich at the expense of citizens, while in office or after leaving it. Some may be most concerned about recognition by foreigners. In all these cases politicians will want something whose pursuit is injurious to citizens.

Such candidate preferences are rarely transparent *ex ante* and candidates are understandably reluctant to reveal them. It is also often difficult to ascertain *ex post* whether elected officials have acted upon them. Elections thus clearly feature the risk of adverse selection as well as moral hazard, and theories of representation are centrally concerned both with selecting the 'most suitable' representatives and with preventing those elected from abusing their powers for ideological purposes or personal advantage. As Mitchell (2000: 336) points out, 'of all the links in the delegation chain from individual voter to Prime Minister, the link from voter to MP may be fraught with the greatest danger.' Similarly, in commenting on agency problems between politicians and bureaucrats, William A. Niskanen (1991: 15) observes that '[m]y judgment is that there is a much more substantial agency problem between politicians and voters'.

The severity of agency problems between voters and representatives is due in part to the institutions that regulate this stage of delegation. Electoral institutions are complex and manipulable: the rules concerning ballot access, the rules that allocate seats among the competing political parties or candidates, and in multimember districts the rules that determine the selection of individual representatives within contending lists. Politicians and political parties often engineer these rules for personal benefit or to render the choices of the voters, for example their preferences over individual candidates, ineffectual. Consider, for example, the practice of gerrymandering legislative district boundaries.

The informational challenges facing voters are also gigantic, since it is very difficult to gather systematic data on all potential representatives. Finally, but perhaps most particularly, agency problems at this stage are due to the great asymmetries of information between 'amateur' voters and full-time 'professional' politicians. Delegation is thus driven by competence concerns as much as by the voters' lack of capacity, and the threat of agency loss is exacerbated by the interaction of these factors. In trying to reduce their informational asymmetries, voters must rely primarily on the screening efforts of political parties, independent interest groups, and mass media. The former mechanism (parties) is likely to be more effective in parliamentary systems, the latter ones (interest groups and media) in presidential ones. The problem, of course, as in all reliance on third parties, is that parties, interest groups, and media may have their own political agendas.

Forming Cabinets

The next step in the chain of delegation is when coalitions of parliamentarians form to select a Prime Minister and cabinet. The rules vary, so that in some countries parliament delegates specifically to a Prime Minister who in turn selects a cabinet, whereas elsewhere parliament selects the cabinet as a whole. Yet, it is very rare for the Prime Minister not to be selected *internally* among the members of parliament, and indeed among the leaders of the largest parliamentary parties. The same rules and expectations apply, though often less strictly, to other cabinet members. In the Westminster model, these are quite rigid requirements; in other systems they are at least conventions or strong regularities.

The information problems at this stage of delegation are generally less formidable than between voters and parliamentarians. Cabinet members are linked to parliamentarians by copartisanship and are often personally familiar to them. Yet, although this delegation relationship involves professional politicians with common backgrounds and experiences, it may entail adverse selection as well as moral hazard. Regardless of how familiar potential cabinet members are, they will have private interests not known to their backbenchers. Once in office, they will generally also have opportunities to act on such interests, even to the detriment of their respective parties. For example, some office holders use the perquisites of office to enrich themselves or at least to support a lifestyle that they would not otherwise have been able to enjoy. In less aggravated cases (as when Mona Sahlin of the Swedish Social Democrats charged personal expenses to her ministerial account), such behaviour may cause embarrassment and electoral liability to copartisans. In more serious cases (as in the cases of Italian politicians such as Bettino Craxi in the 1980s), it may drain the public coffers and/or undermine the popular legitimacy of the regime. Hence, parliamentarians must look for institutional and other solutions to such agency problems at the very core of government. While some accountability mechanisms (confidence procedures) are constitutionally entrenched, for the most part parliamentary democracies have to rely on the more informal policing efforts of parliamentarians and political parties. As we have seen, such accountability is often rendered ineffective by an incentive system that induces parties to close ranks behind their leaders.

Coordinating the Cabinet

Once a Prime Minister has been installed, he or she must coordinate a cabinet of some twenty highly ambitious politicians with their own respective agendas. While the exact composition of the cabinet is typically at least in part up to the Prime Minister, his or her precise authority varies. Although commonly referred to as *primus inter pares*, the Prime Minister's role may in fact be either more or less than that description would imply.[12] In multiparty coalitional systems such as Italy, the Prime Minister's control over cabinet appointments and dismissals is thus often sharply curtailed. Cabinet decision rules vary between hierarchical ones, in which the Prime Minister is entitled to define the 'sense of the meeting', and collegial ones, in which issues are ultimately decided by majority vote.

Andeweg (2000) points out that delegating authority to a team of cabinet members involves its own peculiar challenges. In his words,

> the process of delegation from government to ministers appears to differ fundamentally from delegation processes elsewhere in this democratic chain. The complication is that, as we commonly understand the term, the government, which delegates to heads of departments, also consists of heads of departments (with exceptions for the Prime Minister and ministers without portfolio). In other words, the principal is made up of its own agents (Andeweg 2000: 377).

As Andeweg suggests, the delegation relationship between Prime Minister and other ministers is often not entirely clearly defined. Besides, the Prime Minister may have good reason to worry about agency problems on the part of his line ministers. Even if these ministers share the bond of copartisanship, their personal career incentives may diverge sharply. Indeed, the Prime Minister may literally be the only thing that stands between some of them and the realization of their ultimate career objectives. Hence, a norm that disposes Prime Ministers to appoint to the cabinet their most prominent and ambitious copartisans may entail particularly acute forms of adverse selection. When cabinet members do not even share the common interest that membership in the same political party provides, preference divergence within the cabinet may be even greater. And the anecdotal literature on cabinet politics is full of stories about moral hazard and treachery.

Managing Civil Servants

The final step in our chain of delegation is between cabinet members as head of departments and the civil servants that serve them and implement decisions in their names. These relationships have been the subject of more agency-theoretic scholarship than any of the previous steps. The Westminster model implies a strict hierarchy between ministers and civil servants.[13] Yet, parliamentary administrative structures are not always equally hierarchical. In Sweden, for example, executive agencies are under the authority of the cabinet as a whole, not the individual minister (see Chapter 20). Obviously, this constrains the authority of cabinet ministers as individual principals.

---

[12] Sartori (1994) thus distinguishes between three prime ministerial roles: (1) a *first above unequals*, who can appoint and dismiss cabinet ministers at will and cannot easily be unseated (as in Britain), (2) a *first among unequals*, who can unseat cabinet members but cannot be unseated by them (as in Germany), and (3) a *first among equals*, who has little control over the selection of cabinet members but falls with them (as in Italy).

[13] The strict hierarchy of the classical Westminster model is well captured by Sir Robert Armstrong, former Head of the British Home Civil Service: 'The determination of policy is the responsibility of the Minister (within the convention of collective responsibility of the whole Government for the decisions and actions of every member of it). In the determination of policy the civil servant has no constitutional

Even where civil servants are clearly subordinated to their respective ministers, this agency relationship has its own peculiarities that sometimes constrain the cabinet member. Some civil servants have highly specialized tasks for which extensive professional preparation is necessary. They often benefit from large information asymmetries vis-à-vis their political superiors as well as the scarcity of their skills. Some bureaucracies go far in granting such policy specialists autonomy. The sheer number of agents serving each cabinet member, and the enormous specialization of modern governmental functions, also exacerbate the information asymmetry between principal and agent. Finally, although cabinet members are full-time politicians, many have no professional expertise and hold a particular portfolio for a limited time only. The resulting informational problems led British Labour Party minister Hugh Gaitskell to lament that '[s]ometimes Cabinet meetings horrify me because of the amount of rubbish talked by some Ministers who come there after reading briefs which they do not understand' (Gaitskell, quoted in Hennessy 1986: 45).

Since civil service reforms were introduced roughly a century ago, many European bureaucracies have harboured strong traditions of non-partisanship. This, of course, complicates the alignment of preferences between cabinet members and civil servants (see Huber 2000). Moreover, civil servants typically have tenure and other protections that make them relatively immune to sanctions from the minister or indeed any political superior. More recent civil service reforms have often been motivated by the inefficiencies and rigidities that the classical bureaucracies introduced. One of these problems is the lack of incentive toward effort. Because of the lack of such incentives, leisure-shirking is probably a more serious concern in this delegation relationship than elsewhere in democratic politics.

Combating Information Problems

The brief review in this section has shown the prominence of informational asymmetries between principals and agents all along the parliamentary chain of delegation. Chapter 4 will survey the actual Western European parliamentary systems in much greater detail. Yet, even on the basis of the brief review above, there is ample reason to characterize these asymmetries of information as large, particularly in the first and last of our four stages of delegation. Hence, the choice of oversight mechanisms is consequential. This choice depends on the effectiveness of the available institutions, as well as on the costs of acquiring information before and after the fact. Thus, the less costly information acquisition is *ex post*, and the more effectively the principal can

---

responsibility or role, distinct from that of the Minister. Subject to the conventions limiting the access of Ministers to papers of previous Administrations, it is the duty of the civil servant to make available to the Minister all the information and experience at his or her disposal which may have a bearing on the policy decisions to which the Minister is committed or which he is preparing to make, and to give to the Minister honest and impartial advice, without fear or favour, and whether the advice accords with the Minister's view or not' (Armstrong 1989: 141–2).

impose penalties for lying or misbehaving, the more successfully she can contain moral hazard.

Except for the last stage of delegation, between cabinet ministers and civil servants, political parties are the main vehicles of accountability in parliamentary systems. Parties are instruments by which preferences are aligned before authority is delegated and they serve especially to protect against adverse selection. Institutional checks (constraints or veto gates) are mechanisms by which public policy is constrained later in the policy process, and they guard most effectively against moral hazard. If the dominant agency problem is adverse selection, then, as Lupia points out in Chapter 2, *ex ante* mechanisms of screening and selection have clear advantages. Consequently, the institutions of Westminster (and other) parliamentary democracy have much to recommend themselves. If, on the other hand, moral hazard is the greater concern, there is a stronger case for *ex post* control. If so, in turn, presidential constitutions are at a comparative advantage.

THE BEAUTY OF PARLIAMENTARISM: EFFICIENCY

Let us now summarize the effects of parliamentarism on democratic agency problems. The merits of any constitutional design must be judged partly on the basis of procedural qualities, such as efficiency, coordination, transparency, and credibility. Westminster parliamentarism scores particularly well on the first two of these dimensions. It permits policy coordination and fosters efficiency. The distinctive features of parliamentary delegation—simplicity, indirectness, and cabinet agenda control—generate a set of discernible advantages. One is efficiency, which refers to three salient properties of parliamentarism. First, parliamentarism favours *policy efficiency* in the sense that agents face fewer institutional (external) checks and constraints (veto players). Thus, in the vocabulary of Cox and McCubbins (2001), parliamentarism promotes *decisiveness*. Second, since agents serve only one principal and are thus unlikely to face mutually contradictory or ambiguous demands, parliamentarism fosters *administrative efficiency*. Third, because it gives agents greater inducements to exert themselves on behalf of their principals, parliamentarism implies *incentive efficiency*. The first of these three sources of efficiency follows directly from our definition of parliamentary democracy. Let us, however, briefly consider the other two advantages of parliamentary rule.

First, parliamentary democracy implies advantages in administrative efficiency. The fact that each agent faces a single principal means that agents are less likely to face conflicting demands than under presidentialist or other multiple-principal systems. Agents are less likely to have their hands tied by contradictory requests from two or several principals. Hence, parliamentary systems exhibit greater administrative efficiency than presidential systems, an effect that may be most notable at the stage of policy administration. These effects are consistent with the argument of Terry Moe and Michael Caldwell (1994), who note that for reasons of greater administrative simplicity, environmental and other legislation has been much more successful, and environmental administration much more cost-efficient, under British parliamentarism than under US presidentialism.

Besides reducing constraint and gridlock, the simplicity of parliamentary democracy may induce greater effort among principals and agents alike. In addition to their policy concerns, both principals and agents face trade-offs between work and leisure (Brehm and Gates 1997). Differences in representative institutions affect the effort that agents put into their tasks and principals into monitoring the agents (Aghion and Tirole 1997). Agents exert greater effort when they are given more latitude to choose the means by which to realize their goals. As long as the agents' preferences do not deviate greatly from the public interest, this may be a good thing. For example, to the extent that the task of civil servants is to find technically efficient solutions to coordination problems, extensive oversight and constraint by multiple principals is probably misguided. The relative scarcity of constraints and monitoring thus means that parliamentary democracy is comparatively resistant to leisure-shirking.

Similarly, the institutional simplicity of parliamentary democracy may enhance the principals' incentive to exert effort in monitoring agents. If such oversight allows the principal (e.g. the members of a particular parliamentary committee overseeing an executive agency) to claim exclusive credit, and if their efforts to control their agents are not thwarted by other 'overseers', then these principals should put more effort into their constitutional responsibilities. Hence, parliamentary democracy is at an advantage, particularly compared to collegial presidentialism, in providing incentives for principals to monitor and for agents not to shirk.

These expectations are borne out by the case of Nigeria. When Nigeria returned to civilian rule in 1979, after 13 years of military government, it changed from a parliamentary to a presidential constitution that included numerous checks and balances. Hence, the country offers a relative rare natural experiment in regime change. Whereas the parliamentary First Republic (1960–6) allowed the Northern-dominated majority to run roughshod over the opposition, the presidential Second Republic (1979–83) legislature quickly became embroiled in gridlock and ineffectiveness. What ensued, according to Osaghae (1998: 114), was 'rivalry between the two houses, leading to unnecessary delay and controversies in the passing of bills'. To the chagrin of Nigerian citizens, their politicians increasingly turned to 'opportunistic and self-interested behaviour' (Diamond 1988: 52), in other words, leisure-shirking (or worse).

In addition to these salutary effects of simplicity, parliamentarism benefits from the role that political parties play as devices of preference alignment and screening (see Müller 2000). Party cohesion under a Westminster system allows voters to make reasonably well-informed choices and ensures a certain amount of responsiveness and accountability in government. When governing parties are cohesive and reasonably large (as under single-party majority government), they may also more easily be able to pursue policies favouring encompassing rather than distributional interests (Olson 1982). Finally, as we have seen, parliamentary regimes may be better equipped to deal with problems of adverse selection. To the extent that the main problem in politics is to select the right 'type' of representative, the advantage should lie with regimes that devote more resources to the prior screening of candidates, as is the nature of parliamentarism.

THE ACHILLES HEEL: TRANSPARENCY

Just as parliamentary democracy has identifiable advantages over its competition, so too does it have its weak points. Simplicity has its costs as well as its benefits. One such disadvantage stems from the singular and indirect chain of parliamentary accountability, which increases susceptibility to policy divergence, as the model above demonstrates. Recall that in this model, agency loss is decisively greater under parliamentarism than under either form of presidentialism, and that such agency loss could be particularly severe when the agenda setter is relatively extreme and the reversion point unattractive to the principal.

Indeed, to the extent that the chain of delegation is longer and more indirect that this simple model assumes, the agency loss may be even greater. As Barbara Geddes (1994) argues, a singular chain of delegation is only as strong as its weakest link (see also Lupia, Chapter 2). If legislators, for example, are poor agents of their voters, then it may not at all be desirable to enhance civil servant accountability to them. This is true at least as long as agents do not compete for the favour of their principals. In other words, if principals can bypass a particular link in the chain of delegation, then agency losses in that link are less critical. But what characterizes parliamentary democracy is precisely that such competition does not occur and that principals therefore cannot bypass their agents. Therefore, severe agency loss at any stage of delegation is a particularly serious concern.

Broadly speaking, more complex systems, such as presidentialism or parliamentary systems with more external constraints, favour credible and stable outcomes. In Cox and McCubbins' (2001) terms, they tend to be more *resolute*, which means for one thing that agents are less likely to take action that will make their principals worse off than they previously were. For the same reasons, presidential systems are likely to produce greater policy stability, and they are more able credibly to commit themselves to particular policy goals (such as fiscal rectitude).

Moreover, presidential systems in particular are more likely to *generate transparency*, because they contain mechanisms by which agents are forced to share information and principals can learn. The more principals can learn, of course, the more they can ultimately trust their agents, and the less the likelihood of agency loss. Learning is particularly important in dynamic settings in which poorly informed principals facing repetitive challenges attempt to acquire the requisite information from their agents. The informational perspective on legislative organization identifies some of the preconditions for effective political learning. For example, Gilligan and Krehbiel model the relationship between legislatures and their committee members as a signalling game, in which committee members invest resources in specialization and information acquisition and then use their private information to advise the non-specialist members (the floor) on the quality of pending proposals. The more heterogeneous the preferences of the committee members, the more confidence floor members can have in committee signals. Thus, learning improves with the diversity of the sources of information available to the legislators (Gilligan and Krehbiel 1989; Krehbiel 1991).

These lessons can be generalized to the agency relationships we are considering here. Generally speaking, because they feature multiple agents with potentially divergent preferences, presidential constitutions are more likely to feature the conditions under which principals can rely on the signals they receive from their respective agents, at least insofar as these signals converge. Under parliamentary systems, all else being equal, principals (e.g. parliamentarians) are less likely to be able to rely on the information fed to them by their agents, in part because these agents have homogeneous preferences induced by copartisanship.

Moreover, the informational advantages of presidentialism are reinforced by the fact that more of the policy bargaining between different constitutional actors takes place in the public domain, rather than behind closed doors. In a presidential system, policy bargaining typically takes the form of proposals and counter-proposals that are shuttled back and forth between different chambers or branches of government. In contrast, parliamentary bargaining tends to take place behind close doors in cabinet or in coalition committees or party summits. Thus, political bargaining is displaced from a public to a private arena, where it will be less informative to the citizens. The more bargaining is confined to this sphere of 'invisible politics' (Sartori 1976), to private negotiations within political parties, or within government coalitions, the less transparent the policy process, and the more uncertainty voters may have about their representatives. Thus, transparency is a general liability of Westminster systems, and the lack of transparency may in itself exacerbate the problems of transparency mentioned above.

Thus, comparing the foreign policy of Japan to that of the United States, Peter F. Cowhey notes that

> there are...no built-in checks on reversals of policy promises. This poses problems when trying to limit foreign or domestic demands for politically risky policies. So, the LDP invented a mixture of institutional constraints and self-binding political pledges to manage the political and diplomatic bargaining risks of foreign policy. At the same time, prolonged LDP rule permitted extensive delegation to the bureaucracy. This delegation created a significant veil over the Japanese policy process that reduced the transparency and credibility of foreign policy promises (Cowhey 1995: 209).

In some ways, coalitional parliamentary systems may resemble presidentialism, with its strengths and weaknesses. They may, for example, tend to be more resolute than Westminster systems. Yet, while coalitional parliamentarism (particularly pivotal parliamentarism) also sacrifices much of the efficiency, and particularly the electoral accountability, of the Westminster model, it does not yield the transparency advantages of checks-and-balances presidential systems. In presidential systems, policy bargaining takes place in more public arenas, whereas in parliamentary systems bargaining is more likely to be confined to private, intra-party fora. This is not likely to change under multiparty governments, except that coalition committees or party summits take the place of intra-party policy-making (Strøm and Müller 1999). Indeed, the classical descriptions of consociational democracies, for example, stress the close-knit nature of decision-making circles and the informational asymmetries between governors and the governed (Lijphart 1977; Tsebelis 1990). Thus, a multiparty format is unlikely to help parliamentary democracies reap the advantages of information revelation that characterize presidentialism.

THE PERILS OF CONSTITUTIONAL DESIGN

Policy-making in parliamentary democracies can be understood as a chain of delegation that begins with the voters and ends with the civil servants (or other agents) that implement government decisions. In Chapter 2, Lupia introduced a class of analytical models, principal–agent models, which can illuminate such delegation relationships and generate precise understandings of their effects. In this chapter, I have sought to integrate these insights in a way that helps us understand contemporary parliamentary constitutions.

All political systems imply particular delegation regimes, and any delegation runs the risk of agency loss. But democracies are not necessarily created equal in this sense. Thus, I have shown that parliamentary democracies are better protected against some such problems, such as adverse selection, than against others, such as moral hazard. Yet, the contrast between parliamentary and presidential constitutions is not simply one between a regime designed to combat adverse selection and one focused on moral hazard. There are other values that are tied up in these institutional 'packages'. Thus, the ideal–typical parliamentary constitution is one that promotes efficiency by eliminating redundancies and taking incentives seriously. On the other hand, presidential constitutions promote credibility and transparency by protecting against hasty and potentially ill-considered policy change and by forcing disclosure of the pull and tug of policy-making in the public arena.

The broader lessons are that agency problems are stubborn and that they come in different forms. Democratic delegation is necessary, consequential, and at the same time fraught with danger. Political parties and institutional checks exist in large part for these reasons. In turn, and for better or worse, they affect the policy process in their own ways and sometimes in complex interaction. There is no simple institutional fix for all agency problems. Thus, neither parliamentary nor presidential constitutions can effectively safeguard against dishonest or incompetent public servants. As long as principals and agents differ in their preferences and information, some agency losses must be expected, but such agency losses may come in different forms under different constitutions. And the choices between them represent real trade-offs, as summarized in Table 3.3, which is based partly on the models presented above, partly on the less formalized arguments that I have presented.

Yet, parliamentary systems are by no means all alike, and any serious assessment of their merits and demerits clearly requires more detailed and configurative description and analysis. In order to understand the effects of institutions such as parliamentarism on the policy process, our account thus has to begin and end with that process. We need to map out and understand the democratic policy process all the way from voters to civil servants. If we, for example, think of deviations from the Westminster model in terms of veto players, it is important to realize that a proliferation of institutional veto players (external constraints) has very different consequences from a fragmentation of

Table 3.3. *Regime Form and Agency Loss: A Summary*

| Regime Form | Forms of Agency Loss | | | |
	Policy Divergence	Leisure Shirking	Rent Seeking	Dominant Agency Problem
Westminster Parliamentarism	High; **Less** Susceptible to bias	Low	Moderately high	Moral hazard
Pivotal Parliamentarism	Moderately high; Susceptible to bias	Moderately high	High	Moral hazard
Constrained Parliamentarism	Moderate; susceptible to bias	Moderate	Moderate	Moral hazard
Collegial Presidentialism	Moderately low; Susceptible to bias	High	Low	Adverse selection
Competitive Presidentialism	Low; **Less** susceptible to bias	Moderately low	Moderately low	Adverse selection

the party system (partisan veto players). An increase in the former should under many circumstances enhance *ex post* control and thus counteract problems of moral hazard especially. A fragmentation of the party system, on the other hand, may very well lead to weaker *ex ante* controls and consequently to an increased susceptibility to adverse selection problems and other agency problems. Needless to say, if the goal is to contain agency loss, the former effect is much more desirable than the latter.

To understand parliamentarism, we must thus read its fine print, which is the purpose of the next eighteen chapters of this book, which collectively constitute its bulk. These chapters will take us through the four main links in the chain of delegation, as these steps have been outlined here and elsewhere. The data will be presented in summary cross-national form and further analysed in Chapter 4. The following seventeen chapters provide more configurative portraits of the respective national chains of demo-cratic delegation. Our emphasis will be on identifying mechanisms of delegation and accountability more than agency loss. Thus, these chapters will lay out the national policy process and describe the constraints on policy-making and the boundaries within which it is appropriate to characterize the constitutional actors as agents (directly or indirectly) of the citizens. Each chapter focuses specifically on the role of parties as bonding instruments used to align incentives and permit citizen control of the policy process. In sum, these data provide an unprecedented guide to contemporary European parliamentary democracies, as well as to the larger lessons and broader prospects of democratic representation, at the dawn of the twenty-first century.

APPENDIX

This appendix describes, for each of the three games depicted in Fig. 3.2 and each of the ten preference configurations, the largest (worst-case) and smallest (best-case) agency loss, relative to the principal's ideal point. In each scenario, I assume for simplicity that the status quo and the reversion point are identical and equal to zero. While there may in many cases be a range of conditions associated with either the best-case or worst-case outcome, only one example of each is offered. All references below to distance refer to the absolute policy distance between the ideal points of the respective players. Recall that all models assume complete information, that it is costly to make any proposal, and that if otherwise indifferent, the principal will opt for the reversion point. Therefore, the agency loss will never be greater than P (in case no proposal is made), or $P - \varepsilon$ (in case a proposal is made and accepted).

Preference Configuration I (PC I): $A1 > A2 > P > 0$

Parliamentarism

The best-case scenario is when the distance between the principal and the reversion point (P) is minimal (equal to ε). Then agent 1 will have to propose the principal's ideal point, and agent 2 and the principal will accept. The worst-case scenario occurs when the distance between the principal and agent 1 is just smaller than the distance between the principal and the reversion point (or equal to $P - \varepsilon$). Then agent 1 will propose his own ideal point (A_1), which will be accepted. The agency loss is $P - \varepsilon$.

Competitive Presidentialism

The best-case scenario, with no agency loss, occurs when P is minimal (equal to ε). Then agent 2 will propose the principal's ideal point, and she will accept. The worst-case scenario is when the principal is closer to agent 2 than to the reversion point. Agent 2 will then propose his ideal point (A_2), and the principal will accept. The agency loss will be $P - \varepsilon$.

Collegial Presidentialism

The best-case scenario is when the distance between the principal and the reversion point (P) is minimal (equal to ε). Then either agent will have to propose the principal's ideal point, which will be accepted. The worst-case scenario occurs when the distance between the principal and agent 2 is just smaller than the distance between the principal and the reversion point (or equal to $P - \varepsilon$). Then agent 2 will propose his own ideal point (A_1), which will be accepted. The agency loss will be $P - \varepsilon$.

Preference Configuration II (PC II): $A_1 > P > A_2 > 0$

Parliamentarism

The best-case scenario, with no agency loss, is when the distance between the principal and agent 2 is just smaller (by ε) than that between agent 2 and the reversion point. Then agent 1 will propose P, and agent 2 and the principal will accept. The worst-case scenario is when the distance between agent 2 and the reversion point is minimal (equal to ε). Then agent 1 will propose ε, which will be accepted. The agency loss will be $P - \varepsilon$.

Competitive Presidentialism

The agents' proposals will converge to the ideal point of the principal, and there will be no agency loss.

Collegial Presidentialism

The best-case scenario, with no agency loss, is when the distance between the principal and agent 2 is smaller than that between agent 2 and the reversion point. Then both agents will make acceptable proposals that will converge to the principal's ideal point. The worst-case scenario is when the distance between agent 2 and the reversion point is minimal (equal to ε). Then the agents' proposals will converge to the ideal point of agent 2, which will be accepted. The agency loss will be $P - \varepsilon$.

Preference Configuration III (PC III): $A_1 > P > 0 > A_2$

Parliamentarism
Since agent 2 will veto any proposal greater than 0, and the principal will reject any proposal smaller than 0, no proposal will be made. Hence, the best-case (and worst-case) scenario is the reversion point, under which agency loss is P.

Competitive Presidentialism
The agents' proposals will converge to the ideal point of the principal, and there will be no agency loss.

Collegial Presidentialism
Since agent 2 will not make or accept any proposal greater than 0, and the principal will reject any proposal smaller than 0, no proposal will be made. Hence, the best-case (and worst-case) scenario is the reversion point, under which agency loss is P.

Preference Configuration IV (PC IV): $A_1 > 0 > A_2 > P$

Parliamentarism
Since agent 1 will make no proposal smaller than 0, and the principal will reject any proposal greater than 0, no proposal will be made. Hence, the best-case (and worst-case) scenario is the reversion point, in which agency loss is P.

Competitive Presidentialism
Since agent 1 prefers the reversion point to any proposal that would be acceptable to the principal, any acceptable proposal will come from agent 2, who will indeed propose his ideal point. The best-case scenario is when agent 2 is at a minimal distance, ε, from the principal. The worst-case scenario is when agent 2 is similarly close (distance equal to ε) to the reversion point. The agency loss will then be $P - \varepsilon$.

Collegial Presidentialism
Since agent 1 will make or accept no proposal smaller than 0, and the principal will reject any proposal greater than 0, no proposal will be made. Hence, the best-case (and worst-case) scenario is the reversion point, under which agency loss is P.

Preference Configuration V (PC V): $A_1 > 0 > P > A_2$

Parliamentarism
Since agent 1 will make no proposal smaller than 0, and the principal will reject any proposal greater than 0, no proposal will be made. Hence, the best-case (and worst-case) scenario is the reversion point, under which agency loss is P.

Competitive Presidentialism
The agents' proposals will converge to the ideal point of the principal, and there will be no agency loss.

Collegial Presidentialism

Since agent 1 will make or accept no proposal smaller than 0, and the principal will reject any proposal greater than 0, no proposal will be made. Hence, the best-case (and worst-case) scenario is the reversion point, under which agency loss is P.

Preference Configuration VI (PC VI): $A_2 > A_1 > P > 0$

Parliamentarism

Agent 2 will approve any proposal acceptable to agent 1 and the principal. The best-case scenario is when the distance between the principal and the reversion point (P) is minimal (equal to ε). Then agent 1 will have to propose the principal's ideal point, and agent 2 and the principal will accept. The worst-case scenario occurs when the distance between the principal and agent 1 is just smaller than the distance between the principal and the reversion point (or equal to $P - \varepsilon$). Then agent 1 will propose his own ideal point (A_1), which will be accepted. The agency loss will be $P - \varepsilon$.

Competitive Presidentialism

As under parliamentarism, the precise ideal point of agent 2 is immaterial. The best-case scenario is when the distance between the principal and the reversion point (P) is minimal (equal to ε). Then either agent will propose the principal's ideal point, which will be accepted. The worst-case scenario occurs when the distance between the principal and agent 1 is just smaller than the distance between the principal and the reversion point (or equal to $P - \varepsilon$). Then agent 1 will propose his own ideal point (A_1), which will be accepted. The agency loss will be $P - \varepsilon$.

Collegial Presidentialism

Agent 2 will approve any proposal acceptable to agent 1 and the principal, but will never make a more favourable proposal than agent 1 does. The best-case scenario is when the distance between the principal and the reversion point (P) is minimal (equal to ε). Then agent 1 will have to propose the principal's ideal point, and agent 2 and the principal will accept. The worst case scenario occurs when the distance between the principal and agent 1 is just smaller than the distance between the principal and the reversion point (or equal to $P - \varepsilon$). Then agent 1 will propose his own ideal point (A_1), which will be accepted. The agency loss will be $P - \varepsilon$.

Preference Configuration VII (PC VII): $A_2 > P > A_1 > 0$

Parliamentarism

Agent 2 will approve any proposal acceptable to agent 1 and the principal. Agent 1 will always be able to propose his ideal point and have it accepted. The best-case scenario is when agent 1 is at a minimum distance from the principal, in which case the agency loss is ε. It is $P - \varepsilon$ in the worst-case scenario, when the distance between agent 1 and the reversion point is minimal (equal to ε).

Competitive Presidentialism

The agents' proposals will converge to the ideal point of the principal, and there will be no agency loss.

Collegial Presidentialism

The best-case scenario, with no agency loss, is when the distance between the principal and agent 1 is just smaller (by ε) than that between agent 1 and the reversion point. Then the principal will delegate to agent 2, who will propose P, and agent 1 and the principal will accept. The worst-case scenario is when the distance between agent 1 and the reversion point is minimal (equal to ε). Then either agent will propose agent 1's ideal point (A_1), which will be accepted. The agency loss will be $P - \varepsilon$.

Preference Configuration VIII (PC VIII): $A_2 > 0 > A_1 > P$

Parliamentarism

Since agent 2 will veto any proposal greater than 0, and agent 1 and the principal will reject any proposal smaller than 0, no proposal will be made. Hence, the best-case (and worst-case) scenario is the reversion point, under which agency loss is P.

Competitive Presidentialism

Since agent 2 prefers the reversion point to any proposal that would be acceptable to the principal, any acceptable proposal will come from agent 1, who will indeed propose his ideal point. The best-case scenario is when agent 1 is at a minimal distance, equal to ε, from the principal. The agency loss is ε. The worst-case scenario is when agent 1 is at a minimal distance, ε, from the reversion point, in which case the agency loss will be $P - \varepsilon$.

Collegial Presidentialism

Since agent 2 will not make or accept any proposal greater than 0, and the principal will reject any proposal smaller than 0, no proposal will be made. Hence, the best-case (and worst-case) scenario is the reversion point, under which agency loss is P.

Preference Configuration IX (PC IX): $P > A_1 > A_2 > 0$

Parliamentarism

The principal will approve any proposal acceptable to both agents. The best-case scenario is when the distance between the principal and agent 1 is minimal and when agent 2 is closer to agent 1 than to the reversion point. Then agent 1 will propose his ideal point and the principal accept. The agency loss is ε. In the worst-case scenario, agent 2 is at a minimum distance, ε, from the reversion point. Agent 1 will then have to propose agent 2's ideal point, and the agency loss will be $P - \varepsilon$.

Competitive Presidentialism

As under parliamentarism, the precise ideal point of agent 2 is immaterial. The agency loss is ε in the best-case scenario, and $P - \varepsilon$ in the worst-case scenario.

Collegial Presidentialism

Agent 1 will always make a proposal that agent 2 and the principal prefer to the reversion point. Agent 2 will never make a more favourable proposal than agent 1. As under parliamentarism, the agency loss is ε in the best-case scenario, and $P - \varepsilon$ in the worst-case scenario.

Preference Configuration X (PC X): $P > A_2 > A_1 > 0$

Parliamentarism

The principal and agent 2 will approve any proposal made by agent 1, who will indeed propose his ideal point. In the best-case scenario, the distance between the principal and agent 1 is equal to 2ε. In the worst-case scenario, the agency loss will be $P - \varepsilon$.

Competitive Presidentialism

Both agents will propose, and the principal will accept the larger proposal, which will be agent 2's proposal of his own ideal point. In the best-case scenario, the distance between the principal and agent 2 is minimal and the agency loss equal to ε. In the worst-case scenario, the agency loss will be $P - 2\varepsilon$.

Collegial Presidentialism

Agent 2 will always make a proposal that agent 1 and the principal prefer to the reversion point. Agent 1 will never make a more favouable proposal than agent 2. The best-case scenario is when the distance between the principal and agent 2 is minimal and when agent 1 is closer to agent 2 than to the reversion point. Then agent 2 will propose his ideal point and agent 1 and the principal accept. The agency loss is ε. In the worst-case scenario, agent 1 is at a minimum distance, ε, from the reversion point. Agent 2 will then have to propose agent 1's ideal point, and the agency loss will be $P - \varepsilon$.

REFERENCES

Achebe, Chinua (1983). *The Trouble with Nigeria*. London: Heinemann.

Aghion, Philippe and Tirole, Jean (1997). 'Formal and Real Authority in Organizations'. *Journal of Political Economy*, 105: 1–29.

Aldrich, John (1995). *Why Parties?: the Origin and Transformation of Political Parties in America*. Chicago: Chicago University Press.

Andeweg, Rudy B. (2000). 'Ministers as Double Agents? The Delegation Process Between Cabinet and Ministers'. *European Journal of Political Research*, 37: 377–95.

——and Nijzink, Lia (1995). 'Beyond the Two-Body Image: Relations Between Ministers and MPs', in Herbert Döring (ed.), *Parliaments and Majority Rule in Western Europe*. Frankfurt am Main: Campus and New York: St. Martin's Press.

Armstrong, Sir Robert (1989). 'The Duties and Responsibilities of Civil Servants in Relation to Ministers', in Geoffrey Marshall (ed.), *Ministerial Responsibility*. Oxford: Oxford University Press.

Arrow, Kenneth J. (1951). *Social Choice and Individual Values*. New York: John Wiley.

Bagehot, Walter (1963[1867]). *The English Constitution*. London: Fontana/Collins.

Barro, Robert J. (1973). 'The Control of Politicians: An Economic Model'. *Public Choice*, 14: 19–42.

Bendor, Jonathan, Moe, Terry M., and Kenneth W. Shotts (2001). 'Recycling the Garbage Can: An Assessment of the Research Program'. *American Political Science Review*, 95(1): 169–90.

Bergman, Torbjörn (1993). 'Formation Rules and Minority Governments'. *European Journal of Political Research*, 23: 55–66.

Boix, Carles (1999). 'Setting the Rules of the Game: The Choice of Electoral Systems in Advanced Democracies'. *American Political Science Review*, 93: 609–24.

——(2001). 'Democracy, Development, and the Public Sector'. *American Journal of Political Science*, 45: 1–17.

Brehm, John and Gates, Scott (1997). *Working, Shirking and Sabotage*. Ann Arbor: University of Michigan Press.

Buchanan, James M. (1980). 'Rent Seeking and Profit Seeking', in James M. Buchanan, Robert D. Tollison, and Gordon Tullock (eds.), *Toward a Theory of the Rent-Seeking Society*. College Station: Texas A&M Press.

Carey, John M. (1996). *Term Limits and Legislative Representation*. Cambridge: Cambridge University Press.

Cohen, Michael, March, James G., and Olsen, Johan P. (1972). 'A Garbage Can Model of Organizational Choice'. *Administrative Science Quarterly*, 17: 1–25.

Cowhey, Peter F. (1995). 'The Politics of Foreign Policy in Japan and the United States', in Peter F. Cowhey and Mathew D. McCubbins (eds.), *Structure and Policy in Japan and the United States*. Cambridge: Cambridge University Press.

Cox, Gary W. (1987). *The Efficient Secret*. Cambridge: Cambridge University Press.

——and McCubbins, Mathew D. (1993). *Legislative Leviathan*. Cambridge: Cambridge University Press.

————(2001). 'The Institutional Determinants of Economic Policy Outcomes', in Stephan Haggard and Mathew D. McCubbins (eds.), *Presidents, Parliaments, and Policy*. Cambridge: Cambridge University Press.

Dahl, Robert A. (1970). *After the Revolution?* New Haven: Yale University Press.

Diamond, Larry (1988). 'Nigeria: Pluralism, Statism, and the Struggle for Democracy', in Larry Diamond, Juan J. Linz, and Seymour Martin Lipset (eds.), *Democracy in Developing Countries*. Boulder: Lynne Rienner.

Dicey, A. C. (1959). *An Introduction to the Study of the Law of the Constitution*, 10th edn. London: Macmillan. (First edition 1885.)

Epstein, David, and O'Halloran, Sharyn (1999). *Delegating Powers*. Cambridge: Cambridge University Press.

Esaiasson, Peter and Holmberg, Sören (1996). *Representation from Above: Members of Parliament and Representative Democracy in Sweden*. Aldershot: Dartmouth.

Fearon, James D. (1999). 'Electoral Accountability and the Control of Politicians: Selecting Good Types versus Sanctioning Poor Performance', in Adam Przeworski, Susan C. Stokes, and Bernard Manin (eds.), *Democracy, Accountability, and Representation*. Cambridge: Cambridge University Press.

Ferejohn, John (1986). 'Incumbent Performance and Electoral Control'. *Public Choice*, 50: 5–25.

Geddes, Barbara (1994). *Politician's Dilemma: Building State Capacity in Latin America*. Berkeley: University of California Press.

Gilligan, Thomas and Krehbiel, Keith (1989). 'Asymmetric Information and Legislative Rules with a Heterogeneous Committee'. *American Journal of Political Science*, 33: 459–90.

Goel, Rajeev, and Nelson, Michael A. (1998). 'Corruption and Government Size: A Disaggregated Analysis'. *Public Choice*, 97: 107–20.

Hardin, Garrett (1968). 'The Tragedy of the Commons'. *Science*, 162: 1243–8.

Hennessy, Peter (1986). *Cabinet*. Oxford: Basil Blackwell.

Hernes, Gudmund and Nergaard, Kristine (1989). *Oss imellom*. Oslo: FAFO.

Huber, John D. (1996). *Rationalizing Parliament*. Cambridge: Cambridge University Press.

Kiewiet, D. Roderick and McCubbins, Mathew D. (1991). *The Logic of Delegation*. Chicago: University of Chicago Press.

Krehbiel, Keith (1991). *Information and Legislative Organization*. Ann Arbor: University of Michigan Press.

Lane, Jan-Erik, and Narud, Hanne M. (1992). 'Regjering og nasjonalforsamling: Bemanning av de to statsorganene'. *Norsk Statsvitenskapelig Tidsskrift*, 8: 303–16.

Laver, Michael J. and Shepsle, Kenneth A. (1996). *Making and Breaking Governments*. Cambridge: Cambridge University Press.

Lijphart, Arend (1977). *Democracy in Plural Societies*. New Haven: Yale University Press.

——(1984). *Democracies*. New Haven: Yale University Press.

——(1999). *Patterns of Democracy*. New Haven: Yale University Press.

Linz, Juan J. (1994). 'Presidential or Parliamentary Democracy: Does It Make a Difference?' in Linz, Juan J. and Valenzuela, Arturo (eds.), *The Failure of Presidential Democracy*. Baltimore: The Johns Hopkins University Press.

Lipset, Seymour M. and Rokkan, Stein (eds.) (1967). *Party Systems and Voter Alignments*. New York: Free Press.

Lupia, Arthur and McCubbins, Mathew D. (1994). 'Learning from Oversight: Fire Alarms and Police Patrols Reconstructed'. *Journal of Law, Economics, and Organization*, 10: 96–125.

—— and Strøm, Kaare (1995). 'Coalition Termination and the Strategic Timing of Parliamentary Elections'. *American Political Science Review*, 89: 648–65.

————(2004). 'Coalition Governance Theory: Bargaining, Electoral Connections and the Shadow of the Future', in Kaare Strøm, Wolfgang C. Müller, and Torbjörn Bergman (eds.), *Coalition Governance in Parliamentary Democracies*. Oxford: Oxford University Press.

McChesney, Fred S. (1997). *Money for Nothing: Politicians, Rent Extraction, and Political Extortion*. Cambridge, MA: Harvard University Press.

McCubbins, Mathew D. and Schwartz, Thomas (1984). 'Congressional Oversight Overlooked: Police Patrols versus Fire Alarms'. *American Journal of Political Science*, 28: 165–79.

McKelvey, Richard D. (1976). 'Intransitivities in Multidimensional Voting Models and Some Implications for Agenda Control'. *Journal of Economic Theory*, 12: 472–82.

Manin, Bernard, Przeworski, Adam, and Stokes, Susan C. (1999). 'Elections and Representation', in Adam Przeworski, Susan C. Stokes, and Bernard Manin (eds.), *Democracy, Accountability, and Representation*. Cambridge: Cambridge University Press.

Mattson, Ingvar and Strøm, Kaare (1995). 'Parliamentary Committees', in Herbert Döring (ed.), *Parliaments and Majority Rule in Western Europe*. New York: St. Martin's Press.

Mitchell, Paul L. (2000). 'Voters and their Representatives: Electoral Institutions and Delegation in Parliamentary Democracies'. *European Journal of Political Research*, 37: 335–51.

Moe, Terry M. and Caldwell, Michael (1994). 'The Institutional Foundations of Democratic Government: A Comparison of Presidential and Parliamentary Systems'. *Journal of Institutional and Theoretical Economics*, 150: 171–95.

Montinola, Gabriella R. and Jackman, Robert W. (2002). 'Sources of Corruption: A Cross Country Study'. *British Journal of Political Science*, 32: 147–70.

Müller, Wolfgang C. (2000). 'Political Parties in Parliamentary Democracies: Making Delegation and Accountability Work'. *European Journal of Political Research*, 37: 309–33.

—— and Strøm, Kaare (eds.) (2000). *Coalition Governments in Western Europe*. Oxford: Oxford University Press.

Niemi, Richard G. and Weisberg, Herbert F. (1968). 'A Mathematical Solution for the Probability of the Paradox of Voting'. *Behavioral Science*, 13: 317–23.

Niskanen, William A. (1991). 'A Reflection on Bureaucracy and Representative Government', in André Blais and Stéphane Dion (eds.), *The Budget-Maximizing Bureaucrat: Appraisals and Evidence*. Pittsburgh: University of Pittsburgh Press.

Norton, Philip (1994). *The British Polity*, 3rd edn. New York: Longman.

Olson, Mancur, Jr. (1965). *The Logic of Collective Action*. Cambridge, MA: Harvard University Press.

——(1982). *The Rise and Decline of Nations*. New Haven: Yale University Press.

Osaghae, Eghosa E. (1998). *Crippled Giant: Nigeria since Independence*. Bloomington: Indiana University Press.

Palmer, Matthew S. R. (1995). 'Toward an Economics of Comparative Political Organization: Examining Ministerial Responsibility'. *Journal of Law, Economics and Organization*, 11: 164–88.

Parker, Glenn R. (1996). *Congress and the Rent-Seeking Society*. Ann Arbor: University of Michigan Press.

Rasch, Bjørn Erik (2000). *Demokrati: Ideer og Organisering*. Bergen: Fagbokforlaget.

Riker, William H. (1982). *Liberalism Against Populism: A Confrontation Between the Theory of Democracy and the Theory of Social Choice*. San Francisco: W. H. Freeman.

Riker, William H. and Ordeshook, Peter C. (1973). *Introduction to Positive Political Theory*. Englewood Cliffs: Prentice Hall.

Rokkan, Stein. (1970). *Citizens, Elections, Parties*. Oslo: Universitetsforlaget.

Romer, Thomas and Rosenthal, Howard (1978). 'Political Resource Allocation, Controlled Agendas, and the Status Quo'. *Public Choice*, 33: 27–44.

Rose, Richard and Mackie, Thomas T. (1983). 'Incumbency in Government: Asset or Liability?', in Hans Daalder and Peter Mair (eds.), *Western European Party Systems: Continuity & Change*. London: Sage.

Rose-Ackerman, Susan (1999). *Corruption and Government: Causes, Consequences, and Reform*. Cambridge: Cambridge University Press.

Saalfeld, Thomas (2000). 'Members of Parliament and Governments in Western Europe: Agency Relations and Problems of Oversight'. *European Journal of Political Research*, 37: 353–76.

Sartori, Giovanni (1976). *Parties and Party Systems: A Framework for Analysis*. Cambridge: Cambridge University Press.

——(1994). 'Neither Presidentialism nor Parliamentarism', in Juan J. Linz and Arturo Valenzuela (eds.), *The Failure of Presidential Democracy: Comparative Perspectives*. Baltimore: The Johns Hopkins University Press.

Shepsle, Kenneth A. and Bonchek, Mark S. (1997). *Analyzing Politics*. New York: W. W. Norton.

——and Weingast, Barry R. (1987). 'The Institutional Foundations of Committee Power'. *American Political Science Review*, 81: 85–104.

Shugart, Matthew S. and Carey, John M. (1992). *Presidents and Assemblies*. Cambridge: Cambridge University Press.

Sjöblom, Gunnar (1987). 'The Role of Political Parties in Denmark and Sweden, 1970–1984', in Richard S. Katz (ed.), *Party Governments: European and American Experiences*. Berlin: de Gruyter.

Strøm, Kaare (1990). *Minority Government and Majority Rule*. Cambridge: Cambridge University Press.

——and Müller, Wolfgang C. (1999). 'The Keys to Togetherness: Coalition Agreements in Parliamentary Democracies'. *Journal of Legislative Studies*, 5: 255–82.

——and Swindle, Stephen M. (2002). 'Strategic Parliamentary Dissolution'. *American Political Science Review*, 96: 575–91.

Thies, Michael F. (2000). 'On the Primacy of Party in Government: Why Legislative Parties Can Survive Party Decline in the Electorate', in Russell J. Dalton and Martin P. Wattenberg (eds.), *Parties without Partisans*. Oxford: Oxford University Press.

Tsebelis, George (1990). *Nested Games: Rational Choice in Comparative Politics*. Berkeley: University of California Press.

——(1995). 'Decisionmaking in Political Systems: Veto Players in Presidentialism, Parliamentarism, Multicameralism, and Multipartyism'. *British Journal of Political Science*, 25: 289–325.

——(2000). 'Veto Players and Institutional Analysis'. *Governance*, 13: 441–74.

——(2002). *Veto Players: An Introduction to Institutional Analysis*. Princeton: Princeton University Press and the Russell Sage Foundation.

Weaver, R. Kent and Rockman, Bert A. (eds.) (1993). *Do Institutions Matter? Government Capabilities in the United States and Abroad*. Washington, DC: The Brookings Institution.

Wessels, Bernhard (1999). 'Whom to respresent? Role orientations of legislators in Europe' in Hermann Schmitt and Jacques Thomassen (eds.), *Political Representation and Legitimacy in the European Union*. Oxford: Oxford University Press.

PART II

Survey

4

Democratic Delegation and Accountability: Cross-national Patterns

TORBJÖRN BERGMAN, WOLFGANG C. MÜLLER,
KAARE STRØM, AND MAGNUS BLOMGREN

INTRODUCTION

Contemporary democracies necessitate political delegation from the ultimate principal, the citizens, to all sorts of agents. Chapter 3 identifies three particularly important motivations for delegation, namely problems of (*a*) capacity (since not all citizens have the time or resources to make all important decisions for themselves), (*b*) competence (which is to say that they also do not have the skills to do so), and (*c*) social choice and collective action (which is to say that the members of any large group have trouble reaching and enforcing mutually beneficial agreements among themselves). While the last category may appear somewhat academically arcane, in truth it applies to decision-making in any community. So do, of course, the former two problems, although these seem to have become particularly acute in contemporary advanced democracies, with their technical advancement, expansive governments, and exceedingly complex policy challenges.

As we have also learned in the preceding chapters, delegation poses a myriad of potential problems. The first three chapters of this book have explained how preference divergence and asymmetric information between citizens and politicians can cause agency problems. Preference divergence can stem from conflicting visions about policy but also from leisure- or rent-seeking motivations on the part of politicians. Information problems materialize in two critical forms: adverse selection and moral hazard, which have been discussed in Chapters 2 and 3.

To deal with such problems, democratic constitution makers have devised various mechanisms of political *accountability*. As Arthur Lupia points out in Chapter 2, there are at least two ways to think about accountability: as policy outcomes or processes of control. In the 'outcome' perspective, accountability means that the policy outcomes meet the principal's preferences (whether or not the agent's intentions or hard work were in any way responsible). Viewed in terms of control, on the other hand, the relevant

Most of the credit for this chapter goes to our country experts who have painstakingly collected the information provided in the tables. In addition to those that appear as authors in this volume, we want to thank Indridi H. Indridason and Josep M. Reniu for their invaluable help.

question for accountability is whether principals can effectively direct the behaviour of their agents (whether or not such direction leads to desired outcomes).

Our concern in this and the following chapters, with the exception of the final one (Chapter 23), will largely be with accountability as a procedure, rather than an outcome. As discussed in Chapter 3, accountability implies two kinds of rights that principals have vis-à-vis agents: a right to demand information, and a capacity to impose any or all of three types of sanctions: (*a*) blocking or amending decisions made by the agent (veto power), (*b*) deauthorizing the agent (remove him from office or curtail his authority), and (*c*) imposing specific (monetary or other) penalties on the agent.

To determine when and how to impose sanctions, principals rely on various mechanisms of accountability. An accountability mechanism is any device by which a principal (*a*) can get information about an agent's intentions, skills, and behaviour or (*b*) can sanction or reward the agent. The information can come in oral, written, digital, pictorial, or any other form imaginable. Sanctions can also take many forms, and may include positive rewards such as new tasks, perks, or inducements. Of course, accountability mechanisms may be more or less effective. As information devices, at best they tell the principal what she needs to know. At worst, they provide faulty information about the agent's preferences (the adverse selection problem) or behaviour (the moral hazard problem). As sanctions, at best they ensure that agents behave according to their principals' preferences. At worst, badly designed accountability mechanisms can reward or sanction ineffectively, or, for that matter, so severely that they constrain agents from taking action that the principal would have desired.

Accountability mechanisms vary in the comprehensiveness of the principal's sanctions and right to information, as well as in their exclusiveness. Accountability mechanisms in which the principal's rights are comprehensive and exclusive are classically *hierarchical*. Under multiple principals with less comprehensive rights towards the agent, we speak instead of *plurarchy*. As mentioned in Chapter 3, classical parliamentarism tends to be hierarchical, whereas presidentialism is typically more plurarchical.

Delegation and accountability are two complementary and interdependent aspects of the democratic policy process. We shall refer to this larger policy process as democratic *governance*. We distinguish between government and governance. Government is a set of institutions for public policy-making. Governance is a process that takes place in part in those institutions but also requires a linkage between principals (citizens) and political agents. This chapter examines national governance in European parliamentary democracies. These decisions typically involve a great number of actors interacting formally and informally. Yet, in this chapter and indeed in this volume we are concerned primarily with top-level national governance.

Despite a number of excellent national or cross-national studies of individual mechanisms of delegation and accountability, and even though Western Europe includes some of the best-researched countries in the world, we lack a study that applies a unified perspective to the entire national process of democratic delegation and accountability. Our point of departure is the ideal–typical parliamentary democracy defined in Chapter 3. With the theoretical framework from previous chapters to guide us, we can identify cross-national differences as well as discrepancies between

theoretical models and contemporary realities. To understand parliamentary governance as delegation and accountability, we draw upon both existing research and a
wealth of new information provided by our country experts.

In this and the following chapters we trace the national chains of delegation and
accountability through four stages: (*a*) from voters to parliamentarians, (*b*) from parliamentarians to Prime Minister and cabinet, (*c*) within the cabinet, from chief executive
to individual ministers, and finally (*d*) from individual cabinet ministers to civil servants.
It is important to recall that in this scheme institutions can serve multiple purposes. For
instance, the electoral system is part of the contract design by which voters entrust parliamentarians to act on their behalf. At the same time, the electoral system is also the
main accountability mechanism by which citizens hold politicians accountable.
Moreover, as an accountability mechanism, elections can function both as an *ex ante*
screening device (by allowing voters to gain information on and select competing candidates) and as an *ex post* sanction (by permitting voters to remove MPs from office).

It is not practically possible to give equal attention to all mechanisms of democratic
delegation and accountability that exist in our countries. We are hence forced to make
hard choices and to focus on instruments of democratic accountability, since we believe
that these are generally less well understood than the mechanisms of delegation.
Moreover, as the country chapters (Chapters 5–21) will indeed testify, in parliamentary
democracies political parties play a particularly important role. The chapter that follows
immediately upon the country chapters (Chapter 22) therefore probes further into the
roles of political parties and other mechanisms of citizen control in parliamentary
delegation. Thus, the *combination* of this and the following chapters constitutes
our empirical contribution to a better understanding of contemporary parliamentary
democracies.

In this chapter, we compare and contrast the national chains of delegation and
accountability in the parliamentary democracies of Western Europe, mostly for the
entire post-Second World War period (see Chapter 1). To detail these institutions, we
present twenty comparative tables and four figures. All but four of these tables rely
exclusively on the information provided by our country experts. For the remaining
tables (Tables 4.2, 4.4, 4.17, and 4.19), we rely on secondary sources as well as on constitutions, parliamentary standing orders, and other official documents. Where rules
have changed, we record the year that they went into effect. Note that the end date for
all the tabular information is 1 January 2000, but that the text may also report on more
recent changes. Most notably, the new Finnish Constitution of March 2000 is not covered in the tables. Instead the most important changes in the Finnish Constitution are
covered in the country chapter and in Chapter 22.[1]

---

[1] In the text and tables we sometimes use such common acronyms as PM (Prime Minister) and MP
(Member of Parliament).

RULES OF GOVERNANCE

The rules of parliamentary governance are not particularly secret. Yet, identifying the relevant national rules is not entirely straightforward. Certainly, any serious account must begin with the formal constitution, but it cannot stop there. Some constitutional rules are in practice simply obsolete. Many Western European democracies used to be monarchies in which the heads of state were much more than figureheads, from which constitutional provisions have survived that currently have little meaning and relevance. Hence, we largely ignore the formal rules concerning hereditary monarchs unless these rules shape the expectations of other important political players (such as party leaders or PMs). We also realize that actors not recognized by constitutions may be of greater relevance to the policy process than are some constitutional actors. The prime example is political parties, which are scarcely mentioned in many older constitutions, yet dominate much of the public policy process in Western Europe (Müller 2000*a*).

Constitutional provisions do not always serve the purpose for which they were designed. For one thing, it may be notoriously difficult to pinpoint the 'real' intention behind a certain institutional design (Müller 2002). Furthermore, gifted politicians—masters in the 'art of manipulation' (Riker 1986)—can use institutions in ways not intended or foreseen by their creators. For example, the secret vote in parliament (as used in Italy from the nineteenth century until 1988) originally was invented to protect MPs from external pressure and to allow them to vote according to their conscience. Yet, in the age of party politics it had two kinds of unintended consequences: (*a*) moral hazard for MPs (who could vote against their constituency and/or party without repercussions) and (*b*) less predictable parliamentary outcomes. And the unsuccessful employment of the German constructive vote of no-confidence in 1972 (also by secret ballot) showed that under certain conditions the secret vote can be an instrument by which party leaders control their MPs—exactly the opposite of the original intent (see below).

Strong conventions, which generate expectations and can entail costs for those who violate them, can matter more than written rules. Despite great similarities in formal rules, the Presidents in France and Austria (or for that matter Iceland) perform quite different roles, with the former being the country's leader and the latter essentially a figurehead (see Duverger 1980; Elgie 1999 and below). Hence, we agree with Bogdanor (1988: 5) that it is more important to look at the 'working constitution' than at the written one.

For these reasons, our empirical investigation here goes much beyond the simple collection of seventeen (or, not counting the United Kingdom, sixteen) national constitutions to encompass written rules of different sorts, including ordinary legislation and, for example, parliamentary standing orders. We sometimes also include constitutional practices (strong conventions) that the actors involved understand to be de facto rules that it would be costly to disregard. But since our interest is in identifying rules that have some capacity to induce compliance, there is a real and significant problem in adopting too broad a notion of what constitute rules of governance. We do not wish to count as institutions of governance mere behavioural regularities that reflect habit, tradition, or self-interest. Such patterns of behaviour may persist as long as the actors in question find them profitable or convenient, but have no force of compulsion if that is no longer the case. If so, they are of little analytical use to us. Therefore, for a rule to qualify as a mechanism of delegation or accountability, it must be enforceable. Voters, politicians, or civil servants must expect such rules to be backed up by direct or indirect sanctions from their principals, or from courts or other third parties that can enforce them. Finally, enforcement can rest on the political actors' expectations that if they break the rules, voters will punish them in upcoming elections, or that other relevant parties will reject them as less than trustworthy.

Rules may matter even when they do not seem to be enforced. For example, in the Swedish Riksdag any individual MP has the right to demand a recorded vote. Yet, decisions are often made by acclamation (voice vote) after which the Speaker finds that the 'Aye' or 'No' side has won (on voting procedures, see Saalfeld 1995a). However, it would be incorrect to discount an MP's right to request a recorded vote. Rather, Swedish MPs act in the shadow of this rule. If any of them expected that the voice vote would jeopardize their prospects of winning, they would, without doubt, insist on the recorded vote. Hence, even rules that are not always enforced may directly or indirectly structure behaviour. For that reason, linking observed behaviour to constitutional rules requires in-depth knowledge of political realities.

Thus, democratic governance involves a complex interplay between formal rules and constitutional practice. That is why in a few tables, we account for whether the relevant rule is formal-legal or convention. Where judgement calls have been necessary, we have in the final event relied on the country experts to make them.

MAKING LAWS AND CONSTITUTIONS

Some institutions are more fundamental than others. The rule of law, which most Western European democracies generally respect, implies that most important political decisions require legislative authorization. And within the body of law, constitutional rules are typically privileged. Constitutions (and constitutional practice) provide the basic 'contract design' for delegation between the main democratic principal ('the citizens') and its agents. Among other things, they specify (a) the extent of the power delegated to these agents and (b) how the people can hold them accountable. Constitutions also regulate (c) the relationships between different types of agents, for instance, between parliament and cabinet. Below we describe for each country the procedures for ordinary legislation as well as constitutional amendments, and we account for the organization of the legislature.

Making Laws

Consider first the making of ordinary law. Table 4.1 presents the actors that together with the lower (or only) chamber are constitutionally designated participants in ordinary

Table 4.1. *Decision-making Procedure: Actors and Rules in Ordinary National Legislation*

Country and year	Head of state (Actor 1)	Cabinet (Actor 2)	Lower chamber (Actor 3)	Decision-making procedure in lower chamber			Upper chamber (Actor 4)	Other constitutional actor (Actor 5)	Which actors co-decide? (Refers to actors in previous columns)
				Quorum requirement	Decision rule	Voting procedure			
Austria 1945–2000	Formal	Can propose	Discretionary power	1/3 of all MPs	Simple majority	Anonymous	Suspensive veto[a]	n.a.	n.a.
Belgium 1945–2000	Formal	Can propose	Co-decides	Absolute majority	Simple majority	Recorded	Co-decides	n.a.	3, 4
Denmark 1945–52	Formal	Co-decides	Co-decides	Absolute majority	Simple majority	Recorded	Co-decides	n.a.	2–4
1953–2000	Formal	Co-decides	Co-decides	Absolute majority	Simple majority	Recorded	n.a.	n.a.	2, 3
Finland 1945–2000	Suspensive veto[b]	Can propose	Discretionary power	No	Simple majority	Recorded	n.a.	n.a.	1–3
France 1959–2000	Can refer to constitutional court[c]	Can propose	Discretionary power	No	Simple majority	Recorded	Can propose	n.a.	n.a.
Germany 1949–2000	Formal	Can propose	Discretionary power	Absolute majority	Simple majority	Recorded	Co-decides[d]	n.a.	n.a.
Greece 1975–2000	Suspensive veto[e]	Can propose	Discretionary power	No	Simple majority	Recorded	n.a.	n.a.	n.a.
Iceland 1945–2000	Can refer to referendum[f]	Can propose	Discretionary power	Absolute majority	Simple majority	Recorded	n.a.	n.a.	n.a.

Ireland 1945–2000	Can refer to Supreme Court[g]	Can propose	Discretionary power	20 MPs	Simple majority	Recorded	Can propose	n.a.	n.a.
Italy 1948–87	Suspensive veto[h]	Can propose	Co-decides	Absolute majority	Simple majority	Secret	Co-decides	n.a.	3, 4
1988–2000	Suspensive veto[h]	Can propose	Co-decides	Absolute majority	Simple majority	Anonymous	Co-decides	n.a.	3, 4
Luxembourg 1945–2000	Formal	Can propose	Discretionary power	Absolute majority	Simple majority	Recorded	n.a.	Council of State[i]	n.a.
The Netherlands 1945–2000	Formal	Co-decides	Co-decides	Absolute majority	Simple majority	Recorded[j]	Veto	n.a.	2–4
Norway 1945–2000	Formal	Can propose	Discretionary power	Absolute majority	Simple majority	Recorded[j]	n.a.	n.a.	n.a.
Portugal 1976–2000	Veto[k]	Can propose	Discretionary power	Absolute majority	Simple majority	Recorded	n.a.	Constitutional Tribunal[l]	1, 3, 5
Spain 1978–2000	Formal	Can propose	Co-decides	Absolute majority	Simple majority	Anonymous	Co-decides	Autonomous Communities and popular initiatives[m]	3, 4
Sweden 1945–70	Formal	Co-decides	Co-decides	No	Simple majority	Recorded	Co-decides	n.a.	2–4
1971–4	No role	Can propose	Discretionary power	No	Simple majority	Recorded	n.a.	n.a.	2, 3

Table 4.1. (*Contd.*)

Country and year	Head of state (Actor 1)	Cabinet (Actor 2)	Lower chamber (Actor 3)	Decision-making procedure in lower chamber			Upper chamber (Actor 4)	Other constitutional actor (Actor 5)	Which actors co-decide? (Refers to actors in previous columns)
				Quorum requirement	Decision rule	Voting procedure			
1975–2000	No role	Can propose	Discretionary power	No	Simple majority	Recorded	n.a.	n.a.	n.a.
United Kingdom									
1945–2000	Formal	Can propose	Discretionary power	40 MPs	Simple majority	Recorded	Suspensive veto[n]	n.a.	n.a.

Notes: The table reports the default voting method. In cases where there is a choice between two or more options and no clear default, we report the most restrictive one. The entry 'Can propose' means that the actor has proposal rights but that this proposal is subject to discretionary approval by other actor(s). The entry 'Co-decides' means that two or more actors have to agree on a proposal or it fails. The entry 'n.a.' means not applicable in this case.

An absolute majority is defined as 50% + 1 of all MPs. Simple majority is defined as 50% + 1 of the MPs present and voting. Most countries count a simple majority of 'votes cast', but in Belgium, Denmark, Italy, Luxembourg, Portugal, and Sweden, the counting rule is based on a 'simple majority of valid votes'. The latter counting rule excludes blank votes.

[a] The Bundesrat has suspensive veto power over legislation, that is, it can issue a veto, but the Nationalrat can decide the issue by holding a second vote. In this case the decision rule is simple majority. The quorum requirement in the *Nationalrat* is 50% of all MPs.

[b] The Finnish President has a suspensive veto. Until 1987, the President could delay legislation until a new general election had been held and the new parliamentary majority voted against his veto. From 1987, a President can delay a law for 3 months, after which point the parliament can override the veto in a simple majority vote.

[c] The Prime Minister, the President of the National Assembly, the President of the Senate, and, since 1974, any 60 deputies or senators, hold the same right.

[d] Slightly more than half of the laws, including virtually all important ones, require the consent of both 'chambers'. With regard to the remaining laws, the Bundesrat can delay a bill's passage by a suspensive veto. Such an objection can be overturned by an absolute majority of the Members of the Bundestag. If the Bundestag rejects a regular bill by a two-thirds majority, its veto can only be overturned in a vote in which at least two-thirds of the Bundestag MPs participate and at least 50% + 1 of the Bundestag MPs reject the veto. The budget bill can only be introduced by the cabinet. The Bundesrat may express an opinion, but cannot veto the federal budget. The Bundesrat may express an opinion, but cannot veto the federal budget.

[e] The Parliament can override the veto with absolute majority of all MPs.

[f] If the President in Iceland vetoes a new law, the law is subjected to a referendum in which the people can reject it in a simple majority vote.

[g] The Irish President can either sign a new law or refer it to the Supreme Court to test its constitutionality.

[h] The Parliament can override the veto.

[i] The advice of the Council of State is compulsory (but non-binding) for every bill, proposal, and amendment. The Council of State can decide whether or not legislation must be put to a second vote (Article 59). The Constitution stipulates, in effect, that all bills must pass a second vote in the Parliament no earlier than three months after the first vote. This second vote can only be avoided if plenary sessions of the Parliament and Council of State decide that it is unwarranted. The Council of State thus has a suspensive veto, which in practice is rarely used. The Council of State can also initiate (non-binding) proposals for the amendment of legislation.

[j] In the large majority of cases Dutch MPs vote by the show of hands and voting is recorded by party rather than individual MP. Yet, any individual MP can demand a roll-call vote.

[k] The Parliament can override the veto with absolute majority of all MPs with regard to some policy areas but only with two-thirds majority with regard to others. The number of policy areas requiring a two-thirds majority was increased in the 1982 constitutional reform.

[l] From 1976 to 1982, the Council of Revolution had the power to veto laws it considered unconstitutional. The 1992 constitutional revision abolished the council, and replaced it with the Constitutional Tribunal, which was granted the power to veto laws on account of their unconstitutionality.

[m] Bills can be proposed by the Autonomous Communities or through popular initiatives (500,000 signatures are required).

[n] The House of Lords has the power to delay enactment of a bill (suspensive veto) for a year (de facto for 8 months). Until 1949 this was 2 years.

law-making, and the role of such constitutional actors as the cabinet and the head of state. The respective roles of these actors can range from none to full discretionary power.[2]

The Role of Parliament

There is one constitutional actor that is invariably involved in the ordinary law-making process, namely the parliament. Even if legislatures in parliamentary democracies only rarely actually draft legislation (see Bagehot (1963 [1867]) and Polsby 1975), they are central to the process of creating basic rules for society and politics. Wherever such rule-making begins,[3] it for all practical purposes ends with an Act of Parliament. That is to say, all laws must pass through parliament and be formally adopted by a parliamentary majority. Yet, this parliamentary deliberation may take a variety of forms.

Table 4.1 reports the parliamentary procedures by which laws are made, focusing on those pertaining to the lower chamber. Western Europe features a mixture of unicameral and bicameral parliaments. There are upper chambers in Austria, Belgium, France, Germany, Ireland, Italy, The Netherlands, Spain, and the United Kingdom. Our focus on the lower chambers is based on three considerations: (*a*) their political supremacy in legislation, (*b*) their constitutional role in holding the cabinet accountable, and (*c*) their direct accountability to the people (voters). Historically, upper chambers were introduced to represent estates, sub-national units in federal countries, or groups defined by their social or economic status. Upper houses had longer terms and distinctive electoral systems. Typically, they were designed to be the more moderate (indeed, conservative) chamber.[4]

Often little known and sometimes ignored, the parliamentary *quorum rules* define what is a large enough group of MPs to be decisive. For ordinary legislation, the most common quorum rule is that more than half of all MPs have to be present, but some countries—such as Finland, France, Greece, and Sweden—have no quorum rule. Parliamentary *decision rules* range from 50 per cent plus one of the voting MPs (simple majority) or among all MPs (absolute majority), to two-thirds majorities, or other majority requirements (see Rasch 1995). All countries use simple majority rule (50 per cent plus one of those present and voting) for ordinary legislation. The variation is whether the majority must be based on all votes cast or if 'blank' (spoiled) votes are excluded from the count. On this point, the split is about even. *Voting procedure* refers to whether parliamentary votes are secret (it is not possible to identify how individual MPs voted), anonymous (voting occurs in public but individual votes are not recorded), or recorded (it is possible to identify who voted and how) (Saalfeld 1995a: 531–41). With the exceptions of Austria, Italy, and Spain, all parliaments use recorded votes for ordinary

---

[2] Note, however, that Table 4.1 does not include advisory bodies that provide non-mandatory or non-binding reviews of legislative proposals before they enter into law. Nor do we include constitutional courts or other forms of judicial review that take place mainly after laws have gone into effect.

[3] Austria, Italy, and Spain feature the people's initiative, that is, the right for a predetermined number of citizens to propose legislation.

[4] The Swedish upper chamber, which over time came to be a bastion of the Left, became a notable exception.

legislation. These three countries instead use anonymous votes, which means that the votes of individual MPs may be observed but that they cannot be found in the official parliamentary record.

Upper chambers make the chain of delegation more complex (Table 4.2). The relationship between lower and upper chambers is often complex, not least in Germany where the Bundesrat represents the governments of the federal *Länder*.[5] In bicameral systems, the cabinet is generally accountable to the lower (or first) chamber (such as the House of Commons). In the symmetrical legislatures of Belgium (until 1995), Italy, and Sweden (until 1971), the cabinet is accountable to both chambers, but even here the lower chamber is considered pre-eminent in national law-making (see also Tsebelis and Money 1997; Patterson and Mughan 1999; Russell 2000; Baldwin and Shell 2001).

The main law-making influence of upper chambers stems from their authority to block or substantially delay legislation. Such veto power comes in several shades. The strongest veto power is where legislation cannot be enacted unless positively approved by the upper chamber (the consent requirement). A somewhat lesser version is the mere veto power, in which case a bill is enacted unless vetoed by the upper chamber. This distinction mirrors the one between positive and negative parliamentarism (cf. Bergman 1993). Some constitutions feature both the consent requirement and the veto power, but apply them to different policy areas. To keep things simple, we have in Table 4.1 coded 'veto power' whenever the upper chamber actively or passively can block legislation. In some cases, this power is considerably restricted, as in Austria, where only laws altering the respective jurisdictions of the *Länder* and the federal government require the consent of the upper chamber (the Bundesrat). Even if they lack veto powers, upper chambers may be able to delay legislation, through a *suspensive* veto power or through procedural rules that guarantee the upper house a substantial period for consideration. Since in politics time is often scarce, even the power to delay decisions can be valuable. The one upper chamber that has only delaying power, the British House of Lords, can de facto stall legislation for up to 8 months. Hence, a government in the last 8 months of a parliamentary term depends on the cooperation of the Lords. In a few cases, even the 8-week delay that the Austrian Bundesrat can inflict has proven effective in preventing last-minute government legislation.

Whenever the upper chamber's consent is necessary or it has permanent (as opposed to suspensive) veto power, it is de facto a critical actor. The Italian Senate has exactly the same legislative authority as the Chamber of Deputies. The other upper chamber that is involved in a broad range of legislation, the Dutch Eerste Kamer, cannot initiate

---

[5] It is debatable whether the German Bundesrat is appropriately labelled an 'Upper Chamber'. The Bundesrat represents the governments of the German federal states (*Länder*). Most laws are made jointly by the Bundestag and the Bundesrat. In addition, the Bundesrat can freely veto *national* legislation (subject to Bundestag override), and any national constitutional amendment requires a two-thirds Bundesrat majority (see below). It also has the power to initiate bills at the national level and has done so with increasing frequency. Moreover, Bundesrat members have the right to speak in the Bundestag and often do so on national matters. For example, before the 1998 election SPD leaders Gerhard Schröder and Oskar Lafontaine used their privileges as Bundesrat Members to challenge Chancellor Helmut Kohl in the Bundestag.

Table 4.2. *Strength of Upper Chambers*[a]

Country	Same electoral system as lower chamber	Government accountability to upper chamber	Consent required in all cases	Consent required in some cases/laws/ decisions	Can veto all cases	Can veto some cases	Can delay
Austria							
1945–84	No	No	No	No	No	No	Yes
1984–2000	No	No	No	Yes[b]	No	Yes[b]	Yes[c]
Belgium							
1945–95	No	Yes	Yes	n.a.	Yes	n.a.	Yes
1995–2000	No	No	No	Yes[d]	No	Yes[d]	Yes
Denmark							
1945–53	No	No	Yes[e]	Yes	Yes[e]	Yes	Yes
1953–2000	n.a.	—	—	—	—	—	—
Finland	n.a.	—	—	—	—	—	—
France[f]	No	No	No	Yes[g]	No	Yes[g]	Yes
Germany	No	No	No	Yes[h]	No	Yes[h]	Yes
Greece	n.a.	—	—	—	—	—	—
Iceland	n.a.	—	—	—	—	—	—
Ireland	No	No	No[i]	No[j]	No[i]	No[j]	Yes
Italy	Yes	Yes	Yes	n.a.	Yes	n.a.	Yes
Luxembourg	n.a.	—	—	—	—	—	—
The Netherlands	No	No	Yes	n.a.	Yes	n.a.	Yes
Norway	n.a.	—	—	—	—	—	—
Portugal	n.a.	—	—	—	—	—	—
Spain	No	No	No	Yes	No	No	Yes[e]
Sweden							
1945–70	No	Yes[k]	Yes	n.a.	Yes	n.a.	Yes
1971–2000	n.a.	—	—	—	—	—	—
United Kingdom	No	No	No	No	No	No	Yes[l]

[a] This includes constitutional amendments, but excludes money bills.

[b] Constitutional amendments that introduce shifts of competences between the federal level and the *Land* level require the consent of the second chamber (the Bundesrat).

[c] About 8 weeks.

[d] The Senate has equal rights with the House for initiating and deciding on constitutional amendments and other institutional reforms, regionalist matters, ratification of treaties, and the organization of the judiciary. The Senate is exclusively competent to resolve conflicts between the national and subnational legislatures (Article 77).

[e] Consent not required for the budget which is not considered in this table.

[f] The French Senate has the same legislative powers as the Asemblée nationale until the Cabinet intervenes that can demand a final decision from the Assemblée nationale. The Assemblée nationale can stick to its original decision, accept a compromise drafted by the conference committee, or take on board amendments by the Senate (Article 45).

[g] Laws interpreting the Constitution (*lois auxquelles la Constitution*, institutional acts of Parliament) require the consent of both chambers if they are concerned with the Senate. If the Senate is not affected such laws can be accepted by the absolute majority of *all* members in the Assemblée nationale (Article 46).

[h] Slightly more than half of the laws require the consent of both chambers.

[i] With the support of one-third of the Dàil members the Irish Seanad is entitled to appeal to the President of the Republic and demand a referendum if the Dàil passes a bill of 'national importance' which had been rejected by the Seanad (Art. 27). The President then decides on the holding of such a referendum. Then the bill can not become law until either it passes the referendum or the Dàil passes it again following a general election. In practice Article 27 has never been invoked.

[j] Even constitutional amendments can be passed without consent of the Seanad (Art. 46).

[k] The Lower Chamber was considered more important, but both counted for cabinet formation, stability, and termination.

[l] Two years until 1949, one year since then. Due to the counting rules the delay is de facto 8 months since the time is calculated from the introduction of bills in the House of Commons.

Sources: Country chapters; Constitutions; Arter (1991); Tsebelis and Rasch (1995: 369–70, 372–3); Patterson and Mughan (1999); Russell (2000).

or amend legislation, and is thus much more of a veto player, strictly defined (see the country chapters for details). Although the Dutch upper chamber has comprehensive jurisdiction, the German Bundesrat, whose consent is required for slightly more than half of all legislative acts, is in practice much more influential. Its role in law-making when its partisan majority is different from that of the Bundestag has given rise to the thesis that Germany is a 'grand coalition state' (Schmidt 1996). In the other consent requirement cases, relating to Austria, Belgium, France, Ireland, and Spain, the upper chamber must consent on a few select issues only (see the footnotes to Table 4.2 for details). As Table 4.2 demonstrates, the overall trend is that upper houses have become less important or even abolished (see Longley and Olson 1991). For instance, until its 1995 constitutional reform, Belgium had a very influential upper chamber.[6] Denmark and Sweden abolished their upper chambers in 1953 and 1971, respectively.

The Head of State

Officially, the final stage in the legislative process is often in the hands of the Head of State. Yet, the main Western European pattern is that the Head of State has only a formal role in legislation. Instead cabinets have critical agenda powers, and in practice most items of the parliamentary agenda are government proposals (see Chapter 3). In Denmark and Sweden (until 1975), cabinets formally co-legislate with the Parliament. However, these rules pre-date parliamentary democracy and are of little or no practical importance.

In (ordinary) law-making, the Portuguese President alone has true veto power over legislation enacted by the Parliament. The Finnish President has a *suspensive* veto. Until a 1987 reform, a parliamentary vote to override the presidential veto could be held only after intervening parliamentary elections. Hence, the President's veto could delay legislation substantially (see Chapter 22). Since 1987, the President can delay a law for 3 months, at which point the Parliament can override. If it does not, the law is deemed to have lapsed. Interestingly, this suspensive veto was maintained under the Constitution that came into force in 2000, which otherwise has considerably reduced presidential powers. In Iceland, if the President vetoes a new law, it is subjected to a popular referendum in which it can be abrogated. The Irish President has two options. He (or she) must either sign a parliamentary act into law or refer it to the Supreme Court to test its constitutionality. The French President similarly has the right to appeal legislation to the Constitutional Court.

Constitutions

Constitutions are political meta-rules that distinguish themselves not only by their genesis, but also by their political entrenchment. Nonetheless, they vary a great deal in their comprehensiveness and specificity. In accordance with the literature (e.g. Huber *et al.* 2001: 336–8), we take the number of words to indicate the density of regulation and hence as a proxy for the volume of specially protected rules and rights. If we focus

---

[6] The Belgian constitutional reform of 1995 removed important powers (investiture and no-confidence motions, budget matters, and the right to conduct interpellations of ministers) from the upper chamber.

only on the main constitutional documents, which may not be the only document with constitutional status, their length (in the most recent English translation) varies between 3,600 (Iceland) and 32,600 words (Sweden). While some constitutions (Austria, Germany, and Greece) contain more than 20,000 words, others have fewer than 10,000 (Luxembourg, Denmark, France, and Norway). The mean length of constitutions is around 15,800 words and the median 13,300 words (see also Table 4.4).

Compared to ordinary law-making, more restrictive rules are used for constitutional amendments. In practice, constitutional amendments can be difficult to pass even when the formal requirements are few. Even in the United Kingdom, where passing the functional equivalent of a constitutional amendment closely follows the procedure for ordinary legislation, an important institutional change (such as a reform of the upper chamber) is normally preceded by years of deliberation and debate. Most countries, however, protect the constitution from amendment through one or more special requirements.

Table 4.3 describes the rules for constitutional amendments. In most countries the procedure is much the same as for ordinary legislation. There are two major exceptions. One is that *decision rules* differ, and the second is that in many countries there are *intervening constraints*. The most common decision rule is a two-thirds majority, used in seven countries (Austria, Belgium, Germany, Luxembourg, The Netherlands, Norway, and Portugal). Italy employs an absolute majority rule (i.e. more than half of all MPs must vote in favour). Three Nordic countries (Denmark, Iceland, Sweden), Ireland, and the United Kingdom use the simple majority rule (with some variation in counting invalid or blank votes). In the remaining four countries, the decision rule is contingent upon such matters as the size of the majority in the upper chamber or the authorship of the original proposal (see the footnotes for Table 4.3 for details).

The most common constraint, used in seven countries, is the requirement of an intervening election between two parliamentary votes. In France and Ireland, constitutional amendments are instead put to a referendum. Denmark probably has the most restrictive amendment rules, which require both an election and a referendum. The remaining countries impose no mandatory intervening constraint, but many allow a minority of MPs to subject the amendment to a national referendum. Countries that allow a change of the constitution after only one vote, Austria, Finland, Portugal, and Spain, use a qualified majority threshold to restrict amendments (these rules are detailed in Table 4.3). In the Finnish case, though, an even larger majority (five-sixths) must first agree to use such a procedure (otherwise there must be an intervening election).

Note that in Finland and France, the President can play a significant role in amending the Constitution. In Finland, it is the President who decides, in a plenary sitting of the Council of State and at the suggestion of the Cabinet, whether the government will present any legislative proposal to the Parliament.[7] This has given strong Presidents considerable agenda control over all types of legislation. In France, the President can initiate a constitutional amendment by submitting a proposal to the Parliament. After

---

[7] Note that a major Finnish constitutional reform, which went into effect in March 2000, significantly altered the President's powers. See Chapters 9 and 22 for more details.

Table 4.3. *Decision-making Procedure: Constitutional Amendments*

Country and year	Head of State (Actor 1)	Cabinet (Actor 2)	Lower chamber (Actor 3)	Decision-making procedure in lower chamber			Upper chamber (Actor 4)	Other constitutional actor (Actor 5)	Which actors co-decide (refers to actors in previous columns)	Mandatory intervening constraints
				Quorum requirement	Decision rule	Voting procedure				
Austria 1945–2000	Formal	Can propose	Discretionary power	Absolute majority	2/3 majority	Anonymous	Can propose	Popular initiative[a]	n.a.	No[b]
Belgium 1945–2000	Formal	Can propose	Co-decides	Absolute majority	2/3 majority	Recorded	Co-decides	n.a.	3, 4	Election[c]
Denmark 1945–52	Formal	Co-decides	Co-decides	Absolute majority	Simple majority	Recorded	Co-decides	n.a.	2–4	Election + referendum[d]
Denmark 1953–2000	Formal	Co-decides	Co-decides	Absolute majority	Simple majority	Recorded	n.a.	n.a.	2, 3	Election + referendum[d]
Finland 1945–2000	Suspensive veto[e]	Can propose	Discretionary power	No	2/3 majority[f]	Recorded	n.a.	n.a.	1–3	No
France 1959–2000	Can propose[g]	Formal	Co-decides	No	Simple majority	Recorded	Co-decides	n.a.	3, 4	Referendum[h]
Germany 1949–2000	Formal	Formal	Co-decides	Absolute majority	2/3 majority	Recorded	Co-decides	n.a.	n.a.	No
Greece 1975–2000	None	None	Discretionary power	No	3/5 majority[i]	Recorded	n.a.	n.a.	n.a.	Election

Iceland 1945–2000	Formal	None	Discretionary power	Absolute majority	Simple majority	Recorded	n.a.	n.a.	n.a.	Election[j]
Ireland 1945–2000	Formal	Can propose	Discretionary power	20 MPs	Simple majority	Recorded	Formal	n.a.	n.a.	Referendum[k]
Italy 1948–2000	Formal	Can propose	Co-decides	Absolute majority	Absolute majority	Anonymous	Co-decides	n.a.	3, 4	No[l]
Luxembourg 1945–2000	Formal	Co-decides	Co-decides	3/4 of all MPs	2/3 majority	Recorded	n.a.	Council of State[m]	n.a.	Election[n]
The Netherlands 1945–2000	Formal	Co-decides	Co-decides	Absolute majority	2/3 majority	Recorded[d]	Veto[p]	n.a.	2–4	Election[q]
Norway 1945–2000	Formal	Can propose	Discretionary power	Absolute majority	2/3 majority	Recorded	n.a.	n.a.	n.a.	Election[r]
Portugal 1976–2000	None	None	Discretionary power	No	2/3 majority	Recorded	n.a.	n.a.	n.a.	No
Spain 1978–2000	Formal	Can propose	Co-decides	Absolute majority	2/3 majority[s]	Recorded	Co-decides	n.a.	3, 4	No
Sweden 1945–70	Formal	Co-decides	Co-decides	No	Simple majority	Recorded	Co-decides	n.a.	2–4	Election[t]
Sweden 1971–4	Formal	Co-decides	Co-decides	No	Simple majority	Recorded	n.a.	n.a.	2–4	Election[t]
Sweden 1975–2000	None	Can propose	Discretionary power	No	Simple majority	Recorded	Co-decides	n.a.	2–4	Election[t]

Table 4.3. (Contd.)

Country and year	Head of State (Actor 1)	Cabinet (Actor 2)	Lower chamber (Actor 3)	Decision-making procedure in lower chamber			Upper chamber (Actor 4)	Other constitutional actor (Actor 5)	Which actors co-decide (refers to actors in previous columns)	Mandatory intervening constraints
				Quorum requirement	Decision rule	Voting procedure				
United Kingdom										
1945–2000	Formal	Can propose	Discretionary power	40 MPs	Simple majority	Recorded	Suspensive veto[u]	n.a.	n.a.	No

Notes: The table reports the default voting method. In cases there is a choice between two or more options and no clear default, we report the most restrictive one. The entry 'Can propose' means that the actor has proposal rights but that this proposal is subject to discretionary approval by other actor(s). The entry 'Co-decides' entails that two or more actors have to agree on a proposal or it fails. An absolute majority is defined as 50% + 1 of all MPs. Simple majority is defined as 50% + 1 of the MPs present and voting. Most countries count a simple majority of 'votes cast', but in Denmark and Sweden the counting rule is based on a 'simple majority of valid votes'. The 'latter counting rule excludes blank votes.

[a] 100,000 voters can initiate a constitutional amendment.

[b] A 'total' revision of the Constitution requires acceptance by referendum. In other amendments a one-third minority of the MPs can demand such a referendum.

[c] After a constitutional amendment, Parliament is dissolved, elections are held, and the new Parliament makes the final decision.

[d] The Parliament passes the bill and a new election is called. The new Parliament must accept the bill without amendments and then the bill is submitted to a referendum within 6 months.

[e] The Finnish President has a suspensive veto. Until 1987, the President could delay legislation until a new general election had been held and the new parliamentary majority voted against his veto. From 1987, a President can delay a law for 3 months, after which point the Parliament can override the veto in a simple majority vote.

[f] The Constitution can be changed by two identical decisions with an intervening election. The first decision (before the election) is a simple majority decision. The decision after election must be carried by a two-thirds majority. Alternatively, a two-thirds majority can amend the Constitution in one decision. However, this is only possible if the Parliament first decides to use this procedure by a five-sixths majority.

[g] The French President has the authority to initiate amendments to the Constitution by submitting a proposal to the Parliament. After an amendment has been accepted in both chambers of the National Assembly by two-thirds majority of the MPs present, he can submit it to a joint session of Parliament (National Assembly and Senate) at which it is finally accepted if it is supported by a three-fifths majority of all voting MPs. A referendum is not needed for the amendment to become law under this procedure.

[h] After being proposed and adopted in the legislature, a constitutional amendment that does not emanate from the President is decided upon in a referendum.

[i] A constitutional amendment must be passed by two successive Parliaments with an intervening election. An absolute majority (151 MPs) is required for one of the decisions and three-fifth majority (180 MPs) in the other, irrespectively of order. Before the election, Parliament decides the issue either by a majority of three-fifths (180 MPs out of 300) or by absolute majority of all MPs (151). After the election, the majority required for adoption depends on the size of the majority in favour in the proposing Parliament.

[j] Constitutional amendments must be passed twice in identical form, with an intervening parliamentary election.

[k] Lower chamber passes a Bill—an Act to Amend the Constitution, which decides the wording of the referendum question to be put to the people, who decide the issue. Referendums are decided by a simple majority of valid votes cast.

[l] Constitutional amendments must be passed twice with at least 3 months intervening. When an amendment has been approved by a majority below two-thirds of all members, it can be submitted to popular referendum, if one-fifth of the members of either house or 500,000 voters or 5 regional councils so demand.

[m] The advice of the Council of State is compulsory (but non-binding) for every bill, proposal, and amendment. The Council of State can decide whether or not legislation must be put to a second vote (Article 59). All bills must pass a second vote in the Parliament no earlier than three months after the first vote. This second vote can only be avoided if plenary sessions of the Parliament and Council of State decide that it is unwarranted. The Council of State can also initiate and call for the modification of legislation.

[n] After a constitutional amendment, a declaration is issued by the Parliament; that Parliament is dissolved and the new Parliament makes the final decision after the election.

[o] In constitutional amendments the decision rule is two-thirds majority in the upper chamber.

[p] In the large majority of cases Dutch MPs vote by the show of hands and voting is recorded by party rather than individual MP. Yet, any individual MP can demand a roll-call vote.

[q] Constitutional amendments are proposed by law; these need simple majority. Then, Parliament must be dissolved and the newly elected Parliament must accept the amendments with a two-thirds majority.

[r] Proposals for constitutional amendments are first adopted by simple majority. After the next election, the newly elected Parliament must accept the amendment with a two-thirds majority (of all votes cast).

[s] Constitutional amendments must be approved by a three-fifths majority of each Chamber or, alternatively, by an absolute majority of the Senate and a two-thirds vote in Congress, with a referendum being called upon request of one-tenth of the members of either chamber. A complete revision of the Constitution or amendments affecting basic principles, fundamental rights, or the Crown, require a two-thirds majority of each chamber and ratification by referendum.

[t] The Riksdag has to make two identical decisions, one before a general election to the lower chamber and one after such an election. From 1980, in addition, a minority of one-third can decide that the constitutional amendment should be submitted to a referendum.

[u] The House of Lords has the power to delay enactment of a bill (suspensive veto) for a year (de facto for 8 months). Until 1949 this was 2 years.

both parliamentary chambers have accepted an amendment by a two-thirds majority, the President can submit it to a joint session of parliament at which it is finally adopted if supported by a three-fifths majority of all voting MPs. In contrast to amendment initiatives that emanate from the legislature, a referendum is not needed (but can be held if the President so chooses). In other countries, the Head of State at best has a formal role in constitutional amendments. And in Greece, Iceland, and Portugal, the amendment procedure actually excludes even the cabinet!

What are the implications of different constitutional amendment procedures? In his influential study, Lijphart (1999) ranks democratic constitutions according to their rigidity, based mainly on their supermajority amendment requirements.[8] Lijphart thus considers any supermajority requirement a greater obstacle to constitutional change than the need to solicit the approval of the citizens through referendums or intervening elections.[9] Other studies, however, have considered a wider range of procedural impediments. Lutz (1994) measures the relative difficulty of amendment through an index (the Relative Difficulty of Amendment Process (RDAP) index) that gives a certain number of points to each constitutional amendment requirement. The higher the index, the more difficult are constitutional amendments. Constitutions are most amendable if this only requires the involvement of parliament (*legislative supremacy*) (average RDAP index score 1.23). Next comes a procedure that requires a *double vote* in parliament with an intervening election (average RDAP index score 2.39). The third major category is *legislative complexity*, under which there are multiple paths to constitutional amendment, including the possibility of an *ex post* referendum demanded by a legislative minority, the executive, or a specified number of citizens (average RDAP index score 2.79). Finally, there are constitutions that can be amended only after an intervening *referendum*. These are the constitutions that are most difficult to amend, which is reflected in an average RDAP index score of 4.01 (Lutz 1994: 363).[10] Overall, this index ranges from 0.5 (New Zealand) to 5.1 (United States).

Table 4.4 reports the *minimum* requirements for constitutional amendments, using the RDAP criteria. The conditions listed in Table 4.4 must apply simultaneously (i.e. they are jointly necessary) to permit a constitutional amendment. Thus, political agents that possess the required majority (see also Table 4.3) can in all but two countries (Denmark

---

[8] Lijphart (1999: 218–23) generates four categories of supermajority requirements: (*a*) greater than two-thirds majority, (*b*) two-thirds, (*c*) between two-thirds and ordinary, and (*d*) ordinary majority. To this categorization, Lijphart makes two adjustments. To control for plurality electoral systems, which facilitate supermajorities, Lijphart deducts one rank from their majority requirement score. And to adjust for the effects of strong bicameralism, specifically the lack of intercameral congruence, Lijphart moves such countries up one category (in our sample, this is relevant only for Germany).

[9] Lijphart's classification leads to the following placements of our seventeen countries, from high to low rigidity: (*a*) Germany; (*b*) Austria, Belgium, Finland, Luxembourg, The Netherlands, Norway, Portugal, and Spain; (*c*) Denmark, France (since 1974), Greece, Ireland, Italy, and Sweden (since 1980); (*d*) France (before 1974), Iceland, Sweden (before 1980), and the United Kingdom.

[10] Some of the values that Lutz's rules assign to Western European countries are contestable. For instance, Denmark has a score of 2.75 whereas Ireland's is 3. Yet, we would consider constitutional amendments more demanding in Denmark than in Ireland (see below).

Table 4.4. *Mandatory and Minimum Constraints on Constitutional Amendments, 2000[d]*

Country	Mandatory and minimum constraints on constitutional amendments				Index of relative difficulty of amendment process	Number of words in main constitutional text
	Referendum	Intervening election	Qualified parliamentary majority	Two decisions in Parliament		
Austria			X		0.80	27,900
Belgium		X	X	X	2.85	13,700
Denmark	X	X		X	2.75	6,600
Finland			X[b]		2.30	12,900
France	X[c]		X	X	2.50	7,700
Germany			X		1.60	24,500
Greece		X	X[d]	X	1.80	22,300
Iceland		X		X	2.75	3,600
Ireland	X				3.00	15,000
Italy				X[e]	3.40	12,000
Luxembourg		X	X	X	1.80	5,700
The Netherlands		X	X	X	n.d.	10,700
Norway		X	X	X	3.35	8,100
Portugal			X		0.80	32,000
Spain			X		3.60	17,800
Sweden		X		X	1.40	32,600
United Kingdom					n.a.	n.a.

Index: Lutz (1994: 369).

Number of words: Based on the most recent English translation of the constitutional texts (available in 2000 via http://www.uni-wuerzburg.de/law/ or from the home pages of national governments or parliaments). The word count for Denmark includes the Succession Act, the one for Sweden the Fundamental Law of Freedom of Expression, the Press Act, and the Succession Act, which collectively contain what otherwise is codified in one constitutional document. Numbers are rounded to full hundreds.

Notes:

[a] The figure lists the cases in which the rules are more restrictive than a single majority vote.

[b] The Constitution can be changed by two identical decisions with an intervening election. The post-electoral decision must be carried by a two-thirds majority. Alternatively, a two-thirds majority can amend the Constitution in one decision, but only if the Parliament first adopts this procedure by a five-sixth majority.

[c] After being adopted by the legislature, a constitutional amendment is decided upon in a referendum. Alternatively, the French President has the authority to initiate constitutional amendments by submitting a proposal to the Parliament. After an amendment has been accepted in both chambers by a two-thirds majority of the MPs present, the President can submit it to a joint session of Parliament (National Assembly and Senate) at which it is finally adopted if supported by a three-fifths majority of all voting MPs. A referendum is then not needed for the amendment to become law.

[d] A constitutional amendment must be passed by two successive Parliaments with an intervening election. The proposing Parliament decides the issue either by a three-fifths majority (180 MPs out of 300) or by an absolute majority of all MPs (151). The following Parliament in its first session decides which amendments will be finally adopted. The majority required for adoption depends on the size of the majority in favour in the proposing Parliament. An absolute majority (151 MPs) is required for one of the decisions and a three-fifths majority (180 MPs) for the other, irrespective of order.

[e] Constitutional amendments must be passed by both Chambers twice with an interval of no less than 3 months. An amendment that has been approved by a majority less than two-thirds of all members can be submitted to a popular referendum, if one-fifth of the members of either house or 500,000 voters or 5 regional councils so demand.

and Ireland) change the rules of the game without express popular consent on final decision. In contrast, both of the latter countries' constitutions by implication require a referendum on any changes to the EU treaties. And in both countries such amendments have in fact been rejected when they were first put before the people: in Denmark in 1992 (the Maastricht Treaty) and in 2000 (the euro currency) and in Ireland in 2001 (the Nice Treaty), resulting in considerable embarrassment to the national governments and the European Union.

Lutz notes an interesting and strong relationship between the rules and the actual frequency of constitutional amendments—the more demanding the referendum process, the fewer the amendments. As it turns out, there is also a clear negative correlation between the scope of the constitutionally protected area (as measured by the number of words in the Constitutions) and the relative difficulty of constitutional amendment. In other words, in Western Europe either the constitutionally protected area is large but its protection relatively weak (Portugal or Sweden), or the scope is small but the protection strong (Italy or Norway). (Yet, although we lack quantitative data for Britain, it would clearly score low on both dimensions.) Indeed, the alternatives would not be very appealing. Combining a narrow protected area with permissive amendment rules invites majority tyranny while combining a large protected area with restrictive amendment rules may cause political sclerosis. Thus, political systems may achieve similar entrenchments of fundamental rights and procedures through different means. Focusing narrowly on a single indicator of constitutional rigidity could therefore be misleading.

PARTY COHESION

Before examining in greater depth the chain of delegation in European parliamentary democracies, let us consider the organizations that keep the different links in that chain together. In parliamentary democracies, political parties traditionally perform that function. Chapter 3 has argued that their strength (cohesiveness) is determined by their value to politicians as mechanisms of bonding and to voters as informational economizing devices. Party cohesion is the degree to which the public office-holders of any one party act mutually consistently. As Fig. 4.1 shows, party cohesion results from the individual cost–benefit calculations of the relevant intra-party actors. If many of them find it beneficial to go against the party line, cohesion will be low. These individual calculations, in turn, are based on the politicians' preferences, which presumably include both policy- and career-related goals. If these individual preferences within the

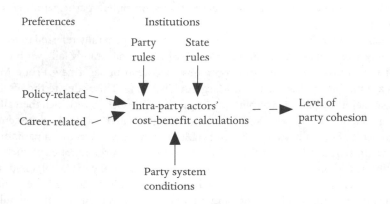

Figure 4.1. The Causes of Political Party Cohesion.

party by and large do not conflict, party cohesion will be high even if no discipline is imposed. Yet, often intra-party preferences are not so well aligned. Under such conditions parties need to be 'strong' in order to be cohesive, as Krehbiel (1993) has pointed out. A 'strong' party can cause its members to follow the party line even if that conflicts with their preferences. And given the negative electoral effects of a lack of cohesion, parties have a collective interest in being strong.

But how can parties achieve such conformity? It is party rules and their interplay with government rules (particularly those that govern the first two steps of the delegation chain) that, under appropriate institutional design, provide the proper incentives. Quite simply, such rules make it more likely that politicians achieve their career and policy goals if they act in line with their party comrades (Müller 2000a). But institutions can also provide the 'wrong' kinds of incentives (as did the secret vote in the Italian Parliament until 1988).

Finally, party system conditions affect the cost–benefit calculations of intra-party actors. Maintaining cohesion is relatively easy for parties in single-party majority cabinets facing strong competition and most difficult for parties in coalition governments characterized by great preference diversity. Single-party cabinets are most likely to feature preference identity within the cabinet (and between the cabinet and the relevant parliamentary party), particularly in majority situations. In contrast, parties in coalition governments are forced to make concessions to the other government parties. So do weak minority governments that have to accommodate other parties in parliament. The greater the concessions, the more strain on party cohesion. Figure 4.1 summarizes our argument.

Western European parties generally display very high levels of parliamentary cohesion, indeed so high that they are hardly ever systematically measured (for some exceptions, see Saalfeld 1995b; Bowler *et al.* 1999; Jensen 2000; Müller *et al.* 2001). And, as Laver and Schofield (1990: 15) have noted, 'parties do in practice tend to go into and come out of government as single actor'. Yet, 51 of 331 Western European coalition cabinets of the 1945–99 period (15.4 per cent) terminated due solely or in part to intra-party conflict (Müller and Strøm 2000a: 586). Thus, in these cases the members of at least one coalition party were not agreed that government participation was worth the price.

In parliamentary voting, the major British parties are generally referred to as models of strength and cohesion (e.g. Sartori 1997). British cabinets rarely fall over intra-party conflict. At most, the same party continues to govern under a new Prime Minister (such as John Major after the fall of Margaret Thatcher). This is due to the often comfortable majorities provided by plurality single-member elections (which then allow for some parliamentary dissent) and to the power, generated by electoral insecurity, of preference alignment between MPs and cabinet members. Given that a parliamentary seat is a prerequisite for executive office, and there are a large number of such executive offices, and since many parliamentary seats are electorally marginal, dissolution is a powerful threat. If elections were called and the incumbents lost, a large number of politicians—members of the government and MPs in marginal seats—would lose political office.

Yet, if anything, many continental European parties seem to outrank the British ones in parliamentary cohesion. Major backbench 'rebellions' (Cowley 2000) are extremely rare events in much of continental Europe, as are parliamentary defeats resulting from a lack of party cohesion. We can, however, identify two countries where the parties are clearly not very cohesive and hence constitute a challenge to governance: France and Italy. In Fifth Republic France, all three parties that have held the presidency and the prime ministership—the Gaullists, the UDF, and the Socialists—are weak. The non-socialist parties are first and foremost vehicles for the personal ambitions of individual politicians. They are characterized by 'the delights and poisons of factionalism, patronage and personal rivalry' (Fysh 1996: 90), as evidenced in the frequent breakdown of party cohesion in presidential elections since the 1970s. More recently they have fissured over European integration. The UDF, which always was a federation of different parties, has split over the issue of cooperation with the Front National (Knapp 2003). The Socialist Party traditionally has harboured several factions (Cole 1989), one of which broke away in the 1990s (creating the Mouvement des Citoyens) (Szarka 1999). More than anything else, the 2002 presidential election witnessed the dramatic inability of the Socialist Party to keep the Left together. Yet, French cabinets manage to survive and govern. Government institutions, in particular the electoral system (which forces political parties into stable alliances) and, as we will see below, government-friendly parliamentary institutions, allow cabinets that achievement.

Italy has similarly weak parties. David Hine (1993: 109) concisely summarizes the impact of factionalism in the so-called first Italian republic: 'The Italian Christian Democratic Party, and to a lesser extent its coalition partners, have deep internal divisions...[These divisions] ensure that authority to make policy is rarely delegated to a cohesive leadership group in government'. Political parties in the so-called second republic seem no stronger. As Verzichelli (2003) has shown, about 22 per cent of the lower-chamber MPs and 20 per cent of the Senators changed their party affiliation in its first two legislative terms. Indeed, since 1945 more coalition cabinets have been terminated due to intra-party conflict than in any other country (seventeen of the first fifty postwar cabinets) (Verzichelli and Cotta 2000), and absenteeism and frequent breakdowns of voting cohesion in Parliament have been characteristic of Italian politics. As yet, it remains unclear whether the parties of the second Italian republic will eventually consolidate and attain greater cohesion than those of the first.

DELEGATION FROM VOTERS TO MPs

Above we have surveyed the procedures by which the parliamentary democracies of Western Europe make fundamental political decisions. In this and the following sections, we shall examine how, and to what extent, citizens can select and control the politicians that make such decisions. We trace this selection and control through the four stages of democratic delegation, beginning with the transfer of authority from voters to members of parliament.

The simple act of voting is the first and fundamental stage of democratic delegation, and elections are the fundamental source of democratic legitimacy and accountability. Though the incumbents of other political offices may be variously selected, in all democracies citizens elect the members of at least one legislative chamber. Under parliamentary democracy, that may be about the extent of their direct delegation. The defining feature of parliamentarism is precisely that the core executive (the cabinet) is *not* popularly elected. Typically, parliamentary systems also feature fewer other directly elected officials (executive offices, judges, etc.) than presidential ones. Thus, parliamentary elections are the linchpin of popular selection and control.

Voters have a tough time delegating effectively. Even under the best of circumstances they have little opportunity to coordinate their behaviour. Moreover, many voters also have scant information about the individual agent (MP) to whom they delegate (see below). After all, voters are the 'amateurs' of representative democracy and politicians the 'professionals'. Thus, great information asymmetries exist, which in turn make agency loss more likely than in situations in which the distribution of information is more symmetrical.

Agency control in this first stage of delegation can thus be exercised either directly by the voters, or indirectly through political parties. Political parties may help voters by aligning the preferences of their representatives. Yet, there is a clear tension here in constitutional design. Mechanisms that help parties control their respective representatives may leave ordinary voters with scant influence, whereas institutions that empower the voters may weaken cohesion and control through political parties. Thus, intra-party candidate choice, for example, may enhance voter control over their elected representatives, but often at the cost of weakening party cohesion. In the classical parliamentary model, this tension has been resolved in favour of the parties, but our survey below will show whether this model still fits the contemporary democracies of Western Europe.

Constitutional and Statutory Rules

Democratic constitutions and other statutory instruments ameliorate agency problems between voters and parliamentarians in various ways, for example, by proscribing particularly inappropriate forms of agency. Such rules may eliminate parliamentary candidates considered morally or experientially unacceptable, such as felons or individuals that have gone through bankruptcy. Table 4.5 details the conditions under which an MP can be rendered ineligible or expelled from parliament. The legal means to expel elected members may reinforce the influence of parliamentary parties. But such eligibility requirements normally eliminate only a small number of potential candidates. And although most parliaments can under certain conditions expel their own members, these conditions are generally restrictive, and in a number of countries the final decision rests not with the parliament but with a court of law. Two mechanisms that might have more bite, term limits and popular recall procedures, are used in none of our countries. No Western European parliamentary democracy limits the number of terms an MP can serve, mandates a retirement age, or permits voters to recall an elected member.

Table 4.5. *The Legal Electoral Connection Between Citizens and MPs*

Country and year	Electoral formula	Smallest constituency	Largest constituency	No. of suppl. seats	Primaries[a]	Intra party pref voting	Inter party pref voting	Does an extra election end the electoral period?	Length of term	Can Parliament expel its members?	Conditions under which an MP loses his/her seat[b]	Rules of ineligibility for parl office[c]
Austria												
1945–8	List PR	3	12	n.a.	No	No	No	Yes	4	No	1, 3, 6, 7, 8	6, 7, 8
1949–70	List PR	3	12	n.a.	No	Yes	No	Yes	4	No	1, 3, 6, 8	6, 8
1971–91	List PR	4	12	n.a.	No	Yes	No	Yes	4	No	1, 3, 6, 8	6, 8
1992–2000	List PR	1	7	n.a.	Yes	Yes	No	Yes	4	No	1, 3, 6, 8	6, 8
Belgium												
1945–8	List PR	2	31	n.a.	No	Yes	No	Yes	4	Yes	1, 2, 3, 4, 5, 6, 8	1, 2, 3, 4, 5, 6, 8
1949–65	List PR	2	32	n.a.	No	Yes	No	Yes	4	Yes	1, 2, 3, 4, 5, 6, 8	1, 2, 3, 4, 5, 6, 8
1966–94	List PR	2	33	n.a.	No	Yes	No	Yes	4	Yes	1, 2, 3, 4, 5, 6, 8	1, 2, 3, 4, 5, 6, 8
1995–2000	List PR	2	22	n.a.	No	Yes	No	Yes	4	Yes	1, 2, 3, 4, 5, 6, 8	1, 2, 3, 4, 5, 6, 8
Denmark												
1945–9	List PR	2	8	31	No	Yes	No	Yes	4	Yes	10	10
1950–2	List PR	2	8	44	No	Yes	No	Yes	4	Yes	10	10
1953–63	List PR	2	11	40	No	Yes	No	Yes	4	Yes	10	10
1964–2000	List PR	2	15	40	No	Yes	No	Yes	4	Yes	10	10
Finland												
1945–50	List PR	1	31	n.a.	No	Yes	No	Yes	3	Yes	4, 8	4, 6, 7
1951–4	List PR	1	33	n.a.	No	Yes	No	Yes	3	Yes	4, 8	4, 6, 7
1955–61	List PR	1	33	n.a.	Yes	Yes	No	Yes	4	Yes	4, 8	4, 6, 7
1962–8	List PR	1	20	n.a.	No	Yes	No	Yes	4	Yes	4, 8	4, 6, 7
1969–71	List PR	1	20	n.a.	Legally required but not binding	Yes	No	Yes	4	Yes	4, 8	4, 6, 7
1972–4	List PR	1	20	n.a.	Legally required but not binding	Yes	No	Yes	4	Yes	4, 8	4, 7
1975–86	List PR	1	24	n.a.	Legally required but not binding	Yes	No	Yes	4	Yes	4, 8	4, 7
1987–94	List PR	1	29	n.a.	Legally required but not binding	Yes	No	Yes	4	Yes	4, 8	4, 7
1995–2000	List PR	1	31	n.a.	Legally required but not binding	Yes	No	Yes	4	Yes	4, 8	4, 7

Table 4.5. (contd.)

Country and year	Electoral formula	Smallest constituency	Largest constituency	No. of suppl. seats	Primaries[a]	Intra party pref voting	Inter party pref voting	Does an extra election end the electoral period?	Length of term	Can Parliament expel its members?	Conditions under which an MP loses his/her seat[b]	Rules of ineligibility for parl office[c]
France												
1959–84	Majority-plurality	1	1	n.a.	No	No	No	Yes	5	Yes	1, 4, 5, 9	4, 5, 6
1985–6	List PR	2	24	n.a.	No	No	No	Yes	5	Yes	1, 4, 5, 9	4, 5, 6
1987–9	Majority-plurality	1	1	n.a.	No	No	No	Yes	5	Yes	1, 4, 5, 9	4, 5, 6
1990–8	Majority-plurality	1	1	n.a.	No	No	No	Yes	5	Yes	1, 2, 4, 5, 9	2, 4, 5, 6
1999–2000	Majority-plurality	1	1	n.a.	No	No	No	Yes	5	Yes	1, 2, 4, 5, 9	2, 4, 5, 6
Germany												
1949–52	List PR	1	43[d]	n.a.	No	No	No	Yes	4	No	1, 2, 3, 7, 10, 11	8
1953–64	List PR	1	89	n.a.	No	No	No	Yes	4	No	1, 2, 3, 7, 10, 11	8
1965–78	List PR	1	80	n.a.	No	No	No	Yes	4	No	1, 2, 3, 7, 10, 11	8
1979–2000	List PR	1	77	n.a.	No	No	No	Yes	4	No	1, 2, 3, 7, 10, 11	8
Greece												
1975–80	List PR	1	25	n.a.	No	Yes	No	Yes	4	Yes	1, 3, 8, 9	4
1981–4	List PR	1	28	n.a.	No	Yes	No	Yes	4	Yes	1, 3, 8, 9	4
1985–8	List PR	1	32	n.a.	No	No	No	Yes	4	Yes	1, 3, 8, 9	4
1989–95	List PR	1	32	n.a.	No	Yes	No	Yes	4	Yes	1, 3, 8, 9	4
1996–2000	List PR	1	38	n.a.	No	Yes	No	Yes	4	Yes	1, 3, 8, 9	4
Iceland												
1945–58	Plurality + PR comb.	1	8	11	No	No	No	Yes	4	No	9	3, 8
1959–70	List PR	5	12	11	No	No	No	Yes	4	No	9	3, 8
1971–86	List PR	5	12	11	No	No	No	Yes	4	No	9	3, 8
1987–2000	List PR	5	18	9	No	No	No	Yes	4	No	9	3, 8
Ireland												
1945–6	STV	3	7	n.a.	No	Yes	Yes	Yes	5	Yes	4, 5, 6, 10	4, 5
1947–2000	STV	3	5	n.a.	No	Yes	Yes	Yes	5	Yes	4, 5, 6, 10	4, 5
Italy												
1946–94	List PR	1	54	n.a.	No	Yes	No	Yes	5	No	1, 3	1, 3, 6
1994–2000	Plurality + PR comb.	1	10	n.a	No	No	No	Yes	5	No	1, 3	1, 3, 6

Luxembourg												
1945–53	List PR	6	20	n.a.	No	Yes	Yes	Yes	6[e]	Yes	3, 4, 8, 11	5, 6, 8
1954–63	List PR	6	20	n.a.	No	Yes	Yes	Yes	5	Yes	3, 4, 8, 11	5, 6, 8
1964–83	List PR	6	23	n.a.	No	Yes	Yes	Yes	5	Yes	3, 4, 8, 11	5, 6, 8
1984–8	List PR	7	25	n.a.	No	Yes	Yes	Yes	5	Yes	3, 4, 8, 11	6, 8
1989–2000	List PR	7	23	n.a.	No	Yes	Yes	Yes	5	Yes	3, 4, 8, 11	6, 8
The Netherlands												
1945–2000	List PR	n.a.[f]	n.a.	n.a.	No	Yes	No	Yes	4	No	3	3, 4, 6, 9
Norway												
1945–52	List PR	3	8	n.a.	No	No	No	No	4	No	3, 4, 12	4
1953–84	List PR	4	13	n.a.	No	No	No	No	4	No	3, 4, 12	4
1985–8	List PR	4	13	n.a.	No	No	No	No	4	No	3, 4, 12	4
1989–2000	List PR	4	15	8	No	No	No	No	4	No	3, 4, 12	4
Portugal												
1976–2000	List PR	5	56	n.a.	No	No	No	Yes	4	Yes	7, 8	3, 4, 6, 8
Spain												
1977–2000	List PR	1	33	0	No	No	No	Yes	4	No	1, 3, 4, 6	3, 4, 6, 8, 9
Sweden												
1945–69	List PR	3	24	n.a.	No	No	No	No	4	No	1, 9	1, 6
1970–4	List PR	2	33	40	No	No	No	No	3	No	1, 9	1, 6
1975–88	List PR	2	33	39	No	No	No	No	3	No	1, 3, 9	1, 6
1989–94	List PR	2	33	39	No	No	No	No	3	No	1, 3, 9	1
1995–6	List PR	2	33	39	No	No	Yes	No	4	No	1, 3, 9	1
1997–2000	List PR	2	34	39	No	No	No	No	4	No	1, 3, 9	1
United Kingdom												
1945–2000	Plurality	1	1	n.a.	No	No	No	Yes	5	Yes	2, 10	3, 4, 5, 6, 8

Note: None of the countries in this study have legally required rules regarding (*a*) term limits, (*b*) mandatory retirement age, or (*c*) legally enforced recall mechanisms.

[a] Response to question whether parties represented in the parliament use primary elections and whether they are legally required.

[b] 0 = None (other than voluntary resignations), 1 = Election annulled, 2 = Campaign or election violation, 3 = Election or appointment to incompatible office. The automatic resignation can be temporal (as, e.g., in Norway and Sweden) or for the rest of the term, 4 = Incompatible occupation, 5 = Bankruptcy or incompatible economic interest, 6 = Insanity, 7 = Membership of illegal organization, 8 = Automatically upon conviction of certain crimes, 9 = By discretionary court decision upon conviction of certain crimes, 10 = By parliamentary decision upon conviction of certain crimes, 11 = By parliamentary decision in the absence of conviction of a crime, 12 = By successful impeachment through special procedure.

[c] 0 = None (other than lack of citizenship), 1 = Election annulled, 2 = Campaign or election violation, 3 = Election appointment to incompatible office, 4 = Incompatible occupation, 5 = Bankruptcy or incompatible economic interest, 6 = Insanity, 7 = Membership of illegal organization, 8 = Automatically upon conviction of certain crimes, 9 = By discretionary court decision upon conviction of certain crimes, 10 = By parliamentary decision upon conviction of certain crimes, 11 = By parliamentary decision in the absence of conviction of a crime, 12 = By successful impeachment through special procedure.

[d] The number of list seats allotted for Northrhine-Westfalia, the largest list constituency in Germany, changes frequently. In the table we report the largest number of constituency seats during the four time periods. The full list is as follows: 1949–52: 43; 1953–6: 72; 1957–60: 88; 1961–4: 89; 1965–8: 80; 1969–71: 78, 1972–9: 75; 1980–2: 76; 1983–6: 75; 1987–90: 72; 1991–3: 75; 1994–2000: 77.

[e] In Luxembourg 1945–53, half of the seats were up for re-election every third year.

[f] In The Netherlands the whole country is one constituency.

Electoral rules more narrowly defined are more critical to the voters' ability to contain agency costs.[11] Such rules define the terms of parliamentarians and their most important *ex post* constraint: re-election. They also regulate the competition between candidates, and between and to some extent within political parties. The classical electoral system, under parliamentary as well as presidential constitutions, was the 'single member district plurality' (SMDP) system. Today, only the United Kingdom retains this system for *all* seats in the national parliament. The typical Western European electoral system is instead List Proportional Representation (PR). The finer details vary, but a large majority of our countries (thirteen out of seventeen countries) use such a system. France is unusual in that although it has experimented with PR, it currently employs a two-stage single member district (SMD) system, which combines a majority principle (SMDM) at the first stage with a plurality rule at the second. Italy has recently moved to a mix of PR and SMDP. Germany formally also features such a combination but since the parties typically place the same candidates at the top of both types of lists, in practice the system functions as PR. Its mixed-member system has nonetheless been a model for many recent electoral reforms (Shugart and Wattenberg 2000). The Irish single-transferable vote (STV) system combines PR with inter-party candidate choice.

Legal rules concerning ballot access are one important way in which the people's representatives are controlled both before and after taking office. Simon Hug (2001: 178–81) has compiled information on the conditions new political parties (i.e. parties not yet represented in parliament) must meet to get on the ballot. His empirical analyses, however, demonstrate that these rules do little to explain the success or failure of new parties. We focus here on the rules that govern the ballot access of individual candidates. Except in Finland, intra-party candidate selection is not strictly regulated by the state. Finnish electoral law, however, (since 1969) requires political parties to hold 'primary elections'. Groups as small as fifteen party members can nominate parliamentary candidates, and when the number of nominated candidates is higher than the district magnitude (the number of representatives elected per district), parties are legally required to let their members vote. In practice, medium-sized and large parties must hold such intra-party elections. Formally, membership influence is somewhat restricted in that the party's district executive body may replace up to a quarter of the candidates put forward by local branches. In practice, however, the district party organizations tend not to avail themselves of this right.[12]

In our PR systems, district magnitude varies substantially both within and across countries. We thus find districts as small as one (1) representative (which obviously does not permit any proportionality in seat distribution), whereas the largest of the German *Länder*, Northrhine-Westphalia, in 1998 elected as many as seventy-seven Bundestag

---

[11] The electoral process is governed by an often complex set of institutions, but the most important rules are those that (*a*) determine which candidates get access to the electoral ballot, and (*b*) translate the popular vote into legislative (or other) representation (Katz 1997). It is common to refer to the former as rules concerning ballot access and the latter as electoral rules (or system) proper. However, like Gary Cox (1997: 38) we wish to avoid that somewhat artificial distinction.

[12] As the country chapters and Table 4.4 show, other European parties have similar candidate selection mechanisms that include 'membership voting'. But since these are not legally mandated, they are not reported here.

members via the *Land* list (70 since 2002) in addition to the MPs elected in single-member constituencies (64 in 2002). In The Netherlands, the whole country is one constituency with 150 members.

A substantial district magnitude is necessary for PR to have many of its putative effects (such as the enhancement of proportionality). In closed-list PR systems, which in our sample includes Germany, Norway, Portugal, and Spain, the leading list candidates of major parties are often very likely to be elected and are thus somewhat cushioned against adverse election results. And the greater the district magnitude, the more effectively parties can use ballot placement to reward or punish incumbent MPs. Thus, district magnitude is an important part of electoral system design, and a large magnitude facilitates centralized party control (Taagepera and Shugart 1989; Cox 1997).

On the other hand, a low district magnitude, and particularly a magnitude of one, is traditionally seen as a key to a strong constituency link, which helps voters identify their representatives and hold them accountable for government policy (e.g. see, Loewenberg and Patterson 1979: 45–8). Do SMD systems therefore ensure greater MP accountability more generally? Such accountability requires both voter information and the ability to coordinate in accordance with popular preferences. SMD electoral systems should have an advantage in informational simplicity compared to electoral systems that link large numbers of voters to large pools of MPs.[13] Based on data from fifteen to nineteen countries from three continents, Norris (2001) shows that voters in SMD systems indeed have a better knowledge of candidates and more contacts with MPs than those in multimember systems, although mixed-member systems outperform both on these criteria.[14] The case also seems straightforward with respect to the ease of coordination. Generally, under SMD it takes comparatively little voter coordination to unseat an unpopular MP. Since there is only one incumbent per district, all that dissatisfied voters need to do is to coordinate on a serious competitor.

Some students of electoral systems (e.g. Mitchell 2000) argue that the high number of 'safe seats' in such SMD systems as the United Kingdom means that in reality only a relatively small subset of seats are contestable. Thus, the Conservative Party is extremely unlikely ever to lose Canterbury, while the Labour Party is equally unlikely to be defeated in several constituencies in South Wales. According to Linton and Southcott (1998: 52, 79) only 114 of the 432 seats (26.3 per cent) in which Labour and the Conservatives were the two leading parties in the 1997 elections were 'marginal' (i.e. a Conservative or Labour lead of less than 10 per cent of their combined vote). In other words, under first-past-the-post (SMD) systems the competitiveness of individual districts matters, and in Britain the geographical distribution of voter preferences diminishes accountability.[15]

---

[13] However, in a case study of the now-defunct Italian Democrazia Cristiana, Golden and Chang (2001) show that intense intra-party competition for preference votes had the unintended consequence of corrupting MPs.

[14] Thus, 76% of German and 69% of Norwegian voters know at least one candidate, compared to 61% of British voters. The picture is more mixed with regard to contacts with MPs. Such contacts are claimed by 15% of the voters in Norway, 13% in the United Kingdom, 11% in Germany, 5% in The Netherlands, and 3% in Spain (Norris 2001: 890–1).

[15] A good summary of the British electoral system debate is in *The Report of the Independent Commission on the Voting System*. London: Stationary Office, 1998 (Cm 4090-I).

The SMD systems present the voters with only one candidate per party. As of 2000, voters in seven countries (Austria, Belgium, Denmark, Finland, Greece, The Netherlands, and Sweden) can select specific candidates from the list of their chosen party. Intra-party preference voting has become somewhat more widespread over the postwar period. It was established in Austria in 1949 and Sweden in 1997, whilst Greece has gone back and forth, but currently also allows for preference votes. Italy, however, has gone in the opposite direction. A 1991 referendum abolished the intra-party preference vote, and in 1994 Italy introduced the single-member plurality system for three-quarters of the MPs while the remainder is elected by closed-list PR. At least in general elections, voters in Ireland and Luxembourg enjoy the privilege of being able to choose both among candidates and parties. The Irish electorate votes for individual candidates in multimember constituencies and can rank candidates from different parties. This often proves highly effective. In 2002, for instance, Fine Gael, the main opposition party, lost its deputy leader and nine out of sixteen of its frontbench team due to such preference voting. Voters in Luxembourg can also rank specific candidates, regardless of party.

Although PR electoral systems increasingly allow for intra-party preference voting, this trend is by no means overwhelmingly strong. Moreover, in practice, relatively few MPs owe their seats in parliament to this instrument. This is in part because intra-party preference voting allows voters only to reward, but not punish, candidates (by striking them out or moving them to the bottom of the list). Thus, leaving aside the STV system, the effects of preference voting range from insignificant to modest. In some countries, where candidates are ranked on party lists, preference voting favours a small subset of candidates that would not otherwise have been elected (as Austria, Belgium, The Netherlands, and Sweden). But as a check on the party leadership, such preference voting is less effective since it is not the people at the top of the list that lose their seat but rather the candidates at the end of the list of the 'safe seats'. And even when only preference votes are decisive and there is no bias in favour of high-ranking candidates (as in Denmark, Finland, Luxembourg, and Italy before 1994), unpopular incumbents can be deselected only if a sufficient number of voters converge on the same replacement candidate. In practical terms this requires intensive coordination and low-ranking list candidates with significant electoral appeal. Yet, the potential effects of preference voting are surely much greater than the actual effects that we have observed thus far.

Intraparty Rules

Since political parties play such a crucial role in the screening of parliamentarians, particularly in closed-list PR systems, Table 4.6 reports on *intraparty* selection rules for all parties that have been represented in the cabinet. Only Icelandic parties hold 'open' primary elections (contests in which the right to vote is not restricted to party members) among candidates from the same party. Note that Icelandic electoral law does not require primaries, which instead reflect the political parties' response to citizens' calls for more openness (see Chapter 12). But while the Austrian People's Party at one time (in 1994) also subscribed to primary elections, this party statute soon became a dead letter, which the party chose not to observe in the early election of 1995 or in the regular one in 1999.

Primary elections defined more permissively as involving a vote among the party members over a list of nominated candidates have become increasingly common. This

Table 4.6. *Party Rules on Candidate Selection*[a]

Country and year	Does any party permit non-members to vote on candidate selection?	Type of involvement of party members in 'primaries'?[b]	Are there parties with term limits?	Are there parties with a mandatory retirement age?
Austria				
1945–66	No	None	No	No
1967–90	No	None	No	Yes
1991–2000	Yes[c]	Conditionally or partially binding[c]	No	No
Belgium				
1945–68	No	Fully binding	No	No
1969–80	No	None	No	Yes
1981–2000	No	None	Yes	Yes
Denmark				
1945–2000	No	None	No	No
Finland				
1959–2000	No	Conditionally or partially binding	No	No
France				
1959–2000	No	None	No	No
Germany				
1949–2000	No	None	No	No
Greece				
1974–2000	No	None	No	No
Iceland				
1945–69	No	None	No	No
1970–2000	Yes	Conditionally or partially binding	No	No
Ireland				
1945–95	No	None	No	No
1996–2000	No	Conditionally or partially binding	No	No
Italy				
1946–2000	No	None	Yes	No
Luxembourg				
1945–2000	No	None	No	No
The Netherlands				
1946–2000	No	None	No	No
Norway				
1945–2000	No	None	No	Yes
Portugal				
1976–2000	No	None	No	No
Spain				
1977–2000	No	None	No	No
Sweden				
1945–2000	No	Non-binding	No	No
United Kingdom				
1945–2000	No	None	No	No

[a] Only parties that have been represented in the cabinet are included.

[b] The categories 'Non-binding', 'Conditionally or partially binding', and 'Fully binding', imply an increasing degree of influence of membership voting. The categories are reported only when half or more of all parties in the respective country use this selection procedure.

[c] Still valid party statue but not observed after 1994.

is the minimal definition of a 'primary election' in Tables 4.5 and 4.6. The country chapters provide further information on membership involvement and the competition for ballot access. Yet, only in a minority of countries does a majority of all relevant parties (here defined as parties that have participated in the cabinet) allow members to vote on candidate selection. Currently at least some of the major parties in Austria, Finland, Iceland, Ireland, The Netherlands, and Sweden permit such membership participation, though again practice does not in all cases live up to their claims.

In the vast majority of parties, MPs formally owe their nomination to subnational party units (constituency organization, district, or *Land* organization). This is true even if we take into account the informal influence of the national party organization, which, of course, is hard to measure. Generally, national party organizations can exercise some influence over subnational candidate nomination, either by special quotas (as in Austria) or by offering the right 'type' of candidate (Gallagher and Marsh 1988; Katz and Mair 1992).[16] Anecdotal evidence suggests that it is much harder for the national party to veto the nomination of specific candidates unless they resort to such dramatic means as expelling MPs from the parliamentary party.

Most studies of parties and candidate selection suggest that there is a significant electoral advantage to incumbency. Not only do incumbents often control the constituency organizations that nominate candidates, but they also benefit from greater name recognition and from past opportunities to claim credit for policy initiatives and constituency service, and generally to advertise themselves to their voters (Mayhew 1974). Except for some green parties, only in Belgium and Italy have established parties imposed term limits on their MPs. Enforcement must rely exclusively on party-internal mechanisms (Müller 2000*a*). Except for some Austrian, Belgian, and Norwegian parties, Western European political parties have also refrained from introducing a mandatory retirement age for politicians. Moreover, incumbents are in a position to take many other steps to enhance their standing with their electorate in ways that are difficult to monitor. These advantages may translate into a significant moral hazard problem internal to political parties and their candidates.

Parliamentary Dissolution and Campaigns

Since Second World War, the Parliaments of Western Europe have been elected for terms of 3–6 years.[17] National law determines whether or not election timing is fixed

---

[16] According to Gallagher (1988: 245) the role of the party centre in candidate selection is (*a*) insignificant in Austria, Belgium, Finland, Germany, Norway, and the United Kingdom, (*b*) significant, but decisive only for a minority of candidates, in Ireland, Italy, and The Netherlands, and (*c*) dominant in France and Greece. This largely conforms with Bille's study of candidate selection in eleven Western European countries (2001: 366). We can add Denmark and Sweden to the first category. The best comparative candidate selection data refer to elections to the European Parliament, for which most countries have a nationwide constituency. When asked to assess the importance of the national versus subnational party organization, candidates in Spain, The Netherlands, Belgium, Italy, and France have ranked the support of the national party organization as more important than that of the local and regional organizations, whereas the opposite is the case in Denmark, Germany, and the United Kingdom. In Ireland the two are rated as equally important (Norris 1997: 222).

[17] In the vast majority of our Western European countries (in twelve cases) Parliament is elected for a 4-year term, whereas currently five countries (France, Ireland, Italy, Luxembourg, and the United Kingdom) have a 5-year term. Sweden and Finland have previously tried 3-year terms and Luxembourg early in the postwar period elected MPs for 6-years.

and predictable, or subject to political manipulation. In fact, in all our states but Norway, the constitution permits early (or extra) parliamentary elections. Under the German Basic Law, such premature termination is severely restricted (although it has occurred twice). Sweden discourages dissolution by requiring that elections be held at predetermined and regular intervals, regardless of any intervening (extra) election. Fixed election dates reduce the information advantages of the incumbents. Even without such institutional means to determine the election date, they can plan the political agenda so that the parliamentary term ends with the enactment or, preferably, implementation, of popular reforms, for example, tax cuts, or at the peak of the business cycle (Nordhaus 1975; Tufte 1978; Willett 1988; Mueller 1989: 277–86). Yet, exogenous political shocks, for example, a sudden economic downturn, can easily bring such plans to nought. Hence being able to schedule parliamentary elections at will is a real boon for incumbents, and the record suggests that governing parties do exploit this advantage (Strøm and Swindle 2002).

Citizen control over parliamentarians may also depend on the rules concerning campaigning and electoral competition. Since political candidates seek to gain support from an electorate that often has little prior knowledge of them, the length of campaigns matters. The longer the campaign, the more opportunities voters have to scrutinize the candidates on offer. In some countries, campaign length is directly or indirectly regulated. Where opportunities for early parliamentary dissolution are either non-existent or tightly circumscribed (see above and Table 4.12), parties and candidates can confidently anticipate election dates and thus schedule their own campaign activities. Where early dissolution is more likely (such as in the United Kingdom, Denmark, or Ireland), direct regulation of campaign duration is more important. The shorter the campaign, the greater the potential incumbency advantage. Table 4.7 shows how the length of political campaigns is regulated. In half of the twelve countries that we can classify, the minimum campaign is shorter than a month, in three (Austria, Germany, and Italy) it is roughly one month, and in three countries (Finland, Luxembourg, The Netherlands) it is considerably longer.

Table 4.7 also includes other legal rules that pertain to the *fairness of interparty competition*.[18] If incumbent politicians are able to manipulate the agenda and stack the deck in their favour, fairness clearly suffers. But while there is agreement on some minimal conditions that make elections free and fair (e.g. one person–one vote, no election-related violence or coercion, no electoral fraud), other normative standards, or at least their operational implications, are less clear. Thus, the rules of competition may systematically disadvantage new competitors and hence sustain a cartel of traditional parties (Müller 1993; Katz and Mair 1995). Three common forms of discrimination are against (*a*) the opposition in general, (*b*) smaller parties, and (*c*) new parties.

Broadcasting and Polling

Fairness demands that all relevant parties have some access to channels of communication with the voters. Given the importance of voter information, media discrimination

---

[18] See Elklit and Svensson (2001) and Choe (1997) for a more comprehensive discussion of free elections.

Table 4.7. *Rules of Electoral Competition*

Country and year	Minimum length of campaign (days)	Public broadcasting time				Commercial advertising permitted?[c]	Restrictions on the publications of opinion polls
		Free time for Parliamentary parties	Allocation[a]	Free time for parties not represented in Parliament	Allocation[b] (in comparison to parl. parties)		
Austria							
1945–68	21	Yes	Proportional	No	n.a.	Not permitted	No
1969–91	32	Yes	Proportional	No	n.a.	Not permitted	No
1992–2000	31	Yes	Proportional	No	n.a.	Not permitted	No
Belgium							
1945–84	n.a.	Yes	Proportional	Yes	Minimum quota	Not permitted	No
1985–91	n.a.	Yes	Proportional	Yes	Minimum quota	Not permitted	Yes
1992–2000	n.a.	Yes	Proportional	Yes	Minimum quota	Not permitted	No
Denmark							
1945–2000	21	Yes	Equal	Yes	Equal	Not permitted	No
Finland							
1945–2000	50	No	n.a.	No	n.a.	Unrestricted	No
France							
1959–76	20	Yes	Proportional	Yes	Minimum quota	Not permitted	No
1977–2000	20	Yes	Proportional	Yes	Minimum quota	Not permitted	Yes
Germany							
1949–2000	30	Yes	Proportional	Yes	Minimum quota	Not permitted	No
Greece							
1975–88	30	Yes	Proportional	Yes	Minimum quota	Not permitted	No
1989–95	30	Yes	Proportional	Yes	Minimum quota	Unrestricted	No
1996–2000	30	Yes	Proportional	Yes	Minimum quota	Unrestricted	Yes
Iceland							
1945–2000	n.a.	Yes	Equal	Yes	Less time (over minimum quota)	Permitted	No
Ireland							
1945–64	21	No	n.a.	No	n.a.	Not permitted	No
1965–76	21	Yes	Proportional	No	n.a.	Not permitted	No
1977–2000	21	Yes	Proportional	Yes	Minimum quota	Not permitted	No

Italy							
1948–75	30	Yes	Equal	No	n.a.	Not permitted	No
1976–92	30	Yes	Equal	Yes	Minimum quota	Not permitted	No
1993–2000	30	Yes	Proportional	Yes	Minimum quota	Not permitted	Yes
Luxembourg							
1945–58	60	n.a.	n.a.	n.a.	n.a.	n.a.	n.a.
1959–67	60	No	n.a.	No	n.a.	Not permitted	No
1968–83	60	Yes	Proportional	Yes	Minimum quota	Not permitted	No
1984–2000	60	Yes	Proportional	Yes	Minimum quota	Not permitted	Yes
The Netherlands							
1945–89	43	Yes	Equal	No	n.a.	Not permitted	No
1990–2000	43	Yes	Equal	Yes	n.a.	Unrestricted	No
Norway							
1945–93	n.a.	No	n.a	No	n.a.	Not permitted	No
1994–8	n.a.	No	n.a	No	n.a.	Not permitted	Yes
1999–2000	n.a.	No	n.a	No	n.a.	Restricted	Yes
Portugal							
1976–94	20	Yes	Proportional	Yes	Minimum quota	Not permitted	Yes
1995–2000	13	Yes	Proportional	Yes	Minimum quota	Not permitted	Yes
Spain							
1977–84	21	Yes	Proportional	Yes	Equal	Not permitted	No
1985–2000	15	Yes	Proportional	Yes	Minimum quota	Not permitted	Yes
Sweden							
1945–59	80	No	n.a.	No	n.a.	Not permitted	No
1960–4	80	Yes	Equal	No	n.a.	Not permitted	No
1965–82	80	No	n.a.	No	n.a.	Not permitted	No
1983–8	50	No	n.a.	No	n.a.	Not permitted	No
1989–2000	35	No	n.a.	No	n.a.	Not permitted	No
United Kingdom							
1945–83	20	Yes	Proportional	Yes	Equal	Not permitted	No
1984–2000	16	Yes	Proportional	Yes	Equal	Not permitted	No

Note: 'n.a.' means not applicable in this case.

[a] The distinction here is between 'equal' allocation of time for all parliamentary parties or an allocation of time 'proportional' to the size of the parties

[b] The distinction here is whether non-parliamentary parties get an 'equal' allocation of time compared to parliamentary parties. Alternatively, do they get an allocation (minimum quota) that is smaller than the allocation for parliamentary parties, but the same for all non-parliamentary parties? The third entry, 'less time', is used when non-parliamentary parties get more than a minimum or equal share of broadcasting time, but they still get less time than parliamentary parties.

[c] This refers only to the purchasing of broadcasting time, not free broadcasting time.

against particular political parties may seriously hamper their ability to compete. But what, exactly, does 'equal access to publicly controlled media' (Elklit and Svensson 2001: 204) mean in practice: equal time for all competitors, or access proportional to their strength in previous elections? And should it include all registered parties or only those already represented in parliament?

While all media may favour or disfavour specific parties, the media owned or licensed by the state are a particular concern. The government can abuse its authority over these media to get preferential treatment or to deny the opposition access. Alternatively, it can allocate at least some minimum public broadcasting time to all political parties. Table 4.7 thus reports on the time public broadcasting corporations provide during which the respective parties can control the content, excluding the corporation's own political reports, interviews, studio debates, etc. Except for three Nordic countries (Finland, Norway, and Sweden), our states do allocate some free public broadcasting time to political parties. Most even grant access to some parties without parliamentary representation.

A related question is whether parties are permitted to purchase (additional) broadcasting time. An unrestricted market in political advertising tends to favour wealthy parties relative to poor ones. Hence, media regulations can be presented as a means to equalize electoral opportunities. On the other hand, such restrictions may disadvantage parties that have poor media access (such as opposition parties or parties disfavoured by the media) and it may enhance the opportunities for media favouritism. Except for Finland, Greece (since 1989), Iceland, The Netherlands (since 1990 and only within limits), and Norway (since 1999 and only on public radio), most Western European countries do not allow parties to purchase advertising time from public broadcasting corporations. Yet, these restrictive rules pertain to the domestic broadcasting corporations and not to the political parties per se. Since television has become international, parties can bypass these restrictions through satellite transmission and channels based in foreign countries and hence not obligated by these rules. Indeed, German political parties have frequently bought television time from private channels based in neighbouring countries that target the German market.

Finally, Table 4.7 details restrictions on the publication of opinion polls prior to or during elections. It has been argued that the manipulative power of polls requires such restrictions. Opponents respond that bans on polling place the public at an informational disadvantage vis-à-vis parties and politicians (Mann and Orren 1992). Although some countries may restrict polls through gentlemen's agreements or other voluntary accords, here we account for formal-legal rules only. Currently such restrictions—most of which were introduced in the 1980s and 1990s—exist in seven of our seventeen countries, including all the Southern European ones. In addition, Belgium had such restrictions for a short time (1985–91), but eventually abolished them. In 2002, France reduced the ban to 2 days, Election Day and the day before that.

Legal Restrictions on Campaign Spending

Governments may also place legal restrictions on campaign spending, ostensibly often to help parties that have comparatively limited financial resources. Campaign law reformers in the United States, for instance, argue that such caps strengthen the power of ideas vis-à-vis the power of money. On the other hand, such caps may help government parties or parties with great media access, which need fewer resources of their own to develop and advertise their policies. The country chapters do give some indication of the problems that new parties face in contesting established ones. However, judging from the country chapters, there is no obvious correspondence between the legal caps on campaign spending in Belgium, France, Greece, Ireland, Italy, Portugal, and Spain, and more favourable conditions for new parties.

Table 4.8 reports how political parties and electoral campaigns are financed, which again has much to do with electoral contestability (allowing entry to new challengers) and fairness. Note that these are data on *direct* and *public* party subventions only, that is, money that goes directly to the extra-parliamentary party and/or the parliamentary party group.[19] Existing studies of direct public party finance freely acknowledge the problems of cross-national comparison (e.g. see Katz and Mair 1992).[20] These problems are truly staggering with regard to private sources of party finance. In this context, we therefore satisfy ourselves with an inventory of when public party financing was introduced and whether parties outside parliament benefit.

As Table 4.8 shows, since the 1970s public party finance has been a universal feature of Western European democracies. One danger of public party finance is that it may help sustain a cartel of established parties and petrify the existing party system (Paltiel 1981: 170). Thus, in some countries (Belgium, Finland, Iceland, Ireland, Italy, Luxembourg, The Netherlands, and the United Kingdom) a quarter of a century or more has passed without any extension of public funding to non-parliamentary parties. Cartelization is less likely if public money is extended to parties not represented in parliament, which is currently the case in seven countries (Austria, Denmark, France, Germany, Greece, Norway, and Sweden). Here, parties with and without parliamentary representation were in most cases granted public subsidies simultaneously or within a few years. However, if anything, the party systems of the former countries have been less stable than those of the latter, which suggests that the exclusion of non-parliamentary parties from state subsidies is not sufficient to freeze party systems.[21]

Controlling Members of Parliament

Delegation from voters to parliamentarians is fraught with potential agency problems. In parliamentary democracies, such agency problems are contained, but sometimes also

---

[19] Thus, we do not cover indirect forms of public party or campaign finance, such as public staff for the party in public office, free telephone access, free mail, or free broadcasting time in 'public service' media.

[20] Drawing on his massive edited volume on comparative party finance (Nassmacher 2001), Karl-Heinz Nassmacher (2002) ranks eight Western European countries according to per capita annual public party finance. Austria (USD 19.00) and Sweden (USD 11.00) stand out, followed by Germany and France (USD 4.90 and 4.20, respectively), whilst Spain, Italy, The Netherlands, and the United Kingdom spend only between USD 1.50 and USD 0.07 per capita.

[21] This is confirmed by more intensive empirical research on the effects of public party finance in a smaller number of countries (Pierre *et al.* 2000; Nassmacher 2001: 191–2).

Table 4.8. *Public Party Finance and Spending Caps*

Country and year	Does public party financing exist?	Public money for parties not in Parliament?	Legal cap on spending?
Austria			
1945–62	No	No	No
1963–74	Yes	No	No
1975–2000	Yes	Yes	No
Belgium			
1945–70	No	No	No
1971–88	Yes	No	No
1989–2000	Yes	No	Yes
Denmark			
1945–64	No	No	No
1965–85	Yes	No	No
1986–2000	Yes	Yes	No
Finland			
1945–66	No	No	No
1967–2000	Yes	No	No
France			
1959–88	No	No	No
1989–2000	Yes	Yes	Yes
Germany			
1949–53	No	No	No
1954–8	Yes	No	No
1959–66	Yes	No	No
1967–2000	Yes	Yes	No
Greece			
1975–83	No	No	No
1984–95	Yes	Yes	No
1996–2000	Yes	Yes	Yes
Iceland			
1945–70	No	No	No
1971–2000	Yes	No	No
Ireland			
1945–62	Yes	No	Yes
1963–96	Yes	No	No
1997–2000	Yes	No	Yes
Italy			
1948–74	No	No	No
1975–92	Yes	No	No
1993–2000	Yes	No	Yes
Luxembourg			
1945–64	No	No	No
1965–2000	Yes	No	No
The Netherlands			
1945–63	No	No	No
1964–2000	Yes	No	No
Norway			
1945–69	No	No	No
1970–4	Yes	No	No
1975–2000	Yes	Yes	No
Portugal			
1976–87	No	No	Yes
1988–2000	Yes	No	Yes

Table 4.8. *(contd.)*

Country and year	Does public party financing exist?	Public money for parties not in Parliament?	Legal cap on spending?
Spain			
1977–84	Yes	No	No
1985–2000	Yes	No	Yes
Sweden			
1945–65	No	No	No
1966–71	Yes	No	No
1972–2000		Yes	
United Kingdom			
1945–74	No	No	No
1975–2000	Yes	No	No

exacerbated, by the presence of political parties. By themselves, electoral systems have quite different consequences for candidate accountability. But because of the central role of political parties, these differences are mitigated and candidate accountability cannot be understood without reference to the strengths and weaknesses of parties (Müller 2000a).

Traditionally, political parties, rather than ordinary voters, have possessed the means to control parliamentarians. And as Katz and Mair (1995) have argued, party elites increasingly rely on the state to fund and support their existence, which reduces their need for and reliance on activists for labour and funds.[22] While this continues to be the case, there are growing chinks in the parties' armour. In many countries political parties have responded to calls for more openness and internal democracy by allowing such reforms as party primaries (Bille 2001) or preference voting. For Western Europe as a whole this remains the exception rather than the rule, but the increase in membership participation and voter choice reflect party efforts to open up and democratize their organizations (or, at least, give that impression). Such reforms may be driven by a growing popular suspicion that delegation through political parties is fraught with as many dangers as delegation anywhere else.

Much of the regulation of elections and campaigns suits the interests of those already in power. Thus, the rules and conventions that govern candidate selection favour incumbents (Somit *et al.* 1994). Campaign rules, the rules of media access, and public funding also have clear incumbency effects. What is interesting, however, is that these discriminate less against newcomers than they help support (or 'prop up') political parties in general. Again, this may reflect the concerns of a cartel of party leaders who sense that their entire 'business' is under siege.

Yet, not all trends in election and campaign regulation display such consistency. For some of the electoral regulations considered in this volume (e.g. the publication of preelectoral opinion polls) there are no clear cross-national patterns. While a few countries, for example, the Iberian democracies, or Germany and Austria, tend to converge, the bulk of the countries cluster differently on the various dimensions. Maybe this reflects the fact

---

[22] Yet, there are empirical studies of Western European party finance that suggest that in some countries public subsidies have been extended without at least some of the detrimental effect ascribed to them (Pierre *et al.* 2000).

that the normative debate is far from conclusive. Moreover, in reality national regulations often do not reflect a coherent view of how elections should be governed, but rather take the form of an ad hoc response to specific problems (e.g. a party finance scandal).

DELEGATION FROM PARLIAMENT TO CABINET

The next stage in the parliamentary chain of delegation is one step removed from the voters: the selection and control of the core executive (Prime Minister and cabinet). Constitutionally, this is a crucial and pivotal phase in the democratic chain of delegation (Müller 2000a: 323–7). In ideal-typical parliamentary systems, MPs are the only directly elected national agents of the people. Parliamentarians in turn directly or indirectly delegate to the Prime Minister and other members of the core executive. These are indeed the only agents directly accountable to parliament, and this very linkage is the crux of parliamentarism.

In the link between parliament and executive, the potential for agency loss is large and obvious. Parliamentarians face problems of adverse selection as well as moral hazard. The many perquisites available to cabinet members may well draw the 'wrong kind' of aspirants. Moreover, even well-intentioned politicians face serious temptations, since parliamentary oversight is often ineffective. Given the myriad of opportunities that cabinet members have to make policy and other decisions, moral hazard may indeed be the most likely agency problem.

Agency loss among cabinet members may take several forms. It is widely known from the scandal sheets and anecdotal evidence (though not extensively documented in the academic literature) that cabinet members often gratify themselves with fancy cars and living quarters, use government airplanes for private trips, host unnecessarily lavish receptions, or make other inappropriate uses of government money. While ministers tend to see such profligacy as 'fringe benefits' for their hard word, if disclosed it usually inflicts damage on their party and may endanger the re-election prospects of their co-partisans (who therefore have an incentive to prevent ministers from such behaviour). And if ministers use their office as a ticket to high society and its indulgences, the bitter fruits of leisure shirking and rent-seeking may follow. In serious cases, cabinet members become 'kleptocrats' (Rose-Ackerman 1999), draining the public coffers for their own benefit (or those of their families and friends). In international comparison, the democracies of Western Europe are probably not the most seriously afflicted, but the incentive for agency loss is nonetheless there.

Even politicians who have previously been loyal partisans may not always be reliable agents as cabinet members. Government ministers have typically reached the peak of their political careers and hence will not self-interestedly act as 'robotic party delegate(s)' but 'opt for a quiet life or establishing a personal reputation as an efficacious decision-maker, both of which might well maximize their post-ministerial career prospects in business or elsewhere in public life' (Dunleavy and Bastow 2001: 3, 6).[23] Under such

---

[23] Blondel shows that in Scandinavia, The Netherlands, Austria, Britain, and France, the ministerial career is 'truly a springboard for a third career' (1991: 170).

circumstances ministers may follow the cues of civil servants, their department's clientele, or the media, whenever doing so seems more rewarding than following the party line or popular preferences. Thus, cabinet members may make policy decisions contrary to the preferences of the parliamentarians that stand behind them.

As this brief discussion makes clear, the link between MPs and ministers, even if they belong to one and the same party, is problematic. This is even more the case in coalition governments where typically no party link exists between the ministers and the majority of MPs. Moreover, recruitment patterns may be such that cabinet members have little in common with MPs. When cabinet ministers are drawn from the pool of MPs they are more likely to share preferences with those members that remain in parliament. In any case, they have gone through the same recruitment processes and share the parliamentary experience. But as De Winter (1991: 48) has shown, in the 1945–84 period 12 per cent of cabinet members in Western Europe were outsiders who had had practically no prior political experience.[24]

Yet, even cabinet members recruited from the ranks of MPs may have interests and incentives not known, and often not acceptable, to their colleagues in parliament. And once in office, they have ample opportunity to act on them. Besides, there is a long-standing argument concerning the skills of MPs as cabinet ministers. According to Richard Rose (1976: 364), the chief skills of MPs 'concern personal relations and the effective oral presentation of ideas'. In the words of Bruce Headey (1974), although former MPs are well qualified to act as 'policy selectors' and 'ambassador ministers,' cabinet members also need to be 'policy initiators' and 'executive minister' (i.e. they must be able to direct a large organization—their department). As Headey (1974) concludes, MPs are not specially trained to serve as department managers and, as Rose (1976: 368) puts it, 'the role for which prior parliamentary work offers least preparation is that of a policy initiator'. To the discomfort of advocates of strong parliamentary government, in which the cabinet members are recruited from parliament exclusively, Rose (1976: 369) concludes that 'there is nothing in parliamentary work that gives this experience to MPs before they become ministers'. MPs may be able to acquire the requisite qualifications prior or parallel to their parliamentary career, for instance, in business. Otherwise, however, limiting the choice of cabinet members to the pool of government MPs may help the willingness of the spirit, but not the strength of the flesh.

Thus, MPs cannot take it for granted that candidates for cabinet positions have the capacity and incentives to act in the parliamentary majority's best interest. Hence, parliamentarians must look for institutional and other ways to screen candidates and ensure accountability at the very core of government. Four mechanisms are particularly spectacular and make for national and often international headlines: cabinet inauguration, no-confidence votes, confidence votes, and parliamentary dissolution. The former two are mechanisms by which the parliamentary majority can seek to control the cabinet through scrutiny and the threat of replacement. The latter two are

---

[24] According to De Winter (1991: 48), 'outsiders' were particularly common in The Netherlands (37.5%), Luxembourg (24.1%), Sweden (21%), and Austria (20.2%), and practically unknown in Ireland (0%), the United Kingdom (2.6%), and Italy (2.4%). Greece, Iceland, Portugal, and Spain were not included in this study.

countervailing powers held by the cabinet (sometimes specifically by the PM or Head of State). They similarly contain threats that can be used to diffuse parliamentary dissent or more generally to align preferences between the cabinet and the parliamentary majority. These four mechanisms can be combined in various ways and we believe that together with the design of the electoral systems, these combinations are the most important variations in delegation design and accountability mechanisms among parliamentary democracies.

Cabinet Inauguration

One of the most celebrated and public events in modern democracies is government inauguration. In parliamentary regimes parliamentarians select, or at least tacitly accept or reject, a PM and his or her cabinet. This is largely a party-dominated process (Andeweg and Nijzink 1995). Thus, parliamentarians—as we stress throughout this book—are constrained by the political parties that select them as candidates and that by virtue of their 'brand name' often guarantee their election. Thus, the distribution of seats and bargaining power among the political parties in parliament usually determines the outcome of the formation process.[25] Yet, the tools (mechanisms) provided by the constitution shape the behaviour of both MPs and political parties in this process.

Contemporary constitutions typically designate the constitutional actor that appoints the PM (a power most commonly vested in the Head of State) and determines whether or not an incoming head of government needs to submit to a vote of investiture. In the latter case, to enhance the ability of parliament to contain adverse selection problems, the constitution may even prescribe a policy statement (government declaration) to be delivered by the presumptive PM. Historically, cabinet appointment was the prerogative of the Monarch. As parliamentary government developed, Parliaments wrested this prerogative out of his control. In some countries Monarchs were replaced by Presidents elected either directly (e.g. Austria, Finland, France, Iceland, Ireland, and Portugal), or by an electoral college composed largely or entirely of MPs (Germany, Greece, and Italy). In the other countries, the Monarch is still the Head of State. With the exception of Sweden (since 1975), where the Speaker of Parliament nominates the PM, their respective constitutions formally leave it to the Monarch to appoint the PM. Although the actual role of the Monarch in government formation is largely formal and symbolic, even the most formal and symbolic involvement can influence coalition bargaining (see Bogdanor 1984; De Winter 1995). Among most Western European republics, the President under normal circumstances similarly plays only a formal role. However, several country chapters identify episodes in which the President has been more consequential in the making of cabinets (and other major political decisions). Clearly, the Presidents of Italy, Portugal, and Austria have a greater role in cabinet appointment than the German President. And the Presidents of France and Finland (until March 2000) have or have had a discretionary role in government formation that clearly exceeds that of their counterparts elsewhere.

---

[25] To date, the most systematic efforts to chart cabinet inauguration processes cross-nationally are Laver and Schofield (1990: ch. 4), Bergman (1993, 1995: ch. 3), De Winter (1995), and Rasch (2001).

Table 4.9 presents the formal rules of cabinet eligibility, appointment, and inauguration. Three eligibility regimes can be distinguished: (*a*) those that require membership in parliament (Ireland, United Kingdom), (*b*) those that permit it, and (*c*) those that treat cabinet office as incompatible with holding a seat in parliament (Belgium since 1995, France, Luxembourg, The Netherlands, Norway, Portugal, and—since 1974—Sweden). Those countries that allow the combination of parliamentary and executive office can be further differentiated according to the behavioural patterns that have evolved (Andeweg and Nijzink 1995: 160). Thus, simultaneous membership (the so-called 'dual mandate') is less frequent in Austria and Finland than in the other countries that permit it.

The bulk of Table 4.9 describes the involvement of Parliament in cabinet inauguration. In Belgium, Germany, Greece, Ireland, Italy, Luxembourg, and Spain, cabinets are essentially inaugurated after they have won an investiture vote in Parliament. The seven countries that require a cabinet to win a majority vote (simple or absolute) in the Parliament before or immediately after (Belgium, Italy, and Luxembourg) it takes office have a positive investiture rule (positive parliamentarism). Elsewhere, the test of a new cabinet's viability is negative: it is up to the Parliament to unseat any cabinet it does not tolerate. Portugal and Sweden (since 1975) have an investiture vote, but the requirement is only that the Prime Minister candidate not lose by an absolute majority. Bergman (1993) refers to this as a negative formation rule (or negative parliamentarism). In the remaining eight countries, there is no inauguration (investiture) vote. Instead it is up to the Parliament, at any time, to unseat the PM (and cabinet).[26]

Among countries that require an investiture vote (either positive or negative), in six cases the Parliament votes on the PM candidate. In Belgium, Italy, and Luxembourg the vote is instead on the full cabinet. In all cases except Ireland and Sweden, the Head of State nominates or appoints the PM (to be confirmed by a vote in Parliament). In Ireland any MP is entitled to propose a Prime Ministerial candidate to the Dáil. The successful candidate for PM then proposes his cabinet members to the Dáil for its approval. The President only gets involved after the investiture vote by formally appointing the PM and the other cabinet members. In Sweden the Speaker of Parliament nominates the PM candidate. Six of the nine investiture countries feature a mandatory screening procedure, in which the designated PM lays out the government's policy programme, presents the proposed cabinet to Parliament, and subjects both to plenary debate and an investiture vote. The investiture countries also differ in their voting rules. Except for Germany, which subscribes to the secret vote, in all investiture countries cabinets are confirmed through a recorded vote.[27]

---

[26] These countries (including Portugal and Sweden) all have negative formation rules. This decision rule contrasts starkly with much of the rational choice literature on coalition formation, which assumes that forming a cabinet (i.e. winning) requires the explicit support of an absolute majority of MPs (Bergman 1995). Yet, as early as the 1920s, Axel Brusewitz (1929) noted the negative formation rule in his account of Swedish parliamentarism.

[27] Only Ireland, Portugal, and Sweden do not require a quorum of at least 50% of their MPs to invest a new cabinet. Decision rules for cabinet inauguration vary considerably. They are most demanding in Germany, Italy, and Spain, where a majority of *all* MPs (50% + 1 MP) is required. Greece and Ireland satisfy themselves with majorities of MPs present and voting.

Table 4.9. *Rules of Cabinet Inauguration, Lower Chamber Rules Only*

Country and year	Cabinet position and membership in Parliament	Appointment by Head of State	Inauguration by Parliament				Parliamentary voting rules		
			Inauguration by parl.	Formal proposal by?	What is proposed?	Mandatory *ex ante* screening of program?	Minimum quorum requirement	Decision rule	Voting procedure
Austria 1945–2000	Compatible	Formal	No	n.a.	n.a.	n.a.	n.a.	n.a.	n.a.
Belgium 1945–1994	Compatible	Formal	Yes	Monarch	Cabinet	Yes	Absolute majority or higher	Simple majority	Recorded
1995–2000	Incompatible	Formal	Yes	Monarch	Cabinet	Yes	Absolute majority or higher	Simple majority	Recorded
Denmark 1945–2000	Compatible	Formal	No	n.a.	n.a.	n.a.	n.a.	n.a.	n.a.
Finland[a] 1945–2000	Compatible	Discretionary role	No	n.a.	n.a.	n.a.	n.a.	n.a.	n.a.
France 1959–2000	Incompatible	Discretionary role	No	n.a.	n.a.	n.a.	n.a.	n.a.	n.a.
Germany 1949–2000	Compatible	Formal	Yes	President	PM	No	Absolute majority or higher	Absolute majority	Secret
Greece 1975–2000	Compatible	Formal	Yes	President	PM	Yes	Equal to or less than half of all MPs	Simple majority	Recorded
Iceland 1945–2000	Compatible	Formal	No	n.a.	n.a.	n.a.	n.a.	n.a.	n.a.
Ireland 1945–2000	Required	Formal	Yes	Individual MPs[b]	PM	No	20 MPs	Simple majority	Recorded
Italy 1948–2000	Compatible	Formal	Yes	President	Cabinet	No	Absolute majority or higher	Simple majority	Recorded

Luxembourg								
1945–2000	Incompatible	Formal	Yes	Monarch	Cabinet	Yes	Absolute majority or higher	Simple majority	Recorded
The Netherlands								
1945–2000	Incompatible	Formal	No	n.a.	n.a.	n.a.	n.a.	n.a.	n.a.
Norway								
1945–2000	Incompatible	Formal	No	n.a.	n.a.	n.a.	n.a.	n.a.	n.a.
Portugal								
1976–2000	Incompatible	Formal	Yes	President	PM	Yes	No	Less than an absolute majority voting against	Recorded
Spain								
1978–2000	Compatible	Formal	Yes	Monarch	PM	Yes	Absolute majority or higher	Absolute majority	Recorded
Sweden								
1945–73	Compatible	Formal	No	n.a.	n.a.	No	n.a.	n.a.	n.a.
1974	Incompatible	Formal	No	n.a.	n.a.	No	n.a.	n.a.	n.a.
1975–2000	Incompatible	No	Yes	Speaker of Parliament	PM	No	No	Less than an absolute majority voting against	Recorded
United Kingdom								
1945–2000	Required	Formal	No	n.a.	n.a.	n.a.	n.a.	n.a.	n.a.

Notes: 'n.a.' means not application in this case.

An absolute majority is defined as 50% + 1 of all MPs. Simple majority is defined as 50% + 1 of the MPs present and voting. Most countries count a simple majority of 'votes cast', but in Belgium and Luxembourg the counting rule is based on a 'simple majority of valid votes'. The latter counting rule excludes blank votes.

[a] The new Finnish constitutional rules for cabinet inauguration that took effect in March 2000 are not included in the table. As for all tables, the cut-off point is January 1, 2000. However, the constitutional changes in Finland are described in the country chapter.

[b] Nominations for the position of 'Taoiseach (PM) are done by individual deputies. The quorum is 20 MPs and the candidate that first secures a majority of those voting wins the vote.

These institutional differences have practical consequences. While they may not determine the outcome of coalition bargaining, they do increase (or decrease) the probability of certain outcomes. When controlling for SMDP systems, which tend to produce single-party majority cabinets, countries with negative parliamentarism tend to have more minority cabinets and a shorter bargaining process than do countries with positive parliamentarism (Strøm 1990; Bergman 1993, 1995; De Winter 1995).

Ex Post *Control Mechanisms*

Let us now consider the *ex post* side of cabinet inauguration, namely the 'no confidence' (also frequently known as censure) procedures directed against incumbent PMs and cabinets. Again, parliamentary majorities can under parliamentary democracy remove the cabinet from power by expressing their lack of 'confidence' (although the specific terminology varies). In some countries, this parliamentary power is simply a strong convention. In other countries, this is laid out in elaborate detail in constitutional articles.

A vote of no confidence is the ultimate 'weapon' that MPs can use against the sitting cabinet, and it is typically tabled by members of the parliamentary opposition. Whether it is directed against the cabinet as a whole or the PM, the consequences are the same, namely that the full cabinet must resign. In most countries, MPs also have the option of targeting individual cabinet ministers and forcing them to resign (at which point the full cabinet can decide to resign too, if it so chooses). Yet, a number of countries (France, Germany, Ireland, Portugal, Spain, and the United Kingdom) recognize only collective cabinet responsibility and hence do not allow such a vote against individual ministers. This probably makes defection harder for government MPs.

There are a number of finer details in no-confidence procedures. Most countries restrict the no-confidence vote to groups of MPs of some specified size (which varies between countries). In a similar vein, most countries specify a minimum period of time that must expire from when the motion is tabled until the actual vote can be held. However, only a few countries restrict the number of no-confidence motions that can be tabled during a parliamentary term or session. Such rationing undermines the principle that the government is responsible to parliament at any time. Some countries use quorum rules as protection against sudden and purely accidental parliamentary majorities, caused by the absence of government MPs. Table 4.10 reports the variation in no-confidence procedures.

No-confidence procedures may require either simple or absolute majorities.[28] Besides, they can be either positive or negative. Negative (or 'ordinary') means that the vote is held on the present government and removes the cabinet from power; positive (or, to use a more common term, 'constructive') means that a majority must specify an alternative government. The constructive vote of no confidence, invented in Germany after the Second World War, stipulates that a head of government can only be removed from office by the

---

[28] Echoing the distinction between positive and negative formation rules, De Winter (1995: 137) distinguishes between positive and negative resignation rules. Positive resignation rules require a motion of no confidence to carry an absolute majority in parliament (i.e. a majority of *all* MPs) while negative resignation rules only require a simple majority (i.e. a majority of those MPs present and voting).

Table 4.10. *Rules of No-Confidence Votes (i.e. Initiative Rests with Parliament)*

Country and year	Directed against		Proposal power[a]	Constraints			Voting rules		
	PM/cabinet collectively	Individual ministers		Time	Time in days	No. of proposals	Quorum requirement	Decision rules	Voting procedures
Austria 1945–2000	Yes	Yes	Min. no. of MPs	Yes	2	No	Equal to or less than half of all MPs	Simple majority	Recorded
Belgium 1945–94	Yes	Yes	Any member	Yes	7	No	Absolute majority or higher	Simple majority	Recorded
Belgium 1995–2000	Yes	Yes	Any member	Yes	7	No	Absolute majority or higher	Absolute majority	Recorded
Denmark 1945–2000	Yes	Yes	Any member	No	n.a.	No	Absolute majority or higher	Simple majority	Recorded
Finland 1945–2000	Yes	Yes	Min. no. of MPs	No	n.a.	No	No	Simple majority	Recorded
France 1959–2000	Yes	No	Min. no. of MPs	Yes	2	Yes	No	Absolute majority	Recorded
Germany 1949–2000	Yes	No	Min. no. of MPs	Yes	2	No	Absolute majority or higher	Absolute majority	Secret
Greece 1975–2000	Yes	Yes	Min. no. of MPs	Yes	2	Yes	Absolute majority or higher	Absolute majority	Recorded

Table 4.10. (*contd.*)

Country and year	Directed against		Proposal power[a]	Constraints			Voting rules		Voting procedures
	PM/cabinet collectively	Individual ministers		Time	Time in days	No. of proposals	Quorum requirement	Decision rules	
Iceland 1945–2000	Yes	Yes	Any member	Yes	2	No	Absolute majority or higher	Absolute majority	Recorded
Ireland 1945–2000	Yes	No	Any member	Yes	3	Yes	Equal to or less than half of all MPs	Simple majority	Recorded
Italy 1948–2000	Yes	Yes	Min. no. of MPs	Yes	3	No	Absolute majority or higher	Simple majority	Recorded
Luxembourg 1945–2000	Yes	Yes	Min. no. of MPs	No	n.a.	n.a.	Absolute majority or higher	Simple majority	Recorded
The Netherlands 1945–2000	Yes	Yes	Min. no. of MPs	No	n.a.	n.a.	Absolute majority or higher	Simple majority	Recorded
Norway 1945–2000	Yes	Yes	Any member	No	n.a.	No	Absolute majority or higher	Simple majority	Recorded
Portugal 1976–2000	Yes	No	Recognized party group or min. no. of MPs	Yes	3	Yes	No	Absolute majority	Recorded

Spain								
1978–2000	Yes	No	Min. no. of MPs	Yes	5	No	Absolute majority or higher	Absolute majority	Recorded
Sweden								
1945–70	Yes	Yes	Any member	No	n.a.	No	No	Simple majority	Recorded
1971–2000	Yes	Yes	Min. no. of MPs	Yes	3	No	No	Absolute majority	Recorded
United Kingdom								
1945–2000	Yes	No	Any member	Yes	1	No	Equal to or less than half of all MPs	Simple majority	Recorded

Notes: n.a. means not applicable in this case.

An absolute majority is defined as 50% + 1 of all MPs. Simple majority is defined as 50% + 1 of the MPs present and voting. Most countries count a simple majority of 'votes cast', but in Belgium, Denmark, Luxembourg, and Sweden (before 1971), the counting rule is based on a 'simple majority of valid votes'. The latter counting rule excludes blank votes.

[a] In the cases which require 'min. no. of MPs', the actual number of MPs varies between countries.

Required majority

	Simple	Absolute
Ordinary	Austria, Belgium (until 1995), Denmark, Finland, Italy, Ireland, Luxembourg, The Netherlands, Norway, Sweden (until 1971), United Kingdom	France, Greece, Iceland, Portugal, Sweden (since 1971)
Constructive	(No cases)	Belgium (since 1995), Germany, Spain

Figure 4.2. Types of No-Confidence Votes in Western Europe.

election of his or her successor; it forces the opposition parties to agree on a joint PM candidate. Logically, we can thus distinguish four types—simple majority, absolute majority, constructive simple majority, and constructive absolute majority—in increasing order of restrictiveness. Figure 4.2 places our seventeen countries accordingly.

More than half of the Western European countries require a vote of no confidence to be carried by the usual (simple) majority (leaving aside some variation in counting blank and invalid votes). Government stability is more strongly protected in the countries in the two quadrants of the right side of Fig. 4.2. This is particularly true when the vote of no confidence needs to be constructive. Since the German constructive vote of no confidence is generally seen to have contributed to the postwar stability of German politics, it has become an export product, which was adopted by Spain in the 1970s, by Belgium in 1995, as well as by several countries not included in this volume. Yet, the German no-confidence vote is by secret ballot, which may jeopardize its restrictiveness.[29] If the most severe threat to government—and indeed to democracy—is that extremists of different stripes may join forces in order to remove a centrist cabinet (as happened most prominently in Weimar Germany; Finer 1946: 1104–6), the constructive vote of no confidence may be a powerful protection.

---

[29] The secret vote did become an issue in the first application of the German constructive vote of no confidence in 1972, though there are different interpretations what actually happened. After several government MPs had resigned from their respective parties and the government seemed to have lost its majority, CDU/CSU leader Rainer Barzel tried to topple Chancellor Willy Brandt through a constructive no-confidence vote. To compromise the secrecy of the vote, however, the coalition parties demanded that the bulk of their MPs abstain and allowed only a few 'secure' supporters of Chancellor Brandt to participate. According to one interpretation it was this tactic that worked: Barzel received 247 votes (while ten 'no' votes and two invalid votes were cast), whereas to be elected he would have needed an absolute majority of 249. Hence, Brandt survived, although in a direct confrontation he might have won fewer votes than Barzel. According to another interpretation the balance was tipped by one allegedly bribed CDU member who, shielded by the secret vote, did not vote for Barzel. In this case the secret vote worked in two ways for Brandt: To the extent that it was undermined it reduced the risk of defection from the Brandt camp, to the extent it worked it allowed defection from the Barzel camp.

Regardless of its specific form, the no-confidence vote is a very powerful accountability mechanism, but it is also a blunt one, and there are at least two circumstances that seriously restrict its use. First, it takes a majority (in some countries an absolute majority) of MPs to succeed. This is hard to achieve for members of the parliamentary opposition, mainly because the MPs of government parties in the vast majority of cases do not want to rock the boat, regardless of how much they may regret the actions of the cabinet or individual ministers. The second problem is that a cabinet is a 'package deal' in policy terms. Removing the PM and cabinet from power also means removing those (if any) parts of the policy package that are favourably viewed by the MPs and substituting those of an alternative cabinet. This consideration, of course, particularly applies to government MPs and explains why they do not want to rock the boat. Yet, even opposition MPs may fare better in policy terms under the incumbent government than under its likely replacement, and they may also face considerable uncertainty about the policy consequences of government removal. Hence, there are few circumstances in which a majority of MPs can be motivated to support a no-confidence motion.

Confidence Votes and Dissolution Powers

Incumbent cabinets are not defenceless against MPs that cause them trouble. In most parliamentary democracies, they have two countervailing institutional mechanisms. Most countries counterbalance the parliament's no-confidence weapon by vesting the PM with the power to invoke a confidence vote (Huber 1996a; Diermeier and Feddersen 1998). The other institutional weapon available to many PMs is to dissolve the parliament.

With confidence votes, the initiative rests with the cabinet. The confidence vote allows the cabinet to demonstrate to the world, and specifically to the parliamentary opposition, that it controls a parliamentary majority. A confidence vote can either formally or informally help the cabinet to overcome parliamentary reluctance to adopt its policy proposals. All our seventeen democracies allow the cabinet thus to tie its fate to the outcome of a parliamentary vote. Even when the constitution or other legislative procedure does not provide for a confidence vote, this mechanism exists by convention. Yet, compared to no-confidence procedures, which sometimes also exist only by convention, the rules governing confidence votes are often more open to interpretation. For all seventeen countries, Table 4.11 specifies whether the confidence vote exists only by convention or in the form of written rules, or both. Table 4.11 also details the formal procedures that exist in seven countries.

About half of our Western European countries do have formal confidence procedures laid out in the constitution or the standing orders of Parliament. In France, Germany, Portugal, and Spain, confidence votes are held only under specified provisions. In Belgium, Greece, and Italy, such provisions exist, but confidence votes can also be held without employing the legally specified process. Only in Belgium can any member of the cabinet invoke a confidence vote. Here a full week (168h) must pass from the time that such a vote is proposed until it is actually held. This period is much shorter in the seven other countries. The (regulated) Belgian vote of confidence (since 1995) is also constructive. If an absolute number of MPs reject the motion, the House of Representatives needs to elect a new PM within 3 days. If it fails to do so, the Cabinet can either remain in office or demand parliamentary dissolution.

Table 4.11. *Rules of Confidence Votes (i.e. Initiative Rests with Cabinet)*

| Country and year | Confidence vote[a] | Explicit and formal confidence vote mechanisms only | | | | | | | |
| | | Subject of vote | | Proposal power | Constraints | | | Voting rules | |
		PM/cabinet collectively	Individual ministers		Time	Time in hours	Quorum requirements	Decision rule	Voting procedure
Austria									
1945–2000	Convention only	n.a.	n.a.	n.a.	n.a.	n.a.	n.a.	n.a.	n.a.
Belgium									
1945–94	Convention only	n.a.	n.a.	n.a.	n.a.	n.a.	n.a.	n.a.	n.a.
1995–2000	Specific regulation and convention	Yes	Yes	Any member of the Cabinet	Yes	168	Absolute majority or higher	Absolute majority	Recorded
Denmark									
1945–2000	Convention only	n.a.	n.a.	n.a.	n.a.	n.a.	n.a.	n.a.	n.a.
Finland									
1945–2000	Convention only	n.a.	n.a.	n.a.	n.a.	n.a.	n.a.	n.a.	n.a.
France									
1959–2000	Specific regulation only	Yes	No	PM only	No	n.a.	No	Simple majority	Recorded
Germany									
1949–2000	Specific regulation only	Yes	No	PM only	Yes	48	Absolute majority or higher	Absolute majority	Secret
Greece									
1975–2000	Specific regulation and convention	Yes	No	Cabinet collectively only	Yes	96	Equal to or less than half of all MPs	Simple majority	Recorded
Iceland									
1945–2000	Convention only	n.a.	n.a.	n.a.	n.a.	n.a.	n.a.	n.a.	n.a.
Ireland									
1945–2000	Convention only	n.a.	n.a.	n.a.	n.a.	n.a.	n.a.	n.a.	n.a.

Country									
Italy 1948–2000	Specific regulation and convention	Yes	No	Cabinet collectively only	Yes	24	Absolute majority or higher	Simple majority	Recorded
Luxembourg 1945–2000	Convention only	n.a.	n.a.	n.a.	n.a.	n.a.	n.a.	n.a.	n.a.
The Netherlands 1945–2000	Convention only	n.a.	n.a.	n.a.	n.a.	n.a.	n.a.	n.a.	n.a.
Norway 1945–2000	Convention only	n.a.	n.a.	n.a.	n.a.	n.a.	n.a.	n.a.	n.a.
Portugal 1976–2000	Specific regulation only	Yes	No	Cabinet collectively only	Yes	72	Absolute majority or higher	Simple majority	Recorded
Spain 1978–2000	Specific regulation only	Yes	No	PM only	Yes	24	Absolute majority or higher	Simple majority	Recorded
Sweden 1945–2000	Convention only	n.a.	n.a.	n.a.	n.a.	n.a.	n.a.	n.a.	n.a.
United Kingdom 1945–2000	Convention only	n.a.	n.a.	n.a.	n.a.	n.a.	n.a.	n.a.	n.a.

Notes: 'n.a.' means not applicable in this case.

An absolute majority is defined as 50% + 1 of all MPs. Simple majority is defined as 50% + 1 of the MPs present and voting. Most countries count a simple majority of 'votes cast', but in Portugal and Spain the counting rule is based on a 'simple majority of valid votes'. The latter counting rule excludes blank votes.

[a] If coded 'convention only' there are no specific provisions in the constitution or parliamentary rules of procedure, but in practice the cabinet can legitimately threaten to resign in the event of a parliamentary defeat.

Table 4.12. *Rules of Parliamentary Dissolution*

Country and year	Constitution permits early dissolution?	Right to dissolve				Automatic constitutional provision	Restrictions on these powers to dissolve
		Head of State	PM	Cabinet	Parliamentary majority		
Austria							
1945–2000	Yes	Dissolution power (not exclusive)[a]	No	No	Dissolution power (not exclusive)[a]	In conjunction with attempts to unseat the Head of State	No
Belgium							
1945–4	Yes	Veto[b]	Can propose[c]	Can propose[c]	No	Pending or following constitutional amendment	No
1995–2000	Yes	Veto[b]	Can propose[c]	Can propose[c]	No	Pending or following constitutional amendment	Time restrictions; dissolution requires majority consent of the House (unless the House introduced but failed to pass a constructive motion of no confidence)
Denmark							
1945–52	Yes	No	Dissolution power (exclusive)[d]	No	No	Pending or following constitutional amendment	No
1953–2000	Yes	No	Dissolution power (exclusive)[d]	No	No	Pending or following constitutional amendment	A new Cabinet cannot dissolve Parliament before it and Parliament have met
Finland							
1945–1990	Yes	Veto[d]	No	No	No	No	Only when Parliament is in session
1991–2000	Yes	Veto[d]	Can propose[c]	No	No	No	Only when Parliament is in session
France							
1959–2000	Yes	Veto[d]	Can propose[c]	No	No	No	Time restrictions; not during emergency or similar
Germany							
1949–2000	Yes	Veto[b]	Can propose[c]	No	No	No	No
Greece							
1975–85	Yes	Dissolution (exclusive)[d]	No	Can propose[c]	No	If Parliament is unable to elect a PM	No
1986–2000	Yes	Veto[b]	No	Can propose[c]	No	If Parliament is unable to elect a PM; if the President resigns	No

Iceland 1945–2000	Yes	Dissolution power (exclusive)[d]	No	No	No	Pending or following constitutional amendment; in conjunction with attempts to unseat the Head of State	No
Ireland 1945–2000	Yes	Veto[d]	Can propose[c]	No	No	No	No
Italy 1948–2000	Yes	Dissolution power (exclusive)[d]	No	No	No	No	Time restrictions; only when Parliament is in session
Luxembourg 1945–2000	Yes	Veto[b]	Can propose[c]	Can propose[c]	No	Pending or following constitutional amendment	No
The Netherlands 1945–2000	Yes	Veto[b]	No	Can propose[c]	No	Pending or following constitutional amendment	No
Norway 1945–2000	No	n.a.	n.a.	n.a.	n.a.	n.a.	n.a.
Portugal 1976–81	Yes	Dissolution power[f] (exclusive)[d]	No	No	No	If Parliament defeated the third cabinet formed in a single legislature	Not during emergency or similar not during an extension of the President's term of office
Portugal 1982–2000	Yes	Dissolution power[g] (exclusive)[c]	No	No	No	No	Time restrictions; not during emergency or similar
Spain 1978–2000	Yes	Formal[h]	Dissolution power (exclusive)[d]	No	No	Pending or following constitutional amendment; if Parliament is unable to elect a PM	Not during emergency or similar time restrictions
Sweden 1945–70	Yes	Veto[b]	No	Can propose[c]	No	No	Time restrictions
Sweden 1971–4		Formal[h]	Dissolution power (exclusive)[d]	No			

Table 4.12. (contd.)

Country and year	Constitution permits early dissolution?	Right to dissolve				Automatic constitutional provision	Restrictions on these powers to dissolve
		Head of State	PM	Cabinet	Parliamentary majority		
1975–2000		No	No	Dissolution power (exclusive)[d]		If Parliament is unable to elect a PM	Time restrictions; the Cabinet cannot dissolve Parliament after it has resigned and is serving in a caretaker capacity
United Kingdom 1945–2000	Yes	Veto[b]	Can propose[c]	No	No	n.a.	No

Notes: For the column on 'Automatic constitutional provision' we have used the following cross-national coding categories: 'Pending or following constitutional amendment'; 'In conjunction with attempts to unseat the Head of State'; or 'If Parliament is unable to elect a PM'. For the column on 'Restrictions on these powers to dissolve' we have used the following cross-national coding categories: 'Time restrictions'; 'Not during states of emergency or similar; or 'Only when Parliament is in session'. When these have not adequately reflected the real variation, the country experts have provided a brief description of the relevant conditions. 'n.a.' means not applicable in this case.

[a] May dissolve on own initiative, but does not have the power to prevent other constitutional agents from dissolving.
[b] Has discretionary power to deny proposal by other constitutional agent, but does not have the power to initiate proposal.
[c] May propose only, subject to discretionary approval of other constitutional agent.
[d] May dissolve on own initiative and has exclusive discretionary power to dissolve.
[f] Formally, dissolution requires support by the Council of the Revolution.
[g] Note, however, that the President can only dismiss the cabinet after 'consulting' with the Council of State.
[h] Formal role only.

Everywhere but in Norway (for reasons explained below), a lost confidence vote can result in the dissolution of parliament. Alternatively, dissolving parliament can be a deliberate choice made by an otherwise secure PM or cabinet (Strøm and Swindle 2002). The conditions under which such dissolution can take place are therefore important. Table 4.12 identifies the rules of parliamentary dissolution. Below, we discuss the roles of the most important players.

Of all parliamentary accountability mechanisms, dissolution allows for the greatest role for the Head of State. In all but two of the sixteen countries that in principle allow parliamentary dissolution, the Head of State can or must be involved (the exceptions are, by convention, Denmark[30] and, since 1975, Sweden). Empirically, we can identify five different types:

1. The Head of State's role is purely *formal* in Spain, and was so in Sweden between 1971 and 1974.
2. In Portugal (since 1982) the Head of State has *proposal power* with respect to dissolution but does not make the final decision.
3. In eight countries the Head of State has or has had *veto power*: he or she can refuse to call early parliamentary dissolution even when it is proposed by other players: Belgium, Germany, Greece (since 1986), Ireland (though only if the PM, who proposes dissolution, has lost the confidence of Parliament), Luxembourg, The Netherlands, the United Kingdom, and Sweden (between 1945 and 1970). There is considerable variation in the role the Head of State actually plays. For example, the Basic Law tightly constrains the German President.[31]
4. Three Presidents, those of Austria, France, and Iceland can dissolve Parliament on their own initiative. Hence, formally, they are *decisive players*, as defined in Chapter 3. Strictly speaking, in Austria dissolution requires a cabinet proposal and Iceland requires the counter-signature of the Prime Minister (although the President is nominally free to appoint and dismiss the cabinet). In Austria, the President's power is not exclusive, as the Austrian Parliament is the only assembly that has the discretionary right to dissolve itself. In France, the President needs to consult with the PM and the Presidents of both chambers of Parliament, but that is merely a formal requirement and the President is the only actor who can dissolve Parliament. All three Presidents are restricted by constitutional clauses that limit their dissolution powers, though the French President faces more severe restrictions. Yet, the Icelandic President has never dissolved Parliament and the Austrian President has not dissolved Parliament since 1930, while presidential

---

[30] Section 32 of the Danish Constitution still states 'The King may at any time issue writs for a new election with the effect that the existing seats be vacated upon a new election'.

[31] Although the German Constitution permits the early dissolution of the Bundestag, the strategic use of this instrument is cumbersome. The two early dissolutions to date have occurred under extraordinary circumstances. The first dissolution took place after the failed no-confidence vote against Willy Brandt in 1972, when there was no government majority but also no alternative majority. The second case happened in 1983 after the change from the SPD–FDP to the CDU/CSU–FDP coalition. The government 'manufactured' a defeat on a vote of confidence in order to legitimize an early election (Poguntke 1999).

dissolutions are a regular feature of French politics (having occurred in 1962, 1968, 1981, 1988, and 1997).

5. According to the letter of their respective constitutions, the Presidents of Finland (from 1991 on the proposal of the PM), Greece (1975–85), Italy (after consultation with the Speakers of both houses of Parliament), and Portugal (1976–81) have the most extensive dissolution powers. These Presidents have (had) the exclusive right to dissolve on their own initiative and are thus dissolution *dictators*.

As we have already seen, Heads of State are not the only actors in the dissolution process. In most countries, the PM has an important role in the dissolution process. Empirically we can distinguish three types.

1. In Denmark, Spain, and Sweden (1971–74), the PM can or could dissolve parliament on his or her own initiative. Moreover, except for automatic provisions, in these countries only the respective PMs can effectively decide to dissolve. According to the terminology developed in Chapter 3, they are dissolution *dictators*.
2. In Finland (since 1991), France, Germany, and Ireland, the PM has the power to propose early dissolution. Formally, this is also true for Belgium, Luxembourg, the United Kingdom and other monarchies. It is then within the discretion of the Head of State to accept or decline such a proposal, though in the monarchies a refusal might precipitate a constitutional crisis.
3. In contrast, the constitutions of Austria, Finland (before 1991), Greece, Iceland, Italy, The Netherlands, Portugal, and Sweden (except 1971–74) do not give a special role to the PM. Here, dissolution power is either in the hands of the Head of State or the full cabinet.

One might naively expect parliamentary government to imply that parliaments themselves could decide to dissolve early. Yet, this is the case only in Austria, where the Parliament is one of two actors that can dissolve in their own right, and to a lesser degree in Belgium, where early dissolution requires either conflict between the Cabinet and Parliament (a failed motion of confidence or a successful no- confidence motion), or a Cabinet resignation, which in turn may be a way to preempt a vote of no confidence by the parliamentary majority.

Constitutional mechanisms do not necessarily tell us the whole story about the practical importance of the four critical powers we have surveyed: investiture mechanisms, no-confidence votes, confidence votes, and parliamentary dissolution procedures. There are cross-national variations in the use of these powers that do not conform to the variation in formal rules. Table 4.13 reports on the actual employment of these four mechanisms for every cabinet formed in the relevant period.[32] We count a new cabinet with every (*a*) general election, (*b*) change of party membership in the cabinet, or (*c*) new PM.[33] Table 4.13 details the actual voting figures for investiture, no-confidence,

---

[32] Note that the term 'cabinet' includes only the PM and those ministers (with or without portfolio) that have voting rights in the government's collective body. In this book, the term 'government' is used in a broader sense to include the junior ministers and other political appointees that resign with the cabinet.

[33] For reasons detailed in that book, we use the same counting rule as Müller and Strøm (2000*b*).

Table 4.13. *Confidence Votes and Early Elections: The Behavioural Record*[a]

Country and year	No. of cabinets formed	No. of investiture votes	No. of no confidence votes	No. of confidence votes (under specific institutional rule only)	No. of early elections
Austria					
1945–2000	22	n.a.	22	n.a.	9
Belgium					
1945–2000	34	34	n.d.[b]	n.a./0[c]	11
Denmark					
1945–2000	31	n.a.	2	n.a.	20
Finland					
1945–2000	45	n.a.	127[d]	n.a.	4
France					
1959–2000	23	n.a.	32	71	5
Germany					
1949–2000	26	18	2	3	2
Greece					
1975–2000	11	10	3	2	6
Iceland					
1945–2000	26	n.a.	1	n.a.	7
Ireland					
1945–2000	22	39	n.d.[e]	n.a.	16
Italy					
1945–2000	52	55	24	232	7
Luxembourg					
1945–2000	17	17	1[f]	n.a.	2
The Netherlands					
1945–2000	23	n.a.	36	n.a.	5
Norway					
1945–2000	26	n.a.	25	n.a.	n.a.
Portugal					
1976–2000	15	11	1	5	4
Spain					
1977–2000	8	8	2	2	6
Sweden					
1945–2000	26	9	2	n.a.	1
United Kingdom					
1945–2000	20	n.a.	26	n.a.	10
Total	427	201	306	315	115

[a] Except for the number of cabinets, the table does not include any data on the cabinets that were still in power on 1 January 2000. 'n.a.' means not applicable in this case, 'n.d.' means no data.

[b] In Belgium, there is no study or inventory of the number of no-confidence votes introduced by the Chambers. It is common practice that the opposition parties, after a government declaration or interpellation, introduce no-confidence motions. However, since the Second World War, not a single government has been forced to resign because of a motion of no confidence.

[c] Not applicable before 1995, 0 since 1995.

[d] The Eduskunta minutes do not list or index no-confidence votes on individual ministers separately from the no-confidence votes that have been directed at the PM/full Cabinet. Nor is this systematically available in the literature. Consequently, the number of no-confidence votes listed here also includes a smaller number of votes directed at individual ministers.

[e] There is no official source or index that lists the number of no-confidence votes.

[f] In Luxembourg, there is no study or inventory of the number of no-confidence votes introduced by the Parliament. Here, we record only the single no-confidence vote on which we have systematic information, precisely because it was successful.

and confidence votes.[34] Except as otherwise noted, Table 4.13 reports only those no-confidence votes that were directed against the PM or the whole cabinet and hence, if successful, would have caused the cabinet's fall.[35] No-confidence data are missing for Belgium, Luxembourg, and Ireland, where no official account is accessible.

Table 4.13 demonstrates considerable variation with regard to all the four accountability mechanisms presented here: investiture votes, no-confidence votes, confidence votes, and early elections. Ireland and Italy alone have had more investiture votes than cabinets. In Ireland the high number of investiture votes results from the separation of the vote for PM from the en bloc vote, which typically occurs only a few hours later, for the rest of the cabinet (Chubb 1982: 183–4). Otherwise, a higher number of investiture votes than cabinets indicates that prospective cabinets occasionally lose investiture votes. This has happened in Italy where five cabinets have not survived their vote of investiture (Strøm 1990: 143), and in Ireland in 1989, when several parties presented unsuccessful Prime Ministerial candidates (O'Leary 1991: 143).

While an investiture vote may be constitutionally required for a cabinet to assume office, other confidence and no-confidence votes are not. Party leaders deliberately schedule them, because they expect to win or to send a signal to the electorate or other political players. Among incumbents, Finnish cabinets are most frequently challenged through no-confidence motions, though most of these are not serious attempts to unseat the cabinet but rather demonstrations of opposition discontent with government policies.[36] In France and Italy, where it is used most often, cabinets frequently put their existence on the line, through the confidence vote, to back up their proposals in Parliament. This mechanism has been most successful in France. If the government invokes Article 49-3, it either provokes the opposition into introducing a no-confidence vote or the relevant government proposal is automatically accepted (without any formal vote in Parliament) (Chapter 9; Huber 1996b). In Italy, the confidence vote was until 1988 less suited to shielding controversial legislation from dissident MPs, because after a successful vote of confidence the government proposal still required a final separate vote (which in a good number of cases was lost, due to the secret vote and factionalism in the governing parties) (Müller-Wirth 1992; Hine 1993: 191–3).

Finally, Table 4.13 identifies whether the Parliament was dissolved early. We define 'early dissolution' to include cases (*a*) in which the cabinet resigned after it was defeated in Parliament, (*b*) in which the cabinet resigned by convention for other constitutional reasons (e.g. the assumption of office by a newly elected Head of State), and in which these events were immediately followed by elections, or (*c*) in which election occurred in the first nine-tenths of the constitutional interelection period (CIEP) (see Strøm and

---

[34] Note that, for obvious reasons, for cabinets in power on 1 January 2000—the end date of our empirical survey—we only record investiture data.

[35] Unfortunately, the Finnish parliamentary records do not allow us to distinguish these no-confidence votes from those directed against individual ministers. To the best of our knowledge, the large majority of the Finnish no-confidence votes recorded in Table 4.13 were directed against the PM or the whole Cabinet, though Table 4.13 also contains a few votes against individual ministers.

[36] As noted above, some Finnish no-confidence motions were directed against individual ministers.

Swindle 2002).[37] Thus defined, early parliamentary dissolution happens most frequently in Denmark, Greece, and Ireland, where this fate befalls about two-thirds of all
cabinets or more. These are countries in which cabinets cannot expect—or do not
want—to serve the maximum term.

The Parliament–Cabinet connection is the defining link of parliamentary government, and the accountability mechanisms that we have just detailed are the most visible
ones. Lupia and Strøm (1995) refer to no-confidence votes and dissolution powers as the
'doomsday devices' of parliamentary democracy. Elections and the different types of
confidence votes are the most important parts of the constitutional structure that shapes
and helps constrain the behaviour of politicians and parties. The country chapters will
place the large variations in these rules and their consequences in historical context.

Parliamentary Questions

Parliamentary democracies also feature a variety of less dramatic ways for parliamentarians to control their agents in the cabinet. In contrast to mechanisms through which
ministers may be directly sanctioned and removed from power, Mény and Knapp (1998:
208–11) refer to these as 'unsanctioned' control mechanisms. Although less dramatic,
these can be important mechanisms in the ongoing parliamentary oversight of the
executive branch. Within the arsenal of such weapons, parliamentary questions occupy
a central position (Wiberg 1995). Parliamentary questions are among the most visible
mechanism by which individual MPs, especially those from opposition parties, can hold
ministers publicly accountable even when there is no immediate prospect of an election or a change of government. Most parliaments feature a variety of procedures
whereby individual members can question the PM, other members of the cabinet,
or—in committees—civil servants.

Questions may take oral or written form, they may or may not effectively force the
relevant cabinet member to respond, and they may or may not allow the questioner to
proceed with more serious parliamentary challenges, such as motions of no confidence. MPs may question ministers for a variety of reasons, involving the desire to get
personal credit for an issue or simply name recognition (Mayhew 1974). Individual MP
motives thus may have little to do with any serious ambition to oversee the cabinet or
enforce the policy preferences of the parliamentary majority. That, however, does not
take away from the importance which MPs and cabinet ministers sometimes attach to
parliamentary questions. Ministerial accountability in this form may indeed reduce the
potential for moral hazard.

Parliamentary questions have three functions: (a) to provide information, (b) to criticize
government action (or non-action), and (c) to test the honesty or ability of cabinet
members. The first function of parliamentary questions is straightforward: MPs,
particularly from the opposition parties, are at an informational disadvantage vis-à-vis
the government. By asking questions they can force cabinet members to share at least
some information with them and indeed the interested public. In many cases, of course,

---

[37] As the country chapter notes, this counting is quite different from the British 'convention', in which
dissolutions in the last year of a government's term are not considered 'early'.

the questioner is not totally ignorant of the plans and actions of the government, often because of the answers to previous ('innocent') questions or because of 'fire alarms', that is, hints from interested parties (co-partisans 'on the ground', interest groups, individual citizens, or even partisan or frustrated civil servants).

The remaining functions of parliamentary questions are less public-spirited. Questions that implicitly criticize government action (or the lack of such) are designed to force the minister to publicly admit inconvenient or embarrassing facts. If—rather than admitting failure or answering evasively—ministers lie to parliament, opposition MPs may be able to convict them. At least in some countries it is a long-standing convention that ministers who have been proven guilty in this respect have to resign or be dismissed by the PM (e.g. see Finer 1946: 975; Woodhouse 1994: 49; Brazier 1997: 273). Since ministers often 'are apt to think that a questioner possesses a larger fund of knowledge than he in fact does' (Finer 1946: 866), they will mostly avoid blatantly lying to parliament. Yet, their answers may not be particularly comprehensive or informative. As Finer (1946: 865) has noted, the British House of Commons is willing to accept 'the substitution of wit for confession'. After all, parliamentary politics is a party game and a minister 'scoring' for his team (party) will be able to rely on the support of his or her teammates as long as he or she does not grossly violate the rules of the game. Nonetheless, there are limits to such evasive tactics and often a series of questions leads the executive to reveal more of its private information than it had intended.

Table 4.14 presents the relevant instruments in broad categories. Written parliamentary questions have existed in most Western European Parliaments throughout the postwar period. In Denmark, however, they were introduced as late as 1947. In Luxembourg, questions have in parliamentary practice existed during the entire postwar period, but were codified in the standing orders only in 1965. In Denmark, France, Ireland, The Netherlands, Portugal, and Sweden, any individual MP may at any time ask a written question about anything that falls within ministerial competence. Except for Ireland, the same countries also permit MPs to ask oral questions. Elsewhere, there are restrictions, though it is difficult to judge their practical importance. There is a minor trend towards allowing MPs to interrupt the Parliament's regular schedule to ask 'urgent' questions. This has happened in Denmark and Greece, and—with the temporary exception of Luxembourg—no country that has allowed such questions has since abandoned them. Apparently, once MPs have been allowed to ask questions to scrutinize cabinet members, it is not easy to constrain their ability to do so. This may be due to the fact that parliamentary rules of procedure enjoy special protection (as in Austria, which requires a two-thirds majority to change them) or to political considerations, such as the public liability of restricting openness.

At the same time, we see trends to rationalize and streamline parliamentary rules of procedure to limit the opposition's capacity for dilatory action. Parliamentarism in the Fifth French Republic and, to a lesser extent, Greece, has always been designed to ensure the government's predominance. Other (partly) restrictive reforms of the parliamentary rules of procedure were adopted in Italy in the 1980s and in Austria in the 1990s.

Table 4.14 also indicates whether the Parliament requires the cabinet to report on major issues that otherwise fall under the latter's authority. Such issues may include investigations that the cabinet is conducting, the performance of state industries, budgetary allocations, or, for example, cabinet conduct in EU affairs. What is scrutinized

Table 4.14. *Parliamentary Accountability of Cabinet*

Year	Parliamentary questions permitted?				Formal reporting requirements	*Ex post* supervision of cabinet[a]
	Written	Oral	Urgent	Other		
Austria						
1945–60	Yes[b,c]	No	Yes[b,c]	No	Yes	Ad hoc committees of investigation or inquiry; audit office(s)
1961–88	Yes[b,c,d]	Yes[b,c,e]	Yes[b,c]	No	Yes	Ad hoc committees of investigation or inquiry; audit office(s)
1989–2000	Yes[b,c,d]	Yes[b,c,e]	Yes[b,c]	Yes[f]	Yes	Ad hoc committees of investigation or inquiry; audit office(s)
Belgium						
1945–88	Yes[f,g,e]	Yes[f,h,e]	Yes[f,h,e]	Yes[f,i,h,e]	No	Permanent committees to supervise ministries; ad hoc committees of investigation or inquiry; audit office(s); minister can be compelled to testify before any parliamentary committee of any type, but can refuse to answer certain questions
1989–2000	Yes[f,g,e]	Yes[f,h,e]	Yes[f,h,e]	Yes[f,i,l,e]	Yes	Permanent committees to supervise ministries; ad hoc committees of investigation or inquiry; audit office(s); minister can be compelled to testify before any parliamentary committee of any type, but can refuse to answer certain questions
Denmark						
1945–6	No	No	No	No	No	No such supervision
1947–71	Yes[j,k,e]	Yes[j,k,e]	No	Yes[b,i,k,e]	No	No such supervision
1972–96	Yes[j,k,e]	Yes[j,k,e]	No	Yes[b,i,k,e]	No	Permanent committees to supervise ministries; ad hoc committees of investigation or inquiry; minister can be compelled to testify before any committee on any matter
1997–2000	Yes[j,k,e]	Yes[j,k,e]	Yes[h,k,e]	Yes[b,i,k,e]	No	Permanent committees to supervise ministries; ad hoc committees of investigation or inquiry; minister can be compelled to testify before any committee on any matter
Finland						
1945–65	Yes[h]	No	No	No	Yes	Permanent committees to supervise ministries; minister can be compelled to testify before any parliamentary committee of any type, but can refuse to answer certain questions
1966–88	Yes[h]	Yes[h]	No	No	Yes	Permanent committees to supervise ministries; minister can be compelled to testify before any parliamentary committee of any type, but can refuse to answer certain questions
1989–2000	Yes[h]	Yes[h]	No	Yes[h]	Yes	Permanent committees to supervise ministries; minister can be compelled to testify before any parliamentary committee of any type, but can refuse to answer certain questions
France						
1959–2000	Yes[j,h,g]	Yes[j,k,c,l]	Yes[j,m,h,l]	No	No	Permanent committees to supervise ministries; ad hoc committees of investigation or inquiry; minister can be compelled to testify before any parliamentary committee of any type, but can refuse to answer certain questions
Germany						
1949–2000	Yes[b,n,i,d]	Yes[j,k,o]	Yes[k]	No	Yes	Permanent committees to supervise ministries; ad hoc committees of investigation or inquiry; audit office(s); minister can be compelled to testify before any parliamentary committee of any type, but can refuse to answer certain questionsGreece

Table 4.14. (contd.)

Year	Parliamentary questions permitted?				Formal reporting requirements	Ex post supervision of cabinet[a]
	Written	Oral	Urgent	Other		
Greece						
1975–85	Yes[g]	Yes[g]	No	Yes[g]	Yes	Ad hoc committees of investigation or inquiry
1986–2000	Yes[g]	Yes[g]	Yes[g]	Yes[g]	Yes	Ad hoc committees of investigation or inquiry
Iceland						
1945–2000	Yes[h]	Yes[h]	Yes[h]	No	No	Permanent committees to supervise ministries; ad hoc committees of investigation or inquiry
Ireland						
1945–97	Yes[j,g]	Yes[b,d]	Yes[b]	No	Yes	Ad hoc committees of investigation or inquiry
1998–2000	Yes[j,g]	Yes[b,d]	Yes[b]	No	Yes	Ad hoc committees of investigation or inquiry; minister can be compelled to testify before any parliamentary committee of any type, but can refuse to answer certain questions
Italy						
1948–82	Yes[k,l]	Yes[k,l]	Yes[k,l]	Yes[k]	No	Permanent committees to supervise ministries; ad hoc committees of investigation or inquiry
1983–2000	Yes[k,l]	Yes[k,l]	Yes[k,p]	Yes[k]	No	Permanent committees to supervise ministries; ad hoc committees of investigation or inquiry
Luxembourg						
1945–82[q]	Yes[f,g,e]	Yes[f,g,e]	Yes[f,k,d,e]	Yes[f,n,u,k,d,e]	Yes	Permanent committees to supervise ministries; ad hoc committees of investigation or inquiry; audit office(s); minister can be compelled to testify before any committee on any matter
1983–9	Yes[f,g,e]	No	Yes[f,k,d,e]	Yes[f,n,u,k,d,e]	Yes	Permanent committees to supervise ministries; ad hoc committees of investigation or inquiry; audit office(s); minister can be compelled to testify before any committee on any matter
1990–2000	Yes[f,g,e]	Yes[f,g,e]	Yes[f,k,d,e]	Yes[f,n,u,k,d,e]	Yes	Permanent committees to supervise ministries; ad hoc committees of investigation or inquiry; audit office(s); minister can be compelled to testify before any committee on any matter
The Netherlands						
1945–2000	Yes[j,c,p]	Yes[j,c,p]	Yes[f,c,p]	Yes[b,c,e]	Yes	Ad hoc committees of investigation or inquiry
Norway						
1945–8	Yes[n,k]	No	No	No	Yes	Permanent committees to supervise ministries; permanent committees with right to read cabinet minutes; audit office(s)
1949–71	Yes[n,k]	Yes[k]	No	No	Yes	Permanent committees to supervise ministries; audit office(s)
1972–80	Yes[n,k]	Yes[k]	No	No	Yes	Permanent committees to supervise ministries; audit office(s)
1981–4	Yes[n,k]	Yes[k]	No	No	Yes	Permanent committees to supervise ministries; audit office(s)
1985–8	Yes[n,k]	Yes[k]	No	Yes[f,k]	Yes	Permanent committees to supervise ministries; permanent committees with right to read cabinet minutes; audit office(s)
1989–2000	Yes[k]	Yes[k]	No	Yes[f,k]	Yes	Permanent committees to supervise ministries; permanent committees with right to read cabinet minutes; audit office(s)

Country / Period						
Portugal						
1976–2000	Yes[j]	Yes[j]	Yes[j]	No	Yes	Permanent committees to supervise ministries; ad hoc committees of investigation or inquiry; minister can be compelled to testify before any committee on any matter
Spain						
1977–2000	Yes[b,n,m,d,e,p]	No	Yes[b,f,g,e,p]	Yes	Yes	Permanent committees to supervise ministries; ad hoc committees of investigation or inquiry; minister can be compelled to testify before any parliamentary committee of any type, but can refuse to answer certain questions
Sweden						
1945–90	Yes[j,k,p]	No	No	No	Yes	Permanent committees to supervise ministries; permanent committees with right to read cabinet minutes; audit office(s); minister can be compelled to testify before any committee on any matter
1991–2000	Yes[j,k,p]	Yes[j,k,p]	No	No	Yes	Permanent committees to supervise ministries; permanent committees with right to read cabinet minutes; audit office(s); minister can be compelled to testify before any committee on any matter
United Kingdom						
1945–78	Yes[n,c,d]	Yes[b,c]	Yes[b,c]	Yes[b,d]	Yes	Permanent committees to supervise ministries; ad hoc committees of investigation or inquiry
1979–2000	Yes[n,c,d]	Yes[b,c]	Yes[b,c]	Yes[b,d]	Yes	Permanent committees to supervise ministries; ad hoc committees of investigation or inquiry; audit office(s)

[a] This column refers to the ways in which the cabinet can be scrutinized by the Parliament. Note that this does not necessarily presume that the Parliament itself must perform the actual audit. The Parliament can also use information collected by another body, such as an audit office, when it conducts this scrutiny. The scrutiny can involve the cabinet as a whole or individual ministers and ministries. The full list of coding alternatives is the following: (1) permanent committees to supervise ministries; (2) permanent committees with right to read cabinet minutes; (3) ad hoc committees of investigation or inquiry; (4) audit office(s); (5) minister can be compelled to testify before any parliamentary committee of any type, but can refuse to answer certain questions; (6) minister can be compelled to testify before any committee on any matter (and there is no explicit right for the minister to refuse to answer).

[b] Restrictions on the right to ask such questions.

[c] The government must respond to at least some types of such questions.

[d] The government must respond to some such questions within a specified time limit.

[e] Parliament can force response to be given by a specified cabinet member.

[f] Restrictions on the conditions under which such questions can be asked.

[g] The government must respond to all such questions within a specified time limit.

[h] The government must respond to all such questions.

[i] Parliamentary debate and motions of no-confidence may follow some such questions.

[j] No restriction on any MP's right to ask such questions.

[k] Government may ignore such questions at will.

[l] Any member of government can give response.

[m] Restrictions on the right of the government to ignore such questions.

[n] Several types of such questions.

[o] Response can even be given by member of the administration.

[p] Any cabinet member can give response.

[q] The right to ask questions was only written into the Chamber's standing orders in 1965, but in practice they existed during the whole period. However, specific time limits for answers and other similar details have existed only since 1965.

varies from country to country. Almost all countries (except Denmark, France, Iceland, and Italy) require the cabinet to bring such reports to the parliament. Belgium initiated such reporting practices in 1989, to combat a relaxed budget routine in which much government money was regularly spent before the Parliament had approved any expenditures.

Ex post parliamentary supervision of the executive includes various kinds of audits. While audit institutions of some kind exist practically everywhere, our country specialists find audit office(s) designed to scrutinize the executive particularly politically relevant in Austria, Belgium, Germany, Luxembourg, Norway, Sweden, and the United Kingdom. Even these audit offices are not overwhelmingly concerned with the cabinet or individual ministers, but tend to concentrate on administrative units and civil servants. Yet, this scrutiny often reveals how well (or badly) the cabinet has managed its civil servants. Pollitt *et al.* (1999) have analysed the audit offices of Finland, France, The Netherlands, Sweden, and the United Kingdom and discovered a trend away from pure financial audit to performance audit. That is to say, audit offices are increasingly concerned with the quality of the public management rather than with mere bookkeeping issues. And they give increasing publicity to the results of their scrutiny, appealing to the media and the general public rather than exclusively to the audited institutions and parliament. If that trend continues, the political relevance of audit offices is likely to increase.

Parliamentary Committees

In many countries parliamentary committees have been important internal fora ever since the inception of parliamentary government. Although their practical influence and importance vary considerably among our seventeen countries, committees are everywhere involved in the production of public policy and of laws in particular. Parliamentary committees also try to supervise policy implementation, and this practice has spread to more countries over time. When they conduct this scrutiny, committees commonly ask whether laws have been effectively implemented. The use (or misuse) of public funds is also a common committee concern.

Table 4.14 reports whether scrutiny takes place in standing (permanent) or ad hoc (temporary) committees. Standing committees perform *ex post* scrutiny in thirteen countries, including Denmark (since 1972) and the United Kingdom (since 1979). Their operations are guided partly by formal rules and partly by conventions. Three criteria give some indication of committee power. The first is whether committees can assume that cabinet ministers will testify before them, which is the case in ten countries: Belgium, Denmark (since 1972), Finland, France, Germany, Ireland, Luxembourg, Portugal, Spain, and Sweden. The second rule is whether ministers in principle are obliged to answer any kind of question that the committees put to them, as is the case in four of these countries (Denmark, Luxembourg, Portugal, and Sweden). In some of these countries, ministers might not be legally required to testify or provide answers. But in practice, ministers appear when they are called and do not simply refuse to answer questions (though they may answer equivocally or evasively). The third criterion is whether parliamentary committees are allowed to read and investigate cabinet minutes, which is the case only in Norway and Sweden. This authority does enhance the relevant committee's status and influence (see the country chapters for details). Cabinet minutes are not always the most exiting and informative documents, but they may illuminate critical executive discussions and decisions.

On the basis of these criteria, we can distinguish four types of parliamentary committee systems: (*a*) the most powerful category, consisting of those that score positively on three (Denmark, Luxembourg, Portugal) or all four (Sweden) of our criteria, or at any rate give committees the most exclusive privilege: access to cabinet papers (Norway); (*b*) a medium degree of committee authority, as in Belgium, Finland, France, Germany, and Spain, which all provide for routine scrutiny and oblige ministers to some degree of cooperation; (*c*) a low degree of formal accountability to standing committees, as in Iceland, Italy, and the United Kingdom, where such committee privileges are generally lacking; (*d*) and finally, Austria, Greece, and The Netherlands, which do not force cabinet members to account to standing parliamentary committees, which instead serve the purpose of legislation exclusively.

Most countries (all except Finland, Norway, and Sweden) provide for executive scrutiny through ad hoc investigative committees set up to investigate (alleged) mismanagement. Investigative committees often have extensive rights, including the authority to call witnesses and to read government papers. Yet, setting up such a committee, defining its task and duration, and making actual use of its investigative prerogatives require decisions that are often highly politicized. With the partial exception of Germany (where the vote of a quarter of the MPs suffices to launch an investigative committee) such decisions are made by majority vote. Since such investigations tend to be a hassle for the governing parties, they are more likely under minority cabinets, when majority coalitions do not impose strict coalition discipline on such matters, when the investigation relates to the conduct of a government (and parties) that have left office, or when public pressure on the parliamentary majority becomes so great that resistance might involve higher (electoral) costs than allowing an investigation. Despite all these limitations, investigative committees have occasionally had great political impact, for instance in Austria, France, Germany, and Portugal (see country chapters).

Across Western Europe the use of scrutiny procedures has increased over time. Denmark launched a major parliamentary reform in 1972 that gave parliamentary committees the right to scrutinize the government. Ireland in 1998 extended to committees the right to have ministers testify before them. In 1979, the British House of Commons established a system of select committees whose main purpose is to oversee government policy. Norway introduced parliamentary committee hearings on a trial basis in 1995, and these procedures have since been given a more permanent status.

Parliamentary Scrutiny of European Union Affairs

With the increasing importance of European integration, parliamentary scrutiny of the government has taken on an additional dimension. The Treaties of Maastricht (which took effect in 1993) and Amsterdam (effective 1999) considerably increased the powers of the European Parliament (EP) to legislate and to appoint and control the

Commission. Yet the Council, made up of national ministers, remains the main legislative body, in which representatives of the fifteen member governments behind closed doors make decisions that bind their national parliaments.

In three main ways, the design of the European Union makes it difficult for national parliaments to control their respective executives. First, the closed nature of Council deliberations creates critical informational asymmetries. Second, the increased application of Qualified Majority Voting (and the reduced use of unanimity procedures) in the Council makes it difficult for national parliaments to force governments to make prior policy commitments. Indeed, since any one state can be voted down in the Council, such commitments may even be pointless. Third, regardless of the Council decision rule, the extensive involvement of national ministers and civil servants in drafting and implementing EU legislation tends to marginalize national parliaments. The resulting information deficit makes it very difficult for domestic MPs to control their governments in European matters. Not surprisingly, the overwhelming majority of both member state MPs and Members of the European Parliament (MEPs) think that national parliamentary control of EU legislation is weak and in need of strengthening (Katz 1999; Müller *et al.* 2001).

In response, national parliaments have sought to create general and encompassing links to the EP, through such avenues as (*a*) regular meetings between the Presidents/Speakers of all fifteen parliaments and (*b*) co-operation between the EP and the national EU Affairs Committees within the Conference of European Affairs Committees of the Parliaments of the European Union [COSAC]. However, their lack of decision-making powers limits these arenas to symbolic gestures and general networking.

Yet, not all is gloom and doom for member state democracy. Domestically, the European Affairs Committees are probably the most important institutional innovation connecting the national Parliament to supranational decision-making. All fifteen EU countries now have EU Affairs Committees that advise and scrutinize their respective government (Bergman 1997). Hence, in such policy areas as foreign policy and agriculture, some national parliamentarians now receive more information than they did when these issues were an exclusively domestic matter (e.g. see Bergman and Damgaard 2000). Yet, there is considerable variation in how domestic legislatures scrutinize Council meetings. The northern European member states have more Euro-sceptical citizens, and their national parliaments are more inclined and better prepared to scrutinize EU proposals (Bergman 2000). Table 4.15 illustrates the cross-national variations reported by the country experts. As the criteria for judging relative influence can vary, expert judgments need to be considered with care. Yet, Table 4.15 is consistent with previous studies (Bergman 1997, 2000; Raunio and Hix 2000; Raunio and Wiberg 2000).

The parliaments of Austria, Belgium, Germany, Greece, Ireland, and Luxembourg allow MEPs to participate in the preparation of national policy prior to Council deliberations. Apparently, in the minds of European politicians, EU issues are beginning to transcend the traditional distinction between domestic and foreign policy. If these countries portend a new trend, then MEPs could become more involved in national politics.

Table 4.15. *National Scrutiny Process before a Decision in the EU Council of Ministers, Lower House only (1993–2000)*[a]

Country and year[b]	Members in the EU Affairs Committee	EU Affairs Committee, jurisdiction includes			Ministers appears before EU Affairs Committee	Degree of involvement		
		Pillar I	Pillar II	Pillar III		Other parliamentary committees	Plenary meetings	Overall estimate of influence on cabinet ministers
Austria								
1995	MP	Yes	Yes	Yes	Yes	Weak	Weak	Moderate
1996–2000	MP + MEP	Yes	Yes	Yes	Yes	Weak	Weak	Moderate
Belgium								
1993–2000	MP + MEP	Yes	Yes	Yes	Yes	Weak	Weak	Weak
Denmark								
1993–2000	MP	Yes	Yes	Yes	Yes	Moderate	Weak	Strong
Finland								
1995–2000	MP	Yes	No	Yes	Yes	Strong	Moderate	Moderate
France								
1993–2000	MP	Yes	Yes	Yes	Yes	Weak	Weak	Weak
Germany								
1993–2000	MP + MEP	Yes	Yes	Yes	Yes	Strong	Weak	Weak
Greece								
1993–2000	MP + MEP	Yes	Yes	Yes	Yes	Weak	Weak	Weak
Ireland								
1993–2000	MP + MEP	Yes	Yes	Yes	Yes	Weak	Weak	Weak
Italy								
1993–6	MP	Yes	No	No	No	Weak	Moderate	Weak
1997–2000	MP	Yes	Yes	Yes	Yes	Weak	Moderate	Moderate
Luxembourg								
1993–2000	MP + MEP	Yes	Yes	Yes	Yes	Weak	Weak	Weak
The Netherlands								
1993–9	MP	Yes	Yes	Yes	Yes	Moderate	Weak	Weak
2000	MP	Yes	Yes	Yes	Yes	Moderate	Weak	Moderate
Portugal								
1993–2000	MP	Yes	Yes	Yes	Yes	Moderate	Weak	Weak
Spain								
1993–2000	MP	Yes	Yes	Yes	Yes	Weak	Weak	Weak
Sweden								
1995–2000	MP	Yes	Yes	Yes	Yes	Moderate	Weak	Moderate
United Kingdom								
1993–97	MP	Yes	No	No	Yes	Weak	Weak	Weak
1998–2000	MP	Yes	Yes	Yes	Yes	Weak	Weak	Weak

[a] Norway and Iceland are excluded from this table because they are not members of the European Union.

[b] Austria, Finland, and Sweden became EU members on 1 January 1995, which is why no data is reported before that date for these three countries.

The EU Affairs Committees vary in jurisdiction, commonly reflecting those of the three EU 'pillars'. All EU Committees have some oversight over their respective governments with regard to the First Pillar, which includes the internal market and other areas of EU decision-making proper. In Common Security and Foreign Policy (Pillar II) and Justice and Home Affairs (Pillar III), there is more variation. In contrast to the supranational First Pillar, these are policy areas in which traditional international decision-making procedures usually apply. Since the formation of the Union on 1 November 1993, almost all EU Affairs Committees have been involved in scrutiny in all three pillars. The Italian and British EU Affairs Committees were until 1997 limited to the supranational EU pillar. The Finnish EU Affairs Committee does not process issues under Pillar II, which is instead a matter for the Foreign Affairs Committee. Nonetheless, the cross-national pattern is clear. The EU Committees, and, to varying degrees, other parliamentary committees have a broad mandate to scrutinize all aspects of EU politics.

But what real influence can national parliaments have on day-to-day policy-making in the Union? Table 4.15 shows that all EU Affairs Committees can ask cabinet ministers to report on upcoming EU Council meetings and on EU legislative proposals. However, with the notable exceptions of Finland and Germany, and to a lesser extent Denmark, Portugal, and Sweden, regular parliamentary committees have limited involvement in the oversight of EU Affairs. EU politics is not shaped by plenary deliberations in parliament, either. Only in Finland and Italy are such deliberations reported to be of more than casual importance in shaping national EU policy.

Our contributors assess the overall parliamentary influence on cabinet ministers in EU affairs as weak, moderate, or strong. 'Weak' signifies a process best characterized as an exchange of information between cabinet ministers and MPs. 'Moderate' represents a case in which the parliament offers input upon which the cabinet normally acts. 'Strong' means that the parliament is actively involved in shaping the country's EU policy and that the cabinet only deviates from that policy if it has strong reasons to do so. Formally, the Austrian Parliament has the most powerful EU Affairs Committee. In practice, however, largely due to the record of minority cabinets, it is the Danish EU Affairs Committee that has most strongly influenced the cabinet, by actually rejecting EU proposals to which the latter had agreed. The EU Affairs Committees in Finland and Sweden also actively scrutinize their governments. Finally, since the late 1990s, the Dutch and Italian Parliaments have become more active and influential. In the remaining countries, influence over national preparation and coordination of EU Affairs resides primarily—if not almost exclusively—with the executive branch.

The cross-national pattern of generally weak parliamentary oversight in EU Affairs applies even to Iceland and Norway. As non-members of the European Union, they adhere to the European Economic Area (EEA) treaty, which extends the internal market for the free movement of people, goods, services, and capital. In addition, EEA member states cooperate with the European Union on the environment, social policy, education, and other issues. Formally, the Parliaments in the EEA states can refuse to ratify new EU legislation. In practice, however, the EEA treaty forces these countries either to follow EU decisions over which they have little control, or to jeopardize the entire EEA agreement. Compared to the EU member states, the Icelandic and Norwegian Parliaments are yet another step removed from the institutions that shape

EU policies. Furthermore, over time, the EEA countries seem to have been progressively marginalized in EU decision-making. At least, that is certainly the view from the EEA states themselves, as Strøm and Narud point out in Chapter 17.

Controlling the Cabinet?

In all our countries, cabinet appointment confers a wide range of resources, as well as extensive control over the parliamentary agenda. Hence, there are informational and resource gaps between the government and the parliamentarians. For democratic governance to work, parliamentarians must be able to breach those gaps and effectively monitor and scrutinize their agents in the cabinet.

Since the inception of parliamentary government, the screening powers of the legislature over the executive have been central to parliamentary control. The selection procedures assure that whoever is appointed PM is at least tacitly acceptable to a majority of MPs. This in practice means that the PM and the cabinet have to be acceptable to the political parties that represent a majority of the MPs. In some countries the formal threshold is set higher than that, and a new cabinet must win a (positive) vote of investiture. After investiture, the ultimate weapon of the Parliament is the no-confidence vote. But as we have noted, although the no-confidence vote is a powerful threat, it is also a blunt one that is often not credible. Hence, other and less dramatic accountability mechanisms ensure some measure of parliamentary control of the cabinet. Parliamentary questions and debates as well as committee investigations are ways by which parliamentarians can try to gather and disseminate information about government activities.

Parliamentary systems feature a number of institutions that strengthen the cabinet's hand in responding to parliamentary oversight. They allow cabinet members to try to force parliamentary compliance by threatening to resign. Most of them also place the right to dissolve parliament and call new elections in the hands of the PM and/or the cabinet. Such rules often allow the cabinet to pick a favourable time for a new election. The fact that such plans sometimes go awry is another matter. Thus, the institutions of parliamentary government include a number of accountability mechanisms but usually also limit their impact in the interest of political stability. And the executive prerogatives that characterize parliamentarism not only enhance the executive's role in governance, but also weaken the incentives for parliamentary oversight.

DELEGATION WITHIN THE CABINET

The cabinet is at the heart of national policy-making under parliamentary democracy. As Rose (1991: 9) puts it: 'Parliament does not in any meaningful sense govern; that is the responsibility of the executive in which a Prime Minister is primus'. Laver and Shepsle (1996: 28–9) characterize the cabinet's role somewhat more comprehensively: '(I)t is the cabinet that symbolizes the apex of political responsibility. It is the Cabinet that is expected to guide affairs of the state by making and overseeing the implementation of policy on important issues. It is the cabinet that is expected to react to and deal with major crises and emergencies. And, perhaps most significantly of all, it is the cabinet whose survival is on the line at election times'.

To understand delegation within the core executive, we must be able to identify a principal, who at the same time is the parliament's agent. Here is where the doctrine of parliamentary democracy is ambiguous: is the principal the PM or the cabinet? The collective responsibility of the cabinet to parliament would suggest that parliament delegates to the cabinet collectively. Moreover, many constitutions vest a set of powers, often critical ones, in the cabinet collectively. At the same, the PM's formal role in the appointment and dismissal of cabinet members would suggest that he is the direct agent of parliament and the master of his cabinet colleagues. Moreover, PMs enjoy additional prerogatives, such as agenda control over cabinet meetings, that suggest their supremacy vis-à-vis the other cabinet members. Yet, in coalition governments the PM's appointment and dismissal powers are almost exclusively formal with respect to the cabinet members from parties other than his or her own. Often PMs are also seriously constrained with respect to the appointment and dismissal of cabinet members from their own party. But then, while the PM's constitutional powers are 'clipped' in forming a coalition government, he or she can occasionally shake off these chains once a cabinet has assumed office, either by exploiting situations in which the coalition partner(s) have little bargaining power (and mostly with regard to relatively minor issues) or by threatening to end the coalition.[38]

Agency problems within the cabinet then depend on the perspective one takes on whose agent the cabinet minister is. We shall generally consider the PM the principal and the other cabinet members the agents. Yet, there are at least five competing forces that pull and tug at cabinet members and cause potential agency problems in their relationship with the PM: party, coalition, faction, department, and personal (though not necessarily political) ambition. As mentioned above, parliamentary government is in large part party government, and nowhere do parties control political recruitment as tightly as with respect to cabinet access (see Strøm 2000). The fusion of the executive and the parliamentary majority, which Bagehot (1963: 65) called the 'efficient secret' of parliamentary government, nowadays very much rests on cohesive political parties. The *party* is relevant even in coalition governments, which account for roughly 60 per cent of the governments covered in this volume. Here, however, each cabinet member is the servant of two masters—his or her party and the coalition. While the respective minister's party generally expects him or her to push party goals, the coalition partners want the minister to be faithful to the coalition agreement (Strøm and Müller 1999). For some government parties, *factionalism* complicates delegation and accountability. If ministers adhere to factional rather than party goals, party leaders have another reason

---

[38] For example, in 1982, when the German coalition between the SPD and the FDP clearly was close to its end, but the alternative coalition had not yet been negotiated, Chancellor Schmidt dismissed the FDP cabinet members and continued in office with a single-party SPD Cabinet until the deal between the FDP and the CDU/CSU was struck.

to worry about agency loss (while for their coalition partners it may either aggravate
or diminish agency problems, depending on their policy distance to the faction relative
to the party). Yet another pull derives from the fact that most cabinet ministers are first
and foremost heads of *government departments*. Lack of department-specific knowledge,
or a deliberate strategy to win their civil servants' support, may transform ministers into
department ambassadors, who promote their ministry's interests rather than government or party policy (Andeweg 1988). Given that the success or failure of ministers
usually is measured against their achievements as department heads, they clearly have
incentives to promote agency interests over other commitments. Moreover, agency
loss may be a function of *personal ambition*. Even if ministers share the bond that
co-partisanship provides, their personal career incentives may be quite different from
those of the PM or the party leader. As King (1975: 230) has noted with regard to Britain,
'every Cabinet contains the Prime Minister's future successors and therefore, probably,
his present rivals'. Indeed, these may be included in the cabinet precisely because they
are the PM's rivals. As cabinet members they share collective cabinet responsibility and
cannot openly criticize government policy (Rose 1976: 356). If anything, personal rivalry
will be greater in coalitions, in particular if the coalition parties actively compete for the
premiership. Finally, agency loss can even result from a *lack* of ambition on the ministers' part (leisure shirking), or from their prioritization of their private interests.

   Agency problems may derive not only from conflicting preferences within the
cabinet, but also from asymmetries of information. Individual cabinet members, particularly in their capacities as heads of departments, are flooded with information and
demands on their attention. Most studies of cabinet decision-making report that 'line'
ministers largely defer to their colleagues on issues outside the jurisdiction of their
respective ministry (Andeweg 2000: 378), at least in part because they have no time and
opportunity to inform themselves about the majority of issues that reach the cabinet.
These shortages of time and asymmetries of information are only slightly less severe
for the PM. For all these reasons, the PM may have good reason to worry about agency
problems within the cabinet.

Prime Ministers and the Policy Process

Although the PM, like all other political principals, must battle agency problems, he or
she is a figure that can wield enormous influence. Figure 4.3, which is a stylized representation of the cabinet policy process, identifies the primary sources of prime
ministerial influence. First, the PM typically plays a major role in the *appointment* of
cabinet members. Second, the PM may in different ways delineate the responsibilities of
each of these ministers. Appointment itself contains an important element of choice with
regard to the *jurisdiction* of ministers. Although sometimes a particular person—typically
a party heavyweight—cannot be excluded from the cabinet, the PM can give him or her
a portfolio of little import or one that controls a jurisdiction in which their preferences
are particularly closely aligned. Moreover, the PM may be able to shift departmental
jurisdictions (or administrative units) from one department to another, or to merge or
split ministries. The departmental structure may influence the proposals to cabinet not

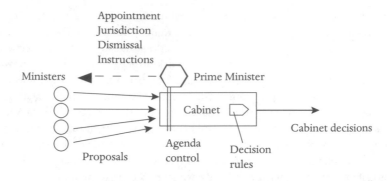

**Figure 4.3. The Policy Process Within Cabinet and (Potential)
Prime Ministerial Powers.**

only because of the preferences of the ministers in charge, but also because different departmental cultures may cause different problem definitions and strategies (hence whether universities are teamed ministerially with either research or education may lead to either research- or teaching-orientated ministry proposals). Third, the PM has *dismissal power* vis-à-vis the other cabinet members. Although this ultimate weapon is not used very frequently in practice, ministers live and work in the shadow of potential dismissal. They can never be safe in their office and hence have incentives to be faithful agents. Fourth, PMs may have the formal right to *instruct* the ministers. These instructions can be procedural (e.g. on the time-priorities of issues) or material (e.g. what general direction a proposal to cabinet should take). Fifth, PMs often have (negative) *agenda control*, which means that they can prevent ministers from bringing issues to the attention of the cabinet. Sixth, the cabinet decision rules may give the PM a special *role in cabinet decision-making*, well beyond having one vote in a body of 10–20 people. Yet, the PM can only use (or, at least, benefit from) many of these rules if he can draw on sufficient *personnel* resources to provide the required information. Below, we therefore survey not only the relevant rules but also the support staff situation.[39]

This range of prime ministerial powers might suggest that under parliamentary government, the cabinet is a strict hierarchy, in which all the individual 'line' ministers are fully and equally subordinated to the PM. And while this is a useful ideal type of cabinet politics, reality is a good deal more complex. Certainly, constitutional rules matter and in some cases do establish a hierarchical command structure. Thus, as Giovanni Sartori puts it, the German Chancellor is 'first above equals' in part because of two institutional rules, the most important of which is the constructive vote of no-confidence. According to Sartori (1997: 107), the premiership system receives 'an additional reinforcement... from the fact that Parliament appoints only the Chancellor, not—as in most parliamentary systems—the full government'.

---

[39] Another power the Prime Minister may hold either unilaterally or share with the cabinet is the right to call a confidence vote. Huber and McCarty (2001) argue that PMs who hold this right enjoy an advantage vis-à-vis those who do not.

Not all PMs are so constitutionally privileged. But then, the power of PMs rests not only on such constitutional foundations, but also on how secure they are in office, or in other words, on how costly it would be to replace them. Thus, in Sartori's typology of Western European PMs, the German-style 'first above equals' is only the second-strongest category. At least the British PM is, as a 'first above unequals', even more powerful in relation to the other cabinet members (Sartori 1997: 103). Yet, the power of the British PM rests less on institutional rules than on party and party system characteristics, more precisely on the dominance of two cohesive and strong parties, which produces stable single-party cabinets. Yet, British PMs remain in office only as long as their respective party considers them an electoral asset (as Margaret Thatcher experienced in 1990; see Jones 1995).

Thus, there are two determinants of prime ministerial power: (*a*) the characteristics of party politics and (*b*) institutional rules (in Sartori's account represented primarily by the constructive no-confidence vote). Sartori considers the former factor more important. Specifically, prime ministerial power depends on 'strong partisan discipline' and a two-party system. Conversely, if these conditions are not present, the PM's constitutional powers are likely to be more formal than real, and going beyond them will be simply impossible.

Party Politics

Party politics is structured in part by the institutions that govern delegation from voters to parliament, as well as delegation from parliament to the cabinet. In this section we take them as given. We have identified two relevant aspects of party politics—party cohesion and party system format. Since we have already discussed party cohesion in a previous section, we concentrate here on the party system. More specifically it is the party composition of the incumbent cabinet and its most likely replacement that affects prime ministerial powers and, more generally, cabinet decision-making.

We distinguish three types of party system, defined by the modes of party competition for government office: two-party systems, two-bloc systems, and pivotal systems (for a similar perspective see Mair 1997: 206–14). Typically countries fall into one of these categories in stable ways, though there are shifts from one type to another. But the important point is the different competitive logics of these respective types.

Two-party systems may have more than two parliamentary parties, but only two are strong enough to compete for government office. They alternate in government in single-party majority or stable minority cabinets (Sartori 1976). In such governments the PM is the leader of the electorally victorious party, thus combining the authority of his party office and that of PM. Elections are contests between alternative PMs, both directly (with the voters voting for the party led by the more appealing prime ministerial candidate) and indirectly (through the effects of leadership on the party and/or the cabinet) (Crewe and King 1994; King 2002). The government party must be careful not to damage the leadership image of the PM and consequently must submit to him or her.

Two-bloc party systems are defined by competition for government office between two blocs of (stably) aligned parties, which often form pre-electoral coalitions. At first sight the logic of party competition seems identical to that of two-party systems. Yet, a bloc of two or more parties is not a party. Typically, there is also electoral competition within each bloc. While the overarching goal for all parties is to win a bloc majority, the individual parties are also concerned about their own strength, which, *inter alia*, may influence their share in the spoils from government office. What does this imply for PMs in two-bloc party systems? On the one hand—except when the office of PM itself is contested among the parties of one bloc (as has occasionally happened among the non-Socialist parties in France)—PMs are safe in office as long as the respective bloc wins. And this safety may allow them to exploit their formal powers. On the other hand, even in well-established blocs, the defection of one party seems more likely than a party split in two-party systems. This is what German Chancellor Helmut Schmidt experienced in 1982, when the FDP—after having fought three elections in alliance with and helped by the SPD—crossed the floor, removed Schmidt from government office, and subsequently contested five elections in alliance with the CDU/CSU.

Finally, in pivotal party systems, the party composition of government is decided not in elections but in negotiations between party leaders. Parties fight elections individually rather than in alliance with other parties. Cabinet composition and the office of PM are up for grabs in (mostly post-electoral) coalition negotiations. Under such circumstances the PM is hardly ever safe. In coalition government an incumbent PM needs not only to appeal to the voters but also keep the coalition partner(s) happy. And the coalition partners have both incentives and means to check the PM. Consequently, he or she is severely constrained from making full use of the institutional prerogatives of office.

Some party systems are hybrids, in which the alternative to single-party government is not a single party but either a solid bloc of parties or a loose coalition, or the alternative to a solid bloc of parties is not a competing bloc but a loose coalition. Such party systems may engender different cabinet dynamics at different times. Another hybrid type is coalition government in which one party has an absolute parliamentary majority (e.g. Austria 1945–49, Germany 1957–60). In such situations, the PM can be expected to be strong, though not as strong as in a single-party cabinet.

A final hybrid type is the weak single-party minority cabinet (the Danish, Italian, and—much less frequently—the Belgian and Finnish cases rather than Swedish Social Democratic minority cabinets). In some respect it resembles a coalition government in a pivotal party system: the PM (and indeed any cabinet member) is insecure and concessions have to be made to other parliamentary parties. In other respects the weak single-party minority cabinet resembles the single-party majority cabinet. The PM presides over party comrades exclusively and they may have even greater incentive to submit to the leader than in majority situations, since they cannot count on majority support in parliament and since as a rule cabinet survival depends on the skills of the PM as negotiator. Therefore, if we consider the PM's power in the cabinet rather than in the political system at large, weak minority single-party cabinets come closer to single-party majority than to pivotal system coalition cabinets.

We now turn to the empirical record. Several party systems have not changed their format. The party systems of the United Kingdom, Spain, and—leaving aside the short period of coalition government—Greece, have always been two-party systems, while—again leaving aside exceptions—those of Iceland, Luxembourg, and The Netherlands have always been pivotal ones. France has consistently been a two-bloc system in the electoral arena, though it has occasionally produced single-party cabinets.

The party systems of Austria, Belgium, Denmark, Finland, Germany, Ireland, Italy, Norway, Portugal, and Sweden have gone back and forth between different party system types. Austria has been a two-party system between 1966 and 1983 and otherwise a pivotal system. Germany has shifted between a pivotal system and a two-bloc system. Typically, a pivotal coalition transformed itself into a bloc of government parties that eventually broke down (as happened in 1982) or was voted out of office (as happened in 1998). Ireland covers almost the full spectrum of party system types, it has been close to two-party (under Fianna Fáil single-party cabinets), two-bloc (under Fine Gael–Labour cabinets), and—since Fianna Fáil became 'coalitionable' and Labour has been in government with both major parties—pivotal.

Norway and Sweden have gone back and forth between two-bloc (with the Social Democrats in office) and pivotal systems (with various government or parliamentary coalitions). Given the fragility and short duration of the Swedish red–green alliance of the 1950s, we consider the party system of that time as pivotal rather than two-bloc. Even when the choice in elections is between Social Democratic single-party government and a competing bloc of non-socialist parties, the internal workings of the 'bloc' are those of a pivotal coalition in Norway and Sweden. This is clear from the facts that it remains a matter of post-electoral negotiations which party will get the premiership (occasionally leading to PMs from relatively small parties—Bondevik and Ullsten) and that the other parties are generally not willing to submit to the PM. Denmark and Italy in its First Republic also have gone back and forth between single-party and coalition cabinets, but the former was never close to a majority. In its Second Republic Italy features blocs of aligned parties contesting elections but less intra-bloc cohesion than other two-bloc systems.

Institutional Powers of Prime Ministers

Even if prime ministerial power depends in large part of party system, it is also a function of a number of institutional choices. Sartori (1997) thus focuses on two features of the relationship between parliament and the cabinet. Borrowing from Bagehot (1963), the *constructive vote of no-confidence* can be labelled the 'efficient secret' of the Bonn Constitution and has been copied in a number of onstitutional reforms since the 1970s, including in our sample Spain and Belgium (since 1995). The second Sartorian dimension is *ministerial accountability*—whether the ministers can be held accountable directly by parliament or only via the PM. As mentioned above, in some countries ministers can indeed be held accountable to parliament only via the PM. That is, parliament can censure an individual minister only by a vote of no confidence in the PM, thereby forcing the entire cabinet to resign. Elsewhere, individual ministers face a double jeopardy: they may be dismissed either by the PM or by the parliamentary majority. Below we shall consider more systematically prime ministerial appointment and dismissal powers, along with other relevant factors that affect the delegation relationships within the cabinet.

Appointment and Dismissal.   Appointment and dismissal powers clearly distinguish the PM from other cabinet members. In Portugal and Sweden (since 1975), the PM formally appoints the other cabinet members. Elsewhere in Western Europe, the PM is the gatekeeper who proposes the other cabinet members (and thus controls the screening of ministers) while the Head of State makes the formal appointment. Given the lack of influence of many Heads of State, this difference may be more formal than real. The major exception is France, where the President exerts great influence on the selection of cabinet ministers in situations of non-*cohabitation* and some influence even in situations of *cohabitation*. On occasion, the President has influenced the appointment process even in Austria and, more frequently, Finland (see the country chapters).

Yet, in coalition systems there are strong conventions that the PM controls the appointment of the ministers from his or her own party only. De facto, the respective party leaders choose the other ministers. In the vast majority of Western European postwar coalition cabinets, each party has been free to fill its own cabinet portfolios (Müller and Strøm 2000a: 574). A seasoned Austrian coalition politician once coined the term the 'chimpanzee principle' for this practice, meaning that the PM would have to accept even a chimpanzee as minister if nominated by the coalition partner. However, in some coalition systems, such as Germany and Norway, the PM has retained some de facto veto power over ministerial nominations.

As we have seen in the preceding section, the constitutional rule, in place in Ireland and the United Kingdom, that ministers must be recruited exclusively from Parliament can considerably constrain the PM's or party leader's choice set. Rose (1976: 363) estimates that a British PM must give ministerial appointment (including non-cabinet positions) to half or more of all MPs who are not obviously unsuited (for reasons of lack of experience, old age, or personal characteristics) for such an appointment (see also Rush 2001: 136). In Ireland the PM seems to be even more constrained. In the words of O'Leary (1991: 137) the PM 'has to choose 30 government and junior ministers from the limited pool of fewer than 90 deputies who support him. At least half of these deputies will be unsuitable for office on grounds of youth, unwillingness to serve, administrative incompetence, or emergent (or fully-blown) senility'. In Italy there is a strong convention that ministers must come from Parliament, and the real selection criteria are quite similar to those at work in Britain (Dogan 1989). The less such constitutional rules and conventions apply, the larger the pool from which PMs and party leaders can select cabinet members. A larger pool should positively affect the PM's ability to find able and willing ministers and thus reduce the potential for agency slack.

With the exception of Italy (where the written Constitution is silent on this point but PMs have been quite effective in getting rid of unwanted ministers without formally involving the Head of State), the PM's formal dismissal powers are the mirror image of his or her appointment powers. In the United Kingdom, the PM's appointment and dismissal powers are de facto identical, though dismissal does not require the formal involvement of the Monarch. In Portugal and Sweden, it is the PM who dismisses ministers, while in most other countries the PM proposes ministerial dismissal to the Head of State.

Cabinet Governance   While appointment and dismissal powers are obviously critical to cabinet delegation, the rules by which the cabinet makes decisions obviously also matter. In reviewing these, recall that parliamentary systems vary greatly in the formality and rigidity of such intra-cabinet rules. In general, they tend to be much less codified than those pertaining to parliament, presumably due to the expectation of greater prefer-ence convergence among members of the cabinet. One of the more formal and critical powers within the cabinet is the ability to determine ministerial jurisdictions. If this is in the hands of the PM, as in Denmark, France, Germany, Greece, Iceland, Ireland, Portugal, Spain, and the United Kingdom, he or she can then shift policy areas or administrative units between ministries in order to have a congenial minister.

Some constitutions also allow PMs to issue binding instructions to their ministers. The best-known example is the *Richtlinienkompetenz* of the German Chancellor. With the exceptions of Ireland and Italy (since 1988), which combine it with individual min-isterial accountability, this authority to instruct ministers exists primarily in systems where ministers are accountable to parliament only via the PM (Germany, Portugal, Spain, and the United Kingdom). The reason may be that this authority conflicts with the constitutional principle of ministerial responsibility and/or accountability. Consequently, the PM's authority is also always limited to general policy guidelines.

The PM is not the only member of the cabinet that may be more than equal. Positions such as the Deputy PM, Minister for Foreign Affairs, and Minister of Finance (or Economy) often carry particular status and influence. Finance ministers often have a position second only to the PM, as there are few government decisions of any signifi-cance that do not have financial implications. As Larsson (1993: 207–8) argues, 'the min-ister of finance can even be regarded as a second Prime Minister, since no other minister is involved in all the aspects of the life of the cabinet in the way the minister of finance is'. While other ministries, such as environmental portfolios, also may have jurisdictions that systematically crosscut those of other line ministries, they typically are not backed up by the institutional powers enjoyed by the PM or the minister of finance.

Table 4.16 identifies the PM's institutional powers in cabinet deliberations. The table employs broad categories. We refer to the country chapter for details and, in particular, for contextual information on the practical relevance of these powers. Recall that in coalition systems all formal powers tend to be circumscribed. As shown in Table 4.16, Belgium, Sweden, and the United Kingdom have no formal cabinet decision rules. In all three countries, the PM summarizes the cabinet consensus and thus has significant discretionary authority. Denmark and Spain have the same decision rule but here it is constitutionally mandated. No vote is actually taken. Finland, France, Germany, Greece, Iceland, Ireland, Luxembourg, The Netherlands, and Norway have a formal majority voting rule, even if some of these countries use it very rarely. In Austria, Italy, and Portugal, cabinet consensus is constitutionally required. Finally, in France, the President rather than the PM defines the cabinet consensus, provided that both belong to the same political alliance. Otherwise, the PM prevails.

Cabinet decision rules can favour the PM over other ministers. Agenda control, which is enjoyed by the PMs of Denmark, Germany, Ireland, Italy, Luxembourg, Portugal, and the United Kingdom, allows the PM to decide the timing of cabinet delib-eration and to preempt issues that would undermine cabinet cohesion. While cabinet decision-making everywhere in reality tends to follow informal and consensual proce-dures, the underlying rules do matter when it is possible for the PM or other cabinet members to impose them. Thus, when these rules allow the PM to summarize and

Table 4.16. *Delegation Within the Cabinet: Prime Ministers and Cabinet Ministers*

Country and year	Formal cabinet decision rule	Actual decision rule	PM right to appoint[a]	PM right to dismiss[a]	Ministers' parliamentary accountability	PM formal right to decide ministry jurisdiction?	PM steering or coordination rights vis-à-vis ministers?	PM full control over cabinet agenda?	Administrative structure under the PM's supervision
Austria									
1945–86	Yes	Unanimity	Through act by President	Through act by President	Direct	No	Yes	No	Civil service staff
1987–2000	Yes	Unanimity	Through act by President	Through act by President	Direct	No	Yes	No	Personal staff (political appointees); civil service staff
Belgium									
1945–2000	No	Consensus defined by PM	No	No	Direct	No	Yes	No	Personal staff (political appointees); civil service staff
Denmark									
1945–63	Yes	Consensus defined by PM	Through act by Monarch	Through act by Monarch	Direct	Yes	No	Yes	None
1964–2000	Yes	Consensus defined by PM	Through act by Monarch	Through act by Monarch	Direct	Yes	No	Yes	Civil service staff
Finland									
1945–2000	Yes	Majority	No	No	Direct	No	No	No	Personal staff (political appointees); civil service staff
France									
1959–2000	Yes	Consensus defined by President	Through act by President	Through act by President	Via PM only	Yes	Yes	No	Personal staff (political appointees); civil service staff
Germany									
1949–2000	Yes	Majority	Through act by President	Through act by President	Via PM only	Yes	Yes	Yes	Personal staff (political appointees); civil service staff
Greece									
1949–2000	Yes	Majority	Through act by President	Through act by President	Direct	Yes	Yes	No	Personal staff (political appointees); civil service staff

Iceland 1945–2000	Yes	Majority	Through act by President	Through act by President	Direct	Yes	No	No	None
Ireland 1945–2000	Yes	Majority	Through act by President	Through act by President	Direct	Yes	Yes	Yes	Personal staff (political appointees); civil service staff; PM occupies specific (PM) portfolio
Italy 1948–87	Yes	Unanimity	Through act by President	No	Direct	No	No	No	None
Italy 1988–2000	Yes	Unanimity	Through act by President	No	Direct	No	Yes	Yes	Personal staff (political appointees); civil service staff
Luxembourg 1945–94	Yes	Majority	Through act by Monarch	Through act by Monarch	Direct	No	Yes	Yes	Civil service staff; PM occupies specific (PM) portfolio
Luxembourg 1995–9	Yes	Majority	Through act by Monarch	Through act by Monarch	Direct	No	Yes	Yes	Civil service staff
Luxembourg 2000									Civil service staff; PM occupies specific (PM) portfolio
The Netherlands 1945–2000	Yes	Majority	No	No	Direct	No	No	No	Civil service staff
Norway 1945–8	Yes	Majority	Through act by Monarch	Through act by Monarch	Direct	No	No	No	None
Norway 1949–55	Yes	Majority	Through act by Monarch	Through act by Monarch	Direct	No	No	No	Personal staff (political appointees);
Norway 1956–2000	Yes	Majority	Through act by Monarch	Through act by Monarch	Direct	No	No	No	Personal staff (political appointees); civil service staff
Portugal 1976–2000	Yes	Unanimity	By PM alone	By PM alone	Via PM only	Yes	Yes	Yes	Personal staff (political appointees); civil service staff
Spain 1978–2000	Yes	Consensus defined by PM	Through act by Monarch	Through act by Monarch	Via PM only	Yes	Yes	Yes	Personal staff (political appointees); civil service staff

Table 4.16. (contd.)

Country and year	Formal cabinet decision rule	Actual decision rule	PM right to appoint[a]	PM right to dismiss[a]	Ministers' parliamentary accountability	PM formal right to decide ministry jurisdiction?	PM steering or coordination rights vis-a-vis ministers?	PM full control over cabinet agenda?	Administrative structure under the PM's supervision
Sweden									
1945–63	No	Consensus defined by PM	Through act by Monarch	Through act by Monarch	Direct	No	No	No	None
1964–74	No	Consensus defined by PM	Through act by Monarch	Through act by Monarch	Direct	No	No	No	Personal staff (political appointees); civil service staff
1975–2000	No	Consensus defined by PM	By PM alone	By PM alone	Direct	No	No	No	Personal staff (political appointees); civil service staff
United Kingdom									
1945–2000	No	Consensus defined by PM	Through act by Monarch	By PM alone	Via PM only	Yes	Yes	Yes	Personal staff (political appointees); civil service staff

[a] Through act by Head of State (Monarch or President) means that the PM/cabinet has the decisive influence, but that, as a formality only, the Head of State must also be involved.

interpret the sense of the meeting, his position will be stronger than when the rules prescribe voting procedures in which each cabinet member may have equal weight. At least theoretically, under a unanimity rule any single minister can prevent a cabinet decision. Majority rule lies somewhere between 'decision-making by interpretation' (Steiner and Dorff 1980) and unanimity.

Prime Ministerial Staff Formal authority may not be sufficient to prevent agency problems within the cabinet. On any particular issue, the respective line minister is likely to have much more detailed knowledge of policy than the PM. In order to offset such problems of asymmetric information, PMs need independent access to information and staff (see Peters *et al.* 2000). Nowadays all PMs except the Icelandic one have their own supporting office and staff. As Table 4.16 shows, significant prime ministerial staffs are a relatively recent development in the Nordic countries. Until the mid-1950s, with a few exceptions, the PMs in these countries had essentially no support staff of their own, except for a custodian and a couple of secretaries. By the mid-1960s, the Danish and Swedish PMs ensured that they had a civil service staff of their own. And by the mid-1970s, the Swedish PM's office began to be filled also by political appointees. Finland is an exception, as is the role of the Finnish President. Yet, relatively limited staffing is not exclusively a Nordic phenomenon. Until quite recently even the Dutch and Italian PMs had relatively limited staff support.

Summary: Institutional Powers Obviously, there is considerable variation in the rights and resources of European PMs. One way to summarize their relative institutional powers is to construct a simple index. Ours contains the two institutional variables stressed by Sartori (1997), the six active prime ministerial powers discussed above and the personnel resources at the PM's disposal. While the institutional rules have remained remarkably stable (we record only one relevant change in the case of Italy, in 1988), the personnel resources of PMs have in many cases increased over the postwar period.

These various powers are not all equally important, as our index will reflect. The first two variables, the constructive vote of no confidence and the parliamentary accountability of ministers via the PM only, are dichotomous. In each case we assign three points when these rules apply, and zero otherwise. With regard to prime ministerial appointment and dismissal powers, we add one point for each of these powers. We have noted fine institutional differences but do not consider them sufficiently important to discriminate between the countries in each main category. Likewise we add one point each for prime ministerial powers in determining ministerial jurisdictions, giving instructions to ministers, and controlling the cabinet agenda. For cabinet decision rules we allocate two points when the PM sums up the cabinet discussion, one point if majority-rule voting applies, and zero if cabinet decisions are made by unanimity. Finally, with regard to personnel resources, we distinguish between two categories of staff—civil servants and political appointees. We score one point for each type of staff resource at the PM's disposal. The maximum index value is thus fifteen. As always, the number of points allocated per dimension, the scoring on each dimension, and the placement of some cases can be discussed. However, the countries identified with institutionally powerful PMs would remain the same if we had weighted each variable identically.

Applying these counting rules to our seventeen countries, we can identify particularly institutionally powerful PMs in Spain (which scores a perfect fifteen points), Germany (fourteen) and the United Kingdom (twelve), followed by the Portuguese (ten), French (nine), and Irish (eight) PMs. The PMs of Belgium and Denmark (who have increased their scores from six to seven points over the postwar period) and Greece and Luxembourg (six) follow. Thanks to increased staffing, the institutional powers of the Swedish PM have increased (from four to six points). Towards the lower end of the spectrum, the powers of the Finnish PM have remained stable (five points), while those of the Italian and Norwegian PMs have increased (from three to five points). The powers of the Icelandic and Dutch PMs have remained unchanged (at four points), whereas those of the Austrian Chancellor, the institutionally weakest PM, have moved up marginally (from three to four points). Recall that formal prime ministerial authority and resources alone do not give us a realistic assessment of their power. As noted above, under favourable conditions PMs may be able to go well beyond their formal powers while under unfavourable conditions (including coalition government) they may be severely constrained.

Assessing Prime Ministerial Power   We can now bring the two determinants of prime ministerial power, party system cohesion and institutional authority, together. Figure 4.4 places each country according to our discussion in the text and Table 4.16. The vertical dimension represents the prime ministerial powers derived from party and party system characteristics, reflecting the three major categories distinguished above (single-party cabinets, 'bloc' coalition cabinets, and coalition cabinets in pivotal party systems). We again use a fifteen-point scheme. This is not meant to indicate that the party and institutional dimensions are of equal importance. We tend to agree with Sartori that the former is more important than the latter. In the party dimension we have given fifteen points to majority and thirteen points to minority single-party cabinets. Countries with a mixed record are placed in-between according to the time spent under the respective type (thus a country is scored at fourteen if there is an even split between majority and minority single-party cabinets). We have given ten points to 'bloc' coalition cabinets, and five points to coalition cabinets in pivotal party systems. Finally, we have adjusted the placement on the basis of party system characteristics by moving systems with less cohesive parties down by two points. Note that the numbering of the respective countries does not indicate a temporal sequence but the relative strength of the PM within different party system configurations. Figure 4.4 covers the entire post-war period. Yet, some of these cabinets were clearly exceptions in the countries' overall record and hence have been introduced with shaded rather than bold symbols.[40] In our discussion we will leave these cases aside.

The horizontal dimension of Fig. 4.4 represents institutional powers. To keep the figure readable we have refrained from reporting temporal variation. The PMs are placed at

---

[40] In Belgium, five cabinets were single-party, two minority, and three majority. Of the former, one (Spaak) lasted for a mere 7 days and the latter all occurred in the early 1950s under the only single-party majority in postwar Belgium. In Finland, four of thirty-seven partisan cabinets were single-party, one in each decade from the 1940s to the 1970s. In Germany three minority single-party cabinets lasted only for a few days and the only majority one dates back to 1960–61.

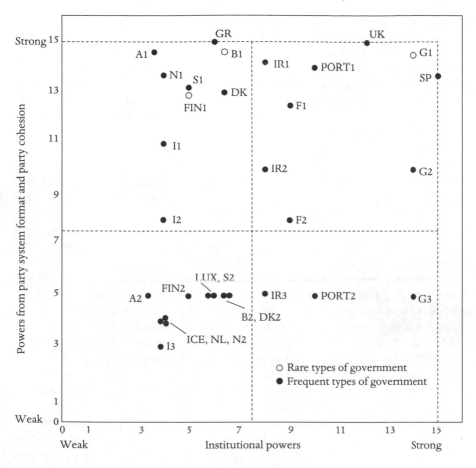

Figure 4.4. **Prime Ministerial Powers in Western Europe.**

the mean within the ranges reported above. None of these temporal variations amounts to more than two out of fifteen points, and the change has always strengthened prime ministerial powers. Hence, Fig. 4.4 slightly underrates the current institutional powers of the Austrian, Belgian, Danish, Italian, Norwegian, and Swedish PMs.

Overall prime ministerial power thus increases along the diagonal from the lower left-hand corner of Fig. 4.4 to the upper right-hand corner. Of course our scheme is a reduction of the real world's complexity. We do not, for example, take into account the different personalities of PMs. Given these simplifications, our classification fits remarkably well with qualitative assessments of prime ministerial power in Western European democracies.

According to Fig. 4.4, the British and Spanish PMs are thus the strongest ones. The Greek PM has fewer institutional powers, but single-party government and cohesive parties have lifted those incumbents who have been party politicians to the apex of prime ministerial power. These placements are in line with most of the empirical literature. King (1991: 43), for example, claims that 'the British Prime Minister is probably able to be more powerful inside his or her own government than any other head of government anywhere else in the democratic world'.[41] Likewise, the placement of Spain can easily be accommodated with Heywood's (1991) account of the Spanish PM's power and Bar's (1997) classification of Spain as a case of 'prime ministerial government'. Finally, our inclusion of Greece among the particularly strong PMs conforms to Koutsoukis' (1994) characterization of the Greek PM as the *'primus solus'*, the 'singularly powerful' head in a 'system of "Prime Minister centrism"' (1994: 273, 280). Those PMs in Portugal, Ireland, France, Denmark, Sweden, Norway, Austria, and even Italy who headed single-party cabinets have more in common with this premier league of PMs than with their compatriots who led coalition governments.

The PM of 'bloc' coalition cabinets in France and—for some time—the German Chancellor and the Irish Taoiseach fall in the upper right quadrant of Fig. 4.4, indicating considerable institutional powers and a cohesive bloc of government parties. Yet, Irish PMs have done better or worse than this placement but German Chancellors only worse. In the lower right hand quadrant of Fig. 4.4 we find PMs who are institutionally relatively strong but who are constrained by coalition government. The German Chancellor stands out here, being more powerful than the Portuguese and Irish PMs under coalition rule and Finnish PMs, who invariably serve in coalition governments. The Italian PM in the Second Republic also ends up in the upper half of Fig. 4.4, but the lack of party cohesion and formal powers do not allow him to play a particularly strong role.

Accounts of the German system all stress the Chancellor's enormous institutional powers. According to Müller-Rommel (1994: 162) 'the Chancellor plays a dominant role in Cabinet decision making', not so much because of direct interference in domestic policy but because this job is effectively done at the pre-cabinet stage by the Chancellor's 450 staff members. The constraints resulting from multi-party cabinets are also generally noted, though the literature lends support to our distinction between pivotal and bloc politics: 'the FDP dares not play fast and loose with a coalition it has established, because a substantial proportion of its own electoral support came from the voters either favouring its formation in the first place or subsequently attracted to the alignment. Why jeopardize that support?' (Smith 1991: 53). In such situations, we have argued, the Chancellor is less restricted than in pivotal systems in the exercise of formal powers. Yet, several German Chancellors have not chaired their respective parties or have maintained rather distant relationships with them (Padgett 1993; Helms 2001), which has increased their appeal to the general public but reduced their grip on their party comrades.

Empirical accounts of the French case stress the role of the President in cabinet decision-making, given the fact that he chairs official cabinet meetings and is involved

---

[41] Three years later, however, King is somewhat more equivocal: 'The British prime minister is, within his own domestic sphere, one of the most powerful heads of government in the Western world, far more powerful than most prime ministers in Western Europe' (King 1994: 210).

in as much of cabinet affairs as he wants to—provided that he belongs to the parliamentary majority. In this situation, the President 'borrows' much of the PM's formal powers, adding them to the considerable ones of his own office (Elgie and Machin 1991; Thiébault 1994). Alone, the PM is then probably weaker than indicated in Figure 4.4, but counting the PM and the President together as a dual Chief Executive, France would probably end up close to Spain and the United Kingdom. Under *cohabitation*, however, our placement seems appropriate.

Likewise, those who have studied the Irish Taoiseach generally stress the powers of the office. Farrell (1994: 79) calls him (as yet there had been no females) the 'master of the Cabinet'. O'Leary (1991: 159) concludes: 'Within his own political system the Irish Prime Minister is potentially more powerful than any other European Prime Minister, with the exception of his British counterpart'. Yet, O'Leary distinguishes between different types of government (single-party versus coalition and majority versus minority) and discusses concomitant variations in prime ministerial power (1991: 156–9). Strikingly, the Irish PM tends to be strong even in coalitions. Yet, as the large majority of these have been 'bloc' rather than pivotal coalitions, we should not be surprised to find a fairly strong PM.

Finally, in the lower left-hand quadrant of Fig. 4.4 we find PMs that neither have strong institutional powers nor are in the comfortable situation of having only co-partisan cabinet colleagues. Leaving aside the exceptions already reported, the Prime Ministers of Iceland, Belgium, Finland, Luxembourg, and The Netherlands belong permanently to this group; those of Austria, Italy, Norway, Sweden, and Denmark only temporarily. At the low end on both dimensions we find the Italian PM under the typical coalition government of the First Republic.

The Austrian Chancellors of single-party governments gave rise to the thesis of prime ministerial government (Welan 1976), and without doubt Bruno Kreisky, leading the centralized and highly disciplined Social Democrats of the 1970s, was among the most powerful PMs of Western Europe. The return in 1983 to coalition politics, however, has occasioned a much more sober assessment of prime ministerial power. While the Chancellor (and party leader) is above the ministers of his own party, he is on not much more than equal terms with the leader of the second coalition party, who de facto assumes many prime ministerial powers with regard to his own team of ministers (Gerlich *et al.* 1988; Müller 1994). Things seem to be similar in Denmark. Schou (1997: 207) notes that in coalition governments the PM's powers 'have to be shared, or at least negotiated, with the leaders of coalition parties'. The Norwegian PM has been labelled a 'political organizer but no superstar' (Olsen 1983: 81). Eriksen (1997) notes differences between prime ministerial powers in single-party and coalition governments along the lines suggested here. The end points of the spectrum of prime ministerial powers are marked by, on the one hand, Einar Gerhardsen's series of single-party Labour cabinets, and, on the other, most PMs in coalition cabinets (Eriksen 1997: 219–21; also Strøm 1994). The Swedish picture is similar, though prime ministerial effectiveness seems to have been limited more by the lack of personnel resources than by intra-party tensions. Mutual trust and a very high degree of preference alignment within the Social Democratic party have tended not to necessitate day-to-day prime ministerial interference in policy-making.[42] PMs in coalition cabinets have been more constrained and have often relied on 'an informal inner cabinet together with the other leaders' (Larsson 1994: 176, 1997).

Finally, we turn to those countries that are placed permanently in the lower left-hand quadrant.[43] Nousiainen (1994: 98) discusses the Finnish PM's role in cabinet decision-making under the heading 'little power but some influence'. PMs cannot use their formal powers vis-à-vis Cabinet members from other parties and are constrained even in relation to ministers from their own party (see also Nousiainen 1997). The Belgian Cabinet seems to feature more intra-party hierarchy, but the PM is largely limited to exercising his powers vis-à-vis the members of his own party. As Frognier (1997: 92) puts it, the PM is 'a *"primus* of the *primi"*—the latter being the Deputy Prime Ministers', who are the leaders of the other coalition parties (see also Timmermans 1994: 117). And concerning The Netherlands, Andeweg in 1991 considered Hans Daalder's judgement, that 'Dutch ministers serve *with*, rather than *under* a Prime Minister', 'as valid today as it was in 1955' (1991: 130).

The Italian PM of the First Republic stands out in our classification as particularly impotent. Indeed, most accounts of the office stress its weakness (e.g. see Cotta 1997: 149). Hine and Finocchi (1991: 79) come closest to a comparative assessment of the Italian PM: 'Compared with Prime Ministers in most parliamentary democracies, few postwar Italian Prime Ministers would rank as powerful leaders'. Even Criscitiello (1994: 197), who generally sees the PM as slightly more powerful, stresses that his powers within the cabinet 'remain limited by the need for coalition bargaining, and by the power of party leaders'. At the same time, by all accounts the powers of the Italian PM have increased since the 1980s, which is consistent with our report.

The Policy Process in Coalition Governments

As we have seen, the PM cannot always act as the principal in cabinet. The most formidable challenge to this status lies in multi-party coalition cabinets. Multi-party cabinets do not have the same mechanisms of preference alignment that exist in Westminster single-party governments. Therefore, the PM must expect that the ministers from other parties will have divergent preferences, induced by a separate linkage to the voters. Whatever the constitution says, these ministers will interpret delegation from parliament as being to the government as a whole. And this will require mechanisms for cabinet coordination other than the PM. Yet, as Andeweg (2000: 383) has noted, coalition governments tend not to be 'models of ministerial equality' but rather to establish some kind of collective leadership.

Table 4.17 summarizes the mechanisms used to manage and ideally to resolve intra-coalition conflict. In accounting for such conflict management mechanisms, we

---

[42] This comes close to the 'ideological-authority version' of prime ministerial government (Dunleavy and Rhodes 1990: 8), in which the PM defines 'a governing ethos, "atmosphere" or operating ideology which generates predictable and determinant solutions to most policy problems'.

[43] We are not aware of any accounts of the roles played by the PMs in cabinet decision-making in Iceland or Luxembourg.

Table 4.17. *Conflict Management Mechanisms in Western European Coalition Governments, 1945–99*

	Number of coalition governments	Number of different coalition institutions	Mechanism for the management of the most common conflicts (in %)		Mechanism for the management of the most serious conflicts (in %)	
			Cabinet-internal	Beyond or outside cabinet	Cabinet-internal	Beyond or outside cabinet
Austria	12	3	100	0	50	50
Belgium	28	3	100	0	32	68
Denmark	14	4	100	0	100	0
Finland	33	3	97	3	58	42
France	14	4	100	0	0	100
Germany	20	6	0	100	0	100
Iceland	17	1	100	0	100	0
Ireland	10	2	20	80	0	100
Italy	32	2	0	100	0	100
Luxembourg	8	3	0	100	0	100
The Netherlands	23	3	61	39	0	100
Norway	7	3	100	0	86	14
Portugal	4	3	50	50	0	100
Sweden	7	2	100	0	100	0

Source: Müller and Strøm (2000b) and data on Iceland provided by Indridi H. Indridason.
Notes: A government is counted with any general election or change in party composition.
Luxembourg: data for the 1964–99 period.

distinguish between routine conflicts, which are likely to emerge frequently, and serious conflicts, which are hopefully more rare but have the potential to lead to a breakdown of the coalition. Furthermore, we distinguish conflict management mechanisms that are cabinet-internal—such as inner cabinets or cabinet committees—and conflict management devices that include party representatives from outside the cabinet, and which in extreme cases can be composed entirely of the latter (coalition committees, party summits). Coalition-internal mechanisms beyond the cabinet itself are generally not backed up by the constitution or indeed by law. Yet, in practice they can be more consequential than the constitutional rules.

The cabinet-dominated systems consist exclusively of Nordic countries. The party-dominated cluster consists of Germany, Ireland, Italy, and Luxembourg. The four mixed cases, which apply both cabinet-internal and cabinet-external conflict management mechanisms, can be subdivided into two categories. Austria and Belgium lean more towards the cabinet-dominated type, while The Netherlands and Portugal display more similarities with the party-dominated type.

On the whole, compared to the previous links in the parliamentary chain of delegation and accountability, within-cabinet delegation is less structured by formal rules. Parliamentary constitutions are largely silent about intra-cabinet relationships, and most countries do with a minimum of other formal rules, relying largely on conventions that allow for more flexibility (Blondel and Müller-Rommel 1997). Hence, parties and individual leaders have ample room to adapt the rules of the game to their needs. The need for flexibility may result in part from the many forces that tug and pull on cabinet ministers, and particularly from the demands for careful management of the preference divergence in multiparty coalition governments. While the doctrines of parliamentary government still largely reflect the Westminster heritage of cohesive single-party governments, constitutional practice must meet the demands of contemporary Western European reality.

DELEGATION FROM MINISTERS TO CIVIL SERVANTS

The final step in the chain of parliamentary delegation is between cabinet members as head of departments and their civil servants. In the US context, scholarship employing principal–agent models has examined such delegation more than any of the previous links. In Western Europe, the information, as well as the analysis, is much more scant.

Civil servants responsible for policy implementation are not only the last players in the chain of delegation. They often also have a crucial and earlier influence, in particular through their role in drafting legislation. And while on politicized issues the impetus for law-making is likely to come from politicians, with respect to many non-politicized topics, civil servants are the ultimate agenda setters vis-à-vis not only their respective minister but also cabinet and parliament. While in each step of delegation the agents are the agenda setters and the principal has the power to accept or reject their proposals, here the agents de facto skip one or two steps of the chain and make proposals to the principal of their principal (the cabinet) and even the cabinet's principal (the parliament). Also, very often civil servants are well placed to protect bills through the various stages of the political decision-making process: with the help of 'house-trained' (captured) ministers they may win the cabinet's support and even be invited to parliamentary committees to give expert testimony and thereby explain the virtues of their proposals (e.g. see Suleiman 1984; Page 1985: ch. 7). For these reasons, it has been claimed that in Western Europe 'the top professional administrators certainly wield more influence in policy-making than do average members of Parliament' (Self 1972: 150). Consequently, Self (1972: 161) maintains that political control over the administration 'does not mean simply (or primarily) making sure that policies which have been met are faithfully executed... It means also establishing an atmosphere in which administrators will continually be aware of political guidelines and constraints'.

Agency Problems

In the classic civil service model that has provided the reference point for Western Europe bureaucracies for more than a century, civil servants are the servants of the state, not of the political masters of the day. They are bound by law and obliged to impartiality. The bureaucratic system of record-keeping, if properly done, allows all who have access to it to pin down political interventions in routine decision processes and hence to establish specific accountabilities. To allow civil servants to resist unreasonable demands from their political masters, they enjoy tenure, a guaranteed (minimal) career based on seniority, and other protections. These features, of course, may exacerbate preference diversity between ministers and civil servants. Civil servants are obliged by (and, it seems, often firmly devoted to) formal and often inefficient administrative procedures. To politicians who 'live and die' within the confines of the electoral cycle, the delay caused by these procedures is often unreasonable and disturbing. Moreover, of all the agents with whom we are concerned in this study, civil servants are most likely to leisure-shirk. If they content themselves with an average career, it is not hard to see why this might be the case. As early as 1944 the House of Commons *Report of the Committee on the Training of Civil Servants* neatly summarized the criticism of the bureaucratic official: 'The faults most frequently enumerated are over-devotion to precedent; remoteness from the rest of the community, inaccessibility and faulty handling of the general public; lack of initiative and imagination; ineffective organization and waste of manpower; procrastination and unwillingness to take responsibility or to give decisions' (quoted from Strauss 1961: 43).

Preference diversity between politicians and civil servants may also lead to the more serious forms of agency loss, namely dissent-shirking and sabotage (see Huber 2000). Why so? In contrast to the other actors in the chain of delegation, civil servants come to office without an electoral mandate. Most are already there when politicians with a mandate from the voters assume public office. Ideally, civil servants are expected to be perfectly neutral towards such a mandate and, within the confines of the law, loyally serve their political masters of the day. In practice, civil servants have their own opinions that may diverge from those of their political superiors on at least two dimensions: the feasibility and the intent of policies.

Civil servants are considered experts in making things happen, that is, in knowing which lever to pull to achieve specific policy outcomes. At least, their ministry or agency will have established procedural wisdoms and routines, and there may be considerable institutional knowledge about the effectiveness of different policy instruments (e.g. see Morstein Marx 1963: 86–90). If politicians are not willing to listen to their civil servants with regard to the choice of policy instruments, this may cause the civil servants to 'undersupply' relevant advice.

Since it is their job to prepare decisions of broad social importance, civil servants are also likely to have their own policy preferences. One source of preference divergence between politicians and (top) civil servants lies in their class background. If the latter overwhelmingly originate from the upper or middle classes, while the former come from or appeal to lower classes, such preference diversity may well result.[44] One classical study of the attitudes of both politicians and bureaucrats has indeed demonstrated relevant differences in ideology and visions of government (Aberbach *et al.* 1981: chs. 5 and 6). Civil servants are (or, at least, were) somewhat to the right of MPs, and they were generally less willing to respond to popular demands and more inclined to defend established policies.

---

[44] For a strong claim, see Miliband (1969: ch. V), who sees the bureaucracy as a major obstacle to socialist reform. Peters (2001: 112–13) shows that 70–80% of senior civil servants in Western Europe have an upper- or middle-class social background.

Administrative Governance

While the civil service in most parliamentary systems is classically hierarchical, different countries have their peculiarities that sometimes constrain the ability of the cabinet member to exercise her will. In most parliamentary systems, civil servants are at least constitutionally subordinated to their respective department heads. Yet, in some countries direct control of civil servants rests with the PM, or with the cabinet as a whole. These are conditions that clearly weaken the authority of line ministers over the civil servants in their respective departments. Moreover, departmental and other civil service staffs are rarely uniformly hierarchical (Page and Wright 1999). In most real-world political systems, the public administration is a very large and complex organization. Regulations concerning personnel appointment and dismissal, for example, are rarely uniform across all hierarchical levels or specialized functions. Thus, there may be multiple categories of public administrators, some with explicitly partisan appointments, others with strictly non-partisan ones. Even among non-partisan personnel, some (e.g. judges) may have much stronger protections against interference or dismissal than others. Some civil servants have highly specialized tasks for which extensive professional preparation is necessary. It is here that we would expect particularly large information asymmetries between bureaucrats and their political superiors. Recognizing the scarcity of their skills, some systems of public administration go far in granting such policy specialists autonomy, whereas others retain a greater degree of subordination and hierarchy. Thus, systems of public administration differ both in the complexity of their hierarchical arrangements and in their promotion of specialization in some deviation from hierarchical principles.

Appointment of Civil Servants

Table 4.18 describes in very condensed form the mechanisms by which civil servants are appointed. If more than one actor is listed, the first-mentioned one proposes (and hence has agenda control) and the last-mentioned one makes the final (or at least the formal) decision. According to the hierarchical parliamentary model, individual ministers appoint the civil servants of their respective departments. Note, however, that the real power of ministers may be limited. In the United Kingdom, for instance, there is very little room for ministerial discretion in appointments.

Yet, the majority of appointment procedures involve two or more actors. All else equal, we would expect that the more constitutional actors are involved in this process, and the more screening takes place, the less the chances that appointments are made on a non-meritocratic basis (e.g. on the basis of private or party connections). This should be particularly true if actors external to the parliamentary chain of delegation get involved in civil servants' appointments and hence function as institutional checks on such delegation.

All countries, except Denmark, Germany, Iceland, and the United Kingdom, involve several constitutional actors in the appointment of high civil servants: the PM, the

Table 4.18. *Rules of Delegation from Cabinet Ministers to Civil Servants*

Country and year	Restrictions on freedom of information law[a]	Agencies under the control of — Minister	Agencies under the control of — Cabinet and/or PM	Are high civil servants appointed in more than one way?	Categories of high civil servants[b]	Who appoints high civil servants? — Category 1	Category 2	Category 3	Category 4
Austria									
1945–73	n.a.	Yes	No	No	n.a.	Minister–Cabinet–President	n.a.	n.a.	n.a.
1974–2000	Privacy; national security; resources; third person	Yes	No	No	n.a.	Minister–Cabinet–President	n.a.	n.a.	n.a.
Belgium									
1945–93	n.a.	Yes	No	Yes	Hierarchical distinctions; distinctions by terms of appointment	Minister–Monarch	Cabinet–Monarch	Minister	n.a.
1994–2000	National security; third person; levels of government	Yes	No	Yes	Hierarchical distinctions; distinctions by terms of appointment	Minister–Monarch	Cabinet–Monarch	Minister	n.a.
Denmark									
1945–63	n.a.	Yes	No	No	n.a.	Minister	n.a.	n.a.	n.a.
1964–70	Privacy	Yes	No	No	n.a.	Minister	n.a.	n.a.	n.a.
1971–2000	National security; recourses	Yes	No	No	n.a.	Minister	n.a.	n.a.	n.a.
Finland									
1945–2000	National security	Yes	No	Yes	Hierarchical distinctions	Minister–President	Cabinet–President	n.a.	n.a.
France									
1959–2000	Third person; levels of government	Yes	No	Yes	Distinctions by terms of appointment	Cabinet–President	Minister	n.a.	n.a.
Germany									
1949–2000	n.a.	Yes	No	No	n.a.	Minister	n.a.	n.a.	n.a.

Table 4.18. (contd.)

Country and year	Restrictions on freedom of information law[a]	Agencies under the control of		Are high civil servants appointed in more than one way?	Categories of high civil servants[b]	Who appoints high civil servants?			
		Minister	Cabinet and/or PM			Category 1	Category 2	Category 3	Category 4
Greece									
1975–85	n.a.	Yes	No	Yes	Distinctions by terms of appointment	Minister–Cabinet	Cabinet	President	n.a.
1986–2000	Privacy; national security; resources; third person; levels of government	Yes	No	Yes	Distinctions by terms of appointment	Minister–Cabinet	Cabinet	President	n.a.
Iceland									
1945–96	n.a.	Yes	No	No	n.a.	Minister	n.a.	n.a.	n.a.
1997–2000	National security; levels of government	Yes	No	No	n.a.	Minister	n.a.	n.a.	n.a.
Ireland									
1945–96	n.a.	Yes	No	Yes	Hierarchical distinctions	Minister	Cabinet	n.a.	n.a.
1997–2000	National security; resources; third person	Yes	No	Yes	Hierarchical distinctions	Minister	Cabinet	n.a.	n.a.
Italy									
1948–2000	n.a.	Yes	No	No	n.a.	Minister–Cabinet	n.a.	n.a.	n.a.
Luxembourg									
1945–2000	Privacy	Yes	Yes	Yes	Hierarchical distinctions; distinctions by terms of appointment	Cabinet–Monarch	Minister–Monarch	n.a.	n.a.
The Netherlands									
1945–2000	National security	Yes	No	Yes	Hierarchical distinctions	Minister–Cabinet	Minister	n.a.	n.a.

Norway								
1945–70	n.a.	Yes	No	Yes	Hierarchical distinctions; distinctions by terms of appointment	Cabinet–Monarch	Minister	n.a.	n.a.
1971–2000	Privacy; national security; resources; third person	Yes	No	Yes	Hierarchical distinctions; distinctions by terms of appointment	Cabinet–Monarch	Minister	n.a.	n.a.
Portugal								
1976–90	n.a.	Yes	No	Yes	Hierarchical distinctions	Minister–Cabinet	Minister–PM	n.a.	n.a.
1991–2000	National security; third person	Yes	No	Yes	Hierarchical distinctions	Minister–Cabinet	Minister–PM	n.a.	n.a.
Spain								
1978–2000	National security; third person	Yes	Yes	Yes	Hierarchical distinctions; functional distinctions; distinctions by terms of appointment	Minister	Minister–Cabinet	Minister–Monarch	Minister–Cabinet–Monarch
Sweden								
1945–74	Privacy; national security; third person	No	Yes	Yes	Hierarchical distinctions; distinctions by terms of appointment	Cabinet–Monarch	Minister	n.a.	n.a.
1975–2000	Privacy; national security; third person	No	Yes	Yes	Hierarchical distinctions; distinctions by terms of appointment	Cabinet	Minister	n.a.	n.a.
United Kingdom								
1945–2000[c]	n.a.	Yes	No	No	Ministers may appoint up to two advisors	Minister	Minister	n.a.	n.a.

Note: 'n.a.' means not applicable in this case.

[a] 'n.a.' here means that there is no freedom of information law. 'Privacy' refers to matters of personal concern only. 'National security' refers to jurisdictional boundaries based on policy distinctions rather than by level of government. 'Resources' refers to restrictions with respect to resource constraints. 'Third person' refers to restrictions because of privacy rights of other citizens. 'Levels of government' refer to restrictions with respect to levels of national government.

[b] Hierarchical distinction (e.g. classes or corps), functional distinction (e.g. specialists versus generalists, policy-making versus implementation), distinctions by terms of appointment (e.g. tenured versus non-tenured).

[c] In 2000, after our 1 January cut-off point, the UK adopted a Freedom of Information Law.

cabinet, or the Head of State. Typically, different combinations of actors have to cooperate in the appointment of civil servants at different ranks. In several countries the
cabinet is in various ways collectively involved in the appointment of civil servants.
While a norm of mutual non-interference may leave civil service appointments at individual ministers' discretion, other cabinet members have an incentive to pay at least
some attention to their collective interests. If revealed, nepotism or other corrupt practices in civil service appointments are likely to inflict damage on the cabinet or the
party as a whole. Cabinet involvement in civil service appointments should help curtail
such ministerial moral hazard. In coalition governments, appointments are likely also
to be scrutinized from a partisan perspective. While in some countries (e.g. The
Netherlands, Finland) coalition governments coexist with a largely non-partisan civil
service, coalition governments in other countries (e.g. Austria, Belgium) have granted
'property rights' over civil service appointments in specific departments to the party in
charge of this portfolio (Müller 2000*b*; see Chapter 22). Even under such circumstances,
however, ministerial appointment powers are likely to be more constrained than under
single-party government.

Appointments violating the norms of meritocracy and due process are most likely if
they serve the collective partisan interests of the incumbents. Such abuses may be
checked if the Head of State is involved, thus denying the parliamentary principal any
monopoly over civil service appointments. This is or was the case in Austria, Belgium,
Finland, France, Greece, Luxembourg, Norway, Spain, and Sweden (until 1975). While
in constitutional monarchies the role of the Head of State in civil service appointments
is symbolic, it can be meaningful under Presidents, particularly in France and at least
previously in Finland and Portugal. Even Austrian Presidents have been willing to use
their final civil service appointment power to prevent the worst excesses of a party
spoils system. Yet, we should not expect republican Heads of State to serve as an effective check on partisanship in civil service appointments. After all, powerful Presidents
typically have been party politicians themselves.

Appointment procedures in six of our countries (Austria, Denmark, Germany,
Iceland, Italy, and the United Kingdom) make no distinction between different categories of high civil servants. The other countries differentiate by one or more of the
following criteria: hierarchy, terms of appointment, and function. Nine countries
(Belgium, Finland, Ireland, Luxembourg, The Netherlands, Norway, Portugal, Spain,
and Sweden) apply different appointment procedures to different ranks of senior civil
servants. This may even be true when the appointment power (as reported in Table
4.18) itself is not affected. Hence, in Denmark, ministers single-handedly retain the
right to appoint even the highest civil servant in their department, the permanent secretary. Yet, a special cabinet committee scrutinizes the candidates and the full Cabinet
must confirm its reports (Nexø Jensen and Knudsen 1999: 233). Different procedures
may pertain to special types of public employees, for example, those with fixed-term
appointments. In the Spanish case, this applies to public jobs abroad and to positions
requiring special qualifications that, in turn, require payment well above the standard
civil service scheme (Molina 1999: 38), whereas in France this label encompasses the
famous *grand corps*. Similar corps exist in Spain (Molina 1999: 41).

Civil Service Governance

Table 4.18 identifies the important lines of authority that run between the PM, ministers, and civil servants. At least formally, the minister–civil servant link varies considerably across Western Europe. In most countries, civil servants in state agencies are accountable directly to the minister. In Sweden, however, Cabinet Ministers have no formal authority over the civil servants in the agencies that implement public policy. This decision-making authority rests only with the full Cabinet. Ministers and ministries prepare and supervise public policy, but the Cabinet as a whole makes all the definitive decisions on public policy implementation. In practice, this distinction is far from strict. Any capable minister or ministry that prepares cabinet deliberations has ample ways to influence (or even pre-determine) the full cabinet decision. But, at the same time, this organizational framework does enhance bureaucratic autonomy, so that civil servants act somewhat more independently in Sweden than where all the decisions are made in the name of the responsible minister (Pierre 1995).

In Luxembourg and Spain, the PM also has an extraordinary influence over civil servants. The civil servants in Luxembourg are under the hierarchical command of the ministers, but there is also a Cabinet position known as the Minister of State, who holds civil servants accountable and to whom citizens can complain. Except for the 1995–99 period (Juncker I), the Minister of State has always been the PM. In Spain, ministers control their agencies, including the civil servants that fall under their jurisdiction. But through the Cabinet's right to issue plans and directives to all state administrative agencies, the PM also has a strong grip on the civil service (see Chapter 19), probably more so than any of his West European counterparts. With these caveats, a cabinet minister in Western Europe is not only a member of a collegial decision-making body, but also the Chief Executive Officer within a specific ministry.[45]

Of course, the ability of cabinet ministers to control their civil servants depends not only on formal rules, but also on the skills and information possessed by the principal relative to the agent. This is where training and career patterns become critical. As Peters (1997: 246) has pointed out, both ministers and civil servants can be either generalists or specialists, with quite different implications for the relationship between them. In his words, 'it would not even be a fair fight', if generalist ministers who are frequently moved from post to post face civil servants with better training who have spent their entire careers in the respective ministry.

Why do ministers tend to be generalists? First, if they are elected politicians they are unlikely to have developed sector-specific specialization before assuming ministerial office. This lack of specialization may be exacerbated by the common practice of

---

[45] Note, however, that we are concerned with national-level policy implementation, and not with the implementation conducted by states, regions, or other subnational communities. For example, given the complexities of German federalism, delegation from ministers to civil servants is more complicated than in most other European countries. If accountability is to include scrutiny of the implementation of all national policy, then in the German case—and many others—subnational bureaucracies must be taken into account.

moving ministers around between different departments. If ministers are moved frequently, they miss the chance of becoming specialists 'on the job'. Rose (1975: 20) has estimated 'the minimum time required for a minister to carry a major new policy within his department' as 'at least three years'—'one year for the minister to understand the techn-ical intricacies of his department sufficiently well to settle the administrative and not unimportant details of a bill, a year to push through Parliament and/or secure Treasury authorization for expenditure, and a year to establish guidelines for administering the resulting policy so that administration can subsequently be routinized and thus delegated to others'. Given that Rose refers to the British case of cohesive single-party governments, 4 years may be more realistic for other political systems. This may even apply to ministers who happen to stay in one particular ministry, if *ex ante* they had reason to expect to be moved around, because under such circumstances they have little incentive to invest in specialization in the jurisdiction of their department.

Unfortunately, we do not have good comparative data on this aspect of ministerial careers. Yet, Table 4.19 contains data on ministerial duration and portfolio stability for fourteen of our seventeen countries. If we assume that a minister must be in charge of one and the same department for 3 or 4 years to become effective, then only Austria, Germany, The Netherlands, and Sweden seem to meet the conditions for effective ministerial governance, though Denmark and Norway also come close. At the low end of the spectrum we find Italy, Finland, Belgium, and France. Note that, except for Finland, these countries also show high levels of bureaucratic politicization.

To the best of our knowledge the literature has not produced a comprehensive cross-national ranking of the specialization of civil servants, based on their training and careers. We expect that civil servants everywhere display a much higher degree of specialization than their political masters.

Table 4.19. *Ministerial Duration and Mobility in Western Europe, 1945–84*

	Ministerial duration (years)	Ministers with a minimum duration of 4 years (in %)	Ministers with two or more different posts (in %)	Ministerial duration per post (years)
Austria	6.0	62	17	4.9
Belgium	3.8	35	45	2.1
Denmark	4.4	88	37	2.9
Finland	3.0	21	33	1.9
France	3.6	33	47	2.0
Germany	5.6	62	36	3.9
Iceland	6.1	60	66	n.a.
Ireland	6.6	71	65	2.9
Italy	3.8	63	58	1.6
Luxembourg	6.8	46	34	n.a.
The Netherlands	4.0	86	21	3.1
Norway	3.9	81	25	2.9
Sweden	5.9	56	29	3.9
United Kingdom	4.8	55	62	2.5

Source: Bakema (1991: 75, 90, 93).

Most parliamentary democracies have legal regulations that aim to prevent political parties from intervening in the delegation between cabinet ministers and civil servants (Müller 2000a). Yet, as the relevant literature (e.g. Page and Wright 1999; Bekke and van der Meer 2000) and the following chapters show, European countries vary not only in the partisan penetration of the civil service (see also Chapter 22), but also with regard to the use of political appointees as a buffer between professional politicians and civil servants. Partisan ties between ministers and their subordinates can help overcome some of their agency problems. Yet, they create problems of their own. Ministers may be too trusting of subordinates with whom they share a party affiliation. Even more critically, they may be loath to intervene when such servants misbehave. There is certainly no reason to expect corrupt practices to be limited to those civil servants that have no party affiliation or one different from the minister.

In practice, the relationship between ministers and civil servants is much less one of command than what the constitution typically suggests. Successful ministers need to convince civil servants of the urgency and relevance of their projects. In so doing they need to provide material and non-material incentives in order to tie civil servants to the policies pursued by the political leadership. In all likelihood, the civil service is not monolithic and ministers may need to get involved in internal disagreements and rivalries among civil servants. In other words, a ministry is an arena that taxes the minister's skills at bargaining as much as command. The New Public Management (NPM) designs, which were introduced in Britain in the 1980s and later diffused throughout Western Europe, greatly enhance the potential for ministerial control. Under NPM schemes ministers control more financial and career incentives and can by tying rewards to outcomes more effectively align the preferences of civil servants with their own. Note, however, that ministers have not been made more accountable to parliament for the acts of their civil servants.

Freedom of Information

Information is a key to the mitigation of civil service agency problems. Since we suspect information asymmetries within governmental organizations, as well as between government officials and citizens, any mechanism that can offset those discrepancies in knowledge may help contain agency problems. Freedom of information laws do precisely that: they lower the cost of information and obligate politicians and civil servants to make information about public decisions available to, in most cases, any citizen. Freedom of information rules thus are not mechanisms that serve the principal in this last stage of parliamentary delegation—cabinet ministers—as much as the ultimate principal, the people. Indirectly, however, such rules impinge on the minister–civil servants relations. They allow third parties access to information and hence increase the likelihood of reliable 'fire alarms' (McCubbins and Schwartz 1984). Thus, they provide incentives to civil servants to behave according to the rules.

Table 4.18 provides information on freedom of information rules regarding citizen and media access to government documents. There is considerable cross-national variation in such access, and the countries that have freedom of information laws differ substantially in their scope and interpretation. While, for instance, the information rights of Swedish citizens are extensive, in Austria they are much more restricted due to concerns for potentially conflicting goals such as the protection of privacy and government efficiency (resource constraints). Thus, many existing laws providing 'open' access to government documents come with considerable restrictions, as reported in Table 4.18. Such caveats notwithstanding, some countries (Finland, France, Luxembourg, The Netherlands, Spain, and Sweden) have long had freedom of information statutes. Beginning in the 1960s, others have opened up such access. Denmark did so in 1964, Norway in 1971, Austria in 1974, Greece in 1986, Portugal in 1991, Belgium in 1994, and, finally, Iceland and Ireland in 1997. The UK adopted such a law in 2000. The remaining countries do not have laws that in this way guarantee freedom of information. Yet, even with the quite restrictive British laws in force until 2000, for example, much government information was provided voluntarily.

Controlling Civil Servants

The last link in the parliamentary chain of delegation, like the first one, connects politician at one end with non-politicians at the other. At this stage, however, politicians are the principals and the 'amateurs'. The potential for agency problems is therefore different, though no less, here than elsewhere in the chain of delegation. While cabinet members do not face the same coordination problems as voters, the fact that the number of agents greatly exceeds that of their principals makes active oversight a challenge. Second, despite the constitutional assumptions of civil service professionalism and neutrality, we have identified a number of potential problems. Of all the agents in the democratic chain of delegation, civil servants are most likely to engage in leisure shirking. Dissent shirking (or even sabotage) can result from preference diversity between ministers and civil servants over the means and ends of policies. Also, at this stage, much of the concern about agency loss focuses on such problems as corruption and patronage.

Traditional remedies have included a greater professionalization of the civil service, more lucrative rewards, or an increase in the number of political appointees. Yet, in the long term these strategies may create as many problems as they solve. In contrast to all other links, there is no consensus in constitutional doctrine or democratic theory that political parties can play a positive role in the relationship between cabinet members and civil servants. One remedy that has been on the rise among advanced democracies is freedom of information laws, which can expose the behaviour of civil servants to public scrutiny and allow ministers to learn from 'fire alarms'. Yet, in contrast to at least some of the institutions that we have previously considered (e.g. electoral systems), our understanding of the various public administration accountability mechanisms, and our ability to compare them across institutional settings, is quite limited. We therefore refer to the country chapters for more configurative descriptions.

CONCLUSION

In this chapter we have mapped out the real-world chain of parliamentary delegation, in Western European societies, that begins with the citizens (the ultimate principals) and ends with civil servants (the ultimate agents). Our data covers the entire period of democracy between 1945 and 2000 in seventeen states (in France since the start of the Fifth Republic). Since constitutions change fairly slowly, these are in almost all cases also the mechanisms that exist early in the twenty-first century. In the chapters that follow we shall discuss how these mechanisms interact in particular polities. But before we delve into this richer picture country-by-country, it is valuable to summarize the main cross-national patterns that emerge.

Below we summarize the empirical patterns that this chapter has uncovered and compare the real world of European parliamentary democracy with our ideal–typical conceptions. Table 4.20 identifies seventeen mechanisms of democratic delegation and accountability, from voters all the way to civil servants, in their ideal–typical form. In the next two columns, Table 4.20 matches these ideal–typical features with the most common real-world mechanisms. The final column identifies the contemporary trend in institutional design and evolution. Note that the most common mechanism often is different from the ideal–typical mechanism, which means that a trend in favour of the most common mechanism actually can be a trend away from the ideal type.

The ideal–typical parliamentary democracy implies a chain of delegation that is indirect, singular, and monopolistic. It is indeed the presumption of hierarchy and control from below that makes parliamentary government democratic. It is also because of the essential role of hierarchy that the principal–agent approach is particularly suited for our study. The principal–agent approach directs attention towards existing elements of hierarchy in representative democracies. If democratic governance ceased to have hierarchical elements, the principal–agent approach might no longer be very relevant, but then neither would the ideals of representative democracy.

To this constitutional design we must add *political parties*. The degree to which parliamentary democracies function as hierarchies is to a large extent determined by how well political parties function as bonding and informational economizing devices. Chapter 3 pointed out that parliamentary systems are generally decisive and characterized by administrative as well as incentive efficiency. They are therefore less prone to leisure shirking than other regime types. When centralized and cohesive, political parties can reinforce hierarchy and fusion and promote efficient delegation. In the classical Westminster model, centralized parties and single-party cabinets all reinforce the hierarchy and fusion of majoritarian democracy.

Though the four stages of parliamentary delegation that we have discussed have many common features, the agency problems that they present are by no means identical. In the first and final step, delegation involves large sets of citizens that are political 'amateurs' and much smaller (relatively speaking) sets of professional politicians. Of course, in the first of these stages, the amateurs are the principal and the professional politicians the agents, whereas in the final stage (cabinet members to civil servants) the

Table 4.20. *Ideal-Typical and Actual West European Mechanisms of Delegation and Accountability: Summary*

Delegation and/or accountability mechanism	Ideal-typical mechanism under party-based parliamentarism	Most common (modal) mechanism in Western Europe, 2000	Major empirical exceptions	Cross-national trend, 1945–2000
Step I: Voter–MP				
Legislative cameral structure	Unicameralism	Bicameralism (9 countries), which, with the exception of Italy, is asymmetrical (i.e. the Upper House is much weaker)	Unicameralism (the Nordic countries, Greece, Luxembourg, and Portugal)	Weakening bicameralism, with Denmark and Sweden moving to unicameralism
Locus of MP candidate selection	By party leaders at the constituency level (elite-dominated/ decentralized)	By party leaders (elite-dominated) at the constituency (district) level (11 countries)	By party leaders at the national level (France, Greece); open primaries (Iceland); membership votes (Finland); advisory membership votes (Ireland and Sweden)	Gradual weakening of party leaders in favour of more membership participation
Preference voting on individual candidates	Closed party lists	Intraparty (7 countries) or interparty (Ireland and Luxembourg) preference voting	Closed party list (Iceland, Norway, Portugal, and Spain); SMD (France and the UK); mixed systems (Germany and Italy)	Moderate increase in preference voting
Step II: Parliament–PM				
Inauguration rule	Positive parliamentarism, that is, cabinet must win majority vote	Negative parliamentarism, that is, parliamentary consent is tacit (10 countries including Finland)	Positive parliamentarism (Belgium, Germany, Greece, Ireland, Italy, Luxembourg, and Spain)	No significant trend (although Finland switched to positive parliamentarism in March 2000)
Parliamentary questions directed at PM and cabinet ministers	Some forms of questions permitted, but restricted use	Urgent, written, and/or oral questions. Restrictions apply in terms of time limits, conditions, and/or number of tabled written questions per MP (11 countries)	Urgent, written, and/or oral questions. No restrictions on individual MPs (Denmark, France, Ireland, The Netherlands, Portugal, and Sweden)	Urgent, written, and oral questions have spread to more countries and become more frequently used

Ex post scrutiny of cabinet affairs	Limited scrutiny rights	Standing committees with rights to scrutinize government documents and to hold hearings. Possibility of setting up ad hoc committees (11 countries)	No ex post scrutiny by standing committees, which have legislative roles only (Austria, Greece, and the Netherlands). Scrutiny by standing committees only (Finland, Norway, and Sweden)	Increase in the right and ability to scrutinize government affairs. Increasing use of ad hoc committees.
No-confidence vote: Who can be targeted	No-confidence motions can be directed against the PM only (with implications for the whole cabinet under collective responsibility)	No-confidence motions can be directed against individual ministers (11 countries)	No-confidence motions can be directed against the PM only (France, Germany, Ireland, Portugal, Spain, and the UK)	No significant trend
No-confidence vote: Decision rule	Absolute majority vote, which counts absentees in favour of the PM	Simple majority (9 countries)	Absolute majority (Belgium, France, Germany, Greece, Iceland, Portugal, Spain, and Sweden)	Trend towards higher thresholds; Sweden switched to absolute majority in 1971 and Belgium in 1995
Parliamentary dissolution: Involvement of Head of State	None or purely ceremonial	Potential involvement beyond pure formality (13 countries)	Dissolution not permitted (Norway); no role for Head of State (Denmark, Sweden); purely formal role (Spain)	Decreasing involvement; Denmark and Sweden have completely abolished (Monarch) involvement
Parliamentary dissolution: PM power	PM can dissolve parliament	PM / cabinet can dissolve parliament (counterbalances parliamentary accountability power) and call an early (or extra) election. In most countries this at least formally requires the consent of the Head of State (9 countries)	Dissolution not permitted (Norway); dissolution powers placed primarily with the Head of State (Austria, Finland, France, Greece, Iceland, Italy, and Portugal)	Weak trend in favour of greater PM power over dissolution, as in Finland in 1991

Table 4.20. (contd.)

Delegation and/or accountability mechanism	Ideal-typical mechanism under party-based parliamentarism	Most common (modal) mechanism in Western Europe, 2000	Major empirical exceptions	Cross-national trend, 1945–2000
Step III: PM–Cabinet				
PM's appointment powers	PM appoints the other cabinet members; Head of State involvement is purely formal	PM is largely limited to appointments from his own party in coalitional systems, especially in pivotal party systems (14 countries); except for France, Head of State involvement ranges from none to mostly formal	Largely unconstrained PMs in single party-governments, particularly in alternational party systems (UK, Spain, Greece)	Stronger prime ministerial powers in coalition systems; decline of Head of State interventions
PM's relationship to party system	PM is undisputed leader of majority party	The PM is weaker vis-à-vis line ministers and party leaders in coalitional systems and in alternational party systems with frequent coalitions (9 countries)	Strong PMs in (effective) two-party (Greece, Spain, the UK) or two-bloc (France) systems, and in alternational systems with frequent single-party cabinets (Norway, Ireland, Portugal, Sweden)	More countries alternate between two-party/bloc and pivotal status and hence between stronger and weaker PMs
PM relation to ministers: Institutional powers	PM has institutional power instrument to control ministers	Strong prime ministerial authority facilitated by rights of jurisdiction, steering, and agenda control as well as cabinet decision rules, and staffing and other resources (14 countries)	Some countries (Austria, Iceland, and The Netherlands) have institutionally weaker PMs	Institutional rules tilting only slightly in favour of PM; drastic increase in staffing and other resources leads to a growing 'presidentialization' of PMs

PM relation to ministers: Dismissal powers	PM has unrestricted dismissal power	Severely constrained dismissal power in coalitional systems (14 countries, some with temporary exceptions)	Almost unrestricted PM dismissal power in single-party cabinets (Greece, Spain, the UK, and episodes in other countries)	No discernible trend
Step IV: Minister–Civil servants Appointment of top-level civil servants	Ministerial control, no competing principal (except for supervision by the PM)	Cabinet coordination common or required. Heads of State are only formally involved (9 countries)	Exclusive ministerial control (Denmark, Germany, Iceland, the UK (with caveats, see text) Some elected Presidents can influence appointments (Austria, Finland, France, and Portugal)	If there is any discernible trend, it is towards greater ministerial influence over appointments, at the expense of the Head of State
Steering and implementation authority	Ministerial control, no competing principal	Ministers have considerable influence, albeit sometimes constrained by coalition partners (14 countries)	Authority over implementation rests with the full cabinet (Sweden); PM has extraordinary influence over civil servants (Luxembourg and Spain)	No discernible trend
Freedom of information act	Civil servants are under the authority and control of the minister, not competing principals. No Freedom of Information Act is necessary	Freedom of Information Act exists, albeit with restrictions for national security, privacy rights, etc. (14 countries)	No such law (Germany, Italy, and the UK)	Strong cross-national diffusion of Freedom of Information legislation.

Note: The most common mechanism often is different from the ideal-typical mechanism, which, for example, means that a trend in favour of the most common mechanism actually can be a trend away from the mechanism suggested by the ideal type.

relationship is the reverse. At any rate, the large numbers of citizens and civil servants involved implies serious issues of coordination, and both of these sets of delegation relationships tend to be fairly heavily and formally regulated. At the same time, however, the relative *ex post* sanctions are fairly weak. Once politicians have been elected to office, voters cannot easily oversee them, and many electoral systems allow no easy sanctions. And while civil servants typically face very detailed contracts and extensive formal screening, there is relatively little that their masters can do to punish them for non-performance *ex post*, even though New Public Management techniques have increased the politicians' capacities vis-à-vis their civil servants (see Peters and Pierre 2001).

The two intervening stages of delegation involve much smaller and more 'intimate' sets of professional politicians. In these relationships, continuous oversight is much more feasible, and the immediate sanctions are much more dramatic and effective. That does not mean that *ex ante* screening is unimportant (e.g. it clearly plays a critical role in the recruitment of cabinet members) but it does imply a greater repertoire of sanctions by which principals can keep their agents in line. At these stages of delegation, principals are further helped by the existence of ever-present, and in most cases cohesive, political parties. Thus, the most formidable challenges in contemporary parliamentary delegation would seem to arise towards the beginning and end of the chain.

Parliamentary democracy in Western Europe is not always what it appears to be, nor does it necessarily conform to the principles of hierarchy, singularity, and indirect control. Certainly, many parliamentary constitutions contain a number of archaic features, so that identifying their real operations may be far from straightforward. Yet, the issues of political delegation and accountability are clearly visible through the patterns that we have identified, and it is also clear that parliamentarism contains strong elements of centralization and hierarchy. At the same time, no such picture can be timeless, and nothing is constant but change.

From a bird's-eye perspective, a number of well-known features of parliamentary democracies appear to be weakening. While constitutional texts are slow to change, there are a number of important changes in the working constitutions. As Table 4.20 shows, some institutional changes favour more direct involvement by the voters (people) and their directly elected representatives (MPs). This is exemplified by the opening up of candidate nomination processes, an increase in preference voting, more scrutiny by parliamentary committees, and more use of parliamentary questions, as well as by the spread of freedom of information laws.

Yet, other forces work in the opposite direction. On most of our seventeen indications, parliamentary democracies exhibit more fusion and hierarchy that they used to a few decades ago. The cross-national trend favours unicameralism, positive parliamentarism, higher thresholds for no-confidence votes, a more critical role for PMs (relative to the Head of State) in parliamentary dissolution, more staff and resources for the PM to monitor ministers, but a lessening of the control of line ministers over civil servants.

The evidence of party decline is more decisive, and particularly striking with respect to the party-in-the-electorate (Chapter 22, see also Dalton and Wattenberg 2000).

But even the institutional features of parliamentary politics nowadays are less conducive to centralized party control. Once on the ballot, contemporary candidates for office are less certain that they will actually be chosen as MPs than was the case early in the postwar period. Not only have the voters become less predictable with regard to their party choice, more candidates are now subject to preference voting. The cross-national tendency towards a more direct link between voters' preferences and candidates for office is the most important change in the relationship between voters and representatives.

A continued erosion of political parties could weaken the chain of parliamentary delegation. Weak and factionalized parties could diffuse authority and muddle accountability. Yet, so far, while voters have gained some influence over candidate selection, while MPs have secured new vehicles of executive scrutiny, and while the public at least potentially has been granted greater access to government documents, parties have strengthened their finances and retain control of the core executive functions.

We now turn to an in-depth look at the parliamentary chain of delegation and accountability in each of seventeen countries. This chapter has shown that even though they share common core features, parliamentary systems are by no means all alike. A serious assessment of their merits and demerits clearly requires more detailed description and a fuller analysis of how they work in practice. That is indeed the purpose of the next seventeen chapters, which collectively will lay out country features, describe the constraints on national policy-making, and discuss the agency relations embodied in their living constitutions. In the final two chapters, we discuss two devices that may protect against agency loss in the long chain of parliamentary delegation, namely political parties and external constraints.

REFERENCES

Aberbach, Joël D., Putnam, Robert D., and Rockman, Bert A. (1981). *Bureaucrats and Politicians in Western Democracies*. Cambridge, MA: Harvard University Press.

Andeweg, Rudy B. (1988). 'Centrifugal Forces and Collective Decision-Making: The Case of the Dutch Cabinet'. *European Journal of Political Research*, 16: 125–51.

——(1991). 'The Dutch Prime Minister: Not Just Chairman, Not Yet Chief?' *West European Politics*, 14(1): 16–32.

——(2000). 'Ministers as Double Agents? The Delegation Process Between Cabinet and Ministers'. *European Journal of Political Research*, 37: 377–95.

——and Nijzink, Lia (1995). 'Beyond the Two-Body Image: Relations Between Ministers and MPs', in Herbert Döring (ed.), *Parliaments and Majority Rule in Western Europe*. Frankfurt am Main: Campus and New York: St. Martin's Press.

Arter, David (1991). 'One Thing Too Many: The Shift to Unicameralism in Denmark', in Lawrence D. Longley and David M. Olson (eds.), *Two Into One. The Politics and Processes of National Legislative Cameral Change*. Boulder: Westview Press.

Bagehot, Walter (1963 [1867]). *The English Constitution*. London: Fontana/Collins.

Bakema, Wilma E. (1991). 'The Ministerial Career', in Jean Blondel and Jean-Louis Thiébault (eds.), *The Profession of Government Minister in Western Europe*. Houndmills: Macmillan.

Baldwin, Nicholas D. J. and Shell, Donald (eds.) (2001). *Second Chambers*. London: Frank Cass.

Bar, Antonio (1997). 'Spain: A Prime Ministerial Government', in Jean Blondel and Ferdinand Müller-Rommel (eds.), *Cabinets in Western Europe*. Houndmills: Macmillan.

Bekke, Hans A. G. M and van der Meer, Frits M. (eds.) (2000). *Civil Service Systems in Western Europe*. Cheltenham: Edward Elgar.

Bergman, Torbjörn (1993). 'Formation Rules and Minority Governments'. *European Journal of Political Research*, 23: 55–66.

——(1995). *Constitutional Rules and Party Goals in Coalition Formation*. Umeå: Umeå University.

——(1997). 'National parliaments and EU Affairs Committees: Notes on Empirical Variation and Competing Explanations'. *Journal of European Public Policy*, 4: 373–87.

——(2000). 'The European Union as the Next Step of Delegation and Accountability'. *European Journal of Political Research*, 37: 415–29.

——and Erik Damgaard (eds.) (2000). *Delegation and Accountability in European Integration: The Nordic Parliamentary Democracies and the European Union*. London: Frank Cass (Also available as a special issue of *Journal of Legislative Studies*, 6(1)).

Bille, Lars (2001). 'Democratizing a Democratic Procedure: Myth or Reality?' *Party Politics*, 7: 363–80.

Blondel, Jean (1991). 'The Post-Ministerial Careers', in Jean Blondel and Jean-Louis Thiébault (eds.), *The Profession of Government Minister in Western Europe*. Houndmills: Macmillan.

——and Müller-Rommel, Ferdinand (eds.) (1997). *Cabinets in Western Europe*, 2nd edn. Houndmills: Macmillan.

Bogdanor, Vernon (1984). 'The Government Formation Process in the constitutional Monarchies of North-West Europe', in Dennis Kavanagh and Gillian Peele (eds.), *Comparative Government and Politics*. London: Heinemann.

——(ed.) (1988). *Constitutions in Democratic Politics*. Aldershot: Gower.

Bowler, Shaun, Farrell, David M., and Katz, Richard S. (eds.) (1999). *Party Discipline and Parliamentary Government*. Columbus: Ohio State University Press.

Brazier, Rodney (1997). *Ministers of the Crown*. Oxford: Clarendon Press.

Brusewitz, Axel (1929). 'Vad menas med parlamentarism.' *Statsvetenskaplig Tidskrift*, 32: 323–34.

Choe, Yonhyok (1997). *How to Manage Free and Fair Elections*. Göteborg: Göteborg University.

Chubb, Basil (1982). *The Government and Politics of Ireland*, 2nd edn. London: Longman.

Cole, Alistair M. (1989). 'Factionalism, the French Socialist Party and the Fifth Republic: An Explanation of Intra-Party Divisions'. *European Journal of Political Research*, 17: 77–94.

Cowley, Philip (2000). 'Can Sheep Bark? British Labour MPs and the Modification of Government Policy'. ECPR paper, Copenhagen, 14–19 April.

Cox, Gary W. (1997). *Making Votes Count*. Cambridge: Cambridge University Press.

Cotta, Maurizio (1997). 'Italy: A Fragmented Government', in Jean Blondel and Ferdinand Müller-Rommel (eds.), *Cabinets in Western Europe*. Houndmills: Macmillan.

Crewe, Ivor and King, Anthony (1994). 'Are British Elections Becoming More "Presidential"?', in M. Kent Jennings and Warren E. Miller (eds.), *Elections at Home and Abroad*. Ann Arbor: University of Michigan Press.

Criscitiello, Annarita (1994). 'The Political Role of Cabinet Ministers in Italy', in Michael Laver and Kenneth A. Shepsle (eds.), *Cabinet Ministers and Parliamentary Government*. Cambridge: Cambridge University Press.

De Winter, Lieven (1991). 'Parliamentary and Party Pathways to the Cabinet', in Jean Blondel and Jean-Louis Thiébault (eds.), *The Profession of Government Minister in Western Europe*. Houndmills: Macmillan.

De Winter, Lieven (1995). 'The Role of Parliament in Government Formation and Resignation', in Herbert Döring (ed.), *Parliaments and Majority Rule in Western Europe*. Frankfurt am Main: Campus and New York: St. Martin's Press.

Diermeier, Daniel and Feddersen, Timothy J. (1998). 'Cohesion in Legislatures and the Vote of Confidence Procedure'. *American Political Science Review*, 92: 611–21.

Dogan, Mattei (1989). 'How to Become a Cabinet Minister in Italy: Unwritten Rules of the Political Game', in Mattei Dogan (ed.), *Pathways to Power*. Boulder: Westview Press.

Dunleavy, Patrick with Bastow, Simon (2001). 'Modelling Coalitions that Cannot Coalesce: A Critique of the Laver–Shepsle Approach'. *West European Politics*, 24(1): 1–26.

Dunleavy, Patrick and Rhodes, R. A. W. (1990). 'Core Executive Studies in Britain'. *Public Administration*, 68: 3–28.

Duverger, Maurice (1980). 'A New Political System Model: Semi-Presidential Government'. *European Journal of Political Research*, 8: 165–87.

Elgie, Robert (ed.) (1999). *Semi-Presidentialism in Europe*. Oxford: Oxford University Press.

——and Machin, Howard (1991). 'France: The Limits of Prime-ministerial Government in a Semi-presidential System'. *West European Politics*, 14(2): 62–78.

Elklit, Jørgen and Svensson, Palle (2001). 'What Makes Elections Free and Fair?', in Larry Diamond and Mark F. Plattner (eds.), *The Global Divergence of Democracies*. Baltimore: Johns Hopkins University Press.

Eriksen, Svein (1997). 'Norway: Ministerial Autonomy and Collective Responsibility', in Jean Blondel and Ferdinand Müller-Rommel (eds.), *Cabinets in Western Europe*. Houndmills: Macmillan.

Farrell, Brian (1994) 'The Political Role of Cabinet Ministers in Ireland', in Michael Laver and Kenneth A. Shepsle (eds.), *Cabinet Ministers and Parliamentary Government*. Cambridge: Cambridge University Press.

Finer, Herman (1946). *The Theory and Practice of Modern Government*, 2nd edn. London: Methuen.

Frognier, André-Paul (1997). 'Belgium: A Complex Cabinet in a Fragmented Polity', in Jean Blondel and Ferdinand Müller-Rommel (eds.), *Cabinets in Western Europe*. Houndmills: Macmillan.

Fysh, Peter (1996). 'Candidates and Parties of the Right', in Robert Elgie (ed.), *Electing the French President. The 1995 Presidential Election*. Houndmills: Macmillan.

Gallagher, Michael and Marsh, Michael (eds.) (1988). *Candidate Selection in Comparative Perspective*. London: Sage.

Gallagher, Michael (1988). 'Conclusion', in Michael Gallagher and Michael Marsh (eds.), *Candidate Selection in Comparative Perspective*. London: Sage.

Gerlich, Peter, Müller, Wolfgang C., and Philipp, Wilfried (1988). 'Potentials and Limitations of Executive Leadership: The Austrian Cabinet Since 1945'. *European Journal of Political Research*, 16: 191–205.

Golden, Miriam A. and Chang, Eric C. C. (2001). 'Competitive Corruption. Factional Conflict and Political Malfeasance in Postwar Italian Christian Democracy'. *World Politics*, 53: 588–622.

Headey, Bruce (1974). *British Cabinet Ministers*. London: George Allen & Unwin.

Helms, Ludger (2001). 'The Changing Chancellorship: Resources and Constraints Revisited'. *German Politics*, 10: 155–68.

Hine, David (1993). *Governing Italy*. Oxford: Oxford University Press.

——and Finocchi, Renato (1991). 'The Italian Prime Minister'. *West European Politics*, 14(2): 79–96.

Huber, John D. (1996a). 'The Vote of Confidence in Parliamentary Democracies'. *American Political Science Review*, 90: 269–82.

——(1996b). *Rationalizing Parliament. Legislative Institutions and Party Politics in France*. Cambridge: Cambridge University Press.

Huber, John D. (2000). 'Delegation to Civil Servants in Parliamentary Democracies'. *European Journal of Political Research*, 37: 397–413.

Huber, John D. and McCarty, Nolan (2001). 'Cabinet Decision Rules and Political Uncertainty in Parliamentary Bargaining'. *American Political Science Review*, 95: 345–60.

——Shipan, Charles R., and Pfahler, Madelaine (2001). 'Legislatures and Statutory Control of Bureaucracy'. *American Journal of Political Science*, 45: 330–45.

Hug, Simon (2001). *Altering Party Systems*. Ann Arbor: University of Michigan Press.

Jensen, Torben K. (2000). 'Party Cohesion', in Peter Esaiasson and Knut Heidar (eds.), *Beyond Westminister and Congress: The Nordic Experience*. Columbus: Ohio State University Press.

Jones, G. W. (1995). 'The Downfall of Margaret Thatcher', in R. A. W. Rhodes and Patrick Dunleavy (eds.), *Prime Minister, Cabinet and Core Executive*. Houndmills: Macmillan.

Katz, Richard S. (1997). *Democracy and Elections*. Oxford: Oxford University Press.

——(1999). 'Representation, the Locus of Democratic Legitimation and the Role of the National Parliaments in the European Union', in Richard S. Katz and Bernhard Wessels (eds.), *The European Parliament, the National parliaments, and European Integration*. Oxford: Oxford University Press.

——and Mair, Peter (eds.) (1992). *Party Organizations*. London: Sage.

————(1995). 'Changing Models of Party Organization and Party Democracy'. *Party Politics*, 1: 5–28.

King, Anthony (1975). 'Executives', in Fred I. Greenstein and Nelson W. Polsby (eds.), *Handbook of Political Science. Volume 5. Governmental Institutions and Processes*. Reading, MA: Addison-Wesley.

——(1991). 'The British Prime Ministership in the Age of the Career Politician'. *West European Politics*, 14(2): 25–47.

——(1994). 'Ministerial Autonomy in Britain', in Michael Laver and Kenneth A. Shepsle (eds.), *Cabinet Ministers and Parliamentary Government*. Cambridge: Cambridge University Press.

——(ed.) (2002). *Leaders' Personalities and the Outcomes of Democratic Elections*. Oxford: Oxford University Press.

Knapp, Andrew (2003). 'Two Pyrrhic Victories? France's Governing Parties, the Ecologists, and the Far Right', in Peter Mair, Wolfgang C. Müller, and Fritz Plasser (eds.), *Changes in Electoral Markets: Party Challenges and Party Responses*. London: Sage Publications.

Koutsoukis, Klemenis S. (1994). 'Cabinet Decision Making in the Hellenic Republic, 1974–1992', in Michael Laver and Kenneth A. Shepsle (eds.), *Cabinet Ministers and Parliamentary Government*. Cambridge: Cambridge University Press.

Krehbiel, Keith (1993). 'Where's the Party?', *British Journal of Political Science*, 23: 235–66.

Larsson, Torbjörn (1993). 'The Role and Position of Ministers of Finance', in Jean Blondel and Ferdinand Müller-Rommel (eds.), *Governing Together*. New York: St. Martin's Press.

——(1994). 'Cabinet Ministers and Parliamentary Government in Sweden', in Michael Laver and Kenneth A. Shepsle (eds.), *Cabinet Ministers and Parliamentary Government*. Cambridge: Cambridge University Press.

——(1997). 'Sweden: The New Constitution—An Old Practice Adjusted', in Jean Blondel and Ferdinand Müller-Rommel (eds.), *Cabinets in Western Europe*. Houndmills: Macmillan.

Laver, Michael and Schofield, Norman (1990). *Multiparty Government: The Politics of Coalition in Europe*. Oxford: Oxford University Press.

——and Shepsle, Kenneth A. (1996). *Making and Breaking Governments*. Cambridge: Cambridge University Press.

Lijphart, Arend (1999). *Patterns of Democracy*. New Haven: Yale University Press.

Linton, Martin and Southcott, Mary (1998). *Making Votes Count. The Case for Electoral Reform.* London: Profile Books.

Loewenberg, Gerhard and Patterson, Samuel C. (1979). *Comparing Legislatures.* Boston: Little, Brown.

Longley, Lawrence D. and Olson, David M. (eds.) (1991). *Two Into One. The Politics and Processes of National Legislative Cameral Change.* Boulder: Westview Press.

Lupia, Arthur W. and Strøm, Kaare (1995). 'Coalition Termination and the Strategic Timing of Parliamentary Elections'. *American Political Science Review*, 89: 648–65.

Lutz, Donald S. (1994). 'Toward a Theory of constitutional Amendment'. *American Political Science Review*, 88: 355–70.

Mair, Peter (1997). *Party System Change.* Oxford: Oxford University Press.

Mann, Thomas E. and Orren, Garry R. (eds.) (1992). *Media Polls in American Politics.* Washington, DC: Brookings.

Mayhew, David (1974). *Congress: The Electoral Connection.* New Haven: Yale University Press.

McCubbins, Mathew D. and Schwartz, Thomas (1984). 'Congressional Oversight Overlooked: Police Patrols Versus Fire Alarms'. *American Journal of Political Science*, 28: 165–79.

Mény, Yves and Knapp, Andrew (1998). *Government and Politics in Western Europe.* Oxford: Oxford University Press.

Miliband, Ralph (1969). *The State in Capitalist Society.* New York: Basic Books.

Mitchell, Paul L. (2000). 'Voters and their Representatives: Electoral Institutions and Delegation in Parliamentary Democracies'. *European Journal of Political Research*, 37: 335–51.

Molina, Ignacio (1999). 'Spain: Still the Primacy of Corporatism', in Edward C. Page and Vincent Wright (eds.), *Bureaucratic Élites in Western European States.* Oxford: Oxford University Press.

Morstein Marx, Fritz (1963). 'The Higher Civil Service as an Action Group in Western Political Development', in Joseph LaPalombara (ed.), *Bureaucracy and Political Development.* Princeton: Princeton University Press.

Mueller, Dennis C. (1989). *Public Choice II.* Cambridge: Cambridge University Press.

Müller, Wolfgang C. (1993). 'The Relevance of the State for Party System Change'. *Journal of Theoretical Politics*, 5: 419–54.

——(1994). 'Models of Government and the Austrian Cabinet', in Michael Laver and Kenneth A. Shepsle (eds.), *Cabinet Ministers and Parliamentary Government.* Cambridge: Cambridge University Press.

——(2000a). 'Political Parties in Parliamentary Democracies: Making Delegation and Accountability Work'. *European Journal of Political Research*, 37: 309–33.

——(2000b). 'Patronage by National Governments', in Jean Blondel and Maurizio Cotta (eds.), *The Nature of Party Government.* Houndmills: Palgrave-Macmillan.

——(2002). 'Parties and the Institutional Framework', in Kurt Richard Luther and Ferdinand Müller-Rommel (eds.), *Political Parties in the New Europe.* Oxford: Oxford University Press.

——Jenny, Marcelo, Steininger, Barbara, Dolezal, Martin, Philipp, Wilfried, and Preisl-Westphal, Sabine (2001). *Die österreichischen Abgeordneten.* Vienna: WUV Universitätsverlag.

——and Strøm, Kaare (2000a). 'Conclusion: Coalition Governance in Western Europe', in Wolfgang C. Müller and Kaare Strøm (eds.), *Coalition Governments in Western Europe.* Oxford: Oxford University Press.

——— (eds.) (2000b). *Coalition Governments in Western Europe.* Oxford: Oxford University Press.

Müller-Rommel, Ferdinand (1994). 'The Role of German Ministers in Cabinet Decision Making', in Michael Laver and Kenneth A. Shepsle (eds.), *Cabinet Ministers and Parliamentary Government.* Cambridge: Cambridge University Press.

Müller-Wirth, Moritz (1992). *Die Debatte um die Parlamentsreform in Italien 1971–1988.* Frankfurt am Main: Peter Lang.

Nassmacher, Karl-Heinz (ed.) (2001). *Foundations for Democracy. Approaches to Comparative Political Finance.* Baden-Baden: Nomos.

Nassmacher, Karl-Heinz (2002). 'Die Kosten der Parteitätigkeit in westlichen Demokratien.' *Österreichische Zeitschrift für Politikwissenschaft,* 31: 7–20.

Nexø Jensen, Hanne and Knudsen, Tim (1999). 'Senior Officials in the Danish Central Administration: From Bureaucrats to Policy Professionals and Managers'? in Edward C. Page and Vincent Wright (eds.), *Bureaucratic Élites in Western European States.* Oxford: Oxford University Press.

Nordhaus, William A. (1975). 'The Political Business Cycle'. *Review of Economic Studies,* 42: 169–90.

Nousiainen, Jaakko (1994). 'Finland: Ministerial Autonomy, Constitutional Collectivism, and Party Oligarchy', in Michael Laver and Kenneth A. Shepsle (eds.), *Cabinet Ministers and Parliamentary Government.* Cambridge: Cambridge University Press.

——(1997). 'Finland', in Jean Blondel and Ferdinand Müller-Rommel (eds.), *Cabinets in Western Europe.* Houndmills: Macmillan.

Norris, Pippa (1997). 'Conclusions: Comparing Passages to Power', in Pippa Norris (ed.), *Passages to Power.* Cambridge: Cambridge University Press.

——(2001). 'The Twilight of Westminster? Electoral Reform and its Consequences'. *Political Studies,* 49: 877–900.

O'Leary, Brendan (1991). '*An Taoiseach:* The Irish Prime Minister'. *West European Politics,* 14(2): 133–62.

Olsen, Johan P. (1983). *Organized Democracy: Political Institutions in a Welfare State—The Case of Norway.* Bergen: Universitetsforlaget.

Padgett, Steven (1993). 'The Chancellor and his Party', in Stephen Padgett (ed.), *Adenauer to Kohl.* London: Hurst.

Page, Edward C. (1985). *Political Authority and Bureaucratic Power.* Brighton: Wheatsheaf Books.

——and Wright, Vincent (eds.) (1999). *Bureaucratic Élites in Western European States.* Oxford: Oxford University Press.

Paltiel, Khayyam Zev (1981). 'Campaign Finance: Contrasting Practices and Reforms', in David Butler, Howard R. Penniman, and Austin Ranney (eds.), *Democracy at the Polls.* Washington, DC American Enterprise Institute.

Patterson, Samuel C. and Mughan, Anthony (eds.) (1999). *Senates. Bicameralism in the Contemporary World.* Columbus: Ohio State University Press.

Peters, B. Guy (1997). 'Bureaucrats and Political Appointees in European Democracies: Who's Who and Does it Make Any Difference?', in Ali Farazmand (ed.), *Modern Systems of Government.* Thousand Oaks: Sage.

——(2001). *The Politics of Bureaucracy,* 5th edn. London: Routledge.

——and Pierre, Jon (eds.) (2001). *Politicians, Bureaucrats, and Administrative Reform.* London: Routledge.

——Rhodes, R. A. W., and Wright, Vincent (eds.) (2000). *Administering the Summit. Administration of the Core Executive in Developed Countries.* Houndmills: Macmillan.

Pierre, Jon (1995). 'Governing the Welfare State: Public Administration, the State and Society in Sweden', in Jon Pierre (ed.), *Bureaucracy in the Modern State: An Introduction to Comparative Pubic Administration.* Cheltenham: Edward Elgar.

——Svåsand, Lars, and Widfeldt, Anders (2000). 'State Subsidies to Political Parties: Confronting Rhetoric with Reality'. *West European Politics,* 23(3): 1–24.

Pollitt, Christopher, Girre, Xavier, Lonsdale, Jeremy, Mul, Robert, Summa, Hilkka, and Waerness, Marit (1999). *Performance of Compliance? Performance Audit and Public Management in Five Countries*. Oxford: Oxford University Press.

Polsby, Nelson W. (1975). 'Legislatures', in Fred I. Greenstein and Nelson W. Polsby (eds.), *Handbook of Political Science. Volume 5. Governmental Institutions and Processes*. Reading, MA: Addison-Wesley.

Poguntke, Thomas (1999). 'The Winner Takes All: The FDP in 1982–1983: Maximizing Votes, Office, and Policy?', in Wolfgang C. Müller and Kaare Strøm (eds.), *Policy, Office, or Votes?* Cambridge: Cambridge University Press.

Rasch, Bjørn Erik (1995). 'Parliamentary Voting Procedures', in Herbert Döring (ed.), *Parliaments and Majority Rule in Western Europe*. New York: St. Martin's Press and Frankfurt am Main: Campus.

——(2001). 'Parlamentariske instrumenter og minoritetsparlamentarisme', Vedlegg 3, Norges offentlige utredninger (NOU) 2001: 3. *Velgere, valgordning, valgte*. Avgitt til Kommunal- og regionaldepartementet 30. januar 2001.

Raunio, Tapio and Hix, Simon (2000). 'Backbenchers Learn to Fight Back: European Integration and Parliamentary Government'. *West European Politics*, 23: 142–68.

——and Wiberg, Matti (2000). 'Does Support Lead to Ignorance? National parliaments and the Legitimacy of EU Governance.' *Acta Politica*, 35: 146–68.

Riker, William H. (1986). *The Art of Political Manipulation*. New Haven: Yale University Press.

Rose, Richard (1975). 'The Making of Cabinet Ministers', in Valentine Herman and James E. Alt (eds.), *Cabinet Studies*. London: Macmillan.

——(1976). *The Problem of Party Government*. Harmondsworth: Penguin.

——(1991). 'Prime Ministers in Parliamentary Democracies'. *West European Politics*, 14(2): 9–24.

Rose-Ackerman, Susan (1999). *Corruption and Government*. Cambridge: Cambridge University Press.

Rush, Michael (2001). *The Role of the Member of Parliament Since 1868*. Oxford: Oxford University Press.

Russell, Meg (2000). *Reforming the House of Lords. Lessons from Overseas*. Oxford: Oxford University Press.

Saalfeld, Thomas (1995a). 'On Dogs and Whips: Recorded Votes', in Herbert Döring (ed.), *Parliaments and Majority Rule in Western Europe*. New York: St. Martin's Press and Frankfurt am Main: Campus.

——(1995b). *Parteisoldaten und Rebellen*. Opladen: Leske + Budrich.

Sartori, Giovanni (1976). *Parties and Party Systems*. Cambridge: Cambridge University Press.

——(1997). *Comparative Constitutional Engineering*. Houndmills: Macmillan.

Schmidt, Manfred G. (1996). 'Germany. The Grand Coalition State', in Josep M. Colomer (ed.), *Political Institutions in Europe*. London: Routledge.

Schou, Tove Lise (1997). 'Denmark', in Jean Blondel and Ferdinand Müller-Rommel (eds.), *Cabinets in Western Europe*. Houndmills: Macmillan.

Self, Peter (1972). *Administrative Theories and Politics*. London: George Allen & Unwin.

Shugart, Matthew Soberg and Wattenberg, Martin P. (eds.) (2000). *Mixed-Member Electoral Systems*. Oxford: Oxford University Press.

Smith, Gordon (1991). 'The Resources of a German Chancellor'. *West European Politics*, 14(2): 48–61.

Somit, Albert, Wildenmann, Rudolph, Boll, Bernhard, and Römmele, Andrea (eds.) (1994). *The Victorious Incumbent: A Threat to Democracy?* Aldershot: Dartmouth.

Steiner, Jürg and Dorff, Robert H. (1980). *A Theory of Political Decision Modes*. Chapel Hill: University of North Carolina Press.

Strauss, E. (1961). *The Ruling Servants*. London: George Allen & Unwin.

Strøm, Kaare (1990). *Minority Government and Majority Rule*. Cambridge: Cambridge University Press.

——(1994). 'The Role of Norwegian Cabinet Ministers', in Michael Laver and Kenneth A. Shepsle (eds.), *Cabinet Ministers and Parliamentary Government*. Cambridge: Cambridge University Press.

——(2000). 'Parties at the Core of Government', in Russell J. Dalton and Martin P. Wattenberg (eds.), *Parties without Partisans*. Oxford: Oxford University Press.

——and Müller, Wolfgang C. (1999). 'The Keys to Togetherness: Coalition Agreements in Parliamentary Democracies'. *Journal of Legislative Studies*, 5(3/4): 255–82.

——and Swindle, Stephen M. (2002). 'Strategic Parliamentary Dissolution'. *American Political Science Review* 96: 575–91.

Suleiman, Ezra N. (ed.) (1984). *Bureaucrats and Policy Making*. New York: Holmes & Meier.

Szarka, Joseph (1999). 'The Parties of the French "Plural Left": An Uneasy Complementary'. *West European Politics*, 22(4): 20–37.

Taagepera, Rein and Shugart, Matthew S. (1989). *Seats and Votes*. Cambridge: Cambridge University Press.

Thiébault, Jean-Louis (1994). 'The Political Autonomy of Cabinet Ministers in the French Fifth Republic', in Michael Laver and Kenneth A. Shepsle (eds.), *Cabinet Ministers and Parliamentary Government*. Cambridge: Cambridge University Press.

Tsebelis, George and Money, Jeannette (1997). *Bicameralism*. Cambridge: Cambridge University Press.

Tufte, Edward R. (1978). *Political Control of the Economy*. Princeton: Princeton University Press.

Verzichelli, Luca (2003, forthcoming). 'Much Ado About Something?'. *Journal of Legislative Studies*.

Verzichelli, Luca and Cotta, Maurizio (2000). 'Italy: From "Constrained" Coalitions to Alternating Governments?' in Wolfgang C. Müller and Kaare Strøm (eds.), *Coalition Governments in Western Europe*. Oxford: Oxford University Press.

Welan, Manfried (1976). 'Die Kanzlerdemokratie in Österreich', in Andreas Khol, Robert Prantner, and Alfred Stirnemann (eds.), *Um Partei und Parlament*. Graz: Styria.

Wiberg, Matti (1995). 'Parliamentary Questioning: Control by Communication?', in Herbert Döring (ed.), *Parliaments and Majority Rule in Western Europe*. New York: St. Martin's Press and Frankfurt am Main: Campus.

Willett, Thomas D. (ed.) (1988). *Political Business Cycles*. Durham: Duke University Press.

Woodhouse, Diana (1994). *Ministers and Parliament. Accountability in Theory and Practice*. Oxford: Clarendon Press.

5

Austria: Imperfect Parliamentarism but Fully-fledged Party Democracy

WOLFGANG C. MÜLLER

INTRODUCTION

Though the Austrian polity deviates from the ideal type of parliamentary democracy as defined in this volume (see Chapter 1), in practice it has nevertheless functioned as a parliamentary system. This is largely due to the strength of party politics, with cohesive political parties being the real actors, using and abusing political institutions. This chapter will argue that political parties ensure that delegation in the democratic chain is successful (because all principals are better off than in a situation without parties), yet they account for agency losses in each stage of the delegation process.

Parliamentarism has been introduced stepwise in Austria (Widder 1979). After the aborted revolution of 1848 and the period of neoabsolutism, a process of gradual parliamentarization began in 1861, though it was not completed during the Habsburg monarchy. In the period 1918–20, assembly government prevailed. The 1920 Constitution established a régime that was almost an ideal-type parliamentary democracy. In 1929, the Constitution was substantially amended as a consequence of the emergence of a strong anti-parliamentary, anti-party spirit. At the end of Second World War, the United States and the Soviet occupation powers as well as the Austrian Communists pressed for a new Constitution, while the Socialist Party called for a return to the Constitution of 1920. Nonetheless the Constitution as amended in 1929 was reintroduced in December 1945, thus replacing the provisional Constitution of April 1945. Since then, the formal framework in which politics take place has been modified by numerous constitutional amendments and constitutional laws and clauses. Its basic architecture has not, however, been substantially changed.[1]

Thanks to Cynthia Kite, Franz Fallend, Michael Schaden, Hubert Sickinger, Emmerich Tálos, and, of course, my fellow editors for comments on earlier versions.

[1] In addition to the *Bundes-Verfassungsgesetz*, which in this chapter is refered to as the Constitution, there are other constitutional laws and clauses with constitutional status within ordinary statute. All of these have the same legal status. They are all equally binding. In 1993 constitutional lawyers counted no less than 63 constitutional amendments, 225 separate constitutional laws, 427 clauses with constitutional rank in ordinary legislation, and 181 state treaties with constitutionally relevant clauses enacted since 1945.

Constitutionally, Austria has since 1929 been semi-presidential, though in practice the parliamentary side has continued to prevail (Müller 1999*a*). Parliamentarism is constrained not only by a constitutionally strong President, but also by federalism, a strong Constitutional Court, direct democracy, consociationalism, and corporatism. The latter two features of postwar Austrian politics are not, however, embedded in the constitutional framework. The parliamentary majority decides the extent to which it will allow these arrangements to tie its hands.

Despite its small size Austria is a federal country. Nine *Länder* constitute a separate level of government between national and local politics. The Constitution contains a general competence clause in favour of the *Länder*, giving them jurisdiction over everything that is not explicitly reserved for the national level, the *Bund*. Yet, the Constitution has reserved the bulk of competencies for the national level (Werndl 1984). After the transfer of competencies to the European Union, there is, de facto, hardly anything left for the *Länder*. However, much national public administration is carried out through the *Land* administrations. With regard to these matters *Land* administrations are subordinated to the federal ministries (Weber 1987).

With the exception of the budget, all types of draft legislation can be introduced in parliament by either chamber, the cabinet, or the people (i.e. 100,000 citizens supporting a People's Initiative). In practice, government proposals and private members' bills from (a minimum of five) Nationalrat MPs prevail.[2] In order to be enacted, constitutional amendments require a quorum of 50 per cent of MPs[3] and the support of a two-thirds majority of the votes cast. The same applies to the Nationalrat's rules of procedure (Article 30) and, since 1962, to school legislation (Article 14 and 14a), which do not have constitutional status. Constitutional amendments are subject to a referendum if one is demanded by one-third of the MPs in one of the two chambers (Article 43). This has, however, never occurred. In contrast, a referendum is obligatory for a 'total revision' of the Constitution (*Gesamtänderung*)[4] (Article 43). This has happened only once. In 1994 a referendum was held on the constitutional amendments required for Austria's accession to the European Union.

To pass, ordinary legislation requires a quorum of one-third of MPs and a majority of the votes cast (50 per cent + 1). A referendum on a law is held before it comes into force if the Nationalrat so decides (Article 43). Even this use of the referendum has occurred only once: a 1978 referendum on the use of nuclear energy (Müller 1998). The process of budget-making differs from normal law making in that it requires the

---

[2] Before 1988 the minimum number of MPs was eight. Bundesrat proposals in parliamentary practice are completely irrelevant. With few exceptions, the people's initiative (*Volksbegehren*) has also been irrelevant with regard to actual law-making. However, it has been quite relevant as a means for party competition (Müller 1998, 1999*b*). The bulk of laws originate from private member initiatives and government proposals. In practice, the distinction between these two ways of initiating a law is blurred by the fact that many private member bills are de facto worked out in government departments.

[3] If not otherwise stated, all references to MPs refer to those of in the Nationalrat.

[4] The Constitution itself does not indicate what constitutes a 'total revision'. Constitutional lawyers and the Constitutional Court have interpreted this clause as referring to amendments that involve changes in one or more of the guiding principles of the 1920 Constitution. These unquestionably include the principles of democracy, federalism, the rule of law, the separation of powers, and liberalism (see Walter 1972: 101–13).

government to submit a proposal at least ten weeks before the end of the budget year. MPs may propose a budget only if the cabinet fails to do so (Article 51).

Although Austria has a two-chamber system, which reflects its federal constitution, it is a very asymmetrical one (Kathrein 1986; Schäffer 1999; Fallend 2000a). The upper chamber, the Bundesrat, represents the *Länder*. Its members are elected by the *Land* diets. The representation system in the Bundesrat takes into account the size of each *Land's* population and party strength. With regard to ordinary legislation passed by the Nationalrat, the Bundesrat can issue only a suspensory veto. This veto can be overridden by the Nationalrat with a quorum of 50 per cent of MPs and a majority of votes cast. By vetoing legislation, the Bundesrat can delay it for, at most, about 2 months. With regard to constitutional amendments, the Bundesrat is more powerful for two reasons. First, since 1984, changes in the distribution of competencies between the national level (*Bund*) and the *Länder* become effective only if the Bundesrat accepts them with a quorum of 50 per cent and a two-thirds majority (Article 44). Second, it can enforce a referendum on any constitutional amendment, if this is demanded by a third of its members. In its own right, however, the Bundesrat cannot block constitutional amendments that do not fall under Article 44. Moreover, there are important decisions that do not involve the Bundesrat at all. In particular, it does not participate in budget-making and other financial acts (Article 42). The Nationalrat and the Bundesrat are politically largely 'congruent' (Lijphart 1999: 207), in the sense that the same parties or coalitions held majorities in both chambers. This is true despite the fact that the representational systems are different enough to have produced different plurality parties in the two chambers (during 19.5 years in the period 1945–2000, including 11.4 years when two parties in the Bundesrat were of equal strength). From 1945 to 2000 the two chambers were politically 'incongruent' only for 5.1 years. Nevertheless, the Bundesrat's limited political relevance is much more a consequence of its lack of formal powers than a result of political congruence. In practice, political parties and non-constitutional bodies consisting of *Land* government representatives are much more important national channels of political influence for the *Länder* than is the Bundesrat (Luther 1986, 1997; Dachs 1996).

At the lowest level of general rules in Austria is the government decree (*Verordnung*). Such decrees are issued by individual ministers or, in rare cases, by the cabinet. Some of them require the consent of Parliament's main committee. According to the Constitution (Article 18), the content of a government decree must, as a rule, already be determined by law. However, the decree may reduce the degrees of freedom contained in the law. It is also possible to introduce *new* rules (which add to those already contained in the law) by decree, however, only if this is specifically authorized by constitutional law (Koja 1986: 141–64).

PARTIES

It is hard to overstate the relevance of parties in Austria. All elections, with the partial exception of local elections in small communities, are structured by parties. All office holders in governmental institutions are party nominees, and, in almost all cases, they are also members and functionaries of their respective parties. Moreover, the major parties have built up huge mass organizations and have colonized large parts of the civil society.

Despite this, the Austrian Constitution mentions political parties only briefly and primarily in a negative sense (by excluding their functionaries and employees from being members of the Constitutional Court). Since 1945, however, official constitutional doctrine as elaborated by academic lawyers and upheld by the courts is that, though the Constitution does not prescribe the role of political parties, it proceeds from the assumption that parties exist and are essential for the functioning of the constitutional system. A 1975 party law contains a constitutional clause stating that the existence and variety ('*Vielfalt*') of political parties comprise major elements of the democratic order of the Republic of Austria, and defines their tasks very generally. While arguably these constitutional provisions serve to legitimize party democracy, MPs and other politicians are not bound constitutionally to their parties.

Before 1975 the actual legal form of the existing parties differed and depended, de facto, on prevailing political power relations. Three parties, the Socialist (Social Democratic since 1991) Party (SPÖ), the Austrian People's Party (ÖVP), and the Communist Party (KPÖ)—the parties that founded the Second Republic in 1945— could afford to have an extra-constitutional status by not falling under one of the organizational forms recognized by Austrian law. As opposed to these 'historic' parties, younger parties like the League of Independents (VdU) and its successor, the Freedom Party (FPÖ), assumed the legal form of an association (*Verein*) in order to avoid any risk (such as being treated as an illegal organization by the authorities) created by their extra-constitutional status. Since 1975, however, 'political party' is a legal form *sui generis*. Party status requires the fulfilling of only minimal formal conditions and provides substantial advantages. To begin with, party status prevents state intervention in internal affairs. Only the courts have the right to ban political parties,[5] and they can do so only for reasons set out in constitutional law. Currently, only Nazi activities come under this rubric. Party status is also a necessary though not sufficient condition for benefiting from major parts of Austria's very generous system of public party finance. However, whether parties get public money, and how much they get, depends entirely on their electoral performance. With the exception of election years, in which subsidies are generally higher, only parties with parliamentary representation receive public funds (for the party organization, the parliamentary party, and their political education institutions). In 1999, an election year, support amounted to more than 720 million ATS (c. 52 million euro) at the national level. Over the typical 4 years' electoral cycle, even more money is given to parties at the subnational levels (Sickinger 1997, 2000a). The allocation between parties is largely proportional, with a bias in favour of small parties. This has, however, been reduced in recent years.

Throughout the postwar period the SPÖ and ÖVP have dominated political life. With the exception of the immediate postwar period (in which the KPÖ was included

---

[5] Strictly speaking the law considers unconstitutional parties as non-existent and public authorities treat them accordingly. If this behaviour is challenged, the courts decide over the existence or non existence of these parties.

in the cabinet) and the 1983–7 period (during which the FPÖ participated in government) only these two parties held government office until 2000. They did so either in 'grand coalition' governments—which were supported by a parliamentary base of up to 95 per cent of the MPs—or in single-party governments (1966–83) (Müller 2000c). Even during the period when the party system essentially functioned as a two-party system, high levels of parliamentary cooperation between the major parties were maintained (Müller 1993, 1997a). Nonetheless, the SPÖ and ÖVP have always competed vigorously with one another, more often checking each other and competing with each other for votes than working together in competition against opposition parties. Since 1986, SPÖ–ÖVP dominance has been reduced considerably by the establishment of new parties (the Greens in 1986 and the Liberal Forum in 1993) and in particular by the spectacular rise of the FPÖ, which won fifty-two seats in 1999 and hence temporarily gained equal status with the ÖVP (but fell back to a mere 18 seats in 2002). Following the 1999 election the ÖVP and FPÖ joined forces in government, causing a major change in the structure of party competition (Müller 2000d).

While the SPÖ has been a very cohesive, disciplined, and centralized party, the ÖVP is more factionalized and decentralized. However, this difference has directly affected only internal decision-making processes. In the parliamentary and governmental arenas both parties have acted cohesively. Parliamentary voting cohesion is generally very high. Indeed, no parliamentary battle has ever been won or lost as a result of a lack of party voting cohesion in parliamentary parties.

The major interest groups traditionally have constituted another set of highly important actors in Austrian politics. Some are public institutions (called 'Chambers'). They are established by law and automatically enrol all potential members. Chambers are legally entitled to issue opinions on proposed legislation. However, the real influence of the major interest groups on public decisions stems from their close link to the traditional major parties, and, indeed, their ability to commit them to their positions in socioeconomic policy-making. Thus the major interest groups have as much influence as the parliamentary majority is willing to grant them. This willingness has been considerably reduced since the 1970s, reaching a new low with the ÖVP–FPÖ governments in office since 2000.

DELEGATION FROM VOTERS TO MPs

Rules of Electoral Competition

Voters delegate to MPs under a set of rules which favour party politics and already established parties. A minimum length for campaigns of roughly 1 month (20 days before 1969) results from various clauses in the electoral law. However, in practice even early elections that were called on short notice (e.g. in 1995) allowed for a campaign of 2 months. There are no restrictions on the publication of opinion polls during campaigns. There has never been a legal limit on campaign spending. Free broadcasting time (abolished in 2002) and financial subsidies from the state are available only to parties that already have established themselves in Parliament. Only in elections years do non-parliamentary parties which have won at least 1 per cent of the votes get a refund towards their campaign costs. Thus the parties with parliamentary representation enjoy a competitive advantage.

Rules of Candidate Selection

There is no public regulation of important features of candidate selection. No primary election is legally enforced on parties, and there are no term limits or mandatory retirement age for MPs. These and other matters are partly regulated by party rules (Müller 1992). It is worth noting that in the 1990s the traditional parties changed their statutes to allow for more direct participation of the party members in candidate selection, with the ÖVP even introducing primaries open to all voters. However, in practice the FPÖ never and the SPÖ and ÖVP only once (in 1994) actually observed their own rules. Even then, the impact of voters and members on the party lists was very limited. Thus, candidate selection is a prerogative of the party bodies, particularly of the district and *Land* party organizations, which nominate the vast majority of candidates. Since the 1960s national party leadership has managed to increase its influence on candidate selection, for example by establishing quotas for 'central requirements'. The FPÖ has managed to increase the centralization of candidate nomination more than any other party in the 1990s, giving particular attention to the media skills of potential MPs.

Generally, candidates must be party members. Only in the 1990s have some parties allowed for exceptions to this rule, and only a few exceptions have actually been made. Most of these candidates eventually joined the party that put them up for election. With the exception of the SPÖ, which since 1968 has a mandatory retirement age of sixty-five (from which exceptions can be made), no major party has such rules, as of 2003.

The Electoral System: Impact on Party Competition

The Constitution requires Austrian elections at all levels to be general, equal, free, and secret. Electoral laws, on the other hand, are ordinary statutes. Therefore, as long as constitutional principles are not violated, election laws can be altered by a simple parliamentary majority. The Constitution sets limits on districting and redistricting by ruling out the establishment of electoral districts that combine parts of different *Länder* (Article 26). Elections to the Nationalrat are to be held every 4 years, or earlier if it so decides.[6] Voters are automatically registered on the basis of their declaration of residence. Voting in Nationalrat elections is generally not compulsory, however, until 1992 the *Länder* had the right (since abolished) to make it so regionally. Three *Länder* had exercised this right and required residents to vote in parliamentary elections.

The constitutional requirement of equality in elections has been interpreted to mean that some form of PR electoral system must be adopted. While respecting this principle, Parliament has made several changes to the electoral law since 1945. The most important ones affected the mechanism by which votes are translated into seats. Accordingly, the postwar period can be divided into three phases (Müller 1996*b*).

---

[6] Other constitutional means to shorten the term of the Nationalrat exist, but have not been used in practice.

From 1945 until 1970, twenty-five electoral districts existed. One hundred and sixty five seats were distributed among the parties participating in the election in two stages, the first of which operated within electoral districts. In the second round the electoral districts were aggregated into four units, and parties' unused votes were counted, provided that they had received at least one seat in the first stage (a *Grundmandat*). Three features tended to make this electoral system a *relatively* 'strong' one (cf. Sartori 1997: 42–4). First, the electoral system worked against small parties since it established a substantial threshold for parliamentary representation—the requirement that parties must win a seat in at least one of the twenty-five relatively small electoral districts. Second, apportionment among electoral districts was (and still is) based on the number of citizens rather than those eligible to vote, thus favouring rural areas (and hence the ÖVP), since they—as a rule—include a higher proportion of children. Third, the fact that the seats distributed in the first stage were cheaper in votes than those distributed in the second stage[7] favoured the big parties, because they received a higher proportion of their seats in the first stage. Thus this electoral system served the interests of the two major parties in general, and the ÖVP in particular, effectively shielding them against competitors. More specifically, the ÖVP's plurality in 1953 and 1959 and its majority in 1966 were manufactured by the electoral system.

In 1970, the SPÖ and FPÖ joined forces to pass a new electoral law, which came into force in 1971. The number of electoral districts was reduced to nine, whose boundaries were identical with the *Länder*. The number of parliamentary seats was increased from 165 to 183, and in the second stage of seat distribution the electoral districts were aggregated into only two units. Not surprisingly, this reform benefited the two parties that introduced it as well as new parties (which faced the same problem as the FPÖ). First, it lowered the threshold of representation by reducing the number of electoral districts and increasing the number of seats. Second, it reduced the impact of distributing seats according to population rather than voters by uniting rural and urban areas in larger electoral districts. Third, it removed the advantage of parties that receive a larger proportion of their seats in the first round of seat distribution (i.e. the big parties) by making these seats more expensive in votes.[8]

In 1992, SPÖ and ÖVP—which had been governing together since 1987—introduced a new electoral law. It divided the nine electoral districts into forty-three regional electoral districts (*Regionalwahlkreise*). Seats are distributed in three stages. First, at the regional electoral district level. In the second stage, at the *Land* electoral district level. The cost of seats in these two stages is identical within each *Land*. In the third stage, seats are distributed at the national level. Only parties that win either one or more seats at the regional electoral district level or at least 4 per cent of the valid votes nationwide participate in the second and third stages. Seats already distributed at the regional and *Land* levels are deducted from the number of seats calculated at the national level. The 4 per cent barrier has raised the threshold for parliamentary representation. In 1999 the Liberal

---

[7] Until 1970, in the first round in each electoral district the number of votes required for a seat was calculated by the Hagenbach–Bischoff system, while the d'Hondt system was used in the second round.

[8] Since 1971, seats in the first round are distributed by the Hare system, while the d'Hondt system continues to be used in the second (or, since 1992, third) round.

Forum missed the required 4 per cent (by 0.35 per cent) and hence lost parliamentary representation, while it would have won several seats under the previous electoral system.

The Electoral System: Impact on Candidate Competition

Throughout the postwar period, candidate selection and ranking by political parties has been extremely important for reducing the number of election alternatives and—via the party vote—determining who will take a seat in Parliament. However, with the exception of 1945, when a pure list system operated, not all discretionary power has rested with the party organization.

In 1949 the possibility of intraparty preference voting was introduced. Until 1970 it was possible for relatively small numbers of voters to change the party lists by re-arranging the ranking of candidates and crossing off candidates (Fischer 1971). Despite its potential power, however, the system was little used. Altogether, only four MPs who were not placed in 'eligible' party list positions were elected to Parliament before the official ballot paper was introduced in 1959. In all four cases the voters had been fooled by intraparty groups that had distributed ballot papers with altered rankings of candidates (Müller 1983).

In 1971 this system was replaced by a system in which the name of the preferred candidate (from the party list) has to be written on the ballot paper. Until 1992, a candidate not ranked among the 'eligible' places of the party list could be elected if he/she won as many preference votes as the number of votes required for a seat. Only once was this system consequential (in 1983) (Müller 1983). In 1990 it was partly used to transform the parliamentary election into a Chancellor election, with the SPÖ campaigning for preference votes for its leader, Franz Vranitzky.[9]

The preference voting system was changed as part of the 1992 electoral reform, the official goal of which was the personalization of elections and hence the improvement of the relationship between the citizens and their representatives. To win a seat at the regional district level it is sufficient for a candidate to win either half as many preference votes as votes are required for a seat, or preference votes amounting to a sixth of the party vote—provided that the party wins enough votes to get a seat in a relevant regional electoral district. If more candidates meet these conditions than there are seats won by their party, then the candidates with the greatest number of preference votes are elected. At the level of the larger electoral districts—equivalent to the Länder and hence the pre-1992 electoral districts—a candidate still needs as many preference votes as the number of votes required to win a seat.

The new system has not had a great impact. While several candidates won enough preference votes in their electoral districts to win a seat in Parliament, all of them had been placed at the top of their party lists. Thus, the preference votes did not change the lists (Müller and Scheucher 1994). Yet, both in 1999 and 2002 one ÖVP

[9] Vranitzky was much more popular than his party and leading his party's lists in all electoral districts he did not depend on preference votes for election to Parliament. Eventually he received enough preference votes to give him seventeen seats (Müller 1990; Müller and Plasser 1992).

candidate was elected by preference votes. Nevertheless, under the 1992 electoral system there has been an increase in intraparty competition, with the preference votes counting in the next candidate selection.

The empirical record of preference voting indicates that Austrian voters think very much in terms of parties rather than individual candidates. Survey evidence compiled since 1980 confirms this. Nonetheless, the increased use of preference voting and the candidates' competition for preference votes has been accompanied by an increase in the role that candidates play in influencing voters' decisions.

In sum, until 1992 the party organizations were virtually free to determine who would obtain a seat in parliament. The 1992 reform has not substantially reduced that freedom. Thus, intraparty candidate selection remains much more decisive than the general election for parliamentary representation.

Potential Agency Problems in the Link Between Voters and MPs

The consequence of this party-dominated recruitment system is that candidates and MPs are normally long-standing party functionaries who have worked their way up in the party organization. There are quite a few MPs who have been professional politicians practically their entire life, beginning with the party youth organization and later taking professional positions in the party, party-controlled institutions, or public sector firms while continuing their political career. Both MPs and political parties display clear and in some respect increasing gaps in social representation (such as occupation) (Müller and Ulram 1995; Fischer 1997: 103). While long-term party screening of MPs minimizes the risk of recruiting political fortune-hunters, these politicians tend to adapt to the subcultures of party organizations and to lose an understanding of what average voters think. Even when this is not the case, MPs know that their position in the party organization is particularly important for their careers (Müller *et al.* 2001). MPs therefore have two principals—their voters and their party (either locally or nationally). MPs have to be concerned about their renomination by the local party organization and, increasingly, also about preference votes.

Ex Post Mechanisms for Holding MPs Accountable

The Constitution does not provide a recall mechanism. Once elected, MPs maintain their seat until the next election unless they lose their eligibility, voluntarily resign, or die in office. According to the Constitution, MPs have a 'free mandate', that is they are 'bound in the exercise of their function by no mandate' (Article 56). This means that MPs are not subordinate to their own parliamentary party group, the extra-parliamentary party organization, or the voters in their electoral district. The only constitutional way to exercise *ex post* control is via elections and candidate selection. This is *grosso modo* an effective mechanism, since most MPs want to be re-elected. Austrian MPs are well paid and used to be able to earn a substantial pension if they served for a minimum of 10 years, which in most cases requires being re-elected twice. Moreover, many MPs have not only *static* but *progressive* ambition (Schlesinger 1991). They aim at promotion within the parliamentary party, appointment to executive office at the national or

Land levels, or, increasingly, nomination to winnable slots on party lists for European elections.

In principle, parliamentary rules of procedure favour *ex post* control of individual MPs. Secret votes, which make it impossible to hold individual MPs accountable, can only be held if a majority of the Nationalrat so decides. Even then, however, a minority of twenty MPs (twenty-five before 1989) is sufficient to enforce a recorded vote. In fact, secret votes have hardly ever been used, except in personnel elections, when they are legally required. In contrast, recorded votes have become more frequently used. As a rule, they are held at the demand of the opposition whenever it wants to demonstrate the government MPs 'lack of responsiveness' vis-à-vis specific groups of voters (Müller *et al.* 2001). Nevertheless, leaving aside issues of great salience and local concern, ordinary voters rarely have the time and interest required to follow politics closely enough to enable them to rationally punish or reward individual MPs in subsequent elections on the basis of their voting record. Instead, voters reward or punish political parties. Thus voters delegate to political parties and leave it to them to exercise *ex ante* and *ex post* control over MPs. Political parties are durable organizations. They collectively seek to preserve their 'brand name'—that is, the party's established reputation (Aldrich 1995: 49). For this reason, parties are even more likely to remain in tune with their voters than are individual MPs.

Political parties have sticks and carrots they can use to make their MPs behave (Damgaard 1995; Müller 2000*b*). Positive incentives include small rewards such as participation in parliamentary delegations travelling to interesting locations and the opportunity to advance within the parliamentary party group (e.g. a better seat in the plenary meeting, more prestigious committee assignments, nomination to more visible speaking positions in plenary debates, etc.) or politics in general. All of these rewards can be withheld from an MP who creates trouble. The ultimate sanctions are deselection as a parliamentary candidate and, even more severe, expulsion from the party. Decisions such as these are extremely serious and are made by relevant bodies in the extra-parliamentary party organization. For many MPs, beyond its obvious consequences for their future political careers, expulsion from the party would have severe social and economic consequences (cf. Michels 1963). The SPÖ and ÖVP have also traditionally required their parliamentary candidates to sign an undated letter of resignation (cf. Duverger 1959: 198). This instrument does not work if the MP actively objects, but in other cases it makes life easier for the leadership. Indeed, there have been cases where not only incumbent MPs but also *all* unsuccessful candidates from that list (who would in sequence fill vacancies in Parliament) resigned from their seat in order to allow their party to make people MPs who had not contested the last election. Moreover, until 1992, all resources of the parliamentary party (i.e. money and staff) were controlled by the parliamentary party, and not by individual MP's (Müller and Steininger 2000). Though MPs now have their own staffs, parliamentary rules of procedure have become increasingly party-based, thus reducing the individual MP's opportunity to act without party support. These changes were not, however, introduced to tighten the parties' grip on their MPs but were a side effect of attempts to 'rationalize' the conduct of parliamentary proceedings. While all these means of party control can be used to control MPs, the most powerful argument for cohesive behaviour by MPs is that a powerful parliamentary party group is a source of considerable gains (cf. Cox and McCubbins 1993; Aldrich 1995; Müller 2000*b*).

DELEGATION FROM PARLIAMENT TO CABINET

Cabinet Installment

According to the Constitution the directly elected federal President appoints the federal Chancellor and, at the proposal of the Chancellor, the other cabinet members and secretaries of state (junior ministers). The Constitution contains no restrictions whatsoever as to who should be invited to form a government or on the government's political composition. However, de facto, the President has little discretion. The government needs parliamentary support in order to survive and govern effectively. The President therefore refrains from appointing a cabinet that is opposed by a parliamentary majority. This, in theory, might still leave some leeway for the President. Potentially, presidential influence increases when alternative majority coalitions can be formed and the coalition preferences of the parties are not (yet) fixed. In practice, however, the President largely has limited himself to ratifying whatever the parties agree to. This means that the President is occasionally pre-empted by public party declarations or even pre-electoral commitments. It is well-established convention that the task of forming a government goes first to the leader or 'Chancellor candidate' of the largest parliamentary party (Welan 1997: 47). With the single exception of 2000, the largest party (and, with one exception, also the first person officially designated the Chancellor candidate by the President) has always succeeded in forming a viable government. On several occasions the President intervened in the government formation process; while exercising some influence, he was not *decisive* (Müller 1999*a*). The most remarkable presidential intervention occurred in the 1999/2000 government formation. It ended by the President swearing in a cabinet he had worked hard to prevent. Indeed, he had never given the formal task of forming a government to the new Chancellor Wolfgang Schüssel. However, the President exercised some influence. He pushed for a preamble to the coalition agreement that obliged the coalition parties to some principles he wanted the government to observe and he rejected two FPÖ ministerial nominees, which no President had done since 1949.

Once it is formed and sworn in, the cabinet must present itself to Parliament (the Nationalrat) within one week after assuming office (Article 70, see Ringhofer 1977: 229). The cabinet does not have to go through an investiture vote; however, it must present an outline of its programme and, by convention, this is followed by a debate. This occasion can also be used to introduce a vote of no confidence. To unseat a government requires a parliamentary majority against it (for details see below). Austria is thus an example of 'negative' parliamentarism, as the burden of proof rests with the opposition (cf. Bergman 1993). Since 1945 only one government—the ÖVP–FPÖ government formed in 2000—had to face a vote of no confidence in connection with its first appearance before Parliament. In addition, only once was an individual minister challenged—unsuccessfully—on such an occasion (Table 5.1).

Table 5.1. *Cabinet Formation, Cabinet Termination, and Early Parliamentary Dissolution: Austria 1945–2000*[a]

No	Cabinet	Date of formation	Investiture votes (iv)	No-confidence votes (ncv)			Confidence votes (cv) under specific institutional mechanism only	Did the cabinet end with an early election?	Who dissolved Parliament in this case?[b]
			n.a.	No. of ncv	Cabinet removed by ncv	Cabinet resigned to pre-empt ncv	n.a.		
1	Renner	45/04/27		—	—	—		n.a.	
2	Figl I	45/12/20		0					
3	Figl II	47/11/20		0					
4	Figl III	49/11/08		0				Yes	Parliamentary majority
5	Raab I	53/04/02		0				Yes	Parliamentary majority
6	Raab II	56/06/29		0				Yes	Parliamentary majority
7	Raab III	59/07/16		0					
8	Gorbach I	61/04/11		0				Yes	Parliamentary majority
9	Gorbach II	63/03/27		0					
10	Klaus I	64/04/02		1	No			Yes	Parliamentary majority
11	Kalus II	66/04/19		1	No				
12	Kreisky I	70/04/21		0				Yes	Parliamentary majority
13	Kreisky II	71/11/04		1	No				

14	Kreisky III	75/10/28	3	No		
15	Kreisky IV	79/06/05	4	No		
16	Sinowatz	83/05/24	2	No	Yes	Parliamentary majority
17	Vranitzky I	86/06/16	0	No		
18	Vranitzky II	87/01/21	2	No	Yes	Parliamentary majority
19	Vranitzky III	90/12/17	3	No		
20	Vranitzky IV	94/11/29	4	No	Yes	Parliamentary majority
21	Vranitzky V	96/03/12	0	No		
22	Klima	97/01/15	1	No		

[a] n.d. = no data (missing data); n.a. or '—' = not applicable in this case.

[b] The question 'Who dissolved Parliament in this case?' in this book's coding scheme can be answered with one of five options. This identifies the main constitutional actor that caused the early election. We have not coded the formal signatory, but rather the person or body that made the real decision: (1) Head of State; (2) Prime Minister; (3) Cabinet; (4) Parliamentary majority; (5) Automatic constitutional provision (e.g. if it is required when a new President takes office, or, for example, if it is required after the adoption of a proposal for constitutional amendments).

The only formal requirement for appointment to the cabinet is that cabinet members must be eligible for the Nationalrat. Cabinet positions are compatible with membership in Parliament, though the latter is not required (Article 70). In practice, Austria is among the countries that have the lowest rate of ministerial recruitment from Parliament (De Winter 1991: 48). For instance, fewer than half of the members of the last grand coalition cabinet (Klima) served in Parliament before first being appointed to cabinet and only five out of twelve members of the ÖVP–FPÖ cabinet in office in September 2000 had a record of parliamentary service. Cabinet members who are not recruited from Parliament tend to come from interest groups or *Land* governments, though recruitment from private industry has become more important over time. The potential agency problem that this can create is mitigated by the fact that cabinet members with different backgrounds share party membership and have often been involved in government in an expert capacity for many years.

Party-Internal Mechanisms of Ex Ante Control

Party control of the cabinet is greater when cabinet ministers have internalized party values and act upon them. The holding of high party office can be used to operationalize the internalization of party values. Empirical data shows that between 1945 and 1987 the average proportion of cabinet members (including secretaries of state) who were, or had been, members of the executive body of their party was 42 per cent. However, there was significant variation among the parties and over time. In the 1990–4 period, 23 per cent of the ÖVP cabinet members had served in the party executive before their first appointment to government while the figure was zero for the SPÖ (Müller, Philipp, and Steininger 1996: 93–4). While party and cabinet are still linked in the SPÖ, the point of entry has changed. Appointment to cabinet has become the springboard for a party career, as exemplified most prominently by Chancellors Franz Vranitzky (1986–96) and Viktor Klima (1996–2000). Both were appointed to cabinet despite the fact that they had not held party office, and both succeeded in becoming party chairman.

Scrutiny of Legislation and Parliamentary Resolutions

Draft legislation is scrutinized via a system of permanent committees, which largely parallels the ministerial structure. These parliamentary committees can demand that ministers appear before them (with their civil servants if ministers so wish). They are exclusively concerned with legislation and function as gatekeepers in the sense that they have the authority to examine government bills (as well as all other types of bills) and to amend them. It is the committee's proposal, rather than the original bill, that is submitted to the plenary meeting. While the task of drafting legislation is, de facto, largely delegated to the government, this scrutiny and amendment power is the Parliament's most important formal *ex ante* mechanism—that is, the one that enables Parliament to avoid policy abdication. Moreover, since 1987 Parliament has become much more active in scrutinizing and amending government proposals, despite the fact that the basic rules covering this process have remained unchanged throughout the postwar period. For the parliamentary party groups of the government parties an informal *ex ante* mechanism is equally important: their policy experts' participation in negotiating draft legislation in the coalition (Müller 1993; Sickinger 2000*b*; Müller *et al.* 2001; Tálos and Kittel 2001).

A reform of the Parliament's rules of procedure in 1975 made it possible for a parliamentary minority to launch an appeal to the Constitutional Court in order to exercise abstract norm control. One-third of the MPs can bring any law before the Constitutional Court, which has the power to invalidate laws that violate the principles of the Constitution. The decisions that subsequently come from the Court are made according to a decision rule that, by its very nature, is quite different from Parliament's. The possibility of an appeal to the Constitutional Court has actually proven to be a quite effective means of control. Not only have several laws been invalidated, the parliamentary majority now tries to anticipate potential appeals by the minority and to pre-empt them by keeping them in mind during the process of drafting legislation. Given tight party discipline in Parliament, appeals to the Constitutional Court, with a single exception, were only launched when the parliamentary opposition held a minimum of a third of the seats. Thus this instrument was not important under grand has already faced government. In contrast, the incumbent ÖVP–FPÖ coalition has already faced more opposition appeals to the Constitutional Court than any previous government.

Parliament has the authority to pass resolutions demanding specific action on the part of cabinet or cabinet members (Article 52). Although these are not actually legally binding, cabinet members' parliamentary accountability makes them, de facto, binding. Between 1971 and 1999, Parliament passed 730 such resolutions, some of which were of great importance—for example, the resolution that fixed the course of Austria's European Union (EU) integration policy (Fischer 1997: 110–1).

Cabinet Accountability

The political accountability of the cabinet is explicitly regulated in the Constitution (Article 74) and in the rules of procedure. If the Nationalrat passes a vote of no confidence, the cabinet (or individual members who have lost Parliament's confidence) must be dismissed by the President (Welan 1967). A motion of no confidence must be sponsored by five MPs (eight before 1988). To pass a vote of no confidence requires a quorum of 50 per cent of MPs and a majority of the votes cast. The cabinet is not accountable to the second chamber, the Bundesrat.

The opposition has regularly introduced motions of no confidence since the mid-1960s to criticize general government policy, particular policies, or individual cabinet members. Table 5.1 summarizes the behavioural record of no-confidence votes (directed against the cabinet or the Chancellor) and parliamentary dissolution.[10] In light of the fact that all but one of the cabinets were majority governments, that coalition

[10] Note that two no-confidence notions were directed against the Vice-Chancellor and leader of the second government party under cabinets Sinowatz and Klima, respectively.

discipline guides voting in parliament (Müller 2000c), and that parliamentary parties are highly cohesive, it is not surprising that all motions of no confidence have failed.

Cabinet members can be held accountable through the Constitutional Court for contravening the law (*Ministeranklage*) (Articles 142 and 143). The act of invoking the Constitutional Court in such cases is political, but the procedure itself judicial (Korinek 1986; Schambeck 1997: 72–80). To bring a minister before the court, a quorum of 50 per cent of MPs must be present in plenary session and a majority of votes cast must support doing so. Given these requirements, it is not surprising that this instrument has had no practical relevance in the postwar period.

In a party democracy, it is not surprising that 'sanctioned' controls have been less effective than 'unsanctioned' mechanisms. The cabinet can be held accountable *ex post* through a range of parliamentary instruments, including several types of questions, formal reporting requirements, committees of investigation, checks by the audit office, and reports by the ombudsman office.[11]

Over the postwar period the instruments by which cabinets can be held accountable have been reformed several times (Auracher-Jäger 1997; Atzwanger and Zögernitz 1999). The rules of parliamentary procedure originally restricted the opposition's opportunity to effectively criticize the government and present alternatives in a way that would attract broad public attention. This has changed since 1961 due to the introduction of new parliamentary instruments, primarily ones of importance to the opposition, and because the number of MPs needed to invoke these instruments has been reduced over time. This trend has continued increasingly, but it has been accompanied by efforts to ration the use of these instruments (Schefbeck 1997).

Written questions, which must be sponsored by five MPs, have throughout the postwar period proved the most important means for scrutinizing the executive. The number of parliamentary questions has increased enormously, particularly as a result of the termination of 'grand coalition' governments in 1966, an event which—for the first time—led to the emergence of a strong parliamentary opposition. Interestingly, the return to grand coalition government in 1987 was also followed by a major increase in parliamentary questions. Compared to the 1971–86 period, the number of written questions per month increased by 183 per cent between 1986 and 1996. In the 1996–9 term more than 6,700 written questions were asked.

The second type of question that has existed throughout the postwar period is the urgent question (*Dringliche Anfrage*), a written question that is motivated orally by its main sponsor during the plenary session in which it is introduced. Following the minister's oral defence, the question is debated. An urgent question originally required the support of twenty MPs, but this was reduced to five in 1988. At the same time, a limit on the number of urgent questions was established: each MP could support two per year until 1996 and one per year thereafter, with an additional minimum annual quota of four per parliamentary party since 1996. Typically the opposition parties exhaust their contingent, and plan to do so irrespective of the political agenda. This led to sixty-nine urgent questions in the 1996–9 term. Urgent questions from the opposition

[11] See Gerlich (1973), Neisser (1986) and Nödl (1995).

typically aim to challenge government policy and to highlight its own alternative proposals. Since 1996, an urgent question can be substituted by an urgent proposal, allowing for a more constructive approach.

In 1961 a question hour was introduced. This is the only time when each individual MP has the right to question ministers before Parliament (without being sponsored by other MPs); however, question time is a scare resource, allowing, for instance, only 255 questions in the 1996–9 term (to be followed by 927 ad hoc questions). In 1988 the Parliament introduced an hour's debate on current subjects. One such debate can be held each week if five MPs (with an alternation of the proposing parliamentary parties) so demand. However, this debate is cancelled if an urgent question is introduced. Generally, the effectiveness of these and other parliamentary instruments has been increased by reforms aimed at giving them more publicity.[12]

Parliamentary questions must relate to executive business (thus excluding legislative and private affairs). Since 1961 cabinet members have been required to answer written questions within 2 months (no time limit existed before.) At a minimum, parliamentary questions require a formal response.[13]

Parliament has always had the power to order the audit office (*Rechnungshof*) to scrutinize a particular branch of the executive. The audit office is formally an auxiliary institution of Parliament charged with exercising financial oversight of the executive branch of government. It is designed to be independent of the parliamentary majority (Widder 1997)[14] and much of its investigative activity is carried out on its own initiative. However, regardless of whether an investigation was conducted at Parliament's request, the audit office always reports its findings and suggestions to Parliament. While it is up to the parliamentary majority to decide whether or not Parliament will act on the basis of audit office reports (e.g., by changing laws, passing resolutions to force the executive to take certain actions, or censuring a minister), reports also have a more indirect impact. Because they provide a wealth of arguments that can be used by the opposition and receive considerable public attention, they put pressure on the government (Müller 1996a: 43–5). A 1975 reform gave any minority of one-third of MPs the right to appeal to the audit office. In 1988 the necessary number of MPs was

---

[12] Since 1996 the number of urgent questions has been limited to one per day. If more than one is put forward, the party that had not asked an urgent question for the longest time is given preference. Since the government parties do not nearly exhaust their contingent they are more likely to be in that position and hence have the chance to buy time, if they find this appropriate.

[13] A cabinet member can respond but not provide a substantive answer for a variety of reasons. While these have not been legislated, parliamentary practice has established the following reasons: (1) if the question goes beyond the questioned minister's jurisdiction, (2) if the information needed to answer the question is impossible or very costly to gather, (3) if the answer to a question would reveal information which must be kept secret in the national interest. However, only in exceptional cases can a minister refuse to an answer by referring to the bureaucracy's obligation to secrecy (Czerny and Fischer 1982: 297; see Neisser 1986: 678–83 for a partly deviating interpretation).

[14] The audit office is linked to Parliament only by the election of its President, who since 1986 is elected for one non-renewable term of 12 years. Although the President—like cabinet members—is accountable to Parliament and can—in principle—be removed using the same procedures (see below), this is unlikely. The parliamentary majority's removal of an inconvenient President would be seen as an illegitimate use of power and would probably be more politically damaging than criticism from the audit office.

reduced to twenty. Minority access to the audit office however has remained rationed. Initially a new minority order required the completion of the previous investigation, later that contingent was increased to two, and since 1993 three, investigations carried out simultaneously.

A parliamentary majority can also set up special investigative committees (Fallend 2000*b*). Each party represented in the Parliament's main standing committee automatically has representation in investigative committees. These committees work under the same rules as criminal courts. They can force witnesses to testify before them, and they have access to government papers. Until 1988 investigative committees worked behind closed doors. The President of Parliament can now grant access to media representatives during testimony of witnesses and experts, which in fact had been done in all cases. In practice, investigative committees have been established only to look into allegations of major abuses of executive power. This happened once in the 1940s, twice in the 1960s, five times in the 1970s, and five times in the 1980s (not counting the re-establishment of investigative committees after elections). Investigations that have been covered by the media have had a particularly important political impact, one that has damaged governing parties. This is one reason why the government majority has not approved new investigative committees in the 1990s. Only after the formation of the ÖVP–FPÖ government in 2000, a new investigative committee was set up in order to look into the business of a ministry previously headed by SPÖ ministers.

In addition to the Parliament's instruments for monitoring the government, the latter is subject to many reporting requirements. Schambeck (1997: 105–8) lists more than sixty reports that the cabinet must regularly submit to Parliament. In many cases a specific law demands a regular report to Parliament—for example, on social security, research, arts, and public debt.

Finally, parliamentary oversight can make use of a weak, that is, unsanctioned, version of institutional checks (cf. Kiewiet and McCubbins 1991). The activities of the audit office that stem from its own initiative (rather than investigations ordered by Parliament) fall under this rubric. Furthermore the ombudsman office (*Volksanwaltschaft*), which was established in 1977 as another auxiliary institution of Parliament, receives citizens' complaints about the administration. In addition to trying to solve these problems by working with the administration, it reports to Parliament and suggests general remedies (Widder 1997). However, both the ombudsman and the audit office can only bark but not bite. That is, they report their findings to Parliament, which must then decide whether to act.

In short, Parliament has many mechanisms to hold the cabinet accountable, but in practice party cohesion and coalition discipline undermine their immediate effectiveness: parties and coalitions continue to support their cabinet members even when convincing criticism is tabled against them (Müller and Bubendorfer 1989). It is only to the extent that parliamentary accountability mechanisms raise public attention to unpopular policies and maladministration that they can produce *indirect* effects. Either these factors enter the voters' evaluations of the government parties or, anticipating such effects, the government parties remove cabinet members who have become an electoral liability or reverse their policies.

Party-Internal Mechanisms of Ex Post Cabinet Control

As a rule, extra-parliamentary party organizations do not try to monitor their cabinet members in 'police patrol' fashion (McCubbins and Schwartz 1984). While cabinet members attend party executive meetings, these are infrequent and cabinet members are not required to systematically report to them. Instead, extra-parliamentary party oversight of cabinet members is largely based on 'fire alarms'. This means that when members of the party executive are alarmed about particular issues, then they question or criticize ministers over these specific issues, and may also demand policy change (Müller 1994). The activities of the parliamentary party vis-à-vis the cabinet come closer to 'police patrol' oversight, at least with regard to legislation.

Many of the 'fire alarms' and 'police patrol' interventions of MPs result, de facto, from compromises, which are a constant feature of coalition politics. While it is easy to detect deviations from a party's ideals, the executive boards of parties and party MPs are less qualified to judge whether their party has exhausted its negotiation potential, thus making compromise a reasonable course of action. As a rule, cabinet members enjoy the benefit of the doubt, especially as long as they enjoy the trust of the party leader.

DELEGATION WITHIN THE CABINET

Division of Labour Between the Cabinet and Individual Ministers

Once the cabinet is appointed, there is a clear division of labour between the cabinet and individual ministers. All tasks of the government rest with individual ministers unless they are explicitly reserved to the cabinet by constitutional or ordinary law. The number of cabinet tasks is relatively small. The most important are:

(a) to propose legislation and the budget to Parliament (Articles 41 and 51);
(b) to provide reports to Parliament;
(c) to make proposals about appointments (including top civil servants' posts and constitutional judgeships) to the President (Articles 65, 67, 147);
(d) to nominate candidates (after agreement with the Nationalrat's main committee) for Austria's most important positions in EU bodies (Article 23c);
(e) to table issues before the Constitutional Court (Article 138–42);
(f) to propose the dissolution of Parliament to the President (Article 29);
(g) to exercise the government's (very limited) emergency decree powers[15] (Article 18);
(h) to veto *Land* legislation (Article 98);
(i) to empower the minister of defence to dispose over the army (Article 80).

---

[15] The cabinet and the permanent sub-committee of the Parliament's main committee jointly propose emergency decrees to the President. The cabinet also countersigns these decrees.

Cabinet Decision Rules

All cabinet decisions are made according to the rule of unanimity.[16] The use of this procedure, which gives each minister (and hence each government party) absolute veto power, is in keeping with the dominant interpretation of the Constitution (Adamovich 1971: 265; Walter 1972: 485–6). However, an alternative interpretation would probably not be unconstitutional (Pfeifer 1964). Welan and Neisser (1971: 100) have argued that the unanimity rule has the status of a constitutional convention (which implies that it might be changed without a constitutional amendment). To avoid potential problems created by conflicting interpretations of cabinet decision-making rules, the post-1987 coalition agreements of the SPÖ–ÖVP coalition have explicitly referred to the unanimity rule. It is still observed under the ÖVP–FPÖ government.

The Power of the Chancellor

The Constitution does not give the Chancellor the power to issue binding directives to the members of the cabinet. Rather, the Chancellor has only a co-ordination competence (Adamovich 1973). Despite attempts by constitutional lawyers to clarify the matter, it remains unclear what is actually meant by the term Chancellor's co-ordination competence. However, in legal terms this authority certainly falls short of the power to issue directives. Despite this, the Constitution gives the Chancellor important hiring and firing powers. The President appoints and dismisses other cabinet members and state secretaries based on proposals from the Chancellor. From a purely constitutional perspective, this implies that members of the government must initially be approved by the Chancellor, and that their position in the government depends on his continued support.

In practice, the powers of the Chancellor are both increased and decreased by party politics (Müller 1997b). In coalition governments, the Chancellor's appointment and dismissal powers, de facto, do not apply to the party (or parties) other than his own. Yet, it seems that Chancellor Schüssel, in coalition with a pariah party since 2000, has been concerned to avoid some particular damaging appointments in his coalition partner's realm. Party autonomy with regard to government positions that it has been granted in coalition negotiations is one of the iron rules of coalition politics in Austria. It is the Vice-Chancellor who, in practice, exercises these powers vis-à-vis the members of his party's ministers and state secretaries. Both the Chancellor and Vice-Chancellor exercise these powers as party leaders.[17] Being party leaders is a very important source of authority, one that increases the Chancellor's and Vice-Chancellor's ability to direct the actions of their parties' government members. However, party leaders are not dictators. Generally speaking, SPÖ leaders have had greater discretion than have ÖVP leaders.[18]

---

[16] See Welan and Neisser (1971), Gerlich, Müller, and Philipp (1988), Gerlich and Müller (1997), and Müller (1997b).

[17] With few short-lived exceptions, the leaders of government parties have always been in cabinet and have held the position of Chancellor or Vice-Chancellor.

[18] The two FPÖ leaders who served in government until 2003 actually fell in disgrace with their party and lost office in less than one term in government.

Finally, the Chancellor is head of an important department with overarching competencies. These include reviewing draft legislation to determine its constitutionality and (until 1997) heading the civil service, the latter of which gave the Chancellor significant influence over civil servant positions and promotions. These competencies can, to some extent, be used strategically to support the Chancellor's position.

Cabinet Coordination

Coordination of cabinet work can be accomplished using either negative or positive instruments. The fact that decisions in cabinet have to be unanimous constitutes an important means for negative coordination. Proceeding from an informal norm of reciprocity, ministers tend not to interfere in the policies of their cabinet colleagues, as long as these policies have no direct impact on their own departments (Müller 1994).

There are both formal and informal positive forms of coordination. The draft legislation review procedure (*Begutachtungsverfahren*) is a formal, permanent means of coordination. Draft bills from individual departments are sent to other ministries (as well as to a variety of interest groups and administrative units), which comment on them. They might also recommend—or even demand—revisions (Fischer 1972; Tálos and Kittel 2001).

Implementation of laws is not usually the responsibility of the cabinet, but that of individual ministers. Coordination of individual ministers' (or parties') implementation activities can, however, be enforced by introducing an 'accord' clause (*Einvernehmens-Klausel*) into a particular law. Such a clause specifies that a particular group of ministers must agree on administrative measures to implement the law (Barfuß 1968). To the chagrin of administrative reformers, coalition governments frequently insert 'accord' clauses into their legislation in order to guarantee interparty consensus in the implementation of relevant laws.

Coexisting alongside these formal instruments are many informal, bilateral contacts between ministers. The cabinet has no authority to make decisions over matters that fall under the competence of individual ministers. In practice, however, non-constitutional bodies such as coalition committees and meetings of the party leaders have done so. Prominent issues are often coordinated—which is not to say formally decided—by the Chancellor (and Vice-Chancellor). Policies that require additional financial expenditures need to be coordinated with the minister of finance.

Formally, all portfolios are equal. Ministers are therefore formally equal—both as portfolio-holders and as members of the cabinet. The exception to this equality is the minister of finance, who is 'more equal' than others in the implementation phase. The finance minister has always had a strong position, one that was further strengthened by a 1986 constitutional amendment (Article 51a–c) and new budget law. These changes gave the minister the authority to spend the reserve budget if economic developments suggest that doing so would be wise. In addition, the ministry of finance closely supervises budget implementation. In this capacity it has the authority to prevent the spending of money already granted by Parliament, if changing economic conditions warrant doing so and if the cabinet agrees.

The Constitution does not require that position-taking in EU bodies by cabinet members or civil servants be preceded by a cabinet decision. In practice, however, government parties and departments have agreed on a more comprehensive coordination mechanism which, by and large, seems to work quite well. There are also provisions for regular coordination on EU matters at the technical and political levels (Müller 2000a; 2001).

DELEGATION FROM MINISTERS TO CIVIL SERVANTS

Federal administration is the responsibility of ministers and all government agencies are subordinated to specific ministers (Article 69). Ministries are established by law and are strictly hierarchically organized. In principle, all decisions are to be made by the minister. However, since it would be rather cumbersome and ineffective to bring all matters to the minister and wait for him or her to make a decision, the minister is entitled to delegate specified groups of tasks to civil servants who then make decisions autonomously, but in the minister's name. A minister may reverse prior decisions delegating power to civil servants, and may also reserve the right to make particular decisions himself/herself. A minister is also entitled to issue a formal order (*Weisung*) to civil servants directing them to act in accordance with his or her will. Furthermore, the Constitution stipulates that civil servants must carry out such an order as long as it does not violate criminal law (Article 20).[19] As a consequence, the minister is constitutionally responsible for all the acts of his or her ministry (Brandtner 1992).

As is true elsewhere, however, the Austrian bureaucracy is actually much more influential than the Constitution suggests (Kneucker 1973, 1981; Neisser 1974, 1997). In general, a minister depends on the cooperation of his or her bureaucracy. If it does not readily provide its expertise, if it 'over informs' or 'under informs' the minister, or if it follows a policy of deliberately limiting the minister's decision-making alternatives to those that follow the department's conventional wisdom, then the minister will have little policy impact and might even suffer political problems. Given this, ministers often try to avoid issuing orders. Indeed, some former ministers claim that they have never issued a formal order. If they want to implement policies, they critically depend on civil servants acting supportively even when they do not intervene.[20] Indeed, the capacity of ministers to actually monitor the behaviour of their civil servants is rather limited. The 'spoils system' is restricted to the positions of minister and secretary of state. Civil servants retain their positions regardless of what cabinet is in office. Ministers may appoint a few personal secretaries and staff members in their personal cabinets that have increased from a total of about thirty in the early 1970s to more than eighty in the 1990s (Liegl and Müller 1999). This is still a quite small number of persons, particularly in light of the fact that many staff members are not concerned with running the department at all, but act as the minister's press secretaries. Nevertheless, some ministers have

---

[19] Constitutional lawyers continue to discuss the precise meaning of 'criminal law' (*strafgesetzliche Vorschriften*) in this context (Koja 1986), but it is nonetheless clear that the limits for not observing ministerial orders are narrowly drawn.

[20] Sometimes, however, formal orders cannot be avoided since some civil servants ask for them in order to avoid responsibility (Neisser 1974: 236).

managed to shelter themselves from their civil servants, heavily relying on their personal staff in making politically important decisions. If anything, these ministers have been less successful than those who tried to work closely with the permanent civil servants.

Despite the absence of a true 'spoils system', partisan loyalty has traditionally helped ensure civil servant support for ministers' policies. Political parties have colonized the civil service, and several departments for decades have been one-party dominions (Müller 1989). Although a civil service reform in 1989 introduced an objective civil service recruitment system, promotions to key positions still reflect political affiliation (Liegl and Müller 1999). And although ties of partisan loyalty do not work in every case, ministers still rely heavily on them. Of course, if ministries change hands from one party to another, the party-politicization of the civil service may aggravate the delegation problem. In such situations ministers might make full use of their organizational powers in order to reorganize the ministry and fill key positions with people who are partisan loyal. This is eased by the fact that since 1996 all appointments to leadership positions in the civil service are made for 5 year terms only. Reversing the politicization of a ministry, of course, requires partisan candidates waiting in the wings, and this has often not been the case when ministries dominated by one political party have been handed over to another. Because there is no tradition of civil servants moving among ministries, ministers must then turn to other strategies in order to exert control over the ministry. These include exploiting personal rivalries and career interests within the civil service, and finding allies among the civil servants to promote specific goals. In any case, contrary to the constitutional prescription of hierarchy and submission, the minister must behave within the ministry very much as he or she would in a genuinely *political* environment.

Not surprisingly, not all ministers have been equally good at directing their departments. They have faced different challenges in terms of the intransigence or support of their ministries, the policy agenda, and—perhaps most importantly—differences with regard to personal skills. While it would be easy to compile a list of ministers widely considered to have been failures, it would be hard to argue that lack of control of their ministries was the single most important factor in their failure. Rather, their behaviour in political arenas *outside* of their ministries has given them the reputation of being unsuccessful.

EXTERNAL CONSTRAINTS

Parliamentarism in Austria is constrained by the presidency, federalism (which was discussed in the Introduction), the Constitutional Court, direct democracy, consociationalism and corporatism, and membership in the EU.

The President

Under the terms set out in the Austrian Constitution, the country is about as 'semi-presidential' as France. In practice, however, the President has never exercised his strongest powers—cabinet dismissal and dissolution of Parliament. The President has exercised only moderate influence in the government formation process. In day-to-day politics, the President can distort the parliamentary chain of delegation with regard to administrative and judicial appointments and in foreign policy. The Constitution allows the President to reject government proposals in these matters, though it does not give him the power to impose alternatives. In a worst case scenario this could lead to stalemate. The Constitution thus requires that the President and government cooperate if the country is to be governed successfully. This has indeed been the norm in postwar Austria, with the President generally accepting the predominance of Parliament (Welan 1997; Müller 1999a).

The Constitutional Court

The parliamentary majority is also constrained by the decisions of the Constitutional Court (*Verfassungsgerichtshof*), which settles disputes about competencies between the branches of the federal government, as well as between the federal level and the *Länder*. More importantly, the Constitutional Court rules on the constitutionality of legislation and government decrees (Welan 1974, 1988). The Court cannot act unless a relevant appeal is brought to it. Until the 1970s the right to appeal to the Constitutional Court was limited to other courts, the cabinet, and the *Land* governments. Since then the right of appeal has been extended. Since 1975, a parliamentary minority in each of the chambers of Parliament has had the right to appeal to the Court, as can any individual personally affected by a law or government decree (Michalitsch 1989).

As far as ordinary legislation is concerned, parliament can 'override' the judgement of the Constitutional Court by raising a law deemed unconstitutional to the status of constitutional law. It can also anticipate problems with the Constitutional Court on a particular piece of legislation and opt to give it constitutional rank from the outset. Doing so requires the support of a two-thirds Nationalrat majority, however this traditionally has posed little problem. With the single exception of the period 1994–5, grand coalition governments have commanded such a majority, and they have frequently used it to bypass or 'override' the Constitutional Court—not least prior to 1966. Austria's single-party governments and the SPÖ–FPÖ coalition between 1966 and 1987 did not control a two-thirds majority in the Parliament. Even during these years, however, the impact of the Constitutional Court was moderate due to the fact that it practised judicial self-restraint. Since the 1980s, however, the Court has assumed a more active role as it has shifted from a formal to a more substantive interpretation of the Constitution. At the risk of oversimplification, under the formal doctrine the Court upheld parliamentary decisions which did not conflict with the text of the Constitution, while the substantive doctrine is based on an interpretation of the underlying principles. Consequently, the Court has become less predictable and even reversed several previous decisions. At the same time, government parties have become more reluctant to 'override' the Constitutional Court. This is partly because doing so is not well received by the public, and partly because one of the government parties usually favours the Court's decision. The Constitutional Court has therefore become a relevant constraint on parliamentary government. This is even more the case under the ÖVP–FPÖ coalition, which does not command a two-thirds majority.

Direct Democracy

Austrian parliamentary democracy is constrained by three instruments of direct democracy: the people's initiative, the consultative referendum, and the referendum (Müller 1998). These instruments have not, however, undermined the primacy of parliamentary democracy or its institutions. In response to an initiative from the people (the *Volksbegehrcn*) the Parliament is obliged only to consider the bill. There is no direct path from an initiative to a referendum. This is because only the Parliament has the authority to call for a legally binding or a consultative referendum. Formally speaking, only the former is binding. In practical terms, however, this is also true of the consultative referendum, the results of which are difficult for Parliament to ignore. As has already been mentioned, the Constitution also provides for an automatic referendum in particular circumstances. A referendum must be held whenever the constitutional undergoes a 'total revision' (Article 44). A referendum must also be held before a federal President can be removed from office (Article 60). Even in these cases, however, the initiative rests with the Parliament. It can always avoid a referendum, though perhaps only at the price of sacrificing major policy or political ambitions.

The Central Bank

The central bank, *Oesterreichische Nationalbank*, is a special form of joint stock company that decides monetary policy (Winckler 1989). While 50 per cent of its shares are owned by the Republic, represented by the cabinet, and 50 per cent held by major interest groups and firms with clear political affiliations, the cabinet has traditionally appointed the majority of its board members. In addition, since 1998 it has also appointed the Governor representing Austria in the European Central Bank. The board of the central bank has always been of the 'grand coalition' type—that is, it is a balance of the ÖVP and SPÖ. This might be seen as a means to guarantee the bank's independence vis-à-vis government types other than grand coalitions. In fact, bank policy has been widely accepted by all governments, as a manifestation of national consensus.

Consociationalism and Corporatism

The central bank is only one example of consociational constraints on rule by the parliamentary majority. Indeed, postwar politics has been characterized by efforts on the part of politicians to build supermajorities and thereby legitimize their decisions. In some cases the demand for supermajorities has been formalized. School legislation is the most prominent example of this practice, with the requirement of a two-thirds majority being added to the Constitution. Even when the country was governed by single-party governments, it was not uncommon that appointments to key positions were roughly proportional. In many cases, parliamentary majorities have been willing to trade some of their potential policy gains in exchange for opposition voting support in Parliament—even in cases when such support was not necessary in order to pass legislation. Such practices have directly or indirectly constrained parliamentary majorities (and to some extent also future ones). However, these constraints have been created by ruling parliamentary majorities and many can be removed relatively easily. That is, there are no hard constraints to doing so. The latter applies even more strongly to corporatist arrangements—that is, the parliamentary majority's acceptance of the practice that particular policies are created via agreements forged between the major interest groups and the government. The maintenance of both consociational and corporatist arrangements is based on rational calculations on the part of the parliamentary majority, and both have been expanded or curtailed when doing so has been judged to be advantageous.

The Impact of the EU

Austria's accession to the EU in 1995 has, de facto, transferred most law-making powers to the EU (MPs themselves estimate that they have lost up to 70 per cent of their legislative power). However, the EU's legislative authority is not exercised without Austria's participation. This raises the question of the extent to which parliamentary democracy is maintained. In other words, how is the process of delegation and accountability extended to the EU? Austria has a constitutional amendment that obliges ministers to coordinate their position-taking in the EU with Parliament, or—more precisely—an amendment that gives Parliament the opportunity to demand that ministers do so (Körner 1994; Khol 1995). Ministers must inform the Nationalrat about EU proposals well in advance of EU decision-making (Article 23e). It is up to Parliament to decide whether to issue its opinion on any particular EU proposal. If it does so, then the minister is obligated to follow the Parliament's will[21] and may deviate from it only when there are 'cogent foreign and integration policy reasons' for doing so and only after the minister has reconsulted Parliament. In EU matters, the Parliament acts through a sub-committee of its main committee, which—in contrast to other permanent committees—meets in public and has an alternating membership, depending on the policy area of the EU proposals.

In constitutional terms, the position of the Austrian Parliament in the European decision-making process is stronger than that of any other national parliament by its capacity to bind ministers to positions it takes concerning upcoming decisions in the Council. In practice, however, its impact has remained rather limited. In 1995, Austria's first year in the EU, the Nationalrat was informed of about 17,317 EU proposals. The main committee chose to deliberate on about 100 of these, and it issued an opinion in no more than 18 cases. In the next 5 years (1996–2000) more than 102,000 EU proposals were submitted to Parliament. The main committee dealt with 152 of them and issued an opinion in 39 cases. Regardless of how one measures, these figures are clearly

---

[21] In the case of matters that need the consent of the other chamber of Parliament—the Bundesrat—(Article 44 [2]), this applies to positions taken by both chambers.

lower than those for Austria's first year of membership and they do not indicate that Parliament has had an important impact on EU policy. Moreover even when the Parliament has acted, interviews with civil servants and interest group representatives suggest that it has not necessarily done so on the most important issues (Falkner and Müller 1998). The policy specialists of the government parties, however, can exercise some influence within the mechanisms of coalition governance.

CONCLUSION

The terms of its Constitution make Austria an imperfect parliamentary democracy. To begin with, voters delegate to two agents: MPs and the President. The cabinet then is appointed by the President and formally accountable to both Parliament and the President. Thus, it has two principals. Individual cabinet ministers are accountable to Parliament and the Chancellor (and indirectly also to the President whose cooperation is required with regard to ministerial appointments and dismissals). These relations are all defined primarily by an initial expression of trust through elections or appointment and by the possibility that incumbents can be removed if they do not satisfy the expectations of their principals. MPs can only be removed in subsequent elections. The President can, in principle, be removed between elections, but in practice this is not particularly likely.[22] In contrast, the cabinet and individual ministers can be held accountable by their principals at any time. However, the Constitution does not give ministers' principals the formal power to issue directives to their agents. The final step in the delegation chain, that from ministers to civil servants, differs with regard to both dimensions. Civil servants cannot be removed from their positions, yet they are obligated to follow the instructions of their political masters.

Political parties and constitutional conventions have made the delegation process more straightforward and akin to parliamentary democracy. The role of the President has largely been limited to ratifying the outcome of the party game. The existence of strong and cohesive parties makes Austria a party democracy par excellence. In reality, voters delegate authority to political parties rather than to individual MPs. Parties then maintain control over MPs (Müller and Jenny 2000). The making and breaking of governments is a party game, as is the process of governing. Individual parties are cohesive. When in government, the party and its representatives in the cabinet are very closely connected to one another. There is fusion of top party and government offices. In some cases the direction of interaction between the two has turned around—that is, rather than giving government positions to party officials, government members were given party offices. As noted above, party is also important for delegation from ministers to civil servants. In short, political parties help make democracy work. At the same time, however, political parties undermine accountability as specified by the design of political institutions. The specific mechanisms to hold politicians accountable largely

[22] It would require first a two-thirds majority in the Nationalrat, then a majority in the Bundesversammlung (that is the Nationalrat and Bundesrat combined), and, finally, a majority in a referendum. If such an attempt failed, however, the Nationalrat would automatically be dissolved.

become ineffective because of the dominance of party loyalty over the formal tasks of political office. It is only when parties anticipate that such behaviour would inflict damage on their electoral prospects—their 'brand name'—that they are ready to hold accountable their members in public office. In effect, this results in delegation being successful (since this form of party democracy leaves the citizens better off than a world without parties), but also in considerable agency losses.

The public is fully aware of the transformation of the process of delegation and accountability due to the existence and activities of political parties. Therefore the agency problems the public discusses are of a very general nature. To the extent that 'shirking' occurs, it is first and foremost attributed to political parties (and to politicians in general). Since the 1980s, parties have increasingly been criticized. Although they are still accepted as a necessary part of a democratic polity, citizens have become much more critical about their actual performance in the delegation process. The two major political parties have responded by implementing organizational and institutional reforms, for instance the introduction of primaries and the 1992 electoral reform aimed at tying voters and MPs closer together. Opposition parties have characterized themselves as 'movements' rather than parties. Institutional reforms that impact on the process of delegation have partly been responses to the new dissatisfaction with party politics. Thus, the numerous reforms of the parliamentary rules of procedure have been prompted in part by the majority's desire to demonstrate its willingness to make possible effective parliamentary scrutiny. Likewise, the establishment of 'objective' civil service recruitment practices in 1989 aimed at demonstrating the government parties' respect for the political neutrality of the civil service. Although the relevance and long-term impact of some of these reforms should not be underestimated, they could not solve the problems caused by the party system. From 1987 until 2000, Austria was locked into a 'grand coalition' government. On the one hand, there was no alternative that a majority of voters and parties found acceptable. On the other hand, electoral responsiveness remained low. Voters had to rely on intraparty and intra-coalition mechanisms of political accountability, to which there were obvious limits. The end of 'grand coalition' government in 2000 has changed the structure of party competition (Müller 2000d). Basically, a two block system of ÖVP–FPÖ versus SPÖ–Greens has emerged, which, in principle, increases electoral accountability.

REFERENCES

Adamovich, Ludwig (1971). *Handbuch des österreichischen Verfassungsrechts*. Vienna: Springer.
——(1973). 'Die Koordinationskompetenz des Bundeskanzlers in verfassungsrechtlicher Sicht'. *Juristische Blätter*, 95: 234–42.
—— and Funk, Bernd-Christian (1980). *Allgemeines Verwaltungsrecht*. Vienna: Springer.
Aldrich, John H. (1995). *Why Parties?* Chicago: University of Chicago Press.
Auracher-Jäger, Barbara (1997). *Die Mechanismen im Nationalrat*. Wien: Verlag Österreich.
Atzwanger, Konrad and Zögernitz, Werner (1999). *Nationalrat-Geschäftsordnung*. Vienna: Manz.
Barfuß, Walter (1968). *Ressortzuständigkeit und Vollzugsklausel*. Vienna: Springer.

Bergman, Torbjörn (1993). 'Formation Rules and Minority Governments'. *European Journal of Political Research*, 23: 55–66.

Brandtner, Werner (1992). 'The Organization of State Administration—An Overview', in Federal Chancellery (ed.), *Public Administration in Austria*. Vienna: Federal Chancellery.

Czerny, Wilhelm F. and Fischer, Heinz (1982). *Kommentar zu Geschäftsordnung des Nationalrates*. Vienna: Österreichische Staatsdruckerei.

Cox, Gary W. and McCubbins, Mathew D. (1993). *Legislative Leviathan*. Berkeley: University of California Press.

Damgaard, Erik (1995). 'How Parties Control Committee Members', in Herbert Döring (ed.), *Parliaments and Majority Rule in Western Europe*. New York: St. Martin's Press.

Dachs, Herbert (1996). 'The Politics of Regional Subdivisions', in Volkmar Lauber (ed.), *Contemporary Austrian Politics*. Boulder: Westview.

De Winter, Lieven (1991). 'Parliamentary and Party Pathways to the Cabinet', in Jean Blondel and Jean-Louis Thiébault (eds.), *The Profession of Government Minister in Western Europe*. London: Macmillan.

Duverger, Maurice (1959). *Political Parties*. London: Methuen.

Falkner, Gerda and Müller, Wolfgang C. (eds.) (1998). *Österreich im europäischen Mehrebenensystem*. Vienna: Signum.

Fischer, Heinz (1971). 'Wahlpunkte und Vorzugsstimmen'. *Österreichische Zeitschrift für Öffentliches Recht*, 22: 95–112.

——(1972). 'Zur Praxis des Begutachtungsverfahrens im Prozeß der Bundesgesetzgebung'. *Österreichische Zeitschrift für Politikwissenschaft*, 1: 35–54.

——(1997). 'Das Parlament', in Herbert Dachs *et al.* (eds.), *Handbuch des Politischen Systems Österreichs*. Vienna: Manz.

Fallend, Franz (2000a). 'Der Bundesrat in Österreich', in Gisela Riescher, Sabine Ruß, and Christoph M. Haas (eds.), *Zweite Kammern*. München: Oldenbourg.

——(2000b). 'Demokratische Kontrolle oder Inquisition? Eine empirische Analyse der parlamentarischen Untersuchungsausschüsse des Nationalrates nach 1945'. *Österreichische Zeitschrift für Politikwissenschaft*, 29: 177–200.

Gerlich, Peter (1973). *Parlamentarische Kontrolle im Politischen System*. Vienna: Springer.

—— and Müller, Wolfgang C. (1997). 'Austria: Routine and Ritual', in Jean Blondel and Ferdinand Müller-Rommel (eds.), *Cabinets in Western Europe*. London: Macmillan.

——,——, and Philipp, Wilfried (1988). 'Potentials and Limitations of Executive Leadership: the Austrian Cabinet since 1945'. *European Journal of Political Research*, 16: 191–205.

—— and Ucakar, Karl (1981). *Staatsbürger und Volksvertretung*. Salzburg: W. Neugebauer.

Kathrein, Irmgard (1986). 'Der Bundesrat', in Herbert Schambeck (ed.), *Österreichs Parlamentarismus*. Berlin: Duncker & Humblot.

Khol, Andreas (1995). 'Demokratieabbau durch EU-Regierungsgesetzgebung?', in Günther Schefbeck (ed.), *75 Jahre Bundesverfassung*. Vienna: Verlag Österreich.

Kiewiet, D. Roderick and McCubbins, Mathew D. (1991). *The Logic of Delegation*. Chicago: University of Chicago Press.

Kneucker, Roul F. (1973). 'Austria: An Administrative State'. *Österreichische Zeitschrift für Politikwissenschaft*, 2: 95–127.

——(1981). 'Public Administration: The Business of Government', in Kurt Steiner (ed.), *Modern Austria*. Palo Alto: SPOSS.

Koja, Friedrich (1986). *Allgemeines Verwaltungsrecht*. Vienna: Manz.

Korinek, Karl (1986). *Ministerverantwortlichkeit*. Vienna: Orac.

Körner, Margit (1994). 'Das EU-Begleit-Bundesverfassungsgesetz—die Mitwirkung der Parlamente von Bund und Ländern bei der Schaffung von neuem EU-Recht'. *Österreichisches Jahrbuch für Politik*, 1994: 513–41.

Liegl, Barbara and Müller, Wolfgang C. (1999). 'Senior Civil Servants in Austria', in Edward C. Page and Vincent Wright (eds.), *Senior Civil Servants in a Service State*. Oxford: Oxford University Press.

Lijphart, Arend (1999). *Patterns of Democracy*. New Haven: Yale University Press.

Luther, Kurt Richard (1986). 'The Revitalization of Austrian Federalism', in Michael Burgess (ed.), *Federalism and Federation in Western Europe*. London: Croom Helm.

——(1997). 'Bund–Länder Beziehungen: Formal- und Realverfassung', in Herbert Dachs *et al.* (eds.), *Handbuch des Politischen Systems Österreichs*. Vienna: Manz.

McCubbins, Mathew D. and Schwartz, Thomas (1984). 'Congressional Oversight Overlooked: Police Patrols Versus Fire Alarms'. *American Journal of Political Science*, 2: 165–79.

Michalitsch, Martin (1989). 'Die Geänderte, Realverfassungsändernde Rechtsprechung des Verfassungsgerichtshofes'. *Österreichisches Jahrbuch für Politik*, 1989: 197–207.

Michels, Robert (1963). *Political Parties*. New York: Free Press.

Müller, Wolfgang C. (1983). 'Direktwahl und Parteiensystem'. *Österreichisches Jahrbuch für Politik*, 1983: 83–112.

——(1989). 'Party Patronage in Austria', in Anton Pelinka and Fritz Plasser (eds.), *The Austrian Party System*. Boulder: Westview.

——(1990). 'Persönlichkeitswahl bei der Nationalratswahl 1990'. *Österreichisches Jahrbuch für Politik*, 1990: 261–82.

——(1992). 'Austria (1945–1990)', in Richard S. Katz and Peter Mair (eds.), *Party Organizations*. London: Sage.

——(1993). 'Executive–Legislative Relations in Austria: 1945–1992'. *Legislative Studies Quarterly*, 18: 467–94.

——(1994). 'Models of Government and the Austrian Cabinet', in Michael Laver and Kenneth A. Shepsle (eds.), *Cabinet Ministers and Parliamentary Government*. Cambridge: Cambridge University Press.

——(1996a). 'Political Institutions', in Volkmar Lauber (ed.), *Contemporary Austrian Politics*. Boulder: Westview.

——(1996b). 'Wahlsysteme und Parteiensystem in Österreich 1945–1995', in Fritz Plasser, Peter A. Ulram, and Günther Ogris (eds.), *Wahlkampf und Wählerentscheidung*. Vienna: Signum.

——(1997a). 'Das Parteiensystem', in Herbert Dachs *et al.* (eds.), *Handbuch des Politischen Systems Österreichs*. Vienna: Manz.

——(1997b). 'Regierung und Kabinettsystem', in Herbert Dachs *et al.* (eds.), *Handbuch des Politischen Systems Österreichs*. Vienna: Manz.

——(1998). 'Party Competition and Plebiscitary Politics in Austria'. *Electoral Studies*, 17: 21–43.

——(1999a). 'Austria', in Robert Elgie (ed.), *Semi-Presidentialism in Europe*. Oxford: Oxford University Press.

——(1999b). 'Plebiscitary Agenda-Setting and Party Strategies'. *Party Politics*, 5: 305–17.

——(2000a). 'Austria', in Hussein Kassim, B. Guy Peters, and Vincent Wright (eds.), *The National Co-ordination of EU Policy: The Domestic Level*. Oxford: Oxford University Press.

——(2000b). 'Political Parties in Parliamentary Democracies: Making Delegation and Accountability Work'. *European Journal of Political Research*, 37: 309–33.

——(2000c). 'Austria: Tight Coalitions and Stable Government', in Wolfgang C. Müller and Kaare Strøm (eds.), *Coalition Governments in Western Europe*. Oxford: Oxford University Press.

——(2000d). 'Das Österreichische Parteiensystem: Periodisierung und Perspektiven', in Anton Pelinka, Fritz Plasser, and Wolfgang Meixner (eds.), *Die Zukunft der Österreichischen Demokratie*. Vienna: Signum.

——(2001). 'Ministerial Government at the European Level: The Case of Austria', in Hussein Kassim, Anand Menon, B. Guy Peters, and Vincent Wright (eds.), *The National Coordination of EU Policy: The European Level*. Oxford: Oxford University Press.

——and Bubendorfer, Heidemarie A. (1989). 'Rule-Breaking in the Austrian Cabinet: Its Management and Its Consequences'. *Corruption and Reform*, 4: 131–45.

—— and Jenny, Marcelo (2000). 'Abgeordnete, Parteien und Koalitionspolitik: Individuelle Präferenzen und Politisches Handeln im Nationalrat'. *Österreichische Zeitschrift für Politikwissenschaft*, 29: 133–52.

——,——, Steininger, Barbara, Dolezal, Martin, Philipp, Wilfried, and Preisl-Westphal, Sabine (2001). *Die Österreichischen Abgeordneten. Individuelle Präferenzen und politisches Handeln*. Vienna: WUV Universitätsverlag.

—— , Phillip, Wilfried, and Steininger, Barbara (1996). 'Austria: Party Government within Limits', in Jean Blondel and Maurizio Cotta (eds.), *Party and Government*. London: Macmillan.

——and Plasser, Fritz (1992). 'Austria: The 1990 Campaign', in Shoun Bowler and David M. Farrell (eds.), *Electoral Strategies and Political Marketing*. London: Macmillan.

—— and Scheucher, Christian (1994). 'Persönlichkeitswahl bei der Nationalratswahl 1994'. *Österreichisches Jahrbuch für Politik*, 1994: 171–97.

——and Steininger, Barbara (2000). 'Not Yet the Locus of Power: Parliamentary Party Groups in Austria', in Knut Heidar and Ruud Koole (eds.), *Parliamentary Party Groups in European Democracies*. London: Routledge.

——and Ulram, Peter A. (1995). 'The Social and Demographic Structure of Austrian Parties, 1945–1993'. *Party Politics*, 1: 145–60.

Neisser, Heinrich (1974). 'Die Rolle der Bürokratie', in Heinz Fischer (ed.), *Das Politische System Österreichs*. Vienna: Europaverlag.

——(1986). 'Die Kontrollfunktion des Parlamentes', in Herbert Schambeck (ed.), *Österreichs Parlamentarismus*. Berlin: Duncker & Humblot.

——(1997). 'Die Verwaltung', in Herbert Dachs *et al.* (eds.), *Handbuch des Politischen Systems Österreichs*. Vienna: Manz.

Nödl, Andreas (1995). *Parlamentarische Kontrolle*. Vienna: Böhlau.

Pelinka, Anton and Welan, Manfried (1971). *Demokratie und Verfassung in Österreich*. Vienna: Europaverlag.

Perthold-Stoitzner, Bettina (1993). *Die Auskunftspflicht der Verwaltungsorgane*. Vienna: Manz.

Pfeifer, Helfried (1964). 'Über die Beschlußfassung der Regierung und die Verantwortlichkeit ihrer Mitglieder'. *Juristische Blätter*, 86: 485–500 and 541–51.

Ringhofer, Kurt (1977). *Die österreichische Bundesverfassung*. Vienna: Verlag des Österreichischen Gewerkschaftbundes.

Sartori, Giovanni (1997). *Comparative Constitutional Engineering*. Houndmills: Macmillan.

Schäffer, Heinz (1999). 'The Austrian Bundesrat', in Ulrich Karpen (ed.), *Role and Function of the Second Chamber*. Baden-Baden: Nomos.

Schambeck, Herbert (1997). *Regierung und Kontrolle in Österreich*. Berlin: Duncker & Humblot.

Schefbeck, Günther (1997). 'Der Nationalrat Zwischen Rechtssetzungsorgan und Tribüne'. *Journal für Rechtspolitik*, 5: 117–35.

Schlesinger, Joseph A. (1991). *Political Parties and the Winning of Office*. Ann Arbor: University of Michigan Press.

Sickinger, Hubert (1997). *Politikfinanzierung in Österreich*. Thaur: Kulturverlag.

——(2000*a*). 'Parteien- und Wahlkampffinanzierung in den 90er Jahren', in Fritz Plasser, Peter A. Ulram, and Franz Sommer (eds.), *Das Österreichische Wahlverhalten*. Vienna: Signum.

——(2000*b*). 'Die Funktion der Nationalratsausschüsse im Prozess der Bundesgesetzgebung'. *Österreichische Zeitschrift für Politikwissenschaft*, 29: 157–76.

Tálos, Emmerich and Kittel, Bernhard (2001). *Gesetzgebung in Österreich*. Vienna: Wiener Universitätsverlag.

Walter, Robert (1972). *Österreichisches Bundesverfassungsrecht*. Vienna: Manz.

Weber, Karl (1987). *Die mittelbare Bundesverwaltung*. Vienna: Braumüller.

Welan, Manfried (1967). 'Das Mißtrauensvotum nach der Österreichischen Bundesverfassung'. *Österreichische Juristen-Zeitung*, 22: 561–69.

——(1974). 'Der Verfassungsgerichtshof—eine Nebenregierung?', in Heinz Fischer (ed.), *Das Politische System Österreichs*. Vienna: Europaverlag.

——, (1988). 'Constitutional Review and Legislation in Austria', in Christine Landfried (ed.), *Constitutional Review and Legislation*. Baden-Baden: Nomos.

——(1997). *Das Österreichische Staatsoberhaupt*. Vienna: Verlag für Geschichte und Politik.

——and Heinrich Neisser (1971). *Der Bundeskanzler im Österreichischen Verfassungsgefüge*. Vienna: Hollinek.

Werndl, Josef (1984). *Die Kompetenzverteilung Zwischen Bund und Ländern*. Vienna: Braumüller.

Widder, Helmut (1979). *Parlamentarische Strukturen im Politischen System*. Berlin: Duncker & Humblot.

——(1986). 'Der Nationalrat', in Herbert Schambeck (ed.), *Österreichs Parlamentarismus*. Berlin: Duncker & Humblot.

——(1997). 'Rechnungshof und Volksanwaltschaft', in Herbert Dachs *et al.* (eds.), *Handbuch des Politischen Systems Österreichs*. Vienna: Manz.

Winckler, Georg (1989). 'Geld und Währung', in Hanns Abele *et al.* (eds.), *Handbuch der Österreichischen Wirtschaftspolitik*. Vienna: Manz.

6

Belgium: Delegation and Accountability under Partitocratic Rule

LIEVEN DE WINTER AND PATRICK DUMONT

INTRODUCTION

The National Congress, the constituent assembly that defined the institutions of the new State, laid down the main features of Belgian parliamentary democracy in 1831. The founding fathers opted for a representative constitutional monarchy with a—for the time—quite liberal Constitution that protected most modern civil rights and liberties.[1]

Apart from the expansion of suffrage (the last significant one occurred in 1948, granting suffrage to women), until 1993 the constitutional form of political representation did not undergo important modifications, despite several waves of reform launched in the 1970s and 1980s. The 1993 reform that completed the transformation of the unitary State into a complex federal system also modified the structure, composition, and functioning of Parliament and the competencies and operation of the federal executive. As these changes were implemented only after the 1995 general elections, it is too early to evaluate their effects. This chapter therefore presents the main features of the postwar representative system and major recent changes, with most behavioural analyses referring to the pre-1995 situation.

The Belgian Parliament has two chambers, a feature that deviates from the singularity principle of delegation. From the beginning, both chambers were symmetrical both functionally (government-making, legislation, control) and organizationally. Due to the democratization of suffrage, their composition has also become very similar.

Until 1995, representatives as well as senators could introduce legislative proposals. To become law, a bill had to go through numerous stages in each chamber: submission to the speaker of the chamber concerned; formal decision by the Plenary Assembly that the proposal will be 'taken into consideration'; committee referral; detailed committee examination(s); amendment and vote; written report by one committee member summarizing the committee debate; referral of the proposal plus the report to the Plenary Assembly of the chamber; plenary debate of the committee version of the bill; amendment by individual MPs and/or the government; vote on the bill—first

---

[1] Basic overviews of Belgian constitutional law and representative institutions include Alen, Tillemans, and Peeters (1992), Alen and Meerschaut (1998), Delpérée and Renders (1998), François (1997). For an English-language introduction to Belgian politics, see Fitzmaurice (1996).

article by article and then in its entirety. If the bill won majority support (of valid votes, excluding blank votes, with half of the members of the chamber present), it was then sent to the other chamber. The latter then referred the bill to its relevant committee, and repeated all the steps in the committee and plenary stages. If the version of the bill approved by the 'first' chamber eventually was also adopted by the second chamber, it was sent to the monarch for royal approval, published by the Official Record, and received the force of law. If the 'second' chamber approved an amended bill, then it was referred back to the 'first' chamber, where all committee and subsequent plenary stages had to be repeated. This process continued until both chambers had adopted the same version of the bill. Hence, there were no rules for stopping the *navette* (shuttle). To save time, the coalition parties exerted strong pressure on their MPs not to modify a bill that had already been accepted by the other chamber. Government bills, including budget bills (see below for detail), were subject to the same procedure, but did not require the bill taken into consideration by the Plenary Assembly.

Amongst the instruments of delegated legislation we find 'royal decisions' (govern-mental decisions aimed at implementing a law approved by Parliament), 'ministerial decisions' (like the previous type but taken by single ministers[2]), 'cadre laws' (which explicitly define only the general principles, to be complemented by specific measures), and 'task laws' (that give the government the power to regulate a matter that normally falls under the competence of the legislature). Finally, in the case of 'special powers', Parliament accords the government large competencies in a broad policy area for a fixed period of time, and decisions taken under such a mandate cannot be altered by Parliament during the same legislative session.[3]

Since the 1960s, Belgium has followed a difficult path toward federalism. A 1993 Constitutional amendment transformed Belgium into a federal country based on three linguistic communities (Flemish, French, and German, a tiny minority) and three regions (Flanders, Brussels, and Wallonia). Since 1995, the Senate has lost several com-petencies. As of 2003 only the House of Representatives can invest or dissolve a government, approve the budget, and conduct interpellations of ministers. All govern-ment bills are introduced in the House. Despite this, the Senate and the House remain equally competent as regards constitutional and other institutional reforms, regional and linguistic matters, ratification of treaties, and the organization of the judiciary. The Senate is exclusively competent for conflicts between the national and regional/ community legislatures.[4] The Senate has the right to discuss and amend bills approved by the House, but the latter has the final word, even on bills initiated by the Senate.[5]

---

[2] In the 1960–85 period, the Belgian Parliament issued 4,058 laws, while the executive issued 40,044 'royal decisions' and 11,951 'ministerial decisions' (Dewachter 1992: 18).

[3] In the postwar period, special powers were accorded in 1965, 1967, 1978, 1982, 1986, 1993, and 1996. They were often valid for several years. In all, the government ruled with special powers for about 15% of the 1926–86 period (Alen 1986).

[4] Conflicts between chambers are solved through *navette* or conference committee.

[5] Except for matters in which the Senate is (equally) competent, the Senate examines bills adopted by the House only if fifteen members request it within one week. The Senate then has one month to examine it and propose amendments. The House can accept or reject the Senate's amendments. If the House adds amendments

Thus, the Senate has evolved into a 'reflection chamber' and a meeting place between the federal and regional/community levels of government.

To protect the rights of regional and linguistic minorities, some bills require qualified majorities of not only a two-thirds majority of the valid votes cast, but also by a majority of valid votes in each linguistic group in each chamber (with a majority of members of each linguistic group present).[6] The laws that are subject to this special procedure are those that implement specific constitutional rules regarding the communities and the regions (i.e. modifying borders, competencies, and/or statutes of the provinces, the communities, and regions). Constitutional amendments have to be approved by a two-thirds majority of valid votes in each chamber, with a quorum of half of the MPs present.

Federalization not only modified the role of the Senate, it created an entirely new chain of delegation in the regions and communities, each of which has its own directly elected legislature, an executive headed by a PM, and civil service. This level of government controls about one-third of overall public spending. After the 1993 reforms, regional competencies include urban planning, environment, local government, housing, and parts of various other sectors. The communities' competencies include nearly all educational matters, culture, parts of health policy, and assistance to families, the disabled, elderly, youth, etc. Almost all these competencies are exclusive. We can therefore focus on federal agents since regional and community actors, in principle, do not interfere in federal policies.

Finally, although laws and royal decisions are formally signed by the Head of State (but always countersigned by at least one minister), his role in legislation and the day to day running of the executive has since the Second World War become redundant. Informally, and especially during the reign of King Baudouin (1950–92), however, the coalition and policy preferences of the King have sometimes proven significant, especially with regard to moral or ethno-regional issues.

POLITICAL PARTIES

The main particularity of the chain of delegation in Belgium, which like Italy is often labelled a partitocracy (De Winter, Della Porta, and Deschouwer 1996), is the overwhelming presence of disciplined political parties. From a two party system during most of the nineteenth century, when the Catholic and Liberal parties opposed each

---

of its own, the Senate has three days to examine them and send the amended bill back to the House. The House then makes a final decision on the bill, if necessary after further amendments. Similar *navette* procedures apply to bills first introduced in the Senate. Again, the House makes the final decision.

[6] Since 1970, linguistic minorities also have the power to delay or block legislation threatening their interest, through the *alarm-bell* procedure. In both chambers, if at least three quarters of the members of a linguistic group introduce an alarm bell motion (after the committee report on a bill and before the final plenary vote), then parliamentary procedure is suspended. The Council of Ministers must then within thirty days propose to the relevant chamber either the original bill or an amended version.

other across the religious divide, the Belgian party system turned to a three-party type with the Socialist breakthrough at the end of the century. It remained that way until at least 1965. The parties' relative strength varied considerably throughout the period, but most of the time the three 'traditional' parties (Christian Democrats, Socialists, and Liberals) together received more than 90 per cent of the total vote and alternately shared governmental offices in different coalition combinations. In the 1960s and 1970s, the number of parties represented in Parliament rose dramatically. The linguistic–regional parties (*Volksunie* in Flanders, *Rassemblement Wallon* in Wallonia, and *Front Démocratique des Francophones* in the Brussels region) came first and even entered governmental coalitions in the 1970s. The growing saliency of the linguistic and regional cleavage divided the Christian-Democrat, Liberal, and Socialist parties, and each traditional party split into two organizationally and programmatically independent Flemish and French-speaking branches (in 1968, 1972, and 1978 respectively). At the end of the 1970s came the ultra-Flemish nationalist and anti-migrant *Vlaams Blok*, the poujadist *Union Démocratique pour le Respect du Travail*, and the Green parties (AGALEV in Flanders and ECOLO in the Francophone areas). Thus, by 1981 fourteen parties were represented in Parliament. During the 1980s, the Communists, the Reassemblement Wallon (RW), and the UDRT lost their last representatives in Parliament. The 1991 general election introduced the latest newcomers, the Francophone extreme-right *Front National*, and the libertarian ROSSEM (which ran only in the 1991 elections). Despite this, until the law on public party finance was passed in 1989, parties did not have any legal status. Even parliamentary parties were not recognized in the parliamentary rules until 1962 (De Winter and Dumont 2000). The extreme fragmentation of the party system (the Rae index reached 0.91 in 1999) expresses a multitude of cleavages and policy dimensions: left–right, clerical–anticlerical, regional–linguistic, materialist–postmaterialist, system–antisystem. There are no national parties left in Belgium, that is, parties that run candidates in all twenty constituencies. All parties are homogeneously Flemish or Francophone, and contest only Flemish or Francophone constituencies (with the exception of the bilingual Brussels-Halle-Vilvoorde constituency).

Due to this fragmentation, since the 1970s cabinets have been rather unstable coalitions of between four and six parties (thirty-four cabinets 1946–2000). The pivotal Christian Democrats (the largest party family until 1987, in power from 1958 to 1999) usually chose either the Socialists or the Liberals as coalition partners (De Winter, Timmermans, and Dumont 2000).

To guarantee a minimal degree of cohesion and stability, governmental parties minimize the interference of other political actors: voters, party rank-and-file, MPs, individual ministers, civil servants, and even the judiciary. Policy-making within parties is highly centralized in the hands of the party executive—mainly the party president and his entourage. Within the government, power is concentrated in the hands of the Prime Minister (PM) and vice-PMs (the government's party heavyweights). Given the instability of multiparty coalitions, parties have invented and to some extent institutionalized particular coalition maintenance mechanisms, such as the inner cabinet (the *Kernkabinet*), the watchdog role for junior ministers and ministerial *cabinets*, party summits, and central patronage committees.

DELEGATION FROM VOTERS TO MPs

Electoral Rules and Electoral Responsiveness

The 150 members of the House of Representatives are elected through proportional representation in twenty multimember constituencies (in the 1948–94 period, there were thirty constituencies and 212 Representatives). Parties in each constituency normally nominate a number of candidates equal to the number of Representatives to be elected (two to twenty-two). In practice, voters only decide the number of seats a party will receive, not who will fill the seats. Voters cannot add names to the lists of candidates. More importantly, the electoral code fixes the way in which seats are distributed among each party's list candidates. There are two alternative ways of casting votes (for the House as well as the Senate): a list vote, endorsing the order of candidates on the list that is presented, and a preference vote. Every candidate whose number of preference votes reaches the eligibility figure (calculated by dividing the party's total constituency vote by the number of seats it won, plus one) receives a seat. Usually, only candidates at the top of party lists do. If the head of the list receives fewer preference votes than this, list votes are added to his preference votes until the required number is reached. This procedure is repeated until all the party's seats have been allocated. However, if all list votes were needed before all the seats have been assigned, then the remaining seats are given to those remaining candidates who have the largest number of preference votes. In practice, voters rarely manage to alter the ordered list (this has happened for less than 1 per cent of all MPs elected since the First World War; Rihoux 1996) in spite of the fact that preference voting has increased from 16 per cent in 1919 to 60 per cent in 1999.

Nonetheless, preference votes are not entirely irrelevant to a candidate's political career. Selectors do take into account a candidate's previous electoral performance. Still, many lists give safe places to privileged candidates—pressure groups representatives, parliamentary specialists, national party leaders, or even ministers—who receive few preference votes, at the expense of candidates with a larger personal vote. The wide use of preferential voting thus does not make MPs electorally accountable to their voters. There are no term limits and there is no mandatory retirement age, or legally enforced recall mechanism: formally an MP only has to resign when he finds himself in a position that violates the criteria of illegibility and of incompatibility of mandates.[7]

The co-optation of thirty-one of seventy-one senators also perverts the simple chain of delegation and accountability. The parties decide whom they will back as candidates for co-optation, and to what extent their electoral popularity will serve as a criterion. Most co-opted senators are candidates who failed to win a seat in the general election, but some co-opted senators do not run in any type of election.

---

[7] In the case of incompatibility (for instance if an MP takes a civil service job) resignation is automatic. In case of post-electoral illegibility violations (for instance when an MP loses his civic rights, a measure usually reserved for a court conviction for a serious crime) the chamber may have to initiate expulsion proceedings. To date, this has never happened, because in every case the MP decided to resign before his chamber could expel him.

These structural constraints undermine the MPs' ability to represent the policy preferences of their respective voters. First, the fragmented party system obliges MPs to position themselves programmatically on more dimensions and issues than ever before. Given their strict obligation to the national party programme, it is not easy to adopt a profile that best suits their specific constituencies. In addition, majority MPs are obliged to honour the coalition agreement. Many MPs try to circumvent this structural handicap by generating electoral support through non-policy related activities—for example, case work, pork barrel politics, and symbolic representation (De Winter 1997).

Candidate Selection

Belgian parties have active and relatively autonomous constituency and local organizations. The constituency parties make most candidate selection and deselection decisions. Interference by national party headquarters is rare. All traditional parties—except for the Francophone Socialists (PS)—gradually shifted away from the poll procedure (a type of primary in which all party members could participate) in the 1960s and early 1970s (De Winter 1980). In most parties, the process is now in the hands of local and constituency party activists, while in the CVP (Flemish Christian Democrats) it is controlled by the three intraparty factions (workers', farmers', and middle classes' organizations).[8] Most parties in the late 1960s and 1970s set an age limit of 65 years for elected mandates, allowing rather generous exceptions. Since the flashlight success of Pensioners Parties in the early 1990s, some parties relaxed or even dropped these limits (Smeets, 1994). Selectors' preferences are influenced by background characteristics as well as the candidates' behaviour inside and outside Parliament. Because of the threat of deselection, selectors can usually sanction an MP who does not live up to their expectations (De Winter 1988).

Political Campaigning and Finance

Most elections are anticipated and held within 40 days after parliamentary dissolution, as required by the Constitution. Hence, election campaigns are rather short. Still, the costs of campaigning have risen exponentially, from 4 million euro in 1974 to about 25 million since 1987. This happened despite the fact that no purchase of broadcasting time is allowed on public or private TV and that parties represented in Parliament (and under certain conditions non-parliamentary parties) are allocated free public broadcasting time, in a quasi-proportional way. A 1985 law that prohibited publication of polls 30 days before election day, was repealed in 1991.

Public financing of parliamentary parties' began in 1971. A comprehensive system of public financing covering extra-parliamentary parties was established only in 1989

---

[8] In ECOLO and AGALEV, as well as in the VLD since 1992, candidates are selected by the regular rank-and-file members. In the Communist Party and the FDF, a national committee decides.

(Iker 1998). In the past, tax-deductible donations could only be made to the party research centres and, since 1985, to specially created party treasury funds. The 1989 legislation on public financing of parties provided all parties represented in both chambers a lump sum plus an additional amount per vote in the most recent elections. New regulations were introduced in order to reduce the costs of campaigning. A number of campaign techniques were also prohibited. Tax deductible gifts were first limited, and then prohibited altogether in 1993. Responsibility for enforcing these campaign restrictions rests with a parliamentary committee. Also the 1993 law almost quadrupled subsidies.

State subsidies are all given to central party offices, which decide how to allocate these funds to different candidates. Hence, even in terms of campaign resources, MPs have grown more dependent on their respective national parties. Other traditional sources of party income are membership dues (still about one out of ten voters is a party member) and contributions from elected officials and parliamentary parties—most of whom transfer the bulk of their resources to central party office (De Winter and Brans 1999; De Winter and Dumont 2000). Finally, government parties can lay claim to a considerable number of the members of the so-called *cabinets ministériels*. These are the personal staffs of ministers and junior ministers (secretaries of state), though the appointments are controlled by parties rather than by individual ministers. In the 1980s, there were roughly 3,000 'cabinetards'; however, their numbers have decreased drastically in the 1990s (partly due to increased public financing of central party offices).

DELEGATION FROM PARLIAMENT TO CABINET

Since the early 1970s Belgium has undoubtedly had the most complex coalition bargaining system in Western Europe, and government formation has become its most crucial policy decision-making stage. The large number of relevant parties increases uncertainty and shirking potential, thus undermining cabinet stability. Hence, in order to reduce agency loss, parties have developed an elaborate set of *ex ante* and *ex post* delegation control mechanisms, which tend to reduce cabinet ministers to pure party agents. Governmental decision-making—since the introduction of coalition government after the First World War (Perin 1960)—is extremely collective (Timmermans 1994: 116–9).

The Formation Process as Ex Ante Control Mechanism

A large number of soft or hard institutional constraints determine the delegation from Parliament to cabinet. Some of these reduce the excessively high number of potential coalition possibilities, others further complicate the bargaining process (Strøm, Budge, and Laver 1994).

1. 'Positive' investiture vote rules (Bergman 1993): the government that is appointed by the Monarch has to gain the confidence of a majority of those voting (excluding blank votes). Until 1995, the quorum was more than half of the members present. Since then an absolute majority of all Representatives must vote in favour.

2. Symmetrical bicameral system: until 1995, a government had to win the investiture vote not only in the House but also in the Senate. Here, the distribution of seats in the Senate was also important for determining the composition of coalitions. Although parties' strengths in both chambers are highly correlated, the occasionally slight incongruence has sometimes been enough to render a particular coalition non-viable.

3. Negative resignation rules: until 1995, in either chamber a simple majority vote in favour of a motion of censure or not supporting a motion of confidence[9] was enough to bring down the government (De Winter 1995), if voted by a majority of MPs. In addition, any government was supposed to step down after a defeat on a major bill, even if it was constitutionally not obliged to do so and the government had not turned the vote into a matter of confidence. Hence, governments needed permanent, unconditional majority support in Parliament. Because a few rebels could provoke fatal accidents, parties strove to build oversized coalitions. Since 1995, the Senate no longer has the power to censure the government. In addition, two types of constructive votes of censure have been introduced: (a) when the House, by an absolute majority of its members, rejects a motion of confidence introduced by the government and within 3 days manages to pass a motion proposing a new Prime Minister, the government has to resign ('constructive rejection of motion of confidence'). If the House does not name an alternative PM, the government can continue or even ask the Monarch to dissolve the House (and thereby automatically the Senate). (b) The House can also take the initiative to unseat the government, by adopting by an absolute majority a motion of censure and at the same time naming a new Prime Minister ('positive vote of censure').

4. Before 1995, the government (formally the King[10]) could dissolve the chambers at any time. The government now requires majority consent of the House[11] in order to dissolve (unless the House introduced but failed to pass a constructive motion of no confidence), which also automatically provokes the dissolution of the Senate.

5. Supermajorities for constitutional amendments or particular bills (see Introduction). As institutional reform has dominated the governmental agenda since the 1960s, any government with the ambition of tackling this issue has needed a two-thirds majority in Parliament and a majority within each linguistic group in the chambers.

[9] Both types of motions could be introduced unrestrictedly by any individual MP (and motions of confidence also by the government, the PM, the cabinet, or an individual minister in case he was under attack) and were to be voted the week following its introduction.

[10] Constitutionally, it is the Head of State, not the PM or the cabinet, that dissolves Parliament. As every decision of the monarch requires the counter-signature of at least one minister, in practice it is the PM (usually in the name of and by a decision of the Council of Ministers) that proposes dissolution and counter-signs the royal decree that dissolves Parliament (Senelle 1983).

[11] A parliamentary majority can only dissolve the House by triggering an automatic dissolution device, such as proposing a constitutional amendment. In fact, when both chambers (by simple majority vote) as well as the Monarch (i.e. the government) declare certain articles (or parts thereof) of the Constitution to be open for revision by the next Parliament, both chambers are automatically dissolved. When the House has dismissed a government by a constructive motion of censure (naming a new PM) but this PM does not manage to form a new government, the Monarch can dissolve the chambers without the consent of the House.

Table 6.1 summarizes the behavioural record with respect to cabinet investiture, no-confidence and confidence votes, and parliamentary dissolution. While an unsuccessful investiture vote occurred against Spaak in 1946, there have been no additional instances since then. Furthermore, though no inventory is kept in Belgium regarding the number of no-confidence votes introduced in the chambers, at no time has a cabinet been removed by such a vote. Nonetheless, eight cabinets have resigned in order to pre-empt a no-confidence vote, for example, Martens VI in 1987. In eleven instances the Parliament has been dissolved and the cabinet ended in an early election, for example, Dehaene I in 1995.

Formally, the making of a new cabinet starts with the King's consultations with the main parliamentary parties. The King can then appoint a *formateur*, though he usually appoints an *informateur* first, or sometimes a mediator if the political situation is exceptionally difficult. In practice, the largest party usually takes the initiative if it is willing to do so.

The electoral responsiveness of coalition bargaining is very low, with parties taking office more often after electoral losses than after gains. Electoral accountability is low as well, as voters are hardly ever called upon to indicate which parties should govern after a government breaks down (De Winter, Timmermans, and Dumont 2000). This lack of electoral responsiveness is due not only to the formal formation rules, but also to two behavioural regularities that stem from the party system:

1. *Political and linguistic symmetry in composing coalitions.* Traditional parties belonging to the same *ideological* family have always been together in government or opposition, despite the fact that since the 1970s they have become fully autonomous. Thus coalitions often include a relatively small surplus party, because it is the sister party of a major coalition party from the other linguistic camp.

2. *Federal/regional symmetry.* As far as numerically possible, coalitions at the regional/community level contain the same parties as the national-level coalition. Because the negotiators at both levels are often identical and, until 1999, elections at both levels were held simultaneously, these negotiators usually managed to link the formation process at the two levels.

The result of interparty negotiations is embodied in the coalition policy programme, which since the late 1960s is usually published as an appendix to the official 'government declaration' delivered in Parliament.[12] It has grown over time (often more than 100 pages) and is frequently referred to as the 'coalition bible' (De Winter, Timmermans, and Dumont 2000). While they are essentially packages of policy agreements, coalition agreements sometimes also contain statements about competencies and behavioural rules the coalition members are expected to follow. The 1992 and 1995 agreements

---

[12] Until 1958 the government declaration was the only written statement presented in both chambers of Parliament. In the early 1960s, the party leaders began to write down the results of the negotiations, though these reports were only published after the cabinet had been sworn in or not at all (Neels 1975). In the 1970s, policy negotiations became more institutionalized and coalition agreements were published immediately after the negotiators had signed them.

Table 6.1. Cabinet Formation, Cabinet Termination, and Early Parliamentary Dissolution: Belgium 1946–2000[a]

No.	Cabinet	Date of formation	Investiture votes (iv)						No-confidence votes (ncv)			No. of confidence votes under spec. inst. mech.[b]	Did the cabinet end with an early election?	Who dissolved Parliament in this case?[c]
			No. of unsuccessful investiture votes	Voting results of successful iv (1: pro gov, 2: against gov, 3: abstentions and 4: other)					No. of ncv[d]	Cabinet removed by ncv[e]	Cabinet resigned to pre-empt			
				1	2	3	4							
1	Spaak	46/03/13	1	90	90	15	n.a.		n.d.					
2	Van Acker III	46/03/31	0	107	91	0	—		n.d.		Yes			
3	Huysmans	46/08/03	0	99	87	0	—		n.d.		Yes			
4	Spaak II	47/03/20	0	148	13	22	—		n.d.		Yes		Yes	Head of State
5	Eyskens	49/08/11	0	125	64	1	—		n.d.				Yes	Head of State
6	Duvieusart	50/06/08	0	108	100	1	—		n.d.					
7	Pholien	50/08/16	0	107	78	0	—		n.d.					
8	Van Houtte	52/01/15	0	103	97	2	—		n.d.					
9	Van Acker IV	54/04/22	0	106	89	1	—		n.d.					
10	Eyskens II	58/06/23	0	106	104	0	—		n.d.					
11	Eyskens III	58/11/06	0	121	85	2	—		n.d.				Yes	Head of State
12	Lefevre	61/04/25	0	147	38	15	—		n.d.					
13	Harmel	65/07/27	0	131	65	0	—		n.d.		Yes			
14	Van den Boeynants I	66/03/19	0	119	81	0	—		n.d.		Yes		Yes	Head of State
15	Eyskens IV	68/06/17	0	115	86	5	—		n.d.				Yes	Head of State
16	Eyskens V	72/01/21	0	124	73	4	—		n.d.				Yes	Head of State
17	Leburton	73/01/26	0	144	53	5	—		n.d.				Yes	Head of State
18	Tindemans	74/04/25	0	100	63	47	—		n.d.					
19	Tindemans II	74/06/12	0	109	79	11	—		n.d.					
20	Tindemans III	77/03/06	n.a.[f]	—	—	—	—		n.d.				Yes	Head of State
21	Tindemans IV	77/06/03	0	165	34	3	—		n.d.		Yes			

n.a.

22	Van den Boeynants II	78/10/20	0	158	28	2	—	n.d.			Yes	Head of State
23	Martens I	79/04/03	0	133	50	5	—	n.d.				
24	Martens II	80/01/23	0	119	52	8	—	n.d.	Yes			
25	Martens III	80/05/18	0	151	29	0	—	n.d.				
26	Martens IV	80/10/22	0	117	47	9	—	n.d.				
27	M Eyskens	81/04/06	0	118	52	4	—	n.d.			Yes	Head of State
28	Martens V	81/12/17	0	114	89	1	—	n.d.				
29	Martens VI	85/11/28	0	114	93	0	—	n.d.	Yes		Yes	Head of State
30	Martens VII	88/05/09	0	140	65	1	—	n.d.				
31	Martens VIII	91/09/29	0	115	60	0	—	n.d.				
32	Dehaene I	92/03/07	0	118	82	0	—	n.d.			Yes	Head of State
33	Dehaene II	95/06/23	0	80	61	1	—	n.d.		0		
34	Verhofstadt	99/07/12	0	90	47	1	—	—				—

a n.d. = no data (missing data); n.a. or '—' = not applicable in this case.

b The government will always (see Tindemans III for an exception) ask for the confidence of Parliament during an investiture vote, and usually when it makes a formal declaration to Parliament (which is an important statement about policy), but until 1995 this was not a codified procedure. Moreover, just like no confidence motions, these votes were not computed by parliamentary services until after the constitutional reform that took effect in 1995. The 1995 reform, which was decided in 1993, introduced an explicit and formal confidence vote procedure.

c The question 'Who dissolved Parliament in this case?' can be answered with one of five options. This identifies the main constitutional actor that caused the early election. We have not coded the formal signatory, but rather the person or body that made the real decision: (1) Head of State; (2) Prime Minister; (3) Cabinet; (4) Parliamentary majority; (5) Automatic constitutional provision (e.g. if it is required when a new President takes office, or, for example, if it is required after the adoption of a proposal for constitutional amendments).

d There is no study nor inventory on the number of no-confidence votes introduced by the chambers. It is common practice that the opposition parties, after a government declaration or interpellation, introduce no-confidence motions. At such occasions, the majority parties introduce an ordinary motion 'passing the order of the day' which has voting precedence over any other motion and a vote is held on this. Since the Second World War, not a single government has been forced to resign because of a motion of no confidence (once it had passed the investiture).

e No Belgian Cabinet was removed by a no-confidence vote.

f In 1977, the PM dismissed two ministers of the RW and replaced them with ministers from the remaining parties of the coalition without offering the resignation of the cabinet and without presenting a new policy declaration to the chambers. This was seen as unconstitutional by many opposition MPs.

concluded with a statement that 'also for all matters not included in the coalition agreement the majority parties have agreed to observe the classic rule of consensus within the cabinet and in parliament'. This means that government MPs and ministers can only launch new policies when their initiative is explicitly approved by the other coalition parliamentary parties or by the full cabinet respectively.[13]

Many other matters are negotiated. First, because the Constitution did not restrict the number of ministers until 1995, the number of government members was decided by coalition negotiators. It has therefore varied considerably, depending on the number of parties and factions in the coalition (Frognier 1993). Second, the governments' coordination mechanisms (e.g. cabinet committees) are also usually decided during coalition formation negotiations. Finally, since the early 1970s, the allocation of patronage has been included in government agreements (De Winter, Frognier, and Rihoux 1996).

The coalition composition and policy agreement become definitive after they have been submitted to the party congresses. Since 1961, the internal rules of almost all parties require that the government composition and policy agreement be approved by its national congress—the party's supreme decision-making body representing the communal or constituency party organization (Dewachter 1987). Congress decisions bind the entire party to the coalition contract. They therefore constitute a central element in coalition maintenance and in the delegation from parties and their parliamentary groups to the cabinet. Any party organ's criticism of the policy of ministers of other parties can be condemned as a breach of party discipline, as long as the policy is in the coalition agreement. Thus, the coalition agreement not only ties coalition parties to each other, but also enhances discipline within each coalition party.

Portfolio distribution is formally the final stage in the formation process. The distribution of portfolios amongst partners is decided first, followed by the nomination of specific ministers. In both cases the party presidents are the main or sole decision-makers. Though the largest party usually claims the office of Prime Minister and most parties have specific portfolio preferences, the portfolio allocation nonetheless involves interparty bargaining to satisfy a complex set of demands. Still, ministers are generally seen as delegates of their party leaders. The fact that ministerial posts often change hands further undermines ministers' opportunity to develop policy expertise and thus autonomy (Frognier 1997). Nearly all ministers are recruited from the Parliament, which hinders the selection of specialists or technicians (De Winter 1991).

Once the PM and ministers have been sworn in by the King, there is a customary parliamentary investiture (until 1995, in both chambers), which has been won by all cabinets except one since 1945. Voting discipline is very high. Since the coalition programme and configuration are approved by the national party congresses before the government is invested, a negative vote by the Parliament majority would openly defy

---

[13] There are also 'specific rules of the game' concerning the way in which parties will deal with controversial policy subjects through postponements or referral to some external committee of experts. Governments may also stipulate that certain delicate policy issues (like abortion or institutional reform) should be decided by Parliament autonomously, without government initiatives or interference. On other issues, the government may reserve for itself the right to initiate legislation (De Winter, Frognier, and Rihoux 1996).

their parties' supreme decision-making bodies. Thus, while some majority MPs do criticize the government programme during the debate preceding the vote of confidence, they rarely dare to cast a negative vote.[14]

Mechanisms of Permanent Party Monitoring of the Government

Even detailed and clear-cut coalition agreements are still statements of intent that coalition parties have to enforce in all internal party policy making institutions. To help ensure adherence to coalition agreements between and within coalition partners, a large and sophisticated set of coalition maintenance mechanisms has been developed over time.

In all parties, nearly all ministers and junior ministers regularly attend the weekly meetings of their party executive. Even more important are their weekly meetings with the party chairman (who, according to party statutes, cannot be a cabinet member) and top party leaders (De Winter 1993). At these meetings, the cabinet agenda is carefully scrutinized, and the positions to be defended by the ministers are defined. Apart from these regular meetings, informal and ad hoc contacts are also important. For instance, when important issues or new facts are unexpectedly raised during a cabinet meeting, the meeting is sometimes suspended in order to allow ministers to phone their party leader for advice, or the matter is deferred to the next meeting.

Ministers have large personal staffs ('ministerial cabinets') paid by the state. The size of ministerial cabinets ranges from several dozens to over 200 members (De Winter, Frognier, and Rihoux 1996). In the traditional parties, most top cabinet members are appointed by party headquarters, including the *chef de cabinet*, the minister's main advisor. This enables party leaders to install their 'men of confidence' as monitoring and information channels in the immediate entourage of their ministers. The *chefs de cabinet* often remain in charge of a department longer than do ministers. As a reward for their party service, they often advance to the top civil service, or become MPs, ministers, or, in exceptional cases, the PM.

The members of the ministerial cabinet prepare their minister's own projects and positions on issues to be raised in upcoming cabinet meetings or in cabinet committees on which the minister serves, formulate potential compromises that the minister can propose, and also prepare the minister's positions for parliamentary appearances. Some advisors specialize in the policy area of another department, usually when a coalition party has a particular interest in a policy area in which it does not have any ministers. Finally, the ministerial cabinet, especially its lower-level staff, is responsible for running the clientelist machinery, especially in the minister's electoral constituency. Dozens of ministers' staff members also work directly and exclusively for the party, and hardly ever show up at the offices of the minister's personal cabinet.

---

[14] In the entire postwar period, an average of only 0.6% of the majority MPs voted against the government in the investiture vote (De Winter, Timmermans, and Dumont 2000).

Parliamentary Monitoring of Government Behaviour Through Legislation

In comparison with the powerful inter- and intraparty tools that parties use to monitor the government, the traditional tools for parliamentary monitoring of the executive (legislation and various oversight devices) seem quite ineffective (De Winter 1998*a*).

In parliamentary systems, Parliament can monitor government behaviour through the role it plays in government legislation (including budget bills). An even more powerful steering tool is for Parliament to pass its own legislation. In spite of the fact that committees in both chambers are specialized and permanent, this potentially strong committee structure (Mattson and Strøm 1995) has not prevented Parliament's role in drafting legislation from becoming redundant. The executive has largely usurped this function. A large majority of successful bills are introduced by the government rather than by individual MPs. However, the declining role of Parliament in legislation has not prevented individual MPs from engaging in a considerable and increasing number of law-initiating activities. The relative decline of the legislative function of Parliament is rather due to the fact that a decreasing proportion of the bills and amendments introduced by MPs becomes enacted. In contrast, government bills and amendments are generally successful.[15]

The low success rate of private member bills is primarily due to the detailed and extensive government agreements. The only private member bills that have a chance to become law are those outside the governmental programme on which members of the coalition parties can nevertheless agree. Hence, successful private member bills are usually of little policy importance and often motivated entirely by a desire to claim credit for specific legislation. Since majority parties occupy most legislative leadership positions and can therefore set its plenary and committee agenda, governmental proposals usually get priority treatment. Finally, given the increasing complexity of the decision-making process and the need for rapid decisions, the executive increasingly resorts to delegated legislation, thus further undermining the legislative role of Parliament.

Monitoring the Cabinet Through Parliamentary Oversight Devices

Apart from budget control, votes of censure, and committees of investigation, the main parliamentary tools of government control are questions and interpellations.[16] Over the past decades the House has become increasingly active with regard to these activities (De Winter 1998*b*). Nonetheless, the majority's duty to promote government stability has considerably undermined Parliament's control function.

There are several different types of parliamentary questions: written questions (introduced and answered in written form), oral questions (introduced in written form

---

[15] The success rate of private member's bills has gone down by about a half during the past three decades. On the other hand, the proportion of private member's bills increased from less than 20% of all approved bills in the 1960s to about one third in the 1990s (De Winter 1998*b*).

[16] There are no formal requirements for the government as a whole to report to Parliament. The chambers can require the presence of ministers and ask them questions and hold interpellations.

and answered orally), and urgent questions (introduced and answered orally).[17] All involve demands for information. They can expose neglect, abuse, or incorrect application of the law. They can force a minister to voice an opinion on delicate matters or to suggest improvements and reform. Yet despite their substantial control potential, about half of the questions are simple demands for information, often inspired by mere vote-or publicity-seeking motives. Moreover, because ministers' responses to questions are not followed by debate, the usefulness of questions for controlling the government and ministers is limited.

Interpellations are the classic and most powerful tool of parliamentary control. They are questions put to the government or a minister on a matter of general importance. The initial question and response can be followed by a motion for debate between the interpellant and the government, which can include a proposal not to grant the government the confidence of the House (since 1995 the Senate no longer holds interpellations). Although in principle matters of local or special interest are not legitimate matters for interpellations, in practice these have become more numerous. By now most interpellations focus on a minor aspect of a particular governmental policy and are inspired by a member's personal electoral concerns. Given their particularistic nature, the House increasingly tends to relegate them to public committee meetings. Only interpellations of a general nature or of exceptional political importance are still held in plenary session. In about one of three interpellations, the interpellant (or another MP) introduces a motion. Members of the opposition usually introduce a motion of censure. The House votes on such motions one week after they are introduced, which—if necessary—gives the government ample time to re-establish the confidence of majority MPs, who thus need not express themselves immediately. This is a face-saving device in case the government's or minister's reply has failed to satisfy the House.

Before reforms in 1989, departmental budget bills (indicating planned expenditures for the coming year) were usually submitted quite late—after the budget year had already begun. Thus, most of the money was spent before the final budget was approved![18] In addition, budget bills were usually rushed through the chambers by the government majority. Parliament's budgetary oversight of the executive therefore became nothing but a farce.[19] Since then, the rules governing the government's budget bill have been changed to strengthen parliamentary oversight. The budget process ends with parliamentary approval of the Law on Accounts, which includes a financial report from the Audit Office. This requires the introduction of a bill to that effect during October following the end of the fiscal (i.e. calendar) year. The vote on this law was originally intended to provide an opportunity to assess governmental policy. Yet

[17] House committees started holding weekly sessions devoted to questions concerning current events. In addition, most questions are now asked in committee meetings rather than in plenary. Committees can summon the minister, ask all questions, and hear any kind of person or group for advice. Committees do not have the right to read cabinet minutes.

[18] Of all departmental budgets approved during the 1976–88 period, only 6.8% were approved on time (Dewachter 1992: 121).

[19] Until the early 1990s, there were over 300 'budget funds' in different ministerial departments. These allowed them to accumulate funds (often by loans) and make expenditures that did not appear in the official budget. Government expenditures therefore tended to expand unnoticed and uncontrolled (Lammens 1993: 101–4).

because passage of the Law on Accounts often occurs several years later, it has become a mere formality, not least because the responsible government is usually no longer in power. In addition, the Audit Office's report evaluates the regularity and legality of governmental expenditures, rather than their efficacy and necessity.

Parliamentary committees of investigation have the same powers as an examining magistrate. Until the 1980s, such committees were quite uncommon because majority MPs—in solidarity with the government—were reluctant to allow investigations that could embarrass a specific minister or the entire government. In addition, even when a committee of inquiry suggested that a minister was politically responsible for certain failures, the minister did not resign as long he was supported by his party. However, while the House created only nine such committees in the entire 1880–1988 period, since then it has established roughly one each year. They have developed into an alternative instrument of parliamentary oversight and get considerable publicity. In addition, regular committees can—in their legislative function—gather advice and documentation from persons or institutions outside the Parliament. However, the number of such hearings remains extremely low.[20]

Finally, since 1993, at the beginning of every parliamentary year the PM holds a 'state of the union' speech, which usually launches a general debate of government plans. Since 1989, before the annual debate (in autumn) on each departmental budget, the minister has to present a policy note (policy goals, budgetary means, timing) which is followed by a debate for his sector for the coming year(s).

Parliamentary Party Discipline and Control

Parliamentary government in Belgium can only function properly if the MPs of the majority parties are able to guarantee permanent support for the government. Until the introduction of the constructive motion of censure in 1995, the cabinet had to mobilize a majority of votes from the majority parties on every single governmental initiative introduced in Parliament (because any defeat would have 'morally' obliged the government to resign). 'Alternative majorities' (that include the votes of some opposition parties and exclude some of the majority parties) might have existed on specific issues, but have never been used in the postwar period (at least on government initiated proposals) because doing so would trigger the downfall of the government. Hence, members of the majority are permanently faced with the dilemma of having to approve governmental actions unconditionally, or forcing the cabinet to resign. Consequently, parliamentary groups were (and still are, in spite of the constructive motion of censure) very disciplined in voting (Langerwerf 1980; Verminck 1986).

---

[20] Parliamentary ombudsmen can serve as an additional tool for overseeing the government bureaucracy. In spite of the introduction of ombudsmen in other public institutions, the House did not establish a parliamentary ombudsman until 1997. One reason for this reluctance was the fact that MPs themselves are very active in constituency casework. The prominence of this role is related to a clientelistic political culture, to the lack of other sources of administrative redress, and to the wide scope of party patronage until the early 1990s (De Winter 1996, 1997). To some extent, this casework has informational spin-offs for legislative oversight, as it reveals the quality of government services.

Formal and informal party constraints further enhance voting discipline. First, the statutes of all parties give supreme authority to the party's national congress, and between congresses to the party executive. In most party executives a majority of members are MPs, but they do not generally consider themselves delegates of the parliamentary party (De Winter and Dumont 2000).

In addition, most party statutes define the role of their public office holders in agency terms: office holders are agents of the party, and they are obliged to carry out the party programme. In almost all parties, MPs must ask permission from their group (leader) to introduce a private member bill or amendment, hold interpellations, or support a bill sponsored by another party. The parliamentary group can explicitly sanction voting rebellions in a variety of ways—from a simple warning to expulsion from committees, the parliamentary party group, and/or the party. The fact that most ministers (until 1995) and party presidents have been members of Parliament, and therefore usually attend parliamentary caucus meetings, has been an additional source of party control over the group's decision-making (De Winter 1993).

The small staffs of individual MPs and the relatively well subsidized party research centres add to the MPs dependency on his party organization. MPs often rely on information provided by their research centre in drafting bills, amendments, and interpellations. For most policy sectors, a group of paid experts and volunteer specialists associated with the party research centres prepare the party's proposals in collaboration with the MPs who specialize in these areas. Thus MPs to a large extent depend on their party's brain trust.[21]

DELEGATION FROM CABINET TO INDIVIDUAL MINISTERS

Rules Concerning Cabinet Composition and Operation

There are no legal texts concerning internal cabinet rules, except for a few articles in the Constitution, such as the 'parity' rule requiring the cabinet to have equal numbers of Dutch and French-speaking members, not taking the PM and the junior ministers into account. Furthermore, ministerial and royal decrees on regional and linguistic matters require the cabinet's consent. Otherwise, there are no fixed rules specifying the types of decisions the cabinet can take.

Yet, at least in some cabinets, a text called 'Practical instructions of the Council of Ministers' has been distributed. The 1985 version (Alen and Dujardin 1986: 532–4), which is still operational, stipulates that the cabinet not only debates and decides on 'overall governmental policy' but also on all bills ministers want to introduce in Parliament, all ministerial decisions with 'important budgetary repercussions', and all matters that could 'jeopardize government solidarity'. The latter rule brings most

---

[21] In addition, MPs depend heavily on the ministers' *cabinet ministériel* in their individual and collective constituency casework. Ministerial cabinets play an important role in pushing the administration to consider an MPs client's case benevolently. More importantly, they control the administration's handling of pork barrel benefits. In addition, parties have increasingly centralized patronage with regard to the recruitment and promotion of civil servants (De Winter 1981). Hence, MPs depend on the ministers and national party headquarters for access to electorally beneficial favours.

matters decided by individual ministers under collective cabinet responsibility and gives coalition parties effective veto power over policies proposed by ministers of other parties. In fact, the objection of one party or minister to a certain policy proposal is sufficient to force a discussion by the full cabinet, followed by a decision taken by consensus. In addition, for each matter that may 'involve the government as a whole', ministers must consult the relevant cabinet committee or the cabinet. Also, ministers are not supposed to make declarations about matters that fall under their colleagues' competencies and that might embarrass them. Even in their own jurisdiction, they must be 'extremely discreet' about making public statements as long as the government has not yet decided the matter! Finally, ministers should not make any declaration or take any action expressing a personal point of view that challenges the government agreement.

By constitutional convention, cabinet decisions are taken by consensus formulated by the Prime Minister. The 1985 principles state that a minister, when he does not agree with a cabinet decision supported by a 'fundamental' majority, has two alternatives: accept it without public dissent, or resign.[22]

These operational rules suggest that Belgian ministers are not at all policy dictators in their jurisdictions.[23] Every policy initiative of any significance must be scrutinized and approved by the cabinet. However, the vague formulations of these rules leave the PM and his Vice-PMs with some discretion (Senelle 1983; Timmermans 1994).

The PM, Vice-PMs, and Cabinet Committees

The PM chairs the cabinet and its secretariat. His main task is one of coordination. He is also responsible for a number of administrative agencies such as the Chancellery (which assists the PM in his coordination tasks and supervises the issuing of public contracts). But more importantly, although formally he has no veto power, the PM controls the agenda—not only what items it will contain, but when and how issues will be raised. This authority gives him considerable power over the ministers (Frognier 1997).

However, vis-à-vis his Vice-PMs, the PM is only a *primus inter pares*. Each coalition party (including, in the most recent governments, the PM's party) usually has one Vice-PM. These Vice-PMs are in charge of large departments and sometimes a second, minor department as well. In addition, they serve as cabinet leaders of their party—and constitute the so-called *Kerncabinet*, chaired by the PM. This inner cabinet, which meets quite regularly, is a forum in which coalition parties reach major decisions on conflictual matters, which the full cabinet then formally ratifies. To assist them in their cabinet leadership role, Vice-PMs are equipped with a 'ministerial cabinet for general policy' of about seventy staff members, who follow the decision-making of other ministers and safeguard the party's interest.[24]

---

[22] Formally the King dismisses ministers. In practice, a PM can only dismiss ministers with the agreement of their party leaders.

[23] Formally the right to determine ministerial jurisdictions belongs to the King, or thus to the government as a whole. Hence, in practice, competencies are decided during the formation negotiations.

[24] In addition the Vice-PMs can rely on a cabinet for each ministerial portfolio they have. Thus, some of them had over two hundred personal staff members.

Until 1992, when they were abolished, cabinet committees prepared its decisions. Cabinet committees included not only the relevant ministers but usually also each coalition party, regardless of the actual departmental competencies. Therefore, each party was fully informed about the decisions that were under preparation. Coordination was assured by the PM, who chaired most of the committees, and by the personal staffs of the ministers.

Junior Ministers

The number and the competencies of junior ministers (a position that has existed since 1960) are decided collectively by the formation negotiators. Until 1991 junior ministers often did not belong to the same party as their senior, or—in the days of the unitary traditional parties—often came from a different linguistic wing of the party (De Winter, Timmermans, and Dumont 2000). In these cases, junior ministers tended to operate as watchdogs over their ministers. The junior ministers' decision-making autonomy was often relatively large and rested on the overall balance of power between coalition parties. This watchdog system led to so many conflicts between ministers and their juniors that since 1991 they have always belonged to the same party. In addition, the most recent governments have reduced the number of junior ministers dramatically.

Interparty Summits, Pacts, and Package Deals

Supporting parties can monitor cabinet decision-making through direct formal and informal contacts between leaders of the party organizations. Such contacts often lead to decisions that are binding for cabinet members. Interparty summits often reach compromises that aggregate a large number of conflictual issues. This reduces the problems of shirking once a party has seen its preferred policies implemented—a problem that is particularly likely to plague large coalitions. In many cases compromises can only be reached by solving 'in one stroke' all or most unresolved problems in a wide variety of policy areas. Sometimes these decisions acquire the status of political pacts, which cannot be amended by the cabinet or by the parliamentary majority (De Winter, Frognier, and Rihoux 1996).

DELEGATION FROM MINISTERS TO CIVIL SERVANTS

The so-called ministerial cabinets[25] are the main link between the minister and his civil servants. The excessive use of ministerial cabinets is partially due to the politicization of the civil service, which often creates tensions when top civil servants belong to

---

[25] The number of *cabinetards* involved in policy-making grew from 108 in 1953 to 325 in 1986 (and decreased to 235 in 1995), while their overall number increased from 750 in 1960 to 2000 in 1987 (Dewachter 1992: 238; Hondeghem 1996: 55). Current estimates of the overall number including all levels of government are at 4,000 (Suetens and Walgrave 2001).

a different party than their minister. In fact, about three out of four higher civil servants are party members (Dierickx and Majersdorf 1993: 151), of which six of ten are Christian Democrats (Tegenbos 1990).

This high politicization of the civil service is a traditional feature of Belgian consociationalism, which became more institutionalized and pervasive during the 1970s due to the fragmentation of the party system (De Winter 1981, 1996). Two types of interparty negotiations govern the distribution of civil service promotions between governmental parties. First, the distribution of top positions (director general and secretary general) is decided by the government collectively. Second, promotions of lower ranks of university-trained civil servants are decided by an unofficial interparty committee, in which each coalition party is represented. For each vacancy, the committee considers the candidates for promotion and the support each one has from a coalition party. In principle, each coalition party has a quota of nominations (approximately proportional to its parliamentary strength) that is usually fixed in a secret protocol annexed to the coalition agreement. Only when there is no partisan candidate does the committee nominate the candidate proposed by the board of directors of the ministerial department.

Given this encompassing politicization, ministers feared that they could not unconditionally rely on the loyalty of their civil servants. Hence, until the early 1990s, ministerial cabinets carried out most policy development, verification of policy implementation, and mediation with interest groups (Hondeghem 1996: 51–8).[26] The civil service, including high civil servants, basically only provided the cabinet with the information necessary for policy planning and policy and department management (except for personnel policy, which was also controlled by the ministerial cabinets).

Many *cabinetards* go back and forth between the ministerial cabinets and the civil service, with cabinet service quickening promotion in the civil service, and the civil service serving as a waiting room for the politically active whose party is in opposition (Dewachter 1992: 237).[27] A similar exchange operates between ministerial cabinets on the one hand, and the judiciary and the public enterprises on the other.

However, since the late 1980s, and especially after the breakthrough of the extreme right in the 1991 'Black Sunday' elections and the subsequent calls for a 'new political culture', there has been a general move towards accountability and depoliticization of the civil service. As a consequence, at the present time, about five of six higher civil servants are appointed on the proposal of the departmental board of directors (Hondeghem 1996: 60). In addition, a code on the relationship between ministers and their administration has expanded the role of the latter. The ministerial staffs are now required to meet regularly with their top civil servants. In the past, ministerial staffs tended to work with civil servants loyal to their party, often bypassing the departments' hierarchy. Higher civil servants have been made more responsible for the management of their departments, are regularly evaluated, and can now be sanctioned (or even fired)

---

[26] Parties (together with trade unions) interfere with the promotion (and often also with the initial recruitment) of personnel at different levels (ranging from the janitor in a public kindergarten to the chairman of the board of directors of SABENA airlines) in other employment sectors too, including public radio and television, public education, (semi-) public and quasi-autonomous enterprises and services, and local government.

[27] Other incentives are the political power these positions give and their better remuneration.

for poor performance. The role of the departmental secretary-general has been enhanced in budgeting, personnel policy, and policy implementation. A college of secretaries-general advises the government and coordinates matters that concern several departments (De Ryck 1994: 473–5). As a consequence, ministers now tend to have much more direct contact with their top civil servants. The emancipation of the higher civil service has been enhanced by the reduction of the size of the ministerial cabinets by half,[28] basically due to the introduction of a constitutional amendment limiting the number of ministers to fifteen, and by the transfer of competencies to regions and communities.[29]

The (lack of) delegation from ministers to civil servants has varied across time and policy sectors. Some departments (finance, defence, and foreign affairs) traditionally managed to maintain a relative high level of autonomy vis-à-vis the ministers and their cabinets. As up to the late 1970s the latter two were not policy sectors of strong partisan conflicts, parties felt less inclined to politicize recruitment.

Finally, in the 1990s several important public enterprises were given more autonomy (airways, telephone, railroad, ferries, post, some public banks and credit institutions, etc.). Management contracts between the minister and 'public managers' heading these enterprises have been concluded. They stipulate the objectives of the service and the financial means allocated by the minister in charge. Managers themselves can decide how to allocate these resources and achieve their goals. However, a government commissioner supervises the manager to ensure that the contract is respected. If it is not, he can ask the minister to annul the manager's decisions. Parliament has no supervisory authority vis-à-vis these enterprises insofar as the latter are only required to submit their annual reports and budgets to Parliament during the following year. This rules out any parliamentary debate on the policy and budgetary options open to these enterprises (Bock and Debroux 1995).

In many of the public enterprises, public stockholding has been reduced to 51 per cent or less (De Ruyter, Michielsen, and Mortelmans 1994). Private sector participation puts a check on direct ministerial or party interference in policy-making and, in particular, personnel recruitment.

EXTERNAL CONSTRAINTS

The Head of State and the Referendum

The democratic accountability of the monarch has grown over time. Constitutionally, legislative power is shared between the two chambers and the monarch—in practice, the cabinet. Every bill signed by the monarch requires the countersignature of a minister

---

[28] The figures reported in note 25 suggest that there has only been a transfer from the federal government to the executives of the regions and communities.

[29] These reforms are part of a wider effort to modernize and democratize the civil service, including a move towards openness. Since 1991, administrative decisions have to contain motivation. Since 1994, citizens can consult administrative documents, even when they do not have a personal interest in them. Still, many restrictions remain. Civil servants are bound by professional secret. Administrative documents deposited in the governmental archives can only be consulted after 100 years. Ministers can decide to make them accessible after 50 years! Thus, even after 1991 one cannot not freely obtain information on the preparation of governmental decisions.

who can be held accountable. The impact of the monarch on cabinet decision-making has gradually become insignificant. The consultative referendum over the King's Question (1950) concluded this process.[30] In addition, the effect of the referendum was so devastating that the potential (re-)introduction of this particular instrument of direct democracy completely disappeared from the political agenda of governments and parties until the early 1990s. By now, the only visible political role of the monarch occurs during cabinet formation and crises.[31]

The National Bank

In comparative perspective, the Belgian National Bank scores low on political autonomy.[32] Although the National Bank is formally autonomous, there has been a rather symbiotic relationship between the Governor and the top echelons of the government. The previous Governor was the previous PM's *chef de cabinet* for several years. His evaluation of the government's socio-economic and budgetary policy often seemed to have been drafted after consultations with the PM and was not viewed by the opposition as an independent opinion.

The Constitutional Courts

Belgian legal culture has traditionally opposed judicial review of the constitutionality of laws. Ordinary courts cannot review the constitutionality of laws, though they exercise judicial control over administrative actions. Only two specialized courts exercise some authority with regard to the constitutionality of legal rules:

1. The Council of State is an advisory court that can express an opinion on the constitutionality of governmental or legislative bills.[33] It does not express an opinion on the policy goals or means of a bill and its decisions are non-binding. Only prior consideration by the Council of State is mandatory: general bills initiated by the

---

[30] The King's Question whether or not Leopold III (1934–50) should remain Monarch given his compromising attitude towards the Nazis during Second World War created a major and violent conflict—Socialists, Communists, and some Liberals were pitted against the Catholic Party, the Church, and other conservative circles. In the 1950 referendum, called by the governments of the day to resolve the issue, the North and the South voted differently: 72% of the Flemings voted in favour of the King, while only 42% of Walloons did so. Overall, 57.6% voted in favour of the King. After violent protests, Leopold abdicated in favour of his son Baudouin.

[31] This is especially true with regard to his role in the nomination of government *formateurs* and *informateurs*. Also, when a governmental crisis is imminent, the King can take time to decide whether or not to accept the resignation of the cabinet. The King has weekly meetings with the PM and regularly receives ministers. Preferences expressed by King Boudouin did carry some weight in ministerial decision-making. His moral judgement was generally appreciated, apart from his refusal in 1988 to sign the bill liberalizing abortion. In order to prevent a major constitutional crisis, the government (with the King's approval) declared the King 'temporarily unable' to exercise his powers. Then, given the presumed incapacity of the King, all the ministers signed the bill, which was instantly promulgated. After 36 hours, the King was found fit to govern again.

[32] In Grilli, Masciandaro, and Tabellini's (1991) classification of central bank political independence, Belgium obtains the lowest score of eighteen countries. In other surveys its position is less dramatic, but still quite low (Eijffinger 1997).

[33] The Council of State consists of thirty councillors nominated by the minister of interior.

government must be submitted to the Council of State by the relevant ministers. The initiative to submit a draft bill may also come from Parliament. In other cases asking for this court's advice is optional. Hence, out of all rules for which an opinion might be requested (bills, amendments, ministerial rules issued by federal, regional, or community executives or parliaments, collective labour agreements, etc.), only 20 per cent are submitted to the Council of State. Although it has no formal legislative power, its advice has gained moral weight since 1970, when constitutional reform began to dominate the political agenda. Nonetheless, when there was a solid consensus between coalition parties, the governmental majority has on occasion not hesitated to pass a bill or amendment that the Council had judged unconstitutional.

2. The Court of Arbitration was established in 1984 in order to determine whether legislative rules issued by federal, regional, and community assemblies were enacted in compliance with the Constitution and its enabling legislation. In 1988 its competencies were enlarged to include reviewing the compliance of legislative rules with fundamental rights enumerated in three constitutional articles: the principles of equality, non-discrimination, and the right to and freedom of education. The Court exercises its jurisdiction through annulment proceedings that may be initiated by the executive or legislative bodies of the federal, regional, or community levels of government or by any legal or natural person. In such cases, the Court's rules are binding. This is not the case, however, when the Court expresses an opinion on prejudicial rulings initiated by ordinary courts. In practice, the Court has interpreted its new competence broadly, including all cases of discrimination and violation by federal, regional, and community legislative assemblies of constitutional rights and other rights granted in international treaties. It has therefore evolved into a genuine constitutional court, though it has limited policy competence.

Recruitment to the courts, and especially the constitutional ones, is heavily subject to party patronage (De Winter 1981). Although there is no strong evidence that judges recruited through party patronage are easily influenced by party pressure, their partisan recruitment and career dependence raise questions about the independence and political neutrality of the 'third branch'.

Neo-corporatism and Pillarization

Interest groups are very influential in Belgium, because they constitute a basic element of each of the three pillars. As three out of four workers, employees, and civil servants are trade union members (1991), Belgium has one of the highest rates of unionization in the world (Arcq 1993). Farmers are also well organized, and membership in mutual health insurance funds is compulsory. These pressure groups influence government decision-making through several hundred formal advisory and co-decisional bodies. Once pressure groups (and the government) have reached an agreement, Parliament's role is limited to formal ratification.[34] In addition to this formal neo-corporatist network,

---

[34] By 1991 trade unions and employers organizations had concluded nearly 30,000 social agreements. Since 1968, these agreements have been legally binding. However, following the economic recession of the

there appears to be an extensive and often secret network of informal negotiations. Clearly, these consultative and (co-)decisional networks undermine Parliament's and the executive's competence in many policy sectors, insofar as the former ratifies and the latter executes decisions taken in the neo-corporatist network (De Winter 1999).

These pressure groups reflect the consociational or pillarized character of Belgian society. In fact, the predominance of traditional political parties (Christian Democrats, Socialists, and Liberals) is partly due to the fact that they aggregate, articulate, defend, and implement the interests of a 'pillar' or 'social world' that includes trade unions, farmer and 'middle class' organizations, socio-cultural organizations, educational and health service networks, press networks, etc. Their strength is due to the fact that policy implementation in many sectors of public life is subcontracted to pillar organizations.

Delegation to the European Union

As one of the founding European Union (EU) members, the Belgian Parliament was the first to create a specific European Affairs Committee (1962) (De Winter and Laurent 1995). The Committee is entitled to get all information on the consequences of the application of the EC Treaties in Belgium and to supervise their application. For this purpose, the Committee received governmental reports on the execution of the treaties, and it could summon ministers to attend committee meetings and answer questions. The Committee drafted a report for the House each time the European Parliament or another European assembly made a decision or resolution that could have implications for Belgian legislation. However, despite its broad competence, the European Affairs Committee had only limited success. Indeed, it limited itself essentially to the role of collecting reports drafted by Belgian members of the European assemblies, but produced only a few reports on European questions. Its share in the overall legislative production of the Parliament was virtually nil. In addition, it usually met only about four times a year and lacked expertise. Therefore, in practice, the Foreign Affairs Committee and other relevant departmental committees usually handled European matters. If necessary, these were handled by the plenary. In the 1979–85 period, the European Affairs committee even disappeared, as the Foreign Affairs committee usurped its competence.

In 1985, the House created the Advisory Committee in charge of European Matters, composed of an equal number of national and European MPs. This Committee can, either on its own initiative or in response to a demand from a Belgian MP or MEP, give advice on EU issues. It receives all texts approved by EU bodies and decides which topics merit discussion and elaboration. The House, which receives committee reports, then decides whether or not to debate them. Similarly, the Advisory Committee also drafts resolutions to be debated by the House in Plenary Assembly. Although formally all legislative texts must be approved by one of the traditional permanent committees, the Committee more and more often takes legislative initiat-ives and regularly holds common meetings with other permanent Committees (External Relationships, Finance, Defence, and Social Affairs).

1970s, agreements between different groups became more difficult to achieve. This enhanced the active role of the government in most traditionally 'corporate' policy sectors.

In practice, the Committee most often discusses texts that have already been ratified by Community authorities. This is not surprising given the fact that the government usually transmits European documents to Parliament very late in the legislative process. Therefore, as executive decisions can only be challenged *ex post facto*, Parliament is reduced to a mere rubber-stamping body, and is forced to transpose Community rules into domestic law more or less automatically.

Different proposals have been suggested to correct this situation. In 1993, an article was added to the constitution specifying that before the government signed any document the chambers were to be kept informed, from the opening round of negotiations intended to revise the EU treaties, about the progress and results of negotiations. Contrary to classic international treaties, the EU Treaties require the preliminary approval of Parliament. Second, a new legislative article states that proposals sent to the European Council of Ministers on regulations and directives from the European Commission are to be transmitted to the chambers. This tool is increasingly used and enables Parliament more regularly to examine EU proposals.

Still, although these rules afford some measure of political control, if the government violates its obligations the only applicable sanction is to inform Parliament. Hence, while the current House and Senate Advisory Committees in charge of European Matters have become more prominent, they remain very dependent on governmental goodwill. Their dependency is due to the executive's monopoly on information and to the lack of transparency that characterizes European decision-making. The Advisory Committees frequently cannot meet their obligations in a timely fashion, usually because the government does not in due course transmit relevant proposals for directives, regulations, or other texts produced by the European Commission.

CONCLUSION

The Belgian partitocracy violates the ideal-type chain of parliamentary delegation in many ways, insofar as political parties play a predominant role at each stage. They channel the delegation of power from voters to MPs, from Parliament to the cabinet, from the collective cabinet to individual ministers, and from ministers to their civil servants. Hence, they might be considered the effective principals in the polity. The voters only determine the relative weight of the parties. The parties themselves choose the individuals who will occupy Parliament and—since electoral responsiveness in coalition formation is very low—they also decide how and with whom to exercise their power. In order to make coalitions function and to maintain their status as principals, they have developed a large number of *ex ante* and *ex post* control and monitoring mechanisms. Therefore, many actors in the parliamentary chain of delegation (including MPs, ministers, and civil servants) have been reduced to mere party agents.

To some extent, partitocracy is unavoidable and even functional for political system stability. Given the extremely high fragmentation, a minimum level of government stability and coherence requires power to be concentrated in the hands of a small number of actors. Autonomous MPs, ministers, top civil servants, and to some extent even judges and courts could 'spoil' the extremely complex and delicate process of delegation, and even contribute to its collapse.

On the other hand, the costs of partitocracy are high, and partitocratic practices carried to their extreme have undermined political legitimacy and governability.[35] Since the 1991 'Black Sunday' elections, institutional reform and democratic refinement have been high on the political agenda. This has produced a large number of institutional reform proposals (De Winter and Brans 1999). The working group coordinated by the Speaker of the House reached a consensus in 1997—but most of its provisions have not yet been enacted and implemented. They include restricting the accumulation of local executive offices by MPs, closing loopholes with regard to private party financing, lowering the ceiling on campaign spending for individual candidates, allowing groups of citizens to introduce a 'popular legislative initiative' to Parliament, re-evaluating and simplifying existing legislation, increasing access to public administrators, increasing the transparency, responsiveness, responsibility, and efficacy of public administration, depoliticizing civil service recruitment and promotions, and drafting a code of conduct for MPs that would curtail their clientelistic intervention in public administration.[36]

The more radical proposals of the opposition parties include electoral system reforms. These include reducing the impact of list votes on the election of MPs; the introduction of a (more) majoritarian system, direct election of members of the executive (from mayors to the PM), and the introduction of a binding referendum. There are also calls for an absolute prohibition against holding multiple public offices, limits on outside occupations for public officials, and term limits.

Hence, mainly since the early 1990s, Belgium has witnessed a gradual decline in the informal system of partitocratic delegation. Thus, some formal agents (the cabinet, top civil servants, some MPs) are gradually reacquiring autonomy. Some of these evolutions will facilitate the restoration of the simple and stepwise chain of delegation, while other aim at introducing direct links between parts of the chain that, in the ideal–typical model, are not adjacent.

REFERENCES

Alen, André (1986). 'De "Bijzonder Machten": Een Nieuwe "Besluitenregering" in België?' *Tijdschrift Voor Bestuurswetenschappen en Publiek Recht*, 41: 123–59.

——and Dujardin, Jean (1986). *Casebook Belgisch Grondwettelijk Recht*. Brussels: Story-Scientia.

——and Meerschaut, Frank (1998). *La Constitution de la Belgique fédérale*. Diegem: Kluwer.

——Tillemans, Bernard and Peeters, Patrick (1992). *International Encyclopaedia of Constitutional Law: Belgium*. Deventer: Kluwer.

Arcq, Etienne (1993). 'Le Taux de Syndicalisation 1982–1991'. *Courrier Hebdomadaire du CRISP*, 1386.

Bergman, Torbjörn (1993). 'Formation Rules and Minority Governments'. *European Journal of Political Research*, 23: 55–66.

---

[35] In the 1990s Belgium had the highest level of public debt of the fifteen EU members (still 114% of GNP at the end of the decade). During the Dutroux affair, it also scored the lowest with regard to citizen satisfaction with the functioning of democracy (Eurobarometer, 47.1).

[36] The Flemish Parliament has in 1997 promulgated such a code, drafted by Dr. De Winter, which has gradually become the standard for similar codes being drafted by other national, provincial, and local assemblies (De Winter and Dumont 2000).

Bock, Isabelle and Debroux, Philippe (1995). *Le Contrat de Gestion, ses Limites et ses Potentialités*. Bruxelles: Services Fédéraux des Affaires Scientifiques, Techniques, et Culturelles.

Delpérée, Francis and Renders, David (1998). *Code Constitutionnel*. Bruxelles: Bruylant.

De Ruyter, Karin, Michielsen, Stefaan, and Mortelmans, Johan (1994). *België Verkoopt. De Stille Privatisering van de Belgische Overheidsbedrijven*. Groot-Bijgaarden: Scoop.

de Ryck, Etienne (1994). 'Ministeries', in Mark Deweerdt, Clem De Ridder, and Roger Dillemans (eds.), *Wegwijs Politiek*. Leuven: Davidsfonds.

Dewachter, Wilfried (1987). 'Changes in a Particracy: The Belgian Party System from 1944 to 1986', in Hans Daalder (ed.), *Party Systems in Denmark, Austria, Switzerland, The Netherlands and Belgium*. London: Pinter.

——(1992). *Besluitvorming in Politiek België*. Leuven: Acco.

De Winter, Lieven (1980). 'Twintig Jaar Polls, of de Teloorgang van een Vorm van Interne Partijdemocratie'. *Res Publica*, 22: 563–85.

——(1981). 'De Partijpolitisering als Instrument van de Particratie. Een Overzicht van de Ontwikkeling Sinds de Tweede Wereldoorlog'. *Res Publica*, 23: 53–107.

——(1988). 'Belgium: Democracy or Oligarchy', in Michael Gallagher and Michael Marsh (eds.), *Candidate Selection in Comparative Perspective*. London: Sage.

——(1991). 'Parliamentary and Party Pathways to the Cabinet', in Jean Blondel and Jean-Louis Thiébault (eds.), *The Profession of Government Minister in Western Europe*. London: Macmillan.

——(1993). 'The Links Between Cabinets and Parties and Cabinet Decision-Making', in Jean Blondel and Ferdinand Müller-Rommel (eds.), *Governing Together*. London: Macmillan.

——(1995). 'The Role of Parliament in Cabinet Formation and Resignation', in Herbert Döring (ed.), *Parliaments and Majority Rule in Western Europe*. New York: St. Martin's Press.

——(1996). 'Party Encroachment on the Executive and Legislative Branch in the Belgian Polity'. *Res Publica*, 43: 325–52.

——(1997). 'Belgian MPs between Party and Voters'. *Journal of Legislative Studies*, 3(3): 128–54.

——(1998a). 'The Belgian Parliament', in George Kurian (ed.), *World Encyclopedia of Parliaments and Legislatures*, Vol. I. Washington, DC: Congressional Quarterly.

——(1998b). 'Parliament and Government in Belgium: Prisoners of Partitocracy', in Philip Norton (ed.), *Parliaments and Governments in Western Europe*. London: Frank Cass.

——(1999). 'Belgium: Insider Pressure Groups in an Outsider Parliament', in Philip Norton (ed.), *Parliaments and Pressure Groups in Western Europe*. London: Frank Cass.

——and Brans, Marleen (1999). 'Belgien. Berufspolitiker und die Krise des Parteienstaates', in Jens Borchert (ed.), *Politik als Beruf*. Opladen: Leske + Budrich.

——, Della Porta, Donatella, and Deschouwer, Kris (1996). 'Comparing Similar Countries'. *Res Publica*, 38: 215–36.

——and Dumont, Patrick (1999). 'The Belgian Party System(s) on the Eve of Disintegration', in David Broughton and Mark Donovan (eds.), *Changing Party Systems in Western Europe*. London: Cassell.

————(2000). 'Belgium: Subjects of Partitocratic Dominion', in Knut Heidar and Ruude Koole (eds.), *Parliamentary Party Groups in European Democracies*. London: Routledge.

——, Frognier, André-Paul, and Rihoux, Benoît (1996). 'Belgium: Still the Age of Party Government?', in Jean Blondel and Maurizio Cotta (eds.), *Party and Government*. London: Macmillan.

——and Thierry, Laurent (1995). 'The Belgian Parliament and European Integration'. *Journal of Legislative Studies*, 1(3): 75–91.

——, Timmermans, Arco, and Dumont, Patrick (2000). 'Belgium: On Government Agreements, Evangelists, Followers, and Heretics', in Wolfgang C. Müller and Kaare Strøm (eds.), *Coalition Government in Western Europe*. Oxford: Oxford University Press.

Dierickx, Guido and Majersdorf, Philippe (1993). *La Culture Politique des Fonctionnaires et des Hommes Politiques en Belgique*. Brugge: Vanden Broele.

Eijffinger, Sylvester C. W. (1997). *Independent Central Banks and Economic Performance*. Cheltenham: Edward Elgar.

Fitzmaurice, John (1996). *The Politics of Belgium: A Unique Federalism*. London: Hurst.

François, Aymé (1997). *De l'Etat Unitaire à l'Etat fédéral. La Dynamique Institutionnelle de la Belgique*. Louvain-la-Neuve: Ciaco.

Frognier, André-Paul (1993). 'The Single Party/Coalition Distinction and Cabinet Decision-Making', in Jean Blondel and Ferdinand Müller-Rommel (eds.), *Governing Together*. London: Macmillan.

——(1997). 'Belgium: A Complex Cabinet in a Fragmented Polity', in Jean Blondel and Ferdinand Müller-Rommel (eds.), *Cabinets in Western Europe*, 2nd edn. London: Macmillan.

Grilli, Vittorio, Masciandaro, Donato, and Tabellini, Guido (1991). 'Political and Monetary Institutions and Public Financial Politicies in Industrial Countries'. *Economic Policy*, 13: 341–92.

Hondeghem, Annie (1996). 'De Politieke en de Ambtelijke Component in het Openbaar Bestuur', in Rudolf Maes and Kathleen Jochmans (eds.), *Inleiding tot de Bestuurkunde*. Brussel: Studiecentrum Open Hoger Onderwijs.

Iker, Laura (1998). 'Evolution des Règles de Financement et de Contrôle des Partis Politiques'. *Courrier Hebdomadaire du CRISP*: 1607–9.

Lammens, André (1993). *Het Bankroet van België*. Antwerpen: Darbo.

Langerwerf, Etienne (1980). 'Het Stemgedrag in het Parlement. Onderzoek in de Kamer van Volksvertegenwoordigers Voor de Periode 1954–1965'. *Res Publica*, 22: 177–88.

Mattson, Ingvar and Strøm, Kaare (1995). 'Parliamentary Committees', in Herbert Döring (ed.), *Parliaments and Majority Rule in Western Europe*. Frankfurt am Main: Campus and New York: St. Martin's Press.

Neels, Leo (1975). 'Regeringsverklaringen en Regeerakkoorden als Documenten van Toenemend Publiekrechterlijk Belang. Een Nieuwe Vorm van Publiek Recht?' *Rechtskundig Weekblad*, 38: 2370–410.

Perin, François (1960). *La Démocratie Enrayée. Essai Sur le Régime Parlementaire Belge de 1918 à 1958*. Bruxelles: Institut de Science Politique.

Rihoux, Benoît (1996). 'Electoral Reform and Electoral Behaviour in Belgium: Change Within Continuity... Or Conversely'. *Res Publica*, 38: 255–78.

Senelle, Robert (1983). *De Ministerraad in België*. Deventer: Kluwer.

Smeets, René (1994). *Ouderen en Politiek*. Leuven: Davidsfonds.

Strøm, Kaare, Budge, Ian, and Laver, Michael (1994). 'Constraints on Cabinet Formation in Parliamentary Democracies'. *American Journal of Political Science*, 38: 303–35.

Suetens, Mik and Walgrave, Stefan (2001). 'Belgian Politics Without Ministerial Cabinets?' *Acta Politica*, 36: 180–205.

Tegenbos, Guy (1990). 'Partijnota: Zes op Tien Hoge Ambtenaren Zijn Kristendemokraat'. *De Standaard*, May 9, 3.

Timmermans, Arco (1994). 'Cabinet Ministers and Parliamentary Government in Belgium: The Impact of Coalitional Constraints', in Michael Laver and Kenneth A. Shepsle (eds.), *Cabinet Ministers and Parliamentary Government*. Cambridge: Cambridge University Press.

Verminck, Mieke (1986). 'Concensus en Oppositie in het Belgisch Parlement Tijdens Een Verkiezingsjaar'. *Res Publica*, 28: 475–87.

7

Denmark: Delegation and Accountability in Minority Situations

ERIK DAMGAARD

INTRODUCTION

After three decades of constitutional struggles between liberals and conservatives—the latter more or less aligned with the constitutional monarchy established by the constitution of 1849—the cabinet's accountability to the lower, or popular, chamber (*Folketinget*) of Parliament was finally accepted in 1901. Danish parliamentary democracy was consolidated in the early twentieth century, but the principle of cabinet accountability was not formally written into the constitution until 1953. The same reform abolished the upper chamber, which historically had served to protect conservative interests.

The prevalent Danish Constitution of 1953 is very short. It does not say much about the formation, operation, and resignation of governments. It does not establish a constitutional court, and while the Supreme Court has claimed the power of judicial review, it has actually been reluctant to invalidate legislative decisions. The Danish Monarch is a prominent figure in the constitutional text, but the functions actually reserved for the Queen or King are only ceremonial. By law the Danish National Bank is an independent institution with responsibility for important aspects of monetary policy, but it is not without links to the world of politics. One-third of the Bank's Council members are MPs elected by Parliament, and the minister of the economy 'oversees' (as it is formally expressed) its activities.

Denmark is basically a small, unitary state with only about 5 million inhabitants. Thus, federalism does not complicate the chain of political delegation. Yet, the Danish public sector is one of the most decentralized in the world, and the government annually bargains with the organizations of local and regional governments ('Kommunernes Landsforening', 'Amtsrådsforeningen') in order to coordinate macroeconomic policy with the activities of individual local and regional governments (Blom-Hansen 1998).

According to the Constitution, legislative power is shared by Parliament and government ('the King'). In reality the head of state (the Monarch) no longer has political influence. However, as will be discussed below, the electorate may, in some instances, have a direct say in the adoption of laws and other decisions. The constitution prescribes that bills must go through three parliamentary readings before a final vote can be taken. The Standing Orders of the Folketing state that a bill may be referred to a committee after the second reading. Committees may receive advice and evidence from various interested parties. The committee in question—usually one of the permanent, specialized committees that reflect the party composition of full Folketing—then reports to the floor, which makes the final decision at the end of the third reading. More than one-half the MPs must be present for a decision to be made, and the decision rule is 50 per cent + 1 of all valid votes cast (ignoring abstentions). The budget proposal is dealt with in the same way as other bills. The government may issue more detailed rules than those adopted in the form of law (delegated legislation), provided that such government decrees are authorized by laws. They are known as 'bekendtgørelser', that is, statutory instruments.

The procedures for amending the Constitution are strongly biased in favour of the status quo. While three readings are required before ordinary bills can be enacted, a much more demanding procedure is required for constitutional changes. A bill to amend the Constitution must first be passed by the Folketing. If the government favours the amendment, it must then call for the election of a new Folketing, which must adopt the identical amendment once again. Finally, the amendment must be submitted to a referendum for approval or rejection within 6 months after its final passage. The amendment is adopted if a simple majority of those voting in the referendum favour it, provided that this majority constitutes at least 40 per cent of the electorate. As these rules obviously give veto power to several players, a high-level of consensus is required to change the Constitution.

Given these observations, Denmark would appear to be rather close to an ideal–typical conception of parliamentary democracy in which voters, Parliament, and government are the crucial actors. However, at least five general features of Danish politics complicate this simple picture. First, Denmark is a small state, heavily constrained by international ties. It is a member of NATO (since 1949) and the European Union (EU) (since 1973) as well as a multitude of other international organizations. These memberships clearly limit the discretion of Danish authorities, but they also create opportunities for security and influence that would not otherwise exist (cf. Dahl and Tufte 1974).[1]

Second, Denmark holds the postwar world record with regard to minority government rule in a parliamentary democracy. Except for 20 months during 1993–4, minority governments have held power in Denmark since 1971 (Damgaard 2000c). Minority governance is bound to affect the nature of parliamentary delegation and accountability in various ways. What does delegation mean when the government does not have the powers of a majority?

Third, although representative democracy and cabinet accountability are core elements in the political system, the Constitution allows for—and in some situations

---

[1] It might be argued that the chain of delegation and accountability only breaks down if a particular instance of delegation is not matched by an appropriate accountability relationship. If delegation, in Robert A. Dahl's terms, is 'a revocable grant of authority' (Dahl 1989:112–4), there need not be any problem. However, if delegation turns out to be an 'alienation' of power, there certainly is a democratic problem. The same reasoning can be applied to domestic state–local/regional government relations, although in this case the Parliament (if not the responsible minister) can at least recall delegated powers. In Kiewiet and McCubbins' (1991) terminology, this delegation is certainly not 'abdication'.

even requires—the holding of referendums. There have been 15 referendums since 1953. These are manifestations of direct democracy in a system in which decision-making is normally reserved for Parliament and government. Thus, the scope of delegation from voters to Parliament is somewhat limited by constitutional rules and practices.

Fourth, organized interests (in addition to those of local and regional governments) are an important feature of Danish politics. Denmark may no longer be quite as corporatist as it was described in the 1960s and 1970s (Christiansen and Rommetvedt 1997), and the Parliament has increased its influence as of 2003 (Damgaard 1994*a*). Nonetheless, interest organizations certainly still play a role in initiating and implementing policy decisions. Bargaining constantly occurs among politicians, groups, and civil servants in many policy areas. In the labour market, the organizations of labour and employers conduct collective bargaining that, to a large extent, regulates salaries and working conditions for most people. In this area, one might say that voters (or at least union members) delegate power not to Parliament but to interest organizations. Alternatively, one can speak about two different channels of delegation and accountability: the 'numerical' and the 'corporate' (cf. Rokkan 1967, 1975).

The fifth, and perhaps most important, modification to the ideal type of parliamentary democracy concerns the role of political parties.

POLITICAL PARTIES

The existing Danish Constitution, like its predecessors from 1920, 1915, 1866, and 1849, does not mention political parties at all. Nevertheless, parties are key actors in mass politics, in Parliament, and in government. They must therefore be integrated in realistic models of parliamentary delegation and accountability.[2] As the parties are very cohesive, or disciplined, one could perhaps argue that they structure delegation and accountability between voters, Parliament, and government, without affecting the parliamentary model. On the other hand, the inclusion of parties probably violates the singularity principle that each agent has only one principal. An individual MP, for example, may act as an agent for his voters as well as for his/her party organization.

Constitutionally, Danish MPs are Burkean free agents insofar as they are bound solely by their own conscience and not by any directives from their voters. In practice, however, they are also party agents (Jensen 1996; Damgaard 1997). MPs generally think that they are perfectly able to represent their party and constituency simultaneously, although these interests might sometimes conflict. While some MPs spend a lot of time on constituency-related matters, on the whole they are party representatives, even if some claim that their own convictions are those that ultimately matter. While this might be true, candidates must nonetheless choose a party in order to become a Member of Parliament in the first place.

That the electoral law recognizes political parties is revealed by the fact that it presupposes the existence of such organized bodies. In fact, the basic structure of party

---

[2] Gunnar Sjöblom (1995) thus describes Danish representative democracy in terms of a 'party government' model.

organization is adapted to the administrative structure of the election law in the sense that parties have national, regional, constituency, and local organizations (Bille 1994). The high degree of organizational uniformity has not, however, been forced upon parties. No law regulating the structure and internal affairs of parties has ever been proposed. Parties are regarded as voluntary, private associations, and—although this has changed—for a very long time they were not interested in direct public subsidies (Bille 1994).

A distinction should be made between the (extra-parliamentary) membership party and the parliamentary party groups (of MPs). The latter are recognized in the Standing Orders of Parliament. Public subsidies for parliamentary party groups were introduced in the mid-1960s in order to improve the working conditions of MPs and party groups in terms of staffing and facilities (Pedersen and Bille 1991). This support has subsequently been expanded. It was not until 1986, however, that a law was passed providing public support to finance the activities and electoral campaigns of membership parties.[3] The parties do not have to account for how the money is spent, but since 1990 they have been required to provide information about their various sources of income (public support, membership fees, organizations, private enterprises, etc.) in gross figures. Since 1996 the names of private donors must also be revealed if the donation is more than DKK 20.000 per year (Elklit and Pade 1996). Finally, while the difference between the two branches of the parties is important, it is worth keeping in mind that in practice they are closely interconnected with respect to staffing and financing (Bille 1994).

Danish political parties and the characteristics of the party system have been described elsewhere (see e.g. Pedersen 1987; Bille 1994; Damgaard 2000c). No single party has commanded a majority since the early twentieth century, and in the postwar period 'only' seven parties have been in government, either alone or in coalition. These seven parties include four 'old parties' and three 'new parties'. The four old ones are the Social Democrats ('Socialdemokratiet', SD), the Social Liberals ('Det Radikale Venstre', RV), the Liberals ('Venstre', V), and the Conservatives ('Det Konservative Folkeparti', KF). The new parties that have participated in government are the Center Democrats ('Centrum-Demokraterne', CD), the Christian People's Party ('Kristeligt Folkeparti', KRF), and the Justice Party ('Danmarks Retsforbund', DR). Parties of the extreme Left and Right have never been in government.

DELEGATION FROM VOTERS TO MPs

The Constitution states that no more than 175 MPs (apart from two elected in Greenland and two in the Faroe Islands) are to be elected to a 4-year term using a proportional representation formula to be set out in the election law. It also states that

---

[3] According to the rules introduced in 1987, each party (or independent candidate) obtaining at least 1,000 votes was entitled to 5 DKK per year per vote obtained in the latest Folketing election. In 1996 the amount per year per vote was increased to 19,50 DKK. Thus, for parties that obtain at least 1,000 votes public funding is exactly proportional to the distribution of the national vote, regardless of whether or not the party wins seats.

in allocating seats among localities, attention is to be paid to number of inhabitants, number of voters, and population density. In geographical terms these rules tend to slightly favour sparsely populated areas. Nationally, the election law assures proportional representation of parties that obtain: (a) at least 2 per cent of the national vote, or (b) the regional quota for one member in two of the three electoral regions (Metropolitan Copenhagen, The Islands, Jutland) into which the country is divided, or (c) at least one regular constituency seat. (The conditions were slightly different 1945–60, cf. Elklit 1993; Elklit and Pade 1996.) Proportionality in the Danish two-tier electoral system is assured by a national allocation rule that applies Hare's quota in combination with the method of the largest remainder. Since 1953 forty adjustment seats are used to ensure that the share of seats a party gets corresponds as closely as possible to its share of the national vote. Only 135 of the 175 seats are thus allocated in the 17 multi-member constituencies (district magnitude 2–15) according to a modified St.-Laguë method.

Danes vote for either a party or a preferred candidate within a party (or for an independent candidate). Thus, voters can influence the election of individual MPs, although the strength of this influence depends on the type of candidate list presented by the parties. Danish parties can present a 'pure party list' with ranked candidates or, if they prefer, an alphabetic list of candidates in which preferential voting can be much more decisive. Individual parties therefore decide how much of a choice the voters have. Increasingly most parties have presented variations of the latter type. Thus intraparty preference voting does occur, despite the fact that there are no primaries in Denmark.

Denmark has no official rules concerning term limits, mandatory retirement age, or recall mechanisms. However, the Danish Folketing can expel a member if it decides that an MP has been convicted of an offence that renders him/her unworthy of being a Member of Parliament. In practice, this happens very rarely.

For purely practical reasons the minimum length of electoral campaigns is 3 weeks. There is no limit on campaign spending. All parties, regardless of size and incumbency, are treated equally by the public service radio and television stations. It is not possible to purchase broadcasting time, but opinion polls may be published at any time (Pedersen and Bille 1991; Elklit and Pade 1996).

Party rules governing candidate selection are fairly similar (Bille 1992). No political party has voter primaries, term limits, or a mandatory retirement age. The only major difference among the parties is that conditional, or partially binding, intraparty primaries are used by the SDs and the CDs. In all parties the local and regional organizations are crucial in the nomination process (Bille 1993). They can hold their elected MP accountable, which is important with regard to the possibility of renomination and re-election. On the other hand, the local party organizations are keen to propose candidates that can attract votes, which means that an individual MP has a considerable advantage if he/she is likely to be an electoral asset. Nevertheless, MPs in most parties also depend on the parliamentary party organization to be re-elected or to advance within the party hierarchy (Damgaard 1995).

As is evident, the nexus of voter, party, and MP relations is quite complex. It can be argued that delegation from voters authorizes party MPs to make decisions in the election period ahead, and that voters are principals in the sense that they can remove MPs from office on election day. In practice, however, while voters do punish or reward individual MPs, they primarily reduce, increase, or leave unchanged the various political parties' seats in Parliament (cf. Nannestad 1989).[4]

DELEGATION FROM PARLIAMENT TO CABINET

Cabinet Formation

According to the Constitution, the Monarch formally appoints the Prime Minister and other ministers. There are no positive constitutional rules governing the cabinet formation process, only informal norms that have gradually evolved during the twentieth century. On the other hand, the Constitution explicitly states that no minister can remain in office if the Parliament has passed a motion of no confidence against him / her. The implication is that Danish cabinets are formed according to the principle of 'negative parliamentarism' (Rasmussen 1972), which does not require a vote of investiture. A government can stay in office as long as it is tolerated by Parliament, that is, if there is no explicit majority against it. Negative parliamentarism generally facilitates minority cabinets (Bergman 1993, 1995), and Denmark is a clear case in point.

Denmark's informal rules governing cabinet formation (Damgaard 2000c) require that the parliamentary parties formally advise the Monarch. If their advice unambiguously points to a majority cabinet or a cabinet with the assured support of a majority in Parliament, then the Monarch is obligated to appoint such a cabinet. If no such majority emerges, the goal is to appoint the minority cabinet most likely to survive. The whole process is one of bargaining among parties, which often prefer that in the first stage a leading parliamentarian is appointed by the Monarch to serve as a 'royal informateur'. When advice from the parties is unclear, it is the acting Prime Minister, and not the Monarch, who is responsible for interpreting it.

Confidence and No-Confidence Votes

Any MP can propose a motion of no confidence addressed to the Prime Minister (the cabinet) or an individual minister during debates on interpellations (see below) or upon general statements by a government about its policy proposals. Otherwise there are no constraints on no-confidence initiatives, and the usual Danish parliamentary voting rules apply. More than half (50 per cent + 1) of the members must be present, and in counting a public and recorded vote abstentions are disregarded (decision rule: 50 per cent + 1 of MPs present and voting 'yes' or 'no', thus ignoring abstentions). Conversely, the Prime Minister may ask for a vote of confidence by declaring, before a vote on a

---

[4] The delegation/accountability relationships become even more complex if one considers MPs to be neither voters or parties agents nor principals, but political representatives with a complex role involving interaction with voters, the interests of which should be taken care of, and independent judgement as to the best decision to make (cf. Pitkin 1967; Eulau and Karps 1977). Note that Esaiasson and Holmberg (1996; cf. Holmberg 1997) talk about 'representation from above' in the similar Swedish case.

proposal under debate, that the government will resign or call elections if the proposal is rejected by Parliament. Governments may also receive a vote of confidence during debates on interpellations and government policy. The procedure is the same for votes of no confidence.

Technically speaking, such matters of confidence are normally settled using a procedure that the Standing Orders, until 1997, termed a 'proposal to pass on to the next item on the agenda (proposal for a resolution on the order of business)'. It is now called a proposal for a 'decision'. This important instrument is very flexible because it allows a parliamentary majority to state its opinion on the government and on policies in any area. It can be used to instruct the government without necessarily phrasing the request in terms of confidence. Unless no confidence is explicitly mentioned, such parliamentary declarations are not legally, though usually are politically, binding. The instrument was frequently used against minority governments between 1982 and 1988 by the so-called 'alternative majority' on defence and security matters, and led to Danish 'footnotes' in NATO documents.

There are no statistics on the number of no-confidence votes taken. They would be difficult to produce insofar as one cannot simply count the number of votes on 'motions for a resolution on the order of business' or 'decisions'. Many of these do not concern confidence as such, and it is often not easy to decide the extent to which they do. What can be said, however, is that since 1945 only two governments have been removed by a no-confidence vote—in 1947 and 1975. In addition, the rejection of the government's budget bill for 1984 was interpreted as a no-confidence vote, and the government called new elections. In 1993 Prime Minister Schlüter resigned, probably anticipating a defeat in Parliament because of a 'scandal' ('Tamilsagen'). However, (minority) governments more commonly resign, or call elections, when they are unable to obtain parliamentary support. Cabinets dissolving Parliament (which cannot dissolve itself) are not required to resign from office. Often they may in fact be able to stay in power after the election.

Although no individual minister has ever been forced to resign by the passage of a motion of no confidence, there are some cases in which ministers have resigned because they anticipated a vote of no confidence (Jens Peter Christensen 1997: ch. 24). Schlüter V in 1993 is one such instance. However, it is often difficult or impossible to establish whether a minister who resigned would actually have been forced out by a no-confidence vote had he not left office voluntarily.

The Prime Minister has de facto power to dissolve Parliament at almost any time, although it is the Monarch who formally dissolves it on the proposal of the PM. The only restriction on the power of dissolution is that a new cabinet cannot dissolve Parliament before it and Parliament have met in a public meeting. In deciding whether or not to dissolve Parliament, the PM must pay attention to the views of coalition partners. For example, in the autumn of 1997 the PM chose not to call elections—although he and his party actually wanted to do so—because of the views of his coalition partner. In all, twenty cabinets have ended in early elections, eighteen of which were dissolved by the PM. Table 7.1 summarizes the behavioural record with respect to cabinet investiture, no-confidence and confidence votes, and parliamentary dissolution.

Table 7.1. *Cabinet Formation, Cabinet Termination, and Early Parliamentary Dissolution: Denmark 1945–2000* [a]

No.	Cabinet	Date of formation	Investiture votes (iv)	No-confidence votes (ncv)			Confidence votes (cv) under specific institutional mechanism	Did the cabinet end with an early election?	Who dissolved Parliament in this case? [b]
			n.a.	No. of ncv	Cabinet removed by ncv	Cabinet resigned to pre-empt ncv	n.a.		
1	Kristensen	45/11/07		1	Yes			Yes	PM
2	Hedtoft I	47/11/13		0				Yes	PM
3	Hedtoft II	50/09/16		0					
4	Eriksen I	50/10/30		0				Yes	Const.
5	Eriksen II	53/04/21		0				Yes	Const.
6	Hedtoft III	53/09/30		0					
7	Hansen	55/02/01		0				Yes	PM
8	Hansen II	57/05/28		0					
9	Kampmann I	60/02/21		0				Yes	PM
10	Kampmann II	60/11/18		0					
11	Krag I	62/09/03		0					
12	Krag II	64/09/26		0				Yes	PM
13	Krag III	66/11/22		0				Yes	PM
14	Baunsgaard	68/02/22		0				Yes	PM

#	Government	Date					
15	Krag IV	71/10/11	0				
16	Jorgensen I	72/10/05	0			Yes	PM
17	Hartling	73/12/19	1	Yes		Yes	PM
18	Jorgensen II	75/02/13	0			Yes	PM
19	Jorgensen III	77/02/15	0				
20	Jorgensen IV	78/08/30	0			Yes	PM
21	Jorgensen V	79/10/26	0			Yes	PM
22	Jorgensen VI	81/12/30	0				
23	Schlüter I	82/09/10	0			Yes	PM
24	Schlüter II	84/01/10	0			Yes	PM
25	Schlüter III	87/09/10	0			Yes	PM
26	Schlüter IV	88/06/03	0			Yes	PM
27	Schlüter V	90/12/18	0		Yes		
28	Rasmussen I	93/01/25	0			Yes	PM
29	Rasmussen II	94/09/27	0				
30	Rasmussen III	96/12/30	0			Yes	PM
31	Rasmussen IV	98/03/11	—			—	—

[a] n.d. = no data (missing data); n.a. or '—' = not applicable in this case.

[b] The question 'Who dissolved Parliament in this case?' can be answered with one of five options. This identifies the main constitutional actor that caused the early election. We have not coded the formal signatory, but rather the person or body that made the real decision: (1) Head of State; (2) Prime Minister (PM); (3) Cabinet; (4) Parliamentary majority; (5) Automatic constitutional provision ('Const.' for example, if it is required when a new President takes office, or, for example, if it is required after the adoption of a proposal for constitutional amendments).

Parliamentary Control Instruments

The Danish Parliament has numerous additional instruments for controlling the cabinet. There are various forms of parliamentary questions, which have been used increasingly over the past decades (Damgaard 1994b). Short questions to be answered in writing or during the weekly 'question time' were introduced in 1947, but written answers only in the early 1960s. Since then such requests have escalated, reaching a level of 3–4,000 in the most recent sessions, whereas only a few hundred questions per year are answered orally. Urgent questions (unprepared questions and answers) were introduced in the fall of 1997, and these are put to the government for 1 hour each Tuesday.

Committees can submit written questions to ministers in connection with bills and draft resolutions under scrutiny, and they have the authority to request the presence of a minister in a committee meeting to answer questions (a 'consultation'). Committee powers were expanded in 1972 when the committee system was completely reformed with the establishment of some twenty permanent, specialized committees with jurisdictions roughly matching the various government ministries. At that time it was emphasized that committees should indeed supervise their respective areas, and that they could address questions to the relevant minister even if no specific proposal was under consideration. Henrik Jensen concluded a comprehensive study on Danish committees in the following way: 'The committees are used as instruments in the political struggle by the committee members qua party representatives, and at the same time the committees structure the behaviour of the actors, that is, the political parties and their representatives on the committees' (Jensen 1995:199).

Legally, ministers can ignore questions because they are only regulated in the Standing Orders (whereas interpellations are mentioned in the Constitution). In addition, they might attempt to delay written answers. In practice, however, they normally answer short questions one way or another. The record is a bit different with regard to questions on topics other than bills and resolutions under consideration. Thus, in 1995/96 about 300 questions out of more than 5,000 had not been answered at the end of the parliamentary session. No regular reports to Parliament are formally required, but according to the Constitution Parliament can use an interpellation to force an oral report on any topic from a minister. The interpellations must be answered by the minister, and the ensuing debate may end with a vote (cf. above on confidence and no-confidence votes).

Since the early 1980s parliamentary majorities have increasingly ordered quasi-judicial investigations of ministerial 'scandals' and administrative problems, a few of which have resulted in the resignation of a minister. The auditing office, which was previously part of the executive branch but now reports to Parliament, has also become a monitor of the activities of government departments. A few years ago, the old impeachment procedure—which dates back to the time before the introduction of cabinet accountability and which had not been used since 1909—was 'rediscovered'. In 1995 it was used to convict a former minister of justice. This trend has been interpreted as a 'judicialization' of parliamentary accountability (Jens Peter Christensen 1997). On the basis of such contentions, Jens Peter Christensen has identified several norms with which ministers must comply, including the duty to 'speak the truth in front of parliament', to 'comply with the rules concerning the disbursement of state funds', to 'comply with acts of parliament', and the duty to 'take action as head of the government administration' (Jens Peter Christensen 1997: 604).

Delegation and Minority Rule

If voter delegation of power to Parliament in Denmark is quite complex, the delegation from Parliament to cabinet is arguably even more so. Cabinets are formed according to informal norms and are almost invariably minority cabinets. The political parties play a game that usually results in a delegation of power that is extremely conditional. Government parties do have a leadership role, but they do not usually control a parliamentary majority necessary to enact their policies. Instead, they must constantly bargain with one or several opposition parties to obtain a legislative majority. This also applies to the budget proposal, which is legally a bill, albeit a rather special one that can be rejected in the final instance if the government has not enlisted sufficient support in advance. The annual bargaining over the budget is therefore very important (Mattson 1996). Note that the Finance Committee of the Folketing has the power to grant money not already authorized in the budget act (*finansloven*). However, spending ministers must first have the approval of the minister of finance. Such grants are then included in the annual supplementary appropriations act.

In contrast to majority coalitions, Danish minority governments are highly dependent on opposition parties. Although majority governments are also ultimately accountable to Parliament, they are clearly less vulnerable. Nonetheless, even majority coalition governments, which have always been of minimal winning size, do not have the power to change the Constitution.

The Danish Parliament clearly does not delegate all its power to the cabinet. Rather, it retains the power to decide, on each single issue, whether or not the government should have its way. There is little variation across policy areas. Even foreign affairs, traditionally an executive domain, is always under close parliamentary surveillance and control. Thus, the government is indeed accountable to Parliament.

DELEGATION WITHIN CABINET

The Danish Prime Minister is more than a *primus inter pares* in relation to the cabinet colleagues from his own party. Although the formal act is carried out by the head of state, the Prime Minister alone appoints and dismisses ministers from his party, and he must approve, at least formally, the ministers proposed by coalition partners because they subsequently become members of 'his' cabinet. Since 1964 the Prime Minister has a small secretariat (cf. Statsministeriet 1988) staffed by civil servants who monitor the various government departments, though they rarely directly interfere in department activities because individual ministers are quite autonomous. Furthermore, since coalition governments have become the rule in Danish politics, there are limits on the Prime Minister's authority over ministers from other parties.

The PM chairs the weekly meetings of the cabinet, which has about twenty members. All politically important topics are dealt with in cabinet meetings, if only to make sure that there is agreement. Interministerial differences will normally be sorted out before an item reaches the cabinet. The agenda is set by the PM, who receives proposals from individual ministers. Items discussed in cabinet meetings include government and private member's bills and draft resolutions, ministerial reports to Parliament, interpellations, questions that might be controversial in Parliament, ongoing bargaining with other parties, important appointments, the establishment of committees, etc. (Olsen 1988).

Except for the special status of the Prime Minister and the important role of the minister of finance over the budgets of spending ministries, Danish cabinet ministers are formally equal and quite powerful within their respective jurisdictions, which in principle are mutually exclusive. However, because irrespective of formal jurisdiction issues are often of interest to more than one minister, interministerial conflicts of interest are not unknown. The decision rule applied in cabinet meetings under such circumstances might best be described as 'consensus as defined by the PM'.

The constitution dictates that ministers' jurisdictions are to be decided by the Prime Minister (formally the Monarch). Therefore, Parliament cannot interfere with the distribution of offices and jurisdictions among the government ministers, although parliamentary majorities have in fact tried to do so. Ministers do not have junior ministers or secretaries of state at their disposal (though several of them have found ways to appoint informal political assistants). 'Cabinet' and 'government' are therefore synonymous terms in Denmark.

Cabinet ministers are the heads of their departments but not dictators within their jurisdictions. They form part of a team directed by the Prime Minister, who also needs to take into account the views of coalition partners. Danish governments are equipped with various mechanisms to coordinate and, if necessary, settle interdepartmental disputes. In addition to regular cabinet meetings, governments have some kind of inner cabinet and a varying number of issue-specific cabinet committees (Olsen 1978; Christensen 1985; Olsen 1988). One cannot say that the cabinet may, if it wants, take decision-making power away from individual ministers, but a minister needs the approval of the Prime Minister and cabinet colleagues for politically important decisions.

It has been argued that longevity in ministerial position and previous parliamentary experience affect the performance of ministers. With the exceptions of the Prime Minister and the minister of foreign affairs, recent analysis has shown a decline in individual ministerial longevity since 1945, and particularly since 1960. Thus, the average period in office between 1945 and 1960 was 3 years and 8 months, whereas it was 2 years and 11 months during 1960–78 (and 2 years and 10 months 1978–94). These figures can be compared to 5 years and 3 months in 1920–40 (Kirk and Knudsen 1996). Kirk and Knudsen argue that as a consequence an increasing proportion of a minister's time in office is spent 'learning the job'. Their proposition that this development has weakened ministers is doubtful, however, because of other factors that also play a role in political leadership. For example, there is no corresponding decline in the proportion of ministers with parliamentary experience before their first ministerial appointment, and in the most recent period only one out of five ministers was not an MP when first appointed minister (Kirk and Knudsen 1997). One might even argue that long-term service in a particular ministry raises the possibility that the minister can become an 'ambassador for the ministry' rather than a political leader, a risk implied in analyses by Christensen (1983). This risk of 'going native' is probably greatest in a system like Denmark's, where cabinet ministers have no political assistants.

Generally speaking, governmental power in Denmark is exercised through individual ministers responsible for their departments. Ministers are quite powerful within their jurisdictions, but also constrained both by the cabinet, which is headed by the Prime Minister, and by their coalition partners. In this sense, the autonomy of ministers in Denmark seems to correspond to a pattern that is fairly common in Western Europe (Laver and Shepsle 1994). The important difference is that Danish governments and ministers are usually in a minority position in Parliament.

DELEGATION FROM MINISTERS TO CIVIL SERVANTS

Traditional Danish administrative policy states that a government minister is responsible for his/her governmental department. While he or she might not be personally responsible for mistakes made by civil servants (cf. below), ministerial accountability is the basic norm. There is a direct line of command from the minister downwards through the administrative bureaucracy. Higher-level civil servants are appointed by the minister, with the support of his/her cabinet colleagues in the cabinet's committee on appointments. Ministers are therefore in a position to control the careers of top civil servants.

Danish civil servants are usually recruited on the basis of merit. This usually requires that they hold a university degree in law, economics, or political science, although special agencies may require more technical degrees. Civil servants are supposed to be politically neutral and to report only to their own minister. Promotions are also granted on the basis of merit.

A large number of problematic cases about the duties and responsibilities of civil servants as opposed to ministers have led to a series of official investigations. A recent summary of the results of these investigations states that civil servants are obliged to 'inform and counsel the minister', to 'warn the minister (the "duty to put the foot down")', and to 'refuse to carry out clearly illegal orders by the minister'. Similarly, the minister's responsibility vis-à-vis civil servants include the duty to 'question his or her civil servants in such a manner that the minister does not deliberately deprive him or herself of knowledge about important factors'. The minister is also obligated to 'respect the division of labour between the minister and the civil servants—including the duty to respect the fact that the professional background and responsibilities of the civil service establish limits on the right of the minister to give instructions'. Finally, the minister must 'respect general principles of administrative law' (Jens Peter Christensen 1997: 604–5).

The relationship between ministers and civil servants is a hotly disputed issue in contemporary Danish government. Because there are no partisan junior ministers or secretaries of state, civil servants are more or less required to perform genuinely political tasks. Civil servants have consistently opposed the idea of introducing junior ministers, and they do in fact willingly give ministers political advice. However, they do not appear publicly in the capacity of political advisors. They might sometimes get into trouble as a result of the dilemma between serving the minister and being an administrative expert of the classical type, but normally the cooperation between civil servants and ministers works to their mutual satisfaction. Only in purely partisan matters will civil servants resist requests to assist their ministers.

The integration of organized interests into the making and implementation of public policy has important consequences for the traditional, judicial, and parliamentary institutions of accountability. 'Delegated administration' in the Danish labour market, agriculture, and cooperative housing, for example, has weakened relationships of political accountability and led to quite a few scandals involving the misuse of public funds during the 1980s and early 1990s. However, none of the cases involved outright corruption (Christensen 1993).

There is really no tradition of state-owned enterprises and nationalized industries in Denmark. However, public corporations organized in accordance with Danish company law, with the central government owning all or part of the shares, do exist, and new ones have increasingly been established over the past two decades. The same is true of public enterprises with their own boards of directors (which are exempted from unrestricted departmental supervision).[5] The whole development may be interpreted as a shift from hierarchical governance towards market governance. Parliamentary and governmental control are thus clearly reduced insofar as there is now less direct accountability to political authorities. Still, note that when the international privatisation movement started in the early 1980s, Denmark had few nationalized industries to privatise (Damgaard 1989; Christensen and Pallesen 1997).

Another development in the past 25 years is a steady process of delegation from political executives to civil servants at lower administrative levels. For example, the reformed budgetary system makes it possible for public institutions to transfer resources from one spending item to another, and to transfer resources from the present year to the next one (Christensen and Pallesen 1997). This obviously reduces financial control from the top.

In sum, ministers are in charge of their departments and ultimately responsible to Parliament. Civil servants are accountable to their minister. As indicated above, however, it is not quite clear whether a minister always controls or directs the behaviour of civil servants. The civil servant may also to some extent represent the interests of the bureaucracy. At the same time, administrative developments in recent decades imply that a number of areas are no longer directly controlled by government ministers. Consequently, they cannot be held accountable for all relevant activities.[6]

---

[5] Thus, in 1975 there were forty-one organizations of one of these two types. By 1995 this number had more than doubled, to eighty-five. In addition some genuine privatization has occurred during the same period (involving a life insurance company and a mining company with a number of associated companies). Furthermore, several existing government organizations have acquired a semi-autonomous status (Christensen and Pallesen 1997).

[6] Moreover, the freedom of information act of 1964 entitled citizens to see government documents in cases to which they were parties. In 1971 a new law introduced a general right (with some exceptions,

EXTERNAL CONSTRAINTS

As mentioned by way of introduction, it has become accepted that Danish courts can rule on the constitutionality of specific pieces of legislation, although the courts have been cautious in their exercise of this authority (cf. Alivizatos 1995). This caution might, however, change in the future. A small step in the direction of judicial activism was recently taken when the Supreme Court (surprisingly) allowed a group of citizens to sue the Prime Minister for having signed the Maastricht Treaty, which, they claimed, violated the Constitution. The PM was acquitted by a High Court in 1997 and by the Supreme Court in 1998. However, there will almost certainly be more future cases, because the Supreme Court also ruled that it alone has the authority to decide on the constitutionality of laws. In 1999 the Court even overruled a law. Consequently, the Danish court system will become more involved in political matters than it has been in the past.

The Danish National Bank must also be taken into account by the government, particularly if its director propounds the opinions of the bank in the media. While it is difficult to measure the Bank's influence, it seems to have been quite important in the making of Danish monetary policy, not least policy with regard to liberalizing international capital flows (i.e. deregulation of foreign exchange control) in the 1980s (Jensen 1989). One study concluded that, from a governmental point of view, the National Bank is 'one of the most influential partners in economic policy' (Bent Christensen 1985: 172). It appears, however, that its influence varies across issues and over time.

A third point to be made is that Danish voters do not delegate all their power to Parliament. The constitution of 1953 requires the electorate to make the final decisions in some matters—including changes in voting age, constitutional changes, and, under certain circumstances, delegations of power to international authorities (in particular when the Parliament passes a bill to that effect by a majority that is smaller than a qualified absolute majority of five-sixths). In addition, decisive referendums on bills passed in Parliament, with certain exceptions (including taxation), can be organized at the request of one-third of MPs. Thus, defeated parliamentary minorities can, in some instances, appeal to the electorate to reverse a parliamentary decision. Finally, Parliament can order consultative referendums. Danish voters, however, have no right to initiate referendums (see Svensson 1996).

Since 1945 there has been one referendum on amending the constitution (1953), five referendums about changing the voting age (1953, 1961, 1969, 1971, 1978), six on the EC/EU (1972, 1986, 1992, 1993, 1998, 2000)[7], and four in 1963 about bills passed by the Parliament—all of which were rejected in referendums. While fifteen referendums in 45 years may not seem to be all that many, the very possibility of a referendum influences the behaviour of parties and MPs, because even legislative majorities must consider the likelihood of its use in any particular situation.

---

including cases involving the personal and economic relations of individuals, state security matters, and internal working documents) for citizens to see documents in cases dealt with by government authorities.

[7] The 1986 referendum on the Single European Act was consultative but actually binding.

In the modern world, a small state like Denmark cannot possibly in any meaningful and realistic sense be 'sovereign'. Therefore, the 1953 constitution introduced a section (§ 20) stating that: 'Powers vested in the authorities of the Realm under this Constitutional Act may, to such extent as shall be provided by statute, be delegated to international authorities set up by mutual agreement with other states for the promotion of international rules of law and cooperation.' This is the constitutional basis for Danish membership in the EC/EU.

Since the very first days of Danish membership (1973), a major issue has been how the Folketing can make sure that the government, acting in the EU Council of Ministers, does not commit the country in ways that the parliamentary majority does not approve. The solution to this problem is the European Affairs Committee (EAC) (previously named the Market Relations Committee). Its role in Danish EU policy-making is that the minister in question obtains a bargaining mandate from the committee, and that the government provides the committee with timely and full information on EU developments. The specific details with regard to the latter have changed over time (see e.g. Arter 1995; Dag Arne Christensen 1997; Sidenius 1997; Sidenius *et al.* 1997), mainly in an effort to further improve parliamentary control, openness, and legitimacy. The Maastricht Treaty and the associated Edinburgh Agreement did not fundamentally alter the parliamentary control system.

The EAC is involved in all EU matters, and it is the only Folketing committee that can give the minister a bargaining mandate. A mandate requires that there is no majority (in Parliament as a whole) against the position proposed by the government. Thus, the Committee delegates power to the government, which is accountable to the Committee and the whole Parliament. Other standing committees also receive information from the government on matters within their jurisdiction (Sidenius *et al.* 1997), for example the committees on the environment, legal affairs, and taxation, but so far only the Committee on the Environment seems to have influenced the decision-making process very actively. Attempts to use plenary sessions for debates on proposed EU-directives and other measures have not been very successful.

CONCLUSION

It is perfectly legitimate to claim that Danish voters delegate power to MPs, who again delegate power to the government, the ministers of which in turn delegate power to civil servants. In each link there is a reversed relationship of accountability: MPs are accountable to the electorate (at the next election in any case), cabinets and ministers are accountable to Parliament at all times, and civil servants are accountable to their minister. *Ex ante* mechanisms of control exist in all these relationships. Voters have a choice among several candidates with widely divergent policy preferences, a majority of MPs decides which government is acceptable, and ministers direct the work of civil servants. Similarly, *ex post* control mechanisms are found in all relationships. Voters may refuse to re-elect MPs, MPs may force cabinets and ministers out of office, and ministers may order changes in administrative rules and decisions.

In all the delegation/accountability relationships mentioned, agents try to anticipate the reactions of their principals. MPs think a lot about how the voters will react at the next election (relevant information is constantly provided by public opinion polls), and they adjust their behaviour and decisions accordingly. Cabinets and individual ministers shape their proposals according to their expectations about how Parliament will react to them, and civil servants adjust their advice and proposals according to their knowledge of the preferences of the ministers.

All of this sounds as if we are talking about an ideal type of parliamentary democracy. Looking at the real world of politics, however, this description leaves out some important aspects. Keep in mind that voters are party voters, and that MPs and ministers are party representatives. Furthermore, MPs and ministers are not only ultimately agents of the voters. The case can be made that MPs and ministers as political leaders play a very active role in relation to voters, when the latter do not actually have clear preferences or goals. On the other hand, Danish voters do not delegate all their power to Parliament. The electorate sometimes decides issues in referendums. As of 2000, voters have actually rejected six of the fifteen proposals that have been submitted to referendums.

The links between Parliament and government in Denmark are more complex than assumed by the ideal model of parliamentary democracy. The cabinets formed are almost always minority cabinets, which implies that the delegation of power to cabinets is very conditional. The parliamentary instruments of control are generally highly effective. This also applies to the very important EU policies of the Danish government. The European Union is certainly a significant environmental constraint on Danish policy-making, and the EAC attempts to preserve national parliamentary influence over EU policy.

While such national actors as the courts and the central bank play important roles in specific incidents, they are generally not as politically important as their counterparts in, say, Germany. The role of organized interests (including local and regional governments) should not be neglected. A recent study on Denmark and Norway has shown a decline in the use of traditional corporatist institutions (interest organization memberships in various boards, councils, and commissions) in the past two decades, but during the same period there has been an increase in the frequency and intensity of informal interest group contacts with public authorities. In particular interest organizations have increased their contacts with parliamentary committees, party groups, and MPs—presumably because the parliaments of the two countries since the 1970s have increased their power vis-à-vis the administration (Christiansen and Rommetvedt 1997).

Though the delegation and accountability perspective is a simplification of reality, it has proved to be useful for a general understanding of Danish parliamentary democracy. Within the limits established by the present analysis a few conclusions can be drawn on possible agency problems in Denmark. First, Danish voters appear to be well represented by MPs through *ex ante* and *ex post* control mechanisms as well as anticipated reactions. The proportional representation election system—with its low barriers for party representation and preferential voting within parties—assures a high level of representativeness. But it does not always assure a congruence of popular and elite policy positions. Although on some occasions the electorate is called upon to make the final decision in a referendum, most decisions must be made by responsible MPs regardless of whether a majority of voters are in favour. After all, MPs are not only agents of the electorate, they are also expected to govern the country.

Second, Danish MPs decide who should be allowed to form the cabinet. Very often the outcome is a minority cabinet in need of external parliamentary policy support. Furthermore, a variety of control instruments is available to MPs and party groups in relation to any cabinet, but these instruments are particularly serious if applied to minority cabinets. In short, the Danish Parliament is a strong principal vis-à-vis the cabinet as agent. On the other hand, government ministers usually have much better access to relevant information than MPs, which they might conceivably use to their own advantage by hiding or misrepresenting information. In the important area of EU policy-making a standard complaint has been that the EAC is informed too late to really influence the Danish policy position. However, various steps have recently been taken to involve the EAC at an earlier stage of EU policy-making.

Third, individual cabinet members are relatively autonomous within their jurisdictions, although they are all collectively responsible to Parliament. However, it is often discussed whether ministers are able to control their own departments, which often work closely with organized and institutionalized interests. The evidence is mixed and the discussion so far inconclusive, but the need for ministers to appoint political assistants has finally been acknowledged (Betænkning 1998).

REFERENCES

Alivizatos, Nicos C. (1995). 'Judges as Veto Players', in Herbert Döring (ed.), *Parliaments and Majority Rule in Western Europe*. Frankfurt am Main: Campus, and New York: St. Martin's Press.

Arter, David (1995). 'The Folketing and Denmark's "European Policy": The Case of an "Authorising Assembly"?'. *Journal of Legislative Studies*, 1 : 110–23.

Bergman, Torbjörn (1993). 'Formation Rules and Minority Governments'. *European Journal of Political Research*, 23: 55–66.

——(1995). *Constitutional Rules and Party Goals in Coalition Formation*. Umeå: Department of Political Science.

Bille, Lars (1994). 'Denmark: The Decline of the Membership Party?', in Richard S. Katz and Peter Mair (eds.), *How Parties Organize*. London: Sage.

——(1993). 'Candidate Selection for National Parliament in Denmark 1960–1990', in Tom Bryder (ed.), *Party Systems, Party Behavior and Democracy*. Copenhagen: Copenhagen Political Studies Press.

——(1992). 'Denmark', in Richard E. Katz and Peter Mair (eds.), *Party Organizations*. London: Sage.

Blom-Hansen, Jens (1998). 'Macroeconomic Control of Subcentral Governments: Experience from America and Scandinavia.' *Government and Policy*, 16: 323–40.

——(2000). 'Still Corporatism in Scandinavia? A Survey of Recent Empirical Findings'. *Scandinavian Political Studies*, 23: 157–81.

Betænkning (1998). *Forholdet mellem minister og embedsmand*. Copenhagen: Statens Information (Betænkning no. 1354).

Christensen, Bent (1985). *Nationalbanken og forvaltningsret*. Copenhagen: Jurist- og Økonomforbundets Forlag.

Christensen, Dag Arne (1997). 'Europautvala i Danmark, Sverige og Noreg: Sandpåstrøningsorgan eller politiske muldvarpar?'. *Nordisk Administrativt Tidsskrift*, 78: 143–62.

Christensen, Jens Peter (1997). *Ministeransvar*. Copenhagen: Jurist- og Økonomforbundets Forlag.

Christensen, Jørgen Grønnegård (1993). 'Corporatism, Administrative Regimes and the Mismanagement of Public Funds'. *Scandinavian Political Studies*, 16: 201–25.

Christensen, Jørgen Grønnegård (1985). 'In Search of Unity: Cabinet Committees in Denmark', in Thomas T. Mackie and Brian W. Hogwood (eds.), *Unlocking the Cabinet. Cabinet Structures in Comparative Perspective*. London: Sage.

——(1983). 'Mandariner og ministre'. *Politica*, 15: 284–304.

——and Pallesen, Thomas (1997). 'Coping with Leviathan: The Mixed Record for Danish Public Sector Reform'. Paper, Annual Meeting of APSA, Washington, 28–31 August.

Christiansen, Peter Munk and Rommetvedt, Hilmar (1997). 'Parliament and Organized Interests in Denmark and Norway'. Paper, IPSA World Congress, Seoul, 17–21 August.

Dahl, Robert A. (1989). *Democracy and its Critics*. New Haven: Yale University Press.

——and Tufte, Edward R. (1974). *Size and Democracy*. Stanford: Stanford University Press.

Damgaard, Erik (1977). *Folketinget under forandring*. Copenhagen: Samfundsvidenskabeligt Forlag.

——(1989). 'Crisis Politics in Denmark 1974–1987', in Erik Damgaard, Peter Gerlich, and J.J. Richardson (eds.), *The Politics of Economic Crisis*. Aldershot: Avebury.

——(1994a). 'The Strong Parliaments of Scandinavia: Continuity and Change of Scandinavian Parliaments', in Gary W. Copeland and Samuel C. Patterson (eds.), *Parliaments in the Modern World*. Ann Arbor: University of Michigan Press.

——(1994b). 'Parliamentary Questions and Control in Denmark', in Matti Wiberg (ed.), *Parliamentary Control in the Nordic Countries*. Helsinki: Finnish Political Science Association.

——(1995). 'How Parties Contol Committee Members', in Herbert Döring (ed.), *Parliaments and Majority Rule in Western Europe*. Frankfurt: Campus, and New York: St. Martin's Press.

——(1997). 'The Political Roles of Danish MPs'. *Journal of Legislative Studies*, 3: 79–90.

——(2000a). 'Minority Governments', in Lauri Karvonen and Krister Ståhlberg (eds.), *Festschrift for Dag Anckar*. Åbo: Åbo Akademi University Press.

——(2000b). 'Parliament and Government', in Knut Heidar and Peter Esaiasson (eds.), *Beyond Westminster and Congress: The Nordic Experience*. Columbus: Ohio State University Press.

——(2000c). 'Denmark: The Life and Death of Government Coalitions', in Wolfgang C. Müller and Kaare Strøm (eds.), *Coalition Governments in Western Europe*. Oxford: Oxford University Press.

——and Nørgaard, Asbjørn S. (2000). 'The European Union and Danish Parliamentary Democracy'. *Journal of Legislative Studies*, 6(3): 33–58.

Elklit, Jørgen (1993). 'Simpler than its Reputation: The Electoral System in Denmark since 1920'. *Electoral Studies*, 12: 41–57.

——and Pade, Anne Birte (1996). *Parliamentary Elections and Election Administration in Denmark*. Copenhagen: Ministry of the Interior.

Esaiasson, Peter and Holmberg, Sören (1996). *Representation from Above. Members of Parliament and Representative Democracy in Sweden*. Aldershot: Dartmouth.

Eulau, Heinz and Karps, Paul D. (1977). 'The Puzzle of Representation: Specifying the Components of Responsiveness'. *Legislative Studies Quarterly*, 2: 233–54.

Holmberg, Sören (1997). 'Dynamic Opinion Representation'. *Scandinavian Political Studies*, 20: 265–83.

Jensen, Henrik (1995). *Arenaer eller aktører? En analyse af Folketingets stående udvalg*. Frederiksberg: Samfundslitteratur.

Jensen, Jesper Bo (1989). *Liberalisering af de finansielle markeder*. Aarhus: Department of Political Science.

Jensen, Torben K. (1996). 'Partidisciplin og indflydelsesstrategier i partigrupperne i Folketinget'. Paper, Nordic Political Science Association Congress, Helsinki, August 15–17.

Kiewiet, D. Roderick and McCubbins, Matthew D. (1991). *The Logic of Delegation*. Chicago: University of Chicago Press.

Kirk, Anders and Knudsen, Tim (1997). 'Danske ministres parlamentariske baggrund og erfaring i perioden 1848–1994'. *Nordisk Administrativt Tidsskrift*, 78: 81–97.

——and Knudsen, Tim (1996). 'Danske regeringers og ministres holdbarhed'. *Nordisk Administrativt Tidsskrift*, 77: 325–39.

Laver, Michael and Shepsle, Kenneth A. (eds.) (1994). *Cabinet Ministers and Parliamentary Government*. Cambridge: Cambridge University Press.

Mattson, Ingvar (1996). *Förhandlingsparlamentarism. En jämförande studie av riksdagen och folketinget*. Lund: Lund University Press.

Nannestad, Peter (1989). *Reactive Voting in Danish General Elections 1971–79*. Aarhus: Aarhus University Press.

Olsen, Søren-Ole (1988). 'Tilrettelæggelsen af regeringsarbejdet', in *Statsministeriet i 75 år*. Copenhagen: Statens Informationstjeneste.

Olsen, Søren-Ole (1978). 'Regeringsarbejdet og statsministeren'. *Nordisk Administrativt Tidsskrift*, 59: 55–62.

Pedersen, Mogens N. (1987). 'The Danish "Working Multiparty System": Breakdown or Adaptation?', in Hans Daalder (ed.), *Party Systems in Denmark, Austria, Switzerland, The Netherlands and Belgium*. London: Frances Pinter.

Pedersen, Mogens N. and Bille, Lars (1991). 'Public Financing and Public Control of Political Parties in Denmark', in Matti Wiberg (ed.), *The Public Purse and Political Parties*. Helsinki: Finnish Political Science Association.

Pitkin, Hanna F. (1967). *The Concept of Representation*. Berkeley: University of California Press.

Rasmussen, Erik (1972). *Komparativ politik 2*. Copenhagen: Gyldendal.

Rokkan, Stein (1967). 'Norway: Numerical Democracy and Corporate Pluralism', in Robert A. Dahl (ed.), *Political Oppositions in Western Democracies*. New Haven: Yale University Press.

——(1975). '"Votes Count, Resources Decide": Refleksjoner over territorialitet vs. funksjonalitet i norsk og europeisk politikk', in *Makt og motiv*. Oslo: Norsk Gyldendal.

Sidenius, Niels Christian (1997). 'Problems Searching a Solution: The Role of the Folketing in Danish European Community Politics', in Guy-Erik Isaksson (ed.), *Inblickar i nordisk parlamentarism*. Åbo: Åbo Akademi.

——, Einersen, Bjørn, and Sørensen, Jens Adser (1997). 'The European Affairs Committee and Danish European Union Politics', in Matti Wiberg (ed.), *Trying to Make Democracy Work. Nordic Parliaments and the European Union*. Stockholm: Gidlunds förlag.

Sjöblom, Gunnar (1995). 'Partistyre, repræsentativt demokrati og politisk magt i Danmark', in Morten Madsen, Hans Jørgen Nielsen, and Gunnar Sjöblom (eds.), *Demokratiets mangfoldighed. Tendenser i dansk politik*. Copenhagen: Forlaget Politiske Studier.

Statsministeriet (1988). *Statsministeriet i 75 år*. Copenhagen: Statens informationstjeneste.

Svensson, Palle (1996). 'Denmark: the Referendum as Minority Protection', in Michael Gallagher and Pier Vincenzo Uleri (eds.), *The Referendum Experience in Europe*. London: Macmillan.

8

Finland: Polarized Pluralism in the Shadow of a Strong President

TAPIO RAUNIO AND MATTI WIBERG

INTRODUCTION

The birth of parliamentary democracy in Finland is closely linked to the struggle for independence. In the aftermath of the 1905 revolution in Russia and a general strike in Finland, the Constitution was rewritten in 1906. The previous Constitution was based on the 1772 Swedish Constitution. The new Constitution established—for the first time in a European country—universal suffrage. At the same time the old four-estate assembly was replaced by a unicameral Parliament, the *Eduskunta*. The first general nationwide parliamentary elections were held in 1907. In the summer of 1917 the Constitutional Committee approved a regulation on parliamentary governance. Following the revolutions in Russia, Finland declared independence in December 1917. Parliamentary governance was consolidated in the 1919 Constitution Act.[1] Section 2 of the Form of Government Act read:

Sovereign power in Finland shall belong to the people, represented by Parliament convened in session. Legislative power shall be exercised by Parliament in conjunction with the President of the Republic. Supreme executive power shall be vested in the President of the Republic. In addition, for the general government of the State there shall be a Council of State comprising the Prime Minister and the requisite number of Ministers. Judicial power shall be exercised by independent courts of law, at the highest instance the Supreme Court and the Supreme Administrative Court.

The inter-war period saw the gradual consolidation of parliamentarism and the main political parties. The short but bloody civil war of 1918 had bitterly scarred the defeated Reds. Of twenty-three cabinets that held office between the declaration of independence and the outbreak of Winter War in late 1939, all but two were built around bourgeois parties.

We would like to thank Heikki Paloheimo (University of Turku) for his assistance in compiling the government data and Voitto Helander (Åbo Akademi) for his encyclopaedic wisdom. For a general overview of the Finnish political system, see Pesonen and Riihinen (2002).

[1] Finland used to have four different laws which together constituted the Constitution. These were the Form of Government Act (1919), the Parliament Act (1928), the Act Concerning Ministerial Responsibility (1922), and the High Court of Impeachment Act (1922). There have not been any major constitutional reforms. A new unified Constitution entered into force in March 2000. Note that this chapter presents primarily the situation under the old constitution. See www.eduskunta.fi for the current version.

The Second World War changed the political situation in Finland, and the leftist parties were brought into the government. Since the war, Finnish parliamentary democracy has been influenced by a number of different constraining factors. The imperative of what—in popular language—was referred to as the 'electoral district of Moscow', cast a long shadow on almost all aspects of Finnish politics for several decades. More recently, membership of the European Union (EU) has since 1995 added a new dimension to Finnish politics. During the 1970s and 1980s, Finland was also a strongly corporatist country (Paloheimo 1990). Another constraint on Finnish parliamentarism is the role of the country's President.

The Finnish system combines parliamentary democracy with a strong presidency and is therefore characterized as semi-presidential (Arter 1987; Nousiainen 1992*b*; Jansson 1993; Hidén and Saraviita 1994). The President has wide-ranging powers, especially in foreign policy. In its 1917 report, the constitutional drafting commission stated that the executive branch should have a fairly independent position based on the authority of the President. Compared with other Western European chief executives, the Finnish President is a strong political player—provided the person who occupies the post chooses to exercise his powers. The post-Second World War Presidents have used their powers in varying degrees, with Urho Kekkonen (1956–81) testing the limits of presidential power more than the others—sometimes even overstepping the formal boundaries of presidential authority.

The legislative initiative is vested in the President, the Council of State—that is, the government, consisting of the Prime Minister (PM) and other ministers—and individual MPs. Private members' bills are commonly proposed, but less than 1 per cent are successful. New laws generally originate in legislative proposals from the Council of State. A government proposal may contain one or more laws or amendments to existing laws. It is the President who decides, in a plenary sitting of the Council of State and at the suggestion of the cabinet, that the government will present a proposal to the Parliament. Following a submission debate, legislative matters require three readings. In the first reading the plenary sends the bill to a special committee for preparation. No decisions are taken concerning the form or content of the law in this reading. These matters are settled in the second reading on the basis of statements by the standing committee. Finally, the bill must either be accepted or rejected by a simple majority in the third reading. This can take place no earlier than the third day after the second reading. Until September 1992 a bill could also be postponed until after the next election if one-third (i.e. sixty-seven) of MPs so decided. Amendments to the Constitution are left in abeyance by a majority of the votes cast. In the first parliamentary session after the elections, the new Parliament must adopt the bill without material alterations with two-thirds of the votes cast. Constitutional amendment can also be declared urgent by five-sixths of the votes cast. In such cases, the bill can be adopted by the same Parliament with two-thirds of the votes cast (see Wiberg 1994*b* and Rasch 1995 for details).

There is also one category of general rules below laws: The decisions of the Council of State (*Valtioneuvoston päätös*). These are given and implemented without parliamentary involvement. Their role is to specify the implementation of laws and decrees, and they therefore contain only technicalities.

POLITICAL PARTIES

Finland's party system has traditionally been characterized by a high degree of fragmentation. As measured by the effective number of parties, Eduskunta is one of the most fragmented parliaments in Europe (see Lane, McKay, and Newton 1997: 163). Multiparty democracy has historically been rooted in the permanence of five main parties (Sundberg 1999).

There is no extreme right-wing party in Finland. The moderate right is represented by the National Coalition (KOK, *Kansallinen kokoomus*), the Swedish People's Party (RKP, *Ruotsalainen kansanpuolue/Svenska folkpartiet*), the Centre Party (KESK, *Suomen Keskusta*), and the Christian Union (SKL, *Suomen Kristillinen Liitto;* since 2001 Christian Democrats, *Kristillisdemokraatit, KD*). Among the leftist parties, the centre-left Social Democratic Party (SDP, *Suomen Sosialidemokraattinen Puolue*) is traditionally the strongest, while the Left Alliance (VAS, *Vasemmistoliitto*) is a collection of socialists and communists of various colours. The rural and peripheral areas are mainly represented by the Centre Party, the Christian Union, and the True Finns (PS, *Perussuomalaiset*, the political successor of the Rural Party, SMP). The Left–Right dimension is the dominant political cleavage in Finland. Other salient and partly overlapping cleavages are centre–periphery, urban–rural, national–international, language (Finnish–Swedish), environmentalism, and secularism–religion. During the 1990s the national–international dimension increased in significance, which also highlighted the centre–periphery cleavage (Raunio 1999). The National Coalition, the Social Democratic Party, the Green League (VIHR, *Vihreäliitto*), and the Left Alliance draw their support mainly from the urbanized southern parts of the country. In popular support, the Green League is one of the strongest environmental parties in Europe, and in 1995 it became the first green party to gain a cabinet seat in Europe. In practice, the small Christian Union and the True Finns have been politically marginalized. No political party has ever gained a parliamentary majority of its own. The all-time maximum Shapley-Shubik voting power of a parliamentary party group in Finland is 0.4, meaning that no single party has ever had more than 40 per cent of the voting power in the Eduskunta (Wiberg and Raunio 1997).

Although parties are not mentioned in the Constitution, in reality they dominate politics. Finnish political parties are cohesive in their parliamentary voting behaviour (Wiberg 2000). Political parties were first legally recognized in the 1969 Party Act, which gave them a privileged status in elections and in the allocation of public funds. Both extra-parliamentary and parliamentary party organizations receive public funding based on the share of seats won in the most recent parliamentary election. Parties that are represented in Parliament have been publicly funded since 1968 and parliamentary party groups since 1967. Parties without parliamentary representation do not get public funding (see Wiberg 1991a). The public support of parties takes two main forms: Money is allocated to the extra-parliamentary party organization (called party support proper) and also to the parliamentary party groups (called public support for parliamentary groups). Paragraph 9 of the Party Law defines the legal basis for Party support as follows: 'Within the limits set by the state budget, a political party represented in Parliament may be allocated financial assistance in order to support the public activity that has been defined in its rules and general programme. Such support must be divided in proportion to the parliamentary seats won by the parties in the most recent parliamentary elections' (Wiberg 1991*a*: 73). Various extra-parliamentary party organizations—such as students', youth, and womens' organizations—get public money both from the state and from (some) municipalities. These kinds of public support amount to more than five times the sums provided directly to the party organizations (party support proper) (see Wiberg 1991*a* and 1997 for details). The Finnish system of public party support is transparent: all relevant documents are available to anyone who asks for them (no need even to be a Finnish citizen). Candidate recruitment is decentralized and based on primaries in district organizations. Otherwise, however, parties are centralized (see Sundberg 1997). Intraparty politics is run by the elected party elite. Responsibility for day to day party business and bargaining with others is vested in the party executive organs.

There is little variation among the parties with regard to internal decision-making and organization.[2] According to the Party Law (1969) and the Law on the Election of the Parliament (1975) all parties must be democratically organized. The national level organization typically includes the party executive committee, the party council, various working committees, and youth, women's, and students' organizations. The chairperson (party leader) is the overall head of the party. He chairs the party executive and has almost always simultaneously held a seat in the Parliament. However, he has seldom been the head of the parliamentary party group. The leader is selected by the party congress, normally for 2–3 years, with no formal term limits. A party congress brings together delegates from throughout the country and is the main forum for approving political programmes. Congress delegates make active use of their right to submit motions. While party congresses usually meet only once every 2 or 3 years, the other national level party organs meet more regularly—at least a few times a year (Sundberg 1994, 1996).

The parliamentary party group is relatively independent from the rest of its party during the legislative term. The internal autonomy of the parliamentary party is very strong because no other party organ meets on a continuous basis. The parliamentary party presents annual reports about its activities to the party's central organs, and party secretaries and/or other staff from the central office attend parliamentary party meetings. However, the ability of party leaders to influence the reselection of MPs is limited because candidates are selected by district branches. Therefore, major parliamentary party groups always include some troublesome MPs with whom the party leadership is not entirely happy. The independence of the parliamentary party also depends upon whether or not the party is in government. The decision to join the cabinet is made jointly by a leading party unit and the parliamentary party. The party executive is more closely involved in the work of the parliamentary party if a party is in the government than if it is part of the opposition (Sundberg 1994; Wiberg 2000).

---

[2] The structure of Finnish parties is analysed in Sundberg (1994, 1996) and Sundberg and Gylling (1992). The internal organization and decision-making of the parliamentary party groups is examined in Wiberg (2000).

Altogether there have been forty-five cabinets since 1945, most of them including non-partisan ministers. The average number of cabinet parties is three. There have also been six caretaker cabinets, the most recent in 1975. Cabinets have normally been over-sized. During the Kekkonen presidency (1956–81), the usually short-lived governments were mainly based on coalitions between the Social Democrats and the Centre. This coalition has occasionally included the Left Alliance and more often the Swedish People's Party and other small parties. The conservative National Coalition was kept out of the government by the President from 1966 to 1987 due to 'general causes'—read 'Moscow'. While this was not publicly stated, it was understood by all relevant players. Since mid-1980s all parties have been *regierungsfähig*, and governments have stayed in office for the whole 4-year legislative term.

DELEGATION FROM VOTERS TO MPs

Except for some adjustments carried out in 1952, 1955, and 1969, the electoral system used in parliamentary elections has remained stable throughout the 80 years that have lapsed since Finland became independent.[3] Electoral turnout, however, has now fallen to below the West European average.

In 1906 the minimum voting age was 24. It was lowered to 21 in 1944, 20 in 1969, and finally to 18 in 1972. Section 14 of the Constitution states that 'Every Finnish citizen who has reached eighteen years of age has the right to vote in national elections and referendums.' With the exception of soldiers, 'everyone with the right to vote and who is not under guardianship can be a candidate in parliamentary elections' (Section 27).

The 200 members of the Eduskunta are elected for a 4-year term. The country is divided into one single-member and fourteen multimember electoral districts. Åland is entitled to one seat regardless of its population. The remaining 199 seats are allocated to the fourteen multimember districts according to their populations. In the 1995 elections district magnitude ranged from 7 to 31 seats per constituency. Finland's traditional provinces form the electoral districts. Each district is a separate subunit and there is no national pool of supplementary seats. The formula used for allocating seats to districts is the method of largest remainders, and the procedure to allocate seats to parties is the d'Hondt method (Kuusela 1995).

Parties, electoral alliances, and other groups present a list of candidates in the constituencies. The voter casts one vote for one candidate. This means that Finnish voters are not restricted to choosing among political parties. They also have the right to choose between candidates. The electorate chooses 200 MPs from about 2,000 candidates. Helander (1997: 75) describes the situation as follows:

'In spite of the decentralised nature of the Finnish electoral system the recruitment process results . . . in a relatively elitist parliament in terms of social background. . . . [S]trong contempt for

---

[3] The electoral system used in both parliamentary and presidential elections is explained in detail in Kuusela (1995) and Nurmi (1990), and Tarasti and Taponen (1996). Developments until the 1960s are covered in Törnudd (1968). Helander (1997) provides a thorough analysis of the recruitment of candidates for parliamentary elections in Finland. For a bibliography of Finnish electoral studies, see Wiberg (1995).

parties and politicians has not been able to change the picture. The professional politicians with skills and other kinds of resources constitute the pool from which the legislators are recruited. The selection process in all its stages results in a more and more elitist outcome. The party members at the first step in the recruitment process are conservative: ...usually prefer to select male, highly educated, urban persons.... The voters are, if possible, even more conservative...'.

The parties have considerable power in selecting candidates, while voters have the power to choose among these candidates. There is no such thing as a safe seat in the Finnish Parliament (Ruostetsaari 2000).

Candidate selection within parties is based on district-level primaries, with the local branches playing a dominant role.[4] Registered political parties and voters' associations with at least 100 persons have the right to nominate candidates, but only political parties can enter into electoral alliances, technical coalitions that present a list of candidates containing no more names than will be chosen from the electoral district. Alliance partners profit electorally from pooling their resources. Yet, although there are some in every election, such alliances have not been particularly prevalent. Prior to the 1969 electoral law the party leadership was able to control the nomination process in the districts. One consequence was that parties tended to nominate the same candidates in several constituencies. (On Åland, political parties have no right to nominate candidates.)

The 1969 law requires parties to use membership voting as a means of selecting candidates. Voting must be undertaken in constituencies where the number of nominees exceeds the official upper limit of candidates the party has the right to nominate. The parties themselves decide how the primaries are to be conducted, but in practice their regulations tend to closely resemble those found in the election law. If party statutes do not include regulations for this purpose, the directives set out in the law must be followed. The law states that a local branch or, alternatively, that a group of at least fifteen members has the right to nominate candidates. A group of at least thirty members from different branches has the same right. The district executive body of the party has the right to replace a maximum of a quarter of the candidates put forward by local branches (Sundberg 1995, 1997). Local primaries are rarely used in small parties, whereas the large parties use them in most electoral districts (see Sundberg and Gylling 1992; Tarasti and Taponen 1996; Helander, Kuitunen, and Paltemaa 1997, for campaign regulations). The minimum length of a campaign is 50 days according to the electoral law. Parties receive no free broadcasting time for their campaigns, but are free to buy time commercially. The publicly owned channels organize the main political debates at no monetary cost to the parties.

During the campaign, the national-level party organization and leadership primarily act as a background resource, providing the local branches with necessary propaganda and giving the party a public face. The actual work of collecting funds and spreading the message is the responsibility of candidates' support groups. While parties must

---

[4] The role of parties in candidate selection is analysed in Sundberg (1995). The study by Helander *et al.* (1997) includes a thorough investigation of candidate selection in the 1995 parliamentary elections.

report to the Ministry of Justice on their use of state subsidies (Wiberg 1991*a*), there is no legal limit on campaign spending. Though this is very difficult to estimate, it appears that total campaign spending increased more than fourfold during the 1980s and 1990s.

DELEGATION FROM PARLIAMENT TO CABINET

The Constitution Act of 1919 was virtually silent on the issue of government formation.[5] The government was required to enjoy the confidence of the Eduskunta and the President was 'to appoint citizens of Finland known for their honesty and ability to serve as members of the Council of State'. The current wording of Section 60 is:

The Government consists of the Prime Minister and the necessary number of Ministers. The Ministers shall be Finnish citizens known to be honest and competent. The Ministers are responsible before the Parliament for their actions in office. Every Minister participating in the consideration of a matter in a Government meeting is responsible for any decision made, unless he or she has expressed an objection that has been entered in the minutes.

The selection of ministers is wholly controlled by party leaders. The parliamentary party group has no formal responsibilities in ministerial selection, and has historically played only a minor role. Government formation decisions have been transferred from the party executive to a larger body of representatives from both the party executive and the parliamentary party group, but it still takes place within the party machinery (see Nousiainen 1996: 113).

Before the new Constitution entered into force in March 2000, the President had a central role in government formation. After the outgoing cabinet had submitted its resignation, the President invited the Speaker of the Parliament and the representatives of the parliamentary parties—starting with the biggest group and ending with the smallest—to bilateral discussions. During this round of consultations, the party groups had an opportunity to express their views on the future government, and it was the duty of the President to assess which was the most suitable partisan solution.

Taking into account these consultations, the President then appointed either a prime ministerial candidate or a third person whose task it is to continue negotiations—primarily with those parties that she or he would like to see included in the cabinet. These negotiations had three aims: to decide (1) which parties would form the government, (2) the government programme, and (3) the allocation of portfolios. In practice the parties first agreed on the distribution of portfolios, and then the parties' parliamentary groups decided which persons would fill them. However, it was not uncommon for the President to influence the selection of individual ministers. The programme was written, or at least formally accepted, only after these negotiations were completed.

After these three issues had been settled, the President—who had constantly been updated on the progress of the negotiations—appointed the incoming cabinet in the

---

[5] The history, legal norms, and political dynamics of government formation are discussed by Jansson (1993) and Nousiainen (1988, 1992*b*, 1996, 1997). The study by Tiihonen (1990) provides an extensive analysis of the development of governmental power in Finland.

last full plenary meeting of the resigning cabinet. The President's influence should not be underestimated. In 1987, the Centre Party and the National Coalition tried to form a coalition government, but President Mauno Koivisto (1982–94) overruled this bourgeois option, indicating that a coalition between the National Coalition and the Social Democrats was preferable. He got his way due to his formal Constitutional powers.

If government formation negotiations failed and building a partisan cabinet was thus impossible, the President had the right to appoint a caretaker cabinet consisting of civil servants. Since 1945 Finland has had six caretaker cabinets, most recently the Liinamaa cabinet in 1975. Moreover, about two-thirds of the remaining postwar cabinets have included professional (i.e. non-partisan) ministers (Tiihonen 1991).

The new Constitution parliamentarized government formation, reducing the role of the President to that of giving the formal seal of approval to the result of the Eduskunta vote. According to Section 61 of the Constitution:

The Parliament elects the Prime Minister, who is thereafter appointed to the office by the President of the Republic. The President appoints the other Ministers in accordance with a proposal made by the Prime Minister. Before the Prime Minister is elected, the groups represented in the Parliament negotiate on the political programme and composition of the Government. On the basis of the outcome of these negotiations, and after having heard the Speaker of the Parliament and the parliamentary groups, the President informs the Parliament of the nominee for Prime Minister. The nominee is elected Prime Minister if his or her election has been supported by more than half of the votes cast in an open vote in the Parliament. If the nominee does not receive the necessary majority, another nominee shall be put forward in accordance with the same procedure. If the second nominee fails to receive the support of more than half of the votes cast, the election of the Prime Minister shall be held in the Parliament by open vote. In this event, the person receiving the most votes is elected.

The government programme is presented in the inaugural meeting of the cabinet, recorded in the minutes of the Council of State, and published in the Official Journal (*Virallinen lehti*). These programmes have become more detailed since the Second World War (Wiberg 1991b). The programmes have usually contained no more than a few hundred words, but the programme of the cabinet appointed in 1995 contained 4,859 words (including appendices), an all-time high. Ministries are expected to develop parliamentary proposals and implement the government programme, and the cabinet as a whole provides reports on what has been achieved. Prior to a 1991 Constitutional amendment, the cabinet was not legally obliged to present its programme in the Eduskunta. Only twice—in 1926 and in 1945—did cabinets voluntarily present their programmes in the Parliament. The new Constitution states: 'The Government shall without delay submit its programme to the Parliament in the form of a statement. The same applies when the composition of the Government is essentially altered' (Section 62). The statement is followed by a debate and a mandatory confidence vote.

The average lifespan of Finnish cabinets remained very short until the early 1980s. For example, there were six different cabinets during the 1954–8 electoral period. However, only twice during the postwar era—in 1972 and 1975—have mid-term government resignations led to early elections. On both occasions President Urho Kekkonen ordered the cabinet to step down and new elections to be held. Since 1983, all governments have survived the whole electoral period of 4 years.

At times, cabinet resignation has been caused by the action of the Eduskunta—either a vote of no confidence following the tabling of an interpellation, or a parliamentary decision against the wishes of the cabinet. Other factors that have led to cabinet resignation include dissolution by the President, the holding of new parliamentary or presidential elections, internal disputes within the cabinet, and foreign policy conditions (Nousiainen 2000).

Until 1991, the President alone had the right—without even consulting the cabinet or the Parliament—to dissolve the Eduskunta and order new elections. During the postwar era the President has exercised this right four times (1953, 1962, 1971, 1975). A 1991 amendment to the Constitution strengthened parliamentarism by requiring explicit prime ministerial consent for dissolving the Eduskunta: 'On the basis of a reasoned initiative by the Prime Minister, the President may, after consulting the Speaker of Parliament and the various parliamentary factions, and at a time when Parliament is in session, dissolve Parliament by ordering that new elections be held.' (Section 27, 22 July 1991/1074). Section 26 of the new constitution consolidated this practice:

The President of the Republic, in response to a reasoned proposal by the Prime Minister, and after having heard the parliamentary groups, and while the Parliament is in session, may order that extraordinary parliamentary elections shall be held. Thereafter, the Parliament shall decide the time when it concludes its work before the elections.

The most common cause of cabinet termination has been the holding of new parliamentary elections. Prior to the Second World War it was not customary for the cabinet to resign following an election. Since then, however, cabinets in office—regardless of the election result—have always submitted their resignation. Similarly, caretaker cabinets have resigned as soon as new elections have been held. Reflecting the strong role of the President, the cabinets also resigned following each presidential election, even if the President was re-elected. During the past two decades, Presidents have allowed the existing cabinets to continue in office after the presidential elections.

Internal disputes have occasionally led to cabinet termination. As a result of such conflict, the cabinet has either resigned or the party composition has changed because a party has left the governing coalition. The latest example of the latter occurred in 1994 when the Christian Union left the Centre-led bourgeois coalition. Foreign policy imperatives refer to situations in which developments abroad lead to cabinet resignation. The only postwar example is from 1958, when pressure from the Kremlin forced the Fagerholm cabinet to step down (Nousiainen 1998: 252).

Table 8.1 shows the composition and duration of Finnish cabinets since 1945. While the average lifespan of Finnish governments is quite short, cabinet duration has increased considerably since the early 1980s. Since then all governments have survived the whole 4 year electoral term. Governments have as a rule been formed by two of the three main parties: SDP, National Coalition, and the Centre. The cabinets have almost without exception been coalitions, and recently have brought together parties from

Table 8.1. *Cabinet Formation, Cabinet Termination, and Early Parliamentary Dissolution: Finland 1945–2000*[a]

No.	Cabinet	Date of formation	Investiture votes (iv) n.a.	No-confidence votes (ncv)			Confidence votes (cv)		Did the cabinet end with an early election?	Who dissolved Parliament in this case?[b]
---	---	---	---	No. of ncv	Cabinet removed by ncv	Cabinet resigned to pre-empt ncv	No. of cv under spec. inst. mech. n.a.	Cabinet removed by failed cv		
1	Paasikivi III	45/04/17		2	No					
2	Pekkala	46/03/26		3	No					
3	Fagerholm I	48/07/29		2	No					
4	Kekkonen I	50/03/17		0						
5	Kekkonen II	51/01/17		0						
6	Kekkonen III	51/09/20		5	No					
7	Kekkonen IV	53/07/09		1	No					
8	Tuomioja	53/11/17		1	No				Yes	Head of State
9	Törngren	54/05/05		0						
10	Kekkonen V	54/10/20		2	No					
11	Fagerholm II	56/03/03		1	No					
12	Sukselainen I	57/05/27		0						
13	Sukselainen II	57/07/02		0						
14	Sukselainen III	57/09/02		1	Yes					
15	von Fieandt	57/11/29		3	Yes					
16	Kuuskoski	58/04/26		0						
17	Fagerholm III	58/08/29		1	No					
18	Sukselainen IV	59/01/13		1	No				Yes	Head of State
19	Miettunen I	61/07/14		0						
20	Karjalainen I	62/04/13		5	No					
21	Lehto	63/12/18		3	No					
22	Virolainen	64/09/12		2	No					

23	Paasio I	66/05/27	3	No	
24	Koivisto I	68/03/22	1	No	
25	Aura I	70/05/14	2	No	
26	Karjalainen II	70/07/15	1	No	
27	Karjalainen III	71/03/26	1	No	
28	Aura II	71/10/29	0	Yes	Head of State
29	Paasio II	72/02/23	1	No	
30	Sorsa I	72/09/04	10	No	
31	Liinamaa	75/06/13	0	Yes	Head of State
32	Miettunen II	75/11/30	1	No	
33	Miettunen III	76/09/29	0	No	
34	Sorsa II	77/05/15	1	No	
35	Sorsa III	78/03/02	3	No	
36	Koivisto II	79/05/26	6	No	
37	Sorsa IV	82/02/19	4	No	
38	Sorsa V	82/12/31	1	No	
39	Sorsa VI	83/05/06	7	No	
40	Holkeri I	87/04/30	12	No	
41	Holkeri II	90/08/28	6	No	
42	Aho I	91/04/26	18	No	
43	Aho II	94/06/28	3	No	
44	Lipponen I	95/04/13	13	No	
45	Lipponen II[c]	99/04/15	—	—	

[a] n.d. = no data (missing data); n.a. or '—' = not applicable in this case.

[b] The question 'Who dissolved Parliament in this case?' can be answered with one of five options. This identifies the main constitutional actor that caused the early election. We have not coded the formal signatory, but rather the person or body that made the real decision: (1) Head of State; (2) Prime Minister; (3) Cabinet; (4) Parliamentary majority; (5) Automatic constitutional provision (e.g. if it is required when a new President takes office, or, for example, if it is required after the adoption of a proposal for constitutional amendments).

[c] At this cabinet formation, an investiture vote was held. However, since the new Constitution that for the first time makes such a vote mandatory actually only went into effect in March 2000, this vote is not reported here.

across the Left–Right dimension. Such government cooperation is partially explained by convergence in party ideologies, notably in economic matters.

There are several ways in which the Eduskunta can exert parliamentary control over the cabinet.[6] The most spectacular is the vote of no confidence. There are no formal regulations concerning the no-confidence vote. The cabinet can be brought down in three ways.

1. By votes of no confidence, which always follow an interpellation. An interpellation involves two separate stages: in the first stage an individual MP initiates or tables it, and in the second the interpellation is presented to the government by the Speaker. Even though an individual member of Parliament can initiate the interpellation, they are usually put forward by a whole party group, often in cooperation with other opposition groups. A minimum of twenty signatures is needed for an interpellation to be presented to the cabinet or an individual minister. The cabinet must respond within 15 days (Helander and Isaksson 1994; Isaksson 1997). Altogether, 236 interpellations were presented during the period 1918–99. During 1945–90 the MPs tabled on average two interpellations per year, while during the period 1990–99 a total of 45 interpellations were tabled (i.e. 4.5 per year). The last cabinet resignation due to a vote of no confidence following an interpellation occurred in 1958 (von Fieandt).

2. By a vote of confidence initiated by the cabinet. In this case the cabinet makes the proposal, understanding that a defeat will lead to its downfall. In these cases it is important that the Eduskunta recognizes the implications of the outcome. The last resignation through a government-initiated vote of confidence took place in 1953 (Kekkonen IV).

3. By a vote of no confidence during a plenary debate. The opposition can, without prior warning, request a no confidence vote. To date, such votes of no confidence have never led to a resignation. However, resignations caused by internal disputes can be seen as a way of pre-empting a defeat in the Parliament.

Table 8.1 summarizes the behavioural record with respect to cabinet investiture, no-confidence and confidence votes, and parliamentary dissolution. Again, while the great majority of Finnish cabinets faced votes of no confidence—indeed a handful of cabinets faced such votes on ten or more occasions—only two cabinets were actually removed by such a vote since the Second World War. A total of four cabinets ended with the dissolution of Parliament and an early election.

The Eduskunta may also indicate that an individual minister no longer enjoys the confidence of the parliamentary majority. On three occasions, a minister has been forced to resign following pressure from the Parliament. The most recent incident was in 1948 when the Constitutional Committee found that the Minister of Interior, Mr Yrjö Leino, had handed Finnish citizens over to Soviet authorities. President Paasikivi sacked Leino immediately.

---

[6] There is relatively little empirical research on control instruments. Wiberg (1994a) contains a thorough examination of the rules and use of parliamentary questions, while the interpellation mechanism has been researched by Helander and Isaksson (1994).

Criticism of individual ministers is commonplace in Finland. However, since the cabinet operates collegially, it usually stands behind the minister. On occasion though, ministers have also made a strategic decision to resign because they have believed that doing so was in their own and/or the government's interest.

Turning from the spectacular to less visible methods of scrutiny, the parliamentary question is a multifunctional instrument. MPs can table three types of questions: (1) written questions (introduced in 1906); (2) oral questions (introduced in 1966); and (3) questions to the Council of State (introduced in 1989). While the first two options are available to individual MPs, questions to the Council of State must be signed by at least four representatives. Cabinet ministers answer the questions during a monthly debate—the Council of State's question hour—which is televised live on the first Thursday of each month. Questions must be on matters that are both 'current' and 'of consequence'. The Speaker's Council, consisting of the Speaker, the Deputy Speakers, and the chairpersons of parliamentary committees, decides which questions are forwarded to the cabinet. All remaining questions lapse (Parliament Act, Section 37b, 23 March 1989/297).

The written questions are processed in the following manner. The MP or group of members that tables the question submits it to the Parliament's central office for evaluation. The central office sends it to the PM's office, which sends it on to the relevant ministry. The minister always presents his or her answer in writing. Questions are to be answered within 21 days. MPs can table questions even when the Parliament is not in session (Parliament Act, Section 37, 26 July 1993/691).

With regard to oral questions, the Speaker's Council decides when the questions are to be answered in the Eduskunta. The difference between the Council of State's question hour and a normal question hour is that while the former focuses on what is topical and highly political, the latter provides the individual representative with a chance to engage in a dialogue with cabinet ministers. A member may submit two oral questions per week. Questions are useful to MPs for a variety of reasons. They offer them a way to act on a specific issue of importance to them. They also make it possible for MPs to send and receive information, get much-needed publicity (particularly in the case of oral questions), and put pressure on the government (Wiberg 1994a).

The actual impact of questioning is hard to measure. However, the steady increase in the number of written questions shows that members find them worthwhile. The number of oral questions, on the other hand, has been declining since the mid-1980s and in particular since the introduction of questions to the Council of State.

The individual MP can submit three types of initiatives: legislative bills, budget motions, and petitionary motions. These motions do not normally proceed any further than the committee stage, and it is extremely rare for a private member's bill to be passed in the plenary. Members can also give plenary speeches. A recent amendment to the Parliament Act gives members the right to propose to the Speaker that a debate be held in the plenary on a topic of her or his choosing (Section 36b, 26 July 1993/691).

According to Section 44 of the Constitution:

The Government may present a statement or report to the Parliament on a matter relating to the governance of the country or its international relations. At the conclusion of the consideration of a statement, a vote of confidence in the Government or a Minister shall be taken, provided that a motion of no confidence in the Government or the Minister has been put forward during the debate. No decision on confidence in the Government or its Member shall be made in the consideration of a report.

Section 46 stipulates that 'The Government shall submit annual reports on its activities to the Parliament and on the measures undertaken in response to parliamentary decisions, as well as annual reports on State finances and adherence to the budget.'

The committee system is the backbone of the Eduskunta. All legislative proposals must be referred to a committee. Committee deliberation is compulsory and committees must report to the plenary on all matters under consideration except on private members' bills and motions. Committees meet behind closed doors. Ministers do not hold seats on committees. Committees can invite ministers to hearings, but cabinet representatives are not legally obligated to appear in person (Wiberg and Mattila 1997).

Since committees are the fora in which the main scrutiny of governmental initiatives takes place, access to information is a vital part of control. Section 47 of the Constitution states that:

The Parliament has the right to receive from the Government the information it needs in the consideration of matters. The appropriate Minister shall ensure that Committees and other parliamentary organs receive without delay the necessary documents and other information in the possession of the authorities. A Committee has the right to receive information from the Government or the appropriate Ministry on a matter within its competence. The Committee may issue a statement to the Government or the Ministry on the basis of the information. A Representative has the right to information which is in the possession of authorities and which is necessary for the performance of the duties of the Representative, in so far as the information is not secret or it does not pertain to a State budget proposal under preparation.

Finally, the Parliament may bring charges against a minister for unlawful conduct while in office. Following an initiative by either the Chancellor of Justice—whose task it is to supervise the constitutionality of law-making and implementation—the Parliamentary Ombudsman, a parliamentary committee (usually the Constitutional Law Committee), or at least five MPs, the Constitutional Law Committee decides whether the charges are to be processed. The final decision rests with the Parliament. On three occasions— 1953, 1961, and 1994—charges led to a total of five ministers being found guilty of illegal acts while in office.

During the past two decades Finnish governments have been strong and stable coalitions. They have, in practice, controlled the Parliament rather than the reverse. These governments have been able to rule without effective dissent from the Eduskunta.

DELEGATION WITHIN THE CABINET

The lack of effective parliamentary opposition to recent governments has increased individual ministers' freedom of action. Delegation of authority to individual ministers has flourished, while their accountability has not been seriously examined on a regular basis.

The PM is the head and chairman of the cabinet. Another minister is deputy PM, and takes her or his place when the PM for some reason is prevented from attending to his duties as the chairman. If the deputy is also unavailable, then the most senior minister acts as chairman. The Prime Minister takes on the duties of the President when the latter is prevented from doing so. The constitution stipulates that the dissolution of the Eduskunta is now dependent on a 'reasoned proposal' by the PM. If the PM resigns, the whole cabinet is dissolved.

In cabinet meetings five members constitute a quorum. The Chancellor of Justice also attends. Decisions are taken by simple majority rule, with each minister having one vote. When the vote is tied, the PM decides the outcome. Since Finnish postwar governments have tended to be broad coalitions, the PM needs to have good bargaining skills because decisions are often based on deals between the coalition parties. Besides these formal weekly plenary meetings, the cabinet also convenes regularly on an informal basis. Such so-called 'evening school' (*iltakoulu*) meetings date from 1937–9 when PM Cajander sought a forum for more relaxed negotiations, with the goal of making it easier to resolve potential problems.

Finland currently has thirteen ministries, each headed by a minister. The PM cannot appoint or dismiss individual ministers without the consent of the government parties. The cabinet used to include at most seventeen persons, but the cabinets appointed since 1995 have included eighteen ministers. Ministers with a portfolio but without a ministry of their 'own' are considered equal to their departmental colleagues. There are no junior ministers in Finland. The first secretary of state (*poliittinen valtiosihteeri*) was introduced in the Prime Minister's office in 1995. He is not directly responsible to the Parliament. Since 1970, all ministers have had their own special political advisers (*erityisavustaja*), who are to be distinguished from the technical secretaries in the ministries.

Individual ministers have strong influence over their fields of competence. While 'matters of wide importance or matters that are significant for reasons of principle, as well as matters whose significance so warrants' are decided in ordinary sessions of the cabinet, the ministers in practice have wide executive powers (Constitution, Article 67). The autonomy of ministers has increased since the 1970s. Moreover, ministers may delegate executive authority to their civil servants. This delegation of authority from the PM and the cabinet as a collegiate body to the individual ministers and their civil servants reflects the increasing workload of the government and the growing complexity of Finnish society.

While individual ministers have gained important powers inside the cabinet, they also bear a collective responsibility for cabinet actions. The Constitution makes this clear: 'The Ministers are responsible before the Parliament for their actions in office. Every Minister participating in the consideration of a matter in a Government meeting is responsible for any decision made, unless he or she has expressed an objection that has been entered in the minutes.' (Section 60).

Besides plenary meetings, the work of the cabinet is coordinated through four statutory ministerial committees (*ministerivaliokunta*). These do not have formal competence to make decisions on the behalf of the whole cabinet. Their role is to speed up cabinet decision-making by preparing initiatives and putting together political package deals, which the cabinet then, in practice, simply rubber-stamps. The titles and composition of these committees are:

1. Cabinet Foreign and Security Policy Committee (*ulko- ja turvallisuuspoliittinen valiokunta*): PM, Foreign Minister, and six other ministers.
2. Cabinet Finance Committee (*raha-asiainvaliokunta*): PM, Finance Minister, and five other ministers.
3. Cabinet Economic Policy Committee (*talouspoliittinen ministerivaliokunta*): PM and a maximum of eight other ministers.
4. Cabinet EU Committee (*EU-ministerivaliokunta*): PM, Minister of Foreign Affairs, and seven other ministers.

The EU-committee is a newcomer, established following Finland's accession to the EU in 1995. All committees are chaired by the PM. The composition of the committees may change depending on their agendas. The cabinet may also decide to set up additional ad hoc committees for the preparation of specific matters.

DELEGATION FROM MINISTERS TO CIVIL SERVANTS

Due to a general rise in media coverage and the gradual decline of the domestic role of the President, the cabinet and especially the PM have become the focus of public attention and scrutiny. In practice, however, individual ministers have strong authority over their respective fields of competence. The minister controls directly agencies in his/her jurisdiction.[7]

By and large the administration is loyal to the government of the day. Civil servants are career bureaucrats. The administration's legalistic tradition produces an ideology of neutrality and impartiality. Measured in terms of the number of people on the payroll, the state is the biggest single employer in Finland. Public administration is divided into three main levels: national, provincial, and municipal.

The national level administration consists of ministries and other central state agencies. 'While holding the office of a Minister, a member of the Government shall not hold any other public office or undertake any other task which may obstruct the performance of his or her ministerial duties or compromise the credibility of his or her actions as a Minister.' (The Constitution of Finland, Section 63.)

Ministers are aided by a permanent secretary (*kansliapäällikkö*), whose task is to oversee the functioning of the ministry.

Ministries are divided into various sections and offices.[8] Since the preparation of issues and actual decision-making is delegated downwards within ministries, the heads of various sections and offices are influential players. Civil servants can be held accountable for actions they undertake in their official duties:

A civil servant is responsible for the lawfulness of his or her official actions. He or she is also responsible for a decision made by an official multi-member body that he or she has supported

---

[7] For detailed analyses of cabinet ministers and parliamentary government in Finland, see Nousiainen (1994, 1997).
[8] For information on ministers and ministries, see Nousiainen (1992a).

as one of its members. A rapporteur shall be responsible for a decision made upon his or her presentation, unless he or she has filed an objection to the decision. (The Constitution of Finland, Section 118)

As a result of the authority that has been delegated to civil servants, control over civil service appointments, especially top-ranking positions, has become a sensitive matter. Excluding those positions filled by the President, appointments are made by the cabinet, individual ministries, and central state agencies.

The President traditionally enjoyed strong appointment powers until the new Constitution entered into force. Following a proposal from the relevant minister, she or he appointed the top civil servants, including the Chancellor and the Assistant Chancellor of Justice; the Archbishop and the Bishops; and the Presidents and Justices of the Supreme Court and the Supreme Administrative Court; army and navy officials; the directors-general of the central state agencies; and—upon nomination by the Council of State—the provincial governors. Based on the Council of State's recommendation, the President appointed other senior civil servants of the central state agencies; the head and the presenting officials in the President's office; and—upon nomination by the competent authority—the highest civil servant in the Council of State, the Supreme Court, and the Supreme Administrative Court. Up to August 1998 the President also appointed university presidents and professors. With regard to his appointment authority, the President is not formally bound by the recommendations of ministers. The new Constitution reduced presidential powers by narrowing the list of persons the president appoints.

Party politics penetrates most levels of administration. Membership in a particular party can facilitate access to influential, well-paid positions. This trend is particularly visible in top jobs within state-owned companies, central state agencies, and ministries, but also exists at the regional and municipal levels. Patronage is not unknown, although it is clearly not a core element of the political system or a major factor in the relationships between the cabinet and supporting parties. Rather, the political culture is primarily legalistic. The spoils system has never been characteristic of the Finnish administration, and administrative formalism sets limits to partisan advantage. Despite this, the allocation of jobs on partisan grounds, both at the national and provincial levels, is a visible form of patronage (Nousiainen 1996: 123).

Many party-based, ad hoc committees—whose overall composition reflected the proportional strength of the traditional political parties—have been replaced by non-partisan policy advisers (*selvitysmies*) appointed by the ministers. These advisors are responsible for formulating policy advice and preparing reforms. This had led to a decline in the connection between partisan politics and policy formulations, while at the same time strengthening the technocratic administrative apparatus, which is less directly accountable to political parties and the MPs.

EXTERNAL CONSTRAINTS

Due to geopolitical realities, Finland has always been subject to external constraints. Although the impact of the Soviet Union often has been overestimated in the Western literature, it is true that Finns found it wise to anticipate the reactions of the country's eastern neighbour during the Cold War.

Domestically, organized interests, such as labour, industry, and farmers, have traditionally not played the same significant role as in Finland's Scandinavian neighbours. Nonetheless, economic and social policy matters are largely handled in a corporatist fashion. The cabinet is the central clearing house for public policies. As Nousiainen (1996: 126) puts it, the cabinet is the only body with enough resources and information to keep the corporatist conglomerate together. It is true, however, that big corporations, both private and public, sometimes control the government rather than the other way around. This occurred particularly in the 1970s and 1980s when Finland was strongly corporatist (Paloheimo 1990).

Among other actors, the Bank of Finland has had a strong and rather independent position, which, of course, has changed with the progressive implementation of Economic and Monetary Union (EMU). While Finland does not have a constitutional court, there are other legal checks on politicians and bureaucrats. The duties of the Parliamentary Ombudsman include controlling the activities of the courts of law and other authorities. It is also the Ombudsman's responsibility to ensure that civil servants and other persons employed by public corporations, as well as other persons responsible for public affairs, uphold the law and fulfil their responsibilities. The Chancellor of Justice is responsible for supervising the upholding of the Constitution and other legislation. He/she supervises public authorities, civil servants, and other persons employed in public corporations and elsewhere who carry out public functions. The purpose of this supervision is to ensure that all these persons uphold the law and carry out their responsibilities without infringing on anyone's legal rights.

National referendums, which are only consultative, have only been used twice: in 1931 on the prohibition of alcohol, and in 1994 on EU membership. There are two other features of political life that have a greater impact on Finnish parliamentary democracy: the President and membership in the EU.

The President is elected for no more than two consecutive 6-year terms. Until 1982, the President was elected by an electoral college of 300 members (301 in 1982), elected by the same proportional system as MPs. A one-time experiment was conducted in the 1988 election involving a mixed two-ticket system of direct and indirect voting. To be elected by a direct vote, a candidate needed to receive 50 per cent of the votes cast. Since no candidate reached this share, the election was passed on to a simultaneously elected electoral college (Nurmi 1990; Kuusela 1995).

A new electoral system for choosing a President was first used in 1994. If a candidate receives more than half of the votes cast, she or he is elected President. If no one receives the majority of the valid votes, a new election is held on the third Sunday after the first election. In the second round, the two persons who received the most votes in the first election run against each other. The candidate who receives the majority of votes is elected President. In the unlikely event of a tie, the election is decided by the drawing of lots.

The President is closely involved in law-making. First, it is up to the President to decide whether a government initiative will be passed on to the Eduskunta for further action. Second, once the Parliament has adopted a proposal, the law must be signed and ratified by the President. The President can refuse to ratify the proposal, or may choose not to sign it within 3 months.

An Act adopted by the Parliament shall be submitted to the President of the Republic for confirmation. The President shall decide on the confirmation within three months of the submission of the Act. The President may obtain a statement on the Act from the Supreme Court or the Supreme Administrative Court. If the President does not confirm the Act, it is returned for the consideration of the Parliament. If the Parliament readopts the Act without material alterations, it enters into force without confirmation. If the Parliament does not readopt the Act, it shall be deemed to have lapsed. (The Constitution of Finland, Section 77)

Since the proposal can become a law without the approval of the President, she or he has only a suspensive veto (Wiberg 1994b). While the President's role is formally strong, in practice the cabinet proposals and parliamentary decisions are honoured by the President. Presidents have supported cabinets that they have appointed. It is very rare that conflicts between these two state organs have become public. The President and the cabinet are engaged in a continuous web of negotiations: they both anticipate each other's moves.

The President makes her or his decisions in meetings of the Council of State. These weekly meetings are normally held on Fridays and chaired by the President. Ministers introduce their proposals, and their ministerial colleagues have the right to participate in debate about the initiatives. However, the final decision always rests with the President, who is not legally bound by the cabinet position, even when the cabinet is unanimous.

The President also has independent executive powers that fall outside the remit of the Parliament. These are regulated by Section 58 of the Constitution. The President is the Commander-in-Chief of the defence forces, though in time of war she or he may turn the command over to another person (Section 128). Foreign policy used to be the exclusive domain of the President. Section 33 of the Constitution Act stated:

The relations of Finland with foreign powers shall be determined by the President. Treaties concluded with foreign states shall, however, be approved by Parliament if they contain provisions within the legislative sphere or if the consent of Parliament is otherwise required by the constitution. Decisions concerning war and peace shall be made by the President with the consent of Parliament.

Membership in the EU has, however, significantly changed the situation.[9] According to Section 93 of the Constitution:

The foreign policy of Finland is directed by the President of the Republic in co-operation with the Government. However, the Parliament accepts Finland's international obligations and their denouncement and decides on the bringing into force of Finland's international obligations in so

---

[9] For analyses of national policy formulation on EU issues, see Murto *et al.* (1996), and previous work by the authors which focuses on the Parliament's involvement in EU matters (Wiberg and Raunio 1996; Raunio and Wiberg 1997, 2000).

far as provided in this Constitution. The President decides on matters of war and peace, with the consent of the Parliament. The Government is responsible for the national preparation of the decisions to be made in the European Union, and decides on the concomitant Finnish measures, unless the decision requires the approval of the Parliament. The Parliament participates in the national preparation of decisions to be made in the European Union, as provided in this Constitution.

The cabinet is the main actor with regard to EU policy formulation and coordination. According to the Consitution, the Parliament and its committees are formally involved in this process, but the cabinet now acts in a European arena that involves many policy areas and this has made effective scrutiny by the Parliament more difficult.

A related issue is that, with regard to EU matters, the respective power of the cabinet, the Eduskunta, and the President is by no means a settled issue. Particularly controversial is the question of representation in EU Summits. President Martti Ahtisaari (1994–2000) indicated that he did not want the President to be sidelined in the making of national EU policy. Under the compromise reached between the government and the President in 1995, the PM always attends EU Summits and the President attends them whenever he or she so wishes. This practice will continue during the presidency of Tarja Halonen, elected in 2000.

The Eduskunta has been an active and influential actor in the formulation of national EU policy. Instead of setting up a special European affairs committee, the Parliament decided to turn a pre-existing committee, the Grand Committee (*Suuri valiokunta*), into a body responsible for coordinating the Eduskunta's positions on EU issues. The Grand Committee handles first and third pillar issues, while the Foreign Affairs Committee deals with second pillar matters. The composition of the Grand Committee (25 MPs and 13 alternates) reflects the parties' strength in the chamber. The minister appears in the Committee in person before and, when required, after the Council meeting. While the Committee does not give legally binding voting instructions to the ministers, it is extremely rare for a minister to act against its wishes. The Finnish system benefits from the delegation of authority to specialized committees. The standing committees are closely involved in the formulation and scrutiny of national policies from an early stage in the policy process, and the final position of the Grand Committee is based on guidelines from the standing committees (Wiberg and Raunio 1996; Raunio and Wiberg 1997, 2000).

CONCLUSION: FORMAL RULES AND INFORMAL PRACTICES

It would be wrong to claim that Finnish constitutional regulations are intolerably far away from reality. Finland is, in fact, a rather well-functioning liberal democracy. While the Finnish Constitution does not even recognize political parties, in reality the Finnish political system is heavily party-centred and government-dominated. The chain of delegation and accountability in Finnish democracy is influenced by a number of constraints relating to political parties, the party system, and the power of various kinds of external agents—for example interest organizations and international actors like the

EU. The main problems for delegation and accountability can be summarized as follows:

1. The direct link from the voters to the legislators is affected by the electoral system. The parties play a major role in selecting the candidates and organizing the elections. The electoral system favours large parties, and the entry of new parties has been made less than easy by the introduction of formal criteria regulating what kind of organization can be registered as a party. Public funding of parties only extends to those parties represented in the Parliament, which similarly supports the cartel of the established parties and narrows the voters' freedom of choice. Declining turnout can also be seen as a manifestation of voters' lack of confidence in the link between the electorate and the representatives.

2. Compared to an ideal type of parliamentary democracy, the link between the legislature and the cabinet was until the enactment of the new Constitution weakened by the fact that Parliament did not have full control over the formation of cabinet, but rather competed with the President for this control. Although cabinets have enjoyed the support of the parliamentary majority during the last decades, Finland has also had a number of non-partisan cabinets who do not run for re-election and are therefore less concerned with *ex post* accountability.

3. With strong majority cabinets, the executive controls the Parliament rather than the other way around. Majority cabinets can have their way since party cohesion and group discipline in the Parliament are strong. This is sometimes also the case with bureaucrats and ministers. The legalistic and somewhat hierarchical Finnish society gives top level civil servants a strong position that can be used to exercise discretion in implementation, as well as to initiate and propose much of the cabinet's—and thereby the parliament's—agenda. Finland has a particularly legalistic political culture which highlights the role of civil servants, who have to some extent run the entire country as an ideologically homogenous and rather closed circle of pragmatic technocrats. While the country has numerous associations, only trade unions have been able to recruit large numbers of rank and file members.

In sum, while it is fair to call the Finnish political system a well functioning representative democracy, parliamentary democracy in Finland is not without its short-comings. It has existed somewhat in the shadow of a strong presidency and important neighbours. Throughout the postwar period, agency problems seem to have been rather significant in the sense that all actors in the delegation game have had at their disposal many resources to aid them in strategic information concealment. More recently, constitutional amendments have strengthened parliamentarism and reduced the powers of the President. Were it not for EU membership, this process would have increased Parliament's ability to ensure cabinet accountability. However, the development is actually, at least in part, itself a consequence of Finland's membership in the EU, which has begun to reshape Finnish democracy.

REFERENCES

Arter, David (1987). *Politics and Policy-Making in Finland*. Brighton: Wheatsheaf.

Helander, Voitto (1997). 'Finland', in Pippa Norris (ed.), *Passages to Power*. Cambridge: Cambridge University Press.

——and Isaksson, Guy-Erik (1994). 'Interpellations in Finland', in Matti Wiberg (ed.), *Parliamentary Control in the Nordic Countries: Forms of Questioning and Behavioural Trends*. Jyväskylä: The Finnish Political Science Association.

——, Kuitunen, Soile, and Paltemaa, Lauri (1997). 'Kansalaisesta aktiiviksi, aktiivista edustajaksi— Tutkimus vuoden 1995 eduskuntavaaleista ja niiden ehdokasasetteluista.' *Valtio-opillisia tutkimuksia* no. 51. Turku: Turun yliopisto.

Hidén, Mikael and Saraviita, Ilkka (1994). *Valtiosääntöoikeuden pääpiirteet*. Helsinki: Lakimiesliiton kustannus.

Isaksson, Guy-Erik (1997). 'Interpellationsmönstret i Finlands riksdag', in Voitto Helander and Siv Sandberg (eds.), *Festskrift till Krister Ståhlberg*. Åbo: Åbo Akademis förlag.

Jansson, Jan-Magnus (1993). *Hajaannuksesta yhteistoimintaan—Suomalaisen parlamentarismin vaiheita*. Helsinki: Gaudeamus.

Kuusela, Kimmo (1995). 'The Finnish Electoral System: Basic Features and Developmental Tendencies', in Sami Borg and Risto Sänkiaho (eds.), *The Finnish Voter*. Tampere: The Finnish Political Science Association.

Lane, Jan-Erik, McKay, David, and Newton, Kenneth (1997). *Political Data Handbook*. 2nd edn. Oxford: Oxford University Press.

Ministerial Responsibility Act (25 November 1922/274).

Murto, Eero, Väänänen, Pekka, and Ikonen, Raimo (1996). *Sisäpiirit EU-Suomessa: unioni ja uudet eliitit*. Helsinki: Edita.

Nousiainen, Jaakko (1988). 'Finland', in Jean Blondel and Ferdinand Müller-Rommel (eds.), *Cabinets in Western Europe*. Macmillan: Houndmills.

——(1992*a*). *Politiikan huipulla. Ministerit ja ministeristöt Suomen parlamentaarisessa järjestelmässä.* Juva: WSOY.

——(1992*b*). *Suomen poliittinen järjestelmä*. Porvoo: WSOY.

——(1994). 'Finland: Ministerial Autonomy, Constitutional Collectivism, and Party Oligarchy', in Michael Laver and Kenneth A. Shepsle (eds.), *Cabinet Ministers and Parliamentary Government*. Cambridge: Cambridge University Press.

——(1996). 'Finland: Operational Cabinet Autonomy in a Party-Centered System', in Jean Blondel and Mauricio Cotta (eds.), *Party and Government*. Macmillan: Houndmills.

——(1998). *Suomen poliittinen järjestelmä*. Porvoo: WSOY.

——(2000). 'Finland: The Consolidation of Parliamentary Governance', in Wolfgang C. Müller and Kaare Strøm (eds.), *Coalition Governments in Western Europe*. Oxford: Oxford University Press.

Nurmi, Hannu (1990). 'A Theoretical Review of the Finnish Parliamentary and Presidential System', in Jan Sundberg and Sten Berglund (eds.), *Finnish Democracy*. Jyväskylä: The Finnish Political Science Association.

Paloheimo, Heikki (1990). 'Between Liberalism and Corporatism: The Effect of Trade Unions and Governments on Economic Performance in Eighteen OECD Countries', in Renato Brunetta and Carlo Dell' Aringa (eds.), *Labour Relations and Economic Performace*. Houndmills: Macmillan.

Pesonen, Pertti and Riihinen, Olavi (2002). *Dynamic Finland: The Political System and the Welfare State*. Helsinki: Finnish Literature Society.

Rasch, Bjørn Erik (1995). 'Parliamentary Voting Procedures', in Herbert Döring (ed.), *Parliaments and Majority Rule in Western Europe*. New York: St. Martin's Press.

Raunio, Tapio (1999). 'Facing the European Challenge: Finnish Parties Adjust to the Integration Process'. *West European Politics*, 22(1): 138–59.

——and Wiberg, Matti (1997). 'Efficiency Through Decentralisation: The Finnish Eduskunta and the European Union', in Matti Wiberg (ed.), *Trying to Make Democracy Work*. Stockholm: Gidlunds.

——(2000). 'Building Elite Consensus: Parliamentary Accountability in Finland'. *Journal of Legislative Studies*, 6(1): 59–80.

Ruostetsaari, Ilkka (2000). 'From Political Amateur to Professional Politician and Expert Representative. Recruitment of the Parliamentary Elite in Finland 1863–1995', in Maurizio Cotta and Heinrich Best (eds.), *The European Representative. 150 Years of Parliamentary Recruitment in Comparative Perspective 1848–1998*. Oxford: Oxford University Press.

Sundberg, Jan (1994). 'Finland: Nationalized Parties, Professionalized Organizations', in Richard S. Katz and Peter Mair (eds.), *How Parties Organize*. London: Sage.

——(1995). 'Organizational Structure of Parties, Candidate Selection and Campaigning', in Sami Borg and Risto Sänkiaho (eds.), *The Finnish Voter*. Tampere: The Finnish Political Science Association.

——(1996). *Partier och partisystem i Finland*. Esbo: Schildts.

——(1997). 'Compulsory Party Democracy: Finland as a Deviant Case in Scandinavia'. *Party Politics*, 3: 97–117.

——(1999). 'The Enduring Scandinavian Party System'. *Scandinavian Political Studies*, 22: 221–41.

——and Gylling, Christel (1992). 'Finland', in Richard S. Katz and Peter Mair (eds.), *Party Organizations*. London: Sage.

Tarasti, Lauri and Taponen, Heimo (1996). *Suomen vaalilainsäädäntö*. Helsinki: Edita.

Tiihonen, Seppo (1990). *Hallitusvalta—Valtioneuvosto itsenäisen Suomen toimeenpanovallan käyttäjänä*. Helsinki: VAPK-Kustannus & Hallintohistoriakomitea.

——(1991). 'The Professionals of Government: Caretaker Cabinets, Professional Ministers and Full-Time Party Politicians', in Matti Wiberg (ed.), *The Political Life of Institutions*. Jyväskylä: The Finnish Political Science Association.

Tornudd, Klaus (1968). *The Electoral System of Finland*. London: Hugh Evelyn.

Wiberg, Matti (1991a). 'Public Financing of Political Parties as Arcana Imperrii in Finland', in Matti Wiberg (ed.), *The Public Purse and Political Parties: Public Financing of Political Parties in Nordic Countries*. Jyväskylä: The Finnish Political Science Association.

——(1991b). 'Analysis and Politics'. *Studies on Political Science* no. 11. Turku: University of Turku.

——(1994a). 'To Keep the Government on Its Toes: Behavioural Trends of Parliamentary Questioning in Finland 1945–1990', in Matti Wiberg (ed.), *Parliamentary Control in the Nordic Countries: Forms of Questioning and Behavioural Trends*. Jyväskylä: The Finnish Political Science Association.

——(1994b). 'Law Production in Finland: Strategic Considerations', in Matti Wiberg (ed.), Rationality in Institutions, *Annales Universitatis Turkuensis* B: 206. Turku: University of Turku.

——(1995). 'Bibliography of Finnish Electoral Research', in Sami Borg and Risto Sänkiaho (eds.), *The Finnish Voter*. Tampere: The Finnish Political Science Association.

——(1997). 'Suomen valtionapuvetoinen puoluetukijärjestelmä', in Sami Borg. (ed.), *Puolueet 1990-luvulla: Näkökulmia suomalaiseen puoluetoimintaan*, Valtio-opillisia tutkimuksia no. 53. Turku: Turun yliopisto.

——(2000). 'The Partyness of the Finnish Eduskunta', in Knut Heidar and Ruud Koole (eds.), *Parliamentary Party Groups in European Democracies*. London: Routledge.

Wiberg, Matti and Mattila, Mikko (1997). 'Committee Careers in the Finnish Parliament, 1945–1994', in Lawrence D. Longley and Attila Ágh (eds.), *The Changing Roles of Parliamentary*

Committees. Appleton: International Political Science Association, Research Committee of Legislative Specialists.

——and Raunio, Tapio (1996). 'Strong Parliament of a Small EU Member State: The Finnish Parliament's Adaptation to the EU'. *Journal of Legislative Studies*, 2: 302–21.

————(1997). 'Where's the Power? Controlling Voting Outcomes in the Nordic Parliaments 1945–95', in Guy-Erik Isaksson (ed.), Inblickar i Nordisk parlamentarism, *Meddelanden från ekonomisk-statsvetenskapliga fakulteten vid Åbo Akademi* A: 470. Åbo: Åbo Akademi.

9

France: Delegation and Accountability in the Fifth Republic

JEAN-LOUIS THIÉBAULT

INTRODUCTION

Delegation and accountability in France must be analysed in the specific context of the 'semi-presidential' regime of the Fifth Republic. This regime grafts a popularly elected President with extensive constitutional powers onto a more or less conventional parliamentary system in which the government (the Prime Minister (PM) and the cabinet) are accountable to the popularly elected legislative chamber, the National Assembly (Article 20 of the Constitution).

The uniqueness of the Fifth Republic rests on the status of the President. The Constitution says that the cabinet is accountable to Parliament (Article 49) but that the President is not (Article 68). However, the strength of the French presidency goes beyond the letter of the Constitution and is only partially a result of the fact that the President of the Republic is directly elected by the voters. Other contributing factors are an institutionally weak Parliament, the majority system for the election of deputies, and the considerable change in public debate brought about by the development of television (Beaud and Blanquer 1999).

The French political system is a flexible one capable of producing a wide variety of combinations of state and partisan power under the presidential authority. Its hybrid rules can be interpreted to suit varying situations, a characteristic that has given the institutions of the Fifth Republic great adaptability. If the President and National Assembly share the same partisan loyalties, then the President has undisputed power. In such situations, the President dominates the exercise of political power. The predominance of the President is based on three elements: the institutional powers of the President, the President's electoral and popular legitimacy, and the President's position as the real leader of the parliamentary majority. The relationship between the President and National Assembly is thus a hierarchical one. The parliamentary majority, the PM, the cabinet, and the administration act under the leadership of the President.

This chain of delegation and accountability links voters to the President, with the President controlling the PM, the cabinet, the administration, and the majority party. De Gaulle asserted the constitutional doctrine supporting this chain of delegation and accountability in a press conference on 14 January 1964, during which he stated:

The indivisible authority of the state is wholly confided to the President by the people, who elected him, and [...] there is no other authority, be it ministerial, civil, military or judicial, which is not conferred or maintained by him. Finally, he adapts his own supreme sphere of action to those to whom he delegates authority. Nevertheless, normally, it is essential to preserve the distinction between the function and sphere of action of the head of state and that of the Prime Minister (quoted from Hayward 1993a: 24).

Three types of agreement are required if the system is to work successfully. First, there must be agreement between the President and the PM. Second, agreement between the assembly majority and the government, based upon the principle of accountability to the assembly, is necessary. The third type of agreement that is necessary is agreement between the President and the parliamentary majority (Duverger 1985).

If the President and the majority in the National Assembly have different partisan loyalties, then the PM is an important holder of executive power and the President's power is more limited than the authority granted him by the Constitution. This situation, popularly known as *cohabitation*, occurred as a result of legislative elections in 1986, 1993, and 1997. In each case the President lost his supporting majority in Parliament.

The idealized chain of delegation and accountability in parliamentary democracy— the one that links voters to Members of Parliament, Members of Parliament to cabinets and the PM, the PM to cabinet members, and individual ministers to civil servants—has been more closely observed in France during the three periods of *cohabitation* (1986–8, 1993–5, and 1997–2002) than when the President and the parliamentary majority were of the same party. During periods of *cohabitation* the President and government proceed from opposing political camps. The PM has undisputed control of the government. The President retains an oversight function with regard to some particularly important matters such as foreign and defence policy as well as some residual areas of responsibility, in particular culture and constitutional affairs (Duverger 1985; Duhamel 1994).

The 'residual area' leaves the President with important constitutional powers. For example, it includes the authority to initiate amendments to the Constitution by submitting a proposal to the Parliament. After an amendment has been accepted in both chambers of the National Assembly by two-thirds majority of the MPs present, he can submit it to a joint session of Parliament at which it is finally accepted if it is supported by a three-fifths majority of all voting MPs. A referendum is not needed for the amendment to become law. In contrast to this, constitutional amendments of parliamentary origin must be subject to a referendum (Article 89) (Duverger 1985; Mény 1991; Duhamel 1994).

The President also has the right to call a referendum—nominally at the 'request' of the cabinet or Parliament—on non-constitutional changes in the organization of political authority on changes in the economic and social policies and the public sector (revision of 1995), or for the ratification of treaties (Article 11). De Gaulle resuscitated the referendum as a means of appealing to the French people over the heads of their parliamentary representatives. After his success with referendums on Algeria in 1961 and 1962, and the issue of the popular election of the President in 1962, de Gaulle opted for another referendum in April 1969. In this referendum, which was about a variety of issues including the restructuring of regional government and reforming the Senate, de Gaulle lost. Only 47 per cent of those voting supported the proposed changes, while 53 per cent opposed. As he had promised in advance, de Gaulle interpreted the defeat as a personal repudiation and resigned. His action serves as a good illustration of the idea that the President should be directly accountable to the people.

Under the Fifth Republic, domestic policy-making is not fundamentally linked to legislation. The executive enjoys vast decree authorities (Huber 1998). The decline of the importance of parliamentary legislation is associated with the subordination of the law-making process to the government. Article 34 of the Constitution specifies the subjects about which Parliament may legislate. These include civic rights, nationality, the criminal code, tax and currency matters, the electoral systems, nationalization and privatization, and the fundamental principles of the organization of defence, local authorities, education, property rights, labour relations, and social security. Another such area is the state budget. Article 37 states that all matters not enumerated in Article 34 are part of the government's regulatory power (decrees) and need not be submitted for parliamentary approval. For Article 34 legislation, the process is as follows: The PM or individual MPs can propose legislation to the Assembly. The government has exclusive initiation rights with respect to financial matters. That is, MPs are not allowed to propose bills or amendments that would reduce public resources or create or increase a public charge (Article 40). The Assembly decides on the matter by a simple majority of all votes cast. There is no formal quorum requirement. The Senate has veto power, but this veto can, upon the request of the cabinet, be overridden by the Assembly with simple majority (50 per cent plus one vote of the votes cast) (Money and Tsebelis 1995). Note that the votes are valid, irrespective of the number of MPs actually present, unless the President of a parliamentary party group asks for a verification of the quorum requirement. Since 1999, the MPs can vote by proxy.

POLITICAL PARTIES

Article 4 of the Constitution of the Fifth Republic for the first time in French history formally acknowledged the existence of political parties. However, the role of political parties was to be confined to 'contributing to the expression of suffrage'. De Gaulle was determined to avoid the re-emergence of the 'party regime'. He never openly admitted that the operation of the French political system required a partisan parliamentary majority supporting the President (Hayward 1993b). A trend towards party government was associated with the emergence in 1962 of a stable majority coalition of parties in the National Assembly. Moreover, party competition was increasingly dominated by the presidency during the 1960s and 1970s. This was reflected in the evolution of the system from a fragmented and undisciplined multiparty system with no stable coalition towards a two-bloc, four-party structure with lasting coalitions (Machin 1993). In this respect, the development of the Fifth Republic has not followed de Gaulle's conception of the presidency and the political system as being above parties (Reif 1987). Rather, political parties structure the relationship between voters on the one hand and both the President and the Parliament on the other hand.

The first step in this process was the emergence of the Gaullist party (earlier under the RPR label, since 2002 under the UMP label) as a presidential party in Parliament (Cole 1993). With its coalition allies, it held a stable majority in the National Assembly between 1962 and 1981. It brought about an unprecedented consolidation of the traditionally fragmented Right. The lack of an alliance between Socialists (PS) and Communists (PCF) meant that the Left suffered from disunity until 1972. In this situation, there was no plausible alternative to a Gaullist government. The presidential, two-bloc system appeared to reach its peak of development in the 1978 parliamentary elections, when the government's Centre-Right forces and the Left opposition created two similar-sized alliances. The Centre-Right alliance included the Gaullist RPR party and the UDF. From 1978 to 1998 the UDF was a confederation of five centrist and moderately conservative parties (Republican Party, Radicals, Christian Democrats, Social Democrats, and Giscard's club, Perspectives et Réalités). In 1998 the UDF split, now consisting of Radicals, Christian Democrats, and Social Democrats. The new Liberal Democracy party consists of the former Republican Party and the Giscard's club, but does not include Mr Giscard d'Estaing himself who stayed with the UDF. The parties of the Left were the Socialist Party and the Communist Party (Bartolini 1984; Machin 1993).

Since 1978, the number and relative strength of the parties have changed. The subsequent stage of the evolution, in 1981, saw the electoral defeat of the Right and a shift in the party balance within the Left. François Mitterrand defeated Valery Giscard d'Estaing in the 1981 presidential elections, and, in the early parliamentary elections immediately called by Mitterrand after his victory, the Left gained a majority for the first time in the history of the Fifth Republic. Further changes took place in the 1980s. In opposition, the Centre-Right parties faced a new challenge on the Right from Le Pen's Front National (FN). On the Left, the alliance of the PS and PCF disintegrated when the PCF left the governing coalition in July 1984. In 1986, the Centre-Right won the parliamentary elections and *cohabitation* brought about a new stage of party development. The re-election of Mitterrand in May 1988, which ended *cohabitation*, marked the beginning of another phase. Early parliamentary elections held in June 1988 led to no clear majority in the National Assembly and minority government of the Socialists (Elgie and Maor 1992). A new *cohabitation* began after the victory of the Centre-Right alliance in the 1993 parliamentary elections. In 1995 Chirac won the presidency, thus ending the second period of *cohabitation*. However, a third *cohabitation* period began in May 1997 after Chirac opted to dissolve the Parliament and hold early elections. The 'plural left' (Socialist, Communist, and Green) won the election, thus depriving Chirac of his parliamentary majority. He regained a majority in the parliamentary elections of 2002 (after his re-election as President). The party system is now more fragmented, and, since the 1990s, is characterized by a partisan presidency and a two-sphere party system—one sphere of presidential contenders (PS, UDF, now UMP, and RPR), and a non-presidential one composed of parties that do not expect to win the presidency in the foreseeable future (Greens, PCF, FN).

Relations between the government and the parties in Parliament have undergone substantial development since the beginning of the Fifth Republic. The periods of *cohabitation* are an obvious example, but changes have occurred also during periods of stable majority support for the President. There has been an increase in collaboration between the two branches in that the government now consults regularly with the party groups that form the parliamentary majority. Considerable political bargaining between the governments and its parliamentary representatives precedes formal policy announcements. The parliament is often encouraged to make the widest possible use of its legislative functions and of its 'right to control governmental policies'. The relations between the deputies and the government are sometimes institutionalized in the form of a liaison committee composed of representatives of the coalition parties that meets regularly with the PM. These meetings are not free of tensions, mainly due to policy conflicts. Sometimes these conflicts are resolved by bargaining; more often the PM decides.

Most of the French political parties used dubious financing methods until the early 1990s. Things have changed with the introduction of new financing laws in 1988, 1990, and 1995 (Drysch 1993; Avril 1994). These laws provide public money for parties in proportion to the number of representatives in both chambers of Parliament, but also for parties which have presented candidates in more than fifty electoral constituencies in the last parliamentary elections. In 1998 a total of FF 526 million was spent for this purpose. These laws also ban corporate donations and place strict limits and disclosure requirements on contributions to political parties. The 1988 law also has introduced a legal cap on campaign spending. Parliamentary parties also enjoy free broadcasting time that is proportionally allocated among them since the beginning of the Fifth Republic, while non-parliamentary parties get a minimum quota of broadcasting time. Parties are not allowed to buy additional broadcasting time. Since 1977 the publication of opinion polls before elections is restricted; however, this law can easily be bypassed by publishing poll results abroad and citing foreign sources for them. Since 2002, the ban on opinion poll publication only applies to the day before the election and election day itself.

DELEGATION FROM VOTERS TO MPs AND THE PRESIDENT

There is a dual chain of delegation and accountability from French voters to political authorities. First, there is a link from the voters to MPs via the legislative elections. In addition, voters delegate to the President of the Republic, who is subsequently accountable to them, via the process of direct presidential election.

Delegation from Voters to MPs

Legislative elections are conducted using a majority system with single member electoral districts. The left introduced a proportional electoral system in 1985, but the Right abolished it and returned to the majority system when they won the parliamentary majority in the 1986 elections.

Balloting usually occurs twice because run-off elections are necessary in the event that no candidate obtains an absolute majority of the votes cast in the first round—which is most often the case (in 84 per cent of the electoral districts in the 1978–97 period) (Goldey 1998: 552). The most important rule with regard to run-off elections is that only candidates who receive 12.5 per cent of the potential votes (originally 5 per cent of the votes cast, 1966–76 10 per cent of the potential votes) are eligible to run in the second ballot (Cotteret and Emeri 1994).

The legislative electoral system has been criticized for encouraging parochialism. The small electoral districts and the two ballots system invite a multiplicity of very different candidates, thus ensuring that elections are characterized by considerable decentralization and by a preoccupation with very local—rather than national—issues. The average number of candidates who ran for election in the first round of balloting was 8.9 for each seat in 1993 and 10.8 in 1997, and 14.7 in 2002. The traditional French view is that a deputy is first and foremost a local representative and spokesman for constituency interests.

The mechanisms by which deputies are selected are also elements of the process of delegation and accountability. In parliamentary democracies political parties play the key role in screening candidates for parliamentary office. However, in the Fifth French Republic, the role of parties in the screening of prospective deputies is weak. Political parties employ local selection devices. The normal career of the French deputy begins in local government. More specifically, a political career on the national scene usually begins in the *commune* and the *département* (local politics). Local government serves as a jumping-off point for politicians with greater ambitions. Of interest in this context is the fact that there is no clear demarcation between local and national politics. Rather, the two are intimately linked. For example, both local and national offices can be held concurrently (Blondel and Thiébault 1991). In the four Parliaments elected between 1978 and 1988 no less than 78 per cent of the MPs held local offices (Knapp 1991). The practice of maintaining multiple mandates was restricted in 1985, when a law was passed limiting those with a parliamentary mandate to holding only one local or regional office. Nonetheless, MPs who are also mayors or local councillors still spend a large part of their time in their constituencies. Even when they are in Paris, they are busy contacting ministries on behalf of their constituents. As a result, parliamentary absenteeism is a major problem for the National Assembly, both in plenary and in committees.

Such a strong commitment by the Members of Parliament to local and regional affairs has many consequences. The deputy who knows that he will face re-election on the basis of his local success will frequently spend much of his energy in obtaining satisfaction for local demands. In this way the MP constantly brings local pressures into the national scene. Another consequence is that their strong local bases makes it practically impossible to dislodge political figures and tends to turn longevity into stagnation (Mény 1991). Political longevity is of great significance for the process of accountability. Many deputies are repeatedly re-elected—anywhere from two to ten times—for 5-year terms. There is no limit on the number of terms an MP may serve, nor is there a mandatory retirement age. Some deputies serve, without interruption, from their first election to the very end of their political career. An incumbent who seeks re-election in his electoral district is difficult to defeat.

Because of their structural weakness, most French political parties do not provide a sufficiently large and solid basis for the recruitment of candidates to a parliamentary seat. A career in local government in many cases is functional in the selection process for national office. The degree of centralization in this process is quite low. It is, above all, in the UDF that the power of the national party organization is greatly limited by the influence of both the leaders of the party parliamentary group and the leaders of the local party organizations. In the other parties, the local roots of candidates are also strong. In the Socialist Party, selection is concentrated at the departmental level. However, the national party organization is sometimes decisive in cases of conflict, thus permitting it to pursue national objectives. In the Gaullist RPR party, the candidate selection process shows the domination of the national party organization outside of Parliament, which wields most of the decision-making power in this area. However, the national organization must always take into account the strong local ties of candidates as well as the demands of its parliamentary group. The latter wants to obtain an assurance of renomination for all deputies facing re-election (Thiébault 1988*a*).

Traditionally, local connections have been less significant for the centralized and well-organized Communist Party. In the past the nomination mechanism was subject to the principle of democratic centralism and amounted to co-optation. The national party organization thus controlled the selection process in its entirety (Thiébault 1988*a*). In recent years, however, the power of the national party organization has declined, and it is now limited by the increased influence of the leaders of the local party organizations.

Participation by party members in the recruitment process varies considerably between the parties. On the Left, a large majority of members are involved, while in the right-wing parties the percentage is much lower. In both cases, the numbers of those who participate represent a negligible proportion of party voters. Although the involvement of party members in the nomination of candidates for legislative elections has increased in recent years, it remains weak. In the electoral arena, there is not much careful *ex ante* screening of candidates by voters and parties. Under the two-ballot electoral system, it is possible to consider the first round of voting as a 'primary' election comparable with an American primary. The left-wing parties systematically use the first round as a 'primary' in this fashion. The left-wing candidate with most votes becomes the bloc's sole candidate in the decisive second round. The parties of the Centre-Right come to an agreement on a common candidate for the first round often in about 80 or 90 per cent of the constituencies. Despite these variations with regard to party practices, it is fair to say that because there is no real 'primary' election regulated by the Constitution or other legislation, there is no general voter participation in the selection process (Thiébault 1988*a*).

Between elections, however, parties or parliamentary party groups have power to sanction representatives, with a rebuke or a blame, but also with the ultimate sanction of expelling the MP from the party. MPs receive party directives coming from outside Parliament. While the formal institution of a whip is unknown, in most cases the discipline of the party parliamentary groups is tight, on important as well as on unimportant matters. Consequently, deputies have very rarely been expelled from their party for flagrantly defying a party directive. The French Fifth Republic is therefore not well equipped to deal with problems of *ex post* accountability of MPs vis-à-vis voters and parties. It also has a weak capacity for *ex post* monitoring.

Delegation from Voters to the President

The French President is also elected under a majority electoral system with two ballots in which run-off elections are necessary unless one of the candidates obtains an absolute majority of the votes cast in the first round. The two top vote-getters in round one run against each other in the second ballot. The system operates in such a way as to make the elections national in character. Thus, the Fifth Republic has changed the nature of electoral campaigning. In particular, it has acquired a national dimension with the presidential election. Modern communications and an apparent simplification of issues have also contributed to this development. The professionalization of campaigning has also changed presidential elections. The use of public opinion polls and public relations experts is now widespread.

In the early years of the Fifth Republic, the Constitution seemed to give priority to the President's role as non-partisan arbitrator. The President was considered to be above party politics. Over time, however, the trend has been towards an increasingly partisan presidency. As mentioned above, de Gaulle saw a clear distinction between presidential elections, in which he avoided party connections, and legislative elections, when he was willing to explicitly support members of his own party. During his years as PM, Pompidou assumed de facto leadership of the parliamentary majority and oversight of party management. He continued to take a very close interest in party affairs even after his election to the presidency in 1969. Pompidou depended upon majority partisan support as his sole claim to presidential power. Giscard d'Estaing emerged in 1974 as a highly partisan figure, a role that was re-enforced when he created the right-centre UDF confederation in 1978. When he was elected President in 1981, Mitterrand was clearly the Socialist candidate in the first ballot and that of the Left in the second ballot. Mitterrand has been the President least inclined to mask his political affiliation (Hayward 1993*a*). However, Chirac also was elected President as a highly partisan figure in 1995.

In the Fifth Republic, the role of parties in the screening of presidential candidates was weak during the 'Gaullist' phase of the regime. But now political parties more and more control the delegation by voters to the President of the Republic. *Ex ante* procedures, that involve party members in the nomination of presidential candidates, may take the form of careful party screening.

The text of the 1958 Constitution clearly implies that the President should not be held accountable for his actions, except in the case of high treason (Article 68). Traditionally, this lack of responsibility had been manifest in the practice of ministers counter-signing President's actions. In doing so, the ministers signal their acceptance of responsibility for the action vis-à-vis the Parliament, thus relieving the President of accountability. His non-accountability is also revealed by the fact that the President is expected to communicate with Parliament only via written messages, but he does not appear in Parliament and his messages are not debated by Parliament.

The authority of the President is based on his popular election and his role in the referendum process. In theory, he is not politically accountable. However, in practice, under particular circumstances, the President may be accountable to the voters through referendums and early parliamentary elections. First, the President can make a referendum a confidence question. The 1969 referendum on the reform of the Senate failed to give de Gaulle the renewed popular mandate that he sought. Having staked his presidential legitimacy and his continued tenure on this vote, he resigned. Second, the President can dissolve Parliament, in an attempt to secure a new majority to implement his presidential programme. After President Chirac's early dissolution led to an electoral victory for the Left in 1997, however, he did not resign. Thus, the Fifth Republic provides mechanisms other than presidential elections by which the President can be held accountable. However, these mechanisms can only be invoked by the President himself, and over the course of the Fifth Republic, the Presidents have been less and less willing to tie their political fate to the use of these mechanisms.

DELEGATION FROM THE PARLIAMENT AND THE PRESIDENT TO THE CABINET

The chain of delegation and accountability applicable to the French cabinet is dual in nature—it originates from both the President and the Parliament.

Delegation from the President to the Cabinet

In non-*cohabitation* situations, the French President is the dominant figure with regard to the rules and conventions governing the formation, inauguration, and resignation of cabinets. The Constitution clearly gives the President the right to appoint the Prime Minister (Ardant 1991). The President's practice of selecting as PM people who have no independent political power base—the notable exceptions being Chaban-Delmas, Chirac, Mauroy, and Rocard—tends to emphasize his dominance over the appointment process. However, the President's freedom of action is limited during periods of *cohabitation*. Nonetheless, even when *cohabitation* strips the President of any real authority over the appointment of the PM, Presidents have symbolically insisted that the appointment remains their prerogative.

The President is not constitutionally empowered to dismiss the PM. However, there is a gap between the formal rules of the Fifth Republic and practice. The dismissals of PM Pompidou (1968), Chaban-Delmas (1972), and Rocard (1991) all confirm the Presidents' assumption of the right of dismissal. Moreover, PMs have always accepted this right. The constitutional convention that PMs offer their resignation to a newly elected President has allowed Presidents Mitterrand and Chirac to appoint new PMs after their victories in the presidential elections of 1981, 1988, and 2002, before parliamentary elections were held. Again, however, the President's authority with regard to the dismissal of PMs is limited during *cohabitation* (Ardant 1991; Wright 1993).

Formally, the President of the Republic appoints the members of the cabinet on the proposal of the PM. In practice, the cabinet composition is negotiated between the two (Wright 1993). The PM constantly has to contend with some ministers whose loyalties are focused on the President. Moreover, in composing the government, the PM has also to be responsive to the requests of his or her party and coalition partners. The outcome of the formation process is normally a coalition composed of the alliance of political parties that won the legislative elections. Most electoral coalitions have been a way to ensure a parliamentary majority. The negotiations take into account the electoral platforms (election manifestos) of the parties in the parliamentary majority. The negotiations focus on the formulation of a government programme and the distribution of ministerial posts. In contrast to many other West European countries, the distribution of portfolios among the parties is not necessarily proportional to their strength in Parliament. Instead portfolio distribution tends to favour the larger parties (Thiébault 1988b). The political parties have no way of screening potential ministerial candidates. Party leaders do not nominate ministers and secretaries of state, nor do parties have any decisive voice with regard to the selection of their cabinet members. The President, at the proposal of the PM, has a role in the screening of potential cabinet members. The formation of governments in France is not a time-consuming process. On average it takes only 1 or 2 days and leads to relatively stable governments.

In non-*cohabitation* situations the President oversees and directs government work. This is due to his role as the true party leader and eased by the fact that some ministers are very close to him. Moreover, the President can draw on his personal staff, amounting to a maximum of twenty-three civilian and thirteen military staff under de Gaulle, forty civilians and six military staff under Pompidou, twenty-four civilians and seven military staff under Giscard d'Estaing, and forty civilians and seven military staff under Mitterrand (Stevens 1993). Finally, the President chairs the regular cabinet meeting, called the Council of Ministers, but he chairs also the interministerial council, that is, the meeting of the President, PM, and some cabinet ministers for the purpose of discussing government policy in special policy areas, in particular defence and foreign policy. However, in *cohabitation* situations, the PM who controls the parliamentary majority can impose his own policies on even the most hostile President.

Delegation from the Parliament to the Cabinet

In this 'semi-presidential' regime, neither political parties nor parliament plays a key role in the process of choosing ministers. This makes the formation procedure quite similar to those which are characteristic of presidential systems (Suleiman 1981; Quermonne and Chagnollaud 1996).

The Constitution requires cabinet members not to hold parliamentary office simultaneously. In contrast to many parliamentary democracies cabinet and legislative offices are strictly incompatible (Article 23). Many cabinet members are former deputies, but some of them are high civil servants who have no experience in the national legislature at all. Recruitment to cabinet is therefore partly internal and partly external to the parliamentary chain of delegation. *Ex ante* control mechanisms, particularly the screening of cabinet members, are much more important than *ex post* mechanisms.

A newly formed cabinet does not immediately appear before the National Assembly to present its program and receive parliamentary approval (Article 49-1).[1] PM Pompidou argued in 1966 that, at any time, opposition parties in Parliament could test the government's support by introducing a censure motion (Article 49-2). The PM also stressed that the government is formed and exists from the moment it has been appointed by the President. Most of Pompidou's successors have followed this precedent and refused to present their programmes and cabinets to Parliament for approval. Despite the fact that

[1] Article 49-1 reads: 'The Prime Minister, after deliberation in the council of ministers, may pledge the responsibility of the government before the national assembly with regard to the program of the government of if it be so decided with regard to a declaration of general policy.'

no formal expression of parliamentary confidence is required before a government takes office, the cabinets led by PMs Chirac (1986), Balladur (1993), and Jospin (1997) used the parliamentary vote in order to demonstrate that they had the support of the parliamentary majority (Table 9.1). In all three cases this was in situations of *cohabitation*.

The cabinet can be held collectively accountable to the Parliament via a vote of no confidence. The National Assembly cannot censure an individual minister. However, the PM can force an individual minister to resign without bringing about a cabinet crisis. He would do so by proposing that the President dismiss the minister. Note that the President can only dismiss ministers if the PM asks him to do so.

Under the Fourth Republic, France suffered from 'government by assembly'. Those who wrote the Constitution of the Fifth Republic deliberately put an end to the subordination of the government to Parliament. For this reason, the Constitution includes strict rules for the use of confidence votes (Articles 49 and 50). Moreover, the President can dissolve the Parliament and call for new elections. This is also possible in the event of a motion of censure against the cabinet (Article 12). The power of dissolution is a personal prerogative of the President, with a restriction that he could not use it twice in the same year. It has only be used five times: twice by de Gaulle (1962 and 1968), twice by Mitterrand (1981 and 1988), and, in the 'British' manner, once by Chirac (1997). Given French political history, it is not surprising that the new Constitution spelled out in detail the conditions under which the National Assembly could dismiss a government. These rules were quite obviously designed as a substitute for disciplined majority voting (Duhamel 1994; Carcassonne 1996; Quermonne and Chagnollaud 1996).

There are three procedures for conducting votes of collective accountability. The first is described by Article 49-1 of the Constitution. The PM can pledge the accountability of the government to the National Assembly with regard to the government's programme or to a declaration of general policy. A simple plurality in support of the government serves as an expression of parliamentary confidence.

Other constitutional rules that enforce the principle of cabinet accountability to Parliament are based upon the presumption that the assembly majority is precarious and must be supported by procedural devices. The main one is found in Article 49-2 of the Constitution. The National Assembly may force the issue of government accountability by conducting a vote on a motion of censure (no confidence). However, there are strict limits to these votes: a vote on a motion of censure is carried out only if it is signed by at least one-tenth of the members of the National Assembly. If the vote fails, the MPs who have supported the introduction of the motion are not allowed to sign another motion of no confidence for the remainder of the parliamentary session (such a session is about 9 months). Moreover, forty-eight hours must pass between the introduction of a motion of no confidence and the vote, allowing for all kinds of 'defence' measures from the side of the government. All this does not encourage the frequent use of this parliamentary instrument, as can be seen from the figures in Table 9.1.

Under this procedure, the government is deemed to have retained the assembly's confidence unless an absolute majority of all members of the assembly supports a censure motion. Only votes favourable to the motion are counted. Under the Fifth Republic, the National Assembly passed a motion of censure only once—the procedure was used to bring down the first Pompidou government in October 1962 (Table 9.1).

Table 9.1. *Cabinet Formation, Cabinet Termination, and Early Parliamentary Dissolution: France 1959–2000*[a]

No.	Cabinet	Date of formation	Investiture votes (iv)[b]	No-confidence votes (ncv)			Confidence votes (cv)[c]		Did the cabinet end with an early election?	Who dissolved Parliament in this case?[d]
			n.a.	No. of ncv	Cabinet removed by ncv	Cabinet resigned to pre-empt ncv	No. of cv under spec. inst. mech.	Cabinet removed by failed cv		
1	Debré	59/01/08		2	No		4	No		
2	Pompidou I	62/04/14		2	Yes		3	No	Yes	Head of State
3	Pompidou II	62/11/28		1	No		0			
4	Pompidou III	66/01/08		1	No		3	No		
5	Pompidou IV	67/04/06		3	No		0		Yes	Head of State
6	Couve de Murville	68/07/10		0			0			
7	Chaban-Delmas	69/06/20		1	No		0			
8	Messmer I	72/07/05		1	No		0			
9	Messmer II	73/04/02		2	No		0			
10	Chirac I	74/05/27		2	No		0			
11	Barre I	76/08/25		0			1	No		
12	Barre II	78/04/03		0			1	No		
13	Mauroy I	81/05/21		0			0		Yes	Head of State
14	Mauroy II	81/06/22		5	No		6	No		

15	Fabius	84/07/17	1	No	4	No	
16	Chirac II	86/03/20	1	No	8	No	
17	Rocard I	88/05/10	0		0	Yes	Head of State
18	Rocard II	88/06/23	6	No	28	No	
19	Mme. Cresson	91/05/16	2	No	8	No	
20	Beregovoy	92/04/02	2	No	4	No	
21	Balladur	93/03/29	0		1	No	
22	Juppé	95/05/17	0		0	Yes	Head of State
23	Jospin	97/06/02	—		—	—	—

[a] n.d. = no data (missing data); n.a. or '—' = not applicable in this case.

[b] In France, there is no investiture vote for the cabinet. The PM, after deliberation in the Council of Ministers (cabinet), may (but is not obliged to) ask for a supporting vote when he pledges the responsibility of the government or presents a declaration of general policy to the Parliament. However, these votes are not reported since the table is designed only to record investiture votes.

[c] The PM may, after deliberation in the Council of Ministers, pledge the government's responsibility on the vote of a bill. The text shall be considered as adopted, unless a motion of censure is voted (Article 49-3 in the Constitution).

[d] The question 'Who dissolved Parliament in this case?' can be anwered with one of five options. This identifies the main constitutional actor that caused the early election. We have not coded the formal signatory, but rather the person or body that made the real decision: (1) Head of State; (2) Prime Minister; (3) Cabinet; (4) Parliamentary majority; (5) Automatic constitutional provision (e.g. if it is required when a new President takes office, or, for example, if it is required after the adoption of a proposal for constitutional amendments).

Another way of holding the government accountable by Parliament is described in Article 49-3 of the Constitution. In this case, the government makes the adoption of a particular bill an issue of confidence. The PM can pledge the accountability of the government before the National Assembly in a vote on legislation for which there is clearly no parliamentary majority. Under this procedure, if no censure motion is introduced or if a censure motion fails to get an absolute majority of votes, then the bill is said to be passed (Article 49-3 of the Constitution). This procedure thus favours the government. It allows for the adoption of a bill for which there is no legislative support whenever an absolute majority of representatives does not want to defeat the government. The deputies know that a vote of censure is likely to lead to the dissolution of the Assembly. This procedure is used only in specific circumstances, including when the parliamentary majority is divided (the Barre government between 1978 and 1981), when the parliamentary majority is only a relative one (the Rocard, Cresson, Bérégovoy cabinets between 1988 and 1993), and when the government is under considerable time pressure (the Chirac government between 1986 and 1988). Rocard used the procedure on twenty-eight proposals in 36 months. Edith Cresson used it on eight proposals in 10 months, and Chirac employed it eight times in 24 months of *cohabitation* (Table 9.1).

Under the Fifth Republic, only opponents vote on confidence and no-confidence motions (Article 49-2 and 49-3). The government does not seek explicit, positive manifestations of confidence from its parliamentary supporters, only implicit, negative acquiescence. This helps the government survive when the majority is divided (as with the Barre governments) or when the government is a minority one (as with the Rocard, Cresson, and Bérégovoy cabinets). This survival is ultimately made possible by a procedural device that counts all non-hostile votes as tacit votes of support. However, it is also fair to say that this draconian safeguard has been superfluous throughout most of the history of Fifth Republic because loyal majorities in the National Assembly have supported stable governments (Huber 1996). For example, because of the loyalty of the left 'plural majority', PM Jospin never used Article 49–3 during his five years in office 1997–2002.

The government can also be held accountable to the Parliament through the use of particular instruments, including parliamentary questions and investigation committees. One way in which Members of Parliament can extract information from the government is to put written and oral questions to the ministers. The government responds to oral questions in the National Assembly every week. Since 1974, due to the initiative of then newly elected President Giscard d'Estaing, this question and answer session is no longer an unproductive reading of prepared and written statements. Instead it is characterized by much of the lively give-and-take typical of the weekly question periods in the British Parliament. Question sessions in the National Assembly attract more viewers than other meetings and both the majority and opposition makes good use of time. A fundamental difference between the Fourth and Fifth Republics is that these question sessions have not become a new 'interpellation' procedure—an instrument used by deputies under the Fourth Republic to harass the government. The existing Standing Orders of the National Assembly (1959) state that exchanges between deputies and the government taking place during a question period may not lead to a vote or a resolution. In the Fifth Republic, cabinets are more likely to resign because of pressure from (or decisions by) the President than because of events that take place in the National Assembly.

The procedure of controlling the executive machinery through the use of ad hoc committees of investigation has rarely been used effectively. In most cases, when the opposition calls for an investigation of something it considers scandalous or improper, the government is able to use its numerical strength in the Parliament to prevent the establishment of a committee of investigation. The investigative procedure is also strictly regulated. The parliamentary majority has the exclusive right to appoint the members of such committees. However, committees cannot ban the press from attending hearings and committee findings must be made public. The President and the PM attempt to prevent Parliament from subjecting their policies to careful scrutiny. Hence, these mechanisms designed to contain moral hazard have hardly been used in the Fifth Republic.

DELEGATION FROM CABINET AND THE PRESIDENT TO INDIVIDUAL MINISTERS

Individual ministers head a ministry. There are no ministers without portfolio (Thiébault 2000). In addition, ministers also collectively participate in the formulation and management of governmental policy. In periods of *cohabitation*, the decision rule in the cabinet is consensus as defined by the PM. However, at other times, when the same party/coalition hold all branches of national government, the content and existence of consensus is defined by the President. This is probably also the general rule intended by the makers of the Constitution.

Since the beginning of the Fifth Republic, greater importance has been attached to ministers' management of departments than to their political and governmental functions. The autonomy and therefore authority of ministers has declined as a result. The cabinet is primarily an administrative body (Thiébault 1988b). Ministers tend to relate to the PM, and also to the President, in a manner akin to that of civil servants. The PM's instructions (*directives*) to individual ministers are often requests to prepare either decrees (executive decisions) to be submitted to the cabinet (Council of Ministers), laws to be sent to the Parliament, or instructions about the preparation of the budget. Individual ministers' power of regulation is largely restricted to implementation of laws, decrees, or budgetary matters (Thiébault 1994).

Delegation from the PM to Individual Ministers

Individual ministers must report to or get the approval of the PM and/or other cabinet members (e.g. the finance minister) for bill drafts within their own jurisdictions. They cannot formulate cabinet policy on their own. The PM has the authority to give instructions (*directives*) to all individual ministers. He or she leads the government by setting out the rules of conduct those individual ministers' must follow. The subordinate character of a ministerial department is underlined by the fact that the PM has the right to dismiss ministers.

The finance minister has a stronger decision-making position. His functions include supervising the activities of other ministers. He must also approve all draft bills involving public expenditures. He shares with the PM the responsibility for reviewing all public spending and thereby of all governmental activities. He also has at his service a financial controller in each ministry. These controllers are responsible for supervising all actions involving public expenditure and for authorizing disbursements.

The main instrument for PM control is the PM's office, which includes the general secretariat of the government and the PM's ministerial staff. The former prepares the agenda for meetings of the cabinet (the Council of Ministers) and the various inter-ministerial meetings. It also prepares notes for the PM and informs him about matters to be discussed. The general secretary attends meetings of the cabinet and keeps the minutes. He notifies all relevant ministers about decisions taken during the Council meetings. Ministers who are responsible for carrying out decisions are required to send the general secretary copies of all their instructions. This makes it possible for the general secretariat to follow up on the implementation of government decisions for the PM. The PM also has an important personal staff. The director of this staff has general duties, notably liaison with the general secretary of the presidency, with whom there is plenty of scope for conflict, though close cooperation is essential (Elgie and Machin 1991; Schramek 2001).

The jurisdictions of all individual ministers are mutually exclusive. Each ministry has its own assigned area of competence and tends to jealously protect it. This leads to such extreme compartmentalization that it is absolutely essential that individual ministers participate in meetings designed to ensure the coordination of government action. Individual ministers have no authority to formulate cabinet policy. Rather, they participate in the making of policies within their field of competence. The most important aspects of policies are then presented at interministerial meetings before policy proposals go on to the full cabinet. Final decisions on matters requiring legislation are normally taken by the cabinet (the Council of Ministers).

Delegation from the President to Individual Ministers

The PM must constantly deal with the reality that some ministers give their loyalty primarily to the presidency. It is also the case that the Constitution gives the President the main responsibility for French foreign and defence policies. He sets policy guidelines and makes decisions on matters of national and international consequence. The minister of foreign affairs is only responsible for the detailed implementation and defence of the President's policy and for routine diplomatic work. The cabinet seldom discusses foreign affairs, though it receives a weekly review of the international situation from the Foreign Minister. The President controls also defence policy through his position as chairman of the defence council. The main responsibility of the minister of defence is to execute the President's decisions (Menon 1994). The President has great freedom over the appointment of the ministers of foreign affairs and defence. Presidents have used their authority to appoint either politically friendly experts (such as diplomats) or personal friends. During periods of *cohabitation* the President seeks to negotiate the appointment of 'technocrats' to these areas, in which he is determined to defend his prerogatives (Wright 1993).

The President may place political and personal friends in other ministerial posts. A number of ministers have been recruited directly from the President's staff at the Elysée. The President might encourage direct links between individual ministers and the Elysée as a way to bypass the PM's control. The PM can therefore rarely count on the unswerving support of his ministerial colleagues. Except during periods of *cohabitation*, the PM's authority over the government is weakened by the President's control of the government's agenda. The President's programme forms the basis of government action. The President might even intervene to impose his wishes with regard to a policy matter without informing the government—or even against the wishes of the ministers most concerned.

The complexities of modern government require coordination between ministries. France has created a system of semi-permanent conflict resolution mechanisms for the purpose of coordinating policy prior to its consideration by the cabinet (Quermonne and Chagnollaud 1996). There are basically three types of institutions. First, there are interministerial *meetings* composed of senior civil servants. These are held at the PM's residence at Matignon, with a member of the PM's ministerial cabinet serving as chairman. A member of the President's staff represents the Elysée. These meetings end with the PM's representative summarizing the discussion. If agreement cannot be reached, the proposals to be decided upon are then sent to the second level, the interministerial *committee*. This committee is usually composed of ministers and secretaries of state. Secretaries of state are junior ministers to whom the respective minister delegates specific tasks. They do not belong to the cabinet and they are subject to orders from their respective minister and the PM. The PM chairs the interministerial committee. It is the PM's main instrument for resolving conflicts.

The third type of cabinet committee, the interministerial *council*, is the most exclusive of these coordinating bodies. It usually consists of a few senior ministers who meet at the Elysée under the chairmanship of the President. The President, the PM, the ministers, and the ministerial cabinet spend a great deal of time at interministerial council meetings, except during periods of *cohabitation*.

DELEGATION FROM MINISTERS TO CIVIL SERVANTS

The Fifth Republic tends to place a great reliance on *ex ante* accountability mechanisms, especially the prior screening of high civil servants. The Constitution involves the President (with the PM) in making appointments of high civil servants. A spoils system at the summit of the French state has been developed. Because both the President and the PM must agree on these appointments, disagreements have to be resolved during the years of *cohabitiation*.

The relationship between ministers and civil servants within a ministry is a direct chain of command. Executive agencies are not autonomous. In practice, the autonomy of individual ministers also appears to be constrained by top bureaucrats in the ministries, but this power does not have a real constitutional basis. Rather it stems from the traditionally strong role of these bureaucrats who tend to have similar training and background and enjoy high status in French politics (Rouban 1999). Nevertheless, formally speaking, heads of departmental divisions are usually directly responsible to the department minister. The interposition of a secretary-general—a bureaucratic head of a ministry similar to the British permanent secretary—between department heads and the minister has been avoided (except in the ministry of foreign affairs).

The direct chain of command reinforces minister control over the political appointment of high civil servants. The minister can make discretionary appointments—although the cabinet formally appoints heads of divisions, and the President and/or PM sometimes get involved in individual appointments. If differences of opinion develop between an individual minister and the head of a division within the ministry, then the situation is usually resolved by promoting the division head or transferring him/her to an equivalent post elsewhere.

Since the beginning of the Fifth Republic, top civil servants have prepared important policy decisions—down to the smallest detail—without consulting Parliament or other elective bodies. They have thus assumed de facto decision-making power over many issues, and as a result there is little or no discussion of these matters in Parliament.

In the relationship between ministers, members of their staff, and administrative personnel, the boundaries separating the initiation and execution of policies are necessarily vague. Among these three groups there exists a considerable degree of homogeneity with regard to function and mentality (Marcou and Thiébault 1996). Both ministers and the civil servants become directly involved in establishing political priorities and thereby in decision-making. However, in many respects, the restoration of governmental authority has strengthened executive control of top civil servants.

Ministerial staffing has been developed in order to help individual ministers manage their departments. All ministers have a staff (usually from ten to twenty persons) that provides the crucial link between the political and administrative executive. The lack of permanent secretaries in most French ministries means that the task of coordinating and directing the work of the various divisions is the responsibility of the ministerial staff. The fact that decision-making has become a more exclusively executive matter under the Fifth Republic has meant that the key members of the ministerial staff are those advisers borrowed from the civil service who are concerned with preparing, coordinating, and supervising the implementation of policy. The overwhelming majority of the members of ministerial staffs are recruited from the senior civil service. About three-quarters of the holders of the most important posts of director and special adviser are recruited from among the 'grand corps', notably from the group of administrative lawyers of the Council of State (see below) and the economic experts in the finance *inspectorate*. This is clear evidence that these two bodies compose a parallel hierarchy to the heads of the ministry's divisions. In addition, it reflects the fact that in France it is considered more important to ensure bureaucratic accountability to ministers than ministerial accountability to Parliament (Beaud and Blanquer 1999).

The director of the ministerial staff has become the de facto element of administrative coordination within the ministry. He receives all documents to be signed by the minister. It is his task to decide which he can deal with himself and which must be referred to the minister due to their political importance. Instructions to senior civil servants from the director of the ministerial staff are considered to be from the minister himself. As well as coordination within the ministry, the director of the minister's staff is also responsible for preparatory coordination between ministries. When a minister cannot attend an interministerial meeting, the director of his staff usually attends in his place. The bulk of ministerial staff consists of specialist advisers and *chargés de mission* that have responsibility for particular areas of the ministry's work.

The staff members perform four main functions. First, they prepare memoranda for the minister on matters to be considered in cabinet. This work might involve conducting basic research on particular questions or actually deciding what the ministry policy ought to be. Second, with regard to the area for which they have responsibility, they coordinate the work of the ministry and conduct its relations with other ministries, the latter of which involves participating in numerous meetings with members of other ministerial staffs. They also meet with interest groups seeking to influence the ministry as well as groups whose support the ministry wants to mobilize in support of ministry policy. Third, they draft outlines of the minister's speeches and interviews. Finally, advisers and *chargés de mission* supervise the implementation of the ministry's policies, which involves maintaining close and frequent contact with senior officials in the ministry (Quermonne and Chagnollaud 1996). The capacity of individual ministers to actually monitor the behaviour of their civil servants, to control them at this stage of the chain of delegation, has become more important. This, in turn, has increased the importance of the ministers' staff.

EXTERNAL CONSTRAINTS

Institutions that are outside the parliamentary and bureaucratic chains of delegation insert themselves in the process of national decision-making. The importance of the President and the use of referendums have already been discussed. Moreover, the President has considerable decree powers under Article 16 of the Constitution, which, however, have been used only once (in 1961) (Huber 1998). Other institutions of interest in this regard include (constitutional) courts, central banks, and international organizations, the latter of which increasingly intervene in the delegation process and limit actors' freedom of action.

These developments have multiplied the constraints on the chain of delegation in France. The influence of the Constitutional Council is now well documented. The establishment of a Constitutional Council in 1958 was part of an attempt by the makers of the new Constitution to protect the innovations of the Fifth Republic from future efforts to undermine them. The champions of the traditional doctrine that the Parliament is the repository of national sovereignty were going to be prevented from successfully eroding the constitutional constraints imposed on Parliament. To this end, the Constitutional Council was created. A novelty in French parliamentary democracy, it was given the authority to decide whether laws passed by Parliament are unconstitutional. A decision in 1971 expanded the Council's power by making it a guardian of civil liberty capable of imposing respect for constitutional rights even on the President and the government. The Constitutional Council has thus become a constraint on the executive organs of government, which are required to act in conformity with the values enshrined in the Constitution and its preamble.

There is also a change in the supervision of policies in some sectors from the State to independent administrative authorities, such as the Higher Council of Broadcasting (CSA).

Government control over the Bank of France was increased by legislation in 1936 and by nationalization of the Bank in 1945. Complete government control over the Bank of France put 'monetary power' at the disposal of the political interests of the cabinet. Relations between the Bank of France and the finance minister have often been even closer than institutional ties suggest because the Bank's governor has often been a finance inspector or a former finance ministry official. However, more recently the Bank has begun to show signs of greater autonomy. The recent more influential position of the governor of the Bank of France can be explained by his long tenure in office and by the fact that he now, under European monetary integration, possesses the autonomous powers of the German *Bundesbank* President (Elgie and Thompson 1998).

The policy process has increasingly adopted an European dimension. The European Union has imposed a general constraint on the cabinet and has set strict parameters within which policies can be developed. In recent years, the French cabinet has lost much of its power to control budgetary and monetary policies.

De Gaulle's conception of a Europe of sovereign states was built on the notion of EC/EU cooperation controlled by national governments. The French position turned more pro-federal under Mitterrand, but French EU policy is primarily seen as a matter for the President and the government and not for the Parliament.

Over the years, the French government has maintained close control over its experts in Brussels. The general secretariat of the interministerial committee for European cooperation (SGCI) sends instructions to Brussels early in the policy formulation and negotiation process. The SGCI is headed by a senior civil servant that is accountable to the PM. Highly centralized administrative coordination also takes place, with a minister especially responsible for European affairs assuming political responsibilities as well. Under the President, the PM seeks to assert control over European policy through the interministerial committee for European cooperation, which is charged with responsibility for high policy. The foreign affairs minister has sought to monopolize supervision of relations between the EC commission and all French ministries. The French foreign ministry plays a decisive role in the key EU decision-making bodies—the Council of Ministers and the Committee of Permanent Representatives—via monthly meetings of EU foreign ministers and the ministry's influence over the preparation and exposition of agreed national positions in France's permanent delegation. The French Parliament has only recently been given a measure of involvement in French EU policy. For years it has only been provided with routine information about the decision-making process. However, some measures have been adopted to better associate the French Parliament with European policies and to introduce some possibilities for control. Accordingly, the cabinet must subject to Parliament's European proposals, when they are likely to affect French legislation. Parliamentary committees for EU affairs have been created and are consulted on such proposals. This system has created an *ex ante* control, before EU rule-making.

CONCLUSION

France has a flexible political system capable of producing various combinations of state and partisan power. If the President and majority in the National Assembly come from the same political party/group, then the relation between them is a hierarchical one. The parliamentary majority, the PM, the government, and the administration all act under the leadership of the President. The idealized chain of delegation and accountability in parliamentary democracy is not observed. Of particular importance is the fact that the President is not accountable to the Parliament. This situation is aggravated by the weakness of parliamentary control. This is a fundamental difference between the French and American systems, the latter of which has been sometimes described as been a 'congressional' regime.

However, if the President and National Assembly majority are of different partisan loyalties, *cohabitation* is conducive to the emergence of the PM as the dominant executive power. In this case the President's power is limited to that given him in the Constitution. The idealized chain of delegation and accountability under a parliamentary regime (which links voters to Members of Parliament, Members of Parliament to the cabinet and the PM, a PM to cabinet members, and ministers to civil servants) is then more closely observed. The government is then collectively accountable to the Parliament rather than to the President.

REFERENCES

Ardant, Philippe (1991). *Le Premier Ministre en France*. Paris: Montchrestien.

Avril, Pierre (1994). 'Regulation of Political Finance in France', in Herbert E. Alexander and Rei Shiratori (eds.), *Comparative Political Finance Among the Democracies*. Boulder: Westview Press.

Bartolini, Stefano (1984). 'Institutional Constraints and Party Competition in the French Party System'. *West European Politics*, 7(4): 103–27.

Beaud, Olivier and Blanquer, Jean-Michael (1999). *La responsabilité des élus*. Paris: Fayard.

Blondel, Jean and Thiébault, Jean-Louis (eds.) (1991). *The Profession of Government Minister in Western Europe*. London: Macmillan.

Carcassonne, Guy (1996). *La Constitution*. Paris: Le Seuil.

Chagnollaud, Dominique and Quermonne, Jean-Louis (1996). *Le Gouvernement de la France sous la 5e République*. Paris: Fayard.

Cole, Alistair (1993). 'The Presidential Party and the Fifth Republic'. *West European Politics*, 16(3): 49–66.

Cotteret, Jean-Marie and Emeri, Claude (1994). *Les systèmes électoraux*. Paris: Presses Universitaires de France.

Drysch, Thomas (1993). 'The New French System of Political Finance', in Arthur B. Gunlicks (ed.), *Campaign and Party Finance in North America and Western Europe*. Boulder: Westview Press.

Duhamel, Olivier (1994). *Droit Constitutionnel et Politique*. Paris: Le Seuil.

Duverger, Maurice (1985). *Le Système Politique Français*. Paris: Presses Universitaires de France.

Elgie, Robert and Howard Machin (1991). 'France: the Limits to Prime Ministerial Government in a Semi-presidential System'. *West European Politics*, 14(2): 62–78.

—————and Maor, Moshe (1992). 'Survival of Minority Governments: The French Case, 1988–91'. *West European Politics*, 15(4): 57–74.

——and Thompson, Helen (1998). *The Politics of Central Banks*. London: Routledge.

Goldey, D. B. (1998). 'The French General Election of 25 May–1 June 1997'. *Electoral Studies*, 17: 536–55.

Hayward, Jack (1993a). 'From Republican Sovereign to Partisan Statesman', in Jack Hayward (ed.), *De Gaulle to Mitterrand. Presidential Power in France*. London: Hurst.

——(1993b). 'The President and the Constitution: Its Spirit, Articles and Practice', in Jack Hayward (ed.), *De Gaulle to Mitterrand. Presidential Power in France*. London: Hurst.

Huber, John D. (1996). *Rationalizing Parliament*. Cambridge: Cambridge University Press.

——(1998). 'Executive Decree Authority in France', in John M. Carey and Matthew Soberg Shugart (eds.), *Executive Decree Authority*. Cambridge: Cambridge University Press.

Knapp, Andrew (1991). 'The *Cumul des mandats*, Local Power and Political Parties in France'. *West European Politics*, 14(1): 18–40.

Machin, Howard (1993). 'The President, the Parties and Parliament', in Jack Hayward (ed.), *De Gaulle to Mitterrand. Presidential Power in France*. London: Hurst.

Marcou, Gérard and Thiébault, Jean-Louis (eds.) (1996). *La Décision Gouvernementale en Europe*. Paris: L' Harmattan.

Menon, Anand (1994). 'Continuing Politics by Other Means: Defence Policy in the French Fifth Republic'. *West European Politics*, 17(4): 74–96.

Mény, Yves (1991). *Le Système Politique Français*. Paris: Montchrestien.

Money, Jeannette and Tsebelis, George (1995). 'The Political Power of the French Senate: Micromechanisms of Bicameral Negotiations'. *Journal of Legislative Studies*, 1: 192–217.

Reif, Karlheinz (1987). 'Party Government in the Fifth French Republic', in Richard S. Katz (ed.), *Party Government: European and American Perspectives*. Berlin: de Gruyter.

Rouban, Luc (1999). 'The Senior Civil Service in France', in Edward C. Page and Vincent Wright (eds.), *Bureaucratic Élites in Western European States*. Oxford: Oxford University Press.

Schramek, Olivier (2001). *Matignon, river gauche, 1997–2001*. Paris: Le Seuil.

Stevens, Anne (1993). 'The President and His Staff', in Jack Hayward (ed.), *De Gaulle to Mitterrand. Presidential Power in France*. London: Hurst.

Suleiman, Ezra N. (1980). 'Presidential Government in France', in Richard Rose and Ezra N. Suleiman (eds.), *Presidents and Prime Ministers*. Washington, DC: American Enterprise Institute.

Thiébault, Jean-Louis (1988a). 'France: the Impact of Electoral System Change', in Michael Gallagher and Michael Marsh (eds.), *Candidate Selection in Comparative Perspective. The Secret Garden of Politics*. London: Sage

——(1988b). 'France: Cabinet Decision-making under the Fifth Republic', in Jean Blondel and Ferdinand Müller-Rommel (eds.), *Cabinets in Western Europe*. London: Macmillan.

——(1994). 'The Political Autonomy of Cabinet Ministers in the French Fifth Republic', in Michael Laver and Kenneth A.Shepsle (eds.), *Cabinet Ministers and Parliamentary Government*. Cambridge: Cambridge University Press.

——(2000). 'France: Forming And Maintaining Government Coalitions in the Fifth Republic', in Wolfgang C. Müller and Kaare Strøm (eds.), *Coalition Governments in Western Europe*. Oxford: Oxford University Press.

Wright, Vincent (1993). 'The President and the Prime Minister: Subordination, Conflict, Symbiosis or Reciprocal Parasitism?', in Jack Hayward (ed.), *De Gaulle to Mitterrand. Presidential Power in France*. London: Hurst.

10

Germany: Multiple Veto Points, Informal Coordination, and Problems of Hidden Action

THOMAS SAALFELD

INTRODUCTION

The German Basic Law of 1949 was a result of historical learning. The experience of five radical regime changes within less than a century, the collapse of the Weimar Republic largely due to deep elite and mass rifts, and National Socialist totalitarianism shaped the Federal Republic's Constitution and the informal norms underpinning it (Pulzer 1995: 7; Paterson 2000: 25). The construction of democratic delegation and accountability was deeply influenced by the desire for political stability and consensus and the need to stamp out dictatorship for good. The resulting constitutional design featured a relatively strong dispersion of political power encouraging bargaining amongst different political and economic elites. I will argue in this chapter that the Basic Law was successful in achieving democratic regime stability, a broad democratic consensus, and a high level of government and policy stability. The downside have been efficiency problems (high transaction costs of policy change) and problems of political accountability and transparency.

Article 20(2) of the Basic Law proclaims the electorate to be the ultimate democratic principal and establishes a democratic chain of delegation and accountability in which all state authority emanates from (but is not immediately exercised by) the people. At the national level, referendums are restricted to decisions about boundary changes between *Länder*, to be held in those *Länder* directly affected by these changes. As far as the initial two links in the process of delegation and accountability are concerned—the link between voters and Members of Parliament MPs, and the government—the Basic Law largely conforms to the ideal type of parliamentary democracy (Strøm 2000: 268–9). Yet, there are considerable deviations, especially at the later stages of delegation. The German federal government is constrained by a large number of actors with veto powers whose authority may be derived from the Constitution or quasi-constitutional norms rather than the electoral process (e.g. the Federal Constitutional Court or the European Central Bank). While the Federal Republic largely fits Strøm's (2000: 268) characterization of a parliamentary system of government as 'a single chain of delegation with multiple links' where—in each link—'a single principal delegates to a single or multiple non-competing agents', German federalism adds at least a strong element of delegation to competing agents, which Strøm (2000: 269) considers to be more typical of presidential regimes.

The provision that each essential norm set by any political actor has to be based on parliamentary legislation is one of the constitutional safeguards for the democratic accountability of policy-makers. The federal government, a parliamentary party, or a group of 5 per cent of the Members of the Bundestag from one or more parties are entitled to introduce bills in the Bundestag. The Bundesrat, the body representing the *Länder* executives, can also initiate bills, but does so infrequently.[1] The Basic Law distinguishes between three types of laws with different procedures and majority requirements:

1. *Constitutional amendments* must be approved by two-thirds of the Members of the Bundestag and two-thirds of the votes of the Bundesrat.[2] Despite this seemingly high threshold the Basic Law was amended 190 times between its proclamation and the summer of 1998 (Busch 2000: 445). Certain constitutional provisions, however, are entirely or partly protected from amendment. Article 79 (3) of the Basic Law prohibits constitutional amendments affecting the federal nature of the German state, the participation of the *Länder* in legislation, and the basic rights and principles laid down in Articles 1 and 20 of the Basic Law. The fundamental rights in Articles 2–19 can be amended, but their essential content may not be encroached upon.

2. A *regular law* is passed by the Bundestag subject to the suspensory veto of the Bundesrat. That is, the Bundesrat can delay a bill's passage by lodging an objection. Such an objection can be overturned by an absolute majority of the Members of the Bundestag. If the Bundesrat rejects a regular bill by a two-thirds majority, its veto can only be overturned in a vote in which at least two-thirds of the Bundestag Members participate and at least 50 per cent plus one of the Bundestag Members reject the veto. The budget is essentially a 'regular law' with some qualifications. Most importantly, only the federal government can introduce the budget bill. The Bundesrat may express an opinion, but cannot veto the federal budget[3] (for a description of the budgetary process see Ismayr 1992: 402–14).

3. By contrast, Bundesrat consent is mandatory for *consent laws*—that is, such laws are subject to an absolute veto that the Bundestag cannot overturn. In effect, more than half of all bills and most important domestic laws are 'consent laws' (Saalfeld 1998a: 50).

After their passage in the Bundestag bills are sent to the Bundesrat. If the Bundesrat rejects a bill in whole or in part, it is usually referred to the conference committee with an equal number of representatives from the Bundesrat and the Bundestag (for details

---

[1] Most scholars do not consider the Bundesrat to be a second parliamentary chamber, but an autonomous state organ in its own right (e.g. see Rausch 1981: 72). Given its involvement in the process of legislation, however, the Bundesrat will be treated as a functional equivalent to a second parliamentary chamber, although it is in reality a representation of the executive branch of the *Land* governments.

[2] Each state has between three and six votes roughly in proportion to its population. State-government representatives always vote in accordance with the instructions of their governments.

[3] However, bills involving taxes to which—completely or in part—federal states or local authorities are entitled require mandatory Bundesrat consent (Article 105[3] of the Basic Law). The same is true with regard to bills concerning the distribution of taxes between the federation and the states.

see Hasselsweiler 1981; Dästner 1995). If the conference committee proposes amendments to a bill, the Bundestag must vote on it again. When the federal government lacks a Bundesrat majority, the conference committee may be a key player in the policy process. A bill comes into force when it is signed by the Federal President and promulgated in the federal statutes. The Federal President has the duty to review the constitutionality of the law. If he decides that a law is materially unconstitutional or that the process of law-making has been unconstitutional, he is required to veto it.[4]

POLITICAL PARTIES

The political parties influence the delegation process at virtually every stage. Not only are they privileged actors in Parliament, their influence in German politics and society is such that Germany has often been referred to as a 'party state' (Grewe 1951) or 'party democracy' (Gabriel, Niedermayer, and Stöss 1997). They provide the most important screening mechanisms for parliamentary and ministerial candidates, although there have been doubts whether they are really a safeguard against 'adverse selection'. Aspiring parliamentarians typically have to go through a long party career before they are nominated for elected office, which is sometimes criticized as creating a systematic bias in favour of career politicians and discouraging candidates with professional experience outside party politics (Scheuch and Scheuch 1993: 50–1).

One distinctive characteristic of the Federal Republic is the high degree of legal codification of party politics (Poguntke 1994). The most important legal sources determining the status of extra-parliamentary parties are the Basic Law, the Political Parties Act, the Federal Elections Act, and the individual parties' constitutions. Of particular importance at the parliamentary level are the Members of Parliament Act,—which was amended in 1994 to include a section on parliamentary parties (especially their financial accountability), the Bundestag's rules of procedure, and the individual parliamentary party groups' rules of procedure.

Article 21 of the Basic Law formally recognizes the crucial role of political parties in the 'formation of the political will of the people' and generally requires that their internal life be organized democratically. The 1967 Political Parties Act requires a number of specific principles of intraparty democracy. For example, it requires all party executive bodies to be elected by conferences of delegates of the rank-and-file membership and limits the number of (not directly elected) ex officio members to a maximum of 20 per cent of the respective body's total membership. The Act thus requires parties to have a democratic chain of delegation and accountability parallel to the one that exists in the polity at large.

Individually the parties contribute to the screening and accountability of elected politicians. Perhaps more importantly, postwar changes in the *party system* have also improved the scope for general electoral accountability. The 1950s and 1960s witnessed a steady concentration of the vote in favour of the two major parties, the Christian-Democratic CDU/CSU and the Social-Democratic SPD. The result was a bipolar coalition system with the liberal FDP frequently in a pivotal position, at least between 1961 and

---

[4] Presidential vetoes have been extremely rare (Saalfeld 1998b: 272–3).

1983. The relative cabinet stability since the mid-1960s and the bipolar structure with an increasingly competitive relationship between government and opposition have provided a more favourable context for electoral accountability than did the ill-fated Weimar Republic. For the first time in German history, the postwar German party system met 'the two key tests of sustaining stable governments and providing for alternation of power' (Paterson 2000: 27).

There are currently five main parties: the Christian-Democratic alliance composed of the Christian Democratic Union (CDU) and the Christian Social Union (CSU, the former's more conservative Bavarian 'sister party'), the liberal Free Democratic Party (FDP), the Social Democratic Party (SPD), the left-libertarian and environmentalist Green Party (Bündnis '90/Die Grünen), and the post-communist Party of Democratic Socialism (PDS), whose support is concentrated in eastern Germany. CDU/CSU, SPD, and FDP have dominated government formation for much of the postwar period. The Green Party has been represented in the Bundestag since 1983 and formed national government coalitions with the SPD in 1998 and 2002. The PDS was represented in the Bundestag as a parliamentary party (_Frakton_) between 1990 and 2002. While the PDS has been involved in two formal coalitions and tolerated a number of minority cabinets at the _Land_ and local levels in eastern Germany, it has remained 'non-coalitionable' federally as the most ideologically left-wing party and one that is seen to have not yet adequately dealt with its past as the ruling party of the communist dictatorship in East Germany between 1949 and 1989. It failed to overcome the 5 per cent threshold of the Federal Republic's electoral law in the 2002 elections.

Although constraints of space do not allow a detailed description of the development of the German party system (Stöss 1986; Mintzel and Oberreuter 1992; Lösche 1993; Roberts 1997), certain key characteristics should be mentioned. First, CDU and CSU are independent parties forming a common parliamentary party in the Bundestag. The alliance is formally renewed after each general election. As a result of the far-reaching codification of party organization and finance, there are no fundamental organizational differences among the main parties, apart from the fact that only CDU and SPD really have a mass membership.[5] The major German parties are not organized in a strictly hierarchical fashion. Some authors have therefore chosen expressions such as 'loosely coupled anarchy' (Lösche 1993) or 'organised anarchy' (Wiesendahl 2000) to describe the organizations of the CDU and SPD and the relatively autonomous coexistence of the different levels of party organization. One consequence is that power is dispersed within the political parties and that governments face high transaction costs in generating the necessary intraparty consensus for policy changes. This, in turn, encourages bargaining in informal bodies.

DELEGATION FROM VOTERS TO MPs

German citizens use their vote to delegate powers to elected politicians at the local, _Land_, national, and European Union (EU) levels. Given the intertwined relations

---

[5] In December 2000 the CDU had approximately 617,000 and the SPD approximately 735,000 members (Sources: reports of CDU and SPD executive committees to the parties' annual conferences).

between the *Länder* and federation (the national level) in German politics, the chains between voters and Members of federal–state Parliaments on the one hand and between voters and Members of the Bundestag on the other must be seen as competitive. The Bundesrat's crucial role in national politics, the importance of *Land* bureaucracies for the implementation of national legislation, the national ambitions of many leading *Land* politicians, the national importance of *Land* elections (which are not considered to be second-order elections like local or EU elections), the existence of legislative 'joint tasks' shared by the federation and the *Länder*, and the existence of 'concurrent' and 'framework legislation' where both the federation and the *Länder* have powers illustrate this point. From the perspective of agency theory, therefore, the Federal Republic has a more complicated chain of delegation and accountability than the ideal-type of parliamentary democracy (Strøm 2000).

Given the crucial and all-pervasive role of political parties in the Federal Republic, the direct electoral accountability of individual Bundestag Members is not as strong as may be the case in the United States. Powerful *ex ante* control mechanisms such as screening and selection of candidates are reserved for the minority of citizens who are active members of the respective candidate's party. Individual candidates rarely expect significant personal electoral rewards or penalties independent of their party's overall fate. Like *ex ante* accountability mechanisms, *ex post* electoral accountability is mediated by the political parties. Nevertheless, electoral competition with candidates from other parties and, crucially, aspirants from within their own parties provides incentives for Members of the Bundestag to share information with voters, especially through constituency 'surgeries' and the local news media at constituency level.

Delegation from voters to MPs is strongly shaped by Germany's electoral system of proportional representation with a two-tier districting system. According to the Federal Elections Act, 299 Members of the Bundestag were in 2002 elected at the lower level by plurality vote in single-member constituencies. Proportionality is achieved through adjustment at the upper level, where an additional 299 deputies were elected from *Land* party lists.[6] Nonetheless, the German system is not completely proportional and discriminates against smaller and new parties. The most important violation of strict proportionality is the 5 per cent clause of the electoral law. Parliamentary representation requires at least 5 per cent of the national vote or three direct constituency mandates (for more detailed accounts of the Federal Republic's electoral system and its evolution see Nohlen 1986; Jesse 1990). As intended by the framers of the electoral law, the 5 per cent threshold contributed considerably to the concentration of the party system during the 1950s. It has effectively barred small anti-democratic parties from national parliamentary representation without completely stifling new competitors, as the Greens since the 1980s and the PDS in the 1990s demonstrate. To some extent, the 'additional-member' electoral system would seem to allow for a 'personal vote' and give

---

[6] Since 1949, the proportionality of the system has been gradually increased. In 1953, the ratio of lower-level mandates (apportioned by plurality vote) to upper-level (adjustment seats to achieve proportionality) was reduced from 60 : 40 to 50 : 50. In 1987 the d'Hondt system of apportionment of upper-level seats to each party was replaced by the more proportional LR-Hare system.

voters an opportunity to employ *ex post facto* sanctions against individual Members of the Bundestag. In practice, however, only a small minority of German voters see the candidates of the parties as the determining factor of their vote (Conradt 2000: 150).

Ex ante (that is, prior to the delegation from voters to Members of Parliament), voters have no direct say in candidate selection. Those who join one of the main political parties have a better opportunity to screen individual candidates and to hold them personally accountable, although the process is in practice often dominated by local and regional oligarchies. Nomination by a party is *the* crucial step to election: 'a candidate can expect to be elected to Parliament if his party places him high up on its state party list' (Patzelt 1995: 58). Paragraph 22 of the Federal Elections Act regulates the nomination of both list and constituency candidates. Candidate selection is strongly dominated by local and regional party elites, 'and it is only in exceptional circumstances that *Land* or federal party leaderships can hope to impose candidates of their own choosing' (Poguntke 1994: 189). Although SPD statutes require 'consultation' with their national executive in the nomination of both constituency and list candidates, and although the state or district executive committees have certain veto rights, these powers are very rarely used. Specific 'recommendations' from the federal or *Land* executive committee about nominations are not welcomed and frequently disregarded (Kaack 1971; Poguntke 1994). Compared to all actors in the electoral process, mid-level regional party elites have the most effective means to screen, monitor, and sanction candidates and incumbents.

The rules of electoral competition have not changed a great deal since 1957. There is no legal document explicitly specifying the minimum length of a campaign. However, provisions of the Basic Law and the Federal Elections Act indirectly point to 30 days as the minimum. According to Article 39(1) of the Basic Law, the Bundestag is elected for 4 years (i.e. 48 months). At the earliest, regular elections are to be held 45 months after the last elections, at the latest 47 months after them. This formulation is the result of a 1976 amendment to the Basic Law (which was first applied in 1980). Between 1953 and 1976, each Bundestag had a fixed term of 4 years unless it was dissolved by the Federal President. It is legally and politically almost impossible and/or very costly for governments to call early elections at a politically convenient time. The constraining effect of competition rules such as the ones mentioned above is compounded by the constitutional provisions pertaining to the early dissolution of Parliament (see below).

There is no legal cap on campaign spending. Public funding of political parties has been generous by international standards and has helped relatively small parties to stabilize their organizations and/or cope with the 'liability of newness'. Between 1967 and 1994, public funding was specifically designed to compensate parties for election expenses as their ability to compete effectively in elections was seen to be in the public interest. All parties that are permitted[7] to put forward party lists (not just parliamentary

---

[7] The Federal Constitutional Court has the power to ban parties and seize their assets if their aims are found to anti-democratic. Parties can only put forward a *Land* list in elections, if their list is supported by the signatures of one per thousand (maximum: 2,000) voters in the respective federal state. Individual constituency candidates need the support of 200 voters in their constituency.

parties) are allocated free public broadcasting time during election campaigns. The parties have to pay for the production costs of advertisements transmitted by commercial stations. In both—public and commercial—systems, the norm for allocating time is proportionality, with a minimum quota for non-parliamentary parties. It is not possible to purchase additional time on the public broadcasting networks. There are no restrictions on the publication of opinion polls, except that exit polls on polling day may not be published until polling stations close.

The regulation of public subsidies to political parties is an important aspect of the Political Parties Act of 1967. In the early 1990s, approximately two-thirds of the parties' considerable income stemmed from public funds. Public party subsidies have been the subject of many legal disputes, and the nature of public funding has been changed a number of times (see Gunlicks 1988; Poguntke 1994; Saalfeld 2000c). Public financing of political parties started with indirect subsidies in the form of tax deductions for donations in 1954. After a number of changes, further amendments to the party laws of 1994 stipulate that parties are entitled to a direct subsidy for each voter and year, and for each euro they receive in membership contributions and donations, as long as the donations originate from natural persons (rather than corporations and interest groups) and do not exceed a certain limit per annum. The allocation formula gives a slight advantage to smaller parties. Direct public subsidies are limited to 50 per cent of a party's total income ('relative limit') and to euro 133 million for all parties combined ('absolute limit'). The latter can be revised in line with the rate of inflation. In order to be eligible for public subsidies, a party must have won at least 0.5 per cent of the vote in the previous Bundestag or European Parliament elections or 1.0 per cent in a *Land* election (Article 18, Parteiengesetz). Especially since the 1980s, a number of high-profile party finance scandals have led to serious criticism of the parties as well as the system of public funding. Nevertheless, the system is fair to smaller parties. Furthermore it has allowed sitting Members of Parliament and their challengers to maintain a relatively well-supported presence in their constituencies and thereby to share information with interested constituents and grass-roots party members. At least for parliamentarians without government office or a high-profile function in their (parliamentary) party, regular constituency work has become a virtual precondition for renomination. It has also allowed MPs and parliamentary parties to employ staff in the federal capital to support their ongoing oversight activities.

Article 38 of the Basic Law underscores the independence of individual Members of the Bundestag vis-à-vis voters, parties, or any other influences. It stipulates that Members are to represent the people as a whole, that they are not bound by any orders or instructions, and that they are subject only to their own conscience. Thus, in constitutional theory the agency relationship between voters and MPs is deliberately designed to grant the agent—the MP—a large degree of autonomy. The relationship between MPs and their parties has been far more contentious. Article 21 of the Basic Law has often been interpreted by leading constitutional lawyers (especially during the 1960s) in such a way as to make Members of Parliament virtual agents of their parties (e.g. Leibholz 1966). Today the predominant view amongst constitutional lawyers is that the Basic Law recognizes parties—inside and outside Parliament—as indispensable elements in the chain of democratic delegation and accountability (although this terminology is not used). Nevertheless, the formal independence of individual Members enjoys equal constitutional status and serves as a corrective against over-powerful parties. The tension between Articles 21 and 38 allows the Federal Constitutional Court to rule on specific conflicts on a case-by-case basis (Arndt 1989: 652–4).

Ex post safeguards against the consequences of oligarchy and agent opportunism, such as term limits or a mandatory retirement age, do not exist. Between 1983 and 1987, however, the Green party used a system of 'rotation', in which every Green Member of the Bundestag was required to resign after 2 years and was replaced by another candidate drawn from the respective Green *Land* list. This practice was considered to be of questionable constitutional status and abandoned for practical reasons.

DELEGATION FROM PARLIAMENT TO CABINET

The agency relationship between MPs and cabinet is complicated. In reality we can distinguish at least three agency relationships, each with its specific problems:

1. Although the 'two-body image' of 'the' Parliament versus 'the' executive is misleading for modern parliamentary systems of government (see King 1976), there is a 'residual' collective parliamentary identity as its majority decisions are treated as decisions of the chamber as a whole. More importantly in our context, there is a vast information asymmetry between parliamentarians serving in government office on the one hand and non-government members on the other. This asymmetry is largely a result of the government ministers' privileged access to the civil service, executive agencies, and scientific advice. The government's informational advantage generally reduces the effectiveness of ongoing oversight and increases the scope for hidden action and thus moral hazard. Like all other West European parliaments, the German Bundestag is affected by such problems.

2. King (1976) attempts to capture the reality of modern parliamentary systems in his distinction between 'intra-party', 'inter-party', and 'opposition' modes of executive–legislative relations, indicating that there are not one but *several* agency relationships, each with their own problems. The first two modes refer to the agency relationships within each government party ('intra-party mode') or within a coalition of parties ('inter-party mode'), the third refers to those parties who do not support the government of the day ('opposition mode'). The most powerful *ex ante* (screening and selection) and *ex post* accountability mechanisms (monitoring, rewards, and punishments) are effectively (if not totally) reserved for the members of the government parties. Due to a higher degree of incentive compatibility between government and government parliamentarians, the Members of the governing parties tend to have easier and timelier access to accurate executive information than Members belonging to opposition parties. The Federal Republic differs from other West European parliamentary democracies in that the informational disadvantage at least of the major opposition parties is usually alleviated by their access to ministerial bureaucracies at the *Land* level. Major opposition parties can often draw on support from 'friendly' *Länder* governments controlled by their own

regional organizations. For such governments the incentives to cooperate with the national opposition may be strong if they compete electorally with government parties at the *Land* level and/or if the head of the respective *Land* government has ambitions on the national level.[8]

3. Legislative–executive relations in Germany are additionally influenced by the ethos of a 'working chamber' contributing to a high degree of institutionalized policy specialization. This specialization is reflected in the importance given to committee work, but also in the emphasis on policy formulation and monitoring through parliamentary working groups, especially in the two major parties. This creates a layer of policy experts within the parliamentary parties with privileged access to executive information. Although this improves the Bundestag's overall capacity for monitoring and other ongoing oversight activities, it also creates additional agency relationships (and problems) between ordinary backbenchers on the one hand and the parliamentary parties' policy experts, who often act on behalf of their parliamentary parties at large, on the other.

Let us now consider some accountability mechanisms in greater detail. The Bundestag as a whole, and the parliamentary majority parties in particular, have three crucial *ex ante* devices at their disposal.

1. The Basic Law requires the election of the Federal Chancellor by an absolute majority of the Bundestag. The formal rules of *government investiture* are laid down in Articles 63, 64, and 67 of the Basic Law. The Federal President proposes to the Bundestag a candidate for the office of Federal Chancellor. To be elected, a candidate must be supported by an absolute majority of all Members of the Bundestag, that is, there is an explicit support requirement of 50 per cent plus one vote of all members entitled to vote and an implicit quorum requirement of 50 per cent plus one of all members. Voting is done by secret ballot. The Federal President must appoint the chancellor-candidate elected by an absolute majority of the chamber. If no candidate receives an absolute majority in the first ballot, there may be an unspecified number of further ballots within 14 days. If no candidate wins an absolute majority within this period, the Federal President may appoint the candidate that has the relative majority of votes or, alternatively, may call an election. As yet, this has never been necessary. Once elected, the Chancellor nominates the members of his cabinet, who are subsequently appointed by the Federal President without separate Bundestag approval. The cabinet ministers' tenure in office ends with the Chancellor's.

2. The election of a Chancellor is only the formal completion of the process of government and, in particular, coalition formation. Leading members of the parliamentary majority parties are closely involved in this bargaining process, as are leaders and relevant experts from the extra-parliamentary party organizations. These actors work out the future government's policies as well as the allocation of cabinet portfolios to particular parties and politicians. The government's policy programme is formally summarized in a coalition agreement and the Federal Chancellor's first government

---

[8] It has to be remembered, for example, that *Land* Prime Ministers and ministers have the privilege to speak in the Bundestag at any time and may be important speakers for the national opposition.

declaration to Parliament. In effect this means that the majority parties agree on a formal contract before the government is elected (cf. Saalfeld 2000b).

3. Although the Basic Law does not require the Federal Chancellor or cabinet ministers to be Members of the Bundestag, all Chancellors except Kurt Georg Kiesinger (1966–9) have been Members at the time of their election.[9] To a slightly lesser extent this is also true for cabinet ministers. The Federal Chancellor and cabinet ministers are thus subjected to informal screening mechanisms in the form of parliamentary apprenticeships. Yet, as ministers are often drawn from *Länder* governments or elsewhere from outside the Bundestag, the average parliamentary seniority of German cabinet members (1949–84: 7.7 years) is markedly lower than in the United Kingdom (12.2), Finland (10.3), Denmark (9.7), and some other West European countries (De Winter 1991: 48). A lengthy pre-ministerial career in party politics—inside or outside the national chamber—provides Members of Parliament with information about a prospective minister's or Chancellor's policy preferences and personal qualities. Even when the Chancellor appoints a minister from 'outside' the usual career stream of professional party politics, the latter is interested in quickly establishing a good working relationship with the relevant experts in the government's parliamentary parties. This usually involves becoming a Member of the Bundestag at the earliest opportunity.

Once elected, the Federal Chancellor and his cabinet are relatively well protected from early dismissal. The President cannot dismiss them unilaterally. The obstacles for the use of the Bundestag's ultimate *ex post* accountability device, removal from office, are relatively high. Against its own will, the government can only be collectively dismissed by the Bundestag, and only through a 'constructive vote of no-confidence' (Article 67 of the Basic Law) against the Chancellor. This means that an absolute majority of the Bundestag Members must not only be willing to depose the Chancellor and his entire cabinet, they must simultaneously elect an alternative candidate. The right to propose such a constructive vote of no-confidence rests with a parliamentary party or at least 25 per cent of all Members of the Bundestag. Forty-eight hours must pass between the proposal and vote. There is no limit on the number of constructive no-confidence votes that can be held. The decision rule for all no-confidence votes is 50 per cent of all Members of the Bundestag eligible to vote plus one. It follows implicitly that there is a quorum requirement of at least 50 per cent of all members of the Bundestag plus one. Voting is by secret ballot.

The right to propose confidence votes (in which the initiative rests with the government) rests with the Federal Chancellor. He or she alone can be the object of such a vote. There are no unregulated confidence votes, that is, the government is under no obligation to resign in the absence of parliamentary support for important government bills or motions. Nevertheless, the fate of Brandt's 1969–72 cabinet demonstrates that the Federal Chancellor may have incentives to seek early elections by 'manufacturing'

---

[9] Kiesinger had served as Prime Minister of the state of Baden-Württemberg before he became Chancellor. Nonetheless, he had considerable prior experience in the Bundestag. He was not atypical for leading German politicians, who have often gained administrative experience in a state government before returning to national politics as a minister or Chancellor.

an unsuccessful confidence motion under such circumstances. Forty-eight hours must pass between the proposal of a confidence vote and the vote itself. If the Federal Chancellor loses a vote of confidence—that is, fails to achieve a majority of 50 per cent of all Bundestag members plus one—he may ask the President to dissolve the Bundestag (Article 68 of the Basic Law). There is no explicit quorum requirement, but it follows from Article 68 that at least 50 per cent plus one of all Bundestag Members must be present and support the Chancellor. Voting is usually, but not necessarily, by secret ballot.

The rules for an early dissolution of the Bundestag are relatively restrictive and require agreement between the Federal Chancellor, the parliamentary majority, and the Federal President. The Basic Law makes it difficult for Federal Chancellors to evade parliamentary accountability by calling early elections and referring issues to 'the people'. The President may dissolve the Bundestag at his own discretion only if the chamber fails to elect a Chancellor by an absolute majority within 14 days of the first (unsuccessful) ballot. If the Chancellor fails to achieve a majority of all Bundestag Members in a vote of confidence, he may ask the Federal President to dissolve Parliament. The Federal President may then dissolve the Bundestag within 21 days, although he is not compelled to do so. Alternatively, the Chancellor may stay in office or request the President to declare a state of legislative emergency. If the Chancellor decides to do nothing, the President cannot dismiss him because the President can only act on the advice of the Chancellor. Neither the cabinet nor the parliamentary majority has any right to initiate an early dissolution unilaterally. There are no automatic constitutional provisions for an early dissolution. *De jure* and de facto it is *extremely* difficult for the Chancellor to bring about an early dissolution of the Bundestag (Ismayr 1999: 22; Niclauß 1999: 29).

Table 10.1 reports some behavioural data on the life of cabinets and Parliaments. Although no Federal Chancellor from Adenauer to Kohl has managed to win the votes of all members of the government parties, not one of the seventeen investiture votes between 1949 and 2000 was unsuccessful. There have been two constructive votes of no confidence, an unsuccessful one against Willy Brandt in 1972 and a successful one against Helmut Schmidt in 1982. No Chancellor has resigned in order to pre-empt a constructive vote of no confidence. Brandt lost a vote of confidence in 1972 in a deliberate attempt by the government[10] to bring about an early dissolution of the Bundestag in the absence of a clear supporting majority (Bracher, Jäger, and Link 1986: 67–76). This step was only possible, however, due to a consensus between government and opposition on the necessity of early elections. A similar event occurred in 1983, when the Kohl government (which commanded a clear parliamentary majority) 'manufactured' a defeat in a vote of confidence, with some government supporters abstaining in order to enable an early dissolution. The reason for this highly exceptional move was the FDP's decision to form a government with the CDU/CSU in 1982, although it had fought the previous (1980) election on the basis of a pre-electoral pact with the SPD. CDU Chancellor Helmut Kohl therefore sought and received a direct mandate from the voters for the new CDU/CSU–FDP coalition. This is a strong indication

---

[10] The members of the cabinet did not vote.

Table 10.1. *Cabinet Formation, Cabinet Termination, and Early Parliamentary Dissolution: Germany 1949–2000*[a]

No.	Cabinet	Date of formation	Investiture votes (iv)					No-confidence votes (ncv)			Confidence votes (cv)		Did the cabinet end with an early election?	Who dissolved Parliament in this case?[b]
			No. of unsuccessful investiture votes	Voting results of successful iv[c] (1: pro gov, 2: against gov, 3: abstentions and 4: other)				No. of ncv	Cabinet removed by ncv	Cabinet resigned to pre-empt ncv	No. of cv under spec. inst. mech.	Cabinet removed by failed cv		
				1	2	3	4							
1	Adenauer I	49/09/15	0	202	142	44	1	0			0			
2	Adenauer II	53/10/09	0	305	148	14	0	0			0			
3	Adenauer III	55/07/23	—					0			0			
4	Adenauer IV	56/02/25	—					0			0			
5	Adenauer V	57/10/22	0	274	193	9	0	0			0			
6	Adenauer VI	60/07/02	—					0			0			
7	Adenauer VII	61/11/07	0	258	206	26	0	0			0			
8	Adenauer VIII	62/11/19	—					0			0			
9	Adenauer IX	62/12/13	—					0			0			
10	Erhard I	63/10/16	0	279	180	24	1	0			0			
11	Erhard II	65/10/20	0	272	200	15	0	0			0			
12	Erhard III	66/10/28	—					0			0			
13	Kiesinger	66/12/01	0	340	109	23	1	0			0			
14	Brandt I	69/10/21	0	251	235	5	4	1	No		1	Yes	Yes	Head of State
15	Brandt II	72/12/14	0	269	223	0	1	0			0			

	Cabinet	Date								
16	Schmidt I	74/05/16	0	267	225	0	0		0	0
17	Schmidt II	76/12/15	0	250	243	1	1		0	0
18	Schmidt III	80/11/05	0	266	222	2	1		No	1
19	Schmidt IV	82/09/17	—	Yes		1	1	Yes	Head of State	0
20	Kohl I	82/10/01	0	256	235	4	0		Yes[d]	1
21	Kohl II	83/03/29	0	271	214	1	0			0
22	Kohl III	87/03/11	0	253	225	6	3			0
23	Kohl IV	90/10/30	—				0			0
24	Kohl V	91/01/17	0	278	257	9	0			0
25	Kohl VI	94/11/15	0	338	333	0	0			0
26	Schröder I	98/10/27	0	351	287	27	1		—	—

[a] n.d. = no data (missing data); n.a. or '—' = not applicable in this case.

[b] The question 'Who dissolved Parliament in this case?' can be answered with one of five options. This identifies the main constitutional actor that caused the early election. We have not coded the formal signatory, but rather the person or body that made the real decision: (1) Head of State; (2) Prime Minister; (3) Cabinet; (4) Parliamentary majority; (5) Automatic constitutional provision (e.g. if it is required when a new President takes office, or, for example, if it is required after the adoption of a proposal for constitutional amendments).

[c] Until 1990, these data exclude the votes of Members for Berlin.

[d] The government defeat was 'engineered' to make early elections possible.

of 'diverted accountabilities' (Strøm 2000: 284). Kohl clearly enjoyed the confidence of a parliamentary majority (i.e. the parliamentary principal), but felt (in tune with public opinion) that his government needed an explicit popular mandate (from the ultimate democratic principal). These two instances of 'manufactured' defeat in a vote of confidence were the only times a cabinet ended with the dissolution of Parliament and the holding of early elections.

Under modern party government the federal government is not primarily an agent of Parliament, but of the majority parties. Anthony King (1976) has captured this fact in his intraparty mode of legislative–executive relations. Despite a high degree of 'incentive compatibility' conflicts of interest between government backbenchers and ministers are not infrequent. Therefore, government backbenchers have incentives to monitor the behaviour of 'their' ministers. This ongoing oversight by the parliamentary majority parties can be very effective as the government depends on their votes and other forms of support.

Backbench influence on the government side is relatively formalized. The two major parliamentary parties (SPD and CDU/CSU) maintain a comprehensive system of working groups shadowing and monitoring the government departments and preparing virtually all decisions of the party caucus in the Bundestag. The smaller parties do not have enough members to achieve a comparable specialization and usually have working groups monitoring more than one government department. The chairs of the specialized working groups are usually experienced, respected, and influential policy experts with privileged access to ministerial information (especially when the party is in government) and are taken seriously by government departments. On the government side they are often key players in coalition committees. On the one hand, this differentiated organization institutionalizes the influence of parliamentary (non-government) elites on cabinet decisions. On the other hand, it contributes to the existence of several 'classes' of MPs with varying degrees of influence and the generation of agency problems within the parliamentary parties.

Such mechanisms of ongoing control within the government parties are effective, but they work largely in private. Their existence has not made the Bundestag an 'informationally efficient' Parliament vis-à-vis the voters, who need more information to evaluate the parties' and candidates' performance. Using an analogy to Krehbiel's heterogeneity principle for committees of the US Congress (1991: 84),[11] one could

---

[11] Keith Krehbiel's (1991) 'information theory' of committees differs from the models proposed by other new institutionalists in that it does not primarily focus on distributional aspects of policy-making ('gains from trade'). Although Krehbiel does not deny that reelection-seeking Members of Parliament care about distributional benefits to their constituencies, he insists that—due to uncertainty in the policy environment—legislators are more severely constrained in obtaining distributional benefits than is suggested in the distributional perspective. His key interest is to analyse rules and procedures providing incentives for individual parliamentarians to develop policy expertise and then to share policy-relevant expertise with fellow legislators, including legislators with competing distributive interests. In this context, he identifies a number of principles that encourage the development of policy expertise and information-sharing. He calls one of his principles the 'heterogeneity principle'. According to this principle, specialists from opposite sides of a policy spectrum are collectively more informative to the other members of the parliamentary chamber than specialists from only one side of the spectrum.

argue that if there is public competition between politically opposing forces, then parliamentarians have incentives to share information with the voters. In parliamentary systems of government, the opposition can be crucial in ensuring heterogeneity and informational efficiency in Krehbiel's sense, if it pursues a 'competitive' strategy vis-à-vis the government. Yet, although the opposition's 'armoury' in the Bundestag is strong by international comparison and has been further strengthened over the years, there have been important countervailing forces preventing the Bundestag from being informationally efficient. The traditional hostility towards party conflict among both German elites and voters (Grosser 1975)—which gives opposition parties little electoral incentive to engage in constant Westminster-type adversarial politics—along with a tradition of cooperative federalism, have favoured consensual policy-making. In this process, the minority often has incentives to influence decision-making in the private atmosphere of parliamentary committees, joint intergovernmental consultative bodies of the federation and the *Länder*, and the conference committee of the Bundestag and Bundesrat rather than to challenge the government in public. This has repeatedly led to criticisms of lacking transparency. Nevertheless, government–opposition relations have generally become more adversarial since the early 1980s. This is not to say that there is no conflict, but that the major German opposition parties have a much wider choice of strategic options than, say, their counterparts in Great Britain whose only real weapon is publicity (Saalfeld 1998a: 62–7).

The Members of the Bundestag have a number of monitoring devices at their disposal, which are designed to ensure ongoing *public* scrutiny. One distinctive characteristic of the Bundestag's rules of procedure is that most of these instruments can be employed by any parliamentary party or any group of Members whose number is equivalent to the size of a parliamentary party (5 per cent of the total Bundestag membership). The main implication of these provisions is that the majority has less power to control the Bundestag's plenary agenda than is the case in more majoritarian systems of government (Döring 1995: 225). The down side of this strong protection of minority rights through privileging the parliamentary parties in parliamentary agenda-setting is that, if they want to speak or ask questions, individual members de facto need the backing of their parliamentary parties (Schüttemeyer 1994: 36–7).

Since 1983, the opposition parties have made more use of parliamentary questions as a means of monitoring the government and forcing public debates than previously. This increased opposition activity is largely a result of the advent of the Greens in the Bundestag and the ensuing electoral competition not only between government and opposition but also between SPD and the Greens as (then competing) opposition parties (Saalfeld 1998a: 63–4). The Bundestag's rules of procedure allow two main kinds of *written parliamentary questions*:

1. The *Große Anfrage* is one of the most powerful instruments available to the opposition parties to extract information from the government and—based on this information—force floor debates on issues of their own choice. Only a parliamentary party or an equivalent number of Members can request them. The government is expected to answer such questions on current issues in writing within three weeks. If

the government refuses, a parliamentary party or an equivalent number of Members can still demand a full plenary debate on the issue. In the vast majority of cases the government responds, and the ensuing parliamentary debate is based on the government's written answer, which is published before the debate takes place (Schäfer 1982: 232–4).

2. *Kleine Anfragen* are—often quite comprehensive and detailed—written questions, which are answered by the government in writing. They are an important means for Members of the Bundestag to collect information, although they do not usually trigger a major plenary debate. Only parliamentary parties or an equivalent number of members can ask such questions. The government is expected to answer within a fortnight, though it also has the option of refusing to answer or giving a confidential reply.

In each regular week, Members of the Bundestag will be collectively allocated up to 180 minutes for *oral questions*. Members of the Bundestag may ask one short question for oral answer per day and up to two questions per week. Although such questions may be tabled by individual members, they are expected to be cleared with the relevant party working groups, executive committees, and whips' offices (Arndt 1989: 670–1). The rules of procedure also allow individual members to ask *'urgent questions'*. Such questions must be submitted to the Bundestag President's office by noon on the day before the question is to be asked. The President decides whether the question at stake qualifies as one of 'urgent public interest'. Questions for oral answer do not attract the same publicity as in the British House of Commons. *Aktuelle Stunden* are short, topical one-hour debates which can be demanded by any parliamentary party or an equivalent number of Members. Since 1983, the use of such short debates has grown considerably, facilitated by procedural reforms and a generally more competitive opposition (Saalfeld 1998a: 63). In 1988 the Bundestag introduced so-called *'cabinet questions'*, initially on an experimental and in 1990 on a permanent basis. Under this procedure, Bundestag Members are allowed to ask specific ministers questions of 'current interest' as well as questions about the preceding cabinet meeting (Schindler 1994: 984–6). *Regular formal reports* from the federal government to the Bundestag have been of growing importance to parliamentary scrutiny and legislation. There are three main types of reports. First, the government has a statutory duty to issue certain reports at regular intervals.[12] Second, a parliamentary resolution can also require the government to present a report. Finally, the government issues reports on its own initiative. The use of such formal reports has increased over time (1949–53: 9, 1987–90: 172, total 1949–90: 1,286) (Schindler 1994: 490–1).

Despite its well-developed floor array of interpellation instruments and information rights, the Bundestag relies heavily on executive *scrutiny by committee*. The function of detailed scrutiny is thus delegated to the parliamentary parties' policy experts serving on the relevant committees *and* playing a leading role in the parliamentary parties' parallel working groups. There are at least four different kinds of parliamentary committees: departmental standing committees, special ad hoc committees, investigative

---

[12] For example, this is true for the half-yearly Report on Integration in the European Communities (Bericht über die Integration in den Europäischen Gemeinschaften), the Annual Report on the State of the Economy (Jahreswirtschaftsbericht), or the Annual Energy Report (Energiebericht), which are all prepared by the Ministry of Economic Affairs.

committees and enquiry commissions. A residual category comprises bodies like the Committee on Election Validation, Immunity and Rules, the Petitions Committee, and the Senior Council. The latter, de facto, is the business (or steering) committee of the Bundestag, which fixes its agenda and timetable, and generally ensures an efficient use of its time, particularly, by avoiding plenary debates on rules.

Until 1969, committees were primarily agents of the chamber and could only make recommendations to the Bundestag on matters expressly referred to them. Since 1969 the Bundestag rules of procedure have also allowed them to examine any other subject in their remit, irrespective of an express referral. Although they do not have independent legislative powers, they have, in practice, considerable influence because their members are the parliamentary parties' experts in the respective policy areas. These experts wield considerable policy influence within their parties, and when they are part of the government majority, they cannot easily be ignored by the government. The committees' powers to obtain independent outside information were strengthened considerably in 1969 when a minority of 25 per cent of the committee members were given the authority to force public hearings (Ismayr 1999: 24).

The committee seats are allocated to the parliamentary parties in proportion to the seat distribution in the chamber. According to paragraph 57 of the Bundestag's rules of procedure, the parliamentary parties nominate committee members. Hence committee members are formally agents of their parties.[13] Once party quotas are established, the actual appointments of committee members, as well as their recall and replacement, are left to the parliamentary parties and merely communicated to the President of the Bundestag. Likewise, committee chairs are proportionally distributed among the parties, and the parties fill their chairs as they wish, although they usually attempt to reach interparty consensus on nominations. The assignment of specific committee chairs is negotiated in the Senior Council.

The Bundestag's principal instruments of executive oversight are its standing departmental committees. The majority of these twenty-one committees (2003) mirror a single government department. Only the remits of the Committees on Appropriations, Justice, and EU Affairs cut across departmental jurisdictions. Under the Basic Law, all committees are entitled to compel the attendance of ministers, as is the Bundestag floor majority. Most committees regularly question ministers and civil servants on issues within their jurisdiction. Departmental standing committees combine a 'watchdog function' of ongoing scrutiny with detailed discussion of draft bills after their first reading. Most German MPs' parliamentary timetables are dominated by work in standing committees and parallel working groups within their parliamentary parties. The overlap that exists between the parliamentary parties' working groups and the Bundestag's standing committees is designed to ensure that the parliamentary parties' agents in Bundestag committees share information with their co-partisans (Saalfeld 2000a: 28–9).

---

[13] Individual Members not belonging to a party are to be nominated for a committee seat by the Bundestag President. However, they do not have the right to vote in committee.

The characteristics and powers of the other Bundestag committees and bodies cannot be described in detail (cf. Saalfeld 1998*b*: 268, 273–4, 276–7). The Bundestag's *investigative committees* can be used to inquire into instances of alleged administrative mismanagement or government wrongdoing. Such committees must be created if at least a quarter of the Bundestag Members request it. *Commissions of Enquiry* are appointed ad hoc and are charged with the task of informing the Bundestag and the public thoroughly on policy issues of a fundamental or long-term importance. In many ways, they resemble the British Royal Commissions. Whereas all other committees of the House consist only of Bundestag MPs, Commissions of Enquiry have the power to appoint outside experts as full committee members with voting rights. The *Petitions Committee* can be directly approached by citizens who have complaints about instances of administrative wrong-doing, but it has no power to investigate matters independent of a specific complaint. In this sense it is exclusively a 'fire alarm' (McCubbins and Schwartz 1984), which can be activated by citizens in the event of implementation problems. A number of special bodies assist the Bundestag in its ongoing scrutiny of government activities. The Parliamentary Commissioner for the Armed Forces has been influenced by the model of the Scandinavian Ombudsman. The Federal Audit Court, among other activities, audits government spending supporting, in particular the work of the Appropriations and Finance committees. The Appropriations Committee has a special Auditing sub-committee.

DELEGATION WITHIN THE CABINET

Delegation within the cabinet is structured by somewhat ambivalent and vague norms in the Basic Law as well as by the political realities of party and coalition government. This has allowed a number of interpretations ranging from a position emphasizing the Federal Chancellor's dominance ('Chancellor democracy') at one extreme to, at the other, a position emphasizing the informational advantages of bureaucrats vis-à-vis elected politicians and arguing that the capacity for policy development de facto rests with the ministerial bureaucracies.

At first glance, the Federal Chancellor appears to be a very powerful principal. The Basic Law grants him considerable *ex ante* controls by empowering him to determine the general policy of the government. Although he is constrained by the Constitution, the federal government's rules of procedure, and the coalition agreement, he does have certain agenda powers, such as the extent to which decisions are delegated to ministers (important issues, including many foreign policy issues, are often unilaterally declared to be 'matters for the leader'), the government's organization, the procedures that have to be followed by the ministers, and the mechanisms for interdepartmental conflict resolution. He bears overall responsibility for the government's policies vis-à-vis the Bundestag. Although cabinet ministers are individually answerable to the Bundestag in parliamentary questions, Müller-Rommel (1994: 160)—putting it somewhat strongly— emphasizes that ministers primarily depend on the Chancellor's confidence: 'ministers are appointed and dismissed by the chancellor. They serve at his pleasure and not that of the Parliament'.

According to the rules of procedure of the federal government, the Chancellor has the right to determine the number and jurisdictions of individual departments, an important discretionary authority. The Federal Chancellor's Office, with a staff of more than 500 civil servants (1994) and headed by a cabinet minister close to the Chancellor, provides him with a considerable monitoring capacity vis-à-vis individual departments. The Office has a system of specialized sections each liasing with, and monitoring the activities of, a number of government departments and trying to minimize agency loss between Chancellor and departments. According to the federal government's standing orders, individual ministries have the statutory duty to keep the Chancellor informed of important policy developments in their departments. Not only does the Chancellor's Office attempt to coordinate the work of the departments, it also serves as the government's secretariat by preparing cabinet meetings and coordinates the activities of the three German intelligence services (Busse 1997: 110–20; Rudzio 2000: 284–9).

Nevertheless, it would be inaccurate to overstate the constitutional and practical importance of the 'Chancellor principle'. First the constitutional norms are ambivalent and give some weight to the 'departmental principle' and the 'cabinet principle' (see below). Second the risk of agency loss in the form of 'departmentalism' is high given the superior information available to the departmental bureaucracies. Finally, the realities of coalition government in Germany render simple models of delegation unrealistic. Coalition government is a constant bargaining process. Bargaining power depends on factors such as the walk-away value of the parties rather than legal norms, voting strength in Parliament, or the Chancellor's formal constitutional position.

Although the Basic Law establishes a 'Chancellor principle', it simultaneously gives cabinet ministers individual responsibility for all matters within their departments' jurisdictions ('departmental principle'). The Chancellor does not have the right to circumvent a minister and intervene directly in a ministry, although most Chancellors in practice have developed a strong interest in foreign and security matters and interfered with the jurisdiction of the foreign ministry (for the Kohl era, see Korte 2000: 7). At the domestic level, however, the experts in the departmental bureaucracies usually enjoy a tremendous informational advantage vis-à-vis elected politicians. Laver and Shepsle (1996: 13) therefore maintain that (generally in Western Europe) 'only the government department with jurisdiction over a particular policy area is effectively equipped to develop feasible and implementable policy proposals in that area and present these to the cabinet for decision', strengthening the position of individual cabinet ministers vis-à-vis cabinet and head of government. In this view, ministers would de facto almost be the agents of 'their' bureaucracies. With specific reference to the (West) German system, Mayntz and Scharpf (1975: 48) assert in a similar vein: 'The political system's capacity for active policy-making is largely a capacity of its ministerial bureaucracy'.

Principals will have some control over agents if they have *ex ante* powers to choose them freely from a pool of suitable competitors, if they can monitor their behaviour, and if they can reward or punish them *ex post facto*. While the monitoring capacity of the Chancellor's office is highly developed, the Chancellor's powers of appointment and dismissal are limited both within his own party and, even more so, vis-à-vis other coalition parties. Within his own party, the Chancellor has to ensure the representation of important ideological factions, socio-economic interests, regions, and the main religious denominations. His influence on the selection of ministerial personnel in his coalition partner's party is even more limited. *Ex post facto*, it can be extremely difficult for a Chancellor to 'discipline' ministers belonging to a different coalition party if they enjoy the support of their own party's leadership. It may even be costly for the Chancellor to punish defiant ministers of his own party, if they enjoy strong intraparty support.

In addition to the 'Chancellor' and 'departmental principles' the Basic Law stipulates a 'cabinet principle'. Certain powers, such as the right to initiate legislation and to appeal directly to the Federal Constitutional Court, are exercised collectively by the federal government. Article 65 of the Basic Law states that differences between members of the federal government are to be resolved by the cabinet as a whole. Thus, the Federal Chancellor has no constitutional right to act as an arbiter. Also, the cabinet must be collectively informed about the appointment of high-ranking civil servants and political appointees to the civil service. Nevertheless, the cabinet as a collective body has tended to be weak. It usually meets only once a week. Its agenda is prepared by the Chancellor's Office. Most conflicts over policy are resolved in interministerial negotiations before an issue is allowed on the agenda by the Chancellor's Office. The formal cabinet decision rule is majority voting, yet such votes are highly exceptional. Differences of opinion are usually resolved at earlier stages, for example in coalition committees or interministerial committees of civil servants. Formal votes are therefore often an indicator of a breakdown of the usual coordination mechanisms and an imminent coalition crisis (Rudzio 2000: 290–3).

There are a number of organizational devices designed to alleviate the impact of departmentalism. Direct interministerial negotiations at the bureaucratic level (including representatives from the Chancellor's Office) are one important device, especially for routine matters. Cabinet committees in the British sense do exist, but are not considered to be important coordination mechanisms (Müller-Rommel 1994: 155). The most important steering bodies are more informal coalition talks and bodies. The reliance on such informal bodies has increased in the past two decades, especially during the Kohl era (1982–98). They usually comprise the Federal Chancellor or his representatives, some cabinet ministers and representatives of the extra-parliamentary party leadership, as well as the leadership and policy experts of the parliamentary parties. The overall direction of policy, important policy decisions, and questions of coalition governance are dealt with in these informal bodies. The cabinet and the parliamentary majority parties are often left with the task of implementing the decisions made in these bodies. Routine matters tend to be dealt with in cabinet; important policy changes are virtually always prepared in coalition talks (Korte 2002: 88–90; Schreckenberger 1994: 334).

These bodies have been effective in reducing the scope for agency loss *within* the government and the transaction costs of coordination between departments, government parties inside and outside Parliament, the *Länder*, and other actors with veto powers in the German political system. Despite a large number of such actors, this system of informal co-ordination has been capable of responding quickly and decisively to important challenges, as in the case of German unification. The disadvantage of informal arrangements is the downgrading of the cabinet's role, a lack of transparency, and a reduction in government accountability vis-à-vis voters and Parliament. The interactions in such informal bodies are difficult for principals to observe and make it difficult to establish the political responsibility for decisions. The fact that the Schröder government (1998–)—after initial attempts to reinstitutionalize the decision-making processes within the constitutional framework of cabinet government and more formalized coalition committees—swiftly returned to the informal system of 'secret governing' (Korte 2002: 88–93) characteristic of the Kohl era, indicates the attractiveness of such a system to incumbents. The return to such a model was partly driven by a desire to reduce public information about internal disagreement, partly because the formal interministerial coordination bodies turned out to be ineffective.

DELEGATION FROM MINISTERS TO CIVIL SERVANTS

As in all political systems, the information asymmetry between elected politicians and civil servants with greater expertise and resources to generate and process information is highly problematic. Generally, there are a number of ways for ministers to enhance bureaucratic accountability and responsiveness in their respective departments: control of top departmental appointments, ability to use 'rewards and punishments' both in promotions and policy decisions, ability to appoint ministerial staff to top-level department positions, and providing clear direction (Dunn 1999). For a number of reasons most of these mechanisms are problematic in the German case.

1. The Federal Ministers often have little direct control over policy implementation. Much of domestic federal legislation is implemented by *Länder* governments or parapublic bodies with considerable autonomy. Unlike the United States government, the German federal government, in most policy areas, cannot rely on its own administrative infrastructure at regional or local levels. The federal bureaucracy accounts for less than one-tenth of all civil servants (for data see Rudzio 2000: 294). Since state civil servants are primarily accountable to their state governments that are, in turn, accountable to regional parliaments, the usual agency problems affecting unitary states are compounded by multiple-principal problems if and when there is a conflict of interest between the federation and the *Länder*. Even many agencies that *are* under direct federal jurisdiction enjoy a considerable degree of autonomy. Several parapolitical bodies such as the Federal Bank or the Federal Employment Office, as well as a large number of corporate bodies, foundations, and institutes, are organized under public law and carry out important policy functions, often in cooperation with interest groups. Some of them play a crucial role in the economic management and in the social welfare sector and 'wield substantial power virtually unchecked by the federal government' (Katzenstein 1987: 58, see below).

2. Despite an increasing tendency for civil servants to be party members (1970: 28 per cent, 1987: 57 per cent), ministers' control over staffing in their departments is limited. In 1967 the introduction of 'parliamentary secretaries of state' (modelled

largely on British junior ministers) did strengthen the political control of departments and liaison between Parliament and the top level of Federal Ministries. In addition, there have always been political appointees to the civil service: ministers may require permanent secretaries and heads of divisions to take 'temporary retirement' replacing them with qualified persons of their own choosing. Compared to the United States or France, however, the number of political appointees is small (1994: 161). In addition, there are relatively few negative sanctions available to ministers. Career civil servants or long-serving public employees cannot easily be demoted or dismissed. Ministers do have some opportunities to use positive incentives, mainly promotions. However, civil service law and the powerful staff councils in the ministries limit even their powers of promotion (Rudzio 2000: 308).

3. This lack of federal control over domestic policy implementation is compounded by two organizational features of the federal bureaucracy itself: The federal bureaucracy 'is a steep hierarchy in which the apex has little control over lower levels' (Katzenstein 1987: 19). Departments have a four-tiered organizational structure. The minister, occasionally (depending on the size and importance of the department) aided by one or two junior ministers, and one or two permanent secretaries are at the top of the pyramid. The second and third levels are the divisions and subdivisions. Sections typically have 3–5 civil servants and represent the fourth level, which is crucial in the process of detailed policy development (Katzenstein 1987: 20; Rudzio 2000: 305).

Given the low level of control the federal government can exercise over policy implementation, it has to rely strongly on *ex ante* control through the detailed drafting of bills after early, comprehensive consultations with all veto players. This approach involves two main sorts of costs: (a) Relatively detailed laws, leaving relatively little discretion to local bureaucracies in the implementation process, may lack the flexibility that is necessary to adjust a piece of legislation to different local conditions. (b) The attempt to reach *ex ante* agreements with the *Länder* and interest groups involved in the running of a number of semi-autonomous para-political bodies (such as the Federal Employment Office or the various social insurance funds) may carry high transaction costs for the government if and when its preferences differ from those of important veto players. Such bargaining also leads to a lack of decision-making transparency.

EXTERNAL CONSTRAINTS

Germany fits the description of a *'constitutional democracy'*. The Basic Law is a constitution which can be enforced by courts and which specifies particular majority requirements for constitutional changes. It requires institutions and incumbents to act on behalf of the constitution and certain interests, even if these diverge from the preferences of the voters: For example, the first twenty Articles as well as Articles 101, 103, and 104 of the Basic Law guarantee fundamental and inalienable rights and liberties which as directly enforceable law bind the legislature, the executive, and the judiciary. Their 'essential content' may not be encroached upon, by either a majority of the voters or a majority of elected Members of Parliament.

The German polity is characterized by a large number of powerful institutional checks on Parliaments and governments both at the national and *Land* levels. The *Federal Constitutional Court* has far-reaching powers of judicial review and is by parliamentarians perceived to be a serious constraint (cf. von Beyme 1998: 105–14). The judges are appointed for a single term of 12 years, or until they reach the retirement age of 68, whichever is earlier. The Federal Government does not have complete *ex ante* control over the appointment of judges to the Federal Constitutional Court. A selection committee of the Bundestag elects only eight of the sixteen judges, the Bundesrat the other half. In both Houses, successful candidates need to achieve a two-thirds majority. Although the judges are, in effect, nominated as a result of bargaining between the major parties, they are very unlikely to behave as party agents. They tend to be quickly co-opted by the norms of the Court and to act independently of the parties that nominated them. The Constitutional Court is not a court of appeal in civil or criminal cases, but a constitutional watchdog for the defence of individual liberty and civil rights. It may consider constitutional complaints brought by individual citizens or organizations claiming that their constitutional rights have been violated. It is the final arbiter of disputes between institutions of the federation, between the federation and the *Länder*, between different federal states, and between other courts. In addition, under the rules governing 'abstract norm review', the federal government, a state government, or a group of at least one-third of the Members of the Bundestag may challenge the constitutionality of any federal or state law, even if this does not involve a particular case arising from its implementation (Goetz 1996: 97–8).

Germany is a *federal republic* in which the sixteen states (*Länder*) enjoy not only autonomous decision-making powers in certain policy areas defined by the constitution, but also considerable legislative and veto powers at the national level. In much of the period between 1969 and 2000, there has been 'divided government' in the sense that the government at the national level did not enjoy clear majority support in the Bundesrat representing the *Land* executives. This is not to say that the national opposition controlled the Bundesrat. The increasing differences between regional party systems (especially after unification) have led to more and more complicated coalition alignments at the *Land* level frequently cutting across the government–opposition divide in the Bundestag, giving rise to a great deal of bargaining and strategic behaviour (König and Bräuninger 1997; Zohlnhöfer 1999). The *Länder* have increasingly responded to the erosion of their own autonomous policy-making powers due to growing dependence on central financial resources and European integration by using their powers to amend or block national legislation in the Bundesrat (von Beyme 1998: 98–9, 141). As a result, the federal government needs to engage in bargaining with the *Länder* in many policy areas in order (a) to get bills passed by the Bundesrat and (b) to get them (and EU legislation) implemented without delay.

Many executive responsibilities are delegated to *nearly autonomous* or *semi-autonomous bodies* such as the Federal Bank, the Federal Employment Office, and numerous other bodies organized under public law to carry out important federal policy functions.[14] The Federal Bank (*Bundesbank*) is one such parapublic institution, which

---

[14] For a more detailed account see Katzenstein (1987: 58–80).

'enjoys a degree of autonomy from the federal government and private interest groups which is more far-reaching than comparable institutional arrangements in the United States, Britain, France, Japan, and Sweden' (Katzenstein 1987: 60). The Bundesbank must support the government's overall economic policy, but only if that policy does not interfere with the bank's overriding statutory duty to safeguard the currency. With the establishment of European Monetary Union most of the Federal Bank's powers to set interest rates have in practice been transferred to the European Central Bank, which adds an additional constraint on economic and fiscal policy for all member states of the European Monetary Union. Critics of independent central banks often focus on their character as agents, whose relationship with democratically elected principals such as MPs or government ministers is (by design) extremely loose, casting doubt on the democratic legitimacy of their often far-reaching decisions. Yet independent central banks may also be important mechanisms to redress information asymmetries in economic policy-making by reducing the government's ability to hide unfavourable information and providing the public with key information on economic policy (Bernhard 1998: 314).

Finally, membership of the EU is a very important constraint on at all levels of Germany parliamentary democracy. EU policy-making involves a great deal of intergovernmental bargaining which may entail some agency loss in the delegation from national Parliaments to governments (Scharpf 1988; Lupia 2000; Saalfeld 2000*d*). Generally the information asymmetry between the federal government and the Bundestag is even greater in EU matters than in purely domestic affairs, making it difficult for the Bundestag to hold the federal government accountable for its role in shaping particular EU decisions (Bulmer 1986: 222, 243). In the German case, the EU-related agency problems are compounded by the existence of simultaneous multiple-agent and multiple-principal arrangements. Interministerial coordination within the federal government has traditionally been weak in EU matters, although the Schröder government (elected in 1998) has strengthened the coordination role of the Ministry of Finance. Yet, in practice neither the Chancellor's Office nor any other ministry exercises effective and detailed oversight over the negotiations between departmental experts in the EU's Committee of Permanent Representatives (COREPER) or other bodies responsible for the preparation of EU legislation. It is not unheard of for different ministries to pursue conflicting policies.[15] This trend has become more pronounced as EU policy has increasingly become domestic in character. In their areas of exclusive jurisdiction, the German *Länder* are represented in the Council of Ministers and other bodies by their own delegates, which adds to the multiple-agent problems. Not only may the lack of interministerial coordination within the German government and between federation and the *Länder* weaken the German bargaining position in the EU; it also undermines government accountability vis-à-vis the Bundestag, as policy responsibility is hard to establish. To some extent the information problems have been addressed in a 1992 constitutional amendment which codifies the Bundestag's and Bundesrat's

---

[15] For example the Ministry for Environmental Protection and the Ministry of Economic Affairs in the field of environmental policy (see Wurzel 2000).

information rights in the area of the EU, and through the establishment of a new EU Affairs Committee of the Bundestag in 1994. Nevertheless, parliamentary monitoring of government policy in Brussels remains highly problematic (Saalfeld 1995). One of the traditional problems of parliamentary scrutiny of EU legislation, the departmental standing committees' strenuous defence of their traditional jurisdictions, has continued to hamper the development of the EU Affairs Committee as an effective instrument of parliamentary accountability. In practice the lack of coordination within the federal government, leading de facto to multiple agents of Parliament with conflicting objectives, is mirrored by competition between different scrutiny committees at the parliamentary level.

CONCLUSION

The Basic Law was designed in 1948/49 to avoid the political divisions and instability experienced under the Weimar Republic (1919–33) and to prevent the abuse of power experienced under National Socialism (1933–45). This led to a constitutional design that is contradictory from the perspective of principal–agent theory. On the one hand, the Basic Law has strengthened the representative system of government, establishing a unified chain of delegation and accountability. Compared to the Weimar Constitution, direct democracy was reduced to a minimum, the powers of the head of state were greatly reduced, and the powers of the Federal Chancellor were strengthened, as was his direct accountability to the Bundestag. Yet, the Basic Law simultaneously created a host of powerful institutional checks on the government, which, de facto, dilute the unitary chain of delegation and accountability and lead to complex, multi-layered agency relationships. The *Land* governments, the Federal Constitutional Court, the Federal Bank, and para-political agencies make, influence, execute, delay, and veto policy. Decisions are frequently compromises between the federal government and some of these various actors. If no compromise is possible, the status quo is preserved increasing the risk of a reduction of the system's problem-solving capacity.

For much of the Federal Republic's history, the incentives to seek consensus and compromise have been strong and beneficial to the country's political stability. Nevertheless, the resulting bargaining processes often take place outside the formal constitutional chain of delegation and accountability. Their multilevel nature and complexity give the federal government additional discretion and opportunities to avoid political responsibility. In the terminology of principal–agent theory, they have created the potential for hidden action and 'moral hazard'. These dangers are compounded by the relatively infrequent alternation in office throughout the postwar period. The revelations about former Chancellor Kohl's party finance practices (1999/2000) triggered the 'biggest scandal in postwar German political history' (Clemens 2000: 25), and can be seen as an—admittedly extraordinary—illustration of this danger.

Given the organizational strength of the German parties, there has not been a rapid decline of *ex ante* screening processes similar to the developments in other Western countries (e.g. see Strøm 2000: 283). Nevertheless the consequences of these party-based selection processes are in dispute as far as they favour professional career politicians without a great deal of experience outside politics.

Although the Bundestag has at its disposal a relatively highly developed arsenal of *ex post* monitoring devices and all the usual dismissal powers, the federal government's negotiations in coalition committees at the federal level, in joint bodies with the *Länder*, and, in particular, at in the EU are difficult to scrutinize. To be sure, parliamentarians of all major parties are involved in these multilevel bargaining processes, but transparency is limited and political responsibility is often difficult to establish—especially for the voters. The virtual 'Grand Coalition' system (Schmidt 1996) with a large number of veto points has ensured political stability but also increased decision-making costs and reduced transparency. At the same time wider access to education and a revolution in the media sector have contributed to a more educated, informed, and critical public. The growing gap between popular expectations on the one hand and consensual, elite-dominated decision-making 'behind closed doors' on the other has arguably contributed to a growing disaffection with representative democracy. As a result of this growing pressure, the governmental agents in the Federal Republic (like most of their counterparts elsewhere in Western Europe) have increasingly faced the problem of 'diverted accountabilities' (Strøm 2000: 284) as government ministers have to serve several (often competing) principals simultaneously: Parliament, their parties, and the voters.

REFERENCES

Arndt, Claus (1989). 'Fraktion und Abgeordneter', in Hans-Peter Schneider and Wolfgang Zeh (eds.), *Parlamentsrecht und Parlamentspraxis in der Bundesrepublik Deutschland*. Berlin: Walter de Gruyter.

Bernhard, William T. (1998). 'A Political Explanation of Variations in Central Bank Independence'. *American Political Science Review*, 92: 311–28.

Bracher, Karl Dietrich, Jäger, Wolfgang, and Link, Werner (1986). *Republik im Wandel 1969–1974: Die Ära Brandt (Geschichte der Bundesrepublik Deutschland*, Volume 5/I). Stuttgart/Mannheim: Deutsche Verlags-Anstalt/Brockhaus.

Bulmer, Simon (1986). *The Domestic Structure of European Community Policy-Making in West Germany*. London: Garland.

Busch, Andreas (2000). 'The Grundgesetz after 50 Years: Analysing Changes in the German Constitution'. *German Politics*, 9(1): 41–60.

Busse, Volker (1997). *Bundeskanzleramt und Bundesregierung: Aufgaben, Organisation, Arbeitsweise*. Heidelberg: Hüthig.

Clemens, Clay (2000). 'A Legacy Reassessed: Helmut Kohl and the German Party Finance Affair'. *German Politics*, 9(2): 25–50.

Conradt, David P. (2000). *The German Polity*, 7th edn. New York: Longman.

Dästner, Christian (1995). *Die Geschäftsordnung des Vermittlungsausschusses*. Berlin: Duncker & Humblot.

De Winter, Lieven (1991). 'Parliamentary and Party Pathways to the Cabinet', in Jean Blondel and Jean-Louis Thiébault (eds.), *The Profession of Government Minister in Western Europe*. Basingstoke: Macmillan.

Döring, Herbert (1995). 'Time as a Scarce Resource: Government Control of the Agenda', in Herbert Döring (ed.), *Parliaments and Majority Rule in Western Europe*. Frankfurt am Main: Campus and New York: St. Martin's Press.

Dunn, Delmer D. (1999). 'Mixing Elected and Nonelected Officials in Democratic Policy Making: Fundamentals of Accountability and Responsibility', in Adam Przeworski, Susan C. Stokes, and Bernard Manin (eds.), *Democracy, Accountability, and Representation.* Cambridge: Cambridge University Press.

Dürig, Günter (ed.) (1994). *Grundgesetz mit Vertrag über die abschließende Regelung in bezug auf Deutschland, Menschenrechtskonvention, Bundesverfassungsgerichtsgesetz, Parteiengesetz und Gesetz über den Petitionsausschuß,* 32nd edn. Munich: Deutscher Taschenbuch Verlag.

Gabriel, Oscar W., Niedermayer, Oskar, and Stöss, Richard (eds.) (1997). *Parteiendemokratie in Deutschland.* Bonn: Bundeszentrale für Politische Bildung.

Goetz, Klaus H. (1996). 'The Federal Constitutional Court', in Gordon Smith, William E. Paterson, and Stephen Padgett (eds.), *Developments in German Politics 2.* Basingstoke: Macmillan.

Grewe, Wilhelm (1951). 'Parteienstaat—oder was sonst?' *Der Monat,* 3(36): 563–77.

Grosser, Dieter (1975). 'Die Sehnsucht nach Harmonie: Historische und verfassungsstrukturelle Vorbelastungen der Opposition in Deutschland', in Heinrich Oberreuter (ed.), *Parlamentarische Opposition: Ein Internationaler Vergleich.* Hamburg: Hoffmann und Campe.

Gunlicks, Arthur B. (1988). 'Campaign and Party Finance in the West German "Party State"'. *Review of Politics,* 50: 30–48.

Hasselsweiler, Ekkehart (1981). *Der Vermittlungsausschuß.* Berlin: Duncker & Humblot.

Ismayr, Wolfgang (1992). *Der Deutsche Bundestag: Funktionen, Willensbildung, Reformansätze.* Opladen: Leske + Budrich.

——(1999). '50 Jahre Parlamentarismus in der Bundesrepublik Deutschland'. *Aus Politik und Zeitgeschichte,* B20: 14–26.

Jesse, Eckhard (1990). *Elections: The Federal Republic of Germany in Comparison.* Oxford: Berg.

Kaack, Heino (1971). *Geschichte und Struktur des deutschen Parteiensystems.* Opladen: Westdeutscher Verlag.

Katzenstein, Peter J. (1987). *Policy and Politics in West Germany: The Growth of a Semisovereign State.* Philadelphia: Temple University Press.

King, Anthony (1976). 'Modes of Executive–Legislative Relations: Great Britain, France and West Germany'. *Legislative Studies Quarterly,* 1: 11–36.

König, Thomas (1998). 'Regierungswechsel ohne politischen Wandel? Ein Vergleich des wirtschaftspolitischen Handlungsspielraums der Regierung Kohl, einer Regierung Schröder, einer Großen Koalition und einer SPD-Alleinregierung.' *Zeitschrift für Parlamentsfragen,* 29: 478–95.

——and Thomas Bräuninger (1997). 'Wie wichtig sind die Länder für die Politik der Bundesregierung bei Einspruchs- und Zustimmungsgesetzen?' *Zeitschrift für Parlamentsfragen,* 28: 605–27.

Korte, Karl-Rudolf (2000). 'Solutions for the Decision Dilemma: Political Styles of Germany's Chancellors'. *German Politics,* 99(1): 1–22.

——(2002). 'The Effects of German Unification on the Federal Chancellor's Decision-Making.' *German Politics,* 11(3): 83–98.

Krehbiel, Keith (1991). *Information and Legislative Organization.* Ann Arbor: University of Michigan Press.

Laver, Michael and Kenneth A. Shepsle (1996). *Making and Breaking Governments: Cabinets and Legislatures in Parliamentary Democracies.* Cambridge: Cambridge University Press.

Leibholz, Gerhard (1966). *Das Wesen der Repräsentation und der Gestaltwandel der Demokratie im 20. Jahrhundert,* 3rd edn. Berlin: Walter de Gruyter.

Lösche, Peter (1993). *Kleine Geschichte der deutschen Parteien.* Stuttgart: Kohlhammer.

Lupia, Arthur (2000). 'The EU, the EEA and Domestic Accountability: How Outside Forces Affect Delegation within Member States'. *Journal of Legislative Studies*, 6(1): 15–32.

Mayntz, Renate and Scharpf, Fritz W. (1975). *Policy-Making in the German Federal Bureaucracy*. Amsterdam: Elsevier.

McCubbins, Mathew D. and Schwartz, Thomas (1984). 'Congressional Oversight Overlooked: Police Patrols versus Fire Alarms'. *American Journal of Political Science*, 28: 165–79.

Mintzel, Alf and Heinrich Oberreuter (eds.) (1992). *Parteien in der Bundesrepublik Deutschland*, 2nd edn. Bonn: Bundeszentrale für Politische Bildung.

Müller-Rommel, Ferdinand (1994). 'The Role of German Ministers in Cabinet Decision Making', in Michael Laver and Kenneth A. Shepsle (eds.), *Cabinet Ministers and Parliamentary Government*. Cambridge: Cambridge University Press.

Naßmacher, Karl-Heinz (1997). 'Parteienfinanzierung in Deutschland', in Oscar W. Gabriel, Oskar Niedermayer, and Richard Stöss (eds.), *Parteiendemokratie in Deutschland*. Opladen: Westdeutscher Verlag.

Niclauß, Karlheinz (1999). 'Bestätigung der Kanzlerdemokratie? Kanzler und Regierungen zwischen Verfassung und politischen Konventionen'. *Aus Politik und Zeitgeschichte*, B20: 27–38.

Nohlen, Dieter (1986). *Wahlrecht und Parteiensystem*. Opladen: Leske + Budrich.

Paterson, William E. (2000). 'From the Bonn to the Berlin Republic'. *German Politics*, 9(1): 23–40.

Patzelt, Werner J. (1995). 'German MPs and Their Roles', in Wolfgang C. Müller and Thomas Saalfeld (eds.), *Members of Parliament in Western Europe: Roles and Behaviour*. London: Frank Cass.

Poguntke, Thomas (1994). 'Parties in a Legalistic Culture: The Case of Germany', in Richard S. Katz and Peter Mair (eds.), *How Parties Organize*. London: Sage.

Pulzer, Peter (1995). *German Politics 1945–1995*. Oxford: Oxford University Press.

Rausch, Heinz (1981). *Parlament und Regierung in der Bundesrepublik Deutschland*, 6th edn. München: Landeszentrale für Politische Bildungsarbeit.

Roberts, Geoffrey (1997). *Party Politics in Germany*. London: Cassell.

Rudzio, Wolfgang (1991). 'Informelle Entscheidungsmuster in Bonner Koalitionsregierungen', in Hans-Hermann Hartwich and Göttrik Wewer (eds.), *Regieren in der Bundesrepublik II: Formale und informale Komponenten des Regierens in den Bereichen Führung, Entscheidung, Personal und Organisation*. Opladen: Leske und Budrich.

——(2000). *Das politische System der Bundesrepublik Deutschland*, 5th edn. Opladen: Leske+Budrich.

Saalfeld, Thomas (1995). 'The German Houses of Parliament and European Legislation'. *Journal of Legislative Studies*, 1(1): 12–34.

——(1998a). 'The German Bundestag: Influence and Accountability in a Complex Environment', in Philip Norton (ed.), *Parliaments and Governments in Western Europe*. London: Frank Cass.

——(1998b). 'Germany', in George Thomas Kurian and Lawrence D. Longley (eds.), *World Encyclopedia of Parliaments and Legislatures*. Vol. 1. Washington, DC: Congressional Quarterly Press.

——(2000a). 'Bureaucratisation, Coordination and Competition: Parliamentary Party Groups in the German Bundestag', in Knut Heidar and Ruud Koole (eds.), *Parliamentary Party Groups in European Democracies*. London: Routledge.

——(2000b). 'Coalitions in Germany: Stable Parties, Chancellor Democracy and the Art of Informal Settlement', in Wolfgang C. Müller and Kaare Strøm (eds.), *Coalition Governments in Western Europe*. Oxford: Oxford University Press.

——(2000c). 'Court and Parties: Evolution and Problems of Political Funding in Germany', in Robert Williams (ed.), *Party Finance and Political Corruption*. Basingstoke: Macmillan.

——(2000d). 'Members of Parliament and Governments in Western Europe: Agency Relations and Problems of Oversight'. *European Journal of Political Research*, 37: 353–76.

Schäfer, Friedrich (1982). *Der Bundestag: Eine Darstellung seiner Aufgaben und seiner Arbeitsweise*, 4th edn. Opladen: Westdeutscher Verlag.

Scharpf, Fritz W. (1988). 'The Joint-Decision Trap: Lessons from German Federalism and European Integration'. *Public Administration*, 66: 239–78.

Scheuch, Erwin K. and Scheuch, Ute (1993). *Cliquen, Klüngel and Karrieren: Über den Verfall der politischen Parteien – eine Studie*. Reinbek bei Hamburg: Rowohlt.

Schindler, Peter (1994). *Datenhandbuch zur Geschichte des Deutschen Bundestages 1983 bis 1991*. Baden-Baden: Nomos.

Schmidt, Manfred G. (1996). 'Germany: The Grand Coalition State', in Josep M. Colomer (ed.), *Political Institutions in Europe*. London: Routledge.

Schreckenberger, Waldemar (1994). 'Informelle Verfahren der Entscheidungsvorbereitung zwischen der Bundesregierung und den Mehrheitsfraktionen: Koalitionsgespräche und Koalitionsrunden'. *Zeitschrift für Parlamentsfragen*, 25: 329–46.

Schüttemeyer, Suzanne S. (1994). 'Hierarchy and Efficiency in the Bundestag: The German Answer for Institutionalizing Parliament', in Gary W. Copeland and Samuel C. Patterson (eds.), *Parliaments in the Modern World: Changing Institutions*. Ann Arbor, University of Michigan Press.

Stöss, Richard (ed.) (1986). *Parteienhandbuch: Die Parteien der Bundesrepublik Deutschland 1945–1980*. Opladen: Westdeutscher Verlag.

Strøm, Kaare (2000). 'Delegation and Accountability in Parliamentary Democracies'. *European Journal of Political Research*, 37: 261–89.

von Alemann, Ulrich (2001). *Das Parteiensystem der Bundesrepublik Deutschland*. Second edition. Opladen: Leske + Budrich.

von Beyme, Klaus (1998). *The Legislator: German Parliament as a Centre of Political Decision-Making*. Aldershot: Ashgate.

Wiesendahl, Elmar (2000). 'Changing Party Organisations in Germany: How to Deal with Uncertainty and Organised Anarchy'. *German Politics*, 8(2): 108–25.

Wurzel, Rüdiger (2000). 'Flying into Unexpected Turbulence: The German EU Presidency in the Environmental Field'. *German Politics*, 9(3): 23–42.

Zohlnhöfer, Reimut (1999). 'Die große Steuerreform 1998/99: Ein Lehrstück für Politikentwicklung bei Parteienwettbewerb im Bundesstaat.' *Zeitschrift für Parlamentsfragen*, 30: 326–45.

11

Greece: 'Rationalizing' Constitutional Powers in a Post-dictatorial Country

GEORGIOS TRANTAS, PARASKEVI ZAGORITI, TORBJÖRN
BERGMAN, WOLFGANG C. MÜLLER, AND KAARE STRØM[1]

INTRODUCTION

The 1975 Constitution gave the Greek President important powers such as the right to dissolve the Parliament and to call a national referendum without the countersignature of the cabinet. In the 1986 Constitutional revision, most of these rights were distributed among the Prime Minister (PM), the cabinet, and the Parliament. The amendments placed most powers in the hands of the PM. This concentration of power in one elected representative must be understood against the backdrop of Greek historical experience. The Second World War was followed by a bitter civil war (1944, 1945–9). The subsequent 1952 Constitution gave the King important powers in government formation. In 1955 King Paul pre-empted a decision by the ruling Conservative Party by naming Constantine Karamanlis, then a senior minister, PM after the death of PM Marshal Papagos. In 1963, without calling for new elections, the King forced Karamanlis to resign. In 1965, a new political crisis broke out when King Constantine II insisted on having a say in the naming of government ministers. At this time, PM Papandreou resigned, even though his party held an absolute majority in Parliament. The trauma that these power struggles inflicted helped bring about the 1967 military *coup d'état* (Legg 1969, 1973; Katsoudas 1987).

The Colonel's regime declared a Republic in 1973 but fell when the Turkish invasion of Cyprus made its position untenable (1974). At this point, Karamanlis was called in from his Paris exile and formed the so-called 'Government of National Unity', which included members from the old conservative and centre parties, personalities from the struggle against the dictatorship, and technocrats. This Government managed in a short period to lay the bases for a liberal political system and to hold free elections (Diamantouros 1984, 1986, 1991; Kaminis 1993). The newly elected Parliament's main task was to draft a new Constitution.[2]

---

[1] Professor Trantas provided a chapter draft on this topic in 1998. The other authors have then revised, updated, and completed the chapter.

[2] The form of Government was settled by a referendum that decided in favour of a Republic.

The Constitution of 1975[3]

Because of the 1967–74 dictatorship, many believe that Greece has an authoritarian political tradition. In fact, dictatorship has been the exception in Greek political history, but the 1967 dictatorship did have a strong impact on subsequent constitutional developments. As the dictatorship was partly caused by the bankruptcy of parliamentary institutions, the new Constitution of 1975 tried to 'rationalize' the political process by reinforcing the executive and limiting the possibility of parliamentary obstruction (Alivizatos 1979, 1990; more generally see Huber 1996: ch. 1).

Article 1 of the Constitution of 1975 states that the government of Greece is a 'parliamentary presidential democracy'. The term 'presidential' emphasizes the republican character of the Constitution, while 'parliamentary' stresses the way in which power is to be exercised. Parliamentarism was deemed so important that Article 110 states that no constitutional amendment may change this feature of Greek democracy. The Constitution gives the Chamber of Deputies a central role in Greek politics. It also endorses the principle that all state organs should be legitimized by the people through Parliament. At the same time, it provides the instruments by which the executive dominates the Parliament.

The original 1975 Constitution was, however, ambiguous as to the balance between the President and the Parliament. The President of the Republic was given certain constitutional powers reminiscent of those of the Fifth Republic French President. He could, for example, preside over the Council of Ministers (the cabinet) and dissolve the Parliament with ease. He had considerable freedom to appoint the PM whenever there was no clear majority in Parliament, and some legislative veto power. During the 1975–81 period, when the conservative party New Democracy (ND) ruled, Presidents Tsatsos and Karamanlis made no use of these powers. Neither stressed the presidential elements of the Constitution. Political tension marked the 1981–5 period of *cohabitation* between President Karamanlis and the socialist government of Andreas Papandreou (Manessis 1985; Clogg 1993). In 1986, a major constitutional reform stripped the President of all prerogatives that could enable him to intervene actively in day-to-day Greek politics. This largely eliminated all constraints on governments with majority support in Parliament.

Some constraints exist, such as judicial review of the constitutionality of laws.[4] This means that the Courts must not apply laws they find contrary to the Constitution. Traditionally, Greece has been a strongly centralized unitary state. Furthermore, local and regional government have been gaining power and influence and this has added a new, albeit still weak, constraint on national decision-makers. International constraints such as the European Union (EU) and the jurisprudence of the European Court of Justice and the European Court of Human Rights have also become more important. However,

---

[3] If not otherwise noted, the presentation draws primarily on Manitakis (1994), Spyropoulos (1995), and Pantélis (1979).

[4] All courts can examine the constitutionality of laws. According to Article 13, § 4 of the Constitution, 'The Courts must not apply laws the content whereof is contrary to the Constitution'. In practice, however, the judgements of the Supreme Civil and Criminal Court and the Council of State prevail over the decisions of other courts. It belongs to the jurisdiction of the Special Highest Court to settle disagreement between two courts over the constitutionality of a law (Article 100, § 1e).

Greece has no second chamber, no federal system, and no constitutional court. Thus, the Greek Government is almost omnipotent, at least in institutional terms.

Law-making and Constitutional Amendments

Formally, legislation is essentially the business of Parliament. The right to legislative initiative belongs to the government or to the individual members of the Chamber of Deputies. The government submits its proposals in the name of the cabinet as a whole and these proposals dominate legislative output. In contrast, bills introduced by individual Members of Parliament (MPs) are seldom successful. The MPs of the governing party do not even make practical use of this right. Opposition MPs introduce legislative proposals, but these are practically doomed because the Standing Orders of the Chamber reserve only 1 day in the month for private member bills. Discussion of a private member bill also demands the accord of the majority in the Parliament, that is, consent by the government party. It is thus not surprising that in the period 1974–98 only two private member bills related to minor issues were passed. There are also other constitutional limitations on the legislative initiatives of individual MPs. For example, private member bills on pension issues are not allowed.

Thus, in practice, legislative initiatives are in the domain of the cabinet.[5] Its power is further enhanced through its right to amend bills that are pending in Parliament, while amendments of individual MPs are procedurally restricted. Amendments are very important in Greek legislative practice. Although the Constitution could be read as forbidding the addition of unrelated provisions in a statute, the Courts have hitherto not enforced such a rule. Until relatively recently, this meant that most bills ended up with a great number of amendments, most of them irrelevant to their nominal subject. By freely adding amendments to pending legislation, all governments have avoided serious problems relating to party cohesion and the implementation of its legislative programme. At the same time, such practices damage the transparency of legislation and usually confer particularistic benefits. The abuse of government amendments goes back to the Constitution 1952, but was perhaps most pervasive after the Socialists came to power in 1981. Since the formation of the Simitis Government in 1996, a serious effort has been made to limit such legislation. Currently, amendments are usually limited to matters that at least belong to the jurisdiction of the ministry that has prepared the bill.

Normally a bill is first introduced in committee[6] and then on the floor.[7] Debate may take place either in Plenum or with the Parliament divided into two sections. The

[5] The preparation of cabinet bills was in the past mostly the work of the civil servants of the relevant ministries. Today the relevant minister's advisers usually prepare bills. It is an established practice that bills, before they are sent to Parliament, are examined by the Central Committee on the Preparation of the Legislation, a committee of experts (usually senior judges and academics) that gives its opinion on the structure and the wording of the bill, but not on its content. The committee functions as an early warning device concerning the constitutionality of the bill.

[6] There are six standing legislative committees, each with a jurisdiction corresponding to a ministry. According to the standing orders, a bill may not be discussed in more than three sessions of the committee. When the deliberations are concluded, the Committee submits a report to the House.

[7] Bills may be and usually are sent to the academic service of Parliament for its opinion concerning the legal technicalities of the bill and also its constitutionality.

latter was common practice up until 1977 but has not been used since then.[8] The bill is first discussed on the floor on principle, then article by article. But if there is an agreement among the parties, as there is with most international agreements, bills are passed after little or no debate. Furthermore, the cabinet can introduce 'extremely urgent' bills directly on the floor. Voting then takes place within one day after a limited debate. With the assent of the Chamber, such a bill can be discussed over a period of 3–5 days.

Historically, opposition MPs commonly misused the quorum requirements to halt government legislation. Hence, the Constitution of 1975 abolished the (formal) quorum requirement for most parliamentary proceedings. If a vote is called, a bill passes when a majority of the MPs present in the Chamber vote in favour. However, the majority in favour of the bill cannot be lower than one-fourth of all MPs (and in the sections two-fifths of the MPs that are members). These rules have led to a situation where often only a few MPs participate in the debates. Sometimes only the minister and one or two MPs from the opposition debate a bill. As the opposition does not usually bother to object, in practice most bills are passed with only a handful of MPs present.

A bill passed by the Chamber is then sent to the President of the Republic who signs it and orders its publication in the Official Journal, and thus it becomes a law. The cabinet, or the PM and the competent minister, must also sign the bill. Almost all acts of the President have to be signed by a person who is responsible before the Chamber. However, on his own, within a month, the President has the right to return the bill to the Chamber for reconsideration and to state his reasons for this. The bill is then discussed in plenary meeting. If a majority of all MPs of passes the bill, then the President is obliged to publish it within 10 days. This is a very weak veto. Furthermore, the fact that strong parliamentary majorities typically support Greek cabinets makes it highly improbable that the veto will be sustained. Thus, the veto has never been used. As Greece has a very strong unicameral tradition, there is no other veto player that can stop a legislative initiative supported by a strong parliamentary majority.

The President of the Republic (in practice the proposing and countersigning minister) has only limited autonomous rule-making powers.[9] This is the right to decree the conditions for the execution of laws. Instead the vast decree power of the Greek executive is delegated by ordinary legislation (Spiliotopoulos 1987). The delegation is to the President of the Republic, though for less important matters to the cabinet, the PM or individual ministers, public bodies, or local authorities. Each law contains a vast number of delegations, which, however, must be specific. This means that the law should provide the general principles and procedural guidelines and specify the time limit

---

[8] The sections are divisions of the Parliament. They are not committees but true legislative organs working within the Parliament. By the absolute majority of the total number of deputies, the 1975/86 Constitution allows Parliament to decide the composition and functioning of the Sections at the beginning of each parliamentary session.

[9] The autonomous decree power was sometimes abused until the early 1990s (when the courts greatly curtailed the practice), as ministers and, sometimes, the cabinet itself set rules without delegation from Parliament. These rules were later ratified by Parliament but until then were legally invalid though nevertheless followed by the administration.

within which the executive must make such authorization. In reality, the parliamentary majorities have given Greek governments much discretion in using their decree power. However, there seems to be a decline in the (mis-)use of this practice.

There is also an *ex post* legislative control mechanism. This is the 'Council of State', which was created after the model of the French *Conseil D' Etat*. It is the Supreme Administrative Court of Greece. Under the Constitution the Council can annul acts and financial decisions by administrative authorities on grounds of abuse of authority or violation of the law. It can also 'clarify' the meaning of a disputed law. The Council is also heard (*ex ante*) when the government issues regulatory decrees.

Amending the Constitution

With the exception of certain key provisions (the republican and parliamentary democratic form of government, separation of powers, basic human rights), the Constitution can be amended. But no amendment can be initiated within 5 years of the most recent amendment. They must also be passed by two successive Parliaments with an intervening election. A proposal to amend the Constitution needs to be sponsored by fifty MPs. Parliament specifies the provisions to be amended and decides on the issue either by a majority of three-fifths (180 MPs out of 300) or by absolute majority of all MPs (151). The following Parliament in its first session decides which amendments will finally be adopted. Consequently, the new Parliament has the power to amend or abolish the provisions of the proposing Parliament. The majority required for adoption depends on the size of the majority in favour in the proposing Parliament. An absolute majority (151 MPs) is required for one of the decisions and three-fifths majority (180 MPs) in the other, irrespectively of order. But it belongs to the new Parliament to decide whether these provisions will be finally revised.

The 5-year time limitation, the required majorities, and the involvement of two consecutive Parliaments make constitutional amendment very time-consuming and difficult. After the Constitution came into force in 1975 there has been only one constitutional amendment (in 1986). But, the Parliament elected in 2000 had to decide which of fifty-seven different amendments to adopt. These proposal concerned a variety of issues, but even if forty-eight of 119 articles were amended the changes have been characterised as a 'vaguely defined modernization' (Alivizatos and Eleftheriadis 2002: 71) that did not change the basic structure of the Greek Constitution.

POLITICAL PARTIES

On the long road to parliamentary democracy, traditional social structures and the existing networks of clientelism were transformed and became the bases upon which political parties were born. The Constitution of 1975 (Article 29) is the first to recognize political parties and guarantee their freedom. Furthermore, it recommends that parties be democratically organized—although this is not an enforceable constitutional requirement—and calls on the state to fund them.

For most of the period since the restoration of democracy, the party system has been a 'two and a half' system (Mavrogordatos 1983, 1984). The Conservative 'New Democracy' Party and the Socialist PASOK have attracted most of the votes (Clogg 1992; Doukas 1994).[10] The Greek Communist Party (KKE) was a third (half) force, but the party has in the last decades experienced major losses. Other smaller parties have emerged, but face tough constraints in the electoral law and the extreme polarization of Greek politics. In 1989 KKE, together with EAR, EDA, and other leftist groups, merged into the electoral alliance 'Synaspismos' ('Coalition'). When 'Synaspismos' participated in a 1989 coalition cabinet with ND, many people argued that it had developed into a new party of the Left. However, the KKE split over the merger in 1991. In the June 1989 election Democratic Renewal (DIANA), a splinter party of ND, was the only party that survived the extreme polarization and gained one seat, due to the high popularity of its leader Constantine Stephanopoulos. After the next (1990) election, the party used its seat to support ND so that the ND could form a government that enjoyed the confidence of the Parliament. In 1993, ND split over the recognition of the Former Yugoslav Republic of Macedonia (Kentrotis 1994). This led to the creation of a new political party called 'Political Spring' (Politiki Anoixi), which won representation in both the 1993 national election and the 1994 European elections, but failed to develop into more than a single-issue party and lost its representation in the Chamber of Deputies in 1996.[11] DIKKI, a small, new party playing on the anger of traditional PASOK voters over the government's EMU-related austerity programme did gain parliamentary representation in that election. Despite the existence of so many small parties, Greek cabinets have except for the period 1989–90 been one-party cabinets (ND 1974–81 and 1990–3, PASOK 1981–9 and since 1993).

The Constitution does not regulate internal decision-making in political parties. The statutes of Greek parties vest authority either in the executive committee or by the party congress. However, all parties are highly centralized. In practice, except for the Communist Party, the party leader makes most major decisions. The congress and the other party organs have only an advisory role and usually merely endorse and legitimize decisions already taken. The major role of the congress is to elect the party leader. However, this can lead to a conflict with the parliamentary group.[12] Regional or

---

[10] On the right there were ultra-conservative, pro-dictatorial, and pro-monarchist parties, while PASOK had ascended at the expense of the old Union of the Centre Party, its successor (EDIK), and the small Social Democratic Party (KODISO). On the left, KKE was challenged by a faction that left the party after the Prague Spring and created the Euro-communist party ('KKE of the Interior', later Greek Left—EAR). KKE also battled with the EDA Party, a cover party for KKE during the pre-dictatorial period when KKE was outlawed, but later a Euro-communist Party. EDA cooperated with PASOK in the 1980s.

[11] In the 2000 election it joined forces with the Conservative Party.

[12] In late 1995, when Papandreou (PM and President of the Socialist Party) collapsed due to failing health, the question of his successor as PM arose. The Constitution states that in such cases the parliamentary group of the majority party elects a new leader who will then be named as the new PM. However, the statute of the Socialist Party (PASOK) states that the PM should be the President of the party, elected by a party congress. Because a congress requires months of preparation, it was proposed that a new PM and acting party

local party organizations are extremely dependent of the central party machine. These levels are primarily an instrument for the implementation of central party decisions and not so much a vehicle for the representation of party members. This is one reason why Greek parties are not fractionalized.[13]

Party finance is a very complicated and hotly debated issue. Except in the small parties on the Left, member contributions make up only a tiny proportion of the party budget. The state pays large subsidies to the parties.[14] These are mostly given to the two big parties, but smaller parties are also financed. The Law on Party Finance provides that parliamentary representation is required for state subsidies but in 1984 ad hoc rules were created to provide financial means to parties that used to have MPs or MEPs. The Law regulates private contributions for candidates but not for political parties.

DELEGATION FROM VOTERS TO MPS

Since 1958 Greece has had a 'reinforced proportionality' electoral system intended to encourage the creation of two big parties that can alternate as the majority party (Penniman 1981). Under the present form of reinforced proportionality (1990), the country is divided into fifty-six electorals districts (Pantélis 1991).[15] The first distribution of seats takes place on the basis of voting in these districts, using the Hagenbach–Bischoff formula. This means that the electoral quota that a party must obtain in order to get a seat is found by dividing the total number of votes by the total number of seats plus

---

President be elected by the party central committee and then ratified by the parliamentary group. This solution was rejected by the parliamentary group, which then proposed Kostas Simitis as PM while the ailing Papandreou remained President. The party crisis continued. Simitis, seemingly with majority support in the parliamentary group, threatened to resign. Threatened with the prospect of new elections, the party congress elected Simitis President. The episode suggests that the parliamentary group does have the muscle to impose its will on the party.

[13] As the two main parties Greek parties (PASOK and ND) have few important policy differences, politics are usually built around political tactics and personal feuds rather than policy. Personality politics dominate the party agenda. This is no surprise considering the omnipotence of the party leader not only in the administration of the party but also in candidate selection and party finances.

[14] It is well known that political parties face economic problems and that many of them are heavily indebted to state banks. State funding was introduced in 1984. Subsidies are predominantly given to parties represented in the Chamber of Deputies or in the European Parliament. According to the 1984 Law on Party Financing, a party is entitled to public financing if it received at least the 3 per cent of the vote in the election (5 per cent for an alliance of two parties, 6 per cent for an alliance of three or more parties) and ran candidates in at least two-thirds of the electoral districts. The law also made it possible for parties that did not meet these qualifications to receive some support if they had met the vote requirement in one of the previous two elections. A later amendment provides public financing for parties that hold at least one seat in the Chamber of Deputies or the European Parliament. The subsidies are divided among the parties largely according to their vote share. Legislation also limits the electoral budgets of individual candidates. However, as is characteristic of Greek politics, after the 1996 election the report of the control commission charged with examining election spending was set aside. Parliament passed a bill that gave immunity to MPs who had overspent and cancelled the heavy fines imposed under the law.

[15] The electoral district is generally the Prefecture. There are five single-member districts. Only 288 MPs are elected in electoral districts. Twelve national seats are divided among the parties on the basis of their share of the national vote using the d'Hondt system.

one. Since 1990, only parties that win 3 per cent of the national vote can win seats in this round. This makes it practically impossible for small regional parties and independent candidates to win a seat.

A second round of seat distribution takes place in thirteen regional electoral districts. It used to be that votes that were not used to fill seats in the first round of seat distribution were transferred to the next round. Only parties that had won at least 17 per cent of the vote went on to the second round (Vegleris 1983). Under the 1990 Electoral Law, not just remaining votes, but all votes and the remaining seats are transferred to the regional level. If after the second distribution there are still unassigned seats, there is a third distribution. In the first phase of this third round, the party with the greatest number of votes nationally automatically gets unassigned seats in those electoral districts in which it got the most votes. In the second phase the total number of votes that each party won and the remaining seats are transferred to a unique national district. As in all previous rounds, the Hagenbach–Bischoff formula is applied. If, after all this, there are still unassigned seats, then they are all awarded to the party that won the largest number of votes.

Under the present electoral system, the plurality party can easily acquire a strong majority in Parliament if its share of the national vote is 1–3 per cent higher than that of the second-largest party. (The exact number depends on the electoral success of the smaller parties.) Smaller parties might field a joint list of candidates in order to under-mine the rules favouring the big parties. To avoid this, the electoral law eliminates possible electoral coalitions of parties by limiting their participation in the second round of seat distribution. Only parties that receive more than 3 per cent of the total vote are allowed to participate. To aid small parties, the so-called 'normalization' procedure takes effect after the third round of distribution. This complex procedure, introduced in 1990, guarantees that smaller parties will not receive fewer than 70 per cent of the seats corresponding to their percentage of the national vote. In practice a considerable number of seats won by the party that came in second are thus given to parties that came in third and fourth. This procedure creates odd discrepancies at the district level. It is now common that a small party that wins only a small proportion of the district votes will get a district seat, while the party that comes in second may not be represented.

Voters cast votes for parties and, if they so prefer, for individual candidates on the party list. Candidates are listed alphabetically. The number of candidate votes allowed depends on the district's electoral population. In larger districts the voter has the chance to vote for two or three candidates. Thus in the end the voters and not the parties determine who will take a seat in Parliament, although the parties control candidate selection. Almost all voters cast candidate votes in addition to the party vote. The personal vote favours candidates who can create clientelist networks and those who have the support of particular interests (Lyrintzis 1984; Tzannatos 1986).[16]

---

[16] In 1985 Papandreou's Socialist government abolished the candidate vote to promote discipline inside the parliamentary group. However, the effort was not very successful because MPs that fell out with the leader had nothing to lose, especially at the end of a legislative period, by coming out openly against the party

Campaign spending by candidates is not regulated. Electoral competition among candidates in larger districts is stiff, and campaign costs are considerable. Hence, successful candidates must have strong financial support.[17] On the other hand, the personal vote does somewhat constrain the power of the party leader.[18]

Party statutes give party leaders responsibility for candidate selection. In practice, however, all sitting MPs are chosen as candidates. Because deputies have usually built a clientelistic network, it can be unwise for party leaders to create conflict with them just before an election. The leader has much more discretion with respect to new candidates. All parties in Parliament have internal advisory procedures. These take the form of proposals by the party prefecture committee,[19] which is usually 'controlled' either by a locally powerful MP or by the party leadership. These proposals do not bind the party leader. In many cases the leader uses such opportunities to 'parachute' into a district political friends or even people without any local or party affiliation.

The Greek Constitution is rich in regulations with regard to who may be elected as an MP. State officials may not be elected in districts in which they have exercised duties in the last 6 months. This rule was introduced to reduce the likelihood that civil servants would use their authority to capture the clientelist networks of local deputies. Its practical importance today is that party officials who serve as general secretaries in ministries or as Presidents/managers of state enterprises cannot be elected. Furthermore, there is incompatibility between the offices of mayor or elected prefect on the one hand and MP on the other. There exist no term limits or mandatory retirement regulations.

DELEGATION FROM PARLIAMENT TO CABINET

Delegation from Parliament to government is highly formalized through the Constitution and the regulation of the Chamber of Deputies. The relevant rules tend to promote government stability and to reinforce the rights of the Government over the Chamber of Deputies. In addition, the party leaders appoint the party's parliamentary spokespersons. The latter do not function as whips but are the permanent representatives of the parliamentary group in the plenary debates. The party leadership also appoints the *rapporteurs* for legislative proposals and the members of parliamentary commissions. The Parliamentary Rules of Procedure also prohibit private member bills that have not been approved by the party leader or the party's parliamentary spokesperson.

---

leadership. The measure seems to have been more useful to the opposition ND leader, Kostas Mitsotakis, than to Papandreou, since Mitsotakis used it to get rid of some old party barons and entrench his position as leader. The candidate vote was reinstated after the 1989 elections.

[17] After the 1989–90 experience, a modification of the electoral law provides that, if the Chamber of Deputies is dissolved before 2 years after the previous election, then the new MPs will be elected according to their list positions.

[18] In addition, there are twelve national deputies elected according to their position on the national party list. The institution of national deputies was intended to facilitate the parliamentary participation of national figures, including distinguished university professors, scientists, entrepreneurs, and also party worthies (e.g. former ministers or party leaders).

[19] In ND the proposal is formulated after a vote of the party members in the district.

The Appointment of a Government, Vote of Confidence, and Vote of Censure

According to the Article 37 of the Constitution, the President of the Republic appoints the PM and, on the PM's recommendation, appoints and dismisses cabinet members. Until 1986, the Constitution gave the President numerous opportunities to select the PM he preferred. This discretion has been eliminated. The Constitution now governs the appointment of the PM under two different circumstances. The first is when a single party has an absolute majority in Parliament, in which case the President has to name the leader of the party, or the person the leader proposes. If, on the other hand, there is no clear majority in the Chamber, or a government loses its majority, the Constitution describes in great detail the steps that the President is to follow in naming a PM.

In such a case, the President must first call upon the leader of the party that holds the greatest number of parliamentary seats to ascertain the possibility of forming a Government enjoying the support of the Chamber of Deputies. If he fails, the President then calls on the leaders of the second and third parties to try to form a government.[20] Each mandate lasts 3 days. If the mandates prove unsuccessful, the President summons all the party leaders. If all efforts to form a party government fail, the President tries to form a government composed of all parties in Parliament for the purpose of holding new parliamentary elections. If even the all-party attempt fails, he then entrusts a President of one of the three Supreme Courts to form a government as broadly acceptable as possible, and to charge it with the task of dissolving the Parliament and carrying out elections. This happened twice during the period 1989–90.[21] Thus the Constitution provides for three attempts to form viable governments and for two methods, to be used subsequently, to install a government selected only for the purpose of organizing elections.

After the government is appointed, it is obliged to ask the Parliament for a vote of confidence within 15 days after the PM has been sworn in. Table 11.1 shows how many votes have been held at the start of a new cabinet. The table also shows the frequency

[20] The Constitution provides that, if two parties have equal number of seats, both parties will be given a mandate to form a government. The party that won the most votes goes first. In addition, an older party has precedence over a newer. A maximum of four exploratory mandates are given.

[21] The elections of June 1989 produced a hung Parliament. After the leaders of the three big parties had failed to form a government, President Christos Sartzetakis then summoned them to a council, where they agreed to form a coalition government composed of the ND party and the Left party Synaspismos. The government was headed not by Mitsotakis, the leader of ND, but by Tzannis Tzanetakis, an ND deputy proposed by Mitsotakis. When the Tzanetakis Government had carried out its programme, it resigned. A new series of exploratory mandates and a party leader council failed to create a new government. The President then gave Grivas, President of the Areios Pagos (the Supreme Civil and Criminal Court), the task of forming a Government in order to dissolve Parliament and carry out elections. Grivas' appointment was accepted by all parties. The elections of November 1989 again resulted in a hung Parliament. After exploratory mandates failed, the President called a party leader council, which agreed to a coalition government of all the parties in Parliament, led by a former Governor of the Bank of Greece, Xenophon Zolotas. The experiment lasted only a few months, after which the parties had their ministers resign. A new set of fruitless exploratory mandates were extended, followed by a council in which party leaders agreed to let Zolotas form a Government for the purpose of carrying out the elections. The Parliament was dissolved and the election was held in April 1990. ND won the election.

Table 11.1. *Cabinet Formation, Cabinet Termination, and Early Parliamentary Dissolution: Greece 1977–2000[a]*

No.	Cabinet	Date of formation	Investiture votes (iv)						No-confidence votes (ncv)			Confidence votes (cv)		Did the cabinet end with an early election?	Who dissolved Parliament in this case?[b]
			No. of unsuccessful investiture votes	Voting results of successful iv (1: pro gov, 2: against gov, 3: abstentions, and 4: other)					No. of ncv	Cabinet removed by ncv	Cabinet resigned to pre-empt ncv	No. of cv under spec. inst. mechanism	Cabinet removed by failed cv?		
				1	2	3	4								
1	Karamanlis	77/11/28	0	171	126	3			0			0			
2	Rallis	80/05/10	0	180	115	4	1		0			0		Yes	Cabinet
3	Papandreou I	81/10/21	0	172	113	2	13		0			0		Yes	Cabinet
4	Papandreou II	85/06/05	0	161	138	1			2	No		1	No		
5	Tzannetakis	89/07/02	0	174	124	1	1		0			0			
6	Grivas[c]	89/10/12	—	—	—	5	—		—			—		Yes	Cabinet
7	Zolotas	89/11/23	0	292	1	5	2		0			0		Yes	Cabinet
8	Mitsotakis	90/04/11	0	152	146	1	2		1	No		1	No	Yes	Cabinet
9	Papandreou III	93/10/13	0	170	129	1			0			0			
10	Simitis I	96/01/22	0	166	123	8	3		0			0		Yes	Cabinet
11	Simitis II	96/09/25	0	161	134	5			—			—		—	

[a] n.d. = no data (missing data); n.a. or '—' = not applicable in this case.

[b] The question 'Who dissolved Parliament in this case?' can be anwered with one of five options. This identifies the main constitutional actor that caused the early election. We have not coded the formal signatory, but rather the person or body that made the real decision: (1) Head of State; (2) Prime Minister; (3) Cabinet; (4) Parliamentary majority; (5) Automatic constitutional provision (e.g. if it is required when a new President takes office, or, for example, if it is required after the adoption of a proposal for constitutional amendments).

[c] Non-partisan cabinet formed for the purpose of holding parliamentary elections only.

of confidence votes, no-confidence votes, and early parliamentary dissolution. This is also discussed further.

By stipulating that a new cabinet can be approved at a threshold lower than absolute majority, the rules favour the formation of a new cabinet. As a part of the inauguration process, there is a mandatory investiture vote (referred to as the mandatory *confidence* vote). As is the case with all explicit confidence votes the cabinet must show that it has the explicit the support of a majority of the MPs that vote. The size of this majority may be no smaller than two-fifths of the total number of all MPs. This could in theory mean that a new cabinet can form on the basis of the active support of 120 MPs, but as shown in Table 11.1, all cabinets have enjoyed the support of more than half of the MPs.[22]

During its lifetime, a cabinet has the right to demand a vote of confidence at any time. The decision rule is the same as the one used for the mandatory investiture vote. However, confidence votes have been requested only implicitly and in connection with the vote on the budget or on a politically important bill. In these cases governments have requested a vote of confidence not so much because it doubted its strength in Parliament, but in order to send a political message.[23]

According to the Constitution, cabinet members are collectively responsible before Parliament for general policy, and individually responsible for actions and omissions within the jurisdiction of their respective departments. Parliament may decide at any time to withdraw its confidence in the government. However, just as in the interest of government stability the Constitution promotes investiture, it also makes it difficult for parliament to pass an vote of no confidence (censure). A motion of censure must be signed by at least one-sixth of the MPs, virtually eliminating the possibility that one of the smaller parties could call for it. And while a majority of 120 MPs is sufficient to pass a confidence vote, a motion of censure demands an absolute majority of all MPs—that is, 151. Furthermore, once a motion of censure fails, a new motion of censure cannot be submitted for 6 months, unless it is signed by a majority of all MPs.

Even the procedure in motions of censure favours the incumbent government. Thus, while debate on the motion is to begin 2 days after it has been proposed in Parliament, the government can ask for immediate debate. In addition, while a vote of censure (no confidence) normally takes place immediately after the debate, it can be postponed for 48 hours at the government's request. To date these procedural privileges have not been used. In practice, motions of censure have only been used to force the

[22] During the 1993–6 legislature there was a greater amount of dissent among the MPs of the two big parties than before. This was probably due to the demise of charismatic party leadership (Karamanlis and Mitsotakis for the ND Party and Papandreou for PASOK). The development was most clear in the PASOK, where an identifiable intraparty opposition to Simitis emerged after the 1996 election. It is no longer rare for MPs to vote against their party instructions in parliamentary committees in the Chamber of Deputies. In most cases (and in particular in the Chamber's plenum) dissenting MPs simply do not show up to vote. This has caused particular difficulties for PASOK because the Simitis cabinet has not always been able to control a legislative majority.

[23] The government has asked for a vote of confidence on only three occasions: in 1987, 1992, and 1998. In the first two cases the government won easily. In 1998 PM Simitis had to threaten early elections to put down a 'mutiny' of some deputies who wanted to give him a 'qualified' vote of confidence. Because of the cross-natural counting rule not to report votes of confidence for cabinets still in power 1 January 2000, this vote is not included in Table 11.1.

government to defend its policies before the Chamber, thus giving opposition parties the opportunity to publicly present their own positions.[24] If the Chamber approved a motion of censure, the President of the Republic would relieve the cabinet of its duties.[25] The rules also reinforce the central role of the Prime Minister. A vote of confidence is essentially a vote of confidence in the PM, because after a cabinet reshuffle no vote of confidence is needed, nor has any government ever requested one. A motion of censure against the PM personally is considered to be a motion against the government.

The President cannot relieve a government (that is the PM) of its duties, except if it resigns or is voted down in Parliament. Nor can the President by himself prematurely dissolve the Chamber of Deputies. He can only do so in a formal act that is requested by the cabinet as a whole or when it is impossible to form a government that enjoys the confidence of the Chamber. In coalitions, all coalition parties must agree. Leaving aside the period 1989–90, all Greek elections have been preceded by a premature dissolution of the Parliament at the cabinet's request. According to the Constitution, dissolving Parliament is justified when the government faces a national issue of such exceptional importance that it demands the renewal of the government's popular mandate. Governments have easily found 'important' reasons to dissolve the Parliament when they have wanted to do so. In all cases, the President has accepted proposals from the government for the dissolution of Parliament.[26]

Mechanisms of Parliamentary Control

As already mentioned, the most important instrument of parliamentary control is the motion of censure that gives the opposition the opportunity to force a full, public debate on government policy. The PM has the right to give a short statement or to make an announcement about government policy at any Chamber meeting. If he does, it is followed by a short debate involving the party leaders. The government can also request a general debate on policy issues. Customarily, at least one or two such debates are held during each ordinary session of Parliament. The practice has been institution-alized, and since 1990 the Standing Orders require the government to ask for such a

[24] There have been only four motions of no confidence under the 1975 Constitution (1988, 1989, 1993, and 1996). All have been won, predictably, by the government. Because of the cross-national counting rule not to report votes of no-confidence for cabinets still in power 1 January 2000, the 1996 vote is not included in Table 11.1.

[25] If two governments have resigned or been voted down by Parliament and the composition of the Chamber does not guarantee governmental stability, the President of the Republic may dissolve the Parliament. The rationale is that the threat of dissolution may keep the Chamber from voting a government out of office. Yet, the President cannot dissolve the Parliament until 1 year has passed since its opening session, except when it is not possible to form a cabinet that enjoys the confidence of the Chamber.

[26] The dissolution of Parliament has practical importance because only in this case is the government entrusted with conducting elections, which is a certain political asset during the campaign. In other cases, this is done by a government headed by a person accepted by all the parties or by one of the Presidents of the three Supreme Courts. In August 1993 the Mitsotakis cabinet lost its absolute majority in Parliament due to the defection of some deputies. While the opposition was preparing a motion of censure, Mitsotakis asked for the dissolution of the Parliament with reference to national security. His proposal was accepted. Although at the time some criticized this as an abuse of procedure, "Mitsotakis' " action was technically correct.

debate at least once per session. The Standing Orders specify that during this debate Greece's relations with the EU are to be discussed. Finally, the Standing Orders give the opposition the right to ask for four such debates per session, two for the strongest opposition party and one for each of the smaller ones.[27] A variety of issues are discussed at each session, with the opposition giving emphasis to economic or foreign policy issues. Many existing laws require the government to submit annual reports to the Parliament on developments in various policy areas (e.g. European integration or drug abuse). In most cases the submission of such a report is followed by a short debate.

The usual instruments of parliamentary control include petitions, questions, and interpellations. Each citizen has the right to petition the Chamber, either through an MP or through the President of the Chamber. MPs can also support a petition sponsored by another MP or the President. Ministers are required to respond to such grievances within fifteen days of it being deposited in the Chamber. If a minister fails to do so, the President of the Chamber makes the petition part of the agenda for debate between ministers and deputies in Parliament.

Each deputy has the right to question ministers on any public issue within the minister's sphere of responsibility. Questions are written and responsible ministers are obliged to answer in written form within twenty-five days. If a minister fails to respond within that period, the question is submitted for debate on the floor of the Chamber, unless the minister responds after the deadline to the deputy's satisfaction. Deputies can also submit 'urgent' questions to the government. Urgent questions must be related to a current issue and are always discussed in the Chamber. Because there are usually many urgent questions, only those allowed by the parliamentary leadership of each party are submitted and only those that are subsequently drawn by lot, as provided in the Standing Orders, are discussed. There is an effort to discuss urgent questions from each opposition party and certain arrangements between the opposition parties seem to facilitate that. Debates on petitions, questions, and urgent questions are short. Debates on questions directed to the PM are longer. Only party leaders may pose such questions.[28]

Parliament can also demand a deposition of files or acts from the government. In this case, the responsible minister is obliged to provide Parliament with files or acts within twenty days unless they are related to a military, foreign policy, or state security secret. Deputies can also pose interpellations to ministers. In contrast to questions, these imply a certain censure of the minister and might lead to a motion of no confidence (something that has never occurred since 1975). An interpellation may follow a question or a demand for a deposition, for example, in cases in which a deputy considers a minister's response to be unsatisfactory. Interpellations are discussed in plenary. An interpellation debate can lead to a more general discussion, for example one that covers other interpellations against the minister. The decision to broaden the debate is made by the

---

[27] During his last period as PM, Papandreou's government was not forced to participate in such a large number of debates, most likely because of his health problems.

[28] Questions directed at the PM were introduced in 1990 and again in 1996. They were abolished during Papandreou's second term as PM (1993–6).

Chamber after a proposal from fifteen deputies. Once a week the Chamber discusses urgent interpellations, typically those favoured by party leaders.

Standing committees also exercise parliamentary control.[29] In 1993 an addition was made through a modification of the Standing Order. The legislative Committees can now, in plenary or, more often, in ad hoc subcommittees, hold hearings with ministers or under-secretaries, as well as with civil servants and officers of the armed forces. An exception is made with regard to defence issues, on which the Minister of Defence has the right to prohibit a hearing. Otherwise hearings are mandatory if they are supported by two-fifths of the members of the subcommittee. In effect, this gives the biggest opposition party the right to demand such hearings, which can be held once a month. After a hearing the subcommittee writes a report, which reviews the issue and includes the committee's conclusions and recommendations. On a proposal from the Government the Chamber can establish other committees, so called ad hoc committees. The leaders of each opposition party have the right to ask for such a committee once a year. Such committees have been created increasingly with bipartisan support (e.g. on drug abuse and social security reform).

An ad hoc committee on state enterprises and organizations is responsible for checking the qualifications of persons nominated by the government to head the most important state enterprises and organizations (e.g. the Public Electricity Corporation, the Greek Organization of Telecommunications, the Bank of Greece, the National Bank of Greece, the Commercial Bank of Greece). The committee has the authority to call persons to a hearing and to make recommendations to the responsible minister on appointments.

The legislation of 1990s allows parliamentary involvement in the oversight of certain sensitive policy issues. Thus, since 1998 the Governor of the newly independent Bank of Greece reports to the Parliament's Standing Committee on Economic Affairs. The newly created (1997) Citizen's Defender (Ombudsman) is named by the government following the proposal of the Parliamentary Committee on Institutional Affairs. Other special oversight agencies include the Commission for the Protection of the Inviolability of Personal Communications, the Commission for the Protection of Personal Data, and the Commission for the Selection of Public Employees.

Some of the traditional instruments of parliamentary control seem to have fallen into disuse. The Constitution requires the Chamber to hold a vote each year on the state's financial statement and the balance sheet of state finances. Although both votes give the Chamber the opportunity to undertake a thorough examination of state finances, in reality the Committee debate and plenary is entirely a formality, if one is held at all. The same is true of the debate concerning the Court of Auditors' annual report on state finances.

---

[29] During the preparation of a bill a standing committee has the right to hold hearings and call civil servants and experts to testify. A proposal to do so is made by the minister or one-tenth of the committee members. Hearings take place in the presence of the responsible minister. If representatives of organizations are called to the hearing, at least one-third must be called at the proposal of the opposition.

The so-called select committees of investigation have fallen into disuse. The Constitution states that such committees can be established by a resolution supported by two-fifths of the total number of MPs, after proposal from one-fifth of all MPs (i.e. 120 and 60 MPs, respectively). On foreign policy and defence matters, an absolute majority is needed (i.e. 151 MPs). Investigation committees were originally seen as essentially a minority right, but the Socialist majority in 1986 interpreted the Constitution as saying that an investigative committee requires the assent of the majority. This basically rendered the institution toothless. To date the majority has agreed to establish investigative committees only in three cases, all involving criminal charges against ministers. However, a recent modification of the Standing Orders provides for the possibility of investigative committees on the management of state enterprises and organizations.

With Chamber support a Greek minister or, usually, an ex-minister can only be brought to trial for crimes committed while in office. After an investigative committee or judicial investigation provides evidence of such criminal acts, the Chamber votes whether to prosecute or creates a committee of interrogation. In the latter case, the Chamber decides by absolute majority of all MPs whether to prosecute only after the committee has reported. If the Chamber votes to prosecute, then it elects a committee of five MPs (plus five substitutes) to act as public prosecutors before the Special Court that, under the Constitution, has jurisdiction in criminal cases against ministers.[30]

DELEGATION FROM CABINET TO INDIVIDUAL MINISTERS

The Constitution states that law must specify the composition and functioning of the cabinet. By decree, the PM may appoint Vice Presidents of the cabinet (Deputy PMs), Ministers, Substitute (or alternate) Ministers, Ministers without portfolio (now formally known as Ministers of State), and Under-secretaries. The Law stipulates that Deputy PM, Ministers, Alternate Ministers, and Ministers without portfolio are members of the cabinet with full voting rights. According to the current law, Under-secretaries are civil servants and not formally members of the cabinet. Under-secretaries are named in almost all ministries and exercise power given them by a joint decision of the PM and the relevant minister.

There are three models for the relations between ministers and Under-secretaries within the ministry. The first model gives the Under-secretary exclusive competence in certain areas. According to the second model, the Under-secretary is generally free to administer certain policy areas but the minister has the right to oppose his decisions. According to the third model the minister and the Under-secretary have concurrent

---

[30] In 1989 the new coalition government brought charges against former PM Papandreou and members of his cabinet. The two spectacular trials that followed were so acrimonious that, although three ex-ministers were convicted, it is now a common belief among politicians that the whole system for prosecuting ex-ministers should be depoliticized. The Socialists, back in power in 1993, tried to get revenge by prosecuting ex-PM Mitsotakis. The charges were eventually dropped.

jurisdiction, meaning that in case of differences of opinion the minister's opinion will be imposed. The PM and the responsible minister make the choice of model, but in practice their room for discretion varies with the political balance within the cabinet and the governing party. The Deputy PMs are not really second-in-command in the hierarchical chain (as their title might imply). Rather they sometimes substitute for the PM in cabinet sessions, and they might occasionally coordinate the work of other ministries. All these arrangements mean that governmental power below the PM is very dispersed. No inner cabinets of senior ministers exists that can challenge the authority of the PM.

As a constitutionally defined body, the cabinet is responsible for proposing and implementing policy and, as mentioned above, it has limited decree power. It is also responsible for nominating certain high officials (e.g. ambassadors, Presidents, and Vice-Presidents of the Supreme Courts). The *formal* appointment takes the form of a presidential decree. In the cabinet, voting takes place only in rare and politically controversial cases, and there is no established voting procedure. In practice, however, decisions are taken on the basis of majority rule, although the opinion of the PM naturally carries particular weight.

Both in legal terms and in practice, the minister is master of his ministry and the cabinet has only the executive powers given to it by law. Politically, however, a minister will rarely ignore the objections of his colleagues, in particular when there is a clear majority against him in the cabinet. Hence, the cabinet as a whole can and does settle a matter politically and impose its will on an individual minister who must either implement the decision or resign.

The Law on the Government provides for the creation of numerous cabinet committees. The Committee on Foreign Policy and Defence is responsible for most executive decisions dealing with the armed forces and the police. The Government Committees act as inner policy-making circles. These cabinet committees' coordinate ministerial activities and they control the way in which ministries exercise their authority.

The Minister is the Chief Executive over the policy areas for which his ministry is responsible. Although alternate ministers and under-secretaries can have specific responsibilities, they are nevertheless politically responsible to the minister. Ministers are not allowed to interfere in the administration of ministries other than their own. Most of the rule-making powers of the cabinet members are delegated to them by the President of the Republic. Ministers are responsible for proposing and countersigning presidential decrees within their jurisdiction. In addition, the Constitution allows the delegation of regulative authority to ministers and other administrative organs (e.g. local authorities and universities) on more specific matters, matters of local interest, or matters of a technical and detailed nature. Some of this delegation of authority (e.g. in environmental protection) is of great practical importance. In many cases ministers publish regulations without prior delegation of authority from Parliament. These decisions are then later ratified by Parliament. Although the Council of State has declared this behaviour unconstitutional, ministers still engage in it, though more recently in a less provocative manner.

Some ministers enjoy particular status. Aside from the Ministers of Foreign Affairs, Justice and Defence, and National Economy, the Minister of Finance plays an important coordinating role, which dates back to the huge crises in state finances of the 1920s, and gives him a virtual veto over all ministerial decisions with budgetary consequences. In every ministry, the Ministry of Finance also has agents who are either civil servants or political appointees and who are responsible for overseeing ministry spending and for ensuring that the budget targets are maintained. No changes in ministerial budgets are legitimate without the countersignature of the Minister of Finance. In addition, the Minister of Finance is the only person authorized to release credits from the budget's reserve funds.

The Minister of Interior (who nowadays also simultaneously has the symbolic position as the Minister of the Presidency of the Council of Ministers) is responsible for the civil service and public administration. In addition, he has special responsibility for the Official Gazette, which publishes all laws, decrees, or governmental and ministerial acts. The Minister thus exercises final overall control over the legislative and administrative output of the government.

These arrangements all support the Prime Minister as the ultimate power within the government. Although he is not formally hierarchically superior to the ministers, he makes proposals to the President of the Republic on appointing and dismissing ministers. (The President is bound by these proposals.) Thus, the Prime Minister is the real master of the cabinet. The Prime Minister also has two additional mechanisms for controlling the day-to-day business of the government: the Office of the PM and the Secretariat of the Government. The Office of the PM, which is directed by a trusted political friend of the PM, engages in policy planning as well as oversight of the Government. Of particular importance is the economic adviser to the PM. The Legal Department of the Office of the PM also plays an important role. According to established practice, a ministerial bill or amendment cannot be introduced to Parliament before the director of the Legal Department (usually a law professor or a judge) signs it. This is a discreet way for the PM to control the legislative initiatives of his ministers without getting involved in conflicts with them.

The Secretariat of the Government exists alongside the Prime Minister's Office and works in close cooperation with it. The Secretariat is not so much a policy-making body as an administrative staff. The Secretary General of the Government is responsible for following the implementation of cabinet decisions. Furthermore, the Legal Office of the Secretariat must before these are signed and published examine all drafts of presidential decrees or regulatory decisions by the government or individual ministers. This allows the PM to extend his control to the regulatory decisions of his government.

DELEGATION FROM MINISTERS TO CIVIL SERVANTS

The Constitution gives civil servants many guarantees concerning their careers and independence (Papadopoulou 1989; Skouris 1994). There are no *permanent* Under-secretaries in the ministries, with the exception of the Ministry of Foreign Affairs, in which the position has not been filled since 1968. The most senior civil servants are the Secretaries General. Because international diplomatic practice so requires, the Ministry of Foreign Affairs has a permanent Secretary-General and one alternate permanent Secretary-General named among its senior diplomats.

The Greek Civil Service used to be organized in a strictly hierarchical and bureaucratic manner. There were ranks connected with the exercise of certain administrative
duties. General directors, alternate general directors, and directors were the top civil
servants. In 1982, the Socialist government eliminated the positions of general director
and alternate general director along with the ranks inside the civil service hierarchy
(Tsekos 1986). These changes have enhanced party patronage (Sotiropoulos 1994;
Spanou 1996). Promotion to the position of directorship became a matter of ministerial
discretion, with ministers' decisions being based on party affiliations. Furthermore,
they only allowed three-year appointments, thus making the highest ranks of the civil
service even more dependent on the minister. When the number of experienced top
civil servants declined, ministers instead began appointing people from outside the civil
service, either experts (e.g. lawyers, political and social scientists, economists) or party
loyalists. When the Conservatives returned to government in 1990, they re-established
the civil servant rank of general director and eliminated time limits on appointments.
In 1993, when the Socialists returned to power, they retained the civil servant rank of
general director but they reintroduced the three-year appointment period.

In addition, a curious form of neo-corporatism has developed within the civil service.
Between the minister and his personal cabinet on the one hand, and the civil service
on the other, a vacuum has emerged due to the absence of top career civil servants.
This vacuum has been filled by civil servants' unions, which have become increasingly
powerful as the liaison between the minister and the civil service cadres.

EXTERNAL CONSTRAINTS

The President of Greece has very little influence in the country's political life. As
mentioned above, if he refuses to sign a decree on political grounds, a government that
enjoys a strong majority in the Chamber can easily override his veto. The same goes for
a proclamation of a referendum. In only one case can he override the cabinet (or more
specifically the Minister of Justice) and this concerns his right to the final word in
pardoning, commuting, altering, or reducing sentences pronounced by the courts of
law. Since 1986, the President can have an important impact on politics only by resigning, since this can force dissolution of the Parliament and new elections. A new
President must be elected with the support of at least two-thirds of all MPs. If this is not
possible in two ballots, then the Chamber can elect a President with the support of a
majority of three-fifths. If the third ballot fails, Parliament is dissolved and a new election called.[31] The President is also important for maintaining the functioning of the institutions of the Republic. In this role the President has often convened councils of the
party leaders to discuss political issues of grave importance, in particular those related
to foreign affairs. The decisions of the council of the political leaders, although not
legally binding on the government, are influential.

---

[31] The new Parliament again tries to elect a President with a three-fifths majority. If this is not possible, a
new vote is held, and this time only an absolute majority is required. Finally, if even this proves impossible,
a President can be elected with a relative majority.

Greek courts can have an important political impact by virtue of their authority to exercise judicial review (Vegleris 1967; Spiliotopoulos 1983; Dagtoglou 1986; Manitakis 1988; Skouris 1988). The Council of State is responsible for examining all drafts of presidential decrees. The control the Council exercises is limited to evaluating the constitutionality and legality of the draft decree and its reports are only advisory. Nonetheless, the examination procedure has acquired weight, because the practice has developed that the President does not sign any decree that does not follow the Council's recommendations. The Legal Office of the Presidency of the Republic determines whether ministers have followed the comments of the Council of State. Furthermore, the Constitution requires that bills providing state pensions must be sent to the Court of Auditors and to the state auditor. Although the comments of the Court of Auditors are not binding, the minister has an incentive to follow them, because otherwise the bill might later be struck down as unconstitutional.

A 1994 Law transformed the political organization of the regions (departments). Rather than prefects appointed by the government, elected prefects and departmental councils now administer departments. New legislation in 1997, which took effect with the October 1998 communal elections, called for the fusion of the thousand[s] of small and medium size communes and the creation of fewer and administratively more competent metropolitan communes. This might lead to communes that are more independent from the central government. These reforms, which are based on a French model, have created some confusion about the competencies of the central, regional, and local government. Handing over partial control of decentralized administrative agencies to elected officials has produced a limited but still important institutional constraint on the government.

Greece lacks a civil society that can balance and limit political institutions. The Greek Orthodox Church is the most important social institution. This is due to the importance Greeks give to their Church as part of their national identity, but also to its social work and financial power. Of particular political importance also is the National Bank of Greece, a private bank company in which the majority stocks are held by the state, the church, and public pension funds. A Governor named by the government administers it. The Governor has in many cases exercised an important behind the scene role bringing market realism in the development of economic policies. Greek trade unions are under party influence. Each party has its own trade union organization. Furthermore, trade unions are more or less financially dependent on state subsidies, a fact that increases the government's influence. In recent years, a degree of influence over government economic policy has been exercised by the Union of Greek Industries and the Union of Greek Banks. The latter is the umbrella organization of industrialists and bankers (state and private).

Although there are no real societal forces that can challenge the parties and their leaders (Papadopoulos 1989), these leaders are nevertheless suspicious of referendums, which may explain why no referendum has been held since 1975. The Constitution of 1975 gave the President of the Republic the power to call a referendum. Although the President has never exercised this power, it was viewed by many as a potential weapon that the President could use to block government policies. Thus it is not astonishing that the 1986 constitutional amendment cut the discretion of the President of the Republic to call a referendum. The Constitution now regulates the cases and the conditions under which a referendum can take place. There are two cases under which an *advisory* referendum might take place. The first concerns a serious national matter, that is a foreign policy question. Such a question can be put before the people when the government proposes this and Parliament so decides by an absolute majority of its members. The second case applies for an act of Parliament that concerns a serious question concerning society. In that case the President can refer the bill to the people, but only if this is supported by a three-fifths majority in Parliament. This rule permits only two such referendums per Parliament and these referendums cannot concern state finances. It is clear that under these rules the possibility of a referendum is extremely limited.

Greek politics is also influenced by international constraints, such as the conflict with Turkey over Cyprus, the status of the Aegean continental shelf, and the limits of the Greek territorial waters. The geopolitical situation became even more complicated after the fall of Communism and during the ensuing conflicts in the Balkans. The geopolitical situation has always made Greece look to foreign powers for protection—primarily the United States. Otherwise, the most important international constraint is the European one. Greece became a member of the European Communities in 1981, and is also a member of the Council of Europe and the European Convention on Human Rights and the European Social Charter, both of which create obligations with regard to legislation and political practices. In recent years the legality of many Greek laws and administrative practices have been tested before the EU and the European Court of Human Rights.

Opinion polls show that Greeks are one of the most pro-community peoples of the EU. Greek European policies are elaborated and implemented largely at the executive level without the participation of Parliament. The introduction of Community law in the Greek legal order is almost exclusively made through executive decrees. In the last few years, the standing Special Committee on EU Issues has begun to play a still very limited but at least more important role. This European Affairs Committee is mostly concerned with policy issues at the European level and not with the day-to-day implementation of European policies in Greece. The Foreign Ministry regularly briefs the committee on European developments and the committee occasionally hears experts. It submits a report to the plenary twice a year, both of which are followed by a debate. Otherwise, the Parliament gets involved only when a parliamentary statute is demanded by the Constitution (i.e. tax legislation) in the implementation of Community legislation. The fact that the implementation of Community law is delegated to the executive means that it is really only when the implementation takes the form of a presidential decree that there does exist a limited *ex ante* control in the form of the required opinion of the Council of State.

CONCLUSION

In Greece, the formal lines of delegation and accountability are clearly defined. The Greek process of delegation is highly institutionalized. The institutionalization is exhaustively regulated in the Constitution. This might suggest that Greece is an exemplary case of delegation and accountability. However, the importance of clientelistic networks should caution against this conclusion. Moreover, the 1975 Constitution meant to 'rationalize' Greek political institutions and nowhere is that clearer than in the relations between the cabinet and Parliament. Not only does the Constitution support cabinet stability, it also gives the cabinet the means to impose its will on Parliament in legislation. The electoral system also contributes to making the Greek government, perhaps after the British, the most powerful among the West European in its relationship to the Parliament. For many years the legitimacy of such an omnipotent executive was seen as unproblematic. Charismatic party leaders dominated the elections and ruled unchallenged over their respective party machines and parliamentary groups. The position of the PM was particularly strong. However, with the passing away of charismatic rulers, divisions inside parliamentary groups may increasingly challenge the dominance of the cabinet and change the institutional power balance in favour of the Parliament.

REFERENCES

Alivizatos, Nicos (1979). *Les institutions politiques de la Grèce à travers les crises, 1922–1974*. Paris: LGDJ.

——(1990). 'The difficulties of "rationalization" in a polarized political system: The Greek Chamber of Deputies', in Ulrike Liebert and Maurizio Cotta (eds.), *Parliament and Democratic Consolidation in Southern Europe*. London: Pinter.

—— and Eleftheriadis, Paulos (2002). 'The Greek Constitutional Amendments of 2001'. *South European Society & Politics*, 7:63–71.

Clogg, Richard (1992). *A Concise History of Greece*. Cambridge: Cambridge University Press.

——(ed.) (1993). *Greece 1981–1989. The Populist Decade*. London: Macmillan.

Dagtoglou, Prodromos (1986). 'Griechenland', in Christian Starck (ed.), *Verfassungsgerichtsbarkeit in Westeuropa*, Vol. 1. Baden-Baden: Nomos (leefloose).

Diamantouros, Nikiforos P. (1984). 'Transition to, and Consolidation of, Democratic Politics in Greece, 1974–1983: A Tentative Assessment', in Geoffrey Pridham (ed.), *The New Mediterranean Democracies: Regime Transition in Spain, Greece and Portugal*. London: Frank Cass.

——(1986). 'Regime Change and the Prospects for Democracy in Greece, 1974–1983', in Guillermo O'Donnel, Philippe C. Schmitter, and Laurence Whitehead (eds.), *Transitions from Authoritarian Rule. Prospects of Democracy*. Baltimore: John Hopkins University Press.

——(1991). 'PASOK and State–Society Relations in Post-Authoritarian Greece (1974–1988)', in Speros Vryonis Jr. (ed.), *Greece on the Road to Democracy: From the Junta to PASOK, 1974–1986*. New Rochelle: Ar. D. Caratzas.

Doukas, George (1994). 'Papandreou in Government Again: a New "Change"?', in Richard Gillespie (ed.), *Mediterranean Politics*, 1: 227–31. London: Pinter.

Huber, John D. (1996). *Rationalizing Parliament*. Cambridge: Cambridge University Press.

Kaminis, Georges (1993). *La transition constitutionnelle en Grèce et en Espagne*. Paris: LGDJ.

Katsoudas, Dimitrios K. (1987). 'The Constitutional Framework', in Kevin Featherstone and Dimitrios K. Katsoudas (eds.), *Political Change in Greece—Before and After the Colonels*. London: Croom Helm.

Kentrotis, Kyriakos (1994). 'Echoes from the Past: Greece and the Macedonian Controversy', in Richard Gillespie (ed.), *Mediterranean Politics*, Vol. 1: 85–103. London: Pinter.

Legg, Keith (1969). *Politics in Modern Greece*. Stanford: Stanford University Press.

——(1973). 'Political Change in a Clientelistic Polity: The Failure of Democracy in Greece'. *Journal of Political and Military Sociology*, 1: 231–46.

Lyrintzis, Christos (1984). 'Political Parties in Post-Junta Greece: A Case of Bureaucratic Clientalism?', in Geoffrey Pridham (ed.), *The New Mediterranean Democracies: Regime Transition in Spain, Greece and Portugal*. London: Frank Cass.

Manessis, Ariostovoulos (1985). 'L'évolution des institutions politiques de la Grèce: à la recherche d'une légitimation difficile'. *Les Temps Modernes*, no. 473: 772–814.

Mantakis, Antonis (1988). 'Fondement et légitimité du contrôle juridictionnel des lois en Grèce'. *Revue internationale de droit comparé*, 40: 39–55.

——(1994). 'Le régime constitutionnel de la Grèce', in Yves Guchet (ed.), *Les systèmes politiques des pays de l'union européenne*. Paris: A. Colin.

Mavrogordatos, George Th. (1983). 'The Emerging Party System', in Richard Clogg (ed.), *Greece in the 1980s*. London: Macmillan.

——(1984). 'The Greek Party System: A Case of "Limited but Polarised Pluralism"?' *West European Politics*, 7(4): 156–69.

Pantélis, Antoine (1979). *Les grands problèmes de la nouvelle constitution hellénique*. Paris: LGDJ.

——(1991). 'Chronique: Droit constitutionnel hellénique'. *Revue Européenne de Droit Public*, 3: 217–32.

Papadopoulos, Yannis (1989). 'Parties, the State and Society in Greece: Continuity within Change'. *West European Politics*, 12(2): 55–71.

Penniman, Howard R. (1981). 'The Modern Greek State and the Greek Past', in Speros Vryonis, Jr. (ed.), *The Past in Medieval and Modern Greek Culture*. Malibu: Undena Publications.

Skouris, Wassilios (1988). 'Constitutional Disputes and Judicial Review in Greece', in Christine Landfried (ed.), *Constitutional Review and Legislation*. Baden-Baden: Nomos.

——(1994). 'Das Recht des öffentlichen Dienstes in Griechenland', in Siegfried Magiera and Heinrich Siedentopf (eds.), *Das Recht des öffentlichen Dienstes in den Mitgliedstaaten der Europäischen Gemeinschaft*. Berlin: Duncker & Humblot.

Sotiropoulos, Dimitrios A. (1994). 'Bureaucrats and Politicians: A Case Study of the Determinants of Perceptions of Conflict and Patronage in the Greek Bureaucracy under PASOK Rule, 1981–1989'. *British Journal of Sociology*, 45: 349–65.

Spanou, Calliope (1996). 'Penelope's Suitors: Administrative Modernisation and Party Competition in Greece'. *West European Politics*, 19(1): 97–124.

Spiliotopoulos, Epaminados (1983). 'Judicial Review of Legislative Acts in Greece'. *Temple Law Quarterly*, 56: 463–502.

——(1987). 'Grèce—Les délégations législatives'. *Revue Française de droit administratif*, 3: 729–31.

Spyropoulos, Philippos C. (1995). *Constitutional Law in Hellas*. The Hague/Boston: Kluwer Law International.

Tsekos, Théodore (1986). 'Changement politique et changement administrative: La haute fonction publique en Grèce avant et après 1981', in Danièle Lochack et al.(eds.), *La haute administration et la politique*. Paris: puf.

Tzannatos, Zafiris (ed.) (1986). *Socialism in Greece—The First Four Years*. London: Gower.

Vegleris, Phédon Th. (1967). 'La Constitution, la loi et les tribunaux en Grèce'. *Annales de la faculté de droit de Liège*, 12: 439–77.

——(1983). 'L'évolution du système et des pratiques électorales en Grèce. Leurs résultats et leurs effets comparés—élections nationales et européennes', in Jacques Cadart (ed.), *Les modes de scrutin des dix-huit pays libres de l'Europe occidentale*. Paris: puf.

12

Iceland: A Parliamentary Democracy with a Semi-presidential Constitution

SVANUR KRISTJÁNSSON

INTRODUCTION

Parliamentary democracy was gradually established in Iceland. Or, as Icelanders prefer to put it, it was 're-established', as the Icelandic Parliament, the Althingi (Alþingi, founded in 930), reclaimed its central position in the Icelandic political system. The process began with the re-establishment of the Althingi in 1845, when Iceland was still subject to Danish rule. The parliamentary majority pressed for Iceland's sovereignty within a union with Denmark, while Danish authorities viewed Iceland as inseparable part of the Danish state. After a long impasse, Christian IX, King of Denmark, came to Iceland in 1874 and unilaterally granted the country a separate Constitution. The Althingi received financial power, subject to the King's veto. Executive power was placed in the hands of one Minister and remained part of the Danish administration until Iceland gained Home Rule in 1904. At that time the Minister became accountable to the Althingi.

The Republic of Iceland has a written Constitution. It was adopted in a national referendum in 1944, when Iceland declared its independence, thereby abolishing the union with Denmark. Centuries of foreign rule, which had begun in 1262, had finally ended. The mythological origins of parliamentary government in Iceland's golden past undoubtedly greatly strengthened the tiny nation's resolve to become an independent nation state. However, myths are seldom particularly conductive to clear thinking about principles of good government in the present.

The principles of Iceland's parliamentary democracy rest partly on a written Constitution, partly on conventions. The constitutional tradition is generally stronger than the written Constitution. Brought about in haste by the pressure of the Second World War, without due deliberation and calm reflection (not to mention the lack of proper consultation with Denmark, which suffered under German occupation), the Constitution of 1944 was only intended to be temporary. The intended full-scale revision has never been achieved, and the Constitution remains full of ambiguities. The separation

The author gratefully acknowledges the helpful suggestions on the text that have been provided by Auður Styrkásdóttir, Indriði H. Indriasson, and the editors.

of powers is vague, as is the constitutional position of the President. According to the letter of the Constitution, the Icelandic President has numerous political powers. In constitutional practice the President's position has varied greatly, mostly due to different circumstances as well as the political skills and role conception of each of the five individuals who have served as Iceland's President.

Evolving informal rules and conventions have often been a substitute for constitutional revisions. In this, today's Icelanders follow the political traditions of the past, when the struggle for independence was primarily a nationalistic one rather than a battle for government reform. The essence of political reform was defined in terms of national sovereignty rather than individual rights. This does not mean that the constitutional and legal framework is unimportant in an analysis of parliamentary government in Iceland. Rather, we must explain the development of the political system in terms of the way in which a changing combination of formal and informal rules affect the action of politics.

One important tradition that sets Iceland apart from its Scandinavian neighbours is its prevailing pattern of patronage. Politics Icelandic-style combines a personal style of politics with a non-bureaucratic, patronage-centred mode of public administration. This has implications for the whole chain of delegation and accountability, from voters to civil servants. Recent efforts to develop corporatist relations have also had an impact on Icelandic parliamentary government.

There are also environmental constraints that affect political behaviour at the national level. The Danish 'heritage' is one factor that has shaped Icelandic politics. NATO's presence on the island has also been a crucial factor affecting the country's political life. Since 1993 Iceland has been formally linked to the European Union (EU) through its membership in the European Economic Area (EEA). This relationship with the EU is an important factor in Icelandic politics. Finally, recent developments at the domestic local level also deserve to be mentioned here. Iceland has a strong unitary state. In recent years, however, there has been a move towards an increasing role for local government. The number of local governments was reduced from 204 in 1990, to 124 in the 1998 local elections. Responsibility for primary schools has been transferred from the central government to local ones. Additional transfers of political responsibility are planned.

National legislation is passed by the Parliament by a simple majority vote. Any MP can propose legislation, as can standing committees and cabinet ministers, who—with few exceptions—are also MPs. A parliamentary quorum consists of an absolute majority (50 per cent + 1 of all MPs) and when voting takes place, the vote of every MP is recorded. In the past, the Parliament's chamber was formally divided into two quasi-chambers. These chambers were not separately elected but in the beginning of each term Althingi divided itself into two chambers for conducting its legislative process. However, since 1991 the Parliament meets as a single chamber. The executive branch proposes most legislation. Formally, proposals come from the cabinet; however, in reality they are usually formulated by the government bureaucracy, interest groups, or, increasingly, in many cases dictated by the requirements of the EEA treaty.

Parliamentary legislation is not subject to review by any constitutional court, but the President can refuse to sign any law passed by the Parliament. Before such a law goes into effect, however, it must be put to the voters in a national referendum. The law is invalidated if a simple majority of those participating vote against it.

Two policy areas are subject to specific procedures that apply only to them, the budget and foreign policy. The budget proposal is processed according to special law, which requires the cabinet to submit the following year's budget as well as a three-year budget plan to the Althingi at the opening of the fall session. With regard to foreign affairs, the cabinet must confer with the foreign affairs committee before the introduction of legislative proposals.

Proposals for amending the Constitution are introduced in the Althingi. If they are approved by a simple majority vote—with quorum requirements identical with those in ordinary legislation—the Althingi is dissolved and a parliamentary election is held. The proposed constitutional amendment becomes a binding law provided that the new Althingi passes it unaltered. An important constitutional amendment in the 1990s is the 1995 addition of a catalogue of human rights to the Constitution.

The use of executive decrees was restricted by constitutional change in 1991. Previously executive decrees were frequently issued and only sometimes did they have to be confirmed in the next session of Althingi. The cabinet can still, with the President's authorization, issue executive decrees. Such decrees must be introduced in the Althingi at the beginning of the next meeting and are invalidated if not passed by the Althingi in 6 weeks time. After a constitutional change in 1991, the Althingi is permanently in session between elections. The Althingi is in recess between meetings and can be called into session at any time. It is up to the individual minister to decide on government regulations. Since the laws have become more open-ended and more complex over time, this has placed more capacity to make general rules in the hands of the ministers.

The government has various means at its disposal to conduct its business without involving the Althingi. The government is entrusted with implementation of legislation, frequently filling the space left by open-ended legislative bills of government decrees.

POLITICAL PARTIES

With regard to political parties, Iceland has basically had a four-party system since the 1930's. The Independence Party (IP) was founded in 1929 by a merger of the Conservative Party (founded 1924) and the Liberal Party (founded 1926). It usually receives about 40 per cent of the vote. The second largest party, the Progressive Party (PP), is located in the centre of the political spectrum. It was established in 1916 and since about 1980 it has received around 20 per cent of the national vote. The Social Democratic Party was founded in 1916 as the political arm of the labour movement. It was organizationally tied to the Icelandic Federation of Labour until 1942. Since that time the SDP was usually the smallest of the four main parties, receiving 14–16 per cent of the vote. Finally, the People's Alliance (PA) is a descendant of the Communist Party and other breakaway groups from the SDP and normally got around 15–18 per cent of the vote, thus making it the third largest party.

Since the early 1980s one or two smaller parties have also been represented in the Althingi. The Women's Alliance (WA) held seats from 1983 (see Styrkársdóttir 1986). Before the parliamentary elections of 1999 a new electoral alliance, the United Front, was formed, composed of four political parties: the PA, the SDP, the WA, and the People's Movement (a social democratic splinter party). It received nearly 30 per cent of the vote. A new Left-socialist party, the Left and Green Party, also fielded candidates in all electoral districts and won close to 10 per cent of the national vote.

The main parties are formally organized as mass political parties. In reality they are rather loose organizations. They do not collect membership dues, nor do they maintain reliable membership lists. Since the 1970's all traditional parties have adopted primaries to select candidates for parliamentary elections (the WA used selection committees for nominations). The primaries have reinforced the cadre-party character-istics of the parties, and have contributed to frequent internal disunity. Primaries have also reduced the parties capacity to formulate policy insofar as they encourage parties to settle for the most general common denominator with regard to taking policy posi-tions. But the established parties have been able to retain their central political role due to the conservative impact of Iceland's proportional electoral system and the very strong tradition of majority coalition cabinets.

On the whole, and in spite of the decentralized candidate selection process and the relatively low level of party cohesion, Icelandic political parties contest elections and form governments as organized entities. They are considerably weaker in policy formulation and decision-making. Thus, as we shall see, the effects of parties are much stronger at the level of delegation from voters to MPs and in the linkage running from Parliament to cabinet than in the delegation chain from cabinet to individual ministers or from ministers to civil servants.

DELEGATION FROM VOTERS TO MPs

The electoral system is part of the Constitution. It has been changed four times in the history of the Republic (1942, 1959, 1987, and 2000). In the period 1971–87, forty-nine of the sixty Althingi members were elected in eight constituencies: thirty-seven in five- and six-member constituencies, and twelve in Reykjavík, the capital. In each constituency, seats were allotted to ranked lists put forward by the political parties according to a simple proportional system (d'Hondt). The eleven remaining seats, the supplementary seats, were allotted to parties that had won at least one seat, the goal being to minimize the difference between each party's proportion of the vote and the party's proportion of seats in the Althingi. The supplementary seats were filled with candidates not elected in the constituencies, but next in line on their party's list.

In 1987 three parliamentary seats were added and new, complex rules of allocation were introduced. These are designed to better obtain the goal of exact proportional representation. As before, the voter selects one of the lists put forward by the political parties. The parties rank the candidates in advance and the voter has little chance of altering the ranking.

The many changes made in the Icelandic electoral system in this century have helped reduce the impact of the personal vote. This has happened in two ways: (1) By moving, in 1959, from a mix of single-member constituencies and proportional multi-member districts to a multi-member Proportional Representative (PR) system; (2) By changing counting rules in such a way that the alterations voters make in the ranking of list candidates weigh less than they used to in the allocation of seats to candidates.

Sometimes the number of such 'preference votes' is high, primarily in the form of crossing out the names of unpopular candidate(s). However, in practice the impact of such attempts is usually negligible. The last time such changes affected the selection of MPs was in the 1946 election when the popular Mayor of Reykjavík defeated a competing candidate who occupied a higher position on the same party list.

While the electoral system is characterized by absence of the personal vote, the opposite is true at the nomination stage. In this case the open primary method means that there is direct voter participation in the selection of candidates for the major political parties.

Primaries in Iceland have two main characteristics. First, party institutions do not screen candidates competing for top seats on the party list. The maximum requirement is that the candidate be a party member, and often the candidate must be endorsed by a small number (20–50) of party members. Secondly, the primaries are generally open. As most parties in most constituencies do not keep records based on dues-paying members, the distinction between party members, party identifiers, and other voters is unclear. Thus no real restriction on participation in primaries can be effectively applied.

Voting in one primary does not legally prohibit participation in another, and the participation rate at primaries is high. On occasion, in some constituencies more voters turn out for primaries than for the ordinary elections. One measure of the participation rate in the primaries is to compare the number of voters in each party's primaries to the total countrywide vote received by the parties in the general election. This percentage ranges from a low of 24 per cent (1991) to a high of 51 per cent (1978). Another indication is to compare the number of votes received by the same party only in those districts holding primaries. The summary percentage then range from 41 to 70 per cent. For an individual party in one district, the lowest percentage is 30 per cent, while the highest is an astonishing 140 per cent (Kristjánsson 1998: 177).[1]

The introduction of primaries in Iceland was a part of party strategy designed to deal with internal party disagreements on nominations and to improve the parties' electoral fortunes. It has indeed helped the four traditional parties to maintain their electoral standing. However, this innovation in party strategy has also had a wide-ranging and lasting impact on the parties as organizations, on the logic of politics and governance, and, ultimately, on the basic issues of democracy—namely, relations between the rulers and the ruled (Kristjánsson 1998).

The parties' role as intermediaries between voters and MPs has greatly decreased in the nearly three decades of primaries. Individual MPs are increasingly free agents. The party organization cannot control them *ex ante* through the process of screening and

[1] According to Gallagher and Marsh (1988), in other West European countries the highest percent of voters participation in nominations was 2.1 % (Belgium). During elections in Iceland from 1971, the percentage of primary elections voters relative to all eligible voters has been as follows: 1971–25%; 1978–32%; 1979–21%; 1983–26%; 1987–16%; 1991–15%; 1995–20% (Kristjánsson 1998: 177).

selecting candidates, nor can they use *ex post* mechanisms—that is, punishing MPs for not following the party line by denying them renomination or rewarding faithful ones by giving them safe or promising seats.

The impact of the open primary on relations between voters and MPs is complex. Thus, it is possible to view the primaries as having strengthened the role of voters as principals. This is of course true in a trivial sense—the winners of an open primary must have a strong personal following; the losers do not. However, there is more to it than this. The open primary also empowers voters by giving them an additional *ex post* device. It enables local voters to press their MP into providing them with extensive and concentrated constituency service, and offers them an opportunity to sanction the MP at the nomination stage.

The rational MP seeking re-election will try to please voters in his electoral district, because he/she knows that the nomination process is open to voter participation. In fact, the nomination stage is inherently more unpredictable and dangerous to sitting MPs than is the general election. In an open primary, there are no safe seats. Everyone can be defeated. Turnovers at the nomination stage are therefore rather frequent and, more importantly, sometimes very unpredictable. In contrast, there are many safe seats on the party lists in the general election. Defeats at this stage are confined to candidates occupying marginal places on the lists.

In short, the primary is by nature a personal vote. As mentioned, the voter can even occasionally select candidates for more than one party. The driving force behind this voting behaviour is not deceitful voters but rather the rules of contest. Candidates in an open primary seek to involve all voters favourable to them in the primary, regardless of whether they are party voters or not.

The open primary fits the prevailing pattern of patronage in Iceland. The informal, personal, and male-dominated political network is enforced by the system of political finance.[2] It has been estimated that during the 1995 parliamentary election—when approximately 170,000 people voted—political parties spent about 230 million Icelandic Krona (roughly 3.3 million US Dollars).[3] There are no restrictions on how much parties can spend in elections or otherwise; nor do political parties have to reveal their income or spending. Public support to political parties has steadily increased and during 2003 is worth about 230 million Icelandic Krona per year. Parties not represented in the Parliament do not get public funding.

Electoral competition is largely unregulated. There are no laws on the fundraising or expenditures of political parties and the parties have as much availability of mass media advertising, including television, as money can buy. Only laws prohibiting the collection and storage of personal information limit the commission and use of public opinion polls.

---

[2] The origins of this informal, personal, and male-dominated political network have been traced to the first decades of the twentieth century (Styrkársdóttir 1998).

[3] Given the fact that the US population is 1,000 times that of Iceland, this is roughly equal to the amount of money spent on all elections in the United States. In the United States in 1997, candidates and parties in search of seats in the US House of Representatives and the Senate spent at least 660 million. The estimate for spending in all elections exceeds 3 billion (*The Economist*, 8–14 February 1997).

The state radio and television provide free and equal broadcasting time to parliamentary parties contesting elections in all electoral districts. Other political parties (newcomers and/or parties that do not run lists in all districts) have no guaranteed access to mass media, although some broadcasting time is allocated to them when contesting local or parliamentary elections.

Given the heavy financial losses parties have suffered as a result of money-losing, now-defunct party newspapers and the high and increasing cost of electoral campaigns, public support to parties does not by any means suffice to cover their expenditures. Thus, most parties are heavily in debt. In 1993 all parliamentary parties except the WA voted in favour of a change in the tax code, which allows private companies to deduct contributions to political parties. The financing of political parties by private interests without any public disclosure reinforces the private nature of governance in Iceland and reinforces the link between special interests and ministers and MPs.

The gradual transformation of the Icelandic political system, from party rule to personal politics, is also manifested at the parliamentary party group level. The MPs have gained more freedom of action; they are agents without any strong party organization to control them. Members of Parliament have extended their freedom of action into new areas, including decisions about whether to support or oppose the cabinet in the Althingi. As a result, the current PM has spoken of the need to create oversized cabinet coalitions to protect the government from defection and opposition by government backbenchers in the Althingi. Many events in the 1990s support the PM's analysis. A minimum coalition gives every government-party MP bargaining power, something that is obviously discomforting for any cabinet.

It is important to note that the developments discussed here should not be taken as indication of a complete collapse of party cohesion and a fatal weakening of parliamentary party groups. Party groups have, in fact, retained a strong degree of cohesion because the parliamentary system provides countervailing incentives. These incentives have to do with the parliamentary form of the relationship between the cabinet and the Parliament.

DELEGATION FROM PARLIAMENT TO CABINET

Since Iceland achieved Home Rule in 1904, ministers have been accountable to the Althingi. Formally, the Althingi is the principal, the Cabinet the agent. However, this seemingly straightforward relationship is complicated by three interacting factors: (1) the absence of formal rules, (2) the tradition of majority cabinet formation, and (3) the role of the President.

The Constitution does not offer much insight into the actual processes and rules influencing the delegation from Parliament to cabinet. The basic rules for cabinet formation and cabinet resignation are not formally spelled out more than that the President appoints a new cabinet. There is no vote of investiture in the Parliament. However, a cabinet already in power, or a particular minister, can be voted out of power by a majority (50 per cent + 1 of all valid votes) in the Parliament with quorum requirements of 50 per cent + 1 of all members. Any individual MP can propose such a vote. Formally, the President can remove the cabinet, but it would be against the basic principles of parliamentary government to do so without prior declaration of non-confidence on the cabinet in the Althingi. There is also a constitutional practice that holds that a cabinet must resign if it loses a vote on a matter to which it has attached its survival, but because of the tradition of majority coalitions the specific meaning of this practice remains unclear.

In sharp contrast to the other Nordic countries—in particular Denmark, Norway, and Sweden (Strøm 1986; Bergman 1995)—Iceland has no tradition of minority cabinets in the post-Second World War era. The 1917–44 period was quite different in this respect—majority coalition cabinets reigned for less than half the time during these years.

The tradition of majority cabinet was born with the Republic in 1944. In that year, an 'oversized' majority cabinet was formed. This government included the party furthest to the right (the IP), the Social Democratic Party, and a radical Socialist party (the United Socialist Party). The cabinet was supported by thirty-two MPs. The opposition was made up of the agrarian Progressive Party, which held fifteen seats, and five IP MPs who had broken ranks with their party. The new cabinet was a response to a cataclysmic event in Icelandic politics. In 1942 the Regent of Iceland—Sveinn Björnsson, who was elected by the Althingi for a 1 year term—appointed a non-partisan cabinet because the parliamentary parties had been unable to form a government. The non-partisan cabinet was in power when a special session of the Althingi at Thingvellir (the site of the old Althingi) proclaimed Iceland's independence and the establishment of the Republic. This historical occasion, which was attended by approximately 20 per cent of the population and broadcast by radio all over the island, was an occasion at which many MPs felt humiliated by their own inability to form a cabinet. Ever since, majority cabinets have been seen as the proper result of cabinet formation. Only majority cabinets are considered to be real parliamentary government. Minority cabinets are, at best, only short-term measures. Given this, MPs are under great pressure to form majority cabinets as soon as possible after elections.

The letter of the Constitution gives the President the right to dissolve the Parliament. The government, however, holds executive power. Thus, in practice, the Prime Minister (PM) proposes parliamentary dissolution to the President. It is then the President's decision to accept or reject such a proposal. The Constitution also gives the President the power to appoint a non-partisan cabinet if the Althingi fails to create a cabinet tolerated by a majority of MPs. This provision has undoubtedly strengthened the collective identity of MPs as part of an institution, the Althingi. In recent years Icelandic political leaders have shown themselves capable of forming cabinets quickly without 'interference' from the President. Given the improvements in the economy—after experiencing great economic instability in the post Second World-War period the country now enjoys a low rate of inflation rate (2–3 per cent)—political leaders have also been under somewhat less pressure to quickly form a cabinet. The role of the President in cabinet formation will remain pro-forma as long as the political parties represented in the Althingi can agree on a majority cabinet. In this sense the Althingi has firmly established itself as the principal over the cabinet.

Table 12.1 summarizes the empirical record of no-confidence votes and parliamentary dissolutions in Iceland. Only once a cabinet had to face a no-confidence vote, Thors IV in 1950. This cabinet was removed by this vote. In addition, seven of twenty-five cabinets were ended by early parliamentary dissolution, mostly by the President.

To understand the relationship between the Althingi and the cabinet, it is necessary to put it into the context of Icelandic history—notably the origins of these two institutions. Kristinsson (1996: 443), has observed:

Parliament has always been a major channel for political patronage. Apart from its important role in deciding the composition of executive committees and boards, its legislative and budgetary powers have been extensively used in the twentieth century to promote narrow constituency interests. The constitution and the law of parliamentary procedure grant a broader scope of manoeuvre to Icelandic parliamentarians than exists in most European countries. There are no restrictions on the right of individual parliamentarians to propose new legislation or amendments to the government budget. Private members bills have always been numerous.

The division of authority and functional responsibilities between the legislature and the executive branch is muddled. For example, the Althingi is heavily involved in executive administration and the cabinet often plays a dominant role in the legislative process, as, for example, with regard to the budget.

In recent years several steps have been taken to sharpen the separation of legislative and executive power. The Althingi has become more effective as an institution, just as individual MPs, in particular opposition MPs, have increasingly turned to parliamentary questions and special extraordinary debates to oversee the ministers and call public attention to issues which they are concerned about. Any MP can request information from cabinet ministers, which they are required to provide. Nine MPs can ask for a report by a minister on a specific public matter. If accepted in a parliamentary vote, the respective minister must submit such report to the Althingi within ten weeks. The Althingi can also audit executive departments and public agencies through the Public Accounting Office, which answers only to the Althingi. The cabinet's scope for issuing executive decrees has also been restricted.

The political parties in the cabinet and the parties' MPs are also intertwined given the fact that in most cases only MPs become ministers. They then continue to serve as MPs and receive salaries for both jobs. In addition, neither MPs nor the ministers are the agents of strong independent party organizations outside the Althingi and the cabinet. In this respect the basic line of conflict between opposing interests is usually not between Parliament on the one hand and the cabinet on the other, but rather between opposition MPs and cabinet MPs, some of whom are also ministers (for a classic article on this general topic, see King 1976).

Foreign policy issues are handled by the Althingi somewhat independently of the pattern of conflict between cabinet MPs and opposition MPs. Here the Althingi sometimes acts more as a principal. Special efforts are made to build a wide consensus in this field that includes MPs in general and members of the Foreign Affairs Committee in particular. Every year the Foreign Minister submits to the Althingi an extensive policy

Table 12.1. *Cabinet Formation, Cabinet Termination, and Early Parliamentary Dissolution: Iceland 1944–2000*[a]

No.	Cabinet	Date of formation	Investiture votes (iv) n.a.	No-confidence votes (ncv)			Confidence votes (cv) under specific institutional mechanism n.a.	Did the cabinet end with an early election?	Who dissolved Parliament in this case?[b]
				No. of ncv	Cabinet removed by ncv	Cabinet resigned to pre-empt ncv			
1	Thors II	44/10/21		0					
2	Thors III	46/06/30		0					
3	Stefansson	47/02/04		0				Yes	Head of State
4	Thors IV	49/12/06		1	Yes				
5	Steinthorsson	50/03/14		0					
6	Thors V	53/09/11		0				Yes	Head of State
7	Jonasson III	56/07/24		0					
8	Jonsson	58/12/23		0				Yes	Const.
9	Jonsson II	59/06/28		0				Yes	Head of State
10	Thors VI	59/11/20		0					
11	Thors VII	63/06/09		0					
12	Benediktsson	63/11/14		0					
13	Benediktsson II	67/06/11		0					
14	Hafstein	70/10/10		0					
15	Johannesson I	71/07/14		0				Yes[c]	Head of State

16	Hallgrimsson	74/08/28	0		
17	Johannesson II	78/09/01	0		
18	Gröndal	79/10/15	0	Yes	Head of State
19	Thoroddsen	80/02/08	0	Yes	Head of State
20	Hermannsson I	83/05/26	0		
21	Palsson	87/07/08	0		
22	Hermannsson II	88/09/28	0		
23	Hermannsson III	89/09/10	0		
24	Oddsson I	91/04/30	0		
25	Oddsson II	95/04/23	0		
26	Oddsson III	99/05/28	—	—	

[a] n.d. = no data (missing data); n.a. or '—' = not applicable in this case.

[b] The question 'Who dissolved Parliament in this case?' can be answered with one of five options. This identifies the main constitutional actor that caused the early election. We have not coded the formal signatory, but rather the person or body that made the real decision: (1) Head of State; (2) Prime Minister; (3) Cabinet; (4) Parliamentary majority; (5) Automatic constitutional provision ('Const.'; for example, if it is required when a new President takes office, or if it is required after the adoption of a proposal for constitutional amendments).

[c] In this particular case the Parliament was dissolved to pre-empt a no-confidence vote.

report. The somewhat special role of the Althingi in the field of foreign policy is explained by several factors:

1. The heritage of the politics of independence, which calls for national unity in defending and promoting the national interest. This emphasis was particularly strong in 'the new national struggle', the extension of Iceland's exclusive fishing zone to 12 miles (1958), 50 miles (1972), and finally 200 miles (1975).
2. In most instances foreign policy is less tied to the politics of patronage. MPs have less need to worry about serving local and particular interests, and can identify more with the Althingi as an institution for promoting the common Icelandic good.
3. The foreign policy dimension cross-cuts the Left–Right dimension of party politics, thus making possible unconventional alliances among parties. Thus the Social Democratic Party and the IP worked closely together in supporting Iceland's membership in NATO and the stationing of American troops in Iceland. Since 1999 the leaders of the IP and the Left and Green Party have voiced similar arguments against Iceland's membership in the EU, invoking fears of the loss of national sovereignty to a supranational organization as an unacceptable price of entry.

DELEGATION FROM CABINET TO INDIVIDUAL MINISTERS

The executive government in Iceland is generally characterized by three main features:

1. The separation of power between the Althingi and the executive remains unclear.
2. Individual ministers are highly independent.
3. The civil service has a low degree of autonomy.

Together these characteristics produce a highly individualized style of executive government.

As a note of curiosity, one could say that when Iceland got Home Rule in 1904 there was no delegation and accountability problem within the cabinet because there was only one minister! The minister was formally a member of the Danish State Council, but he was independent of the Danish Parliament and did not resign when Danish governments did so.

In 1917 the number of ministers increased to three. Europe was at war and many Icelanders felt that the executive branch should be strengthened in this time of emergency. Some also wished to increase the cabinet's capacity to direct and control the civil service. The composition of the Althingi also played a role. No party majority existed, which necessitated the formation of a coalition cabinet (Kristinsson 1994).

With three ministers the question of cabinet decision-making rules inevitably arose. The Althingi debated this issue in 1920. The proposal for the new Constitution had originally contained the principle of majority voting in cabinet meetings, but the Althingi removed this clause. The cabinet has no formal decision rule but majority voting is rarely used and in some cabinets not at all. Generally the cabinet is not collectively responsible. Rather, executive responsibility is held by individual ministers (Kristinsson 1994).

The Oddsson cabinet formed in 1999 included twelve ministers. The mean of the five most recent cabinets through the Oddsson cabinet is 10.4. The central government organization is divided into twelve departments, with a total combined staff of 366 people in 1993. The largest departments are Finance (79), Education (66), and Foreign Affairs (51) (Kristinsson 1994: 63). Each minister also has one personal assistant, who comes to the ministry with the minister and leaves with him/her as well. Icelandic ministers thus have a good possibility to control their departments, if for no other reason than because of their small size.

The formal rule for appointments and dismissals of ministers is that this is the prerogative of the President. In practice he/she generally does so only on the initiative of the PM. The PM also defines the jurisdictional boundaries between the ministries. However, the leadership of coalition cabinets is inherently more complicated than that of single-party majority cabinets. In the latter case, the PM is faced with the task of providing leadership for a group of ministers who are not members of the same party, but without the formal rule of collective cabinet responsibility to aid him in this task. In Iceland the last single-party majority cabinet ruled from 1924 to 1927. Since then majority coalitions have included ministers from two, three, and—in one case—four political parties. The life expectancy of cabinets is generally negatively related to the number of parties included in them. Most two-party cabinets last the full electoral term, while no three-party cabinet has lasted the normal term of 4 years.

Some PMs have (in the 1980s and 1990s) had great success in keeping their coalitions together, while others have failed. Two of the successful PMs were Progressive Party leader (1979–94) Steingrímur Hermannsson and Davíd Oddsson, leader (since 1991) of the Independence Party. Why do some party leaders succeed as PM while others fail? On this point, available research only allows for a tentative answer. However, the following account, based on eyewitness information, is a reasonable answer. The similarities between Oddsson's conception of the PM's role and Hermannsson's approach are striking. In Oddsson's case we find that he clearly saw the position and function of the PM to be very different from the office of the Mayor of Reykjavík, a post he held for 9 years (1982–91):

The job of the Prime Minister as a leader is completely different from that of the mayor. It is mostly concerned with co-ordinating the views of individuals with different background. I do not have the supreme power; I mean the direct power to command, which I possessed as mayor. Each cabinet minister has full power over his department. Formally the Prime Minister can not command him to do anything. Consequently my power as Prime Minister consists as influence rather than the power to command, although both types clearly coexist. (*Frjáls verslun* nr.1 1996: 32–9)

In the same interview Oddsson also emphasized the importance of personal contact with his cabinet ministers, of making himself accessible to them at all times. This allows the PM to coordinate and influence. It also 'forces' cabinet ministers to consult with the PM. Ministers cannot hide behind the cover of not being able to reach the PM.

The Oddsson cabinet does not use majority voting. Consensus had usually emerged before cabinet meetings, while in the case of serious disagreement on jurisdiction between ministers the PM made the final decision. Oddsson also made a sharp distinction between the power of the PM as such and the position of the PM as his/her party leader. The PM does not select the ministers from his partner(s) party(ies), nor is he politically responsible for their conduct in office. In practice ministers are delegates of their respective party, and they are not politically accountable to the PM. In his conception of the PM's powers and his operating style as PM, Oddson follows in the footsteps of PM Hermannsson.

From the outside it appears to be the case that successful PMs displayed political skills in three arenas. They were successful by (1) forming and maintaining coalition cabinets, (2) preserving a strong position in the parliamentary party, and (3) winning parliamentary elections. For Icelandic PMs, the first two of these skills can be the most important. When they fail it is often because they lack in skills of coalition management and maintenance.

The cabinet is not a collective body dominated by the PM, but rather a council of highly independent ministers. The prevalence of coalition cabinets further complicates the PM's role, while at the same time absolving him of political responsibility for ministers from his coalition partner(s). The successful PM adjusts to the formal and informal rules of the game, not by establishing clear chains of delegation and accountability but by carefully learning on the job. Those who approach the PM's role in purely a formal fashion will quickly fail.

DELEGATION FROM MINISTERS TO CIVIL SERVANTS

In the context of delegating to civil servants, the comments of Charles Cobb, former United States ambassador to Iceland, are worth citing:

Icelandic politics is both fast-paced and very personal in nature. In most countries political parties are institutionalised organisations; a bureaucracy controls everything. As a result all things move at slow speed; developments and changes take place at the speed of a snail. In Iceland policy is deliberated for one evening and implemented the next day....In the U.S. cabinet secretaries always express the same view on issues of the day. Members of the government do not publicly disagree. Great emphasis is placed upon this rule of conduct. Cabinet ministers have two choices; either they speak on behalf of one common policy, the President's policy, or they resign...The Icelandic situation is very different; it is quite common for Cabinet ministers to publicly disagree on policy. Such behaviour is considered acceptable so far as I can observe. (*Morgunbladid*, 9 Jan 1992)

The dominance of the minister over his/her ministry starts with his/her power to hire civil servants. As Oddsson has put it: 'The power of the individual minister in hiring people is absolute.' (*Frjáls verslun* 1996). Each minister also actively cultivates contacts outside the ministry, including ones with individuals, companies, and interest groups. All ministers make themselves available for personal appointments. Anyone can request an appointment to discuss something with a minister. Some people might be required to wait a long time for such an appointment, but the waiting time is not as long as that for seeing some medical specialists or getting an operation in a hospital! An individual might even call a minister on the telephone, even at home. (He will find the number in the phone book.)

The argument is not that anyone can get a minister to do his/her bidding at any time. What is important here is that ministers are highly accessible. Most people, companies, and interest groups can get the minister's attention. This access undercuts the authority of the civil service hierarchy and decreases the autonomy of the civil service. Ministers can oversee and control civil servants by cultivating the relevant 'customers' of public service.

Ministers have powerful incentives to nurture outside contacts. To start with, ministers are by convention almost invariably also MPs and as such they are in constant danger of not being re-elected. As noted above, the nomination stage is particularly hazardous given the prevalence of open primaries in all but one of the major political parties. The open primary is a personal vote. To survive under such circumstances, ambitious MPs, such as the ministers, must emphasize constituency service.

The ministers run their departments and have full formal control of the civil servants under their own jurisdictions. Civil servants, who are of only one type, that is, career civil servants, are accountable direct to the minister. The greatest restrictions to their rule come from outside the government departments. The unclear division of power between the Althingi and the executive branch of government cuts both ways. It enables ministers to play a crucial role in the preparation and interpretation of legislation, but also allows for direct involvement of the Althingi in executive functions.

Sometimes the minister and the ministry work together in order to decrease the scope of administrative discretion and strengthen bureaucratic autonomy. This is most obvious in the case of decisions regarding the size and distribution of fishing quotas, which are among the most important decisions made by government agencies at any given time. Given their importance, the Department of Fisheries has issued detailed and transparent rules to govern such decisions.

EXTERNAL CONSTRAINTS

Parliamentary democracy became the basic constitutional principle of the Republic established in Iceland and it remains dominant today. However, parliamentary government has evolved in response to several factors external to it (or at least to its ideal-type).

From the beginning the parliamentary system was mixed with another constitutional principle, that of semi-presidential government. The parliamentary system established its identity partly in power struggles—first with the Regent and then with the President. The political parties also contributed to the development of a coherent parliamentary system with the Althingi as the pivotal institution. Nevertheless, the principles of delegation and accountability were poorly developed within this system, because the logic of Iceland's patronage system embedded political relationships in a social system of mutual exchange and favours. A number of important changes have occurred over time.

One change is that a new form of governance has emerged—that is, corporatism without parties.

A very comprehensive corporatist agreement, termed The National Consensus, was reached early in the year 1990. This consensus, which was initiated and formulated in great detail by the employers' association and the labour unions, included agreements on wage-raise policies. The role of the cabinet was primarily to get the necessary legislation through parliament, pay the bill from the budget, and keep the employees' wage settlements in line with those included in the National Consensus. (Kristjánsson 1998: 180)

This type of decision-making, which was repeated in 1998 when a new comprehensive proposal on pension funds was approved in a similar procedure, pushes both the Althingi and the executive branch to the sidelines of policy-making and allows interest groups to dominate.

Parliamentary government is also affected by the constitutional provision of the national referendums and by international factors such as NATO membership and the country's formal relationship with the EU, through the EEA. The Constitution automatically calls for a national referendum under three sets of circumstances:

1. A resolution to unseat the President has been passed by a three-quarters majority in the Parliament. The President is immediately stripped off his official power, but his impeachment must be ratified in a national referendum. If the President wins the referendum he reclaims full authority and the Althingi is immediately dissolved.
2. The President has refused to sign legislation passed by the Parliament. In this case the legislation goes into effect, but must be ratified in a national referendum. This law is rescinded if a majority of those participating in the referendum vote against it.
3. Parliament has passed a proposal changing the status of the national state Lutheran church. This decision must be put to a vote among the whole electorate.

The Althingi alone can initiate national referendums other than in these three situations. It can simply attach a clause to any law that it passes stating that the law's coming into effect is contingent upon its acceptance in a national referendum.

In the history of the present Constitution, no national referendum has been held. This should not, however, lead to the conclusion that national referendum is insignificant in the Icelandic political system. First, the constitutional provisions with regard to the holding of referendums clearly bypass the chain of delegation and accountability characteristic of the ideal model of parliamentary government. Through national referendums, the power to resolve fundamental conflicts between the Althingi and the President is vested with the people. Second, from time to time demands are raised for national referendums to settle controversial issues. Such demands have been voiced inside and outside the Althingi. These demands often include references to the fact that the national referendum has been used five times in Iceland. It was used twice (in 1918 and 1944) to decide Iceland's relationship with Denmark and to approve the basic constitution. It was used in 1908 and 1933 to settle the issue of whether or not to prohibit alcohol. Finally, in 1916 a proposal for compulsory civic work for young men was defeated in a national referendum. Given the rather large gap that now exists between the formal Constitution and constitutional practice, it is possible that a national referendum has the potential to shift the balance of power between the parliamentary majority and the President.

Another issue that has affected the country's democratic chain of delegation and accountability is the NATO base on Iceland. Iceland occupied a strategically crucial position during the Cold War. The country's political leaders quickly developed great skill at turning this position into dollars and cents. The US and other NATO governments used economic assistance and favours to facilitate Iceland's acceptance of the stationing of US troops on Iceland in the face of strong domestic resistance. Iceland's political leaders also successfully pursued the goal of repeatedly extending Iceland's fishing limits, from 12 miles in the late 1950s to 200 miles in 1975. In this struggle Iceland 'defeated' both Great Britain and West Germany, both of whom lost their traditional rights to fish in Icelandic waters. The mobilizing of the Icelandic population was important for securing this outcome, but so was the government's masterful manipulation of 'the American connection'. The government hinted at a reconsideration of its NATO membership and the defence agreement with the United States. The US promptly used its political leverage to help settle the dispute.

More recently, Iceland's membership in the EEA has created an important environmental constraint on its political system. Iceland signed the treaty without changing its Constitution and without holding a national referendum. The government argued that the agreement did not curtail Iceland's sovereignty or change the constitutional status of its national institutions. Despite these claims, the position of the country's political institutions has indeed been altered insofar as Iceland must fulfil obligations established by the agreement but has no real influence in EU policy-making. In fact, Icelandic legislation must conform to the rules and regulations established by the EU in all areas covered by the EEA agreement (see Kristjánsson and Kristjánsson 2000).

Prior to the adoption of the EEA agreement, in 1991, pressure from the European Commission of Human Rights and the European Court of Human Rights played a very important role in the decision of the Althingi to change the judicial system in order to separate the executive and judicial role of the local magistrates. Environmental 'pressure' thus helped to bring about the most fundamental revision of the Icelandic judicial system since 1874. In connection with this, Icelanders increasingly have both the means and the will to seek redress for their grievances against the domestic institutions with actors and institutions outside of the nation state—often by emphasizing their rights as established by Iceland's membership in European and international organizations and institutions. The increasing concern for codified citizen rights is also evident in the 1995 constitutional change, adding fifteen new clauses covering the full range of human rights. The judiciary, notably the Supreme Court, has in several cases in the 1990s ruled against the acts of the Althingi and the Cabinet on Constitutional grounds.

CONCLUSION

One can fruitfully place the parliamentary system of Iceland in two contexts: the domestic level and the environment outside the boundaries of the nation state. On the domestic level, clearer delegation has developed within the Icelandic parliamentary system, in particular due to the sharper definition of the Althingi as the principal institution which, in turn, delegates power to the executive branch. At the same time, the parliamentary system has lost much of the coherence previously provided by patronage-oriented political parties. The political system has thus become more complex.

Organizationally weak political parties survive in the electoral arena, partly by abnegating their collective responsibility for offering the voters a choice between clear alternatives. Individual MPs, on the other hand, are now more directly accountable to the voters.

The increasing accountability of individual MPs, and clearer definition of the Althingi as separate from the executive, is more than matched by countervailing developments. Of particular importance in this regard is greater pluralism in society as a whole as various actors—including firms, professionals, interest groups, government institutions, mass media—have gained considerable autonomy from (party) politics. Neither individual MPs nor political parties prepare or initiate the most important laws passed by the Althingi. The government bureaucracy and specialists play a key role in the political system. A clear example of this is the fact that the preparation and enactment of the state budget is predominantly in the hands of the cabinet, particularly the Ministry of Finance.

With regard to the environment beyond the nation state, the picture is rather clearer. Political leaders in Iceland are subject to increasing constraints at a time when they have fewer opportunities than before to 'milk' external relations for the country's benefit as well as their own. Other Icelanders—as individuals and members of groups or firms—share these constraints to some degree, but they have also gained considerable leverage on Icelandic politicians. Icelandic citizens now have better chances of redressing grievances against their own government by external means.

Now that the Cold War has ended, the EEA agreement is Iceland's most important treaty. EEA membership involves costs and benefits for the country as a whole. From the point of view of the average citizen, the opportunities clearly outweigh the new constraints. For rulers, the picture is more mixed. Their opportunities to participation in and exert influence on decision-making at the European level are extremely limited, while at the same time the constraints they are subject to are considerable. They face both direct constraints due to the EEA agreement and other international agreements and indirect ones because of the new opportunities citizens have to make their own government more accountable by making use of the external commitments binding the Icelandic nation state.

REFERENCES

Bergman, Torbjörn (1995). *Constitutional Rules and Party Goals in Coalition Formation*. Department of Political Science. Umeå University.
The Economist (1997). February 8–14.
Frjáls verslun (Icelandic journal) (1996): 1, 32–9.
Gallagher, Michael and Marsh, Michael (eds.) (1988). *Candidate Selection in Comparative Perspective*. London: Sage.
King, Anthony (1976). 'Modes of Executive-Legislative Relations: Great Britain, France and Germany'. *Legislative Studies Quarterly*, 1: 37–65.
Kristinsson, Gunnar H. (1994). *Embættismenn og stjórnmálamenn*. Reykjavík: Heimskringla.
——(1996). 'Parties, States and Patronage.' *West European Politcs*, 19(3): 433–57.

Kristjánsson, Svanur (1998). 'Electoral Politics and Governance: Transformation of the Party System in Iceland, 1970–96', in Paul Pennings and Jane Erik Lane (eds.), *Comparing Party System Change*. London: Routledge.

——and Kristjánsson, Ragner (2000). 'Delegation and Accountability in an Ambiguous System: Iceland and the European Economic Area (EEA)', in Torbjörn Bergman and Erik Damgaard (eds.), *Delegation and Accountability in European Integration: The Nordic Parliamentary Democracies and the European Union*. London: Frank Cass.

Morgunbladid (Icelandic daily newspaper) (1992): 9 January.

Strøm, Kaare (1986). 'Deferred Gratification and Minority Governments in Scandinavia'. *Legislative Studies Quarterly*, 11: 583–605.

Styrkársdóttir, Audur (1986). 'From Social Movement to Political Party: The New Women's Movement in Iceland', in Drude Dahlerup (ed.), *The New Women's Movement*. London: Sage.

——(1998). *From Feminism to Class Politics*. Department of Political Science. Umeå University.

13

Ireland: 'O What a Tangled Web…'— Delegation, Accountability, and Executive Power

PAUL MITCHELL

INTRODUCTION

Given that the political histories of Britain and Ireland are inextricably linked it is perhaps not surprising that the governing institutions of independent Ireland are an adaptation of the Westminster system, and that both countries continue to have much in common. On the other hand, the new Irish state was established by revolutionary secession from the United Kingdom and the circumstances of its birth helped shape its institutions and political parties.

Sinn Féin, which had won a resounding victory at the 1918 election to the Westminster Parliament (taking 73 of the 105 seats on the island of Ireland), refused to attend that Parliament and instead established in 1919 its own revolutionary assembly, Dáil Éireann. The ensuing war of independence from Britain resulted in a military truce and subsequently 'Treaty' between the two sides during 1921. The terms of the Treaty, which 'went much further than conceding Home Rule, but stopped well short of permitting complete separation' (Coakley 1999: 16) led to a bitter civil war (1922–3) that the anti-Treaty forces lost. This division is of more than historical interest since the pro- and anti-Treaty sides constituted the origins of the two parties that came to dominate independent Ireland, Fine Gael and Fianna Fáil, respectively. Thus the new Irish state was created in 1922 by a partial secession from the United Kingdom that resulted in a partition of Ireland into two political entities.

The new state was conceived as a parliamentary democracy with many features such as the organization of Parliament, procedures for law-making, and the administrative structure clearly inherited from Westminster. Nevertheless, Irish political institutions were designed as a variation on rather than a carbon copy of the Westminster model. The most important institutional divergence from Britain was the adoption of limited government by a written Constitution (first in 1922 and superseded by the current 1937 Constitution) protected by a Supreme Court and developed by judicial interpretation and popular referendum. The 1937 Constitution was enacted by the people in a referendum as a demonstration of popular sovereignty.[1] Other important institutional

---

[1] Ireland, or rather southern Ireland, officially became a republic in 1948 but is henceforth referred to for simplicity as 'Ireland'.

innovations enshrined in the Constitution include the adoption of proportional representation by means of the single transferable vote for all parliamentary elections and a directly elected President as Head of State.[2]

The constitution clearly establishes (in Article 15) that Ireland is a parliamentary democracy. The national parliament (Oireachtas) consists of the President, Dáil Éireann (House of Representatives), and Seanad Éireann (Senate). The government is responsible to Dáil Éireann (Article 28.4.1) and unlike countries such as the United States or France its members must be members of the national Parliament. The President appoints the Taoiseach (Prime Minister) and members of the government who must have the prior approval of Dáil Éireann (Article 13.1-2). The indirectly elected Seanad has very limited powers; from a prospective government's perspective the balance of forces in the Dáil is decisive.

Westminster norms are most evident in the Irish pattern of law-making and general parliamentary behaviour. Irish practice conforms closely to the British style of an adversary relationship between government and opposition, a practice that perhaps makes for better theatre than reasoned reflection. As Farrell (1983: 256) states, governments and oppositions in Ireland have 'remained committed to a traditional, and largely artificial, parliamentary mock battle in which the real prize is less the issues of politics than the opportunity to either retain or gain governmental power'.

The Oireachtas has 'the sole and exclusive power of making laws for the State' (Article 15.2.1), though of course the parliamentary majority can only enact laws consistent with the Constitution. Any provisions declared repugnant to the Constitution by the Supreme Court are invalid (Article 15.4.2).[3] In reality the Oireachtas' 'sole and exclusive' legislative authority is seriously amended by membership of the European Union (EU). At least domestically, however, the national Parliament is virtually unchallenged by other levels of government. Unlike many other European countries local government in Ireland was not constitutionally recognized or protected (until 1999). It was traditionally fairly weak and under-resourced. Indeed the central government has on occasion—and for partisan reasons—even postponed local government elections.[4]

The process of law-making in Ireland is very similar in intent and practice to that of Westminster (see Dooney and O'Toole 1992; Gallagher 1999b). Each bill must pass a number of stages in both houses of Parliament and is then sent to the President who must either sign it into law or refer it to the Supreme Court to test its constitutionality.

---

[2] Note that the electoral system is protected by the Constitution and thus can only be changed by referendum. The electoral system and presidency are discussed in sections below.

[3] Any citizen can test the constitutionality of any law, treaty, or action of the Parliament and government by bringing a case before the high court, or in an appeal against its decision, before the Supreme Court. The citizen must establish, however, that she has *locus standi*—that she is in someway affected by the action or law (Gallagher 1999a: 83). Gallagher (1999a: 83) comments that 'in Ireland, judicial review has proved to be the main method by which the constitution has been developed'. In addition, the President (Article 26) can elect to refer a bill passed by the Oireachtas directly to the Supreme Court to test its constitutionality rather than sign it into law. Of course while judicial interpretation often serves valuable functions the dilemma is that judges of the Supreme Court are not accountable to anybody.

[4] In 1999 the voters in a referendum approved of a constitutional amendment recognizing the existence of local government and requiring local elections at least once every 5 years (Gallagher 1999a: 81).

The bill is formally introduced in one of the houses which constitutes the first stage of the legislative process. The second crucial stage is the debate on the general principle of the bill. This is the main partisan event that largely determines whether the bill will be passed. The third stage is a detailed examination by the relevant committee at which amendments that do not conflict with the general principle of the bill may be proposed.[5] The fourth stage is the report stage at which further new amendments can be made. The final fifth stage is the formal passing of the bill, which is then sent to the other house where the same stages are repeated.[6]

Although most (non-money) bills can be introduced in either house, the Dáil and Seanad are in no sense equal. While some powers are shared (e.g. the impeachment of a President), in law-making the Dáil is pre-eminent. In essence the most that the Seanad can impose on an ordinary bill is a delay of 90 days. If the Seanad fails to pass a bill that has already passed through the Dáil or proposes amendments unacceptable to the lower house, the Dáil prevails. Following the delay the bill is 'deemed to have been passed by both Houses of the Oireachtas' (Article 23.1 of the Constitution). In the case of money bills (the Chairman of the Dáil determines what constitutes a money bill) the Seanad's powers of delay are reduced to just 21 days. If the Seanad rejects a bill and the Dáil overrules its objections the Seanad can invoke the 'Article 27 procedure' (Gallagher 1999b: 200), whereby a majority of the Seanad plus one-third of the Dáil can petition the President not to sign the bill on the grounds that it 'contains a proposal of such national importance that the will of the people thereon ought to be ascertained' (Article 27.1). If the President accedes to such a petition the bill cannot become law until either it passes a referendum or the Dáil passes it again following a general election (Article 27.5.1). However, no Article 27 petition has ever been presented to the President, partly because the government usually controls a majority in the Senate.[7] Given that the Senate is relatively powerless and rather bizarrely composed, some parties, such as the Progressive Democrats, have called for its abolition or reform (e.g. see Lynch 1996; Laver 1996b; Coakley and Manning 1999).

As in other parliamentary democracies the formal position that the legislature makes laws and the government executes them, elides the reality that the government (at least a majority government) largely controls the legislature. Most bills are government bills

---

[5] In practice the relevant minister decides whether a proposed amendment is consistent with the principle of the bill. Since committee assignments are proportionate to party strength, majority governments could in any case out vote the opposition on any committee. In addition, committee decisions can be overturned by the Dáil (Gallagher 1999b: 196).

[6] Any member may demand a quorum which is twenty TDs. The decision rule is simple plurality (50 % + 1 of those voting). Actually in practice it is 50 % since in the event of a tie there is a strong convention that the Ceann Comhairle (Speaker) will vote with the government.

[7] Government control of the upper house is facilitated by the fact that an incoming Taoiseach (following an election) nominates eleven of the Seanad's sixty members. The importance of this prerogative was demonstrated during the 1994–7 government which was the first time that one coalition replaced another without an election. This meant that the new government formed in 1994 inherited the eleven 'Taoiseach's nominees' of the previous government, so that the combined opposition had a majority in the Seanad. 'The result was a major change in the manner in which Senate business was conducted…The government suffered two defeats on legislation and avoided defeat on other occasions by either conceding on issues or by postponing them altogehter' (Coakley and Manning 1999: 200).

and certainly only bills supported by the government have much prospect of being enacted. In Ireland the government's privileged position in the legislature has constitutional foundation through Article 17.2 that states that no provision involving revenue or spending can be passed by the Dáil unless it has been recommended by the government in a message signed by the Taoiseach. This stipulation is 'clearly motivated by the fear that were it not in force, parliament might vote for the spending of money but against government efforts to raise it' (Gallagher 1999*b*: 187–8).

Apart from an 'Article 27 referendum' any proposal to amend the Constitution must be initiated in the Dáil and passed (or deemed passed) by both houses before being submitted to the people for a decision in a referendum.[8] Referendums are decided by a majority of valid votes cast. The frequency of referendums has been increasing: while only two occurred before 1968, twenty more took place between 1968 and 1998, averaging about one a year in the 1990s (see Gallagher 1996*a*: 90). Most referendums have fallen into three broad categories: institutional issues (for example electoral laws); European integration (accession to EC, ratification of the Single European Act, Maastricht and Amsterdam Treaties); and finally, moral issues (abortion, divorce). Electoral behaviour during referendum campaigns also appears to be progressively less determined by the positions of the political parties (Gallagher 1996*a*). Interest groups and well-organized single issue movements have dominated some recent referendum campaigns, with parties playing a relatively low-key role, sometimes because they themselves are internally divided. However, on controversial, especially 'moral' issues referendums may help insulate rather than undermine the party system (Sinnott 1995; Gallagher 1996*a*). In sum, the referendum device is an important but occasional parallel chain of delegation and accountability, which despite having some life outside of parties is nevertheless structured by them since only Parliament can authorize a referendum and the government determines the wording of the question. In all other areas of parliamentary and executive behaviour, parties and especially their leaders play the dominant role.

POLITICAL PARTIES

Political parties are neither presumed nor protected by the Constitution. While various offices and institutions are constitutionally mandated, including an Uachtarán (President), Taoiseach (PM), Tánaiste (deputy PM), and Dáil, political parties are not even mentioned. This fact and the relative lack of statutory regulation mean that Irish political parties have been essentially private organizations, though there are some signs that this is beginning to change due to new legislation designed to regulate party finances. The state plays no role in regulating party membership, candidate selection, the internal organization, or the election of party leaders. General election campaigns

---

[8] Thus citizens cannot initiate referendums. Although Parliament (or in reality the government) initiates and determines the wording of the proposed ammendment to the Constitution, 'parliament does not vote on the substance of the proposal, only on the question of whether the proposal should be put to the people' (Gallagher 1996*a*: 88).

must be a minimum of 3 weeks and a maximum of 4 weeks. As of 2003, there are no restrictions on the publication of opinion polls during elections, though several governments have considered restrictions. The state does play some role in providing financial subsidies and access to election broadcasting. While Ireland introduced a more explicit system for the state financing of political parties in the 1990s, it has indirectly financed parties through subsidies to parliamentary groups (block grants) and individual deputies (travel expenses, secretarial, and research assistants). By 1989 David Farrell (1994: 235) estimated that the total amount of state aid for deputies and their parties (excluding broadcasting) was about £4 million. A series of corruption scandals in the 1990s stimulated concern about the private financing of parties and led to *The Electoral Act 1997*, a piece of legislation that Laver and Marsh (1999: 157) suggest is 'destined to have a fundamental impact on party politics in modern Ireland'. Essentially, much more public money will be given to parties and candidates (based on their past and present electoral performances, but weighted in favour of opposition parties) in order to reduce their reliance on anonymous donors. 'The 1997 Act relies entirely upon making political donations transparent, rather than upon regulating either the size or the source of acceptable donations' (Laver and Marsh 1999: 157). The new law also places clear limits on how much individual candidates and parties can spend during elections. In addition free political commercials on national TV during elections represent an important hidden public subsidy to parties. These are allocated to parties proportionally based on votes in the previous election.[9]

Irish parties are generally very cohesive and disciplined and in most respects are increasingly centralized under the direction of the party leaderships (Gallagher 1985; Mair 1987; D. Farrell 1994; Laver and Marsh 1999). Candidate selection is a partial exception since ordinary party members are reluctant to cede their only real power, but even here the party head offices exert considerable influence by promoting certain candidates or imposing an additional candidate on the constituency (more below). In general though, most powers in the parties lie with the leadership and to a lesser extent the parliamentary party. In all parties members of the parliamentary party can hope to influence policy and in most cases they elect the party leader.

For most of its history Irish politics has been dominated by three parties: Fianna Fáil, Fine Gael, and the Labour party. Much confusion results from the difficulty of assigning Fianna Fáil and Fine Gael to the standard ideological families of European politics. Unfortunately there is no easy answer. In comparative terms both parties are best regarded as parties of the centre or centre-right. They are not, however, clearly members of the two principal centre-right families in Europe, the secular conservatives or the Christian Democrats (see Mair 1999: 129–31). Content analyses of party manifestos and expert surveys suggest that there has been considerable movement between these two parties and they have even on occasion appeared to leapfrog each other in

---

[9] In 1965 (the first televised election) free broadcasting time was allocated to parties with at least seven TDs. In 1977 the allocation rule was changed to parties or groups with at least seven candidates, though the amount of time is based on votes at the last election and the geographical distribution of candidates (Farrell 1992). Parties cannot purchase additional time.

ideological space (see Mair 1986, 1987; Laver 1992, 1994, 1998; Laver and Hunt 1992; Benoit and Laver 2003). However, most commentators would probably rank the parties from Left to Right as follows: Sinn Féin, the Greens, Democratic Left,[10] Labour, Fianna Fáil, Fine Gael, and the Progressive Democrats as the most right-wing party.

Of these seven parties only five have ever been in government (exceptions are Sinn Féin and the Greens) and three—Fianna Fáil, Fine Gael, and Labour—have dominated government tenure.[11] The history of the post-1945 party system is conveniently divisible into three periods: before 1973, 1973–89, and after 1989 (Mitchell 2000b). Before 1973 Ireland had a multiparty system in which the typical election produced a single-party (though quite often minority) government. Fianna Fáil governed for most of these decades, including two separate periods of continuous sixteen-year rule (1932–48, 1957–73).

During the second period (1973–89) the logic of competition remained Fianna Fáil versus 'the rest', but 'the rest' consisted of just two parties (Fine Gael and Labour). Thus, during these sixteen years Fianna Fáil single-party governments alternated with 'the coalition'. The third period began in 1989 when Fianna Fáil transformed the bargaining environment by entering its first executive coalition, ceding two cabinet seats to the Progressive Democrats. Since that time Ireland has been governed by six successive coalitions, thus breaking the earlier pattern of alternating single-party and coalition governments. Indeed, until 2002, no government since 1969 had been elected to a second successive term so that alternation, and coalition reshuffles, have become the norm in the 1990s. From 1948 to 1997 there have been eight single party governments and eight coalitions. While Ireland has some history of minority governments (six in the same period accounting for 27 per cent of duration), the recent pattern of coalitions replacing coalitions suggests that the incidence of minority administrations will decline, since most coalitions build towards a majority.[12]

The primary constraint on all parties and leaders in the parliamentary and governing arenas are the legislative resources at their disposal, that is, the Members of Parliament that they can count on.

DELEGATION FROM VOTERS TO MPs (TDs)

Ireland's candidate-centred electoral system can be expected to influence the incentives and loyalties of deputies (TDs) in a manner that may attenuate the agency losses we normally expect to characterize the relationship between voters and their representatives. Electoral institutions by definition structure the delegation relationship between

[10] In early 1999 Democratic Left ceased to be a party and merged with the Labour Party. This consolidated party has retained the name the Labour Party.

[11] Indeed in the period 1973–97 the Labour party was in government longer than any other. The figures for tenure in government in days (and years) are as follows: Labour, 4,810 days (13.4 years); Fianna Fáil, 4,330 (12); Fine Gael, 4,155 (11.5), Progressive Democrats, 1,183 (3.3); Democratic Left, 892 (2.5). Note the PDs were only founded in 1985 and DL in 1992.

[12] Minority coalition governments do occur and were formed in 1948, 1981, and 1997. Nevertheless, 83 per cent of coalition duration (1948–97) has been in majority governments (Mitchell 1999b: 252).

voters and Members of Parliament (Mitchell 2000*a*). In most systems of proportional representation each voter's principal decision is to choose between rival party lists. Although many countries' list systems have intraparty preference voting, electors nevertheless usually vote first for the party, and their vote may help elect an individual whom they oppose. The central feature of Ireland's electoral system (proportional representation by single transferable vote (STV)) is that the electorate votes directly for individual candidates in multimember constituencies.

The adoption of STV in Ireland owes much to the electoral reform debate in Britain in the nineteenth century. Reformers such as John Stuart Mill and Thomas Hare opposed strong political parties, and for this reason 'the single transferable vote had for them a particular attraction in being a personal and not a party system of voting' (Carstairs 1980: 194). Similar reservations about the role of political parties existed in Ireland with the result that the party affiliation of candidates was not even listed on the ballot paper until 1965 (Sinnott 1999: 100).[13] Thus there was (and is) a normative preference amongst the electorate for a pattern of (small district) constituency representation similar to the Westminster plurality system, but without the latter's pronounced disproportionality at national level. This is not to suggest that the rules governing the electoral system are uncontentious. Indeed, Fianna Fáil single-party governments have twice attempted to replace STV with the plurality system. On both occasions (1959 and 1968) the proposed electoral reform was rejected in a popular referendum, the second time quite decisively (60.8 per cent against, 39.2 per cent for). While there are still periodic calls for electoral reform, there is little prospect of any fundamental change, especially after the Constitutional Review Group (Whitaker *et al.* 1996) did not recommend changing the electoral system. Thus STV is likely to be retained.

Two principal aspects of STV are of importance to delegation and accountability between the electorate and their representatives. First, it is a preferential electoral system in which voters have the opportunity to rank individual candidates in constituencies with a very small district magnitude (since 1947 between three and five seats).[14] This typically means that only two or three of a major party's candidates have much chance of being elected and that the voters alone decide which of the party's candidates are successful. A frequent result is intense intraparty competition at all levels of electoral campaigning and candidate selection. From the perspective of individual candidates the electoral threat from intraparty competition is tangible and severe. For the 1948–77 period Carty found that on average 30 per cent of all seat turnovers at general elections were intraparty, with incumbents losing to party colleagues (Carty 1983: 115).[15] This

---

[13] Antipathy to political parties clearly was not the only or main reason for the largely uncontested adoption of STV in Ireland. The British Proportional Representation Society proposed STV as a way of easing the Home Rule crisis, arguing that it would guarantee the representation of minorities. Irish Nationalist leaders were persuaded of the merits of STV over first-past-the-post and in any case tended to equate PR with STV since there was a 'profound ignorance' concerning list system PR (Gallagher 1987: 27).

[14] TDs are elected for 5 years. There are no term limits or mandatory retirement age, though in principle a member could be expelled for corruption, electoral offences, or bankruptcy.

[15] Gallagher has re-examined this threat at the 1987, 1989, and 1992 elections. Of the 33 Fianna Fáil incumbents that were defeated twenty were displaced by party colleagues. In Fine Gael ten of the thirty-three

provides incentives towards constituency service since three or four candidates of one party (with limited ideological differentiation feasible) compete for the two or three seats that the party can realistically hope to win.[16]

The second relevant feature of STV is that preference voting is not limited to an intraparty choice: voters can (and do) vote across party lines. As Gallagher (1987: 41) says: '[u]nder list systems with preferential voting, deputies would need to concern themselves only with the support of those who will, or might, vote for their party, whereas under STV even the fifth or sixth preference of a supporter of another party could be important, so that deputies need to be concerned about their reputation in every voter's eyes'. This creates incentive for candidates to try to attract lower preferences from partisans of other parties, and clearly has important consequences in terms of democratic accountability.

One of the sophisticated (and unique) aspects of STV is that votes cannot help an individual candidate unless they explicitly express a preference for him or her (Gallagher 1988: 128). Thus the electorate can easily punish an incumbent deputy without having to abandon the party.[17] Prominent politicians can and do lose their seats. Leading politicians from the smaller parties are particularly vulnerable: at the June 1997 election, one cabinet member and three junior ministers lost their seats and one party leader only survived on the final count. At election time there is nowhere to hide. There is nothing equivalent to the 'safe' spots near the top of a party's list that exist in non-preferential electoral systems.

Candidate Selection

The individual accountability of incumbent deputies at elections, enhanced in Ireland by the voters' ability to desert an individual without abandoning the party, is one institutional control that should help contain agency losses. With rival party colleagues active in their constituencies and after their seats, deputies cannot afford to stray too far from the interests of their constituents, the ultimate principals.

However, the primary mechanism for containing agency losses in the delegation chain from voters to representatives is clearly political parties and partisanship (Müller 2000). It is difficult though not impossible to get elected without the support of an established

---

defeated TDs lost to running mates. Thus, the risk of being ousted by a party colleague (if you belong to Fianna Fáil or Fine Gael) is real. This very rarely applies to other parties since they typically run single candidates in each constituency. In the same elections no incumbents of other parties were defeated by a running mate (Gallagher 1996b: 510).

[16] The electoral incentive towards candidate differentiation does not of course necessitate that constituency service be the method of competition. Candidates could compete as effective legislators, ministers, or take up distinctive ideological positions if these were thought highly valued by voters.

[17] Assuming that the party has nominated more than one candidate. An important (and often overlooked point) is that the degree of choice in an STV electoral system crucially depends on nomination strategies. For example, since the smaller parties typically nominate a single candidate in each constituency there is no intraparty choice. A substantial degree of choice depends on parties nominating more candidates than the seats they expect to win.

party. Independents and minor party candidates are elected at every election—which is unusual in Europe—though in fairly small numbers. For 1944–97 an average of 6.8 such deputies were elected at each election. For the more recent period between 1981–97, on average, 3.5 per cent of parliamentarians were independents or minor party candidates. Thus 96 per cent of all members of the Dáil belonged to the established parties (Fianna Fáil, Fine Gael, Labour, Democratic Left, and Progressive Democrats).

Hence, selection as a candidate by one of the main parties is the primary route to a political career. The choice of candidates that the electorate have the opportunity to reward or punish is largely predetermined by the political parties in the 'secret garden' of candidate selection (Gallagher and Marsh 1988). In practice candidate selection is entirely a matter for the parties. There are no constitutional or legal provisions relating to candidate selection for general elections.

The main Irish parties have broadly similar methods of candidate selection. First, just like most parties in Europe candidate selection is a power retained by the parties and their members: there are no primaries in which ordinary voters play a role. Second, candidates are chosen at constituency level by selection conventions composed of delegates representing the constituency party branches. Thus, a considerable number of party members are involved in selection through their role as convention delegates, the number depending on the size of the party. For example, Gallagher (1988: 121) reports that the average Fianna Fáil convention is about 220 delegates (varying from 40 to 440), whereas the Labour Party average is about fifty delegates (varying from 20 to about 200).[18] Selection is by election, with most parties (though not Fianna Fáil) using STV. However, in 1996 Fine Gael introduced an important reform whereby all members in a constituency of at least 8 weeks' standing (who belong to a branch that has been registered for at least 3 months) could participate and vote at candidate conventions. The introduction of 'one member, one vote' by Fine Gael stimulated competitiveness, increased attendance, and generally enlivened selection conventions for the 1997 election. For example, in the party leader's constituency of Meath, eight candidates sought the three available places on the party ticket, and 845 members (out of almost 950 eligible) actually voted (Galligan 1999: 63).

Behavioural Effects of Candidate Selection and STV

The formal rules, while important, do not capture the full dynamics of candidate selection. A strong strategic influence is the impact of 'localism', of which there are several

---

[18] Differences of detail are as follows. In Fianna Fáil selection conventions are held at which each branch can have three delegates. Election is by an elimination system for each place to be filled. The national leadership can add or delete a candidate. From 1945 until 1996 Fine Gael also used a branch delegate system in which each branch was entitled to a number of delegates proportionate to its size (see above). In the Labour Party, selection conventions are held in which each branch is entitled four delegates and voting is by STV secret ballot. The Progressive Democrats' generally use one-member-one-vote but their procedures are flexible so that they occasionally use branch delegate conventions, as they did in 1997 in Limerick East (Galligan 1999: 61). Voting is by STV secret ballot. The Greens allow all ordinary members in a constituency to participate in candidate selection by a postal vote.

reinforcing aspects. First, the one personal quality that a prospective candidate must have is strong local connections. Irish electoral behaviour is quite different from the pattern in Britain where *parachutage* is widely practised.[19] In Ireland, a Dublin candidate standing in Kerry or Donegal would do well to save his or her deposit. No party would select a candidate without a strong local base. Thus, it is not really possible to test whether voters insist on strong local connections, because the parties hardly ever select candidates without them (Gallagher 1988: 130). What is clear is the selectors' strong preference for local candidates, which is not entirely surprising. The selectors want to reward members of the local organization, and the national party largely acquiesces since it is in their interest to have local party workers campaigning enthusiastically for the party's candidates. Thus, most prospective parliamentary candidates have assiduously endeavoured to build a local political machine, one aspect of which is holding local office. Of deputies elected in 1997, 74 per cent were members of a local authority before their initial election (O'Sullivan 1999: 191). Indeed, virtually the only way of acquiring a local pedigree without building a strong local base is to 'inherit' the seat from a relative, quite a frequent practice in Ireland (Gallagher 1988: 139).[20]

Second, in electoral systems featuring multimember constituencies, the selectorate often attempt to 'balance the ticket' according to various criteria such as gender, race, locality, or ideological persuasion. In Ireland, it is well known that selection conventions attempt to balance the geographical dispersion of their candidates (Marsh 1981a,b; Gallagher 1988). If a party selects three candidates it is highly unlikely that it will pick three individuals whose bases are all in the north-west corner of the constituency—even if they are the 'best' candidates. Parties attempt to geographically distribute their candidates throughout the constituency both to maximize their vote, and to contain negative aspects of intraparty competition stimulated by two or more party candidates concentrating on the same part of the constituency.

While the candidates are mostly selected locally by the convention, all the national party leaderships reserve the right to determine the number of candidates nominated and the right to veto or add to the list of candidates selected locally. In practice the parties rarely veto the local selection of candidates since this would lead to considerable resentment. Increasingly, however, the central leadership will add a candidate to those selected locally if it believes that doing so provides a competitive advantage. Since incumbents' seats are most vulnerable to party colleagues, some deputies attempt to lessen the danger by having fewer and weaker candidates selected, a practice known as 'quota-squatting'. Of course, such defensive tactics are not in the interests of party leaders. Therefore, they increasingly add an additional candidate if they believe the party's constituency ticket to be too uncompetitive (or if one of their favoured candidates

---

[19] *Parachutage* is the French term for the imposition of non-local candidates by the national party leaderships. Indeed it is Britain that is exceptional in that it is the only country in Europe where many candidates were 'outsiders' when they were first selected.

[20] Of the 166 deputies elected in 1992, 39 (23%) were related to a present or former TD. More significantly, in 26 cases (16%) the relationship was judged sufficiently close to have made a difference (such as a son or daughter taking over a seat from a parent) (Gallagher 1993c: 73). This pattern was repeated in 1997 (O'Sullivan 1999: 190).

failed to get selected). Even then, however, party leaders attempt to do this sensitively, and usually add a local candidate, often someone who was unsuccessful at the selection convention. The nature of STV facilitates the leadership's intervention. As Gallagher (1988: 129) points out, 'Under STV the national executive can add a name without displacing anyone' or pushing anyone further down a list. All of a party's candidates are formally equal.

The fact that candidate selection is largely controlled locally might suggest that deputies are free to do as they please as long as they look after local interests, a delegation relationship that is principally between voters and individual TDs. And certainly there is an element of truth to this: some rebels can survive sanction by the national leadership if they remain locally popular (see footnote 21). Nevertheless, Irish voters are primarily party voters, and loyalty to a party usually outweighs local orientations (as evidenced by transfer patterns; see Gallagher 1977; Marsh 1981b; Carty 1983; Sinnott 1995). Even if a local TD has built up an elaborate personal election machine, he or she will often find that loyalty is contingent on remaining within the party (Gallagher 1988: 133).

Party discipline in the legislature is strong. Apart from deputies' general commitment to their parties (which should not be underestimated), they know that promotion will be denied if they oppose the leadership and that if they repeatedly vote against the party line in Parliament they will lose the party whip. Persistent rebellious behaviour could lead to deselection or expulsion from the party, in which case the deputy loses his primary electoral asset, the party label. Moreover, incumbents know that deselection will most likely end their political careers. Mair (1987: 67) states that 'a survey of the relatively poor electoral results of candidates who leave established parties and attempt to win seats as independents suggest that there is not much life outside party, and that the prior success of these individuals derived mainly from their original party affiliation'.[21]

In summary, localism, while important, usually does not override partisanship. Loyalty to party results in disciplined party voting in Parliament and structures electoral behaviour. Thus, the chain of delegation is mixed: while it primarily flows between voters and parties, the nature of STV means that voters can punish individuals without deserting party.

DELEGATION FROM PARLIAMENT TO CABINET

While the legislatures of parliamentary democracies are officially sovereign, in practice legislatures and executives are not even equal. In most countries majority governments with disciplined parties are in an ascendant position to Parliament. In terms of its relationships with the executive branch, the role of the legislature can be reduced to two

---

[21] Counterexamples are few and therefore relatively exceptional. In 1997 two prominent politicians from the largest parties (Michael Lowry and Jackie Healy-Rae) stood as independents after they were denied nominations. Both of them topped the polls in their respective constituencies. Thus, while this is unusual, the election of independents in Ireland means that there may be some life after party.

main sets of functions. The first are the institutional powers of the legislature in the 'making and breaking' of governments (Laver and Shepsle 1996). The defining characteristic of parliamentary democracies is that the government is at least accountable to the legislature. The cabinet is linked to the legislature by a series of 'tests', investiture votes, confidence motions, and dissolution powers, by which a parliamentary majority can select or terminate a government at will (assuming that Parliament is in session). Of course in many countries the legislature has the important *ex ante* screening power that cabinet members must be members of the legislature. In Ireland all cabinet members must be members of one of the houses of Parliament and no more than two can be from the Senate. In addition the Constitution stipulates that the Taoiseach, Tanaiste (deputy PM), and Finance Minister must be members of the Dáil (Article 28.7.1). In practice, all cabinet members are selected from the Dáil, the last exception occurring in 1981. Of course these 'hire and fire' powers have an all or nothing quality that provide little opportunity to influence ongoing policy-making. Thus the second role of Parliament is to monitor, investigate, and generally exercise legislative oversight of the executive powers of government.

Inauguration, Dissolution, and Confidence Procedures

The Irish Parliament plays a direct role in inaugurating governments through a vote of investiture. The formal rules are that the President on the nomination of the Dáil appoints a Taoiseach (PM). The Taoiseach then nominates the other members of the government who are then appointed by the President in a ceremony in which they receive their seals of office (Article 13). Despite the protocol the President plays virtually no discretionary role in government formation. The only thing that really matters is the balance of political forces in the lower house of Parliament (Dáil Éireann). To take office a prospective government must win an investiture vote by a majority of those voting.

The typical procedure is as follows. The Dáil is dissolved and an election is held within 30 days (Article 16.3.2 of the Constitution). The new Dáil then assembles within 30 days of polling day (Article 16.4.2). The first items of business are nominations for the election of Dáil officers, in particular the Ceann Comhairle (Chair) of the Dáil. Following this, nominations open for the position of Taoiseach (PM) and nominees must be proposed and seconded by individual deputies.[22] Usually the vote is a formality since either a single party has a majority or substantial coalition bargaining will already have occurred. However, since Ireland has become a fully-fledged coalition system, government formation has become more complex. Thus, in 1989—for the first time ever—the Dáil failed to elect a Taoiseach at its first meeting. After the leader of Fianna Fáil had failed to be appointed, the leaders of Fine Gael and Labour were nominated, although without a prior coalition agreement there was no prospect of their election. All nominees for Taoiseach were rejected. The Dáil was adjourned to

---

[22] The quorum is twenty and the vote is won by a candidate securing a majority of those voting.

allow further time for negotiations between the parties. After 2 weeks (and one more unsuccessful meeting of the Dáil) a government was finally elected, the first ever Fianna Fáil-led coalition government.

It is generally expected that once formed a government will govern without much 'interference' from Parliament. Of course all governments must be able to win periodic votes in Parliament. But while legislative defeats might be an irritation, only lost confidence motions are terminal. In Ireland the Constitution (Article 28) specifies that the Taoiseach must resign from office if he ceases to retain the support of a majority in the Dáil (and if this happens all other members of the government are automatically deemed to have resigned).

In practice no-confidence motions are fairly rare and some that do occur are a form of symbolic protest by the opposition rather that a realistic attempt to topple the government. Strong party discipline means that most governments can survive no-confidence motions with impunity. Any TD can propose a no-confidence motion. Confidence motions are not explicitly in the parliamentary rules of procedure. It seems that they must be governed by the rules pertaining to all motions. In confidence votes the quorum is twenty and the decision rule is a simple majority of those voting.[23] Of course the strategic context changes if the government lacks an overall majority, thereby empowering the legislature. Only two Irish governments have ever been dismissed by the Dáil. The first was in November 1982 when the Fianna Fáil minority government was defeated on its own confidence motion (proposed by the Taoiseach) after the Workers' Party withdrew its external support (Mitchell 1996: 123–4). Similarly in November 1992 another Fianna Fáil minority government lost a confidence motion the day after its coalition partners, the Progressive Democrats, had resigned (Mitchell 1993: 113).

Nevertheless, the fact that the Dáil has only directly brought down two governments underestimates the confidence procedure as an institution framing parliamentary government. For example, Gallagher counts at least eight other occasions (August 1927, 1938, 1944, 1951, 1957, January 1982, 1987, and 1994) when governments opted for an election rather than face almost certain defeat on a confidence motion (Gallagher 1999b: 183). Table 13.1 includes the resignation of the Haughey IV cabinet in this group.

While the President plays only a formal role with regard to the inauguration of governments he or she does have one potentially important discretionary power in relation to dissolutions. In normal circumstances, when a Taoiseach requests the President to dissolve the Dáil and hold an election, the latter is required to do so (Article 13.2.1 of the Constitution). However, according to Article 13.2.2, the President 'may in his absolute discretion refuse to dissolve Dáil Éireann on the advice of a Taoiseach who has ceased to retain the support of a majority in Dáil Éireann' (see Gallagher 1988; Laver 1996a). Constitutional ambiguity arises because it is not clear (and is not specified in the Constitution) what should count as evidence that the Taoiseach has lost the Dáil's

---

[23] The Dáil's Standing Orders (SO) say 'All motions to be put on the order paper for any day, shall be in writing, signed by a member, and shall reach the clerk not later than 11 a.m. on the fourth preceding day' (SO 28), though by permission of the Ceann Comhairle motions may be made on shorter notice. Dáil standing orders also stipulate that: 'No member shall re-open a discussion on a question already discussed during the preceding six months' (SO 51), which seems to limit the frequency of such motions.

confidence. Losing an explicit confidence motion or suffering defeat on the Finance Bill would certainly count but other situations are less clear-cut. For example, if one of the coalition partners essential to the government's majority resigns, could the President use this as tangible evidence that the government has lost the confidence of the Dáil and hence refuse to dissolve? While this has never been tested, to conclude otherwise would undermine presidential discretion since a Taoiseach faced with certain defeat on a confidence motion could always ask for a dissolution (Laver 1996a). On the other hand, the President by using this power could encourage coalition renegotiation after a government falls as an alternative to the traditional resort to an election. While no President has yet exercised this power, it could become a source of controversy if Ireland were to experience a period of coalition turbulence and government instability.

Table 13.1 summarizes the behavioural record with respect to cabinet investiture, no-confidence and confidence votes, and parliamentary dissolution.

The tables shows that, while unsuccessful investiture votes have generally been rare in Ireland, a total of six unsuccessful votes occurred both before the Haughey IV cabinet in 1989 and the Reynolds II cabinet in 1993. No data exists on the number of no-confidence votes held during each cabinet, but two cabinets were forced to resign because they lost no-confidence votes, and six cabinets resigned to pre-empt a no-confidence vote. On sixteen occasions early elections were held after the Taoiseach dissolved Parliament.

Parliamentary Scrutiny and Monitoring

One informed observer claimed in the early 1990s that the Irish government enjoys a 'virtual immunity from informed review or criticism' (O'Halpin 1993: 191).[24] While perhaps a slight exaggeration, there is little doubt that compared to some other countries the government in Ireland has had the whip hand in Parliament–executive relations. The government has a near-monopoly on legislative initiative and through the Standing Orders effectively controls the Dáil's timetable and order of business. For example, Standing Order 86 allows a minister without any prior notice to pre-empt private member's time (that is, opposition time) and substitute government business, the content and order of which is determined by the Taoiseach (Farrell, B 1994: 75).

Parliamentarians can certainly extract some information from ministers via parliamentary questions and committee oversight, but their ability to do so is heavily constrained by strong—many would say excessive—doctrines of cabinet confidentiality and executive secrecy. Traditionally, the chairman of the Dáil rules out of order questions that relate to internal cabinet discussions, and ministers have a multitude of devices to avoid answering questions. Nevertheless, each year TDs put thousands of parliamentary questions to ministers. There are three categories of questions: written, oral, and urgent. Oral questions must be submitted three working days in advance, but since ministers take 'question time' in rotation, the TD must wait until it is the relevant

---

[24] This has begun to change in the last few years. See section on 'Executive Secrecy', and Connolly and O'Halpin (1999).

Table 13.1. *Cabinet Formation, Cabinet Termination, and Early Parliamentary Dissolution: Ireland 1944–2000*[a]

No.	Cabinet	Date of formation	Investiture votes (iv)						No-confidence votes (ncv)[b]			Confidence votes (cv) under specific institutional mechanism[c]	Did the cabinet end with an early election?	Who dissolved Parliament in this case?[d]
			No. of unsuccessful investiture votes	Voting results of successful iv (1: pro gov, 2: Against gov, 3: abstentions, and 4: other)					No. of ncv[e]	Cabinet removed by ncv	Cabinet resigned to pre-empt ncv			
				1	2	3	4							
1	de Valera VI	44/06/09	0	77	49	11	1		n.d.	No		n.a.	Yes	PM
2	Costello I	48/02/18	1	75	68	3	1		n.d.	No	Yes		Yes	PM
3	de Valera VII	51/06/13	1	74	69	3	1		n.d.	No			Yes	PM
4	Costello II	54/06/02	1	79	66	1	1		n.d.	No	Yes		Yes	PM
5	de Valera VIII	57/03/20	0	78	53	15	1		n.d.	No				
6	Lemass I	59/06/23	0	75	51	20	1		n.d.	No			Yes	PM
7	Lemass II	61/10/11	0	72	68	3	1		n.d.	No			Yes	PM
8	Lemass III	65/04/21	0	72	67	4	1		n.d.	No				
9	Lynch I	66/11/10	0	71	64	8	1		n.d.	No			Yes	PM
10	Lynch II	69/07/02	0	74	66	3	1		n.d.	No			Yes	PM
11	Cosgrave I	73/03/14	0	72	70	1	1		n.d.	No			Yes	PM
12	Lynch III	77/07/05	0	82	61	4	1		n.d.	No				
13	Haughey I	79/12/11	0	82	62	3	1		n.d.	No			Yes	PM
14	FitzGerald I	81/06/30	0	81	78	4	3[f]		n.d.	No	Yes[g]		Yes	PM
15	Haughey II	82/03/09	0	86	79	0	1		n.d.	Yes			Yes	PM
16	FitzGerald II	82/12/14	0	85	79	1	1		n.d.	No	Yes		Yes	PM
17	Haughey III	87/03/10	1	83	82	1	0[h]		n.d.	No			Yes	PM
18	Haughey IV	89/07/12	6[i]	84	79	2	1		n.d.	No	Yes		—	—
19	Reynolds I	92/02/11	0	84	78	3	1		n.d.	Yes			Yes	PM

20	Reynolds II	93/01/12	6[j]	102	60	3	1	n.d.	No	Yes	—	—
21	Bruton	94/12/15	1	85	74	6	1	n.d.	No	—	Yes	—
22	Ahern I	97/06/26	0	85	78	2	1	—	—	—	—	PM

[a] n.d. = no data (missing data); n.a. or '–' = not applicable in this case.

[b] In Irish politics, the distinction between 'no-confidence' and 'confidence' votes is not very relevant. They essentially mean the same thing. This is because if the opposition parties propose—or even threaten to propose—a no-confidence vote, the cabinet has agenda control and will immediately pre-empt this attempt by announcing a confidence vote.

[c] While there is no constitutionally defined mechanism for a confidence vote procedure, as in other countries this possibility exists by convention. In this context, it can be interesting to note that only two cabinets have failed such a 'confidence vote'. These are Haughey II, which ended in November 1982, and Reynolds I, which ended in November 1992.

[d] The question 'Who dissolved Parliament in this case?' can be answered with one of five options. This identifies the main constitutional actor that caused the early election. We have not coded the formal signatory, but rather the person or body that made the real decision: (1) Head of State; (2) Prime Minister; (3) Cabinet; (4) Parliamentary majority; (5) Automatic constitutional provision (e.g. if it is required when a new President takes office, or, for example, if it is required after the adoption of a proposal for constitutional amendments).

[e] There is no official source or index that lists the number of proposed no-confidence votes. This means that short of going through the entire parliamentary record, this data is not available anywhere.

[f] Two Irish Republican prisoners were elected on an abstentionist ticket (at the time of the NI hunger strikes). Thus, in 1981 the effective size of the Dáil was reduced by 2 to 164. The third 'other' was the Ceann Comhairle whose vote was unnecessary.

[g] FitzGerald I was defeated on its budget. According to strong convention this is equivalent to loosing a CV. In these cases the government must resign—otherwise it would immediately lose an explicit ncv.

[h] After the vote was tied 82–82 (with a key independent, Tony Gregory, abstaining) the Fianna Fáil leader became Taoiseach on the casting of the vote of the Ceann Comhairle.

[i] In 1989 the Dáil for the first time ever was unable to elect a PM (Government) at its first post-election meeting. After electing the Chairman of the Dáil, the leaders of the three largest parties were sequentially nominated as PM and were all defeated. The Dáil also failed on its second meeting. Only during the third post-election meeting did the Dáil, after a coalition deal, appoint a PM. Deciding how many unsuccessful formation attempts to count is difficult. Given two inconclusive meetings of the Dáil one might count two unsuccessful investiture attempts (the failed nomination of the candidate of the largest party on two occasions) or six (failed nomination of candidates of three largest parties on two occasions). For cross-national comparability, six is the appropriate answer in terms of project consistency. Even if some of these 'failures' were merely symbolic (e.g. the Labour leader had no chance whatsoever of being elected PM), nevertheless the nomination was made and a vote was held in each.

[j] Same as previous note.

minister's day. While oral questions allow the TD to ask a 'supplementary' question many oral questions are not answered due to time constraints (the order in which oral questions are taken is decided by lottery). Partly because of this many (by the 1980s most) questions seek a written reply, which must be provided within three working days (Gallagher 1993b: 136–7). TDs can also ask 'private notice questions' for which the minister receives no prior notice. The Dáil Standing Orders allow questions relating to 'matters of urgent public business', but these are subject to the permission of the Ceann Comhairle. Gallagher (1993b: 137) calculated that in the mid-1980s there were on average (per annum) about 2,000 oral questions, 8,700 written questions, and 40 private notice questions.

While such questions are of some value in eliciting information, they do not adequately function as an *ex post* mechanism of monitoring government policy. Farrell notes that 'there is a well established principle that the chair [of the Dáil] has no power to compel a minister to answer a question or a supplementary question' (B. Farrell 1994: 75). Nevertheless, practical political limitations exist in the extent to which ministers can avoid answering questions (see Gallagher 1999b). Dáil question time is a showpiece event covered by the media so that a minister continually refusing to answer a question risks stimulating suspicion that he or she has something to conceal. More generally, in an adversarial Parliament a minister 'performing well' turns hostile questions to the government's advantage rather than merely refusing to answer them.

In many countries the real business of detailed and continuous legislative scrutiny takes place in parliamentary committees. Before the 1980s Ireland had no real experience of committee oversight of government behaviour. The few committees that did exist were mainly of a 'housekeeping' character rather than a serious effort to hold government to account. Since then, repeated efforts to introduce a more comprehensive committee system have had limited success. This is partly because ministers and backbenchers have lacked the appropriate incentives to devise powerful committees and partly because of a prevailing (Westminster type) expectation that it is the 'job of government to govern' free of too much 'interference'. Nevertheless, attempts to reform the committee system continue.

Irish committees lack power because their institutional foundations are weak. Governments have typically preferred to avoid too active scrutiny, while the opposition that hopes soon to be the government has incentives to collude (see Gallagher 1999b). Backbenchers, aware that committees are weak, have found more profitable ways to spend their time. Committees have been institutionally impoverished in a number of respects. First, while the 1980s and 1990s saw a significant growth in the number and activities of committees, there are no permanent Standing Committees. Committees (whose partisan composition is proportional to party strength in the Dáil) are established anew at the beginning of each Parliament and their number and functions vary. Thus, there is no sense in which Irish committees establish 'property rights' over jurisdictions. Second, they have no real *ex ante* agenda or *ex post* veto powers: they consider government bills. In Ireland, the decisive plenary stage of a bill *precedes* the committee stage of deliberation, which means that the broad principle of the bill has already been politicized and decided. If the minister rejects suggested amendments the bill normally will pass unamended. Third, most Irish committees (at least those set up before the mid-1990s) tended not to directly shadow government departments but rather to cover a bundle of jurisdictions that cut across departments (this was changed after the 1997 election so that now there is a committee monitoring each department).[25] Fourth, committees have lacked powers to compel ministers and civil servants to attend and give evidence, and more generally have lacked administrative resources. Finally, individual incentives have militated against the development of very strong committees. When push comes to shove, TDs prioritize loyalty to party over loyalty to committee for reasons dear to their hearts: promotion and re-election. Since committees do not distribute 'goodies', TDs do not expect electoral credit in their constituencies for good committee work. Indeed, they anticipate that too much time devoted to committees could be electorally counter-productive, or even suicidal. Nevertheless, committees do appear to be very gradually gaining in prestige and influence and play an increasing role in developing specialist knowledge and creating 'information efficiencies' (Krehbiel 1991).

DELEGATION WITHIN THE CABINET

The Taoiseach is the boss both formally and in practice. He (to date all have been men) has the constitutional right to hire or fire any member of the government. The Taoiseach's ministerial nominees will be appointed by the President providing that they have been previously approved by Dáil Éireann (Article 13.1.2). For majority governments this is a formality. The Taoiseach's power over ministerial selection is amended during coalition governments, so that the leaders of the other governing parties pick their own ministers.[26] Similarly the Taoiseach can fire any member of the government 'for reasons which to him seem sufficient' (Article 28.9.4) though again in practice a Taoiseach cannot fire a minister of another party without that party leader's consent. While ministers are not dismissed very frequently, the Taoiseach's power is always manifest. Thus, the delegation relationship is not so much from cabinet to minister as from Taoiseach (and other governing party leaders) to individual ministers, since the latter serve at the former's pleasure.

Irish cabinets contain fifteen ministers (all governments since 1973 have filled this constitutional maximum) who are both collectively responsible for the work of all government departments and individually responsible for virtually all the actions of their own department. The style of cabinet decision-making is structured by Article 28.4.2 of the Constitution: 'The Government shall meet and act as a collective authority, and shall be collectively responsible for the Departments of State administered by the members of the Government'. The cabinet acts as a clearing house for most major decisions and the doctrine of collective cabinet responsibility 'normally denies ministers the right to record

[25] The new committee system is also a source of patronage in that there are four paid positions (Gallagher 1999*b*).

[26] Technically, the nominees are recommended to the Dáil as members of the government rather than to particular departments, a point that was made clearly to the Dáil by Eamon de Valera in 1944 (Chubb 1983: 60). This underlines the Taoiseach's power to alter assignments or jurisdictions at will.

private dissent, let alone public opposition, to cabinet decisions' (Farrell 1993*a*: 174). This collective responsibility of the cabinet is reinforced by a doctrine of executive secrecy.

Nevertheless, there is a difference between the cabinet being formally collectively *responsible* for government decisions and extensive use of actual collective *decision-making* (Laver and Shepsle 1994: 298, 1996). There is a far-reaching division of labour in government and this gives decision-making a departmental structure in which each cabinet minister has considerable agenda powers to determine which policies and policy options are brought to cabinet for a formal decision. And cabinet ministers have considerable discretion as the unequivocal heads of their departments. This role is established by the Ministers and Secretaries Act 1924 (and subsequent amendments) whereby the minister is legally a 'corporation sole', and can be sued in that capacity. 'The effect of this is that the acts of a department are the acts of its minister, for which he alone is responsible ... in effect, the minister *is* the department' (Dooney and O'Toole 1992: 115).[27] However, while energetic and determined ministers no doubt have considerable scope to shape the policies of their departments, this autonomy should not be exaggerated. Particularly during coalitions party leaders cannot afford to allow full ministerial discretion since they would then lose all input in jurisdictions in which they did not control the minister. Parties have strong incentives to underwrite the credibility of their key policies—and attempt to commit their coalition partners to them—by negotiating their inclusion in the coalition policy document and subsequently policing these promises by a variety of devices designed to monitor progress towards the party's goals (see also Strøm 1998; Mitchell 1999*a*).

The Irish cabinet has not made extensive use of cabinet subcommittees (which are established on an ad hoc basis) and as a collective body appears to at least 'see' an extraordinary volume of papers. Farrell (1993*a*: 173) estimates that about 800 papers a year are handled by the cabinet, as compared to about 60–70 in Britain, where much more is delegated to cabinet committees. The Taoiseach controls the cabinet agenda through the government secretariat (the Department of the Taoiseach), and the cabinet usually meets once a week. There is no quorum, and in any case voting is not common. In addition the Minister for Finance clearly has a special role in exercising financial control over other departments. The Finance Minister is briefed on every proposal that comes before the cabinet and prior to this all submissions to the government 'must have been presented in advance to the Department of Finance so that that department may include its comments and advice to the government' (Dooney and O'Toole 1992: 234). After the Taoiseach, Finance is clearly the most important ministry and norms of mutual non-intervention do not apply to it.

In conclusion, the attempt to contain agency losses between individual ministers and their party leader relies heavily on their assumed incentive compatibility through their co-partisanship and their shared electoral goals. Leaders, ministers, and MPs of the same party *do* usually sink or swim together. Thus, though some ministers are more forceful or more able than others, they are generally agents of their parties and in practice (especially when in government) the party leader is the arbiter of the party interest. He or she

---

[27] The 'corporation sole' principle was partially amended in 1997. See section titled Delegation from Ministers to Civil Servants.

can, after all, fire any of them. However, while some commonality of interest may develop between coalition partners, they have different policy priorities and often suffer diverging electoral fates. Agency losses are a continuous problem in that a party is likely to be interested in the policy outputs (and electoral credit if available) of departments controlled by cabinet ministers belonging to their governing partners. While intervention in other ministries is a decidedly uphill task, a party cannot simply abandon a key party policy simply because it does not control the relevant minister. The increased frequency of coalition governments has led to the evolution of enforcement mechanisms by which parties attempt to safeguard their key interests. These range from contract design, in which parties negotiate the inclusion of brand identity items in the coalition policy document, to the detailed tracking, reporting, and monitoring of all departments by policy advisors and junior ministers in an attempt to ensure that party policies are being implemented in *all* ministries (see section titled Delegation from Ministers to Civil Servants). Smaller parties have been more enthusiastic about these enforcement mechanisms than larger ones. This might reflect their policy-driven profiles, but also indirectly testifies to the considerable agenda powers inherent in controlling ministries. Quite simply, large parties control more of the government agenda by virtue of the fact that they control more ministries, so that ancillary enforcement mechanisms that essentially attempt to compensate for less direct control (fewer portfolios) are less crucial to the big guns. In short, delegation relationships are more complex in coalition governments: they are a tangled web of agents monitoring other agents.

DELEGATION FROM MINISTERS TO CIVIL SERVANTS

While civil servants are in a general sense servants of the public they are more directly agents of the minister. Indeed, in Ireland 'the minister in charge of each department is legally the employer of all staff in that department' (Dooney and O'Toole 1992: 109). Most civil servants are recruited by means of competitions held by the Civil Service Commission. The minister in each department appoints all civil servants from names submitted by the Commission, subject to the posts being made available by the Finance ministry. The one exception is the Secretary of each department (the top civil servant), who is appointed by the cabinet on the recommendation of the relevant minister. As noted, Irish ministers were traditionally regarded as 'corporation soles': the minister *is* the department. Civil servants had no legal basis for issuing a decision in their own names and the minister is responsible for virtually everything done by her department. This position has been somewhat transformed by the Public Service Management Act 1997, 'which for the first time identified the role and responsibilities of senior civil servants and distinguished their responsibilities from those of the minister. The Act gave a public, legal accountability to the Secretary General of each government department' (Connolly and O'Halpin 1999: 264).

Evidence concerning senior civil servant's potential for independent influence on the political process is mostly anecdotal. Brian Farrell (1994), one of the few to have interviewed cabinet ministers about such matters, generally judges the civil service's influence as quite extensive. While some ministers claimed to be able to identify quite easily civil servants engaging in delaying and blocking tactics, many others were frustrated by the difficulty of forcing their agents to do their bidding.

As coalition politics has evolved ministers have increasingly resorted to political advisors—often people familiar with the civil service—whose chief characteristic is their direct loyalty to the minister. Thus, unlike the civil service, these advisors should not shirk their responsibility or engage in hidden actions, because, if carefully selected, their incentive structure should closely correspond to that of their principal, the minister. Their tenure depends entirely upon keeping the minister in power. These advisors are of two types. One is the ministerial political advisor who acts (in the words of senior civil servants) as 'a replication of the minister in many respects, as an extension of his political personality, as an extra pair of eyes and ears, doing for him what the minister would do for himself if he had the time' (Dooney and O'Toole 1992: 39).

Many civil servants were very unhappy, however, with a 1993 innovation whereby the incoming Fianna Fáil–Labour government created a new set of appointments in which each cabinet minister would appoint a 'programme manager'. These were senior political appointments operating within the civil service, but accountable directly to the minister rather than part of the normal line management of a department (O'Halpin 1997: 81). Whereas political advisors look after the minister generally, the programme manager's central task was to submit policy implementation to detailed tracking, to overcome bureaucratic and political obstacles to policy delivery, and generally to make sure that the party's policies were actually implemented. Thus, apart from overcoming civil service obstacles, a key function of the programme manager was to enable the Labour Party to 'maximise its strength in a coalition and to exercise its influence across a range of issues, including those where Labour ministers had no direct responsibility but on which the party itself had some view or definite policy position' (O'Halpin 1997: 80). Labour's programme managers met weekly as a group with party officials and TDs to monitor the progress of the party's policy. The programme managers are agents of their respective ministers: their job is to protect the minister against agency losses vis-á-vis the permanent civil service. In effect they constitute an attempt to compensate for the information asymmetry that favours the civil service in increasingly complex policy areas.

These appointments were repeated by the next government in 1995–6 but scaled down by the 1997 Fianna Fáil–Progressive Democrat coalition, partly because the PDs in particular had criticized the creation of the new political appointees as wasteful. However, the practice is likely to re-emerge since it was generally quite successful, and more to the point popular with most ministers who welcomed the addition of a senior operative unequivocally loyal to themselves.

'EXTERNAL' CONSTRAINTS

The Impact of 'Foreign Affairs'

Two sets of 'external' events are of particular importance to representative politics in Ireland: Northern Ireland and the EU. While the status and future of Northern Ireland has long been one of the biggest problems facing the Irish government, the special relationship with Britain has improved dramatically in the 1980s and 1990s. After the Anglo-Irish Agreement of 1985 and especially following the negotiating breakthroughs in 1998, the Irish government has become increasingly involved in North–South cooperation at all political and administrative levels (see Mitchell and Wilford 1999). Nevertheless, despite its intrinsic importance, increased involvement in Northern Ireland affairs imposes responsibilities rather than serious constraints on Irish policy makers in Dublin.

The same cannot be said of the EU. Like other member countries, the Irish Parliament's 'sole and exclusive' legislative authority is seriously amended by membership of the EU. Nevertheless, and unlike its larger neighbour, Ireland has generally been an enthusiastic member of the European club. Yet despite Ireland's active participation in the development of European institutions, a domestic democratic deficit in terms of a lack of accountability has occurred in relation to EU decision-making. In 1973 the Oireachtas established the Joint Committee on the Secondary Legislation of the European Communities, ostensibly to compensate for the pooling of sovereignty implied by membership. In practice, however, although 'its reports were often of high quality... the Oireachtas generally showed little interest in them' (Gallagher 1993b: 139). In addition, the government undertook to place two reports a year before Parliament but 'these reports generally arrive too late for parliament to give serious consideration to the issues they raise' (Keatinge and Laffan 1999: 339). However, a Joint Committee on European Affairs was created in March 1995 with a deputy from the governing coalition as chairperson. This committee like others in Ireland has no real binding power on government. EU membership, however, has dramatically affected the work of most departments and the civil service. One obvious effect has been to increase the domestic stature and importance of the Foreign Affairs ministry, which plays a key coordinating role.

Executive Secrecy

Ireland traditionally adhered strictly to doctrines of collective cabinet responsibility and executive secrecy. While some privacy of cabinet discussion is usually considered prudent, when applied rigorously these doctrines constitute an important constraint on executive accountability. This became a problem of public concern in the 1990s as the Irish political establishment was rocked by a series of scandals. Matters came to head in 1992 during a Tribunal of Enquiry into the Beef Industry, which among other things was investigating whether there had been improper links between some senior ministers and business interests (see Collins and O' Raghallaigh 1995; O'Toole 1995). The Supreme Court (in 1992) declared that the Tribunal could not have access to cabinet discussions; the Court thereby established a constitutional right to absolute cabinet confidentiality. Even the cabinet could not waive this right. The Chief Justice declared that 'confidentiality is a constitutional right which, in my view, goes to the fundamental machinery of government and is, therefore, not capable of being waived by any individual member of the government' (Farrell 1993a: 175, 1993b). A former Taoiseach, Garret

FitzGerald, argued that the Supreme Court decision 'turned a valuable political convention into a dangerous constitutional ban of an absolutist character' (*The Irish Times*, 18 October 1997).

The Irish political class is still struggling with such issues of executive accountability. A number of senior ministers have been forced to resign and former Taoiseach Charles Haughey has admitted improperly accepting a 'gift' of over one million pounds. Further scandals necessitated further tribunals of investigation, which found themselves hamstrung by the confidentiality ruling and by their inability to compel witnesses to testify. In an unsatisfactory attempt to deal with the first of these problems, a referendum on cabinet confidentiality was narrowly passed (53 per cent to 47) in November 1997. It enshrined this doctrine in the Constitution while at the same time allowing the High Court to authorize disclosure in inquiries by official tribunals.[28] Related reforms are gradually moving Ireland from a position of almost total executive secrecy to gradual and limited openness. New electoral laws now govern and limit campaign spending and require financial disclosure. The establishment of a 'Standards in Public Office Commission' was announced in June 1998 as a permanent investigative tribunal, replacing the previous pattern of ad hoc individual enquiries. The head of the Commission is to have the powers of a High Court judge and will investigate complaints against politicians and examine financial donations to deputies and parties (*The Irish Times*, 13 June 1998). A *Freedom of Information Act* was passed in 1997, although with twelve significant exemptions. Nevertheless, every department has now trained designated civil servants as freedom of information officers and citizens have a new legal right to information, or failing disclosure, to a justification. Connolly and O'Halpin (1999: 267) comment that the Act 'represents a reversal of the presumption of secrecy that has underpinned Irish government...It is, for example, in practice a far more powerful investigative instrument than a parliamentary question...' Legislation has also been introduced allowing committees to compel testimony from senior public servants and grant immunity to certain witnesses.[29] These reforms are overdue and essential if tribunals, courts, and parliamentary committees are to have the opportunity to exercise effective *ex post* scrutiny of politicians' behaviour in government.

CONCLUSION

In terms of the 'bigger picture' the newly independent state of Ireland established in the 1920s has been remarkably successful. The political forces initially engaged in a bitter civil war subsequently managed to abandon violence in favour of peaceful alternation in office and there have been no serious threats of democratic breakdown or regime instability. Political institutions, parties, and norms of parliamentary behaviour were quickly institutionalized in a manner considered legitimate and reasonably efficient.

---

[28] Many who voted 'no' did so because they felt that the amendment was much too restrictive, not because they were in favour of confidentiality.

[29] The Committees of the Houses of the Oireachtas (Compellability, Privileges, and Immunitiies of Witnesses) Act 1997.

Ireland approximates the ideal–typical singular chain of command characteristic of Westminster type political systems. Voters traditionally expect to cast a decisive judgement on the government; Parliament and executive closely interlock and share personnel; and the executive branch is headed by a Prime Minister who, while not omnipotent, is clearly the boss. Of course some deviations from a pure Westminster system have been noted. Most obviously TDs are elected by a form of proportional representation that places multiple agents in mutual competition in fairly small districts. This design is unpopular with some politicians, ultimately one suspects because it renders them more accountable to their constituents than they perhaps might like. Additional deviations from the Westminster model include a written Constitution as a check on executive power, and increasingly a behavioural shift towards coalition governments.

Nevertheless, Irish governments (at least majority governments) have not been heavily constrained or monitored by other institutions and agencies, least of all by Parliament. It is tempting to conclude that the Irish political system has been strong on delegation and too weak on accountability. While the system generally appears to have been quite successful, the recent and ongoing attempts at reform need to constrain agents and hold them accountable for their actions in government.

REFERENCES

Benoit, Kenneth and Michael Laver (2003). 'Estimating Irish Party Policy Positions Using Computer Wordscoring: The 2002 Elections', *Irish Political Studies*, 18:1, forthcoming.

Carstairs, Andrew McLaren (1980). *A Short History of Electoral Systems in Western Europe*. London: George Allen and Unwin.

Carty, R. K. (1983). *Party and Parish Pump: Electoral Politics in Ireland*. Brandon: Mercier Press.

Chubb, Basil (1983). *A Source Book of Irish Government*. Dublin: The Institute of Public Administration.

Coakley, John (1999). 'The Foundations of Statehood', in John Coakley and Michael Gallagher (eds.), *Politics in the Republic of Ireland*, 3rd edn. London: Routledge and PSAI Press.

——and Manning, Maurice (1999). 'The Senate Elections', in Michael Marsh and Paul Mitchell (eds.), *How Ireland Voted 1997*. Boulder: Westview Press.

Collins, Neil and O' Raghallaigh, Colm (1995). 'Political Sleaze in the Republic of Ireland'. *Parliamentary Affairs*, 48: 697–710.

Connolly, Eileen and O'Halpin, Eunan (1999). 'The Government and Governmental System', in John Coakley and Michael Gallagher (eds.), *Politics in the Republic of Ireland*, 3rd edn. London: Routledge and PSAI Press.

Dooney, Sean and O'Toole, John (1992). *Irish Government Today*. Dublin: Gill and Macmillan.

Farrell, Brian (1983). 'Coalitions and Political Institutions: The Irish Experience', in Vernon Bogdanor (ed.), *Coalition Government in Western Europe*. London: Heinemann.

——(1993a). 'The Government', in John Coakley and Michael Gallagher (eds.), *Politics in the Republic of Ireland*. Dublin: Folens and PSAI Press.

——(1993b). '"Cagey and Secretive": Collective Responsibility, Executive Confidentiality and the Public Interest', in Ronald J. Hill and Michael Marsh (eds.), *Modern Irish Democracy*. Dublin: Irish Academic Press.

—— (1994). 'The Political Role of Cabinet Ministers in Ireland', in Michael Laver and Kenneth A. Shepsle (eds.), *Cabinet Ministers and Parliamentary Government*. Cambridge: Cambridge University Press.

Farrell, David (1992). 'Ireland', in Richard S. Katz and Peter Mair (eds.), *Party Organizations: A Data Handbook on Party Organizations in Western Democracies, 1960–90*. London: Sage.

—— (1994). 'Ireland: Centralization, Professionalization and Competitive Pressures', in Richard Katz and Peter Mair (eds.), *How Parties Organize*. London: Sage.

Gallagher, Michael (1977). 'Party Solidarity, Exclusivity and Inter-Party Relationships in Ireland, 1922–77: the Evidence of Transfers'. *Economic and Social Review*, 10: 1–22.

—— (1985). *Political Parties in the Republic of Ireland*. Manchester: Manchester University Press.

—— (1987). 'Does Ireland Need a New Electoral System?' *Irish Political Studies*, 2: 27–48.

—— (1988). 'Ireland: The Increasing role of the Centre', in Michael Gallagher and Michael Marsh (eds.), *Candidate Selection and Comparative Perspective: The Secret Garden of Politics*. London: Sage.

—— (1993a). 'The Constitution', in John Coakley and Michael Gallagher (eds.), *Politics in the Republic of Ireland*. Dublin: Folens and PSAI Press.

—— (1993b). 'Parliament', in John Coakley and Michael Gallagher (eds.), *Politics in the Republic of Ireland*. Dublin: Folens and PSAI Press.

—— (1993c). 'The Election of the 27th Dáil', in Michael Gallagher and Michael Laver (eds.), *How Ireland Voted 1992*. Dublin: Folens and PSAI Press.

—— (1996a). 'Ireland: the Referendum as a Conservative Device?', in Michael Gallagher and Pier Vincenzo Uleri (eds.), *The Referendum Experience in Europe*. London: Macmillan.

—— (1996b). 'Electoral Systems'. Appendix 4 of *Report of the Constituition Review Group*. Dublin: The Government of Ireland.

—— (1999a). 'The Changing Constitution', in John Coakley and Michael Gallagher (eds.), *Politics in the Republic of Ireland*, 3rd edn. London: Routledge and PSAI Press.

—— (1999b). 'Parliament', in John Coakley and Michael Gallagher (eds.), *Politics in the Republic of Ireland*, 3rd edn. London: Routledge and PSAI Press.

—— and Michael Marsh (eds.) (1988). *Candidate Selection and Comparative Perspective*. London: Sage.

Galligan, Yvonne (1999). 'Candidate Selection in 1997', in Michael Marsh and Paul Mitchell (eds.), *How Ireland Voted 1997*. Boulder: Westview Press.

Keatinge, Patrick and Laffan, Brigid (1999). 'Ireland: A Small Open Polity', in John Coakley and Michael Gallagher (eds.), *Politics in the Republic of Ireland*, 3rd edn. London: Routledge and PSAI Press.

Krehbiel, Keith (1991). *Information and Legislative Organisation*. Ann Arbor: University of Michigan Press.

Laver, Michael (1992). 'Coalition and Party Policy in Ireland', in Michael Laver and Ian Budge (eds.), *Party Policy and Government Coalitions*. London: Macmillan.

—— (1994). 'Party Policy and Cabinet Portfolios in Ireland 1992: Results from an Expert Survey'. *Irish Political Studies*, 9: 157–64.

—— (1996a). 'The Government Formation Process in Ireland: Implications for the Constitutional Role of the President, the Government and the Dáil'. Appendix 1 of *Report of the Constitution Review Group*. Dublin: Government of Ireland.

—— (1996b). 'Notes on a New Irish Senate'. Appendix 7 of *Report of the Constitution Review Group*. Dublin: Government of Ireland.

—— (1998). 'Party Policy in Ireland 1997: Results from an Expert Survey'. *Irish Political Studies*, 13: 159–71.

Laver, Michael and Hunt, W. Ben (1992). *Policy and Party Competition*. New York: Routledge.

——and Marsh, Michael (1999). 'Parties and Voters', in John Coakley and Michael Gallagher (eds.), *Politics in the Republic of Ireland*, 3rd edn. London: Routledge and PSAI Press.

——and Shepsle, Kenneth A. (1994). 'Cabinet Members in Theoeretical Perspective', in Michael Laver and Kenneth A. Shepsle (eds.), *Cabinet Ministers and Parliamentary Government*. Cambridge: Cambridge University Press.

————(1996). *Making and Breaking Governments: Cabinets and Legislatures in Parliamentary Governments*. Cambridge: Cambridge University Press.

Lynch, Kathleen (1996). 'Seanad Éireann'. Appendix 6 of *Report of the Constitution Review Group*. Dublin: Government of Ireland.

Mair, Peter (1986). 'Locating Irish Parties on a Left–Right Dimension: An Empirical Enquiry'. *Political Studies*, 34: 456–65.

——(1987). *The Changing Irish Party System: Organisation, Ideology and Electoral Competition*. London: Frances Pinter.

——(1999). 'Party Competition and the Changing Party System', in John Coakley and Michael Gallagher (eds.), *Politics in the Republic of Ireland*, 3rd edn. London: Routledge and PSAI Press.

Marsh, Michael (1981*a*). 'Localism, Candidate Selection and Electoral Preferences in Ireland: the General Election of 1977'. *Economic and Social Review*, 12: 267–86.

——(1981*b*). 'Electoral Preferences in Irish Recruitment: The 1977 Election'. *European Journal of Political Research*, 9: 61–74.

Mitchell, Paul (1993). 'The 1992 General Election In The Republic of Ireland'. *Irish Political Studies*, 8: 111–17.

——(1996). *The Life and Times of Coalition Governments: Coalition Maintenance by Event Management*. Ph.D. Dissertation. Florence: European University Institute.

——(1999*a*). 'Coalition Discipline, Enforcement Mechanisms and Intra-Party Politics', in Shaun Bowler, David Farrell, and Richard S. Katz (eds.), *Party Cohesion, Party Discipline and the Organization of Parliaments*. Ohio: Ohio State University Press.

——(1999*b*). 'Government Formation: A Tale of Two Coalitions', in Michael Marsh and Paul Mitchell (eds.), *How Ireland Voted 1997*. Boulder: Westview Press.

——(2000*a*). 'Voters and Their Representatives: Electoral Institutions and Delegation in Parliamentary Democracies'. *European Journal of Political Research*, 37: 335–51.

——(2000*b*). 'Ireland: From Single-Party to Coalition Rule', in Wolfgang C. Müller and Kaare Strøm (eds.), *Coalition Governments in Western Europe*. Oxford: Oxford University Press.

——and Wilford, Rick (eds.) (1999). *Politics in Northern Ireland*. Boulder: Westview Press and PSAI Press.

Müller, Wolfgang C. (2000). 'Political Parties in Parliamentary Democracies: Making Delegation and Accountability Work'. *European Journal of Political Research*, 37: 309–33.

O'Halpin, Eunan (1993). 'Policy Making', in John Coakley and Michael Gallagher (eds.), *Politics in the Republic of Ireland*. Dublin: Folens and PSAI Press.

——(1997). 'Partnership Programme Managers in the Reynolds/Spring Coalition, 1993–4: An Assessment'. *Irish Political Studies*, 12: 78–91.

O'Sullivan, Mary-Claire (1999). 'The Social and Political Characteristics of the Twenty-Eighth Dáil', in Michael Marsh and Paul Mitchell (eds.), *How Ireland Voted 1997*. Boulder: Westview Press.

O'Toole, Fintan (1995). *Meanwhile Back at the Ranch: The Politics of Irish Beef*. London: Vintage.

Sinnott, Richard (1999). 'The Electoral System', in John Coakley and Michael Gallagher (eds.), *Politics in the Republic of Ireland*, 3rd edn. London: Routledge and PSAI Press.

——(1995). *Irish Voters Decide: Voting Behaviour in Elections and Referendums Since 1918*. Manchester: Manchester University Press.

Strøm, Kaare (1998). 'Institutions and Strategy in Parliamentary Democracy: A Review Article'. *Legislative Studies Quarterly*, 23: 127–43.

Whitaker, T. K. *et al.* (1996). *Report of the Constitution Review Group*. Dublin: Government of Ireland.

14

Italy: Delegation and Accountability in a Changing Parliamentary Democracy

LUCA VERZICHELLI

INTRODUCTION

The Italian political system has usually been described as a stable parliamentary democracy with proportional representation rules and a fragmented party system. About 10 years ago, this image was undermined by a deep crisis whose consequences, after several years of political turmoil, are still not clear. In this Chapter I discuss the constitutional and historical context of parliamentary democracy in Italy, starting from the 'classic' model set out in the republican Constitution of 1948. Of course, parliamentary democracy began much earlier, under the so-called *Liberal Italy* (1861–1924). The old Constitution marked the birth of an elective Parliament without changing the 'private' nature of the monarchic government[1] and without introducing broad political participation.[2] After 20 years of Fascism (1924–43), the entire political landscape was fundamentally altered—including the party system, the political class, and the predominant political cultures.

The constituent assembly elected in 1946 represented a complicated constellation of parties. Nevertheless, the new *carta* was approved by a large majority (around 90 per cent) of assembly members. Many strands of thought influenced the contents of the 1948 Constitution, which turned out to be both inflexible and long. Left parties and the Christian Democrats, despite the great differences between them, supported the introduction of social rights and welfare principles. In addition, the Constitution included basic liberal principles. Institutionally, after long debate, a parliamentary model prevailed. This choice signalled the dominance of mass parties, which would set the conditions for Italy's consensus democracy. The parties (or party factions) occupied all institutional levels, thus serving as the gatekeepers of democratic consolidation (Morlino 1991).

---

[1] The *Statuto albertino* was issued by the King of Piedmont in 1848 and then extended to the unified state. Article 5 of the *Statuto Albertino* stated that 'the executive power belongs to the King'. Article 65 added that 'the King appoints and dismisses his ministers'.

[2] Less than 5% of the population had the right to vote before the first extention of the suffrage in 1882. Until the reform of 1912, which introduced universal male suffrage, only about 10% of the population had the right to vote.

The 1948 Constitution provides the two Chambers with *symmetrical* legislative powers. Both chambers have to approve all legislative items. A quorum of 50 per cent +1 of the MPs is required, even though it is not checked by default. Both chambers feature similar procedural options: an abbreviated procedure by committee (*Commissione in sede legislativa*) can be applied, with the exception of constitutional amendments, electoral laws, delegations to cabinet, ratification of international treaties, and Budget laws.[3]

The President of the Republic has the power of promulgation (Article 73),[4] thus he is formally involved in the legislative process, while the cabinet has only limited powers of initiative and the authority to issue decrees on specific urgent issues (Article 77). A decree loses its legislative force unless Parliament approves it within 60 days. However, cabinets have traditionally reiterated the same decrees, challenging the majority to accept its initiatives (De Micheli 1997).

Constitutional amendments and budgetary policy (after 1978) do not follow this legislative process. The budget consists of a number of documents written by the cabinet (the Treasury and the Prime Minister (PM)) and approved by the Parliament during its autumn budgetary session. One of them is the formal *budget law*, which includes the final balance for the current year and the estimate for the next. All authorizations to change the existing expenditures and revenues have to be recorded in the Financial Bill (*Legge finanziaria*). A decade after the 1978 budget reform, the unsatisfactory results (and rising deficit) convinced Parliament to reinforce the cabinet's power, shorten the budgetary session, and constrain parliamentary amendments (Hine 1993: 180–7). According to Article 138 of the Constitution, constitutional amendments have to pass two votes in each chamber, with the second vote held at least 3 months after the first. If an amendment is approved by a majority smaller than two-thirds of all MPs, then a referendum on the amendment can be requested by one-fifth of MPs or by five (of twenty) Regional Councils.

The legislative procedures, which do not follow the ordinary process, also include the referendum provided by the Constitution (Article 75), which allows citizens to abrogate ordinary laws. There have been few changes in the legislative process since 1 January 1948. The most important transformations have been due to non-constitutional reforms. For example, the *anonymous* vote (1988) has replaced the dominance of secret voting in Parliament. On the other hand, the rise of strong party government and the cleavage between 'Atlanticists' and Left parties rapidly changed the conditions for the implementation of some provisions of the Constitution. Government parties, in an effort to increase the freedom of action of their fragile majorities, tried to reduce the Constitution's power-dispersing system of checks and balances (Hine 1993: 157)

---

[3] The abbreviated procedure has been heavily used, especially in the past, typically to produce an output called little-laws (*leggine*), micro-sectional pieces of legislation decided by variable majorities inside the committees (Di Palma 1977; Capano and Giuliani 2002*b*).

[4] Article 73 of the Constitution states that the President must sign new laws within 1 month of their approval, less if the Chambers declare the legislation urgent. Article 74 also states that the President may request a reconsideration by means of a message to both Houses, but if the Houses reapprove a law then it must be promulgated.

and delayed the actual creation of important institutions contained in the Constitution (the Constitutional Court, until 1958, the referendum, until 1970, and above all the regional autonomies, also until 1970). Paradoxically, Left parties, after favouring a centralized political system, pushed for 'regionalization' to strengthen their local and administrative power. The delay in the implementation of the Constitution distorted some of the intentions behind its provisions, thus making institutional mechanisms more flexible than one would expect given the formal Constitutional framework.

Political scientists and constitutional lawyers have paid particular attention to the problem of *party government* (see further). In contrast, institutional evolution has been largely unexplored. The usual image of Italian democracy is therefore relatively static: formally, the framework of parliamentary democracy has not changed, despite strong public demand for institutional and administrative reforms over at least the past fifteen years. However, in reality, the institutional structure has always been flexible (Calandra 1996). In this writer's view, this flexibility is connected to cycles of party government (Pasquino 1987; Verzichelli and Cotta 2000). In a broad sense, the success or dominance of different governance styles has been linked to different stages of Italian party government and, specifically, to the political formulas that supported the fifty-one cabinets of the 1945–98 period. In particular, we can identify a number of small changes related to parliamentary delegation and ministerial accountability.

The literature illustrates this flexibility in the practice of governing Italy. Maurizio Cotta (1994) shed light on the dynamics of the interaction between Parliament and cabinet. Using a revised Lijphart model (Lijphart 1984), he discovered the alternation between 'majoritarian' phases (during the 1950s and the 1980s) and 'proportional' ones. Majoritarian phases have been characterized by a clear distinction between cabinet and parliamentary opposition, a relatively strong PM, and greater cabinet autonomy. In the proportional phases, a progressive integration of the (Left) opposition has been visible both in the legislative process and in appointments, and Parliament has prevailed over a constrained cabinet. Pasquino (1987) and Vassallo (1994) confirm the existence of a historical evolution of party government. The latter, in particular, observes changes in the ruling party's ability to control the political agenda and appointment processes. Four phases of party government have been manifest in postwar Italy. Interestingly enough, Vassallo raises doubts about Italian institutional stability, asserting that some constitutional prerogatives (for instance the role of the PM during government formation) have been implemented in quite different ways at different times.

Differently from the publications quoted above, I will discuss whether the empirical record makes it possible to consider Italy as a good approximation of the ideal type of parliamentary delegation and accountability. Hence, I review the Italian delegation process as established in law and discuss whether or not significant modifications actually have occurred. If we want to understand 'delegation and accountability' in Italy, we must first assess to what extent the republican experience fits parliamentary democracy's ideal type. In the conclusion I return to the theoretical framework to discuss whether this model of delegation and accountability is applicable to the Italian case, not least in the light of recent changes.

POLITICAL PARTIES: THE TRADITIONAL GATEKEEPERS

Italian politics after Second World War was deeply influenced by a fragmented multi-party system and by the powerful role of those parties. A strong polarization between two permanent oppositions and the governmental centre was the basic characteristic of a polarized, multiparty system (Sartori 1976). The Left was dominated by the largest Communist party in Western Europe (PCI), while the small but stable neo-fascist party (MSI) was the main actor on the Right. The DC (Christian Democrats) dominated that part of the political spectrum from which governments came. It was flanked by the so-called secular parties (*partiti laici*): the Liberals (PLI) on the Centre-right, and the Social Democrats (PSDI) and the Republicans (PRI) on the Centre-left. Finally, the Socialist party (PSI) was always a middle-sized party, acting as a second power in both the Left opposition (until 1963, when it distanced itself from PCI) or in the governmental arena. A broad literature has analysed the impact of parties in the recruitment of parliamentary elites (Cotta 1979), the distribution of cabinet positions (Calise and Mannheimer 1982), or policy-making (Pasquino 1987). But how (and to what extent) have political parties influenced democratic delegation in Italy?

Traditional interpretations argue that a strong *party government* rapidly transformed parliamentary democracy in Italy by filling all political institutions with politicians from governing parties, a *ceto politico* selected and formed by traditional mass parties. Under this view, political parties worked mainly as office-seeking and/or patronage agencies (Vassallo 1994; Cotta and Verzichelli 1996). However, it is important to keep in mind (Panebianco 1982) that Italy's traditional parties have produced different types of politicians and exercised different degrees of control over their voters (Cotta 1979). In general terms, DC and PCI represent two alternative models. In the first case, a factionalized party (with discipline progressively enforced at the elite level) could control the selection of politicians on the basis of a checks-and-balances logic between different 'electoral forces' (territorial patrons and national factions) and a powerful central elite. Parliamentary seniority was the basic requisite for a Christian Democratic leader both to enter government (Calise and Mannheimer 1982) and to influence the party. On the other hand, the 'apparatus model' of recruitment of the Communist Party implies centralized candidate selection. Parliamentary turnover (i.e. regular replacement of party MPs) and circulation between representative institutions and positions within the party organization were the dominant methods used to secure this control, and served to concentrate recruitment and selection decisions in the hands of a small group of leaders. The Communist model implied a minor role for voters. Party elites were responsible for selection and elected politicians could be indirectly sanctioned by that same elite. In the other model, different party actors (individuals, local elites, national elites) and voters were all involved in a bargaining process in the first step of delegation. The DC's procedure is more interesting in the present context because, for a long time, it was the most important 'constraint' on the linkages we are studying here (i.e. the delegation between electorate and governmental MPs and between governmental MPs and cabinet). Of course, this procedure is particularly relevant to relationships among DC voters and politicians, but even other parties in government had similar selection methods.

The Role of Political Parties

As gatekeepers in the system of representation, parties also influenced political life insofar as they acted *instead of* institutional actors. This is not always clear with regard to legislation, where party discipline was traditionally balanced by a polycentric Parliament dominated by committees (Di Palma 1977). However, parties could directly influence some decisions about the life of government, for example, prompting a cabinet crisis via actions outside the parliamentary arena. They also participated (as parties rather than parliamentary groups) in summits aimed at monitoring cabinet activities. In addition, they influenced relationships inside the cabinet, for example by opposing initiatives of ministers from another party, or defending explicitly the action of 'their' ministers during a conflict with the PM about a specific policy competence. (For convenience I refer to the Italian head of government as PM, though the correct title is President of the Council of Ministers.)

Significant changes have taken place in the last decade. Party penetration of society has declined since the mid-1980s (Bardi and Morlino 1994; Morlino and Tarchi 1996), as has party control over the executive (Vassallo 1994; Verzichelli and Cotta 2000). A long phase of political turmoil started with the sudden emergence of a regionalist movement in the north of the country (1992) and persisted with the electoral revolutions of 1994 and 1996 (Bufacchi and Burgess 2001). The old political class was suddenly delegitimized, due to the discovery of a huge party-financing underworld, and, consequently, most of the traditional parties were eliminated and others were forced to undergo a dramatic transformation with regard to both ideology and organization.

Nevertheless, the introduction of a new electoral system and the consolidation (with the 2001 elections) of a bipolar competition system (Newell 2002) could only partially reduce the role of parties. They are quite remarkably distanced from the past, but they are still a crucial force, able to intervene between the voters and their agents and capable of influencing other links of the delegation process.

DELEGATION FROM VOTERS TO MPs: THE WEAK LINK

The Electoral Systems

In keeping with the consensus democracy model, the electoral connection between citizens and MPs in Italy was long governed by a PR system. Until 1992 two different PR systems enabled many parties to get at least a few seats in Parliament. The electoral system for the lower chamber was pure PR, based on multimember constituencies and a national distribution of the remainders (*corrected quota system*). Three or four 'mega-constituencies' in different areas of the country increased proportionality. Elections to fill the 315 Senate seats were based on a single-member district system at the first stage, but the majority required to win a seat was so high (65 per cent of the constituency vote) that the normal outcome was a second stage, in which all seats were proportionally distributed (*d'Hondt method*) on a regional basis. In elections to the lower chamber voters chose from among parties: symbols for each party list, not candidates, were printed on the ballot. Voters could exercise a preference vote by writing in a maximum of four names from the party lists. Although preference voting was not mandatory, it was widely used by voters (especially DC voters) to determine the internal ranking on each list. On the other hand, the single-member competition for the Senate gave only the 'illusion' of personal voting. Parties were not encouraged to form electoral cartels (because of the impossibly high threshold) and commonly imposed their own candidates in each constituency. Therefore, in reality, there were no significant differences—in terms of selection process, electoral campaign, or party results—between the two electoral systems.

In the early 1990s a strong pro-majoritarian movement, supported by local and second rank politicians from different parties, promoted a referendum that abolished preference voting in lower chamber elections. Though the referendum had few practical consequences, it was rich in symbolic meaning. The 1992 elections were technically different from the previous ones, but still 'proportional'. However, major change was on its way. A real reform was introduced in 1993 (after another referendum had definitively killed the old electoral system). In the elections of 1994 and 1996, 25 per cent of deputies and senators were elected proportionally on regional bases and 75 per cent through a single-member plurality system.

Campaigns and Party Financing

Apart from election rules, delegation from voters to MPs has not been regulated in detail. The constitutional principle stating that MPs are national representatives (Article 67) serves as a reminder of the absence of a direct relationship between territory and representative. More importantly, there are no formal obligations with regard to candidate selection, which has traditionally been 'delegated' to parties (Wertman 1988).

Even electoral campaigns used to be fully dominated by parties. Or better, until 1993, campaigns were completely unregulated. There were a few norms guiding the use of broadcasting time during the last part of campaigns, but these were substantially cooperative and exclusionary—securing equal time for each parliamentary party and excluding other challengers. The reform of public television in 1976 introduced a minimum allocation of broadcasting time for all parties, including those 'extra-parliamentary' ones that presented their own lists in three-quarters of national electoral districts. Electoral activities remained largely unregulated. In 1993, a new set of rules introduced a financial cap on individual campaigns, a more proportional and controlled distribution of broadcasting time, and regulations concerning the publication of opinion polls. In addition, public subsidies for campaign expenditures to individual candidates (and not to parties) were introduced, together with a set of new rules about transparency and disclosure of campaign activities (e.g. contacts, personnel, and expenditures). Thus, the institutional and legal environment, which was very stable during the first 45 years of democratic competition, underwent change designed to limit some party privileges (Fusaro 1994). However, the effects of these changes are still unclear.

Since the 1970s parliamentary parties have also benefited from public subsidies. Significant amounts of money have been distributed to national parties through the 'public party financing programme'.[5] The funds are distributed proportionally based on national electoral support (Bardi and Morlino 1994). At the beginning of the 1990s public contributions to parties reached 100 billion lira per year, representing 40–90 per cent of the overall income of each party. A 1993 referendum abrogated the 1974 party finance law and introduced a new system of public financing based on the principle of 'electoral reimbursement' (of campaign costs). The distribution of funds was still proportional and the parliamentary parties were still the beneficiaries. A subsequent law (no. 157 of 1999) confirmed the same principle and quadrupled the annual volume of subsidies (Pujas 2000). In general, after 1974, two important features continue to characterize the public financing of political parties: First, a party needs to enter the Parliament in order to receive public funds. Second, money is always distributed proportionally.

In parliamentary recruitment, the common pattern for most parties was 'local involvement' in the selection of nominees, but strong 'central control' (Wertman 1988). During the period popularly known as the *first republic* (1948–1994), candidate selection was entirely controlled by parties, which could easily prevent any genuine, direct participation by voters—and to a large extent, by party members as well. Consequently only a very small percentage of voters were involved in candidate selection, which was largely a process of bargaining between local executives and national elites,[6] and intraparty competition was very limited. A significant exception was competition among Christian Democratic list of candidates. However, this competition did not take place according to transparent mechanisms, but was governed by informal agreements among strong candidates (the so-called *cordate*). The Socialist party occasionally also manifested a high degree of factionalism, but internal competition was controlled by national leaders. In fact, most party statutes reserved a 'quota' of parliamentary slots for party executives (Bardi and Morlino 1994).

The recent transformation of the party system and the shake-up of the old parliamentary establishment have changed the political professionalism of MPs (Verzichelli 1998, 2002), but recruitment continues to be centralized. In no party are voters or members directly involved in determining parliamentary nominees, and very few have added rules about term limits or retirement age. The relative weakness of the principal (the voter) and the hidden information controlled by the agent (the MP) thus seem to characterize this delegation process. Already before the 1990s, certain external constraints had progressively changed the opportunities for political parties to limit the

---

[5] Law no. 195/1974 introduced an annual subsidy to all parties that won at least one seat in Parliament or 2% of the valid votes nationwide. A 1978 referendum to abrogate this law was supported by only about 40% of voters. The law was amended several times (in 1978, 1980, and 1981), though none of these were significant changes. Other funds subsidized parties running for European and local elections (Law 422/1980).

[6] Interparty differences did, of course, exist. PCI members had little opportunity to control candidate selection since the involvement of the national executive began very early in the process. DC local elites had some power, which was reflected in the structure of the traditional candidate list: a top group of candidates (maybe with some national names), a second group of 'local' and 'strong' incumbents, and finally the rest of the nominees in alphabetical order. For a more detailed description see Wertmann (1988).

prerogatives of the voters and thus protect the privileges enjoyed by their elites.[7] But the real change happened only with the electoral revolution of 1994. Since this election, a remarkable instability of parliamentary parties and a high degree of party indiscipline have characterized parliamentary life, thus impeding efforts to enhance citizen control (Verzichelli 2003). A decisive step towards the consolidation of the new party system occurred with the 2001 election, but this is not a sufficient condition to argue that constituency control and individual accountability of MPs have emerged. Yet, a rather unusual lack of incumbency power persists after three applications of a _first past the post_ electoral system (Verzichelli 2002).

At the end, while the old _partisan_ model of political recruitment is still at work, a clear _decay of information_ (Strøm 2000), due to a deep and persistent crisis of the party system, seems to endanger the tools of _ex ante_ voter control of politicians.

DELEGATION FROM PARLIAMENT TO CABINET: A SLOW CONSOLIDATION

Constitutional Features

Formal mechanisms of government formation have remained unaltered since the establishment of the Italian Republic. After _consultations_ involving parties and institutional personalities, the President of Republic appoints the PM and, on advice of the PM, the other members of the cabinet. In reality, parties have been the key negotiators, reducing the role of institutional actors and imposing their own nominees (Verzichelli and Cotta 2000). According to Article 92 of the Constitution, Parliament is not formally consulted during the first phase of the process. Nonetheless, during preliminary consultations, the President of Republic typically invites the speakers of the chambers and the former Presidents of the Republic to discuss the political situation. Party leaders and parliamentary whips (_capi-gruppo parlamentari_) also participate in the consultations. This practice can be seen as a screening procedure designed to find a stable parliamentary majority, though it does not seem to be terribly important in the appointment process.

Italy features positive parliamentarism (Bergman 1993) insofar as the Constitution requires that governments win a mandatory vote of confidence in both Chambers of Parliament within 10 days of the appointment of ministers (Article 94). The investiture vote was debated for a long time by those who drew up the Constitution and remains a complicated matter for scholars. The Constitution aims to give the cabinet a strong parliamentary legitimization. The two-Chamber investiture vote requirement was intended to force the Government to establish a stable majority in each chamber. In reality, the symmetrical political configuration of the two chambers, a consequence of the PR voting systems, made the second vote (in the Senate) unnecessary and

---

[7] A good indicator can be the consolidation of the abrogative referendum, which is discussed below. Another progressive sign of change is the emergence of a number of parliamentary actors with different form of 'anti-party' message: the Radicals (1976), the Greens (1983), other minor formations between 1987 and 1992, and a more conspicuous number of politicians elected by the new parties after 1992 (Verzichelli 2000a).

predictable.[8] The situation is a bit different since the electoral reform of 1993.[9] This is partly due to a minor rule difference between the two chambers with regard to the distribution of the seats under the proportional quota (Katz 1996), but it is also caused by uncertainty in the party system in the wake of the breakdown of the old *partitocracy*. In the past, the roll-call votes of confidence were characterized by a high degree of party discipline. During the chaotic phase of the transition that started in 1992, however, individual MPs changed their partisanship, parties changed their coalition strategies, and some parliamentary groups split (Verzichelli 2003).

In addition to the inauguration vote, there are two types of confidence votes in Italy: the no-confidence motion (*mozione di sfiducia*), which can be introduced by MPs, and the confidence motion (*mozione di fiducia*), which is an instrument of the government. The former, which can be directed against a single minister or the whole cabinet, must be signed by at least one-tenth of the members of either house and can be voted on 3 days after its submission. The quorum requirement is the simple majority (50 per cent + 1 of MPs), while the majority requested to censure a cabinet member or the entire cabinet is 50 per cent + 1 of the MPs present and voting.[10] The same rules apply to the confidence motion, which can be tied to a single piece of legislation like bills or resolutions (*questione di fiducia*).[11] The cabinet has to request a confidence vote at least twenty-four hours before the scheduled vote on the relevant legislation.

The Practice of Parliamentary Government

In the past, Parliament rarely used the no-confidence instrument. Polarization between the Communists and neo-fascists in opposition was the main reason. However, its use has increased in the late twentieth century and in 1995 a no-confidence motion against an individual minister was passed for the very first time. In contrast, many *franchi tiratori* ('snipers')—majority MPs who voted against their government on a secret ballot— have often helped the opposition reject cabinet proposals.[12] Cabinets, on the other

---

[8] The order in which the chambers hold the vote of confidence alternates: the Chamber goes first after one election, then the next time the Senate votes first.

[9] In 1994 Berlusconi had a stable majority in the lower chamber (366 yes and 245 no in the inauguration vote), but was forced to gain support from some independents in the Senate (and even the vote of one MP elected from the Popular party) to obtain a very slight majority (159 votes to 153). Prodi's difficulties (1996) arose in the Chamber, where he won the vote of confidence thanks to the external support of the neo-communist party (322 votes to 299). In the Senate, MPs from the coalitional parties were sufficient. After the 2001 elections, a solid majority supports the Berlusconi II cabinet in both the chambers. However, an important difference is that at the Senate the votes of the Northern League can be necessary to pass the cabinet's initiatives.

[10] In the Chamber of Deputies, this means the majority of MPs who actually vote, while in the Senate the rule is the positive vote of the majority of the MPs who are present at the moment of the vote. Thus, in the Senate abstention is in effect counted as a vote against the government.

[11] The regulations of the lower Chamber forbid the use of this motion in cases of parliamentary investigation, personal questions, or the modification of internal regulations. The latter eruption (internal regulations) applies to the Senate as well.

[12] This did not usually occur on confidence motions, but the *franchi tiratori* often acted in the first secret vote held after the confirmation of confidence. The abrogation of the secret vote in 1988 (with the exception of voting on decisions about individuals) eliminated the phenomenon.

hand, used to verify their support in different arenas, especially in summits with party leaders from the majority parties. Cabinet resignations very often occurred before a vote on a parliamentary resolution, thus pre-empting a no-confidence vote. Hence the prevalence of the so-called *extra-parliamentary crisis*: a resignation directly announced to the President of Republic, before a decisive parliamentary vote. Even when a cabinet was sent back to Parliament to verify its majority or when there was a 'threat' of possible defeat, the PM preferred to resign in anticipation—perhaps in order to obtain a new appointment.

In contrast, the cabinet often uses the confidence motion to support its legislative initiatives. As already mentioned, this special procedure can be applied to normal legislation (with few exceptions). A vote on a piece of legislation 'marked' by a request of confidence is conducted according to the normal voting procedure (under existing rules, a non-secret vote without a roll-call). Cabinets have employed the confidence motion more than 230 times in either or both Chambers between 1948 and 2000 and the practice increased in the 1990s. For example, the government's annual financial bill and proposed economic reforms are often amended in Parliament. The cabinet has begun turning passage of these pieces of legislation into confidence votes to pressure its parliamentary majority to accept the original proposals.

The lack of balance in the use of confidence votes (i.e. rarely by MPs, often by governments) shows the gap between the actual delegation process and the one formally envisaged in legislation, including the Constitution. The repeated use of confidence motions, for instance, indicates the 'ambitiousness' of a government seeking to control parliamentary behaviour in particular policy areas, even when Parliament has not delegated authority in those policy areas to the government.

Table 14.1 summarizes the behavioural record with respect to cabinet investiture, no confidence and confidence votes, and parliamentary dissolution. The table shows that unsuccessful investiture votes have been rare; only five have occurred in the postwar era, the most recent before the formation of the Goria cabinet in 1987, when the five-party coalition was living a period of crisis due to the conflict between the DC and PSI. Numerous cabinets have faced votes of no confidence, but no cabinet has been removed through such a vote, though several have resigned to pre-empt one. The number of confidence votes, as noted above, has been large, although only the Prodi government in 1998 was removed by a failed confidence vote. Seven cabinets ended in early elections, after having been dissolved by a parliamentary majority.

A final constitutional tool to delegate legislative powers is the legislative delegated decree (*decreto delegato legislativo*). It enables the Parliament to give the cabinet the power to legislate in a given matter. A clear '*ex ante*' control is provided by Article 76 of the Constitution: 'the exercise of the legislative function may be delegated to the government only after having established principles and criteria, for a limited period of time and for specific objects'. In practice, there are very few delegated decrees, though in recent years there has been an increasing tendency to resort to them. For example, a 1992 delegation of authority allowed the cabinet to produce an important decree on public finance. In addition, both the technocratic cabinets (Ciampi 1993; Dini 1995) and the political ones (Prodi 1996; Belusconi 2001) implemented important delegated decrees. According to most observers, this is clear evidence of growing cabinet power (Calise 1994).

Table 14.1 Cabinet Formation, Cabinet Termination, and Early Parliamentary Dissolution: Italy 1945–2000[a]

No.	Cabinet[b]	Date of formation	Investiture votes (iv)					No-confidence votes (ncv)			Confidence votes (cv)[c]		Did the cabinet end with an early election?	Who dissolved Parliament in this case?[d]
			No. of unsuccessful investiture votes	Voting results of successful iv[e] (1: pro gov, 2: against gov, 3: abstentions, and 4: other)				No. of ncv	Cabinet removed by ncv	Cabinet resigned to preempt ncv[f]	No. of cv under spec. inst. mech.	Cabinet removed by failed cv		
				1	2	3	4							
1	Parri	45/06/21	—	—	—	—	—	—			—		—	—
2	De Gasperi I	45/12/09	—	—	—	—	—	—			—		—	—
3	De Gasperi II	46/07/13	0	398	53	7	n.a.	0			—			
4	De Gasperi III	47/02/02	0	292	53	1	n.a.	0			—			
5	De Gasperi IV	47/05/31	0	274	231	4	n.a.	0			—			
6	De Gasperi V	48/05/23	0	346	167	0	n.a.	0			1	No		
7	De Gasperi VI	50/01/21	0	314	89	12	n.a.	0			3	No		
8	De Gasperi VII	51/07/26	0	291	175	42	n.a.	0			3	No		
9	De Gasperi VIII	53/07/16	0	263	282	37	n.a.	0			0			
10	Pella	53/08/17	1	315	215	44	n.a.	1	No	Yes	0			
11	Fanfani I	54/01/18	0	260	303	12	n.a.	0			0			
12	Scelba	54/02/10	1	300	283	1	n.a.	1	No	Yes	8	No		
13	Segni I	54/07/22	0	293	265	12	n.a.	1	No		7	No		
14	Zoli	57/05/19	0	305	255	11	n.a.	0			1	No		
15	Fanfani II	58/07/01	0	295	287	9	n.a.	0			1	No		
16	Segni II	59/02/15	0	333	248	1	n.a.	0			0			
17	Tambroni	60/03/25	0	300	293	0	n.a.	1	No		0			
18	Fanfani III	60/07/26	0	310	156	96	n.a.	1	No		2	No		
19	Fanfani IV	62/02/21	0	295	195	83	n.a.	2	No	Yes	2	No		
20	Leone I	63/06/21	0	255	225	119	n.a.	0			0			
21	Moro I	63/12/04	0	350	233	4	n.a.	1	No		25	No		

Table 14.1 *Continued*

No.	Cabinet[b]	Date of formation	Investiture votes (iv)	Voting results of successful iv[e] (1: pro gov, 2: against gov, 3: abstentions, and 4: other)				No-confidence votes (ncv)			Confidence votes (cv)[c]		Did the cabinet end with an early election?	Who dissolved Parliament in this case?[d]
			No. of unsuccessful investiture votes	1	2	3	4	No. of ncv	Cabinet removed by ncv	Cabinet resigned to preempt ncv[f]	No. of cv under spec. inst. mech.	Cabinet removed by failed cv		
22	Leone II	68/06/24	0	263	252	88	n.a.	0			0	No		
23	Rumor I	68/12/12	0	351	247	2	n.a.	0			3	No		
24	Rumor II	69/08/05	0	346	245	6	n.a.	0			2	No		
25	Rumor III	70/03/27	0	348	239	0	n.a.	0			4	No		
26	Colombo	70/08/06	0	348	231	1	n.a.	0			0			
27	Andreotti I	72/02/17	1	n.d.	n.d.	n.d	n.a.	0			0		Yes	Parl. Maj.
28	Andreotti II	72/06/26	0	329	288	0	n.a.	0			2	No		
29	Rumor IV	73/07/07	0	371	242	0	n.a.	0			4			
30	Rumor V	74/03/14	0	343	231	0	n.a.	1	No		1	No		
31	Moro II	74/11/23	0	355	226	19	n.a.	0			3	No		
32	Moro III	76/02/12	0	287	220	60	n.a.	0		Yes	0		Yes	Parl. Maj
33	Andreotti III	76/07/29	0	258	44	303	n.a.	0			4	No		
34	Andreotti IV	79/03/20	0	n.d.	n.d.	n.d	n.a.	0			0		Yes	Parl. Maj.
35	Cossiga I	79/08/04	1	287	242	65	n.a.	1	No	Yes	1	No		
36	Cossiga II	80/04/04	0	335	271	0	n.a.	0			3	No		
37	Forlani	80/10/18	0	362	250	9	n.a.	0			5	No		
38	Spadolini	81/06/28	0	369	247	0	n.a.	1	No		8	No		
39	Fanfani V	82/12/01	0	349	244	15	n.a.	0		Yes	8	No	Yes	Parl. Maj.
40	Craxi	83/08/04	0	361	243	3	n.a.	2	No		34	No		
41	Fanfani VI	87/04/17	0	131	240	193	n.a.	0			0		Yes	Parl. Maj.
42	Goria	87/07/28	1	371	237	0	n.a.	0			6	No		
43	De Mita	88/04/13	0	366	215	2	n.a.	0			6	No		
44	Andreotti V	89/07/23	0	371	200	3	n.a.	1	No	Yes	7	No		

45	Andreotti VI	91/04/13	0	339	207	0	n.a.	2	No		4	No	
46	Amato	92/06/28	0	330	280	2	n.a.	1	No		15	No	
47	Ciampi	93/04/29	0	309	60	185	n.a.	1	No	Yes	12	No	Parl. Maj.
48	Berlusconi	94/05/11	0	366	245	0	n.a.	3	No	Yes	3	No	
49	Dini	95/01/17	0	302	39	270	n.a.	1	No	Yes	9	No	Parl. Maj.
50	Prodi	96/05/18	0	322	299	0	n.a.	1	No		33	Yes	
51	D'Alema	98/10/21	0	333	281	3	n.a.	1	No		2	No	
52	D'Alema II	99/12/22	0	310	301	9	n.a.	—	No		—	No	

a n.d. = no data (missing data); n.a. or '—' = not applicable in this case.

b The definition of a cabinet in this cross-national project is more restrictive than the conventional Italian counting rule. If the latter rule had been used, some of the cabinets listed in the table (Moro I, Andreotti III, Spadolini, and Craxi) would count as more than one 'cabinet'.

c The data presented in this column refers only to votes held under the specific confidence vote (Questioni Di Fiducia) that is defined by the rules of procedure for the Lower Chamber (Art. 116) and the Senate (Art. 161). With this tool, cabinets 'force' a parliamentary chamber to support a particular cabinet proposal.

d The question 'Who dissolved Parliament in this case?' can be anwered with one of five options. This identifies the main constitutional actor that caused the early election. We have not coded the formal signatory, but rather the person or body that made the real decision: (1) Head of State, (2) Prime Minister, (3) Cabinet, (4) Parliamentary majority (In Italy the Constitution gives the President the exclusive right to dissolve Parliament, but in these cases it was the parliamentary majority that asked for a dissolution). (5) Automatic constitutional provision (e.g. if it is required when a new President takes office, or, for example, if it is required after the adoption of a proposal for constitutional amendments).

e The results presented below are for the Lower Chamber only (and not for the Senate).

f This includes resignations after presentation or announcement of a possible no-confidence motion by a group of MPs.

Parliamentary Accountability of the Cabinet

Italy's constitutional fathers were keen to give the Parliament a set of screening and investigative powers. These tools of accountability, similar in both chambers, consist of opportunities to put written and oral questions to the government, as well as to initiate urgent interrogations. Both chambers also have investigative powers, via both permanent and ad hoc committees. Under the Constitution (Article 96), ministers are collectively responsible for cabinet decisions and individually responsible for those of their own ministries. It is, however, the PM who is directly involved in answering questions related to the government's general political programme. These control mechanisms have traditionally been used very extensively (even by government MPs), thus ensuring continuous contact between the legislature and executive.[13] On the other hand, to safeguard the activity of the cabinet, the PM or an individual minister can delay his/her response or simply avoid answering.

Another instrument in the hands of MPs is supervision of cabinet activity. The Constitution does not provide a direct monitoring device (such as scrutiny of cabinet minutes). Nonetheless, every legislative committee can investigate executive administrative action in its area of competence. Committees can invite ministers and junior ministers to present periodic reports. A few bicameral committees (committees for vigilance and control) supervise cabinet action on specific issues (e.g. telecommunications, distribution of resources to local governments, information agencies, and security). In sum, many potential mechanisms of parliamentary control exist. How well they function depends upon a variety of factors, including the organization of the executive, the personalities of cabinet leaders, and the strength of the coalition that supports the government. Two crucial events in the evolution of parliamentary control were the 1971 reform of parliamentary procedures and the reorganization of the legislative bureaucracy during the 1980s. The former reform introduced a more effective control, some consultative 'advice' on governmental appointments and cabinet activities. The latter made the MPs more effective (especially in technical fields such as budgetary policies) in checking and responding to cabinet proposals.

No comprehensive study has been conducted of formal and informal interaction between the cabinet and legislators in the whole law-making process. Nonetheless, variation from one policy issue to another seems to grow with the passing of the time (Di Palma 1977; Capano and Giuliani 2002). In at least two areas the initiative is clearly in the hands of the cabinet: foreign affairs and the budget (since the 1978 financial bill). In the former case, Italy's limited international role has made executive predominance less and less important. Moreover, after that the constraints introduced by the Maastricht Treaty and then by the stability pact, budgetary policy has become the real 'test' of cabinet strength. The cabinet has since become increasingly effective (Cotta and Verzichelli 1996), thus confirming its progressive strengthening since the 1980s (Calise 1994). Today, the government is clearly the initiator in other areas as well. The

---

[13] Every week there is at least one question period in each Chamber. Answers must be delivered within two (for oral questions) or three (for written questions) weeks.

'technocratic' and political cabinets of the 1990s were able to conclude important pieces of labour legislation and reforms of the welfare system. The cabinet also increasingly appears to be in control of Italy's *European policies* (including security and public order, regulatory policies, and communications). The 'new dualism' created by cabinet and Parliament at the sunset of the *partitocratic* age (Pitruzzella 1997) implies a stronger cabinet role in ordinary policy-making and a clear dominance for the Parliament with regard to institutional reform.

Another feature emerged recently, corroborating the new image of executive–legislative relations depicted by the analysts (Capano and Giuliani 2002): the growing screening role of legislative committees, more and more involved in the (cooperative) work of 'improving' the quality of the cabinet proposals, but less and less engaged as 'alternative sources of legislation' through the use of direct legislative power and the consequent production of *leggine*. This feature, which has to be interpreted in the direction of a more rational application of the 'delegation and accountability rule', was already noticed at the end of the *first republic*, especially observing the work of so-called 'horizontal committees'[14] Today, up-to-date information about legislative behaviour and outcomes confirm this trend (De Micheli 1997; Capano and Giuliani 2003).

Another important issue is the role of extraparliamentary actors. With the delegitimation of national and partisan political elites, regions and the President of the Republic have in recent years become increasingly active. In particular, regions, which used to have very little legislative influence, have begun to exercise their constitutional prerogatives in national legislation—for example, by proposing legislative initiatives or promoting abrogative referendums. Furthermore, during the 1990s, two active Presidents sought to influence agenda-setting in a number of ways (see the section on 'External Constraints' below).

Legislatively, the Italian cabinet has always been very active, interpreting broadly its constitutional responsibility to promote 'urgent and necessary' decrees with the force of law (Article 77). The use of this decree authority, which increased progressively until the early 1990s (De Micheli 1997; Capano and Giuliani 2002),[15] best enables the cabinet to impose its political programme when faced with a fragmented Parliament. On the other hand, Parliament can respond with strong counter-force. Each decree has to be put to a vote no later than 60 days after its publication. This form of parliamentary control has been used in very different ways. The parliamentary response to cabinet decrees has varied with the subject matter of the decree and the strength of the cabinet that proposed it. Recently, Parliament has tended to delay the adoption of cabinet decrees and, occasionally, to reject them (Della Sala and Kreppel 1998).

In sum, the cabinet is a strong institutional agent by virtue of its constitutional authority. This authority is counterbalanced by the parliamentary instruments discussed earlier, which give the chambers the power to enforce parliamentary control.

[14] Namely, they are the Budget committee and the Institutional Affairs committees. Thy are called 'horizontal' because their main task is to monitor the reliability of all the proposals on the parliamentary agenda with the existing norm concerning budgetary and constitutional constraints.

[15] A recent judgement of the Constitutional Court limited to the use of the reiterated decrees by the cabinet.

These countervailing forces have continued to evolve historical perspective: the institutionalization of the typical measures of cabinet accountability, for instance, required a certain time (Cotta 1994; Furlong 1996). The same has been true for the increasing delegation of legislative power to the cabinet. Potential agency losses have emerged in the decline of parliamentary screening and selection mechanisms during cabinet formation (especially under the recent transitional phase) and in the absence of effective institutional checks on the cabinet. This has to do with the flexibility of the legislative–executive relationship in the long cycle of Italian republican experience (Cotta and Verzichelli 1996). Generally speaking, the cabinet remains relatively constrained. However, the effectiveness of the principal (i.e. the Parliament) depends upon the locus of interparty bargaining and the influence of 'third powers' like the President.

DELEGATION WITHIN CABINET: STILL AN UNCERTAIN RESPONSIBILITY

Cabinet Structure

The complexity of the executive institutions is created by the Constitution, which solemnly states that: 'The government of the Republic consists of the President of the Council, and of the Ministers, who together constitute the Council of Ministers'. Three institutions are made into one. This institution has three different types of responsibilities as well as three actors all seeking to control the others in a complicated game of checks and balances.

According to the Constitution, the PM sets the guidelines of the cabinet agenda. Article 95 states that the President of Council of Ministers conducts and is responsible for the general policy of the government. He is to ensure the unity and consistency of the political and administrative programme 'by promoting and coordinating the activity of ministers'. The same article states that all the ministers 'are collectively responsible for the decisions of cabinet, and individually for their own ministries' acts'. This constitutional provision links each minister both to an individual political agenda setter (the PM) and to a collective actor (their respective ministries). Therefore, this cabinet model is a mixed one: it cannot *tout court* be a collective government, because each minister has a clear sector of responsibility. It is not a pure collegial government either, because the PM is not absolutely a *primus inter pares* (Andeweg 1993). The progressive use of the PM's constitutional prerogatives to set policy guidelines and, above all, the changes provoked by the reform of this office in 1988 (see below), particularly the creation of a policy staff and the strengthening of the PM's agenda coordination powers, have implied a significant change in the delegation process, without fully resolving the nature of the Italian PM.

From about twenty ministers in the early postwar period (roughly fifteen portfolios plus a variable number of ministers without portfolio), the size of the cabinet has progressively increased to more than thirty. If one counts junior ministers—who are appointed on the basis of party (and faction) proportionality—then more than

100 political appointments were made when the last Andreotti government came to power in 1991. It is easy to explain the increasing cabinet size with reference to the enlargement of the governing coalition and the balance among governing parties (Verzichelli and Cotta 2000). The presence of a Vice-PM is a clear example: this position exists in some multiparty cabinets in order to balance the appointment of a 'strong' leader from the largest party as PM. However, after 1992 the size of the government has declined. The number of ministries and the number of ministers have both been reduced. The number of junior ministers has also been reduced, particularly in the technocratic cabinets, and the total number of political appointments is now down to about seventy. Nonetheless, the 1997 reform, providing a remarkable reduction of ministerial structure and a more functional link between executive units and legislative committees, has been implemented in a rather 'shy' mode.

The PM-designate has the formal right to propose ministers to the President of Republic, that is, the right to submit a name for each ministry. Much more complicated is the question of who has the right to dismiss ministers. The Constitution is silent on this point, and since there is no example of a minister being removed at the request of the PM, many observers argue that the PM does not have this power. Technically, the only mechanism to remove a minister is the individual no confidence motion in Parliament, but in practice other instruments have always been used: the cabinet reshuffle, the minister's resignation with no substitution (in this case, the PM generally takes on the portfolio responsibility *ad interim*), and in some cases a full cabinet crisis followed by the birth of a very similar cabinet.

All ministers take part in the weekly meetings of the Council, but only portfolio ministers have a full right to vote on all items. The golden rule among cabinet members is unanimity. Nonetheless, reforms in the 1980s gave the PM some limited opportunity to get his proposals passed by an absolute majority vote.

These characteristics push the Italian cabinet in a collective direction. At the same time, however, the Constitution provides an opportunity for government by committee by permitting the creation of collegial bodies *inside* the cabinet. Despite this, together with the cabinet *councils* established in the 1980s, only a few interministerial committees have been active.

The reduction of this network into a distinction between the 'collegial' responsibility of the cabinet and the 'autonomy' of each minister—the traditional legalistic approach—is of very limited use. Empirical analyses describe a system in which every minister has a different set of resources and confronts a different set of opposing powers depending on the nature of the department and his or her political 'mandate'. Some ministers are asked to make policy decisions (particularly the former 'troika' of economic ministers, who were forced to work together). Others, the more generalist politicians, control important areas of policy implementation, for example, agriculture, communications, or industrial relations, in addition to operating as 'watch-dogs' with regard to the PM's political programme. A third type of cabinet figure is the 'specialized' minister who works in a specific policy area with limited political autonomy. This kind of minister seems to have become more common, not only in the 'technocratic governments' but also in the political cabinets where, some observers argue, a new configuration characterized by a stronger PM is emerging (Fabbrini 2001).

Independently of the type of ministerial appointment, party control was tradition-ally a defining cabinet feature. Until the end of the 1980s, parliamentary seniority and party background were the natural prerequisites for a cabinet appointment. The pro-portional representation of parties (and the DC and PSI factions) was the most impor-tant criterion, which killed all initiatives aimed at specializing the ministers. As a result, the typical government had a unifying element (the *partyness* of personnel) and a vari-able one—that is, the experience and competence (and interest) of each minister. Therefore, ministers with quite different individual roles were characteristic of cabinets under the *first republic*. In contrast, a certain continuity seems to characterize the polit-ical execut-ives of the period from 1994 (the centre-right Berlusconi cabinet in 1994, the centre-left cabinets between 1996 and 2001, and again a Berlusconi cabinet in 2001). Nevertheless, there are some indications of a return to party government: for instance, the use of majority summits among coalition parties (including those who provide external support) and the creation of an informal *directorium* of leaders of the coalition parties (Criscitiello 1996). Another related sign is the re-emergence of intraparty nego-tiations (e.g. among heads of parliamentary groups, party experts, and individual min-isters) on specific policy issues before the meetings of the cabinet. All these actions traditionally promoted the cabinet as a collective body and reduced the powers of indi-vidual ministers (Cassese 1981). At the same time, however, they limited the PM's ability to control and coordinate the cabinet. On the other hand, 'majoritarian reforms' have had some obvious effects. The PM is now 'indirectly chosen' by the voters as leader of his elec-toral cartel and his role of coordinating of ministers seems to be slowly increasing. These limited changes can be interpreted as a transformation of the government decision-mak-ing process in a more hierarchical direction (Andeweg 1993): the PM seems to have strengthened his political authority, while other ministers have become more accountable with regard to the management of their specific competencies (Fabbrini 2001).

The PM and Ministerial Accountability

How does the PM interact with his ministers on a day-to-day basis, and to what extent are they subject to *ex ante* or *ex post* controls designed to ensure their accountability? To illuminate these matters, it is necessary to analyse the PM's real powers to control other administrative actors. The weakness of the Italian political executive has always been seen as evidence that the country's political institutions are flawed. Reforming the role and increasing the authority of the PM was on the political agenda throughout the 1980s. Before the rise of a presidential (or semi-presidential) proposal, which had found little support among the traditional parties, the most relevant reform proposal of the 1980s was a form of 'hierarchical' parliamentary democracy in which the cabinet (and the PM) would have greater freedom of action. This debate did not lead to constitutional reform, though it caused important developments such as the informal creation in 1986 of a more exclusive sub-cabinet, including the most important ministers: the cabinet council (*consiglio di gabinetto*).[16] This was followed by a new law (400/1988) which re-enforced the PM's control over the cabinet agenda and provided him with political instruments to coordinate the actions of ministers. The same reform allowed the PM to give instructions to implement cabinet directives and to suspend temporarily a ministerial initiative in order to bring it up in a subsequent cabinet meeting.

Law 400/1988 authorized the creation a prime ministerial staff (Hine and Finocchi 1991) in order to support the PM's constitutional coordination role. Yet, it did not clarify the PM's real impact as a policy coordinator. As David Hine argues (1993: 197), this touches on a central issue in Italian parliamentary democracy. The strengthening of the Prime Minister should imply not only new 'positive' power for the PM to direct the ministerial team, but also 'negative' power to limit ministers' own actions. The actual situation with regard to the PM's power is currently quite unclear. He is more than a *primus inter pares* but is still unable to hold ministers accountable on a day-to-day basis.

The evolution of the role of the PM clearly has important consequences for policy formulation and implementation. The PM can ask his personal staff to raise questions and to provide independent data that can be compared with information from ministers. He can review the operation of departments and coordinate intracabinet disputes. On the other hand, in particular policy areas, such as administrative reform, the prerogatives of the PM appear not to have been effectively enforced and have not significantly enhanced his control over the administrative actions of the ministers.

Recent practices do not have much in common with the classic vision of collegial government, insofar as they establish a new hierarchy inside the cabinet. On the other hand, the governmental process has retained a collegial structure, something that seems appropriate given Italy's fragmented polity. In particular, the PM's enforcement authority makes individual ministers more *accountable* (and not purely administratively) when they are *delegated* authority to draft a legislative act or conduct a preliminary investigation. At the same time, some *super-ministers* tend to have the same role of coordinator over specific issues—for instance, the Treasury Minister on economic issues— as the PM has over government policy in general.

The traditional fragmentation of the Italian government remains the most evident obstacle to delegation based on specific departmental functions and prime ministerial steering and coordination. Recent experience suggests a paradox. While technical and 'temporary' governments were strongly directed by their respective PMs (with the evident support of the Head of State), PMs from the 'political' cabinets (Berlusconi, Prodi, and even D'Alema) seem, for different reasons, to have been weaker. The constitutionally based logic of cabinet collegiality, developed during the first decades of the Republic (Criscitiello 1994), is still present. In sum delegation within the cabinet is fluid. Despite the formal division of labour provided by constitutional and ordinary norms, different circumstances make the real game quite uncertain. Some of these

---

[16] The size of *consiglio di gabinetto* was flexible. The practice was to include all the financial and economic ministers, the foreign office, and the defence ministers. Another informal rule was to include at least one representative from each coalition party.

circumstances are directly connected with the fragmented nature of the Italian multi-party coalitions, which increases the number of veto points within the government. Others are due to the different degree of accountability by individual ministers whose competencies, duties, and policy autonomy are rather flexible over the time. Again, the idea of *coalition cycles* (where each cycle includes caretaker, weak, consolidated, and critical cabinets) can help explain these variations (Verzichelli and Cotta 2000). But one can also discern a slow process of change, based on attempts to rationalize and enforce delegation within the executive. An excellent example is provided by the Treasury Minister, who has greatly increased (specially during the 1990s) his autonomy from spending ministers and also become much more accountable to the PM.

Yet, the reforms of the past and those currently in progress cannot remove the risk of agency losses. Particularly weak links remain in the definition of the ministerial competencies (on the side of *ex ante* delegation) and in the real impact of the reports to the PM (on the *ex post* side of accountability).[17]

DELEGATION FROM MINISTERS TO CIVIL SERVANTS: COMMUNICATION PROBLEMS

A wide variety of departments and agencies, under direct or indirect cabinet control, have emerged in Italy since the postwar reconstruction. The main reason was the dominance of the administrative system (Hine 1993), which was made possible by the consolidation of a huge class of professional bureaucrats capable of translating and interpreting the difficult 'language' of law. A second reason is the continuity of administrative elites. The new political class of the late 1940s had to make compromises with the top bureaucrats who had survived the regime change. From that moment on, control over bureaucratic recruitment became an important source of political struggle.

In principle, all positions in public administration are filled in open, public examination. In reality, this method is used at low and middle levels, while the small, central top administration (*dirigenza generale*) is directly appointed by the cabinet. Other basic principles are that officials are to have generalist backgrounds and that administrative uniformity is to apply to the whole civil service. Administrative unity means that all posts other than the central top administration formally belong to a single class, even if different levels of skill and pay exist.[18] With the passing of time these general rules have been weakened. Specialized training was introduced in some administrative branches as early as the 1970s in the form of mandatory enrolment at a school for the higher civil service (*Scuola superiore di pubblica amministrazione*). Later reforms introduced

---

[17] As mentioned earlier, the implementation of the reform of the cabinet structure has not been very easy. Other measures to reduce the public administration bill, both using the contracting-out system and creating of specialized agencies, are still under discussion.

[18] In the past there were eight functional divisions. Doormen or workers, recruited without a particular educational title, made up the first four divisions. The middle ones were composed of office workers, who generally held a high school diploma. Heads of sections, who held advanced degrees, were found in the two highest divisions. Recent reforms reduced this fragmentation to three basic levels corresponding to educational requirements.

opportunities for mobility between sectors and more differentiated positions—for example, part-time jobs and external consultants.

In 1992, the total number of civil servants in Italy exceeded 2 million (10 per cent of the active population) (Cassese and Franchini 1994). Thus, the great size of the bureaucratic staff is a dominant characteristic of Italian public administration. A demand for a more efficient public administration existed as early as 1950 and has become a serious priority in the past two decades. According to many observers the bureaucracy's central problem is administrative heterogeneity. Jobs and personnel are distributed among about twenty departments, not including the PM's staff, which includes the secretaries of ministers without portfolio. This implies the co-participation of ministers and administrative agencies in designing, implementing, and monitoring common policies and programmes (Hine 1993: 226). The Italian administration also has two clusters of 'peripheral' bureaucracies that are not specifically analysed here—the local bureaucracies (at the communal, provincial, and regional government levels) and state-holding companies.

The top bureaucratic elite is selected by the cabinet. Both individual ministers and/or the PM have the right to propose nominees. Higher civil servants are closely connected to their ministers, though in most cases it is not possible to speak about real accountability. Cabinet instability and political fragmentation mean that the administrative elite are relatively free to act and, to some extent, avoid ministerial orders. A 'new' minister can discover that he faces senior civil servants who have much more experience than he has, and who want to maintain their autonomy from 'generalist' politicians. The latter, on the other hand, have tools to control the careers of civil servants and the ministry budgets. However, they cannot use these tools until they have successfully consolidated their positions inside their departments. A minister's ability, political skills, personal power, and even charisma can therefore have a major impact on his relationship with the civil servants in his ministry.

The Constitution states that every agency responds directly to its minister, but there are important exceptions. In particular, one branch of the Treasury bureaucracy—the General Accounting Office—has complete autonomy to contact other ministers and to make proposals about their budget planning. In this case, *ex post* mechanisms of control over administrative behaviour have been weak and there have been several cases of conflict between the administration and political leadership.

The relationship between ministers and bureaucrats has been fairly stable despite important, though partial, public sector reforms. One of these reforms has resulted in the decline of the traditional administration of nationalized firms, based on multi-sectoral holding companies controlled by the government. Starting in the 1980s, with the implementation of privatization programmes and the creation of independent regulatory agencies, this sector was significantly reduced in size and its management given more autonomy. From the late twentieth century there have been a series of direct attempts to reform the administration. This wave of small reforms has given new 'agents' (specialized civil servants and governmental agencies) a certain autonomy. An ordinary law recently introduced the notion of higher civil servants' *independence* from their 'political nominator' (e.g. ministers in the case of general directors of departments, regional governments in the case of local bureaucrats). This innovation is aimed at reducing the likelihood that a political principal will act instead of the responsible administrative agent (*potere di avocazione*). At the same time, the simplification of the bureaucratic structure might make it easier for ministers to supervise civil servants. To balance the 'independence' of civil servants, legislative decree no. 29/1993 introduced the idea of 'senior staff responsibility': higher civil servants are directly accountable to their minister for actions that are not explicitly included in the powers delegated to them.[19]

To what extent have these arrangements helped to facilitate delegation and accountability between ministers and civil servants? At least two further developments seem to be necessary. The first is the consolidation of a new administration based on a smaller number of departments and the creation of functional agencies, a step related to the need to decentralize the administrative machine. The second step involves a general reform of the recruitment of higher civil servants, including a reduction in the number of permanent positions, the introduction of skilled staffs, and the implementation of a system of evaluation. In the absence of such structural changes, the links between executives and civil servants will continue to be characterized by unsatisfactory and incomplete delegation to agents and weak sanctions in the hands of the political principal. The notion of administrative 'neutrality' and loyalty to the government of the day can easily hide the fact that complicated games of coordination and competition go on inside as well as among departments. The absence of specific legislation to make information about administrative behaviour freely available increases the likelihood that this situation can develop and persist.[20]

EXTERNAL CONSTRAINTS

I already mentioned the influences of some external actors on the chain of delegation and accountability. Here I will discuss the weight of these actors. The President of Republic, who under Article 87 of the Constitution represents national unity, may send messages to both houses of Parliament, promulgate laws, and issue decrees. The same article lists other presidential prerogatives as commander of the armed forces, head of the High Council of Judiciary, etc.—but these are not directly related to the parliamentary chain of delegation. The President is not formally invested with strong powers related to the crucial link between cabinet and Parliament. On the other hand, because he formally appoints ministers and dissolves the houses of Parliament, the Constitution gives him a limited opportunity to exert influence.

The decade 1992–2001 has been referred to as a time of 'semi-presidential management of the Italian transition' (Calandra 1996: 473; Pitruzzella 1997: 244), that is to say a period bringing no real change in the rules of the game[21] but, in the meantime,

---

[19] The same law adopted an open system of evaluation for senior staff via the introduction of an evaluation team (*nuclei di valutazione*) in each administrative unit.

[20] Important steps have been taken in this direction, in particular the adoption of a law about transparency in public administration (Law no. 241/1990) and the introduction of measures to simplify administrative procedures (1993). Nonetheless, implementation will probably take a long time.

[21] A proposal passed by a *bicamerale* committee in June 1997 endorsed a 'weak' semi-presidentialism: a directly elected President with a 6-year term, who has responsibilities in matters of foreign and defence

discovering the possible practical evolution of the Presidential role. There is evidence that supports this characterization: the active participation of the President in bringing about institutional reforms, his active role in government formation (i.e. he proposes some candidates for cabinet positions), and his increasing participation in setting the policy agenda—by means of messages to Parliament, summits with members of government, and even explicit requests for policy initiatives. It is true that the President was not irrelevant in the past, either.[22] The difference between the old style of presidency and the 'transitional' one probably lies in the degree of engagement. At one time the President, who was never fully autonomous, occasionally acted as a 'tool' to promote the policy goals of some political group (e.g. a DC faction). Today the President has become an initiator of important change, by taking advantage of the disappearance of parties as 'engines' of political life (Cotta 1996; Pasquino 1997).

A similar development has occurred with regard to the role of the central bank. For a decade after its 'divorce' from the Treasury in the early 1980s, *Bankitalia* played a subordinate role in economic policy-making. Its leader (the *governatore* and his advisers) were 'guardians' of economic soundness, but their suggestions were often rejected by the executive. When the old ruling class was destroyed by political crisis, the central bank had the opportunity to assume a significant role in determining the guidelines of economic policy, and some of its important figures have even assumed powerful government roles.[23]

While the changed roles of actors like the President and the central bank are evidence of important differences between the *first republic* and the thereafter, transition, the popular referendum has undergone much slower, incremental change. Since 1970, when an ordinary law established the referendum,[24] Italy has witnessed an increasing number of requests to abrogate legislation. The Constitutional Court, which has to verify that these requests conform with legislation, has interpreted constitutional norms quite rigidly, and has therefore approved very few referendums. Over time, however, the Court has become more flexible, approving, for instance, referendums about the electoral systems which, by abrogating existing rules, could create dangerous gaps in legislation. Since the end of the 1980s voters have approved some referendums (and thus abrogated laws). It is interesting to consider which actors use the referendums. The referendum was first used in 1974 when Catholics (who are not directly

policy. As envisaged in the proposal, the President could be dismissed by a qualified majority in Parliament. This proposal did not become law because the government and the centre-right opposition could not reach an agreement, and all decisions concerning the new form of government were postponed to the next legislature (the one begun in 2001).

[22] President Gronchi, for instance, had a significant influence during the rise of a centre-left coalition in the early 1960s, while President Pertini tried several times to balance the relationship between the DC and its 'secular' allies by appointing a PM who was not a Christian Democrat.

[23] Carlo Azelio Ciampi and Lamberto Dini, technical Prime Ministers during the 1990s, were both top leaders of *Banca d'Italia*. Interestingly, both decided to remain in politics: Ciampi as 'expert' economic minister (and then as President of the Republic) and Dini (who started a new party in 1996) as Foreign Minister in the Prodi cabinet.

[24] Law 352/1970 introduced the referendum. Article 75 of the Constitution forbids the use of referenda on fiscal and budgetary legislation, amnesties, and the ratification of international treaties.

represented by the Christian Democrats) were mobilized to oppose the legalization of divorce. Later, small and unconventional minorities (e.g. radical parties, the new Left, the Greens) used the referendum to oppose the 'consociative' legislation of 'national solidarity'. During the 1990s, abrogative referendums have been called for by groups representing 'societal forces' (meaning industrialists, associations) as well as by individual politicians such as Mario Segni, who was able to transform himself from a second-tier DC politician to the leader of the pro-majoritarian movement. In 1995, regional councils also began exercising their constitutional right to request abrogative referendums on some pieces of legislation.

Between 1974 and 1987 nine proposals of abrogation were rejected by referendum. Among them were a proposal to abolish divorce (introduced in 1970), an attempt to rescind the law on abortion, and a proposal to cancel a reduction of wage-indexation decided in 1984. The first two proposals were supported by the Christian Democrats, the last one by the Communists. In 1987 five referendums passed. Three of them called for a reduction in the use of nuclear energy. In 1991 and 1993 it was the proportional electoral system to be changed by the popular vote. All the other seven referendums held in 1993 were successful, abrogating various pieces of legislation. The most significant 'anti-party' outcome was the abrogation of a large part of the 1974 law on party financing. Moreover, three ministries were abolished (among them, the famous *Ministero delle partecipazioni statali*, which had been a crucial agency for party control over economic resources) and important reforms introduced in the health system (giving more competencies to the regional governments) and drug detention.

In 1995, five out of twelve referendums passed. With the reconstruction of a bipolar political spectrum, a clearer pattern of alliances between societal and political forces emerged, but with mixed results. Some 'neo-liberist' proposals by the radicals and by the industrialists (and strongly supported by the centre-right leader Silvio Berlusconi) cancelled old privileges of the national trade unions (namely, the automatic union affiliation and the special quota reserved for these organizations). The Left and the unions avoided an even worst result, as some other proposals were rejected. On the other hand, the same actors (plus a number of other political and non-political promoters) failed to gain a majority for the so-called 'anti-Berlusconi' referendum: two proposals to abrogate legislation from the 1980s on television network concessions and the use of paid television advertisements for political purposes.

In the last three rounds of referendums, in 1997 (7), 1999 (1), and 2000 (7), a lack of voter quorum (50 per cent + 1 of the registered voters) has resulted in three consecutive failures. Even the proposal to abrogate the party ballot in lower chamber elections did not reach the quorum (neither in 1999 nor in 2000), despite the (formal) support of the most important parties. This appears to be a clear sign of decay for an important 'external' democratic tool which has been crucial in reshaping the democratic chain of delegation.

In addition to its role in screening referendum proposals, the Constitutional Court decides on controversies about the constitutionality of laws, acts emanating from the regions, and also on conflicts between constitutional powers (Article 134).

Its capacity to scrutinize legislation is subject to a request by an ordinary court. Nevertheless, the impact of the Constitutional Court's doctrine has become important, with the passing of the time, in 'challenging' Parliament to reduce, rearrange, or abrogate contradictory norms. This has been facilitated the progressive autonomy of 'non-political' judges.[25]

Writing before the 1990s, nobody would probably have listed the Regional and local governments among the 'external actors' impacting the line of delegation and accountability at the national level in Italy. The constitutional statement providing accountable elected councils in all the regions, in fact, was implemented only in 1970, and the local executives were never particularly able to influence *high politics*. The situation was suddenly changed since the beginning of the 1990s: a new law regulating the local election system introduced the direct election of Mayors and Presidents of Provincial Executives. At the same time, Regional offices (particularly the Executive Presidents) increased their political visibility, incrementally using their constitutional and political means (for instance, the *committee of the President of Regional Executive*) with a great deal of autonomy. This phase of *devolution* has come to a first result at the end of the decade: in 1999 a new regional election system was adopted, introducing at this level also the direct election of the chief executive. Even more importantly, the Constitutional law no. 1/2001 reformed the whole title V of the constitution and introduced a real 'subsidiarity principle', thus deepening the legislative and administrative powers of local and regional governments. The creation of a full-fledged federal system is on the political agenda and sub-national actors will probably be of increasing importance.

A sixth important and changing external constraint is supranational actors. The evolution of the European Union (EU) since (at least) 1993 has had important consequences for the parliamentary delegation process. In the 1990s national governments have been able to strengthen their role in the legislative process due to European developments. However, Parliament has recently reacted against its subordination. A 1989 law requires the cabinet to report on Italian participation in the European Council every 6 months. Via the annual 'Community law' (*Legge comunitaria*), the Parliament authorizes the cabinet to adopt European directives (Furlong 1996). In 1997 the Parliament's EU affairs committee became a full legislative committee in both chambers. It was given a broader jurisdiction, including common foreign and security policy. A cabinet representative has to report to the committee before EU Council meetings. The involvement of other committees (or the plenary meeting) in EU matters appears to depend upon the political classes' interest in the policy questions being discussed in Brussels.

Though it is difficult to evaluate the impact of recent changes it seems clear that Italian politics has been transformed by the introduction of a number of 'national' and 'supranational' constraints. Given that Italy is still undergoing political transition, their long-term impact is not yet clear.

---

[25] According to the Constitution (Article 135), the Court consists of fifteen judges. Five are appointed by the President of the Republic, five are elected by Parliament, and five by the supreme courts. The judges are appointed for a period of 9 years and cannot be re-elected.

CONCLUSION

Parliamentary democracy in Italy has always shown much more flexibility than one would suspect given its rigid constitutional framework, as it has continuously adapted to changing circumstances. Traditionally, a partisan parliamentary class representing different political traditions controlled the individual actors who collectively formed the government. Bargaining among (and inside) parties reduced the opportunities for well-defined delegation relationships. Another evident deviation from the ideal-type of a parliamentary democracy was visible in the last link in the chain, where the ability of the cabinet to coordinate the bureaucracy has always been limited.

During the last decade, the crisis of old parties and the delayed consolidation of a new party system has changed the political framework. In the wake of the decline of the established political class, voters and other principals—for example, the PM vis-à-vis his ministers—have regained some of their powers to hold their agents accountable. The previously powerful intervening actor—the political parties—have lost some of their prerogatives. However, a new set of external forces has begun to assert itself. The final outcome is, at the moment, unclear, but we can argue that, despite the extraordinary expectations raised between 1992 and 1994, another incremental change, rather than a revolutionary one, has occurred. Thus, the recent transitional phase is another example of the adaptability of the 'old' constitutional order.

In theory, the legal framework provided by the Constitution established a set of mechanisms which formed a chain of delegation. With the exception of the link between voters and MPs, the mechanisms of control in the hands of principals were well defined. In reality, however, the structure worked in very different ways. As has been explained above, the major limitations on interpreting Italian parliamentary democracy as a chain of delegation and accountability have to do with two critical links. The first is delegation from the cabinet to individual ministers who sometimes act autonomously and competitively. The second problem is the lack of accountability of many civil servants.

In general, the whole chain has suffered as a result of the weak institutionalization of delegation mechanisms, as the story of executive–parliamentary relations illustrates. The reasons for this weakness are to be found in the historical circumstances of Italy's democratic experience, in particular a highly fragmented, polarized polity and a society with deep cleavages. Throughout the history of the Republic voters have not been active and effective principals, and the political class—strongly linked to parties—has not been held accountable. On the other hand, the distance between political and civil society also explains the lack of *ex post* control mechanisms in the hands of cabinet ministers vis-à-vis civil servants. That is to say, ministers do not enjoy the benefit of attentive social interests ('fire alarms') who continuously monitor the performance of government agencies.

Several environmental factors have constrained democratic delegation and accountability. The first is the legacy of party rule born during a war of liberation and resulting in a high level of *partitocracy*. The second factor is the continued existence of an administrative and legal system born in a proto-democratic era and consolidated under

Fascism. The third is extreme fragmentation, which reproduced—in a different political framework—the same polarization that existed before Fascism. The combined impacts of these factors created conditions that permitted the distortion of parliamentary delegation. In particular, parties, factions, and groups had to secure a place at the centre of the political system, which has usually been a 'proportional' legislative arena. This explains the persistence (despite some fluctuation) of the centrality of Parliament (Cotta 1990). David Hine confirms that 'despite counter-powers—constitutionally entrenched regionalism, direct democracy, constitutional review of legislation etc.— Italian parliament is widely thought of as considerably more important, in relation to other parts of the political system, than are most European legislatures' (Hine 1993: 166). Even today such a judgement could hardly be refuted. But, party system realignment and the progressive implementation of the Constitution made this 'strong' parliamentary democracy mutable enough in practice. Good examples of this flexibility are the changes in parliamentary monitoring mechanisms, or even the variability of the cabinet's autonomy (Cotta and Verzichelli 1996).

The transition of the 1990s has to be seen as a profound change in the delegation process. Evidence of this is the increase in voters' *ex post* control and the enforcement of some governmental powers. In a sense, the turmoil of Italian politics began with an explicit request for a more appropriate system of delegation and accountability, in particular a system making the political class and the executive more accountable. It is much harder to say whether the actual reforms are moving in the right direction. Flexibility remains a typical feature of constitutional life in Italy: the political executive led by Berlusconi rapidly failed, in 1994, in favour of a technical cabinet. After the election of 1996, another cabinet whose leadership had been strongly legitimized by the popular vote, the centre-left government of Prodi, was the first example of a cabinet terminated through a parliamentary rejection of a confidence motion.

The solidification of the new party system seems to be a precondition for the definitive consolidation of stable government, as is a new relationship between political and administrative elites. Nobody can say what the 'face' of the future system will be until all the 'noise' abates. In particular, we do not know if a new form of parliamentary democracy will be created, or whether there will be a different type of delegation based on an alternative institutional model.

REFERENCES

Andeweg, Rudy (1993). 'A Model of the Cabinet System: The Dimension of Cabinet Decision Making Processes', in Jean Blondel and Ferdinand Müller-Rommel (eds.), *Governing Together: The Extent and Limits of Joint Decision-Making in Western European Cabinets*. London: Macmillan.
Bardi, L. and Morlino L. (1994). 'Italy: Tracing the Roots of the Great Transformation', in R. S. Katz and P. Mair (eds.), *How Party Organise*. London: Sage.
Bergman, Torbjörn (1993). 'Formation Rules and Minority Governments'. *European Journal of Political Research*, 23: 55–66.
Bindi, Federiga M. (1996). 'Italy: In Need of More EU Democracy', in Svein S. Andersen and Kjell A. Eliassen (eds.), *The European Union: How Democratic Is It?* London: Sage.

Bufacchi, V. and Simon Burgess (2001). *Italy after 1989. Events and Interpretations*. London: Palgrave.

Calandra, Piero (1996). *I Governi della Repubblica. Vicende, Formule, Regole*. Bologna: Il Mulino.

Calise, Mauro (1994). *Dopo la Partitocrazia*. Torino: Einaudi.

——and Mannheimer, Renato (1982). *Governanti in Italia. Un Trentennio Repubblicano*. Bologna: Il Mulino.

Capano Giliberto and Marco Giuliani (2002). 'Governing Without Surviving? An Italian Paradox: law-making in Italy 1987–2001'. *Journal of Legislative Studies*, 7(4): 13–36.

——(2003). 'The Italian Parliament: in Search of a New Role?' *Journal of Legislative Studies*, forthcoming.

Cassese, Sabino (1981). *Esiste un Governo in Italia?* Roma: Officina.

——and Franchini, Carlo (1994). *L'amministrazione Pubblica Italiana. Un Profilo*. Bologna: Il Mulino.

Cotta, Maurizio (1979). *Classe Politica e Parlamento in Italia*. Bologna: Il Mulino.

——(1990). 'The Centrality of Parliament in a Protracted Democratic Consolidation: The Italian Case', in Ulrike Liebert and Maurizio Cotta (eds.), *Parliament Consolidation in Southern Europe*. London: Pinter.

——(1994). 'The Rise and Fall of The Centrality of the Italian Parliament', in G. W. Copeland and S. C. Patterson (eds.), *Parliaments in the Modern World*. Ann Arbor: The University of Michigan Press.

——(1996). 'La Crisi del Governo di Partito all'Italiana', in Maurizio Cotta and Pierangelo Isernia (eds.), *Il Gigante dai Piedi di Argilla. La Crisi del Regime Partitocratico in Italia*. Bologna: Il Mulino.

——and Verzichelli, Luca (1996). 'Italy: Sunset of a Partitocracy', in Jean Blondel and Maurizio Cotta (eds.), *Parties and Government*. London: Macmillan.

Criscitiello, Annarita (1994). 'The Political Role of Cabinet Ministers in Italy', in Michael Laver and Kenneth A. Shepsle (eds.), *Cabinet Ministers and Parliamentary Government*. Cambridge: Cambridge University Press.

——(1996). 'Alla Ricerca della Collegialità di Governo. I Vertici di Maggioranza dal 1970 al 1996.' *Rivista Italiana di Scienza Politica*, 26: 365–89.

Della Sala, Vincent and Kreppel, Amie (1998). 'Dancing Without a Lead: Legilsative Decrees in Italy', in John M. Shugart and Matthew S. Shugart (eds.), *Executive Decree Authority*. Cambridge: Cambridge University Press.

De Micheli, Chiara (1997). 'L'attività Legislativa dei Governi al Tramonto della Prima Repubblica'. *Rivista Italiana di Scienza Politica*, 27: 151–88.

Dente, Bruno (1990). 'Introduzione', in Bruno Dente (ed.), *Le Politiche Pubbliche in Italia*. Bologna: Il Mulino.

Di Palma, Giuseppe (1977). *Surviving Without Governing*. Berkeley: University of California Press.

Fabbrini, Sergio (2001). *Tra Pressioni e veti. Il Mutamento Politico in Italia*. Roma Bari: Laterza.

Furlong, Paul (1996). 'The Italian Parliament and European Integration. Responsibilities, Failures and Successes', in Philip Norton (ed.), *National Parliaments and the European Union*. London: Frank Cass.

Fusaro, Carlo (1994). 'Media, Sondaggi e Spese Elettorali'. *Rivista Italiana di Scienza Politica*, 24: 427–64.

Hine, David (1993). *Governing Italy. The Politics of Bargained Pluralism*. Oxford: Oxford University Press.

——and Finocchi, Renato (1991). 'The Italian Prime Minister'. *West European Politics*, 14(2): 79–96.

Katz, Richard S. (1996). 'Electoral Reforms and the Transformations of Party Politics in Italy'. *Party Politics*, 2: 31–53.

Lijphart, Arend (1984). Democracies: Patterns of Majoritarism and Consensus Government in Twenty-One Countries. New Haven: Yale University Press.

Morlino, Leonardo (1991). 'Introduzione', in Leonardo Morlino (ed.), *Costruire la Democrazia. Partiti e Gruppi in Italia*. Bologna: Il Mulino.

——and Tarchi, Marco (1996). 'The Dissatisfied Society: The Roots of Political Change in Italy'. *European Journal of Political Research*, 30: 41–63.

Newell, James (2002) (ed.), *Berlusconi's Victory: The Italian 2001 Elections*. Manchester: Manchester University Press.

Pasquino, Gianfranco (1987). 'Party Government in Italy. Achievements and Prospects', in Richard S. Katz (ed.), *Party Governments. American and European Experiences*. Berlin: De Gruyter.

Panebianco, Angelo (1982). *Modelli di Partito*. Bologna: Il Mulino.

Pitruzzella, Giovanni (1997). *Forme di Governo e Trasformazioni della Politica*. Roma: Laterza.

Pujas, Veronique (2000). 'Party Financing and Mass Media: Peculiarities of the Italian Case', in Mark Gilbert and Gianfranco Pasquino (eds.), *Italian Politics*, edn. New York: Berghahn Books.

Sartori, Giovanni (1976). *Parties and Party Systems. A Framework for Analysis*. Cambridge: Cambridge University Press.

Strøm, Kaare (2000). 'Delegation and Accountability in Parliamentary Democracies'. *European Journal of Political Research*, 37: 261–89.

Vassallo, Salvatore (1994). *Il Governo di Partito in Italia (1943–1993)*. Bologna: Il Mulino.

Verzichelli, Luca (1998). 'The Parliamentary Elite in Transition'. *European Journal of Political Research*, 33: 121–50.

——(2002). 'Da un ceto Parlamentare all'altro. Il Mutamento Nelpersonale Legisaltivo Italiano', in R. D'Alimonte and S. Bartolini (eds.), *Maggioritario Finalmente? La Transizione Elettorale 1994–2001*. Bologna: Il Mulino.

——(2003). 'Much Ado about Something ? Parliamentary Politics in Italy amid the Rhetoric of Majority Rule and an Uncertain Party System'. *Journal of Legislative Studies*, forthcoming.

——and Cotta, Maurizio (2000). 'Italy: From "Constrained" Coalitions to alternating Governments?', in Wolfgang C. Müller and Kaare Strom (eds.), *Coalition Governments in Western Europe*. Oxford: Oxford University Press.

Wertman, Douglas (1988). 'Italy: Local Involvement, Central Control', in Michael Gallagher and Michael Marsh (eds.), *Candidate Selection in Comparative Perspective*. London: Sage.

15

Luxembourg: A Case of More 'Direct' Delegation and Accountability

PATRICK DUMONT AND LIEVEN DE WINTER

INTRODUCTION

The Grand Duchy of Luxembourg was created by the Great Powers at Vienna in 1815 and became a unified constitutional parliamentary monarchy under its first liberal constitution in 1848. The Constitution created a unicameral Parliament of deputies directly elected in a two-round majoritarian system with restricted voting rights. Democratization was temporarily reversed when the reactionary Constitution of 1856 created a non-elected Council of State with an important legislative role.

During the First World War,[1] the Grand-Duchess Marie-Adelaïde exercised the monarch's prerogatives to dissolve the Parliament and keep the Catholic Party (Party of the Right) in power without a parliamentary majority. Following the turmoil provoked by this decision, a 1919 referendum settled the future form of the State in favour of the monarchy. The Constitution of 1919 was a decisive democratic improvement. It stipulated that sovereignty rests with the nation, introduced universal suffrage for men and women, and created a new electoral system—list proportional representation (PR).

Environmental Constraints

Ever since its creation, Luxembourg's small size has heavily influenced its choices. First, it accounts for the unitary Constitution. Second, militarily weak and dependent on foreign markets, Luxembourg has always participated in (or even initiated) international political and economic agreements. From the German Confederation (1815–66) and the Zollverein (1842–1918) to the 1921 Union économique belgo-luxembourgeoise (UEBL) and the 1944 Benelux Treaty on the Customs Union, the country has always been associated with international cooperation and economic integration. Luxembourg's participation

We thank former Prime Minister Pierre Werner for his generous comments on a draft chapter. We also wish to thank Mrs Maryse Baustert, Mr Ben Fayot, and Mr Etienne Schneider.

[1] Despite its neutrality, Luxembourg was occupied during Second World War. Yet, domestic civil authorities continued to function, as German military authorities worked along with them. The Grand Duchy adopted a neutral policy to avoid making the occupation worse, but the behaviour of Grand Duchess Marie-Adelaïde (and the Catholic government) was widely seen as pro-German.

in transnational economic and political structures is widely supported by the population. For example, popular attitudes towards European integration have always been much more positive than the EU average (Eurobarometer 48, Autumn 1997).

Legislative Process

Since 1848, the Constitution stipulates that both the unicameral Parliament (the Chamber of Deputies) and the monarch (in practice, his government)[2] have the right to initiate legislation and that the assent of the Parliament is required. The Grand Duke signs and promulgates all bills, but a member of the cabinet responsible for implementing them must countersign. The Grand Duke has not used his formal veto power after the Second World War. The Council of State, designed in 1856 as the legal advisor to the government, has a right of initiative, as well as a much broader role in the legislative process. First, it gives compulsory advice on each bill or amendment. Though the advice is non-binding, voting in Parliament cannot take place until it is received. Second, it can decide whether or not legislation must be put to a second vote (Article 59). The Constitution stipulates, in effect, that all bills must pass a second vote in the Parliament no earlier than 3 months after the first vote. This second vote can only be avoided if plenary sessions of the Parliament and Council of State decide that it is unwarranted. The Council of State thus has a suspensive veto, which in practice is rarely used (Als and Philippart 1994).

Until 1990, the parliamentary Standing Orders required a vote to authorize the consideration of a legislative proposal before the proposal could be sent to the Council of State. Since 1990, the Speaker of the House decides on behalf of the Parliament, and then submits the proposal to the relevant committee as soon as the advice of the Council of State is received. Legislative proposals are considered in one or several permanent specialized committee(s) (introduced by the 1965 revision of the Standing Orders),[3] or in a special ad hoc committee. The committee(s) in charge draft(s) a report that is (are) then discussed in a plenary session. Under the urgency procedure, a bill can go through committee and plenary deliberation even if the advice of the Council of State has not yet been received, but the Parliament will nevertheless have to wait for this advice before the final vote. More than half of the MPs must be present for voting to be valid. Voting is done article by article. If any amendments are accepted (by the successive voting procedure), then they must be sent to the Council of State. When the Parliament receives the Council's advice on the amendments accepted, a new 'statutory vote' on the articles and amendments is held, followed by a vote on the entire bill. As with the first vote, a quorum of half of all MPs plus one is required, and a bill is passed

---

[2] For simplicity and to avoid awkwardness, we use the male pronoun when we refer generically to the monarch, a minister, or a legislator. During the period of interest, males were indisputably overrepresented in these positions.

[3] Before 1965 the Parliament was divided into three central sections, chosen by lot. The sections were not specialized, and within a particular section the opposition might form a majority. Bills were examined simultaneously by the three sections, then by a group formed by the sections' *rapporteurs*, before plenary deliberation. This system was gradually replaced by specialized committees, which in some fields (e.g. agriculture, finance) have been in use since before 1945.

if 50 per cent plus one of all valid votes are cast in favour of the bill (blank votes are not counted). If the Council of State demands the second, so-called 'constitutional vote', the Parliament has to wait at least 3 months before definitively adopting the bill (with the same quorum and decision rule). On government-initiated legislative proposals, including budget bills, the *avant-projet de loi* is examined first by the Council of State. The latter may introduce modifications or even a counter-proposal (by urging the government to legislate or to modify the existing legislation, the Council of State even has a right of initiative). If it agrees with the Council of State, the government may ask the Council to draft the amendments itself. The definitive proposal is then submitted to the Grand Duke for authorization to introduce it in Parliament. The rest of the procedure is the same as for parliamentary initiatives.

A 1924 law established other legislative actors—the elected professional chambers (see below). While they are not enshrined in the Constitution, and therefore failing to consult them would not constitutionally nullify the law, in practice the Parliament usually waits for their (non-binding) advice before holding a final vote. Hence, they play an important role on bills relating to particular professional interests, including appropriations in the national budget. In contrast to laws, governmental decrees ('Grand Ducal decrees' and 'regulations', see below) passed without the advice of the professional chambers can be rendered null and void.

Since 1966, the government may also consult the Economic and Social Council (see below) on broader economic, financial, and social legislation. Although this body also has the right to make proposals to the government based on the reports it drafts at the government's or its own initiative, it plays no part in any compulsory phase in the legislative process. Its main function is rather to help reconcile divergent interests (e.g. conflicting advice from the professional chambers). A 1977 government bill created the 'tripartite committee' (see below) for crisis management. It issues advice when one of three well-defined unemployment thresholds is reached. Not only is this process compulsory, but in practice its recommendations are also binding. The Parliament does not take part in this interchange between labour and government representatives. In principle, it remains sovereign and may accept, refuse, or modify the deals made by this committee but in practice it is required to ratify agreements and to formalize them into law. This new legislative procedure is therefore a more serious deviation from pure parliamentary democracy than the others are.

The constitutional amendment process has two stages. First, a declaration of revision enumerates all articles to be amended, without specifying the nature of the change. Parliament is dissolved immediately after passing this declaration. The normal quorum and decision rules apply. Once a new Parliament has been elected, the constitutional articles mentioned in the declaration of revision can be amended through a parliamentary vote in which three-quarters of all MPs are present, and two-thirds of the votes (blank votes excluded) are cast in support of the amendments. International treaties negotiated and signed by the government (officially the Grand Duke) must be ratified by the Parliament. Since 1956, international agreements that involve transfers of authority to supranational organizations are subject to the same quorum and decision rule as constitutional amendments.

Otherwise, the powers of the Grand Duke (*in casu* his government) are constitutionally limited to the making of decrees and regulations necessary to the execution of laws. He cannot suspend a law or dispense with its execution, nor initiate autonomous regulations on matters that have not been legislated. 'Grand Ducal decrees' are governmental decisions aimed at implementing an act of Parliament, whilst 'Grand Ducal (or public administration) regulations' are decrees limited to administrative or policing matters. Both of these instruments are adopted in the Council of Ministers, signed by the Grand Duke and countersigned by a minister, and finally published in the official journal. For either type of governmental decree to be promulgated, the advice of the corresponding professional chamber(s) must have been requested and received. Administrative and policing regulations must also receive the advice of the Council of State, except if the Grand Duke invokes an urgency provision. Finally, if it is stipulated in the law, instruments issued in the execution of the law may be submitted to the Parliament's *Commission de travail* (working committee, *Conférence des présidents* since 2000) for advice. 'Ministerial decrees (or regulations)' are supplementary rules for the execution of a law issued by a single minister. The nonconformity of all these decrees and regulations to a law can be sanctioned by the courts. Other specific executive decrees are used for the implementation of European directives (see below). Finally, by adopting a bill called *loi habilitante*, Parliament delegates to the government its competencies in specific policy areas for a fixed time. The government can then take important measures in these fields through Grand Ducal regulations (see below).

Featuring an indirect chain of delegation and a reasonable correspondence to the singularity principle, the Grand Duchy of Luxembourg thus presents a number of characteristics that approximate the ideal type of parliamentary democracy. The country is a unitary parliamentary monarchy with a unicameral Parliament, and it has never used a referendum in the postwar period. Yet, a number of domestic institutions and policy-making procedures do deviate from this ideal–typical picture. Another constraint has been the country's involvement in international organizations and arrangements that continuously reduce its sovereignty and thus the significance of the national chain of delegation and accountability.

POLITICAL PARTIES

Because political parties are not legally recognized, they receive no governmental subsidies for central party offices, which are very poor in both infrastructure and personnel. Parliamentary groups (which must include at least five MPs) were recognized in the Parliament's Internal Rules in 1965 and have since received state support to maintain offices and staff.[4]

A four-party system existed from the 1920s to the early 1980s. Socialists, Liberals, and Catholics became structured parties between 1902 and 1914, while the Communist Party was founded in 1921. The system was rooted in a two-dimensional cleavage structure.

---

[4] A 'technical group' was created in 1990 for parties that did not have enough MPs to form a parliamentary group.

The socio-economic class cleavage was superimposed upon the older clerical/anti-clerical one, which as early as 1848 pitted Catholics against Liberals (Hearl 1987). Language has never been a conflict issue, although the country lies at the crossroads of the Roman and German worlds.

The CSV (Christian Democrats) has always been the largest party in Parliament, usually followed by the Socialists, Liberals, and Communists (in that order). Between 1968 and 1989, when new parties first performed better than the KPL (Communists), the four traditional parties' combined share of the vote dropped from 99.6 per cent to 80.2 per cent. The Greens appeared in 1984, fought the 1989 elections on two separate tickets, but reunited in 1993. The *Aktiounskomitee fir Demokratie a Rentegerechtegkeet* (ADR) was created in 1987 as a pressure group for increased private sector pensions. It has subsequently become a single-issue, populist party. The Communist Party lost parliamentary representation in 1994, but re-entered Parliament in 1999 (one seat) under the name of *Déi Lénk* (DL), an alliance of the KPL and a number of extreme-left organizations.

From 1945 onwards, Luxembourg's party system has shared all the features of Sartori's 'moderate pluralism' (Sartori 1976: 173). All governments have been coalitions, and centripetal competition has favoured the most centrist party (CSV), which typically has governed in coalition with Socialists or Liberals. However, the small ideological distance between relevant parties has enabled all possible two-party coalitions (CSV–LSAP, CSV–DP, but also DP–LSAP from 1974 to 1979) to emerge. The Communist Party, the only anti-system party, was excluded from all coalition negotiations after 1947. Furthermore, Luxembourg has displayed extraordinary cabinet and prime-ministerial stability. The five most recent governments have all served full terms, and there have been only nine Prime Ministers since 1919.

Parties influence the chain of democratic delegation at various stages and to various degrees. Candidate selection takes into account both the segmented nature of Luxembourg's society and the specific features of the electoral system. Each of the three traditional parties is part of and seeks to represent an extensive network, a more or less integrated 'pillar' of social organizations. Parties also try to recruit local notables and media figures not strongly associated with the 'pillars' to benefit from *panachage* (see below). Candidate selection is a decentralized process in which the initiative rests with the constituency party and lists are adopted nationally. All constituency party members,[5] or delegates of the lowest party institution, ratify the selection. There are no retirement age limits, but during its stint in opposition (1974–9), the CSV decided to refresh not only its ideology but also its personnel by introducing a party statute stipulating that not more than two-thirds of the candidates could be more than 40 years old.

---

[5] Closed primaries are used only by the Greens. Within the KPL, the CSV (a quarter of whose lists are drafted by the national party officials), the LSAP, and the DP, final candidate selection decisions are made nationally, though national organs rarely reject the constituencies' candidates. The major exception occurred in 1974 when DP President Thorn drafted the party's lists. In 1999 the Socialists began to use closed primaries to choose their national *Spitzenkandidat* and the *Spitzenkandidaten* of the four constituencies.

The electoral system (see below) reduces the importance of partisan candidate selection and even implies that, once elected, MPs are accountable to their constituency voters. This gives MPs an important incentive to pay attention to local interests (to bring home 'pork', to attend social constituency events, etc.). MPs who deviate from their party's national policy positions to protect their constituency do not usually have to worry about losing their seat in the next election. Candidates of traditional parties (especially the CSV and the LSAP) who are officially supported by pressure groups may occasionally deviate from party positions considered harmful to the group. However, rebellion against the party as a whole would provoke harsh reactions in the powerful partisan press and rejection by the 'pillar'. Hence, party splits in parliamentary voting are rare.

Permanent monitoring and reporting enhance party cohesion in legislation. Private members' bills are subject to the approval of the parliamentary group, which also decides on party voting discipline. Hence, an MP's voting discretion is usually very narrow: either he complies with the group's decision, or he declares in advance in a group meeting that he wants to abstain. Parliamentary party meetings are attended by several different party organs: national MPs and their parliamentary staff, MEPs, the party's government members, and leaders of the party organization. In the traditional parties, members of the Council of State, representatives of newspapers that support the party, as well as representatives of sub-organizations (e.g. youth and women's organizations) are also invited. These meetings are not public. In coalition government parties, the meetings also serve as preparatory sessions before the 'inter-fractional' (or coalition parliamentary group) meetings (see below), and thus help to assure coalition loyalty in Parliament.

Political parties more effectively structure the link between Parliament and cabinet than the one between voters and MPs. Although cabinet ministers have frequent meetings with their respective party presidents, the Prime Minister (PM) or the vice-PM is the real leader of each party's ministerial team. A party president customarily resigns this position when he becomes PM or vice-PM. During the late 1960s and early 1970s, party organizations were more influential and managed to solve coalition conflicts through 'inter-fractionals'. Since the 1980s, when almost all coalition party heavyweights have had cabinet positions and parliamentary groups have received generous financial aid, the national party leadership outside the cabinet has become less influential than the party's cabinet and parliamentary team. Finally, political parties affect the link between cabinet and civil servants through political nominations and promotions for top civil service appointments (see below).

DELEGATION FROM VOTERS TO MPs

Voting in Luxembourg is compulsory for all citizens aged eighteen or older.[6] The country is divided into four electoral districts, and MPs are elected for a five-year term (the

---

[6] The minimal voting age was lowered from twenty-one to eighteen in 1972.

number of terms they can serve is not limited).[7] Until 1954, the term was 6 years, with half of the Parliament—two of the four constituencies—up for re-election every 3 years. Elections were held in the southern and eastern constituencies at the same time, with the central and the northern district constituting the other pair. Before 1989, the number of seats in each constituency was linked to total population figures. Today the Constitution stipulates a fixed number of parliamentary seats, 60, which can only be changed through a constitutional amendment. A law passed by a constitutional majority determines the allocation of seats to the four constituencies. Since 1989, the south has elected twenty-three MPs, the centre twenty-one, the north nine, and the east seven. Proportionality is determined within the four districts, not nationally. Articles 136, 137, and 138 of the Electoral Code establish a first allocation of seats as follows: the total number of valid constituency votes is divided by the total number of seats plus one and rounded up in order to produce an electoral quota (the Hagenbach–Bischoff quota). After each list has received as many seats as the number of times its total vote meets the quota, the remaining seats are filled through a largest average method. This formula discourages newcomers in the two smallest constituencies.

As Hearl (1987) puts it, 'Luxembourg possesses a unique and ingenious electoral system, which not only ensures party proportionality but also makes every successful candidate's seat dependent upon his personal vote rather than upon party preference'. As a convention, parties do not rank their candidates, but list them alphabetically. Moreover, if the voter casts a straight party vote list by ticking the appropriate cell, each candidate is awarded one vote, regardless of party rankings. The voter can also choose specific candidates, either from the same party or from a variety of parties (*panachage*). Voters who opt for preferential voting, whether intraparty or interparty, may cast a maximum of two votes for each candidate (though the maximum number of preference votes equals the total number of constituency seats). Since the 1970s preferential voting has increased, from 31.3 per cent of the votes cast in 1979 to 41 per cent in 1999, with the proportion of interparty *panachage* jumping from 18 per cent of the total vote in 1979 to 29 per cent in 1999. Traditionally, those parties (DP and CSV) that presented well-known candidates benefitted most from *panachage*. Parties based on a well-defined ideology or/and local structures rather than specific candidates (KPL and LSAP) had more disciplined and 'exclusive' electorates. The 1994 and 1999 election figures, however,

---

[7] Apart from death, voluntary retirement, and the end of term or dissolution, there are various conditions under which an MP can lose his seat. First, there are six positions constitutionally incompatible with the mandate of MP (Article 54 of the 1848 Constitution): minister, member of the judiciary, member of the *Chambre des comptes*, district commissioner, finance civil servant, and active army member. A seventh one (member of Council of State) was added in 1948. According to a 1968 amendment to the 1924 electoral law, an MP who accepts an incompatible position is to be removed from his seat (Article 101). Article 102 of the electoral law stipulates that MPs cannot be the parents, close relatives, or spouses of other MPs. Since 1985, Article 100 enumerates more extensively than the Constitution the incompatible public positions (including the Railways Company). Since 1984, the European MP mandate is also incompatible with the national one. Absentees can also lose their seat in Parliament if they in two consecutive parliamentary years fail to attend at least half of the meetings. The 1911 law on parliamentary enquiries stipulates that an MP can be imprisoned and lose his voting and eligibility rights for 5–10 years after the Chamber has lifted his immunity. MPs can also be temporarily expelled from Parliament for a maximum of six sessions if they prove to be trouble-makers.

reflect a new trend: the LSAP has now become the party that relies most on inter- and intraparty *panachage* votes (45.2 per cent), and the DP won the 1999 elections after 15 years in the opposition by mobilizing a proportion of list votes (above 60 per cent) it had never reached before. The newer parties, the Greens and the ADR, constantly had a figure of party votes higher than 60 per cent, but whilst for the former this proportion decreased in 1999, the latter recorded a high of 73.9 per cent such votes (Centre de Recherche et d'Information Socio-Politiques 1995; Centre de Recherche Public, Gabriel Lippmann 2000).

Since 1974, the Liberals have chosen a *Spitzenkandidat* (top candidate) to lead their campaign, win support for the party list, help people identify their candidates for PM and ministerial portfolios, and attract a maximum of voters through *panachage*. The remainder of the party list is presented in alphabetical order. Other parties subsequently adopted this strategy—CSV in 1979, LSAP in 1984, followed by the nontraditional parties in 1994. As expected, the *Spitzenkandidaten* score better than other candidates, and their electoral fate is seen as a genuine popularity contest. Since preferential votes determine who gets elected, the voters decide which candidates become MPs. Hence, parties have less influence over the composition of their parliamentary group than they do in most countries with list systems.

Party organizations do not appear in any legal document and are not considered to be legal entities. It is therefore impossible for the state to finance them or to control their resources or campaign expenses. Only parliamentary groups, and therefore only parties that are already represented in Parliament, get financial support to hire personnel. Since 1999, political parties represented in Parliament receive public subsidies for electoral campaigns, but there is no legal cap on campaign spending. As campaigning has become increasingly costly, in both financial and manpower terms, richer candidates (or parties) backed by extra-parliamentary organizations stand a better chance of winning. Moreover, the fact that the main newspapers are either owned by or friendly to a particular party benefits these parties.[8] The publication of opinion polls is forbidden in the month preceding the elections. Electoral campaigns last between two (parties must introduce their lists at least sixty days before the elections) and three months (the maximum time between a parliamentary dissolution and the elections).

Several fairness rules govern broadcast time on national radio and television. Parties that are not represented in Parliament are given time according to the number of lists and candidates they are presenting (the minimum is a two-min spot), while the others are granted time in proportion to their parliamentary strength. However, governing parties tend to generate publicity by sponsoring cultural or sports events. Since broadcast time cannot be freely purchased, this kind of publicity usually advertises a specific candidate rather than the party.

Luxembourg's electoral system not only influences the link between voters and MPs: the Grand Duke usually asks the leader of the largest party to form a new government,

---

[8] Until 1999, it was impossible for a party to buy space for political advertisement in a newspaper outside its pillar. In 1999, the leading newspaper (the Catholic *Luxemburger Wort*) first opened its pages to parties other than the CSV. The other newspapers decided to follow the same policy.

but the junior partner is almost always the traditional party that has made gains relative to the previous election. Moreover, coalition parties usually select ministers on the basis of their personal electoral success. This direct link between electoral success and office, for parties as well as *ministrables*, rests on convention rather than law. It represents a deviation from the simple and indirect chain of delegation common in parliamentary democracy. Together with the growth of *panachage* voting, these conventions make cabinet ministers accountable not only to the parliamentary majority, but also to the voters. Accordingly, cabinet ministers try to promote their constituency interests, sometimes against the will of their formal principal, the parliamentary majority.

DELEGATION FROM PARLIAMENT TO CABINET

According to the Constitution, the Grand Duke nominates and can dismiss ministers. In practice, his power has been very weak since 1945, and he only nominates the *formateur*. The selection of ministers is left to the coalition parties, although the *formateur* can propose names for his own party. By drafting comprehensive coalition agreements before the cabinet takes office, parties strongly condition the policy link between Parliament and government. Although the coalition composition generally respects the will of the voting majority, government formation is controlled entirely by political parties.

Since 1848, ministers may not simultaneously hold seats in Parliament, although they have the right to attend parliamentary meetings. The principle of internal selection of ministers is widely respected, and almost all cabinet members over the past 50 years have come from the Parliament. Symbolic of ministerial accountability, the Parliament has the right to require ministers to appear at any time. The first democratic Constitution introduced the notion of ministerial responsibility. This very general provision (in so far as it fails to spell out the authority to which the ministers are accountable or the nature of their responsibility) reflects the fact that the Grand Duke is non-responsible (Article 45 requires that a minister must countersign all his acts). However, two other articles stipulate that only the Parliament has the right to accuse ministers, thus implying their accountability to the Parliament alone. Although the matters for which a minister can be held accountable have never been spelled out in law, the convention is that political accountability to the Parliament exists, and that certain types of votes imply dismissal.

Formation, Maintenance, and Resignation: Rules, Structures, and Behaviour

To open negotiations with a particular party, the *formateur* has to respect the decision of his party's National Council or enlarged party executive. In all three traditional parties, the party executive decides over the potential coalition partner. This proposal is then endorsed by the National Council or enlarged executive (Dumont and De Winter 2000). The leaders of the negotiating teams are in contact with their respective party executives throughout the bargaining process. In a meeting before the party rank-and-file they eventually defend the concessions made in the joint policy programme and portfolio allocation. Except in the DP, a national congress expressly convened for the occasion must positively endorse this agreement. A veto (or even the anticipation of one) by any party congress means that negotiations have failed. In practice, however, the party congress has always ratified the agreement, and mostly without a hitch (Dumont and De Winter 2000). Once approved, coalition agreements bind all coalition parties and all decision-making organs within each party.

By convention, a parliamentary investiture vote takes place after the reading of the governmental declaration and the subsequent debate. Luxembourg uses a positive formation rule (Bergman 1995: 40–55) in which a relative majority must actively support the government (i.e. 50 per cent of the MPs plus one must be present, and 50 per cent plus one of the votes cast, blank votes excluded, must support the government). Because party discipline is rigorously enforced in investiture votes, dissident government MPs tend to express their discontent by verbally opposing certain provisions of the coalition agreement, rather than by voting against the agreement as a whole. Investiture votes can be seen as a screening procedure in the delegation from Parliament to cabinet. However, the investiture motion introduced by majority MPs is purely a formality. In the postwar period, no government has lost such a vote of confidence, and there have been very few abstentions.

Motions of confidence and no confidence are not institutionalized or regulated. In practice, when Parliament refuses to pass a governmental bill, it can be considered a personal defeat for the competent minister. If he decides to resign, then cabinet solidarity—among ministers of the same party or in the form of collegial accountability (see below)—brings down the government. Parliamentary action has brought down only two cabinets: one after a majority turned a vote on a specific motion into a question of confidence (1958), and another when a cabinet resigned to pre-empt such a vote (1966). In the first case an information mission unsuccessfully tried to avoid an early parliamentary dissolution. In the second case, the coalition partners (CSV and LSAP) managed to re-form a cabinet without early elections. Under this new cabinet, Parliament was nevertheless dissolved one year before the normal end of its term, the second premature dissolution in Luxembourg's postwar political history. Table 15.1 summarizes the behavioural record with respect to cabinet investiture, no-confidence and confidence votes, and parliamentary dissolution.

The Parliament's vote on the government's annual budget bill is considered to be a vote of confidence, because under the Constitution the Parliament is sovereign with regard to state finances. The budget vote thus serves as another *ex ante* control over the government's annual program. However, the influence of the Parliament over the budget seems even lesser than with regard to the 'investiture vote'. This is due in part to the practice of 'debudgetizing'—taking expenditures off-budget—which deprives Parliament of its power to oversee large parts of state spending by providing subsidies to semi-public bodies like the Social Security agency, but also by creating special investment funds for telecommunications, roads, etc. Parliament's budget authority is also undermined by the fact that it does not have the requisite resources for a thorough scrutiny of the annual budget bill (1,000–1,500 pages of highly technical articles). In short, the Parliament cannot in this case effectively control its agent. In addition, the government might deliberately hide information from the Parliament through, for example, obscurely labelled budget items.

Table 15.1. *Cabinet Formation, Cabinet Termination, and Early Parliamentary Dissolution: Luxembourg 1945–2000* [a]

No.	Cabinet	Date of formation	Investiture votes (iv)						No-confidence votes (ncv)		Cabinet resigned to pre-empt ncv	Confidence votes (cv) under specific institutional mechanism (n.a.)	Did the cabinet end with an early election?	Who dissolved Parliament in this case? [b]
			No. of unsuccessful investiture votes	Voting results of successful iv (1: pro gov, 2: against gov, 3: abstentions, and 4: other) [c]					No. of ncv [d]	Cabinet removed by ncv				
				1	2	3	4							
1	Dupong I	45/11/14	0	44	0	0	0		n.d.	No				
2	Dupong II	47/03/01	0	34	16	1	0		n.d.	No				
3	Dupong III	48/07/14	0	n.d.	n.d.	n.d.	n.d.		n.d.	No				
4	Dupong IV	51/07/03	0	40	11	1	0		n.d.	No				
5	Bech I	53/12/29	0	n.d.	n.d.	n.d.	n.d.		n.d.	No				
6	Bech II	54/06/29	0	n.d.	n.d.	n.d.	n.d.		n.d.	No				
7	Frieden	58/03/29	0	31	19	1	0		1[e]	Yes			Yes	Head of State
8	Werner I	59/03/02	0	43	10	2	0		n.d.	No				
9	Werner II	64/07/15	0	33	23	0	0		n.d.	No	Yes		Yes	Head of State
10	Werner III	69/02/06	0	30	23	4	0		n.d.	No				
11	Thorn	74/06/15	0	n.d.	n.d.	n.d.	n.d.		n.d.	No				
12	Werner IV	79/07/16	0	46	18	0	0		n.d.	No				
13	Santer I	84/07/20	0	40	19	0	0		n.d.	No				
14	Santer II	89/07/14	0	38	22	0	0		n.d.	No				
15	Santer III	94/07/13	0	n.d.	n.d.	n.d.	n.d.		n.d.	No				
16	Juncker	95/01/26	0	34	26	0	0		n.d.	No				
17	Juncker II	99/08/07	0	—					—					—

[a] n.d. = no data (missing data); n.a. or '—' = not applicable in this case.

[b] The question 'Who dissolved Parliament in this case?' can be answered with one of five options. This identifies the main constitutional actor that caused the early election. We have not coded the formal signatory, but rather the person or body that made the real decision: (1) Head of State, (2) Prime Minister, (3) Cabinet, (4) Parliamentary majority, (5) Automatic constitutional provision (e.g. if it is required when a new President takes office, or, for example, if it is required after the adoption of a proposal for constitutional amendments).

[c] No investiture vote was taken for most of the inter-election period cabinets (1953, 1958, 1995). For the 1948, 1954, and 1979 cabinets, votes were taken by the 'hands up' procedure and the Speaker simply stated by looking at the show of hands that 'the proof (of the necessary majority) was doubtless' and that the motion was thus adopted.

[d] The reason for the lack of data on no-confidence votes is the same as in Belgium (see Chapter 6). In addition, most motions do not get to the voting stage due to the so-called 'simple motion' presented by majority MPs that has priority on all others. If they do pass and a vote is held, data are not kept separately from the votes over other types of motions.

[e] Result of the no-confidence vote: 30 yes, 17 no, 3 abst.

Dissatisfaction with parliamentary budgetary oversight has led to various reform efforts. Since 1985 the PM has during the first half of each year been required to present a general policy statement on the state of the nation. The rationale is to bring the Parliament into the budget process long before the final debate and vote on the bill. Until 1993 the State of the Nation address was actually followed by a debate on each ministerial department's budget. A second reform was implemented in 1994 when the Parliament's audit office (*Chambre des Comptes*, since 2000 *Cour des comptes*) acquired more autonomy and the resources needed to produce independent analysis and information.

Governments tend to dominate other legislation as well. Bills proposed by the opposition can be stopped at different procedural stages and are unlikely to be put to a vote. More generally, behavioural or structural factors ensure that only an insignificant number of private members' initiatives ever become law. The Parliament's lack of resources (including personnel, expertise, and documentation) helps explain why very few private bills are even introduced. In addition, an MP's right of initiative is also, to various degrees (depending on the strictness of party and parliamentary group statutes), subject to the approval of his parliamentary group (*Fraktion*). Majority MPs are further constrained by the coalition agreement, while the actions of opposition MPs are influenced by their knowledge that any initiative will probably be blocked. In short, MPs generally do not invest much time in drafting bills because there is little prospect that they will be passed.

Majority parties dominate all parliamentary bodies, including the Chair (Speaker), the *Commission de travail* (Parliament's business committee), and all parliamentary committees. Control of the prestigious position of Speaker is part of the government formation negotiations.[9] Although the Parliament's Standing Orders stipulate that the Speaker acts on behalf of the Parliament and in correspondence with the Parliament's will, the degree of non-partisan leadership depends on the Speaker's own inclinations. The Speaker has a number of important, exclusive competencies, most notably the authority to judge the acceptability of private bills, motions, and questions. In practice, he uses this authority consensually, since he is allowed to evaluate only the form and not the content of legislative acts. The Speaker never makes decisions that go against the will of one or more majority parties.

The *Commission de travail* is a permanent committee designed to help the Speaker organize parliamentary business. It proposes the parliamentary agenda to the Speaker, prepares agreements between political groups, gives mandatory advice on certain Grand-Ducal draft regulations, allocates debate and interpellation time, etc. The Committee is made up of the Speaker of the Parliament and the chairmen of the political groups. Representatives have as many votes as their party has seats in the Parliament while the Speaker has none. Even if the Committee usually decides issues consensually, it is clearly controlled by the parliamentary majority and the government. A representative of the government (usually the top civil servant who serves as Secretary-General of the

---

[9] The Speakership has with one exception gone to the party that holds the most seats in Parliament (the CSV since 1945).

Council of Ministers) attends all the meetings of the *Commission de travail* to ensure that the plenary agenda is drafted in full compliance with government interests. Thus, although government bills are not formally given agenda priority, the government can in practice always assure that its interests come first.

On permanent parliamentary committees, parties are represented in proportion to their strength in the Parliament. Committee chairmen and vice-chairmen are elected by committee members at the beginning of each parliamentary year, while committee composition normally remains the same throughout the legislative term. Committee competences generally correspond to the main ministerial departments, and almost all chairmanships go to majority MPs (usually from the same party as the minister who heads the corresponding department).[10] Since committees have no deadline for their reports to the plenary (unless the Speaker proposes one), majority members can block opposition bills by voting against the relevant report, setting the committee agenda, or failing to attend meetings so that no quorum exists. For these reasons, private member bills often 'die' at the committee stage. Provisions in these bills, which majority parties find interesting, are sometimes reintroduced in governmental bills.

Finally, inter-fractional meetings (meetings of coalition parliamentary groups) further promote coalition cohesion on government-sponsored legislation. Although not institutionalized in the parliamentary Standing Orders, these meetings serve to verify that all government projects comply with the coalition agreement and to eliminate any parliamentary initiative that violates it. Even though there are no official barriers prohibiting majority MPs from exercising their parliamentary initiative, coalition governance rules in practice limit its effectiveness. Since voting discipline in Parliament depends on the results of inter-fractional meetings, the initiatives of dissident MPs are never voted upon.[11] 'Inter-fractionals' were often used in the 1970s, when cabinets did not have comfortable parliamentary majorities. Such meetings became more structured (with regard to frequency, thematic agenda, etc.) in 1984–5. Although they might seem to increase MP involvement in the legislative process, inter-fractionals actually remove the decision-making process (at least on delicate political issues) from Parliament. This is because only coalition MPs are informed and because their behaviour is constrained by strict voting discipline.

The low success rate of private members' bills is also due to the fact that the Council of State must give mandatory advice on every bill or amendment. Due to limited time and resources, this politicized body gives priority to government bills, and thus 'kills' private members' bills through delays. Moreover, by invoking urgency (with parliamentary approval), the government can speed up the legislative process. In matters deemed to be urgent, the Council of State is not asked to give mandatory advice before the final vote (see below).

[10] The petitions committee, which has no corresponding ministerial department, is normally chaired by an opposition representative.

[11] 'Extraordinary' inter-fractional meetings can be held at the request of the PM. Nicknamed 'the fire brigade', they were convened most often during the crisis years of the late 1960s, but have since been rare. They have traditionally dealt with issues such as the interpretation of the coalition agreement. They have also been held when the Council of Ministers has been unable to resolve a conflict.

Parliament may, through a bill supported by a simple majority, grant the cabinet 'special powers' for a limited time (though government must report to the Parliament). The government is only allowed to legislate on a restricted number of subjects and in accordance with certain fundamental guarantees. This provision was first used in 1915 to preserve the country's economic interests in wartime. It was later used in response to the Great Depression of the 1930s, again in 1939 to promote the country's interests in wartime, and then in 1946 to facilitate reconstruction. Over time this practice of transferring legislative authority has become a 'regular' (rather than 'crisis') technique of governance. In fact, while until the late 1950s Parliament tended to grant special powers to the government unanimously, since then only majority MPs vote in favour. While the original intent of special powers was at times ignored until the 1960s, since then it has been abused every year, even though in truth Luxembourg's socio-economic problems have not been so severe as to justify the granting of special powers year in and year out.

Tools for Parliamentary Control

To say the least, the accountability mechanisms discussed so far and the working of the legislative process do not protect the principal against agency loss. Increasingly, therefore, Parliament has devised a number of instruments aimed at reducing the risks of hidden action and hidden information. MPs may use these tools at any time, thus allowing for continuous, day-to-day oversight of the cabinet.

Interpellations are instruments of accountability that require the government to engage in a public debate about its policy. Interpellations can be introduced by any MP, can be addressed to a particular minister or to the cabinet as a whole, and must—in theory—be answered within six months. They can be followed by a vote on the text of a motion (for instance, holding a minister responsible). However, the government has the right to refuse an interpellation demand, or, in agreement with the *Commission de travail*, to change an interpellation request into a parliamentary question in order to avoid a vote. Interpellations have mostly been used during political turmoil (as new instruments of social policy and in response to economic crisis)—for example, in the aftermath of the Second World War and, to a lesser extent, during the 1960s and 1970s. They were used most frequently (twenty-six times) in the 1940s and least often (only once) in 1974–5 and 1988–9. Under the DP–LSAP government from 1974 to 1979, no interpellation was ever answered. The average number of interpellations has not exceeded ten per year.

Parliamentary questions are demands for information from a specific ministry or about a specific cabinet decision. They can be answered by the responsible minister. With regard to urgent questions (the urgent procedure), if the Speaker accepts the question, and if the minister agrees that there is urgency, then the minister must reply at the time that the Speaker designates, or in written form within a week. For normal questions, the formal deadline for responding is one month. The questions and answers are published in parliamentary documents. A 1990 reform gave MPs the right to put their questions to ministers orally if they have not replied within one month.

The number of parliamentary questions has increased dramatically over the last thirty years, to more than 500 in the two most recent (1989–94 and 1994–9) legislative terms, with a peak of 717 in the 1990–1 session. One reason for this increase might be publicity. Most questions are communicated to the press when they are introduced in the Parliament. No question can be asked during committee meetings because they work behind closed doors. Ministers, on the other hand, do not seek publicity for their written replies. If ministers do not answer within the allotted time, then they must inform the Speaker and explain why they have missed the deadline and when an answer can be expected. Although there is no other legal recourse at the disposal of MPs, ministers do tend to reply.[12]

A new type of question was created in 1990 in order to introduce the possibility of a debate between an MP (or group of MPs) and a minister. After having asked his question and hearing the ministers' reply, the MP can ask a brief follow-up question related to the reply. Since 1991, there has been an average of fifteen questions with debate per year.[13] A monthly 'question hour' was introduced in the late 1990s. During that hour, six questions (three for the majority, three for the opposition) on subjects of general interest contained in the most important government statements (the governmental declaration, the state of the union, or the foreign affairs declarations) are directed at the government. At least as regards the questions of the opposition the government does not have much time to prepare its replies (eight minutes per question), as questions may be transmitted by MPs to the Speaker only three hours before question time.

Another tool of parliamentary control open to MPs is the introduction of a motion. These are motivated statements approving or disapproving specific government actions, or even calls for the government to resign. In response to motions attacking the cabinet, majority MPs usually introduce a 'simple motion', a call to 'return to the business of the day'. Since it is up to a majority of MPs to decide which motion has priority, the simple motion is voted on before all motivated motions. If the former is accepted, the latter are defeated.

Since the beginning of the 1990s, different forms of parliamentary debate have been introduced in the Parliament's Standing Orders. A 1990 reform introduced the debate on current matters (*débat d' actualité*). At least five MPs or the government itself can request such a parliamentary debate on a specific subject of general interest. The *'Commission de travail* decides if the proposal will be treated as a standard question or as a debate on current matters, in which case the government is requested to reply in written form before a deadline. An average of three such debates have been held per year. Since 1990, five or more MPs can ask for a *débat d' orientation* on issues under consideration in a particular ministry. This debate can be prepared in a committee. If the demand is supported by at least fifteen deputies, then the debate is automatically placed on the parliamentary agenda. A ministry cannot be the subject of more than one orientation debate per year. On average, less than two debates of that kind are held a year.

---

[12] In the most recent legislative term (1994–9), the rate of reply was 94 %.
[13] In contrast to other types of questions, the number of these questions that can be asked during each legislative session is limited. Each parliamentary group can ask twice as many questions as it has members.

A final type of parliamentary debate introduced in the early 1990s is a public debate on the government's foreign policy.

Accountability mechanisms also exist in parliamentary committees. Ministers and civil servants may be called upon by a parliamentary committee to answer questions in connection with the committee's scrutiny of a government bill. Moreover, Article 64 of the Constitution gives Parliament investigative powers, for which it may seek expert reports and/or call witnesses to testify. A 1911 law gives the parliamentary committee of investigation the same powers as a criminal law judge. After almost half a century of disuse, three parliamentary investigations have been held in the postwar era. In 1989, following a parliamentary investigation, a minister was found guilty by the Parliament and forced to resign. A third instrument is described in Article 24 of the Standing Orders, which stipulates that a committee can, in order to prepare its legislative work, by majority vote seek information and advice from persons or institutions not belonging to Parliament. Because parliamentary committees already benefit from the advice of one or several professional neo-corporatist chambers, such hearings are not very frequent. Hearings with a greater scope may be requested by parliamentary committees and organized in plenary meetings. They do not have to be linked to a particular bill, but rather are aimed at gathering general information from a wide range of pressure groups and citizens' associations. The Parliament decides whether or not the hearing will be public. Because such hearings are time-consuming, only four were held before the 1990s.

DELEGATION WITHIN THE CABINET

Cabinet Internal Organization

The Grand Ducal decree of 1857 (since amended seven times) about the organization of the government stipulates that all decisions that need the consent of the Grand Duke are to be discussed and decided collectively by the cabinet (Majerus 1990: 174). The PM chairs the Council of Ministers (cabinet meeting), sets the agenda, and coordinates ministerial departments. Yet, the PM is not legally a hierarchical chief over the other ministers (Bodry 1996). Although it is not a formal rule, either the PM or the vice-PM acting on the PM's behalf may nevertheless call for a cabinet discussion of any departmental issue. This authority follows from the PM's responsibility scrupulously to verify that all ministers' proposals conform to the coalition agreement (see below). Thus, a minister's individual responsibility is residual in the sense that the management of his department's competencies are subject to collective deliberation. Even if consensus is always sought in the Council of Ministers, it is not required. Decisions can be made by majority rule. In recent years, this has only occurred with regard to non-political questions (i.e. appointments). Ministers who do not vote in favour of a particular decision can excuse themselves from collective responsibility by recording their opposition in the written report of the cabinet meeting. In this event, dissident ministers cannot be held legally or politically accountable for the cabinet decision. If the dissident minister is the minister responsible for implementing the decision, he is only responsible for executive acts following the decision.

Since the cabinet is small, there is no institutionalized inner cabinet (though informal contacts between the two coalition leaders—the PM and the vice-PM—take place very frequently). Specialized ministerial committees are sometimes created, but only on very pragmatic grounds. Recent examples include European affairs, employment, and information policy. Even when there is a special committee, however, all issues are discussed and decided in the cabinet.

The position of junior minister was created in the 1950s to give ministers in very large or highly compartmentalized departments an efficient, day-to-day assistant. These Secretaries of State never belong to a party other than the minister's.

Ministerial portfolios are concentrated in a few hands, all of whom have clear partisan identities. Even PMs commonly head one or two departments beyond the Ministry of State. Parties are very important in this regard, as they seek ministerial competencies that are particularly important to their own electorate or departments that are highly visible and have large budgets.

Government Agreements

Compliance with the coalition agreement is essential to cabinet stability. Apart from regular elections, the main cause of cabinet resignation in Luxembourg is intra-coalition conflict (though this has not occurred since 1968). The cabinet's great respect for the agreement has several explanations. First, ministers are all very familiar with the agreement because most of them helped negotiate the government themselves. While they know in advance that they are almost certain to get a ministerial post, however, they do not know for sure which portfolio they will receive. Hence, most negotiators participate in all plenary bargaining sessions and understand the spirit of policy intentions on any topic. Second, and perhaps most importantly, ministers are constantly monitored by the PM and the vice-PM, who are the guardians of the execution of the coalition pact.

Changing the PM does not trigger the drafting of a new coalition agreement, nor does it automatically lead to a new governmental declaration or investiture vote. Partners may take the opportunity to amend the agreement, but extensive revisions are rare, since the equilibrium reached during the formation of the preceding government is difficult to maintain in renegotiations.

DELEGATION FROM MINISTERS TO CIVIL SERVANTS

Civil service positions are awarded on the basis of competitive exams. The candidates with the best results may choose their department from among those that have vacancies. Politicization in the middle and lower career levels is very low. However, top civil service appointments and promotions are highly politicized, despite the formalism of the process (collective cabinet decisions signed by the Grand Duke for appointment of the five *administrateurs généraux*, the top civil servants who collectively cover all ministries). Cooperation between government and the civil service is assured via the appointment of about fifty government advisers organized in a four-level hierarchy, who become the ministers' personal staffs. Most are drawn from the top civil service to ensure that they have the requisite experience. They keep their civil servant status and often continue their careers after they leave their political posts. Other advisers are private sector experts who become 'civil serviced' without having taken an exam. A General Secretary of the Council of Ministers is chosen from among the more than 400 civil servants in the Cabinet Office. Because most of these 'promotions' are made along party lines, those who are assigned to a department other than the one in which they were previously working are likely to be reassigned to much less attractive positions if their parties are not part of the subsequent government. Screening and selection (*ex ante*) procedures thus also intervene in the relationship between ministers and civil servants to ensure the former that their agents will not go against their preferences.

Ministers head one or more departments, while the Minister of State heads the entire government administration.[14] The accountability of civil servants working in ministries is thus doubly indirect: They are accountable for their doings neither directly nor via their departmental minister. Rather, citizens complain to the Minister of State, not to the relevant minister. Individual ministers are nevertheless politically accountable to the Parliament for the actions of their civil servants, and as such may be asked to respond to parliamentary enquiries. On the other hand, MPs are only provided information from the civil service through the government as intermediary. The problem of hidden information, specifically the problem of obtaining information for the purpose of holding the government accountable, is a constant concern of parliamentary committee members. Orders to withhold (or delay) information come from cabinet ministers, and the politicization of the top civil service means that ministers are obeyed, despite the fact that hearings and the consultative advice of professional chambers (third-party testimonies) are designed to mitigate this potential information problem.

We noted earlier that the government's legislative predominance and the parliament's lack of resources reflect the fact that law-making requires increasingly diversified competencies. In Luxembourg, the civil service and through it the executive branch have the necessary human and financial resources to perform the functions assigned to them. As a result, the government's legislative initiatives and responses to parliamentary questions and interpellations are well thought-out and professionally drafted by civil servants. Thus, successful delegation from ministers to civil servants tends to reinforce agency loss between the legislature and the executive.

EXTERNAL CONSTRAINTS

There are a number of external actors who intervene in the chain of parliamentary delegation and accountability in Luxembourg. The first three discussed below have a potential impact, though in practice they do not constrain the delegation process. The other three lead to serious deviation from the ideal-type of parliamentary democracy. Keep in mind that the effects of the creation of a Constitutional Court in 1997 cannot yet be judged.

---

[14] The Ministry of State has always been held by the PM, except for the 1995–9 period (Juncker I).

Head of State

The Grand Ducal decree of 1857 stipulates that all decisions that need the consent of the Grand Duke are taken collectively by the cabinet and countersigned by a minister. These decisions include all bills passed by the Parliament, Grand-Ducal decrees, and high-level appointments. Yet, the powers of the Head of State are purely formal, and in practice he cannot act autonomously in public life. Yet, the Grand Duke retains the right to be consulted by his ministers. He occasionally influences the country's political choices, most effectively in times of political crisis. In general, political leaders appreciate his mediation.

The National Bank

Even before the introduction of the Euro, due to the UEBL, most central bank functions were located abroad. In practice, however, this had never prevented governments from pursuing country-specific policies. Luxembourg has no National Bank in the classical sense, since fixed parity made the relationship of the Luxembourg franc with other currencies the responsibility of the Belgian National Bank. Neither the BNB nor the *Caisse d'Epargne de l'Etat*, the two institutions allowed to issue money, had much weight in government policy-making. There have been instances in which Belgian monetary decisions have not been followed by the Grand Duchy.[15] Revisions of the UEBL treaty have given Luxembourg greater domestic powers (e.g. the right to maintain its own public debt policy) than did the original.

The Referendum

Direct democracy is enshrined in the Constitution (Article 51), but in practice no referendums have been held since 1937. Referendums are formally held only at the request of the Parliament. Only three questions have ever been subject to a referendum, two in 1919 and one in 1937. Even though past referendums can be interpreted as non-binding, the question of their decisive or consultative character is not answered in any legal document. The uncertainties associated with the referendum helps explain why parliamentary majorities refrain from using it.

The Council of State

No final vote on legislation can be taken without the advice of the Council of State, which, in other words, has veto powers (see above). It can also modify or even replace a bill with a 'counter bill' by amending proposed bills or amendments coming from Parliament or the government. The Council of State also has something close to a suspensive legislative veto. All laws are subject to a so-called 'second constitutional vote' three months after the first one, unless the Chamber of Deputies and the Council

---

[15] On the other hand, in 1982 the Martens government devalued the Belgian franc without even warning the Luxembourg government.

of State deem it unnecessary. This second constitutional vote is intended to give the Parliament time to reflect (and thus compensates for the absence of a second chamber). In fact it has rarely been used during the postwar period. The Council of State always justifies its decision that a second vote is not necessary with a reference to the urgency of the matter at hand. However, when the opinion of the Council of State fundamentally diverges from the Parliament's—on average, almost once each year—the Council refuses to grant an exemption.

The twenty-one members of the Council of State are appointed by the Grand Duke (i.e. *in casu* the government), either on his own or on the basis of a list of three candidates proposed either by the Chamber of Deputies or by the Council of State itself. As a result, the Council of State is highly politicized and in effect colonized by the three traditional parties. The Council meets behind closed doors.

(Neo-)Corporatism

Since 1924, there have been five professional chambers in Luxembourg: agriculture, labour, commerce, private employees, and craftsmanship. In 1964, a sixth chamber was added for civil servants. These bodies were created to represent all economic forces. Each chamber is directly elected by those who work in the corresponding field. All wage earners and independent workers are obliged to pay dues to their respective chamber, and all who pay have the right to stand as candidates for election. The chamber(s) give advice on bills and governmental decrees concerning their particular professional interests. The cabinet must have received this advice before it can approve a decree or a budgetary bill, although it does not have to follow it. Nonetheless, the Parliament never neglects the chambers' views on matters that significantly affect them.

A 1966 law created a Economic and Social Council of thirty-five members: twenty eight appointed by the Council of Ministers on the basis of proposals from professional organizations in twelve sectors (e.g. small companies, steel industry, banks, transport, insurance, agriculture), and seven independents four of whom are selected by the twenty-eight, three by the cabinet. All members serve four-year terms. The Council studies economic, social, and financial issues and can initiate studies on its own or at the request of the government. During the first trimester of each year, the government asks the Council's advice on the government's report on the economic, social, and financial evolution of the country and on its related policy programme. The government can ask for advice on matters of general interest and on questions of principle on which the professional chambers have expressed divergent views. In the latter case, the Council must provide a 'single and coordinated' opinion.

The Luxembourg model of neo-corporatism is based on mixed committees both at the national and at the individual company level ('*cogestion*' was introduced in 1974 for large companies) and has evolved with the unfolding of the steel industry crisis. A 1977 law triggered the formation of the 'Tripartite Co-ordination Committee', whose task is to give advice on unemployment measures. Consisting of four members of the government, four employers' representatives, and four union delegates, and presided over by the PM, it meets whenever one of three unemployment thresholds is reached. Since

1977, it has given advice on other politically delicate matters and has helped social partners reach consensus. In theory, the Chamber of Deputies is free to ignore agreements reached in the Tripartite Committee, but in general it considers itself bound to ratify them. As a result, this tripartite structure gives economic interests ('social partners') the power to block the government's socio-economic proposals. The golden age of the model was between 1977 and 1983. Its importance has since declined (Govaert 1997; Hoffman 1996), but it remains an important feature of Luxembourg's consensus democracy.

The European Union

As a founding member of the ECSC and the EEC, Luxembourg has always favoured European integration. Constitutional engineering to allow a (temporary) transfer of national sovereignty to international cooperation dates from the 1954–6 period. The national implementation of EU directives and the expansion of the EU's policy competence certainly constrain Luxembourg's governments. The 1992 Maastricht Treaty is a good example. The right of all EU citizens to participate in European and local elections in Luxembourg violated Articles 52 and 107 of the Constitution. Neither of these was included in the June 1989 declaration of revision prepared for the purpose of amending the Constitution. Nonetheless, the Treaty was adopted with its unconstitutional provisions after the three traditional parties agreed that the relevant articles would be declared open for revision in 1994.

Since the adoption of the Maastricht Treaty, constraints on national power as a consequence of EU membership have become more visible to the population. Experts denounced the government's actions in the press, and some associations were created to defend and promote respect for the Constitution. Many Luxembourgers also worry that European fiscal harmonization will damage the economy. The fact that the new Constitutional Court (1997) does not judge the conformity of laws transposing international treaties into national law is another indication of the special treatment awarded to European integration, and thus of its seriousness as an external constraint.

Delegation to the European Union is done in a very pragmatic and decentralized way. First, Luxembourg only has specific national interests in a limited number of policy areas in which the EU has competence. In addition, because of its small size, civil service hierarchy generates less cumbersome decision-making procedures within ministerial departments in Luxembourg than in most other European countries, especially with regard to EU matters. In particular, within each technical ministry a few civil servants (often only one) are responsible for both preparing and implementing European legislation. Direct and informal contacts between the competent minister and the civil servant in charge take the place of more formal routines and allow for flexibility. The individual department is responsible for implementing European legislation in its field of competence.

The decentralized procedure notwithstanding, EU issues are channelled through the Ministry of Foreign Affairs to ensure that all necessary information is communicated to ministerial departments, the Foreign and European Affairs Committee of the Parliament, and European institutions. The parliamentary committee, composed of both national MPs and MEPs, does not seem to have much impact on European policy. Although there are few persons in Luxembourg with competence in EU matters, coordination in EU bodies mostly occurs along party lines.

Through 1995, over 90 per cent of EU directives had been transposed into Luxembourg's legal order through four types of executive decrees that do not require parliamentary participation (Carlier 1995). Legislation is only used when a European directive introduces a new obligation, or if the subject matter is one that the Constitution vests exclusively in the legislature. Apart from these objective criteria, the scope of economic and political changes included in the directive might be taken into account. Luxembourg's cumbersome legislative procedure, which has difficulty operating within EU deadlines, justifies the use of governmental decrees and thus further enhances cabinet predominance vis-à-vis the Parliament.

CONCLUSION

Luxembourg seems to fit rather well the simple and indirect chain of delegation and accountability of parliamentary democracies. Strøm's proposition that this chain might be most applicable to small, homogeneous, and stable societies in which principals have greater faith in their screening procedures is thus confirmed in this case. Deviations from the ideal-type do exist, but almost all the links in the chain display features of delegated power to an agent and accountability mechanisms aimed at controlling the agent's actions. Political parties play an important role, but they serve to channel the delegation process from one actor in the classical chain to another, rather than distort it. External actors, on the other hand, create some deviations from the singularity principle. While a direct link between voters and ministers is discernible, this is not only a result of an evolution found in most parliamentary democracies (Strøm, Chapter 3), but also due to structural and conventional arrangements in Luxembourg.

Between voters and MPs, the electoral system assures a representation that is relatively immune to party discretion, and that approximates the ideal-type of parliamentary delegation. However, long-standing conventions aimed at creating a high level of responsiveness (e.g. the largest party is almost always in government, its junior partner is usually the traditional party that had the best election performance, and ministers are usually those persons who got the most preference votes) and increasing *panachage* voting have tended to establish a direct link between voters and cabinet ministers. This presence of multiple principals could increase the likelihood of failed delegation.

Majority parties structure the link between Parliament and cabinet. Because parties dominate all parliamentary bodies, draft comprehensive coalition agreements, and set up very strict ministerial accountability mechanisms towards their party and the coalition as a whole, the executive is free from parliamentary interference in the implementation of coalition policies. Even though accountability tools at the Parliament's disposal have increased, they are not sufficient to counter the downgrading of Parliament, even with respect to legislative initiative. The power delegated by the principal is not balanced by effective accountability mechanisms to the Parliament as a whole, but rather the executive is formally responsible to the parliamentary majority

(majority parties)—which is consistent with the model of parliamentary democracy. These features account for the extraordinary stability of cabinets in Luxembourg. External constraints such as the Council of State, neo-corporatism, and EU membership further reduce the role of Parliament, but also create deviations from the singularity principle of delegation and accountability.

The link between cabinet and individual ministers is probably the one that deviates most from the ideal model presented in this volume. Collective decision-making reduces the scope of matters that are effectively delegated. *Ex ante* mechanisms—the comprehensive coalition agreement, the screening and selection procedure during negotiations—and *ex post* mechanisms—permanent monitoring of the PM and vice-PM on behalf of the cabinet and as party leaders—serve to make the process different from the ideal-type, as delegation is limited, while accountability requirements are high.

Finally, the delegation between ministers and civil servants is in keeping with the ideal model. Top civil servants are important both in implementation and in policy-making. This delegation of power is necessary in a country in which all ministers hold multiple portfolios and cannot be specialized in all fields. Accountability is ensured by the politicization of nominations and promotions of top civil servants, and by the coordination tasks performed by ministerial advisers.

REFERENCES

Als, Nicolas and Philippart, Robert L. (1994). *La Chambre des Députés. Histoire et lieux de travail.* Luxembourg: Chambre des Députés du Grand-Duche de Luxembourg.

Bergman, Törbjorn (1995). *Constitutional Rules and Party Goals in Coalition Formation.* Umea: Umea University, Department of Political Science.

Bodry, Alex (1996). 'La fonction de Premier Ministre dans le système politique du Luxembourg'. *Bulletin du Cercle François Laurent*, 1: 3–27.

Carlier, Katty (1995). *Autonomie et pouvoir d'appréciation de la Chambre luxembourgeoise dans l'application du droit communautaire.* Dissertation. Départment des Sciences Politiques et Sociales, Université Catholique de Louvain-la-Neuve.

Centre de Recherche et d'Information Socio-Politiques (CRISP) (1995). *Les élections au Grand-Duché de Luxembourg. Données sur les scrutins de 1974, 1979, 1984, 1989 et 1994. Résultats et comportements.* Etude réalisée pour la Chambre des Députés du Grand-Duché de Luxembourg. Bruxelles: CRISP.

Centre de Recherche Public–Gabriel Lippmann (CRPGL) (2000). *Les élections au Grand-Duché de Luxembourg: Rapport sur les élections législatives du 13 juin 1999.* Etude réalisée pour la Chambre des Députés sous la direction de F. Fehlen and Ph Poirier. Luxembourg: CRPGL.

Dumont, Patrick and De Winter, Lieven (2000). 'Luxembourg: Stable Coalitions in a Pivotal Party System', in Wolfgang C. Müller and Kaare Strøm (eds.), *Government Coalitions in Western Europe.* Oxford: Oxford University Press.

Eurobarometer 48 (Autumn 1997). European Commission.

Govaert, Serge (1997). 'Le Grand-Duché de Luxembourg: Une stabilité trompeuse?' *Revue Internationale de Politique Comparée*, 4: 585–99.

Hearl, Derek J. (1987). 'Luxembourg 1945–82. Dimensions and Strategies', in Ian Budge, David Robertson, and Derek Hearl (eds.), *Ideology, Strategy and Party Change.* Cambridge: Cambridge University Press.

Hoffman, André (1996). 'Le modèle luxembourgeois: un instrument de régulation en crise'. *Cahiers Marxistes*, 201 (April–May): 39–51.

Majerus, Pierre (1990). *L'Etat Luxembourgeois. Manuel de droit constitutionnel et de droit administratif.* Luxembourg: Imprimerie Saint-Paul.

Sartori, Giovanni (1976). *Parties and Party Systems: A Framework for Analysis*. Cambridge: Cambridge University Press.

Numerous brochures edited by the *Service Information et Presse du Gouvernement.*

16

The Netherlands: Rules and Mores in Delegation and Accountability Relationships

ARCO TIMMERMANS AND RUDY B. ANDEWEG

INTRODUCTION: THE CONSTITUTION AND BEYOND

The Constitutional Framework

The government and the two Houses of Parliament together make up the constitutional legislative power of The Netherlands. The two Houses of Parliament are not equal in this respect, however. Only the popularly elected *Tweede Kamer* (Second Chamber, or Lower House) is granted the constitutional power to initiate or amend legislation. Ministers and individual MPs can propose bills, which must be approved by a simple majority (votes are public), with a quorum rule of 50 per cent plus one. The *Eerste Kamer* (First Chamber, or Upper House), which is elected by an electoral college composed of all provincial councillors, lacks the right to initiate or amend legislation, which underlines the fact that the constitutional engineers intended it to be a *chambre de réflexion*. Once legislation is approved in the Lower House, the *Eerste Kamer* is mainly a potential veto player, as it can only approve or reject bills at large. If approved, the bill has to be signed by the monarch and countersigned by a minister to become law.

For bills fixing departmental budgets and for constitutional revisions, a special legislative procedure is required. Bills containing proposals for the annual budget can only be submitted by government ministers, which is done formally on the third Tuesday of September. Before that date, ministers draft their respective budgetary proposals according to an internal schedule drawn up by the cabinet. Changes of the Constitution can be proposed by ministers and members of the Second Chamber. As with ordinary legislation, both Houses of Parliament must approve proposals for a revision of the Constitution by simple majority. This is followed by a second reading, after at least the Second Chamber has been dissolved and newly elected. In this second reading a two-thirds majority is required in both Houses. As in other cases, the quorum requirement is 50 per cent plus one vote. In practice, the second reading is usually held after regular elections in order to avoid cutting short the government's term of office by calling special elections.

The Dutch Constitution is based on the principle of representative democracy. This does not mean, however, that Parliament alone is responsible for public policy-making.

The most obvious other policy-making body is the government. The Constitution mentions both Parliament and the government as the legislative powers, and in practice the government usually takes the initiative. In addition to formal legislation, the government produces executive decrees, which flesh out formal legislation. This kind of 'pseudo legislation' has become more important over time, and already in the early 1970s one observer took this as a reversal of the doctrine of Trias Politica: the executive (government) has become the main legislative power (Koopmans 1970). With only few exceptions, Parliament is not involved directly in the making of these decrees, and it takes highly alert MPs to bring these decrees within the scope of effective parliamentary control.

The Netherlands has been described both as a consociational democracy and an example of neo-corporatism. Both concepts are closely related. Catholic, Protestant, and Socialist groups have emerged and formed networks of subcultural organizations. This feature of Dutch political life is widely known as pillarization. Although the social pillars have eroded to a large extent, their leaders still share responsibility for governing the country in a culture of compromise and cooperation. In specific policy areas such as socio-economic policy and education policy, the leaders of the relevant subcultural networks also work together, often in special institutional arrangements such as tripartite advisory councils. The Socio-Economic Council, in which representatives of employers organizations, trade unions, and government appointed experts meet, is a typical example.

Extending the Scope of Delegation and Accountability

Both consociationalism and neo-corporatism emphasize the predominance of elites. Indeed, the opportunities for citizen involvement are relatively limited. As mentioned already, only the Lower House of Parliament is directly elected by the citizens. There are no direct elections for any executive office. The decisiveness of elections is low. For example, the composition of the government depends less (at least less directly) on how voters reward or punish parties than on the relative positions and strategies of these parties (Timmermans and Andeweg 2000: 364–5). The elected Prime Minister is still one of the unrealized desiderata of institutional reformers. Even provincial governors and local mayors are appointed by the central government. A proposal to amend the Constitution to introduce a binding referendum in the form of a popular veto over certain forms of legislation was narrowly defeated in the First Chamber during the proposal's second reading in 1999.

The infrequent and often half-hearted attempts to increase the role of citizens in national politics contrasts with the relative ease with which parts of national sovereignty are given up to EU policy-making bodies. The transfer of powers from national political institutions to the European level, in particular to a supranational body such as the European Commission, goes beyond delegation. Formally, a minister's actions within intergovernmental bodies such as the European Council of Ministers remain within the scope of delegation and accountability at national level, but the abolition of the unanimity rule for certain decisions has weakened effective control by the national Parliament.

POLITICAL PARTIES AND CONSTITUTIONAL PRINCIPALS AND AGENTS

Political parties have their own chains of delegation and accountability that go beyond the Constitution and may also cut across the formal constitutional relationship between Parliament and cabinet. Yet, parties are not mentioned in the Constitution, there is no law on parties, and the term 'party' does not even figure in the electoral law. In the Dutch system of political minorities, policy-making usually involves interparty bargaining. In this context, constitutional bodies such as government and Parliament are arenas as much as they are principals and agents. Parties condition the chain of delegation through their strategies and through mostly unwritten rules that have emerged within and between them.

The four main parties with stakes in these arenas are the Social Democrats (PvdA), the Christian Democrats (CDA), the Liberal Conservatives (VVD), and the Liberal Democrats (D66) (see Timmermans and Andeweg 2000). With the exception of D66, the social and ideological roots of these parties date to the early years of the twentieth century, much like similar parties in other European parliamentary democracies. In their present form, however, all main parties are postwar organizations. The PvdA and the VVD were formed in the immediate postwar years, as modern versions of the pre-existing Social Democratic and Liberal parties. D66 began as a democratic reform party in 1966, while the CDA was created through a merger of two smaller Protestant and one Catholic party in 1980.

These relatively centralized and disciplined parties also dominate the governmental arena. All postwar Dutch cabinets have been composed of at least two but more often three or more parties. In these cabinets, the Christian Democrats (before 1980 mainly the Catholic party) long took a pivotal position, having been in office continuously from 1917 to 1994. Dutch government coalitions often control more than a simple majority in Parliament, although the number of minimum winning coalitions has increased since the late 1960s.

DELEGATION FROM VOTERS TO MEMBERS OF PARLIAMENT

Electoral Engineering in a Quasi-Multiple District System

The formal election procedure in the Dutch system of proportional representation (PR) is that the voter expresses a preference for an individual candidate from a party list in one of nineteen electoral districts. In reality, however, the electoral system does not produce a real relationship of delegation between voters in a particular district and an individual MP. For the distribution of the 150 seats in the Second Chamber, all nineteen districts are combined into a single nationwide district, and district votes are aggregated to one national party vote. The districts mainly play a role in the organization of the elections (supervising of polling stations, counting votes, etc.), and the party vote in a particular district determines what share of the seats that the party has won nationwide will be filled by candidates from the district list. Until the 1960s, the electoral districts had some practical relevance, as the larger political parties presented different lists (and list leaders), if not in each electoral district, then at least in different regions of the country. Probably under the impact of the electronic media, the scale of electoral campaigns has become national, and the names topping parties' lists are now the same in all nineteen districts. If the remaining names on the lists differ from one district to another, this is to allow a party to nominate a larger number of candidates nationwide than the maximum (thirty for new parties; twice the number of seats currently held with a maximum of eighty for parties already represented) that it is permitted in an individual district. Most candidates are nominated in several districts, though their ranking on the lists varies across districts.

Parties as Intermediaries Between Voters and Candidates for Parliament

There are few legal constraints on the nomination of candidates: they must have Dutch nationality, be at least 18 years old, and not deprived of their voting rights by the courts. Some positions are incompatible with being an MP (minister, membership of the Upper House, the Council of State, and the General Accounting Office), but this is checked before taking office and does not stand in the way of being a candidate. The position of a candidate on a party list is determined by the party alone. The procedure differs among the parties, and here a regional element comes into play. Most parties have party organizations at the level of the electoral district, and these district organizations play an important role in deciding the ranking of candidates below the national list leader and other top candidates (Koole and Leijenaar 1988; Hillebrand 1992). This was the case particularly in the Social Democratic PvdA, which—in keeping with a proposal to introduce 'real' electoral districts into the electoral system—implemented a decentralized party nomination procedure. However, the party has 're-nationalized' the nomination procedure in order to secure a proper balance of expertise in different policy areas within the parliamentary party. Even under the new procedure, however, the chairmen of the district organizations are involved in drawing up the list.

There is no legal term limit nor mandatory retirement age for MPs, and none of the four main parties formally limits the number of terms an individual Member of Parliament may serve, nor does any party have a mandatory retirement age for MPs. Recent experience shows, however, that strategic concerns induce party leadership to effectively remove incumbent 'veteran' MPs from their lists. This happened for instance when the CDA drew up its party list in the fall of 1997. Often to their frustration, long-serving MPs were told by the party leadership not to apply for another term. This course of action was not restricted to the largest opposition party, but also occurred in two of the three coalition parties (PvdA and D66).

As Hillebrand (1992) shows, ordinary party members have little direct influence on the composition of party lists. In 1986, 16 per cent of local chapters of the Christian Democratic CDA were never convened to discuss the nominations. In the Liberal Conservative VVD, 40 per cent of the chapters did not meet for this purpose, nor did 61 per cent of PvdA chapters. When meetings were held, attendance was low. The Liberal Democratic party, D66, uses a different nomination procedure in which the ordering of the list is determined in a postal ballot among all members. Even here, however, participation is low. Only 36 per cent of the members returned their ballot in 1986. It should also be noted that only about 2.5 per cent of the electorate is a member of a political party. This means that 97.5 per cent of voters do not have any opportunity to influence the composition of their party's list.

Once election manifestoes are written and party lists are set, active campaigning can begin. The minimum length of election campaigns is forty-three days, which is the maximum time that the Electoral law permits between the deadline for nominating candidates and voting. Although there is no legal maximum on campaign spending by parties, they face clear budgetary constraints. The main source of income for parties' campaign budgets is party membership contributions. The steady decline in party membership over the last twenty-five years has therefore limited the amount of money available for election campaigns. This has created pressure to increase government subventions for the parties. In 1998, a new law introduced direct subsidies to parties, but earmarking the money for research, youth organizations, etc; that is, not for campaigning.

The access of parties to public broadcasting is strictly regulated; party political broadcasts are limited to three minutes each time. The public channels are not open for the unrestricted purchase of broadcasting time. The total broadcasting time per season (September through August) is determined by a regulatory agency (*Commissariaat voor de Media*) and depends in part on the number of parties represented in Parliament. The total time is allocated equally among the parties. Each parliamentary party has approximately one hour of broadcasting time per election period. Since it can be used only in three minutes blocks, a party can make about twenty broadcasts per election season. A complex lottery at the beginning of the season determines the timing of the party broadcasts, so as to ensure that all parties get some prime-time slots. In contrast to public channels, commercial channels are open to parties on a simple 'pay per minute' basis. In 1998, for the first time, some parties made very modest use of this opportunity.

Apart from party propaganda, the media continuously report on how the parties are doing in opinion polls. They also organize their own polls. There are no restrictions, legal or otherwise, on the publication of poll results. The only results that are kept secret are the polls on the government's popularity that are commissioned by the Government Press Office. However, this information is not very different from the polling results that are made public.

Fixed Party Lists and Preference Voting

The success of the parties' election campaigns is determined in a zero-sum game for parliamentary seats. At least in terms of the institutional arrangements governing voting, subgames within parties may also take place. This is because voting arrangements include the possibility of preference voting. A vote for the list leader implies agreement with the party's ordering of the candidates, as all votes in excess of the electoral quota are transferred down the list. Preference votes, that is, votes for other candidates than the list leader, can reduce the effect of this mechanism on the actual allocation of seats to party candidates.

In practice, however, preference voting does not constitute a direct link between voters and an individual MP, even though they have gradually increased to over

20 per cent of votes cast. Research has revealed that the main reason for preference voting is to choose a female candidate (the list leaders of most parties are male). Regional representation is the second most important motivation (Hessing 1985).

Occasionally, preference voting may indicate voter disagreement with the ordering of the candidates on the party list. Sometimes this disagreement takes the form of *ex post* accountability. In 1986, for example, about one-third of the VVD electorate cast a preference vote, primarily to support incumbent MP Theo Joekes, who had fallen out with the party leadership over his role in a Parliamentary Inquiry. He had criticized one of his party's cabinet ministers. When he was relegated to an unelectable position on the party list, a campaign started to get him elected in defiance of party leaders, with the result that he retained his seat.

However, it is not always disagreement with the party's list of candidates that creates an incentive for preference voting. It may be used also to signal discontent with party policy more generally, as in 1952, when a political weekly launched an appeal to vote for the seventh candidate on the party list as a sign of opposition to the country's defence policy. Less often, preference voting might be meant to show support for the party's choice of candidates. For example, in 1986 a significant number of PvdA voters cast their votes for Wim Kok, the intended successor of long-time party leader Joop den Uyl.

The real impact of preference voting on who wins a seat in Parliament is quite small. Since 1945, only a few candidates have obtained a seat due to preference voting. The threshold for obtaining a seat via this process has only gradually been reduced from 50 per cent of the electoral quota within one of the administrative electoral districts to the current 25 per cent of the electoral quota nationwide. Moreover, parties do not always allow their candidates to campaign for preference votes. In some cases parties do not even allow their candidates to accept election on the basis of preference voting without the party's consent—for example, candidates are required to sign undated letters of resignation. Increasing the impact of preference votes is controversial. In 1989, the government rejected a proposal to bring the threshold down from 50 to 25 per cent, on the grounds that this would transfer too much influence from the parties to voters (Proceedings of the Second Chamber 1987–8, 20264 no. 3: 59). In 1993, an advisory committee rejected the abolishment of a threshold because it would create more intra-party competition, decrease job security of incumbent MPs, and hinder the balance of expertise within parliamentary parties (De Koning Commission 1993: 28).

The absence of a personal relationship between voters and MPs is generally felt to be one of the system's shortcomings. In the 1960s and early 1970s, proposals to intro-duce PR within multimember districts were rejected because doing so would make nationwide party representation less proportional. In the 1990s, advocates of electoral reform have sought to circumvent this objection by advocating variations on the German electoral system, which combines nationwide PR with the election of at least some candidates in single or multimember districts. These proposals have failed because they have been deemed to be too complicated or to have other undesirable side-effects (Andeweg 1997a: 239–44).

As a result, there is little or no delegation directly from voters to MPs. There are no provisions for recall elections, and especially when an incumbent MP is placed relatively high on the party list in subsequent elections, there is no way in which voters can hold the individual MP accountable. Voters tend to vote for a party rather than an individual candidate, and even in the rare event of an MP being elected through preference voting, the MP does not know who his/her voters are. For the members future political career, it is probably wiser to try to impress those within the party who have power over the party lists than to rely on preference voting. The chain of delegation is therefore indirect: voters delegate to parties, and parties are, or contain, the selectors to whom MPs are responsive. It is this interposition of the party in the chain of delegation between voter and MP that has led to rejections of American models of representation (Thomassen 1994; Andeweg 1997*b*).

DELEGATION FROM PARLIAMENT TO CABINET

The constitutional link between Parliament and the government most clearly distinguishes parliamentary democracies from other kinds of systems. As in most parliamentary systems with a written Constitution, the Dutch Constitution delegates general policy-making competence to the government, and it grants control powers to Parliament. In this section we discuss the specific forms that these governing and control powers take as instruments of delegation and accountability, as well as their relevance in practice. Before the coexistence of the two bodies is considered, however, we consider the way in which the government, the non-elected body, is formed.

Ex Ante *Control: The Formation and Inauguration of Cabinets*

The Constitution stipulates that government ministers are appointed by Royal decree (Article 43), but other than that, the rules pertaining to the formation of Dutch governments are not explicitly mentioned in legal documents such as the Constitution. In 1965, for example, a new coalition was formed after a cabinet crisis, without calling new elections. This came to be seen as undemocratic and has not been repeated (except for short-lived interim governments), but politicians and constitutional scholars disagree over the question of whether this practice (no new coalition without new elections) has now become part of the unwritten Constitution. The formation of a new government starts when the Queen instructs a *formateur* or *informateur* to explore the possibility of forming a government that can look forward to fruitful cooperation with the States General (the two Houses of Parliament). With the exception of caretaker governments, this 'fruitful cooperation' has meant the building of majority government coalitions. The conventional sequence in the negotiation process goes from the formation of a party combination (coalition) through discussions of specific policies (coalition agreement) to the allocation of portfolios and, finally, to the nomination of cabinet ministers and junior ministers.[1] There is, however, overlap between these 'stages', as interparty negotiations in any stage are influenced by expectations about claims of parties later on.

---

[1] In contrast to countries such as Belgium and France, there are few patronage appointments in the Dutch government formation process.

The norm of 'fruitful cooperation' between the government and Parliament is rather vague, but an appreciation of it is crucial for understanding the mechanisms of delegation and accountability in legislative–executive relationships. The most general interpretation of this norm is that the government should be able to obtain the support of a majority of MPs when the bills that it submits to Parliament are put to a vote. The norm also has a more qualitative meaning, however, which is that the government parties should form a stable coalition in Parliament, a coherent governmental majority (Timmermans 1991). One Liberal parliamentary party leader once referred to this as 'strategic monism' (Nijpels 1984).[2] Whatever label is used, the important point is that the second interpretation of the norm concerns relationships between parties rather than between individual MPs. Government viability is essentially a matter of relationships between prospective coalition parties.

The most visible way in which a government majority is built prior to the inauguration of the government is through the drafting of a coalition policy agreement. The practice of drafting and publishing coalition agreements dates back to 1963 (Bovend'Eert 1988). Coalition agreements are usually made *for* rather than *by* the government. In particular, they are constructed by prominent members in the parliamentary party groups that are included in the nascent coalition. The forging of agreements is not just an internal party ritual as Luebbert (1986) asserts, but is a serious affair, particularly for negotiators who may become cabinet ministers. MPs tend to see negotiations on a coalition agreement as a major opportunity to influence coalition policy. Moreover, the informal setting of government formation talks facilitates agreement on politically sensitive matters, or the establishment of procedural arrangements to deal with such matters (Peterson *et al.* 1983; Timmermans 1998). It is important to appreciate that coalition agreements are not really an *ex ante* control mechanism in the hands of Parliament as such. Commitments established by a written agreement are between coalition parties and not between formal constitutional bodies. For this reason, an agreement might function as an *ex ante* control mechanism mainly because it predetermines part of the new government's agenda. Though parliamentary party groups say they cement the coalition through a written agreement (and opposition parties criticize the coalition agreements as interfering with parliamentary deliberations), this is insufficient to speak of one united principal. Indeed, explicit policy commitments made before the government is sworn in might even bring the parliamentary parties (and individual MPs) of the coalition into an agent position, as such commitments might tie their hands once government decisions are to be voted on in Parliament.

Other *ex ante* mechanisms controlled by the coalition parties are the screening of candidates for ministerial portfolios. These are typically internal party affairs. Although there have been of cases in which a particular minister candidate has been unacceptable to another party, a party's autonomy in selecting and screening internal candidates for office usually extends to the nomination of ministers. In most cases, candidates include people who have been party spokespersons in the government formation process

---

[2] Ironically, when this party prominent was in the government, a conflict between a party colleague in the cabinet and the party's parliamentary group led to the premature resignation of the government in 1989.

(people who, almost without exception, are MPs), but ministers are also recruited from outside Parliament. Article 57 of the Constitution prohibits ministers from simultaneously holding seats in Parliament.[3]

After an often protracted process of government formation, the inauguration of governments illustrates the complex interplay of parties and constitutional bodies. A party's involvement in the formation of a government activates an internal chain of delegation and accountability within the party. Drafts of the coalition agreement, for example, are scrutinized and often amended by the parliamentary groups. The overall outcome of the negotiations (coalition agreement and portfolio allocation) will be voted on at a special party congress (PvdA, D66), or scrutinized by party councils (CDA and VVD) and/or the parliamentary group (VVD). Within the constitutional arena, the government formation is formally concluded when the Head of State signs the Royal Decrees appointing the ministers, but the new Prime Minister countersigns these decrees (including the one pertaining to his own appointment) (Article 48), and in that way the formation of the government falls under the general responsibility of the government to Parliament (Article 42). There is no formal investiture vote. The Prime Minister reads the 'Government Declaration' (usually a summary of the coalition agreement) in Parliament, followed by a parliamentary debate. At the end of the debate, opposition parties may introduce a motion of no confidence in the new government. As long as such a motion is not approved by a majority, the government is assumed to have Parliament's confidence (i.e. negative parliamentarism; see Bergman 1993).

Ex Post *Control: Operation and Termination of Cabinets*

Historically, many of the formal rules pertaining to the relationship between Parliament and the government date back to the constitutional revision of 1848. Before that revision, the King's legislative power was relatively unconstrained. Under the new Constitution, ministers are responsible before Parliament (Article 42 of the current constitution). The revised Constitution also gave Parliament greater authority to enact and amend legislation and to control the government. Parliament's new authority extended to approving the annual budget and amending it, and increased its right to information (by giving Parliament the authority to hold inquiries and to put urgent questions to the government). The government was given the right to dissolve Parliament (by Royal Decree). This can be interpreted as a mechanism to put conflicts between principal and agent to the ultimate democratic principal, the electorate. It is now generally accepted that the government cannot dissolve Parliament more than once in any given conflict.

As noted in the introduction, the government and the two Houses of Parliament jointly pass legislation. The government initiates much more legislation than the Second Chamber does; at least three-quarters—and in some years over 90 per cent—of all bills are drafted by ministers. Moreover, many laws give the government (usually

---

[3] The exception is the period between elections and the inauguration of the new cabinet, when a minister remains a member of the outgoing government even if he or she has been elected to parliament.

individual ministers) considerable discretion to issue executive orders containing more detailed policies. Control and accountability rules are particularly significant with respect to this second category of government activity, in which broadly worded laws are fleshed out without direct parliamentary involvement. This government legislative activity is beyond the reach of the veto power exercised by the First Chamber, which can only approve or reject bills at large—an authority that is actually used only infrequently, even for formal legislation. Delegation and accountability rules in the relationship between Parliament and the government apply equally to all policy areas.

The two main categories of parliamentary instruments for holding governments accountable are reporting requirements and sanctions (March and Olsen 1995: 162–7). Parliament (i.e. individual MPs, groups of MPs, or the Second or First Chamber as such) has a variety of ways to exercise its control function. Individual MPs can ask oral and written questions, which first are screened by the parliamentary leadership of most parties. In the Second Chamber, over a thousand written questions are asked each year. The government can only refuse to provide the information asked for with an appeal to *raison d'état*, which it rarely does. The same applies to parliamentary committees requesting information during the committee stage of the legislative process. Formally, urgent questions followed by an emergency debate (*interpellaties*) can only be put to the government if a majority supports them. In practice, however, the informal rule governing urgent questions is that the majority requirement is not (ab)used by coalition parties to prevent the opposition (which is always a minority in the Netherlands) from asking questions. On average there are just over ten *interpellaties* per annum, but there is quite some variation in this number. A parliamentary majority is also required for setting up a parliamentary inquiry, in which ministers, civil servants, and citizens can be required to answer questions under oath, but here there is no informal rule allowing a minority to start an inquiry. From 1945 to 2002 there were only seven inquiries.

Individual ministers are directly accountable insofar as there is no formal way in which they can hide behind the Prime Minister. In practice, however, the Prime Minister may defend an individual minister, which transforms the issue into one of collective cabinet responsibility, thus making it more difficult for Parliament to render a negative political verdict on the minister. Since 1945, nine individual cabinet ministers have resigned after they were censured by Parliament, or in anticipation of such a censure. With respect to parliamentary sanctions, a formal vote of no confidence does not exist. What constitutes an indication of no confidence (as well as confidence) is largely a question of how the government interprets the contents of parliamentary amendments and motions (i.e. parliamentary statements). Individual MPs can initiate motions and legislative amendments (although a motion cannot be considered without the support of at least five MPs).[4] An important difference between countries which have a formal vote of no confidence and ones that do not is that, in the latter case, Parliament cannot formally enforce a minister's/government's resignation. Actions that we

---

[4] This is the constitutional rule for the Tweede Kamer. Members of the Eerste Kamer do not face such a support threshold when they submit motions to a plenary vote. This is remarkable because in most other respects the Eerste Kamer has fewer competences.

consider motions of no confidence are those that express 'disapproval' (which is the commonly used terminology) of the behaviour of a minister or (more rarely) a whole government. Most no-confidence motions proposed between 1981 and 1997 were rejected (see Table 16.1). Although we have no systematic information about the number of no-confidence motions in the period before 1981, we do know from parliamentary history that few were approved and/or led to the resignation of a minister or of the government. Only twice between 1945 and 1981, in 1960 and 1966, did the government resign after a motion approved by a parliamentary majority was interpreted as a vote of no confidence.[5] In 1951 and more recently in 1989, the government resigned after a motion was tabled but before the Parliament had voted. In both cases, the motion criticizing the government had been introduced by one of the coalition partners, indicating that the coalition had broken down.

Whether or not parliamentary sanctions are used to bring down governments, the Constitution limits a government's term to four years, or more precisely, it states that elections must be held every four years (governments remain in office after an election until a new government is formed, which usually takes several months). While the Constitution does not explicitly give Parliament the power to end the term of a government (i.e. it does not contain a motion of no confidence), the government can dissolve Parliament (Article 64). However, the early dissolution of Parliament is rarely brought about by conflict between the government and Parliament as an institution. When the Parliament is dissolved prematurely, it is more often a consequence of the escalation of a conflict within the governing coalition. Table 16.1 summarizes the behavioural record with respect to confidence votes and parliamentary dissolution. As shown in the table, a total of seven cabinet have ended in parliamentary dissolution and early elections. In October 2002, the Balkenende cabinet (formed after the 2002 elections) also ended prematurely, and early elections were held in January 2003.

What other working rules exist in these two arenas of coalition politics? There is a rich literature on the tension in coalitions between the need to cooperate and maintain coalition cohesion, and each party's desire to profile itself. Most of this literature emphasizes the strategic aspects of interparty relationships, although some recent work has begun to consider institutional constraints (Strøm, Budge, and Laver 1994; Müller and Strøm 2000). Moving beyond formal constraints such as the majority requirement and the procedures for fixing the budget and engineering constitutional revisions, rules pertaining to party interaction during a government's term have evolved. These rules are endogenous to the political system and concern mainly the 'peaceful coexistence' of coalition parties. An example of such an unwritten rule is that outgoing governments or caretaker governments should leave politically controversial issues to the new government formed after parliamentary elections.

One of the rules relating to interparty relationships that has evolved since the 1960s is that parties must observe the coalition agreement.[6] We previously referred to the

---

[5] In the case of 1960, however, cabinet resignation was revoked, while in 1966 the MP who tabled the motion was reported to have said that he had not intended to bring down the government.

[6] The rule has evolved, though it was written down in the first published coalition agreements in 1963 and 1965. Later the rule was implicit (Timmermans 2003).

Table 16.1. *Cabinet Formation, Cabinet Termination, and Early Parliamentary Dissolution: The Netherlands 1945–2000*[a]

No.	Cabinet	Date of formation	Investiture votes (iv) (n.a.)	No-confidence votes (ncv)			Confidence votes (cv) under specific institutional mechanism (n.a.)	Did the cabinet end with an early election?	Who dissolved Parliament in this case?[b]
				No. of ncv[c]	Cabinet removed by ncv	Cabinet resigned to pre-empt ncv			
1	Schermerhorn	45/06/24		0					
2	Beel I	46/07/03		0				Yes	Const.
3	Drees I	48/08/07		1	Yes[d]			Yes	Cabinet
4	Drees II	51/03/15		0					
5	Drees III	52/09/02		0					
6	Drees IV	56/10/13		0					
7	Beel II[e]	58/12/22		0				Yes	Cabinet
8	De Quay	59/05/19		1	No[f]				
9	Marijnen	63/07/24		0					
10	Cals	65/04/14		1	Yes				
11	Zijlstra[g]	66/11/22		0				Yes	Cabinet
12	De Jong	67/04/05		0					
13	Biesheuvel I	71/07/06		0					
14	Biesheuvel II[h]	72/08/09		0				Yes	Cabinet
15	Den Uyl	73/05/11		0					
16	Van Agt I	77/12/19		1	No				
17	Van Agt II	81/09/11		0					
18	Van Agt III[i]	82/05/29		1	No			Yes	Cabinet
19	Lubbers I	82/11/04		4	No				

Table 16.1. (contd.)

No.	Cabinet	Date of formation	Investiture votes (iv) (n.a.)	No-confidence votes (ncv)			Confidence votes (cv) under specific institutional mechanism (n.a.)	Did the cabinet end with an early election?	Who dissolved Parliament in this case?[b]
				No. of ncv[c]	Cabinet removed by ncv	Cabinet resigned to pre-empt ncv			
20	Lubbers II	86/07/14		12	No[j]	Yes		Yes	Cabinet
21	Lubbers III	89/11/07		5	No[k]				
22	Kok	94/08/22		10	No				
23	Kok II	98/08/03		—		—		—	—

[a] n.d.=no data (missing data); n.a. or '—'=not applicable in this case.

[b] The question 'Who dissolved Parliament in this case?' can be answered with one of five options. This identifies the main constitutional actor that caused the early election. We have not coded the formal signatory, but rather the person or body that made the real decision: (1) Head of State; (2) Prime Minister; (3) Cabinet; (4) Parliamentary majority; (5) Automatic constitutional provision ('Const.'; for example, if it is required when a new President takes office, or after the adoption of a proposal for constitutional amendments).

[c] Systematic data exists only for period from 1981.

[d] The Liberal party VVD tabled a motion of no confidence. This motion was never actually voted on, but all observers agree that it did not have majority support. Before the vote, the only VVD minister (against the policy of whom his own party's anger was directed) felt that he could not stay in a cabinet in which his own party no longer had confidence, even if the cabinet still had majority support. When he resigned, all other ministrers decided to resign as well.

[e] Caretaker cabinet until elections scheduled after the breakdown of the previous cabinet (Drees IV) could be completed.

[f] No-confidence vote in December 1960 obtained majority, but cabinet resignation was later revoked.

[g] Caretaker cabinet until elections scheduled after the breakdown of the previous cabinet (Cals) was defeated in Parliament.

[h] Caretaker cabinet until elections scheduled after the breakdown of the previous cabinet (Biesheuvel I).

[i] Caretaker cabinet until elections scheduled after the breakdown of the previous cabinet (Van Agt II).

[j] Only one no-confidence vote obtained a majority, but this was after the cabinet had already resigned and was outgoing. Ironically, cabinet resignation was the result of one party leaving just before a no-confidence motion was to be voted on in the Parliament.

[k] One 'no-confidence vote' addressed to two ministers was approved, but this was when the cabinet was outgoing after the parliamentary elections were held.

coalition agreement as an *ex ante* control mechanism because it specifies in advance a large part of the government's scope of activities. What parties say that they will do and want the government to do are important, but these are only statements of intent. For this reason, coalition agreements can only have a real meaning if there are also *ex post* controls for enforcing the agreement during the government's term. Since agreements are not contracts, enforcement is the business of the coalition parties themselves. The rule that parties must observe the coalition agreement is a rule of interparty (as well as intraparty) loyalty or discipline (Andeweg and Bakema 1994). It is an institutional rule because it involves mutual expectations. It is reciprocal because those who break the rule might be punished by the other(s). In the parliamentary arena, coalition discipline combines the positive rule that coalition parties should be cooperative with the negative rule that they should not form ad hoc legislative coalitions with non-coalition parties, except in those cases in which the coalition agreement explicitly allows it. Within the cabinet, the rule may be sustained by the collective responsibility of ministers (see the next section). If ministers are politically responsible for decisions taken by colleagues from a different party, then this may increase compliance. Ministers can, in principle, try to exploit their discretionary power and covertly follow their own preferences when the agreement is to be implemented—which is a form of agency loss (see Laver and Shepsle 1996; Shepsle 1996). However, the likelihood of this happening seems to depend, at least in part, on the extent to which ministers have been involved in the process of negotiating the agreement. Ministers who are confronted with the agreement as a fait accompli are more likely to act in ways that are contrary to it. Ministers who participated in negotiations seem to have a higher degree of commitment to the agreement and be less vulnerable to departmental pressures.

To say that the rule of faithfulness to coalition agreements is important is not to say that it is always observed. The first empirical work on this subject reveals that agreements in The Netherlands are frequently broken, although sometimes policy arrangements are so opaque that it is difficult to say whether or not particular decisions taken by the cabinet or in Parliament are in keeping with the agreement (Timmermans 1998). The relevant point here is that perceived deviations from a coalition agreement often lead to conflict within the coalition, which indicates that the principle that agreements must be observed is a relevant institutional rule of coalition behaviour.

Returning to delegation from Parliament to the government with regard to the issues included in a coalition agreement, parliamentary parties appear to be as committed to them as is the government. This is illustrated by the fact that coalition agreements often explicitly mention the issues on which MPs from the coalition parties are exempted from coalition discipline (Timmermans and Andeweg 2000: 373). It has even become a matter of mutual expectation that issues not explicitly mentioned in the agreement—neither as clear-cut policy decisions nor as matters on which coalition partners are free to act as they choose—are subject to the same regime of coalition discipline. Thus, the individual coalition parties' freedom to challenge proposals supported by a majority within the cabinet is rather limited. D66, for example, found this out in December 1997, when as a governing party it opposed a cabinet proposal for agricultural reform but subsequently was accused of putting the survival of the coalition at stake (*De Volkskrant* 16 December 1997).

The coalition agreement and the working rules that have emerged to sustain the governmental majority also serve to condition (and often to constrain) the use of parliamentary instruments. For example, amendments to government bills win majority support (which requires the support of at least one coalition party) in only one-third of cases, this despite the fact that many legislative amendments have no important substantive consequences. If coalition parties are loyal and if the intentions spelled out in the policy package are carried out, the opposition parties are effectively relegated to a marginal position. This clearly illustrates that working rules in coalition governance are fundamentally different from the formal constitutional rules pertaining to executive–legislative relations.

DELEGATION WITHIN THE CABINET

Rules of Delegation and the Role of the Prime Minister

It is only since 1983 that the Dutch Constitution has recognized the existence of a Council of Ministers, which 'shall consider and decide upon overall government policy and shall promote the coherence thereof' (Article 45), and of a Prime Minister who 'chairs the Council of Ministers' (Article 45). Although the Constitution allows for ministers without portfolio, these are exceptions. Practically all cabinet ministers head a department. The Constitution does not regulate the size of the cabinet, but it has never included more than sixteen members.

To the extent that individual ministers have delegated powers, these come from the Council of Ministers (cabinet) rather than from the Prime Minister. As the formateur of the new government, the Prime Minister formally nominates ministers for appointment by the Queen, but he has real influence only over his own party's nominations (in his capacity as party leader). The Prime Minister cannot change the departmental jurisdictions of ministers, dismiss ministers, or unilaterally reshuffle the cabinet, nor can he issue policy directives to individual ministers. In the case of a tie vote in the cabinet, the Prime Minister casts the decisive vote; however, this is of limited importance since the cabinet rarely takes decisions by voting. The Prime Minister heads the Department of General Affairs, but most of its officials work in the Government Press Office or the semi-autonomous Scientific Council for Government Policy. He has only a dozen policy advisers, all career civil servants, each of whom focuses on a few policy areas, but who lack formal monitoring competences.

The influence of the Prime Minister is sometimes much greater than that which comes from his limited formal powers or small staff, and some commentators argue that there has been a trend towards a stronger premiership in recent years (cf. Andeweg 1991). This is based partly on the increased external role of the Prime Minister (EU summitry, press conferences), although greater visibility connected to external responsibilities does not automatically imply greater political power. A more important reason for this trend is that, as the need for coordination grows with the complexity of modern government, so to does the acceptance of a more powerful Prime Minister to serve as coordinator. Nonetheless, even if this has led to a more influential

Prime Minister, his role is still mostly reactive, more like an arbitrator than a true policy activist (Blondel 1988). Moreover, the norms and rules relating to this more influential role are still emerging.

The Dutch government has permanent cabinet committees, but they have no delegated powers and they do not delegate power to ministers. With a few insignificant exceptions, these committees are only authorized to prepare items for discussion within the cabinet. Only a few of these committees meet frequently. All ministers are welcome to attend committee meetings in which they are interested. Civil servants also serve as members of cabinet committees. The Dutch cabinet also has a number of informal committees, some of which are more important than the formal ones. While most of these are ad hoc, some are more or less permanent. The group of ministers with responsibility for socio-economic policy (called the 'triangle' or the 'pentagon' depending on the number of ministers involved) has even been accused of forming a de facto inner cabinet. Of course, even if this informal committee does reach agreement, decisions are not binding on other ministers unless they have been channeled through the cabinet.

Formally speaking, delegation from the cabinet to individual ministers is accompanied by detailed supervision. The Standing Orders of the Council of Ministers spell out which ministerial decisions are to be submitted to the cabinet for prior approval. These include all proposals for legislation and regulation, all important appointments, the creation of committees or advisory councils, and in general any decision that might impact on other ministers' policies or might have major financial or political consequences. When in doubt, a minister is expected to consult the Prime Minister. Since ministers' decisions eventually become public, it is difficult to ignore this rule. Moreover, the rule is not merely pro forma. The Dutch Council of Ministers not only meets frequently, it actually debates and amends proposals, even against the wishes of the sponsoring ministers.

The Tacit Rule of Mutual Non-Interference

The limited formal powers of the Prime Minister and the tradition of substantive debate within cabinet have increased the potential relevance of the rule of mutual non-interference as a form of coordination without hierarchy. This tacit rule, which has emerged over time, puts an important procedural constraint on ministers in cabinet meetings. It states that ministers should participate in the debate primarily when their own departmental interests are at stake, because they otherwise risk encroachment by other ministers on their own departmental turf.

Such 'negative coordination' is often referred to in ministerial memoirs and studies of cabinet government, both in The Netherlands and elsewhere. Nevertheless, there are hardly any empirical studies of its actual relevance to cabinet decision-making. A detailed study of the minutes from Dutch cabinet meetings during 1968 (a year for which the minutes were accessible) reveals that about 80 per cent of all ministerial contributions to cabinet debate can be traced to the speaker's own departmental portfolio (Andeweg 1990). This confirms the relevance of the rule of mutual non-interference, but it also shows its limitations. After all, one-fifth of all contributions to cabinet discussions involve crossing portfolio boundaries—that is, ministers speak about matters not related to their own department. The amount of 'barrier crossing' varied widely among the ministers; a few did not even seem to be aware of the rule, while others rarely spoke on matters outside their departmental portfolio.

The importance of non-intervention is likely to be declining for two reasons. First, the international economic recessions in the late 1970s and 1980s ended a long period of growing government expenditure. As a result, the setting of ministerial budgets has become more zero-sum in character. Despite the risk that intervention will provoke reciprocal action by colleagues, a study of financial decision-making in the cabinet between 1975 and 1986 concludes that ministers have become more aggressive in this respect, thus weakening the significance of rule of non-intervention for cabinet decision-making (Toirkens 1988).

A second factor that has eroded the non-intervention rule is the politicization of cabinet since the 1960s. Today, ministers are not only departmental heads, but also prominent politicians and representatives of their party. In that role, they also have a legitimate interest in portfolios that are entrusted to a minister from another party. For that reason weekly party gatherings are held on the eve of cabinet meetings, attended by the ministers of a coalition party, the leaders, its parliamentary groups in the two Houses of Parliament, and the party president, and intended to prepare a common political strategy for next day's cabinet meeting. In order to provide some 'positive coordination' where the 'negative coordination' of mutual non-interference no longer applies, new mechanisms have developed. The Prime Minister and the Deputy Prime Minister(s)—that is, the leaders of the other coalition parties inside the cabinet—meet each Wednesday with leaders of the parliamentary groups of the coalition parties in the Second Chamber. These meetings bring together a kind of 'coalition committee' to deal with politically controversial decisions. When ministers wear their party hat instead of their departmental hat, the cabinet is operating in its political mode and delegation to individual ministers is less important because, by definition (given coalition government), not all governing parties can be in charge of all portfolios. Apart from relaxing the rule of mutual non-interference, a party might try to influence the policies of a department controlled by another party, provided that it has a junior minister (state secretary) in that department. Most, though not all, junior ministers are appointed to departments led by a minister from a different party, but in practice they rarely act as 'watchdogs'. When portfolios are distributed, it is usually the case that each party is given a minister in each of the main policy areas (socio-economic, foreign affairs, culture, and education, etc.).

In the ideal-type chain of delegation, delegation is from the cabinet to individual ministers, and it is from this perspective that we have discussed cabinet decision-making. However, it is an empirical question whether this is always the direction in which delegation takes place. The cabinet is not only a body with a set of institutional rules that prescribe how ministers should execute and implement its decisions. In a looser sense, the cabinet is also an arena in which individual ministers act as delegates of their department and of their party. From our description of the cabinet as a political coalition it is clear that the parties are the principals, and that the ministers take on the role of party agents.

The importance of this for cabinet outcomes has increased since the 1960s. Perhaps less obvious is the fact that ministers quite often 'go native' and become departmental ambassadors to the cabinet. Especially new ministers are often targets of such attempts by high-ranking department officials who seek to co-opt them. This brings us to the question of the relationship between ministers and their departmental organizations.

DELEGATION FROM MINISTERS TO CIVIL SERVANTS

Ministerial Responsibility, Civil Service Loyalty, and their Limits

The relationship between ministers and the administrators in their departments is probably the purest case of delegation in the whole chain from voters to policy implementation. Ministers are responsible for all public-policy related activities of their civil servants', including decisions involving the use of discretionary power. Civil servants are supposed to be loyal to their minister. This rule of loyalty is considered to be so self-evident that explicit arrangements for the public accountability of civil servants to their ministers do not exist.

The civil service is organized along functional departmental lines. Formal internal departmental structures are hierarchical in accordance with the classical Weberian model. Departments are not staffed by a minister's political affiliates, and in general recruitment of department officials is based on expertise in the department's policy area or in more general management practices. There have been efforts to rotate top civil servants among departments increasingly in order to avoid over-compartmentalization in the administrative management of departments.

Some civil servants have powers granted to them directly by law. Tax inspectors, for example, can determine an individual citizen's tax liability, just as university professors determine students' grades without ministerial interference. Much more important, however, are the powers delegated to civil servants by their department minister. For example, every year Justice Department officials, acting on behalf of the Minister of Justice, make some 30,000 decisions regarding the naturalization of immigrants. Over 600,000 decrees setting student scholarships are issued on behalf of the Minister of Education (Scheltema Commission 1993: 36). These ministers may provide civil servants with decision-making guidelines, but they are rarely cognizant of specific decisions, despite the fact that they are fully responsible for each and every one of them.

Dutch ministers have few control instruments, despite the fact that they must, of necessity, delegate considerable authority. It is physically impossible for a minister to actually monitor the behaviour of his/her numerous departmental civil servants. There is considerably more continuity in the civil service than in cabinet, even though Dutch cabinets are relatively stable (on average they remain in office for about three years), and ministerial careers may continue beyond a particular cabinet (the average ministerial career lasts almost four years; see Bakema 1991: 93). Furthermore, departmental decisions often require a level of technical expertise that most ministers do not have. None of this is necessarily peculiar to the Netherlands, but it seems to be more pronounced here than in most other countries. Civil servants are highly specialized (and are recruited on this basis), and in most cases they spend their entire career within a single department. The asymmetry in expertise between ministers and their departmental staffs might be limited by the fact that Dutch ministers are also recruited in part on the basis of policy-specific expertise (recall that ministers can be recruited from outside Parliament). Another factor that may limit the expertise asymmetry is that Dutch ministers are often single post ministers (within Europe only Austrian ministers are less mobile across departments; see Bakema 1991: 90). In practice, however, a minister's relevant expertise seems to be less useful in helping him/her control the department, and more useful to top civil servants seeking to co-opt the minister. That is, it seems to increase the likelihood that the minister will become an ambassador for the department. This leads to a paradox about the 'weakness' and 'strength' of ministers. Even if departmental civil servants want a minister who is susceptible to their policy beliefs and can be influenced, at the same time they prefer a 'strong' ambassador who can get things done in cabinet.

Departments are completely staffed by career civil servants. There are no party political appointments or ministerial *cabinets*. When top civil service positions are vacant, party allegiance does matter. However, the pervasive rule of proportionality among the main political parties prevents a minister from exclusively appointing party friends. As of 2003, only Deputy Prime Ministers have a small personal *cabinet*. However, it is supposed to focus on external activities (to help coordinate their party's ministers), rather than to monitor the department to ensure that it is faithfully carrying out ministerial policy. Ordinary ministers are allowed to hire a political adviser, but if they do so the adviser's job is primarily to serve as a liaison with the party or with Parliament. In short, ministers—including the Prime Minister—have no source of regular, policy-specific advice and support other than their departmental officials.

All of what has been reported here about the nature of decisions, required level of policy expertise, broad ministerial responsibility, and limited instruments of control, is fuel for the argument that ministerial responsibility is a fiction. In fact, there have been proposals to limit ministerial responsibility by introducing the criterion of reproachability. This means that Parliament should only hold a minister responsible (and censure him/her) when she/he is actually at fault, that is, when a policy failure is due to the minister's own policy guidelines, or to his neglect of departmental management. Opponents of such a 'narrow' interpretation of ministerial responsibility have pointed out that this would create situations in which civil servants are accountable to no one.

The practical 'solution' for reducing the gap between the fiction of full ministerial responsibility and the reality of civil servants' discretion was to transfer responsibility for some public tasks from departments to other (semi-public) organizations. The proposal intended to create so-called 'core departments' of a size more amenable to ministerial supervision (Wiegel Commission 1993). These core departments were to be formed by decentralizing tasks (transferring from central to provincial and municipal governments), by privatization, and by splitting off parts of departments to create new, quasi non-governmental organizations (quangos). While there are examples of all three strategies, their overall importance should not be overestimated.

EXTERNAL CONSTRAINTS

The institutional factors affecting the democratic chain of delegation and accountability that have been discussed so far are internal to the delegation process, such as political parties or the structure of the civil service. There are also 'constraints' or institutional factors relevant to delegation, which are external to the formal chain of delegation. While there is a whole range of possible and more or less stable external influences on delegation and accountability, we will limit this discussion to those influences mentioned in the introductory chapter which have immediate relevance in The Netherlands.

Representative Democracy and the Referendum

In June 1997, a parliamentary majority voted in favour of a proposal to change the Constitution to make it possible to hold referendums at the national and local level. The proposal was a response to demands for more popular involvement in policy-making, and it has been much debated because the established parliamentary parties (PvdA, CDA, and especially the VVD) see it as a threat to their role as intermediary organizations. This explains why the proposed amendment involves the introduction of a corrective referendum (cf. Andeweg 1997a). Of all types of referendum this is the one least likely to thwart the chain of delegation and accountability. In a corrective referendum the influence of voters is essentially negative (it is also known as the popular veto). Citizens cannot propose legislation, but they can block the promulgation of legislation that has been approved by Parliament. The emphasis of a corrective referendum is thus on *ex post* control over the whole chain. It involves accountability rather than delegation. The proposal was narrowly defeated in its second reading in the First Chamber, in May 1999, which caused a cabinet crisis. The crisis was resolved when the coalition parties agreed to introduce the corrective referendum without changing the Constitution (this bypassing the need for a qualified majority). This means that the outcome of referendums will not be binding formally, although it would seem unlikely that Parliament will ignore the outcome if all the high thresholds for calling a referendum are passed.

The Judiciary

A fundamental principle of the *Rechtsstaat* is that the judiciary remains outside the formal chain of delegation and accountability, or at least outside that part of the chain in which relationships are political. Looked at this way, the courts are a constraint by virtue of their authority to judge the legality and constitutionality of government decrees and actions in court cases. Legislation approved by Parliament is not subject to judicial review, not even if there have been procedural errors in the legislative process. The absence of judicial review does not remove the judiciary as a constraint on the delegation process, as so much of government policy is laid down in decrees rather than laws (see Van Koppen and Van Kate 1994). In addition to the 'ordinary' judiciary, the Council of State acts as the highest administrative court. In practice, the administrative courts deal primarily with the implementation of government policy, which is often the task of subnational governments. They are therefore less important as a constraint on delegation and accountability at the national level.

European Union, Delegation, and National Accountability

To what extent are Dutch ministers who participate in the European Council of Ministers agents of the national Parliament (as distinct from the European Parliament)? To what extent are these ministers accountable to the special parliamentary committee, the European Affairs Committee? These questions are really about whether an important and, in part, external supranational actor—the European Union—can be controlled by national political actors. Our focus here is on a new national institutional arrangement, the European Affairs Committee.

The European Affairs Committee was created in 1986 (see Van Schendelen 1995). Its main function is to facilitate the provision of information on European policy-making to the Second Chamber. As is true for other parliamentary committees, the European Affairs Committee can submit issues to Parliament for plenary debate. Parliamentary committees can propose amendments to bills, though this authority is much less relevant to the European Affairs committee, given its focus on supranational regulation and its national consequences. The European Union Treaty (1993) gives both Houses of Parliament the right to vote on draft decisions on Third Pillar matters which are under consideration by the EU Council of Ministers and which, if adopted, are directly binding on member states. With regard to the European Affairs Committee's authority to control the government's EU policy, the instruments available to it are the same as those available to the Parliament at large. In practice, these control instruments are used as cautiously with regard to European policy issues as they are for any other policy area.

To relate this discussion to the broader issue of delegation to EU and national control, it should be said that in practice delegation and control are only marginally affected by the activities of the European Affairs Committee, or by the actions of any other public institution involved in the European legislative process. In addition to this well-known 'democratic deficit', an 'implementation gap' is seen to exist (Richardson 1996). This is because the scale and magnitude of delegation gives appreciable discretion to national actors charged with implementation of EU directives.

CONCLUSION

To the extent that the ideal-type chain of delegation is a normative model, it should perhaps be thought of as a cycle, in which the policy output of the system of representative government is evaluated by voters. If the ideal-type model starts with voters, it should thus also end with voters. In the idea of democratic delegation and accountability, elections are prominent features. It is through elections that politicians are held accountable by the voters on the basis of their judgements about the extent to which their policy preferences have been followed, misunderstood, or ignored since the last election. To the extent that many voters consider the government to have misunderstood or ignored their preferences, voters can be said to have experienced agency loss.

Although this can and often does occur within the administrative sphere as well, in the Dutch case it is the politicians who are held accountable, at least once every four years. We conclude our contribution by highlighting the most important deviations from this ideal–type chain or cycle of delegation and accountability in the Netherlands.

The most striking deviation concerns the interposition of political parties as key actors in the chain. The various roles of parties cut across the formal chain at several points (voters–MPs, MPs–cabinet, cabinet–ministers, sometimes ministers–civil servants as well). Parties may even be seen as political actors in broader policy coalitions that extend beyond the formal political bodies in parliamentary democracy. All these actual roles and linkages involving parties are sometimes seen as harmful to the ideal type, as for example, in Lord Bryce's *cri de coeur* about the 'Decline of Parliament'. However, a good argument can be made that parties have not usurped power, but rather have saved the parliamentary system of government. In institutional terms, it is not true that parties constrain the operation of the chain of delegation; in fact, they facilitate the operation of the system of representative democracy. Indeed, they have been key actors in the creation of the system, for example, by pressing for universal electoral suffrage, which was granted in 1919. The ideal-type relationship between voters and individual MPs probably would not have survived the shift to a mass electorate, and for this reason the responsible party model is perhaps more appropriate as a point of departure for studying modern parliamentary democracy.

Second, the empirical picture not only differs from the norm; it is also considerably more complex than the ideal type. This complexity creates its own delegation problems and forms of agency loss. Arrows in the empirical chain or cycle do not point unambiguously in one direction, and the scheme contains numerous loops reaching beyond the constitutional system. The main reason for this deviation from the ideal type is that, in practice, the various elements within the chain are not only institutions but also arenas in which struggles for power and policy take place. This is most clearly the case with regard to Parliament and cabinet, where incumbents are constrained not only by these bodies' institutional rules, but also by the institutional rules of other organizations, such as parties and departments, which also see these incumbents as agents. For example, ministers not only represent the cabinet in Parliament, they also represent their departments and their parties within the cabinet.

This complexity is not only a matter of level of analysis and conceptual confusion; it is a real problem for parliamentary democracy insofar as delegation 'down' the chain (starting with voters) has no monopoly. Signals from the opposite direction may jam signals from the citizens as initial principals. Parliamentary democracy seems to allow only for input into the system, not for 'withinput'. Even the validity of inputs from citizens is problematic in the Dutch case. The crucial normative feedback loop in which policies and politicians are subject to the judgement of voters is often obfuscated. The outstanding example of this is the weak relationship between electoral shifts and the subsequent results of the government formation process, in which parties winning parliamentary seats often fail to obtain a seat at the cabinet table.

Coalition politics also creates ambiguity in the relationship between Parliament as principal and the cabinet as the agent, and this manifests itself through the practice of formulating and enforcing coalition agreements. Ostensibly, Dutch cabinets are bound by the comprehensive and detailed coalition agreements drafted and adopted by the parliamentary groups. In this case, the governing majority in the Second Chamber, and not the Second Chamber as a body, acts as the principal. In fact, the informal character of policy negotiations during cabinet formations seriously limits the potential of Parliament to function as a genuine principal with regard to major policy issues. But even if parliamentary groups are very important actors in coalition formation negotiations, the commitments they make also tie their own hands, or at the very least limit the possibility that they can take initiatives on politically sensitive issues once the cabinet is in office. Indeed, on such matters the rules of the game related to coalition agreements prevent individual coalition parties in Parliament from forming ad hoc legislative coalitions with non-coalition parties. At the same time, coalition agreements often leave appreciable discretion to ministers on matters below the sphere of high coalition politics. Particularly with regard to departmental matters, information asymmetries between cabinet and Parliament (or between individual ministers and MPs) exist and hidden action occurs. On such matters, parties in Parliament (perhaps with the exception of small and impotent opposition parties) are not inclined to complicate the lives of ministers by making hidden actions public.

All this led to demands for more direct democracy in the 1960s and 1970s. Today, this same problem has led to renewed demands for procedures that bypass the chain of delegation and establish direct links between citizens and policies. This is to be accomplished by introducing judicial review, through the introduction of a referendum (see the previous section on External Constraints), and by creating new accountability arrangements that give people a voice in the performance of public organizations (citizens' charters, etc.). Alongside such reform suggestions, public agencies increasingly take recourse to non-legislative policy instruments, for example, covenants with private actors in specific policy areas. The possible result of these developments is not the reform of the chain of delegation running through Parliament, but a hollowing out of the parliamentary system of government.

REFERENCES

Andeweg, Rudy B. (1990). 'Tweeërlei Ministerraad; besluitvorming in Nederlandse kabinetten', in R.B. Andeweg (ed.), *Ministers en Ministerraad*. The Hague: SDU.

—— (1991). 'The Dutch Prime Minister: Not Just Chairman, Not Yet Chief?' *West European Politics*, 14(2): 116–32.

—— (1997a). 'Institutional Reform in Dutch Politics: Elected PM, Personalized PR, and Popular Veto in Comparative Perspective'. *Acta Politica*, 32: 227–57.

—— (1997b). 'Role Specialisation or Role Switching? Dutch MPs between Electorate and Executive'. *Journal of Legislative Studies*, 3(3): 110–27.

—— and Bakema, Wilma E. (1994). 'The Netherlands: Ministers and Cabinet Policy', in Michael Laver and Kenneth A. Shepsle (eds.), *Cabinet Ministers and Parliamentary Government*, Cambridge: Cambridge University Press.

Bakema, Wilma E. (1991). 'The Ministerial Career', in Jean Blondel and Jean-Louis Thiébault (eds.), *The Profession of Government Minister in Western Europe*. London: Macmillan.

Bergman, Torbjörn (1993). 'Formation Rules and Minority Governments.' *European Journal of Political Research*, 23: 55–66.

Blondel, Jean (1988). 'Cabinet Structures and Decision-Making Processes in Western Europe.' *European Journal of Political Research*, 16: 115–23.

Bovend'Ecrt, P.P.T. (1988). *Regeeraccoorden en Regeringsprograms.* 'S-Gravenhage: SDU.

De Koning Commission (1993). 'Het Bestel Bijgesteld.' *Proceedings of the Second Chamber 1992–3*, 21427, no. 36–7.

Hessing, R.C. (1985). 'Bij Voorkeur: een Onderzoek naar het gebruik van voorkeurstemmen.' *Acta Politica*, 20: 157–76.

Hillebrand, Ron (1992). *De Antichambre van het Parlement; kandidaatstelling in Nederlandse politieke partijen* (with English language summary). Leiden: DSWO Press.

Koole, Ruud A. and Leijenaar, Monique H. (1988). 'The Netherlands: The Predominance of Regionalism', in Michael Gallagher and Michael Marsh Candidate (eds.), *Selection in Comparative Perspective*. London: Sage.

Koopmans, T. (1970). 'De rol van de wetgever', in *Honderd jaar rechtsleven. Nederlandse Juristenvereniging.* Zwolle: Tjeenk Willink.

Laver, Michael and Shepsle, Kenneth A. (1996). *Making and Breaking Governments*. Cambridge: Cambridge University Press.

Luebbert, Gregory M. (1986). *Comparative Democracy. Policymaking and Governing Coalitions in Europe and Israel.* New York: Columbia University Press.

March, James G. and Olsen, Johan P. (1995). *Democratic Governance*. New York: Free Press.

Müller, Wolfgang C. and Strøm, Kaare (eds.) (2000). *Coalition Governments in Western Europe*. Oxford: Oxford University Press.

Nijpels, E. T. M. (1984). 'Over monisme als strategie'. *Liberaal Reveil*, 15: 4–7.

Peterson, Robert L., De Ridder, Martine M., Hobbs, J. D., and McClellan, U. F. (1983). 'Government Formation and Policy Formulation in Belgium and the Netherlands'. *Res Publica*, 18: 49–82.

Richardson, Jeremy (1996). 'Eroding EU policies: Implementation Gaps, Cheating and Re-steering', in Jeremy Richardson (ed.), *European Union: Power and Policy-Making*. London: Routledge.

Scheltema Commission (1993). 'Steekhoudend Ministerschap; betekenis en toepassing van de ministeriele verantwoordelijkheid'. *Proceedings of the Second Chamber 1992–3*, 21427, no. 40–1.

Shepsle, Kenneth A. (1996) 'Political Deals in Institutional Settings', in Robert A. Goodin (ed.), *The Theory of Institutional Dessign*. Cambridge: Cambridge University Press.

Strøm, Kaare, Budge, Ian, and Laver, Michael, J. (1994). 'Constraints on Cabinet Formation in Parliamentary Democracies'. *American Journal of Political Science*, 38: 303–35.

Thomassen, Jacques J. A. (1994). 'Empirical Research into Political Representation: Failing Democracy or Failing Models?', in M. K. Jennings and T. E. Mann (eds.), *Elections at Home and Abroad. Essays in Honor of Warren E. Miller*. Ann Arbor: University of Michigan Press.

Timmermans, Arco (1991). 'Königreich der Niederlande', in Winfried Steffani (ed.), *Regierungsmehrheit und Opposition in den Staaten der EG*. Opladen: Leske+Budrich.

—— (1998). 'Policy Conflicts, Agreements, and Coalition Governance'. *Acta Politica*, 33: 409–32.

—— (2003). *High Politics in the Low Countries*. Aldershot: Ashgate.

—— and Andeweg, Rudy, B. (2000). 'The Netherlands: Still the Politics of Accomodation?', in Wolfgang C. Müller and Kaare Strøm (eds.), *Coalition Governments in Western Europe*. Oxford: Oxford University Press.

Toirkens, José (1988). *Schijn en werkelijkheid van het bezuinigingsbeleid 1975–86*. Alphen aan den Rijn: Tjeenk Willink.

Van Koppen, P. J. and Van Kate, J. (1994). 'Judicialisation of Politics in the Netherlands. Towards a Form of Judicial Review'. *International Political Science Review*, 15: 143–53.

Van Raalte, E. (1977). *Het Nederlandse Parlement*. 'S-Gravenhage: SDU'.

Van Schendelen, M. P. C. M. (1995). 'From Founding Father to Mounding Baby'. *Journal of Legislative Studies*, 1: 60–74.

Wiegel Commission (1993). 'Naar Kerndepartementen; kiezen voor een hoogwaardige en flexibele rijksdienst'. *Proceedings of the Second Chamber 1992–3*, 21427, no. 51–2.

17

Norway: Virtual Parliamentarism

KAARE STRØM AND HANNE MARTHE NARUD

INTRODUCTION

Norway is an old and stable democracy, but not originally a parliamentary one. The Norwegian Constitution of 1814 is currently the oldest living codified constitution in Europe and indeed second only to that of the United States in the democratic world. Contrary to Denmark and Sweden, Norway has not in recent decades fundamentally overhauled and updated its Constitution. Consequently, it is silent on many aspects of modern governance (such as the role of political parties), and on other issues there are major discrepancies between formal constitutional provisions and contemporary practice. The 1814 Constitution was a separation-of-powers construction, under which considerable powers were vested in the monarch. Contrary to the intentions of the founding fathers, however, the Head of State in practice became occupied by the dual monarchy of Sweden and Norway. Hence from the 1870s on, liberals became increasingly vociferous in their demands for cabinet accountability to the *Storting* (the Parliament). In 1884, they through impeachment forced this reform upon a recalcitrant cabinet of conservatives loyal to the king. Under such duress, the conservatives gradually accepted the realities of parliamentary government. Thus, although Norwegian democracy has in practice been parliamentary since 1884 or shortly thereafter,[1] the written Constitution gives scant recognition to this practice. It is important to note, however, that long-standing practice has given parliamentary government the status of a constitutional convention (*sedvanerett*). The most controversial political reform of the nineteenth century thus became a non-issue in the twentieth.

Although parliamentarism is not well entrenched in the formal Constitution, Norway does conform to most key features of parliamentary government. During the struggle over parliamentary government, the battle cry of Johan Sverdrup and his Liberal Party was 'all power in this assembly', meaning the Storting. Although the Liberals may not have realized their goal in full, they have come far in terms of the

We are grateful to Bjørn Erik Rasch, Eivind Smith, Lars Svåsand, Henry Valen, and the co-editors for valuable information and comments.

[1] Nordby (2000) claims that the Conservatives did not fully accept the principles of parliamentary government until 1905.

formal distribution of authority in Norway, which places few and relatively weak constraints on the parliamentary majority.

Under the Norwegian Constitution, all legislative authority is exercised by the people through Parliament (Article 49). The same constitutional article specifies that the Storting consists of two divisions: the *Odelsting*, with three-quarters of the total number of members, and the *Lagting*, with one-quarter. These two divisions of the Storting are not truly independent chambers, since they are jointly elected. The assignment of individual representatives to the Odelsting or Lagting occurs when the Parliament first convenes after an election, on the first weekday in October. The members of the Lagting are then elected by the parliamentarians at large, and the remaining members assigned to the Odelsting. In reality, party leaders negotiate the membership of the two divisions, and since the advent of parliamentary government interparty proportionality has prevailed. Thus, the parties' relative strength in the two divisions is effectively identical, and the majorities in the two divisions very rarely diverge. The division of the Storting into two quasi-chambers thus has virtually no consequence for legislation. Note also that the Storting is so divided only when it deliberates on non-financial bills.

Bills can be introduced by any member of the Odelsting, and there is no requirement of a second sponsor. In reality, however, government bills, known as propositions (*proposisjoner*), dominate the legislative agenda. Non-financial bills must be approved by the Odelsting and the Lagting separately by a simple majority of those present and voting. If the Lagting twice fails to approve the bill adopted by the Odelsting, the bill goes to a plenary session, which must pass the bill by a two-thirds majority (Article 76). After legislation has successfully passed the Storting, it is signed by the King and Prime Minister in a formal cabinet meeting (Article 78). The Constitution thus technically gives the King and the Prime Minister *ex post* veto power. However, parliamentarism has made this power a pure formality. The volume of Storting legislation has gradually increased. At the end of the nineteenth century, it passed an average of twenty laws per year. This has after Second World War grown to about ninety. Between 1989 and 1994, it ranged from 76 in 1989–90 to 155 in 1992–3 (Østbø 1995: 88).

Budgetary bills are decided by the Storting in plenary sessions. The budget proposal (*Stortingsproposisjon* No. 1) is always the first bill introduced by the government when the annual Storting convenes in October. Since 1961, the budget year begins in January and thus coincides with the calendar year, and budget deliberations therefore dominate the fall session of the Storting.

Constitutional amendments must be introduced during one of the first three years of a legislative term and then be adopted in one of the first three years of the subsequent parliamentary term. Thus, the voters will always be consulted between the time that a constitutional amendment is proposed and the final parliamentary vote. Ordinary constitutional amendments are considered by a plenary session of the Storting and require a two-thirds majority (Article 112). Constitutional amendments that involve a transfer of sovereignty to an international organization face an even more rigorous requirement. According to Article 93, passed in 1962 in the wake of Norway's first application for European Union (EU) (then EEC) membership, such amendments must command a three-quarters majority.

Outside the Parliament, there are few domestic constraints on the legislative policy process. A Constitution that provides for centralized government and singular institutions has proven to be conducive to parliamentary governance. Norway is a unitary state, and the constitutional status of subnational government is weak. Members of Parliament are the only national agents elected by the people. And although some constraints exist on delegation and accountability through the parliamentary chain, Norway is in practice a fairly pure case of parliamentary democracy.

Although the formal Constitution vests a number of powers in the cabinet (formally the King), much of this authority has been eroded by convention. Yet, as we will discuss below, the cabinet retains significant legislative and appointment powers. More importantly, it has strong legislative agenda powers. Moreover, in practice Parliament delegates much of its policy-making authority to executive agencies (*fullmaktslovgivning*).

At the level of the central government, two additional constraints on legislative authority need to be mentioned, although neither is particularly strong by international standards. One is the referendum mechanism. Since the Norwegian Constitution does not mention referendums, they can only be consultative. Only six national referendums have in fact been held, the most recent being the 1972 and 1994 EU membership referendums. Second, the Supreme Court has established a doctrine of judicial review, but the courts are in practice very reluctant to challenge the constitutionality of parliamentary decisions. A less constitutionally entrenched, but in practice more significant, constraint is the practice of remiss (*høring*) in legislative matters. This practice, which is embedded in ordinary legislation, provides a right for affected interests, such as government agencies, institutions, and interest organizations, to be consulted on legislative initiatives of significant concern to them.

POLITICAL PARTIES

Though political parties were not recognized by Norwegian law until well into the twentieth century, formal party organizations have existed since the 1880s, and looser parliamentary clubs began forming a couple of decades before that. The two original parties, the Liberals (*Venstre*) and the Conservatives (*Høyre*) date back to 1883, when they represented the two sides in the battle over parliamentary government. The Labour Party (*Arbeiderpartiet*) followed in 1887, reflecting the beginning of Norwegian industrialization. All other parties that currently enjoy parliamentary representation date from the twentieth century. The Centre Party (*Senterpartiet*) and the Christian People's Party (*Kristelig Folkeparti*) both broke away from the Liberals before the Second World War. The Socialist Left Party (*Sosialistisk Venstreparti*) and the Progress Party (*Fremskrittspartiet*) both formed in the wake of the destabilizing 1972 European

Community (EC) referendum, although the former built on a precursor, the Socialist People's Party (*Sosialistisk Folkeparti*), that was founded in 1961.

The party system has been defined around six dimensions of conflict, determined by economic, geographical, and cultural circumstances (see Rokkan 1967, 1970; Valen and Rokkan 1974). The class cleavage and the urban–rural divide were determined by economic conflicts in the labour market and the commodity market, respectively. A territorial cleavage between centre and periphery partly overlaps with three cultural cleavages: a socio-cultural conflict between two different versions of the Norwegian language, a moral conflict articulated by the teetotalist movement, and a religious conflict originally pitting the liberal leadership of the Lutheran state church against a revivalist lay movement. A number of cleavages have thus influenced Norwegian party politics. Although the labour market (Left–Right) conflict has in the twentieth century dominated and generated a bloc division between Socialists and non-socialists, the cleavages cross-cut in a complex and dynamic fashion.

Through the 1960s Norway had one of the most stable party systems in Western Europe. With the first EC referendum in 1972, however, Norway began to experience more party system fragmentation and volatility than at any time since the 1920s. After the early 1970s about one out of three voters changed partisanship from one election to the next, as compared to the 1960s when the corresponding figure was about one out of four (Valen and Urwin 1985). In the 1993 Storting election, individual volatility reached almost 44 per cent, a proportion that was virtually unchanged in 1997 and 2001.

Norwegian parties, both those on the Left and those on the right, traditionally had strong mass membership organizations. For many years about fifteen per cent of the electorate were dues-paying members, according to reports from party headquarters (Svåsand 1985: 49–53). In some smaller parties, particularly the Centre Party, the ratio of members to voters has at times been as high as one in three. However, national election surveys indicate that during the 1990s party membership declined to around 10–11 per cent (see also Svåsand, Strøm, and Rasch 1997). In such parties as the Labour Party and the Liberals, it had the late 1990s come closer to 5 per cent than to double digits (*Aftenposten*, 16 July 1998). According to the parties' own records, the Labour Party and the Conservatives (the two largest membership organizations) both lost about one-third of their gross membership figures between 1993 and 1999, whereas the smaller parties all suffered somewhat smaller losses.

The parties are well provided for financially. Public financing of political parties was first introduced in 1970, and has since increased greatly in volume. The largest part of these subventions goes to the national party organizations. The total volume of such aid was 8 million NOK in 1970, increasing to 21 million in 1980, and almost 59 million in 1990. By 1997, it had passed 100 million, and in 1999 it stood at close to 119 million. Only registered parties that gain at least 2.5 per cent of the national vote are favoured in the funds distributed nationally. There are also province-level and local subsidies, in total almost 100 million in 1999. The distribution of all these funds is largely proportional to the electoral support of the party. Public subsidies make up an ever-increasing share of party finances. The Labour Party, for example, in 1997 received more than 41 million NOK from the government, whereas the unions contributed around 10 million

NOK, and individual members only just over one million. Similarly, public funds accounted for 71 per cent of the Centre Party's revenue and 70 per cent of that of the Conservatives (*Aftenposten*, 16 July 1998).

Norwegian parties are critical players at most stages of the policy process. As the section on Delegation from Voters to Parliament will show, they control the selection of candidates for parliamentary office to a greater extent than in any other Nordic country. In the legislative arena, party cohesion is very high, and the same is the case in the cabinet. In coalition governments, the most serious disagreements have tended to be handled by party leaders, rather than through formal cabinet channels. It is only in the civil service that party control is significantly less prominent. Though there are frequent tales of partisan promotions at high levels of the civil service, the administration is by and large professional and non-partisan. Partisan quotas or favouritism would be considered illegitimate. During the period of social democratic dominance, Labour Party members and sympathizers gained a disproportionate share of top-level appointments in state enterprises including the Norwegian Broadcasting Corporation (NRK). With Labour's vote share declining and privatization gaining support, however, the importance of such partisan preferences seems to be decreasing. All in all, Norwegian voters have become less enamoured with their parties, but there is as of yet little evidence that the parties have suffered significant decline in their control of the democratic chain of delegation.

DELEGATION FROM VOTERS TO PARLIAMENT

The Electoral System

Delegation from voters, the ultimate principals, to their representatives in Parliament is surely one of the most exhaustively studied and debated phenomena in politics, and for good reason. Norway is no exception, as electoral reform was on the political agenda for most of the twentieth century. The rules by which Members of Parliament (the *Storting*) are selected and held accountable are embodied in legislation of different status. Some of these rules are contained in the Constitution; others are spelled out in ordinary legislation, the most important of which is the Election Law of 1 March 1985 (Overå and Dalbakk 1987; Aardal 2002).[2] Unlike most parliamentary systems, legislative terms are constitutionally fixed at four years, and there is no provision for early parliamentary dissolution. Nor does the Constitution provide any mechanism for the recall of individual representatives, or specify conditions under which a representative would lose his or her seat. Parliament does not have the right to expel its own members. There are no term limits or any mandatory retirement age, even though parties do not commonly nominate candidates who will turn seventy during the parliamentary term. Thus, the independence of the elected representatives is very strongly protected.

Three principles established by the constitutional assembly in 1814 have had a lasting effect upon the electoral system (Valen 1981, 1985; Matthews and Valen 1999). First, basic principles, such as the definition of constituencies and the apportionment of seats,

---

[2] Prior to that date, the relevant legislation was contained in separate laws concerning parliamentary elections and nominations, both of which were adopted in 1920 (Valen 1985).

were incorporated into the Constitution. Since constitutional amendments require a two-thirds parliamentary majority, this decision made reapportionment or electoral reform very difficult. Second, the constitutional assembly decided that peripheral regions should be overrepresented compared to central areas. And third, the assembly decided that urban and rural areas should vote separately, with a seat allocation in the ratio of 1:2. This latter provision, which originally favoured urban areas and gradually came to overrepresent rural ones, was abolished as late as 1952. From then on, each of the 19 provinces, including both urban and rural areas, has been a separate constituency.

Norway has since 1920 employed proportional representation (PR). Until 1952, a d'Hondt formula was used in a single-tier system with relatively small-magnitude districts. Since 1952, Norway has used a modified St. Laguë system with somewhat greater district magnitude. The total number of seats has been increased incrementally, from 150 to 155 in 1972 (effective with the 1973 elections), and to 157 in 1985. The main purpose of these increases has been to ease the under-representation of such areas of population growth as the Oslo region. Only in 1988 (effective with the 1989 elections), however, was complex districting introduced, when eight adjustment seats were created. Since then, there have been 157 first-tier seats and a pool of eight national second-tier seats.[3]

The 2002 report of an Electoral Reform Commission provided the impetus for significant institutional reform. The total number of seats was increased to 169, and the number of adjustment seats raised from eight to nineteen. The geographical apportionment of seats was removed from the Constitution and subjected to periodic adjustments based on census figures. Yet, the deliberate overrepresentation of rural areas was retained. The Commission's recommendation of personal preference voting was, however, rejected by the Storting. The reforms are effective as of the 2005 election.

As in the case of adjustment seats, the demand for greater partisan proportionality ('fairness') was the main argument when the Storting reintroduced apparentement (listeforbund) in 1985, after it had been abolished in 1949 (Matthews and Valen 1999). This reform greatly benefited the non-socialist coalition parties. Apparentement was removed again in 1988, and this time prohibited by constitutional amendment. Yet, demands for strict geographical proportionality in representation ('one person, one vote, one value') were never seriously considered until the Electoral Reform Commission of 2002.

Rules of Electoral Competition

Since Norwegian parliamentary terms are fixed, election dates are perfectly predictable, and no legislation is needed to regulate the length of parliamentary election campaigns. Nor are there many other explicit regulations concerning electoral competition. Though political parties enjoy generous public subsidies, there is no official regulation of campaign spending. Nor is there any provision of free broadcasting time to the parties. Since commercial television is relatively new in Norway, paid TV advertisements

---

[3] Supplementary seats, allocated to parties which are under-represented on the basis of constituency representation, are given to provinces in which the respective parties have the highest remainders (in raw numbers) of 'unused' votes. The highest remainders tend to be found in large and under-represented constituencies.

have only recently become an issue. The debate on this topic was triggered by a 1997 election campaign incident in which the Progress Party attempted to purchase such time on Norway's premier commercial television channel, TV2. The consumers' ombudsman intervened and stopped the advertising, but the Market Council later reversed this decision, creating a situation of legal ambiguity. Hence, in July 1999 the Storting passed a new law permitting political advertising on radio but not on television. Previously, the political parties were not allowed to advertise in any of the broadcast media, the main argument being that it would favour the most resourceful parties and groups. Those in favour of political advertising, on the other hand, pointed to the fact that such advertising was already allowed in the print media as well as on the internet.

Another issue that has only recently been regulated is campaign polling. Until 1994, the only restrictions on polling and the publication of poll results were unofficial gentlemen's agreements between the parties and the polling organizations. Before the 1994 EU membership referendum, however, Parliament banned the publication before the polls were closed of surveys conducted on election day. In addition, restrictions were introduced on exit polling, as no voter surveys or interviews were permitted inside the polling station or in its immediate surroundings. From 1995 on, these restrictions have been applied to ordinary local and national elections as well.

Rules of Candidate Selection

Norwegian election law regulates the nomination of candidates in the nineteen constituencies. Slates of candidates presented in each district must contain at least as many candidates as there are seats to be filled in the constituency, and the deadline for submission is July 1 in the year of the election (which are invariably held in September). Registered parties have the right to present slates in any constituency.[4] Groups that are not registered parties need the signatures of at least 500 eligible voters within the constituency (province) in question (Overå and Dalbakk 1987). The candidates on each list are ranked in the order in which their party wishes to see them elected. The voters are permitted to change the list by crossing out the name of one or more of the nominated candidates, but in practice, such changes have no impact on the final result, since such a large number of voters have to make the same move in order to overrule the default ranking. In fact, the voters have never successfully changed the rank ordering of any party in a Storting election (Valen 1988: 211).

Until 2002, the election law required electoral lists to be decided by party conventions in each constituency. These decisions could not be overruled by public authorities or by national party bodies. However, the conventions could submit the list to a referendum among party members, in which case the result of the referendum would be final. Such a referendum, however, has never been held (Valen 1988: 212). Likewise, voter or member primary elections have never been employed.

---

[4] In order to be registered, a party must submit a petition signed by at least 3,000 eligible voters, who need not, however, be party members. A party's registration lapses if it does not present candidates in any constituency in two successive elections (Overå and Dalbakk 1987).

The law gave all parties monetary incentives to select their candidates in each constituency (province) by conventions of delegates elected by the parties' dues-paying members in the province's subdivisions. These nomination procedures were not mandatory, but if the party used them, the national government would fund the provincial conventions. In general, the parties tended to follow the law, except in Oslo, where distances are so small that expenses for nomination meetings are negligible (Valen 1988: 212; Valen *et al.* 2002).

The organizational procedures for candidate selection do not differ much from one party to the next. In each locality the delegates are elected by majority vote. These meetings normally take place 6–9 months before the election. In all parties the typical nomination committee asks incumbents whether they are available for renomination, though in recent years it has become more common for interested incumbents to be turned down for renomination (see below). Normally the first draft of the nomination committee's list is sent out to the local branches for comments. All parties report that local organizations carry a great deal of weight when the committees draw up their lists (Valen 1988: 213; Valen *et al.* 2002). Although it is difficult to identify the precise party arena in which the key decisions are made, it is clear that the candidate selection process in Norway is decentralized. As Valen (1988: 228; Valen *et al.* 2002) points out, the process is not one of oligarchic selection directed from the top of the political parties. Rather, the ultimate decision lies with the constituency party organizations.

Consequences: Party Government?

There is ample evidence of *ex ante* screening of candidates for the Norwegian Parliament, and political parties play a critical role in this process. Successful independents are very rare; in fact, since the Second World War only two candidates not affiliated with the established parties have been elected to the Storting.[5] Screening devices are largely similar across parties. Only dues-paying party members are allowed to participate in candidate selection meetings. Of these, only one out of three actually do.

As in most parties in other countries (Ranney 1981), incumbency is an important criterion for reselection in all parties. So is service in local government, which traditionally has been an important credential for Norwegian parliamentarians. Among representatives serving between 1945 and 1985, 58 per cent had prior experience from local government, and 30 per cent had indeed been mayors of their respective municipalities. Over time, the proportion of local councillors has increased (to 85 per cent for the 1981–85 term), whereas the percentage of mayors has decreased (Eliassen 1985: 123). Norwegian parties also attain a high degree of social representativeness, reflected traditionally in a comparatively high

---

[5] The independents are Anders Aune and Steinar Bastesen. Aune was in 1989 elected as a representative of a local non-partisan slate (*Folkeaksjonen Fremtid for Finnmark*) in the province of Finnmark. He did not run for re-election in 1993. Bastesen, a controversial and outspoken whaling captain, was elected from Nordland on the slate of the Coastal People's Party (*Kystpartiet*) in 1997 and re-elected in 2001. Interestingly, both independents have been elected from northern provinces, a fact that may reflect a peripheral protest vote.

proportion of working-class parliamentarians and, during the 1990s, in a representation of women that approaches 40 per cent (Raaum 1995; Skjeie 1997).

A Nordic study from the late 1990s indicates that the predominant long-term trend has been the replacement of farmers and blue-collar workers with career politicians. In 1996 only 10 per cent of Norwegian MPs came from blue-collar occupations, whereas almost 80 per cent had a white-collar career and only 5 per cent a farming background (Narud and Valen 2000: 88). In addition, the legislature has been intellectually professionalized, expressed through the increased level of education among the representatives. In the period from 1945 to 1961, 34 per cent of the MPs had a higher education, a percentage that between 1961 and 1985 increased to 46 (Eliassen and Pedersen 1978; Eliassen 1985:120). In 1996 the proportion of MPs with higher education had reached 63 per cent, as compared to only 23 per cent of the electorate (Narud and Valen 2000: 88). Public sector employees and party functionaries have become increasingly over-represented. Whereas about two-thirds of the Norwegian labour force belong to the private sector, only about one-third of the parliamentarians are drawn from this sector. Variations exist, however, between the parties. The proportions of blue-collar workers and women are higher in the Socialist parties than in the non-socialist ones, and the former parties also recruit proportionately more MPs from the public sector. Overall, the recruitment patterns of the parties are what we might expect from their ideologies and platforms (Narud and Valen 2000: 90–1).

Party dominance and the absence of preference voting, primary elections, or recall mechanisms give ordinary citizens very limited opportunities to affect candidate selection, or to sanction representatives once they have been elected. Parties, on the other hand, are in a strong position to control their representatives, since ballot access is so much under their control. To the extent that delegation is to work, therefore, political parties must be its primary vehicles. Does delegation from voters to parliamentarians actually work? One indicator might be the willingness of the voters to re-elect those representatives that run for re-election. Here, the record has traditionally been quite favourable for Norwegian politicians. Their major obstacle has been getting their party's nod, and most party organizations have let interested parliamentarians accumulate up to three or four (four-year) terms of seniority. However, the picture has changed somewhat. Legislative turnover has increased since the early 1970s. Elections of particularly high turnover have coincided with periods of high electoral volatility and corresponding changes in the partisan vote shares (Narud 1998; Matthews and Valen 1999). Notable examples are the elections from 1969–77 and 1989–93, which were strongly influenced by the EU membership debate. Yet, since 1977 retirements for 'natural reasons' (i.e. death, illness, or old age) have become less common, whereas the number of 'other' retirements (e.g. voluntarily retirement or deselection) has increased. Tellingly, in the run-up to the 1997 elections, several leading parliamentarians, including the parliamentary leader of the Conservative Party, were either deselected or given less favourable ballot placements than they had previously enjoyed.

On the other hand, the political trust and satisfaction reported by Norwegian voters suggests that delegation has long worked quite well. In the 1985 election survey,

89 per cent of Norwegian respondents claimed to be satisfied or very satisfied with the way democracy worked in their country. In a similar 1984 Eurobarometer survey, the highest such proportion was 73 per cent in (West) Germany. Similarly, confidence in politicians has quite consistently been higher than in such societies as Sweden and the United States, and cynicism comparatively low (Aardal and Valen 1989: 276–81). In the mid-1980s, however, political trust began to decline markedly (Miller and Listhaug 1990; Aardal and Valen 1997: 72), only to recover in the 1990s. In a 1995 Eurobarometer survey, Norway scored second only to Denmark with a trust level of 82 per cent (Aardal _et al._ 1999).

DELEGATION FROM PARLIAMENT TO CABINET

More than a hundred years ago, Bagehot already identified executive selection as the most important function of the British Parliament (Bagehot 1963 [1867]; see also Cox 1987). This stage of delegation may be either _internal_ or _external_. In a 'pure' form of parliamentarism, the delegation from Parliament to cabinet is internal, in that only Members of Parliament may be appointed to the cabinet. In many contemporary parliamentary systems including Norway, however, this process is external, as the members of the cabinet need not, and indeed may not, simultaneously hold parliamentary seats (for a cross-national survey, see Andeweg and Nijzink 1995).

Cabinet Formation

Formally, the Norwegian Constitution gives the King wide discretion to appoint the members of the cabinet, which is still formally known as the King's Council. In practice, however, the King has exerted no influence on the composition of any cabinet since 1928, and it is questionable whether he could constitutionally exercise any such authority today.[6] In reality, when he formally calls upon someone to form a new government, the King always follows the advice of the leaders of the parliamentary parties. In practice, the choice of a Prime Minister-designate has rarely been difficult. The use of informateurs has no codified place in the Norwegian Constitution, and the practice has been rare indeed. In the postwar period, there is only one notable case.[7] If the recent trend toward party system fragmentation and coalition fluidity continues, however, it is not inconceivable that a stronger tradition of informateurship may develop.

---

[6] In 1928, King Haakon VII called upon the leader of the Labour Party, the largest party in Parliament, to form a new government. The King's decision was in accordance with established procedure, but contrary to the advice of the outgoing Prime Minister and the President of the Storting (Nordby 2000: 105). The result was the formation of the first Socialist government in Norwegian history (see Björnberg 1939). The government proved short-lived but the King's behaviour did much to solidify his support among Norwegian Social Democrats.

[7] In the difficult cabinet crisis of 1971, when a bourgeois majority coalition had just broken down over the EC issue and the Prime Minister's conduct in this area, the King formally gave the President of the Storting, Conservative Bernt Ingvaldsen, the mandate of investigating the opportunities for another non-socialist coalition. It was obvious that the role of Ingvaldsen, a senior, right-wing, and somewhat formal member of his party, was purely that of an informateur. At any rate, his efforts failed for no fault of his own, and the informateur institution has never again been used.

Because of the absence of formal rules and mechanisms, Norwegian government formation is best described as 'free-style bargaining'. The most obviously important procedural rule is what Bergman (1993) calls 'negative parliamentarism', that is, the rule that governments can be invested and sustained as long as there is no explicit majority vote of opposition in Parliament. Norwegian parliamentary procedure contains several more or less formal rules that contribute to this practice: (1) There is no formal vote of investiture, and governments are assumed to have the confidence of the Storting until the opposite has been demonstrated. (2) The Prime Minister is neither formally nor by convention expected to hand in his (or her) resignation at the end of a parliamentary term or on any other formal occasion (e.g. the accession to the throne of a new King). (3) Moreover, the prevailing interpretation of confidence and no-confidence votes is permissive and allows the cabinet to remain in office under circumstances in which it might otherwise have to resign (see below).

The Cabinet Record

The fluidity and informality of the Norwegian Constitution has a permissive impact on coalition bargaining. Specifically, it has favoured the formation of numerically weak governments. Norway is one of the world's leaders in the frequency of minority governments, especially from the 1970s onwards (Strøm 1990). Prior to 1961, the Labour Party dominated Norwegian elections, and the country experienced stable, single-party, majority governments. The 1961 election, however, deprived the Labour Party of a parliamentary majority, which it has never again recaptured. After that watershed, Norwegian cabinets have more often than not been 'undersized', and coalitions have been less common than single-party cabinets. Moreover, in most cases in which (non-socialist) coalitions *have* formed, the coalition-building process has stopped short of a majority. Even in these cases, then, some 'coalition avoidance' has taken place. While this record no doubt has multiple causes, part of the explanation surely lies in the permissive institutional rules concerning government formation and confidence.

From the first postwar election in 1945 through to the end of 1999, there were twenty-six cabinets: eighteen single-party administrations and eight coalitions. Nine cabinets included parties that collectively controlled a majority of the seats in the Storting, whereas seventeen were minority cabinets. Most of these relied on ad hoc parliamentary support; only one (Willoch I 1981–3) had stable and prenegotiated support from two parties ostensibly in the parliamentary opposition, namely the Christian People's Party and the Centre Party.

While the composition and size of Norwegian governments have changed substantially over the postwar period, other patterns of cabinet formation have remained stable. There has been no peacetime coalition between Socialist and non-socialist parties. In fact, the Norwegian Labour Party is the only major social democratic party in Western Europe that has never entered a cabinet coalition with any bourgeois party. Labour has eschewed coalitions not only with non-socialist parties, but also with the smaller parties to its left. In several campaigns, the Labour Party has indeed made a campaign issue out of its resistance to coalition politics (reminiscent of the historical 'anti-coalition' stance of the Irish Fianna Fáil). Thus, a Socialist government has since 1961 meant a Labour minority cabinet. Non-socialist cabinets, on the other hand, have with one exception (Willoch I [1981–3], a purely Conservative administration) been coalitions of at least three parties (Rommetvedt 1984). Yet many coalitions, including all since 1985, have been minority cabinets.

Confidence and No-Confidence Votes

The no-confidence mechanism has evolved in Norway by convention. The right of the parliamentary majority to dismiss the cabinet has been recognized since the constitutional crisis of 1884. No-confidence motions may be brought against individual ministers or against the cabinet collectively. The precise wording used in motions of no confidence always include a statement that 'the government does not enjoy the confidence of the Storting'. Statements to the effect that Parliament 'regrets' some executive action are also commonly taken to signal no confidence (Hansen and Mo 1994: 118). No-confidence motions can be introduced by any member and need no second sponsor. They are voted upon in plenary sessions. There are no restrictions on the number of such motions or on the time when they can be presented. To be adopted, no-confidence motions need a simple majority (50 per cent + 1) of those present and voting. Members who are present in the chamber are not permitted to abstain on confidence votes, or on any other parliamentary votes for that matter. A quorum must be present, and votes are recorded.

The procedures concerning confidence motions are much like those related to no-confidence votes. Confidence motions may be presented by individual ministers, or by the Prime Minister on behalf of the cabinet as a whole. As in the former case, there are few specific regulations in the parliamentary standing orders. Since 1905, however, the constitutional convention has evolved that individual ministers or cabinets that lose confidence votes are required to resign (Hansen and Mo 1994: 118; Nordby 2000). While Norwegian governments must therefore resign if a parliamentary majority adopts an unambiguous motion of no confidence, it may choose to stay in office in case of a 'negative majority.' That is to say, if two or more different motions of no confidence collectively gain the votes of a parliamentary majority, but no single motion has majority support, the government may choose to resign but is under no obligation to do so (Stavang 1968, 1971; Hansen and Mo 1994: 118–9). Thus, although the formal Constitution recognizes no such rule, the government may in practice choose to interpret its relationship to the Storting as governed by a 'constructive' vote of no confidence.

The government is not expected to hand in its resignation in the event of a parliamentary defeat, unless the bill has been made the subject of a motion of confidence or no confidence. Even defeats on major legislative initiatives (e.g. parts of the budget) need not lead to the cabinet's resignation, and over time Norwegian governments (especially minority cabinets) have tolerated more and more parliamentary defeats. Interestingly, the Brundtland cabinets of the 1990s (1990–6) suffered parliamentary defeats with increasing regularity (Rommetvedt 1996), while at the same time Labour government became steadily more, rather than less, entrenched.

Motions of confidence or no confidence are by no means exceptional. Between 1945 and 2000, more than fifty no-confidence motions were introduced, as were sixteen motions of confidence (see Table 17.1). However, on only one of the former occasions did the motion of no confidence actually succeeded and the government resign. That was the case of Gerhardsen VI, which was defeated by a coalition of all the other parliamentary parties (seventy-six votes to seventy-four) on a no-confidence motion introduced in the wake of the Kings Bay tragedy. The occasion was that the government had withheld from Parliament information concerning a fatal accident, to which negligent safety precautions had contributed, in a government-operated coalmine in Spitsbergen (Karmly 1975). There has been no case in which a cabinet has resigned in anticipation of a defeat on a no-confidence vote. Two cabinets have resigned after losing confidence votes: Lyng in 1963 and Willoch III in 1986. Lyng, who came to power without a parliamentary majority upon Gerhardsen's resignation, deliberately provoked his own immediate defeat by requesting a vote of confidence on his budget (Strøm 1990: 223). Willoch was defeated when he attached a confidence motion to his attempt to raise gasoline taxes to meet a drastic shortfall in government revenue following the collapse of world oil prices in 1986. His proposal was voted down by a coalition of the Socialist opposition and the Progress Party.

In general, the use of no-confidence motions has been somewhat cyclical. The Kings Bay vote was the eighteenth after 1945. Fourteen of these came prior to 1961, when the Labour Party enjoyed a parliamentary majority and there was virtually no chance that a no-confidence motion would be adopted. During the 10 years that followed Kings Bay, on the other hand, there were very few no-confidence votes, but their incidence increased substantially after the Socialist Left and the Progress Party gained parliamentary representation in 1973. Brundtland's (minority) cabinets between 1986 and 1996 attracted a relatively large number of such motions, thirteen in total.

Confidence motions have been much less frequent, particularly under Labour governments. Between 1945 and 1963, only two confidence motions were presented by the succession of cabinets under Gerhardsen and Torp. Non-socialist cabinets have used this procedure somewhat more liberally (e.g. Borten five times and Willoch three), but confidence votes remain a rather rare occurrence in the Norwegian Parliament. After Willoch's defeat in 1986, for example, there was no such vote until Bondevik invoked the procedure on his revised budget proposal in June 1998.

Parliamentary Oversight and Questions

Parliamentary oversight of the executive takes place through a variety of means. The most prominent of such mechanisms in the Storting are the standing committees and various forms of parliamentary questions. All matters requiring substantive Storting decisions are referred to a standing committee for scrutiny, discussion, and negotiation. Each representative is a member of one and only one standing committee with a fixed membership and jurisdiction. Under normal circumstances, members serve on the

Table 17.1. *Cabinet Formation, Cabinet Termination, and Early Parliamentary Dissolution: Norway 1945–2000* [a]

No	Cabinet	Date of formation	Investiture votes (iv) n.a.	No-confidence votes (ncv)		Cabinet resigned to pre-empt ncv	Confidence votes (cv) under specific institutional mechanism n.a.	Did the cabinet end with an early election? n.a.
				No. of ncv	Cabinet removed by ncv			
1	Gerhardsen II	45/11/05		5	No			
2	Gerhardsen III	49/10/10		0				
3	Torp I	51/11/19		1	No			
4	Torp II	53/10/12		4	No			
5	Gerhardsen IV	55/01/22		1	No			
6	Gerhardsen V	57/10/07		3	No			
7	Gerhardsen VI	61/09/11		4	Yes			
8	Lyng	63/08/28		0				
9	Gerhardsen VII	63/09/25		0				
10	Borten I	65/10/12		1	No			
11	Borten II	69/09/07		1	No			
12	Bratteli I	71/03/13		0				
13	Korvald	72/10/18		1	No			
14	Bratteli II	73/10/16		7	No			

15	Nordli I	76/01/15	1	No
16	Nordli II	77/09/11	3	No
17	Brundtland I	81/02/04	0	No
18	Willoch I	81/10/14	3	No
19	Willoch II	83/06/08	1	No
20	Willoch III	85/09/08	1	No
21	Brundtland II	86/05/09	6	No
22	Syse	89/10/16	1	No
23	Brundtland III	90/11/03	2	No
24	Brundtland IV	93/09/13	5	No
25	Jagland	96/10/25	0	No
26	Bondevik	97/10/17	—	

[a] n.d. = no data (missing data); n.a. or '—' = not applicable in this case.

same committee throughout the four-year parliamentary term,[8] and re-elected representatives often retain their committee assignments. In general terms, the jurisdictions of parliamentary committees tend to mirror those of the ministerial departments, though exceptions to this rule have become increasingly common (Rommetvedt 1996).

Each of the standing committees engages in various forms of oversight of the executive agencies under its jurisdiction. For most of the post-1945 period, the Storting has had one standing committee with more general and oversight functions. Until 1972, this was the Protocol Committee, which was a committee established as early as 1814 and authorized to read and audit cabinet minutes. Under the early separation-of-powers Constitution, this was a powerful committee, but under parliamentarism it gradually faded into obscurity. By the 1950s, members complained publicly that service on the committee gave them stomach aches (Sejersted 2000: 176). In 1972, this dreaded committee assignment was abolished and its oversight functions divided between the various other permanent committees. This reform proved to impede efforts at coordination, which in 1981 led to the establishment of another centralized oversight committee, the Control Committee, which also took over responsibility for constitutional affairs (Hansen and Mo 1994: 28–30). Yet, the fact that the members had their primary committee assignment elsewhere weakened this new committee, and in 1992 it was reorganized once again and put on a par with other committee assignments. This latest reorganization ushered in a renaissance for the Control Committee during the 1993–7 parliamentary term, when the committee vigorously scrutinized a string of executive 'scandals' (Sejersted 2000).

Parliamentary questions have long played an important role in Norwegian parliamentarism, and their importance has tended to increase over time. As Rasch notes, 'parliamentary questions are in fact used quite extensively as a means of controlling the executive. This is not because the legislators necessarily intend to control. Rather, control is realized as a by-product of behaviour motivated primarily by an attempt to reach other (less collective) aims related to—or derived from—the electoral arena' (Rasch 1994: 247–8; see also Kuhnle and Svåsand 1984). Some form of parliamentary questions have been asked in the Storting as far back as 1885 (the year after the introduction of parliamentary government), and interpellations found their way into the Rules of Procedure in 1908. A regular question time, held every Wednesday beginning at 11 a.m., was established in 1949 (Rasch 1994: 254–5).

Several other types of parliamentary questions have since evolved. For a long period of time, 'long' questions (which allowed the questioner and responding minister five minutes each) coexisted with short ones, but in 1989 the former were abolished. An October 1996 reform instituted two additional forms of parliamentary questions: a spontaneous question time (up to 1 hour in duration) and written questions to be answered in writing (Rasch 1998). The former of these allows for the most immediate and spontaneous debate between cabinet members and MPs, as the questions are not known in advance. Finally,

---

[8] Members of the Storting who are appointed to the cabinet must relinquish their seats to their respective deputies as long as they serve in the cabinet. If they return to the Storting before the end of the term, however, they are not guaranteed reassignment to the same committees on which they served before their cabinet appointments.

the Parliamentary standing orders permit representatives to raise urgent questions during the daily adjournment debate. Known as 'questions at the conclusion of the meeting', such inquiries are rare. Ordinary questions remain by far the most numerous (Rasch 1998: 9).

Outside their own ranks, members of the Storting possess more specialized vehicles of oversight, such as the Auditor General and the various parliamentary ombudsmen. The Auditor General's Office (*Riksrevisjonen*) traditionally engaged in more technical review of the government's expenditures and financial dispositions. During the 1980s, however, these audits became more comprehensive and often critical. From 1993 on, these more incisive audits were increasingly seized upon by a reformed and emboldened parliamentary Control Committee. At the same time, the Auditor General's Office began issuing separate review of particularly important and controversial government agencies. Thus, there have in recent years been strong synergies between the Storting's Control Committee and the Auditor General's Office, and their simultaneous emergence as important fora of *ex post* scrutiny of the executive branch is no mere coincidence (Sejersted 2000).

The Parliamentary Ombudsman for Civilian Affairs is an institution established in 1962 to investigate administrative abuses against ordinary citizens. The Ombudsman is a quasi-judicial institution that reports to Parliament. The Ombudsman cannot assess penalties, but does report on inappropriate practices and may propose reforms and various forms of redress. This institution has since its inception virtually displaced Parliament itself as a forum for petitions and individual casework concerning government agencies. The EOS Committee, which was established in 1995 and reports to Parliament, is a forum for the scrutiny of secret (intelligence) services. Finally, the Storting may appoint independent commissions of inquiry. Until recent years, most investigative commissions were in fact appointed by the cabinet, though often after consultation with Parliament. Since 1985, however, there have been at least four important commissions of inquiry established by the Storting itself (Sejersted 2000: 178).

Thus, there is no doubt that parliamentary scrutiny of the Norwegian executive has become more intense since the 1990s, and that it has found an increasing number of effective institutional vehicles. Compared to Denmark, Sejersted (2000: 179) argues that the Norwegian Parliament has focused less strictly and stringently on legal criteria. Instead, the Norwegian Parliament has more and more jealously defended its right to be properly informed by executive agencies, and critical scrutiny of individual ministers has often focused on whether they have neglected to inform Parliament properly about executive actions under their jurisdiction. Through this growing activism, the Norwegian Parliament has also increasingly focused on *ex post*, rather than *ex ante*, control of the executive branch. The main factor that limits the effectiveness of such parliamentary scrutiny is the bluntness (and hence lack of credibility) of the key sanctions that can be imposed: no-confidence votes and impeachment (see below).

DELEGATION FROM CABINET TO INDIVIDUAL MINISTERS

The Norwegian cabinet is in the 1814 Constitution formally recognized as the Council of State. Article 12 of the Constitution prescribes that the cabinet consist of a Prime Minister and at least seven other members. In practice the number of cabinet members in Norway has since 1945 varied between thirteen and nineteen, with a secular trend toward larger size. Junior ministers, known as secretaries of state (*statssekretær*) and personal advisers (*personlig rådgiver*), were first appointed in 1949. As of September 2000, there were forty-six such appointees altogether. The cabinet normally meets three times per week, with all formal decisions (Royal Resolutions) being made on Fridays in the Council of State, in which the King is present. Council of State meeting are very largely ritualistic, typically lasting only 30–45 minutes and containing no real debate on the issues under consideration. Decisions of the Council of State require the signatures of both the King and the Prime Minister. More substantive discussions take place in the King's absence in the Monday and Thursday cabinet meetings, which last 2–3 h, as well as during the informal cabinet luncheons on Fridays.

Cabinet Authority

The cabinet (Council of State) enjoys extensive powers under the Norwegian Constitution. It is the supreme, collective leadership of the central administration. In the form of bills and white papers, it initiates and prepares most legislation that is subsequently adopted by the Parliament. It can issue decrees with the force of law when Parliament is not in session. It is routinely granted broad implementation powers through regular legislation. It is in charge of a large system of public enterprises. It is an institution to which citizens can appeal under certain circumstances. And it is a branch of government with certain other constitutional prerogatives, such as appointment powers. Within certain limits, the cabinet can delegate authority, most commonly to the individual ministries. Yet some decisions, such as certain appointments, are constitutionally required to take place in the Council of State.

The Prime Minister

The prime ministership is the only cabinet office established by the Constitution. Yet the Norwegian Prime Minister is, in the words of Johan P. Olsen (1983: 81), a 'political organizer but no superstar'. The Prime Minister is the head of the cabinet, but his (or her) powers are otherwise vaguely described. His or her responsibilities include countersigning all decisions of the Council of State, preparing the cabinet agenda, chairing meetings, and casting a double vote in case the King is absent (rarely the source of any real power). The Prime Minister has the right to request information from any cabinet member, but he cannot issue orders, change ministerial jurisdictions, dissolve Parliament, or, technically, dismiss ministers. In reality, there has been substantial variation in the freedom of choice enjoyed by Prime Ministers in selecting and dismissing cabinet members. At one extreme, Einar Gerhardsen is considered to have been the 'strongest' Prime Minister of the postwar period in the discretion with which he could select his cabinet team. Gro Harlem Brundtland approached a similar status during her last years as Prime Minister. At the other extreme, Prime Ministers in coalition cabinets have had virtually no opportunity to select the members representing the other parties

(Olsen 1983; Eriksen 1988*b*). Only Willoch appears to have appropriated some veto powers in this respect.

The Prime Minister is in charge of the Prime Minister's office. This used to be a very small operation, as the Prime Minister had virtually no administrative help in the immediate postwar period. When Einar Gerhardsen formed his first cabinet in 1945, his staff consisted of two civil servants (one lawyer and one economist), three clerical employees, and a chauffeur (Berggrav 1997: 15). In 1956, the office was reorganized and professionalized, and by the mid-1980s it had grown to a size of approximately thirty employees (Berggrav 1985). When Bondevik took office in 1997, he employed six political appointees (four secretaries of states and two political advisers), thirty-five civil servants, and eight chauffeurs, for a total of forty-nine employees (Berggrav 1997: 41). The staff is divided into an administrative office, an economic office, and an international office. The Prime Minister's office has an important function in preparing the cabinet agenda. It also performs coordination functions, such as meetings to which both political appointees and civil servants may be summoned, as well as ceremonial liaison functions vis-à-vis the King.

Cabinet Members

The general rule, spelled out in Article 2 of the standing orders of the cabinet (*Regjeringsinstruksen*), is for each cabinet member to be the administrative head of some ministry. (The Prime Minister heads his or her own office, but after the Second World War no Prime Minister has been in charge of any regular ministry.) Occasionally, though, ministers without portfolio have been appointed. This was most notably the case in the years of reconstruction immediately following the Second World War, when as many as three ministers without portfolio served simultaneously. It is even more rare for any department to be represented by more than one cabinet member, although this again has occasionally happened in periods of administrative reorganization. Thus, Norway neatly fits one favourable condition for ministerial autonomy: being the head of a ministry is to all intents and purposes a necessary and sufficient condition for membership in the cabinet.

Though cabinet members may have close ties to Parliament, they cannot serve as representatives while they hold cabinet office. Nor is it expected that cabinet members have prior parliamentary experience. Between 1945 and 1978, 52 per cent of all Norwegian cabinet ministers had no prior parliamentary experience (Olsen 1983: 93). This proportion was especially high in the early postwar Labour governments under Gerhardsen. Particularly in ministries with distinctive and well-organized clienteles (e.g. agriculture, fisheries), it is considered much more desirable for cabinet members to have good interest group ties than to have parliamentary experience. Prime Ministers and Finance Ministers, however, tend to have extensive previous parliamentary experience.[9]

---

[9] Recent Labour cabinets have occasionally violated this expectation. When Gro Harlem Brundtland first became Labour leader and Prime Minister in 1981, one of the most serious criticisms leveled against her was precisely her relative lack of parliamentary experience. Similar criticisms were directed against Prime Minister Jagland, who had limited parliamentary experience and no cabinet experience when he took over in 1996.

Cabinet Rules and Procedures

Cabinet decision-making rules and procedures have evolved to reflect the practice of parliamentary government. These rules are not highly codified, but certain conventions can be identified. Since the formal Constitution still reflects the formalities of the cabinet as the 'King's Council', there are few hard-and-fast rules for cabinet decision-making. All cabinet meetings are chaired by the Prime Minister, who is also in charge of preparing the agenda. Yet any minister can request that the Prime Minister put an issue on the agenda, and such requests are not denied. This represents a change since the early Gerhardsen days, when there was no set agenda, and when cabinet members spoke in declining order of seniority. In those days, the most junior ministers sometimes had to leave without having an opportunity to present even the most pressing matters (Olsen 1983).

A quorum of more than half the cabinet members must be present for a formal decision to be made. The fact that decisions of the Council of State require the signature of the Prime Minister technically gives this person veto powers. In practice, however, the influence of the Prime Minister is never exercised in this way, nor is there even any known example of a _threat_ of a prime ministerial veto. The implicit decision rule practiced most commonly seems to be general unanimity. Decision-making processes in the cabinet are characterized by a strong search for consensus. Formal votes are rarely taken, although they do occur. In order to avoid divisive votes, ministers make use of extensive consultations before controversial issues are brought before the cabinet. There is indeed a norm not to bring controversial issues (those known to be contested by at least one other minister) before the cabinet until all other means of resolution have been exhausted. If disagreements persist after cabinet debate, recourse is generally had to one of five mechanisms of resolution: (1) reconsideration by the minister responsible for the issue, (2) further extra-cabinet negotiations between the parties (ministers) involved in the dispute, (3) referral to a committee of undersecretaries of state (see above) or civil servants, (4) the appointment of a cabinet committee, often including the Prime Minister, or (5), in the case of a coalition government, negotiations between party leaders (Eriksen 1988b: 191).

In matters of dispute, the cabinet can make its decisions by majority vote (Berggrav 1985: 31). Majority decisions are rarely publicized, but a dramatic illustration of this practice occurred in the early months of the Bondevik I government (1997–2000), when the government had to appoint a new bishop of Oslo, traditionally the head of the college of bishops in the Norwegian Lutheran church. All church authorities, as well as the Minister of Church and Education (a member of the Christian People's Party), recommended in favour of Odd Bondevik, an incumbent bishop who happened to be the Prime Minister's cousin. The two other coalition parties, however, preferred Gunnar Stålsett, a former leader of the Centre Party and a more liberal theologian. Stålsett won the cabinet vote ten to eight, with the Prime Minister recusing himself. (Nonetheless, Bishop Bondevik had the last laugh, as the other bishops defied tradition and elected him, rather than Stålsett, head of their college.)

Under coalition governments, the members of the coalition meet regularly for government conferences. Occasionally the parliamentary leaders are invited to take part.

The government conferences are considered to be informal gatherings, and no constitutional rule exists for decision-making or for setting the agenda (Berggrav 1994). Moreover, there is no formal conflict resolution mechanism, like an inner cabinet or coalition committee. Conflicts within the coalition government are discussed at the government conferences, and in situations where no agreement can be reached, individual ministers have the opportunity to dissent. Normally, the other cabinet members will be informed about the dissent on the preceding government conference. If more serious policy disagreements occur within the coalition, the matter will be discussed in party summits consisting of cabinet members and party leaders. The reports from the government conferences are to be found in the central government's archives, and they are normally only made public after forty years unless *all* parties of the former coalition government consent to do so (Berggrav 1994).

Ministerial Accountability

In Norway, ministers bear two kinds of responsibilities for their actions and those of their subordinates. One is a *constitutional* responsibility for any illegal or unconstitutional behaviour on the part of the cabinet or the minister individually, including any non-compliance with acts of Parliament or any withholding of information to which Parliament is entitled. A minister may also be constitutionally responsible for the actions of a subordinate, such as a civil servant, if negligence is shown in the instruction or oversight of this subordinate. A formal protocol is kept of Council of State decisions, and individual ministers can request that their dissent from cabinet policy be registered in this document. This is the only way they can escape *legal* responsibility for cabinet decisions they consider 'unconstitutional or injurious to the realm'. However, except for parliamentary scrutiny, the cabinet protocol is confidential, and a registered dissent is no *political* excuse for public criticism of cabinet decisions.[10]

Violations of the constitutional responsibilities of ministers are punishable by impeachment, but since the dramatic and unsuccessful impeachment proceedings against Prime Minister Abraham Berge in 1926–7, this extreme instrument has fallen into disuse. In recent years, ministers guilty of major violations of the law have tended to resign and face regular criminal prosecution. Thus, during the 1980s two ministers (one Conservative and one Labour) resigned under suspicion of embezzlement. Both were subsequently convicted.

A more pressing concern for most cabinet ministers is their *political* responsibility to the Storting. This is a form of collective responsibility shared by all members of the cabinet and all other political appointees in the ministries. Whereas ministers can escape some forms of constitutional responsibility by registering their dissent from

---

[10] Not all cabinet decisions are formal and binding. Technically, cabinet ministers and their subordinates are bound only by the formal decisions of the Council of State and not by the more informal agreements reached in other cabinet meetings. Yet this distinction must be considered more formal than real. Individual cabinet members would be ill advised to ignore or sabotage any cabinet decision, regardless of whether it has been ratified in the Council of State.

Council of State decisions, there is no way for an individual minister to exempt himself from his political responsibility to the parliamentary majority.

Ministerial Norms and Behaviour

Surveys of ministers show that most of them focus their energies on matters pertaining to their own ministries. Eriksen (1988a) reports from a survey of thirty-five ministers that they on average devoted almost two-thirds of their time (64 per cent) to departmental matters, whereas an average of 22 per cent of their time was spent in or in preparation for cabinet meetings. Most ministers thus choose the role of specialist, but some exceptions apply. Occupants of the ministries of finance, municipal affairs, and environmental affairs tend to spend more time on issues pertaining to other ministries. And the Prime Minister, of course, does not even have his (or her) own ministry. Also, ministers from smaller parties in coalition cabinets are more likely than ministers in single-party governments to spend time on matters outside their own jurisdiction. This appears particularly to have been the case with ministers from the Centre Party in the Willoch cabinets (Eriksen 1988a: 44).

The prevailing specialist orientation is reinforced by the workload cabinet ministers are under, by patterns of recruitment and experience, and by the norms of cabinet meeting deliberation. Most cabinet members feel severely overworked, and many report that they have little time to invest in matters concerning other ministries. Between 1945 and the late 1970s, three-quarters of all ministers served in only one ministry during their political careers, while only seven persons served in three or more ministries, the prime ministership included. There was substantial variation across ministries, however, as 73 per cent of all finance ministers had headed at least one other ministry, as had more than half of all Prime Ministers and ministers of defence, trade, justice, and foreign affairs (Olsen 1983: 92).

DELEGATION FROM MINISTERS TO CIVIL SERVANTS

The Norwegian civil service was in its initial form an inheritance from Denmark. As one of the few social organizations with professional expertise, it played a major role in the political and economic development of Norway in the nineteenth century. Throughout the development of the Norwegian civil service, there has been an ongoing debate over the merits of a centralized and hierarchical, versus a decentralized and professional, administrative structure. In organizational terms, this has been a debate over whether the civil service should be organized around a smaller set of hierarchical departments under strong political control (traditionally known as the 'Danish model', although Denmark itself has in recent decades deviated somewhat from these principles) or in the form of a larger set of more autonomous and professional agencies under less direct political control (the 'Swedish model'). In practice, the Norwegian administration has become a hybrid of these two models. The former principle is embodied in a structure of departments, the latter in a set of directorates (direktorater). The Danish model dominated initially, but from about 1850 on an increasing number of directorates were

established. This process was reversed after the introduction of parliamentary government in 1884, when the parliamentary majority wished to bring the civil service under
stricter political control. Since the Second World War, there has been no consensus on
either of these two basic principles, and a pragmatic balance has evolved that places
Norway somewhere in between Denmark and Sweden in this respect. As of 2001, there
were seventeen departments and seventy-five directorates in the Norwegian central
administration (Christensen *et al.* 2002).

Since the early 1980s, the total number of civil servants in the Norwegian central
administration has hovered between 3,000 and 4,000, numbers that had increased
slightly over the previous decade. Over a longer period of time, most of the growth in
the central administration has occurred in the directorates. Thus, between 1945 and
1991, the number of departmental positions increased by 70 per cent, whereas the corresponding growth in the directorates amounted to no less than 210 per cent
(Christensen and Egeberg 1994). There are two classes of Norwegian civil servants:
higher civil servants (*embetsmenn*) and ordinary civil servants (*tjenestemenn*). According
to Article 28 of the Constitution, higher civil servants must be appointed by the King
in a formal cabinet meeting. Their tenure is also strictly protected, in that they can only
be dismissed if found guilty of malfeisance in a court of law. Ordinary civil servants
have lesser protections, but in practice Norwegian civil servants of both categories have
always tended to be professional and non-partisan.

Under professional civil services systems such as the Norwegian one, politicians have
very little *ex post* control over the civil servants to whom they delegate. Certainly, civil
servants cannot be hired or fired at will. Accountability takes place in two ways: (1)
Civil servants have explicitly designed contracts that prevent them from taking various
types of hidden or arbitrary action; and (2) all decisions taken in the executive branch
explicitly carry the authorization of the head of department. A great deal of formal
authority is therefore placed in this minister's hands. *Ex ante* controls, on the other
hand, are quite strong, in that the credentials that are required of civil servants tend to
be quite substantial.

Since the late 1960s, *ex post* control has been facilitated by legislation designed to open
the administration up to third-party oversight. The Administrative Procedures Act
(*Forvaltningsloven*) of 1967 established a right for affected interests to be consulted before
the administration adopts a general rule that significantly impacts upon them. The
Freedom of Information Act (*Lov om offentlighet i forvaltningen*) of 1970 (implemented in
1971) gave citizens a general right of access to administrative documents.

EXTERNAL CONSTRAINTS

As mentioned in the introductory section, Norway is in practice a fairly pure parliamentary democracy. Although some constraints exist on delegation and accountability
through the parliamentary chain, these are modest compared to many other European
nations. Below we discuss four sources of domestic constraint on the national chain of
delegation, namely subnational governments, direct democracy, judicial review, and
corporatism. Roughly speaking, these are listed in increasing order of importance. Yet,

it is important to note that none of these constraints is of major importance in cross-national perspective, and that most of them exist by virtue of delegation from Parliament.

Norway is a unitary state. Although local government was established as early as 1837 and enjoys broad support and participation, it has weak constitutional support. Local governments have weak taxation powers, and much of their revenue comes in the form of transfers from the national government. Although some of their responsibilities have remained fairly constant since the early nineteenth century, others have changed, and the central (national) government has frequently changed these terms. Provincial governments, of which there are nineteen, are even weaker. Following a reform in the 1970s, each province now has an elected government, but their jurisdictions are narrow (mainly parts of higher education), and several parties have in recent years called for reductions in their authority or the abolition of provincial governments altogether. Thus, subnational government is largely dependent on authority and funds delegated by the national government and poses no significant constraint on the latter.

Nor does direct democracy. Since Norwegian independence in 1905, only six national referendums have been held: two in 1905 on national independence and on the form of new Norwegian state (monarchy versus republic), two in the interwar period over prohibition, and most recently the 1972 and 1994 EU membership referendums. Because the Norwegian Constitution does not mention national referendums, they can only be consultative, although in practice Parliament has never failed to follow the will of the majority.[11] Yet, there is no constitutional requirement that referendums be held on any particular issue (including constitutional amendments), nor any mechanism by which any institution except Parliament can call such an event. Thus, Parliament is constrained by direct democracy only to the extent that it decides to submit itself to this mechanism.

Judicial review, however, is a less optional constraint on the national government. More strongly than either Denmark or Sweden, Norway has established a doctrine of judicial review. In fact, the Norwegian tradition of judicial review postdates only that of the United States, and in developing this practice Norwegian legal authorities relied heavily on American doctrines (Smith 1993: 32). Judicial review was not clearly and explicitly established in the 1814 Constitution, but evolved gradually through a series of Supreme Court decisions. Smith (1993: 158–9) argues that the practice can be traced back to the 1840s, that it is clearly evident from 1866 on, and that it is first explicitly articulated in a 1890 Supreme Court decision. The latter decision inaugurated the 'golden age' of judicial activism in Norway. From about 1930 until the mid-1970s, however, this activism subsided, and the courts became extremely reluctant to challenge the constitutionality of government

---

[11] Before the EU membership referendum in 1994, representatives of several anti-EU parties did suggest that they would not feel obligated by a narrow pro-EU majority. However, the popular response to this stance was largely negative, so that it is unclear whether the anti-EU representatives would in fact have followed through on their threat to disregard the popular vote.

decisions. Yet, in a widely recognized 1976 decision ('*Kløfta-saken*') upholding private property rights against government regulation, the Norwegian Supreme Court ushered in another era of increased judicial activism.

A less constitutionally entrenched, but in practice equally significant, constraint lies in the Norwegian version of *corporatism*. In cross-national surveys (e.g. Lijphart 1999), Norway is typically ranked among the most corporatist countries in the world. Norwegian corporatism has two main manifestations: (1) a practice of remiss *(høring)*, of consulting affected interests in legislative and administrative matters, and (2) a structure of permanent and temporary boards and committees on which such interests are represented. The remiss procedure provides a right for affected interests, such as government agencies, institutions, and interest organizations, to be consulted when legislative initiatives of significant concern to them are prepared. Interestingly, guaranteed access for affected interests and freedom of information were embedded in ordinary legislation passed under a non-socialist coalition government (Borten) in 1967 and 1970 (see above). Thus, although corporatist practices were most vigorously advanced by Social-Democratic governments, such forms of decision-making enjoyed fairly broad cross-partisan support from the 1950s through to the 1970s.

The appointment of government boards and committees with interest group representation became a regular feature of Norwegian politics in the years following the First World War and expanded greatly during the social-democratic era from the mid-1930s on. The 261 (192 permanent and 69 temporary) committees that existed in 1936 gradually grew to 1,141 (912 permanent and 229 temporary) by 1976, the high point of Norwegian corporatism. As the counter-cyclical expansionary economic policies of the late 1970s failed, however, doubt crept into the governing Labour Party concerning the wisdom of strengthening the 'iron triangles' of Norwegian politics through corporatist practices. Such doubts were much more openly articulated by the Conservative Willoch government that came to power in 1981 and began to dismantle many of the organizational forms of corporatism (Nordby 1994: 71). By 1994, the number of government committees had thus declined to 673 (611 permanent and 62 temporary), even though the practice of creating new such bodies has never been totally abandoned. Yet, it makes sense to see Norwegian corporatism as a historical phenomenon rather than a permanent feature, and as a delegative instrument chosen by political parties rather than an alternative to them. Finally, although corporatism has its roots in the pre-Labour era, its heyday coincides with the period of social-democratic ascendancy.

Yet, the most interesting and important contemporary constraint on the parliamentary chain of delegation may lie in Norway's international commitments and especially in the effects of European integration. This statement may sound paradoxical since, unlike most other Western European states, Norway is not a member of the EU and thus has not transferred sovereignty to this transnational organization. Nonetheless, Norway's membership in the European Economic Area (EEA) does entail some constraints on the authority exercised through the parliamentary channel of representation.

In the early 1990s the possibility of EU membership raised the question whether such a commitment would affect existing parliamentary institutions. In the Storting, European issues have traditionally been the domain of the Foreign Affairs Committee, and after the defeat of the 1994 membership referendum, this is still the case. The Storting has decided that the government's consultation with the Storting on EEA matters shall take place with the EEA Commission (Myhre-Jensen and Fløistad 1997). Some criticism has been raised against the government concerning the lack of information given to the Storting on EU issues (Christensen 1997). Also, critics have pointed to the short deadlines given to the Storting on matters related to the EEA agreement. In addition, the process of handling EEA matters is rather closed since the documents from the meetings are not made public. Overall, the Storting's capacity to control government activities in this area is rather limited.

Sejersted (1996: 125) argues that the Storting has been weakened in two ways. First, the EEA means a massive transfer of real, if not always formal, power from the Storting to the Community institutions, through the EEA organs. Second, it has led to a shift in the balance of power at the national level, weakening Parliament and strengthening the cabinet and the administration, as well as the courts. Sejersted contends that it is primarily the legislative function of the Storting that has been weakened by Europeanization, whereas the financial and budgetary functions are less affected. Unlike Parliaments in the member states, the Storting has not transferred any formal legislative powers. Compared to full membership, he argues, the EEA agreement creates less favourable conditions for parliamentarism, since the formal status of the Agreement camouflages the real transfer of power, and so keeps the Storting from introducing necessary reform.

CONCLUSION

Norway is not the epitome of parliamentary government. In fact, the 1814 Constitution was drawn up to establish a very different kind of regime, a separation-of-powers system. Only gradually, informally, and incompletely has the Constitution been transformed into a parliamentary one. It still lacks some of the typical features of parliamentarism, such as parliamentary dissolution powers. Nonetheless, delegation of authority follows the parliamentary pattern fairly closely. This, however, is largely due to two interrelated factors: the strength of party government and a strong reliance on *ex ante* controls over agents. *Ex post* controls, on the other hand, though increasingly important, are much less well institutionalized. Nonetheless, the performance of Norwegian democracy has traditionally kept most of its citizens happy.

Whether this happy outcome can be maintained is an entirely different matter. Both of these features of Norwegian parliamentarism, political party government and *ex ante* controls, have been eroded by recent developments in the Norwegian polity. Though political parties so far maintain effective control of candidate selection as well as policy-making in the Storting, they are rapidly declining as vehicles of mass participation, and their previously high level of popular support is slipping (Strøm and Svåsand 1997). Given these developments and the clear trend toward more open candidate selection processes in other Nordic countries, it is an open question how long Norwegian parties can maintain their strict control of parliamentary politics. The weakening of *ex ante* controls has occurred simultaneously with the decline of parties, and the two phenomena are in many ways interrelated. It is also in part the reflection of the rise of new parties, such as the Progress Party and the Socialist Left, that reject many traditional forms of social control. But the increasing difficulty of relying on *ex ante* mechanisms is also driven in part by the emergence of a more diverse and competitive, and less transparent, society. In some form, Norwegian politicians seem to recognize these developments and to respond to them by strengthening mechanisms of *ex post* control (e.g. committee hearings and more rigorous audits), particularly in the parliamentary arena. Their success or failure in these endeavours could have a major effect on the future trajectory of Norwegian democracy.

REFERENCES

Aardal, Bernt (2002). 'Electoral Systems in Norway', in Bernard Grofmen and Arend Lijphart (eds.), *The Evolution of Electoral Systems and Party Systems in the Nordic Countries*. New York: Agethon Press: 167–224.

——, in cooperation with Valen, Henry, Narud, Hanne Marthe, and Berglund, Frode (1999). *Velgere i 1990 årene*. Oslo: NKS Forlaget.

—— and Valen, Henry (1989). *Velgere, Partier og Politisk Avstand*. Oslo: Central Bureau of Statistics.

—— —— (1997). 'The Storting Elections of 1989 and 1993: Norwegian Politics in Perspective', in Kaare Strøm and Lars Svåsand (eds.), *Challenges to Political Parties: The Case of Norway*. Ann Arbor: University of Michigan Press.

Andeweg, Rudy B. and Nijzink, Lia (1995). 'Beyond the Two-Body-Image: Relations Between Ministers and MPs', in Herbert Döring (ed.), *Parliaments and Majority Rule in Western Europe*. New York: St. Martin's Press.

Bagehot, Walter (1963 [1867]). *The English Constitution*. London: Fontana/Collins.

Berggrav, Dag (1985). 'Regjeringen', in Trond Nordby (ed.), *Storting og regjering 1945–1985: Institusjoner—rekruttering*. Oslo: Kunnskapsforlaget.

—— (1994). *Slik styres Norge: Kongen, regjeringen og Stortinget i norsk statsliv*. Oslo: Schibsted.

—— (1997). 'Statsministerens kontors historie siden 1945', in Dag Berggrav (ed.), *Maktens høyborg*. Oslo: Grøndahl Dreyer.

Bergman, Torbjörn (1993). 'Formation Rules and Minority Governments'. *European Journal of Political Research*, 23: 55–66.

Björnberg, Arne (1939). *Parliamentarismens utreckling i Norge efter 1905*. Uppsala: Almqvist & Wiksell.

Christensen, Dag Arne (1997). 'Europautvala i Danmark, Sverige og Noreg'. *Nordisk Administrativt Tidsskrift*, 78: 143–62.

Christensen, Tom, Egeberg, Morten., (1994). 'Sentraladministrasjonen—en oversikt over trekk ved departement og direktorat', in Tom Christensen and Morten Egeberg (eds.), *Forvaltningskunnskap*, 2nd edn. Oslo: TANO.

Christensen, Tom, Egeberg, Morten., Larsen, Helge O., Lægreid, Per, and Roness, Paul G. (2002). *Fovalting og politikk*. Oslo: Universitetsforlaget.

Cox, Gary W. (1987). *The Efficient Secret*. Cambridge: Cambridge University Press.

Eckhoff, Torstein and Smith, Eivind (1997). *Forvaltningsrett*, 6th edn. Oslo: TANO.

Eliassen, Kjell A. (1985). 'Rekrutteringen til Stortinget og Regjeringen 1945–1985', in Trond Nordby (ed.), *Storting og regjering 1945–1985: Institusjoner—rekruttering*. Oslo: Kunnskapsforlaget.

—— and Pedersen, Mogens (1978). 'Professionalization of Legislatures: Long-Term Change in Political Recruitment in Denmark and Norway'. *Comparative Studies in Society and History*, 20: 286–318.

Eriksen, Svein A. (1988a). *Herskap og tjenere*. Oslo: TANO.

—— (1988b). 'Norway', in Jean Blondel and Ferdinand Müler-Rommel (eds.), *Cabinets in Western Europe*. London: Macmillan.

Hansen, Guttorm and Mo, Erik (1994). *Om Stortingets arbeidsordning*. Oslo: Stortinget.

Karmly, Dag (1975). *Kings Bay-saken*. Oslo: Gyldendal.

Kuhnle, Stein and Svåsand, Lars (1984). 'Spørreordningene og politiske profiler i Stortinget 1977–1981', in Ole Berg and Arild Underdal (eds.), *Fra valg til vedtak*. Oslo: Aschehoug.

Lijphart, Arend (1999). *Patterns of Democracy*. New Haven: Yale University Press.

Matthews, Donald and Valen, Henry (1999). *Parliamentary Representation. The Case of the Norwegian Storting*. Columbus: Ohio State University Press.

Miller, Arthur H. and Listhaug, Ola (1990). 'Political Parties and Confidence in Government: A Comparison of Norway, Sweden, and the United States'. *British Journal of Political Science*, 29: 357–86.

Myhre-Jensen, Kjell and Fløistad, Brit (1997). 'The Storting and the EU/EEA', in Matti Wiberg (ed.), *Trying to Make Democracy Work*. Stockholm: The Bank of Sweden Tercenary Foundation and Gidlunds Förlag.

Narud, Hanne Marthe (1998). 'Norwegen: Professionalisierung zwischen Parteien- und Wahlkreisorientierung', in Jens Borchert (ed.), *Politik als Beruf. Die politische Klasse in westlichen Demokratien*. Opladen: Leske & Budrich.

—— and Valen, Henry (2000). 'Does Social Background Matter?', in Peter Esaiasson and Knut Heidar (eds.), *Beyond Westminister and Congress. The Nordic Experience*. Columbus: Ohio State University Press.

Nordby, Trond (1994). *Korporatisme på norsk 1920–1990*. Oslo: Universitetsforlaget.

—— (2000). *I politikkens sentrum: Variasjoner i Stortingets makt 1814–2000*. Oslo: Universitetsforlaget.

Olsen, Johan P. (1983). *Organized Democracy*. Oslo: Universitetsforlaget.

Overå, Oddvar and Dalbakk, Steinar (1987). *Den Norske Valgordningen*. Oslo: Sem & Stenersen.

Raaum, Nina Cecilie (1995). 'The Political Representation of Women: A Bird's Eye View', in Lauri Karvonen and Per Selle (eds.), *Women in Nordic Politics: Closing the Gap*. Aldershot: Dartmouth.

Ranney, Austin (1981). 'Candidate Selection', in David Butler, Howard R. Penniman, and Austin Ranney (eds.), *Democracy at the Polls*. Washington, DC: American Enterprise Institute.

Rasch, Bjørn Erik (1994). 'Question Time in the Norwegian Storting—Theoretical and Empirical Considerations', in Matti Wiberg (ed.), *Parliamentary Control in the Nordic Countries: Forms of Questioning and Behavioural Trends*. Jyväskylä: The Finnish Political Science Association.

—— (1998). 'Electoral Incentives to Control Government Ministers'. Paper prepared for presentation at the International Conference on the Significance of the Individual Parliamentary Member in Parliamentary Politics, Budapest, July 1–5.

Rokkan, Stein (1967). 'Geography, Religion and Social Class: Crosscutting Cleavages in Norwegian Politics', in Seymour Martin Lipset and Stein Rokkan (eds.), *Party Systems and Voter Alignments*. New York: Free Press.

—— (1970). *Citizens, Elections, Parties*. New York: David McKay.

Rommetvedt, Hilmar (1984). *Borgerlig samarbeid*. Stavanger: Universitetsforlaget.

—— (1996). 'Norwegian Parliamentary Committees: Performance, Structural Change and External Relations'. Paper presented at the International Conference on the Changing Roles of Parliamentary Committees, Budapest, June 20–22.

Sejersted, Fredrik (1996). 'The Norwegian Parliament and European Integration—Reflections from Medium Speed Europe', in Eivind Smith (ed.), *National Parliaments as Cornerstones of European Integration*. London: Kluwer.

—— (2000). 'Stortingets kontrollfunksjon'. *Nytt Norsk Tidsskrift*, 17: 173–85.

Skjeie, Hege (1997). 'A Tale of Two Decades: The End of a Male Political Hegemony', in Kaare Strøm and Lars Svåsand (eds.), *Challenges to Political Parties: The Case of Norway*. Ann Arbor: University of Michigan Press.

Smith, Eivind (1993). *Høyesterett og folkestyret*. Oslo: Universitetsforlaget.

Stavang, Per (1968). *Parlamentarisme og maktbalanse*. Oslo: Universitetsforlaget.

—— (1971). 'Negativt fleirtal i norsk parlamentarisme'. *Lov og rett*, 145–66.

Strøm, Kaare (1990). *Minority Government and Majority Rule*. Cambridge: Cambridge University Press.

—— and Lars Svåsand (eds.) (1997). *Challenges to Political Parties: The Case of Norway*. Ann Arbor: University of Michigan Press.

Svåsand, Lars (1985). *Politiske partier*. Oslo: Tiden.

——, Strøm, Kaare, and Rasch, Bjørn E. (1997). 'Party Organization', in Kaare Strøm and Lars Svåsand (eds.), *Challenges to Political Parties: The Case of Norway*. Ann Arbor: University of Michigan Press.

Valen, Henry (1981). *Valg og Politikk*. Oslo: NKS-forlaget.

—— (1985). 'Valgsystemet', in Trond Nordby (ed.), *Storting og regjering 1945–1985: Institusjoner— rekruttering*. Oslo: Kunnskapsforlaget.

—— (1988). 'Norway: Decentralization and Group Representation', in Michael Gallagher and Michael Marsh (eds.), *Candidate Selection in Comparative Perspective*. London: Sage.

——, Narud, Hanne Marthe, and Skare, Audun (2002). 'Norway: Party Dominance and Decentralized Decisionmaking', in Hanne Marthe Narud, Mogens Pedersen, and Henry Valen (eds.), *Party Sovereignty and Citizen Control*. Odense: Odense University Press.

—— and Rokkan, Stein (1974). 'Norway: Conflict Structure and Mass Politics in a European Periphery', in Richard Rose (ed.), *Electoral Behavior: A Comparative Handbook*. New York: Free Press.

—— and Urwin, Derek W. (1985). 'De Politiske Partiene', in Trond Nordby (ed.), *Storting og Regjering 1945–1985*, Vol. 2. Oslo: Kunnskapsforlaget.

Østbø, Ivar Buch (1995). *Stortinget: All Makt i denne sal*. Oslo: Schibsted.

18

Portugal: Changing Patterns of Delegation and Accountability under the President's Watchful Eyes

OCTAVIO AMORIM NETO

INTRODUCTION

An elected Parliament has long been a part of Portugal's political landscape. It was first established after the Liberal revolution of 1820. Throughout the nineteenth century, however, parliamentary life in Portugal was markedly oligarchic and clientelistic. In 1910, with the foundation of the Republic, Parliament had for the first time an opportunity to assert itself as an institution responsive to popular demands. But the so-called First Republic fell prey to radicalism, instability, and coup attempts, and soon foundered. Its final collapse in 1926 led to the emergence of a corporatist authoritarian regime—known as the *Estado Novo* (New State)—under the personalistic leadership of António de Oliveira Salazar. This non-democratic regime held power for decades. However, it was badly hurt by its participation in colonial wars in the 1960s, and was finally toppled in April 1974 in a revolution led by the armed forces. The April 1974 Revolution, also dubbed the Revolution of the Carnations, paved the way for a quick, albeit rocky, transition to democracy. Elections for a national constituent assembly were held in 1975. In 1976 a democratic Constitution was promulgated, and free and fair presidential and parliamentary elections were held. Thus, 1976 is the first year of actual parliamentary democracy in Portugal's history.

Any analysis of the chain of delegation and accountability in Portugal's democracy must consider the political role played by the Chief of State. The 1976 Constitution established a popularly elected President of the Republic, and endowed this office with extensive powers over government formation and termination, the survival of the legislative assembly, and policy-making. Constitutional reforms enacted in 1982

The author acknowledges the support of a University of Umeå grant that financed the fieldwork in Portugal on which this study is based. The author is grateful to Mário Bacalhau, Cristina Leston-Bandeira, Arend Lijphart, Pedro Coutinho Magalhães, Antonio Ortiz-Mena, Matthew S. Shugart, and the book editors for their useful comments and suggestions, and to Manuel Braga da Cruz, Margarida Guadalpi, and José M. Magone for kindly sharing their data on Portugal's political institutions.

reduced some of the powers of the President and enhanced those of the Parliament and the cabinet. Despite this, the Chief of State has retained an important role in policy-making.

The law-making process in Portugal displays the following features. Individual MPs and the cabinet can initiate bills in the unicameral *Assembleia da República* (Assembly of the Republic). In the Portuguese constitutional jargon, the bills sponsored by MPs are called *Projetos de Lei* (Projects of Law), and those presented by the cabinet are denominated as *Propostas de Lei* (Proposals of Law). The approval of any bill requires a quorum of 50 per cent plus 1 of all MPs and the support of a majority of those voting. The budget process is identical to that of law-making. As for constitutional amendments, they can only be proposed by MPs, and require a two-thirds majority of all MPs to be enacted.

Additionally, in Portugal the Constitution endows the cabinet with the power to issue decrees, which enables the latter to unilaterally legislate in policy areas that are not constitutionally under the jurisdiction of the Assembly.[1]

A unique feature of the 1976 Portuguese Constitution relative to its Western European counterparts was that it granted the President the power to veto both bills approved by the Assembly of the Republic and decrees of the cabinet (Articles 139, 277, and 278). A President's veto could be overridden by an absolute majority of the members of the Assembly of the Republic (Article 139: 2). However, paragraph 3 of the same Article stated that a two-thirds majority of those present was required to override a president's veto on the following matters: (1) boundaries between the public, private, and cooperative sectors; (2) foreign affairs; and (3) rules governing elections. Moreover, the President had an absolute veto over administrative decrees issued by the cabinet (Articles 138: 2, 278). Also, the president had the power to exert what the Constitution calls pre-emptive control of constitutionality. After consulting with the Council of the Revolution[2] on the constitutionality of a legal document, the President could veto international treaties, cabinet decrees, and laws passed by the Assembly (Article 277). If the Council of the Revolution ruled that a legal document was unconstitutional, then the President was required to veto it (Article 278).

The 1982 constitutional revision actually enhanced the President's prerogatives with regard to his or her veto right. After the revision a two-thirds majority is required to override a President's veto in a larger number of policy areas than was the case under the 1976 Constitution. The new areas were state of siege and state of emergency,

---

[1] The Constitution, Article 164, defines a wide set of policy areas over which Parliament has absolute legislative jurisdiction, such as basic education, the referendum regime, organization of the Constitutional Tribunal, organization of national defence, state of siege and state of emergency regimes, organization of political parties and associations, the electoral system of local legislative assemblies, and appointment of members to European Union (EU) organs. It should be noted that the government has an exclusive right to introduce legislation on its internal organization and functioning.

[2] The Council of the Revolution institutionalized the role of the military as guardians of the democratization process. This role was enshrined in the 1976 Constitution, which, in Article 142, determined that the Council have the functions of advising the President and ensuring the regular functioning of the democratic institutions faithfully in the spirit of the 1974 Revolution. The Council was presided over by the President, and was composed of the PM and high-ranking military officers.

organization of national defence, organization of the armed forces, and organization of the Constitutional Tribunal (Article 139: 3).[3] The revision also strengthened the President's prerogatives with regard to the pre-emptive control of constitutionality. With the elimination of the Council of the Revolution, from 1983 on the pre-emptive control has been performed by the Constitutional Tribunal upon a request by the President (Article 278).

In acknowledgement of the fact that Portugal deviates from a typical parliamentary democracy because of the role played by the President, Portugal experts and comparativists have aptly classified the country's system of government as semi-presidential (Duverger 1980; Cruz 1994; Frain 1995; Sartori 1997) or *premier*-presidential (Moreira 1989; Shugart and Carey 1992).[4] This system has helped Portugal consolidate its young democracy because it proved to be flexible enough to respond quickly to challenges posed by an unstable and ideologically polarized multiparty system in the early phase of democratization. When the parties finally achieved a stable pattern of interaction among themselves and with voters in the mid 1980s, Portugal's democracy managed not only to become institutionalized but also to promote high rates of economic growth and an unprecedented process of social change and modernization. Such achievements are evidence that Portugal's parliamentary chain of delegation, despite all the complexity created by an elected President, seems to be responding well to the demands of voters. This is what will be argued below.

POLITICAL PARTIES

Despite the fact that political parties did not play any part in the governing of Portugal during three-quarters of the twentieth century, since the April 1974 Revolution Portuguese elites have managed to successfully build a stable system of national political parties. According to Bruneau (1997: 1), 'In no other country, ... , have political parties played anywhere near as important a role in the democratization [process] as in Portugal'. Such a role is enshrined in the Constitution. Article 153 grants political parties monopoly over the presentation of candidates for parliamentary elections, and Article 51 prohibits the organization of parties with regional scope and goals.

Since 1976 four parties have emerged as the key contenders for the popular vote: the *Partido Social Democrata* (PSD—Social Democratic Party), the *Partido Socialista* (PS—Socialist Party), *Centro Democrático e Social* (CDS—Social Democratic Centre Party), and the *Partido Comunista Português* (PCP—Portuguese Communist Party). Four parties have been members of at least one cabinet: the PSD, PS, CDS, and the tiny *Partido Popular Monárquico* (PPM—Popular Monarchy Party).

The PSD was founded right after the April 1974 revolution as the representative of the Right in the new regime. The PSD drew support from a variety of social groups

---

[3] The role and composition of the Constitutional Tribunal will be explained in the section on External Constraints.

[4] A semi-presidential or *premier*-presidential system has the following attributes: (1) a president elected by popular vote, (2) endowed with considerable powers, and (3) a PM and a cabinet accountable to Parliament and invested with executive functions.

and political forces formerly associated with the *Estado Novo*, including liberals, university student movements, masons, and Catholic associations (Frain 1997: 78). In order to survive in the radical post-revolutionary environment, its leaders were forced to shift the party's programme to the left of the median position of party members and sympathisers (Frain 1997: 83). The contradiction between the conservative political leanings of the party's core constituencies and the more leftist tone its leaders have adopted in order to increase the party's electoral appeal has left its mark on the PSD. According to Frain (1997: 83), the PSD is not ideologically unified, and therefore it is highly factionalized: '...liberals, technocrats, populists, social democrats all find a place in the PSD'. Factionalism within the party has been further worsened by the strong personalities of its leaders—a characteristic trait of Portuguese political culture—and the clashes stemming from this.

Despite the many internal conflicts that resulted from factionalism, PSD leaders were wise enough to devise a decentralized and democratic organizational structure that could accommodate the diversity of its elites and at the same time ensure strong party identification at the mass level (Frain 1997: 85). Moreover, the fact that the PSD was in the opposition in the first years of the new democratic regime further helped to hold its factions together (the PSD entered the cabinet for the first time in 1980). In addition, when the PSD formed a minority single-party government in 1985 the desire to hold on to power helped to constrain and appease its factions. The party's victories in the 1987 and 1991 elections—in which it won absolute majorities—had a similar positive effect.

The PSD joined seven of the the fifteen cabinets formed between 1976 and 2000— once as a coalition partner, three times as the member of an electoral alliance, and three times as the leader of single party minority or majority governments. It entered the cabinet for the first time in January 1980, as the major partner in a winning electoral alliance with the CDS and the PPM—the so-called *Aliança Democrática* (Democratic Alliance). This alliance formed two additional cabinets during the 1980–3 legislature before being dissolved after the 1983 elections. It was replaced by a government coalition, the *Bloco Central* (Central Block), composed of the two largest parties, the PS and PSD. In the 1985 elections the PSD won 35.2 per cent of the seats in the Assembly of the Republic, which made it the country's largest parliamentary party. The PSD then formed a single-party minority government. In the 1987 election the PSD achieved its greatest electoral success, winning an absolute majority of 59.2 per cent of the seats in parliament. This allowed it to form the first single-party majority government in Portugal's democratic history. In 1991 the PSD repeated its strong electoral performance, managing to retain an absolute majority of seats in the Assembly (58.7 per cent). It therefore continued to single-handedly run the government. In the 1995 election the PSD finally lost its majority, and had to give up government power to the PS.

The PS was founded in 1973 by a group of exiled Portuguese Socialists in Germany. Its first programme called for a classless society and for the nationalization of key industries (Sablosky 1997: 59). This ideological programme made the PS the pivotal party in post-revolutionary Portugal and during the democratization period. Like the PSD, factionalism and clashes among its leaders have also plagued the PS. However, unlike the PSD, the PS has a vertical and centralized organizational structure. The party is controlled from the top, which makes it difficult to achieve efficient coordination of its leaders, factions, and rank-and-file. According to Sablosky (1997: 62), over time the complicated organizational structure proved a weakness as the PS failed to develop a strong cadre of middle level managers.'

A number of factors led the PS to moderate its initial ideological radicalism and move towards the centre of the ideological spectrum. These include the party's participation in the first democratic governments, its decision to 'Europeanize' in the late 1970s, and electoral defeat from the mid-1980s to the early 1990s. Its ideological transformation, combined with an economic downturn in the mid-1990s, contributed to the PS's increasing popularity and made it possible for the party to win both the 1995 and 1999 parliamentary elections and the 1996 presidential race.

The PS was the dominant party during the first years of the new democratic regime. It formed a single-party minority cabinet in 1976 and a coalition government with the CDS in 1978. This coalition soon collapsed. However, because of the highly polarized atmosphere of the late 1970s the parliamentary parties were unable to agree on the composition of a new government. The parties' failure to agree led to a period of sixteen months of undisguised presidential rule, during which President Ramalho Eanes appointed three non-partisan cabinets. The period of presidential rule was followed by the liberal governments of the Democratic Alliance. The PS returned to power in 1983 in a government coalition with the PSD. The latter's rise to dominance in the mid-1980s deprived the PS of government power for a period of 10 years. The party finally regained power after the 1995 elections, this time leading a single-party near majority government. After the 1999 elections, the Socialists were returned to power, again forming a single-party near majority cabinet.

The CDS[5] was founded in 1974 by individuals closely linked to some of the elites of the old regime, particularly elites in the universities, public administration, and business. Its leaders placed the party to the right of the PSD (Robinson 1996). During its first years the CDS was basically a party dominated by notables. Over time, however, it was able to develop a decentralized party structure (Frain 1997: 86). The CDS has been Portugal's fourth largest party and participated in one coalition government (in 1978 with the PS), and in the three Democratic Alliance cabinets between 1980 and 1982.

DELEGATION FROM VOTERS TO MPs

As mandated by Article 149 of the Constitution, MPs are elected in twenty multi-member districts on the basis of proportional representation and the D'Hondt method of seat distribution for a four-year term.[6] Article 151 states that candidates are put forth by parties, and Article 152 that MPs represent the country and not their districts. The 1979 Electoral Law, Article 15, mandates that parties are to present their candidates on closed lists.

---

[5] In January 1993 the CDS changed its label to CDS–PP (Popular Party).

[6] Eighteen districts are located in continental Portugal. The Madeira and Açores Islands have one district each, and there are two districts for Portuguese emigrants, one for those in Europe, and the other for those outside the continent.

According to the comparative literature (Katz 1980; Carey and Shugart 1995), closed list-proportional representation electoral races are mainly won by party organizations, not candidates. This is because the fate of individual candidates depends on the electoral success of their party label and their place on the party list. It is presumed that the better the reputation the candidate has with the party leadership, the higher on the list he or she will be placed. It is further believed that candidates' dependence on the electoral performance of their party lists will both strengthen the party leadership and generate strong incentives for individual candidates to cultivate a party vote.

The Portuguese case largely corroborates the comparative literature. By all accounts, the national party leadership is the most important actor in the selection of candidates for parliamentary elections (Cruz 1995: 175–219; Frain 1997; Freire 1997; Sablosky 1997). There is no institutionalized form of involvement of either voters or ordinary party members in candidate selection. Moreover, there are no term limits nor a mandatory retirement age for MPs. These aspects further enhance the party elite's control over party activities. However, the ability of the national leaderships to shape electoral lists varies across parties. This is partially explained by the different organizational structures of the parties, as indicated in the previous section. Because left parties are more centralized, their national leaders are stronger than their centre and right counterparts. Compelling evidence of such variation is provided by Freire (1997: 42). In the fourth Parliament elected after the establishment of democracy (1985–7), 23.9 per cent of MPs elected from the PS and 17.1 per cent from the PCP occupied posts on the national committee of their parties. Comparative figures for the PSD and CDS were 6.9 per cent and 12.2 per cent, respectively.

Voter surveys seem to confirm the hypothesis that closed list-proportional representation fosters a party vote. Opinion polls show that Portuguese voters have an increasing attachment to parties. In a 1979 national survey, 32.8 per cent of respondents said that parties were very necessary. This same question was put to voters in 1993, and this time an impressive 66.8 per cent of respondents said that parties were very necessary (Bacalhau 1997: 121). In 1993 voters were also asked why they voted for a party. The most frequent response, given by 81.4 per cent of respondents, was 'I vote for the party that is closest to my ideas'—which indicates a strong ideological commitment to parties. After reviewing extensive data from four public opinion polls over fifteen years, Bacalhau (1997: 136) concludes that Portuguese parties '...have emerged as the key actors in politics.'

In addition to candidate selection mechanisms and electoral incentives, institutional aspects concerning electoral competition, party finance, and legislative organization also contribute to the strength of parties in Portugal. Legislative campaigns tend to be rather short. They lasted twenty days in the elections held between 1976 and 1991. In the election in 1995 the campaign period was only thirteen days. It is safe to say that the shorter the campaign period, the heavier the candidates' reliance on their party labels to win electoral races. Moreover, parliamentary parties are endowed with substantial public resources. They have free broadcasting time allocated in proportion to their seat shares, whereas non-parliamentary parties receive a minimum quota of time. Since 1988 parliamentary parties have started to receive public financing. Each receives annually an amount equivalent to 1/225 of the national monthly minimum salary for each vote obtained in the last election for the Assembly of the Republic. For legislative campaigns an amount equivalent to 2,500 national monthly salaries are given to parties which have fielded candidates for at least 51 per cent of the seats, and have won at least 2 per cent thereof. Twenty per cent of that amount are equally distributed, and the remaining 80 per cent are divided according to vote share. According to Katz and Mair (1995), by entrenching the parliamentary parties in the structure of the state, the grant of such public resources to the former helps to cartelize the party system. Portugal can be safely listed as another evidence of such a phenomenon.

Finally, as argued by Leston-Bandeira (1998: 146), individual MPs are endowed with meager resources in the Assembly of the Republic to do their legislative work. An elo-quent indicator of this provided by this author is that since 1991 a typical MP has to share an office with four other colleagues. Consequently, as MPs are deprived of the means to independently operate in Parliament in an efficient manner, the role of party leaderships is considerably strengthened in the organization of legislative activities. Hence, party discipline is very tight in the Assembly. Significantly, all parties have enshrined party discipline in voting decisions in their statutes (Cruz 1995: 193).

In short, political parties are the central agents of Portuguese voters in the electoral and legislative arenas. However, as stressed by some authors (Bruneau and Macleod 1986: 146–64; Cruz 1995: 269–96; Leston-Bandeira 1998), the flip-side of the strength and centrality of nationally-oriented political parties is that MPs have weak links and scarce contact with voters. As MPs are elected through constituencies, such pattern of relationship generates agency loss to voters. Yet, given that Portugal is a small and homogeneous country, this loss can be said to be rather small.

DELEGATION FROM PRESIDENT TO CABINET AND FROM PARLIAMENT TO CABINET

In Portugal's system of government the national electorate designates two agents to whom the cabinet is accountable: the President and the Assembly of the Republic. Because the chain of delegation and accountability in this regime is more complex than that of a typical parliamentary system, delegation from the President to the cabinet will be described separately from that of the Parliament to the cabinet. In addition, the insti-tutional rules regulating the relations among the Chief of State, the Parliament, and the cabinet have undergone important changes since the promulgation of the 1976 Constitution, particularly after the 1982 constitutional reforms. This also speaks in favour of separate subsections for these two delegation–accountability chains.

Delegation from the President to Cabinet

As noted above, the 1976 Constitution established a popularly elected President of the Republic,[7] and endowed the office with extensive powers. Under Article 190 the

---

[7] Portuguese Presidents are elected by majority run-off for a five-year term of office. They are constitu-tionally prohibited from serving a second, consecutive term.

Prime Minister (PM) was appointed by the President after consultations with the Council of the Revolution (which the President himself presided over) and the parliamentary parties, and bearing in mind the electoral results. Cabinet members were appointed by the President at the recommendation of the PM. Articles 193 and 194 established that the cabinet and the PM were politically responsible to the President. Moreover, the President could dissolve the Assembly of the Republic if the Council of the Revolution supported such an action. However, there were restrictions on these powers to dissolve: the Assembly could not be dissolved under a state of siege or a state of emergency, and during an exceptional extension of the President's term of office. There were also automatic constitutional provisions on parliamentary dissolution in case Parliament voted down a confidence motion or cast a no-confidence vote on the third government formed in a single legislature.

Endowing a popularly elected Chief of State with such an array of formal powers in the context of the instability that characterized party politics in Portugal in the first years of the democratic regime had a straightforward consequence: the President became a major player in domestic politics. Portugal's first democratic President was General Ramalho Eanes, the hero of a counter-coup staged in 1975 against a communist uprising. This counter-coup decisively smoothed the path from revolution to democracy. A forceful character, General Eanes assumed the presidency in 1976 intent on making himself heard in the governance of the country.

Additionally, as stressed by Sousa (1983: 14), Article 190—which stated that the President should consult with the Council of the Revolution and parties in the selection of a government—was not binding, which gave Eanes greater discretion in government formation. In fact, he had so much discretion that after the failure of two PS-led governments and disagreements among the parties over the composition of a new government, between 1978 and 1979 he appointed three non-partisan cabinets, staffed by independents. This show of presidential autonomy was obviously opposed by the parties, and gave rise to the Democratic Alliance. The Democratic Alliance government managed to restrain Eanes somewhat. However, in order to place strict limits on Eanes's actions and amend the proto-socialist economic articles of the Constitution with which he was identified, a constitutional revision was necessary (Bruneau and Macleod 1986: 120).

On 30 September 1982 a revised Constitution was promulgated. The revision abolished the heavily militarized Council of the Revolution and replaced it with a 'civilianized' Council of State. Since this constitutional amendment the President's power has been reduced in many important respects. Now the President can only dismiss the government when such a measure is essential to ensure the 'regular functioning of the democratic institutions', and after consulting with the Council of the State. Furthermore, the Assembly of the Republic cannot be dissolved during the first six months after the election of a President nor during the last six months of a President's term. The President is explicitly prohibited from exercising pocket vetoes, that is to say, he or she cannot refuse to sign the promulgation of a bill approved by the Assembly (Article 139: 1,4). This means that if the Chief of State dislikes a bill, he or she must bear the cost of explicitly issuing a veto. In addition, presidential elections are not to be held within ninety days of a parliamentary election (Article 128). The original Constitution required at least sixty days between presidential and parliamentary elections.

It was noted in the introduction of this chapter that the president's power was actually enhanced by the 1982 revision with regard to his veto right. Since then the veto has been the touchstone of presidential power in Portugal, and should be understood as a kind of *ex post* mechanism to control the cabinet and the Parliament. No other popularly elected President in Western Europe has this kind of reactive power, not even the powerful French Chief of State. Furthermore, Portuguese Presidents, unlike their Austrian and Icelandic counterparts, have not abdicated their powers. For example, President Mário Soares (1985–95), a Socialist, vetoed key policy initiatives of the centrist cabinets led by PM Cavaco Silva, who Soares 'cohabited' with during his two terms in office (Cruz 1994: 255–6; Frain 1995: 668; Magone 1997: 42). By using his veto powers—which he did particularly frequently during his second term—Soares was able to push Cavaco Silva's policy initiatives closer to the preferences of the median voter in the presidential election, which leaned to the left. Thus, Portuguese Presidents must be seen as more than figureheads. They actually affect government policy by exercising their formal powers and political clout. During situations of 'cohabitation', Portuguese Presidents are stronger than their French counterparts by virtue of their veto power. Mário Soares was certainly more influential in domestic policy-making in 1985–95 than was Mitterrand in 1986–8 and 1993–5 and than Chirac has been since 1997. On the other hand, when the President and PM come from the same party, French Presidents are definitely stronger than their Portuguese colleagues. The current Portuguese President Jorge Sampaio and former Prime Minister Antonio Guterres are both Socialists, and because of this Sampaio kept a lower profile than his predecessor, Mário Soares. In sum, despite the 1982 Constitutional revision, Presidents have managed to retain an important policy-making role, albeit a negative one, mainly due to their ability to block the governmental agenda through the use of the veto.

Delegation From Parliament to Cabinet

As noted above, the Constitution states that the President appoints the PM after consulting with the parliamentary parties and taking into consideration the electoral results. This last clause was not binding in the first years of the democratic period, as witnessed by the appointment of three non-partisan governments that were of pure 'presidential inspiration', to use the expression common in Portuguese political parlance. However, since the formation of the first Democratic Alliance government in 1980 a constitutional convention has been established: the largest parliamentary party should lead the government. The President appoints the cabinet ministers upon the PM's recommendation, and the latter appoints the junior ministers and the state secretaries.

Once a new PM is selected, he or she submits a governmental programme to the Assembly of the Republic for approval. Article 234 of the Assembly's *Regimento Interno* (standing orders) allows any parliamentary party or at least 25 per cent of all MPs to propose the rejection of the programme when it is under consideration. To reject the government's programme requires that an absolute majority of the members of the

Assembly vote against it. The cabinet also has the right to request a vote on a motion of confidence, and an absolute majority of all MPs is needed for approval. With the exception of the first and third governments led by Mário Soares and the first Guterres cabinet, the opposition has always proposed the rejection of the programme of incoming governments. Yet it has managed to reject only one, that of PM Nobre da Costa, which led to his dismissal by President Eanes. And the only cabinet that fell because of a failed motion of confidence was precisely the first Mário Soares cabinet.[8]

The practice of requesting a vote to reject the government's programme after the appointment of a PM can be considered as a strong convention in Portugal. Moreover, as the rejection of a programme can lead to the dismissal of the cabinet, Bergman (1993: 58) defines such convention as a kind of informal negative investiture vote. For this author, 'according to the negative rules, the onus is not on the government to prove that it is supported by the parliament. Rather it is left to the parliament to prove that the government is not tolerated' (Bergman 1993: 57). This is precisely the nature of Portugal's vote to reject the government's programme.

In addition, students of Portuguese politics agree that those negative rules facilitated the formation of minority and presidential cabinets in the 1976–87 period (Sousa 1983; Moreira 1989; Cruz and Antunes 1990). However, these same cabinets had difficulty passing legislation because, obviously, parliamentary majorities could not be put together without the cooperation of opposition parties. In addition, the factionalism that plagued the largest parties in the early years of the new democratic regime affected governments' ability to make policy. Of course, with the emergence of majority (or near majority) single-party governments in 1987 these difficulties disappeared.

As regards the Parliament's accountability mechanisms vis-à-vis the cabinet, two periods can be identified, between 1976–87 and 1987–95. In the first period—which was characterized by fragile, majority-coalition cabinets, minority cabinets, and presidential governments—parliamentary actors held the executive accountable by means of an *ex ante* non-institutional mechanism: that is, coalition bargaining. In other words, given that during this period no cabinet could count on a stable legislative majority, parliamentary party leaders and MPs had plenty of freedom to trade support for the cabinet for cabinet support of opposition policy preferences.

In the second phase—in which single-party majority cabinets have dominated—there has been an impressive growth in the use of some *ex post*, formal, institutional mechanisms to hold the government accountable. The works of Cruz (1995: 175–219) and Cruz and Antunes (1990), and Leston-Bandeira (1995, 1996, 1998), all show a marked increase in the use of interpellations by the opposition. In the era of single-party majority cabinets the bargaining power of opposition parties simply evaporated. Their natural response to this new strategic situation was to activate the institutional mechanisms at their disposal. The Constitution stipulates that each parliamentary party may request two interpellations per legislative session. In the 1987–91 and

---

[8] For comprehensive data on the record of confidence and no-confidence motions, and proposals for rejection of governmental programmes, see Matos (1992).

1991–95 legislatures, both under majority single-party cabinets, the average number of interpellations per legislative session was 5.5 and 6.3, respectively, as compared to 1.3, 3.0, and 3.5 in the first three democractic legislatures.

Another institutional mechanism that has been intensively used by the opposition in the era of single-party majority cabinets is the committees of inquiry. According to Leston-Bandeira,

the committees of inquiry have become the most visible and popular means of scrutinising government, in particular the discussion on the proposal to establish a committee. In fact, as António Vitorino has pointed out, the proposal for an inquiry often constitutes a "formal charge against the government, likely to put forward conclusions", transforming its discussion into one of the "most lively and polemic parliamentary debates". (Leston-Bandeira 1998: 156)

In the 1991–5 legislature the average number of proposals for committees of inquiry reached its peak, 8.3. It should also be noted that the lowest averages correspond to the legislatures during most of which minority or presidential cabinets were in office: 0.5 in 1976–80, and 4.0 in 1985–7.

Yet, as also observed by Leston-Bandeira (1998: 155), the use of a classical parliamentary control instrument—written questions—has declined with the rise of single-party majority cabinets. Under the 1985–7 legislature, the average number of written questions per legislative session peaked at 2,388.5, but decreased steadily in the next legislatures. Leston-Bandeira contends that this trend is due not only to single-party majorities but also to a rather low rate of answers.

A key problem concerning Portugal's chain of delegation concerns how majority parliamentary parties control their own single-party cabinets. As mentioned in the introduction, the Constitution endows the cabinet with the power to issue decrees. For obvious reasons, the cabinet has been prone to use this instrument of legislative decision-making authority. Between 1977 and 1993, the total number of laws passed by the Assembly of the Republic was 1,249 while the number of decrees issued by the executive was 8,451 (Magalhães 1994: 19). According to Antunes (1988: 82), up to 1987 the Assembly frequently modified the decrees issued by the executive. However, from 1987 to 1991, that is, during the first single-party majority government of Cavaco Silva, the proportion of executive decrees modified by Parliament plummeted to a low of 4 per cent, while no decree was rejected (Magalhães 1995: 98). This author interprets this as indicative of a diminishing role for the Parliament in legislative decision-making.[9] In the language of the principal–agent model, Magalhães can be said to be arguing that the Parliament has abdicated some of its law-making powers to the executive. However, this is not necessarily true. It is only correct if those who hold cabinet posts are entirely at odds with their party's MPs in terms of policy preferences. If ministers and MPs have similar policy preferences, which is very likely in a system in which the executive is dependent on the confidence of Parliament, then the fact that few executive decrees are modified or rejected can be seen as evidence that there is an efficient delegation mechanism from the majority to the cabinet under single-party majority governments.

---

[9] Leston-Bandeira (1998: 152–4) makes a similar point in her analysis of cabinet decrees in Portugal.

Further evidence that such a mechanism exists is that under single-party majority cabinets the Assembly of the Republic passed more laws delegating legislative authority for the executive to speedily deal with relevant matters constitutionally falling under the legislative jurisdiction of the Parliament than it did during the years of majority coalition government and single-party minority governments (Magalhães 1995: 107; Leston-Bandeira 1998: 152). According to the first author, during the 1987–91 legislature and the first half of the 1991–5 one, one-third and one-half, respectively, of the relevant laws enacted by the Assembly were *Leis de Autorização Legislativa* (authorization of powers bills). However, in passing such laws Parliament does not hand a carte blanche to the cabinet. On the contrary, the Assembly defines the scope and time limit for government action, thus establishing *ex ante* mechanisms of control. The efficiency of legislative delegations is suggested by the following indicator: under the 1987–91 legislature the passing of authorization of powers bills took on average eighty-three days, while the average length of time required to pass a standard executive-initiated bills was four months (Magalhães 1995: 107).

Finally, the cabinet is held accountable by means of *moções de censura* (no confidence votes). Article 194 of the Constitution stipulates that at least one-quarter of the membership of the Assembly and any parliamentary party can initiate a no confidence vote on the cabinet's execution of the governmental programme or on any matter of national interest. The approval of a no-confidence vote by an absolute majority of all members of the Parliament leads to the dismissal of the cabinet (Article 195). The first government led by Cavaco Silva (1985–7), a single-party minority one, was terminated by a vote of no confidence initiated by the *Partido Democrático Renovador* (PRD— Democratic Renewal Party), a centre-left party. The PS, which had been cooperating with the government in Parliament, decided to join forces with the PRD in order to avoid running the risk of losing voters to it. The no-confidence motion passed by a vote of 134 votes to 108. Additionally, the Mota Pinto cabinet resigned in order to pre-empt a no-confidence vote in Parliament.

Table 18.1 reports the behavioural record with regard to investiture votes, confidence and no confidence votes, and early dissolution of Parliament.

Other than the motion that led to the resignation of the first Cavaco Silva cabinet, no other motions of no confidence have been voted on in Parliament. A total of five confidence votes have occurred since 1976, though only the first Soares cabinet has been removed by a failed vote of confidence. Four cabinets have ended in early elections following the dissolution of Parliament, most recently in 1987, as of 2003.

DELEGATION WITHIN CABINET

The executive branch is the least studied organ of the Portuguese state during the democratic period. There are only two academic works on this subject—an article by Portas and Valente (1990) that examines the relationship between the PM and cabinet ministers on the basis of interviews with twenty-three former ministers, and the first volume of Amaral's *Curso de Direito Administrativo* (A Course in Administrative Law),

Table 18.1. *Cabinet Formation, Cabinet Termination, and Early Parliamentary Dissolution: Portugal 1976–2000*[a]

No.	Cabinet	Date of formation	Investiture votes (iv)					No-confidence votes (ncv)			Confidence votes (cv)		Did this cabinet end with an early election?	Who dissolved Parliament in this case?[b]
			No. of unsuccessful investiture votes	Voting results of successful iv[c] (1:pro gov, 2:against gov, 3:abstentions, and 4:other)				No. of ncv	Cabinet removed by ncv	Cabinet resigned to pre-empt	No. of cv under spec. inst. mech.	Cabinet removed by failed cv		
				1	2	3	4							
1	Soares I	76/07/23	—[d]	—	—	—	—	0			1	Yes		
2	Soares II[e]	78/01/23	0	141	43	73	—	0			0			
3	Nobre de Costa[f]	78/08/29	1	71	141	40	—	0			0			
4	Mota Pinto	78/11/22	0	109	45	0	—	0		Yes	0			
5	Pintassilgo	79/07/31	0	33	79	125	—	0			0			
6	Sá Carneiro I	80/01/03	0	128	120	0	—	0			1	No	Yes	Head of State
7	Sá Carneiro II[g]	80/10/05	—	—	—	—	—	0			0			
8	Balsemão I[h]	81/01/09	0	134	98	0	—	0			1	No		
9	Balsemão II[i]	81/09/04	0	126	97	0	—	0			1	No	Yes	Head of State
10	Soares III[j]	83/06/09	—[k]	—	—	—	—	0			1	No	Yes	Parl. Maj.
11	Cavaco Silva I	85/11/06	0	86	88	65	—	1	Yes		0		Yes	Parl. Maj.
12	Cavaco Silva II	87/08/17	0	146	30	54	—	0			0			
13	Cavaco Silva III	91/10/31	0	134	15	65	—	0			0			

| 14 | Guterres I | 95/10/28 | —ˡ | — | 115 | — | 2 | — | — | 0 | — |
| 15 | Guterres II^m | 99/10/25 | 0 | — | — | 113 | — | — | 0 | — |

[a] n.d.=no data (missing data); n.a. or '—'=not applicable in this case.

[b] The question 'Who dissolved Parliament in this case?' can be answered with one of five options. This identifies the main constitutional actor that caused the early election. We have not coded the formal signatory, but rather the person or body that made the real decision: (1) Head of State; (2) Prime Minister; (3) Cabinet; (4) Parliamentary majority (Parl. Maj.); (5) Automatic constitutional provision (e.g. if it is required when a new President takes office, or, for example, if it is required after the adoption of a proposal for constitutional amendments).

[c] Two Portuguese rules are very important to note here. One is that the Portuguese decision rule is that the cabinet and its program is rejected only if an absolute majority votes against the proposed cabinet programme. The other is that one-quarter of all MPs can request that an inauguration vote be held. This can be done within three days of when the government presented its programme. Thus, within three days there could potentially be a series of votes in which different parliamentary minorities requested each vote. The vote results that are provided here are those of the first vote to reject the government's programme, except for Cavaco Silva II. For this cabinet, the vote results of the first vote are missing. In this case, the vote results of the second vote are presented instead.

[d] No vote was taken. This was because the opposition parties thought that it would be strategically unwise to show some form of discontent by even requesting a vote.

[e] PM Mário Soares was dismissed by President Ramalho Eanes after the CDS (Social Democratic Center Party) bolted the cabinet.

[f] PM Nobre da Costa was dismissed by President Ramalho Eanes.

[g] This is a new cabinet only because a general election was held. After the election, PM Sá Carneiro and his cabinet simply continued in office and no new vote was necessary. PM Sá Carneiro later died in office.

[h] PM Balsemão resigned alleging that he was being opposed by his own coalition partners.

[i] PM Balsemão resigned after his coalition, the Democratic Alliance (AD, which includes PSD, CDS, and PPM), was defeated in local elections.

[j] PM Soares resigned after some ministers of the PSD (Social Democratic Party), the coalition partner of the PS (Socialist Party), quit the cabinet.

[k] No vote was taken. This was because the opposition parties thought that it would be strategically unwise to show some form of discontent by even requesting a vote.

[l] No vote was taken. This was because the opposition parties thought that it would be strategically unwise to show discontent against a cabinet that just had enjoyed a great electoral success.

[m] There was no roll-call; instead there was a show of hands. The vote results presented here assume that party discipline was perfect.

published in 1992. This section and the section titled Delegation from Ministers to Civil Servants, will rely heavily on these two sources. According to Article 203 of the Constitution, once a government's programme has been adopted by the Assembly of the Republic, the cabinet defines the general guidelines of governmental policy. The PM conducts and coordinates the government (Article 204). The PM is thus the chief of the government, and in this capacity he or she is required to sign all administrative acts of the government.[10]

In addition, the appointment of each ministry's general director (its highest civil servant) is made jointly by the PM and the relevant minister. Under coalition governments, the Vice-PM also signs the directives appointing general directors (Amaral 1992: 225, footnote 1). Individual ministers are charged with carrying out the policies established for their ministries. That is to say, they are Heads of Department, and are in charge of all administrative and organizational aspects of their ministries, even the pettiest matters (Amaral 1992: 230–1). Amaral also notes (1992: 233) that another key ministerial responsibility is to propose policies, although the Constitution is mute on this point.

In their study of Portugal's executive power, Portas and Valente (1990) discovered that, in general, ministers have great autonomy within their policy jurisdictions and concentrate their work on them. The ministers that the authors interviewed reported that they seldom informed their colleagues about the policies they were pursuing. They also confirmed that there is an informal rule stipulating that 'a minister does not discuss the projects of other ministers'. Moreover, all interviewees agreed that the PM's intervention in the affairs of their portfolios were minimal.

Portas and Valente identified three distinct patterns of what they dubbed *discussão política* (policy debate), each one connected to a particular type of government. First, in coalition governments, policy debates were conducted outside the cabinet in private, informal exchanges among the coalition partners. In presidential cabinets, policy was basically discussed in meetings between the President and the PM, though some of the most important ministers were eventually invited to participate in these meetings. Finally, the first elected majority government (the first Democratic Alliance government under the leadership of Sá Carneiro) established an inner cabinet—composed of the PM, the Vice-PM, the adjunct minister, the defence minister, and the adjunct state secretary—to deal with political strategy.

Conventional wisdom in Portugal says that decision-making in the single-party majority governments led by Cavaco Silva between 1987 and 1995 was largely centralized in the hands of the PM in comparison with other Portuguese cabinets. The technocratic profile of Cavaco Silva, an economics professor, certainly contributed to this decision-making style.

---

[10] The *Gabinete da Presidência do Conselho de Ministros* (office of the presidency of the cabinet) provides the PM with support services for the coordination of interdepartmental affairs, and is the umbrella of many State Secretariats that deal with specific policy issues.

DELEGATION FROM MINISTERS TO CIVIL SERVANTS

All civilian ministries in Portugal have the same structure, which tends to be rigid and highly hierarchical. Each ministry has a general director, who is the head of the ministry's civil service and is jointly appointed by the PM and the relevant minister. General directors appoint service directors and are their immediate superiors. Below this are the chiefs of divisions, who are appointed by their immediate superiors, the service directors. Finally, the chiefs of divisions appoint the bureau chiefs.

General directors are the highest-ranking civil servants, and are accountable to the cabinet via the minister in charge of their respective ministry. Service directors, chiefs of division, and chiefs of bureaus do not report directly to either the cabinet or the minister. They are accountable to their immediate superiors. That is to say, a service director is only accountable to the general director; likewise, a chief of division is only accountable to the service director; and a chief of bureau to the chief of division. Thus, on paper, Portugal has a completely vertical chain of command within bureaucracies.

According to Portas and Valente (1990), the relationship between ministers and general directors tends to be rather conflictive. In interviews, some former ministers report that general directors are a 'major obstacle' or a 'conservative force'. They also complain about the poor quality of bureaucrats' work and the great amount of time general directors wasted on various labour problems. Although Portas and Valente only interviewed a relatively small number of former ministers, their findings largely corroborate the conventional wisdom of scholars but also of 'the man on the street'—about the limited competence of the Portugal civil service. This is no surprise given the powerful legacy of the clientelistic and patrimonial practices prevalent in the old authoritarian regime and the fact that the Portuguese civil service in general is not highly skilled (Magone 1997: 128).

Although there have been great improvements in public administration as a result of modernization prompted by high economic growth and Portugal's entry into the European Union (EU), the country's bureaucracy still suffers from the impact of decades of unrestrained patrimonialism. From the point view of the government, patrimonial practices and legacies are a major source of agency loss because they mean that bureaucrats respond to the demands of people other than their constitutional principals.

EXTERNAL CONSTRAINTS

The key external constraint on Portugal's parliamentary chain of delegation and accountability is the EU. The process of democratic consolidation in Portugal was intimately linked to the process of integrating the country with the rest of Europe. In the words of Magone (1996: 152), 'The accession to the EC was seen as the only way to consolidate the very young Portuguese democracy.' Portugal applied for European Community membership in March 1978, and finally became a member in 1986. The decision to join the EU began to have a big impact on domestic policy-making in the late 1980s. Thus, not long after a democratic Parliament had begun to take root in

Portuguese political life, it was faced with the challenge of dealing with a supranational institution. Magone (1996: 157) reports that by 1990 Portugal was already the most successful EU country in terms of enacting national legislation to complete the Single European Market.

Unsurprisingly, the Assembly of the Republic did not take the lead in the process of European integration. Given how busy it was with the domestic side of the democratic consolidation agenda, the Parliament was content to let the cabinet run the show in the early phase of the integration process. Only in 1987 did it pass a law on parliamentary monitoring of Portugal's EU policies. This law was replaced by a new one in 1988, that was, in turn, superseded by yet another in 1994. These laws all aimed at establishing legal mechanisms of parliamentary control over the government's EU policies. The 1988 law established a Committee on European Affairs, which was granted some prerogatives to participate in decisions on EU matters. The 1994 version mandates that the government must submit an annual report on EU matters to the Assembly, an *ex post* mechanism of control. Overall, the three laws have helped to improve the Assembly's information-gathering capacity and enhance its influence over EU affairs. 'Nonetheless, the largest share of EU-related laws has been enacted by the cabinet via executive decrees' (Magone 1996: 155). Yet this should not be seen as evidence that Parliament has abdicated its role in EU affairs. Rather, as argued in the section on Delegation from Parliament to Cabinet, the use of executive decrees can be considered as an efficient delegation mechanism from the majority to the cabinet.

The other significant external constraint on Portugal's parliamentary chain of delegation and accountability is the Constitutional Tribunal. It was created in 1982, and was charged with the pre-emptive control of constitutionality. Upon a President's request, the Tribunal must, within twenty days, rule whether a law approved by the Assembly or a cabinet decree is constitutional. Up to 1997 the Constitution stipulated that this tribunal be composed of thirteen judges, ten elected by the Parliament and three appointed by the ten Parliament-elected judges for a renewable six-year term of office. In 1997 the term was increased to nine years but it is no longer renewable. Candidates for the Parliament-elected judgeships must be sponsored by at least twenty-five MPs and at most fifty.

The Constitutional Tribunal has been active in Portugal's political life. Between April 1983 and May 1993 it ruled over twenty-seven requests made by Presidents, and twenty were deemed unconstitutional (Magone 1997: 52). According to this author, the Tribunal has reviewed important pieces of legislation approved by sizeable parliamentary majorities, such as the anti-corruption law, the law on incompatibilities, and the Official Secrets Act, all passed in 1993, that is, under the second majority single-party cabinet led by Cavaco Silva. It should be noted though that judicial review in Portugal is not based solely on judges' technical concerns with the legality of parliamentary acts. After extensively surveying all the votes cast by the Constitutional Tribunal members on the forty-seven rulings passed by the court between April 1983 and March 1998, Magalhães and Araújo (1998) conclude that there is a 'party connection' underlying those votes. Their statistical analysis clearly shows that in their voting decisions the judges are politically responsive to the agendas of the parties that have supported their appointment to the Tribunal. At any rate, it is safe to affirm that the Constitutional Tribunal is a relevant check on parliamentary majorities in Portugal.

Finally, referendums have increasingly become a new formal external constraint in Portugal. In 1991 a constitutional amendment introduced the referendum as a new policy-making procedure. According to the ordinary law that regulated it, referendums could be proposed by either the cabinet or the Assembly on 'relevant issues of national interest', except for constitutional amendments, budgetary, fiscal, and monetary policies, and policy areas over which Parliament had absolute legislative initiative (see footnote 2). Additionally, the law established that (1) no electoral quorum was required for a referendum to be valid; (2) referendums were to be subject to judicial review before they were voted on; and (3) referendum results were binding on the cabinet and Parliament. However, between 1991 and 1997 no referendum was held.

In 1997 a constitutional amendment allowed citizens to propose a referendum which, however, has to be approved by Parliament before it can be held. And in 1998 a new law regulating the referendum regime was passed. This law was very similar to its 1991 version. The only major change it brought about was to stipulate that a turnout of 50 per cent + 1 of registered voters was required for a referendum decision to be valid. In 1998 two referendums on very relevant issues were held: one on abortion rights, proposed by the PSD, and the other on decentralization, sponsored by the PS. Both were defeated. Thus, so far the referendum can be considered only a *potential* external constraint on Portugal's chain of delegation and accountability.

CONCLUSION

Portugal's blend of semi-presidentialism or *premier*-presidentialism with multipartism has created a regime capable of generating a wide variety of governing solutions: presidential, single-party minority, majority coalition, near majority single-party, and single-party majority cabinets. On the one hand, this flexibility has helped consolidate one of Western Europe's youngest democracies. On the other, it is indicative of how complex the country's delegation process is. The 1982 constitutional revision simplified the delegation process because, for all practical purposes, it eliminated the possibility of presidential government. However, despite the reduction in presidential prerogative brought about in 1982, Presidents have remained important in policy-making, particularly due to their use of the presidential veto, which is a unique characteristic of Portugal's institutional design vis-à-vis its Western European partners.

The second cohabitation period between President Mário Soares and Prime Minister Cavaco Silva showed how important the veto can be. Soares used it as an *ex post* mechanism to influence Cavaco Silva's policy initiatives. This feature of Portuguese political life means that the country's system of government deviates considerably from the unity principle of delegation and accountability in the ideal-type chain. The national electorate selects two agents—the President of the Republic and the Assembly of the Republic—both of whom have the institutional means necessary to respond to their principal's demands, although to differing degrees.

Has this characteristic of Portuguese democracy created agency problems for the voters? It certainly had in the early 1980s, when at a certain point President Ramalho Eanes proved to be too meddlesome in parliamentary politics. Not surprisingly, some of the powers of the presidency were curtailed in the 1982 constitutional revision. However, since then there have not been significant calls to further reduce presidential power. Moreover, the presidency has remained a prestigious and coveted office. In this sense, it is plausible to say that Portuguese voters seem to be now satisfied with their two competing but unequal agents.

Finally, it should also be emphasized that the President has an absolute veto over cabinet decrees and the right to request that the Constitutional Tribunal review bills approved by Parliament. As for cabinet decrees, they make the Portuguese executive very strong in comparison with most of its Western European counterparts by virtue of its monopoly over legislative initiative in many policy areas. Some observers argue that the legislative prerogatives of the cabinet have rendered the Assembly of the Republic almost voiceless in key aspects of national policy-making. In this chapter it was argued that this is not necessarily the case, and that parliamentary majorities have been able to devise efficient *ex ante* and *ex post* mechanisms to hold the executive accountable. Yet it should be conceded that this topic needs further theoretical and empirical study. What is indisputable, though, is that the President's absolute veto over cabinet decrees constitutes an important constraint on the powerful Portuguese cabinet. It should also be viewed as a creative institutional solution to a recurrent problem in parliamentary regimes, namely, unchecked executives created by the fusion of legislative and executive power in the cabinet. Likewise, the President-activated Constitutional Tribunal can be considered as a sensible constraint on potentially perverse consequences of single-party parliamentary majorities.

REFERENCES

Amaral, Diogo Freitas do (1992). *Curso de Direito Administrativo*, Vol. I. Coimbra: Livraria Almedina.

Antunes, Miguel Lobo (1988). 'A Assembleia da República e a Consolidação da Democracia em Portugal'. *Análise Social*, 24: 77–95.

Bacalhau, Mário (1997). 'The Political Party System in Portugal: Public Opinion Surveys and Election Results', in Thomas C. Bruneau (ed.), *Political Parties and Democracy in Portugal: Organizations, Elections, and Public Opinion*. Boulder: Westview Press.

Bergman, Torbjörn (1993). 'Formation Rules and Minority Governments'. *European Journal of Political Research*, 23: 55–66.

Bruneau, Thomas C. (1997). 'Introduction', in Thomas C. Bruneau (ed.), *Political Parties and Democracy in Portugal: Organizations, Elections, and Public Opinion*. Boulder: Westview Press.

—— and MacLeod, Alex (1986). *Politics in Contemporary Portugal: Parties and the Consolidation of Democracy*. Boulder: Lynne Rienner Publishers.

Carey, John M. and Shugart, Matthew S. (1995). 'Incentives to Cultivate a Personal Vote: A Rank Ordering of Electoral Formulas'. *Electoral Studies*, 14: 417–39.

Cruz, Manuel Braga da (1994). 'O Presidente da República na Génese e Evolução do Sistema de Governo Português'. *Análise Social*, 29: 237–65.

Cruz, Manuel Braga da (1995). *Instituições Políticas e Processos Sociais.* Lisbon: Bertrand Editora.

—— and Antunes, Miguel Lobo (1990). 'Revolutionary Transition and Problems of Parliamentary Institutionalization', in Ulrike Liebert and Maurizio Cotta (eds.), *Parliament and Democratic Consolidation in Southern Europe: Greece, Italy, Portugal, Spain and Turkey.* London: Pinter.

Duverger, Maurice (1980). 'A New Political System Model: Semi-Presidential Government'. *European Journal of Political Research,* 8: 165–87.

Frain, Maritheresa (1995). 'Relações entre o Presidente e o Primeiro-Ministro em Portugal: 1985–1995'. *Análise Social,* 30: 653–78.

—— (1997). 'The Right in Portugal: The PSD and CDS/PP', in Thomas C. Bruneau (ed.), *Political Parties and Democracy in Portugal: Organizations, Elections, and Public Opinion.* Boulder: Westview Press.

Freire, André (1997). 'Lógicas de Recrutamento Político: Caracterização Sócio-Política dos Parlamentares Eleitos entre a Constituinte de 1975 e as Legislativas de 1995'. *Secretariado Técnico dos Assuntos para o Processo Eleitoral,* working paper.

Katz, Richard S. (1980). *A Theory of Parties and Electoral Systems.* Baltimore: Johns Hopkins University Press.

—— and Mair, Peter (1995). 'Changing Models of Party Organization and Party Democracy: The Emergence of the Cartel Party'. *Party Politics,* 1: 5–28.

Leston-Bandeira, Cristina (1995). 'Controlo Parlamentar na Assembleia da República: A Translação de Poder da IV para a V Legislatura'. *Legislação: Cadernos de Ciência da Legislação,* 12: 121–51.

—— (1996). 'O Impacto das Maiorias Absolutas na Actividade e na Imagem do Parlamento Português'. *Análise Social,* 31: 151–81.

—— (1998). 'Relationship between Parliament and Government in Portugal: An Expression of the Maturation of the Political System', in Philip Norton (ed.), *Parliaments and Governments in Western Europe.* London: Frank Cass.

Magalhães, José (1994). 'A Constituição e as suas Revisões, a Lei e a Justiça', in António Reis (ed.), *Portugal: 20 anos de Democracia.* Lisbon: Círculo de Leitores.

Magalhães, Pedro Coutinho (1995). 'A Actividade Legislativa da Assembleia da República e o seu Papel no Sistema Político'. *Legislação: Cadernos de Ciência da Legislação,* 12: 87–119.

—— and Araújo, António de (1998). 'A Justiça entre o Direito e a Política: O Comportamento Judicial no Tribunal Constitucional Português'. *Análise Social,* 33: 7–53.

Magone, José (1996). 'The Portuguese Assembleia da República: Discovering Europe', in Philip Norton (ed.), *National Parliaments and the European Union.* London: Frank Cass.

—— (1997). *European Portugal: The Difficult Road to Sustainable Democracy.* New York: St. Martin's Press.

Matos, Luís Salgado (1992). 'O Sistema Político Português e a Comunidade Européia'. *Análise Social,* 27: 773–87.

Moreira, Adriano (1989). 'O Regime: Presidencialismo do Primeiro-Ministro', in Mário Baptista Coelho (ed.), *Portugal: O Sistema Político e Constitucional 1974–1987.* Lisbon: Instituto de Ciências Sociais da Universidade de Lisboa.

Portas, Paulo and Valente, Vasco Pulido (1990). 'O Primeiro-Ministro: Estudo sobre o Poder Executivo em Portugal'. *Análise Social,* 25: 333–49.

Robinson, Richard A. H. (1996). 'Do CDS ao CDS-PP: O Partido do Centro Democrático Social e o seu Papel na Política Portuguesa'. *Análise Social,* 31: 951–73.

Sablosky, Juliet Antunes (1997). 'The Portuguese Socialist Party', in Thomas C. Bruneau (ed.), *Political Parties and Democracy in Portugal: Organizations, Elections, and Public Opinion.* Boulder: Westview Press.

Sartori, Giovanni (1997). *Comparative Constitutional Engineering: An Inquiry into Structures, Incentives, and Outcomes*, Rev. edn. New York: New York University Press.

Shugart, Matthew S. and Carey, John M. (1992). *Presidents and Assemblies: Constitutional Design and Electoral Dynamics*. Cambridge: Cambridge University Press.

Sousa, Marcelo Rebelo de (1983). *O Sistema de Governo Português Antes e Depois da Revisão Constitucional*. Lisbon: Cognitio.

19

Spain: Delegation and Accountability in a Newly Established Democracy

CARLOS FLORES JUBERÍAS

INTRODUCTION: THE BASIC CONSTITUTIONAL FEATURES OF THE SPANISH POLITICAL SYSTEM IN A HISTORICAL PERSPECTIVE

Article 1.3 of the 1978 Spanish Constitution proclaims that 'The political form of the Spanish State is the Parliamentary Monarchy'. Despite the fact that both the Spanish monarchy and Parliament are multisecular institutions—the first dating back to the times of the Visigothic settlers, the second to the Middle Ages—no such statement ever appeared in any previous Spanish Constitution. This, despite the fact that Spain has gone through almost a dozen Constitutions in the last two centuries, almost all of which have attempted to accommodate both institutions.

The Constitution's proclamation arguably puts Spain 'at the forefront of other monarchic States' (Álvarez Conde 1990: 51), since it 'clearly reveals a design to rationalize a parliamentary regime, expressing through written law what in [other] European monarchies has been the outcome of an evolutionary and consuetudinary process' (Sánchez Agesta 1980: 211). Although Article 1.3 of the Constitution has undeniably greatly clarified the role and relationship between the Crown and the Parliament (see Bar Cendón 1979; Torres del Moral 1983), the novelty of the Constitution on this particular point should not lead us to forget the long process of evolution that preceded it.

A Parliamentary form of government was introduced early in the process of modern constitutional evolution of Spain. To overcome the tensions, disputes, and discontinuities that existed under the 1812 Constitution, the 1834 Royal Statute introduced formulas for collaboration between Parliament, cabinet, and the Crown. These were subsequently developed by ordinary legislation and unsanctioned constitutional conventions. Thus, after 1834 the Council of Ministers was formally recognized, the holding of both a cabinet appointment and a parliamentary seat became accepted practice, collaboration between Parliament and the Crown developed, the principle that the cabinet cannot stay in office without the Parliament's confidence was accepted, and the vote of confidence and the motion of censure were introduced (Tomás Villarroya 1982: 35). These developments were gradually codified in subsequent constitutional texts, as well as complemented by other practices—the Speech of the Crown, the use of interpellations, the selection of ministers from the majority party—that are also characteristic of parliamentary government.

However, through the first decades of the twentieth century, Spanish parliament-arism was to a large extent distorted by royal meddling, military influence, the absence of numerous basic political liberties, weak party structures heavily influenced by local party bosses or 'caciques', and by periodic and widely accepted rigging of parliamentary elections. Hence, it was not until the short-lived second Republic that an authentic par-liamentarism emerged, one based on a broad recognition of civil liberties, a well devel-oped party system, and free and competitive elections. However, the 1931 Constitution, which featured a strong Prime Minister (PM) alongside a powerful President and allowed for a deeply divided Assembly, proved 'unable to channel the aggregated impact of an explosive political participation, a deteriorated economic situation, very strong social tensions and the appeal to violence by significant minorities' (Martínez Sospedra 1988: 51). It collapsed after only five years. During the long parenthesis of Francoist authoritarianism, the Head of State enjoyed sweeping powers (Zafra Valverde 1973: 200). Hence, a true parliamentary form of government was delayed until 1978.

The introduction of a true parliamentary government was not the only innovation of the 1978 Constitution. The proclamation of one of the broadest sets of individual, political, and social rights in Western constitutionalism, the reintroduction of the Crown and the Senate, a new attempt to create an efficient judicial review, and above all devolution, became the hallmarks of the new Spanish democracy. The creation of 'el Estado de las Autonomías' (see Flores Juberías 1998), a heterogeneous set of nineteen territorial entities with different degrees of self-government, albeit very similar institu-tions, was a huge task which took a decade and a half. In fact, although the process of community creation and institution building is now completed, the task of transferring competence remains unfinished. This process has substantially changed the way in which the country is governed. The regional chain of delegation and accountability now runs parallel to the national one.

EU membership has also dramatically changed the Spanish political system (see Muñoz Machado 1993). Since Spain joined the European Community in 1986, Spanish policies have had to accommodate EU requirements in a wide range of fields, national law has come under the jurisdiction of the European Court of Justice, and decision-making on many issues has shifted from Madrid to Brussels. Difficulties involved in scrutinizing decisions adopted in the many EU forums and in holding EU bureaucrats accountable—the so-called 'democratic deficit'—has provoked scepticism and distrust. Many citizens feel that the chain of delegation goes well beyond their national institutions, while accountability does not.

POLITICAL PARTIES: THE RAPID CONSOLIDATION OF VOTERS' PREFERENCE

The 1978 Constitution was the first in Spain's history to include an explicit reference to political parties. This was not unexpected since parties played a key role in the transition, and other European constitutions had already paved the way for such a recognition (see García Cotarelo 1985: 142–88). Hence, Article 6, a part of the almost unamendable

Preliminary Title (see Rodríguez Díaz 1989), proclaims that 'Political parties express democratic pluralism, assist in the formulation and manifestation of the popular will, and are a basic instrument for political participation'. The article also states that the creation and activities of political parties should be free so long as they obey the Constitution and the law, and commands that 'their internal structure and operation must be democratic'.

The key role of parties throughout the transition and the idea—widely accepted— that strong parties are a precondition for a stable democracy quickly transformed Spain into a 'party democracy'. It has even been argued that Spain has become a 'party state', 'the structure, performance, and real disposition of which is conditioned by the party system in a relatively autonomous way in relation to its formal juridical configuration' (García-Pelayo 1986: 90).

Perhaps the most telling evidence regarding the preponderance of parties in Spain lies in the fact that their legal regulation was, until the law 6/2002 on political parties was passed, limited to the six articles that comprised the 4 December 1978 Law, a text that left most basic aspects of party activity virtually unregulated and provided no effective guarantee for the constitutional requirement of internal democracy (Cascajo Castro 1992: 192–3).

The configuration of the Spanish party system took place at the 1977 elections, and since then the 1982 and 1996 parliamentary elections have been, by far, the most decisive events in its evolution. The June 1977 elections—the first competitive ones since 1936— reduced the extravaganza of parties, fronts, alliances, and coalitions that emerged after General Franco's death (see Equipo de Estudios 1976) to more manageable propor- tions. Adolfo Suárez's Union of the Democratic Centre (UCD) won the election, while the Spanish Socialist Worker's Party (PSOE) led by Felipe González came a close sec- ond. To the right, some prominent francoist ministers embraced the reformist strategy and rallied behind Manuel Fraga inside the Popular Alliance (AP). Most of the radical Left converged in the Spanish Communist Party (PCE). These two forces polled slightly less than 10 per cent of the vote each.

The situation created by the 1977 elections was largely reproduced two years later in the first post-constitutional elections, but changed dramatically in 1982 (see Penniman and Mujal-León 1985) when the UCD disbanded after suffering a huge loss to the PSOE. The UCD, a loose conglomerate of former francoist cadres and local bosses, with a few moderate opposition figures, was deeply marred by factions. These factions only accepted the leadership of Adolfo Suárez as a matter of convenience (Huneeus 1985). Hence, when the party was forced to transform its election platform into policies on several key issues, its weak cohesion quickly eroded (see Attard Alonso 1983). In contrast to this, the PSOE, which developed strong organizational links while in opposition, was able to carry out an ambitious set of reforms once it took office. This ability to act was made possible by the undisputed leadership of Felipe González, the party's comfortable majority in both houses of Parliament and its dominance in most local and regional governments, and a favourable European environment (see García Cotarelo 1992).

Popular support for González began to decline in the early 1990s when economic performance began to falter and several corruption scandals erupted. In the meantime, the former AP—now renamed the Popular Party (PP)—had transformed itself into a more centrist group, dismissed most of the 'Old Guard', and reinforced its internal organization under the leadership of José María Aznar. The new PP forged comprom-ises with some minor regionalist parties, courted the stronger nationalist forces in Catalonia and the Basque Country, and increased pressure on the Socialist Party as part of its strategy for driving González out of government.

After mustering only a plurality of seats in Congress in the 1993 elections (see Martínez Cuadrado 1996: 149–72), the PSOE was forced to form a minority government with the external support of the Catalan nationalists. In the regional and local elections of 1995, the Socialists were badly beaten by the PP in most important cities and regional Governments (see Martínez Cuadrado 1996: 295–328). Discredited by corruption, and affected by Gonzalez's announced retirement, the party lost the 1996 elections to the PP, which took over the government.

However, throughout its first term in office the new PP government was able to control only a plurality of seats and therefore needed the support of the Catalonian Convergence and Union (CiU) and (to a lesser extent) the Basque Nationalist Party (PNV) and both parties are ideologically right of centre and defend the historical rights of their respective territories. Both have been in power in their respective autonomous governments since they were first established. It was not until the sweeping victory in the 2000 elections that José María Aznar was able to govern with the comfortable backing of an absolute majority of both houses of parliament.

Generally speaking, the Spanish party system can be characterized in terms of five features (Martínez Sospedra 1996: 250–6):

1. Two basic cleavages of class and centre/periphery, but no longer any serious religious division.
2. An authoritarian political culture which explains low party membership ratios, negative views of politics—especially at the national level—and a preference for a strong, paternalistic State.
3. A rather stable distribution of political preferences since 1977, with more than four-fifths of the voters defining themselves as either centre-right, centre, or centre-left, the latter usually being the largest segment (Montero 1995: 105).
4. Parties that abandoned their responsibilities for political socialization once democracy appeared sufficiently consolidated and mass mobilization no longer necessary.
5. And, therefore, parties characterized by low levels of social penetration and party identification, a party membership with more interest in paid jobs in public administration than grassroots activity, and the development of elitist and vote-seeking electoral strategies (Share 1999).

DELEGATION FROM VOTERS TO MPs: HOW ARE THE *CORTES* ELECTED, AND HOW DO THEY PERFORM?

Considering the huge concentration of power in a single person that characterized Franco's regime, creating a strong, popularly-elected executive capable of ruling even against the wishes of Parliament was unthinkable during the transition. The 1978

Constitution envisioned an essentially parliamentary system, largely inspired by the German model, in which Parliament was the only depository of national sovereignty. Under the Constitution the Prime Minister could not be invested nor remain in office without the confidence of the Lower House of Parliament. In addition, there was virtually no possibility of holding a referendum to allow voters to disavow Parliament. Given this, Parliament was bound to become—at least theoretically—the central site of political decision-making.

However, this view of Spain as a paradigm of parliamentary government is superficial. Spanish political parties have turned out to be fairly oligarchic—and in quite a few cases even rather personalistic—organizations, and this tendency has tainted both the way Parliament conducts its affairs and the way it is elected.

The electoral system governing the election of the Congress—the only house to which government is accountable—is spelled out in Article 68 of the Constitution and codified in the 19 June 1985 Electoral Law (see Cazorla Prieto 1986; Fernández Segado 1986). Since this Law reproduces most of the essential features of the provisional electoral system used in 1977, 1979, and 1982, and since it also regulates the basis of the electoral systems used in the autonomous communities and locally, Spanish electoral processes are characterized by a high degree of continuity and uniformity.

Congress is composed of 350 deputies elected for four-year terms in secret balloting in universal, free, equal, and direct elections, open to all Spanish citizens age eighteen or older. The electoral district is the province. Each province has at least two seats, with the remaining 248 being distributed in proportion to the population. Madrid and Barcelona return thirty-four and thirty-one deputies respectively, while the smallest districts—like Soria, Teruel, or Segovia—elect only three. The African cities of Ceuta and Melilla are the exception, returning one deputy each.

Candidates must be nominated by parties or party coalitions and must be included in a closed, blocked list. Nomination by voters themselves is cumbersome and therefore infrequent. To date, primaries have been used only by the Socialist Party to select candidates for the 1998 and 1999 regional elections and for the general election of 2000. However, in several cases internal disputes forced candidates who had succeeded in the primaries to resign before the elections, usually in favour of candidates favoured by the party apparatus.

Seats are awarded by the d'Hondt formula to parties and coalitions that get more than 3 per cent of the vote at the district level, and candidates are elected in the order that they appear on the party or coalition list. Thus, voters cannot influence the order in which individual candidates are elected.

The legal formula for the distribution of seats among districts has created serious malapportionment, one that benefits the smaller, largely rural, provinces at the expense of larger, urban ones. While there is a deputy for every 26,000 voters in Soria, in Madrid there is only one for every 124,000 voters. This imbalance benefits right-of-centre parties, which enjoy substantial support in the overrepresented provinces of central Spain. Moreover, this distribution of seats has encouraged the creation of many small districts—with only three to five deputies—and only a few large ones; namely Madrid, Barcelona, Valencia, and Seville. With such a low district magnitude, disproportionality is bound to be rather high. This obviously favours larger parties, severely punishes smaller ones, and seems difficult to reconcile with the constitutional requirement embedded in Article 68.3.

Other features of the electoral system, for example, campaign financing, also favour larger, well-established parties. Spanish parties raise very little money from private sources—that is, via gifts, donations, or membership fees—because the 1987 Law on Party Finance severely limits private donations and income from membership fees is negligible (del Castillo 1992: 156–62). The bulk of party financing comes from public funds, largely through annual allocations from the State budget. These are distributed among parliamentary parties in proportion to the votes and seats won in the most recent election. Special allocations of State funds, similarly on the basis of previous electoral results, take place with each local, autonomic, parliamentary, or European election (see Arceo Vacas 1993). Finally, there is funding for parliamentary groups in the Cortes, autonomous legislatures, and local assemblies. Since all three sources of income are basically allotted to parliamentary parties, the lack of financial resources is a severe handicap for new groups. The only exception is free advertising during election campaigns when every party running candidates has the right to free radio and television time. But since the amount and hourly distribution of this free advertising time is based on the parties' parliamentary representation, the final outcome is virtually the same (see Solér Sanchez 2001: 123–67).

In light of the party finance rules, the only chance for new parties to survive seems to be by splitting other parties and attracting crossover MPs. Yet this appears to be increasingly infeasible. Though in the late nineties a number of parties—including the New Left, a pro-socialist splinter from the communist-dominated United Left— got some political leverage through such strategies, Spanish parties have become increasingly disciplined. The gradual dissolution of the UCD between the 1979 and the 1982 elections and the Popular Alliance's failure to form stable and cohesive parliamentary groups after 1982 and 1986 have motivated party leaders to strengthen party discipline outside and especially inside parliament.

Outside parliament, the lack of any constitutional or legal regulation of candidate nomination has enabled parties to adopt whatever rules they prefer. These are extremely ambiguous in the Socialist Party, completely centralist in the PP, and slightly more democratic only in the case of United Left (Barrat i Esteve 1995: 125–38). Hence, candidates are often faithful party members who understand that their nomination and re-election to parliament depend less on voters than on the party leadership. Inside parliament, it is the party leadership that determines the agenda of the parliamentary group and selects which deputies will speak for the group in committees and plenary. In government parties, party leadership also ensures the swift passage of government bills and, more broadly, maintains stable parliamentary support for the Cabinet.

Article 79.3 of the Constitution provides some guarantee of the independence of deputies and senators by proclaiming that their vote is personal and cannot be delegated. Moreover, Article 67.2 prohibits the imperative mandate. However, this prohibition has historically been aimed to prevent voters from instructing representatives about what to do, or even from removing them from office before the end of their term. Therefore, it is mostly a relic, unable to affect the way representatives interact with their parties (Punset 1992: 125–6). In this interaction, the position of the representatives in the Spanish Congress vis-à-vis their party leadership is rather weak. While deputies cannot legally be forced to vote against their will or compelled to give up their seats if they dissent (Santaolalla 1992), parties have nevertheless developed a series of practices that greatly limit this independence of mind and put recall essentially in the hands of their party leaders. These practices include requiring their candidates to fill in a resignation document with a blank date and imposing fines on deputies who fail to vote along party lines.

DELEGATION FROM PARLIAMENT TO CABINET: 'RATIONALIZED PARLIAMENTARISM'

Despite the fact that the Spanish political system is constitutionally defined as a parliamentary monarchy, the Constitution had created a strong executive, one quite able to become the central pole of the state (Alzaga 1978: 429). Álvarez Conde (1990: 487) even characterized the Prime Minister (or 'Presidente del Gobierno') as 'the central axis of our political regime'.

This latter descriptive assertion is justifiably made about the Prime Minister, and not about the cabinet as a whole, since the position of the former is constitutionally reinforced vis-à-vis that of the other cabinet members in three main ways. First, the PM is the only member of the executive directly elected by Congress. He drafts the government's agenda and presents it to the legislature, and he plays the key role in the formation and operation of the cabinet. The PM proposes the appointment and dismissal of ministers, directs the government's action, and coordinates the functions of its other members. He is the only member of the executive who is directly accountable to Congress, and the only one authorized to dissolve the legislature. In addition, he is usually the undisputed leader of the largest party in parliament, which means that in addition to his constitutional powers he has a significant degree of political authority. It could be well said that the chain of delegation links not Parliament to cabinet, but Congress to PM in the first instance, and then PM to the cabinet.

The prominence of the PM can be traced, as mentioned above, to the process of cabinet formation itself (see Revenga Sánchez 1988). The government as a whole is constitutionally obliged to resign after general elections, whenever the PM loses a confidence vote in Congress, or upon the resignation or death of the PM (Articles 101.1 and 114.1). It is the King who proposes a candidate for PM. However, the King must consult representatives designated by the political groups represented in parliament, and must make his proposal through the President of the Congress of Deputies (Article 99.1). At a second stage, the proposed candidate is required to submit to the Congress of Deputies the political program of the government he intends to form and to obtain the confidence of an absolute majority of its members in a first vote, or a plurality in a second vote held forty-eight hours later (Article 99.2-3) and with a majority of members in attendance. If the two voting rounds fail to invest the proposed candidate, the King proposes new candidates until one succeeds. If no candidate has obtained the confidence of Congress within two months of the first investiture vote, the King is to dissolve both houses and call new elections (Article 99.4-5). This is the only exception to Article 115.3 of the Constitution, which prohibits a second dissolution of Parliament before a year has passed since the previous one. The constitutional provision is designed to provide stability for newly constituted governments, not to allow endless post-election negotiations.

It has been a subject of occasional debate whether the King has any discretion in proposing a candidate for PM. The matter certainly depends on the election outcome, and in particular on whether there is clear—or at least an unmatched—support for a particular candidate over all others. Since this has always been the case, there is no evidence about what might happen in a situation in which politically divergent alternatives appeared equally feasible. Anyway, in Spain 'the existence of governments lacking the support of the majority of the House is perfectly possible, since this has been consciously sought by the makers of the constitution, in their efforts to promote political stability' (Bar Cendón 1985a: 182).

Congress can withdraw its confidence in the PM at any time, thus forcing his immediate resignation. This can happen either on a motion from the House or on a PM's motion, because the Spanish Constitution authorizes both votes of confidence and votes of no confidence, that is, motions of censure.

The basic characteristics of the vote of confidence are set out in Article 112, which states that 'The President of the Government, after deliberation by the Council of Ministers, may pose before the Congress of Deputies the question of confidence on his program or on a declaration of general policy. Confidence shall be taken as granted when a plurality of the deputies vote for it'. Article 114.1 adds that if Congress denies its confidence to the government, then the government is to submit its resignation to the King, and a new PM will be designated pursuant to the provisions of Article 99. As in other parliamentary systems, the vote of confidence is aimed at allowing the government to confirm the confidence expressed in the investiture vote. In addition, it also compels parliamentary parties to define their positions, especially in the case of minority governments or cabinets supported by a loose coalition of parties.

Several aspects of this procedure deserve consideration. To begin with, the initiation of the vote of confidence depends entirely on the PM, since the cabinet only has the right to deliberate upon proposals from the PM, but not to veto them. This is obviously derived from the fact that only the PM—and not the cabinet—receive Congress confidence upon investiture. As regards the object of the vote, the Spanish procedure is different from the French and German models, both of which allow a vote of confidence to be linked to approval of a government bill. Confidence is, in such cases, granted or withdrawn on the basis of level of support for a programme or general policy declaration submitted by the government. However, the programme or policies in question do not automatically become law upon a positive vote, thus ensuring that the confidence vote cannot become an extraordinary law-making procedure. Third, the government only needs the support of a plurality of deputies to stay in office—not an absolute majority. This feature is in keeping with the investiture vote, but probably transforms the institution into 'a mere formality, devoid of any interest' (Torres del Moral 1992: 231). Finally, the Spanish vote of confidence also contrasts with those of other European states in that it does not provide grounds for parliamentary dissolution. If the PM loses the confidence of Congress, he has no choice but immediate resignation.

The Spanish regulation of the no-confidence vote closely follows the precedent of the German *Grundgesetz*, although the consequences of failure are not exactly the same. The German experience was familiar to Spanish constitution-makers, but imitation is not the only explanation for its adoption. Vírgala Foruria (1988) has argued that the 1977 party system made single party majority cabinets unlikely. Given this expectation, the two largest parties (UCD and PSOE) preferred constitutional rules including no-confidence vote procedures, favourable to the formation and maintenance of single-party minority governments.

The vote of no-confidence must be initiated by at least one-tenth of the deputies. It must be motivated and propose an alternative candidate for Prime Minister. The proposal cannot be put to a vote until five days after its presentation, and alternative motions may be presented during the first two days of this period. Adoption of a vote of no confidence requires the support of an absolute majority of the deputies (Article 113.1-3) and forces the entire government to resign. Since the alternative candidate proposed in the vote of no-confidence is understood to have the confidence of the house, the King must appoint him PM (Article 114.2). If the proposal is unsuccessful, its signatories cannot present another one during the same parliamentary session (Article 113.4).

One of the most criticized feature of the constitutional regulation of the no-confidence vote (e.g. see Vírgala Foruria 1988: 242–5) is the possibility of introducing alternative motions—that is, motions proposing alternative candidates—immediately after a first motion has been proposed. Such a plurality of candidates might complicate deliberations and make it more difficult for the opposition to agree upon a joint strategy. In reality, alternative motions are unlikely. It is true that the number of deputies whose signature is required to propose such a motion is not very high in comparison to the number required for other regulations. Yet, given the configuration of the Spanish party system, only the major opposition parties—PSOE in 1980, the Popular Alliance in 1987—have actually been able to use this mechanism.

The most controversial regulation governing the no-confidence vote is found not in the Constitution, but rather in Congress's Standing Orders. It deals with the debate that precedes the vote on a no-confidence motion. The regulation stipulates that the debate is opened by one of the signatories of the motion, which may speak as long as he/she likes. The alternative candidate speaks second, again without any time limit. After a pause, representatives of those parliamentary groups willing to intervene are given a chance to speak. These procedural rules mean that the sitting PM plays an entirely secondary role in the parliamentary process to the alternative candidate.

Table 19.1 reports the behavioural record with respect to investiture votes, votes of confidence and no-confidence, and parliamentary dissolution.

The only case of an unsuccessful investiture vote occurred before the Calvo-Sotelo cabinet in 1981. Parliament twice voted on motions of no confidence, and twice voted on motions of confidence, but in no instance was a cabinet removed by such a vote. Six cabinets ended in early elections following the dissolution of parliament by the PM, for example the González IV Cabinet in 1996.

Table 19.1. *Cabinet Formation, Cabinet Termination, and Early Parliamentary Dissolution: Spain 1977–2000*[a]

No.	Cabinet	Date of formation	Investiture votes (iv)						No-confidence votes (ncv)			Confidence votes (cv)		Did the cabinet end with an early election?	Who dissolved Parliament in this case[b]
			No. of unsuccessful investiture votes	Voting results of successful iv (1: pro gov., 2: against gov., 3: abstentions, and 4: other)					No. of ncv	Cabinet removed by ncv	Cabinet resigned to pre-empt ncv	No. of cv under spec. inst. mech.	Cabinet removed by failed cv		
				1	2	3	4								
1	Suárez I[c]	77/06/17	n.a.	n.a.	n.a.	n.a.	n.a.		0			0		Yes	PM
2	Suárez II	79/04/04	0	183	149	8	10		1	No		1	No	Yes	PM
3	Calvo-Sotelo	81/02/25	1	186	158	0	6		0			0		Yes	PM
4	González I	82/12/01	0	207	116	21	6		0			0		Yes	PM
5	González II	86/07/23	0	184	144	6	16		1	No		0		Yes	PM
6	González III	89/12/05	0	167	155	6	22		0			1	No	Yes	PM
7	González IV	93/06/10	0	181	165	1	3		0			0		Yes	PM
8	Aznar	96/05/05	0	181	166	1	2		—			—		—	—

[a] n.d. = no data (missing data); n.a. or '—' = not applicable in this case.

[b] The question 'Who dissolved Parliament in this case?' can be anwered with one of five options. This identifies the main constitutional actor that caused the early election. We have not coded the formal signatory, but rather the person or body that made the real decision: (1) Head of State; (2) Prime Minister; (3) Cabinet; (4) Parliamentary majority; (5) Automatic constitutional provision (e.g. if it is required when a new President takes office, or, for example, if it is required after the adoption of a proposal for constitutional amendments).

[c] The formal rules for investiture went into effect only with the new Constitution of 1978.

The Spanish Parliament also enjoys a number of secondary control mechanisms commonly found in other parliamentary systems. These are granted either by the Constitution or by the Standing Orders. Both houses, not only Congress, have a rich panoply of unsanctioned control methods. These include submitting written or oral questions to be answered in plenary or committee, proposing interpellations (i.e. questions leading to debate and sometimes even a vote), passing non-legislative resolutions, forming inquiry committees, and requesting the appearance of ministers and other government officials in plenary or in a committee.

For three reasons, the extent to which these instruments actually increase government accountability to Parliament is uncertain. First, the relevance of these unsanctioned control methods is closely linked to the actual effectiveness of the major control device—the no-confidence vote. Since the latter is quite unlikely to succeed, the actual value of the other controlling devices is significantly reduced too. As Martínez Sospedra (1983: 225) puts it, 'rendering the vote of no confidence useless actually leads to the degradation of the remaining control mechanisms'.

Moreover, the legal regulation of many of these mechanisms appears to be aimed more at protecting the government than at holding it accountable to Parliament. To mention only the clearest example of this, Articles 40 and 52 of the Congress' Standing Orders require a plenary vote in order to form an inquiry committee; mandate that the party composition of its members must mirror the composition of the Congress and that decisions of the committee must be taken by weighted vote; and, finally, stipulate that the committee's final report must be debated in plenary and put to a vote. Given these provisions, it should not be very difficult for the government, which, by definition, enjoys broad support in plenary, to boycott the work of unwelcome committees or even to veto the formation of the most annoying ones. This way—in the words of Torres del Moral (1992: 208)—'the real nature of the institutions we are analysing is in fact reversed, up to the point that they become, instead of means for the parliamentary control over the government [...] a mere exercise of governmental tolerance towards parliament or even,...governmental control over parliament'.

Finally, the very existence of a party democracy, which has transformed the way Parliament works, has also affected the way in which these control mechanisms actually operate. While opposition parties are bound to put all these mechanisms to use in an effort to scrutinize government performance, government parties are likely to request a minister to appear or to pose a question only when doing so will serve to publicize positive achievements. In both cases, as in most other parliamentary systems, the opposition and the majority act more with an eye towards swaying public opinion than in an effort to influence fellow MPs.

DELEGATION FROM CABINET TO INDIVIDUAL MINISTERS: *KANZLERDEMOKRATIE*

The pre-eminence of the Spanish PM over his ministers derives from his privileged position as the only member of the government directly elected by and directly accountable to Congress. This pre-eminence is also revealed in the way the cabinet is formed and operates. The PM alone is responsible for the appointment and dismissal of ministers, and he directs the work of the government and coordinates the actions of its other members.

The freedom with which the PM appoints ministers is almost unlimited. Congress has no constitutional right to scrutinize the PM's proposals, and the King's role is a mere formality. In addition, since the PM is usually the undisputed leader of the majority party, ministerial appointments do not have to reflect to the views of parliamentary groups or party notables. They usually reflect the PM's personal inclinations more than anything else. In fact, only during the first UCD Governments, when Adolfo Suárez had to deal with a highly fragmented party, did factions become major players in the power struggle, asserting control over specific policy areas via ministerial appointments. More commonly, ministerial nominations are not revealed until after the investiture vote, and they are made only after the PM himself has decided whom he wants to appoint. This practice is supported by the Law 50/1997, which repeats the laconic wording of Article 100 of the Constitution, stating that ministers 'shall be appointed and dismissed by the King at the proposal of its President'.

A closely related issue, which illustrates the ever-increasing powers of the Spanish PM, has to do with the determination of ministries. Since 1957 variations in the number, denomination, and competencies of ministerial departments have needed to be established by law. During the turbulent Transition, Royal Decree-Law 18/1976 allowed such variations to take place via successive decrees passed by the Council of Ministers. Once the Constitution entered into force, Royal Decree-Law 22/1982 and Law 10/1983 returned to the practice of requiring legislative authorization. Despite these precedents, the new Law 6/1997 has gone so far as to allow the PM—not the government as a whole—to determine the number, denomination, and competencies of ministerial departments and Secretaries of State. He does so by issuing Royal Decrees in his own name. Hence, the freedom the PM enjoys with respect to selecting and removing ministers extends to the configuration of his cabinet and the basic inner structure of government departments.

Regarding the PM's leading role within the cabinet, Articles 2 and 3 of Law 50/1997 add several additional powers to the wide range of authority already granted by the Constitution. The law makes the PM's broad constitutional mandate of 'direct[ing] the Government's action and coordinat[ing] the functions of its other members' more concrete by spelling out a list of responsibilities. These include representing the government; drafting its political agenda; determining both national and foreign policies and verifying their implementation; directing defence policy and commanding the armed forces; calling, presiding over, and setting the agenda for meetings of the Council of Ministers; solving conflicts of attribution that arise between ministerial departments; providing instructions for the ministers; and entrusting the Deputy PM (when such positions have been created) with the appropriate tasks.

Considering this sweeping enumeration of prime ministerial power, it may be hard to appreciate the so-called 'principle of collegiality' and 'departmental principle'—both of which are articulated alongside the 'prime ministerial leadership principle' in the exposition of the motives of Law 50/1997. The former stems in part from the constitutional provision contained in Article 108, which states that '[T]he Government in its political conduct is collectively accountable before the Congress of Deputies'. It is codified in Law 50/1997, which spells out the functions of the Council of Ministers. Among them, Article 5 lists drafting government bills and the state budget; passing Royal Decree-Laws and Royal Legislative Decrees; negotiating and concluding international treaties, and forwarding them to parliament when necessary; declaring states of alarm and emergency, and proposing to Congress that it declare a state of siege; issuing public debt and borrowing money as authorized by law; passing regulations for the implementation of laws; creating, reforming, or suppressing executive organs within ministerial departments; and adopting programmes, plans, and directives for all state administrative agencies.

The way in which the Council of Ministers exercises all these competencies is strongly determined by three elements. One is the primacy of the PM, who calls, presides over, and determines the agenda for Council meetings. Another one is confidentiality. Cabinet members are legally required to keep their deliberations secret—to the extent that they must swear to do so when they take their oath of allegiance. Minutes of meetings only record cabinet decisions, not the preceding debates. Finally, the lack of formality is also remarkable. Many issues clearly regulated in other institutions—for example, quorum requirements, voting mechanisms, guarantees for minorities, debate procedures—are simply unregulated. As López Calvo (1996: 206) has argued, this has much to do with the fact that Spanish democracy has no experience with coalition governments. It is bound to change once this possibility materializes. Until then, the Council of Ministers appears elusive to both legal regulation and scholarly research.

The so-called 'departmental principle' aims at giving each minister autonomy and responsibility within the scope of his jurisdiction. The Constitution itself, in Article 98.2, requires that the leadership and coordinating functions of the PM should be performed 'without prejudice to [the ministers'] competence and direct responsibility' for the management of their respective departments. However, the scope of these responsibilities is not clarified by Article 4 of Law 50/1997, which basically grants the ministers the power to issue regulations and to carry out the government's business in their respective areas of competence, but always 'in conformity with the decisions adopted at the Council of Ministers and the guidelines from the President of the Government'.

The corollary of this devaluation of ministerial autonomy is, obviously, a parallel devaluation of ministers' individual political responsibility, at least in its most relevant dimension—political censure by Congress. Some scholars (e.g. see Vírgala Foruria 1988: 289–308) have argued that since ministers' responsibility before Congress is not expressly ruled out by the Constitution, it could very well derive from Article 98.2. It is seen as potentially useful in cases in which individual ministers or their subordinates commit important political mistakes in managing their departments with regard to discretionary matters. Nevertheless, the Standing Orders of Congress have never provided any specific procedure for censoring an individual minister, probably on the assumption that if the minister's conduct is supported by the PM the appropriate mechanism is a vote of no confidence. If, on the other hand, the minister does not have the PM's support, then it is the PM who should dismiss him. Thus, the only way Congress can criticize an individual minister appears to be by passing a non-binding, resolution on the minister's policies (see Fernández Segado 1985: 239–91). Motions of this kind have been proposed and voted on several times, but since none has ever passed it is impossible to tell whether such a resolution might force the PM to remove the minister.

In conclusion, while one might expect the operation of Spanish governments to exhibit a balance between the principles of prime ministerial leadership, collegiality, and departmental autonomy, it does not do so. López Calvo (1996: 195) notes that 'while the Council of Ministers has a collegial "appearance" it is in fact an organ in which this principle yields to the monocratic principle'. In short, the Spanish cabinet is a clear-cut example of *Kanzlerdemokratie* (see also Bar Cendón 1985*b*: 48).

DELEGATION FROM MINISTERS TO CIVIL SERVANTS: THE CHIMERA OF A POLITICALLY NEUTRAL ADMINISTRATION, AND AN ADMINISTRATIVELY NEUTRAL GOVERNMENT

Perhaps the only scenario in which the relationship between government and administration does not involve a potential for agency problems is when the spoils system has penetrated the state structures so deeply that there are no administrative posts awarded to neutral and professional civil servants. However, since it is easy to anticipate the endless problems that such a situation might create, it is more useful to consider the problematic agency relationship between government and administration.

Article 97 of the 1978 Constitution puts the administration—civilian and military— under the direction of the government. However, this appearance of total and unconditional submission to the executive partially disappears as a result of language found in Article 103.1, which proclaims that 'the Public administration serves the general interest with objectivity', establishes the principles of 'efficacy, hierarchy, decentralization, deconcentration, and coordination', and orders the administration to remain subject to the rule of law.

The idea that the government leads and the administration simply implements policies is a gross oversimplification. To begin with, the border between government and administration is not easy to draw. Many high-ranking officials in a variety of administrative categories are required to possess a technical expertise, but also need to retain the minister's—or even the cabinet's—confidence. The line separating politicians and political appointees from civil servants is rather permeable. In addition, the public administration has its own set of values and interests. These are often quite different from those that the government promotes and seeks to implement. Finally, the administration sometimes has significant autonomy protected by the law.

For those reasons, prudent separation and mutual respect between government and administration seems highly advisable. This is what Garrido Falla's (1979) formula 'a politically neutral administration, and an administratively neutral Government' means. Of course, the political neutrality of the administration must not become a blatant neglect of the principles, values, and goals enshrined in the Constitution; and the neutrality of the government in purely administrative affairs cannot relieve it from the task of providing leadership.

The general administration of Spain is functionally divided across ministerial lines. Within each department, the Minister and the Secretaries of State are the highest decision-makers. Under them are the directive organs—under-secretaries, general secretaries, technical general secretaries, general directors, and deputy general directors. While Ministers and Secretaries of State are almost exclusively political appointees, appointments of directive organs must involve a consideration of professional competence and experience. While the role of the former is defined as establishing plans of action for agencies under their command, the role of the latter is to develop and implement those plans.

While the political attributions of ministers are largely spelled out in Article 4 of Law 50/1997, those having more to do with the administrative organization and operation of departments are carefully enumerated in Articles 12 and 13 of Law 6/1997. Some of these cover the internal organization of departments, others deal with financial matters, but most of them are about the chain of delegation and accountability. Ministers have the power to appoint and dismiss directive organs in their departments and those public agencies subordinate to the departments. They also propose appointments in cases in which appointments are formally made by the cabinet. They provide subordinates with concrete instructions, delegate competencies to them, and regulate departmental staff. The latter responsibility involves creating new positions as needed and even deciding on salary matters. In short, Ministers, and Secretaries of State appear to be the hinges in the effective articulation of government and administration, or the links that connect the chain of delegation from the cabinet to the entire administration.

Articles 105 and 106 of the Constitution are extremely important with regard to accountability. Article 105 addresses the principle of citizen participation in the administration. It states that citizens have the right to be heard, either directly or through organizations and associations recognized by law, with regard to administrative decisions that affect them. It also gives citizens the right to access the administrative archives and registers except where doing so affects the security and defence of the state, the investigation of crimes, or the privacy of persons. Finally, Article 105 requires the legislature to regulate procedures covering administrative actions and those guaranteeing, where appropriate, the hearing of interested persons (see Sánchez Morón 1980). All of these rights have been further developed in law.

Article 106 establishes the principle that the administration is responsible for its actions and, therefore, that '[p]rivate individuals, under the terms established by the law, shall have the right to be compensated for any harm they suffer in any of their property and rights, except in the cases of force majeure, whenever such harm is the result of the functioning of the public services'. The guarantees relevant to this principle are provided by the fact that the legality of administrative acts falls within the jurisdiction of the Spanish courts (see Blasco Esteve 1981).

EXTERNAL CONSTRAINTS: DIRECT DEMOCRACY, JUDICIAL INDEPENDENCE, REGIONAL SELF-GOVERNMENT, AND EUROPEAN INTEGRATION

The Spanish political system includes a number of highly important institutions which operate outside the specific process of delegation and accountability that has been described thus far—that is, the core of which is the chain linking people, Congress, PM, cabinet, and administration. The political relevance of these institutions and the extent to which they influence the parliamentary system varies significantly, but should not be underestimated.

The fact that the Franco regime frequently used direct democracy, namely the referendum, to popularly ratify key political decisions made direct democracy suspect to many of the framers of the 1978 Constitution. This led to a regulation that Torres de Moral (1992: i. 106) calls 'cautious and stingy'. The Constitution does provide for several kinds of referendums, namely those mentioned in Articles 92 (of advisory nature, about important political decisions), 151.1 (in order to ratify the decision to become an autonomous community), 151.2.3 (in order to ratify a Statute of Autonomy), 152.2 (in order to amend a Statute of Autonomy), 167.3 (facultative, in order to ratify a constitutional amendment of secondary importance), and 168.3 (compulsory, in order to bring about a complete revision of the Constitution or to make a more specific but still significant constitutional amendment).

But this enumeration of referendums is deceptive. This is evidenced by the fact that in more than twenty years, only one referendum has been called—leaving aside those referendums strictly necessary to set in motion a new Autonomic State. During these years, decisions as important as joining the European Union and NATO, ratifying the Maastricht Treaty and participating in the EMU, the legalization of divorce and abortion, the professionalization of the armed forces, and even a constitutional amendment have all been implemented. However, not once did the government invoke the constitutional provision that states that 'political decisions of special importance may be submitted for an advisory referendum of all the citizens'.

Lack of political will among parliamentary parties and the absence of popular pressure largely explain why direct democracy has become almost a mirage in the new Spanish democracy. However, the Constitution itself sets the tone for this marginalization. The authority to call for a referendum rests entirely with the state. Autonomous communities cannot hold regional referendums. Advisory ones can take place only if the PM proposes them and he is supported by an absolute majority in Congress, an institution that can be expected to be reluctant to support such experiments. Last but not least, advisory referendums merely 'advise' Parliament and the government, who might choose to ignore it, though doing so might be somewhat politically risky (see Pérez Sola 1994).

'Justice emanates from the people and is administered in the name of the King by Judges and Magistrates who are members of the judicial power and are independent, irremovable, responsible, and subject only to the rule of the law'. This statement, found in Article 117.1 of the Constitution, clearly implies that members of the judiciary should be kept outside the chain of delegation and accountability, and that the structure, operation, and administration of the Courts and Tribunals is to be linked to popular will and parliamentary majorities only through the law.

However, the Constitution also created a specific organ for the governance of the Judiciary—the General Council of the Judicial Power (GCJP) (see Terol Becerra 1990). It is composed of twenty members appointed by the King for a term of five years, and is chaired by the President of the Supreme Court. Article 122.3 requires twelve of the twenty members to be judges and magistrates from all the judicial categories, while the remaining eight are proposed by Parliament—four by a three-fifths majority of the Congress and four by the three-fifths majority of the Senate. These persons are to be lawyers and jurists of recognized competence and more than fifteen years experience.

The constitutional design of the GCJP meant that it was bound to be politicized to some degree. From the beginning it was assumed that the councilmen designated by Parliament, despite their legal background, would likely behave in a partisan manner, but it was expected that this tendency would be counterbalanced by the independence of elected judges and magistrates. This assumption crashed in 1985 when Parliament passed the Organic Law 6/1985 on the Judicial Power, which provided a daring interpretation of the wording of Article 122.3. The new Socialist majority understood that the Constitution required that twelve of the councilmen be judges and magistrates, without prohibiting that these twelve were elected by Parliament. The Organic Law on Judicial Power explicitly gave Parliament the authority to elect all twenty members of the GCJP, albeit while respecting the professional categories and experience requirements stated in the Constitution. In one of the most controversial decisions, the Constitutional Court declared that this interpretation seriously undermined the intention of the framers of the Constitution, which was to make the Council reflect the tendencies and attitudes of judges and magistrates. The Court acknowledged, however, that the Law was nonetheless compatible with the strict wording of the Constitution. However, since Article 119.2 of the Organic Law on the Judicial Power also established that members of the Council cannot be removed from office and that they are immune to mandates or instructions, it could be said that parliamentary delegation has entered the domain of the judiciary, while accountability has not. A Popular Party sponsored amendment passed in 2001 stating that Councillors have to be proposed by the professional associations of judges and magistrates has not entirely changed the nature of the system, but has reinforced the role of the legal profession in the nomination of the Council.

As discussed earlier, the creation of autonomous communities following the provisions of Title VIII of the Constitution significantly changed the way Spain is governed. It has created a duplication of the chain of delegation and accountability insofar as autonomous communities have created their own legislatures, cabinets, Presidents, and administrative agencies, and have reproduced among them a parliamentary-type regime similar to the one at the national level.

The autonomous communities created since 1978 are quite similar to one another, not least because the Constitution itself provided a summary description of what these institutions should look like. As regulated by Article 152.1, the institutional framework for autonomous communities must include a legislative assembly elected by universal suffrage and proportional representation, a cabinet with executive and administrative functions, and a President elected by the Assembly from among its members and politically responsible before it. The President chairs the cabinet and embodies the supreme representation of the community and of the state within the community.

The parliamentary systems created by the autonomous communities differ from the national system on three major counts. First, their legislatures are unicameral. Second, the functional division between the Head of State and the Chief of the Government does not exist because the President of the autonomous community assumes all the competencies granted to the executive power. Finally, only a few of them have the right to dissolve their legislature, a right that the PM enjoys at the national level.

For the purpose of this analysis, the structure of the autonomous communities' institutions are less interesting than the issue of how their existence influences the chain of delegation and accountability nationally. In principle, their impact was to be noticed through their participation in the Senate. After all, the upper chamber is constitutionally defined as 'the chamber for territorial representation'. However, this expectation has proved unrealistic in light of the fact that Senators designated by the autonomous Parliaments make up only about one-fifth of all Senators and that even these are not subject to instructions from their governments (see Flores Juberías 1999). The image of a German-type upper house in which every territory might voice and defend its claims is alien to the existing Spanish system. Autonomous communities have therefore chosen to interact with the central government through non-constitutional means, including bilateral meetings at various levels, interparty negotiations, and lobbying of all kinds (Parejo 1988).

Finally, European integration has also implied substantial changes in the chain of delegation and accountability, involving a dramatic decline in the ability of both the Spanish people and the Spanish Parliament to hold policy-makers accountable for their decisions. EU membership has altered the way both the legislature and the government operate and interact (see Muñoz Machado 1993), the relationship between autonomous communities and the central institutions of the state (see Soriano 1991), and even the role of the national judiciary (see Ruiz-Jarabo Colomer 1993).

In order to minimize the dangers created by a lack of timely and sufficient information about EU policies, Law 47/1985 and subsequently Law 8/1994 created the Congressional and Senatorial Joint Committee on the European Union. The Committee comprises Deputies and Senators, the exact number being determined by the Boards of both houses. Parliamentary groups are represented in proportion to their respective size in the houses of Parliament. The powers of this Committee appear to be far-reaching. The Committee is to be provided with legislative proposals from at the European Commission. It can debate EU proposals and call plenary sessions to discuss them. It has a right to information from the government on EU institutions and their activities and a right to information on the government's EU positions. Finally, it can hold bilateral meetings with European Parliament deputies. Nonetheless, it is difficult to see how a simple parliamentary committee, however powerful and zealous of its duties, can fight a tendency as seemingly powerful as the increasing distance between the governing and the governed. The complexities of the European Union have only served to highlight and aggravate this tendency.

CONCLUSION: LOTS OF DELEGATION, LESS ACCOUNTABILITY, AND VICE VERSA

If we were to underline a feature of the chain of delegation and accountability able to characterize Spanish parliamentarism, our attention ought to perhaps focus on the imbalance between these two mechanisms. Regarding the chain that links voters with Members of Parliament, and Members of Parliament with the Prime Minister, the impression is that there is a lot of delegation and very little accountability. Voters simply cannot influence the actions of their representatives, much less remove them from office before the expiration of their term. Though the Parliament—or at least the Congress of Deputies—has mechanisms designed to hold the PM and his cabinet politically accountable, the more imposing these devices are on paper, the less effective they appear to be in reality. This applies not only to *ex post* control mechanisms, but also to those that operate *ex ante*. It is only necessary to remember that prime ministerial candidates do not have to disclose their cabinet appointments before the investiture vote or to recall that voter influence on candidate nomination is virtually non-existent.

When we look at the other half of the chain—the part that links the PM, cabinet ministers, high-ranking officials, and civil servants of all ranks—the observation has to be the opposite: delegation shrinks, while accountability soars. The powers of the PM over his cabinet are indeed sweeping. Its structure, composition, agenda, and even survival depend entirely on him. Much the same could be said about each minister with regard to most domestic aspects of his department, and even about lower administrative units and their heads. Here, delegation appears closely related with accountability, ready to disappear as soon as accountability renders negative results.

In the end, the overall impression is an extreme concentration of power and authority in the hands of the PM. He has become 'the central axis of our political regime'—at least as long as he is capable of remaining party leader and his party is able to maintain a sufficiently large majority.

REFERENCES

Álvarez Conde, Enrique (1990). *El régimen Político Español.*, 4th edn. Madrid: Tecnos.

Alzaga, Óscar (1978). *La Constitución española de 1978. Comentario sistemático.* Madrid: Ediciones del Foro.

Arceo Vacas, J. L. (ed.) (1993). *Campañas Electorales y Publicidad Política en España.* Barcelona: PPU.

Attard Alonso, Emilio (1983). *Vida y muerte de UCD.* Barcelona: Planeta.

Bar Cendón, Antonio (1979). 'La monarquía parlamentaria como forma política del Estado español', in *Estudios sobre la Constitución Española de 1978.* Zaragoza: Universidad de Zaragoza.

——(1985a). 'Artículo 99. Nombramiento del Presidente del Gobierno', in Óscar Alzaga (ed.), *Comentarios a las leyes Políticas.* Madrid: EDERSA. Vol. VIII, 135–89.

——(1985b). 'La estructura y funcionamiento del Gobierno en España: una aproximación analítica', in Antonio Bar Cendón (ed.), *El Gobierno en la Constitución Española y en los Estatutos de Autonomía.* Barcelona: Diputació de Barcelona.

Barrat Esteve, Jordi (1995). 'Los procesos de selección de candidatos en los partidos políticos'. *Cuadernos Constitucionales de la Cátedra Fadrique Furió Ceriol,* 13: 95–143.

Blasco Esteve, Avelino (1981). *La responsabilidad de la Administración por los actos administrativos.* Madrid: Civitas.

Cascajo Castro, José Luis (1992). 'Controles sobre los partidos políticos', in José Juan González Encinar (ed.), *Derecho de partidos*. Madrid: Espasa-Calpe.

Cazorla Prieto, Luis María (1986). *Comentarios a la Ley Orgánica de Régimen Electoral General*. Madrid: Civitas.

Del Castillo, Pilar (1992). 'Financiación de los partidos políticos: La reforma necesaria', in José Juan González Encinar (ed.), *Derecho de partidos*. Madrid: Espasa-Calpe.

Embid Irujo, A. (1987). *Los parlamentos territoriales*. Madrid: Tecnos.

Equipo de Estudios (1976). *Lucha política por el poder. Grupos políticos en la actualidad*. Madrid: Elías Querejeta.

Fernández Segado, Francisco (1985). 'Las mociones de reprobación y la responsabilidad política individual (un paradigma de la dinamicidad del Derecho Parlamentario)', in *I Jornadas de Derecho Parlamentario, Vol. I*, Madrid: Congreso de los Diputados: 239–91.

——(1986). *Aproximación a la nueva normativa electoral*. Madrid: Dykinson.

Flores Juberías, Carlos (1998). 'Regionalization and Autonomy in Spain: The Making of the "Estado de las Autonomías"', in Markku Suksi (ed.), *Autonomy: Applications and Implications*. The Hague: Kluwer.

——(1999). 'A Chamber in Search of a Role: The Senate of Spain', in Samuel C. Patterson and Anthony Mughan (eds.), *Senates: Bicameralism in the Contemporary World*. Columbus: Ohio State University Press.

García Cotarelo, Ramón (1985). *Los partidos políticos*. Madrid: Editorial Sistema.

——(1992). *La década socialista*. Madrid: Espasa-Calpe.

García-Pelayo, Manuel (1986). *El Estado de partidos*. Madrid: Alianza Editorial.

Garrido Falla, Fernando (1979). 'Constitución y Administración'. *Revista Española de Derecho Administrativo*, 20: 5–11.

Huneeus, Carlos (1985). *La Unión de Centro Democrático y la transición a la democracia en España*. Madrid: CIS-Siglo XXI.

López Calvo, José (1996). *Organización y funcionamiento del Gobierno*. Madrid: Tecnos.

Martínez Cuadrado, Miguel (1996). *La democracia en la España de los años noventa*. Barcelona: Ariel.

Martínez Sospedra, Manuel (1983). *Aproximación al Derecho constitucional español. La Constitución de 1978*. Valencia: Fernando Torres Editor.

——(1996). *Introducción a los partidos políticos*. Barcelona: Ariel.

Montero, José Ramón (1995). 'Sobre las preferencias electorales en España: fragmentación y polarización (1977–1983)', in Pilar del Castillo (ed.), *Comportamiento político y electoral*. Madrid: CIS.

Muñoz Machado, Santiago (1993). *La Unión Europea y las mutaciones del Estado*. Madrid: Alianza Editorial.

Parejde, Luciano (1988). 'El Gobierno de la Nación y los Gobiernos Je las Autonamías territoritales. Una problema de articulacion'. *Documentación Administrativa*, 215: 137–71.

Penniman, Howard and Eusebio Mujal-León (eds.) (1985). *Spain at the Polls, 1977, 1979 and 1982: A Study of National Elections*. Durham: Duke University Press.

Pérez Sola, Nicolás (1994). *La regulación constitucional del referéndum*. Jaén: Universidad de Jaén.

Porras Nadales, Antonio (1987). 'El Consejo General del Poder Judicial según la STC 108/1986, de 29 de julio, sobre la Ley Orgánica del Poder Judicial'. *Revista Española de Derecho Constitucional*, 19: 225–44.

Punset, Ramón (1992). 'Prohibición de mandato imperativo y pertenencia a partidos políticos', in José Juan González Encinar (ed.), *Derecho de partidos*. Madrid: Espasa-Calpe.

Revenga Sánchez, Miguel (1988). *La formación del gobierno en la Constitución española de 1978*. Madrid: Cívitas.

Rodríguez Díaz, Ángel (1989). *Transición política y consolidación constitucional de los partidos políticos.* Madrid: Centro de Estudios Constitucionales.

Ruiz-Jarabo Colomer. D. (1993). *El juez nacional como juez comunitario.* Madrid: Cívitas.

Sánchez Agesta, Luis (1980). *El sistema político de la Constitución española de 1978.* Madrid: Editora Nacional.

Sánchez Morón, Manuel (1980). *La participación del ciudadano en la Administración.* Madrid: Centro de Estudios Constitucionales.

Santaolalla López, Fernando (1992). 'Partido político, grupo parlamentario y diputado', in José Juan González Encinar (ed.), *Derecho de partidos.* Madrid: Espasa-Calpe.

Share, Donald (1999). 'From Policy-Seeking to Office-Seeking: The Metamorphosis of the Spanish Socialist Workers Party', in Wolfgang C. Müller and Kaare Strøm (eds.), *Policy, Office, or Votes? How Political Parties in Western Europe Make Hard Decisions.* Cambridge: Cambridge University Press.

Soler Sanchez, Margarita (2001). *Campañas electorales y democracia en España.* Castellón: UJI.

Soriano, José Eugenio (1991). *Comunidades autónomas y Comunidad Europea.* Madrid: Tecnos.

Terol Becerra, Manuel J. (1990). *El Consejo General del Poder Judicial.* Madrid: Centro de Estudios Constitucionales.

Tomás Villarroya, Joaquín (1982). *Breve historia del constitucionalismo español.* 2nd edn. Madrid: Centro de Estudios Constitucionales.

Torres del Moral, Antonio (1983). 'La monarquía parlamentaria como forma política del Estado español', in Pablo Lucas Verdú (ed.), *La Corona y la Monarquía Parlamentaria en la Constitución de 1978.* Madrid: Universidad Complutense.

——(1992). *Principios de Derecho Constitucional Español*, Volumes I and II, 3rd edn. Madrid: Servicio de Publicaciones de la Facultad de Derecho de la Universidad Complutense.

Vírgala Foruria, Eduardo (1988). *La moción de censura en la Constitución de 1978.* Madrid: Centro de Estudios Constitucionales.

Zafra Valverde, José (1973). *Régimen político de España.* Pamplona: EUNSA.s

20

Sweden: From Separation of Power to Parliamentary Supremacy—and Back Again?

TORBJÖRN BERGMAN

INTRODUCTION

In 1917 the Swedish King was forced to finally accept that the *Riksdag*, and not he, was the ultimate authority upon which the cabinet's political existence rested (Lewin 1992; Stjernquist 1997; von Sydow 1997). While this event firmly established a parliamentary democracy, it was not accompanied by a change of the written Constitution. Until 1975, Sweden was formally governed under the 1809 Constitution, according to which the Parliament shared political power with the King and his cabinet. On 1 January 1975, a new Constitution went into effect. In contrast to its predecessor, it stipulates an almost ideal–typical single chain of delegation and accountability from the people to civil servants. In this chapter, I present the institutional mechanisms that define this chain and I show that it is challenged by new *ex post* institutional checks that have grown stronger over time.

Let's begin by examining the new Constitution and basic legislative procedures. One impetus for reform was of course the large discrepancy between written statutes and practice. Formally, the King still presided over cabinet sessions, appointed high civil servants and could dissolve the Riksdag. As Head of State he was the supreme military commander. All of these powers were already, before a series of reforms that took place in the 1970s, primarily symbolic and obsolete. But many West European countries have old-fashioned Constitutions so this alone was not the reason behind the reform. There were also two other main reasons (Bergman 1995).

A second reason for reform was that the King still enjoyed a role, albeit very limited, in cabinet formation, cabinet resignation, and parliamentary dissolution. This was a source of embarrassment for the ruling Social Democratic Party. Its party programme had since 1911 called for a Republic. While Social Democratic leaders knew that the

I would like to acknowledge the late Nils Stjernquist who was a constant source of knowledge and inspiration on the chapter topic. I would also like to thank Hans Hegeland, Cynthia Kite, Ingvar Mattson, my fellow editors, and my colleagues at the research seminar at the Department of Political Science, Umeå University for their helpful comments on various drafts of this chapter.

idea of abolishing the monarchy was unpopular with most voters, the party's official support for a Republic provided the leadership with an incentive to favour a major constitutional reform (Bergman 1995). A third reason behind the reforms was that the opposition parties had their own motives for a large-scale reform. They wanted to abolish the First (or Upper) Chamber and increase the proportionality of the electoral system. In both cases, they argued, existing institutional arrangements favoured the Social Democratic Party at their expense (von Sydow 1989).

With the 1970 elections, a partial constitutional reform enhanced the proportionality of the electoral system. And on 1 January 1971, the upper (First) chamber of the Riksdag was abolished (von Sydow 1989). The same constitutional reform also introduced formal rules for a no-confidence vote against the cabinet. After that, the constitutional debate focused on the monarch, resulting in a new Constitution that took away most of his symbolic powers (Bergman 1999).[1] In addition to performing the ceremonial duties of a Head of State in international relations, the monarch now only opens new sessions of the Parliament and chairs an advisory board on foreign affairs. The Constitution places the Riksdag at the centre of representative democracy (Article 1: 4).

With these reforms, the legislative process also changed. Up to 1970, to legislate, a simple majority was needed in each of the two chambers. The cabinet (formally the King) had to consent with these majorities for the law to pass. With regard to budget decisions, taxes, and state expenditures, the Riksdag alone had decision-making powers. If the two chambers disagreed, the total number of votes for and against in each chamber were summed up and the combined majority won the vote. In addition, under the 1809 Constitution, the cabinet had broad powers to legislate by decree. This included laws that governed the public sector and such matters as citizenship. While this legislative authority originally was quite broad, over time the cabinet delegated more and more authority to the Parliament (Lagerroth 1955: 180–4; Andrén 1968: 270–2, 429–59; Kungl. Maj:ts proposition nr 90 år 1973: 201–26).

This reversed form of delegation, from the cabinet to the Parliament, ended with the new Constitution. In 1975, all legislative and budgetary powers were taken over by the Riksdag (Holmberg and Stjernquist 1980). Legislative initiatives from the cabinet or from one or more MPs are referred to a Riksdag committee. This is mandatory. The committees can also initiate legislative proposals on their own. After committee deliberation, the plenary chamber votes on committee proposals. The formal decision is taken by a simple majority of all members present and voting. There is no quorum rule.

With the exception of European Union (EU) law, from January 1995 when Sweden became a member, only the Riksdag can pass a law. Both the cabinet and state agencies can issue binding statutes below the level of a law. However, on some specific matters, such as Civil Law, Criminal Law, laws on Local Authorities, and Electoral Law, the Riksdag cannot delegate to the cabinet the power to issue decrees. Over these matters cabinet can only issue instructions on how the law should be implemented. In other areas, the cabinet can issue decrees (regulations) within the framework of existing law. State agencies can issue binding regulations only if such authority is explicitly delegated

---

[1] Until 1980 the monarch had to be male. Since 1980 females of the royal family can also inherit the throne.

from the Riksdag and/or the cabinet (Holmberg and Stjernquist 1980: 244–5, 293–8, 2000: 123–44).

There is no constitutional court or federalism that limits the Riksdag's power. There is, however, an *ex ante* procedure that involves a Law Council (*Lagrådet*) consisting of High Judges. The cabinet or a Riksdag committee can ask this Council to scrutinize a legislative proposal. The Council can recommend that the Riksdag reject all or parts of a government proposal because it conflicts with the Constitution, is inconsistent, or because it conflicts with already existing law (Article 8: 18). The Riksdag is free to decide whether or not to follow the recommendation. Because it is only advisory, the scrutiny process is a relatively weak *ex ante* constraint. However, the mechanism can become important *ex post* because courts and public authorities must not implement laws or other regulations that conflict with the Constitution (Article 11: 14). The prerogative to set aside unconstitutional statutes existed in practice until 1979 when the Riksdag decided to incorporate it in the written Constitution (Holmberg and Stjernquist 1980: 250). However, if the statute is contained in either a law—and therefore by definition issued by the Riksdag—or a regulation issued by the cabinet, it is only if the conflict with the Constitution is 'obvious' that courts and other authorities can refuse implementing the statute. It is hypothetically possible that a court could refuse to implement a law on the grounds that the law council considers it unconstitutional, even if the Riksdag had decided to adopt it anyway. In practice, however, courts and public authorities have been very restrictive in invoking their right not to implement laws and other regulations (Holmberg and Stjernquist 1980: 397–9, 2000: 144–7, 190–5).

A simple parliamentary majority can change any existing restrictions on the Riksdag's decision-making authority. All that is required is an intervening election between decisions (Article 8: 15). From 1980, however, a minority of 10 per cent of the MPs (currently thirty-five MPs) can ask the Riksdag to subject the constitutional amendment to a decisive referendum. If a third of all MPs support such a motion, the referendum must be held at the next general election. If a majority of those voting in the general election also participate in the referendum and the anti-amendment side wins, the proposed amendment is rejected. Otherwise, the incoming Riksdag is free to adopt or reject the proposed amendment at will (Article 8: 15).

There are also other important constraints that are formally external to the ideal–typical singular chain of parliamentary democracy. Two of the most important constraints have to do with increasingly autonomous local and regional governments and European integration. Neo-corporatist patterns of interest-intermediation and the use of advisory referendums also impact on the chain. We will return to these constraints later on, but let us for now focus on the organizations that link one step to the next in the democratic chain, that is, political parties.

POLITICAL PARTIES

Political parties were first mentioned in the partial constitutional reform that went into effect on 1 January 1971 (Holmberg and Stjernquist 1980: 143). The 1975 Constitution defines political parties as 'any association or group of voters which appears in an election under a particular designation' (Article 3: 7).[2]

On the dominant Left–Right dimension, in the traditional Scandinavian five party system (Berglund and Lindström 1978), the parties has been aligned as follows: the Communist Party (from 1990 the Left Party), the Social Democratic Party, the Centre Party (the former Agrarian Party) the Liberal Party, and the Conservative (or Moderate) Party.[3] In 1988, 1994, and 1998, the Green Party was elected to the Riksdag. In 1991, when the Green Party lost representation, two other parties were elected. One was a populist right-wing party, New Democracy, which lost all of its representation in the following (1994) election. The Christian Democratic Party, on the other hand, managed to stay represented in the Parliament. In 1998, with 11.8 per cent of the total vote, it became the fourth largest party after the Social Democrats, the Conservatives, and the Left Party. The Green, Centre, and Liberal Parties each received around 5 per cent of the total vote (Allmänna Valen 1998).

The Social Democrats have controlled most cabinets, but not because of a lack of party competition (Bergman 1995). Competition has in fact been fierce and the parties have often split into two competing blocs, the Socialist (the Communist and Social Democratic Parties) and the non-socialist blocs (the other three traditional parties). In 2003, the Green Party cooperates with the 'Socialist' bloc and the Christian Democratic Party belongs to the 'non-socialists'. A split among the voters has mirrored the party blocs.

Traditionally, voters have had fairly stable party preferences and voted very much according to class. However, in the early 1970s, voting patterns began to change. Fewer voters have a stable preference for one party and many voters decide which party to vote for late in the election campaign. At the same time there has been growing distrust of political parties, political institutions, and politicians in general (Gilljam and Holmberg 1995; Holmberg 1999). The share of the population with party membership also used to be comparatively very high. In 1990, the political parties had a total of 1.4 million members. The Social Democratic Party alone had about one million members out of a population of a little more that eight million. However, this was largely a consequence of the fact that the Social Democratic Party allowed local unions to register their members collectively as party members. Under pressure from the opposition

---

[2] In Sweden, there are four documents with 'constitutional' status. In this study, the specific individual Articles that are mentioned all come from the Instrument of Government, which is the act that defines the main state institutions and the relationship between these institutions (The Constitution of Sweden 2000). The other three fundamental laws are the Act of Succession, The Freedom of Press Act, and The Fundamental Law of Freedom of Expression. For an amendment, parts of the Riksdag Act also require two decisions and an intervening election. However, this Act can also be changed by one decision if more that three-quarters of voting MPs vote in favour. For the change to be passed, however, the three-quarters majority must also include more than half of all MPs, that is, currently more than 175 MPs must vote in favour.

[3] Except for the relative positions of the parties of the 'middle', the Centre and the Liberal Parties, the alignment has been very stable. However, the predominance of the Left–Right dimension has been weakened by alternative conflict issues such as the nuclear power program in the 1970s and early 1980s, ecology more generally in the 1980s, and conflict over EU-membership and an awakening moral–religious dimension in the 1990s (Oscarsson 1998).

parties and union members, the Social Democratic Party abolished this practice in the early 1990s. In 1999, the parties had slightly over four hundred thousand members, of which about 40 per cent were Social Democrats. Most of the loss of members in the 1990s stems from the changed Social Democratic practice concerning union members, but the numbers also reflect the trend that the political parties in the early and mid-1990s lost members and that they have trouble attracting new ones (Bäck and Möller 1997: 112; Gidlund and Möller 1999: 26). These problems do not necessarily mean that the parties are moribund. They remain well organized and open to membership influence, at least in cross-national comparison (Sannerstedt and Sjölin 1994; Widfeldt 1997). But the challenges to political parties are real enough and their legitimacy has been questioned during the 1990s (Petersson *et al.* 2000).

In spite of their problems, political parties remain important for the democratic chain. The parties nominate candidates for elections and make authoritative decisions in the cabinet and Riksdag. They also select representatives to other bodies that participate in the preparation and implementation of public policy. Cabinets have traditionally relied heavily on government appointed commissions to prepare policy proposals (Larsson 1994). In these commissions, representatives from all Riksdag parties—often MPs—work with technical experts and sometimes with representatives of organized interests to prepare the cabinet's policy proposals. These proposals are published as official reports to government. This policy-preparation process has been very important and, even though its importance has declined in recent years, commissions remain influential. There is also a *remiss* system by which reports from these commissions are scrutinized by state agencies, other levels of government, and organized interests, before the proposal returns to the cabinet and Riksdag (Heclo and Madsen 1987: 13; Ruin 1996). Party representatives also serve on the boards of agencies, where they oversee public policy implementation. While board members are formally appointed by the cabinet, it is usually the political parties, and often their parliamentary groups, who in practice decide who will be appointed (Birgersson and Westerståhl 1992; Isberg 1999). The political parties are thus involved at every step of the delegation chain. Their importance is most obvious when they nominate candidates for political office, when they run electoral campaigns, and in the relationship between the Riksdag and the cabinet. The role and influence of political parties is less obvious and less important further along the chain, but the Swedish parties are involved in all its steps. Well organized and cohesive, they take part in the commissions that prepare cabinet proposals, in decision-making, and in policy implementation. With this in mind, we now turn to the constitutionally mandated chain of parliamentary democracy.

DELEGATION FROM VOTERS TO MPs

The system by which Swedish voters select their representatives has been proportional since 1909. The First (or Upper) Chamber was indirectly elected. Election results to regional assemblies determined each party's share of the First Chamber seats. Since the 1970 elections to the first unicameral Riksdag, the multimember constituencies elect between two and thirty-four representatives. A national pool of second-tier (or supplementary) seats is distributed among the parties to increase the overall proportionality between votes and seats. The national pool is 39 of 349 seats (Article 3: 6). The system excludes from the Riksdag parties that fail to get at least 4 per cent of the vote nationally or 12 per cent in one constituency. With 4 per cent nationally, a party shares in the distribution of the national pool of supplementary seats. A party elected only because it is particularly strong (12 per cent or more of the vote) in one or a few multimember constituencies is not included in the distribution of the national pool of seats. The restrictive threshold for a constituency seat has meant that no party has been elected on the basis of this rule alone.

Although voting is not mandatory, turnout reached over 90 per cent in the four elections between 1973 and 1982. In recent elections turnout has tended to decline, falling dramatically to 81.4 per cent in 1998. This is the lowest for any election since 1958, when turnout was 77.4 per cent (Allmänna Valen 1998).

With the 1998 elections, a 'positive' preference vote was introduced. The new election law is designed to let voters pick a candidate from a party. If the individual preference vote for a particular candidate is 8 per cent or more of the party's total number of constituency votes, then that candidate moves to the top of list (which otherwise remains unchanged). If more than one candidate gets more than 8 per cent, the one with the most preference votes moves to the top of the list and fills the party's first seat in that constituency. In the 1998 elections, about 30 per cent of voters used the preference vote, but most of these went to candidates already at the top of the party list. The direct effect of the preference vote was that 12 (of 349) MPs were elected in place of candidates ranked higher on their parties' lists (SOU 1999: 136).

While the new electoral law allows voters to have a say in which candidates are elected from the party list, it also gave the parties full control over the list itself. The new electoral system does not allow voters to add or cross-out candidates, which the previous system did. Consequently, the new electoral law has also eliminated the possibility for factions or groups within a party to present their own list, unless it is approved by the party organization. In earlier elections, competing lists within the same party could determine MP selection. Thus, while giving voters a greater role in choosing candidates from parties' lists, the new rules also give party organizations more control over ballot access in the first place.

Once elected, the MPs mandate is individual. A party cannot remove an MP from his seat. This means that he or she can leave the party, join another party, or work alone. An MP cannot, however, simultaneously hold a Riksdag seat and serve in the cabinet (or as Speaker). If an MP serves in the cabinet (or as Speaker), an alternate member is temporarily called to fill the MPs seat. Aside from this, an MP can only be removed from his position if the election is annulled or if a court of law finds him or her unsuited to serve (Article 4: 7). This would happen if the MP has been convicted of a serious crime. MPs have a limited form of immunity from prosecution, which covers acts they commit when they vote and speak in the Parliament. This immunity can be lifted by a majority of five-sixths of the MPs present and voting (Article 4: 8). In all other circumstances, Swedish MPs are not protected from prosecution in regular courts (Holmberg and Stjernquist 1980).

Party Funding and Candidate Nominations

The new preference vote added to the amount of national legislation covering political parties, but otherwise the legislation is minimal. The Constitution and the election law focus on electoral rules and procedures. In other areas political parties are free to regulate themselves. For example, there is no legislation concerning binding primaries, term limits, or a mandatory retirement age. Nor are there regulations for the maximum length of electoral campaigns or any legal caps on campaign spending (Pierre and Widfeldt 1992; Bäck and Möller 1997).

Since 1966, political parties have received public financing (Gidlund 1983; Pierre and Widfeldt 1992). Before 1972, only parties with seats in the Parliament were eligible for such funding. Since 1972 all parties that get more than 2.5 per cent of the national vote as well as parties that lose all their seats in the Riksdag (regardless of election performance) get public support. In 1997, the eligible parties together received more than 213 million SEK (Riksdagen i siffror 1996/1997). In 2000, the corresponding figure was about 246 million SEK.

The political parties do not hold primaries that are legally enforceable or bind the party organization. The nomination process within the parties is free from state regulation. All parties allow their local and regional (constituency) organizations to decide how to nominate candidates for Parliament. The parties also have a practice of non-binding primaries (provval) in which members vote on a preliminary list of candidates. While used rather infrequently some thirty years ago, today they are in widespread use (SOU 1972: 17; Back and Berglund 1978: 103–8; Pierre and Widfeldt 1992: 817–18; Bäck and Möller 1997).

The national party has had little say in candidate selection. While party elites sometimes ask regional level party organizations to place a particular candidate high on the party's list of candidates, these requests are not always granted. Until 1970, candidates to the Second Chamber had to reside in their constituency (Holmberg and Stjernquist 1980: 159). First Chamber candidates did not, and this made it somewhat easier for party leaders to hand-pick suitable candidates. However, the regional constituencies often resisted these attempts (e.g. see, Myrdal 1982: 105). One general exception to the regional constituency's autonomy in candidate selection is that all national parties in the last twenty years or so have begun to promote a more equal proportion of men and women on the party lists. The proportion of women elected to the Riksdag has since 1985 been above 30 per cent, and after the 1994 and 1998 elections above 40 per cent (Allmänna Valen 1998).

When regional party organizations select candidates, other social background characteristics are also important. This includes long and tested service in local and regional party functions and place of residence (geographic location) within the regional constituency. The parties also have their own traditions and principles for candidate selection. For example, for the Social Democrats, a trade union career has been meritorious (Andrén 1968: 70–4; Birgersson and Westerståhl 1992; Bäck and Möller 1997: 111–23). MPs are also held accountable at the regional and local level of the party organization. If regional or local party members and party boards are displeased with an MP's performance, they can demote or remove this person from the list in the next election. Still, candidates who are highly ranked in one election tend to remain high in subsequent ones.

In spite of constituency supremacy over nominations, once elected MPs see themselves more as party than as constituency representatives. Their main concern lies with national level policy-making, and constituency interests are seen as complementary to their main role as party representatives (Esaiasson and Holmberg 1996; Bäck and Möller 1997: 119–20). In addition, the parliamentary party groups are both cohesive and influential in shaping the policies that the MPs promote (Hagevi 1999; Isberg 1999). Party competition over executive office provides strong incentives for such behaviour. This leads us to the next step in the delegation chain.

DELEGATION FROM PARLIAMENT TO CABINET

To varying degrees, depending mainly on whether or not the cabinet controls a Riksdag majority, the opposition parties are able to influence policy decisions via parliamentary committees. Among MPs, the three most prestigious committees are the Finance Committee, the Foreign Affairs Committee, and the Committee on Constitutional Affairs (Hagevi 1998: 69–82). Since most cabinets have not controlled a parliamentary majority, the committees have often been arenas for building legislative majority coalitions. All standing committees have full time administrative staffs and are authorized to take legislative initiatives of their own. They are specialized in areas that roughly correspond to the jurisdictions of government ministries, and committee chairs are distributed roughly proportionally among the parliamentary parties (Arter 1999). Riksdag committees thus rank high in international comparisons of relative influence (Strøm 1990; Mattson and Strøm 1995). In spite of the consensual style of policy-making that these arrangements facilitate, government positions come with resources and influence, and they are highly valued and sought after by the political parties.

Negative Parliamentarism

One of the most important institutional features (contract design) of Swedish parliamentary democracy is its 'negative' parliamentarism (Bergman 1993). 'Positive' parliamentarism requires that an incoming cabinet demonstrate explicit parliamentary support, typically by a simple majority in an investiture vote. In negative parliamentarism, the coming to power of a new cabinet requires only tolerance by a parliamentary majority, not active support. Typically, the Head of State appoints the new PM and no investiture vote is held.

Within the category of negative parliamentarism, the Swedish formation rules are unusual in two ways. First, since 1 January 1975 the Head of State (the monarch) is excluded from the cabinet formation process. Second, Sweden has a 'negative' investiture vote in the Riksdag. A candidate for PM is proposed by the Speaker of the Riksdag. Before a new cabinet can assume power, a vote must be held, but the Speaker's candidate for PM succeeds unless more than half of the members of the Riksdag (175 MPs) vote against him or her. All candidates proposed by the Speaker since 1975 have been approved on the first vote.

Compared with the formation process before 1975, the new voting rule has had two important consequences. First, the parties are now forced to show openly whether or not they tolerate a new cabinet before it forms. Abstention effectively means tacit support for a new cabinet. Second, the party groups in the Riksdag have become more involved in the formation process. Previously, the bargaining process was more easily kept within a small circle of leaders. Since the MPs now have to attend a vote on the new cabinet, party leaders consult more widely to ensure that their MPs are willing to vote for or against a particular candidate. While such consultations are largely limited to the parliamentary party groups, the trend has been towards broader consultations. The Liberal Party has held explicit pre-electoral discussions of potential coalitions at party conferences, and the Centre Party is known to have a time-consuming internal decision-making process. Overall, however, cabinet formation and dissolution have been decided largely by party leaders and not by party organizations, party conferences, or membership votes (Bergman 1995).

No-Confidence Votes

As mentioned above, from 1917 to 1971, the principle that the cabinet must resign if the parliamentary majority no longer tolerates it existed only by convention (Andrén 1968). The partial constitutional reform that went into effect in 1971 introduced formal rules for a no-confidence vote against the cabinet. According to the written rule, an absolute parliamentary majority (50 per cent + 1 of all MPs) is needed to bring down the cabinet (Article 12: 4). One practical effect of this voting rule is that it promotes cabinet stability. Even minority cabinets with a relatively small support base in the Parliament can be stable since abstentions are, in practice, counted as support for the incumbent cabinet.[4]

A no-confidence vote can be directed at individual ministers, but if one is directed against the PM the whole cabinet must resign if he loses (Article 6: 5–7). Attempts to use this procedure against the PM occurred in 1980, 1996, 1998 and again in 2002, but none was successful. In 1985 a vote was held on an individual minister, the Minister for Foreign Affairs. This motion of no confidence also failed (Holmberg and Stjernquist 2000: 201). In fact, the opposition parties never expected to win. Instead, opposition parties have used these motions to demonstrate their discontent with the cabinet or the minister. A minister or a PM who believes that he might lose a vote of no confidence is likely to resign before the vote is actually held. This happened in June 1988, when the Minister of Justice resigned to avoid censure (Holmberg and Stjernquist 2000: 201).

---

[4] Here cabinet stability should be understood only in a formal sense, that is, the voting rule makes it difficult to unseat a cabinet already in power. This does not have to mean that a particular cabinet is free from internal conflict or that it has a stable parliamentary base in the Riksdag.

Confidence Votes

There are no formal procedures by which a cabinet can test or demonstrate its ability to govern by winning a crucial vote in the Parliament. If a cabinet wants to show that it can govern, it can attach such an importance to any policy vote in the Riksdag. In this case, presumably the cabinet will choose a policy vote that is important enough to motivate the resignation of the cabinet. If the cabinet loses the vote, it has two options, neither of which is constitutionally mandatory but yet considered politically necessary. It can call an extra election or it can resign, in which case the Speaker will start a new government formation process.

The only explicit confidence vote held in the postwar era occurred in 1990. The ruling Social Democratic cabinet linked its survival to an economic austerity package designed to deal with inflation and a growing budget deficit. It lost the vote and formally resigned. In this case, however, there was no alternative cabinet ready to be formed, and after a brief cabinet crisis the same cabinet continued in power (Bergman 1995).[5]

Parliamentary Dissolution

Other mechanisms that govern the relation between an incumbent cabinet and the Parliament are parliamentary dissolution rights. The most important cornerstone of parliamentary democracy is the Parliament's power to remove the cabinet from power. Another way of terminating a conflict between the cabinet and the parliamentary majority is an early parliamentary dissolution. Under the Swedish Constitution of 1809, dissolving Parliament was one of the King's prerogatives. Once the parliamentary principle was established, it was accepted that the cabinet as a whole controls this power. However, as late as the 1960s some constitutional experts argued that the King could refuse a cabinet's request to dissolve the Riksdag. Others disputed this claim (see Bergman 1995). The constitutional reforms of the 1970s removed all doubt about the King's role in parliamentary dissolution by completely abolishing it.

There are two ways in which the Riksdag can be dissolved. The first is if the Speaker proposes four successive prime ministerial candidates and each is voted down by more than half of the MPs. In this case, new Riksdag elections must be held within three months (Article 6: 3). Second, the cabinet has discretionary power to dissolve the Riksdag by a regular cabinet decision (Article 3: 4) though there are some restrictions on this power. The cabinet cannot dissolve Parliament during the first three months after an election. Nor can it dissolve the Riksdag after it has resigned and is serving in a caretaker capacity (SOU 1967:26: 184–8, 1972:15: 126–7, 1987:6: 127–33; Holmberg and Stjernquis 1980).

In Sweden, even if an extra election is held the ordinary election must be held at the constitutionally mandated date. This effectively decreases the incentive to hold extra

---

[5] Because of the restrictive counting rule used for this volume, in comparative terms this formal resignation and regaining of power does not count as a cabinet formation.

elections. In the postwar period, only one extra election has been held. This was in 1958 when the parties were deeply divided over the creation of mandatory public pension funds (see Molin 1965). In 1973, 1978, and 1981 extra elections were discussed as possible solutions to cabinet crises, but in each case this was ruled out since regular elections would have to be held quite soon thereafter (Särlvik 1983: 130–2; Hadenius, Molin, and Wieslander 1993: 263–81).

Table 20.1 summarizes the behavioural record until 1 January 2000 with respect to cabinet investiture, no-confidence and confidence votes, and parliamentary dissolution. Until 1975, no Riksdag vote was held when a new cabinet formed. From 1975, a cabinet investiture vote occurs only after the former PM has resigned—or has been voted out of office—and the Speaker has suggested a new PM. Until 2000, inauguration votes had been held only nine times. In three of these cases, the cabinet received fewer than half of the votes cast, but in no case did the Riksdag reject a candidate presented by the Speaker. As noted above, the no-confidence votes directed at PMs have all been unsuccessful. The empty column under confidence votes is because Sweden does not have a constitutionally mandated process for such votes. The informal practice concerning such confidence votes was discussed above. Finally, the thesis (above) that the rules governing parliamentary dissolution make an early election unlikely is supported by the fact that in the entire postwar period there has only been one early election (1958). That decision was de facto made by the cabinet.

Parliamentary Scrutiny of Cabinet and Individual Ministers

The Constitution contains a section (Chapter 12) on parliamentary control of the cabinet and the administration. This chapter includes the no-confidence vote. However, no-confidence votes are rare and the bulk of the chapter regulates ordinary parliamentary control mechanisms. As is explained below, the Constitution gives the MPs the right to ask the cabinet questions and to inquire about government affairs. The Riksdag auditors are authorized to investigate public affairs, and the standing Committee on Constitutional Affairs has important scrutiny powers, some of which give it legal authority.

One of the ways in which MPs can hold cabinet ministers accountable is by asking questions about issues that fall under their jurisdiction (Andrén 1968; Holmberg and Stjernquist 1980; Sterzel 1998: 220–3). This option is predominately used by opposition MPs. In researching and preparing debates on such questions, ministers are favoured because access to information is asymmetric. A minister is assisted by the ministry staff and has resources far beyond those of an opposition party or an individual MP. Nonetheless, MPs find asking questions useful. It forces a minister to devote some attention to a particular issue, to provide the MP with information, and sometimes also to act. For the MP, asking questions is also beneficial because it often attracts media attention, not least from the MPs own constituency.

A question about a matter whose importance might prompt a general debate is called an interpellation (Holmberg and Stjernquist 2000: 201–2; see also Wiberg 1994).

Table 20.1. *Cabinet Formation, Cabinet Termination, and Early Parliamentary Dissolution: Sweden 1945–2000*[a]

No.	Cabinet	Date of formation	Investiture votes (iv)						No-confidence votes (ncv)			Confidence votes (cv) under specific institutional mechanism	Did this cabinet end with an early election?	Who dissolved Parliament in this case?[b]
			No. of unsuccessful investiture votes	Voting results of successful iv (1: pro gov, 2: against gov, 3: abstentions, and 4: other)				No. of ncv	Cabinet removed by ncv	Cabinet resigned to pre-empt ncv	n.a.		
				1	2	3	4						
1	Hansson	45/07/31	n.a.					0					
2	Erlander I	46/10/11	n.a.					0					
3	Erlander II	48/09/19	n.a.					0					
4	Erlander III	51/10/01	n.a.					0					
5	Erlander IV	52/09/21	n.a.					0					
6	Erlander V	56/09/26	n.a.					0					
7	Erlander VI	57/10/31	n.a.					0					
8	Erlander VII	58/06/01	n.a.					0				Yes	Cabinet
9	Erlander VIII	60/09/18	n.a.					0					
10	Erlander IX	64/09/20	n.a.					0					
11	Erlander X	68/09/15	n.a.					0					
12	Palme I	69/10/14	n.a.					0					
13	Palme II	70/09/20	n.a.					0					
14	Palme III	73/09/16	n.a.					0					
15	Fälldin I	76/10/07	0	174	160	0	15	0					
16	Ullsten	78/10/13	0	39	66	215	29	0					

Table 20.1. (contd.)

No.	Cabinet	Date of formation	Investiture votes (iv) No. of unsuccessful investiture votes	Voting results of successful iv (1: pro gov, 2: against gov, 3: abstentions, and 4: other)				No-confidence votes (ncv) No. of ncv	Cabinet removed by ncv	Cabinet resigned to pre-empt ncv	Confidence votes (cv) under specific institutional mechanism n.a.	Did this cabinet end with an early election?	Who dissolved Parliament in this case?[b]
				1	2	3	4						
17	Fälldin II	79/10/11	0	170	174	1	4	1	No				
18	Fälldin III	81/05/19	0	102	174	65	11	0					
19	Palme IV	82/10/07	0	179	0	147	23	0					
20	Palme V	85/09/15	—					0[c]					
21	Carlsson I	86/03/12	0	178	0	159	12	0					
22	Carlsson II[d]	88/09/18	—					0					
23	Bildt	91/10/03	0	163	147	23	16	0					
24	Carlsson III	94/10/06	0	180	26	130	13	0					
25	Persson I	96/03/21	0	178	0	154	7	1	No				
26	Persson II	98/09/20	—					—			—		

[a] n.d. = no data (missing data); n.a. or '—' = not applicable in this case.

[b] The question 'Who dissolved Parliament in this case?' can be answered with one of five options. This identifies the main constitutional actor that caused the early election. We have not coded the formal signatory, but rather the person or body that made the real decision: (1) Head of State; (2) Prime Minister; (3) Cabinet; (4) Parliamentary majority; (5) Automatic constitutional provision (e.g. if it is required when a new President takes office, or, for example, if it is required after the adoption of a proposal for constitutional amendments).

[c] The table column for 'No. of ncv' deals only with votes directed against the PM and thereby the cabinet as a whole. However, in February 1985 there was also vote of no confidence against the Foreign Minister (Lennart Bodström). Also this motion failed to get the support of the required absolute majority of all MPs.

[d] In 1990 Carlsson II put an informal confidence motion on the parliamentary agenda. The cabinet failed the vote and resigned, but there was no alternative cabinet solution and the same cabinet returned to power. Please note that this event does not meet our strict cross-national standard for counting either confidence votes or a new cabinet.

While ministers are not formally required to do so, they answer almost all interpellations and questions. If an interpellation/question is delayed or not answered, the
minister must inform the Riksdag as to the reasons why. An MP has no formal right to
get an answer from a particular minister. Even if the question is directed at a specific
minister, it can be answered by one of his cabinet colleagues. In the 1990s attempts have
been made to make the debates livelier. Since 1991 there are weekly televised sessions
in which questions are answered directly by a subset of ministers and since 1996 written
questions (but not interpellations) only receive a written answer (Riksdagens årsbok
1990/91: 20–3; KU 1995/96: 18).

The Riksdag can also scrutinize cabinet reports. The practice of sending cabinet
reports to Parliament has increased over time. The Parliament now receives reports on
the various commissions that prepare government policy, the state-owned enterprises,
and on EU affairs. In addition, the Parliament has its own Parliamentary Audit Office
(*Riksdagens Revisorer*). While much smaller than the government's audit agency, it
nonetheless provides the Riksdag with an autonomous source of information. The
Riksdag also appoints Ombudsmen who are entitled to scrutinize all state and local
government agencies, issue recommendations, and even to prosecute civil servants that
do not follow laws and regulations. The number of actual prosecutions has decreased
over time, but the number of cases examined by the Ombudsmen has increased.
Ombudsmen often issue critical reports. The reports are often influential, but because
their recommendations are not necessarily followed, complaints have been heard about
the relative 'toothlessness' of the Ombudsmen as an oversight mechanism (Petersson
and Söderlind 1993: 113, 115–8; Sterzel 1998: 226–9; Holmberg and Stjernquist 2000).

The Riksdag Committee on Constitutional Affairs produces annual reports on how
cabinet ministers conduct their official duties. The Committee is allowed access to cabinet minutes and documents. The Committee can also question individual ministers on
any matter that has to do with his/her portfolio. The plenary session of the Riksdag
receives the Committee report on the cabinet minister's conduct and votes on whether
or not to support any critique that the Committee may direct against the cabinet or
minister. There is a certain amount of party posturing in these reports, but they also
serve an important function, both as a preventive measure and as a way to scrutinize
ministerial behaviour. The Committee has influenced how the cabinet fulfils its constitutional duties, not least on more technical matters of cabinet procedure (Holmberg
and Stjernquist 1980: 401–4, 2000: 203–4; Sterzel 1998: 213–7).

Its legal authority to decide whether or not to prosecute individual ministers for
unlawful acts committed in office reinforces the authority of the Committee on
Constitutional Affairs. Such acts are narrowly defined as wrongful actions that
a minister could do only because he was a minister. Prosecution has never been an issue
in the postwar period (Holmberg and Stjernquist 2000: 204–5). Nonetheless, the
possibility of prosecution gives the Committee extraordinary measures and status as
the most important body for scrutinizing the conduct of cabinet and ministers.

In the step connecting MPs to the cabinet, Swedish institutional arrangements
(contract design) are such that they make it relatively easy to form a cabinet (i.e. the
absence of a positive vote requirement) and difficult to unseat a cabinet already in

power (e.g. the mandated period between regular elections and the absolute majority requirement for a vote of no confidence). Cabinet positions come with administrative resources and agenda-setting powers and the political actions of MPs are very much focused on influencing cabinet proposals (*ex ante*). *Ex post* instruments, such as parliamentary questions, are also used, partly to demonstrate to the home constituency that its concerns are taken care of, but play a minor role in the Riksdag.

DELEGATION WITHIN THE CABINET

Until 1975, the King formally approved all cabinet appointments that in reality were made by the PM. Since 1975, constitutionally, the PM is free to appoint and dismiss other ministers on his own and at will, although he can of course be constrained by intraparty concerns or by coalition partners. In contrast, collegiality and consensus is the practice (and the norm) in policy decisions within the cabinet.

Including the PM, the cabinet has had between sixteen and twenty-two ministers. As of 2000 there were twenty cabinet ministers (Hadenius, Molin, and Wieslander 1993: 372–80; Holmberg and Stjernquist 2000: 109). It is the cabinet as a whole that rules the country (Article 1: 6) and handles foreign affairs (Article 10: 1). Much of its influence stems from its role as the body in which leaders of the governing party/parties prepare most of the Riksdag's decisions. The cabinet also has the final say over many top-level state appointments and is in charge of the state bureaucracy. For issues that fall outside the jurisdiction of the courts, it is also the highest body in the state-administrative appeals process.

The Constitution does not provide much guidance as to cabinet organization. There are a few broad rules. The cabinet collectively decides on the jurisdiction of each ministry by decree (Article 7: 1). A quorum of five or more ministers is necessary to hold a formal meeting of the cabinet (Article 7: 4). Finally, with the exception of some issues concerning national defence, all cabinet level decisions must be taken at formal cabinet meetings (Article 7: 3).

The Government Office (the Chancery) consists of the cabinet (or PM) office, the individual ministries (currently ten ministries), and the Government Administration Office. Excluding the Ministry for Foreign Affairs, there were about 1,800 employees in the early 1990s. More than half were civil servants, legal experts, and similar employees. About one-tenth were part of the commission system, while roughly one-quarter were assistants and clerical staff. About a hundred were political appointees who resign with cabinet. By 31 December 1999 the total number of employees was 2,281 while the number of political appointees was seventy-five (Petersson 1994: 89; Holmberg and Stjernquist 2000: 116–7).

Individual cabinet members (ministers) are normally heads of their departments. The exception is that some ministers are responsible for preparing certain policy areas (e.g. elementary and secondary schools within the Ministry of Education), but do not head a ministry of their own. These are ministers 'without portfolio' (in 2000 there were nine such ministers). While such ministers used to be mainly responsible for the formal–legal aspects of policy drafting, today these ministers have much the same tasks as those who head a ministry.

Cabinet level decisions are made only at formal cabinet meetings. Unless individual ministers explicitly reserve themselves against a particular decision, all ministers are formally responsible for all cabinet decisions.[6] Nonetheless, constrained only by law and general cabinet procedure, the heads of individual ministries are in charge of their ministries. In this capacity, individual ministers prepare many decisions that are never discussed, but simply accepted by their fellow ministers at the formal cabinet meetings (Andrén 1968: 299–311; SOU 1972:15: 150; Kungl. Maj:ts proposition nr år 1973: 179–86; Holmberg and Stjernquist 1980; T. Larsson 1986: 181–6).

The decision rule within the cabinet is best described as consensus defined by the PM. Under the 1809 Constitution, the King formally made all cabinet decisions himself, which is one explanation for the traditional lack of a formal cabinet decision rule. Establishing a decision rule was discussed during the constitutional reforms of the 1970s, but in the end it was left to individual cabinets to decide such matters (Holmberg and Stjernquist 2000: 120–1; for a case study see S. E. Larsson 1986: 185–208). With regard to cabinet decision-making, the PM obviously has considerable agenda power. He has his own staff to initiate and coordinate policy-making.

Compared to the early postwar period, the PM's resources to monitor other ministers have increased quite dramatically. When PM Tage Erlander first arrived in his new office in 1946, his entire staff consisted of a secretary and one assistant. In the mid-1950s he began to have an advisory support staff of his own. However, it was not until 1964 that he began to build a formal office that included a junior minister (or state secretary, *statssekreterare*). This followed a 1963 incident in which the PM only learned about the capture of a Soviet spy after some of his ministers had already been informed. By 1976, with the coming to power of the first postwar non-socialist coalition, the PM's office became an arena for coalition coordination and problem solving (T. Larsson 1986: 181–95). During the 1991–4 coalition, in addition to civil servants and the PM's personal staff, the PM's office contained a separate coordinating unit for each of the four coalition partners and played a central role as a conflict-resolution mechanism (Bergman 2000).

In a formal sense, all ministers, including the PM, have the same weight in cabinet decision-making. The 1975 Constitution allows the PM to appoint a Deputy (Article 7: 8). This possibility is used only occasionally and the position is primarily honorary. Instead, after the PM, it is the Ministry of Finance that has had a dominant role relative to other departments (Larsson 1994; Mattson 1998). In fact, the Finance Minister, who is

---

[6] The importance of collective decision-making in the cabinet can go beyond the role of the PM and individual ministers. A tradition of collective cabinet responsibility may force coalition partners and individual ministers to defend cabinet policies with which they disagree. This can have practical importance and, for example, create a disincentive to join a coalition unless there is an assurance that its policies will be acceptable (e.g. see Laver 1992: 47–8, on the case of Ireland).

responsible for preparing the state budget, generally has had a better capacity to monitor other ministries than the PM himself (Larsson 1990: 154). It is only in the 1990s that there has been a major shift in resources and monitoring capacity in favour of the PM's Office.

In sum, as the first among equals in the King's cabinet, before 1975 the PM had to act through the King to appoint his ministers. Today the screening and selection procedures are directly in the hands of the PM. In addition, the PM has many informal ways and nowadays a large staff to help steer the cabinet. Constitutional design also limits the autonomy of individual ministers who must pass all major decisions by their colleagues in the cabinet. This constitutional requirement is likely to favour policy-cohesive cabinets.

DELEGATION FROM MINISTERS TO CIVIL SERVANTS

In contrast to most other countries, individual ministers are in Sweden not in charge of the state agencies that implement public policy (Holmberg and Stjernquist 1980, 2000). State agencies fall under the authority of the cabinet, and not under an individual ministry responsible for a particular policy area (Article 7: 3). In addition, neither the cabinet nor the minister can stipulate how an agency or a civil servant should in particular cases implement law or exercise powers of the state over individuals. This is a matter reserved for the civil servants that implement law and exercise state authority (Article 11: 7). Matters of misuse and abuse by agencies or civil servants are to be handled by the courts or by the cabinet in an appeals process. However, the boundary between the cabinet and the ministries on the one hand and the 'autonomous' agencies on the other is not clear and precise, but an area of constitutional debate (Holmberg and Stjernquist 1980, 2000; Petersson and Söderlind 1993: 73–9).

Ministers have been known to complain about their inability to direct agencies and about occasional resistance among the ministerial civil servants and state agencies to cuts in funding or major policy shifts. For example, the 1976 shift from a Social Democratic cabinet to a three party (non-socialist) coalition cabinet faced resistance from some civil servants (Pierre 1995). In general, however, individual ministers 'talk to', 'consult with', and 'exchange information' with the agencies that implement policy in their area. In practice they also control the preparation of policy decision and the agency budgets within the framework decided by the Riksdag. Ministers also control nominations to the highest positions in the agencies, all of which gives them ample opportunity to influence civil servants (Petersson and Söderlind 1993).

Until 1965 it was not possible to fire high civil servants. Today this constitutional protection remains for judges in a limited form only. It is possible for the agency super-vising the court system to fire judges with the support of a court of law (Article 11: 5). Under the old (1809) Constitution, some high civil servants, such as heads of central agencies and county governors, were appointed in the name of the Head of State, while other appointments were made by the state agency itself (Andrén 1968: 385–93). The hierarchical distinction between different categories of civil servants in terms of appointment still exists, but now the dividing line is between those appointed by the cabinet and those who are not (Article 11: 9). For the latter there is a merit system and regular career positions for which one applies. For the former, the cabinet has the discretion to appoint a qualified candidate of its choice. There is a tendency for these positions, for example as county governors, to be a reward for long and faithful service, although not necessarily to a person representing the party in power. Governments fill these positions with candidates from each political camp, but are also sometimes critiqued by the opposition parties (be they Socialist or non-socialist) for over-representing those with partisan connections to the government (e.g. see, KU 1995/96:30: 52–6).

Further evidence that the dividing line between ministries that prepare and agencies that implement is not completely strict is that the cabinet can decide that minor policy decisions or allocation of funds will be handled by a ministry instead of an agency. One such example is aviation regulation, which grew over time from a desk in a ministry to its own agency (Andrén 1968: 339). This practice continues and it is not unusual that the cabinet delegates to one of its ministries the task of deciding on the distribution of funds according to principles laid down by the cabinet (KU 1991/92: 30: 78–80). Taken together, individual ministers have numerous channels through which to enforce their will. Nonetheless, the utility of a particular ministerial portfolio might be more restricted in Sweden than in a system in which each minister exercises a more formal and direct control over implementing agencies.

In addition, civil servants exercise more rather than less influence over policy today than they did early in the postwar period. In fact, when asked what group in society over time had increased its power the most, MPs mentioned civil servants second only to the mass media (Esaiasson and Holmberg 1996: 200–2). Civil servants now take more policy initiatives and their influence has been increasing both at the proposal stage and in implementation (Wallin *et al.* 1999).

In spite of the scandals and corruption cases that do occur in the public sector, in comparative perspective the Swedish bureaucracy remains largely corruption-free (Andersson 1999). Agencies and administrative agencies that exercise 'police-patrol' *ex post* monitoring facilitate this. The National Audit Office (*Riksrevisionsverket*) is empowered to scrutinize both how state institutions manage their funds and how they perform their duties. The cabinet also appoints an Ombudsman (*Justitiekanslern*) to supervise the state administration. His office investigates complaints by the public and he serves as a prosecutor in cases concerning civil servants accused of abusing their public duties and in cases concerning free speech (SOU 1993: 37).

While agencies under both the cabinet and the Riksdag serve as *ex post* controls of policy decisions and their implementation, the cabinet agencies are better funded and staffed than the Riksdag's Parliamentary Audit (*Riksdagens revisorer*) Office (Petersson and Söderlind 1993). The main audit office, the National Audit Office, is both under the control of the cabinet and dependent on a budget allocated via the cabinet. It has also been shown to be more sensitive than the Riksdag's Parliamentary Audit Office to ministerial interests. The Parliamentary Audit also has constitutional protection (Article 12: 7). The problem with this Audit, however, is that the Riksdag does not have well-developed routines for making use of its findings (Ahlbäck 1999).[7]

---

[7] The Riksdag has decided that in 2003 there will be one major audit agency in Sweden. It will be placed under the Riksdag and not under the cabinet.

'Fire-alarm' type monitoring of civil servants is made easier by constitutionally guaranteed access to public documents. There are of course exceptions; the publication of some material can lead to prosecution. This includes material that threatens national security, harassment of a population group, child pornography, and libel. Government documents that refer to sensitive matters, for example in foreign policy, defence, commercial relations, and personal integrity, are to be kept secret. Nonetheless, the main principle is free public access to all documents in the public sector. In addition, the Freedom of the Press Act, which has constitutional status, gives every citizen the right to publish any written material. The same Act allows all citizens, including public officials, freely to provide information to the mass media (Petersson 1994: 173–8).

Public access to government documents helps prevent misuse and abuse of government offices and government power. With the help of such sources, media can draw attention to acts of potential wrongdoing. One area in which this has occurred is with regard to cases of immigration and asylum-seekers, where public attention has led authorities to change earlier decisions and foster public sector reforms. Other such areas include the export of weapons and the practice of state agencies conducting some of their business through 'private' companies that they fully or partially control via stock holding (Petersson and Söderlind 1993: 266, 273–6).

In sum, civil servants have served their political masters rather well. There has been an element of *ex ante* screening and selection of civil servants on the basis of their preferences. Some of this has to do with the long tenure of power enjoyed by the Social Democrats. But more important and influential is the strong tradition of relative administrative autonomy and bureaucratic integrity. This relatively favourable evaluation is helped by constitutional guarantees for freedom of information and access to public sector documents for both the citizens and the press. There are also working *ex post* supervising institutions such as the Ombudsmen. However, it is noticeable that elected representatives (MPs), the cabinet, and individual ministers play a rather limited role in *ex post* monitoring. As principals they have tended to rely on civil servants for policy initiative and development. Monitoring of civil servants that implement policies has been less of a concern.

EXTERNAL CONSTRAINTS

Parliamentary democracy is embedded in a context in which organized interests influence the democratic policy-making chain. In Sweden, as in other small West European nation-states, a system of democratic corporatism has been very important (e.g. see Katzenstein 1985). While the literature has often focused on the organizations representing labour and capital, a broad variety of organized interests have been influential through their close ties with the state administration. The particularly strong ties between the Social Democrats and the blue-collar union federation, the LO (Landsorganistationen), is an often noted feature of Swedish politics (Back and Berglund 1978; Bäck and Möller 1997; Feldt 1991; Strøm and Bergman 1992; Petersson 1994; Teorell 1998).

There are actually two articles in the Constitution that *might* be considered to support a corporatist system. One (Article 7: 2) states that cabinet decisions must be properly prepared and that this can involve the consultation of both individuals and associations. The other (Article 11: 6) provides the possibility of permitting individuals, companies, associations, and foundations to manage the implementation of state policy. If allowed by law (i.e. by the Riksdag), this can include decisions concerning the benefits and/or obligations of individual citizens. Yet, these provisions do not mean that Sweden has a corporatist Constitution. On the contrary, as noted above, Sweden has an almost ideal–typical parliamentary Constitution. What the two statutes actually show is that the corporatist system was long seen as a natural and uncontroversial part of Swedish politics.

Corporatism of course deviates from the ideal democratic chain of delegation and accountability, and a problem has been the lack of public accountability. That is, rather anonymous interest group representatives serve on government commissions and on the boards of state agencies, yet these groups are not accountable to the electorate.[8] In the early 1990s, the corporatist system is reported to have diminished in importance (Lewin 1994; Petersson 1994: 162–5), partly as a consequence of new relations between the major organized interests in the labour market. These new relations are in turn, very much a consequence of the fact that groups representing business have opted out of the system by refusing to appoint representatives to the commissions that prepare cabinet proposals and the boards that implement public policy (Rothstein and Bergström 1999).

While the impact of neo-corporatism as a constraint in many respects has weakened, the importance of other constraints has increased. The direct and single chain of parliamentary democracy has been affected by increased local government spending and by the new power relations between central and local governments that have accompanied this expansion (Petersson 1994: 122–40; Häggroth and Peterson 1999; Stjernquist 1999). The importance of local governments in welfare spending has roots back before the Second World War. But since the early 1970s, it has been national policy to give local (and regional) governments increasingly greater responsibility and greater autonomy for welfare provisions in the social sector (schools, health, etc.). In terms of social expenditure and personnel, the Swedish welfare *state* is very much a function performed by *local* governments. In fact, about 70 per cent of total government consumption occurs at these levels. Simultaneously, the national level government has moved from steering by detailed instructions to a system of general policy targets. In the process, it has become increasingly difficult for the national government to promise certain services or public sector reforms. Today it is very much up to the local governments to actually decide and implement these promises.

Referendums also constrain the parliamentary chain of delegation. Advisory referendums were held both in 1955 (left- or right-hand side traffic) and in 1958 (public and mandatory pension funds). Prior to this, the referendum had only been used in 1922

---

[8] It is, however, not entirely clear that a system more characterized by lobbying and pluralism guarantees that elected officials are more accountable to the general public.

(prohibition of alcohol). In 1980 the national nuclear power programme became the next subject to be tried in a national referendum. In 1994 membership in the EU was decided in a referendum. Formally, these referendums have all been advisory but each time the political parties have promised to follow the wishes of the majority—at least to the extent that it has been possible to identify such a majority. However, a problem with advisory referendums is that it is up to the political parties to interpret and implement the advice they receive. This includes the issue of for how long a referendum result is valid. To make the referendums mechanism decisive would not solve these problems. Instead the use of both kinds of referendums tends to make the power relations that are implied by the ideal type of parliamentary democracy more diffuse. Other important trends work in the same direction.

Indirectly, constitutional adherence to the ideal type of parliamentary democracy assigns a particular role to the courts. While few would dispute the importance of autonomous courts that are able to resist pressure from powerful politicians, an ideal parliamentary democracy assumes that the courts have a more limited role than they have in an ideal–typical separation-of-powers system. Traditionally, the distinction between state administration and the court system has been weak in Sweden. This is at least partly because of roots that go back to a system in which the Kings' rule over the country involved both having power over the state administration and being the administrative appeal authority (Brunsson, Sonneyby, and Wittenmark 1990). Both courts and judges have been reluctant to play an active role relative to the parliamentary system of government. As mentioned, the courts' have constitutional authority to refuse to allow implementation of laws that they find are unconstitutional (Article 11: 14). However, until the 1980s, the option was hardly ever used as courts and judges have wanted not to appear political in what was a system where democratic politics had priority over legalism (Board 1991; Petersson *et al.* 1999).[9]

There is now more of a constitutional debate over the proper role of the courts. Much of the impetus for an increase in judicial activism seems to stem from developments outside Sweden, such as the role of courts in European integration. One important European development is associated with the Convention on Human Rights and the European Court of Human Rights in Strasbourg (Petersson 1994: 120–1). The European Court of Human Rights has questioned the traditional Swedish system of cabinet-appeal rather than court-appeal in administrative matters such as the appeals process for professional licensing and procedural rules concerning the expropriation of property. Following European Court decisions, appeals on such matters have been transferred from the cabinet to administrative courts of justice (Petersson and Söderlind 1993: 262–4; Holmberg and Stjernquist 2000: 195–6).

An obviously significant external constraint is the EU. On 1 January 1995, Sweden became one of fifteen EU member states. The strong and central position of the

---

[9] This debate has been fuelled by domestic legal cases in the 1990s. Two examples are from 1996. In one decision a court of first appeal declined to implement a 1946 law about the complete ban of political uniforms. In the other, the court at the last (second) level of appeal (the Supreme Court) decided not to recognize a punishable offence on the grounds that the law was not based on proper delegation from the Riksdag (Holmberg and Stjernquist 2000: 190–5).

European Court of Justice within European integration has helped foster a new and more active role for national courts. EU membership also has other political and constitutional consequences. Sweden stayed outside of the Economic and Monetary Union (EMU) in 1999 and prior to a referendum in September 2003 opinion polls show that a majority of Swedes oppose membership. However, the Social Democratic cabinet and most opposition parties have been eager to meet the strict budget and finance criteria for EMU membership. They have also decided to change Central Bank rules to give it greater autonomy from direct and short-term influence by elected representatives (Mattson 1998).

EU membership was accompanied by an institutional innovation in the Riksdag.[10] The European Affairs Advisory Committee (*EU-nämnden*) was created for the purpose of monitoring the cabinet when it represents Sweden in the EU Council of Ministers. This committee allows the Riksdag to scrutinize ministers, but it does not have the full formal status of a regular Riksdag committee. The Committee does not have the right to make policy initiatives on its own or to refer issues to the full chamber, but is still considered important. This is shown by the fact that opposition parties send high-ranking MPs to meetings between cabinet ministers and the Committee. Together with the important developments reported above, EU membership is reshaping the Swedish chain of parliamentary democracy. In fact, today the de facto Constitution exhibits a 'dualism' between the ideal–typical national constitution and the treaties of the EU (Algotsson 2000).

CONCLUSION

While far from perfect, for much of the postwar period the Swedish chain of democratic delegation and accountability has not been affected by serious agency problems. Fierce electoral competition between two clearly defined blocs and two alternative visions of society allowed voters to be reasonably sure that elections would impact on the direction of national politics. At the same time, the minority status of most cabinets allowed for moderation in policy decisions. Many interests have been included in the process and well-organized and influential parties have linked together the various steps of the constitutionally mandated parliamentary democracy. In addition, *ex post* mechanisms have worked fairly well. The courts, Ombudsmen, audit offices, and specific agencies have uncovered misuse of state authority and funds. Policy implementers are far from flawless, but there has been comparatively little patronage or outright corruption. Public access to state documents and media scrutiny has helped secure a strong tradition of openness and transparency. This has meant that supervision through active 'police patrolling' and 'fire alarm' reporting from voters and media have been met by the formulation of new policy in the cabinet and in the Riksdag.

Since the late 1980s, however, Swedish politicians have increasingly been faced with distrust, lower electoral turnout, and a loss of party members. The parties have tried

---

[10] For more on the Swedish committee see Hegeland (1999), Hegeland and Mattsson (1997); for a comparison with the Danish committee, see Hegeland and Matsson (1996); for a broad EU-comparison, see Bergman (1997); for a study of the impact of the EU on national democracy in Sweden and the other Nordic countries, see Bergman and Damgaard (2000).

to respond by increasing their state funding and allowing voters more say in the choice of individual MPs. It does not seem to have reversed the trend. This, in turn, might have something to do with the increasingly complex and diffuse political system. It is possible that the growing discrepancy between de facto power relations and the ideal–typical Constitution contributes to a declining popular trust in politicians and political parties.

Early in the twentieth century, parliamentary democracy developed within a Constitution based on separation of powers. By the mid-1970s the last remnants of this Constitution disappeared. At about the same time, a new separation-of-powers system began to develop. There is once again a considerable discrepancy between the written rule and the 'living constitution' (constitutional practice). At the beginning of the new century, national politics has lost a considerable amount of leverage over local governments, which show growing signs of developing disparate solutions to local problems and economic scarcity. In addition, European integration has furthered the development of a pattern of governance more characterized by power sharing with the courts. And important parts of national-level decision-making authority have been transferred to the EU. As a result of these tendencies, the formerly (and still constitutionally) sovereign Riksdag is no longer the supreme focal point in a unitary chain. These developments do not render parliamentary democracy unimportant or uninteresting. On the contrary, the challenge is to develop a further understanding of how the recent changes impact on the national chain of delegation and accountability, which continues to be the fundamental basis of democratic legitimacy.

REFERENCES

Ahlbäck, Shirin (1999). *Att kontrollera staten. Den statliga revisionens roll i den parlamentariska demokratin.* Ph.D. Dissertation, Department of Political Science, Uppsala University.

Algotsson, Karl-Göran (2000). *Sveriges författning efter EU-anslutningen.* Stockholm: SNS Förlag.

Allmänna Valen (1998). *Del 1: Riksdagen* (1999). Stockholm: Statistiska centralbyrån (SCB).

Andersson, Staffan (1999). *Hederlighetens pris: en ESO-rapport om korruption.* Stockholm: Departementsserien 1999:62.

Andrén, Nils (1968). *Svensk statskunskap.* Stockholm: Liber.

Arter, David (1999). *Scandinavian Politics Today.* Manchester: Manchester University Press.

Bäck, Mats and Möller, Tommy (1997). *Partier och organisationer,* 4th edn. Stockholm: Publica.

Back, Pär-Erik and Berglund, Sten (1978). *Det svenska partiväsendet.* Stockholm: Almqvist och Wiksell.

Berglund, Sten and Ulf Lindström (1978). *The Scandinavian Party System(s).* Lund: Studenlitteratur.

Bergman, Torbjörn (1993). 'Formation Rules and Minority Governments'. *European Journal of Political Research,* 23: 55–66.

——(1995). *Constitutional Rules and Party Goals in Coalition Formation: An Analysis of Winning Minority Governments in Sweden.* Ph.D. Dissertation, Department of Political Science, Umeå University.

——(1997). 'National Parliaments and EU Affairs Committees: Notes on Empirical Variation and Competing Explanations'. *Journal of European Public Policy,* 4: 373–87.

——(1999). 'Trade-Offs in Swedish Constitutional Design: The Monarchy Under Challenge', in Wolfgang C. Müller and Kaare Strøm (eds.), *Policy, Office, or Votes? How Political Parties in Western Europe Make Hard Decisions.* Cambridge: Cambridge University Press.

Bergman, Torbjörn (2000). 'Sweden: When Minority Cabinets are the Rule and Majority Coalitions the Exception', in Wolfgang C. Müller and Kaare Strøm (eds.), *Coalition Governments in Western Europe*. Oxford: Oxford University Press.

——and Damgaard Erik (eds.) (2000). *Delegation and Accountability in European Integration: The Nordic Parliamentary Democracies and the European Union*. London: Frank Cass. (Also published as a special issue of the *Journal of Legislative Studies*, 6(1).)

Birgersson, Bengt Owe and Westerståhl, Jörgen (1992). *Den svenska folkstyrelsen*, 5th edn. Stockholm: Publica.

Board, Joseph B. (1991). 'Judicial Activism in Sweden', in Kenneth M. Holland (ed.), *Judicial Activism in Comparative Perspective*. London: Macmillan.

Brunsson, Karin, Sonneby, Claes, and Wittenmark, Lars (1990). *Beslutsmaskinen—en bok om regeringskansliet*. Lund: Studentlitteratur.

The Constitution of Sweden (2000). *The Fundamental Laws and the Riksdag Act*. Stockholm: Riksdagen.

Esaiasson, Peter and Holmberg, Sören (1996). *Representation From Above: Members of Parliament and Representative Democracy in Sweden*. Aldershot: Dartmouth.

Feldt, Kjell-Olof (1991). *Alla dessa dagar... i regeringen 1982–1990*. Stockholm: Norstedts.

Gidlund, Gullan M. (1983). *Partistöd*. Lund: Liber CWK Gleerup.

——and Möller, Tommy (1999). *Demokratins trotjänare. Lokalt partiarbete förr och nu*. Stockholm: Fritzes offentliga publikationer (SOU 1999: 130).

Gilljam, Mikael and Holmberg, Sören (1995). *Väljarnas val*. Stockholm: Norstedts Juridik.

Hadenius, Stig, Molin, Björn, and Wieslander, Hans (1993). *Sverige efter 1900: En modern politisk historia*, 13th edn. Stockholm: Bonnier Alba.

Hagevi, Magnus (1998). *Bakom riksdagens fasad*. Göteborg: Akademibolaget Corona.

——(1999). 'Parliamentary Party Groups in the Swedish Riksdag', in Knut Heidar and Ruud Koole (eds.), *Parliamentary Party Groups in European Democracies*. London: Routledge.

Häggroth, Sören and Peterson, Carl-Gunnar (1999). *Kommunalkunskap. Så fungerar din Kommun*. Stockholm: Hjalmarsson & Högberg Bokförlag.

Heclo, Hugh and Madsen, Henrik (1987). *Policy and Politics in Sweden: Principled Pragmatism*. Philadelphia: Temple University Press.

Hegeland, Hans (1999). *Riksdagen, Europeiska unionen och demokratin*. Licenciatavhandling, Statsvetenskapliga Institutionen, Lund: Lunds Universitet.

——and Mattson, Ingvar (1996). 'To have a Voice in the Matter: A Comparative Study of the Swedish and Danish European Committees'. *The Journal of Legislative Studies*, 2: 198–215.

————(1997). 'The Swedish Riksdag and the EU: Influence and Openness', in Matti Wiberg (ed.), *Trying to Make Democracy Work: The Nordic Parliaments and the European Union*. Stockholm: The Bank of Sweden Tercentenary Foundation & Gidlunds Förlag.

Holmberg, Erik and Stjernquist, Nils (1980). *Grundlagarna med tillhörande författningar*. Stockholm: PA Norstedt & Söners förlag.

————(2000). *Vår författning*, 12th edn. Stockholm: Norstedts Juridik AB.

Holmberg, Sören (1999). *Representativ demokrati*. Stockholm: Statens offentliga utredningar 1999: 64.

Isberg, Magnus (1999). *Riksdagsledamoten i sin partigrupp. 52 riksdagsveteraners erfarenheter av parti-gruppernas arbetssätt och inflytande*. Stockholm: Gidlunds Förlag.

Katzenstein, Peter J. (1985). *Small States in World Markets: Industrial Policy in Europe*. Ithaca: Cornell University Press.

KU (1991/92:30). *Konstitutionsutskottets betänkande 1991/92:KU30 (1992 Granskningsbetänkande)*. Stockholm: Riksdagen.

KU (1995/96:18). *Konstitutionsutskottets betänkande 1995/96:KU18 (1995 Reform av spörsmålsinstituten)*. Stockholm: Riksdagen.

KU (1995/96:30). *Konstitutionsutskottets betänkande 1995/96:KU30 (1996 Granskningsbetänkande)*. Stockholm: Riksdagen.

Kungl. Maj:ts proposition nr 90 år (1973). *Förslag till ny regeringsform och ny riksdagsordning, m.m.* Stockholm: Riksdagen.

Lagerroth, Fredrik (1955). *Moderna författningar mot historisk bakgrund*. Stockholm: P. A. Norstedt & Söners Förlag.

Larsson, Sven-Erik (1986). *Reagera i koalition. Den borgerliga trepartiregeringen 1976–1978 och kärnkraften*. Stockholm: Bonniers.

Larsson, Torbjörn (1986). *Regeringen och dess kansli*. Lund: Studentlitteratur.

——(1990). 'Regeringens och regeringskansliets organisationsstruktur, berednings- och beslutsformer under 150 år', in *Att styra riket—regeringskansliet 1940–1990, Departementshistoriekommittén*. Stockholm: Allmänna Förlaget.

——(1994). 'Cabinet Ministers and Parliamentary Government in Sweden', in Michael Laver and Kenneth A. Shepsle (eds.), *Cabinet Ministers and Parliamentary Government*. Cambridge: Cambridge University Press.

Laver, Michael J. (1992). 'Coalition and Party Policy in Ireland', in Michael J. Laver and Ian Budge (eds.), *Party Policy and Government Coalitions*. London: Macmillan.

Lewin, Leif (1992). *Ideologi och strategi*, 4th edn. Stockholm: Norstedts Juridik.

——(1994). 'The Rise and Decline of Corporatism: The Case of Sweden'. *European Journal of Political Research*, 26: 59–79.

Mattson, Ingvar (1998). *Den statliga budget processen—rationell resursfördelning eller meningslös ritual?* Stockholm: SNS Förlag.

——and Strøm, Kaare (1995). 'Parliamentary Committee', in Herbert Döring (ed.), *Parliaments and Majority Rule in Western Europe*. Frankfurt am Main: Campus and New York: St. Martin's Press.

Molin, Björn (1965). *Tjänstepensionsfrågan. En studie i svensk partipolitik*. Göteborg: Akademiförlaget.

Myrdal, Gunnar (1982). *Hur styrs landet?* Stockholm: Rabén & Sjögren.

Oscarsson, Henrik (1998). *Den svenska partirymden: Väljarnas uppfattningar av konfliktstrukturen i partisystemet 1956–1996*. Ph.D. Dissertation, Department of Political Science, Göteborg University.

Petersson, Olof (1994). *Swedish Government and Politics*. Stockholm: Publica.

——, Hernes, Gudmund, Holmberg, Sören, Togeby, Lise, and Wängnerud, Lena (2000). *Demokrati utan partier?* Stockholm: SNS.

——and Söderlind, Donald (1993). *Förvaltningspolitik*, 2nd edn. Stockholm: Publica.

——, von Beyme, Klaus, Karvonen, Lauri, Nedelmann, Birgitta, and Smith, Eivind (1999). *Democracy the Swedish Way*. Stockholm: SNS.

Pierre, Jon (1995). 'Governing the Welfare State: Public Administration, the State and Society in Sweden', in Jon Pierre (ed.), *Bureaucracy in the Modern State. An Introduction to Comparative Public Administration*. Cheltenham: Edward Elgar.

——and Widfeldt, Anders (1992). 'Sweden', in Richard S. Katz and Peter Mair (eds.), *Party Organizations*. London: Sage.

Riksdagen i siffror 1996/1997 (1997). Stockholm: Riksdagen.

Riksdagens årsbok. Riksmötet 1990/91 (1991). Stockholm: Riksdagen.

Rothstein, Bo and Bergström, Jonas (1999). *Korporatismens fall och den svenska modellens kris*. Stockholm: SNS.

Ruin, Olof (1996). 'Sweden: From Stability to Instability', in Jean Blondel and Maurizio Cotta (eds.), *Party and Government*. London: Macmillan.

Sannersted, Anders and Sjölin, Mats (1994). 'Folkstyrets Problem', in Anders Sannerstedt and Magnus Jerneck (eds.), *Den moderna demokratins problem*. Lund: Studentlitteratur.

Särlvik, Bo (1983). 'Coalition Politics and Policy Output in Scandinavia: Sweden, Denmark and Norway', in Vernon Bogdanor (ed.), *Coalition Government in Western Europe*. London: Heinemann.

SOU (1967:26). *Partiell författningsreform. Betänkande av grundlagberedningen.*Stockholm: Justitiedepartementet. Statens offentliga utredningar (Official report to the government).

SOU (1972:15). *Ny regeringsform. Ny riksdagsordning. Betänkande avgivet av Grundlagberedningen.* Stockholm: Justitiedepartementet. Statens offentliga utredningar (Official report to the government).

SOU (1972:17). *Nomineringsförfarande vid riksdagsval. Undersökning utförd av Dan Brändström på uppdrag av Grundlagberedningen.* Stockholm: Justitiedepartementet. Statens offentliga utredningar (Official report to the government).

SOU (1987:6). *Folkstyrelsen villkor. Betänkande av folkstyrelsekommittén.* Stockholm: Justitiedepartementet. Statens offentliga utredningar (Official report to the government).

SOU (1993:37). *Justitiekanslern—en översyn av JK:s arbetsuppgifter m.m.* Stockholm: Justitiedepartementet. Statens offentliga utredningar (Official report to the government).

SOU (1999:136). *Personval 1998—en utvärdering av personvalsreformen.* Stockholm: Justitiedepartementet. Statens offentliga utredningar (Official report to the government).

Sterzel, Fredrik (1998). *Författning i utveckling.* Uppsala: Iustus förlag.

Stjernquist, Nils (1997). *Tvåkammartiden. Sveriges riksdag 1867–1970.* Stockholm: Riksdagen.

——(1999). 'Huruledes särskilda menigheter må för egna behov sig beskatta', in Lena Marcusson (ed.), *Festkrift till Fredrik Sterzel.* Stockholm: Iustus Förlag.

Strøm, Kaare (1990). *Minority Government and Majority Rule.* Cambridge: Cambridge University Press.

——and Bergman, Torbjörn (1992). 'Sweden: Social Democratic Dominance in One Dimension', in Michael Laver and Ian Budge (eds.), *Party Policy and Government Coalitions.* Basingstoke: Macmillan.

Teorell, Jan (1998). *Demokrati eller fåtalsvälde? Om beslutsfattande i partiorganisationer.* Ph.D. Dissertation, Department of Political Science, Uppsala University.

von Sydow, Björn (1989). *Vägen till enkammarriksdagen. Demokratisk författningspolitik i Sverige 1944–1968.* Stockholm: Tiden.

——(1997). *Parlamentarismen i Sverige. Utveckling och utformning till 1945.* Stockholm: Gidlunds förlag.

Wallin, Gunnar, Ehn, Peter, Isberg, Magnus, and Linde, Claes (1999). *Makthavare i fokus.* Stockholm: SNS Förlag.

Wiberg, Matti (1994). *Parliamentary Control in the Nordic Countries. Forms of Questioning and Behavioral Trends.* Helsinki: The Finnish Political Science Asociation.

Widfeldt, Anders (1997). *Linking Parties with People? Party Membership in Sweden 1960–1994.* Ph.D. Dissertation, Department of Political Science, Göteborg University.

21

The United Kingdom: Still a Single 'Chain of Command'? The Hollowing Out of the 'Westminster Model'

THOMAS SAALFELD

INTRODUCTION

The main features of Britain's partly-written but uncodified, 'ancient and ever-altering constitution' (Bagehot 1963: 59), sometimes summarized as the 'Westminster model of democracy' (e.g. Lijphart 1999: 9), are highly correlated with Strøm's (2000: 268) ideal–typical definition of parliamentary democracy as a 'single chain of delegation with multiple links' where '[i]n each link, a single principal delegates to a single or multiple non-competing agents'. Voters delegate powers to Members of Parliament (MPs) through elections, which—due to the plurality electoral system—are largely an intense competition between two major parties for an overall majority in the House of Commons and—consequently—control of the government. General elections are practically contests between two rivalling teams supporting alternative candidates for the post of Prime Minister (PM). The cabinet, dominated by the PM, is at the apex of decision-making. A highly professionalized, non-partisan civil service with a low level of autonomy is designed to avoid bureaucratic drift. As long as the cabinet enjoys majority support in the House of Commons, the constitutional features of the Westminster model (see below) ideally ensure that the government's ability to carry out its policies is maximized and not constrained by any significant domestic institutional checks.

Although the evolving British practice has always differed from this ideal type, the model does capture some essential elements of the Westminster system. The strictly unitary chain of delegation and accountability, which is generally believed to be typical of the Westminster model, is designed to minimize the efficiency and transparency losses caused by multiple principals and agents observed in other Western democracies (Moe 1984: 768–9). It avoids confusion about political responsibility, as power is not shared among a large number of actors with veto powers (see also Thies 2000: 241–7).

I owe thanks to Bill Jenkins, Lord Norton of Louth, Colin Seymour-Ure, and the editors of this volume for their helpful comments on an earlier draft. Any error or opacity remaining is the author's responsibility alone.

At least since the 1970s a number of authors have argued, however, that the price of these desirable properties is too high, that the system does not ensure accountability, because it lacks checks and balances, does not sufficiently guarantee civil liberties, and is, in effect, an 'elective dictatorship' (Hailsham 1976). I will argue in this chapter that due to constitutional change since the 1970s the ideal type of the Westminster model has become a less and less accurate description of British politics. The privatization and marketization of the 1980s and 1990s, for example, has weakened the link of delegation and accountability between ministers and executive agencies. Furthermore, the ambitious constitutional reform programme initiated during Prime Minister Tony Blair's first term in office entails at least the potential for the creation of a number of veto points and institutional checks that may dilute the single chain of democratic delegation and accountability.

The main sources of Britain's uncodified Constitution are statute law, common law, constitutional conventions, and so-called 'works of authority', that is, constitutional interpretations by leading scholars. The Constitution can therefore be amended by a simple Act of Parliament[1] or, simply, by incremental change in the interpretation and application of constitutional conventions. The constraints on the government are mainly informal: 'Without a written Constitution', as Michael Foley (1999: 50) points out, 'the British system has grown to be dependent upon a range of customs, protocols and traditions that prevent the gaps and ambiguities of the constitution from being exploited by governments. Even when government has the power to overcome the system's checks and balances, it normally remains obligated to the social restraints of "club government"...' The perception that the informal norms of 'club government' may no longer ensure accountability have partly been the impetus for the 1997–2001 reforms. Despite its partly-written nature, there is agreement on certain 'pillars' of the Constitution. The first three pillars constitute and reinforce the single chain of delegation and accountability outlined above, the fourth can be said to dilute it:

1. O. Hood Phillips (1978: 5) calls the *sovereignty of Parliament* 'the one fundamental law of the British Constitution'. According to Albert V. Dicey (1959: 39–40), parliamentary sovereignty means that Parliament defined as Crown-in-Parliament has 'the right to make or unmake any law whatever; and, further, that no person or body is recognized by the law of England as having a right to override or set aside the legislation of Parliament'. Given the dominance of the House of Commons in the trias 'Crown-in-Parliament'—the reduction of the monarch's role to a ceremonial figure head and the reduced role of the upper house as a revising chamber with limited delaying powers—this means de facto sovereignty of the House of Commons and of the government its majority supports.

2. Another important pillar of Britain's Constitution is *parliamentary government* with a 'close union, the nearly complete fusion of the executive and legislative powers' (Bagehot 1963: 65). In Britain's parliamentary system of government, the cabinet

---

[1] This includes legislation about the length of the parliamentary term. For example, the maximum length of time a Parliament can sit was reduced from seven to five years in the Parliament Act 1911.

depends on the confidence of Parliament, although under normal circumstances the cabinet clearly dominates Parliament (Lijphart 1984: 7).

3. *Unitary government* is a logical consequence of the sovereignty of Parliament, which can devolve powers to subnational tiers of government and take away those powers whenever its majority chooses to.

4. Norton (1994: 69) also considers the treaties constituting the *European Union* (EU) to be part of the Constitution. Although British ministers (answerable to the British Parliament) are crucially involved in the passage of EU legislation, the increasing use of qualified majority voting and the incorporation of the European Convention of Human Rights into British law can potentially undermine Parliament's sovereignty.

The vast majority of bills (approximately 80 per cent) passed by the House of Commons are government bills. Whoever initiates a bill—the government, back-benchers, or a member of the upper house—the government is the key legislative actor. Parliamentary deliberations on most bills, and on all finance bills, begin in the House of Commons.[2] A bill is typically subject to three readings. It is usually examined by a parliamentary committee following the second reading, that is, after the stage at which a vote is taken on the principle of the bill (see Norton 1993b: 75). After the third reading, the bill goes to the House of Lords (if it originated in the Commons). Despite some evidence of increased assertiveness of the House of Lords since the first stage of its reform in 1999 (cf. Blackburn and Kennon 2003: 710), in practice it is still generally accurate to say that 'most amendments prove acceptable to the other chamber and, in the event of a clash, the House of Lords usually defers—though not always immedi-ately—to the elected chamber' (Norton 1993b: 77). Once both Houses have approved a bill, it is sent to the Queen who, by constitutional convention, gives her Royal Assent.

The policy areas subject to a significantly different legislative process are those that fall under Royal Prerogative powers, the budget, money bills, and delegated legislation. *Royal Prerogative powers* vested in the monarch include the right to declare war or peace, the power to pardon convicted criminals, the right to dissolve Parliament, the power to approve international treaties[3], and the right to confer Honours upon citizens. In practice, ministers acting as advisers to the Crown exercise these powers. So-called *money bills*, as certified by the Speaker, become law one month after leaving the Commons, whether approved by the Lords or not. This also applies to the *budget*, whose passage largely follows the regular legislative procedures albeit with a number of qualifications: First, all proposals for expenditure or taxation must be demanded or recommended by the government (formally by the Crown) before they can be con-sidered. Second, all charges must first be considered by the House of Commons but must also be embodied in legislation for approval by both Houses of Parliament. Third,

---

[2] Nevertheless, a number of bills each session are introduced in the House of Lords, mainly to reduce the imbalance in the workload of the two Houses.

[3] Treaties do not require approval by either House of Parliament, and in the great majority of cases they are not debated in Parliament. However, under what is known as the 'Ponsonby rule', when a treaty requires ratification the government does not usually proceed with ratification until more than twenty-one days have passed since the date on which the text of the treaty was laid before Parliament.

supply must be voted annually (Blackburn and Kennon 2003: 730–1). *Delegated legisla-tion* is another area in which the process of legislation differs from ordinary public bills. Delegated legislation is law made by ministers exercising powers given to them by a parent Act. A joint committee of both Houses of Parliament considers delegated legislation laid before Parliament, with a view to determining whether the attention of the House should be drawn to it. With very few exceptions, delegated legislation cannot be amended by either House. The government may, however, be persuaded to withdraw and reintroduce a defective measure. The Parliament Acts do not apply to delegated legislation, so the Commons cannot override the Lords in this field (Griffith and Ryle 1989: 244–6).

POLITICAL PARTIES

Political parties are key actors in the British political system, which has classically been characterized as 'responsible party government' (Pulzer 1987). Parties offer choices over competing policies and leaders. They have a virtual monopoly in the recruitment of government personnel and play an important role in the screening of parliamentary candidates. The parliamentary majority party delegates powers to its leadership, which forms the government, and ensures a degree of internal accountability. The opposition parties have incentives to subject the government's activities to continuous criticism and thereby contribute to a degree of public accountability (for a general discussion see Müller 2000). Since the 1960s, three important developments have been particularly important as far as the role of political parties is concerned:

1. Since the early 1970s the British party system has changed significantly as a result of changes in voting behaviour. This had serious implications for the electoral account-ability of the Conservative governments of the 1980s. The decline of class voting, greater electoral volatility, regional disparities in voting behaviour, and the crisis of the Labour Party all led to a drastic decline in the combined vote share among the two major parties. The main beneficiaries have been the Liberal Party (until 1981), the SDP/Liberal Alliance (1981–7), and, since 1988, the product of the merger of these two parties, the Liberal Democrats. In addition, the regionalist parties in Scotland and Wales have gained as a result of the declining electoral fortunes of the two major par-ties (Kavanagh 1994). Under a first-past-the-post electoral system these developments, especially the split in the anti-Conservative vote from 1974 onwards, led to a Conservative hegemony which lasted for almost two decades (cf. Kavanagh 1994: 601–2, 608–9). The Conservative Party was protected from the consequences of adverse electoral swings, although its vote share never surpassed 43 per cent. Today the situation is reversed. The Conservative defeats of 1997 and 2001 were of a magnitude that it may take several Parliaments to draw the appropriate organisational lessons and develop a credible electoral strategy, with similar negative implications for the (*ex post*) electoral accountability of the Labour government.

These developments have had obvious, and serious implications for democratic delegation and accountability. The threat of losing the majority—which had been high until the end of the 1970s due to an electoral system capable of transforming relatively small electoral swings into considerable changes in seat allocation—ceased to be as powerful a constraint on government parties. Frequent alternation of power—one of the conditions that lend legitimacy to strong majority rule in the absence of extensive checks and balances (Lijphart 1984: 22)—was no longer guaranteed. Especially the eighteen years of uninterrupted Conservative government (1979–97) eventually provided powerful arguments for the constitutional reforms of 1997–2001, particularly with regard to limiting 'governmental excess'. In the eyes of many critics the scale and radicalism of the Thatcher government had turned 'the anxiety over "ungovernability" in the 1970s ... to a fear of governmental over-capacity as Margaret Thatcher appeared repeatedly to prevail over the system's checks and balances' (Foley 1999: 50).

2. Since the 1960s, both major parties have undergone a number of radical organizational changes affecting intraparty democracy. These changes did not result from changes in the law, but from internal developments. Following the electoral defeat in 1979 the Parliamentary Labour Party (PLP) lost its monopoly of selecting the Labour leader, initially to an electoral college including representatives of the PLP, trade unions and other affiliated organizations, and the Constituency Labour Parties (1980–92), and later to the Labour Party membership.[4] In 1994, Blair was the first party leader to be elected by a ballot of all individual party members, Labour MPs, and MEPs (cf. Seyd 1998). Also, sitting Labour Members of Parliament were made more accountable to the members of their respective Constituency Labour Party (CLP). Mandatory reselection of sitting Labour MPs between 1980 and 1990 meant that sitting Labour MPs were routinely obliged to go through the process of being reselected by their constituency party before each general election. Although the *compulsory* reselection of sitting MPs was abolished in 1990, the involvement of affiliated organizations (mainly trade unions) and constituency activists in candidate selection and leadership election was significantly enhanced through the 1980 changes to the Labour Party constitution. Labour leaders Neil Kinnock (1983–92), John Smith (1992–94), and Tony Blair (1994–) pushed through a number of further organizational reforms strengthening the direct link between leadership and members at the expense of intermediary bodies and organizations such as the National Executive Committee (NEC) and, more importantly, the trades unions (see Kelly 1994; Fisher 1996; Seyd 1998).

In the Conservative Party, the main organizational innovation was the introduction in 1964 of leadership elections by the parliamentary party and the establishment of formal rules for the dismissal of the Conservative leader by the parliamentary party. As a result, the Conservative Parliamentary Party became the 'principal' who elected and dismissed Conservative leaders. After the 1997 electoral defeat, the new leader of the Conservative Party, William Hague, initiated further reforms introducing the first unified party organization which integrates all three levels of the party: parliamentary party, Central Office, and extra-parliamentary party organization (see Webb 1994: 110). In 1998 the Parliamentary Conservative Party decided that future party leaders

---

[4] Between 1981 and 1993, the PLP had a weight of 40% the affiliated organizations of 30%, and the CLP 30%. Since 1993, each of the three electoral bodies has had one-third of the votes.

would be elected by the rank-and-file party members. The parliamentary party would remain the most important 'screening device' as only candidates supported by at least 25 per cent of the parliamentary party will be eligible for election. The parliamentary party will also retain its powerful *ex post* sanctions against the leader (Peele 1998: 146–7). Iain Duncan Smith was the first Conservative leader to be directly elected by the party rank-and-file in 2001.

3. Since the second half of the 1960s, deputies in both major parliamentary parties have become more assertive vis-à-vis their respective leaders. During the first two decades after the Second World War the two major parliamentary parties were highly disciplined even when intraparty preferences were rather heterogeneous. Philip Norton's (1981: 225–31) work shows that—although cohesion remained high—government backbenchers in the 1970s were increasingly willing to challenge their leaders and—if necessary—risk a government defeat in the division lobbies. The threat of a government resignation lost its power. Cowley's (2001), Cowley and Norton's (1999), and Cowley and Stuart's (2000) studies demonstrate that this trend has continued to the present day. From the late 1960s onwards government backbenchers have thus demonstrated their willingness to employ sanctions (cross voting in both major parties and the removal of two leaders in the Conservative Party) so as to strengthen the government's accountability to the parliamentary majority party.

DELEGATION FROM VOTERS TO MPs

The 659 Members of the House of Commons (2001) are elected in single-member districts using a simple plurality 'first-past-the-post' electoral system with powerful, well-known implications for party competition and government accountability. It reduces the number of parties with effective parliamentary representation to just two, one of which tends to get a clear overall majority of seats. If the parties are almost equally strong, this tends to enhance competition and electoral accountability. Voters have a relatively direct influence on the composition of the next government. They do not have to grant a great deal of discretion to their agents in Parliament. In multiparty systems in which no single party enjoys an overall majority, MPs may have some discretion in selecting a government (De Winter 1995: 117–19). In Britain, MPs may influence the choice of parliamentary leaders, but the voters effectively retain the right to elect the government. Yet, critics of the first-past-the post system point at least to three problems:

1. The system is widely seen to be unfair (even amongst those who defend it) and distorts electoral competition in favour of the two major parties. The threshold for entry to the House of Commons is very high. This 'enables national parties to ignore many political movements and the demands they voice' (Budge 1996: 25).
2. If the vote against one of the major parties is split, this major party is likely to be in a hegemonic position. This reduces the chance of government alternation with problematic consequences for democratic accountability, as the long years of Conservative dominance (1979–97) demonstrate.

3. The aggregate outcome of elections may be so irrational that some authors have described elections as 'the other National Lottery' (Weir and Beetham 1999: 45). The usual examples are the 1951 and 1974 elections, where the party with the highest aggregate number of votes lost the election.

One of the most important advantages of the first-past-the-post system is the potentially close personal link between MPs and their constituents. This is particularly important in the absence of administrative courts and other redress mechanisms for citizens. In theory, the system would also allow voters to hold individual MPs accountable. Yet, although Members' constituency work has increased in the past decades and may significantly effect their re-election chances, the effect is generally moderate (Norton and Wood 1993: 141). Voters cannot effectively punish MPs except at the high cost of deserting their preferred party.

Although divided and hesitant on changes to the electoral system the Blair government set up an Independent Commission on the Voting System under Lord Jenkins to make recommendations for electoral reform. This commission reported in 1998 and recommended a form of proportional representation (alternative vote with top-up seats), but the government did not decide to adopt the recommendations. For all regional (Scotland, Wales, Northern Ireland, Mayor of London) and European elections, different forms of proportional representation are now used. This constitutes a significant departure from the Westminster model at the regional and European levels.

One of the peculiarities of British bicameralism is the fact that the upper house has no direct agency relationship with the electorate, although as a revising and delaying chamber it can have considerable influence on legislation. It consists of hereditary peers, persons who have been awarded a lifetime peerage by the monarch on the PM's recommendation ('life peers'), and Bishops of the Anglican Church, as well as current and former Law Lords, the most senior judges of the country. The Conservative Party has traditionally held at least a plurality of the seats in the chamber. In January 1999 the House of Lords Act, the first stage of the Lords reform proposed by the Blair government, removed the automatic right of the hereditary peers to sit in the upper house. More than 700 hereditary peers lost their seats overnight, although under the so-called 'Weatherill amendment' ninety-two hereditary peers retained their seats until the second stage of reform which failed in 2003 when none of the six alternative proposals for the second stage put to both Houses achieved a parliamentary majority in both the Commons and the Lords. The status quo of a largely appointed chamber with residual hereditary element prevailed therefore. The rejection of all proposals stipulating various percentages of elected members in these votes led to an outcome close to the Blair government's ideal point of an entirely appointed Upper House. The House of Lords is therefore likely to remain less accountable to the voters and hence of inferior democratic legitimacy.

The Constitution and electoral laws do not call for primaries. Nor do electoral laws prescribe intra-party candidate preference voting. The maximum length of the term of the House of Commons is five years. However, the PM can request the monarch to dissolve the House of Commons at any time before the end of its term. There is no term limit for MPs and no mandatory retirement age. Aliens and persons under 21 years of age are disqualified from being elected. Further disqualifications include lunacy, bankruptcy, treason, criminal convictions with a sentence of more than 1 year, conviction of corrupt practices at elections, holding certain offices (e.g., in the civil service or the armed forces), and membership of the House of Lords. There is no legally enforced recall mechanism, though the House of Commons will expel a Member if one of the qualifications listed above applies (Blackburn and Kennon 2003: 67–8). Members lose their seats if they are convicted of criminal charges or treason, if they are certified insane for more than six months, or if they go bankrupt. Members of the House of Commons who, by inheritance or appointment, become Peers of England, Scotland, Great Britain, or the United Kingdom must resign their seats (see Griffith and Ryle 1989: 92).[5]

The rules of electoral competition are relatively simple. According to the Representation of the People Act of 1918, section 21(3), twenty full days must pass between the proclamation of the dissolution of the old Parliament and the first meeting of the new. During this interval, a general election is held (Griffith and Ryle 1989: 180). In 1983, this law was amended to reduce the minimum period to sixteen days. This implies an even greater advantage for a PM who has the power to dissolve Parliament at any time. Individual candidates' campaign spending is severely limited. Until 1998 there was no legal cap on spending by the parties. The reforms of 1998 introduced limits for the parties that will apply for the 365 days prior to a general election and the four months prior to other elections (Blackburn and Kennon 2003: 69). During the campaign, both parliamentary and non-parliamentary parties receive free broadcasting time. The allocation is largely proportional. The main opposition party (Her Majesty's Official Opposition) receives the same amount of time as the party of government. Non-parliamentary parties that contest a minimum of fifty constituencies are allocated broadcasting time in proportion to the number of candidates fielded.[6] There is no unrestricted purchase of broadcasting time. The publication of opinion polls is not restricted except for the publication of exit polls on polling day.

Public party financing is limited. Until 1975, there were no public subsidies to either parliamentary or extra-parliamentary parties, except the salaries (since 1911) and allowances (especially for office costs) paid to MPs, and salaries paid to the Leader of the Opposition both in the Commons and the Lords, the Opposition Chief Whip, (Commons and the Lords) and two Assistant Whips from the main Opposition party in the Commons (Blackburn and Kennon 2003: 173). Since 1975, the opposition parliamentary parties have received some public subsidies. The distribution of these subsidies between the opposition parties is roughly proportional to their share of seats now calculated on the basis of a formula consisting of the number of votes and seats (for data see Blackburn and Kennon 2003: 171). The amounts were increased in the 1998 party

[5] Irish Peers may sit in the House of Commons.

[6] In the 1997 general election there were seven such parties: the Referendum Party, the Natural Law Party, the Pro-Life Alliance, the Liberal Party, the British National Party, the Green Party, and the Socialist Labour Party.

finance reform, which also grants both government and opposition parties support for the development of policies for inclusion in their election manifestos from an annual fund of £2 million (Blackburn and Kennon 2003: 172; Hazell *et al.* 2000: 255).

Candidate selection is mainly governed by the parties' constitutions. None of the major parties constrains candidate selection through term limits or a mandatory retirement age. Both parties rely partly on formal procedures and, most importantly in our context, partly on informal screening devices *before* the actual selection process starts. A prospective candidate's activities in the party, previous political record outside Parliament (e.g. in local government), and general political and personal reputation help the parties assess his or her suitability and reduce the danger of adverse selection (cf. e.g. Rose 1987: 75). In both parties, the formal selection process is carried out by the local Constituency Parties, whereas the party leadership retains certain rights to screen and/or veto candidates. The Conservative Party's Central Office controls admission to the pool of prospective candidates, but has no veto over candidates once they have been adopted by the constituency party (see Fisher 1996: 45). In the Labour Party central *ex ante* controls are weaker than in the Conservative Party. Yet, Labour's National Executive Committee has the power to veto candidates after they have been adopted by the Constituency Labour Party, a right that they have used with greater frequency since the mid-1980s (Kelly 1994: 34; Fisher 1996: 73–4). Thus, *ex post* central control over candidate selection seems to be more far-reaching in the Labour Party than in the Conservative Party. The choice of a closed-list system of proportional representation for elections to the European Parliament in 1999 has enhanced the powers of the party head-quarters in such elections.

DELEGATION FROM PARLIAMENT TO CABINET

In the delegation of powers from Parliament to cabinet, the former is in a weak position. The information asymmetry between government ministers and backbench MP is extreme. The government is aided by the civil service, which has a vastly superior capacity to generate and process information. Ordinary MPs, by contrast, have comparatively little independent information. Their resources in terms of research and secretarial assistance are modest by international standards, let alone in comparison to the government. While MPs may be aided by consultants, interest groups, or press coverage, their ability to generate information independently remains severely limited, especially on the opposition benches (cf. Commission to Strengthen Parliament 2000: 34). Although a great deal of government information is disclosed voluntarily, access to information remains restricted by far-reaching secrecy laws and norms and depends, to some extent, on the government's good will. Until 1989, section 2 of the Official Secrets Act of 1911 protected all government information from unauthorized disclosure. Thus, in principle all unauthorized disclosures of official information were criminal offences. This section was repealed in 1989. Although the Official Secrets Act of 1989 decriminalizes most disclosures, 'Government practice, the civil service code of discipline and the operations of the civil law of confidence continue to promote a highly secretive ethos' (Oliver 1991: 173). The Freedom of Information Act passed in 2000 has been widely criticized as containing too many exemption provisions to reduce significantly the problems of information asymmetry and accountability (cf. Forman 2002: 291–5; Hazell *et al.* 2000: 257). Flinders (2001: 329) concludes that the Freedom of Information Act 2000 represents little more than a statement of good intentions rather than freedom of information. Given this framework and the traditional Whitehall culture of secrecy with regard to policy advice to ministers, the power of parliamentarians and non-parliamentary bodies to limit agency loss in the delegation from Parliament to the government remains severely constrained. The information asymmetry is compounded by the government's (usual) control over the parliamentary majority and, hence, over the Commons' timetable (Griffith and Ryle 1989: 297).

To a considerable extent, the delegation from Parliament to cabinet is shaped by conventions and informal rules rather than by explicit constitutional provisions. These fundamental rules have changed very little during the postwar period. By convention ministers must sit in Parliament. The PM and most ministers nowadays must be members of the House of Commons. This convention provides the basis for the Commons' most important *ex ante* control: parliamentary screening. A British minister, as Richard Rose (1987: 73) points out, 'is a professional politician before he is a Secretary of State…Before being placed in charge of a ministry, nearly every officeholder has spent an adult life in party politics; a decade or two in the distinctive confines of the House of Commons, and often years as a subordinate junior minister.' Their extra-parliamentary and parliamentary apprenticeships offer MPs (especially those from the same party) 'low-cost' information about the preferences and abilities of a prospective minister. With an average parliamentary 'apprenticeship' of 12.2 years (1945–84), Britain has the longest informal screening process in Western Europe for cabinet ministers (De Winter 1991: 48).

Informal screening procedures and the election of party leaders are critical because the House of Commons does not have a formal role in appointing the PM or selecting the cabinet. Government formation is largely determined by electoral outcomes (see above). Ministers are selected *from*, and not *by*, Parliament, remain in it, and depend on it for financial resources and the passage of legislation. The monarch has a degree of discretion only if there is no clear overall majority in the Commons.[7] In this case, after a period of negotiations between the parties, the monarch summons the person deemed most likely to command a majority in the House.

Once a government has taken office, one of the most powerful *ex post* devices at the disposal of the House of Commons is its right to express its lack of confidence through a vote of censure. By convention, a government that loses a vote of no confidence resigns. Since 1945, the only no-confidence motion carried against a government was the one against James Callaghan's government on 28 March 1979 by 311 votes to 310. The Prime Minister immediately advised the Queen to dissolve Parliament (Griffith

---

[7] As long as the Conservative leaders 'emerged', the monarch had also some discretion in situations in which there were doubts about the majority party's leadership. In 1923, after the death of Andrew Bonar Law, the monarch effectively determined the leadership of the Conservative Party by summoning Stanley Baldwin (and not Lord Curzon).

and Ryle 1989: 42). Votes of no confidence are directed against the PM and the cabinet collectively, not against individual ministers. A single MP can propose such a vote. By convention (as with any substantive motion), at least one day's notice is required for the motion to appear on the Order Paper. Once put to the House, it is then debated and, if necessary, settled by a division. A debate on any no-confidence motion will normally take precedence over the normal business of the day. There are no formal constraints on the number of no-confidence proposals that can be proposed per session. Quorum requirements are the same as for any other motion (Limon, McKay et al. 1997).

The government itself can call for a vote of confidence. This has happened only three times between 1945 and 1999, while there were twenty-seven votes of no confidence called by the opposition (Butler and Butler 2000: 201). The motivation for a vote of confidence has usually been to consolidate a government's parliamentary support in the face of considerable opposition within its own ranks. The rules guiding the use of confidence motions are similar to the ones for no-confidence motions. They are largely guided by convention. The object of the vote is the PM and his or her whole cabinet, not an individual minister. The right to propose a confidence motion rests, in effect, with the PM. By convention, at least one day's notice is required for the motion to appear on the Order Paper, although in exceptional cases it could be called without notice. The motion is then debated and settled using a division, if necessary. There is no specific quorum requirement.

Table 21.1 summarizes some behavioural data on the life of cabinets and Parliaments. The dissolution of Parliament is partly governed by law, partly by constitutional conventions and the Royal Prerogative. A Parliament ends by a Royal Proclamation, which also orders the issue of writs for the election of a new Parliament. In most cases, 'the time chosen is one which the Prime Minister considers most likely to result in a victory at the election. But the Prime Minister may advise dissolution because the Government is defeated when seeking a vote of confidence. Alternatively the Opposition may carry a motion of no-confidence in the Government or of censure. Also the Government may say in advance that it regards a particular vote as one of confidence' (Griffith and Ryle 1989: 43). By convention the monarch dissolves Parliament on proposal of the PM only, and not in his or her own right. Although only the PM can request dissolution, he or she cannot dissolve Parliament unilaterally but needs the assent of the monarch. While the monarch by convention accedes to this request, it cannot be taken for granted. The monarch must decide for herself that no one else could form a government without dissolution, particularly when Parliament was elected very recently.[8] Applying the cross-national counting rules employed in this volume, a total of nine cabinets ended in early elections after the PM dissolved Parliament. Note, however, that British standards are much more relaxed—cabinets are not expected to sit until the very end of the parliamentary term. Hence, by conventional British standards only the cabinets Attlee II, Wilson I, and Wilson III were ended by early parliamentary dissolution.

[8] For example, it has been suggested that in 1974 Wilson might have been denied a dissolution if he had asked for it only a month or two after forming a government.

Table 21.1. Cabinet Formation, Cabinet Termination, and Early Parliamentary Dissolution: United Kingdom 1945–2000[a]

No.	Cabinet	Date of formation	Investiture votes (iv)	No-confidence votes (ncv)			Confidence votes (cv) under specific constitutional mechanism	Did the cabinet end with an early election?	Who dissolved Parliament in this case?[b]
				No. of ncv	Cabinet removed by ncv	Cabinet resigned to pre-empt ncv			
			n.a.				n.a.		
1	Attlee I	45/07/26		1	No				
2	Attlee II	50/03/01		0				Yes[c]	PM
3	Churchill II	51/10/26		1	No				
4	Eden I	55/04/06		0				Yes	PM
5	Eden II	55/06/07		2	No				
6	Macmillan I	57/01/10		0				Yes	PM
7	Macmillan II	59/10/20		2	No				
8	Douglas-Home	63/10/13		0					
9	Wilson I	64/10/16		3	No			Yes	PM
10	Wilson II	66/04/18		3	No			Yes	PM
11	Heath	70/06/29		2	No			Yes	PM
12	Wilson III	74/03/04		0				Yes	PM
13	Wilson IV	74/10/22		0					
14	Callaghan	76/04/05		3	Yes				
15	Thatcher I	79/05/04		4	No			Yes	PM

Table 21.1. (*contd.*)

No.	Cabinet	Date of formation	Investiture votes (iv) n.a.	No-confidence votes (ncv)			Confidence votes (cv) under specific constitutional mechanism n.a.	Did the cabinet end with an early election?	Who dissolved Parliament in this case?[b]
				No. of ncv	Cabinet removed by ncv	Cabinet resigned to pre-empt ncv			
16	Thatcher II	83/06/15		1	No			Yes	PM
17	Thatcher III	87/06/12		1[d]	No				
18	Major I	90/11/28		1	No				
19	Major II	92/04/27		2	No				
20	Blair	97/05/02		—	—	—		—	—

[a] n.d. = no data (missing data); n.a. or '——' = not applicable in this case.

[b] The question 'Who dissolved Parliament in this case?' can be anwered with one of five options. This identifies the main constitutional actor that caused the early election. We have not coded the formal signatory, but rather the person or body that made the real decision: (1) Head of State; (2) Prime Minister; (3) Cabinet; (4) Parliamentary majority; (5) Automatic constitutional provision (e.g. if it is required when a new President takes office, or, for example, if it is required after the adoption of a proposal for constitutional amendments).

[c] In the United Kingdom it is common to refer to early dissolutions as only those which occurred within the first three years of a Parliament's life, which would be Atlee II, Wilson I, and Wilson III. However in this cross-national project we have standardized the term early elections to refer only to those that occurred in the first 90% of the constitutionally mandated maximum term of Parliament.

[d] This vote of no confidence took place on 22 November 1990 in the wake of Thatcher's failure to gain a clear majority when her leadership was challenged. It sounded the death knell for Thatcher's leadership of both the party and by default the country; within the week the Conservative Party had a new leader and the country a new Prime Minister.

The government's accountability vis-à-vis Parliament is largely governed by the constitutional convention of *individual ministerial responsibility*. The principle is enshrined in the Questions of Procedures for Ministers (QPM):

Each minister is responsible to Parliament for the conduct of his or her Department, and for the actions carried out by the Department in pursuit of Government policies or in the discharge of responsibilities laid upon him or her as a Minister. Ministers are accountable to Parliament, in the sense that they have a duty to explain in Parliament the exercise of their powers and duties and to give an account to Parliament of what is done by them in their capacity as Ministers or by their Departments. This includes the duty to give Parliament, including its Select Committees, and the public as full information as possible about the policies, decisions and actions of the Government and not to deceive or mislead Parliament and the public. (Hennessy 1995: 34–5)[9]

The House of Commons has a number of instruments at its disposal to hold the cabinet accountable. Parliamentary control in the Commons does not usually involve a realistic threat to overthrow the government, but rather is a matter of subjecting the government to effective parliamentary scrutiny and criticism. 'The government legislates and the two Houses criticize and publicize' (Crick 1970: 41). Bernard Crick's widely accepted interpretation of the role of Parliament is consistent with Keith Krehbiel's theoretical work on information in the US Congress. According to Krehbiel (1991: 84), parliamentarians have an incentive to share information with the voters if there is public competition between politically opposing forces. In the Westminster system, the parliamentary opposition generally pursues a 'strictly competitive' rather than a 'coalescent' strategy (Dahl 1967), and thus ensures a high degree of 'heterogeneity' in Krehbiel's sense. Although parliamentary debates often have very little direct impact on government legislation, controversial debates between government and opposition provide voters—the ultimate democratic principals—as well as interest groups and parliamentarians with important information on government policy. Nevertheless, empirical studies (Dunleavy, Jones, and O'Leary 1990; Dunleavy *et al.* 1993) show that if speeches and questions in the House of Commons are taken as indicators, direct prime ministerial accountability to the House of Commons has declined in the postwar period.

Debates on legislation, which occupy much of the Commons' time, are an opportunity for Members to question government policy. Yet, the government via its majority is able to curtail such debates using closure motions or 'allocation of time motions' (also known as the 'guillotine'). Nevertheless, there are limits on the government's ability to deprive the opposition of reasonable opportunity for criticism. If the government wants to get its business through without obstruction, it will seek some degree of agreement with the Official Opposition about the scheduling and length of debates.

A number of *ex post* monitoring instruments allow the House of Commons—the Official Opposition in particular—to question ministers. The most important ones are debates on the Address (the Queen's Speech), debates held on the twenty 'Opposition

---

[9] I am quoting passages from the 1994 version. The Blair government has amended some of the details of this document.

days', debates on motions of censure, parliamentary questions, debates on private Members' Bills, adjournment debates, motions for recess, and departmental select committees. The *Queen's Speech* from the Throne sets out the government's business for the session. On the second day, the Leader of the Official Opposition determines the issues for debate in his reply, which is usually a general attack on the government's policy. More important in quantitative terms are the twenty *Opposition Days* per session. On seventeen of them, the largest opposition party (Her Majesty's Official Opposition) chooses the topics for debate, on three days the choice of topics is made by the second largest opposition party. Again, these debates allow the Opposition to break the government's usual agenda-setting monopoly and to force the government to account for its policies on issues determined by the Opposition. By convention, if the Official Opposition tables a *motion of censure* on the government, the government provides time for it to be debated. Finally, there are *emergency adjournment debates* under Standing Order No. 20. These allow backbenchers and the opposition leaders to bring urgent issues of their choosing before the House. While the introduction of *private Members' bills* is severely limited (there is a ballot each session and there are bills introduced under the 'ten minute rule' and there is a possibility for 'ordinary presentation' of private Members' bills), their first (and, if granted, second) reading gives Members an opportunity to bring an issue onto the parliamentary agenda.[10]

While the instruments mentioned above help to limit the government's monopoly control over the parliamentary agenda, their information value is limited. Yet redressing the information asymmetry between government and opposition is critical for effective scrutiny and accountability. Although the number *of oral questions to ministers* has increased dramatically during the postwar period, only a minority of MPs think they are well-suited to get hard-to-obtain information (Franklin and Norton 1993: 107). Ministers answer oral questions in a rota from Mondays to Thursdays.[11] Until 1997, PM's Questions were scheduled from 15:15 to 15:30 every Tuesday and Thursday. In 1997, the new Labour government changed this to thirty minutes every Wednesday. Although Prime Ministers and ministers often fear Question Time, its value as a source of information is limited. In particular, ministers have ample opportunity to give evasive answers. They can also refuse to answer on grounds of national security and often encourage government backbenchers to ask so-called 'planted questions' with no other purpose

---

[10] Standing Order No. 14 allows twenty private members' bills per parliamentary session to be drawn in a ballot. The ballot establishes an order of priority enabling those successful in it to use the limited private Members' time on Fridays. Private Members' bills can also be introduced by 'ordinary presentation' according to Standing Order No. 57. Such bills are not likely to be high up the list on private Members' bills on Fridays. Finally there is a possibility to introduce private Members' bills under Standing Order No. 23, otherwise known as the Ten Minute Rule. The Ten Minute Rule allows a brief speech in favour of the Bill by the Member introducing it as well as a speech by one Member opposing the motion. This has to be made in the House after Question Time (at or shortly after 3.30 p.m.) on Tuesdays and Wednesdays.

[11] A 'rota' simply means that not all ministers are questioned on the same day. Ministers from two Departments answer questions concerning their departments on one day. On the following day, questions to two other departments are being answered by ministers from these departments. And so on. So there is a relatively established (if not inflexible) 'sequence' in which departments can expect to have to answer questions, that is, each department has to answer questions approximately once every two weeks.

than to allow a government minister to put his or her own view on the record and—as the time for questions is severely limited—'squeeze out' critical questions. Refusal or inability to give an answer will, however, invariably be exploited by the Opposition and may lead to considerable public embarrassment in front of television cameras. Answers to oral questions demonstrate debating skills, but the scoring of partisan points dominates over the extraction of information. Since the number of questions usually exceeds the time available for oral answers, many oral questions have to be answered in written form. In addition, MPs may ask *questions for written answer*, which are printed in the Official Report ('Hansard') together with a department's answer. Despite their inflationary use and limited effectiveness as a device to obtain information, backbenchers' questions may serve a very important, unintended function: they often provide *ministers* with low-cost information about policy implementation (Chester 1981: 189). Thus, parliamentary questions fulfil a purpose similar to McCubbins and Schwarz's (1984) 'fire-alarm controls', a function that is often under-estimated in the literature. The resources of departmental select committees have been improved over the years, most notably under Robin Cook as Leader of the House and the cabinet minister in charge of the modernisation of Parliament in 2002 (Blackburn and Kennon 2003: 770).

The House's most important instruments for holding the government accountable are *select committees*. There are different kinds of select committees (cf. Norton 1981: 127–37). We are particularly interested in those specializing in *ex post* scrutiny of the policies and administration of a particular department. In 1979, for the first time in the history of the House of Commons, a near-comprehensive system of departmentally related select committees was set up. These committees have the authority to call persons to appear before the committee, to request papers and records, and to scrutinize government policy. They conduct their inquiries largely in the style of McCubbins and Schwarz's (1984) 'police-patrol controls' and are (with an occasional exception) not involved in legislation (see Drewry 1989).

Although the departmental select committees have had little impact on specific government policy, they have carried out thousands of investigations into the government's and government agencies' policy implementation and expenditure. These reports provide the Members of the House of Commons and the interested public with highly valuable, 'low-cost' information and have greatly improved government accountability. Nevertheless, there are severe limits on their activities. The select committees can invite Members of either House of Parliament to appear before them, but cannot compel them to do so. As a consequence of Parliamentary Privilege, the select committees may order a private individual to answer its questions (and enforce its order), yet it has no authority to order a Member to appear. This authority resides with the full House of Commons. Of course, a minister's refusal to cooperate may be brought to the attention of the House and thus cause embarrassment. Although select committees often send for specific civil servants, the minister usually decides which civil servant will represent the department in a committee hearing. Also civil servants are guided by the rather restrictive *Memorandum of Guidance for Officials Appearing before Select Committees* (the so-called 'Osmotherly Rules'). These guidelines limit, among other things, the disclosure of advice given by civil servants to ministers, interdepartmental exchanges concerning policy, and alternative policy options (see Woodhouse 1994: 177–217). In sum, therefore, Woodhouse concludes:

The reform of the select committee system has increased the amount of government information made publicly available; it has also provided a routine departmental accountability, and at times allows a parliamentary input into policy-making. However, in situations where the government considers it politically expedient to withhold information, even if this appears to obstruct a committee's inquiry, then the power of select committees to send for persons, papers, and records is of little consequence. (Woodhouse 1994: 217)

Finally, the government is bound by a number of formal reporting requirements, the most important of which relate to the budget. The Chancellor's annual budget speech is a necessary prerequisite to the renewal of the government's right to tax the populace. The budget debate therefore provides an opportunity for Parliament to examine the government's short-term economic forecast and its medium-term Financial Strategy. In 1998 the Labour government under Blair improved the quality of reporting by introducing a Pre-Budget Report which is presented in the November of the year preceding the new budget. In addition, it increased the information about the spending and performance of individual Departments by splitting the Departmental Reports up into two, one published in spring includes the department's resource estimate for the coming year. The second report, published in autumn, will report on the previous financial year, including progress against its Public Service Agreement targets (Blackburn and Kennon 2003: 453).

DELEGATION WITHIN THE CABINET

The mechanisms of delegation and accountability within the cabinet have long been interpreted in different, sometimes contradictory ways, although there seems to be agreement that the traditional interpretation of the Constitution as 'cabinet government' (Jennings 1959) is outdated:

1. One influential interpretation is that postwar British politics has witnessed a transformation from cabinet government to prime ministerial or even 'quasi-presidential' government (cf. Crossman 1963: 51). The PM is de facto seen as the ministers' principal with considerable autonomous *ex ante* and *ex post* control mechanisms at his or her disposal.
2. The opposite conclusion is often reached by scholars who emphasize the tendency towards fragmentation of decision-making and departmentalism. The superior expertise in the departments and policy networks around them renders any hierarchical principal–agent construction an illusion (cf. Rhodes 1997).
3. A number of authors (e.g. Norton 1993a) have tried to resolve the apparent tension between the first two interpretations by identifying different prime ministerial leadership styles, some more autocratic, others more reliant on cabinet as a 'team'.

4. The research on the 'core executive' in Britain in the 1990s (e.g. Rhodes 1997; Smith 1999) criticizes the traditional focus on the respective resources of PMs and cabinet ministers in isolation from each other and further actors in the political system. Smith (1999: 105) argues that '[t]he Prime Minister can neither govern...nor actually make decisions without dependence on a whole range of other actors and institutions...What the Prime Minister does is play a tactical game that creates the necessary alliances for achieving goals'.

The constitutional convention of 'collective responsibility' can be said to bolster the PM's position. This principle implies that 'each minister accepts responsibility for the decisions of the whole Cabinet. Inside the Cabinet, a Minister may argue for a different course of action but he is expected not to express public disagreement with the course decided on though dispensation may be given to a Minister on a matter particularly affecting his constituency' (Griffith and Ryle 1989: 23). Collective responsibility requires ministers either to accept responsibility for government policy or to resign. Together with the PM's powers of patronage and appointment, the convention of collective responsibility is a powerful instrument to reduce agency losses vis-à-vis individual ministers. In particular, it is a device to limit the negative consequences of departmental specialization and executive fragmentation (the increasing tendency towards decision-making in cabinet committees or specialized 'policy communities' around departments) (King 1994: 207; Rhodes 1997). Yet, the doctrine of collective responsibility impedes, by limiting the effects of political heterogeneity as a source of political information, cabinet's accountability vis-à-vis Parliament (cf. Krehbiel 1991: 84). Dawn Oliver (1991: 57), for example, argues that the conventions of collective responsibility shield cabinet's operation from public scrutiny 'rather than to expose it to public or political accountability for these matters'.

Cabinet (including its various committees) is the classical institutional device to limit the coordination problems caused by 'departmentalism' and related forms of agency loss. It is the body in which, in constitutional theory, most important decisions are taken; it plans the business of Parliament, arbitrates disputes between departments, and oversees and coordinates government policies. Yet its effectiveness as a coordination body is in dispute. As so often in British political practice 'there are no constitutional precepts or legal statutes governing the operation of the cabinet, rules are partly derived from past practices' (Burch 1988: 21). The PM has the formal right to determine the jurisdiction of Ministries and to create new Ministries. In constitutional theory, the PM is *primus inter pares*, although in practice he or she usually clearly dominates. Votes are hardly ever taken in cabinet. Although practice has varied among different premiers, '[t]he usual approach is for the Prime Minister to sum up the sense of the meeting and if this is not challenged it forms the basis for the Secretariat's recording of the decisions reached' (Burch 1988: 22). The PM has the right to appoint and dismiss cabinet ministers. There are no serious constitutional limits on his power of appointment and dismissal, although ministers have to be, or become, MPs or Members of the House of Lords. In addition, PM's usually seek to ensure the representation of influential intraparty factions and currents. Party leaders with a significant political following within the party and other political heavyweights—sometimes referred to as 'big beasts of the jungle' (King 1994: 219–23)—cannot easily be ignored when a PM forms a cabinet, nor can they be dismissed without political cost.

It is often argued that cabinet lost in importance under Prime Ministers Thatcher and Blair. Thatcher also dismantled a number of further 'integrative arrangements' (Gray and Jenkins 1998: 327) such as the Civil Service Department or the Central Policy Review Staff that coordinated government policies across departmental boundaries. In the Thatcher years, coordinating responsibilities increasingly fell to the Treasury and the Cabinet Office. The Cabinet Office, with a staff of approximately 2,200 (1994), provides the PM with a regular bureaucratic structure to monitor and coordinate departmental matters. It is made up of the Cabinet Secretariat and the Office of Public Service (OPS). The Cabinet Secretariat organizes the flow of business through the cabinet and its committees. It also provides policy analysis to the PM independent of individual departments (Moe and Caldwell 1994: 188–9; Burch and Holliday 1996: 32–4), although as a source of policy advice the PM's Policy Unit in 10 Downing Street is more important. The Policy Unit contains a relatively small number of personal advisers outside the formal government structure who assist the PM in policy formulation and in monitoring the departments' activities. The Blair government has continued to expand the size and role of the Policy Unit, a trend that began under Prime Ministers Thatcher and Major (Smith 1999: 190).

Yet coordination did not necessarily improve. Rhodes (1995) argues persuasively that the textbook assertion of growing tendencies towards prime-ministerial government in Britain is inaccurate. He (1988: 76) maintains that 'Ministers responsible for domestic departments are, to a substantial degree, sovereign in their own turf. Co-ordination is achieved (if at all) and conflicts resolved (or at least suppressed) in and by cabinet *and* its multifarious committees, supplemented by bureaucratic mechanisms'. John Major's (1990–7) introduction and strengthening of a Deputy PM with no departmental responsibilities as well as the traditional appointment of cabinet office ministers serving without portfolio seeking to strengthen the PM's strategic leadership capacity and achieve a higher degree of interdepartmental coordination.

DELEGATION FROM MINISTERS TO CIVIL SERVANTS

In British constitutional theory, politicians decide on policy, whereas officials give advice and implement policy (Griffith and Ryle 1989: 27–8; Smith 1999: 107). The model of the British civil service is very much one of 'neutral competence' (Moe and Caldwell 1994: 187), in which highly professional civil servants serve the party in power. In such a system, based on merit and seniority, ministers' *ex ante* powers in the form of political appointments, screening, or contract design are generally low, despite a stronger effort under Thatcher and Blair to politicize key civil service positions. Since British ministers tend to be 'generalists' (Rose 1987: 81) and—due to relatively frequent cabinet reshuffles (Hennessy 1989: 492)—hold a portfolio for only a few years, the information asymmetry between ministers and civil servants, and the scope for hidden information and hidden action, is considerable. The frequency of ministerial reshuffles may limit the tendency for ministers to become agents of their departmental bureaucracies and strengthen the PM's control over potential rivals. At the same time, however, the fact that the average minister can expect to be in his or her particular post for less than two years (Rose 1987: 83), is a disincentive to investing time and effort in the acquisition of specialized knowledge about their departmental briefs.

British ministers do not have ministerial 'cabinets' or 'policy units' of politically appointed civil servants and/or outside advisers to support them. Ministers may appoint up to two specialist outside advisers. Also governments and individual ministers have since the Thatcher years relied more extensively on outside 'think tanks'. Nevertheless, ministers remain 'exceptionally dependent on independently appointed bureaucrats not only for policy implementation but also for policy advice' (Budge 1996: 43). One of the strongest resources of departmental ministers is arguably their legitimacy derived from the democratic process, which is usually accepted by civil servants constrained by statutory norms and their own professional ethos (Smith 1999: 117–22).

Civil service accountability has traditionally been made more difficult by the secretive nature of British government and administration. Despite the 1989 reform of the Official Secrets Act, for example, the policy advice civil servants give to ministers remains confidential. Given the large number of exempted areas and lack of enforceability, the Freedom of Information Act 2000 is likely to fundamentally improve information on decision-making within government departments and enhance civil service accountability (Flinders 2001: 309–38).

Apart from a drastic reduction in the size of the civil service, the Thatcher and Major governments (1979–97) reorganized the civil service in a radical way. In 1988, the Thatcher government's 'Efficiency Unit' proposed a major restructuring ('Next Steps') of central government departments. The civil service in Whitehall was to focus primarily on ministers' core needs, such as policy development and relations with Parliament. The actual implementation of policy was to be placed in the hands of specialized executive agencies, which were usually to remain part of the relevant departments and to be headed by a Chief Executive (see below). By 1997, approximately four-fifths of the nearly 500,000 civil servants were employed in about 200 executive agencies (Gray and Jenkins 1998: 320, 328).

The main objective of the 1988 reforms was to increase managerial efficiency. Democratic accountability was not a major consideration. Nevertheless, the Next Steps programme had important implications for civil service accountability. Ministerial *ex ante* controls (via screening, appointment, and contract design) were strengthened. This was a significant departure from the traditional British career system where promotion from lower to higher ranks depends on performance at lower levels and is 'largely in the hands of civil servants' (Page 1992: 38). The setting of 'measurable' performance targets and reporting duties improved on going oversight. A Chief Executive, who is appointed on a fixed-term contract after an open advertisement and public competition, heads each agency. For the first time, high-ranking administrative positions were open to applicants from outside the civil service, thus enhancing the minister's choice of agent. The use of fixed-term contracts also increases the minister's opportunities to 'punish' unsuccessful Chief Executives *ex post facto*.

Chief Executives are directly answerable to the ministers of their sponsoring departments. The agencies they manage are set up under a 'policy and resource framework', that is, a very specific set of instructions devised by the relevant parent department. This solution comes close to the notion of a 'contract' in principal–agent theory. These frameworks allow ministers to retain decisions over strategy or policy and set performance targets, whereas the Chief Executive decides how the strategy or policy objectives will be implemented. The policy and resources framework sets out the policy, budget, specific targets, and results to be achieved. The agencies' staff continues to be civil servants.

These radical changes have enhanced what Woodhouse (1994) describes as 'internal' accountability, that is, the Chief Executive's responsibility through the departmental hierarchy to the parent minister. External accountability includes accountability to the Houses of Parliament. Woodhouse (1994) and other observers (e.g. Drewry 1994: 594) conclude that the introduction of Next Steps agencies has enhanced parliamentary accountability, because MPs can question the Chief Executives directly on operational matters. The precise formulations of framework documents which include performance targets 'are a potentially invaluable starting point for parliamentary monitoring and scrutiny' (Drewry 1994: 594). Woodhouse (1994: 259) therefore concludes that there is 'a significant progression in personal accountability' as a result of the creation of the Chief Executive.

Nevertheless the reforms have reduced ministerial accountability for policy implementation vis-à-vis Parliament. Ministers are still directly responsible to Parliament for policy. Yet the increasing reliance on executive agencies in policy implementation has on occasion been used by Ministers to avoid political responsibility and accountability to Parliament where the distinction between policy and implementation is imprecise (Flinders 2001: 52–5). Also overall co-ordination of the multitude of agencies has become more problematic (see below) reducing the identifiability of administrative responsibility.

EXTERNAL CONSTRAINTS

It is the essence of the Westminster model that there are hardly any formal institutional checks on the democratically elected government. The *monarch*, as Head of State, is no longer a constraint. The doctrine of sovereignty of Parliament implies that the *Courts* are not able to challenge Acts of Parliament. Nevertheless, the centrifugal pressures of the New Public Management have increased the use of contracts and legal or quasi-legal agreements and led to an increased role of the judiciary as an enforcement mechanism in the UK since the 1980s. In addition, judges—who had traditionally acted within the limits set by parliamentary legislation and sought to ensure that ministers have not acted beyond the powers Parliament has delegated to them—have become more active since the 1980s and decided cases by reference to fundamental rights rather than upholding the will of Parliament. The Human Rights Act 1998—incorporating the

European Convention of Human Rights 1951 into British law—has reinforced this trend 'with potentially fundamental consequences for traditional mechanisms of accountability' (Flinders 2001: 155) in the Westminster system replacing, as Flinders (2001: 158) claims, parliamentary with judicial accountability in some areas. Although the Act does not empower the courts to strike down legislation, they can issue 'declarations of incompatibility'. The exercise of such declarations is identical in process, if not in effect, to a judicial review of primary legislation (Blackburn and Kennon 2003: 759). Thus, the developments of the 1980s and the Human Rights Act 1998 (which has come into force in 2000) have strengthened judicial accountability significantly and increased the demands for a separation of judiciary and parliament and even the creation of a supreme court (cf. Blackburn and Kennon 2003: 759–60).

The three major devolution Acts of 1998 set the framework for new institutions in Scotland, Wales, and Northern Ireland. In 1999 the citizens in Scotland and Wales followed Northern Ireland in electing regional assemblies by proportional representation, which in turn (delayed and repeatedly interrupted in the case of Northern Ireland) elected regional executives.[12] The Scottish Parliament and the Northern Ireland Assembly have law-making and limited tax-varying powers. The National Assembly of Wales, by contrast, only enjoys powers of secondary legislation and is entirely dependent on an annual block grant from London. Initially these assemblies and the regional governments emanating from them are unlikely to be a serious institutional check on the sovereignty of Parliament. The piecemeal nature of this reform is indicated by the fact that to date (2003) the English regions do not have equivalent representative assemblies. To what extent devolution will generate a momentum of its own and the assemblies will incrementally develop into serious institutional checks remains to be seen.

Between 1948 and 1997, the *Bank of England* was not an independent actor as is the American Federal Reserve or the German *Bundesbank*, constraining the government's economic policy. The Governor of the Bank of England was and still is, appointed by the government. Monetary policy and interest rates were controlled by the Treasury, which instructed the Bank of England. One of the first decisions of the incoming Labour government in 1997, however, was to transfer the determination of interest rates to a Monetary Policy Committee, which is chaired by the Governor of the Bank of England and includes representatives of the Bank of England as well as academic experts. Since May 1997, therefore, the Bank of England has had a more independent role in the setting of interest rates, although the Chancellor of the Exchequer still sets global targets for inflation. Critics of this transfer of authority have pointed out that it delegates key economic decisions to an unelected and democratically unaccountable body. Yet, as William Bernhard (1998: 314) emphasizes, an independent central bank can be an important source of information on the direction and

---

[12] In none of the three assemblies does a single party control an overall majority. The Northern Ireland Assembly is characterized by a complicated power-sharing system between the main Unionist and Roman-Catholic parties. At the time of the writing (2003), the Scottish and Welsh Executives are based on a formal coalition between the Labour Party and the Liberal Democrats.

consequences of government economic policy. In their public justification of monetary decisions, independent central banks frequently comment on government policy, provide alternative economic analyses and forecasts, and force governments to be more open about the inflationary effects of their policy choices.

Referendums were held by the Labour governments in the 1970s. Nonetheless, they were exceptional instruments entirely in the hands of the government. The Blair government has made use of the referendum (on the election of regional assemblies for Scotland and Wales in 1997, and an elected Mayor for London as well as the peace process in Northern Ireland in 1998) and has promised to do so in the future (Britain's entry into European Monetary Union). It is important to note, however, that a referendum is held exclusively at the request of the government of the day. In addition, a referendum in Britain is, strictly speaking, only advisory in character. Obviously, however, a popular vote on a policy issue creates a certain degree of pressure on the government.

A more serious domestic constraint on the government is the existence of 'policy communities'. Rhodes (1997: 3) argues that the Westminster model 'no longer provides either an accurate or comprehensive account of how Britain is governed' and suggests that 'interdependence, a segmented executive, policy networks, governance and hollowing out' characterize the British state. This makes the British political system more reminiscent of a 'differentiated polity' than the traditional Westminster model with its 'strong cabinet government, parliamentary sovereignty, Her Majesty's loyal opposition and ministerial responsibility' (Rhodes 1997: 7). From the 1970s onwards, empirical research has generated considerable evidence (e.g. Richardson and Jordan 1979; Jordan 1981; Rhodes 1997) that this development, which accelerated during the 1980s and 1990s, has led to a situation in which more central control is exerted, 'but over less' (Rhodes 1997: 3), and where democratic accountability has become increasingly problematic. In particular, the Westminster model grossly overestimates government autonomy (Rhodes 1997: 3). Although Conservative governments between 1979 and 1997 attempted to eliminate all traces of neo-corporatism, interest groups and professional bodies have remained important players in many policy areas simply because their expertise and cooperation are needed. Policy is often made in sectoral policy networks composed of central government departments, professions, voluntary organisations, and other key interests. Privatization and the establishment of regulatory bodies supervising privatized industries, the establishment of Next Steps agencies, and a host of special-purpose bodies with considerable resources and operational discretion have replaced hierarchical coordination and have turned governing into a more complex bargaining process. This poses problems for democratic delegation and accountability as the bodies in charge of monitoring and regulating privatized services and semi-autonomous agencies are highly dependent on information provided by the regulated (Rhodes 1997).

A key international constraint on the British government is its membership in the *EU*. Britain's entry into the European Economic Community in 1973 has added a new political and judicial dimension to its Constitution. The 1972 European Communities

Act provided that, in the event of a conflict between the provisions of EC law and domestic UK law, the former was to prevail. This obviously sits ill with the doctrine of parliamentary sovereignty and explains why many British politicians and constitutional lawyers find it difficult to accept any strengthening of supranational elements in the EU's decision-making process. In order to scrutinize EC/EU legislation, both British Houses of Parliament have set up scrutiny committees. The House of Commons has a European Scrutiny Committee, which identifies politically significant EU documents and European Standing Committees which carry out detailed scrutiny, often with relevant ministers in attendance (Blackburn and Kennon 2003: 352). The European Scrutiny Committee consists of sixteen MPs. It has the power to investigate Pillar I, II, and III matters and can refer a matter either to a European Standing Committee or (more rarely) the House as a whole. Reports from the European Standing Committees are rarely debated. Legally, the reports do not bind the government. Nevertheless, the government has to make sure that its positions on EU policies are, at a minimum, acceptable to its own backbenchers. The Select Committee of the House of Lords, with its six specialised sub-committees, has better resources with regard to members' expertise, staff, advisers, and time. Therefore, it has generally been considered the more effective scrutiny committee. Nevertheless, documents often do not reach the committees in both Houses in time for them to be considered and reported on before agreement is reached in the Council of Ministers. As a result, the theoretical control these committees have over ministerial actions often cannot be exercised in practice. The government therefore agreed in 1980 that a minister would have to justify the adoption of a document in the Council of Ministers without prior debate in the House of Commons (cf. Griffith and Ryle 1989: 438).

CONCLUSION

The 'core' of the Westminster chain of democratic delegation and accountability has remained tremendously stable in a country whose economic and political institutions have undergone considerable change since 1979. As a result of the electoral system, the voters' aggregate choice, mediated by disciplined political parties, continues to have a very direct impact on the selection of the government of the day. Normatively, this may justify the fact that government, as the agent of Parliament and the electorate, faces few domestic political constraints. Accountability relies heavily on informal screening. MPs, the voters' agents, and government ministers, Parliament's agents, undergo lengthy screening outside and inside Parliament before they are elected or selected for public office. Parties are the most important 'screening agents' in this context.

However, outside the core of the chain, British government has witnessed major changes. Voting behaviour has changed since the 1960s. The Labour Party, as the Conservative Party's main opponent, slipped into a deep crisis during the 1970s and 1980s. These changes contributed to a long spell of Conservative hegemony between 1979 and 1992 with no alternation in government and negative implications for *ex post* electoral accountability.[13] If it is true that 'the basic check on any British Government is the general election' (Crick 1970: 38–9), then this development was highly problematic given that the British political system lacks many of the usual formal constitutional checks and balances found in more decentralised systems. In addition, the nature of government has changed during the Thatcher and Major years (1979–97). The state withdrew from many of its previous duties via privatization, market testing and 'Compulsory Competitive Tendering'. The regulatory bodies that were set up to monitor the performance of market arrangements and 'framework documents' defining the duties of Next Steps agencies make fascinating objects of study for those interested in delegation and accountability. These changes have led to stronger political control over smaller government. Governing has become considerably more complex as a result of the creation of highly inter-dependent networks of ministerial and semi-autonomous actors. This effect was compounded by Britain's entry into the EU and the latter's own institutional development towards more supranational decision-making.

With the election of the Blair government in May 1997, Britain seemed to be at the beginning of a new phase of dramatic constitutional change: The newly created assemblies for Scotland, Wales, and Northern Ireland were elected by proportional representation, as were the British Members of the European Parliament (1999). Following the referendum in May 1998 and elections in June 1998, Northern Ireland had an elected assembly and an executive based on a broad coalition of all major protestant and Roman Catholic parties with considerable powers until it was suspended in 2002. The first stage of the reform of the House of Lords has been implemented, although the government's plan to transform it into an appointed chamber in the second stage failed in 2003 due to lack of support in both Houses. Any 'democratisation' of the selection process to the Upper House even if it is only the diminution of the hereditary principle will enhance its democratic legitimacy and inevitably strengthen its role as a political actor. The Blair government began to feel this with a large number of government defeats in the House of Lords on important pieces of legislation. Attempts to modernize the House of Commons have been more modest and largely in line with the traditional majoritarian character of the Westminster Model (Blackburn and Kennon 2003: 741–78).

'A political party when in opposition tends to become enthusiastic about constitutional and parliamentary reform, the more so the longer they remain in opposition' (Blackburn and Kennon 2003: 749). This may explain the initial reformist zeal of the Labour government under Blair after 18 years of opposition. With the manifest weakness of the Conservative opposition in the first two terms of the Blair government, the latter's short-term incentives to tie its own hands were quickly diminished, however. Blackburn and Kennon (2003: 766) therefore spoke of the 'halting nature' of the reform process. This observation primarily refers to parliamentary reform, but can be generalised for the entire constitutional-reform process. The half-hearted Freedom of Information Act, the piecemeal nature of devolution, the non-implementation of electoral reform proposals at the national level, and the failed second stage of the reform of the House of Lords are cases in point. Nevertheless, devolution may well generate

---

[13] In this respect, the situation was similar to one that existed between 1931 and 1945.

a momentum of its own and lead to general decentralisation. The greater independence enjoyed by the Bank of England in setting interest rates and the Human Rights Act have created serious new constraints on the British government. Combined with the effects of the New Public Management and its repercussions for executive accountability, Europeanisation and globalisation, these constitutional reforms have moved the United Kingdom decidedly away from the ideal type of the Westminster model.

REFERENCES

Bagehot, Walter (1963). *The English Constitution*. Introduction by R. H. S. Crossman. Glasgow: Fontana (first published 1867).

Bernhard, William T. (1998). 'A Political Explanation of Variations in Central Bank Independence'. *American Political Science Review*, 92: 311–28.

Blackburn, Robert and Andrew Kennon with Michael Wheeler Booth (2003). *Griffith and Ryle on Parliament: Functions, Practice and Procedures*. Second edition. London: Sweet & Maxwell.

Budge, Ian (1996). 'Great Britain and Ireland: Variations on Dominant Party Government', in Josep M. Colomer (ed.), *Political Institutions in Europe*. London: Routledge.

Burch, Martin (1988). 'The United Kingdom', in Jean Blondel and Ferdinand Müller-Rommel (eds.), *Cabinets in Western Europe*. Basingstoke: Macmillan.

—— and Ian Holliday (1996). *The British Cabinet System*. London: Harvester Wheatsheaf.

Butler, David E. and Butler, Gareth (2000). *Twentieth-Century British Political Facts 1900–2000*. Eighth edition. Basingstoke: Macmillan.

Chester, Norman (1981). 'Questions in the House', in Stuart A. Walkland and Michael Ryle (eds.), *The Commons Today*, rev. edn. London: Fontana.

Crick, Bernard (1970). 'Parliament in the British Political System', in Allan Kornberg and Lloyd D. Musolf (eds.), *Legislatures in Developmental Perspective*. Durham: Duke University Press.

Commission to Strengthen Parliament (2000). *Strengthening Parliament*. Report by Lord Norton. London: Conservative Party.

Cowley, Philip (2001). *Revolts and Rebellions*. London: Politico's.

—— and Norton, Philip (1999). 'Rebels and Rebellions: Conservative MPs in the 1992 Parliament'. *British Journal of Politics and International Relations*, 1: 84–105.

—— and Stuart, Mark (2000). 'Can Sheep Bark? British Labour MPs and the Modification of Government Policy'. Paper presented at the Fourth Workshop of Parliamentary Scholars and Parliamentarians, Wroxton College, Oxfordshire, 5–6 August.

Crossman, Richard (1963). *Introduction to Walter Bagehot: The English Constitution*. London: Fontana.

Dahl, Robert A. (1967). 'Patterns of Opposition', in Robert A. Dahl (ed.), *Political Oppositions in Western Democracies*. New Haven: Yale University Press.

De Winter, Lieven (1991). 'Parliamentary and Party Pathways to the Cabinet', in Jean Blondel and Jean-Louis Thiébault (eds.), *The Profession of Government Minister in Western Europe*. Basingstoke: Macmillan.

——(1995). 'The Role of Parliament in Government Formation and Resignation', in Herbert Döring (ed.), *Parliaments and Majority Rule in Western Europe*. Frankfurt am Main: Campus and New York: St. Martin's Press.

Dicey, Albert V. (1959). *An Introduction to the Study of the Law of the Constitution*, 10th edn. London: Macmillan (first published 1885).

Drewry, Gavin (1989). *The New Select Committees*, 2nd edn. Oxford: Clarendon Press.

Drewry, Gavin (1994). 'The Civil Service: From the 1940s to "Next Steps" and Beyond'. *Parliamentary Affairs*, 47: 583–97.

Dunleavy, Patrick, Jones, G.W., Burnham, Jane, Elgie, Robert, and Fysh, Peter (1993). 'Leaders, Politics and Institutional Change: The Decline of Prime Ministerial Accountability to the House of Commons, 1868–1990'. *British Journal of Political Science*, 23: 267–98.

———, and O'Leary, Brendan (1990). 'Prime Ministers and the Commons—Patterns of Behaviour, 1868 to 1987'. *Public Administration*, 68: 123–40.

Fisher, Justin (1996). *British Political Parties*. London: Harvester Wheatsheaf.

Flinders, Matthew (2001). *The Politics of Accountability in the Modern State*. Aldershot: Ashgate.

Foley, Michael (1993). *The Rise of the British Presidency*. Manchester: Manchester University Press.

——(1999). *The Politics of the British Constitution*. Manchester: Manchester University Press.

Forman, F. N. (2002). *Constitutional Change in the United Kingdom*. London: Routledge.

Franklin, Mark N. and Norton, Philip (1993). 'Questions and Members', in Mark N. Franklin and Philip Norton (eds.), *Parliamentary Questions*. Oxford: Clarendon Press.

Gray, Andrew and Jenkins, Bill (1998). 'Ministers, Departments and Civil Servants', in Bill Jones (ed.), *Politics UK*, 3rd edn. Manchester: Manchester University Press.

Griffith, J. A. G. and Ryle, Michael (1989). *Parliament: Functions, Practice and Procedures*. London: Sweet & Maxwell.

Hailsham, Lord (1976). *Elective Dictatorship*. London: BBC.

Hazell, Robert *et al.* (2000). 'The British Constitution in 1998–99: The Continuing Revolution'. *Parliamentary Affairs*, 53: 242–61.

Hennessy, Peter (1995). *The Hidden Wiring: Unearthing the British Constitution*. London: Indigo.

——(1989). *Whitehall*. London: Fontana.

Hood Phillips, O. (1978). *Constitutional and Administrative Law*, 6th edn. London: Sweet & Maxwell.

Jennings, Ivor (1959). *Cabinet Government*. Cambridge: Cambridge University Press.

Jordan, A. Grant (1981). 'Iron Triangles, Woolly Corporatism and Elastic Nets: Images of the Policy Process'. *Journal of Public Policy*, 1: 95–123.

Kavanagh, Dennis (1994). 'Changes in Electoral Behaviour and the Party System'. *Parliamentary Affairs*, 47: 598–612.

Kelly, Richard N. (1994). 'Power and Leadership in the Major Parties', in Lynton Robins, Hilary Blackmore, and Robert Pyper (eds.), *Britain's Changing Party System*. London: Leicester University Press.

King, Anthony (1994). 'Ministerial Autonomy in Britain', in Michael Laver and Kenneth A. Shepsle (eds.), *Cabinet Ministers and Parliamentary Government*. Cambridge: Cambridge University Press.

Krehbiel, Keith (1991). *Information and Legislative Organization*. Ann Arbor: University of Michigan Press.

Lijphart, Arend (1984). *Democracies: Patterns of Majoritarian and Consensus Government in Twenty-One Countries*. New Haven: Yale University Press.

——(1999). *Patterns of Democracy: Government Forms and Performance in Thirty-Six Countries*. New Haven: Yale University Press.

Limon, Donald and McKay, W. R. *et al.* (eds.) (1997). *Erskine May's Treatise on the Law, Privileges, Proceedings and Usage of Parliament*. 22nd edn. London: Butterworths Law.

McCubbins, Mathew D. and Schwartz, Thomas (1984). 'Congressional Oversight Overlooked: Police Patrols versus Fire Alarms'. *American Journal of Political Science*, 28: 165–79.

Moe, Terry M. (1984). 'The New Economics of Organization'. *American Journal of Political Science*, 28: 739–77.

——and Caldwell, Michael (1994). 'Institutional Foundations of Democratic Government: A Comparison of Presidential and Parliamentary Systems'. *Journal of Institutional and Theoretical Economics*, 150: 171–95.

Müller, Wolfgang C. (2000). 'Political Parties in Parliamentary Democracies: Making Delegation and Accountability Work'. *European Journal of Political Research*, 37: 309–33.

Norton, Philip (1981). *The Commons in Perspective*. Oxford: Martin Robertson.

——(1993a). 'The Conservative Party from Thatcher to Major', in Anthony King et al. (eds.), *Britain at the Polls 1992*. Chatham: Chatham House.

——(1993b). *Does Parliament Matter?* Brighton: Harvester Wheatsheaf.

——(1994). *The British Polity*, 3rd edn. New York: Longman.

Norton, Philip and Wood, David M. (1993). *Back From Westminster: British Members of Parliament and Their Constituents*. Lexington: University Press of Kentucky.

Oliver, Dawn (1991). *Government in the United Kingdom: The Search for Accountability, Effectiveness and Citizenship*. Buckingham: Open University Press.

Page, Edward C. (1992). *Political Authority and Bureaucratic Power: A Comparative Analysis*. Hemel Hempstead: Harvester Wheatsheaf.

Peele, Gillian (1998). 'Towards "New Conservatives"? Organisational Reform and the Conservative Party'. *Political Quarterly*, 69: 141–7.

Pulzer, Peter (1987). 'Responsible Party Government—What Has Changed?', in Herbert Döring and Dieter Grosser (eds.), *Großbritannien: Ein Regierungssystem in der Belastungsprobe*. Opladen: Leske+Budrich.

Rhodes, R. A. W. (1988). *Beyond Westminster and Whitehall*. London: Unwin-Hyman.

——(1995). 'From Prime Ministerial Power to Core Executive', in R. A. W. Rhodes and Patrick Dunleavy (eds.), *Prime Minister, Cabinet and Core Executive*. Basingstoke: Macmillan.

——(1997). *Understanding Governance: Policy Networks, Governance, Reflexivity and Accountability*. Buckingham: Open University Press.

——(2000a). *Transforming British Government, Volume 1: Changing Institutions*. Basingstoke: Macmillan.

——(ed.) (2000b). *Transforming British Government, Volume 2: Changing Roles and Relationships*. Basingstoke: Macmillan.

Richardson, Jeremy J. and Jordan, A. Grant (1979). *Governing under Pressure: The Policy Process in a Post-Parliamentary Democracy*. Oxford: Martin Robertson.

Rose, Richard (1980). 'British Government: The Job at the Top', in Richard Rose and Ezra N. Suleiman (eds.), *Presidents and Prime Ministers*. Washington, DC: American Enterprise Institute.

——(1987). *Ministers and Ministries: A Functional Analysis*. Oxford: Clarendon Press.

——(1991). 'Prime Ministers in Parliamentary Democracies', in G. W. Jones (ed.), *West European Prime Ministers*. London: Cass.

Royal Commission on Reform of the House of Lords (2000). *A House for the Future*. Royal Commission Report by Lord Wakeham. London: Stationery Office.

Seyd, Patrick (1998). 'Tony Blair and New Labour', in Anthony King et al., *New Labour Triumphs: Britain at the Polls*. Chatham: Chatham House.

Smith, Martin J. (1999). *The Core Executive in Britain*. Basingstoke: Macmillan.

Strøm, Kaare (1997). 'Democracy, Accountability, and Coalition Bargaining. The 1996 Stein Rokkan Lecture'. *European Journal of Political Research*, 31: 47–62.

——(2000). 'Delegation and Accountability in Parliamentary Democracies'. *European Journal of Political Research*, 37: 261–89.

Thies, Michael F. (2000). 'On the Primacy of Party in Government: Why Legislative Parties Can Survive Party Decline in the Electorate', in Russell J. Dalton and Martin P. Wattenberg (eds.),

Parties without Partisans: Political Change in Advanced Industrial Democracies. Oxford: Oxford University Press.

Webb, Paul D. (1994). 'Party Organizational Change in Britain: The Iron Law of Centralization?', in Richard S. Katz and Peter Mair (eds.), *How Parties Organize: Change and Adaptation in Party Organizations in Western Democracies*. London: Sage.

Weir, Stuart and Beetham, David (1999). *Political Power and Democratic Control in Britain*. London: Routledge.

Woodhouse, Diana (1990). 'Ministerial Responsibility in the 1990s: When Do Ministers Resign?' *Parliamentary Affairs*, 46: 277–92.

——(1994). *Ministers and Parliament: Accountability in Theory and Practice*. Oxford: Clarendon Press.

PART III

ANALYSIS AND CONCLUSION

22

Dimensions of Citizen Control

KAARE STRØM, WOLFGANG C. MÜLLER, TORBJÖRN BERGMAN, AND BENJAMIN NYBLADE

INTRODUCTION

Representative democracy means delegation, and delegation implies the risk of agency problems. Parliamentary democracy is a particular delegation regime, a way to structure the democratic policy process, and an attempt to solve agency problems. We can thus think of parliamentarism both as a set of constitutions that share a single, fundamental property (the cabinet's responsibility to the parliamentary majority), and as a broad ideal type. We have referred to the former conception as parliamentary government and to the latter as parliamentary democracy. The preceding eighteen chapters have demonstrated wide ranging differentiation within the real world of parliamentary government in delegation designs and accountability mechanisms. Moreover, they have provided a stepping stone for further analysis of the relationship between democratic institutions and political representation.

Chapter 4 accounts for the accountability mechanisms that permit direct or indirect citizen control of their representatives. We refer to checks that are contained in this parliamentary chain of delegation, such as direct legislative oversight of the cabinet, as *internal constraints* on these various agents. The problem with parliamentary democracy, as noted in Chapter 3, is that due to institutional weakness or the lack of incentives, such internal constitutional devices are not always effective. Therefore, in this and the concluding chapter, we focus on two additional mechanisms by which democratic societies can contain agency problems: *political parties* and *external constraints*. Political parties and external constraints can complement internal accountability mechanisms, as well as one another. Yet, their respective functions and comparative advantages differ.

Political parties, as Chapter 3 has pointed out, are first and foremost a mechanism to align preferences between voters and politicians, and between office-holders along the chain of delegation. As pointed out in Chapters 3 and 4, modern parliamentary systems rely on cohesive and centralized political parties to induce policy agreement along their long and indirect chain of delegation. Parties earn their ability to induce cohesion through their ability to capture and disperse parliamentary agenda powers and other political rents (Diermeier and Feddersen 1998). This capacity is in turn influenced by institutional and party system features (see Chapter 4). Cohesive parties serve especially as an *ex ante* screening device, by which politicians with appropriate beliefs, values, and skills can be selected for public service. Parties are therefore well suited to combating the agency problems of *adverse selection*.

External constraints, on the other hand, variously check politicians once they have been placed in office. In contrast to internal accountability mechanisms, external constraints do not derive their authority directly from the national representatives of the people, the Parliament, and within the constitutional chain of delegation. We shall explore their forms and functions below. The virtue of external constraints as a vehicle of *ex post* accountability is precisely that preferences do *not* get aligned, so that the overseers retain some distance from the office-holders and some motivation to scrutinize their behaviour. External constraints are therefore the weapon of choice against *moral hazard* among elected politicians and civil servants. In reality, of course, it is more accurate to think of the differentiation between internal and external constraints as a continuum, since some constraints are more directly related to the parliamentary chain of delegation than others. Such finer distinctions will indeed be drawn below.

Our investigation of political parties and external constraints focuses on variation across space and time. We will demonstrate substantial cross-national variation in the range of accountability mechanisms employed in democratic representation. Whereas some democracies primarily seek to contain agency losses between voters and politicians through the alignment of preferences generated by political parties, others rely much more on external checks.

Less obviously, perhaps, there is also clear-cut evidence of intertemporal variation. The most important trend among West European democracies is a shift in the importance of *ex ante* versus *ex post* controls. There has been a decline over time in the importance of *ex ante* controls. At the same time, external constraints in general, and *ex post* mechanisms in particular, have been enhanced. Yet, important cross-national differences persist on these two dimensions as well as within the chain. Thus, contemporary parliamentary democracies have almost as many differences as they have commonalities.

Our exploration of these issues falls into three parts. All build on the knowledge that we have accumulated in previous chapters, as well as on relevant and complementary secondary sources. Thus, in the next section we examine the strength of political parties and their value as vehicles of citizen control. In the following section we look at external constraints on democratic agents. Finally, in the concluding section we provide a joint and comparative assessment of the current state of political parties and external constraints as instruments of citizen control.

EX ANTE CONTROLS AND COHESIVE POLITICAL PARTIES

Ex ante controls are typical of the classical model of parliamentary democracy, and a feature closely bound up with strong political parties and cohesive party government (see Chapter 3). For parties to help citizens control their agents, they must function as vehicles of mutual gain between voters and politicians. On the one hand, parties must lessen the agency problems that voters face. In other words, it must be easier to contain agency loss within political parties than in the polity at large. That, in turn, requires that certain conditions be met. First, partisanship must be associated with systematic and relatively transparent differences in the bundles of goods and policies that governments produce. Second, party labels and the policy differences that they represent must bear some relationship to the preferences of the voters. Third, voters must have a way of holding the representatives of any given party responsible for its performance in office. We can think of these three conditions jointly as the voters' incentive conditions, the circumstances in which they are willing to rely on party labels in their voting decisions. Only if all three conditions hold can the voters' incentive condition be satisfied, and only then does it make sense for them to attach themselves to partisan labels.

But parties must also serve the purposes of the politicians that would form them. Thus, for politicians to submit to party discipline and invest in partisan brand names, partisanship must offer them tangible and predictable benefits. Parties must help politicians control the flow of governmental decisions and dispersals (Aldrich 1995), and they must help politicians get re-elected (or, perhaps, elevated to higher office) (Schlesinger 1991; Cox and McCubbins 1994). These, in essence, are the politicians' incentive conditions. If all these conditions are met, then citizens can rely on parties to screen and sanction candidates for political office and thus reduce their agency costs (and politicians can count on citizens to support them). Indeed, these conditions will structure our discussion of political parties below.

We should think of parties here in a broad sense that may include coalitions of formally independent organizations. What matters is whether they provide reliable and useful information to the voters and credible incentives to politicians. Thus, Christian Democrats have arguably attained a higher degree of partyness in Belgium and Germany, where they have been organizationally divided, than in First Republic Italy, where they formed a single but uncohesive organization.

Parties structure the first step in the chain of delegation by offering programmes (if only in the loosest sense) and candidates committed to these programmes. When parties establish meaningful 'brand names' (reputations), they allow voters to economize on the information they must acquire. To protect their reputations political parties have a strong incentive to deliver once elected. Indeed, the claim that they can control the 'downstream' formulation and implementation of policy is part and parcel of the commitment of parties to their voters. And cohesive political parties allow the voters to observe the behaviour of their representatives once they are elected. Parties reward politicians who toe the party line and discipline those who do not. Generally, without parties, politicians would be less able to achieve their career and policy goals (Müller 2000a). If this were not true, we would see far more successful independent candidates. Political parties thus play a critical role as 'bonding arrangements' (Cox and McCubbins 1994) in parliamentary systems.

Traditionally, parties effectively reduced agency costs by bringing together voters and candidates with similar policy preferences. They reduced uncertainty about the 'types' of politicians on offer and thus helped citizens contain their adverse selection problems. European mass parties had their origins in the distinctive subcultures that had emerged in most industrializing nation states by the early twentieth century. Thus, parties brought together candidates and voters from the industrial working class, the

Catholic subculture, particular language communities, or the agricultural sector, just to name a few. The common identities and transparencies of those social segments helped assure voters that they had representatives that shared their values. Thus, political parties reduced the risks of adverse selection. As long as the issue dimensions of democratic politics largely reflected the same social cleavages, citizens could generally trust their agents.

Yet, the ability of contemporary political parties to meet these conditions is a matter of considerable scepticism (e.g. see Dalton and Wattenberg 2000). Sweeping and fundamental social change has eroded some of their foundations, such as the trust that voters traditionally placed in parties, elected representatives, and indirect delegation of political power. As old communities have withered, societies have become more differentiated, and new issue concerns have arisen; parties have trended toward 'catch-all' profiles (Kirchheimer 1966). While this has helped traditional parties stay electorally competitive, it may have reduced the value of their 'brand names' to the voters.

Political parties have many facets that affect their effectiveness as instruments of bonding and preference alignment. Following V. O. Key's (1964) conception, we can distinguish between the party in the electorate, the party organization, and the party in government. These are mutually interdependent aspects of modern political parties. Yet, they are not equally important for the viability of parties as mechanisms of citizen control. Instead, it is useful to think of their interdependence as hierarchical. Unless parties impose some kind of cohesion on government policy-making, it would make little sense for voters to identify with them, or for activists to offer them their services or funds. The party in government is thus fundamental. Without governmental parties, neither the politicians' nor the voters' incentive condition could be satisfied. Yet, the electoral party is almost equally critical, at least from the politicians' perspective. If voters paid no heed to party labels, politicians would find limited use for governmental parties. The (extraparliamentary) party organization is less crucial to party government, as it is simply one way to organize the exchange between politicians and voters. While there is no doubt that extraparliamentary party organizations can play an important role in screening political candidates, as well as in raising funds and providing campaign labour, they are not essential to the core functions of political parties. Indeed, cadre parties used to do without much in the form of extraparliamentary (voluntary) organization, as do indeed many newer parties.

While Key's three facets of political parties are thus at least partially interdependent, and while each tells us something important about party strength, they are not equally important for citizen control of their representatives. Hence, the party in government will be our central concern, followed by the electoral party. In the next section, however, we begin by examining variation across time and space in the importance of contemporary parties, in their different facets, as agents of the citizens.

Electoral Parties

The principal normative role of political parties in democratic societies is to align preferences between citizens and their political agents. For this to happen, electoral parties must meet several conditions. Voters must attach themselves to them on the basis of common policy preferences, and these citizen attachments must in turn drive voting behaviour. Moreover, voters must be faced with a set of parties that is reasonably stable and transparent, and that permits the voters to hold the occupants of government office to account.

We turn first to the latter concern, the degree to which electoral parties facilitate stable and transparent citizen representation and accountability. For parties to be effective instruments of citizen control, the party system needs some measure of stability over time. Party systems in which individual parties are very short-lived, or volatile, do not satisfy this condition. The greater the electoral volatility, of course, the lower the stability of the party system, and the less effectively voters can attach themselves to parties with predictable policy consequences, or subsequently hold them to account.

Table 22.1 contains comparative data on our seventeen countries that enable us to assess the evolution of electoral party strength. Thus, Table 22.1 reports net electoral volatility for parliamentary seats between the first two postwar elections (or, in the cases of newly established regimes, the first two elections to which this measure can be applied, that is, the second and third democratic elections) and the two most recent ones.[1] In the majority of cases volatility has indeed increased over the second half of the twentieth century, in some cases substantially (e.g. France and The Netherlands). More specifically, in many countries volatility decreased in the early post-1945 period, but has then trended clearly upwards since about the 1960s (see Dalton and Wattenberg 2000). All but one of the countries in which volatility has not increased are those with relatively recent authoritarian pasts (Italy, Spain, Germany), in which the early turbulence reflects party system consolidation. Because of this late democratic start, party systems in these countries were not 'frozen' until the 1960s or later (Lipset and Rokkan 1967), and the onset of destabilization was delayed (to roughly the 1990s in Germany and Italy, whereas in Spain it has not yet occurred). Finally, note that while in the early period net volatility varied sharply across nations, there are now virtually no countries in which volatility is very low.

A related concern is the extent to which the parties on offer are willing and reliable vehicles of popular representation. Parties may fail in this respect either if they are primarily protest movements with no serious intention of making policy, or if they have not developed the organizational capacity to do so effectively and cohesively. If parties that are uninterested in, or unsuitable for, executive office make up a large segment of the party system, then the voters' ability to hold governing parties to account is severely curtailed. Interparty competition suffers, and electoral accountability is diminished. Of course, we cannot always identify which parties are suitable and reliable and which ones are not. In the real world, experience is typically the best guide. Thus, the larger the segment of the party system that has actually served in the executive branch,

---

[1] We measure volatility in seats rather than votes because the former measure captures electoral system effects and relates more directly to parliamentary bargaining. If we had comparable cross-national data on gross (individual) volatility, it would certainly add to our understanding of party system stability. The evidence we do have, however, is highly consistent with our results here in that it shows significant trends towards instability (e.g. Dalton 2002).

Table 22.1. Party Strength in the Electorate

	Net volatility (in seats)			Share of parliamentary seats held by non-governing parties[b]			Party identification (or closest equivalent)			Deviation from uniform swing for cabinet parties[d] (entire period)
	First two postwar elections[a]	Two most recent elections (in 1990s)	Change	1950–4 or earliest period	1995–9	Change	In first two surveys[c]	In recent survey	Change	
Austria	6.97	8.20	1.41	10.91 (1953)	32.24	21.33	67	52 (2000)	−15	0.42
Belgium	7.93	9.39	1.46	3.30 (1950)	16.00	12.70	50*	55* (1992)	5	0.63
Denmark	14.56	11.73	−2.83	12.58 (1950)	20.11	7.53	52	50 (1998)	−2	0.40
Finland	6.75	11.50	4.75	0.00 (1951)	5.00	5.00	57	51 (1991)	−6	0.50
France	22.37	43.16	20.79	14.31 (1959)	0.86	−13.45	59*	52* (1992)	−7	0.23
Germany	14.19	8.67	−5.52	5.95 (1953)	5.38	−0.57	78	64 (1998)	−14	0.44
Greece	12.84	8.17	−4.67	12.00 (1977)	6.67	−5.33	—	63* (1992)	n/d	0.22
Iceland	5.77	8.73	2.96	17.31 (1953)	41.27	23.96	80	73 (1995)	−7	0.52
Ireland	10.42	13.25	2.83	10.88 (1951)	8.43	−2.45	61*	39* (1994)	−22	0.19
Italy	21.36	14.69	−6.67	38.64 (1953)	47.14	8.50	78*	60* (1994)	−18	0.50
Luxembourg	7.49	7.61	0.12	7.69 (1951)	16.67	8.98	61*	48* (1992)	−13	0.57
The Netherlands	4.50	19.67	15.17	10.00 (1952)	16.00	6.00	38	28 (1998)	−10	0.70
Norway	9.00	18.18	9.18	2.00 (1953)	21.21	19.21	66	42 (1997)	−24	0.24
Portugal	6.74	15.03	8.29	19.20 (1980)	6.52	−12.68	—	67* (1992)	n/d	0.11
Spain	27.86	8.29	−19.57	14.00 (1977)	15.14	1.14	—	41* (1992)	n/d	0.0
Sweden	8.70	13.90	5.20	2.17 (1952)	28.94	26.77	64	42 (1998)	−22	0.16
UK	9.12	16.95	7.83	1.92 (1950)	11.53	9.61	93	91 (1997)	−2	0.0

* Eurobarometer Data

[a] For France we consider the Fifth Republic; for Greece, Portugal, and Spain the first two elections after the democratization of the 1970s.

[b] Non-governing parties 1995–99 are those that neither participated in the most recent government (1 January 2000) nor participated in government in at least two legislative terms during the entire postwar period. In the earlier period (starting 1950), the number refers to the share of seats belonging to parties that existed in Parliament in the year listed (1950 for Denmark, 1980 for Portugal, etc.) and that have not been in government during at least two different parliamentary terms since then, nor were in government at the end of the period (1 January 2000).

[c] These surveys begin between 1964 (UK) and 1983 (Iceland), but most are from the 1970s.

[d] Calculated as the proportion of cabinets in which parties in government experience divergent electoral results in the subsequent election.

Sources: Party ID: Dalton 2000: 25 and personal communication with the author; Eurobarometer Data; Schmitt and Holmberg 1995; Mair *et al*. 1998: 200; Jenssen 1999; Holmberg 2000: 41. Net volatility, share held by non-governing parties, uniform swing: Comparative Parliamentary Democracies Data Set (January 2002).

the more we trust parties to be effective instruments of democratic governance, rather than empty vessels for rent-seekers or vehicles for popular protest. Our measure of representational capacity is the share of parliamentary seats held by 'non-governing parties'. In Table 22.1, non-governing parties are identified as those parties that have neither held executive office in at least two different legislative terms over the postwar period, nor participated in the most recent government covered in our sample (as of 1 January 2000).[2] As with volatility, we report these shares for two cuts in time, the early 1950s (or the earliest meaningful period) and the late 1990s. On this variable, European countries range widely from those that contain only very insignificant non-established (often anti-system) parties (the United Kingdom or Germany), to those where such parties have always been (Italy), or have become (Sweden), important components of the party system. The temporal trend is very clear and unmistakable: non-governing parties have become stronger since the 1950s. Only France, Portugal, and Greece constitute notable exceptions from this trend (while there has been little change in Germany, Ireland, and Spain).[3] Thus, on this dimension as well, the established party systems of Western Europe have been shaken, and the most consolidated party systems have experienced the greatest shocks. These changes would on the whole seem to make the same party systems less reliable as instruments of citizen control.

The data we have presented above reflect the supply side of electoral parties: the extent to which established parties facilitate citizen attachment. Let us now consider the demand side, the extent to which voters are willing to attach themselves to political parties and rely on such organization to influence public policy. Table 22.1 contains information on the evolution of party identification (or the closest equivalent—see Katz 1985) over the last few decades. While the different measures and periods do not allow for a strict comparison, the overall message is clear: party identification has generally declined (for a more extensive analysis, see Dalton 2000). Indeed, party identification has fallen in every single country for which we have intertemporal data, except Belgium. Granted, party identification remains very high in the United Kingdom, the birthplace of parliamentary democracy, where the decline since the earliest surveys is negligible. But for most other countries the drop is around ten percentage points, and party identification has declined even more in some countries in Northern and Central Europe. In Norway, Sweden, and Ireland particularly, the decline in party identification has been truly major—more than twenty percentage points.

Finally, consider the tendency of citizens to hold politicians accountable in the way that political parties in the classical Westminster model facilitate. In other words, do voters actually treat the occupants of the cabinet, whether single-party or coalitional, as if they constituted a single, cohesive political unit? Our indicator of such behaviour, *uniform swing*, is a score that can vary between 0 (zero) and 1. We score each election separately as follows: If at election time all cabinet parties meet the same fate (they all

[2] We have adopted this latter qualification to extend the benefit of the doubt to newer parties in states that have either recently democratized or experienced substantial party system transformations (Italy).

[3] Moreover, Jean-Marie Le Pen's triumph in the first round of the 2002 French presidential election suggests that non-established parties have prospered even here.

gain or lose votes relative to the previous general election), we score the election as 0 (no deviation from uniform swing). If, on the other hand, at least two governing parties experience different fates (i.e. one loses and the other gains), then we score that observation as 1 (non-uniform swing). For each country, we have then computed the mean over all elections between 1945 and 2000. Because of the limited number of observations in some countries, we have not attempted to identify a trend.

Quite obviously the United Kingdom and Spain, with their exclusive records of one-party governments, exhibit no deviation from uniform swing and thus score 0. Other countries that have very few coalition governments, such as Portugal and Greece, also have very low scores. Conversely, however, it is not true that all coalitional systems exhibit high scores. Our highest sample score, for The Netherlands, is 0.70. This means that in more than two-thirds of all Dutch elections, the voters have rewarded the governing parties differentially. Other countries that score relatively high are Belgium, Luxembourg, Finland, Iceland, and Italy. In these countries, voters do not treat the executive parties as a cohesive bloc and simply 'throw the rascals out' or keep them in, but discriminate between them. In many cases, however, such discrimination on the part of voters coexists with a low degree of responsiveness of cabinet formation to electoral verdicts (Strøm 1990). In other words, whether a particular party has just been rewarded or punished by the voters has little effect on its prospects of gaining executive office.

On the other hand, Ireland, Norway, Sweden, and particularly France have significant records of coalition government, but much greater uniformity of swing than the countries mentioned above. These differences basically reflect our distinction between pivotal and alternational (bloc) party systems, as governing coalitions in the latter type of system have greater electoral cohesion than those in the former. To the extent that they do, they also facilitate electoral accountability.

In sum, the evidence in Table 22.1 suggests two things. First, there is obviously considerable cross-national variation in the extent to which the electoral parties of Western Europe facilitate accountability to the citizens in the ways of the Westminster model. Yet, even though electoral parties in Spain, for example, come as close to the Westminster ideals as they ever did, overall the established parties of Western Europe have lost a significant part of their grip on the voters. Parties have become less stable and reliable instruments of popular governance, and the voters have become less loyal and committed. It is difficult and perhaps futile to establish cause and effect, to determine whether voters have become more fickle because the party system is less conducive to their influence, or vice versa. It is perhaps more useful to say that to the extent that a Westminsterian equilibrium once existed, it is now in most countries not much in evidence.

Party Organizational Strength

We now shift our attention to political parties as voluntary and non-governmental organizations, as parts of 'political society' (Linz and Stepan 1996: 8). European parties are more than aggregations of voters; historically many have also been powerful social movements. Parties have built extraparliamentary strength in part for self-interested reasons. Enrolling citizens as members and committing themselves to intraparty democracy allows parties to present themselves as organizations controlled by their members rather than by professional politicians. Party members are also likely to be loyal voters and increase the party's communication capacity. Furthermore, party members provide financial resources (dues and contributions) and inexpensive campaign labour (see Scarrow 1996: 42–5). To the extent that parties attract volunteers, activists, and sympathizers, they may be greatly helped in their efforts to control political recruitment and thus to screen aspiring politicians. And when such screening is effective, agency problems, particularly adverse selection, may be contained. Yet, as Epstein (1967) points out, extensive extraparliamentary organization is not a requisite for electoral success, and it is not even clear that parties always derive net benefits from developing such organizations. Nor is it obvious that dense extraparliamentary organizations facilitate citizen control: they may instead render party leaders more responsive to their activists than to the voters. For citizen control, the net benefits of strong extraparliamentary organization are therefore much more questionable than those of strong governmental and electoral parties.

These reservations noted, Table 22.2 contains two key indicators of party organizational strength, namely membership density (the number of party members as a percentage of the total electorate), reported where available for several decades since the 1950s, and state subsidies to political parties. There is good reason to treat membership numbers with caution and scepticism. Such figures are notoriously unreliable, and there can be no doubt that

Table 22.2. *Party Organizational Strength: Membership Density and Finance*

	Membership density				Public subsidies by end of			State subsidies in '000s US'$: mean volume, 1980s
	1950s or 1960s	1970s[a]	1990s[b]	Change from earliest date to 1990s	1960s	1970s	1980s	
Austria	23.9	25.9	17.1	−6.8	Yes	Yes	Yes	3,866
Belgium	9.8	10.0	7.6	−2.2	No	Yes	Yes	n/d
Denmark	15.7	14.0	3.1	−12.6	Yes	Yes	Yes	262
Finland	16.4	17.2	10.5	−5.9	Yes	Yes	Yes	3,902
France	7.5	1.9	1.9	−5.9	No	No	Yes	n/d
Germany	2.9	3.7	3.2	0.3	Yes	Yes	Yes	23,099
Greece	—	3.2	6.8	3.6	n/a	No	Yes	n/d
Iceland	—	—	—	—	No	Yes	Yes	n/d
Ireland	—	4.6	3.4	−1.2	Yes	Yes	Yes	162
Italy	13.9	12.8	3.2	−10.7	No	Yes	Yes	n/d
Luxembourg	—	—	—	—	Yes	Yes	Yes	n/a
The Netherlands	11.4	4.4	2.2	−9.2	Yes	Yes	Yes	17
Norway	16.0	12.8	7.9	−8.1	No	Yes	Yes	1,614
Portugal	—	4.3	4.0	−0.3	n/a	No	Yes	n/d
Spain	—	1.2	3.4	2.2	n/a	Yes	Yes	n/d
Sweden	23.4	19.6	7.1	−16.3	Yes	Yes	Yes	3,325
UK	10.0	6.2	1.9	−8.1	No	Yes	Yes	n/d

[a] 1980s for Greece, Portugal, and Spain.
[b] 2000 for Portugal and Spain.
n/a = Not applicable.
n/d = No data available.

Sources: Membership density: Scarrow 2000: 90; Mair and van Biezen 2001. State subsidies: Chapter 4, Table 4.6. Mean subsidies 1980s (prices standardized at 1987 levels): Farrell and Webb 2000: 117.

political parties in a variety of countries have systematically over-reported their true membership. Sometimes public subsidy schemes or other public policies even give them incentives to report inaccurately. Moreover, institutional reforms can render trends in reported members misleading. In some countries, such as Sweden and Norway, the switch from collective trade union affiliation to individual membership (in the social-democratic parties) has thus exaggerated the magnitude of membership decline.

Such considerations notwithstanding, there can be no doubt that membership decline is pervasive. Membership densities have declined almost everywhere. Moreover, this decline has in many cases been rapid and seemingly accelerating. The drop-off in party membership has been particularly severe in Italy, The Netherlands, and northern Europe. Consider, for example, the dramatic and recent downturns reported in Denmark and The Netherlands, where membership densities have shrunk to one-fifth or less of early postwar levels. In Sweden it has been estimated that if membership numbers shrink at their current rate, there will be no party members left by 2013 (Petersson *et al.* 2000). Only the more recent democracies of Greece and Spain, plus Germany, report an overall increase of membership. In the latter case, the positive trend is caused by the CDU's organizational efforts in opposition in the 1970s. If we had considered only the last two decades, we would have found a negative trend even for Germany.

Political parties rely on some mixture of different inputs such as voluntary (and often free) labour on the one hand, and capital on the other. To some extent financial contributions, which need not come from party members, can substitute for rank-and-file labour. There can be no doubt that politics, and campaigning particularly, has become more capital-intensive and less labour-intensive. Indeed, in Western Europe the state has become the greatest and single most import-ant contributor to political parties. Table 22.2 shows that by the end of the 1980s government subsidies to political parties had been introduced in all parliamentary democracies of Western Europe (see also Chapter 4). Yet, as the last column suggests, European democracies vary widely in the volume of subsidies they provide.

While public funding may help political parties survive as campaign organizations, it is less clear that they can sustain their role as vehicles of broad political socialization, recruitment, and screening. The doubts that our data have nurtured concerning the health of contemporary party systems therefore apply as much to extraparliamentary as to electoral parties. Yet, in the former case it is less clear that these trends are inimical to citizen control of their agents.

Parties in Government

Yet, the most critical aspect of party strength lies in the governmental party. Many Western European political parties began as parliamentary organizations (they were 'internally created', according to Duverger 1954), and this function is still critical to the prevailing model of parliamentarism (Frognier 2000). In order for parties to deliver policy outputs or rents, they clearly have to control access to the highest political offices in the land. And citizen control of public officials would be hollow indeed, if the parties through which it operated excluded cabinet-level officials. To be sure, elite-level representative politics in Western Europe is party politics, and the closer we come to the apex of national policy-making, the more clearly this is true.[4] European parties are strong in Parliament and in the cabinet, where they display a high degree of cohesion and leave little room for non-partisanship. In this respect, there is not much cross-national variation (see Strøm 2000).

Tables 22.3 and 22.4 present a variety of indicators of partisanship in the cabinet and the rest of the executive branch. Two of these, reported in Table 22.3, refer to the composition of the cabinet itself. One is the overall incidence of single-party cabinets, measured in the proportion of time that such cabinets have held office. The second and

Table 22.3. *Partisan Influence in Government*

	Single party dominance		Partisanship importance for appointments to		
	Single-party cabinets, percentage of time	Single-party majority cabinets, percentage of time	Leading civil service positions	Other civil service positions	Management of state enterprises
Austria	33.9	30.9	Strong	Moderate	Strong
Belgium	9.2	8.4	Strong	Strong	Strong
Denmark	41.5	0	No	No	No
Finland	10.7	0	No	No	No
France	17.6	4.4	Strong	Moderate	Strong
Germany	2.9	2.5	Strong	Moderate	Moderate
Greece	96.2	77.5	Strong	Strong	Strong
Iceland	2.3	0	Strong	Strong	Strong
Ireland	56.3	30.2	No	No	No
Italy	17.6	0	Moderate	Moderate	Strong
Luxembourg	0	0	Strong	Moderate	Strong
The Netherlands	0	0	No	No	No
Norway	79.9	30.6	No	No	Moderate
Portugal	62.2	46.6	Strong	Strong	Strong
Spain	100	37.2	Strong	Strong	Strong
Sweden	73.6	3.8	Moderate	No	No
UK	100	98.9	Moderate	No	Moderate

Note: Percentage of time of single-party cabinets is based on time in which a government was in power in each country 1945–1999, not including governments in power at the end of the dataset. When the current regime is of more recent origin than 1945, only this period is covered.

Sources: Cabinet data: Comparative Parliamentary Democracies Dataset (January 2002). Partisanship: authors' judgement on the basis of country chapters and Kristinsson (1996), Page and Wright (1999), Beeke and van den Meer (2000), Müller (2000*b*);

---

[4] See Blondel and Cotta (1996, 2000) for attempts to disentangle party and government.

Table 22.4. *Party Cohesion in Government*

	Mean coalition discipline 1950–74 (rank)	Mean coalition discipline 1975–99 (rank)	Cabinet termination over party conflict, raw number 1950–74 (total number of cabinet terminations)	Cabinet termination over party conflict, % of all cabinets 1950–74 (rank)	Cabinet termination over party conflict, raw number 1975–99 (total number of cabinet terminations)	Cabinet termination over party conflict, % of all cabinets 1975–99 (rank)
Austria	1.0 (12)	1.1 (12)	5 (9)	55 (2)	2 (8)	25 (9)
Belgium	2.4 (4)	2.9 (3)	7 (14)	50 (4)	8 (13)	62 (3)
Denmark	1.0 (12)	1.0 (13)	1 (15)	7 (13)	2 (13)	15 (14)
Finland	2.6 (3)	2.0 (5)	10 (21)	48 (5)	4 (12)	33 (6)
France	2.4 (4)	1.5 (8)	4 (10)	40 (7)	4 (12)	33 (6)
Germany	1.1 (10)	1.0 (13)	8 (15)	53 (3)	1 (9)	11 (15)
Greece	n/a	1.3 (9)	n/a	n/a	2 (10)	20 (11)
Iceland	1.8 (6)	1.9 (6)	3 (12)	25 (9)	2 (9)	22 (10)
Ireland	1.1 (10)	1.0 (13)	2 (9)	22 (11)	7 (11)	64 (2)
Italy	1.8 (6)	2.3 (4)	16 (25)	64 (1)	12 (18)	67 (1)
Luxembourg	3.0 (1)	3.0 (1)	3 (8)	38 (8)	0 (4)	0 (17)
The Netherlands	3.0 (1)	3.0 (1)	5 (12)	42 (6)	2 (7)	29 (8)
Norway	1.2 (9)	1.2 (11)	3 (12)	25 (9)	1 (11)	9 (16)
Portugal	n/a	1.9 (6)	n/a	n/a	4 (10)	40 (4)
Spain	n/a	1.0 (13)	n/a	n/a	3 (8)	38 (5)
Sweden	1.3 (8)	1.3 (9)	1 (11)	9 (12)	2 (12)	17 (12)
United Kingdom	1.0 (12)	1.0 (13)	0 (12)	0 (14)	1 (6)	17 (12)
Mean (Median)	1.7 (1.6)	1.7 (1.3)		34 (.39)		30 (.25)

Source: Comparative Parliamentary Democracies Dataset (January 2002).

somewhat more restrictive measure is the frequency of single-party majority cabinets, similarly measured. As Table 22.3 indicates, there is considerable variation in the extent to which the cabinet has had the internal cohesion and parliamentary support that characterizes the Westminster ideal type. The British system indeed has a perfect or close-to-perfect score on both indicators of executive partyness, as one majority party almost invariably controls the cabinet. Spain too has had exclusively one-party cabinets, but far fewer have been majoritarian. Countries such as Germany, Iceland, Luxembourg, and The Netherlands, on the other hand, have had virtually no single-party cabinets. The Scandinavian countries have their own rather distinct record of frequent single-party cabinets but very few majoritarian ones.

Our next two measures of executive party cohesion, reported in Table 22.4, have been designed to capture the extent to which even multiparty government may foster cohesive executive policy-making. One is the cohesiveness of the agreements, formal or informal, into which coalition parties enter. In the larger project of which this book is a part, country specialists have scored all coalition cabinets on a common scale according to the degree of policy cohesion exhibited. For each cabinet, the respective country specialist has scored the coalition rules governing policy cohesion on a four-point scale, from the most comprehensive and committal (scored 1) to the most informal and partial (scored 4). We consider policy cohesion broadly as pertaining to ordinary legislation as well as to other parliamentary decisions (e.g. appointments to various executive offices and agencies). For each country, we report two scores, one reporting the mean for all cabinets and both dimensions (legislation and other decisions) 1950–74 and the second the same for the 1975–99 period. The data are drawn from ongoing research, from which preliminary results have been published (Strøm and Müller 1999). All single-party cabinets have been given the lowest score, indicating the highest level of party cohesion. Countries that have experienced frequent single-party governments therefore also tend to score high (low numerical values) on cabinet cohesion.

Conversely, however, typical coalitional systems do not always exhibit particularly low levels of cohesion. While this is largely true of the Benelux countries, it is clearly not true in Austria and Germany, which combine a tradition of coalition government with a record of high cabinet cohesion. And Ireland, Denmark, and Norway, which tend to alternate between single-party and coalition cabinets, nonetheless feature the high levels of policy cohesion more typical of the former. Again, we see significant differences in cohesion between alternational and pivotal multiparty systems, with some of the former almost indistinguishable from the two-party systems.

Yet, official commitments to coalition discipline may in some cases be little more than pious hopes. Just as the safest bars may not be those that post signs prohibiting fights or weapons, the most cohesive coalitions may not be those that have the strictest official rules. Therefore, Table 22.4 reports not only on rules promoting cabinet discipline, but also on their effects. Thus, we report the proportion of all cabinets whose termination was caused by either intraparty or interparty conflict (rather than, for example, by constitutional requirements or personal factors, such as ill health or retirement). These data have been drawn from Müller and Strøm (2000) and ongoing research. Note that every single country reports such cases of cabinet 'breakdown' for partisan reasons, though the United Kingdom only one. In some countries, including Belgium and Italy, the majority of all cabinet terminations are caused by party conflict. In other countries, even where coalitions occasionally form, such terminations are rare (Denmark and Sweden). While overall there is no clear trend toward greater or lesser cohesion, we do find such patterns in individual countries such as Austria (where it has increased) and Ireland (where it has decreased).

As a final part of our examination of government partyness, we consider the strength of partisanship in the public administration. Parties presumably face conflicting motivations concerning public-sector appointments. Generally, partisan appointments may help parties pursue redistributive goals but jeopardize government efficiency and electoral support. Where parties have significant preference divergences among themselves, they may favour party patronage, whereas on the other hand efficiency concerns often militate against such solutions, and certainly against the more benighted forms of patronage politics. Parties are often conflicted about such appointment policies. When first coming to office, for instance, reformist parties may be attracted by the opportunity to appoint 'their own people' to key positions at the same time that they know that doing so may jeopardize their comparative advantage among the voters. Strategic interaction between political parties may also influence such decisions. Geddes (1994) suggests that the more competitive the party system, the greater the likelihood of civil service reform and non-partisanship.[5]

It is difficult to map the importance of partisanship in government appointments. This is generally considered the least legitimate extension of partisanship. Consequently, the available information is soft and often incomplete. Nonetheless, in Table 22.3 we have sought to classify our seventeen countries on three dimensions of party involvement in civil service and other public-sector appointments. We distinguish between strong, moderate, and no significant partisanship. These scores are based on our reading of the country chapters and additional available information detailed in the table source notes. Note that the information provided here is impressionistic, since we lack the kind of observational data on which we otherwise rely.

The country chapters and the sources consulted for Table 22.3 suggest that partisanship in executive appointments has declined in some countries (e.g. Belgium) in which it long served to reward party activists more than to allow political parties to control the policy process. Conversely, there has been a trend towards partisanship in key civil service appointments, and the public sector more generally, in some countries with a strong previous record of non-partisanship, such as the United Kingdom. In sum, therefore, the cross-national trend seems to be towards convergence rather than towards greater or lesser partisanship overall. Parliamentary democracies appear to converge on a relationship between political parties and civil servants that largely favours administrative independence, but that is leading some countries (such as Britain) towards greater policy cohesion.

---

[5] Note, however, that according to Manow (2002), interparty competitiveness has not depressed the level of patronage politics in Western Europe.

Summary

Overall, the available data suggests a general decline in the functions that political parties play in facilitating citizen control of their agents. We can perhaps best capture the extent of partisan decline by considering the overall changes that have taken place since the early postwar period. For most of our indicators, we can easily identify how the respective countries would have scored in the 1950s (or a similarly early date) relative to the 1990s. Thus, with regard to party identification, seven countries—Austria, Finland, France, Ireland, Luxembourg, Norway, and Sweden—that previously would have ranked above the current cross-national mean (54.4) have now fallen below this level. Only one country (Belgium) has moved in the opposite direction. Similarly, five countries—Austria, Belgium, Iceland, Norway, and Sweden—have experienced a strong increase in the electoral support drawn by non-established parties, whereas only France and Portugal have seen a significant decline in the support for such parties. Membership density has fallen in twelve of the fifteen countries for which we have data, and in some of these the decline has been truly dramatic. Only two countries, Greece and Spain, have experienced a moderate increase.

The evidence is thus consistent and fairly striking. Though on all three dimensions examined here Western European party systems differ significantly from one another, it is clear that parties are on the whole less well equipped to facilitate citizen control than they were in the mid-20th century. This is most obvious with respect to electoral and extraparliamentary parties. Political parties today have a weaker grip on the electorate, and membership in party organizations is falling, in some cases drastically. Apparently, citizens are less content to rely on party 'brand names' than they were in the early decades after the Second World War. This trend is strongest in northern Europe and much weaker or non existent in those southern European countries that have democratized in the latter half of twentieth century. Yet, it is less clear that the party in government has lost in significance. Governmental parties maintain much of their cohesion and thus their ability to bond and discipline politicians. Their influence over legislators and cabinet ministers is still strong.

EXTERNAL CONSTRAINTS

Principals and agents within the democratic chain of delegation, the representatives of the people, are simultaneously bound by their popular mandates as well as by various other obligations and restrictions, which we generically refer to as *constraints*. We refer to those constraints that are formed by institutions that are themselves agents in the parliamentary chain of delegation as *internal*. They have been detailed in Chapter 4. In this section, we shall focus instead on constraints that are *external* to the parliamentary chain of delegation. The country chapters (Chapters 5–21) demonstrate that such constraints on popular representatives are in fact quite important. In this section, we review these constraints and summarize their importance, which, as we shall see, has on the whole increased further.

The most important constraints that have been discussed by our contributors are the following: international (here particularly the European Union (EU)), societal, subnational, executive (i.e. those associated with the role of the Head of State), central banks, judicial, and direct democratic. Below we proceed in the same order, from the most general and indirect constraints to those that are more direct and specific. In each case, we assess the relevance of these constraints cross-nationally and over time. Differences between countries or differences over time result from two developments. One is deliberate constitutional design: institutions that serve as external checks can be created, abolished, or reformed. The second source of change is informal political adaptation, which may result from political self-interest, from convenience, from bandwagon effects, or from no obvious motivation at all. For example, packing institutions intended to constrain parliamentarians with party appointees can have the effect of aligning preferences and hence undermining the very rationale of these institutions. Conversely, freeing institutions from such partisanship can make external checks effective without any change in formal institutions.

International Constraints: The European Union

The constituent parts of the ideal–typical Westphalian world are states with internal as well as external sovereignty. Accordingly, no state faces any international or supranational constraints on the representation of popular preferences. Needless to say, although this may be (or at least may have been) a useful way to simplify our understanding of the world, it does not describe contemporary European realities. National decision-makers are not free to represent the interests of their domestic constituents without international interference. Indeed, those constraints have since the 1980s in many ways become markedly more intrusive.

The international environment not only constrains national policy-making in part through voluntary international agreements, but also through more formal organizations and confederations through which states have agreed to pool or transfer sovereignty. The seventeen country chapters mention a variety of significant bilateral relationships, such as the ones between the United Kingdom and the Irish Republic or between Belgium and Luxembourg. Some states, such as the Nordic countries, have more encompassing regional ties. Most also share common security arrangements, such as NATO membership. Yet, by far the most general and significant international constraint on all but two of our countries (Iceland and Norway) is their common membership in the European Union (EU). And even in the latter two cases, relations with the EU, channelled through the European Economic Agreement (EE-A), are among the most important constraints on the autonomy of national policy-makers. Hence, in this section, we focus on one international constraint: the EU.

Since the 1957 Treaty of Rome, member states have increasingly delegated decision-making powers to the EU. Proponents of closer integration promote this supranational 'pooling' of legislative and budgetary powers as coordination necessary to promote peace, stability, and economic growth. It is also a way to deal with problems that know no national boundaries, such as crime or environmental pollution. But these developments also raise concern about the national Parliaments' ability to scrutinize their respective governments in EU affairs, and about the resulting informational asymmetries that affect the national policy process. Thus, for national representatives of the people,

European integration is Janus-faced. It can promote favourable and efficient policy-making but it also complicates the mandate and accountability of national political agents.

The less bargaining power a member state has within the Union, the greater the constraint on its autonomy. EU institutions operate according to a complex set of rules of weighted voting, under which large members have more power than smaller ones, though not in proportion to their population.[6] Thus, the constraint imposed by EU membership is inversely related to the country's population. As a simple measure of this international constraint, Table 22.5 reports the voting power of each member state in the EU's most critical body, the Council of Ministers, under the qualified majority rule.[7] For our measure of bargaining power, we use the Banzhaf index, as advocated by Felsenthal and Machover (2001; see also 1998).[8] Table 22.5 shows that the four largest countries, Germany, France, the United Kingdom, and Italy, are clearly less constrained by the Union than are the smaller states.

The use of voting power indices to measure the relative power of EU member states is controversial. Garrett and Tsebelis (1999a,b, 2001) are thus critical of the use of voting indices in studies of EU decision-making. These authors (2001: 101) criticize the implicit assumption that all potential voting alliances have the same *ex ante* likelihood of forming, since 'some Council members tend to hold extreme views (such as the United Kingdom) whereas others are generally more centrally located (such as Germany)'. Yet, Italy's dramatic shift under Berlusconi in 2001–2, from a strongly pro-integrationist position to pronounced scepticism, shows that member states' preferences need not be stable. The same might happen to Austria if the Freedom Party were to gain a stronger influence over government policy. National preferences within the EU will vary with the Union's evolving membership and political agenda, as well as with domestic political developments (Marks and Wilson 2000). Therefore, we see no compelling reason to assume that some countries are doomed to be preference outliers. Yet, we do recognize that our measure in Table 22.5 gives only a very partial depiction of decision-making power within the EU.

Societal Constraints

In this volume, our main focus has been on the constitutional structure of the national, supranational, or subnational government. Of course, in a study of decision rules in

---

[6] Certainly, the smaller member states have more representatives in the European Parliament and much more voting power in the Council than they would have under proportional representation based on population size. In that respect, Luxembourg, for example, is extremely advantaged compared to the largest member state, Germany.

[7] Clearly, policy-making in the EU is exceedingly complex, and as Garrett und Tsebelis (2001) point out, this focus on the Council neglects the agenda-setting power of the Commission. Yet, we believe the Council's role to be critical and know of no simple and superior alternative measure of the voting power of the various members. Hence, the index included in Table 22.5 is intended as a heuristic measure of 'one of the most crucial factors' (Hosli 1996: 256) that explain EU decisions.

[8] Felsenthal and Machover (1998) maintain that the Banzhaf index alone measures the a-priori influence (I) of voters in a voting body (based on a voter's ability to affect whether the bill will be passed or defeated). In contrast, its main alternative, the Shapley–Shubik index, is said to measure a voter's expected relative share in some prize (P) a winning coalition can divide among itself. For a critique of this measure, see Garrett and Tsebelis (2001: 99).

Table 22.5. *International, Societal, and Subnational Constraints*

	European Union		Index of coporatism (0–3)	Index of federalism and decentralization (1–5)	Subnational government consumption (1995–6) (0–100)[b]
	Number of votes in the Council	Voting power in the Council under qualified majority rule[a]			
Austria	4	0.0479	3	4.5	66
Belgium	5	0.0587	1	5	35
Denmark	3	0.0359	3	2	71
Finland	3	0.0359	3	2	69
France	10	0.1116	0	1.2	48
Germany	10	0.1116	1	5	89
Greece	5	0.0587	0	1	29
Iceland	n/a	n/a	1	1	40
Ireland	3	0.0359	0	1	52
Italy	10	0.1116	0	1.3	49
Luxembourg	2	0.0226	1	1	35
The Netherlands	5	0.0587	2	3	55
Norway	n/a	n/a	3	2	60
Portugal	5	0.0587	0	1	18
Spain	8	0.0924	0	3	63
Sweden	4	0.0479	3	2	71
UK	10	0.1116	0	1	36

[a] This measure is the standardized Banzhaf index based on the qualified majority rule (62 out of 87 votes).
[b] This index is the proportion of local and regional government final consumption in relation to general government final consumption.
n/a = non-applicable (not EU member states).

Sources: European Union: Nurmi and Meskanen 1999: 167; Index of federalism: Lijphart 1999: 189; Index of regional and local consumption: Lane and Ersson 1999: 188. With the exception of Luxembourg (data from 1992) updated via personal communication with Ersson. Index of corporatism: Lane and Ersson 1999: 23.

national parliamentary systems, such an emphasis makes a great deal of sense. Most formal constraints on the power of those authorized to govern through parliamentary elections, or indirectly authorized through the former, can in fact be located in that constitutional structure. Yet, we would be remiss in describing the institutions of post-Second World War Western Europe without considering the constraining effects of actors, networks, and agreements that extend beyond these formal institutions. Our contributors have pointed to a range of social institutions, in many cases components of civil society, that place important constraints on those empowered in the national chain of delegation. These social institutions can roughly be divided into three categories: corporatist arrangements, consociational structures, and communities of faith.

Corporatism

During the 1930s, corporatism, or more specifically what Schmitter (1974) and others call 'state corporatism', was seen as an alternative to parliamentary democracy, as a form of political decision-making most fervently championed by those who least favoured parliamentarism. After the Second World War, corporatism, now more likely in its 'societal' or 'liberal' variety, became a complement, rather than a competitor, to parliamentary democracy, especially in such central and northern European societies as Austria, Sweden, Norway, Belgium, and Luxembourg, and by some accounts The Netherlands and Germany. Corporatist practices in these countries were in large part associated with the emergence of strong social-democratic governing parties (especially in Scandinavia) and with a postwar economic compromise between capital and labour (especially in central Europe) (Katzenstein 1985).

Unfortunately, the literature has not settled on a clear, operational definition of corporatism (Williamson 1989). The phenomenon is sometimes understood to refer to the strength and organizational unity of economic producer groups, sometimes to the ways in which such groups interact with one another and the government in economic (and other) policy-making. In this volume we are interested in corporatism to the extent that it impinges on the parliamentary chain of delegation. Corporatism then means that decisions formally made by constitutional actors are instead routinely resolved through negotiations between producer groups and the state. Hence laws and executive decisions, mostly in the areas of social and economic policies, are partly made outside the parliamentary chain. Likewise, implementation of government policies can be delegated to state-licensed interest groups.

The extent and ways in which corporatism constrains parliamentary institutions and decision-makers are less clear-cut than in the cases of some other types of constraints. To some extent, corporatism has much in common with consultative referendums: these decision-making mechanisms are not constitutionally entrenched and have no binding force. Yet, parliamentarians resort to them at some peril, since it is difficult to ignore the results without appearing high-handed or undemocratic. Moreover, corporatist consultations can acquire the force of a normative expectation, which politicians may later find costly to violate. In some countries, corporatism rests on more solid legal foundations, as it has found statutory underpinnings in countries such as Austria, Norway, and Sweden. While these laws do not require that Parliament adopt policy compromises reached through corporatist bargaining, they do require interested parties, among which economic producer groups often figure prominently, to be heard before government proposals are even introduced in Parliament. Nonetheless, a retreat from corporatism is far more feasible than, for example, a reversal of federalism or EU membership.

During the 1970s, corporatism was widely depicted as economically efficient and as a force in its ascendancy. Since the late 1980s, a much more sober assessment has tended to dominate. Corporatism, many would argue, is in decline, and the cases that were previously proudly hailed as corporatist economic successes, such as Sweden and Austria, have increasingly put in much less impressive macroeconomic performances or abandoned much of the corporatist edifice. These two countries were ranked numbers two and three, respectively, on Lijphart's (1999: 177) index of corporatism.[9] Table 22.5 lists an alternative index, by Lane and Ersson (1999), which places Austria in one group with four of the Nordic countries (Denmark, Finland, Norway, and Sweden). The

---

[9] Lijphart (1999) actually refers to his index as one of 'interest group pluralism' and clearly refers to corporatism as the opposite pole. Our rankings thus represent an inversion of this scale.

Netherlands is placed thereafter, while Belgium, Germany, and Luxembourg are placed with the fifth Nordic country (Iceland). Remaining countries are scored as having no significant corporatist intermediation. While this classification is less discriminating than some other rankings, it has the advantage of grouping countries in robust clusters.

While the contributors to this volume have not been centrally concerned with the fate of corporatism per se, they do suggest that its trajectory is not uniform across countries. In Austria and Sweden, corporatist practices seem to have fallen into long-term decline. Privatization (in Austria) and European integration (in both countries) have reduced the scope for government intervention in the policy areas most relevant to producer groups. In Austria, the long-term decline in the legislative influence of interest groups was accelerated in 2000 by the replacement in government of the pro-corporatist Social Democrats by the anti-corporatist Freedom Party (Tálos and Kittel 2001). In Sweden, business associations have since the early 1980s opted out of the system of interest representation through government commissions and executive boards, and the whole remiss system has declined in importance (Rothstein and Bergström 1999; Chapter 20). Similar, though less dramatic, developments have taken place in Denmark (Iversen 1999; Blom-Hansen 2001). In Finland, on the other hand, corporatist practices evolved somewhat later and were particularly prevalent in the 1970s and 1980s, but have since fluctuated more. In Norway (ranked number one by Lijphart), corporatist practices were reduced under the non-socialist governments of the early 1980s. In the 1990s, however, social-democratic governments once again invoked the cooperation of unions and business in comprehensive wage bargaining and in the crafting of tax and social security reform. This concertation was generally successful in the early 1990s, but had lost most of its effectiveness by the end of the decade. At the same time, the number of consultative committees and boards has continued to decline. And, as in other Scandinavian countries, the effectiveness of corporatist bargaining has been weakened by labour fragmentation, as white-collar organizations have grown at the expense of the traditional blue-collar sector and gradually severed the unions' organizational ties to social democracy. On balance, therefore, it seems fair to say that in Norway, like the other leading countries in this respect, corporatism has since the 1970s withered (though not completely died). Thus, cross-nationally, corporatism is an external constraint whose importance has declined.

Consociationalism and Communities of Faith

In some countries, corporatism has long coexisted with consociational practices, which are mechanisms for conflict resolution that entail (1) grand coalition government, (2) mutual veto, (3) proportionality in government appointments and contracts, and (4) segmental autonomy (Lijphart 1977). Consociationalism has particularly been featured in plural societies divided along linguistic, ethnic, or religious lines. As Müller points out in Chapter 5, Austria is a prime example of consociationalism as well as corporatism. Post-Second World War politics has been based in large part on accommodations between the two dominant 'Lager' in Austrian politics: the social-democratic working class and the largely rural, Catholic segment. Austrian consociationalism has been characterized by grand coalition government and proportionality, even when such arrangements have not been numerically necessary. As Müller also stresses, however, the constraints imposed by consociationalism (as well as by corporatism) are largely voluntary ones adopted by parliamentary majorities, which parliamentary majorities have also been able to discontinue. Following the surge in support for the populist-right Freedom Party, Austrian politicians have indeed dismantled many of the edifices of consociationalism as well as corporatism. The same decline is in evidence in other formerly consociational countries (Luther and Deschouwer 1999). One reason may be that traditional social cleavages have lost much of their meaning.

Other forms of societal constraint can in some societies be found in the armed forces or in powerful communities of faith. In Portugal, the armed forces played a key role in overseeing civilian institutions during the first few years after the 1974 Revolution. In many Latin American countries, of course, the constraining role of the military has been much more freely acknowledged, and many cases of military intervention have indeed been defended on precisely such tutelary grounds (Loveman 1993).

In most of contemporary Europe, however, the military takes a back seat in importance to civilian institutions such as the Church. In Greece, the Greek-Orthodox Church ranks among the most important social institutions. The Church is an important national symbol, which stands as a bulwark against Islam as well as against Greece's traditional foe, Turkey. The Church is also important because of its financial power and social work. Something quite similar could be said about the position of the Catholic Church in Ireland. By most measures, Ireland has Europe's most devout population, and, given Ireland's tragic and conflictual past, the Church is important politically as well as spiritually. No major party in Ireland is openly anti-clerical, and only in recent years has the Church lost some of its influence on moral and social issues (Coakley 1999).

Most societal constraints differ from other external checks in that their influence is felt particularly at early stages of the policy process. They correspond to some form of agenda control, rather than *ex post* veto power. Note also that corporatism and consociationalism especially are associated with strong, rather than weak, political parties. Hence, corporatism is probably best understood as a form of voluntary delegation by political parties with close ties to particular economic producer groups. Finally, most of these forms of societal constraint seem to have diminished in importance over the past couple of decades, as societies have become more differentiated and social identities more plastic. In sum, then, societal constraints have distinctively structured European parliamentary politics. They have provided social foundations for political parties and simplified citizen *ex ante* control by contributing to the alignment of preferences. Their decline is therefore not evidence of a strengthening of party control of popular representatives, but rather the contrary.

Subnational Constraints

The national chain of parliamentary delegation is impacted not only by supranational constraints but also by subnational ones. The most common type of subnational constraint is federalism, in which there are at least two levels of government, each of which has some constitutionally protected area of jurisdiction in which it is makes final decisions (Riker 1964, 1975). States that do not meet these criteria are either unitary, in which all final authority is vested in the central government, or confederal, if all ultimate authority rests in the lower levels of government.[10] Federalism has a number of putative virtues, such as the ability to accommodate social diversity and particularly geographically concentrated minorities (Lijphart 1977). It may also foster policy experimentation and competition among its subunits and thus a choice of policy environments for its citizens. Such policy choice may yield benefits in economic efficiency (Tiebout 1956). Weingast (1995) has very interestingly expanded on this point, arguing that the economic benefits of federalism accrue specifically under 'market-preserving federalism,' in which subnational governments have the primary regulatory responsibility, the central government ensures a common market without internal discrimination, and subnational governments face a hard budget constraint (do not control the money supply). On the other hand, federalism may exacerbate regional inequalities, and some studies suggest that fiscal decentralization, at least in many less developed societies, may be associated with corruption and poor service delivery rather than beneficial competition (Treisman 2000).

According to the singularity principle (see Chapter 3), a parliamentary democracy should effectively be a unitary state, with no constitutional constraints on the power of the national government. Most Western European democracies are indeed unitary, though we need to recognize exceptions as well as caveats. Table 22.5 presents Lijphart's (1999) index of federalization. Three states covered in this volume are currently federal: Germany, Austria, and Belgium. The former two have been so ever since their current constitutions were adopted. Belgium, on the other hand, has followed a gradual path towards devolution, with a fully federal constitution adopted in 1993. The Belgian and German federalisms reserve significant exclusive or joint powers for subnational governments, whereas in the Austrian case federalism is more apparent than real. Thus Lijphart scores Austria below the other two federal states on decentralization. Although the formal Constitution reserves residual powers for the nine states (*Länder*), actual constitutional practice has vested more and more power in the central government (and, increasingly, EU institutions) (Chapter 5).

While not fully federal, the Italian and Spanish Constitutions reserve significant powers for subnational governments, whose structure is incongruent (i.e. constitutional powers vary significantly across subnational units). Italy and Spain both have particular regions that enjoy an enhanced, and constitutionally entrenched, autonomy. These peculiarities of constitutional structure reflect deliberate compromises based on historical diversity and fierce regional rivalries. In fact, demands for increased autonomy or even secession were significant as late as the 1970s in Italy and the 1980s in Spain, after constitutional autonomy had been secured. In both countries the regions were able to make additional gains in their competences in the 1990s (Colomer 1998; Lane and Ersson 1999: 175–8). And even in historically centralist France, the Socialist governments of the 1980s introduced regionalization policies (Schmidt 1990).

---

[10] Strictly speaking, since they lack internal sovereignty, confederal governments are not states. Since they also are not represented in this volume, we shall in the following disregard them.

Historically, the most purely unitary states, and hence the closest approximations to our ideal type of parliamentary democracy, have been found in northern Europe: in Britain and Scandinavia. While this picture remains largely accurate, even here the supremacy of national political institutions has been challenged. The most obvious case, of course, is the United Kingdom, where devolution of powers to directly elected assemblies in Scotland and Wales was among the first notable achievements of the first Blair government (1997–2001). The Nordic countries have not seen any similar development. Yet, as Bergman (Chapter 20) points out, in their implementation of the welfare state Swedish local governments have become increasingly autonomous from the central government. And the central government's share of tax revenue is no higher in Sweden than in the United States (Lijphart 1999: 193).

In fact, the degree of fiscal decentralization in the Nordic countries is such that Lijphart (1999) classifies all but Iceland as 'unitary and decentralized'. Hence, Table 22.5 includes a measure of decentralization in public spending. The variation across Western Europe in the degree to which the subnational rather than the national level expends tax money is striking. More than half of total government consumption occurs subnationally in all Nordic countries but Iceland, in The Netherlands, Spain, and in two federal states: Austria and Germany. Ireland and Italy also spend about half of the money at the regional and local levels of government. Belgium, the third federal state, spent only about one-third of public moneys subnationally about the time that the new federal Constitution went into effect (1995).

Presidential Powers

The parliamentary systems of Western Europe are roughly evenly divided between monarchies and republican constitutions. In their formal constitutions, the Head of State generally plays an important role. Recall that before parliamentary systems were *democracies*, they gradually became *parliamentary* by wresting constitutional powers away from the monarch and vesting them with the parliamentarians, however democratically the latter may have been elected (Bendix 1978). Even in most contemporary European republics, the Head of State is still a counterweight to the power of the parliamentary majority.

This constraint on popular representation is a feature of virtually all the countries represented in this volume. Only in Sweden has the king been entirely emasculated, as the 1975 Constitution does not even leave him a formal role in the policy process. In most other monarchies (Belgium, Denmark, Luxembourg, The Netherlands, Norway, Spain, and the United Kingdom), however, the role of the monarch is almost strictly ceremonial. Despite the crucial role of the Spanish King in establishing and defending the transition to democracy, none of these Heads of State is a serious policy-maker or constraint on popular representation. Only in Belgium has the monarch actively inveighed on national policy, and even there the 1950 referendum on the 'king's question' effectively relegated him to the sidelines of national politics (see Chapter 6).

Under republican constitutions, the constraining force of the Head of State is likely to be more real (see Elgie 1999). Compared to other executives, directly elected Presidents are at an advantage in popular legitimacy, as in this respect they can claim to be on equal terms with Parliament. Given that Parliament normally does not speak with one voice, a directly elected President may even see himself (or herself) as superior, particularly if the parliamentary majority is small (or unstable) or the President close to the median voter. We therefore expect popularly elected Presidents to be particularly significant constraints on parliamentary policy-making.

Presidential powers fall into a number of distinct areas. First, many Heads of State are vested with more or less significant powers to appoint and dismiss the Prime Minister and other cabinet members. Most Presidents have a variety of other appointment powers. Presidents may also be authorized to dissolve Parliament and call new elections. Furthermore, the Head of State may be allowed to participate directly in policy-making, through veto powers or the authority to issue decrees or other legislative instruments. Some Presidents can call a popular referendum, and some have the power to initiate judicial review. Table 22.6 reports on the selection and powers of Western Europe's republican Heads of State.

In Table 22.7, we present a scoring scheme for presidential powers, building on Shugart and Carey's (1992: ch. 8) additive index, as further developed by Metcalf (2000). Our scheme is based on a total of seven presidential powers relevant to parliamentary systems. In each category, a constitution can score a maximum of four points if the President can single-handedly employ the respective power (i.e. if the President is essentially a dictator in this domain). The more the President is constrained, the fewer points are given, and, of course, no points accrue if the President does not have the respective authority at all. These scores are then added up across categories. As Shugart and Carey (1992: 149) admit, such an additive index is far from perfect but, as they maintain, 'it is preferable to a purely nonquantitative, impressionistic ranking or no assessment of comparative presidential powers at all'.

As always, our concern is with enforceable powers, and we seek to discount those that are not. In so doing, our point of departure is the various constitutions. Yet, identifying enforceable powers is a particular challenge with respect to parliamentary Presidents. One reason is that the discrepancy between the letter of the constitution and political feasibility can be astonishingly large. As Duverger (1980) and the country chapter (Chapter 12) point out, it seems to be particularly huge in Iceland, where the formal Constitution grants the President much broader powers than has been reflected in political practice. France is at the opposite extreme, in that the President under unified government (in non-*cohabitation* situations) is stronger than the Constitution seems to imply.

One cause of this discrepancy between the letter of the constitution and political practice may be that presidential authority often includes dramatic and highly consequential 'emergency' powers that are rarely exercised. Whether the President then truly has the discretion to use them often cannot be determined through observation. Yet, we should be careful not to jump to the conclusion that such powers cannot be exercised. For example, many constitutions grant the President the right to refuse a Prime Minister's request for parliamentary dissolution. Yet, in practice we hardly ever observe such a course of events. But as Strøm and Swindle (2002) argue, this non-occurrence need not indicate that the President is powerless to refuse dissolution, but

Table 22.6. *Presidential Selection and Political Powers (2000)*

	Election	Right (with discretion) to dissolve parliament	Right (with discretion) to appoint Prime Minister	Right (with discretion) to dismiss government	Other relevant powers (in the President's own right, i.e. without prior proposal)
Austria	Direct popular	On the proposal of the Cabinet only[a]	Yes	Yes	No
Finland	Direct popular	On the proposal of the Prime Minister only[c]	No	No	Foreign policy; veto power in legislation[b]
France	Direct popular	Restricted[d]	Yes	Yes[e]	Foreign policy; defence policy; can initiate constitutional review[f]
Germany	By majority of Members of the Federal Convention, consisting of the Members of Parliament (Bundestag) and an equal number of delegates elected by the Land Parliaments	No[g]	No	No	No
Greece	By two-thirds majority of Members of Parliament[h]	No[i]	No	No	Can, by resignation, force new parliamentary election; veto power in legislation[j]
Iceland	Direct popular[k]	Counter-signature of the Prime Minister required	Yes	Yes	Veto power in legislation[l]
Ireland	Direct popular	On the proposal of the Prime Minister only	No	No	Can initiate constitutional review; gatekeeper for minority referendum[m]
Italy	By two-thirds majority of members of the electoral college—consisting of the members of both chambers and three delegates from each of the 20 regions[n]	Restricted[o]	Yes	No	No
Portugal	Direct popular	Restricted[p]	Yes	Yes[q]	Veto power in legislation; gatekeeper for referendums; can initiate constitutional review[r]

[a] The President can dissolve Parliament only once for any one reason (Art. 29), but the Constitution does not include implementing provisions for this qualification.

[b] Special role in foreign policy (Section 93). The President has suspensory veto power in the law-making process. The veto can be overridden by Parliament by a second vote without special majority requirements. A presidential veto may delay the coming into force of law by more than three months (Section 77).

[c] On the basis of a 'reasoned proposal by the Prime Minister', 'after having heard the parliamentary groups' (Section 26).

[d] If the Parliament has been dissolved, no further dissolution is allowed within the year following the election of a new Parliament (Art. 12).

perhaps rather that the Prime Minister recognizes this constraint and refrains from requesting dissolution when he knows that the President will disallow it.

Appointment

Even in parliamentary systems, the Head of State typically has a range of appointment powers, the most important of which is the authority to appoint the Prime Minister and other members of the cabinet. Presidential appointment powers in parliamentary systems are by definition constrained by the fact that the President must appoint a cabinet that is at least tolerated by Parliament. Thus, the President cannot succeed if a cohesive parliamentary majority firmly opposes his or her choice. Hence, few European Heads of State have been able to pick and choose their Prime Ministers.

Yet, it has not been unusual for Presidents in some of our countries to exert significant influence on prime ministerial and cabinet appointments. This has most notably been the case in the French Fifth Republic, when the President's coalition has also controlled the parliamentary majority (Thiébault 2000). But France is not unique. In Italy, the appointments of the Amato (1992–3), Ciampi (1993–4), and Dini (1995–6) cabinets, which were crucial in the transition from the 'first' to the 'second' republic, were largely due to the President (Pasquino and Vassallo 1995; Verzichelli and Cotta 2000). Italian Presidents had influenced prime ministerial selection even before that time,

---

Table 22.6 notes continued

e This right is not contained in the Constitution but it has become an established convention that the government offers its resignation to a newly elected President. Furthermore, Presidents have always succeeded at any time in removing Prime Ministers who belonged to the same party-political alliance as the President.

f Special role in foreign and defence policy (Art. 14 and 15).

g The President has discretion to dissolve Parliament only when it fails to elect a Chancellor with the majority of all MPs (Art. 63) or when the Chancellor fails to win a majority of all MPs in a vote of confidence (Art. 68).

h Election by two-thirds majority of all MPs in the first and second ballots, or three fifths of all MPs in the third ballot. If no President can be elected in three ballots, Parliament is dissolved.

i The Constitution prescribes the President's dissolution right in great detail so that the only possible discretionary act is *not* to dissolve if two governments have resigned or were defeated in Parliament and no stable government can be formed (Art. 41).

j By his own resignation the President may force the dissolution of Parliament, given the supermajority required for his (or her) election and the rule that Parliament is automatically dissolved if it cannot elect a new President in three attempts (Art. 32 (4)). The President has suspensory veto power in the law-making process that can be overridden by Parliament with an absolute majority (a majority of all MPs) only (Art. 42).

k A note of curiosity only: At the time of writing, the Icelandic President is the only West European Head of State who is a Professor of Political Science.

l Presidential veto in legislation. A bill vetoed by the President becomes valid, but is submitted to a referendum for approval or rejection (Art. 26).

m Except for constitutional amendments, urgent legislation, and money bills (Art. 26).

n Elected by a two-thirds majority of the members of the electoral college in the first three ballots, or by a simple majority of the electoral college after the third ballot.

o Not during the last six months of the presidency, unless these six months coincide entirely or in part with the last six months of the term of any of the chambers of Parliament (Art. 88).

p Not during the first six months after a parliamentary election and not during the first six months of the presidency (Art. 133, 172).

q Only 'to safeguard the proper functioning of the democratic institutions' (Art. 195 (2)).

r Decides (with discretionary power) on the holding of referendums proposed by Parliament or the government (Art. 115). Has veto power in some policy areas; the veto can be overridden only by a two-thirds majority in Parliament (Art. 139). The initiation of constitutional review is regulated in Art. 278.

Sources: Country chapters; Constitutions; Shugart and Carey 1992; Elgie 1999.

Table 22.7. *Presidential Power Scores*

	Appointment	Cabinet dismissal	Parliamentary dissolution	Veto	Decree	Referendum	Judicial review	Total
Austria	2	2	3.5	0	0	0	0	7.5
Finland 1945	4	2	4	1	0	0	0	11
Finland 1991	4	2	3.5	1	0	0	0	1C.5
Finland 2000	0	0	0	1	0	0	0	1
France	2	2	3	0	1	1	2	11
Germany	1	0	1	0	0	0	0	2
Greece 1975	2	2	4	2	0	4	0	14
Greece 1986	0	0	0	2	0	0	0	2
Iceland	4	4	4	1–3	1	1	0	15–17
Ireland	0	3.5	0	0	0	0	3	5.5
Italy	1	0	3	1	0	0	0	5
Portugal	2	2	3	2 or 3	0	1	4	14–15

Notes: The final column is an additive index of the other columns, which are scores of presidential powers (the higher the score, the more powerful the President). For sources and coding explanation, see the chapter text.

exploiting bargaining failures and internal splits and rivalries in the now-defunct Democrazia Cristiana (Hartmann and Kempf 1989: 140–2; Hine 1993: 99, 320 note 26). Presidents representing smaller parties have often facilitated the cabinet participation of their respective parties. Yet, the most notorious case of presidential intervention was the premiership of Fernando Tambroni (1960), who was hand-picked by President Giovanni Gronchi and survived precariously for four months with neo-Fascist support until severe left-wing riots brought down his government (Mack Smith 1997: 439–40). Finnish Presidents 'have determined which parties are "eligible" for entrance into a cabinet, put pressure on parliamentary groups and hesitant ministerial candidates, and expressed a clear opinion concerning the coalition base' (Nousiainen 2000: 271). In 1987, President Koivisto decisively influenced the formation of the unusual coalition of Conservatives and Social Democrats and the selection of Prime Minister Harri Holkeri.

Presidents have exerted particular influence over cabinet formation when the party system has been fragmented or the dominant parties uncohesive. This has either led to party-based cabinets, with the party composition strongly influenced by the President, or to technical (non-partisan) cabinets. Portugal, for example, saw three presidential cabinets in 1978–9 (Magone 2000). Yet, Presidents do not always succeed. Austrian President Thomas Klestil tried to return a 'grand coalition' government in 1999–2000 but eventually had to swear in the cabinet he had tried to avoid. Italian President Gronchi's 1960 intervention, mentioned above, was a notorious embarrassment.

The list that we have compiled comprises most of the postwar exceptions to parliamentary dominance over cabinet appointments. The Presidents of Ireland and Finland (since March 2000) have at best formal duties in cabinet appointment. In the case of Greece, Article 37 of the 1976 Constitution already tightly circumscribed presidential appointment powers by providing more precise constitutional appointment instructions than any other Western European constitution (see Chapter 11). The 1986 constitutional amendment removed what limited discretion had remained in the hands of the President (Article 37). Thus, the cross-national norm is that presidential appointment powers are merely formal and only under special circumstances become more than that.

In Table 22.7, because of regime differences and some ambiguities in the original coding scheme, we score presidential appointment powers somewhat differently from Shugart and Carey (1992: 152–3) and Metcalf (2000). One reason is that formal presidential appointment powers interact with the rules of cabinet inauguration, specifically the distinction between positive and negative parliamentarism. Presidents are most powerful when they make cabinet appointments directly and when there is no required subsequent investiture vote (negative parliamentarism). Thus, we score Presidents who can at least formally select individual ministers four under negative and three under positive parliamentarism, and Presidents who can appoint ministers only on the proposal of the Prime Minister two under negative and one under positive parliamentarism. Figure 22.1 contains the appropriate placements of countries with scores between one and four.

Cabinet Dismissal

Cabinet dismissal is the flip side of cabinet appointment. Yet, while appointing cabinets is a normal duty of Heads of State, terminating them at will is not. According to

Appointment of cabinet members

		On proposal by Prime Minister	Directly by President
Parliamentarism	Negative	2 Austria, France, Greece (until 1986), Portugal	4 Finland (until 2000), Iceland
	Positive	1 Italy, Germany	3 (No cases)

Figure 22.1. Appointment Powers of Western European Presidents.

Kaltefleitner (1970: 52–7), presidential dismissal, dissolution, and legislative powers should in parliamentary democracies be 'reserve powers' exclusively, to be applied only if the parliamentary policy chain malfunctions. Moreover, Presidents should use their powers to stabilize the incumbent government. By and large, Western European Presidents behave accordingly. Formally, the Presidents of Austria, Portugal, Finland (until the new Constitution of March 2000), and Greece (until 1986) have (had) discretionary constitutional authority to dismiss the whole cabinet, while individual ministers may be dismissed on the request of the Prime Minister only. Constitutional practice shows that the French President can be added to this list. But all these Heads of State face restrictions on their respective dismissal powers. The single exception is the Icelandic President, who can dismiss individual ministers unilaterally and without restrictions. The Presidents of Germany, Italy, Ireland, Finland (since March 2000), and Greece (since 1986) do not have dismissal power.

Cabinet dismissal makes sense only if an alternative government can be formed and that, in turn, may require a different composition of Parliament. Hence, presidential dismissal power normally goes together with the authority to dissolve Parliament. All four Presidents with dismissal power also have dissolution power, though there are restrictions detailed in our tables.

We score Presidents who without parliamentary consent can dismiss individual ministers or the entire cabinet as four. Presidents whose dismissal power is restricted by the need to get parliamentary consent receive the score three. Those who are limited in the use of this power to specific conditions (such as 'a threat to the democratic institutions') get the score two. Presidents who can only dismiss the entire cabinet, or who can dismiss individual ministers only at the request of the Prime Minister, score one. Presidents without any of these powers have been scored zero.

Parliamentary Dissolution

In all but one (Norway) of our seventeen countries, Parliament can be dissolved before the end of its regular term, or, as it is sometimes called, the constitutional inter-election period (CIEP). Though there are many forms of dissolution power (see Chapter 4; Strøm and Swindle 2002), the Head of State often plays an important role, at least formally. Yet, in most parliamentary democracies, the President's dissolution power is constrained. Moreover, in practice the President's dissolution right is of greater relevance if he or she is free to appoint and dismiss the government.

According to the formal constitutions, only the Icelandic, Greek (until 1986), and Finnish (until 1991) Presidents enjoy unrestricted dismissal powers. The respective constitutions simply assert the President's right or are very unspecific about the conditions that permit dissolution. Hence, the Greek 1975 Constitution allowed dissolution if the President considered that Parliament 'was not in harmony with popular feeling' (Article 41). Between 1991 and 2000, the Finnish President was restricted by the requirement of a 'reasoned initiative by the Prime Minister' and consultations (Section 27). Likewise, the Irish President can dissolve Parliament on the advice of the Prime Minister (Article 13). The Austrian President faces only a very soft constraint in the vague clause that Parliament can be dissolved 'only once for the same reason'. The President can do so only on the proposal of the cabinet (which, however, the President appoints and can single-handedly dismiss). The Presidents of France, Italy, and Portugal have to engage in non-binding consultations, but are more seriously constrained by various time restrictions (see Table 22.5). Finally, the only specific situation in which the German President can dissolve the Bundestag is when it fails to elect a Chancellor by a majority of all MPs (Article 63) or when the Chancellor fails to win an absolute majority in a vote of confidence (as with Helmut Kohl in 1983). Since 1986 and March 2000, respectively, the Greek and Finnish Presidents have no dissolution powers.

In accordance with Shugart and Carey (1992) and Metcalf (2000), in Table 22.7 we score a President with unrestricted dissolution authority as four. If there are restrictions with regard to frequency or timing within the President's or Parliament's term, the score is three. A score of two means that parliamentary dissolution can occur only after a presidential election. If dissolution is only allowed as a response to specific events (e.g. when the cabinet loses the confidence of Parliament), we report the score as one. Finally, if the President has no dissolution power, the score is zero. If a President can dissolve only upon the request of the cabinet or Prime Minister, we reduce the score by 0.5 points.

Legislative Veto Power

Although parliamentary Heads of State may most forcefully exert their authority by appointing or dismissing Prime Ministers or calling elections, they may also play a more direct role in the policy process. This role typically takes two forms: legislative veto powers on the one hand, and decree powers on the other. We shall consider them in succession. In their study of presidentialism, Shugart and Carey (1992) distinguish between package and partial vetoes. No Western European President has the latter and stronger veto power: a partial (line-item) veto. The package veto power exists in five of our cases: Finland, Greece, Iceland, Italy, and Portugal. The value of such veto powers obviously depends on the conditions under which they can be overridden. In Finland, the presidential veto can be overridden by simple majority. While this holds true for the whole postwar period, the veto powers of the Finnish President have declined over time. Until the 1987 constitutional reform, the President could delay legislation until overridden by a newly elected Parliament. Provided that there was no early dissolution, the delay hence could be several years. And, of course, there was the chance that a new parliamentary majority would share the President's preferences. Under the post-1987 rules, however, the President can delay legislation for three months only. Yet, the Finnish President has not let the veto fall into complete disuse. Anckar (1990: 36) reports sixty-four vetoes for the 1919–78 period; Nousiainen (1998: 354) seventy vetoes 1919–95. However, none of these vetoes has caused great conflict. The most frequent presidential rationale has been formal (relating to due legislative process or aspects of the bill's drafting) or financial, and all but six (four of which occurred in 1990) were sustained by Parliament.[11]

In Italy the President can veto ('request a new deliberation', Article 74), but a second vote with exactly the same majority in both chambers is sufficient to override. Although in practice Presidents make very limited use of their suspensive veto (specifically, Sandro Pertini seven times in his presidential term 1978–85, his successor Francesco Cossiga four times in the first two years of his term), their vetoes are generally sustained by Parliament and the bills amended accordingly. In most cases, Italian presidents have intervened to block bills that lacked the necessary revenue provisions (Hartmann and Kempf 1989: 149).

The Portuguese President has stronger veto powers. On certain issues specified in the Constitution, his veto can be overridden only by a two-thirds parliamentary majority.[12] The 1982 constitutional reform actually enhanced presidential veto powers by extending the number of policy areas in which an override requires a two-thirds majority (Chapter 18). As noted in Chapter 18, the Portuguese President has made relatively frequent use of the veto, particularly in situations of 'cohabitation.'

Building on Metcalf (2000), in Table 22.7 we score a presidential veto that cannot be overridden as four, whereas three means override by extraordinary majority, two override by an absolute majority of the whole parliamentary membership, one override by a simple majority of quorum, and zero no veto powers. Iceland does not fit this scheme. The President can veto legislation, but this does not prevent the legislation from coming into force, and it triggers not another vote in Parliament, but a referendum. Depending on the nature of the President's conflict with Parliament, we therefore score this power in the range between the one and three.

Decree Powers

A less dramatic, but often more significant, presidential prerogative is the power to issue decrees or administrative orders. By presidential decree powers Shugart and Carey (1992: 151) refer to the ability of the President 'to make new laws or suspend old ones without the power of decree first having been delegated through enabling legislation'. Presidents in Western European parliamentary democracies generally do not possess far-reaching decree powers. There are, however, two exceptions. Article 16 of the French Constitution grants the President the right to 'take the measures demanded' when 'the institutions of the Republic, the independence of the nation, the integrity of

---

[11] Thanks to Matti Wiberg for clarifying this point.
[12] A two-thirds majority is required for organic laws on foreign relations, issues of private or public ownership, and some election rules (Article 139).

its territory, or the fulfilment of its international commitments are under grave and immediate threat and when the proper functioning of the Constitutional governmental authorities is interrupted'. And Article 28 of the Icelandic Constitution allows the President to issue provisional laws 'in case of urgency' and when Parliament is not in session. These must not contradict the Constitution and need to be submitted to Parliament as soon as it convenes. Yet, both of these decree powers are comparatively weak, as reflected in Table 22.7.

Referendum

In a later section, we shall examine direct democracy as an external constraint on the parliamentary chain of delegation. Here, we note that under some constitutions Presidents, as intimated above, are empowered to call such referendums. Thus, in Greece until 1986, the President could single-handedly proclaim referendums 'on crucial national issues' (Article 44). Since that time, however, the President has had only a formal role in the referendum procedure. In France and Portugal, the President decides on the holding of referendums but only upon a cabinet proposal. We have already considered the authority of the Icelandic Head of State: it is reactive only, conditional upon a piece of legislation that does not find the President's approval. Otherwise the Icelandic Constitution features only automatic referendum provisions. Hence, in practice the Icelandic President has monopoly agenda control over referendums. In Table 22.7 we apply the codings established by Shugart and Carey (1992) as revised by Metcalf (2000).[13]

Judicial Review

Judicial constraints on parliamentary power will be discussed at length below. Sometimes, a Head of State may be instrumental in imposing this constraint through his power to submit legislation to review by a constitutional court prior to promulgation. The Presidents of France, Ireland, and Portugal can thus initiate constitutional review. Until 1974 the French President shared that right with the Prime Minister and the Presidents of both chambers. Since then even a parliamentary minority enjoys this power. In Ireland the President alone can appeal to the constitutional court, yet she is restricted by the exclusion of certain matters from judicial appeal.[14] The President of Portugal has an exclusive but unrestricted right to pre-promulgation constitutional appeal. In Table 22.7, we apply the same coding rules as Metcalf (2000).[15]

---

[13] If the President acting alone can call a referendum (i.e. he is a dictator or at worst a decisive player), we score it a four. The score is two if presidential powers are 'restricted'. Metcalf (2000: 671) understands this as a 'shared' power 'where either the President or the assembly acting alone can propose referendums', that is, when each is a decisive player. The score is one if the President and the cabinet must agree on the use of the referendum (both are veto players). Finally, zero means that the President has no authority to call a referendum.

[14] Up to the end of 1998, the Irish President had appealed to the constitutional court on twelve occasions (Gallagher 1999: 83).

[15] If the President has exclusive power to refer legislation to a constitutional court prior to promulgation, the score is four. If the right is shared and either the President, the cabinet, or a majority of the assembly (or its presiding officer) can request judicial review, the score is two. If the right is shared so that the President, the cabinet, or some parliamentary minority can invoke judicial review the score is one. Finally, if the President has no such authority, the score is zero (Metcalf 2000: 672).

Summary
Table 22.7 presents an overview of all these presidential powers, employing our revised version of the indices of Shugart and Carey (1992) and Metcalf (2000). Note that few Western European Heads of State have substantial legislative or judicial powers, but that many are more significantly involved in the making and breaking of cabinets and the calling of elections. According to formal powers, the presidential rank order sees the Icelandic President on top, neatly reflecting the country's geographical position between parliamentary Europe and presidential America. The Portugese President is next in formal powers and clearly outranks the Icelandic one in the actual exercise of these powers. Even the Presidents of Finland and Greece had considerable powers in earlier decades, but are now among those least favoured. In contrast, the French President has held on to his powers and is well known to exercise them to the extent that the political situation allows. The Presidents of Austria, Ireland, and Italy all hold some important formal powers. In terms of their real impact on parliamentary politics, however, the Italian President ranks first and the Irish last. Finally, the German Head of state has been rendered particularly powerless because of the painful history of the presidency during the Weimar republic. Overall, then, although the Constitutions of newly democratic Greece and Portugal featured powerful Presidents, the longer-term trend has been towards a weakening of the formal and real powers of Western European Heads of State, including the Presidents.

Central Banks

The Head of State is not the only actor within the executive branch that may constrain the parliamentary policy process. In a number of countries, various executive agencies have been granted significant autonomy. Foremost among these, particularly since the early 1990s, have been national banks. The Blair government's move in 1997 to grant effective autonomy to the Bank of England is perhaps most widely known, but it is not the only example and certainly not the most far reaching. The most consequential such development, of course, is related to the growing scope of EU jurisdiction, and specifically the introduction of the European Monetary Union (EMU) and the European Central Bank, which is as independent as any national central bank (de Haan and Eijffinger 2000). Yet, the evolution of more autonomous central banks is not restricted to the 'euro zone' (the EMU states), as Norway and Sweden demonstrate (and we might have been able to refer to more such cases, had our survey covered a larger number of non-EU countries).

Table 22.8 reports two existing measures of central bank independence, both based on the Cukierman–Webb–Neyapti index for the 1960s and the 1980s. The index numbers reflect very little change. Note, however, that more recent developments, such as the reforms in Belgium and Spain in the early 1990s, and in the United Kingdom in 1997, all of which enhanced the independence of central banks, have not been captured in these data. Greater central bank independence is thus a significant, and well recognized, institutional development that serves to constrain parliamentary policy-making.

Table 22.8. *Central Bank Independence*

	1960–71	1980–9	Change: Column 2– Column 1
Austria	0.65	0.61	−0.04
Belgium	0.15	0.17	0.02
Denmark	0.50	0.50	0
Finland	0.28	0.28	0
France	0.36	0.24	−0.12
Germany	0.69	0.69	0
Greece	0.51	0.55	0.04
Iceland	0.34	0.34	0
Ireland	0.44	0.44	0
Italy	0.25	0.25	0
Luxembourg	—	0.33	—
The Netherlands	0.42	0.42	0
Norway	0.15	0.17	0.02
Portugal	—	0.41	—
Spain	0.09	0.23	0.14
Sweden	0.29	0.29	0
UK	0.43	0.27	−0.16

Notes: Legal central bank independence; range from 0 (low independence) to 1 (high independence).

Source: Cukierman *et al.* (1994), table A-1.

Judicial Constraints

Our ideal–typical conception of parliamentary democracy privileges the voice of the people, in that we assume democratic representation to be rooted in popular sovereignty, in the idea that government policy ultimately should reflect popular preferences. Yet, there is a significant alternative or complementary conception of democracy as a way of protecting and promoting a bundle of civic and political rights and liberties. This vision privileges instead a constitutional order that protects and promotes the choices and preferences of the constitutional framers. Among the most serious constraints on democracy as popular sovereignty are thus the institutions that serve to protect constitutional (or liberal) democracy. Foremost among them are constitutional and other important judicial institutions.

During the second half of the twentieth century, Western states evolved toward a rights-oriented vision of democracy, a trend that is very visible in our sample. This judicialization of parliamentary democracy has taken a number of different but mutually reinforcing forms. One is the increased access to constitutional courts, and the growing number of constitutions that have established such courts. A second important trend has been the increasing activism of new as well as established constitutional or supreme courts. A third has been the growing willingness of ordinary courts to challenge demo-cratically elected authorities. Finally, but certainly not least, the EU member states, and even the EEA countries, have been profoundly affected by the growing authority of the European Court of Justice and other supranational judicial institutions, particularly those entrusted with the enforcement of the European Convention of Human Rights (ECHR).

Increased Access to Constitutional Courts

The US Supreme Court established its powers of judicial review through its decision in *Marbury v. Madison*. In twentieth-century constitutions, such powers have instead tended to be explicitly designed. Modern constitutional courts were invented by Hans Kelsen to guarantee the superiority of the constitution over ordinary laws, hence constitutional democracy (Stone Sweet 2000). The Austrian Constitutional Court, established in 1920, became the model. Since then, many parliamentary democracies have established consti-tutional courts and hence accepted limitations on parliamentary sovereignty. While the German Bundesverfassungsgericht, established in 1949, the Italian Corte Constituzionale, included in the 1948 Constitution, and the French Conseil constitutionnel, established in 1958, had national antecedents, they clearly were major steps towards constitutional democracy. The new democracies in southern and central Europe likewise have estab-lished systems of constitutional review. Of the countries covered in this volume, Spain has chosen a fully fledged constitutional court, while Greece and Portugal have established more restricted forms of judicial review. Of the older democracies, Belgium in the course of federalization in the 1980s expanded its system of judicial review.

In France and Austria access to the constitutional court significantly increased in the 1970s. A 1974 French constitutional amendment gave access to the Constitutional Council (which was previously restricted to the President of the Republic, the Prime Minister, and the Presidents of the two chambers of Parliament, positions which until 1981 were all filled by members of the government majority) to any group of sixty deputies or senators. While between 1959 and 1974 the Council was called on to give no more than nine decisions on the constitutionality of law, the figure rose to forty-seven in the 1974–81 period, sixty-six in the first period of Socialist government (1981–6), twenty-six during the first cohabitation (1986–8), and forty-six during the sec-ond Socialist government (1988–93) (Wright 1999: 99). 'Today', Wright (1999: 99) con-cludes, 'all major controversial laws and all annual budgets end up in the Council'.

A 1975 Austrian reform of parliamentary procedure made it possible for one-third of the MPs to appeal to the Constitutional Court to exercise abstract norm control. Since then, even personally affected individuals have been able to appeal directly to the Court to challenge the constitutionality of a law or government decree. Behavioural change has not been as dramatic as in France. Nevertheless, these new rules have allowed the parliamentary opposition or affected citizens to test before the Constitutional Court the constitutionality of virtually every controversial law.

Increased Judicial Activism

The judicialization of parliamentary politics has been caused not just by institutional reforms, but also by a greater willingness among existing courts to use powers that they have long enjoyed. Since 1951, for example, the German Constitutional Court 'has developed into a fiercely independent institution and has struck down large numbers of statutory provisions and administrative regulations' (Kommers 1997: 56). Between 1951 and 1991, it declared 198 federal laws invalid or incompatible with the Constitution (Landfried 1992: 52). While there is no clear trend toward more invalidations over time, this may well be due to the power of anticipated reaction and parliamentary law-making 'in the shadow of the court' (Kommers 1997: 56). This interpretation is supported by surveys of the role orientations of constitutional court judges, which between 1972 and 1983 show a significant shift from 'norm enforcement' to 'development of law' (Landfried 1992: 54).[16]

In Denmark, the High Court and the Supreme Court have since the 1990s shown less judicial restraint. In Norway, the Supreme Court in 1976 resurrected its doctrine of judicial review by ruling against the government in a property rights case (see Chapter 17). From the 1960s on, the Dutch Supreme Court, the Hoge Raad der Nederlanden, 'allowed itself more and more to develop the law by broadly interpreting the codes and statutes. In this process, the Court grew from an insignificant, non-political body to a politically powerful institution' (van Koppen 1992: 80). In Belgium (see Chapter 6), judicial review was in the 1980s enlarged by the creation and subsequent 'upgrading' of the Court of Arbitration, which has evolved into a genuine constitutional court, though with limited jurisdiction. Even in Britain judicial review, though in very limited ways, has increased (Drewry 1992; Sterett 1994).

The French Constitutional Council, initially conceived less as a constitutional court than as the executive's 'cannon aimed at Parliament' (F. Luchare, quoted from Stone 1992: 60), has since 1974 'widened and deepened the scope of its action' (Wright 1999: 99). Annulments of government laws in part or whole have become more frequent, from two (out of nine) cases in 1959–73, to fourteen (out of forty-six) in 1974–80, and forty-nine (out of ninety-two) in 1981–7 (Stone 1992: 58). Through January 2002, the Jospin government had had eight of its laws invalidated (*The Economist*, 26 January 2002). These annulments have included cornerstones of the governments' legislative programmes (Stone 1992). Similarly, the Austrian Constitutional Court has since the 1980s assumed a more active role, shifting from a formal to a more substantive interpretation of the Constitution. At the same time, it has become less predictable and even reversed several previous decisions. The Court has invalidated a long list of important laws, leading in some cases to significant losses of revenue as well as substantial additional expenditures.

Over the years, the Italian Constitutional Court has also invalidated a substantial number of laws (Volcansek 2000: 27–9). However, increasing judicial activism can be inferred most clearly from the battle between the government and the Court over decree laws and the Court's role in the referendum process. The Court initially prac-tised judicial restraint in upholding the government's policy of recycling decree laws that had not been accepted by Parliament within the constitutionally prescribed

---

[16] The respondents in this survey were asked the following question: 'Do you think that your work as a judge of the Constitutional Court consists primarily of norm enforcement or of the development of the law?'

sixty-day period. However, in 1996 it declared all recycled decree laws unconstitutional (Volcansek 2000: ch. 2). And whereas as late as 1987 and 1991 the Court favoured the government parties by blocking referendums that were likely to undermine party rule, in 1993 it changed its ruling and allowed a referendum challenging the Senate's electoral system, eventually leading to the transition to the so-called second Italian republic (de Franciscis and Zannini 1992: 77; Volcansek 2000: ch. 6).

In some cases, increased judicial activism reflects a greater willingness on the part of judges to challenge politicians. In other cases, it may be due to an increasing incongruence between the political orientation of the judges and the parliamentary majority. In Austria, until the formation of the ÖVP–FPÖ coalition in 2000, all judges had been nominated by one of the traditional government parties, the SPÖ and the ÖVP. Hence, their growing willingness to challenge government policies and to give up judicial restraint first and foremost indicates greater independence. In Italy, judges became more willing to disregard the wishes of their nominating parties when the political system came under siege and particularly after the traditional parties collapsed (Volcansek 2000). In France, the various alternations in the partisanship of Presidents and parliamentary majorities since 1981 have led to frequent political incongruence between the government of the day and the Constitutional Council. Hence, a left-wing government may be confronted with a right-wing Council, or vice versa (Wright 1999: 115). Finally, the increased power of constitutional courts is reflected in the anticipation of court decisions by Parliaments, and in the reduced scope for parliamentary decision-making under the Constitution as interpreted by the courts. By these mechanisms, 'legislators are gradually placed under the tutelage of the constitutional court' (Stone Sweet 2000: 194).

Ordinary Courts

Even ordinary courts may significantly constrain the parliamentary chain of delegation, for example, by placing restrictions on individual politicians. Since the 1980s the number of spectacular cases of legal action against incumbent politicians has dramatically increased. Without doubt Italy's 'clean hands' investigation is the most prominent case (Nelkin 1996a,b). Yet, there have been important cases even in France (Wright 1999: 104, 110–2), Germany, Spain, Belgium, and Austria.

International Judicial Impact

The ECHR has now been ratified in its entirety and incorporated into domestic law by most of the countries under consideration in this volume. This is a relatively recent phenomenon. The United Kingdom, for example, had not fully accepted all articles until 1966 and France not until 1981. At the same time, the effective number of rights that the ECHR guarantees has been increased. In particular, the European Commission of Human Rights and the European Court of Human Rights have developed a sizeable body of 'established case-law'. This has imposed more specific limits on each state's ability to apply national laws at its own discretion. Judicial activism has led to the 'discovery' of several new human rights (or at least extensions of the meaning and scope of the existing rights). Hence, 'civil rights' have been interpreted to encompass social welfare as well as environmental benefits (Storey 1995: 144–5).

Table 22.9. *Judicial Constraints (2000)*

	Strength of judicial review (Lijphart)	Degree of court politicization (Alivizatos)	Judicial discretion (Cooter & Ginsburg)
Austria	3*	3	n/d
Belgium	3*	3	3.5
Denmark	2	1	n/d
Finland	1	1	n/d
France	3*	4	3.7
Germany	4*	4	3.46
Greece	2	2	n/d
Iceland	2	1	n/d
Ireland	2	2	n/d
Italy	2.8*	4	3.33
Luxembourg	1	1	n/d
The Netherlands	1	2	4.2
Norway	2	1	n/d
Portugal	2*	3	n/d
Spain	3*	3	2.0
Sweden	2	2	2.5
UK	1	2	2.1

Notes: Low scores indicate judicial restraint, high scores judicial activism or discretion; Lijphart scale: Belgium since 1984, before that 1.5; Italy since 1956, before that 2.0. *Centralized judicial review by special constitutional courts.

Sources: Lijphart 1999: 226; Alivizatos 1995: 575; Cooter and Ginsburg 1996: 300.

Table 22.9 presents three attempts to measure the relevance of judicial constraints cross-nationally. Lijphart's 'strength of judicial review' variable aims to capture both judicial review and the degree of judicial activism (Lijphart 1999: 225–6).[17] Alivizatos' (1995: 567) 'politicisation of courts' measure (1975–94) is meant to capture 'to what extent they influence the decision-making process' (with scores ranging from 1=judicial self-restraint to 4=judicial activism).[18] Finally, Cooter and Ginsburg's (1996) 'judicial discretion' scores are based on the judgements of 'a small number of comparative law scholars' who have rated the judicial 'adventurousness' of various countries on a five-point scale (with 5 being the highest and 1 the lowest score). There is a high degree of consistency between the three measures, although Lijphart's classification fits best with the interpretations of our country experts.

---

[17] Lijphart's entries are scored as follows: 4=strong judicial review, 3=medium-strength judicial review, 2=weak judicial review, 1=no judicial review. An asterisk in the table indicates centralized judicial review by special constitutional courts.

[18] Alivizatos (1995: 567).

Direct Democracy

The final constraint on parliamentary policy-making that our contributors have identified is direct democratic instruments. European states generally became parliamentary long before they became fully fledged democracies: the cabinet's accountability to the parliamentary majority was established before popular sovereignty was truly entrenched. A constitution based on parliamentary sovereignty is thus not necessarily conducive to direct popular decision-making. The contrary might more commonly be the case, as our two historical cases from Chapter 1 (Britain and Sweden) illustrate. In the United Kingdom, the referendum has no well-established place in the constitutional order, and it is only since Britain joined the EU that even consultative referendums have been held. Although direct democracy has been somewhat more common in Sweden, Swedish governments have on two different occasions, after 1955 over right-hand-side driving and after 1980 over nuclear power, effectively ignored referendums that had equivocal or inconvenient outcomes.

Conversely, Switzerland is clearly not parliamentary while at the same time the undisputed European leader in its reliance on direct democracy. In fact, the tension between parliamentary and referendum democracy has never been fully resolved. In the 1920s, Hans Kelsen suggested direct democracy as a remedy against the democratic deficiencies of parliamentarism (see Chapter 1), an idea that has more recently been forcefully championed by Ian Budge (1996; see McLean 1989 for a more sceptical view).

Forms of Direct Democracy

Direct democracy comes in a variety of forms. Such votes may be mandated by the constitution under particular conditions, for example, whenever a constitutional amendment is passed. Alternatively, a referendum may be held at the discretion of either the parliamentary majority, a parliamentary minority of a certain size, the chief executive, or it may be put on the agenda through the collection of citizen signatures. Such referendums may have the power of rescinding a recently enacted law (an abrogative referendum) or of enacting a new one (an initiative). Finally, referendums may be either binding or non-binding (in the latter case, advisory or consultative).

Several countries have since the 1960s broadened the scope of direct democracy. At the same time, reforms have strengthened the power of citizens to initiate direct democratic processes. Austrian (1963) and Italian (1970) legislation has provided implementing provisions for the consultative initiative (Austria) and the abrogative referendum (Italy) and hence made these instruments practically useful. Austria has preserved parliamentary supremacy, but reforms have introduced new forms of direct democracy and eased access to existing ones (Müller 1998; Chapter 5). The Italian referendum, included in the 1947 Constitution but without enabling legislation, in practice became available to citizens and regions in 1970. Since then, with a few exceptions, any existing law can become the subject of an abrogative referendum. Portugal, which in 1991 introduced the referendum controlled by the government and parliamentary majority, followed Italy's lead: a 1997 constitutional amendment and a new referendum law (1998) introduced the popular initiative (leading, upon parliamentary consent, to a referendum) (see Chapter 18). Similarly, after long debate, The Netherlands in 2001 introduced the abrogative (consultative) referendum on the demand of at least 300,000 voters (Andeweg 1997; Chapter 16). These developments were preceded by a considerable expansion of subnational direct democracy in Germany: by the mid-1990s all German *Länder* had introduced state initiatives and referendums and most also a variety of local direct democratic instruments (Scarrow 1997).

Table 22.10 describes the direct democratic institutions in place in 2000. We do not distinguish between binding and consultative referendums since, at least in the short run, even consultative referendums are hard to ignore and hence severely constrain politicians. Some of the direct democratic institutions described in Table 22.10 have been in existence over the whole postwar period. Others are more recent. Thus, the Danish abrogative referendum (upon the demand of one-third of the Members of Parliament (MPs)) was introduced in 1953, when the current Constitution came into force (Qvortrup 2000a). Likewise, the Swedish referendum on constitutional amendments dates from the late 1970s and went into effect in 1980. In Portugal, the referendum on laws was introduced in 1991. The scope of the French referendum was broadened by a 1995 constitutional amendment.

The Use of Referendums

Referendums have not simply become a more widespread constitutional option. There is also clear evidence that this option is more frequently exercised. Several countries thus report an increased frequency of direct democracy. Across the OECD countries as a whole, the number of national referendums increased from a total of eighteen over the period 1965–9 to eighty-four in the years 1990–4 (Strøm 2000: 187). Table 22.11 shows that the number of referendums has more than doubled in the 1990s compared to the preceding decades. Most of this increase, however, is due to the frequent referendums in Italy and Ireland. Though less consequential, there was a major increase in the number of (consultative) initiatives in Austria (Müller 1999). On the other hand, eight countries—Belgium, Germany, Luxembourg, Greece, Iceland, The Netherlands, Spain, and the United Kingdom—did not have a single national referendum during the 1990s.

Nationally concentrated as it may be, there could be several reasons for this increased incidence of popular consultations. In part, it may be driven (as in the Swedish nuclear power referendum) by a desire among elected politicians to rid themselves of a 'hot potato' by handing it over to the voters. If this is indeed the main cause of referendums, and if it is the parliamentary majority or the executive that decides whether and when to hold them, then the increased use of this instrument clearly does not represent much of a popular challenge. This is even more true if the parliamentary majority/executive calls referendums only when it is reasonably confident of winning.

With such concerns in mind, Qvortrup (2000b) has examined whether referendums are controlled by the government and whether they are hegemonic (i.e. produce a pro-government outcome). Although we should keep in mind that the distinction between controlled and non-controlled referendums is not always easy to draw (Smith 1976), Qvortrup reports that the great majority of Western European referendums (seventy-four out of ninety-five) have not been government-controlled, and that a sizeable minority (thirty-seven out of ninety-five) have had an anti-hegemonic outcome. In individual

Table 22.10. *Direct Democratic Institutions in Western Europe (2000)*

	Obligatory referendum on constitutional amendment	Minority right to demand referendum on constitutional amendment	Referendum on legislation on the demand of the parliamentary majority (constitutional provision or established practice)	Abrogative referendum on ordinary legislation on the demand of citizens or the parliamentary minority	Popular initiative (leading to referendum) or consultative initiative (leading to decision in Parliament)
Austria	On major amendment	Yes	Yes	No	Consultative initiative[a]
Belgium	No	No	No	No	No
Denmark	On any amendment	n/a	Yes	Parliamentary minority[b]	No
Finland	No	No	Yes	No	No
France	No[c]	Yes[d]	Yes	No	No
Germany	No	No	No	No	No
Greece	No	No	Yes[e]	No	No
Iceland	On major amendment[f]	No	No[g]	No	No
Ireland	On any amendment	n/a	Yes	No	No
Italy	No	Yes[h]	No	Citizens[i]	Consultative initiative[j]
Luxembourg	No	No	Yes	No	No
The Netherlands	No	No	No	No	No
Norway	No	No	Yes	No	No
Portugal	No	No	Yes	No	(Popular)[k]
Spain	On major amendment	Yes[l]	Yes	No	Consultative initiative[m]
Sweden	No	Yes[n]	Yes	No	No
UK	No	No	Yes	No	No

[a] In Austria, 100,000 citizens or one-sixth of the citizens in each of three *Länder* can propose legislation.

[b] In Denmark, the delegation of powers to international authorities requires a super-majority of five-sixths of MPs. If the majority required for passing ordinary bills is obtained but not the required super-majority, a referendum is held on the demand of the government. On other matters, which exclude the rules that govern the rights and duties of the monarch, civil liberties, financial bills, and other issues, a referendum is held on the demand of one-third of MPs. The bill is rejected when a majority of those participating in the referendum vote against it, provided that they constitute no fewer than thirty percent of those entitled to vote.

[c] In France, the referendum is obligatory unless the constitutional reform has been submitted to Congress (that is, both houses of Parliament meeting in joint session) by the President on the Prime Minister's proposal and approved there by a three-fifths majority of the votes cast.

[d] In France, implicitly, a minority of two-fifths of the MPs can force a referendum on any constitutional change. See note c.

[e] According to the Greek Constitution, the referendum should be concerned only with issues 'of crucial importance'. The respective laws have to be proposed by two-fifths of all MPs and accepted by three-fifths of all MPs.

countries, of course, the picture can diverge. Thus, Finland, France, Norway, Sweden, and the United Kingdom have seen more controlled than non-controlled referendums. On the other hand, in Denmark and Italy particularly, the government has lost a large number of such votes. And the Norwegian government of the day has lost both referendums on EU membership.

Direct democracy, then, is a quite straightforward constraint on the parliamentary chain of delegation, and one that has historically shown little affinity with parliamentary democracy. Specifically, the use of the initiative indicates that the respective issues are not decisively processed through the parliamentary channel. Hence, we can consider the initiative as a kind of *ex ante* lever affecting the parliamentary issue agenda. Likewise, obligatory referendums on constitutional amendments as well as abrogative referendums are clearly *ex post* checks on parliamentary decisions.

The increasing real-world relevance of direct democracy is indisputable. Many European countries have experienced a political debate over the referendum and other instruments of direct democracy. Perhaps with the singular exception of Italy, the debate has tended to favour direct democracy. Specifically, there is considerable demand to introduce new forms of direct democracy or to strengthen already existing ones (Gallagher and Uleri 1996). Opinion polls have tended to show that the majority of citizens support this claim (e.g. Austria, Germany).

Recent attempts to reform the rules for initiating a referendum have begun to undermine the cabinet's agenda control. While this certainly is the case in Italy (since 1970), there have been moves in this direction even in Portugal (since 1998) and The Netherlands (since 1999). Moreover, the frequency of referendums seems to be driven primarily by popular demand (rather than by elite 'supply' of inconvenient issues), and this mass demand will be difficult for elected politicians to resist. The challenge of direct democracy, however, is not specific to parliamentary democracies. As Table 22.12 shows, the use of direct democracy has increased even more in Switzerland than in the Western European parliamentary systems. Likewise, it has become more prominent in those US states in which it is featured (Cronin 1989; Zimmerman 1997; Bowler *et al.* 1998; Dubois and Feeney 1998; Gerber 1999; Bowler and Donovan 2000).

---

[f] In Iceland, any change of the status of the national Lutheran church must be approved in a referendum.

[g] In Iceland, a referendum is held only in case of conflict over legislation between Parliament and the President.

[h] In Italy, an abrogative referendum is held on the demand of one-fifth of the members of either chamber of Parliament or 500,000 voters or five regional Councils.

[i] In Italy, 500,000 voters or five regional councils can demand a referendum on the total or partial repeal of a law or of an act having the force of law.

[j] In Italy, 50,000 citizens can initiate legislation.

[k] In Portugal, a referendum is held only on the condition of approval by the Parliament.

[l] In Spain, a partial revision of the Constitution is subject to a referendum when it is demanded by one-tenth of the members of either chamber of Parliament.

[m] In Spain, the Constitution permits 500,000 citizens to propose legislation. This initiative is not applicable to organic laws, taxation, or international affairs, nor to the royal prerogative of pardon.

[n] In Sweden, a referendum is held on the demand of one-third of all MPs.

Sources: Country chapters; constitutions; Gallagher and Uleri 1996.

Table 22.11. *National Referendums, 1940–2000*

	1940–9	1950–9	1960–9	1970–9	1980–9	1990–9	2000	Total
Austria	0	0	0	1	0	1	0	2
Belgium	0	1	0	0	0	0	0	1
Denmark	0	2	6	3	1	3	1	16
Finland	0	0	0	0	0	1	0	1
France	4	1	4	1	1	2	0	13
Germany	0	0	0	0	0	0	0	0
Greece	1	0	1	2	0	0	0	4
Iceland	2	0	0	0	0	0	0	2
Ireland	0	1	2	5	4	10	0	22
Italy	1	0	0	3	12	32	7	55
Luxembourg	0	0	0	0	0	0	0	0
The Netherlands	0	0	0	0	0	0	0	0
Norway	0	0	0	1	0	1	0	2
Portugal	0	0	0	0	0	2	0	2
Spain	1	0	1	2	1	0	0	5
Sweden	0	2	0	0	1	1	0	4
United Kingdom	0	0	0	1	0	0	0	1
Total parliamentary democracies	9	7	14	19	20	53	8	130
Switzerland	17	43	26	81	60	100	6	333
Total	26	50	40	100	80	153	14	463
No. of countries using referendums	6	6	6	10	7	10	3	14

Note: Only the last two Greek and the last three Spanish referendums were held during the most recent transition to democracy or under democratic Constitutions.

Source: Setälä 1999: 333 (Updated for 1999 and 2000 from various sources, including the EJPR Data Yearbook and personal communication in the case of Ireland).

Table 22.12. *Mean Annual Number of Referendums, 1940–99*

	Switzerland	Italy	Other 16	All 18
1940–9	1.7	0.1	0.8	2.6
1950–9	4.3	0	0.7	5.0
1960–9	2.6	0	1.4	4.0
1970–9	8.1	0.3	1.6	10.0
1980–9	6.0	1.2	0.8	8.0
1990–9	10.0	3.2	2.1	15.3
1940–99	5.5	0.8	1.2	7.5

Source: Setälä 1999: 335 (Updated from various sources, see Table 22.11).

CONCLUSION: CROSS-NATIONAL PATTERNS

This chapter has further highlighted the substantial variation in accountability regimes among real-world parliamentary systems. Indeed, there are three dimensions of citizen control along which such regimes differ. One is the constitutionally mandated chain of citizen control that was the focal point of Chapter 4 and the country chapters. Even though all parliamentary democracies share the few essential features that were outlined in Chapter 3, by no means do they have identical working constitutions. In our seventeen polities, there is everywhere an *indirect and singular* chain of national policy-making, but these respective chains are made up of different electoral systems, different types of parliamentarism (positive or negative), different rules for no confidence votes (although such votes exist everywhere), and different distributions of dissolution powers, to mention only some of the variations. The country-specific chains promote different degrees of *agenda control* by the agents. Although traditionally, parliamentary democracy has been characterized by strong *ex ante* partisan control of democratic agents, and by comparatively fewer and weaker *ex post* constraints, there is significant variation along these dimensions as well. Thus, a more complete picture of parliamentary democracy in modern governance must, as our country chapters have done, also take into account cross-national variation and intertemporal shifts in partisan influence and external constraints.

Partisan cohesion and external constraints help us understand accountability under contemporary parliamentary democracy. While, classically, the parliamentary chain of policy-making was designed without much regard to political parties, in the present world political parties play a crucial role everywhere. Indeed, the classic Westminster model combines the ideal–typical parliamentary institutions with two strong and cohesive parties competing to control them. With an indirect, single, and unidirectional chain and two dominant and cohesive parties competing for power, voters can be reasonably sure that they can ensure accountability by voting the current leaders out of power. However, in polities in which the party systems are more fragmented and/or the parties less cohesive, and where government portfolios are distributed through post-electoral negotiations, citizen policy control through political parties may be harder to achieve. The way in which political parties coexist with the parliamentary chain thus partly determines the way in which accountability works. Similarly, in a polity where there are few subnational, societal, or international constraints on decision-making, the constitutional chain will be more decisive for national policy-making than in a polity in which political decision-making is heavily circumscribed by constraints outside of the parliamentary chain. The partisan and external constraint dimensions are thus tremendously important for how parliamentary government works in the real world.

While the partisan and external constraints dimensions are analytically distinct, there is reason to believe that to some extent they are mutual substitutes (see Chapter 3). Thus, under strong and cohesive party government, *ex post* constraints may be redundant. Yet, as we have noted, political systems evolve only gradually and may not equilibrate to a political optimum. Thus, for example, even when institutional checks are deliberately designed to compensate for decaying partisan controls, it takes time both to recognize this decay and to design and establish the appropriate institutional response. Conversely, when decision-making institutions are freed from partisan control, the occupants may need time to entrench and make use of their freedom. For these reasons, we should not expect a neat trade-off between partisan control and external constraints. We shall return to this point in Chapter 23.

Political Parties

It remains for us systematically to summarize the importance of the two additional dimensions of citizen control. Consider first partisan control. Table 22.13 draws together the cross-national variation presented earlier in the chapter, and particularly the most recent observations. We have discussed partisanship under three rubrics: the electoral party, the party organization, and the party in government. As argued above, we consider the party in government the most critical facet of partisan control, followed by the party in the electorate, while the extraparliamentary organization is the most dispensable component. In Table 22.13, the seven indicators of the strength of partisanship reflect this hierarchy: four pertain to the party in government, three to the electoral party. Each indicator has been introduced previously in this chapter. Together they provide a summary picture of the state of 'partyness' in our seventeen democracies. We normalize each measure by taking the maximum observed value (showing the greatest partisan influence) and setting it equal to one, whereas the minimum observed value is set equal to zero. All observations in between are then scored proportionally. We have generated a simple additive index of partisanship by summing the scores on the seven indicators and dividing the sum by seven.

There is good reason in our data as well as in the literature to question the ability of contemporary political parties, even in their erstwhile strongholds, to perform many of their traditional functions as mechanisms of citizen control (Dalton and Wattenberg 2000). Earlier in the chapter we have shown that the party-in-the-electorate, in particular, has declined throughout Western Europe. Yet, the magnitude of this decline is by no means the same everywhere. To put it bluntly, even if the parties are dying, they are certainly not all dying equally fast! In fact, partisan rule remains strong in a number of countries.

In our summary, one country stands out in terms of party strength: the United Kingdom, which has the highest score on four of seven indicators of party strength and cohesion. There are indications that the extraparliamentary organizations have eroded, but otherwise the Westminster model remains strong. Only in one measure of partisan influence is the United Kingdom weak, namely the extent to which partisanship permeates the public administration. This contrasts with the country that comes in a close second, Greece, in which partisanship is also much more prominent in government appointments. The other more recent democracies of southern Europe, Portugal, and Spain, are next in line in partyness. All of these are clearly alternational party systems.

The Netherlands and Italy, whose edifice of 'partitocrazia' virtually collapsed in the early 1990s, receive the lowest scores. Interestingly, it is the smaller, multiparty

Table 22.13. *Partisan Influence on Parliamentary Delegation: Summary*

Country	Party in the electorate			Party in government				Total	
	High party identification	Low share of parliamentary seats for non-governing parties	High degree of uniform electoral swing for all cabinet parties	High proportion of single-party majority cabinets	High coalition discipline (1975–99)	Low partisan conflict (1975–99)	High partisan influence over of government country appointments	Mean	Ranking of country
Austria	0.38	0.32	0.4	0.31	0.95	0.63	0.83	0.55	7
Belgium	0.43	0.67	0.1	0.08	0.05	0.07	1	0.34	15
Denmark	0.35	0.58	0.43	0	1	0.78	0	0.45	11
Finland	0.37	0.91	0.29	0	0.50	0.51	0	0.37	14
France	0.38	1	0.67	0.04	0.75	0.51	0.83	0.60	6
Germany	0.57	0.90	0.37	0.03	1	0.83	0.67	0.62	5
Greece	0.56	0.87	0.69	0.78	0.85	0.70	1	0.77	2
Iceland	0.71	0.13	0.26	0	0.55	0.67	1	0.47	9
Ireland	0.17	0.84	0.73	0.31	1	0.04	0	0.44	12
Italy	0.51	0	0.29	0	0.35	0	0.67	0.25	16
Luxembourg	0.32	0.66	0.19	0	0	1	0.83	0.43	13
The Netherlands	0	0.67	0	0	0	0.57	0.17	0.18	17
Norway	0.22	0.56	0.66	0.31	0.90	0.87	0.17	0.53	8
Portugal	0.62	0.88	0.84	0.47	0.55	0.40	1	0.68	3
Spain	0.21	0.69	1	0.38	1	0.43	1	0.67	4
Sweden	0.32	0.39	0.77	0.04	0.85	0.75	0.17	0.47	10
UK	1	0.77	1	1	1	0.75	0.33	0.84	1

Notes: For three variables (party ID; share for non-governing parties; and partisan influence over appointments), the entries are based on the most recent data for each country. For the other four variables we use national means for all or parts of the postwar period (uniform swing; single majority cabinets; coalition discipline; and partisan conflict). The entries are based on tables presented earlier in this chapter. Partisan influence over appointments is a composite of the three measurers that were presented in Table 22.3. For example, Belgium has a score of one (high influence) because partisan influence is coded as strong on all three measurers in Table 22.3. Denmark, on the other hand, is scored at zero because there is no indication of partisan influence on appointments on any of the three measurers in Table 22.3. For all seven indicators, numbers are normalized so that the country with the highest level of partisan influence in each category is scored 1, and the country with the lowest is scored 0.

democracies of the Belgium, Finland, and Luxembourg that come closest to Italy and The Netherlands in the weakness of partisan control. This larger group of countries is also furthest from the Westminster models ideal of a government controlled by either of two alternating parties or blocs. Instead, these low-partisanship countries are clearly pivotal.

In Greece and the other newer democracies of southern Europe, Portugal, and Spain, political parties are thus comparatively strong. There may be many reasons that party democracy thus seems to be more vital in southern Europe than in the north. In states that have relatively recently experienced dictatorship, the collective memory of less attractive alternatives to parliamentary democracy may still be fresh, and political parties may benefit from the role that they played in opposition to dictatorship or in the transition to democracy. And although some dominant parties, particular PASOK in Greece and the PSOE in Spain (see Share 1999), have clearly established patronage networks, they may simply have had less time to sully their reputations. Moreover, party attachments may be fed by societal conflicts that are still more present than the more archaic cleavages of the longer lived parliamentary democracies. In any case, the real impact of the strength or weakness of partisan influence can only be assessed in relation to the larger picture of citizen control.

External Constraints

The role of external constraints in promoting citizen control is more complex than that of political parties. When political actors and institutions that are not directly or indirectly the agents of the citizens impinge on the national policy process, they become *external constraints* on parliamentary democracy. External constraints can serve any number of purposes, some of them decidedly undemocratic. In this volume, however, we have focused on how external constraints can help citizens control their agents. Thus, the democratic purposes of external constraints include protecting rights and liberties, facilitating the provision of public goods, checking the power of particular agents, dispersing power in general, and enhancing political transparency. External constraints can take quite a number of different forms. Some, such as corporatism, are *societal*, whereas others, such as autonomous central banks, are *technocratic*, and yet others, such as directly elected presidents and popular referendums, are *democratic*. Clearly, only the last form represents control of elected politicians by ordinary citizens themselves. Yet even the other forms would be ineffective without citizen support.

We have throughout much of this book generally associated partisanship with *ex ante* citizen control and external constraints with *ex post* mechanisms. Yet, external constraints can in fact affect the national policy process both before and after the act of delegation. For instance, when a court of law or the voters in a referendum strike down a piece of legislation after it has been enacted and promulgated, they function as an *ex post* institutional check (or veto player) on the parliamentary representatives. In other cases, however, referendum voters and court opinions can have advisory purposes, or they can narrow the range of options of the parliamentary majority (Stone Sweet 2000), or as *powerful players* influence the legislative process *ex ante*. Yet, most of the external constraints that we have discussed are first and foremost *ex post* institutional checks. Table 22.14, constructed in analogue fashion to Table 22.13, contains seven indicators of external constraint.[19]

Note that the southern European countries are not particularly externally constrained. One might have expected their modern and largely republican constitutions to feature many constraints (e.g. referendum devices) commonly associated with contemporary constitutional design. Instead it is the smaller countries of nothern and central Europe that exhibit the most significant sets of external constraints on their national policy processes. Austria, Finland, and Iceland are the most prominent cases. Denmark, Ireland, and, as the first of the major countries, Germany, follow suit. The United Kingdom is at the other end of the scale, quite apart from most other European countries in its lack of external constraint, but followed most closely by Belgium.

As in the cases of partisanship, we see definitive temporal trends in the importance of external constraints. Clearly, as shown by the tables presented earlier in the chapter, the significance of judicial, direct democratic, subnational, and international constraints have increased. On the other hand, corporatism, consociationalism, and other societal constraints have mostly been in decline, as have some measures of partisan influence and organization. Interestingly, it is thus the constraints that are most inimical to partisan control that have particularly grown in importance, whereas the societal constraints, which have traditionally helped parties perform their screening functions, have decayed with them.

To be sure, the two dimensions of citizen control (partisan preference alignment and external constraints) are not mutually exclusive, since no modern democracy is completely without either. And having more of one does not necessarily condemn you to less of the other. For example, the United States increasingly seems to feature strong partisanship as well as strong external constraint. And as noted above, partisanship and societal constraints may in fact reinforce one another. Nevertheless, since partisan *ex ante* mechanisms and external constraints are to some extent rival and substitutable mechanisms of citizen control, we expect an overall negative association between the two.

Figure 22.2 plots the most recent observations of all of our seventeen countries on both dimensions. Note that countries that score high on one dimension, such as Britain and Greece on partisan influence, or Denmark on external constraints, tend to be low on the other. Thus, the two countries that exhibit the highest degrees of partisan control are

---

[19] On our first indicator, international constraints, the scoring of the non-EU member states, Iceland and Norway, reflects our interest in the EU as a constraint on national governments. This constraint, we argue, is least among states that do not belong to this organization. Therefore, we score Norway and Iceland as minimally constrained on a par with the larger member states (France, Germany, Italy, and the United Kingdom). While in the internal market they are significantly constrained by EU decision-making, outside the internal market (and the EEA agreement) national policy-makers in these countries do not face the same constraints as those in the EU member states. On the other hand, to a larger extent than for the member states, the national government remains the highest level at which political accountability can be exercised.

Table 22.14. *External Constraints on Parliamentary Delegation: Summary*

Country	Restrictions on voting power in EU Council[a]	Subnational government consumption[b]	Corporatism[c]	Presidential powers[d]	Central bank independence[e]	Strength of judicial review[f]	Strength of referendum institution[g]	Mean	Ranking of countries
Austria	0.72	0.68	1	0.5	0.85	0.67	1	0.77	1
Belgium	0.59	0.24	0.33	0	0	0.67	0	0.26	16
Denmark	0.85	0.75	1	0	0.63	0.33	0.75	0.62	2
Finland	0.85	0.72	1	0.07	0.21	0	0.25	0.44	6
France	0	0.42	0	0.73	0.13	0.67	0.50	0.35	10
Germany	0	1	0.33	0.13	1	1	0	0.50	4
Greece	0.59	0.15	0	0.13	0.73	0.33	0.25	0.31	13
Iceland	0	0.31	0.33	1	0.33	0.33	0.25	0.36	9
Ireland	0.85	0.48	0	0.43	0.52	0.33	0.5	0.45	5
Italy	0	0.44	0	0.33	0.15	0.60	0.75	0.32	11
Luxembourg	1	0.24	0.33	0	0.31	0	0.25	0.30	15
The Netherlands	0.59	0.52	0.67	0	0.48	0	0	0.32	12
Norway	0	0.59	1	0	0	0	0.25	0.31	14
Portugal	0.59	0	0	0.93	0.46	0.33	0.50	0.40	7
Spain	0.22	0.63	0	0	0.12	0.67	1	0.38	8
Sweden	0.72	0.75	1	0	0.23	0.33	0.50	0.50	3
UK	0	0.25	0	0	0.19	0	0	0.06	17

Notes: The entries are based on tables presented earlier in this chapter. Numbers are normalized so that the country with the highest level of external constraint in each category is scored 1, and the country with the lowest is scored 0.

[a] Based on the Banzhaf index from Table 22.5. Norway and Iceland (not EU members) are coded as having minimal constraints in this category.

[b] Based on the proportion of local and regional government final consumption in relation to general government final consumption, Table 22.5.

[c] Based on the Lane and Ersson corporatism index, Table 22.5.

[d] Based on the total presidential power score, Table 22.7.

[e] Based on the central bank independence index, Table 22.8, 1980–9.

[f] Based on Lijphart's index of judicial review from Table 22.9.

[g] Based on the number of types of referendum that are available in each country, Table 22.10. For example, Austria has all forms of referendums (coded as 1) while Belgium (coded as 0) has no referendums at the national level.

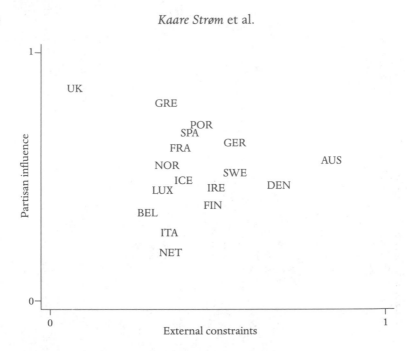

Figure 22.2. Two-dimensional Map of Citizen Control.

Notes: Countries are listed using abbreviations that are identical to Lijphart's (1999); The data is taken from Tables 22.13 and 22.14; The measures are correlated at −0.14 (Pearson's r).

simultaneously at the low end of external constraints. Indeed, our two summary indices correlate negatively, though at the relatively weak level of −0.14 (Pearson's correlation).

Yet, countries that are low on one dimension need not be high on the other. There are countries, most notably Austria, that are well endowed with both dimensions of citizen control. And, more ominously, there are those that are lacking in party cohesion as well as external constraints. Italy, for example, scores comparatively low on both dimensions of citizen control, and so does The Netherlands. While post-fascist Italy is one of the clearest cases of the trend away from partisan control and towards external constraint, it also appears that since the early 1990s the evolution of institutional checks has not kept pace with the collapse of partisanship. On the other hand, the majoritarian Italian electoral reforms of the 1990s represent a fascinating attempt to strengthen party cohesion at the same time that institutional constraints are becoming increasingly effective.

In addition to Italy, the Benelux countries are the most prominent cases of weakness on both dimensions. While the level of partisan influence varies somewhat, external constraints are in all these four countries rather weak, as they have largely ceremonial Heads of State and mostly feeble judicial institutions. In fact, the weakness of both dimensions of citizen control in these countries depresses the association between these two dimensions in our entire sample. Outside of these four countries and Austria, the negative correlation between partyness and external constraints is substantially higher (-0.68).

Note that our placements on these two dimensions do not simply reproduce established scholarly distinctions, such as between Westminster and consensus democracies (Lijphart 1999), between proportional and majoritarian systems (Powell 2000), or between those with few versus many veto players (Tsebelis 2002). One of the more interesting results here is the differentiation among political systems that have traditionally been classified as consociational (Lijphart 1977). Two of the systems that have been most clearly consociational, Belgium and The Netherlands, score low on partisan influence as well as on external constraints. So does Italy, a country that at least in the period of the 'historic compromise' between the Communist Party and the Christian Democrats was considered a candidate for inclusion in the consociational category (Pappalardo 1981). Austria, on the other hand, scores high on both dimensions. And it is striking that none of these systems exhibit the apparent trade-off between the strength of partyness versus external constraints that characterizes the other countries in our sample. We return to these results in Chapter 23.

In sum, there are persistent and essential cross-national differences between European parliamentary democracies along both dimensions of citizen control.[20] Our investigation in this chapter also leads us to conclude that there are very important intertemporal trends among West European democracies in the relative significance of partisanship versus external constraints. Most notably, there has been a decline in the strength and cohesion of political parties and an enhancement of international, subnational, judicial, and direct democratic external constraints. In most respects, these changes strengthen *ex post* controls and weaken *ex ante* screening devices. In comparison with presidential democracies, existing parliamentary democracies still favour *ex ante* accountability mechanisms. Consequently, they still protect more effectively against adverse selection than against moral hazard. But as parliamentary democracies evolve, these contrasts may fade. As the external constraints of parliamentary systems are strengthened, they may become less reliant on partisan screening of politicians. At the same time, however, some of the distinctive virtues of parliamentarism, such as efficiency and simplicity, may become less compelling. It remains to be seen what overall effects different forms of parliamentary democracy have on the quality of democratic representation. Those are among the topics of the final chapter.

REFERENCES

Aldrich, John H. (1995). *Why Parties? The Origin and Transformation of Political Parties in America*. Chicago: The University of Chicago Press.

Alivizatos, Nicos (1995). 'Judges as Veto Players', in Herbert Döring (ed.), *Parliaments and Majority Rule in Western Europe*. Frankfurt: Campus and New York: St. Martin's Press.

---

[20] Hadenius (2001) reaches similar conclusions on the cross-national variation but places less emphasis on the trends that we identify here.

Anckar, Dag (1990). 'Democracy in Finland: The Constitutional Framework', in Jan Sundberg and Sten Berglund (eds.), *Finnish Democracy*. Jyväskylä: Finnish Political Science Association.

Andeweg, Rudy B. (1997). 'Institutional Reform in Dutch Politics'. *Acta Politica*, 32: 227–57.

Bekke, Hans A. G. M. and van der Meer, Frits M. (eds.) (2000). *Civil Service Systems in Western Europe*. Cheltenham: Edward Elgar.

Bendix, Reinhard (1978). *Kings or People: Power and the Mandate to Rule*. Berkeley: University of California Press.

Blom-Hansen, Jens (2001). 'Organized Interests and the State: A Disintegrating Relationship? Evidence from Denmark'. *European Journal of Political Research*, 39: 391–416.

Blondel, Jean and Cotta, Maurizio (eds.) (1996). *Party and Government*. Houndmills: Macmillan.

—— —— (eds.) (2000). *The Nature of Party Government*. Houndmills: Palgrave.

Bowler, Shaun and Donovan, Todd (2000). *Demanding Choices. Opinion, Voting, and Direct Democracy*. Ann Arbor: University of Michigan Press.

—— —— and Tolbert, Caroline J. (eds.) (1998). *Citizens as Legislators: Direct Democracy in the United States*. Columbus: Ohio State University Press.

Budge, Ian (1996). *The New Challenge of Direct Democracy*. Cambridge: Polity.

Coakley, John (1999). 'Society and Political Culture', in John Coakley and Michael Gallagher (eds.), *Politics in the Republic of Ireland*. London: Routledge.

Colomer, Josep M. (1998). 'The Spanish "State of Autonomies": Non-Institutional Federalism'. *West European Politics*, 21(4): 40–52.

Comparative Parliamentary Democracies Data Set (January 2002). This data set combines the institutional mechanisms detailed in Chapter 4 of this book with the behavioural data that is published in Wolfgang C. Müller and Kaare Strøm (eds.) (2000). *Coalition Governments in Western Europe*. Oxford: Oxford University Press.

Cooter, Robert D. and Ginsburg, Tom (1996). 'Comparative Judicial Discretion: An Empirical Test of Economic Models'. *International Review of Law and Economics*, 16: 295–313.

Cox, Gary W. and McCubbins, Mathew D. (1994). 'Bonding, Structure, and the Stability of Political Parties: Party Government in the House'. *Legislative Studies Quarterly*, 19: 215–31.

Cronin, Thomas E. (1989). Direct Democracy. *The Politics of Initiative, Referendum, and Recall*. Cambridge, MA: Harvard University Press.

Cukierman, Alex, Webb, Steven B., and Neyapti, Bilin (1994). *Measuring Central Bank Independence and Its Effect on Policy Outcomes*. San Francisco: ICS.

Dalton, Russell J. (2000). 'The Decline of Party Identifications', in Russel J. Dalton and Martin P. Wattenberg (eds.), *Parties without Partisans*. Oxford: Oxford University Press.

—— (2002). *Citizen Politics*. 3rd edn. New York: Chatham House.

—— and Martin P. Wattenberg (eds.) (2000), *Parties without Partisans*. Oxford: Oxford University Press.

de Franciscis, Maria Elisabetta and Zannini, Rosella (1992). 'Judicial Policy-Making in Italy: The Constitutional Court'. *West European Politics*, 15(3): 68–79.

de Haan, Jakob and Eijffinger, Sylvester C.W. (2000). 'The Democratic Accountability of the European Central Bank: A Comment on Two Fairy-tales'. *Journal of Common Market Studies*, 38: 393–407.

Diermeier, Daniel, and Feddersen, Timothy J. (1998). 'Cohesion in Legislatures and the Vote of Confidence Procedure'. *American Political Science Review*, 92: 611-21.

Drewry, Gavin (1992). 'Judicial Politics in Britain: Patrolling the Boundaries'. *West European Politics*, 15(3): 9–28.

Dubois, Philip L. and Feeney, Floyd (1998). *Lawmaking by Initiative: Issues, Options and Comparisons*. New York: Agathon Press.

Duverger, Maurice (1954). *Political Parties*. London: Methuen.

—— (1980). 'A New Political System Model: Semi-Presidential Government'. *European Journal of Political Research*, 8: 165–87.

Elgie, Robert (ed.) (1999). *Semi-Presidentialism in Europe*. Oxford: Oxford University Press.

Epstein, Leon D. (1967). *Political Parties in Western Democracies*. New York: Praeger.

Farrell, David M. and Webb, Paul (2000). 'Political Parties as Campaign Organizations', in Russel J. Dalton and Martin P. Wattenberg (eds.), *Parties without Partisans*. Oxford: Oxford University Press.

Felsenthal, Dan S. and Machover, Moshé (1998). *The Measurement of Voting Power. Theory and Practice, Problems and Paradoxes*. Cheltenham: Edward Elgar.

—— —— (2001). 'Myths and Meanings of Voting Power: Comments on a Symposium'. *Journal of Theoretical Politics*, 13: 81–97.

Frognier, André-Paul (2000). 'The Normative Foundations of Party Government', in Jean Blondel and Maurizio Cotta (eds.), *The Nature of Party Government*. Houndmills: Palgrave.

Gallagher, Michael (1999). 'The Constitution', in John Coakley and Michael Gallagher (eds.), *Politics in the Republic of Ireland*, 3rd edn. London: Routledge.

—— and Uleri, Pier Vincenzo (eds.) (1996). *The Referendum Experience in Europe*. Houndmills: Macmillan.

Garrett, Geoffrey and Tsebelis, George (1999a). 'Why Resist the Temptation to Apply Power Indices to the European Union'. *Journal of Theoretical Politics*, 11: 291–308.

—— —— (1999b). 'More Reasons to Resist the Temptation of Power Indices in the European Union'. *Journal of Theoretical Politics*, 11: 331–8.

—— —— (2001). 'Even More Reason to Resist the Temptation of Power Indices in the EU'. *Journal of Theoretical Politics*, 13: 99–105.

Geddes, Barbara (1994). *Politician's Dilemma: Building State Capacity in Latin America*. Berkeley: University of California Press.

Gerber, Elisabeth R. (1999). *The Populist Paradox*. Princeton: Princeton University Press.

Hadenius, Axel (2001). *Demokrati—en jämförande analys*. Stockholm: Liber.

Hartmann, Jürgen and Kempf, Udo (1989). *Staatsoberhäupter in westlichen Demokratien*. Opladen: Westdeutscher Verlag.

Hine, David (1993). *Governing Italy*. Oxford. Oxford University Press.

Holmberg, Sören (2000). *Välja parti*. Stockholm: Norstedts Juridik.

Hosli, Madeleine O. (1996). 'Coalitions and Power: Effects of Qualified Majority Voting in the Council of the European Union'. *Journal of Common Market Studies*, 34: 255–73.

Iversen, Torben (1999). *Contested Economic Institutions*. Cambridge: Cambridge University Press.

Jenssen, Anders Todal (1999). 'All That is Solid Melts into Air: Party Identification in Norway'. *Scandinavian Political Studies*, 22: 1–27.

Kaltefleitner, Werner (1970). *Die Funktionen des Staatsoberhauptes in der parlamentarischen Demokratie*. Opladen: Westdeutscher Verlag.

Katz, Richard S. (1985). 'Measuring Party Identification with Eurobarometer Data: A Warning Note'. *West European Politics*, 8(1): 104–8.

Katzenstein, Peter (1985). *Small States in World Markets: Industrial Policy in Europe*. Ithaca: Cornell University Press.

Key, V. O. (1964). *Politics, Parties, and Pressure Groups*. New York: Crowell.

Kirchheimer, Otto (1966). 'The Transformation of the Western European Party Systems', in Joseph LaPalombara and Myron Weiner (eds.), *Political Parties and Political Development*. Princeton: Princeton University Press.

Kommers, Donald P. (1997). *The Constitutional Jurisprudence of the Federal Republic of Germany*, 2nd edn. Durham: Duke University Press.

Kristinsson, Gunnar Helgi (1996). 'Parties, States and Patronage'. *West European Politics*, 19(3): 433–57.

Landfried, Christine (1992). 'Federal Policy-Making in Germany: the Federal Constitutional Court'. *West European Politics*, 15(3): 50–67.

Lane, Jan-Erik and Ersson, Svante (1999). *Politics and Society in Western Europe*, 4th edn. London: Sage.

Lijphart, Arend (1977). *Democracy in Plural Societies*. New Haven: Yale University Press.

—— (1999). *Patterns of Democracy: Government Forms and Performance in Thirty-Six Countries*. New Haven: Yale University Press.

Linz, Juan J. and Alfred Stepan. (1996). *Problems of Democratic Transition and Consolidation*. Baltimore: Johns Hopkins University Press.

Lipset, Seymour Martin, and Rokkan, Stein (eds.) (1967). *Party Systems and Voter Alignments*. New York: Free Press.

Loveman, Brian (1993). *The Constitution of Tyranny: Regimes of Exception in Spanish America*. Pittsburgh: University of Pittsburgh Press.

Luther, Kurt Richard and Deschouwer, Kris (eds.) (1999). *Party Elites in Divided Societies*. London: Routledge.

Mack Smith, Denis (1997). *Modern Italy: A Political History*. Ann Arbor: University of Michigan Press.

Magone, José M. (2000). 'Portugal: The Rationale of Democratic Regime Building', in Wolfgang C. Müller and Kaare Strøm (eds.), *Coalition Governments in Western Europe*. Oxford: Oxford University Press.

Mair, Peter and van Biezen, Ingrid (2001). 'Party Membership in Twenty European Democracies, 1980–2000'. *Party Politics*, 7: 5–21.

——, Müller, Wolfgang C., and Plasser, Fritz (eds.) (1998). *Parteien auf komplexen Wählermärkten*. Vienna: Signum.

Manow, Philip (2002). 'Was erklärt politische Patronage in den Ländern Westeuropas? Defizite des politischen Wettbewerbs oder historisch-formative Phasen der Massendemokratisierung'. *Politische Vierteljahresschrift*, 43: 20–45.

Marks, Gary and Wilson, Carole J. (2000). 'The Past in the Present: A Cleavage Theory of Party Response to European Integration'. *British Journal of Political Science*, 30: 433–59.

McLean, Iain (1989). *Democracy and New Technology*. Cambridge: Polity Press.

Metcalf, Lee Kendall (2000). 'Measuring Presidential Power'. *Comparative Political Studies*, 33: 660–85.

Müller, Wolfgang C. (1998). 'Party Competition and Plebiscitary Politics in Austria'. *Electoral Studies*, 17: 21–43.

—— (1999). 'Plebiscitary Agenda-Setting and Party Strategies'. *Party Politics*, 5: 305–17.

—— (2000a). 'Political Parties in Parliamentary Democracies: Making Delegation and Accountability Work'. *European Journal of Political Research*, 37: 309–33.

—— (2000b). 'Patronage by National Governments', in Jean Blondel and Maurizio Cotta (eds.), *The Nature of Party Government*. Houndmills: Macmillan.

—— and Strøm, Kaare (eds.) (2000). *Coalition Governments in Western Europe*. Oxford: Oxford University Press.

Nelkin, David (1996a). 'A Legal Revolution? The Judges and Tangentopoli', in Stephen Gundle and Simon Parker (eds.), *The New Italian Republic*. London: Routledge.

—— (1996b). 'Stopping the Judges', in Mario Caciagli and David I. Kertzer (eds.), *Italian Politics. The Stalled Transition*. Boulder: Westview Press.

Nousiainen, Jakko (1998). *Suomen poliittinen järjestelmä*. Helsinki: WSOY.

—— (2000). 'Finland: The Consolidation of Parliamentary Governance', in Wolfgang C. Müller and Kaare Strøm (eds.), *Coalition Governments in Western Europe*. Oxford: Oxford University Press.

Nurmi, Hannu and Meskanen, Tommi (1999). 'A Priori Measures and the Institutions of the European Union'. *European Journal of Political Research*, 35: 161–79.

Page, Edward C. and Wright, Vincent (eds.) (1999). *Bureaucratic Élites in Western European States*. Oxford: Oxford University Press.

Pappalardo, Adriano (1981), 'The Conditions for Consociational Democracy: A Logical and Empirical Critique'. *European Journal of Political Research*, 4: 365–90.

Pasquino, Gianfranco and Vassallo, Salvatore (1995). 'The Government of Carlo Azeglio Ciampi', in Carol Mershon and Gianfranco Pasquino (eds.), *Italian Politics. Ending the First Republic*. Boulder: Westview Press.

Petersson, Olof, Hernes, Gudmund, Holmberg, Sören, Togeby, Lise, and Wängnerud, Lena (2000). *Demokratirådets rapport 2000: Demokrati utan partier?* Stockholm: SNS.

Powell, G. Bingham, Jr. (2000). *Elections as Instruments of Democracy. Majoritarian and Proportional Visions*. New Haven: Yale University Press.

Qvortrup, Mads (2000*a*). 'Checks and Balances in a Unicameral Parliament: The Case of the Danish Minority Referendum'. *Journal of Legislative Studies*, 6(3): 15–28.

—— (2000*b*). 'Are Referendums Controlled and Pro-hegemonic?' *Political Studies*, 48: 821–6.

Riker, William H. (1964). *Federalism: Origins, Operation, Significance*. Boston: Little, Brown.

—— (1975). 'Federalism', in Fred I. Greenstein and Nelson W. Polsby (eds.), *Handbook of Political Science. Volume 5. Governmental Institutions and Processes*. Reading, MA: Addison-Wesley.

Rothstein, Bo and Bergström, Jonas (1999). *Korporatismens fall och den svenska modellens kris*. Stockholm: SNS.

Scarrow, Susan (1996). *Parties and Their Members*. Oxford: Oxford University Press.

—— (1997). 'Party Competition and Institutional Change: The Expansion of Direct Democracy in Germany'. *Party Politics*, 3: 451–72.

—— (2000). 'Parties without Members?', in Russell J. Dalton and Martin P. Wattenberg (eds.), *Parties without Partisans*. Oxford: Oxford University Press.

Schlesinger, Joseph. A (1991). *Political Parties and the Winning of Office*. Ann Arbor: University of Michigan Press.

Schmidt, Vivien A. (1990). *Democratizing France*. Cambridge: Cambridge University Press.

Schmitt, Hermann and Holmberg, Sören (1995). 'Political Parties in Decline?', in Hans-Dieter Klingemann and Dieter Fuchs (eds.), *Citizens and the State*. Oxford: Oxford University Press.

Schmitter, Philippe C. (1974). 'Still the Century of Corporatism?' *Review of Politics*, 36: 85–131.

Setälä, Maija (1999). 'Referendums in Western Europe—A Wave of Direct Democracy'. *Scandinavian Political Studies*, 22: 327–40.

Share, Donald (1999). 'From Policy-Seeking to Office-Seeking: The Metamorphosis of the Spanish Socialist Workers Party', in Wolfgang C. Müller and Kaare Strøm (eds.), *Policy, Office, or Votes?* Cambridge: Cambridge University Press.

Shugart, Matthew Soberg and Carey, John M. (1992). *Presidents and Assemblies*. Cambridge: Cambridge University Press.

Smith, Gordon (1976). 'The Functional Properties of the Referendum'. *European Journal of Political Research*, 4: 1–23.

Sterett, Susan (1994). 'Judicial Review in Britain'. *Comparative Political Studies*, 26: 421–42.

Stone, Alec (1992). *The Birth of Judicial Politics in France. The Constitutional Council in Comparative Perspective*. Oxford: Oxford University Press.

Stone Sweet, Alec (2000). *Governing with Judges. Constitutional Politics in Europe*. Oxford: Oxford University Press.

Storey, Hugo (1995). 'Human Rights and the New Europe: Experience and Experiment'. *Political Studies* (Special Issue), 43: 131–51.

Strøm, Kaare (1990). *Minority Government and Majority Rule*. Cambridge: Cambridge University Press.

Strøm, Kaare (2000). 'Parties at the Core of Government', in Russell J. Dalton and Martin P. Wattenberg (eds.), *Parties without Partisans*. Oxford: Oxford University Press.

—— and Müller, Wolfgang C. (1999). 'The Keys to Togetherness: Coalition Agreements in Parliamentary Democracies'. *Journal of Legislative Studies*, 5(3–4): 255–82.

—— and Swindle, Stephen M. (2002). 'Strategic Parliamentary Dissolution'. *American Political Science Review*, 96: 575–91.

Tálos, Emmerich and Kittel, Bernhard (2001). *Gesetzgebung in Österreich*. Vienna: WUV-Facultas.

Tiebout, Charles M. (1956). 'A Pure Theory of Local Expenditures'. *Journal of Political Economy*, 64: 416–24.

Thiébault, Jean-Louis (2000). 'France: Forming and Maintaining Government Coalitions in the Fifth Republic', in Wolfgang C. Müller and Kaare Strøm (eds.), *Coalition Governments in Western Europe*. Oxford: Oxford University Press.

Treisman, Daniel (2000). 'The Causes of Corruption: A Cross-national Study'. *Journal of Public Economics*, 76: 399–457.

Tsebelis, George (2002). *Veto Players: How Political Institutions Work*. Princeton: Princeton University Press.

Van Koppen, Peter J. (1992). 'Judicial Policy-Making in the Netherlands: The Case-by-Case Method'. *West European Politics*, 15(3): 80–92.

Verzichelli, Luca and Cotta, Maurizio (2000). 'Italy: From "Constrained" Coalitions to Alternating Governments', in Wolfgang C. Müller and Kaare Strøm (eds.), *Coalition Governments in Western Europe*. Oxford: Oxford University Press.

Volcansek, Mary L. (2000). *Constitutional Politics in Italy. The Constitutional Court*. Houndmills: Macmillan.

Weingast, Barry R. (1995). 'The Economic Role of Political Institutions: Market-Preserving Federalism and Economic Development'. *Journal of Law, Economics, and Organization*, 11: 1–31.

Williamson, Peter J. (1989). *Corporatism in Perspective*. London: Sage.

Wright, Vincent (1999). 'The Fifth Republic: From the Droit de l'État to the État de droit?' *West European Politics*, 22(4): 92–119.

Zimmerman, Joseph S. (1997). *The Recall: Tribunal of the People*. Westport: Praeger.

23

Challenges to Parliamentary Democracy

KAARE STRØM, WOLFGANG C. MÜLLER, AND
TORBJÖRN BERGMAN

INTRODUCTION

In previous chapters we have examined, configuratively as well as cross-nationally, the successive stages in the constitutional chain of delegation and accountability of Western European parliamentary democracies. Throughout this book, we have deliberately addressed accountability as *a process of control* more than accountability as *an outcome (agency loss)*. Yet, both aspects are obviously important. Hence, in the first section of this chapter we take a closer look at democratic accountability outcomes. Subsequently, we draw together the main lessons of this study. In the third and final section, we conclude by placing our study in the context of current large-scale societal challenges. As we move from one section to another, we also move from specific to more general problems. In all three sections, we aim to facilitate further scholarship on a number of critical and still under-researched lines of inquiry.

UNDERSTANDING AGENCY LOSS

We begin with the perennial problem of agency loss. Agency loss is the damage suffered by a principal because an agent lacks the skill or incentives to complete the tasks delegated to him, or in other words the difference between the policy obtained through delegation and the principal's most desired (and feasible) outcome. Those who delegate hope that their transfer of authority will be successful, but all forms of delegation have their problems.

There are two basic ways in which agents can 'go wrong' and generate agency loss. They can be unable to satisfy the principal and/or they can be unwilling to do so. In the former case, the agent may simply be unfit, for example because the qualifications required for getting the job are systematically different from the demands of the job itself. Or perhaps the principal has inflated demands that no earthly agent could satisfy. For example, mass surveys often show that the typical voter at the same time favours larger government expenditures and lower taxes. There may indeed be a range of such circumstances in which, for no lack of trying, the agent is incapable of meeting the principal's demands. But just as importantly, agents may fail to satisfy the principal because they have their own goals and agendas. They may disagree with the principal about policy objectives, or about the costs they are willing to incur to reach these goals, or they may simply be more interested in their own private affairs.

In this section, we assess agency loss under parliamentary government in five problem areas: leisure shirking (though our discussion of this issue will be only preliminary), policy divergence, policy coordination, rent extraction, and satisfaction with democracy. Briefly put, leisure shirking means that the agent fails to achieve the best possible outcome for the principal due to a lack of effort. Policy divergence means that the agent pursues policies that differ from those that the principal most prefers. Policy coordination problems arise when agents make mutually conflicting decisions, or when the same agent makes inconsistent choices across policy areas or over time. Rent extraction means that the agent exploits his political authority to obtain private benefits for himself or others, rather than to further the principal's policy agenda. Finally, a low satisfaction with democracy simply means that, for whatever reason, the citizens are dissatisfied with their agents. This is our broadest and more encompassing measure, which serves to complement the previous and more specific ones. The level of popular satisfaction presumably reflects a bundle of different assessments, as well as the implicit citizen trade-offs between different values such as efficiency and accountability, and the historically conditioned performance expectations of citizens in particular polities.

There are two basic yardsticks for assessing the extent of agency loss. One is to compare the observed agency loss to some ideal analytical (or normative) standard, as we have done in Chapters 2 and 3. The other approach is empirical and comparative. In this chapter, we opt for the latter, comparative approach.

Our theoretical arguments in previous chapters generate two kinds of comparative expectations. On the one hand, we expect the agency problems of parliamentary democracies to differ systematically from such regime types as presidentialism. Thus we expect, based on the argument in Chapter 3, that in parliamentary systems, the problems of policy divergence and rent extraction will be more salient than those of leisure shirking and policy coordination. Its simplicity, and specifically the singularity of its constitutional design and the agenda control it vests in the cabinet, render parliamentary democracy susceptible to policy shirking and rent extraction. At the same time, the same features make parliamentary democracy decisive, which should enhance policy coordination, and incentive-efficient, which in turn should reduce the incidence of leisure shirking.

On the other hand, within the class of parliamentary systems, we also expect systematic differences corresponding to the design of mechanisms of citizen control. Not all parliamentary democracies have the same propensity for agency loss. Each country-specific chain of parliamentary policy-making has specific features that affect the principals' ability to select, monitor, or sanction agents and thereby also the amount of agency slippage. Since the combination of such factors is specific to each country, the variation in agency performance may well be larger within the worlds of parliamentarism and presidentialism, respectively, than between the two. We thus expect the severity of different agency problems to differ according to the particular design of the democratic chain of delegation and accountability, for example, the parliamentary oversight capabilities.

In this study, our focus is on performance differences among parliamentary systems. Although we in some contexts contrast parliamentary and presidential polities, our focal point below is clearly the variation among parliamentary systems. The problem with classical parliamentarism, as we have argued in previous chapters, is that 'internal' mechanisms of accountability are unlikely to be effective unless reinforced by at least one of two general mechanisms: (1) cohesive, competitive political parties, or (2) effective external constraints. Given the limitations of our data (see below), we shall in this section focus on the latter two mechanisms of citizen control. In general, we expect that, all else equal, the stronger and more competitive political parties are, and the more highly developed the institutions of external constraint, the smaller the overall observed agency losses. Yet, we do not necessarily expect these effects to be equally strong or uniform across the various dimensions of agency loss.

Below we confront these expectations with some simple and preliminary evidence on agency loss in parliamentary systems. For each measure of agency loss that we consider, we examine the effects of each of the two vehicles of citizen control (partisanship and constraint). We employ OLS regression analysis to probe into the empirical relationship between citizen control mechanisms (our independent variables) and the various expressions of agency loss (our dependent variables). Statistical techniques permit us to scrutinize the relationship between regime characteristics and agency loss more systematically than a simple descriptive account of the dependent variables would allow.

Our sample imposes severe restrictions. Although we have used what we consider to be the best available evidence, many of our theoretical concepts are inherently difficult to capture operationally. Thus, the preferences of neither principals nor agents are observable, and our informational assumptions are not easily verified, either. Another concern is that reliance on overly broad operationalizations of our explanatory variables might well obscure some of their critical effects. For example, while party cohesion in the cabinet may have salutary effects, we are not sure that a partisan civil service will have the same consequences. Consequently, rather than the summary indexes of partisan and external constraint influence derived in Chapter 22, we shall employ some of the indicators on which these dimensions are based.

Yet, we are severely limited in the extent to which we can thus disaggregate our analysis. With only seventeen national observations, our statistical estimates can be highly susceptible to any further loss of observations. Because of missing observations, some of the individual indicators accounted for in the previous chapter are therefore less suitable for our use, even if they are clearly defined and measured.

Our independent variables hence include two of the indicators that we judge to be the most important components of each of our two citizen control dimensions. For all four of these, we have complete cross-national data. To capture partisan influence we rely on the extent to which *non-governing parties* are represented in Parliament (Table 22.1) and the measure of *partisan conflict* (Table 22.4). The former variable captures the extent to which the political parties in that system are vehicles of policy cohesion in government, rather than, for example, protest movements. The higher the proportion of government-tested parties, the more likely it is that an alternative government could be formed among the opposition parties. Hence, we take this as a measure of the *competitiveness* of the party system. The greater the proportion of parties with cabinet experience, the more competitive the system. The other partisanship item is the proportion of cabinets that have dissolved because of intraparty or interparty conflicts, which serves as our measure of partisan *cohesion*. Note that we are concerned with partisanship in a broad sense, as homogeneity in observed behaviour, induced by electoral incentives, more than with formal organizational status.

Similarly, we include two measure of external constraint. The index of central bank autonomy is an obvious candidate to capture the *credibility* gains often associated with political constraint. Specifically, central bank independence is a vehicle for solving fiscal time-inconsistency problems. One problem with many such indices, however, is missing data, particularly for the smaller countries. Fortunately the Cukierman, Webb, and Neyapti (1994) index in Table 22.8 provides data for all our countries. Since the formation of a European Central Bank and the European Monetary Union (EMU) has imposed a transnational constraint on central banks, we have opted for central bank independence indicators for the period up to the early 1990s, when the coordination of these policies began in earnest. Our second external constraints measure is designed to tap the effects of intergovernmental *competition* and veto gates inherent in 'fiscal federalism'. The final independent variable, subnational government consumption from Table 22.5, thus measures the relative volumes of subnational versus national public spending. Thus, the former measure captures constraint as checks, the latter as partition.

Given our data limitations, we cannot control for anything like the range of exogenous variables that might affect the relationship between these institutional characteristics and agency loss. Therefore, we confine ourselves to two control variables whose face validity is particularly strong, namely the level of economic development and the national population size. There is a voluminous literature, beginning in its modern incarnation with Lipset (1959), that demonstrates the positive influences of economic development, which we measure conventionally as Gross Domestic Product (GDP) per capita, on democratic performance.

Development is likely to reduce democratic agency problems for at least two major reasons. First, economic development tends to generate a variety of economic opportunities outside the public sector and thus a host of more constructive alternatives to political rent seeking and leisure shirking (see below). Second, economic development tends to boost literacy and educational achievement, which enhances the information that citizens possess vis-à-vis their governors, and which in turn helps reduce the information asymmetries that are all too dramatic in many poor communities. More specifically, GDP is typically positively associated with citizen access to alternative sources of information and communication. Likewise, the 'political society' of nongovernmental organizations is likely to grow along with GDP. All of this allows more effective citizen participation and constrains the politicians' ability effectively to control the public agenda.

Our second control variable is population size, which we expect to be negatively correlated with most aspects of political performance. Because it hinges so much on the availability of information, agency control is easier in small and homogenous societies than in larger and more heterogeneous ones. A small society such as Iceland is much more likely to be politically transparent than for example India, which should make it systematically easier for principals to oversee their agents. Political philosophers going back to Plato and Aristotle have praised the governance virtues of smallness.[1] Although contemporary scholarship on the systemic effects of size has produced inconsistent results,[2] we find it plausible for size to affect agency loss, not least though its effects on informational transparency.

Our control measures in all the analyses below are therefore GDP per capita and population size (logged). While numerous other controls could be imagined, the size of our sample (seventeen countries at most) requires parsimony. Given this small sample size, and the fact that we essentially include the universe of stable European parliamentary systems, we also relax our expectations concerning statistical significance. As the degrees of freedom in our regression estimates can fall as low as ten (in the estimate of errors), it becomes very difficult to reach conventional levels of statistical confidence, and we shall comment on estimates that do not meet these standards but still seem substantively meaningful. Of course, readers can consult our results and judge for themselves how meaningful the various estimates are.

For each of our agency loss measures, we estimate six different models: one for each of our four citizen control variables entered separately, one in which we include all four of these plus our two control variables (population size and GDP per capita), and a final model (model six) in which we delete all variables that in the full model (model five) are not significant at the 0.1 level in a one-tailed test (or the 0.2 level in a two-tailed test). This corresponds to a t-statistic of 1.37 in a model with ten degrees of freedom (Gujarati 1995: 809).[3]

Leisure Shirking

Consider first the agency problem that is perhaps the most difficult to measure, and which we have decided not to pursue in quantitative terms, namely leisure shirking. Leisure shirking refers to situations in which the agent deliberately chooses not to exert the effort necessary to succeed. This may, of course, be because he prefers a quiet life of leisure to work. Putnam (1993: 5) describes the regional government of Puglia in southern Italy as staffed by prototypical leisure-shirking officials. Reportedly, the functionaries are 'indolent' and 'likely to be present an hour or two each day and to be unresponsive even then' and, as a local mayor has put it, 'they don't answer the mail, they don't answer the telephone'.

[1] In *Federalist* No. 10, however, Madison turned the argument on its head and argued that size, because it is associated with a greater variety of parties and interests, helps protect against majority tyranny.

[2] Dahl and Tufte (1973: 40) agree with Madison that increases in population size entail a greater number of organizations and subunits and a more complex policy-making process, but warn that other factors, such as socio-economic development, might interact. Political participation, or the citizens' sense of democratic efficacy, does not seem to vary cross-nationally (though possibly within countries) with size (Dahl and Tufte 1973: 65; see also Anckar 2000).

[3] In the estimates for two of our agency loss measures (Tables 23.2 and 23.4), model five has only one significant independent variable. In these cases, we do not report model six simply because it would be identical to one of the bivariate models.

Public officials in Southern Italy are not unique in this respect. The 'prevalence of absenteeism' in the French Parliament, as noted, for instance, by Anthony King (1976), is a closely related phenomenon. As *Le Monde* put it in the 1970s, some MPs arrive from the provinces Wednesday morning and go home Thursday night. Not much seems to have changed since these lines were written (Knapp and Wright 2001: 147). Absenteeism has been a frequent phenomenon in Italy, too (Hine 1993: 170), and it seems to be even more widespread in the European Parliament (Nugent 1999: 240).

Yet, low attendance rates need not be an indicator of leisure shirking in the narrow sense. Many MPs serve large and distant constituencies. Very often French MPs have been mayors who have devoted their time and energy to local rather than national politics. Moreover, a study of the Austrian Parliament shows that those MPs who are neither very active in Parliament nor in constituency work often have other demanding obligations, for example, as interest group representatives (Müller *et al.* 2001). Thus, when public officials shirk some political responsibilities, it may be because they are attending to others.

Nonetheless, these multiple demands on the time of MPs mean that they are not fully living up to the obligations resulting from their role in the parliamentary chain of delegation while typically still getting full financial compensation. It is also noteworthy that the most notorious cases of political leisure shirking are found in constituencies with low political transparency (as in the European Parliament), ineffective interparty competition (as in most of the Italian south), or both.

Leisure shirking is in many cases an individual-level phenomenon without great political ramifications. As with many forms of democratic agency loss, it may be particularly prominent in less transparent societies where citizens have little information about their public officials. It is perhaps most politically troubling when coupled with a clientelistic network of rent extraction, for example, when public officials shirk because their appointments were never based on any consideration of their qualifications in the first place. Yet, important as it may be, we have only scarce and anecdotal information on leisure shirking by public officials and hence cannot attempt to assess its relative incidence or importance in the countries under scrutiny in this volume. This again underscores how empirically under-researched this phenomenon is. As Chapter 3 has argued, due to the efficiency of individual incentive schemes, leisure shirking should be less prevalent in parliamentary systems (particularly Westminster systems) than in presidential ones. That is to say, because politicians in parliamentary systems are less constrained, they should also be less tempted to slack off. Because of the asymmetries of information, we expect that leisure shirking is also more characteristic of poor and diverse societies than of relatively smaller states boasting high levels of public information. While certainly a relevant concern even in Western Europe, we suspect that it is not the region's most critical agency problem.

Policy Divergence

Policy (or dissent) shirking means that the agent is implementing policies that are not in line with the preferences of the principal not for lack of effort, but because the agent pursues his own policy objectives that differ from those of the principal. This is certainly a common complaint among citizens: that politicians, rather than being lazy or incompetent, have their own policy agendas and ignore those of the voters. Yet, while this has also been a concern among political scientists of many stripes, empirical documentation of such slack has been a stubborn problem. While analytically we can distinguish agency loss that occurs because of constraint from cases due to either laziness or wilful shirking on the agent's part, these phenomena are often indistinguishable to the observer. Thus, while we may be able to identify policy divergence between principal and agent, we cannot always tell whether it is due to shirking on the latter's part.

One approach has been to identify specific commitments that particular governments have made to their voters and then examine, often in case studies, whether such 'pledges' are indeed kept (Rose 1984). This research points to considerable variation between governments.[4] A second approach has been to examine the policy process in more aggregated and often comparative terms and investigate whether variation in partisan control of the government (or parliament) can systematically be linked to differences in policy output (e.g. see Castles 1982; Boix 1998; Garrett 1998).

As a rule in such studies, however, the parties' differential policy preferences are *assumed* rather than empirically established. Typically, authors assume that parties of the left, for example, care more about fighting unemployment than about inflation, more about providing services than about balancing budgets, more about social welfare than national defence, more about redistribution than about tax relief. While all these assumptions may on the whole be correct, they remain rather stylized depictions of political parties, and authors in this tradition rarely actually examine the kind of 'contracts' that parties offer the voters. Klingemann, Hofferbert, and Budge (1993) seek to merge these two traditions by first identifying government budget priorities from party manifestoes and then investigating the impact of such programmatic concerns on budgetary allocations. Although their research design has been controversial (Laver and Garry 2000), they report significant cross-national differences.

A fourth approach, which has become increasingly common since the mid-1980s, is to measure policy divergence between voters and governments based on expert or mass survey placements on standardized policy scales. In one of the most notable exemplars of this tradition, Powell (2000) measures the ideological distance between government and citizens on a ten-point left–right scale (see Table 23.1). While each

---

[4] Often researchers have looked to election platforms ('manifestoes' in British parlance) to identify such policy commitments. The differences between governments in pledge fulfilment are enormous. There are cases such as the Thatcher government that have a remarkable record of implementing fairly radical programmes. Even with regard to these governments, however, careful observers can identify policy sectors (such as the containment of social welfare expenditures) in which the government (for better or worse) backed away from its initial policy commitments. On the other hand, some governments clearly and visibly abandon their manifesto promises. The Spanish Socialists (PSOE) of the 1980s promised Keynesian economic stimulation, significant income redistribution, vastly increased social expenditures, and withdrawal from NATO. Once in power, the PSOE abandoned each of these commitments. Share (1999: 97) speaks of a 'blatant abandonment of the 1982 electoral pledges'. Yet, both governments were returned to office several times and Mrs Thatcher and Mr Gonzalez went on to become particularly long-lived Prime Ministers. Thus, it is not obvious that religious commitment to campaign promises is critical to retrospective voter assessments.

Table 23.1. *Policy Distance Between Government and Median Citizen in Western Europe*

Country	Distance between government and median citizen		
	Early 1980s	Early 1990s	Mean distance
Austria	—	1.0	1.0
Belgium	1.3	0.4	0.85
Denmark	1.1	2.3	1.7
Finland	0.8	1.2	1.0
France	1.6	2.5	2.05
Germany	1.7	0.9	1.3
Greece	0.7	0.6	0.65*
Ireland	0.4	0.2	0.3
Italy	0.8	1.2	1.0
Netherlands	1.4	0.2	0.8
Norway	2.3	1.0	1.65
Portugal	1.6	2.2	1.9*
Spain	0.1	0.4	0.25
Sweden	1.7	1.6	1.65
UK	2.3	2.4	2.35
Mean	1.3	1.2	

Note: Mean of citizen self-placement for Greece and Portugal. Powell (2000) compares voter self-placements with expert placements of political parties. Since we lack expert placements for Greece and Portugal for three of the four periods we use voter placements of political parties. The asterisk (*) signifies that these are our calculations of the average difference, not Powell's.

Source: Powell 2000: 180–1, 184–5; Gunther and Montero 2001: 104, 107.

placement on this scale may well mean different policies in different countries, it at least allows comparison of citizen preferences with those of the parties competing in the same country. The closer the citizens and government parties are on this scale, the more successfully elections generate *representational congruence* (2000: 163). Powell places parties on this scale with the help of expert surveys, and citizens by their self-placement in mass surveys (see Table 23.1).

We have added Greece and Portugal to the data provided by Powell (2000), leaving out only the two smallest states in our investigation, Iceland and Luxembourg. Since these countries are not included in the expert surveys used by Powell (2000), namely Castles and Mair (1984) and Huber and Inglehart (1995), our data for Greece and Portugal are not identical to those for the other countries. Greece and Portugal are represented by the mean (rather than the median) citizen self-placement, and the positions of the government parties are inferred from voter rather than expert placements.[5]

---

[5] Voters and experts do not always place parties fully consistently. Thus, in the early 1990s the Portuguese government party, the PSD, was rated 6.4 on the left–right scale by experts but 7.7 by voters (Huber and Inglehart 1995; Gunther and Montero 2001). Yet, other party placements show much greater consistency between experts and voters. Thus, the Spanish PSOE was placed at 3.6 by experts and 3.9 by voters in the early 1980s, and at 4.0 by experts and at 4.3 by voters in the early 1990s. On the whole, the country-specific data tend to be consistent over time.

Powell's normative yardstick is the absolute policy distance between the government and the median voter, who represents 'the only policy that would be preferred to all others by a majority of voters' (2000: 163). In his calculation of government positions, Powell weights parties by their numbers of seats and reports two figures for each country: one representing the early 1980s and the other the early 1990s. In our sample, the countries included in Table 23.1 range from a smallest observed distance of 0.1 points to a maximum of 2.5. Among the fourteen countries for which we have data for both periods, Greece, Ireland, and Spain consistently exhibit low policy distance, whereas France, Portugal, and the United Kingdom are at the opposite end of the scale. We find no temporal trend in policy divergence. From the 1980s to the 1990s, policy divergence increased in Denmark and France but decreased in The Netherlands and Norway. In aggregate (giving equal weight to each country), there is almost no difference in representational congruence between the early 1980s and the early 1990s.

In Table 23.2, we present a standardized set of regressions results with this measure of policy divergence (government–citizen policy distance) as the dependent variable.

Table 23.2. *OLS Regressions on Government–Citizen Policy Distance*

Independent variables	Model 1	Model 2	Model 3	Model 4	Model 5
Dimensions of citizen control					
Non-governing parties	−0.01				0.00
(seats in Parliament)	(0.02)				(0.02)
Party conflict		−1.39			−2.19*
		(1.11)			(1.48)
Central bank			−0.53		−0.72
independence			(1.38)		(1.74)
Sub-national				−0.01	−0.02
government				(0.01)	(0.02)
consumption					
Control variables					
Population (logged)					0.18
					(0.24)
GDP per capita (logged)					0.53
(thousands US$)					(1.97)
Constant	1.29***	1.65***	1.40**	1.53**	−5.33
	(0.36)	(0.41)	(0.55)	(0.68)	(20.91)
R-squared	0.01	0.11	0.01	0.02	0.28
Adj. R-squared	−0.07	0.04	−0.06	−0.06	−0.27
N	15	15	15	15	15

Notes: Table does not include Iceland and Luxembourg.
*** $p < 0.01$; ** $p < 0.05$; * $p < 0.1$ (one-tailed tests).
Standard errors in parentheses.

Sources: Government–citizen distance: Table 23.1; Central Bank Independence: Cukierman, Webb, and Neyapti (1994), Table 22.4 (1980–9); Other dimensions of control: Chapter 22; Control variables: World Development Indicators, http://www.worldbank.org/data/.

The independent variables in the first four models include our four indicators of citizen control entered separately. The fifth specification includes all these measures simultaneously and adds our two control variables (population and GDP per capita).

Although strong mechanisms of citizen control should generally have desirable effects, it is not clear that we should expect them to be associated with low policy divergence. As Chapter 3 has shown, policy divergence can be relatively large in pure Westminster systems, as strong and cohesive parties allow even non-centrist cabinets to dominate policy-making. And while strong external constraints can pull government policy in particular directions, this pull will not always be centrist. Activist courts, for example, are likely to have civil libertarian commitments that may or may not mirror those of the median voter. And independent central banks may not favour popular preferences for cheap money.

The results in Table 23.2 display only a weak linear relationship between our two citizen control dimensions (party influence and external constraints) and voter–government policy distance. The only one of our four indicators that in the full model registers a statistically significant effect is party cohesion. Thus, systems with significant intra-cabinet conflict (low executive cohesion) have governments closer to their median voters. Also, external constraints are consistently negatively related to policy divergence (i.e. strong constraints are associated with governments that are close to their voters), but these effects are statistically insignificant. Moreover, statistically speaking no specification of the model has any meaningful explanatory power. Thus, in sum the strength of citizen control mechanisms has little discernible impact on the policy divergence between voters and politicians.

Weak as our results are, they are at least minimally consistent with Powell's (2000) finding that policy divergence is comparatively higher in majoritarian than in consensus democracies. Majoritarian systems tend to score low on our measure of party conflict (see Chapter 22), which means that all else equal they should also exhibit greater policy divergence. Majoritarian designs tend to harbour fewer conflicts within the cabinet but can also mean a larger policy distance between governments and citizens. But note that this test considers only the absolute policy distance between citizens and governments, and not the direction of this distance. In other words, we have considered only the problem of representative efficiency, but not that of *bias* (see Chapter 3). In a one-shot setting, of course, efficiency is simply the absolute value of bias, and a priori there seems to be no reason to prefer, say, a rightward deviation to a leftward one. Hence, a simple focus on efficiency seems entirely appropriate.

If, however, we consider policy divergence in a particular polity over time, there is much to be said for also considering direction, or what we have referred to in Chapter 3 as bias. For example, is it better always to have a modest, but directionally consistent distance between citizens and governors (e.g. because the government is consistently slightly to the left of the median voter), or would we prefer a government that tends to be a bit more distant (less *efficient* in the terminology introduced in Chapter 3) but less biased, in the sense that its occupants alternate between being to the left of the median voter and being to the right? Someone that prefers the latter may take a more favourable view of alternational party systems (such as the British one, or the French), compared with pivotal ones (such as Italy 1945–92 or Belgium). In alternational systems, policy divergence at any one time may be substantial, but at least the direction of this slippage varies over time. Thus, in the early 1980s left-wing British voters may have felt as distant from their national government as conservative French voters felt from theirs, but two decades later at least the tables in both places had been turned. In pivotal systems, efficiency may be greater but bias more consistent. For close to a half-century after Second War, Italian voters not enamoured with Christian Democracy had little to be hopeful about. And although on economic issues, the Italian Christian Democrats were probably a good deal closer to the median voter than either Thatcher or the early Mitterrand, Italians who cared greatly about other policy dimensions, such as family policy or clericalism, could understandably feel that they were forever saddled with a national government that represented their interests very poorly.

Policy Coordination

Agents can fail their principals not only by pursuing policy positions at odds with them, but also by failing to coordinate their various policy positions in a productive fashion. There are, of course, many ways in which policy coordination can fail: mutually contradictory decisions may be taken on related issues, government revenues and expenditures may be out of synchronization, decisions taken one day may counteract those adopted the day before.

In this subsection we shall focus on one particularly salient and relatively well-researched topic, namely budgetary policy coordination. One of the benchmarks of such coordination is fiscal discipline, which we here take to mean the avoidance of any build-up of government debt. While there may be circumstances in which it is in the short run desirable, or at least not particularly troubling, to operate a government without a balanced budget, there is ample reason to worry about the accumulation of budget deficits and the long-term build-up of public debt. Specifically, government borrowing drives up interest rates and hence 'crowds out' productive private sector investments, adversely affecting economic growth.[6] Moreover, public borrowing may have redistributive effects, causing long-term income transfers from taxpayers to the holders of government bonds. Finally, excessive debt burdens can impair the government's capacity to make short-term interventions in the economy even when otherwise this would be beneficial, for example to smooth a sudden downturn in the business cycle (Franzese 2002: 51).

Thus, in most cases the accumulation of public debt is due to government weakness and myopia and points to a lack of coordination. It therefore serves as our measure of policy coordination. Mounting levels of public debt have been a serious concern in many developing countries, as well as not a few prosperous European ones. Indeed, concern with fiscal indiscipline was sufficient to cause the leaders of the European Union to build fairly restrictive (albeit, as time has shown, not terribly enforceable) requirements into the Maastricht Treaty that paved the way for the EMU.

---

[6] See Franzese (2002: 50–1) for a theoretical discussion of the crowding-out thesis.

There is ample reason to believe that institutional design matters to fiscal perform-ance. Thus, Persson and Tabellini (2000: 345) note that 'political and institutional fac-tors play an important role in shaping public debt policy'. The causes of high public debt levels may include political instability, that is, frequent turnover in government, which can have at least three detrimental effects. First, incumbents that feel threatened are likely to resort to government borrowing to 'create a constituency for re-election'. Second, the costs of future spending cuts are not fully internalized by the political decision-makers because they have good reason to assume that they will no longer be in office when these costs come due. Third, incumbents who assume that they will not be returned to office may attempt to pre-empt the spending decisions of incoming governments by leaving them nothing but debt (Persson and Tabellini 2000: ch. 13; see also Franzese 2002: ch. 3).

These institutional explanations relate partly to the agents' inability and partly to their lack of willingness to avoid accumulating government debt. Either way, we inter-pret them as shortcomings in citizen control of their political agents. The ill effects of instability can most effectively be counteracted if political agents can be induced to adopt longer time horizons, or (second-best) if they can be constrained from acting on their short-term interests. Stable, encompassing, and cohesive political parties are one vehicle by which politicians may be induced to extend their time horizons. Institutional features may similarly shift their focus to future concerns or at least prevent them from acting solely on their contemporaneous ones. Thus, although the effects of political instability afflict both parliamentary and presidential regimes, the fixed electoral terms of the latter make them somewhat less vulnerable to short-term opportunism. Moreover, Persson, Roland, and Tabellini (2000) argue that because they have more cohesive gov-ernment structures that contain fewer checks against spending increases, parliamentary democracies are more prone to overspending than are presidential ones.

Our main concern here, however, is with the variation that might exist among parlia-mentary systems. Thus, we expect fiscal discipline to be positively correlated with both dimensions of citizen control. Party influence should serve as at least a partial protec-tion against the ills of government instability and opportunism, and external constraints should strengthen government credibility. Of course, central bank independence is typ-ically adopted expressly for the purpose of mitigating some of these parliamentary credibility problems. Fiscal federalism may have similar effects, as it constrains the spending power of central governments, and since sub-national governments are often subject to more effective fiscal restrictions than national ones.

Our operational measure of budgetary coordination is the level of public debt in 1992, the period just before the European Union's transnational commitments to fiscal recti-tude began to take effect. There was considerable variation in government indebtedness among West European parliamentary systems. As Table 23.3 shows, Luxembourg had a very small debt in relation to its GDP. For nine of the other countries, however, the debt was greater than half of GDP. Among these, Belgium and Italy both had staggering debts well above the value of their entire GDP (see Franzese 2002: 25).

Table 23.4 reports the relationships between our measures of citizen control and pub-lic debt. Of the four independent variables, party conflict is by far the most influential

Table 23.3. *Public Debt (as a Percentage of GDP) in Western European Parliamentary Democracies, 1992*

Country	Public Debt (percent of GDP)*
Austria	58
Belgium	129
Denmark	71
Finland	41
France	46
Germany	44
Greece	99
Iceland	47
Ireland	94
Italy	118
Luxembourg	5
The Netherlands	80
Norway	36
Portugal	60
Spain	54
Sweden	71
UK	47

Source: OECD Economic Outlook, June 1999. Luxembourg data from Eurostat: http://europa.eu.int/comm/eurostat/Public/datashop/print-product/EN? catalogue=Eu.

Note: *Central government gross financial liabilities as a percentage of GDP, 1992.

determinant. When entered separately, party conflict alone explains half of the cross-national variation in public debt. The full model confirms the same pattern. Moreover, adding other explanatory variables only weakens the adjusted coefficient of determination. Thus, cabinet cohesion powerfully constrains fiscal indiscipline and is far and away our most powerful predictor. The effect of party competition (our first indicator in the model) is in the same direction, but statistically insignificant.

Unexpectedly, external constraints such as Central bank independence and fiscal federalism have much weaker and less consistent effects. When entered separately, both have the expected negative associations with public debt, but neither effect is close to significance. In the full model, however, the effect of central bank independence is reversed, though still insignificant. Thus, when other effects are accounted for, central bank autonomy is counter-intuitively associated with high (rather than low) levels of public debt! We can only suggest two factors that may account for this surprising result (but note again the lack of statistical significance). One is that in some countries (the United Kingdom and Norway, for example) co-partisanship alone long sufficed to discipline politicians. Thus, until the late 1990s strong fiscal discipline in these countries coexisted with very weak central banks. A second possibility, which is not inconsistent with the first, is endogeneity: perhaps central bank reform is disproportionately likely

Table 23.4. *OLS Regressions on Public Debt (as a Percentage of GDP)*

Independent variables	Model 1	Model 2	Model 3	Model 4	Model 5
Dimensions of citizen control					
Non-governing parties,	0.50				0.57
(seats in Parliament)	(0.61)				(0.49)
Party conflict		120.08***			108.61***
		(27.37)			(34.73)
Central bank			−5.00		41.04
independence			(53.04)		(43.19)
Subnational				−0.30	−0.19
government				(0.43)	(0.38)
consumption					
Control variables					
Population (logged)					2.59
					(5.07)
GDP per capita (logged)					−17.03
(thousands US$)					(35.51)
Constant	55.93***	29.25***	65.53**	80.19***	148.13
	(13.15)	(9.62)	(20.86)	(23.89)	(408.90)
R-squared	0.04	0.56	0.00	0.03	0.66
Adj. R-squared	−0.02	0.53	−0.07	−0.03	0.46
N	17	17	17	17	17

Standard errors in parentheses.

Notes: ***$p < 0.01$; **$p < 0.05$; *$p < 0.1$ (one-tailed tests).

Sources: Debt: For the year 1992, OECD Economic Outlook, June 1999. Luxembourg data on debt comes from Eurostat: http://europa.eu.int/comm/eurostat/Public/datashop/print-product/EN?catalogue=Eurostat&product=1-eb070-EN&mode=download; Central bank independence: Cukierman, Webb, and Neyapti (1994), Table 22.4 (1980–9); Other dimensions of control: Chapter 22; Control variables: World Development Indicators, http://www.worldbank.org/data/.

precisely in countries that have experienced some serious fiscal indiscipline. If this is true, then we must be careful not to mistake cause for effect. Our data do not permit us to examine these possibilities more closely, and we shall therefore close on our main result in this section: we find significant evidence that policy coordination (here: fiscal discipline) can be promoted by party cohesion, but much less reason to draw any conclusion about the effects of external constraints.

Political Rent Extraction

It is easy to think about agency loss that takes the form of ineffective agents: politicians that fail to do what the principal would have most preferred. Yet, sometimes the problem is that agents do too much, rather than too little. A classical problem in modern government is to keep political offices from degenerating into havens for those who most ardently seek power for the sake of self-enrichment. We refer to such action generally as rent extraction.[7] Since rent extraction is generally considered suspect, if not illegal, it is typically concealed. As Djankov *et al.* (2000: 17) note, 'Measuring rents is inherently extremely difficult, especially across countries.' Yet, rent seeking is a massive problem worldwide. Various studies have estimated that in some countries such distortions may account for up to 50 per cent of GDP (for reviews see Tollison 1997; Mueller 2004).

Much rent extraction occurs through government regulatory activities. Even though in recent years market imperatives have become much more important in the countries included in this study, government intervention for the purpose of redistributing wealth to political allies is still rampant in many societies. It has been argued, for instance, that not only in Russia and the former Soviet bloc, but also in Western democracies, industrial privatization has been carried out in ways that have systematically benefited entrepreneurs aligned with the incumbent governments (Feigenbaum, Henig, and Hamnett 1999).

One notorious avenue of rent extraction has gone through government control of market entry. Government regulation of entry is, in principle, compatible with a number of theories about the role of government. It could function as a protection for consumers against predatory competition (which Shleifer and Vishny 1998, refer to as the 'helping hand' theory), it could be a way for powerful interests to erect barriers against competitors (the 'grabbing hand' theory) (Stigler 1971), or it could be a way for ambitious politicians to milk affected interests for 'contributions' (the 'tollbooth' theory) (Shleifer and Vishny 1998).

Empirically, Djankov *et al.* (2000) have marshalled evidence on market entry regulation in seventy-five countries, seeking to ascertain how easy or difficult market entry (i.e. starting a new firm) is and to establish the economic, social, and political causes of the cross-national differences. Their indicators of regulation are the number of bureaucratic procedures that have to be completed in starting a new business (which in their sample range from two to twenty overall), the number of workdays that have to be spent (from 2 to 174), and the overall costs involved, measured relative to annual per capita GDP (from 0.4 to 260 per cent).

Examining a wide range of policy output variables, the authors find that stricter regulation of entry is not associated with higher-quality products or with better pollution or health outcomes. Hence, the data do not support a 'helping-hand' view of entry regulation. Nor do the authors find higher levels of regulation to be associated with greater profits or with impediments to competition. Hence, the evidence does not support the 'grabbing-hand' view, either. Yet, Djankov and associates do find stricter regulation to be positively associated with corruption as well as with the size of the unofficial economy. These results support the *tollbooth view* of regulation, which, as the authors put it, means that politicians and bureaucrats themselves are the beneficiaries of the market distortions they introduce, because they receive campaign contributions, other 'favours' (for instance, jobs put at their disposal to be allocated according to political criteria), or bribes.

---

[7] Rent extraction is based on distortions of the market–government intervention that cannot be justified as a remedy for market failure (e.g. see Mueller 1996: 11).

Among the countries included in *Delegation and Accountability in Parliamentary Democracies*, differences in entry regulation exist and are in some cases considerable. The number of bureaucratic procedures ranges from four to sixteen, the number of work days required from 11 to 154, and the costs involved in starting a new business from 0.1 to 0.48 per cent of per capita GDP. And for the fifteen countries on which we have data, the bivariate (Pearson) correlations between the three measures are all significant (at the 0.05 level) and vary between 0.64 and 0.75. Thus, these measures consistently indicate significant and systematic variation in entry regulation even within Western Europe.

One particularly serious form of rent extraction is corruption—the trading of public benefits for private favours. Corruption has many causes (e.g. see Rose-Ackerman 1999; Treisman 2000). It may be a product of adverse selection as well as moral hazard, as some corrupt officer-holders may have intended all along to abuse their power for venal purposes, whereas others probably at the outset had more admirable ambitions.[8] The opportunity costs for public officials certainly seem to be a critical factor: where the alternatives are plentiful and yield acceptable rewards, corruption is likely to be less prevalent. This problem is particularly severe in societies in which the public sector is the only, or dominant, avenue for social betterment. The great prevalence of corruption, particularly (but certainly not exclusively) in poor societies, is a sad testament to the power of these forces (see Ridley and Doig 1995; Della Porta and Mény 1997; Rose-Ackerman 1999).

Table 23.5 summarizes our data on entry regulations and corruption for the seventeen countries in our sample. The first two columns present each country's score for 1998 and 2000 on the Corruption Perceptions Index developed by Transparency International. The last three columns present three operationalizations of entry regulations: the number of procedures required to start a new business, the time spent in days, and the costs in percent of GDP per capita. For comparative purposes, Table 23.5 also contains entries for five other Western democracies, three of which are parliamentary (Australia, Canada, and New Zealand), one the archetypical presidential system (United States), and the final one Switzerland with its unique directorial government.

As suggested by Table 23.5, political regulation of economic entrepreneurship is more extensive in Austria, France, Greece, Italy, Portugal, and Spain than in Denmark, Finland, Sweden, and the United Kingdom, to list those countries that score most consistently on the various indicators. In line with these results, Djankov *et al.* (2000) find that countries with more open access to political power, greater constraints on the executive, and greater political rights have fewer entry regulations. Yet, political rent extraction is not the only possible explanation for the differences recorded. Differences in legal traditions appear to have a strong impact, with English or Scandinavian legal origin leading to fewer regulations than French or German origin.

---

[8] As we have pointed out in previous chapters, the adverse selection problem is that powerful government offices may attract particularly power-hungry aspirants. The moral hazard problem is that agents controlling a large and powerful government may be tempted secretly to use these resources for purposes that the principal never intended and would not have approved.

Table 23.5. *Political Corruption and Rent Extraction*

Country	Corruption Perceptions Index (CPI) 1998 (from 1 to 10; 10 = clean)	CPI 2000	Entry regulation		
			Number of procedures	Time in days	Costs in % of GDP per capita
Austria	7.5 (11)	7.7 (9)	12 (12)	154 (15)	0.45 (14)
Belgium	5.4 (15)	6.1 (15)	8 (8)	42 (7)	0.10 (7)
Denmark	10.0 (1)	9.8 (2)	5 (4)	21 (3)	0.01 (3)
Finland	9.6 (2)	10.0 (1)	4 (1)	32 (6)	0.01 (2)
France	6.7 (12)	6.7 (13)	16 (15)	66 (9)	0.20 (11)
Germany	7.9 (10)	7.6 (10)	7 (6)	90 (12)	0.09 (6)
Greece	4.9 (16)	4.9 (16)	13 (14)	53 (8)	0.48 (15)
Iceland	9.3 (4)	9.1 (4)	n.d.	n.d.	n.d.
Ireland	8.2 (9)	7.2 (11)	4 (1)	25 (5)	0.11 (8)
Italy	4.6 (17)	4.6 (17)	11 (10)	121 (14)	0.25 (12)
Luxembourg	8.7 (7)	8.6 (8)	n.d.	n.d.	n.d.
The Netherlands	9.0 (5)	8.9 (6)	8 (8)	68 (10)	0.19 (10)
Norway	9.0 (5)	9.1 (4)	6 (5)	23 (4)	0.02 (4)
Portugal	6.5 (13)	6.4 (14)	12 (12)	99 (13)	0.31 (13)
Spain	6.1 (14)	7.0 (12)	11 (10)	83 (11)	0.13 (9)
Sweden	9.5 (3)	9.4 (3)	4 (1)	17 (2)	0.03 (5)
United Kingdom	8.7 (7)	8.7 (7)	7 (6)	11 (1)	0.01 (1)
Australia	8.7	8.3	3	3	0.02
Canada	9.2	9.2	2	2	0.01
New Zealand	9.4	9.4	3	17	0
Switzerland	8.9	8.6	12	88	0.13
United States	7.5	7.8	4	7	0.01

Note: n.d. = no data available; ranks in parentheses.

Sources: Corruption indexes: Transparency International (TI) http://www.gwdg.de.
Entry regulations: Djankov *et al.* 2000.

There are strong cross-national correlations between entry regulation and corruption. Countries deemed to be most corrupt are also much the same that have the most restrictive entry regulation. For two entry measures, procedures and costs, there is a high and statistically significant correlation (−0.69 and −0.67, respectively) with the TI corruption index. (The coefficients are negative because in the TI index high scores mean low corruption.)[9] Yet, there are certainly individual exceptions. On two of three indicators, the United Kingdom is the least regulated of our countries, whereas it is not rated as exceptionally 'clean'. Austria and The Netherlands, on the other hand, appear

---

[9] Political corruption (the 2000 index) co-varies least strongly with the measure for entry regulations in days. The correlation is −0.5 and barely significant at the 0.05 level (0.054).

more regulated than corrupt, whereas the Belgian case is the opposite. Switzerland is similar to The Netherlands: it has about the average level of perceived corruption, but demands much more of a start-up firm. The former 'old dominions' present a pattern similar to Britain: comparatively clean (more so than Britain, actually) and modestly regulated. By European standards, the United States is a middling country in perceived corruption, but the regulatory burden on small businesses is light. Compare Austria and the United States. They are almost identical with respect to perceived corruption, yet the differences in market entry are enormous, with the regulatory process lasting only 7 days in the United States, as against 154 days in Austria. If rent extraction is more directly reflected in market regulations than in societal corruption, then such practices appear to be much more prevalent in Austrian politics than they are in the United States.

In Table 23.6 we examine the predictors of rent extraction as measured by the percent of per-capita GDP required to start a new business. Generally, external constraints have important and notable effects. Yet, our two measures of external constraints point in different directions. While central bank independence seems to

Table 23.6. *OLS Regressions on Entry Regulation (as a Percentage of GDP)*

Independent variables	Model 1	Model 2	Model 3	Model 4	Model 5	Model 6
Dimensions of citizen control						
Non-governing parties	0.00				0.004*	0.004*
(seats in Parliament)	(0.00)				(0.003)	(0.002)
Party conflict		0.12			0.06	
		(0.22)			(0.19)	
Central bank			0.42**		0.57**	0.64***
independence			(0.24)		(0.22)	(0.19)
Subnational				−0.003*	−0.004*	−0.005***
government				(0.002)	(0.002)	(0.002)
consumption						
Control variables						
Population (logged)					0.00	
					(0.03)	
GDP per capita (logged)					−0.25	
(thousands US$)					(0.25)	
Constant	0.14**	0.12*	0.01	0.35***	2.59	0.16*
	(0.07)	(0.08)	(0.09)	(0.12)	(2.70)	(0.10)
R-squared	0.01	0.02	0.20	0.18	0.66	0.61
Adj. R-squared	−0.06	−0.05	0.13	0.11	0.41	0.51
N	15	15	15	15	15	15

Standard errors in parentheses.
Notes: Table does not include Iceland and Luxembourg.
***$p < 0.01$; **$p < 0.05$; *$p < 0.1$ (one-tailed tests)

Sources: Entry regulation: Table 23.5; Central bank independence: Cukierman, Webb, and Neyapti (1994), Table 22.4 (1980–9); Other dimensions of control: Chapter 22; Control variables: World Development Indicators, http://www.worldbank.org/data/

Table 23.7. *OLS Regressions on the Corruption Perceptions Index (2000)*

Independent variables	Model 1	Model 2	Model 3	Model 4	Model 5	Model 6
Dimensions of citizen control						
Non-governing parties	0.00				−0.02	
(seats in Parliament)	(0.03)				(0.02)	
Party Conflict		−4.90***			−3.35**	−3.63**
		(1.75)			(1.70)	(1.52)
Central bank			−0.44		−3.45*	−3.18*
independence			(2.77)		(2.11)	(1.87)
Subnational				0.04**	0.05***	0.05**
government				(0.02)	(0.02)	(0.02)
consumption						
Control variables						
Population (logged)					−0.51**	−0.43**
					(0.25)	(0.18)
GDP per capita (logged)					−0.13	
(thousands US$)					(1.74)	
Constant	7.72***	9.20***	7.91***	5.69***	17.09	14.47***
	(0.70)	(0.61)	(1.09)	(1.13)	(19.98)	(2.76)
R-squared	0.00	0.34	0.00	0.20	0.70	0.68
Adj. *R*-squared	−0.07	0.30	−0.06	0.14	0.53	0.57
N	17	17	17	17	17	17

Notes: ***$p < 0.01$; **$p < 0.05$; *$p < 0.1$ (one-tailed tests).
Standard errors in parentheses.

Sources: Corruption Perceptions Index: Table 23.5; Central bank independence: Cukierman, Webb, and Neyaph (1994), Table 22.4 (1980–9); Other dimensions of control: Chapter 22; Control variables: World Development Indicators, http://www.worldbank.org/dat.

increase entry costs, fiscal federalism (sub-national government consumption) has the opposite effect. The former result is unexpected, and we can only speculate as to why central bank independence and rent extraction go together. Thus, note that countries such as Austria and Greece, with comparatively independent central banks, lose a high proportion of their GDP to regulation costs, while the three Scandinavian ones and the United Kingdom have relatively little entry regulation and at the same time less independent central banks (at least as of the 1980s). A time-series analysis might help sort out such relationships that look anomalous in a purely cross-sectional regression, but the question will have to await further study. In contrast, the second external constraints variable, subnational government consumption, has the expected negative effect on political rent extraction, which is consistent across all the specifications in Table 23.6. Thus, the evidence suggests that fiscal federalism helps contain rent extraction, a result that conforms well to our expectations.

Our results also suggest that strong partisanship tends to reduce rent seeking, though these results are less striking. Inter-party competition significantly constrains entry regulation even when we control for other predictors and thus does seem to help make governments cleaner. Party cohesion in government, on the other hand, has only a weak and insignificant constraining effect on political rent extraction.

Table 23.7 reports the determinants of perceived corruption, as measured by the 2000 Corruptions Perceptions Index. Note that on this index, a high score signifies a comparatively 'clean' country. Table 23.7 reports significant effects for one indicator of partisanship as well as for both measures of external constraint. Party cohesion has a consistent and significant influence. The less cohesion in government, the more corruption. This is in line with our findings on entry regulation and matches our theoretical expectations: governments harbouring severe internal conflict are less capable of serving as citizen agents than governments that work together smoothly. When the variables are entered separately, party cohesion also explains a greater portion of the variance in corruption than any other predictor.

The estimates for central bank independence suggest a positive relationship with agency loss which, again, is not in accordance with our expectations. The country-specific factors discussed above may be relevant even here. Or one might suspect endogeneity problems. Given the substantial and increasing adverse effects of a loss of monetary credibility, corruption-ridden countries may historically have taken the lead in trying to inoculate themselves through policies of monetary autonomy.

On the other hand, as we expected, our second measure of external constraints, subnational government spending, is negatively associated with corruption. The relationship exists both when the variable is entered by itself and in the full model. Thus, as in several other domains, fiscal federalism helps contain democratic agency loss, here in the form of outright (perceived) corruption.

Satisfaction with Democracy

The final part of our analysis of agency loss will focus on a particularly broad measure of agency problems, namely public satisfaction with democratic institutions. Given the multiple dimensions of agency, plus the variation that may exist in the preferences of the principals, it is difficult to establish the relative importance of any of the specific measures of agency loss that we have discussed above. In some societies, citizens may care greatly about any policy divergence between governments and citizens but be relatively unconcerned with the amount of rent extraction that goes on. In other societies, the situation might be the opposite. We therefore conclude our discussion of agency loss by examining some of the more subjective performance evaluations of democratic delegation by the ultimate principal, the citizens.

At first glance, the data on public assessment of democratic institutions and officials are not uplifting. In many advanced industrial democracies, trust in politicians, political parties, and political institutions such as Parliament has declined over the late twentieth century. Citizens have become less satisfied with *all* types of representative democracies, a tendency that clearly extends to most of the parliamentary democracies with which this book is concerned. Dalton (1999: 63–4) investigates trust in politicians through a series of surveys of fourteen advanced democracies from the 1970s through the 1990s. With the exception of The Netherlands and, to a lesser extent, Denmark and

Norway, trust in politicians has declined everywhere. In addition, Newton and Norris (2000: 57) show that between the early 1980s and the early 1990s confidence in five public institutions—police, legal system, armed forces, Parliament, civil service—declined significantly in the United States, Japan, and all Western European parliamentary systems except France (non-significant decline) and Iceland (statistically significant increase in confidence). Newton and Norris (2000: 72) also conclude that 'our research provides substantial support for theories that focus on the performance of governments and political institutions to explain citizens' declining confidence in them'. It is possible that these trends in public confidence have since been affected by such cataclysmic events as those of 11 September 2001, but the well-documented longer-term trajectory has for quite some time worried students of representative democracy.

Paradoxically perhaps, while Western publics have evidently become less trustful of politicians and political institutions, they are at the same time more and more unanimous in their support for democracy. Klingemann (1999) argues that political support for democracy, as a regime type, is analytically and empirically distinct from the distrust that is attached to the performance evaluation of specific institutions. Analysing a much larger set of countries than we consider here, he finds 'no evidence of growing dissatisfaction with democracy as a form of government' (Klingemann 1999: 56).

Table 23.8 summarizes data from several surveys on public confidence in parliamentary and judicial institutions in European parliamentary democracies. These data allow us to compare these two types of institutions, as well as to track trends in their relative support over time. If parties and the parliamentary channel of delegation have in fact been weakened, we might expect this to be reflected in declining levels of public confidence. In fact, although the overall trend is down, public confidence in parliamentary institutions is in many places holding up quite well. When the latest available numbers for the 1990s are compared to the first available numbers from the 1980s or early 1990s, confidence in Parliament has actually gone up considerably in Denmark, The Netherlands, and Portugal. It has elsewhere mostly stayed about the same, and only in Germany (after re-unification) and Norway is the drop in double digits. The core institution of parliamentary democracy, the national legislature itself (with the most obvious and understandable exception of Italy in the early to mid-1990s), by and large has held its position quite well (see Table 23.9). For sure, parliaments are in most countries less trusted than the judiciary, but this discrepancy is much greater in Northern Europe (e.g. Denmark, where it is about forty points) than in the South (e.g. Spain, where it is virtually non-existent). Moreover, the differential in public confidence between Parliament and the judiciary has declined just about everywhere.

Table 23.9 provides more summary information. Because we use slightly different sources, the numbers reported in Table 23.9 are not identical to those in Table 23.8. In most cases, the differences between the two sources are marginal, though in some, such as Finland, the discrepancies are actually remarkably large.[10] The advantage of these additional data sources is that Table 23.9 also includes a particularly broad

[10] If we compare the 'confidence in Parliament' column for 1996 in Table 23.8 with the equivalent column for mid-1990s in Table 23.9, the difference between the two observations is 22 percentage points.

Table 23.8. *Trust in Parliament and the Judiciary in West European Parliamentary Systems*

	Confidence in Parliament, 1981[a]	1990	Change in confidence in Parliament, 1990–81	Confidence in Parliament, 1996	Confidence in judiciary, 1981	1990[b]	Change, in confidence in judiciary, 1990–81	Parliament minus judiciary, 1981	1990
Austria	n.d.	50	n.d.	48	n.d.	33	n.d.	n.d.	17
Belgium	39	43	4	42	58	45	−13	−19	−2
Denmark[c]	36	42	−6	62	80	79	−1	−44	−37
Finland	65	n.d.	n.d.	55	84	n.d.	n.d.	−19	n.d.
France	56	48	−8	46	57	58	1	−1	−10
Germany[d]	52	51	−1	39	67	65	−2	−15	−14
Greece	n.d.	n.d.	n.d.	56	n.d.	n.d.	n.d.	n.d.	n.d.
Iceland	56	53	−3	n.d.	69	67	−2	−13	−14
Ireland	53	50	−3	53	58	47	−11	−5	3
Italy	30	32	2	29	43	32	−11	−13	0
Luxembourg	n.d.	n.d.	n.d.	67	n.d.	n.d.	n.d.	n.d.	n.d.
The Netherlands	45	54	9	68	65	63	−2	−20	−9
Norway	78	59	−18	n.d.	84	75	−9	−6	−16
Portugal	n.d.	34	n.d.	48	n.d.	41	n.d.	n.d.	−7
Spain	49	43	−6	45	50	45	−5	−1	−2
Sweden	47	47	0	47	73	56	−17	−26	−9
United Kingdom	40	46	6	37	66	54	−12	−26	−8

Notes: n.d. = No available data.

Newton and Norris (2000: 56) report World Value Survey data that is marginally different.

[a] 1984 for Iceland.

[b] 1991 for Austria.

[c] This entry is for the 1980s and from Newton and Norris (2000: 56).

[d] West Germany before 1990.

Sources: Listhaug and Wiberg 1995: 304–5, Ulram 2000: 123; Norris 1999: 81.

Table 23.9. *Confidence in Democratic Institutions*

	Satisfaction with democratic performance, 1995	Change in satisfaction with democratic performance, 1995 minus 1991	Confidence in Parliament			Change in confidence in Parliament, early 1990s minus early 1980s
			Early 1980s	Early 1990s	Mid-1990s	
Austria	63	n.d.	n.d.	n.d.	n.d.	n.d
Belgium	54	2	38	42	n.d.	4
Denmark	83	9	36	42	n.d.	6
Finland	52	n.d.	65	34	33	−31
France	47	4	55	48	n.d.	−7
Germany[a]	67	1	51	50	29	−1
Greece	28	−6	n.d.	n.d.	n.d.	n.c.
Iceland	n.d.	n.d.	48	54	n.d.	6
Ireland	70	14	52	50	n.d.	−2
Italy	19	0	30	30	n.d.	0
Luxembourg	77	0	n.d.	n.d.	n.d.	n.d.
The Netherlands	71	9	45	53	n.d.	8
Norway	82	9	77	59	69	−18
Portugal	40	−35	n.d.	n.d.	n.d.	n.d.
Spain	41	−15	48	38	37	−10
Sweden	55	n.d.	47	47	45	0
United Kingdom	46	−14	40	44	n.d.	4
United States	n.d.	n.d.	52	45	30	−7

Notes: Columns 1 and 2 are Eurobarometer data, from Klingemann, in Norris 1999: 50, 52; Columns 3–6 are World Values Surveys data, from Newton and Norris 2000: 56.
[a] West Germany before 1990.

Sources: Norris 1999; Newton and Norris 2000.
n.d. = No data available.

measure of citizen assessment, namely satisfaction with overall democratic performance. Comparing these survey items across our various countries, the overall picture is quite clear. Public distrust is directed more against parliamentary institutions, and presumably even more against specific politicians and parties, than against democracy as such. Under traditional forms of parliamentary democracy, where accountability has largely been managed through *ex ante* mechanisms involving political parties, this is still very problematic. Tables 23.8 and 23.9 also suggest that although confidence in specific institutions (read: courts in particular) is down, we find no downward trend in overall satisfaction with democracy (although the data in Table 23.9 cover only two time points in the 1990s) or specifically with parliaments.

Table 23.10 presents regression models of our most recent data on satisfaction with overall democratic performance (1995) in sixteen parliamentary democracies (excluding Iceland, for which data are missing). The models reveal a number of interesting relationships. Of our four citizen control dimensions, fiscal federalism has the most

Table 23.10. *OLS Regressions on Democratic Satisfaction (1995)*

Independent Variables	Model 1	Model 2	Model 3	Model 4	Model 5	Model 6
Dimensions of citizen control						
Non-governing parties	−0.17				−0.38	−0.44*
(seats in Parliament)	(0.41)				(0.29)	(0.25)
Party conflict		−43.99**			−6.81	
		(21.84)			(18.49)	
Central bank			22.04		11.99	
independence			(31.14)		(22.88)	
Subnational				0.41*	0.38**	0.44**
government				(0.24)	(0.20)	(0.17)
consumption						
Control variables						
Population (logged)					−4.38*	−4.91*
					(3.13)	(2.83)
GDP per capita (logged)					39.57**	38.12**
(thousands US$)					(19.63)	(17.04)
Constant	58.64***	69.13***	47.88***	34.08**	−289.08	−265.78
	(8.24)	(7.82)	(12.34)	(13.56)	(231.83)	(200.73)
R-squared	0.01	0.22	0.03	0.17	0.74	0.73
Adj. *R*-squared	−0.06	0.17	−0.03	0.11	0.57	0.63
N	16	16	16	16	16	16

Standard errors in parentheses.
Notes: Table does not include Iceland.
***$p < 0.01$; **$p < 0.05$; *$p < 0.1$ (one-tailed tests).

Sources: Democratic satisfaction: Table 23.9; Central bank independence: Cukierman, Webb, and Neyapti 1994, Table 22.4 (1980–9); Other dimensions of control: Chapter 22; Control variables: World Development Indicators, http://www.worldbank.org/data/

consistent and significant effect on popular satisfaction with democracy. The more decentralized the polity, the higher the citizens' satisfaction. Given that fiscal federalism means that spending decisions are made closer to the citizen (e.g. in the city council rather than the national parliament), but that policies may vary significantly from one sub-national government to the next, this result suggests that citizens value local control of the political decision-making process more than policy uniformity.

Central bank independence has the same positive sign but is not significant. Party cohesion and competition both have the expected signs (that is to say, cohesive and competitive parties are associated with high levels of satisfaction), but these results are only significant in one model specification each. Note, however, the significant effects of both control variables. Models five and six both reveal that citizens in small countries are more satisfied than those in more populous ones, as indeed we expected. Moreover, there is a strong tendency for people in richer countries to be more satisfied with democracy than those who live in poorer ones. Altogether, Table 23.10 reports that coupled with these control variables, our measures of citizen control explain a large portion (up to 63 per cent) of the variance in democratic satisfaction.

Summary

We have seen that our measures of citizen control are in many cases predictably associated with the various agency problems that we have examined. Even in our small sample, the estimated effects of individual parameters are in many cases, but far from always, statistically significant. For all performance (agency loss) criteria except one, the explanatory power of our overall model is sizeable, as the adjusted coefficient of determination in at least one specification consistently exceeds 0.40. The exception is policy divergence, where we find little systematic relationship between citizen control mechanisms and political outcomes. Interestingly, although there is some modest evidence that polities with cohesive Westminster-like parties exacerbate problems of policy distance between governors and the governed, no specification of our model is able to explain any significant part of the variation in such policy divergence.

On the other hand, even though these effects are not always statistically significant in our sample, we find quite systematic evidence that party cohesion and competition contain other forms of agency loss. In fact, our estimate of the effect of executive cohesion shows the expected sign (meaning that cohesion constrains agency loss) in all nine of these specifications, whereas the direction of the estimates for inter-party competition similarly conforms to expectations in nine out of ten cases.

In other words, the evidence strongly and broadly suggests that cohesive and competitive political parties and governments help reduce the risks of democratic delegation. Specifically, executive cohesion strongly and significantly reduces the risks of corruption and fiscal indiscipline. Party competition, on the other hand, reduces rent extraction and promotes general satisfaction with democracy. Such salutary effects, then, are associated with the Westminster model of democracy, which according to our results deserves much greater respect than it has received in much of the recent literature. Yet, the positive effects of electoral competition and cohesion do not strictly depend on a pure two-party format. Even alternational multiparty systems may under certain circumstances fit the bill. Pivotal, polarized, and fragmented party systems, however, do not.

Our estimates for external constraints do not both exhibit the same consistent and plausible coefficients. Contrary to our expectations, central bank independence is in many specifications associated with higher, rather than lower, reports of agency loss. Above, we have speculated as to what these findings may reflect. Fiscal federalism, on the other hand, constrains agency loss in every one of our thirteen specifications, even though a number of these results are not statistically significant. On the whole, fiscal federalism seems most effective in containing rent extraction and corruption. Thus, external constraints are probably most effective when they pit 'ambition against ambition', without the constraining effects of party cohesion. This is generally more likely with respect to rent extraction than, for example, policy divergence. Thus, Bagehot and Madison were both right: party cohesion and external constraints each have their virtues.

Finally, our control variables demonstrate that country-specific and demographic properties may have systematic effects on democratic delegation that should not be ignored. Small and wealthy countries have populations that are more satisfied with their democracies, and small countries also have fewer corruption problems. These are, at least in part, rather straightforward effects of the greater political transparency that such societies afford. These effects should not be mistaken for consequences of the political institutions that these same societies may happen to have. Even under identical political structures, we should expect Switzerland, Luxembourg, or Norway to solve their democratic delegation problems more successfully than, for example, Russia or even Spain. Such results do not suggest that political agents in the former sorts of countries are necessarily more virtuous than those in the latter, nor do they in themselves prove the superiority of their institutional arrangements. Constitutional designs that have proven successful only in small and rich countries, such as social corporatism (Katzenstein 1985) or perhaps consociational democracy (Lijphart 1977) may not pass muster under more demanding circumstances.

WHAT HAVE WE LEARNED?

Let us now look back at the broader lessons of this study. In the introductory chapters, we identified the problems of democratic delegation in parliamentary democracies and suggested that principal–agent models offer a coherent, rigorous, and parsimonious way to understand a host of these challenges. A morass of competing definitions has hitherto prevented students of constitutional design from fully understanding the virtues and vices of parliamentary democracies. In contrast, by spelling out a few analytical conceptions we have been able to demonstrate the main differences between alternative constitutional designs. Working from the ideal types, we have developed models that illustrate fundamental differences between parliamentarism and presidentialism, as well as critical distinctions within the family of parliamentary systems. Throughout the twenty-three chapters of this book, we have shown that this rational choice-based approach can facilitate large-scale empirical and comparative research and generate a coherent and comprehensive understanding of the policy process in modern democracies. In this study, we have applied such models specifically to parliamentary systems, but of course they apply equally well to other regime types, such as presidential ones.

Parliamentary Democracy

As we have shown in the introductory chapter, students of democratic institutions have long realized both intuitively and empirically that political delegation is problematic. Yet, they have taken different positions on the severity of the problem and on whether indeed it is possible to found popular government on delegation. John Stuart Mill (1984 [1861]) viewed political delegation through representation as preferable to other forms of government, whereas Michels (1962 [1915]) thought delegation through party organizations in the long run unsustainable, as political leaders will eventually cease to serve those whom they ostensibly represent. Mosca (1947) saw parliamentary delegation as feasible only if checked by outside actors and institutions of the kinds that we have called external constraints (courts, audit offices, etc.). Kelsen (1926) likewise considered electoral accountability by itself insufficient to solve the democratic moral hazard problem, but advocated instead the remedies of direct democracy and interelectoral participation. Ostrogorski (1907) and Schmitt (1969 [1923]) went so far as to warn against the detrimental impact of political parties on the constitutional principles of democracy.

Our delegation approach captures many of these most central concerns of the classical writers on democratic constitutional design. Yet, showing that this particular conceptual apparatus can be applied to parliamentary systems is not in itself the ultimate scholarly achievement. There is in principle any number of ways to understand parliamentary institutions. The challenge is not only to show that any particular framework can faithfully and effectively represent the concerns of those who have thought long and hard about the problems, but also to demonstrate the value it adds to the existing wisdom.

We find that value added especially in three properties of our approach: generality, parsimony, and deductive rigour. In terms of generality, Chapter 1 shows that the problems associated with political representation or delegation at different stages of the policy process have often been studied in mutual isolation and in different discourses. We, instead, suggest that similar agency problems pertain to each of the links in the chain of delegation that we have identified. Although specific problems of representation may be particularly acute at different stages of the policy process, they can all be captured in a single, coherent framework.

Nor is this framework ominously complex and inscrutable, and this is where the virtue of parsimony lies. The problems of delegation stem from two basic sources, namely differences between principals and agents in preferences and/or information. Similarly, we have argued that agency problems under incomplete information manifest themselves in two critical forms: adverse selection and moral hazard. And our survey of the institutional remedies have focused on *ex ante* verses *ex post* controls, and specifically on the roles of political parties and external constraints in giving flesh and blood (and enforcement power) to such control devices.

Finally, one of the chief virtues of the principal–agent approach is the fact that it allows us to model political delegation relationship in precise and rigorous ways. Such models in turn allow us to predict the consequences of specific institutional designs, or to compare the performance of different institutions across a variety of assumptions about the preferences and information of political principals and agents, as we have begun to do in Chapter 3. While we hold this potential to be a profoundly important virtue of principal–agent models, it is one that we have only begun to realize here. Yet, we confidently expect such analysis to yield rich fruits in future research.

Merits and Demerits

For those interested in the merits of parliamentary democracy, our study contains both good and bad news. The good news is that evidently the harshest critics of parliamentary democracy have not been correct. Delegation in the form of parliamentary democracy with cohesive and influential political parties and effective constraints can be successful. Our contributors testify that the constitutional chain of delegation in most instances has worked reasonably well. Levels of popular satisfaction with democracy are high across most Western European parliamentary systems. Whatever disenchantment exists is rarely directed at democracy or parliamentarism as such. Thus, a well-designed set of parliamentary delegation and accountability mechanisms can evidently foster successful democratic delegation, at least when critical circumstances (such as prosperity and peace) are favourable.

It is less obvious that we can draw similarly upbeat conclusions about the merits of parliamentary systems versus other democratic constitutions. As Chapter 1 shows, parliamentary democracy has often been celebrated as superior to presidentialism. Generally, parliamentary democracy is seen as more efficient and responsive than its main rival, and less susceptible to democratic breakdown. Presidentialism, in contrast, allegedly can be marred by gridlock and inertia, and the fixed term of the executive can lead to 'rigidity' when presidents stay in power after having lost the support of the legislature. On the other hand, proponents of presidentialism point out that parliamentarism can be prone to haste rather than contemplation, more at risk for executive instability, and more likely to promote government profligacy than to protect the pockets of the taxpayers.

While this is not an empirical study of presidential democracies, our approach enables us to bypass much of the anecdotal discussion and to pinpoint critical analytical distinctions between these two regime types. Comparatively speaking, parliamentary systems, and especially those of the Westminster type, tend to be more susceptible to the agency problems of policy divergence and rent extractions than to those of leisure shirking and policy coordination. The latter problems are more particularly associated with presidential regimes. It is the simplicity, and specifically the singularity, of parliamentary democracy that renders it comparatively susceptible to the former types of agency loss. Yet, the same features render parliamentary democracy decisive, which enhances policy coordination, and incentive-efficient, which reduces the incidence of leisure shirking.

These are analytical results and expectations, and only future research can show whether indeed these trade-offs exist between the virtues of parliamentary and presidential constitutions. Yet, these trade-offs are not associated simply with the larger choice between parliamentary and presidential constitutions, but pertain also to institutional choices within the family of parliamentary systems. Our research shows considerable institutional variation among parliamentary systems. The analytical device of the classical Westminster model yields good insights into the parliamentary regime type. But at the same time, it is only a rough approximation and one that most parliamentary systems (and even the United Kingdom) resemble less and less. As the summary table in Chapter 4 (Table 4.20) helps illustrate, parliamentary design entails a number of variations and trade-offs. For each indicator, our countries manifest different choices. While some choices promote expedient delegation, others provide accountability to the principal and yet others support stability by promoting counterbalancing powers in the hands of the Prime Minister.[11]

While we have not yet tested our expectations concerning the differences between parliamentary and presidential systems, we have been able to examine the effects of institutional variation within the parliamentary camp. Our results show that in most contexts, institutional mechanisms of citizen control do have meaningful and often predictable consequences. And some of the more precise patterns are noteworthy. Parliamentary systems with cohesive, competitive parties and/or effective external constraints generally perform better than those without these features. Inter-party competition can apparently foster policy coordination, as evidenced by our data on public debt. Together with external constraints on national governments, partisan cohesion and competition can also contain rent extraction and enhance democratic satisfaction.

Our empirical results thus suggest that a government prone to infighting is more likely to cause agency loss than one that is not. Parliamentary democracies that approximate the Westminster or alternational multiparty model demonstrate that partisan conflict in the executive, for example, is not an inherent problem in parliamentary democracy, even though it may be a contingent feature of many parliamentary systems. Instead the agency loss experienced in a particular country is a result of its mix of a particular constitutional chain, party system, and external constraints. Pivotal multiparty systems without effective external constraints would seem to be the least desirable form of parliamentary government.

Trends in Parliamentary Governance

In addition to specifying the trade-offs of delegation that are manifest in West European constitutions, our survey, as summarized in Chapter 4, has identified three major trends. One is that the parliamentary chain of delegation itself is changing.

---

[11] To exemplify, a strong Prime Minister may promote efficient delegation, but accountability on a day-to-day basis is perhaps better assured if he has fewer powers. Similarly, granting the PM liberal parliamentary dissolution powers may ensure stability, but at the price of weakening his accountability to his immediate democratic principal, the parliamentary majority.

The speed of change is not overwhelming, but voters in many countries have gained more direct influence over candidate selection and parliamentary elections through membership referendums within parties and preference voting in general elections. Parliaments are moving in the direction of getting more power over less. There is in many countries far more room for parliamentary questions and committee scrutiny than there used to be prior to the 1970s or 1980s. But at the same time, many policy issues have been shifted to the supranational arena, and thus national executives have gained in relative power at the expense of their legislatures.

Some part of the power-shift in favour of the cabinet stems from the central role of national executives in EU decision-making, but the trend was visible even before that EU influence became salient. Above all it favours Prime Ministers, who throughout Western Europe have acquired more staff and larger administrative resources than they had in the early years after Second World War and who have become a greater focus of media and voter attention even for purely domestic reasons. In this respect at least, it is possible to talk about a 'presidentialization' of premierships all over Western Europe. The final step in the chain of delegation is also changing as ministers keep their formal powers but in many cases release their agents from the strict control and micromanagement implied by more classical models of parliamentary democracy. We will return to this point later when we discuss the contemporary challenges facing all representative democracies.

The second and third trends, weaker parties and stronger constraints, were discussed in detail in Chapter 22. Suffice it here to say that the decline of political parties, especially in electoral and membership terms, entails a serious challenge to traditional parliamentary democracy and especially the Westminster model. So does the general enhancement of external constraints. These developments fundamentally change the constitutional principles of delegation and accountability. As Strøm explains in Chapter 3 and our empirical chapters demonstrate, cohesive and competitive political parties can promote both efficiency and accountability. Weakened political parties first and foremost mean that the link between citizens and their political agents becomes less transparent. In some ways, weakened political parties may revive the spirit of many constitutions and specifically the individual responsibility of political agents. Thus, this development may enhance the independence of the civil service or the constraining force of agents that are no longer 'tied-in' by partisan bonds. But at the same time the atrophy of political parties can leave citizens with less information and fewer political cues. Just consider the consequences of MPs regularly changing party affiliation between elections, as has been pervasive in Italy since 1994.

Understanding Political Institutions

One final lesson of this study is to suggest modifications to the understandings of political institutions that tend to dominate political analysis. We firmly believe that any serious such effort must recognize that institutions have consequences. This is not a novel insight, and indeed it is one supposition that has united the otherwise quite distinct literatures that have appeared since about 1980 under the banner of the 'new institutionalism'. But it is important to determine precisely why institutions have consequences, as this will help us understand what institutions are and when they will be effective. Institutions are consequential in large part because there are rewards and punishments associated with the behaviour that they regulate. These rewards may be impersonal and universal, as for example, when market institutions help buyers and sellers engage in transactions for mutual gain. More generally, institutions may induce or sustain particular beliefs and expectations that in turn sustain collective goods and/or have distributional consequences. Or institutional consequences may manifest themselves in much more personalized and particular forms, as when the occupants of public offices are given discretionary power to reward, permit, block, or punish political behaviour.

Yet institutions not only have consequences, they also have purposes driven by the preferences of their occupants. And unless one understands the purposes of political institutions, one may well draw misguided inferences about their consequences. This is less frequently recognized, even by institutionalists. Saying that institutions have purposes is not tantamount to adopting a functionalist mode of analysis. We do not want to argue that institutions invariably produce certain systemic goods, or that there is some organic process by which institutions get 'naturally' selected to help polities survive and prosper. Nor do we want to argue that institutions historically have been selected in a fully instrumental fashion, or in the glorious light of a complete understanding of their consequences. Yet, institutions are chosen and sustained by political actors for specific purposes, albeit often in haphazard and chaotic ways, and no doubt often under expectations that later turn out to be wildly erroneous.

Whatever their genesis, one powerful purpose of modern democratic institutions is to further citizen preferences and contain the behaviour of their political agents. Needless to say, these purposes do not exhaust the consequences of democratic institutions. Nor are these purposes necessarily stable over time. In some cases, such as the US Constitution, the democratic purpose was present from the inception. In others, such as the British one, it may have gradually imposed itself over the course of a long period of time.

While this commitment to institutional consequences and purposes may sound exceedingly general and abstract, it does have quite specific implications for our understanding of parliamentary (and other) democracies. To help spell those out, let us briefly consider two other deservedly influential and powerful accounts of contemporary democratic institutions, namely those of Lijphart (1977, 1984, and 1999) and Tsebelis (2002). While we owe a great deal to each of these authors, there are also important ways in which our understanding of democratic institutions differs from theirs, respectively.

Consider first Lijphart's seminal work. While, like Lijphart, we find the Westminster model a greatly helpful benchmark for institutional analysis, we miss in his analysis a consideration of what we take to be one of the main purposes of such democratic institutions—the containment of agency problems. In Lijphart's analysis, democratic institutions serve to give representation to popular preferences, and particularly it seems, those associated with the interests of specific, often demographically defined, social groups such as ethnic, linguistic, or religious minorities. But while we would certainly not deny that political institutions of representation serve this purpose, it seems to us imperative to consider the problems of agency loss that any such representation may entail.

In Lijphart's view, the virtues of democratic representation hinge decisively on the access of agents from different social groups to the policy process. While this may be a necessary condition for stable and successful democracy, it seems to us far from sufficient. What is missing from this analysis is a consideration of the agency slack which these agents may exploit. If adverse selection or moral hazard is a significant political problem, then institutions of political representation need mechanisms by which the democratic principals can control or even throw out the 'rascals'—their political agents. In his analyses, Lijphart fails to identify such mechanisms of within-group agency control, or to differentiate between systems that have them and those that do not.

Consider the author's conception of Westminster, or majoritarian, democracy. Lijphart (1999: 31) considers its fundamental properties, majority rule and adversarial competition, principles of exclusion (see also Lewis 1965). We agree. But whereas Lijphart seems to understand this principle as actual *ex post* exclusion of democratic principals, we see it instead as *ex ante* excludability of agents. In other words, the key to Westminster democracy is not that some voters *must* be kept out, but rather that some politicians *can* be so treated. And this potential to exclude agents serves precisely to protect the ultimate principals, the citizens. The competitive nature of Westminster democracy is its strongest mechanism of political accountability. As this volume has amply demonstrated, Westminster democracy certainly has its share of problems, but it is important to recognize the democratic purpose of its party cohesion, competition, and hierarchy.

Agency problems are also missing from one of Lijphart's (1977) contrasting models, consociational democracy. In the plural societies in which consociationalism was originally observed, voters are divided into mutually distinct and often antagonistic social groups or segments. The purported virtue of consociationalism is that within such a system, group leaders are able to take more accommodating positions than those most favoured by their respective supporters. But this is unlikely to be the case unless the voters either do not know what their respective leaders are doing, or are unable to influence or displace them. As Tsebelis (1990, ch. 6) has shown in his game-theoretic reconstruction, the benign effects of consociational democracy seem to hinge on high voter information costs and/or a monopoly of political representation (i.e. no effective electoral competition) within each social segment. In other words, consociationalism works best if there are substantial barriers to entry for political entrepreneurs (new parties) and/or regular citizens are systematically in the dark about elite decisions.

These are fragile and counter-intuitive conditions for a successful democratic order. If political agents are at all self-interested, then a situation of poorly informed principals with no effective choice over their agents is one that positively invites such agency problems as rent extraction, leisure-shirking, and possibly corruption. It is therefore no surprise that consociational or quasi-consociational countries such as Belgium, Austria, and Italy score high on many of our indicators of agency loss, and especially those having to do with rent extraction, corruption, and policy coordination. For much the same reasons, we suspect, the same countries have also harboured some of the strongest populist right-wing protest parties in Europe. While such parties no doubt feed on xenophobia and alienation, their success is greatly enhanced when they can cast themselves in the role of opponents of a detached and cozy cartel of career politicians (see Rose 2000).

The fact that out of these countries, Austria appears better governed overall, may reflect its superior combination of effective external constraints and cohesive and competitive political parties, compared with other consociational systems.

Let us now turn to Tsebelis' (2002) powerful and already very influential veto player analysis of political institutions. While we find the veto player approach a parsimonious and highly effective way to analyse political institutions, we again believe that there is more to political institutions than Tsebelis here allows, and that what is missing from his analysis is not simply 'embellishment and detail'. Tsebelis identifies two types of veto players: institutional and partisan ones. He argues that if they are properly identified, partisan and institutional veto players are mutually substitutable. We believe not. Chapter 3 in this volume critiques this assumption, which seems to neglect both the differential consequences and purposes of parties and institutional checks.

On the consequence side, we need to recognize the existence of many kinds of privileged players, such as *dictators, veto players, decisive players*, and merely *powerful players* (see Chapter 3). Strøm and Swindle (2002) have shown that at least for parliamentary dissolution decisions, such finer distinctions do in fact systematically matter. Dictators, for example, have stronger powers and effects than other veto players. More generally, institutional effects depend on the actual rewards and punishments that different kinds of veto players can impose, and here partisan and institutional veto players clearly differ (the latter also among themselves). Institutional veto players typically have constitutionally guaranteed and discretionary powers. These have often been vested in them precisely so that they can ignore the immediate desires of elected officials or the majority of voters. They may even have been selected precisely on the basis of preferences that deviate from those of the median voter. They may have a specific and well-defined mandate, such as upholding the constitution or attaining a target rate of inflation. Party leaders, on the other hand, have only such powers as their elected representatives are willing to give them, which ultimately depend on the voters' preferences and tolerance. Thus, compared with partisan ones, institutional veto players typically have greater authority as well as different purposes.

Tsebelis seeks to explain the consequences of different institutional designs for policy stability or change. He argues that the greater the number of veto players, and the greater the diversity of their preferences, the greater the constraints on policy change. While we would add that the type and specific authority of the relevant players also matter, we generally concur. But if one is interested not only in whether policy change is likely, but also in whether in the process the policy makers would serve the interests of their democratic 'masters', then it is not only helpful, but critical, to distinguish between different kinds of powerful (veto) players. Thus, if institutional and partisan veto players were truly mutually substitutable, then a polity with a fragmented party system and little external constraint could be equivalent to one with a small number of cohesive parties and several strong external constraints. Both might have the same number of veto players and the same dispersion of preferences. For democratic delegation, however, there is every reason to believe that these two categories of political systems differ. In the former case, we would expect to see very weak control of political agents and a high risk of agency loss, in the latter very strong control and a much lower risk of slippage.

CONTEMPORARY CHALLENGES: MIND THE GAP

Parliamentary democracies are changing, in large part because their environment is changing, too. We shall close this chapter (and book) by considering the major challenges to democratic delegation that lie ahead, as far as we can foresee the trends that are under way. There are two basic variables that can drive a wedge between democratic principals and agents, namely differences in preferences and information. These, then, are the sources of the critical challenges to representative democracies. While preference divergence between principals and agents has always been, and will no doubt continue to be, a critical issue in all democratic polities, the most critical challenges ahead may turn out to involve discrepancies in information. This is in large part due to the great contemporary changes in the ways in which information is conveyed, accessed, and evaluated.

As we mentioned in the introduction to this chapter, the classical design of parliamentary democracy harbours a potential transparency problem that stems from the very rationale for representative politics. One reason to delegate is that principals cannot or will not pay the costs of acquiring all the information and skills necessary to perform specific tasks on their own. Less-informed principals leave matters in the hands of better-informed agents. For delegation to be successful, principals want their agents to be as well informed as possible so that they can make decisions that have the highest possible likelihood of leading to beneficial results. Yet, things are not quite so simple.[12] Because of the moral hazard problem, they also do not want the gap in information (information asymmetry) between themselves and their agents to be insurmountable.[13] Hence, adverse selection and moral hazard have been governance problems as long as citizens have chosen representatives to make decisions in their place. They will remain problems as long as representation continues to be a fact of life. But even though these problems are indeed general and timeless, their particular forms, and their comparative urgency, are not.

The Information Revolution

In some ways information would seem to be the least of our worries, as we are living in an age in which knowledge is much more easily accessible than ever before. As Robert A. Dahl (1989) notes, new particularly electronic technology offers enormous opportunities for enhanced communication and public information. 'By means of telecommunications virtually every citizen could have information about public issues

---

[12] For example, principals may differ in their preferences over different informational desiderata. Some may particularly value agents that are articulate, well educated, and knowledgeable (though social scientists are probably prone to overestimate the importance of such concerns among the voters). Others want politicians that are willing to go along and get along. Yet others put a premium on managerial efficiency.

[13] Thus, several information-related conditions should hold. These conditions can occasionally be mutually contradictory, or at least work at cross-purposes. If principals are too ignorant, or if their costs of acquiring information are too high, then it is dangerous for them to delegate to agents that do not share their preferences. It may also be difficult for ignorant principals to figure out what the skill level of the agent actually is.

almost immediately accessible in a form (print, debates, dramatization, animated cartoons, for example) and at a level (from expert to novice, for example) appropriate for the particular citizen' (Dahl 1989: 339).

In addition, the citizenries of contemporary advanced democracies are better educated than ever. In most European societies the 1960s and 1970s were critical decades in the expansion of educational opportunities. By the mid-1990s, the proportion of adult citizens (25 to 64-year-olds) who had completed at least an upper-secondary education had surpassed 50 per cent in most OECD countries and 80 per cent in some. At the same time, in many countries about a fourth or a fifth of the same cohorts had completed a higher education (Norris 2000: 48–9). Of course, among the youngest of these adults, the numbers were in many cases even significantly higher.

The information revolution has not stopped before the doors of politics. Indeed, with a few mouse clicks it is now possible to get access to an abundance of government and parliamentary papers, official information about the lives and actions of politicians, as well as media reports about them. This information-education revolution has greatly enhanced the volume of information available to voters and has in many cases empowered principals of all kinds vis-à-vis their political agents. Access to all this new information should lessen the informational asymmetries that trouble the relationship between citizens and governors.

Yet, the effects of the information revolution may not be quite so simple or benign. For one thing, given the overwhelming amount of available information it is difficult to filter out 'noise' and get to the core of what is relevant. Informational overload means that even better-educated citizens are often unwilling to search for information and consider it the politicians' obligation to deliver by the door. Perhaps the information-education revolution in the end has done more to raise expectations than to satisfy demands for transparency. To put it in the words of media studies, voters seem more 'over-newsed but under-informed' than ever before.

This huge increase in the available information forces many individuals to look for shortcuts and simple and appealing solutions. Given the oceans of available information, citizens may once again need to rely on agents to help them navigate. But by relying on such experts, citizens leave themselves just as exposed to agency problems as when they relied on more traditional sources of information. And the leading practitioners of the new profession of political spin-doctors have acquired remarkable skills in manipulating news and the public agenda (Entman and Bennett 2001: 469; Street 2001). To make things worse, the traditional sources of information may no longer be available.

The Decay of Traditional Information Devices

As the information revolution has progressed, traditional sources of information have atrophied. As we detailed in Chapter 22, recent developments have undercut many well-established devices to structure and economize on information, as well as the organizations that benefit from the control of such information. Information cues, such as party labels, are in many countries losing much of their meaning. In Western Europe, cohesive and centralized political parties have been at the core of democratic politics, and political accountability has largely been based on their prior screening and selection of public officials. In the electoral arena, this has taken the form of careful party screening of candidates and great attention to ascriptive social representation. In Parliament, leaders have been chosen on the basis of experience, co-partisanship, and seniority. In short, principals have been able to use *ex ante* screening to choose well-known and well-tested partisan agents.

Such mechanisms are most likely to be effective when the agents' abilities and preferences are readily observable or predictable from their background and previous experience. They lose their usefulness if prior experience becomes irrelevant for the tasks at hand, or if classification by observable demographic criteria (e.g. ethnicity or class background) ceases to provide useful cues about the preferences and skills of potential agents. Today, this is precisely the problem: ascriptive information and prior experience provide less useful information about political agents than they once did, and whatever value such information has diminishes more rapidly. This is a great liberating development, by which citizens are increasingly able to define their own identities, but it is also one that weakens traditional foundations of political knowledge.

Consequently, class voting, as well as voting along other ascriptive lines (e.g. ethnicity, faith, language, or race), is generally in decline (Dalton 2002). More and more voters are likely to plump for those politicians and parties that offer appealing solutions, regardless of whether or not they have the traditional credentials for a political career. They seem increasingly willing to elect representatives, such as Jesse 'the Body' Ventura in the United States or Silvio Berlusconi in Italy, who have not gone through the traditional partisan screening process (Strøm 1997).[14] Even Tony Blair was a remarkable departure from most previous British prime ministers in the fact that he had had no previous cabinet experience. Yet, the most spectacular case is Pim Fortuyn, who within a few months established himself as a leading force in Dutch politics. Even after his assassination his list finished second in the 2002 general election.

In short, citizens seem to consider prior political experience less important than previously, and the traditional mechanisms to select political leaders and thus to exercise *ex ante* control have become less effective. If most parties appeal to the general electorate rather than to particular groups and claim to have roughly the same goals, voters increasingly have to make their choices on the basis of the candidates' personal qualities or perceived technical competence. This has paved the way for political outsiders. Although he is an extreme case, Silvio Berlusconi is said to have reached the apex of Italian politics because his status as the country's richest man was seen both as evidence of his skills and an indication that he would not need to steal the people's money. At the same time, voters are prepared to abandon at short notice politicians who do not deliver what they have promised. A fickle, sceptical, and often not very well-informed electorate is the result.

Thus, the information revolution is not just about the emergence of new sources of political information, but also about the decay of traditional ones. But even if the

---

[14] See Mair, Müller, and Plasser (2003) for a more comprehensive discussion of this phenomenon in Western Europe.

effects of the former development were to trump those of the latter (as may well be the case), democratic societies are not necessarily home free. Although reliable political information is relatively inexpensive and widely available, it seems to be more unevenly distributed among the citizens (Norris 2000).[15] And in advanced democracies the widening gap between the well informed and the poorly informed may become as much of a challenge as any other inequality.

Increasing Complexity: Europeanization and Globalization

Contemporary information problems are also exacerbated by the increasing complexity of democratic policy-making. The problem is that more decisions are taken in arenas that are more difficult to observe, that is to say, internationally and in particular within the EU. To understand the growing problems of asymmetric information, we therefore need to consider such challenges as Europeanization and globalization.

In Western Europe, the growing importance of the European Union is an important source of such complexity. Decision-making at the EU-level has gained considerably in importance since the 1980s in particular. The great majority of our countries (fifteen out of seventeen) are members of the European Union and hence directly affected by the ever-increasing shift of competencies to the community level. Yet, even the two remaining states (Iceland and Norway) are severely affected by the great majority of EU decisions as they are required to adapt 'autonomously' in order to maintain their membership in the European Economic Area (EEA) (on the consequences of European integration for the national chain of delegation, see Bergman, Müller, and Strøm 2000; Bergman and Damgaard 2000).

The multi-level decision-making process in the European Union is much more complex than those of most traditional nation-states. With the Commission as an external agenda setter and the resulting draft legislation being discussed over an extended period in several hundred committees, the decision-making process is hard to oversee for ministers even within their own jurisdictions and much more so for parliamentarians. Unlike domestic policy processes, it is also very difficult to stop or reverse. Package deals (logrolling) in the European Union can further undermine the transparency of the policy process and hence increase information problems, sometimes even for the line ministers over whose heads Prime Ministers strike such deals.

Few voters participate in European elections, and fewer understand the complexities of EU decision-making. Thus, voters no longer know to whom they have delegated, or who is entitled to make decisions for them. Consequently, the European Union is often seen as an anonymous Brussels machine dominated by bureaucrats and lobbyists. This undermines the legitimacy of EU policies, and perhaps also of government policy in general. Yet, one might argue that the European Union has always relied on output legitimacy and that its so-called legitimacy deficit can be redressed not by strengthening

---

[15] See, however, Lupia and McCubbins (1998) who argue that information shortcuts can compensate for such lack of political knowledge.

process control but by improving its output efficiency (Majone 1998, 2001*a*, *b*; Scharpf 1999).[16]

As this volume demonstrates, the constitutions of the member states have to varying degrees been adapted to the increasing importance of EU politics. Yet, even under the best of circumstances reforms such as the introduction of parliamentary EU affairs committees cannot fully compensate for the decline in parliamentary power. European integration quite simply involves a decline in the capacity of national politicians to affect policy outcomes that matter to their citizens. Even though the same trends, we hope, increase the overall capacity of governments to deal with many serious problems (environmental protection, international crime), growing agency problems could under unfavourable circumstances consume the potential for gains in effectiveness.

All of this suggests that politicians at all stages of the chain of delegation suffer from information deficiencies vis-à-vis the European Union. Of course, the information problems of ordinary citizens are much greater, and politicians variously try to exploit them. Hence, government members claim credit for popular EU policies, blame the European Union for unpleasant developments or regulations, and leak fabricated information about their heroic defence of national interests in Brussels. In contrast, opposition politicians take positions that are popular nationally but have no chance of finding support in the European Union. Of course, this strategy is particularly attractive for EU-sceptical parties.

Information problems can become even more acute when governments respond to globalization by acting in international settings that are even less transparent than the European Union. For example, decisions made in the World Trade Organization (WTO) often have substantial domestic consequences but little transparency. Had not the WTO become the bogeyman of some militant NGOs, even the best-informed voters might never have learned about the relevance of decisions made there.

Finally, serious information problems may arise when decisions are made anonymously in world markets (Held *et al.* 1999: chs. 3–5). Such decisions, which are typically exogenous to the national political decision-making systems and hence cannot be controlled by politicians, may still be extremely consequential. Specifically, the liberalization of financial markets since the 1980s has accelerated the speed by which such market decisions impact on national polities, leaving politicians little scope and less time for manoeuvre. Yet, it is the national political office holders that, if lucky, benefit from market developments, or, if unlucky, pay the bill. In either case, however, democratic accountability is deprived of its rational basis. In a nutshell, more and often particularly consequential decisions are taken outside the national chain of delegation. At the same time citizens continue to hold politicians accountable for outcomes they may not control, as indeed politicians claim credit for those outcomes that suit them.

---

[16] Such proposals have included further strengthening the European Parliament, the direct election of the Commission and Council Presidents, the creation of a second chamber of the European Parliament consisting of delegations from national Parliaments, and the introduction of European referendums (e.g. see Abromeit 1998; Grande 2000).

Citizen Demands and Leadership Responses

Voters are more difficult to please than ever. In Hirschman's (1970) terms, they increasingly opt for exit strategies. Not only is loyalty to political parties in retreat, but the declining number of party members (see Chapter 22) indicates that the same applies to 'voice'. In other words, voters increasingly behave like consumers shopping around for the best short-term deal. This may not in the long run produce the best politicians. Indeed, one might ask whether the main problem in democratic delegation is that the principals, and not the agents, fail to respect their 'contracts' (see Gilardi and Braun 2002: 157).

We can readily observe the growing fickleness of European voters. Over the second half of the twentieth century, there was a gradual rise in electoral volatility (Lane and Ersson 1999: 128) and, more specifically, an increasing tendency for incumbent (cabinet) parties to lose votes relative to the previous election (Müller and Strøm 2000: 589). As Narud and Valen (2004) show, over the entire 1945–2000 period incumbent cabinet parties in the countries covered in this volume slipped an average of 2.59 per cent of the total vote. As a general trend, such losses have increased monotonically over time. The average losses of incumbent cabinets were fairly low in the 1940s (0.10 per cent) and the 1950s (1.08 per cent). By the 1980s the mean electoral setback of incumbent cabinets had reached 3.88 per cent. Still, these losses further escalated and indeed almost doubled in the 1990s, to 6.28 per cent.

How do politicians react to the greater volatility and impatience of citizens? Political parties have had to change their traditional patterns of recruitment and candidate selection. These developments are not altogether novel. Some of their effects were first observed with the emergence of the catch-all party in the 1950s and 1960s (Kirchheimer 1966). Parties putting a premium on consistent ideological appeals and/or appeals to specific socio-demographic groups have become a distinct 'minority programme'.

But changes in citizen demands drive not only party organization and long-term strategy, but also shorter-term tactics. As electoral volatility and dissatisfaction grow, politicians face progressively greater incentives to anticipate and satisfy the voters' desires, even when elections are not imminent. This responsiveness to the voters can, however, cause politicians to have divided loyalties—that is, to try to serve several competing principals simultaneously. Thus, when party leaders negotiate over government formation or termination, they not only anticipate the reactions of parliamentarians and the party organization, but increasingly also those of the electorate. They avoid not only strategies that fail to satisfy the parliamentary majority, but also those that find little favour with the voters. Thus, one response to increasing distrust is for party elites to establish a more direct link to the electorate.

Demands for greater accountability have in some cases changed the basic rules of parliamentary government. One striking example is a convention that since the 1970s has developed in The Netherlands, where it has become established practice that no new cabinet coalition can form unless the voters have endorsed the parties through a new electoral mandate. Thus, when one coalition resigns in the middle of a parliamentary term, it is no longer acceptable for another government simply to replace it.

There is no constitutional requirement in The Netherlands (or in most other parliamentary states) that a government resignation must be followed by a parliamentary dissolution.[17] On the contrary, this practice has developed in the absence of any formal rule (Timmermans and Andeweg 2000: 364) and despite the absence of any pre-election agreement to consult the voters before altering the party composition of the executive.

Indeed, under strictly stepwise accountability there should be no need for a new election. The Prime Minister is accountable only to the parliamentary majority, and it is the task of the latter, not the voters, to generate a new government. Nevertheless, such renegotiation without the involvement of the voters is apparently becoming increasingly rare, not only in The Netherlands. Even though the demand for a direct and transparent accountability between the highest executive offices and the voters is not entirely novel, its growing strength challenges the step-wise construction of parliamentary democracy.

Political parties have tended to respond to such demands by giving their cabinet members, and Prime Ministers in particular, more policy discretion (Blondel and Cotta 1996, 2000). We have noted in Chapter 4 a trend towards the 'presidentialization' of Prime Ministerships. At the same time, politicians are becoming less willing to control their agents, or at least to accept responsibility for their actions. Increasingly, elected politicians refrain from directly instructing their civil servants. Instead they try to evaluate the outcomes these agents produce and then punish or reward them on this basis.

Governments in many European countries have thus begun to restructure their relations with the civil service. According to New Public Management doctrine, it is no longer sufficient for a civil servant to observe administrative regulations in every detail, to follow the specific instruction of his or her superiors, and not to steal public money. Rather, accountability relates to the civil servant's performance in attaining the agency's goals. Here at least two different approaches can be distinguished. The 'let the managers manage' approach implicitly trusts civil servants 'to exercise their judgement intelligently, to employ their flexibility with prudence, and to be motivated primarily by the intrinsic rewards of public office'. This approach is largely based on *ex ante* controls, that is, on finding the right people to empower on these terms. In contrast, the 'make the managers manage' approach provides civil servants with 'specific, tightly written performance contracts that leave little room for trust'. Hence performance improvement is motivated by very extrinsic rewards (Behn 2001: 30) and the use of *ex post* control mechanisms.

In sum, there is every reason to mind the gap between citizens and their political representatives. Contemporary parliamentary democracies are faced with a tension that critically impinges on democratic agency relations. This is the tension between a more demanding citizenry and a world in which external constraints are becoming increasingly important. This tension leads to a situation in which citizens increasingly demand government accountability, while at the same time many political institutions

---

[17] The trend towards greater reliance on parliamentary dissolution parallels what happened in Britain during the evolution of parliamentary government (Cox 1987).

are becoming insulated from popular control. The challenges also include mastering the institutional complexity and cognitive demands of Europeanization and Globalization.

At the same time, the decay of traditional information shortcuts means that political information is cheapened in more ways than one, and that knowledge of the past becomes systematically less helpful in controlling the representatives of the people. While the decay of traditional information sources exacerbates the problem of adverse selection, social disintegration may intensify moral hazard. And if traditional mechanisms of *ex ante* agent control are breaking down everywhere in the western world, the resulting agency loss may be particularly severe under parliamentary systems that have relied heavily on such devices. It is no great surprise that citizens are becoming progressively more critical of those who hold power.

"These are daunting prospects, and the solutions are not obvious. Students of political institutions and governance certainly cannot solve the perennial problems of political delegation once and for all. It is unlikely that we even fully understand the contemporary twists on these issues and their implications. Yet, we can remind policy makers that the institutional menu is extensive, and that parliamentary democracies have responded to serious challenges before."

REFERENCES

Abromeit, Heidrun (1998). *Democracy in Europe*. New York: Berghahn Books.

Anckar, Carsten (2000). 'Size and Party System Fragmentation'. *Party Politics*, 6: 305–28.

Bergman, Torbjörn and Damgaard, Erik (eds.) (2000). *Delegation and Accountability in European Integration: The Nordic Parliamentary Democracies and the European Union*. London: Frank Cass.

——, Müller, Wolfgang C., and Strøm, Kaare (eds.) (2000). 'Special issue: Parliamentary democracy and the chain of delegation'. *European Journal of Political Research*, 37: 3.

Behn, Robert D. (2001). *Rethinking Democratic Accountability*. Washington: Brookings Institution Press.

Bendor, Jonathan, Glazer, Ami, and Hammond, Thomas H. (2001), 'Theories of Delegation', *Annual Review of Political Science*, 4: 235–69.

Blondel, Jean and Cotta, Maurizio (eds.) (1996). *Party and Government*. Houndmills: Macmillan.

——— (eds.) (2000). *The Nature of Party Government*. Houndmills: Palgrave-Macmillan.

Boix, Carles (1998). *Political Parties, Growth, and Equality*. Cambridge: Cambridge University Press.

Castles, Francis G. (ed.) (1982). *The Impact of Parties*. London: Sage.

——and Mair, Peter (1984). 'Left-Right Political Scales: Some "Expert" Judgements'. *European Journal of Political Research*, 12: 73–88.

Cukierman, Alex, Webb, Steven B., and Neyapti, Bilin (1994). *Measuring Central Bank Independence and Its Effects on Policy Outcomes*. San Fransisco: ICS.

Cox, Gary W. (1987). *The Efficient Secret*. Cambridge: Cambridge University Press.

Dahl, Robert A. (1989). *Democracy and Its Critics*. New Haven: Yale University Press.

——and Tufte, Edward (1973). *Size and Democracy*. Stanford: Stanford University Press.

Dalton, Russell J. (1999). 'Political Support in Advanced Industrial Democracies', in Pippa Norris (ed.), *Critical Citizens*. Oxford: Oxford University Press.

——(2002). *Citizen Politics*, 3rd edn. Chatham: Chatham House Publishers.

Della Porta, Donatella and Mény, Yves (eds.) (1997). *Democracy and Corruption in Europe*. London: Pinter.

Djankov, Simeon, La Porta, Rafael, Lopez-de-Silanes, Florencio, and Shleifer, Andrei (2000). *The Regulation of Entry*. National Bureau of Economic Research, Cambridge, MA, Working Paper 7892.

Entman, Robert M. and Bennett, W. Lance (2001). 'Communication in the Future of Democracy: A Conclusion', in W. Lance Bennett and Robert M. Entman (eds.), *Mediated Politics*. Cambridge: Cambridge University Press.

Feigenbaum, Harvey, Henig, Jeffrey, and Hamnett, Chris (1999). *Shrinking the State*. Cambridge: Cambridge University Press.

Franzese, Robert J. Jr. (2002). *Macroeconomic Policies of Developed Democracies*. Cambridge: Cambridge University Press.

Garrett, Geoffrey (1998). *Partisan Politics in the Global Economy*. Cambridge: Cambridge University Press.

Gilardi, Fabrizio and Braun, Dietmar (2002). 'Delegation aus der Sicht der Prinzipal–Agent-Theorie'. *Politische Vierteljahresschrift*, 43: 147–61.

Grande, Edgar (2000). 'Post-National Democracy in Europe', in Michael Th. Greven and Louis W. Pauly (eds.), *Democracy Beyond the State?* Lanham: Rowman & Littlefield.

Gujarati, Damodar N. (1995). *Basic Econometrics*, 3rd edn. New York: McGraw-Hill.

Gunther, Richard and Montero, José R. (2001). 'The Anchors of Partisanship', in P. Nikiforos Diamandouros and Richard Gunther (eds.), *Parties, Politics, and Democracy in the New Southern Europe*. Baltimore: Johns Hopkins University Press.

Held, David, Anthony McGrew, Goldblatt, David, and Perraton, Jonathan (1999). *Global Transformations*. Cambridge: Polity.

Hine, David (1993). *Governing Italy*. Oxford: Oxford University Press.

Hirschman, Albert O. (1970). *Exit, Voice, or Loyalty*. Cambridge, MA: Harvard University Press.

Huber, John and Inglehart, Ronald (1995). 'Expert Interpretations of Party Space and Party Locations in 42 Societies'. *Party Politics*, 1: 73–111.

Katzenstein, Peter J. (1985). *Small States in World Markets*. Ithaca, NY: Cornell University Press.

Kelsen, Hans (1926). *Das Problem des Parlamentarismus*. Vienna: Braumüller.

King, Anthony (1976). 'Modes of Executive–Legislative Relations: Great Britain, France, and West Germany'. *Legislative Studies Quarterly*, 1: 11–36.

Kirchheimer, Otto (1966). 'The Transformation of the Western European Party Systems', in Joseph LaPalombara and Myron Weiner (eds.), *Political Parties and Political Development*. Princeton: Princeton University Press.

Klingemann, Hans-Dieter, Hofferbert, Richard I., and Budge, Ian (1993). *Parties, Policies, and Democracy*. Boulder: Westview Press.

——. (1999) 'Mapping Political Support in the 1990s: A Global Analysis', in Pippa Norris (ed.), *Critical Citizens: Global Support for Democratic Governance*. Oxford: Oxford University Press.

Knapp, Andrew and Wright, Vincent (2001). *The Government and Politics of France*, 4th edn. London: Routledge.

Lane, Jan-Erik and Ersson, Svante (1999). *Politics and Society in Western Europe*, 4th edn. London: Sage.

Laver, Michael and Garry, John (2000). 'Estimating Policy Positions from Political Texts'. *American Journal of Political Science*, 44: 619–34.

Levitt, Malcolm and Lord, Christopher (2000). *The Political Economy of Monetary Union*. Houndmills: Macmillan.

Lewis, W. Arthur (1965). *Politics in West Africa*. London: George Allen and Unwin.

Lijphart, Arend (1977). *Democracy in Plural Societies*. New Haven: Yale University Press.

Lijphart (1984). *Democracies*. New Haven: Yale University Press.

——(1999). *Patterns of Democracy*. New Haven: Yale University Press.

Lipset, Seymour Martin (1959). *Political Man. The Social Bases of Politics*. Garden City: Doubleday.

Listhaug, Ola and Wiberg, Matti (1995). 'Confidence in Political and Private Institutions', in Hans-Dieter Klingemann and Dieter Fuchs (eds.), *Citizens and the State*. Oxford: Oxford University Press.

Lupia, Arthur and McCubbins, Matthew D. (1998). *The Democratic Dilemma*. Cambridge: Cambridge University Press.

Mair, Peter, Müller, Wolfgang C., and Plasser, Fritz (eds.) (2003, forthcoming). *Political Parties in Electoral Markets: Challenge and response in Contemporary Western European Democracies*. London: Sage.

Majone, Giandomenico (1998). 'Europe's "Democratic Deficit": The Question of Standards'. *European Law Journal*, 4: 5–28.

——(2001a). 'Two Logics of Delegation'. *European Union Politics*, 2: 103–22.

——(2001b). 'Nonmajoritarian Institutions and the Limits of Democratic Governance: A Political Transaction Cost Approach'. *Journal of Theoretical and Institutional Economics*, 157: 57–78.

Michels, Robert (1962 [1915]). *Political Parties*. New York: Free Press.

Mill, John Stuart (1984 [1861]). 'Considerations on Representative Government', in John Stuart Mill (ed.), *Utilitarianism. Liberty. Representative Government*. London: Dent.

Mosca, Gaetano (1947). *Elementi di scienza politica*, 4th edn. Bari: Gius Laterza & Figli.

Mueller, Dennis C. (1996). *Constitutional Democracy*. Oxford: Oxford University Press.

——(2004). *Public Choice III*. Cambridge: Cambridge University Press.

Müller, Wolfgang C. and Strøm, Kaare (2000). 'Conclusion: Coalition Governance in Western Europe', in Wolfgang C. Müller and Kaare Strøm (eds.), *Coalition Governments in Western Europe*. Oxford: Oxford University Press.

—— et al. (2001). *Die österreichischen Abgeordneten*. Vienna: WUV-Fakultas.

Narud, Hanne Marthe and Valen, Henry (2004). 'Coalition Membership and Electoral Performance in Western Europe', in Kaare Strøm, Wolfgang C. Müller, and Torbjörn Bergman (eds.), *Coalition Governance in Parliamentary Democracies*. Oxford: Oxford University Press (forthcoming).

Newton, Kenneth and Norris, Pippa (2000). 'Confidence in Public Institutions: Faith, Culture, or Performance?' in Susan J. Pharr and Robert D. Putnam (eds.), *Disaffected Democracies*. Princeton: Princeton University Press.

Norris, Pippa (1999). 'The Political Regime', in Hermann Schmitt and Jacques Thomassen (eds.), *Political Representation and Legitimacy in the European Union*. Oxford: Oxford University Press.

——(2000). *A Virtuous Circle: Political Communications in Postindustrial Societies*. Cambridge: Cambridge University Press.

Nugent, Neill (1999). *The Government and Politics of the European Union*, 4th edn. Houndmills: Macmillan.

Ostrogorski, M. (1907). *Democracy and the Organization of Political Parties*. London.

Persson, Torsten and Tabellini, Guido (2000). *Political Economics*. Cambridge, MA: MIT Press.

——, Roland, Gérard, and Tabellini, Guido (2000). 'Comparative Politics and Public Finance'. *Journal of Political Economy*, 108: 1121–61.

Pollack, Mark A. (2002), 'Learning from the Americanists (Again): Theory and Method in the Study of Delegation', *West European Politics*, 25(1): 47–66.

Powell, G. Bingham, Jr. (2000). *Elections as Instruments of Democracy*. Cambridge, MA: Harvard University Press.

Putnam, Robert D. (1993). *Making Democracy Work*. Princeton: Princeton University Press.

Ridley, F. F. and Doig, Alan (eds.) (1995). *Sleaze: Politicians, Private Interests, and Public Policy*. Oxford: Oxford University Press.

Rose, Richard (1984). *Do Parties Make a Difference?* 2nd edn. London: Macmillan.

——(2000). 'The End of Consensus in Austria and Switzerland'. *Journal of Democracy*, 11: 26–40.

Rose-Ackerman, Susan (1999). *Corruption and Government*. Cambridge: Cambridge University Press.

Scharpf, Fritz (1999). *Governing in Europe. Effective and Democratic?* Oxford: Oxford University Press.

Schmitt, Carl (1969 [1923]). *Die geistesgeschichtliche Lage des heutigen Parlamentarismus*. Berlin: Duncker & Humblot.

Share, Donald (1999). 'From Policy-Seeking to Office-Seeking: The Metamorphosis of the Spanish Socialist Workers Party', in Wolfgang C. Müller and Kaare Strøm (eds.), *Policy, Office, or Votes? How Political Parties in Western Europe Make Hard Decisions*. Cambridge: Cambridge University Press.

Shleifer, Andrei, and Vishny, Robert W. (1998). *The Grabbing Hand. Government Pathologies and Their Cures*. Cambridge, MA.: Harvard University Press.

Stigler, George L. (1971). 'The Theory of Economic Regulation'. *Bell Journal of Economics and Management Science*, 2: 3–21.

Street, John (2001). *Mass Media, Politics and Democracy*. Houndmills: Palgrave.

Strøm, Kaare (1997). 'Democracy, Accountability, and Coalition Bargaining'. *European Journal of Political Research*, 31: 47–62.

——and Swindle, Stephen M. (2002). 'Strategic Parliamentary Dissolution.' *American Political Science Review*, 96: 575–91.

Timmermans, Arco and Andeweg, Rudy B. (2000). 'The Netherlands: Still the Politics of Accommodation?', in Wolfgang C. Müller and Kaare Strøm (eds.), *Coalition Governments in Western Europe*. Oxford: Oxford University Press.

Tollison, Robert D. (1997). 'Rent seeking', in Dennis C. Mueller (ed.), *Perspectives on Public Choice*. Cambridge: Cambridge University Press.

Treisman, Daniel (2000). 'The Causes of Corruption: A Cross-national Study'. *Journal of Public Economics*, 76: 399–457.

Tsebelis, George (1990). *Nested Games: Rational Choice in Comparative Politics*. Berkeley: University of California Press.

——(1995). 'Decisionmaking in Political Systems: Veto Players in Presidentialism, Parliamentarism, Multicameralism, and Multipartyism'. *British Journal of Political Science*, 25: 289–325.

——(2002). *Veto Players: An Introduction to Institutional Analysis*. Princeton: Princeton University Press and the Russell Sage Foundation.

Ulram, Peter A. (2000). 'Civic Democracy. Politische Beteiligung und politische Unterstützung', in Anton Pelinka, Fritz Plasser, and Wolfgang Meixner (eds.), *Die Zukunft der österreichischen Demokratie*. Vienna: Signum.

Index

BITTERSWEET

www.rbooks.co.uk/daniellesteel

*Published outside the UK under the title PASSION'S PROMISE